Tenth Edition

FIELDS *of* READING

Motives for Writing

NANCY R. COMLEY ▫ DAVID HAMILTON ▫ CARL H. KLAUS
ROBERT SCHOLES ▫ NANCY SOMMERS ▫ JASON TOUGAW

e with e-Pages

Paired Readings and Casebooks in *Fields of Reading*

Arts and Humanities

Social Sciences

Sciences

Casebooks

TENTH EDITION

Fields of Reading

Motives for Writing

Nancy R. Comley | Queens College, CUNY

David Hamilton | Univeristy of Iowa

Carl H. Klaus | University of Iowa

Robert Scholes | Brown University

Nancy Sommers | Harvard University

Jason Tougaw | Queens College, CUNY

BEDFORD/ST. MARTIN'S

Boston • New York

For Bedford/St. Martin's
Developmental Editor: Stephanie Butler
Associate Production Editor: Kellan Cummings
Senior Production Supervisor: Nancy Myers
Assistant Production Manager: Joe Ford
Senior Marketing Manager: Molly Parke
Editorial Assistants: Emily Wunderlich/Nick McCarthy
Copy Editor: Diana George
Photo Researcher: Naomi Kornhauser
Permissions Manager: Kalina K. Ingham
Art Director: Lucy Krikorian
Text Design: Castle Design
Cover Design: Marine Bouvier Miller
Cover Art/Cover Photo: Detail of *New City* (2002) by Matthew Northridge, courtesy of the artist and KANSAS, NYC
Composition: Westchester Book Group
Printing and Binding: RR Donnelley and Sons

President, Bedford/St. Martin's: Denise B. Wydra
Presidents, Macmillan Higher Education: Joan E. Feinberg and Tom Scotty
Editor in Chief: Karen S. Henry
Director of Development: Erica T. Appel
Director of Marketing: Karen R. Soeltz
Production Director: Susan W. Brown
Associate Production Director: Elise S. Kaiser
Managing Editor: Shuli Traub

Library of Congress Control Number: 2012945313

Manufactured in the United States of America.

7 6 5 4 3 2
f e d c b a

For information, write: Bedford/St. Martin's, 75 Arlington Street, Boston, MA 02116 (617-399-4000)

ISBN 978-1-4576-0891-9

Acknowledgments
Acknowledgments and copyrights are continued at the back of the book on pages 721–25, which constitute an extension of the copyright page. It is a violation of the law to reproduce these selections by any means whatsoever without the written permission of the copyright holder.

Preface

The tenth edition of *Fields of Reading: Motives for Writing* builds on and extends the reimagining of the previous edition, as a lively new text that maintains the book's original—and well-received—premise: that good readings representing major divisions of the curriculum and major rhetorical approaches will lead to good writing and to great classroom discussions. Recognizing the needs of today's students (and instructors), this new edition reflects several additional premises:

- that students learn to write more effectively when their writing contributes to cultural conversations, the stakes of which they understand. For this reason, Making Connections questions, Paired Readings, and Casebook apparatus emphasize the conversations among essays and invite students to participate in those conversations.
- that students learn through continuous writing, both informal and formal, in a variety of styles and modes. With this in mind, the tenth edition offers more opportunities for focus on all stages of the writing process.
- that we are living through a cultural moment in which new media are transforming the relationship among reading, writing, and thinking—a transformation students are poised to understand and benefit from as they move through college and life. New online selections, the e-Pages for *Fields of Reading*, ask students to apply the critical-thinking skills they will develop by reading the essays and completing the exercises in the printed book to other kinds of content they will engage with in school and beyond: video, audio, infographics, and interactive Web content. e-Pages can be accessed at **bedfordstmartins.com/fieldsofreading/epages**.
- that research is key to a college education. Therefore, this edition offers opportunities for research in the apparatus of many readings, particularly in the Casebooks, as well as in the MLA and APA style guides.
- that students learn most effectively when they immerse themselves in a topic and explore it from a variety of disciplinary and rhetorical viewpoints. The three Casebooks included are intended to achieve that kind of immersion and create a foundation for research.
- that students learn about their own writing by focusing on the language and rhetoric employed by other writers. This is why each major field in the book now includes Paired Readings that focus on language and rhetoric in the given discipline. Furthermore, we have included a model student essay in each of the major disciplines that reflects a strategy for writing in that particular field.

We believe this new edition of *Fields of Reading* is an excellent cornerstone for today's composition classroom because it bridges innovation and tradition by employing emerging approaches to literacy and education in combination with enduring ideas about the written word.

As with previous editions, *Fields of Reading* introduces students to the writing and thinking they will do in college—writing and thinking motivated by genuine intellectual questions and problems. We emphasize, as always, readings in the arts and humanities, in the social sciences, and in the sciences (the major divisions of the curriculum), and we include pieces representing *Fields*'s four major rhetorical modes: reflecting (considers past experience), reporting (conveys information), explaining (makes sense of knowledge), and arguing (debates controversial ideas and issues). For this edition, we continue to emphasize conversations among writers, both explicit and implicit. We have arranged the seventy-seven readings so as to invite students into such conversations, highlighting the particular and unique perspectives offered by writers working from various professional backgrounds, disciplinary methods, and writing traditions.

In the spirit of fostering engaged reading and writing, the question sets following each reading reflect active—and interactive—classroom pedagogy. By engaging students directly with formal and informal writing assignments, we hope to encourage them to build new and flexible thinking and writing skills. Likewise, the accompanying *Instructor's Manual* is designed to help instructors stimulate active learning in the classroom. Throughout, it offers support for teaching rhetorical technique and writing craft, so that instructors can better help students take advantage of online (and other) resources and become reflective and critical users of those resources.

Features of the Tenth Edition

Memorable, well-crafted writing from inside and outside the academy
Seventy-seven readings include works from classic essayists like Frederick Douglass, Barbara Ehrenreich, and Oliver Sacks and engaging contemporary writing by Sherry Turkle, Mark Bittman, and Jhumpa Lahiri. New e-Pages include online selections to further expand the range of pieces in the book.

A flexible organization
Readings are categorized into parts based on broad academic fields, concluding with three Casebooks that bring essays on compelling topics from across the curriculum into conversation with one another. Essays are also identified as belonging to one of four major rhetorical categories—reflecting, reporting, explaining, and arguing—and an alternate thematic table of contents highlights the range of fascinating issues covered in the book.

Editorial apparatus that builds critical thinking, research, and writing skills
Questions following each essay test students' comprehension, help them connect the essay to other ideas in the book and given discipline, and guide them in their own writing.

New to This Edition

New readings address a balance of personal, professional, and academic issues that engage students.
For example:

- Mona Eltahawy reflects on the pros and cons of being connected on Twitter, both professionally and in her personal life.
- Jose Antonio Vargas tells a harrowing tale of hiding his status as an illegal immigrant while becoming an acclaimed journalist.
- Richard Feynman argues for a passionate, almost humanistic, approach to academic pursuits in the sciences.

New Paired Readings focus on the important role language plays in each major academic division: in the experience of writing online (arts and humanities), media bias (social sciences), and scientific literacy (sciences).
Additional Paired Readings address debates that relate to student life as well as professional degrees. For example, Roy C. Selby Jr. and Richard Selzer offer different perspectives on the ways medical professionals perceive and react to their patients.

Three new Casebooks help students connect personally to academic conversations and larger cultural discussions.

- Each Casebook is arranged around a question that can be used as the starting point for researched papers, arguments, and analyses: How Is the Internet Changing Who We Are? What Is the Value of a College Education? and What Do We Really Know about Gender?
- New Casebook-wide essay and multimedia projects ask students to join in the conversation presented in each Casebook.

More editorial help for students allows them to join academic conversations with more coverage of active reading, research practices, and example student writing.

- An expanded Introduction to Writing covers active reading and writing strategies, with examples of note-taking, journaling, and drafting.
- The research section—including new coverage of APA style in addition to MLA—offers students the conceptual and practical guidance they need to write and research in any discipline.
- Student essays in each discipline provide documented models of how college writers can enter the academic conversation. Accompanying apparatus helps students connect their own writing to the practice of reading.

New integrated e-Pages offer online selections that expand the scope of the readings beyond traditional print essays.
Ten compelling multimodal selections help enrich cultural conversation among the disciplines and give students new ideas to think and write about. An illustrated chart that explains why our brains may be making us unhappy, a documentary film trailer showing how the representation of women in the media has

kept them from positions of power, and a humorous video exploring the concept of Internet memes are among the e-Pages students can access with the purchase of a new book. (See inside front cover for details, or go to **bedfordstmartins.com/fieldsofreading/epages**.)

You Get More Digital Choices for *Fields of Reading*.

Fields of Reading doesn't stop with the book. Online, you'll find both free and affordable premium resources to help students get even more out of the book and your course. You'll also find convenient instructor resources, such as downloadable sample syllabi, classroom activities, and even a nationwide community of teachers. To learn more about or order any of the products below, contact your Bedford/St. Martin's sales representative, e-mail sales support (sales_support@bfwpub.com), or visit the Web site at **bedfordstmartins.com**.

Companion Web site for *Fields of Reading* at bedfordstmartins.com/fieldsofreading

Send students to free and open resources, choose flexible premium resources to supplement your print text, or upgrade to an expanding collection of innovative digital content.

Free and open resources for *Fields of Reading* provide students with easy-to-access reference materials, visual tutorials, and support for working with sources.

- Five free videos of real writers from VideoCentral
- *TopLinks* and *AuthorLinks* with reliable online sources
- *Research and Documentation Online* by Diana Hacker

VideoCentral is a growing collection of videos for the writing class that captures real-world, academic, and student writers talking about how and why they write. VideoCentral can be packaged with *Fields of Reading* for free. An activation code is required. To order VideoCentral packaged with the print book, use ISBN 978-1-4576-4337-8.

Re:Writing Plus gathers all of Bedford/St. Martin's premium digital content for composition into one online collection. It includes hundreds of model documents, the first-ever peer-review game, and VideoCentral. *Re:Writing Plus* can be purchased separately or packaged with the print book at a significant discount. An activation code is required. To order *Re:Writing Plus* packaged with the print book, use ISBN 978-1-4576-4336-1.

i-series

Add more value to your text by choosing one of the following tutorial series, free when packaged with *Fields of Reading*. This popular series presents multimedia tutorials in a flexible format—because there are things you can't do in a book. To learn more about package options or any of the products below, contact your Bedford/St. Martin's sales representative or visit **bedfordstmartins.com.**

ix visualizing composition 2.0 (available online) helps students put into practice key rhetorical and visual concepts. To order *ix visualizing composition* packaged with the print book, use ISBN 978-1-4576-4335-4.

i•claim: visualizing argument (available on CD-ROM) offers a new way to see argument—with six tutorials, an illustrated glossary, and over seventy multimedia arguments. To order *i•claim: visualizing argument* packaged with the print book, use ISBN 978-1-4576-4334-7.

i•cite: visualizing sources (available online as part of *Re:Writing Plus*) brings research to life through an animated introduction, four tutorials, and hands-on source practice. To order *i•cite: visualizing sources* packaged with the print book, use ISBN 978-1-4576-4332-3.

Instructor Resources

You have a lot to do in your course. Bedford/St. Martin's wants to make it easy for you to find the support you need—and to get it quickly.

The *Instructor's Manual for Fields of Reading* is available in PDF format and can be downloaded from **bedfordstmartins.com/Catalog/product/fieldsofreading tenthedition-comley.** Invaluable for new and experienced instructors alike, this manual contains an introduction that outlines four approaches to teaching, as well as comprehensive answers to the new questions that appear at the end of every selection. Also included are suggestions for interactive classroom activities and further topics for classroom discussion.

The *Fields of Reading Instructor's Edition* includes a full copy of the text, plus the *Instructor's Manual* bound into the middle of the book.

***TeachingCentral* (bedfordstmartins.com/teachingcentral)** offers the entire list of Bedford/St. Martin's print and online professional resources in one place. You'll find landmark reference works, sourcebooks on pedagogical issues, award-winning collections, and practical advice for the classroom—all free for instructors.

***Bits* (bedfordbits.com)** collects creative ideas for teaching a range of composition topics in an easily searchable blog. A community of teachers—leading scholars, authors, and editors—discuss revision, research, grammar and style, technology, peer review, and much more. Take, use, and adapt the ideas and pass them around. Then, come back to the site to comment or share your own suggestions.

Bedford Coursepacks allow you to easily integrate our most popular content into your own course management systems. For details, visit **bedfordstmartins.com /coursepacks.**

Acknowledgments

For their detailed responses to the ninth edition of *Fields of Reading* and their suggestions for improving the book, we are grateful to the following reviewers: William Carney, Cameron University; Peter Caster, University of South Carolina Upstate; Kathleen Crosby, North Carolina Central University; LaDawn Edwards, Kirkwood Community College; Maryann Feola, the College of Staten Island/CUNY; Shirley Frank, York College/CUNY; Esther Godfrey, University of South Carolina Upstate; Karl Hendricks, University of Pittsburgh; Stacey Kaplan, University of Oregon; Linda Lawliss, College of the Desert; Valerie Levy, Rutgers University, Newark; Amy Lynn, University of Oregon; Kate Quick, University of Alaska Fairbanks; Sarah Ray Rondot, University of Oregon; Jennifer Rowan, Middle Tennessee State University; Kathleen Schroeder, California State University, San Bernardino; John Walser, Marian University; Leanne Warshauer, Suffolk County Community College; Steven Werkmeister, Johnson County Community College; David Wright, Mt. Hood Community College; Sharon Yang, Worcester State University

Finally, we would like to thank our editor, Stephanie Butler, who guided us through this revision of *Fields of Reading*. We'd also like to thank other staff members of Bedford/St. Martin's for their help and encouragement with this edition and along the way, in particular, Thomas Broadbent, who originally signed us up with St. Martin's Press, College Division, and Nancy Perry, now Editorial Director of Custom Publishing, who first worked with *Fields* and has remained a friend of the project. We are grateful to Joan Feinberg, co-President, Macmillan Higher Education; Denise Wydra, President, Bedford/St. Martin's; Karen Henry, Editor in Chief; and Erica Appel, Director of Development in New York. John Sullivan and Steve Scipione, executive editors in Boston, provided excellent counsel along the way; Molly Parke, Senior Marketing Manager, offered astute advice about the vagaries of the textbook market; and Emily Wunderlich and Nick McCarthy, editorial assistants, provided invaluable assistance with tasks big and small. Kellan Cummings, our project editor, and Shuli Traub, Managing Editor, saw the book through from manuscript to final proofs with the assistance of copy editor Diana George and proofreaders Ginny Perrin and Liz Byer. Nancy Myers, Senior Production Supervisor, and Joe Ford, Assistant Production Manager, both kept production on time and on track. Barbara Hernandez, the text permissions researcher, and Naomi Kornhauser, the art permissions researcher, secured invaluable rights. We were fortunate to have the editorial services of Elizabeth Bachner, who helped us with the task of writing new apparatus for the book, as well as material for the *Instructor's Manual*.

Finally, we appreciate the writers and artists who let us publish their work and put them into conversation with one another for the purpose of further engagement and further study across disciplines, modes, and generations.

Contents

Part 2 Arts and Humanities

Part 5 Casebooks

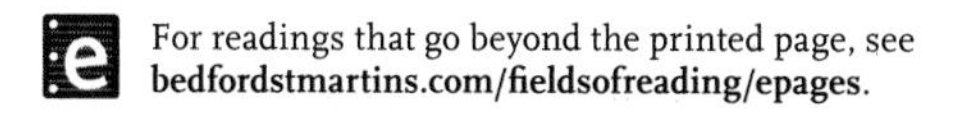
For readings that go beyond the printed page, see **bedfordstmartins.com/fieldsofreading/epages**.

Thematic Contents

Contemporary Issues and Experiences

for readings that go beyond the printed page, see **bedfordstmartins.com/fieldsofreading/epages**.

Cultures in Contact and Collision

Education

Ethics, Values, and Beliefs

Family

Gender and Women's Experiences

Health, Disease, and Medicine

History and Interpreting the Past

Human Portraits

Identity

Interpreting the Body

Life and Death

The Media

Observing and Understanding the World

Race

Violence and War

Part 1
An Introduction to Writing

From Reading to Writing

Fields of Reading is an introduction to the basic work of college—the reading, discussion, thinking, and writing that stimulate and challenge the minds of students and faculty alike. The writing included here explores timely questions within three broad areas of academic study: arts and humanities, social sciences, and sciences. For readers in all disciplines—and for reading beyond this anthology—it seems that the more we learn about social life, identity, and the nature of the universe, the more unanswered questions emerge: What will climate change mean for the future of the planet? How will a globalized economy affect the daily lives of people from various cultures? How is technology transforming social and political life? Is brain science on the verge of solving the mysteries of the self? How does language shape knowledge or identity? What is writing good for? What role will the Internet play in addressing questions like these? How will it change who we are and how we learn?

The readings within are intended to provoke you to think and write about these kinds of questions—questions that will inevitably arise throughout your college course work. Thus we begin with a few observations about the relationship of reading and writing, and the importance of each in various academic fields. Later in the Introduction, we will discuss the characteristics of the modes of writing covered in this book—reflecting, reporting, explaining, and arguing. The last section of the Introduction covers research, a process vital to the work you will do throughout your higher education.

Conversations across the Disciplines

Take, as an example, a single writer in this reader: Barack Obama, the forty-fourth president of the United States. His speech "A More Perfect Union" (p. 355) embodies a conversation involving a multitude of other texts and writers, some of which are also collected here. Obama's title is a deliberate reference to the preamble of the United States Constitution: "We the people, in order to form a more perfect union . . . ." In fact, the speech begins by quoting the preamble. In less direct ways, however, it's also a response to the work of other writers, including Thomas Jefferson's Declaration of Independence (p. 300) and Martin Luther King Jr.'s "Letter from Birmingham Jail" (p. 341). Obama's influential speech on the future of race relations was shaped culturally, historically, and rhetorically by the words and deeds of Jefferson and King. Jefferson, a slave owner, was one of the central thinkers to craft the language on which the nation was founded. King's heroic efforts to argue—and fight—for civil rights in the 1960s made it possible, forty years later, for the nation to elect its first biracial president.

Obama wrote his speech in response to a controversy. His former pastor, Rev. Jeremiah Wright, had made inflammatory statements about the legacy of slavery and the state of race relations in contemporary American culture. Many in the press and in politics questioned Obama's judgment—and his patriotism—as a result of Wright's words. Rather than defend himself personally, Obama took the opportunity to assess and explain the complex state of race relations today, in the wake of both slavery and the civil rights movement. The speech was widely applauded as a brilliant *rhetorical* move, becoming a defining moment in his campaign—and, ultimately, in American politics and culture. Its success was due, in large part, to the ingenious way that Obama responded to—and reframed—the words and ideas of Wright, Jefferson, and King.

At the same time—and in a larger sense—it would be impossible to know the true number of texts that gave essence to Obama's speech. We know that Obama is an avid reader; the words he ultimately delivered were his, but they were surely informed by his lifetime of reading, in more ways than he could even know himself. In this sense, the speech is a moment in a conversation at least two hundred years old (if not older).

Every piece of writing, including your own, is part of a conversation like this. For example, Oliver Sacks's "The Man Who Mistook His Wife for a Hat" (p. 446), which tells the story of a man whose visual experience is profoundly altered by brain damage, can be understood as an implicit response to Plato's classic "The Cave" (p. 104), in which the philosopher suggests that the visual experience of human beings represents a mere shadow of reality. Plato's text might also be understood in dialogue with any number of other texts, including physician Lewis Thomas's "The Corner of the Eye" (p. 427) or Dudley Clendinen's "The Good Short Life" (p. 73). All these texts are about how we know what we think we know, based on firsthand observation. Thomas's essay is philosophical and scientific, whereas Clendinen's is personal and political. While each of these texts is very different in terms of focus, style, and rhetoric, they can be understood as pieces of an ongoing conversation—one that shapes and documents the world we inhabit.

Conversations among texts take many forms and can address almost any topic, often involving writers from very different eras or cultures. George Orwell entered into a centuries-old conversation on language with his essay "Politics and the English Language" (p. 313). Its concern for the degradation of language as propaganda—social, political, and commercial—bears witness to increasingly insidious ways of promoting doubtful versions of the truth. Brooke Gladstone ("The Great Refusal," p. 325) uses a contemporary medium—the graphic narrative—to address twenty-first-century versions of Orwell's questions, focusing on questions about journalistic language and the merits and pitfalls of striving for objectivity with language. James Baldwin (p. 131) and Gloria Anzaldúa (p. 167) do not address Orwell's particular concerns, but their reflections on black English and the "border language" Chicano Spanish add to an ongoing conversation about the nature of language and its place in culture. We have recognized this conversation and given it shape throughout the various editions of this reader by selecting Orwell's essay for an early edition, adding Baldwin and Anzaldúa later, and bringing Gladstone into it now.

Like Obama, Jefferson, and King, or Plato, Sacks, and Thomas, we can think of Anzaldúa, Baldwin, Gladstone, and Orwell as taking part in a long-running conversation. A conversation about politics, race, public perception, and nationhood belongs primarily to the social sciences; one about the physical makeup of the planets, to the sciences; and one about the English language, to the humanities. It's important to remember, however, that these subjects are relevant in more than one discipline. Writing as beautiful as that of Martin Luther King Jr. is likely to be studied in the humanities as well as the social sciences; Plato's text asks questions about perception and cosmology, but it does so in philosophical terms (and philosophy itself is sometimes categorized among the social sciences and sometimes among the humanities); and debates about language and culture belong to the social sciences as well as the humanities.

While the academic disciplines overlap, the written conversations most of us enter into in college and professional life tend to occur within such disciplinary structures as economics, history, biology, or political science. The writing in each of these fields is often very different. Consequently, writing has long been recognized as a subject that deserves close attention across the university curriculum. English majors write analytical essays and creative fiction and nonfiction; marketing majors write briefs and ad copy; psychology and physics majors write literature reviews and lab reports. And while all that writing springs from a core facility with a language, in our case English, it also takes significantly diverging forms as writers specialize. This book attempts to illustrate the core of usage that generates most of our writing as well as something of the paths toward specialization our writing can follow.

How to Use This Book

Parts Two through Four of this book each represent one of the broad areas of academic study: Arts and Humanities, Social Sciences, and Sciences, respectively. Each part contains articles that focus on individual fields of study, such as English, political science, and physics. Many of these readings address noteworthy or controversial topics within each discipline that will give you opportunities to engage with, respond to, and argue with the topic and the author. You may well find, however, that individual readings speak to one another in unexpected ways.

Paired Readings

In addition, we've included three paired readings in each of the academic areas. For example, in the Arts and Humanities section, we've paired two essays that focus on religious belief: Marjane Satrapi's "The Veil" (p. 184) and Paul Bloom's "Is God an Accident?" (p. 194). In her graphic narrative, Satrapi reflects on her childhood ideas about God; Bloom argues for a new understanding of the origins of religious belief. Although both authors focus on people's personal relationships with religion, they do so with very different tones and emphases; and although most readers will probably notice certain common themes in these two essays, individual readers will probably make their own unique connections. In this sense, the conversation taking place between these two readings might provoke your own original thinking and writing.

The same is true with the paired readings in the other two sections. In the Social Sciences section, for example, Susan Sontag argues for a philosophical consideration of war photography (p. 366), and recent veterans reflect on the Iraq War in the series of accounts collected in "Soldiers' Stories: Dispatches from Iraq" (p. 374). In the Sciences section, Natalie Angier's "The Canon" (p. 489) reports on how scientists conceive of their discipline as a "state of mind" rather than a "body of facts," while Thomas W. Martin's "Scientific Literacy and the Habit of Discourse" (p. 501) argues about the importance of designing science education so that it teaches "habits" that enable students to develop a scientific state of mind. We encourage you to enter the conversations taking place among these pairs of writers—to respond to them, evaluate them, and extend them.

Casebooks

Part Five of this book is made up of three "casebooks," each of which includes six or seven readings that address common themes and questions: "How Is the Internet Changing Who We Are?" (p. 553), "What Is the Value of a College Education?" (p. 625), and "What Do We Really Know about Gender?" (p. 679). Notice that each casebook is framed by a question, the kind of question that motivates scholars and writers to conduct research in the search for answers, for knowledge. Of course, such research leads to more new questions than definitive answers, but that's what makes the pursuit of knowledge continuously exciting. The readings in each of these sections were chosen because they offer various approaches to similar questions and a variety of rhetorical modes and academic disciplines. In a sense, these casebooks represent the work of the university in miniature: We've brought together readings that represent the range of inquiry you're likely to encounter in college, and we've done so in such a way that foregrounds the implicit connections among divergent texts and ways of thinking. Such interconnections are what make the intellectual life of college stimulating; it will be up to you to make the most of them. Often, you will do that through writing.

Writing and Thinking: The Rhetorical Modes

In this reader, we have tried to represent the variety of writing, or rhetorical modes, within each of the academic areas. *Reflecting, reporting, explaining,* and *arguing* are strategies that writers use to achieve varying purposes within their fields. For instance, a science writer may want to *explain* how a new experiment sheds new light on long-held assumptions about the firing of neurons or the nature of an atom, but that same science writer might, in another situation, want to *reflect* on the process or implications of that discovery. She chooses her form of writing to suit the particular needs of her task or assignment. It is not that each mode of writing is completely different from all the others; obviously, the lines between them blur, and most writing blends several ways of paying attention and thinking. In fact, the set of them makes sense as a continuum, in which one kind of writing leads naturally to another.

Nonetheless, *reflecting, reporting, explaining,* and *arguing* are distinct modes of writing, and each mode requires writers to practice somewhat different writing strategies. One important goal of this reader is to give you the opportunity to learn from strong examples of writing in each mode, so you can practice the strategies at work in these examples.

The word *reflection* means "bending back," as in reversing the direction of a ray of light. And so we associate this practice with looking back on an event or an idea or a finding, after we have gained some distance from it. The word suggests that moment of tranquility, after the storm, when we are better able to understand what the original drama was about. A *report* gathers information—from observation, interviews, lab experiments, or archives—and delivers it to an audience. Presumably, the writer of a report holds back his or her own judgment to let readers decide what they think of this information. An *explanation* usually focuses on a technical—or at least complex—phenomenon, situation, issue, or problem. The writer of an explanatory essay is usually an expert on a given topic, whether it's the science of genetics or the art of writing. *Argument* is the art of persuasion, of introducing a topic about which your reader may think very differently from you, and attempting to persuade him or her to take your views seriously or even change his or her mind.

Of course, just as the academic disciplines overlap, so do the rhetorical modes. Mark Edmundson *reflects* on his experience teaching in a classroom in the essay "On the Uses of a Liberal Education" (p. 630), but the piece also makes an *argument* about the effect of consumer culture on teaching; Marjane Satrapi's graphic narrative "The Veil" (p. 184) is *reporting* on life in Iran after the Islamic Revolution, but it's also *reflecting* on that experience. As you read essays in the various modes—and practice writing your own—it's instructive to think about the distinct effect of each mode and to remember that the modes overlap.

The Writing Process

Writers don't generally think to themselves, "I'm going to sit down and write a reflective (or reportorial or explanatory or argumentative) essay today." While most finished writing can be categorized somewhere along this rhetorical continuum, most writing happens more unpredictably—and, you might say, more organically—than this. Writing involves a process of thinking over time, in stages. By the time a piece of writing reaches an audience, it's likely to have gone through many stages of exploratory writing, drafting, and revision. Writers often discover their own purposes—or motives—through an informal and sometimes chaotic process of exploratory writing.

The questions and assignments that follow each reading in this book are designed to engage you in this process. *Reading* questions will challenge you to think carefully about a writer's ideas and rhetoric and push you to learn from them. *Exploratory Writing* questions will give you the opportunity to respond to the readings informally, pursuing inspiration for your own ideas and your own writing. *Making Connections* questions will help you find the implicit conversations happening among multiple readings. Finally, *Essay Writing* questions will ask you to write for an audience—sometimes in direct response to what you've read, sometimes using what you've read as a model for a certain kind of writing, and sometimes using what you've read as a point of departure for your writing.

The writing of any given essay (or report or poem or case history or screenplay) begins well before the writer sits down to compose the opening paragraph. Writing begins with reading or conversation or observation. In that sense, writing often develops unconsciously, as ideas percolate in the mind of the writer—often long before he or she plans to write them down. Any given writer will develop his or her own process, and this reader is designed to encourage you to develop yours. The process of most writers will involve some of the following stages:

- Reading (or rereading)
- Observing events, remembering experiences
- Discussing reading, events, or experiences
- Exploratory writing (usually informally, sometimes in a journal or on a blog)
- Organizing and drafting
- Revising
- Editing and proofreading

Reading to Write

Before writing in response to a text, whether that response is direct (as in Obama's response to the preamble to the U.S. Constitution) or indirect (as in Oliver Sacks's response to Plato's "The Cave"), it is important to reread the text thoroughly. That reading will be more productive if it's active, done with a pen or pencil in hand. You might take notes in the margins or, if you don't want to scribble in your books, on a separate sheet of paper. If you're reading on an e-reader or e-reader app on a tablet or smartphone, make use of the highlighting and note-taking features. The device will collect the text you highlight and your notes. If you're reading an article from a Web site or an online database, record your questions and comments in a blank document open on your computer screen. (Make sure to note at the top of the page the title and sourcing information for the piece.) Instead of highlighting important quotes, copy and paste them into your document, making sure to use quotation marks so that you don't mistake excerpts for your own words later. No matter what format your notes take you might make lists of ideas you want to explore further, note interesting language or vocabulary, and identify important stylistic or rhetorical strategies. Such active reading will shape your relationship to the text in a new way. It will help you "own" that text—and, ultimately, give you greater confidence when you respond to it.

As the digital age envelops us in stream after stream of media, we've come to live in a world of texts that we pass by with remarkable speed. This can make revisiting them difficult (or impossible). Still, we listen to certain music over and over, see movies or YouTube videos two or three times, and return to familiar Web sites. Revisiting allows us to become connoisseurs of detail and notice what we had not noticed before. Similarly, you can't really come to know Satrapi or King or Thomas or Obama or any other writer from a single reading. And when it comes to *your* writing, you will write better by rewriting—which is to say, by rereading yourself. You will also find that a given reading will acquire new meanings after you've read another piece by another writer that addresses similar questions. (Orwell, for example, may read differently after you've read Anzaldúa.) Ultimately, rereading means rethinking.

With all this in mind, it's a good idea to read with a pen in your hand, with sticky notes at your side—anything that helps you make your reading active and critical. Think of reading as part of a conversation. The notes you make, the questions you ask in the margins, and the passages you mark are the first contributions you'll make to that conversation. For example, take a look at one reader's response to a passage from Richard Feynman's "The Value of Science" (p. 395).

Interesting language from a scientist

For Feynman, hard facts seem secondary to questions, mystery, and strangeness.

*What about Jekyll and Hyde? Frankenstein? Or even Michel Gondry (*Eternal Sunshine*)?*

> The same thrill, the same awe and mystery, come again and again when we look at any problem deeply enough. With more knowledge comes deeper, more wonderful mystery, luring one on to penetrate deeper still. Never concerned that the answer may prove disappointing, but with pleasure and confidence we turn over each new stone to find unimagined strangeness leading on to more wonderful questions and mysteries—certainly a grand adventure!
>
> It is true that few unscientific people have this type of religious experience. Our poets do not write about it; our artists do not portray this remarkable thing. I don't know why. Is nobody inspired by our present picture of the universe?

Notice how actively this hypothetical reader engages with Feynman's writing, noting reactions and highlighting key words and sentences along the way. The reader is sometimes intrigued, sometimes puzzled. He sometimes agrees with Feynman and is excited by his ideas, but he also disagrees with the author at times. All of these observations will give the reader something to respond to when it comes time to write. The notes demonstrate the first moment when the active reader starts to become a writer. In fact, the roles of reader and writer are blurred for anybody who approaches reading and writing as a conversation.

Exploratory Writing

Observation, memory, and discussion are as important to the writing process as reading. This is one reason writers tend to keep journals (or, perhaps, blogs). A journal or a blog gives a writer a place to reflect on experience, using informal language to explore ideas and sort out responses to experiences, memories, and conversations. Exploratory writing will often raise questions or concerns that a little reading will help illuminate. This kind of exploration gives writers a chance to rehearse their ideas about the conversations they'll enter when they write for an audience.

Rethinking is a fundamental aspect of writing. Our first response to a text or an idea or a question is important because it often represents a complex, unconscious reaction. But that first response is rarely the whole story. If we're writing for an audience, the ideas we write about require careful consideration. Exploratory writing can help us get our minds around an issue or a writing project. It can help us sort through complex materials, find a focus, or come up with a plan for writing.

Exploratory writing can take the following forms:

- **A journal or blog.** The writer reflects on a given topic in a concentrated but informal way.
- **Freewriting.** The writer engages in free association on paper, in a word-processing program, or on a tablet or smartphone, writing down whatever comes to mind, regardless of sense, order, or meaning. (This kind of writing can lead to unpredictable insights.)
- **Lists, charts, or diagrams.** The writer begins to sort through or organize information.
- **Writing through conversation.** The writer asks others to be a sounding board for rough ideas while he takes notes, documenting or responding to these conversations in writing.
- **Generating questions.** The writer articulates the central questions that provide the motives for writing about the topic at hand.

The student who critically read Richard Feynman's essay was drawn to Feynman's statement about artists and insight. As the student reread the piece (p. 395) and his annotations, (example on p. 8) he noticed his strong reaction and expanded on it in his writing journal:

> Feynman's take on science as a "religious experience" that is thrilling is an interesting one, but his dismissal of artists to do the same puzzles me. I couldn't help but think of Michel Gondry and Charlie Kaufman's *Eternal Sunshine of the Spotless Mind,* where exploration of love and pain is portrayed through the science of the brain. It doesn't get much more mysterious than that! Sure, science ends up being the enemy in that the characters learn that a physical erasing of memory from the brain can't truly undo the indelible mark of love or loss, but the mining of individual

psychologies and the fictional science that facilitates it creates the emotion and magic in the film.

This journal entry helped the student transition from his role as reader to that as writer. Based on this informal writing, he decided to explore artistic portrayals of science and compare them to Feynman's descriptions in his own paper.

Every writer will develop a slightly different process for exploring ideas, and the process may even vary from situation to situation, but most writers will engage in some of the preceding practices. See what works best for you. The strategies you adopt will most likely evolve over time. The important thing is to develop strategies for thinking and rethinking before—and as—you write.

Drafting

Drafting an essay involves both organizing ideas and finding language that conveys your meaning. A good draft will have a beginning, a middle, and an end. It will contain much of the evidence and much of the thinking that will eventually form the finished work. But a draft is just that—a draft. It's a first attempt to flesh out your ideas fully. That first attempt will usually involve some messy thinking, some disorganization, and some language that doesn't quite work. The draft may also demonstrate that you need more—or better—evidence. While a draft may be less than fully developed or polished, it gives you something to work with—a body of words, ideas, and evidence in need of revision.

The academic paradigm has always been that first we do our research and then we write it up. In a broad sense, this is true: You need to discover what you're going to write about. You need a purpose and a sense of direction. You need to organize your thoughts. Sometimes that's easier said than done. In many instances, the traditional outline is all but impossible to create until a writer has done a first draft, sorting through ideas and sifting through texts.

Often we don't recognize our real subject until we have written pages and pages. Then suddenly we make a connection or an imaginative leap, and we see where we are going. When conceiving and composing his essay "Bad Food? Tax It, and Subsidize Vegetables," Mark Bittman (p. 294) may have considered several other proposals in response to his objections about American eating habits before concluding that taxing unhealthy foods and subsidizing vegetables was the best solution. He might have considered food education programs or advertising campaigns that emphasize the health risks of junk food (much like antismoking ads). Like any writer, Bittman would have had to consider a variety of alternatives until his "eureka" moment occurred. At that point, he knew what to pare from his writing and how to develop what remained. The excitement of writing often comes in such moments of discovery, which, once made and recognized, dictate the organization of the work.

In his essay "The Eureka Hunt" (p. 431), Jonah Lehrer explains recent scientific research on "the insight experience." Scientific investigation about eureka moments has demonstrated that "before there can be a breakthrough, there has to be a mental block." Where there is excitement and discovery, there is also frustration and block. That's part of the process, so don't worry if you get stuck. Keep at it. Writing through the block can lead to discovery.

To sum up, drafting is an important step in the writing process, but making the most of a draft usually requires serious revision.

Revising

Revision in the root sense means "to see again." While your draft will represent much of your thinking on a topic, in most cases it will require substantial rethinking—of ideas, language, evidence, and organization—before it's ready for an audience. That is, you'll need to see it again very clearly before it's ready to enter into a public conversation on your topic.

Because it can be difficult to get enough perspective on your own writing to really rethink it, it's a good idea to get some distance from your draft before you revise. You can do this by setting it aside and taking a few days off from it. You can also get some distance by asking yourself certain questions about your draft, such as the following:

- Is my essay focused? Is it clear what it's about? Is it clear why my topic is significant?
- Is my evidence relevant and convincing?
- Is my essay well organized? Does it unfold appropriately for the purpose I'm trying to achieve?
- Is my language clear and polished?

If possible, it's also a good idea to get feedback from others—teachers, peers, friends, or family members. To get useful feedback, it is helpful to ask your readers very specific questions about your writing:

- What do you, as a reader, think I'm really trying to say?
- Is my motive for writing clear? Does the draft indicate a purpose and show why my topic is important?
- Where is the essay strongest? Where is it weakest? Why?
- Do you ever get confused by my language or reasoning? Where and why?
- What do you want to know more about?

Questions like these can help readers give you the information you need to gain a new perspective on your own writing. They can help you see your own writing the way you might see another's—with critical distance.

Once you've received and sifted through feedback from others, it will be up to you to use your judgment about how to revise. It's helpful to be very clear about your own motives. Why are you writing? Why is your topic important enough for others to read about it? If you know that, you'll gain control of the process, you'll have a better sense of what evidence you need to accomplish your purpose, and you'll have a clearer sense of how to organize that evidence. If you know what your mission is, you'll be in a good position to know when you've accomplished it.

Take a look at one student writer's revision of the introductory paragraph of an essay entitled "All the News That's Fit to Print?" (p. 45), which you can read in Researching to Write, the last section of Part One.

FIRST DRAFT

The writer begins with a process, not her topic.

The writer claims that the coverage is not "in-depth," but there isn't much detail about what that means.

I read every article related to the environment in the *New York Times* for two weeks. I was surprised and disappointed by what I found. The world's leading newspaper, I learned, does not offer in-depth coverage of environmental issues. While the *Times* does publish a lot of articles on the subject, especially when Earth Day rolls around, these articles are often short and they tend to offer bad news without much analysis. According to my research, they sensationalize the environment, but they don't really deal with scientific or social issues in any depth.

Now, compare the first draft to the student's revised version.

REVISED DRAFT

This new opening makes a claim about the media, not the writer's process. Two intriguing titles from newspaper articles will get readers' attention.

The subject of "environmental health" is a more focused topic than the general issue of poor media coverage.

The media, more often than not, bear bad news about the environment. Headlines like, "Hermaphrodite Frogs Found in Suburban Ponds" or "High Rice Cost Creating Fears of Asia Unrest" are commonplace in today's press. Tragic, discouraging reports have become so standard that most readers simply brush them off as just another catastrophic headline. It is not always mentioned, but environmental health is usually at the root of these disastrous stories. For two weeks, I followed the *New York Times*, keeping a record of all the stories either directly or indirectly related to the environment. At first, I had my doubts about finding many articles, since despite its great importance, environmental health frequently does not receive the attention it deserves. As I began collecting stories, I did find articles related to environmental issues, although in most,

The writer tells us about her process after she introduces her topic.

Her new thesis focuses on the fact that the newspaper doesn't offer enough "in-depth" coverage, rather than suggesting it doesn't offer any at all.

the environment was not the primary focus. I continued to follow the *Times* after I stopped collecting articles, and noticed that as Earth Day approached, more pieces were about environmental issues. This trend culminated in the *New York Times Magazine* "Green Issue," released on Earth Day. The bulk of the magazine focused on innovative green technologies (virtually all of which have yet to break into the mainstream) and possible strategies for reducing human impact on the planet. The magazine was informative and interesting, but it is unfortunate that the environment receives that kind of in-depth news coverage only once a year.

Notice that many of the writer's ideas are represented in her first draft, but that the writing is dry and lacks detail. When she revises, she adds new details that add complexity to her argument. The result is a new thesis. She started out arguing that the *New York Times*'s coverage of the environment lacked depth; upon revision, she makes a subtler and more truthful claim: "it is unfortunate that the environment receives that kind of in-depth news coverage only once a year." In the process, her writing became livelier and more engaging. She achieved two important goals, improving both her sentence-level prose and her general argument.

Editing

Be sure to save time for editing. If revision means rethinking a piece of writing, editing means polishing it so that it's ready for an audience. Editing means looking closely at sentences and at formatting. It means eliminating typos and misspellings, yes, but it also means carefully considering your phrasing to determine whether sentences actually say what you mean them to say.

As with revising, it may be useful to get help from other people when you edit. Others will spot your typos, misspellings, and clunky phrases more readily than you will. By the time you're ready to edit, you've been working with these words so long they can start to seem almost invisible to you. You might ask someone to read your nearly finished draft with a colored pen or pencil in hand, circling or marking any problem spots. If you do this yourself, either imagine that you're another person reading your writing or read your piece out loud. This can help you become aware of problems you might miss otherwise.

Either way, it's important to imagine a reader when you edit. Clunky writing—writing that doesn't quite express your ideas or that expresses them awkwardly—will confuse readers, slow them down, and make them skeptical about your authority as a writer. When you edit, aim to communicate clearly and directly. Pay attention to the details. A worthy goal is to make the hard work of writing appear effortless to readers. That's an illusion, of course, but one that readers appreciate.

Your Process

Most writers develop their process through trial and error—experimenting until they find a sequence of stages that works for them. You should do the same. Remember, nearly every writer engages in a process of developing ideas, drafting, and revision. The professional journalist will receive feedback from an editor; the playwright will workshop a play and revise based on feedback from audiences and producers; the trial attorney will rehearse a closing statement with colleagues until it's just right. Good writing—writing readers want to read—is almost always the product of a long process. Great writers often make writing look easy, but that's because their readers are seeing only the product of a generally labor-intensive process.

To grapple with the hard work of writing, authors tend to form communities, often in the form of writing groups or online discussion groups or blogs. It's valuable to step away from a piece of writing—share it with peers, get feedback, engage in some social interaction—before returning to the sometimes lonely confrontation with the words on the page. Think of your instructor and the other students in the class as such a community. Don't worry if the writing sometimes feels difficult—that's part of the process. Instead of worrying, talk to your peers or your instructor about the process. Such a conversation will almost always be about your ideas or the process of developing your ideas. In many cases, you'll solve a problem or achieve a breakthrough just by talking. Then you'll be ready to go back to the words on the page and revise.

Writing across the Curriculum

After this course, as you travel through your college's curriculum, you will be asked to write in a variety of forms and with a variety of styles suitable for one discipline or another. In some sense, you'll need to learn to write anew for each of those specific contexts. Many of the methods you learn, practice, and develop in this course will be helpful in those courses, but many of them will also need to be adapted or revised to work in the new context. This book is intended to introduce you to accessible examples of writing from the major disciplines—forms you'll repeatedly encounter as you continue through college.

While the academic disciplines do overlap, they also involve specialized language and ways of thinking. In the sciences, generally, the quest is for facts that are demonstrable through some kind of experimental research. Once an experiment produces consistent results through observation, the results receive attention from other scientists and the public, which influences future research and public policy. Therefore, it makes sense for the facts to be discovered first and then written up. In the humanities, however, the idea is less distinguishable from the sentence in and by which it is formed, so research blends more with writing. Writers in the social sciences tend to bridge the approaches common in the sciences and the humanities. Some social scientists work with quantitative data, some with qualitative analysis, and some with a combination of the two. In your college course work, you'll find that some instructors will ask you to gather all your data and then "write it up," while others will ask you to use writing as a process of discovery, refining your ideas—and often gathering new evidence through research—throughout that process.

In your writing for class assignments and the world beyond, be aware that the rules of the game will vary somewhat—sometimes quite a lot—from one field to another. An audience familiar with the rules of computer science will have different expectations from one familiar with the rules of art history or sociology or gender studies. As you read and write in various disciplines, you'll develop the agility to move from one to another, anticipating the expectations of your readers. The goal is to become a flexible writer, comfortable with a variety of contexts, disciplines, and rhetorical modes.

The Modes Explained

Reflecting, reporting, explaining, and arguing, or modes of writing, as we suggested earlier, can describe a wide range of texts in all of the academic disciplines. Literary writers tend to be associated with reflecting, historians with reporting, scientists with explaining, and political scientists with arguing. But that's far from the whole story. A scientist like Oliver Sacks (p. 446) devotes considerable portions of his writing to reflecting on the lives of his patients; a literary writer like Marjane Satrapi (p. 184) uses the tools of graphic narrative to report, in a distinctive way, on life in Iran under the Islamic Republic; and so on.

In this section we will survey writing in each of the four modes, always with an eye toward helping you read them effectively, understand the techniques and rhetoric associated with them, and experiment with employing their strategies in your own writing.

Reflecting

The "reflecting" essays in this reader focus on disparate topics — for example, a slave's experience learning to read and write, an illegal immigrant's struggle to both succeed and stay hidden, and the nature of the universe. Reflective writing relies heavily on personal experience and memory, treating them as sources of knowledge and understanding. We recount memories to make sense of them for ourselves and for others. Reflective writers do this publicly for an audience interested in reading about the lives and memories of others, often as a way of reflecting on their own experience as well.

George Orwell's "Shooting an Elephant" (p. 229) is a good example of an essay in which the writer reflects on a personal experience in a way that invites readers to think about its larger implications. In the following passage, which comes from the third paragraph of the essay, Orwell presents himself in a reflective frame of mind:

> One day something happened which in a roundabout way was enlightening. It was a tiny incident in itself, but it gave me a better glimpse than I had had before of the real nature of imperialism — the real motives for which despotic governments act. Early one morning the sub-inspector at a police station at the other end of the town rang me up on the phone and said that an elephant was ravaging the bazaar. Would I please come and do something about it? I did not know what I could do, but I wanted to see what was happening, and I got on to a pony and started out.

In the opening sentence, Orwell looks back to an enlightening event, and in the second sentence, he gets more specific by letting us know that this single incident gave him new insight into "the real nature of imperialism." Having announced the general significance of this event, he begins to narrate its particulars, recalling what happened that day: the phone call informing him that an elephant was loose in the marketplace; the request that he, as a police officer, do something about it; and his journey to the scene.

This alternation between recalling things and commenting on their significance is typical of the reflective writing in this reader. In some cases, however, the event reflected on is not confined to a single time and place. It might involve a more general condition sustained over weeks or even years. Sometimes, too, the element of personal experience is crucial as the writer addresses a larger topic. In "The Corner of the Eye" (p. 000), for example, physician Lewis Thomas reflects on the relationship among human beings, the planet earth, and the cosmos: "The overwhelming astonishment, the queerest structure we know about so far in the whole universe, the greatest of all cosmological scientific puzzles, confounding all our efforts to comprehend it, is the earth." Thomas's reflections go on to articulate his implicit argument: If we spend too much time looking straight ahead, we will miss out on some of life's greatest pleasures and overlook some of the universe's greatest puzzles. In the course of this reflection, Thomas invokes faint stars, Bach, artificial intelligence, language, metaphors, and the big bang, making his discussion more philosophical than personal. Nonetheless, it is reflective in the classic sense of *looking back*. While Orwell looks back on his personal history, Thomas surveys the history of the universe and human attempts to understand it.

Whether the subject of reflective writing is a dramatic moment in one's own life or the history of the universe, it tends to involve memory. In Orwell's essay it's personal memory, and in Thomas's case, it's historical memory. Reflective writing also tends to involve examining something particular (such as the shooting of an elephant or a Bach fugue) for the purpose of drawing broader conclusions—often personal, ethical, or philosophical ones. As a reader of reflective writing, you should always be attentive to the details of a writer's recollected experience as well as to the ways they illuminate the broader questions the writer is exploring. And in your own reflective writing, you should make sure that you convey both dimensions of your experience—what happened, and what the events enabled you to understand.

WRITING REFLECTIVE ESSAYS

A reflective essay is usually composed of a combination of the following elements:

- a detailed account of past experiences or events (personal, historical, or cultural)
- observations about the larger significance of these experiences or events
- a narration of how the writer either came to understand that significance or was somehow changed by the experiences or events in question

You should include these elements in your own reflective writing; just remember, however, that while they may sound relatively straightforward, they can be employed and combined in a variety of unexpected ways. Orwell and Thomas, for example, combine these elements with very different results. Still other essays included in this reader—for example, Frederick Douglass's "Learning to Read and Write" (p. 67) uses a series of events to make a statement about slavery and freedom—show how these elements can produce a range of results depending on the writer's subject, tone, evidence, and structure.

Your own memory and experience will be your primary source for much reflective writing. But once you have recalled something in detail and made sense of it for yourself, you are still faced with the problem of how to present it to readers in a way that will catch their attention, keep them reading, and invite them to reflect. Given that your readers are probably not familiar with your experience, you must select and organize your material so that you provide a readable account of it. Writing about an experience is different from remembering one. You can think of yourself as a tour guide, leading readers through an archive or a museum of your own experience. Your *point of view*—the physical and mental standpoint from which you tell your story—is crucial in reflective writing. Tell a story that will get readers to pay attention to the details—and emphasize the uniqueness of your reflection about the significance of those details. When you expand your story to include more detail, you will probably also begin to uncover subtleties of understanding that you might otherwise have missed.

As you organize your thoughts, your chosen subject will suggest ways of presenting itself clearly and meaningfully. If your reflections are focused on a single event, you will probably want to write a straightforward narrative, telling your readers what happened in a relatively direct way. Though you cover the event from beginning to end, your narrative should emphasize the details that you consider most striking and significant. In "Shooting an Elephant" (p. 229), Orwell devotes the largest segment of his piece to covering the brief instant when he finds himself on the verge of having to shoot the elephant despite his strong desire not to do so. In fact, he devotes one-third of the essay to those few moments of inner conflict because they bring about one of his major insights— "that when the white man turns tyrant it is his own freedom that he destroys." In writing about a memorable event of your own, you could make your story build similarly toward some kind of climax or surprise or decisive incident, which leads to a moment of insight upon which you would want to focus.

If your reflections center on a particular person, you might want to emphasize description as much as narrative, offering a portrait of this person that reveals his or her character in a variety of contexts or situations. Though you may rely heavily on narration, you will not be able to cover incidents in as much detail as if you were focusing on a single event. Instead, you should isolate the most striking details from each incident you choose to recall.

If your reflections are focused on a particular problem or issue, you may need to combine narration, description, and explanation, bringing together your recollections of numerous events and persons to reveal the nature of the problem. You might survey the problem chronologically from beginning to end, or you might begin with a high point and circle around it, developing its context as you explore your understanding of that experience.

Whatever the subject of your reflection, it's a good idea to devote at least a couple of paragraphs to stepping back and drawing broad conclusions from the details you've been narrating, describing, or explaining. You may also want to tell the story of how you came to understand these conclusions yourself. Paragraphs of this type often come toward the end of a reflective essay (whereas in an argumentative essay, they tend to come near the beginning). Nevertheless, there is no formula for reflective writing. The important things to consider are how you'll reveal connections between the particular and the general, how you'll use details to get readers invested in your reflections, and how you'll illuminate the subject at hand by drawing conclusions that will surprise readers. In a reflection, the uniqueness of the writer's perspective is fundamental. You will enlighten readers by offering them a glimpse of your experience and showing them how it led you to see the world in a strikingly new way.

Reporting

The "reporting" selections in this reader include a teacher describing the troubled backgrounds of the prisoners she instructs, a brain surgeon detailing the progress of a delicate operation, and a historian offering an account of the plague that swept through medieval Europe. Informative writing is basic to every field of endeavor. A reportorial writer organizes and synthesizes material drawn from various sources: interviews, articles, books, public records, and firsthand observation. Working from such varied sources, the reportorial writers represented here all provide detailed accounts of their subjects.

Though reporting depends on a careful gathering of information, it is by no means a mechanical and routine activity consisting simply of getting some facts and writing them down. Whereas reflective writing emphasizes *point of view*, newspaper editors and criminal investigators often say that they want "just the facts"—yet they know that the facts are substantially shaped by the point of view of the observer or investigator. Every writer stands at a particular point in space and time, as well as in thought and feeling. Where we stand will shape the tone in which we write, direct the choices we make about what to include, and even determine how we perceive the subject we're writing about.

A reporter's point of view often goes unnoticed, but as a student of writing, you will learn a great deal by training yourself to notice the clues that help you see how a writer's perspective shapes his or her take on a given topic. See the next page for three frames from Marjane Satrapi's "The Veil" (p. 184), the story of Iran's Islamic revolution told from the perspective of a child.

Satrapi's written text begins with a simple statement: "In 1979 a revolution took place. It was later called 'the Islamic Revolution.'" The image in the first frame depicts the revolution through an image of men and women, dressed in simple black clothing, their fists raised. The starkness and simplicity of this image might well be understood to represent a child's-eye view of a complex sociohistorical event. A child might well notice the drama, anger, and collective force of a revolution without understanding its ideology or social implications. But in the next frame, Satrapi switches gears. We follow her to school, in 1980, "the

From Marjane Satrapi's "The Veil"

year it became obligatory to wear the veil." The faces of the children in the second frame seem curious, perhaps perplexed, or even fearful. The obligatory veil is something new, and the girls aren't sure what to make of it. In the third frame, they are learning what to make of it. Satrapi depicts several girls putting the veil to unexpected uses: as a jump rope, a set of reins, and a disguise, for example. She depicts herself and her peers as playful rebels. They may not understand the causes or the results of their country's revolution, but they are resisting its new rules. This is a report, but it's a highly personalized one, based on the experience of a child and told using the tools of the adult graphic novelist she would become.

Of course, a graphic novel is a particularly distinctive—and even unexpected—form to use for reportorial writing. Perhaps the most common forms of reporting belong to the journalist and the historian, two kinds of writers often thought of as objective observers of events or facts. In "Nickel and Dimed: On (Not) Getting By in America" (p. 243), journalist and activist Barbara Ehrenreich reports on an experiment—or mission—she undertook. She decided to leave her life behind and "plunge into the low-wage workforce." Her goal was to find out how 30 percent of Americans manage to live on very low wages. Like all reporters, Ehrenreich needed to do her research, interview people, and collect data from a variety of sources. However, Ehrenreich took a radical approach to collecting data: She became a member of the workforce she was interested in writing about. She worked as a waitress and a house cleaner—among other things—and discovered for herself just how difficult it was to survive on the wages she earned. She describes her endeavor as "a purely objective, scientific sort of mission," appropriate to the purpose of her ambitious project. However, she also recounts her surprise that "despite the scientific detachment I am doing my best to maintain, I care." Despite her goal of objectivity as an investigative journalist, Ehrenreich's method got her personally involved with her subject. Thus, Ehrenreich builds reflection and her own point of view into her reporting.

Historian Barbara Tuchman's report on the bubonic plague in medieval Europe is perhaps a more traditional example of reportorial writing. But even this historical account is shaped by its writer's perspective. Tuchman is known for her careful research and lively writing. In "'This Is the End of the World': The Black Death" (p. 257), Tuchman's perspective on the plague is both detailed and gripping. While the essay itself doesn't reveal much about its writer, its accessible tone and suspenseful structure are likely shaped by her experience as a teacher, historian, and writer. Tuchman knows how to hook her audience, as you can see from the graphic details in her first sentence: "In October 1347, two months after the fall of Calais, Genoese trading ships put into the harbor of Messina in Sicily with dead and dying men at the oars." Tuchman transports readers to a distant time—an October over 660 years ago—and invites us to witness a shocking event: ships pulling into a harbor manned by ghoulish crews. If you keep reading, you'll learn that this event turned out to be an early indication of a devastating plague that would kill between one-third and two-thirds of Europe's population. Far from being a dry account of dates and names, Tuchman's report on the plague balances specificity and narration to get readers involved in her story. From her perspective as a teacher and writer, she knows that it's her job to get her audience invested in her report.

The purpose of reporting is in one sense straightforward and self-evident. Whether it involves a firsthand account of some recent happening or the documented record of a long-past sequence of events, reportorial writing informs readers about various subjects that may interest them but that they cannot possibly observe on their own. As you can see from the examples above, writers use reporting for a combination of purposes—to provide information; to convey their attitudes, beliefs, or ideas about that information; and to influence the views of their readers. This range of purposes is not surprising. Whenever we make a report, we do so because we believe that the subject is important enough to share with others. And presumably we believe the subject to be important because of what we have come to know and think about it. So when we are faced with deciding what information to report and how to report it, we inevitably base our decisions on these ideas. At every point in the process of planning and writing a report, we act on the basis of our particular priorities for conveying information about the subject.

WRITING REPORTORIAL ESSAYS

A reportorial essay tends to involve the following elements:

- information gathered through observation, interviews, or research
- an introduction or overview of that information
- a detailed discussion of some of that information
- a detailed analysis or reflection on that information

When you write your own reportorial essays, you'll need to strike a balance between shaping your material in ways that will get readers interested or engaged and letting the details speak for themselves. It may help to take a cue from the writers in this reader. Notice how Satrapi, Ehrenreich, and Tuchman combine the various elements of a report and strike this balance in their own ways.

Your choice of topic and your motives for writing about it will usually guide you as you write a report. The material you write about is likely to shape the choices you make about the tone, structure, and contents of your essay. If the information concerns a single event or covers a set of events spread over time, the most effective method is probably narration—that is, telling a story in a more or less chronological order, as Ehrenreich does. If your assignment were to synthesize what is known, up to that moment, about a complex public event, you would need to look at a wider series of events, as Tuchman does. If your assignment is to report on firsthand experience, you might adopt a stance that emphasizes your perspective at the time of the events in question, as Satrapi does.

Once you have settled on a basic form, you should then devise a way of selecting and arranging your information to achieve your purposes effectively. You will need to review all the material you have gathered to determine what you consider to be the most important information to report. Some bits or kinds of information will strike you as more significant than others, and these are the ones that you should feature. Likewise, you will probably find that some information is simply not important enough to be mentioned. To help achieve your purposes, you should also give special thought to the perspective from which you will present your information to the reader. Do you want to present the material in the first or the third person? Do you want to be present in the piece, as Satrapi and Ehrenreich are? Or do you want to be invisible, like Tuchman? Your answer to these questions will depend, to some extent, on whether you gathered the information through your own firsthand observations and want to convey your own reactions to them. Look, for example, at "A Delicate Operation" by Roy C. Selby Jr. (p. 529). Although Selby must have written this piece on the basis of firsthand experience, he tells the story in the third person, removing himself almost completely from it except for such distant-sounding references to himself as "the surgeon." Selby is critically important to the information in this report, yet he decided to de-emphasize his presence so as to focus our attention on the operation itself.

Your challenge will be to report on your "data"—the materials you have gathered on your topic—in a way that gets readers involved and offers enough details to help readers understand the data fully. To do this, you might draw on some of the other modes of writing. For example, some reflecting might help you make sense of your data or your relationship to it (as in Ehrenreich's case), or some explaining might help readers understand the complexity of your data (as in Tuchman's case). In reportorial writing, perspective shouldn't dominate. It may enliven the writing and shape the choices you make, but it shouldn't interfere with the careful reporting of details. Your job, as reporter, is to synthesize details and deliver them to readers in a form that illuminates your subject.

Explaining

The "explaining" essays we've collected in this reader are written by specialists who aim to help nonspecialists understand phenomena as various as the origin of the universe, the significance of urban legends, differences between generations, and the nature of altruism. Explanation is an essential kind of writing in every academic field and profession. Facts, after all, do not speak for themselves; figures do not add up on their own. To make sense of a subject, we need to see it in terms of something that is related to it—the changing colors of autumn leaves in terms of light from the sun and the distribution of nutrients within a tree or the content of urban legends in terms of the immediate circumstances in which they are told.

To help us understand a subject, explanatory writers examine it in terms of some relevant context that will shed light on its origin and development, its nature and design, its elements and functions, its causes and effects, or its meaning and significance. For example, in her essay "Why Leaves Turn Color in the Fall" (p. 442), Diane Ackerman explains the phases leaves undergo as they change color:

> A turning leaf stays partly green at first, then reveals splotches of yellow and red as the chlorophyll gradually breaks down. Dark green seems to stay longest in the veins, outlining and defining them. During the summer, chlorophyll dissolves in the heat and light, but it is also being steadily replaced. In the fall, on the other hand, no new pigment is produced, and so we notice the other colors that were always there, right in the leaf, although chlorophyll's shocking green hid them from view. With their camouflage gone, we see these colors for the first time all year, and marvel, but they were always hidden there, hidden like a vivid secret beneath the hot glowing greens of summer.

Ackerman's purpose here is to explain how and why leaves change color, and beginning in her opening sentence, she offers relevant information about the process. Her careful attention to detail gives readers the information they'll need to understand her explanation. Drawing from the fields of botany and chemistry, she notes that "chlorophyll dissolves in the heat and light" of summer but is "steadily replaced," while in the fall "no new chlorophyll is produced." After explaining how and why leaves change color, Ackerman concludes that "we see these colors for the first time all year, and marvel, but they were always hidden there, hidden like a vivid secret beneath the hot glowing greens of summer." The information that Ackerman draws on from botany and chemistry allows her to offer a knowledgeable, systematic, and instructive explanation for a philosophical question: How is it that leaves *look* green in the summer if the colors of autumn leaves are in them already?

For an example of another style of explanatory writing, look at Oliver Sacks's "The Man Who Mistook His Wife for a Hat" (p. 446). Sacks, a neurologist, offers the results of a case study, which entails the close observation of an individual subject over time. Because the subject of a case study is by definition unique, the study cannot be replicated by other researchers. A case study must therefore be written in sufficient detail to document the observer's understanding of the subject and to enable other researchers to draw their own conclusions about what has been observed. This is exactly what Sacks does when he tells the story of Dr. P., a musician and painter with unusual symptoms:

> He saw all right, but what did he see? I opened out a copy of the *National Geographic* magazine and asked him to describe some pictures in it.
>
> His responses here were very curious. His eyes would dart from one thing to another, picking up tiny features, individual features, as they had done with my face. A striking brightness, a color, a shape would arrest his attention and elicit comment—but in no case did he get the scene-as-a-whole. He failed to see the whole, seeing only details, which he spotted like blips on a radar screen. He never entered into relation with the picture as a whole—never faced, so to speak, *its* physiognomy. He had no sense whatever of a landscape or scene.

It must have been obvious to Sacks that in explaining his patient's case, he needed to illustrate and demonstrate the man's symptoms. Readers need the details to understand Dr. P.'s surprising symptoms. Sacks is careful to include enough concrete evidence to be convincing. But notice also that he includes interpretive sentences toward the end of the paragraph, where he's seeking to explain Dr. P.'s puzzling behavior. Sacks's method could be accurately described as a series of detailed explanations punctuated by moments of interpretation and reflection. For readers to understand such a startling case, they need a lot of explanation and a little interpretation. That's exactly what Sacks delivers.

In Dr. P.'s paintings, Sacks sees evidence of "visual agnosia, in which all powers of representation and imagery, all sense of the concrete, all sense of reality, were being destroyed." Sacks decides to wait until nearly the end of the essay, when readers have an intimate sense of Dr. P.'s unusual symptoms, to define *visual agnosia*, his central term. His goal seems to be to ease nonspecialists into his tale before overwhelming them with medical terminology.

Once the definition is established, Sacks describes the process of uncovering the mystery behind Dr. P.'s unusual behavior. He shows, through description and dialogue with Dr. P. and his wife, the remarkable things Dr. P. can do (his extraordinary musical ability, for example) and the ordinary things he cannot do (such as recognize the faces of his wife and friends). Sacks is able to diagnose Dr. P.'s condition, but the diagnosis doesn't satisfy him. For Sacks, the diagnosis reveals the limitations of neurological and psychological explanations of what appear to be neuropsychological disorders when those sciences overlook "the judgmental, the particular, the personal." In the process, Sacks defines something larger: the limits of cognitive neurology and psychology, suggesting that they, too, may suffer from "an agnosia essentially similar to Dr. P.'s." Without some attention to the particular life of the person, the diagnosis will miss crucial details that may help the patient live a better life—which is, after all, an important goal in medicine. In this sense, Sacks's explanatory essay contains an implicit argument about the ethics and efficacy of medicine that doesn't account for the self of the patient.

Explanatory writing serves a wide range of academic, professional, and public purposes. Rules and regulations or guidelines and instructions are familiar examples of explanation that tell people how to carry out many of the practical and public activities of their lives. As you can see from comparing the essays of Ackerman and Sacks, explanations can vary widely in their forms. Textbooks—such as the one you are reading right now—as well as simplified presentations of highly specialized research (like a newspaper article that describes the results of the newest diet study) are common examples of explanatory writing that help people understand a particular body of information and ideas. Scholarly research papers, government documents, and other technical presentations of data and analysis, though less familiar to the general reader, are important kinds of explanation that advance knowledge and inform decision making. As a reader of explanations, you must be flexible in your approach, always willing to move through unfamiliar territory on the way to understanding the subject being discussed.

WRITING EXPLANATORY ESSAYS

An explanatory essay tends to combine the following elements:

- the presentation of specialized knowledge through concrete examples or evidence
- definitions of key terms
- detailed descriptions of a process, an object, or an idea
- an attempt to shed light on a concept not previously understood

In planning a piece of explanatory writing, you should review your research materials, thinking about how these materials might direct the approach you take with regard to the elements listed above. As a writer of explanations, you must keep in mind that your goal is to instruct readers and to help them understand what they didn't previously. This means you will have to choose your language and organization carefully so that your concept is clear. In every case, it is important to imagine what your readers will and won't know—and to do the careful work of appropriately defining terms, illustrating with concrete details, and demonstrating cause-and-effect relationships.

When you write an explanatory essay, you are likely to combine several methods, as Sacks does, and your approach will shape your essay's organization. Consider, for instance, the way people explain how to get somewhere. Often they'll give an overview of where the place is situated, a step-by-step set of movements to follow and places to look for, brief descriptions of prominent guideposts along the way, a review of the original directions, and possibly a remark or two about misleading spots to avoid. Similarly, when you explain something in writing, you'll want to help readers get from one place to another in a particular subject matter. As with the other modes, there is a range of explanatory writing, and writers in various fields will pick and choose from the methods of explaining we've described here. You should do the same. Let your topic and your purpose guide the choices you make, keeping in mind that your goal is to help readers without specialized knowledge understand a topic you understand more fully than they do. Your job, in short, is to explain.

Arguing

In the "arguing" selections we've included, you will find authors taking positions on numerous (and often controversial) subjects—from the benefits of television to the status of African American English, from the meaning of war photographs to the problematic measurement of human intelligence. No matter what their academic fields or professions, these writers energetically defend their positions on the issues and questions they address. Like any of us, they are especially fired up when their views are pitted against the beliefs of others. So you will find these writers are vigorously engaged in the give and take of argument. As a consequence, you will find yourself having to weigh the merits of competing positions in debates about controversial issues.

Some of the distinctive qualities of argument are clear in the following paragraphs from Martin Luther King Jr.'s "Letter from Birmingham Jail" (p. 341):

> I think I should indicate why I am here in Birmingham, since you have been influenced by the view which argues against "outsiders coming in." I have the honor of serving as president of the Southern Christian Leadership Conference, an organization operating in every southern state, with headquarters in Atlanta, Georgia. We have some eighty-five affiliated organizations across the South, and one of them is the Alabama Christian Movement for Human Rights. Frequently we share staff, educational, and financial resources with our affiliates. Several months ago the affiliate here in Birmingham asked us to be on call to engage in a nonviolent direct-action program if such were deemed necessary. We readily consented, and when the hour came we lived up to our promise. So I, along with several members of my staff, am here because I was invited here. I am here because I have organizational ties here.
>
> But more basically, I am in Birmingham because injustice is here. Just as the prophets of the eighth century BC left their villages and carried their "thus saith the Lord" far beyond the boundaries of their home towns, and just as the Apostle Paul left his village of Tarsus and carried the gospel of Jesus Christ to the far corners of the Greco-Roman world, so am I compelled to carry the gospel of freedom beyond my own home town. Like Paul, I must constantly respond to the Macedonian call for aid.

King's letter is one of the finest statements of democratic values that our country has yet produced; these are the first few paragraphs of an argument that continues for several pages. Like many arguments, King's is a response to an opposing viewpoint. In this case, eight Alabama clergymen had published a statement calling King's actions "unwise and untimely." He was also accused of being an "outside agitator." King counters that accusation immediately by outlining his affiliations with the South, with Alabama, and even with Birmingham. He has ample reason, he argues, to be "here," a word he places unhesitatingly in the first sentence of the first paragraph quoted above and then four more times in the last two sentences of that paragraph.

From this point on, King's argument expands to include larger and larger ideas about justice. "I am in Birmingham because injustice is here," he writes, opening his next paragraph by pivoting on "here," a word that becomes a rhetorical feature of the essay. Calling on biblical parallels to indicate that religious leaders are always "here," confronting need and injustice, King asserts first that all U.S. citizens have every right to converge on whatever "here" they identify as necessary. In the argument that follows, he expands on that idea. However local they may have been, the clergymen who had objected to his intervention had not been "here" at all—not with King, not on the side of justice. Nor had most white clergy or sympathetic white moderates been "here." Almost everyone had displaced King's "here" to some more distant "there," distant in time as much as in place, so much so that the "[s]hallow understanding from people of good will" distressed King almost as much as the overt antagonism of segregationist authorities.

Argumentative writing pervades our lives. We encounter it in political speeches, newspaper editorials, syndicated columns, and letters to the editor, which typically debate the pros and cons of some public issue, be it local taxes or national defense. But arguments crop up in less obvious places every day: in the many brochures, TV ads, and spam e-mails we are confronted with, urging us to vote for one candidate, support a cause, or buy a product. Argument is fundamental in the judicial process, is crucial in the legislative process, and serves the basic aims of the professional and academic worlds, testing ideas and theories by pitting them against one another. Argument is an important activity in the advancement of knowledge and society.

The broad range of argumentative writing can be understood by considering the kinds of issues and questions that typically give rise to disagreement and debate. The most basic sources of controversy are questions of fact—the who, what, when, how, and where of things. Intense arguments over questions of fact can develop in any field, especially when the facts in question have a significant bearing on a subject. Stephen Jay Gould's essay "On Women's Brains" (p. 704) is one such questioning of fact. An earlier scientist had argued that women were less intelligent than men—an assertion Gould challenges by rereading the evidence the previous researcher had offered.

Argumentative writing is possible because any two people confronted with the same set of "facts" may disagree about what they mean. There is no disputing that Paul Broca weighed more than four hundred human brains and found that male brains were, on average, noticeably weightier than female brains. But how to account for that difference is an open question that allows several possible answers; and even if those questions were to be settled, there is no verifiable correlation of brain size with intelligence. What brain size *does* correlate with reliably enough is height; taller people have larger brains than shorter people. Men tend to be taller than women, and so their brains are larger. However, the average weight difference between the male and the female brain, Gould observes, "is exactly the average difference between a 5 foot 4 inch and a 6 foot 4 inch male in Broca's data. We would not (especially us short folks) want to ascribe greater intelligence to tall men."

Beliefs and values are also the stuff of argument. In fact, arguments over values are integral to the formation of society and so determine much about how we live. Nothing illustrates that better than this well-known passage from the Declaration of Independence (p. 300):

> We hold these truths to be self-evident, that all men are created equal, that they are endowed by their Creator with certain unalienable Rights, that among these are Life, Liberty and the pursuit of Happiness. That to secure these rights, Governments are instituted among Men, deriving their just powers from the consent of the governed. That whenever any Form of Government becomes destructive of these ends, it is the Right of the People to alter or to abolish it, and to institute new Government, laying its foundation on such principles and organizing its powers in such form, as to them shall seem most likely to effect their Safety and Happiness.

In this crucial passage, Thomas Jefferson and his congressional colleagues directly challenged several fundamental assumptions about the rights of people and the sources of governmental power that were held by the British king and by many British people and others throughout the world. Only in this way was it possible for them to make the compelling case for their ultimate claim that the colonies should be "FREE AND INDEPENDENT STATES . . . Absolved from all Allegiance to the British Crown."

Though Jefferson and his colleagues did not outline a new system of government in the Declaration itself, the document illustrates the fact that conflicts over beliefs and values influence questions of policy and planning—and therefore shape the lives we are able to live. For an argument to be strong, it must be motivated by a genuine dilemma. Two people may well look at the same evidence and draw different conclusions. A strong argument takes a position—one that is plausible without being too obvious—with regard to one of these dilemmas. The good news for argumentative writers is that the world we live in offers dilemmas like these at just about every turn.

WRITING ARGUMENTATIVE ESSAYS

An argumentative essay tends to combine the following elements:

- an introduction to a conversation, debate, or controversy about facts, beliefs, or values
- an explanation of why that conversation or debate is important
- a thesis statement, made near the beginning of the essay, that demonstrates the writer's position in clear, straightforward terms

- evidence that helps the writer illustrate, support, and develop this position
- analysis of and reflection on that evidence
- the discussion (and often discrediting) of counterarguments that represent opposing points of view

When you write an argumentative essay, remember that your job is to persuade readers. To do so, your writing will need to be clear and readable, and your evidence and analysis will need to be convincing.

The statement of an argument is often called a *thesis* (or, in the sciences, a *hypothesis*). If you want to evaluate your own argument, it's a good idea to test your thesis. Ask yourself if it's *arguable.* In other words, could two reasonable people disagree about it? If an argument is too obvious—for example, "The earth orbits the sun"—then few people are likely to disagree about it. While it's worthwhile to explain how and why the earth orbits the sun, there's not much point in making an argument that it does. Then ask yourself if your thesis is *plausible.* Will it convince some readers? The argument "The earth orbits Venus" may be arguable, but it's not plausible. The trick of making a solid argument is to find the middle ground between originality and plausibility. Getting that balance right generally requires some trial and error (as does most writing).

In any piece of argumentative writing, your primary purpose is to persuade readers that your thesis deserves consideration. Some readers, of course, will agree with you in advance, but others will disagree, and still others will be undecided. In planning a piece of argumentative writing, you should begin by examining your material with an eye toward discovering the issues that have to be addressed and the points that have to be made to present your case persuasively, especially to readers who oppose your position or who are undecided. This means that you will have to deal not only with issues that you consider relevant but also with matters that have been raised by your opponents. In other words, you need to consider plausible *counterarguments* and show readers that you have considered all sides of the controversy, as King does right from the start by confronting the issue of "outside agitators" rather than ignoring it.

After you have identified the crucial points to be addressed, you will need to make a convincing case with respect to each of the points. Some methods for doing so are important no matter what point you are trying to prove. Every argument requires evidence. Sometimes this basic concern for providing readers with appropriate evidence will lead you into the activity of reporting. In his attempt to demonstrate the right of the colonies "to throw off such Government," Jefferson provides a lengthy and detailed list of "injuries" that the king of Great Britain inflicted on the colonies. Often evidence also requires some explaining. Gould, for example, explains several possible reasons for the size discrepancy between the male and female brain. Height is one possible reason. Another is the probable manner of death. Prolonged illness will wither a brain and reduce its size, and women—especially in the mid-nineteenth century, when Broca worked—were more likely than men to die at advanced ages of lingering illnesses. Sometimes personal reflection becomes its own kind of evidence, as in King's reflections on how and why he came to Birmingham. In other words, the lessons you learn writing in the other three modes will come in handy when you are ready to discuss the evidence for an argument.

Evidence alone will not be persuasive to readers. It's the writer's job to analyze evidence in ways that show *how* it supports or illustrates an argument. For example, having made the general claim that "a long train of abuses" entitles people "to throw off such Government," and having cited a long list of abuses that Great Britain had inflicted on the colonies, Jefferson concludes that the colonies "are Absolved from all Allegiance to the British Crown." Because he has analyzed his evidence so effectively, his conclusion is convincing enough to shape our thinking more than two centuries after he wrote it. But that doesn't mean everybody would agree with Jefferson. Great Britain did not accept Jefferson's premises, so it did not accept his conclusions, logical though they were. Other countries of the time took a different view of the matter. The most common reaction to an argument we dislike is to challenge the premises on which it is founded. Many today would take issue with some of Jefferson's premises—for example, the fact that some citizens were defined as more "equal" than others. Keep the possibility of disagreement in mind when you write—as well as when you read. It's likely that you'll disagree with arguments made by writers represented in this reader. Take the opportunity to examine the premises of these arguments, and pay attention to the rhetorical moves the argumentative writers make. This will help you make your own arguments in response to theirs.

When you write an argumentative essay, you are taking part in a conversation on a subject about which people are likely to disagree. In Jefferson's and King's declarations of democratic principles, and in other selections in this reader, you will see how different writers use the various resources of language to produce some very striking and compelling arguments. You will learn from these essays just by reading them. It's likely that the strategies these writers use will creep into your writing without your even realizing it. At the same time, it can be helpful to study their strategies so that you'll both be able to identify the premises of a writer's argument and recognize when a writer invokes a counterargument or uses personal reflection as evidence. The more you recognize rhetorical elements like these in the writing of others, the easier it will become to experiment with them in your own writing.

Reflecting, Reporting, Explaining, Arguing

A central premise of this book is that writers learn by reading good writing. You can learn a great deal about your own writing by reading *as a writer.* Whatever modes they write in, the writers included here demonstrate a range of successful techniques for conceiving a writing project, engaging an audience, and exploring ideas. Notice how writers invent their own strategies, putting their own stamp on the modes in which they write. Notice how the modes sometimes overlap, or how the methods of one may help accomplish the goals of another. Great writing is inventive and dynamic on the one hand, and composed of time-tested techniques on the other. You'll want to learn from these techniques; do some experimenting of your own, and strive to become a flexible writer, able to adapt to a wide range of writing modes and contexts. The reading questions, classroom activities, and writing assignments that accompany the readings are designed to get you actively engaged in the process of reading the way writers do, responding with ideas of your own, writing in a variety of modes, and using a variety of techniques. As we mentioned earlier, you will continue the process of becoming a writer throughout college—and, beyond that, in your chosen profession. Learning to write is a continuous process—one that's never completely finished. We hope that this course and this book will be an important step in your process.

Researching to Write

Research can take a variety of forms: browsing through a bookstore or the Internet, interviewing people, scrolling through notes, or using research databases—just to name a few. How much and what kind of research is needed will be determined by the question at the heart of a writer's inquiry and his or her goals for the writing project.

Many of the readings contained in this book—especially the paired readings and casebooks—will provoke you to ask questions whose answers will require some research. In this section, we will offer you resources and advice for making the research process—no matter what the project—manageable and productive. You will learn to develop a research question, use the Internet (including search engines, library databases, and newspapers and magazines) effectively, evaluate sources, and organize your ideas and materials.

We will also offer strategies for writing as well as guidelines for documenting your work, such as how to incorporate quotations, paraphrase sources, document sources, and format a Works Cited list (MLA) or a Reference list (APA).

Developing a Research Question

A strong research question is one that can't be answered off the top of your head, or with a quick look at an encyclopedia or a dictionary. It can be adequately answered in a single assignment or semester. For example, the question "Where was Thomas Jefferson educated?" is probably too narrow, whereas "What were the many accomplishments of Jefferson's presidency?" is probably too ambitious. A more productive and manageable question lies somewhere in the middle—for example, "How did Thomas Jefferson's education influence some of his most important decisions as president?"

A question such as this contains a blueprint for the kinds of research you'll conduct to answer it. You'll need to know where Jefferson went to school and something about what he learned there. You'll also need to know something about the major decisions Jefferson had to make during his presidency. Biographies can help with both questions, but they may not be enough. You may need to find books and articles by historians about the period when Jefferson was president and some of the major political issues of that time. Then you'll need to choose two or three decisions and learn more about these, again probably from books and articles by historians.

Throughout the process, you'll need to evaluate your topic. Is it too narrow? Is it too broad? You might decide that it makes the most sense to narrow the topic to a single decision Jefferson had to make—perhaps a particularly tough decision. This would make it easier to answer your question, and it would ensure that the question is a significant one, since tough decisions are generally more interesting and important than easy ones. In short, be open to letting your topic and your question evolve as you learn more about it.

Using the Internet Effectively

Whatever your topic or question, a Web search is probably going to be your first step. Of course, the Web contains vast collections of information and data on a multitude of topics. Although some of this information is useful and reliable, some of it is misleading or downright false. While the Internet itself is not organized to help you sort out what's useful and what's misleading, some of the tools you'll use to navigate it are. It's a good idea to be aware of the various tools available and to understand how they'll help you find different kinds of sources.

RESEARCH TOOLS

- **Search engines** like Google and Yahoo! organize information based on how frequently sites on a given subject are visited. So, a search for *"Thomas Jefferson"* will bring up Web sites containing Jefferson's name. Most of these won't help you much if you're researching how Jefferson's education might have influenced an important decision he had to make. If you add a search term and try *"Thomas Jefferson"* and *education*, you'll get closer. (Note that quotation marks around a multiword search term will look for Web sites in which those words appear in the exact order you've indicated.) You might also try *"Thomas Jefferson"* and *presidency*; *"Thomas Jefferson"* and *influential decisions*; or *"Thomas Jefferson"* and *important decisions*. You will get a lot of hits with any of these searches, but it will be up to you to sort out what's reliable or valuable and what's not. (See "Evaluating Sources" on the following page.)
- **Google Scholar** is a specialized search engine that surveys academic publications. Your hits will most likely be written by professional historians or writers associated with a college or university. You will still get more information than you need, and most of it won't address your research question directly. Therefore, you'll have to use your judgment in choosing sources that will help you understand—and write about—your topic.
- **Library databases** are even more specialized, since most academic disciplines have developed particular databases to serve their needs. Your school's library most likely has subscriptions to several of them. There are also databases, such as Lexis/Nexis, that search articles from newspapers and magazines. Consult your instructor or a librarian about which databases might help you find what you're looking for. In many cases, the full text of articles that appear in your search will be available online, but you may have to seek out the print archives in your school or local library for some harder-to-find pieces.
- **Newspapers and magazines** very often have their own Web archive, and it's often a good idea to go straight to it. You can find the publication's

title through a conventional search engine—for example, by typing *"The Washington Post"* or *"The Economist"* into Google. If the publication has its own Web site, it will usually be one of the first few hits you get. Most of these archives are searchable. To read full articles from these archives, you may have to pay a fee; before doing so check with your school's librarian, as many universities have access to online archives or print collections of major publications.

Evaluating Sources

A good source is both useful and reliable. If you're looking for information on Thomas Jefferson's education, and come across an article from an academic journal discussing his ideas on architecture, the information is reliable but probably not useful. In contrast, a Web site with a bias—for example, one that uses Jefferson's educational theories to promote home schooling or one that cites his ownership of slaves to defend the institution of slavery—might seem useful, but is probably not reliable. Yet another potential source, the Web site of Jefferson's alma mater, the College of William and Mary, contains some interesting information about his education. Of course, the college is probably using Jefferson's time there to promote itself, so while its Web site may be a valuable source of information by itself, it won't be enough for your purposes. A thorough research project would need to compare the information from a site meant to promote an institution or person against accounts offered in other sources that offer different perspectives.

There are some questions you can ask yourself about any given source that will help you evaluate it:

- What questions is the source asking? How do these questions overlap with my own questions?
- Is the source affiliated with an organization? If so, is the organization reliable? Is it likely to have a bias or special interest in the subject?
- Is the source authored by an individual? If so, who is it? What is the author's background? What are the author's credentials? Is it likely that the author has a bias or special interest in the subject?
- If the source is a Web site, what is the suffix? Is it .com, .org, .net, or .edu? What does that suffix tell you about the source?
- What role might the source play in the essay you're developing? Would you quote it directly, consult it for background information, or incorporate facts or data that it offers?

These questions will help you form judgments about the sources you find. Ask them—and keep asking them—throughout the evaluation process. It's a good idea to keep notes on these questions for each source, either on index cards or in a file on your computer. As your research develops, it's likely that your own interest and point of view regarding the reliability and usefulness of certain sources will evolve. The important thing is to ask the questions and use your judgment. If you're not sure about your own judgment, ask someone you trust—a friend or classmate, an instructor, a librarian—to take a look at your source, and discuss some of the questions above.

Organizing Your Ideas and Materials

Once you are confident about your research question and you've gathered most of your evidence, you might want to sketch your essay. An essay sketch is looser and more flexible than an outline, but it also represents your ideas in more detail. It's a good idea to make one before you write a draft, as it will help you sort out your ideas and serve as a blueprint for writing.

The essay sketch that follows represents the thinking and organizing for a student essay featured later in this section, "All the News That's Fit to Print?" by Margaret Donaldson (p. 45). You might use this format to sketch your essay, or modify it to suit your own needs.

What is your topic?

Coverage of environmental issues in the *New York Times.*

What is your research question?

How thorough is the *New York Times*'s coverage of environmental issues during a single week? How representative is this of press coverage of the environment more generally?

What's your best guess about how you'll answer your research question? (The answer will be your preliminary thesis, or hypothesis.)

I propose that examining every page of the *New York Times* for a single week and looking for articles on environmental issues will reveal that the paper pays lip service to environmental issues but does not address the crisis with enough thoroughness or substance. This lack of thoroughness and substance is representative of mainstream press coverage of the environment.

List several pieces of evidence you may use in your essay, including the *names of your sources, relevant citation information (or page numbers),* and, where appropriate, *notes on the role those sources might play in your essay.* (You may want to include the actual quotations.)

- Four front-page articles printed during the week in question: (1) March 28, 2008: "Harlem to Antarctica for Science, and for Pupils," by Sara Rimer; (2) March 29, 2008: "High Rice Cost Creating Fears of Asia Unrest," by Keith

Bradsher; (3) March 31, 2008: "As Jobs Vanish and Prices Rise, Food Stamp Use Nears Record," by Erik Eckholm; (4) April 8, 2008: "$8 Traffic Fee for Manhattan Gets Nowhere," by Nicholas Confessore.

- Felicity Barringer, "Group Seeks E.P.A. Rules on Emissions from Vehicles." Note: This will be helpful in a discussion of articles on state-level responses to environmental problems.
- Diane Cardwell, "Faster, Maybe. Cheaper, No. But Driving Has Its Fans": "Despite the threat of traffic jams, honking horns, and the urban version of road rage, these New Yorkers choose to drive, whether to shave time off their commutes, run their errands with less hassle, or have a few moments to themselves inside mobile oases." Note: This article will be helpful in showing the paper's strengths in covering environmental issues, because it is critical of the choice to commute by car in a city with plenty of mass transit.
- Jennifer Conlin, "Going Green in the Blue Mountains." Note: This article is typical of much of the paper's coverage. Ironically, it encourages extravagance while paying lip service to environmentalism.

Write a draft of your introduction.

For two weeks, I followed the *New York Times,* keeping a record of all the stories either directly or indirectly related to the environment. I had my doubts about finding many articles, since despite its great importance, environmental health frequently does not receive the attention it deserves. As I began collecting stories, I did find articles related to environmental issues, although in most, the environment was not the primary focus. I continued to follow the *Times* after I stopped collecting articles, and noticed that as Earth Day approached, more pieces were published about environmental issues. This trend culminated in the *New York Times Magazine* "Green Issue," released on Earth Day. The bulk of the magazine focused on innovative green technologies (virtually all of which have yet to break into the mainstream) and possible strategies for reducing human impact on the planet. The magazine was informative and interesting, but it is unfortunate that the environment receives that kind of in-depth news coverage only once a year.

Incorporating Quotations

For most research essays, you will want to quote many of your sources directly. Choose your quotations carefully. Be sure they help you advance your discussion of your research question and that they say something you could not say more effectively in your own words. Also, be sure to integrate the quotations. You want to make sure it's clear why you've included them. Following a few simple guidelines will help you do so:

- Always introduce quotations with a signal phrase or sentence that gives readers the information they need to understand what the source is.
- Always include a citation, formatted according to the guidelines of the citation style you're using for the essay. (Later in this section, we discuss MLA and APA style. See "Documenting Sources" below.)
- Always follow up a quotation with some discussion or analysis that makes it clear to readers how the quotation relates to the discussion at hand.

Paraphrasing Sources

It sometimes makes more sense to paraphrase a source rather than to quote it directly. In fact, in some academic fields, this is very common. In the social sciences, for example, presenting a piece of information or data from a source is often more important than quoting direct language (whereas in the humanities, it's often crucial to quote the language of a source). Paraphrasing can also help you make a complex or difficult source more accessible to readers.

When you paraphrase, it's important that you represent your source accurately.

- Be sure you read and reread the source until you are confident of its meaning.
- Convey that meaning in your own words. Be sure to cite the source, just as you would if you were quoting it. (See "Documenting Sources," below.)
- Introduce your source and offer some discussion or analysis that links it to the general project of your essay—again, just as you would do when quoting a source directly.

Documenting Sources

Writers document their sources to let readers know where they found their information. This not only reassures readers that the source is trustworthy but also gives them the opportunity to find that source for themselves if it sparks their interest. You will almost surely be asked to use a variety of citation "styles" in the various courses that you take in college. The most common styles include those promoted by the Modern Language Association (MLA), the American Psychological Association (APA), and *The Chicago Manual of Style* (*Chicago*). We offer guidelines for MLA and APA style documentation here. Be sure to check with your professors about what style they prefer. (It's a good idea to own a good writing manual or handbook that includes detailed information about all three of the major documentation styles.)

MLA Style

Documentation in MLA style consists of two interrelated components — in-text citations and a list of Works Cited.

In-text Citations

The in-text citations in an MLA-style research paper point interested readers to the list of Works Cited at the end of the paper. There are several types of parenthetical citations you can use to accomplish this goal.

PARENTHETICAL CITATIONS

A *parenthetical citation* is just what it sounds like: a citation, in parentheses, that tells readers a little about your source. If you introduce your source with a signal phrase that includes the author's name, then in most cases all you need in parentheses is a page number. For example:

> Pollan writes, "For us to wait for legislation or technology to solve the problem of how we're living our lives suggests we're not really serious about changing—something our politicians can't fail to notice. They will not move until we do" (19).

If the example above did not include the author's name in the signal phrase, then it would require his name in the citation. For example:

> An argument can be made that "for us to wait for legislation or technology to solve the problem of how we're living our lives suggests we're not really serious about changing—something our politicians can't fail to notice. They will not move until we do" (Pollan 19).

In short, most parenthetical citations include either just a page number or an author's last name and a page number. That's because the parenthetical citation will lead readers to your Works Cited list, at the end of your essay. The goal is to provide the information readers will need to locate the source there with as little fuss as possible. With that in mind, keep your parenthetical citations simple, so that they don't interrupt the flow of your writing. No commas or other punctuation is necessary within the parentheses.

OTHER COMMON FORMS OF PARENTHETICAL CITATIONS

You're likely to use some of the following common forms of citation in writing MLA-style research papers.

Citing a Work by Two Authors

> If we hope to understand the economy, "we must pay attention to the thought patterns that animate people's ideas and feelings" (Akerlof and Shiller 1).

Citing a Work with an Unknown Author

> A recent opinion article in the *New York Times* makes the argument that wealthy nations of the world must work together to solve the current economic crisis ("The Economic Summit" A28).

Citing an Indirect Source

If you draw on a statement made by one author that is quoted in the work of another author, be sure to indicate this by including the abbreviation *qtd. in* (for "quoted in"). For example:

> According to psychoanalyst and Holocaust researcher Dori Laub, "Bearing witness to a trauma is . . . a process that includes the listener" (qtd. in Hornstein 167).

Citing an Electronic Source

In many cases, online sources don't include page numbers of any kind. In this case, just include the name(s) of the author(s). For example:

> According to one critic, "The more that the earth's sinks are stressed, the harder it is to find ways of disposing of pollution" (Buell).

Readers will see that this is an online source when they go to your Works Cited list.

Sometimes online sources will include paragraph, section, or screen numbers. In cases such as this, use the abbreviation *par.*, the abbreviation *sec.*, or the full word *screen*, followed by the appropriate number. If the citation includes the name of the author, include a comma after it (and before the abbreviation). For example:

> One author makes the point that "As a child, Blake viewed the world in the light of what Wordsworth, in his 'Ode: Intimations of Immortality,' would later call a 'visionary gleam'" (Vulte, sec. 1).

Citing a Long Quotation from a Source

There are some special formatting details to keep in mind when you quote more than three lines from a source. A quotation of four or more lines should be "blocked"—meaning it should start on a new line and be indented ten spaces. The parenthetical citation for a blocked quotation should come after the end punctuation. For example:

> Literary critic James Wood ends his recent and influential book *How Fiction Works* with the following claim:
>
> > Realism, seen broadly as truthfulness to the way things are, cannot be mere verisimilitude, cannot be mere lifelikeness, or lifesameness, but what I must call lifeness: life on the page, life brought to different life by the highest

> artistry. And it cannot be a genre; instead, it makes other forms of fictions feel like genres. For realism of this kind — lifeness — is the origin. (247)

The Works Cited List

Your list of Works Cited will usually include many different types of sources, from books and periodicals to material you found online. You will need to pay quite a bit of attention to format. MLA style requires abbreviations for time designations, geographic names, publishing houses, and some scholarly terms. Consult the *MLA Handbook for Writers of Research Papers*, Seventh Edition, for a comprehensive list.

FORMATTING A WORKS CITED LIST

Your Works Cited list will include all the works you cite in your essay. Use the following guidelines to be sure you format your list accurately:

- Begin on a new page, after the last page of your essay; number the Works Cited page as the next page of your essay.
- Do not number the entries in your Works Cited list.
- Center your heading, *Works Cited*, one inch from the top of the page; do not boldface or italicize the heading, underline it, or use quotation marks.
- Double-space the list.
- List entries alphabetically, according to author's last name. If a source does not list an author, alphabetize it according to the first major word of the title.

The following Works Cited entries give examples of most sources you will need to cite. Follow their formats exactly, according to the kind of source you are citing.

Listing Books

Books by One Author

List the author, last name first. Italicize the title. Include the city of publication, the publisher's name, and the date of publication (use abbreviations for *University Press*, as in *Princeton UP* or *U of California P*).

> Wood, James. *How Fiction Works*. New York: Farrar, 2008. Print.

Books by Two or Three Authors

List authors in the order on which they appear on the title page of the book. List second and third authors with first names first.

> Akerlof, George, and Robert J. Shiller. *Animal Spirits: How Human Psychology Drives the Economy, and Why It Matters for Global Capitalism*. Princeton: Princeton UP, 2009. Print.

Books by More Than Three Authors

List only the first author, followed by a comma and the abbreviation *et al.* (meaning "and others").

Adritti, Rita, et al. *Test Tube Women*. London: Pandora, 1984. Print.

Two or More Books by the Same Author

List two or more books by the same author in alphabetical order, according to title. For each entry after the first, use three hyphens, followed by a period, instead of the author's name.

Pollan, Michael. *The Botany of Desire: A Plant's-Eye View of the World*. New York: Random, 2002. Print.

--- . *In Defense of Food: An Eater's Manifesto*. New York: Penguin, 2008. Print.

--- . *The Omnivore's Dilemma: A Natural History of Four Meals*. New York: Penguin, 2006. Print.

Edited Book

Fleck, Ludwig. *Genesis and Development of a Scientific Fact*. Ed. Thaddeus J. Trenn and Robert K. Merton. Chicago: U of Chicago P, 1979. Print.

Revised Edition

Comley, Nancy, et al. *Fields of Reading: Motives for Writing*. 10th ed. New York: Bedford, 2013. Print.

Anthology

Andrew Carroll, ed. *Operation Homecoming: Iraq, Afghanistan, and the Home Front, in the Words of U.S. Troops and Their Families*. New York: Random, 2006. Print.

Work in an Anthology

McIntyre, Vestal. "Mom-Voice." *Boys to Men: Gay Men Write about Growing Up*. Ed. Ted Gideonse and Rob Williams. New York: Da Capo, 2006. 223-42. Print.

More Than One Work in the Same Anthology

List each essay separately with a cross-reference to the entire anthology.

Bahr, David. "No Matter What Happens." Gideonse and Williams 69-88. Print.

Gideonse, Ted, and Rob Williams, eds. *Boys to Men: Gay Men Write about Growing Up*. New York: Da Capo, 2006. Print.

McIntyre, Vestal. "Mom-Voice." Gideonse and Williams 223-42. Print.

Listing Periodicals

JOURNALS

A *journal* is a periodical aimed at a very specific audience (often experts in a field—for example, literary history, artificial intelligence, or cattle farming). Because of this, journals often contain specialized language that can be difficult to read, but since they represent the latest research in a particular field, they're important for many research projects.

Article in a Journal with Continuous Pagination throughout an Annual Volume

Olutayo, A. O., and O. Akanle. "Fast Food in Ibadan: An Emerging Consumption Pattern." *Africa: The Journal of the International African Institute* 79 (2009): 207-27. Print.

Article in a Journal with Separate Pagination in Each Issue

Beldecos, A., et al. "The Importance of Feminist Critique for Contemporary Cell Biology." *Hypatia* 3 (Spring 1988): 61-76. Print.

MAGAZINES AND NEWSPAPERS

Because magazines are usually designed for a general audience, they are generally easier to read than journals. When it comes to a magazine article, it's a good idea to evaluate your source by finding out what you can about the magazine's reputation and the background of the article's author.

Article in a Monthly or Bimonthly Magazine

A magazine article will often not appear on consecutive pages, as in the example that follows, but may begin on page 48, skip to page 73, and continue on page 75. In cases like this, include the number of the first page, followed by a plus sign.

Ruch, Sarah. "The Power of Greens." *Organic Gardening* Feb./Mar. 2009: 641+. Print.

Article in a Weekly Magazine (Signed or Unsigned)

Max, D. T. "The Unfinished: David Foster Wallace's Project." *New Yorker* 9 Mar. 2009: 48–61. Print.

"Obama Abroad." *The Nation* 2 Apr. 2009: 3. Print.

Article in a Newspaper

Gumbrecht, Jamie. "Global Peace Walk Ends with a Bang." *Atlanta Journal-Constitution* 6 Apr. 2009: 1B. Print.

Listing Internet Sources

Complete source information is sometimes tricky to find online. When citing Internet sources, include whatever information you can find: the title of the Web site (italicized), the date of publication (if available), the date you accessed the source, the author (if there is one), the Web site's host organization, and so on. Note that some of the following examples include only date of access; in these cases, publication dates were not available. The MLA considers articles from newspaper- and magazine-sponsored Web sites to be nonperiodical publications cited only on the Web. (See the example below from the *Atlantic*.) However, the Works Cited listing for a newspaper or magazine article—or a scholarly journal—that you access through an online database should include complete print and electronic publication information.

Nonperiodical Publication Cited Only on the Web

Shenk, Joshua Wolf. "What Makes Us Happy?" *The Atlantic.com*. Atlantic Monthly Group, June 2009. Web. 20 July 2012.

Nonperiodical Publication on the Web Cited with a Print Publication Date

James, William. *The Varieties of Religious Experience: A Study in Human Nature*. New York: Longman, 1911. *Google Book Search*. Web. 20 May 2012.

A Work on the Web with Publication Data for Another Medium besides Print

What to Do on a Date. Dir. Ted Pesha. Coronet Instructional Films, 1950. *Internet Archive*. Web. 20 May 2012.

Scholarly Journal

Baptiste, Ian E. "Wages of Niceness: The Folly and Futility of Educators Who Strive to *Not* Impose." *New Horizons in Adult Education and Human Resource Development* 22.2 (2008): 6-28. Web. 20 May 2012.

A Periodical Publication in an Online Database

Velleman, J. David. "The Genesis of Shame." *Philosophy and Public Affairs* 30 (2001): 27-52. *JSTOR*. Web. 20 May 2012.

E-mail

Hann, Joelle. "Re: Copyediting." Message to Jason Tougaw. 24 Mar. 2012. E-mail.

Listing Other Nonprint Sources

Material Accessed on a CD-ROM, DVD, Diskette, or Tape

"Consciousness." *The Oxford English Dictionary*. 2nd ed. New York: Oxford UP, 2005. CD-ROM.

Television or Radio Program

"DIY Universe." *Radiolab*. WNYC. 26 Mar. 2009. Radio.

Videotape, Movie, Record, or Slide Program

Persepolis. Dir. Marjane Satrapi and Vincent Paronnaud. Sony Pictures, 2007. DVD.

Sample Student Research Paper Using MLA Style

The following student essay, by Margaret Donaldson, responds to an assignment that asked students to track the publication of articles in a single newspaper (in this case, the *New York Times*) on a single issue and report on their findings. Because of the requirements of the assignment, Donaldson's sources are almost all articles from the newspaper (with the exception of the one book she cites). Many research essays will focus on a greater variety of sources, but that will depend on the questions at hand and what kinds of sources help answer these questions. In addition, while Donaldson's instructor allowed her to use personal opinion in her essay, other instructors do not. Check with your instructor—and read the assignment carefully—if you're not sure.

Donaldson 1

Margaret Donaldson
English 101
Professor Greene
May 2008

All the News That's Fit to Print?

The writer begins with a hook and then establishes a motive: to explain that "environmental health" is often at the root of media stories about environmental catastrophe. She then presents the research required to demonstrate this.

The media, more often than not, bear bad news about the environment. Headlines like, "Hermaphrodite Frogs Found in Suburban Ponds" or "High Rice Cost Creating Fears of Asia Unrest" are commonplace in today's press. Tragic, discouraging reports have become so standard that most readers simply brush them off as just another catastrophic headline. It is not always mentioned, but environmental health is usually at the root of these disastrous stories. For two weeks, I followed the *New York Times,* keeping a record of all the stories either directly or indirectly related to the environment. At first, I had my doubts about finding many articles, since despite its great importance, environmental health frequently does not receive the attention it deserves. As I began collecting stories, I did find articles related to environmental issues, although in most, the environment was not the primary focus. I continued to follow the *Times* after I stopped collecting articles, and noticed that as Earth Day approached, more pieces were about environmental issues. This trend culminated in the *New York Times Magazine* "Green Issue," released on Earth Day. The bulk of the magazine focuses on innovative green technologies (virtually all of which have yet to break into the mainstream) and possible strategies for reducing human impact on the planet. The magazine is informative and interesting, but it is unfortunate that the environment receives that kind of in-depth news coverage only once a year.

The writer describes her research process. This is not always necessary — or pertinent — but here it clarifies how and why she found the sources under discussion.

Thesis statement

Environmental issues receive minimal front-page coverage: The four stories I found there are connected to environmental matters, but none spotlight the environment as the main issue. The National and Business sections had the most reports linked to the

Donaldson 2

environment, with nineteen articles and three briefings each. Most of these articles are concerned with oil, which is not surprising considering the major role oil plays in the formulation of American policy. The oil reports highlight rising costs, oil spills, and the search for new oil reserves, but there were no articles about alternative fuels or efforts made to alleviate our national addiction to oil. At the same time, these reports all have to do with the negative aspects of oil addiction. Many might criticize the *Times* for its lack of alternative-fuels coverage, focusing more on issues related to oil. Nevertheless, I do not think it is a bad thing to give considerable attention to all the problems created by our reliance on oil; hopefully, it will lead readers to the conclusion that we must reduce overall fuel consumption.

The writer introduces a quotation with a signal phrase, including the author and title of the article she quotes.

The writer uses a parenthetical citation, announcing the author's name in the signal phrase. She includes the page number in parentheses.

The writer offers a three-part analysis: (1) The newspaper offers adequate coverage of "environmental degradation"; (2) However, that coverage doesn't focus enough on the root of the problems; and (3) Focusing on the root of the problems might motivate people to help solve them.

For example, in a Business section article titled "Fuel Costs Just Part of Airlines' List of Woes," Jeff Bailey writes, "Record-high fuel prices and the industry's fragile finances have led to a new round of bankruptcies among smaller carriers" (C1). Bailey goes on to explain that as airlines shrink, demand stays high, and "flights are growing more crowded and unpleasant" (C1). In my opinion, articles like this one imply to readers that their lifestyles cannot be maintained without a cheap oil supply. This leads me to the conclusion that we must decide whether to continue relying on oil—the availability of which causes so many problems, and promises to create more—or transition to alternative fuels. Moreover, because our current lifestyles cannot be sustained without cheap oil, a change of lifestyle is in order. I think the *Times*, particularly in the National and Business sections, gave adequate coverage to the effects of environmental degradation, like high prices and resource shortages. Unfortunately, it rarely made it clear that our inattentiveness to the environment is one of the root causes of those problems. More attention might create more motivation to preserve the few resources that are left.

The writer uses transitional language to move from a discussion of one type of source to another.

The writer analyzes her source by comparing it to other articles that focus on similar problems and issues.

The writer uses transitional language.

Donaldson 3

While most of the reports I found were related to environmental degradation, a few were about steps being taken to restore environmental health. For example, William Yardley writes, in an article titled, "For Seattle Shoppers, Paper or Plastic Could Come with a 'Green Fee,'" that Seattle Mayor Greg Nickels is hoping this proposal will "reduce waste, reduce production of paper and plastic, and encourage still more people here to be faithful to their bumper-sticker gospel: 'Think Globally, Act Locally'" (A10). Another environmental effort is reported in Felicity Barringer's "Group Seeks E.P.A. Rules on Emissions from Vehicles." Barringer writes of "a coalition of states, cities, and environmental groups . . . seeking to force the Environmental Protection Agency to regulate emissions of heat-trapping gases from new cars and trucks or show that such regulation is unnecessary" (A16). Both these articles were printed in the National section. I think it is excellent that states are taking environmental matters into their own hands, given the lethargic attitude of the federal government. Most of the articles that focused on oil were either about corporations or the federal government. Reports on efforts to protect the environment were more concerned with the roles played by individual states. States feel the effects of environmental degradation more quickly than the federal government and are therefore more apt to make changes that benefit their communities. That states are willing to bypass the federal government to attempt environmental protection reform is an indicator that the national government is not fulfilling its duties.

In addition to providing commentary on the degradation of the environment and efforts to conserve, the *Times* also did stories about excessive consumption by Americans. Each week, a special section called "Escapes" includes a column titled, "Your Second Home." These weekly stories range in topic from tips on buying a second home to forgoing a vacation home and purchasing a recreational vehicle. The article "A New View Every Day" by Steve Bailey claims, "If you can live with the price of fuel, a well-maintained RV can keep you comfortable, whether you're in Death

Donaldson 4

The writer draws attention to her own point of view—and even her bias. Depending on the assignment, this can be an effective strategy. Some college assignments, however, may discourage writers from doing this. Check with your instructor.

Valley, the Everglades, or a Wal-Mart parking lot" (F2). Personally, I think it is ridiculous to promote the use of an RV or the purchase of a second home when articles just pages earlier detail the social and economic turmoil created by industry's addiction to oil. The headline news, geared more toward the international community, regularly describes food crises and natural disasters around the world. Features like "Your Second Home" provide Americans with opportunities to escape the hardships of the real world, supporting the disproportionate standard of living between global regions.

The writer refers to the photos that accompanied the newspaper article she discusses.

"Faster, Maybe. Cheaper, No. But Driving Has Its Fans" by Diane Cardwell also features excess consumption. The story was on the first page of the New York Report section, next to three large photographs of New Yorkers and their comfortable sedans. I liked this article, as opposed to "Your Second Home," because while it emphasizes the popularity of automobiles, Cardwell draws more attention to the utter ridiculousness of commuting in a car while living in New York City, a place with ample access to mass transit. Cardwell writes, "Despite the threat of traffic jams, honking horns, and the urban version of road rage, these New Yorkers choose to drive, whether to shave time off their commutes, run their errands with less hassle, or have a few moments to themselves inside mobile oases" (B1). The story was quite critical of the automobile culture, citing the hassles of driving in New York, especially high parking fees and congestion. Nevertheless, all the interviewees refused to consider life without their cars. Eugene Yates of the Bronx, who lives two blocks away from a train station, says, "I hate standing up when I get in the train station. Then you got to wait on the train, then the train is late, then it's this, then it's that. I can't stand the hassle" (B1). I am ashamed to hear these words from a fellow American. The real hassle will come when Manhattan begins flooding as a direct result of climate change.

The writer makes a strong and emotional claim—almost in the style of an editorial. The strategy is effective because she has established her essay as an opinion piece substantiated by evidence, and the claim is clearly linked to that evidence.

In contrast, efforts by New York to limit automobile congestion in the city received significant attention during the two weeks I collected articles. This issue was covered on the front

The writer presents a contrasting point.

The writer notes how one type of source—articles from the Opinion section—is different from the others. It focuses more intently on environmental problems.

The writer considers a new source—the weekly features sections.

Donaldson 5

page, but the headline was disappointing: "$8 Traffic Fee for Manhattan Gets Nowhere" (Confessore A1). I found the best reports about the shot-down traffic-fee proposal in the editorial section of the newspaper. I particularly enjoyed reading this section because it is the area of the paper where journalists are allowed to not only express opinions, but also offer ideas for solutions. For example, after the congestion pricing proposal lost, contributor Gene Russianoff suggests conducting a "detailed environmental review of all options for reducing traffic" (A25), including driving-day restrictions and mandated carpooling. The same day, contributor Owen D. Gutfreund proposes "adjusting tolls to take into account the vehicle's cost and fuel efficiency and the wear and tear on roads that different cars cause" (A25). Elsewhere throughout the paper, the *Times* did not give the environment much space. But in the Opinion section, it came up repeatedly, in editorials, op-eds, and letters; there was even a cartoon about nuclear power. People are concerned about the environment, and the *Times* Opinion contributors are writing about it. Unfortunately, calls for change do not seem to be getting anywhere. I hope the time comes soon when we can stop talking about change and actually start working toward it. Nevertheless, discussion is obviously necessary, and I felt the Opinion section did a decent job of including commentary on environmental issues.

Articles pertaining to "green culture," which probably appealed more to the average reader than the usual depressing headlines, could be found in the various Weekly Features sections. One such article, titled "Latest College Reading Lists: Menus with Pho and Lobster," by Michael S. Sanders, discusses the trend of serving higher-quality, healthier, more sustainably grown food in college dining halls. In a related story called "Good News about Rising Food Prices," journalist Kim Severson writes, "[i]f American staples like soda, fast-food hamburgers, and frozen dinners don't seem like such a bargain anymore, the American eating public might turn its attention to ingredients like local fruits and

Donaldson 6

vegetables, and milk and meat from animals that eat grass" (F1) as the price of cash crops like corn and soy rises. Both these stories were published in the Dining In special insert.

Similarly, the special Travel section insert featured the article "Going Green in the Blue Mountains" by Jennifer Conlin. Conlin writes, "Lying under a thick patchwork quilt, breathing in the fresh mountain air, I felt like a true eco-traveler as I listened reverently to a morning medley of nature streaming through my window: the chirping of a cockatoo, the scuffle of a passing lizard, the rustling of leaves . . ." (1). Articles like this one, as well as the two food features mentioned above, appeal to the indulgent desires of many upper-middle and upper-class citizens. They advocate extravagance, but only as long as it is "green." On the other hand, I do not find anything inherently wrong with these articles; at least they are trying to provoke some sort of environmental consciousness in even the most self-indulgent readers.

Special inserts also made room for advances in environmental technology. A Tech Innovation insert boasted four environmental articles, all explaining new green technologies. I found "A Cleaner, Leaner Jet Age Has Arrived" by Matthew L. Wald to be the most interesting. According to Wald, "the industry is scrambling to build greener airplanes — to save weight and improve engine efficiency, with an eye toward reducing operating costs and emissions" (2). It is comforting to know that efforts are being made to design technologies that will enable people to live in a more sustainable way, and it is also encouraging to see people get credit in reputable publications, like the *New York Times,* for working toward a more sustainable future.

After discussing several pieces of research, the writer draws a conclusion.

Nonetheless, I was somewhat unimpressed with the overall coverage given to the environment. The National and Business sections did contain reports related to environmental issues, but few discussed environmental issues like global warming or sustainable options in great detail. Granted, there were quite a few editorials written by contributors in the Opinion section, and feature stories were periodically published in special inserts. But the environment is crucial to our future, and perhaps we should pay regular — not periodical — attention to it. Moreover, excepting the one-time Tech Innovation insert, few articles explored options for reducing environmental degradation.

That is where the *New York Times Magazine* "Green Issue" stepped in. Its pages had many examples of ways we could reduce our carbon footprint. Its brief articles covered topics that ranged from green-jobs programs to the slow food movement to skyscrapers that double as gardens. These short articles were extremely interesting and provided hope for the future. However, it eventually becomes monotonous to keep discussing the future, when we face real climate change issues now. The short articles focus primarily on new technologies, while the "Not-So-Free Ride" piece by Stephen J. Dubner and Steven D. Levitt proposes regulation in the form of taxes at the tolls and the pump, as well as insurance programs that offer discounts for driving less. This article reminded me of George Monbiot's book *Heat: How to Stop the Planet Burning.* Monbiot writes, "Manmade global warming cannot be restrained unless we persuade the government to force us to change the way we live" (xv). I think Monbiot makes a valid point, but I also believe we will have a very hard time persuading the government to force us to change our lifestyles when we show no serious desire to change.

If no one else is changing, why should I? Michael Pollan does an excellent job in his "Why Bother?" article answering this question, which everyone seems to be asking these days. Pollan writes, "For us to wait for legislation or technology to solve the problem of how we're living our lives suggests we're not really serious about changing — something our politicians can't fail to notice. They will not move until we do" (19). If everyone waits for everyone else to take action, nothing will get done. In his article, Pollan brings up the significance of individual action, a heavily debated issue. Throughout this past semester, I have said in my

The writer paraphrases a source.

The writer brings in a new kind of source — a book — to contextualize her discussion of the newspaper's coverage of environmental problems.

The writer offers an evaluation of her source when she introduces it.

The writer contextualizes her discussion within the course for which she writes the essay. This may not always be appropriate, but in this case it is consistent with the assignment.

reaction papers that government legislation is the key to reversing climate change and establishing a more sustainable world; that we must do much more than change our lightbulbs, as Al Gore suggested in his film, *An Inconvenient Truth*. But now I have come to the realization that there is no key to reversing climate change, which Pollan makes clear in his article. It is going to take more than regulation, and it is going to take more than technology. That is why working toward a more sustainable world is so daunting, and why virtually no one, including governments, corporations, and individuals, has truly taken significant steps toward solving this problem. We must stop speculating about global warming while putting off taking significant action against it. There are no instant solutions, but we can make great strides by increasing governmental environmental regulation and putting into practice the sustainable technologies we already have. That said, individual action is essential, because without individual action, there is no way legislative or technological advances can be made.

In her conclusion, the writer offers a reflection on her thesis, with a twist. She makes it explicit that her position changed as she spent time carefully evaluating and synthesizing her sources.

At first, I was irritated that very few articles in the *New York Times* exclusively focused on environmental issues. The motto of the *Times* is "All the news that's fit to print." One would assume that environmental news should not only be fit to print, but receive considerable attention, as a healthy planet is crucial to human existence. The *Times* does a good job reporting the devastating effects of environmental degradation, like food shortages and natural disasters. But the bad news is already incorporated into our daily lives, while the good news is still just a feature, fit for a special insert or a weekly magazine, but not for the front page. The media may bear bad news, but if we want positive coverage, we need to create some positive news. There will not be environmental change until we actually implement the changes suggested in special features. If living "green" were a common lifestyle, there would be no need for a "Green Issue." When we make sustainable living and environmental preservation a priority, then it will cease to be a special feature, becoming a front-page headline and a way of life.

Donaldson 9

Works Cited

Bailey, Jeff. "Fuel Costs Just Part of Airlines' List of Woes." *New York Times* 10 Apr. 2008, late ed.: C1+. Print.

Bailey, Steve. "A New View Every Day." *New York Times* 11 Apr. 2008, late ed.: F2. Print.

Barringer, Felicity. "Group Seeks E.P.A. Rules on Emissions from Vehicles." *New York Times* 3 Apr. 2008, late ed.: A16. Print.

---. "Hermaphrodite Frogs Found in Suburban Ponds." *New York Times* 8 Apr. 2008, late ed.: F2. Print.

Bradsher, Keith. "High Rice Cost Creating Fears of Asia Unrest." *New York Times* 29 Mar. 2008, late ed.: A1+. Print.

Cardwell, Diane. "Faster, Maybe. Cheaper, No. But Driving Has Its Fans." *New York Times* 31 Mar. 2008, late ed.: B1+. Print.

Confessore, Nicholas. "$8 Traffic Fee for Manhattan Gets Nowhere." *New York Times* 8 Apr. 2008, late ed.: A1+. Print.

Conlin, Jennifer. "Going Green in the Blue Mountains." *New York Times* 6 Apr. 2008, late ed., Travel sec.: 1+. Print.

Dubner, Stephen J., and Steven D. Levitt. "Not-So-Free Ride." *New York Times Magazine* 20 Apr. 2008, late ed.: 40+. Print.

Gore, Al, narrator. *An Inconvenient Truth*. Dir. Davis Guggenheim. Lawrence Bender Productions, 2006. Film.

Gutfreund, Owen D. "Pick on the Big Guys." Editorial. *New York Times* 9 Apr. 2008, late ed.: A25. Print.

Monbiot, George. *Heat: How to Stop the Planet Burning*. Cambridge: South End, 2007. Print.

Pollan, Michael. "Why Bother?" *New York Times Magazine* 20 Apr. 2008, late ed.: 19+. Print.

Redniss, Laura. Cartoon. *New York Times* 28 Mar. 2008, late ed.: A23. Print.

Russianoff, Gene. "Take Alternate Route." Editorial. *New York Times* 9 Apr. 2008, late ed.: A25. Print.

Sanders, Michael S. "Latest College Reading Lists: Menus with Pho and Lobster." *New York Times* 9 Apr. 2008, late ed.: F1+. Print.

Donaldson 10

Severson, Kim. "Good News about Rising Food Prices." *New York Times* 2 Apr. 2008, late ed.: F1+. Print.

Wald, Matthew L. "A Cleaner, Leaner Jet Age Has Arrived." *New York Times* 9 Apr. 2008, late ed., Technology sec.: 2. Print.

Yardley, William. "For Seattle Shoppers, Paper or Plastic Could Come with a 'Green Fee.'" *New York Times* 5 Apr. 2008, late ed.: A10. Print.

APA Style

In the APA documentation style, the text of the paper must include author-date citations, usually in parentheses. The paper also must include a list of references.

In-text Citations

APA style uses in-text citations for the same reason that MLA style does: to help your readers recognize information from various sources and be able to match the citation to an entry in the list of sources at the end of your paper.

BASIC FORMATS FOR IN-TEXT CITATIONS

When citing sources in a paper using APA style, refer to research in the past tense (that is, "A survey of households showed . . ." or "A study of gentrification patterns revealed . . ."). Provide the author and publication date of the source. Only if using a direct quotation include the page number.

If you refer to the author and publication date as you write about a source, your reader will know when research was conducted and will be able to easily find the details in the reference list at the end of your paper. For example:

> In 2010, Betancur reported that Latino communities in Chicago often fragment when housing prices are affected by gentrification.

Another way to provide the needed information would be to put the year in parentheses:

> Betancur (2010) studied gentrification in Latino communities in Chicago and found that ethnic groups threatened with displacement often fragment along economic lines.

Or you could put both author and date in parentheses:

> Recent research on gentrification has focused on the tensions that develop as some members of an ethnic group stand to benefit from rising property values, while others face displacement (Betancur, 2010).

Just remember that the reader will want to connect what you write with the original source as easily as possible.

Whenever you quote directly from a source, be sure that author, year, and page number or numbers for the quotation are all included.

> Betancur (2010) asserted that "the real tragedy of gentrification was not market displacement *per se*, but community disintegration" (p. 399).

OTHER COMMON FORMATS FOR IN-TEXT CITATIONS

You're likely to use some of the following common forms of citation in writing APA-style research papers.

Citing a Work by Two Authors

If a source has two authors, include both in your parenthetical citations, connected by an ampersand (&).

> Supporters of gentrification have frequently drawn on distorted images of minority youth culture to support an argument that displacement of ethnic groups will create safer, more wholesome communities (Wilson & Grammenos, 2005).

Citing a Work by More than Three Authors

Social scientists often conduct research collaboratively, and they try to include all the authors in parenthetical references to give them their due. If a source has three to five authors, include them all when you first cite the source: (Chambers, Onishi, & Fisher, 2010). Subsequently, you can shorten the citation to the first author followed by *et al.*: (Chambers et al., 2010). Only when a work has six or more authors can you leave authors out in the first citation. In those cases, give the name of the first author followed by *et al.*: (Kendler et al., 2011).

Citing a Work with an Unknown Author

Sometimes a source has no author indicated. In those cases, include the first few words of the reference: in quotations if it is an article or Web page, italicized if it is a book.

> A study of global attitudes since the attacks of September 11, 2001, found that people in a majority of countries feel China is more powerful than the United States ("From hyperpower," 2011).

Citing an Indirect Source

If possible, track down all of the sources that you use, even if you discovered one through another source. However, if you want to quote from a source included in a secondary source, but cannot obtain the original, use the phrase "as cited in" and provide a citation to the secondary source. For example:

> An anonymous resident called them "the meanest streets" in *On Duty Magazine* (as cited in Betancur, 2010, p. 305).

Citing a Quotation from an Electronic Source without Page Numbers

Often, electronic sources do not have page numbers. When paragraph numbers are provided, use them in place of page numbers with the abbreviation *para.* If the paragraphs do not have visible numbers, include the heading for the section in which the quote occurs (or a shortened heading if it is too long to cite in its entirety) and count the number of paragraphs following the heading to indicate in which one the quoted material is found. For example:

> As the components of an open communication system overlap, collaboration "allows for a free exchange of ideas that moves the areas of common agreement and difference of opinion among participants to the forefront" (Mackey, 2011, "A Model for Transparent Design," para. 3).

Citing a Long Quotation from a Source

If a quotation is more than forty words, display it as a block indented a half inch from the left margin (the same as a paragraph indentation). Do not put quotation marks around the blocked quotation. End with a period followed by the author, year, and page number or numbers in parentheses. For example:

> In *The Upside of Irrationality*, the author explores the importance of meaning in one's work.
>
> > In the end, our results show that even a small amount of meaning can take us a long way. Ultimately, managers (as well as spouses, teachers, and parents) may not need to increase meaning at work as much as ensure that they don't sabotage the process of labor. (Ariely, 2010, pp. 81–82)

Citing Personal Communications

Conversations, interviews, personal e-mail messages, and anything else that can't be located by your reader is not included in the reference list. Cite them in the text only by providing the name of the source, the phrase "personal communication," and the date. For example:

> "The company marketing campaign was a huge success," according to C. Johnson (personal communication, October 24, 2011).

The Reference List

When you are using APA style, many of your sources may be periodicals you found either in print or online. You are not limited to using those sources, however, and, just as with essays using MLA style, you will need to pay careful attention to format.

FORMATTING A REFERENCE LIST

Begin your Reference list on a separate page with the title References, centered. List all of the sources you cite in your paper in alphabetical order by author or, if no author is indicated, by the first significant word in the title. The list should be double-spaced and entries should have a hanging indent.

APA style requires that you include the Digital Object Identifier (DOI) for electronic sources that have them. Since 2000, DOIs have been assigned by an international agency that creates unique numbers to identify articles or books from participating scholarly and scientific publishers. While not all electronic sources have DOIs, those that do have them usually include them in the publication information, and they often can be found in the upper or lower right-hand corner of the first page of journal articles. Make sure you keep track of these numbers when you see them in the course of your research.

The following Reference list entries give examples of most sources you will need to cite. Follow their formats exactly, according to the kind of source you are citing.

Listing Books and Periodicals

Books by One Author

List the author's last name and first-name initial or initials. Put the year of publication in parenthesis, then the title in italics, capitalizing only the first word in the title and subtitle and any proper nouns. End with the place of publication and publisher.

> Ehrenreich, B. (2002). *Nickel and dimed: On (not) getting by in America.* New York, NY: Holt.

Books by More than One Author

List authors' last names and initials, linking them with an ampersand (&). Include up to seven authors. If there are more than seven, list the first six, add an ellipses, and then the final author.

> Guerrero, L. K., & Floyd, K. (2006). *Nonverbal communication in close relationships.* Mahwah, NJ: Erlbaum.

If your reference list includes more than one source by the same first author, arrange them by year, with the earliest first. If there is an entry that has the same first author, but includes additional authors, arrange them after the single-author entries. If you have two publications by the same author or authors published in the same year, arrange them alphabetically by title (excluding the *A*, *An* or *The* that may begin the title).

Edited Book without an Author

> Brummett, B. (Ed.). (2008). *Uncovering hidden rhetorics: Social issues in disguise.* Los Angeles, CA: Sage.

Book with a Translator and/or Editor

> Freud, Sigmund. (1966). *Complete introductory lectures on psychoanalysis.* (J. Strachey, Ed. and Trans.). New York, NY: Norton.

Article or Chapter in a Book

Clark, L. B., & Payne, L. A. (2011). Trauma tourism in Latin America. In K. Bilbija & L. A. Payne (Eds.). *Accounting for violence: Marketing memory in Latin America* (pp. 99–126). Durham, NC: Duke University Press.

Revised Editions

Montiel, P. (2011). *Macroeconomics in emerging markets.* (2nd ed.). Cambridge, England: Cambridge University Press.

Electronic Book

Cite as you would a printed book and add a DOI, if available, or "Retrieved from" and a URL.

Mahiri, J. (2011). *Digital tools in urban schools: Mediating a remix of learning.* Ann Arbor, MI: University of Michigan Press. Retrieved from http://hdl.handle.net/2027/spo.10329379.0001.001

Article in a Journal with a DOI (Digital Object Identifier)

Capitalize the first word in an article title, italicize and capitalize the words in the title of the journal, add the volume number in italics, the issue number in parentheses, and the page numbers. The DOI appears last. Rules for listing multiple authors are the same as for books (see "Books by More than One Author," p. 58).

Kendler, K. S., Lindon, J. E., Loken, E. K., Pedersen, N. L., Middeldorp, C. M., Reynolds, C., . . . Gardner, C. O. (2011). The impact of environmental experiences on symptoms of anxiety and depression across the lifespan. *Psychological Science 22,* 1343-1352. doi: 0.1177/0956797611417255

Article in a Journal without a DOI

If there is no DOI, include the URL of the publisher and state "retrieved from" (even if you found the article from a different sourece). In this case, the article was retrieved from a library database, but an Internet search for the journal title provided the publisher's URL.

Mumm, J. (2011). Redoing Chicago: Gentrification, race, and intimate segregation. *North American Dialogue 14*(1): 16–19. Retrieved from http://onlinelibrary.wiley.com/journal/10.1111/%28ISSN%291556-4819

Magazine Article

Include the year and issue date as well as volume, if available.

Knee, J. A. (2011, July/August). Why content isn't king. *The Atlantic, 308*(1), 34–38.

Magazine Article Found Online

If the article was found online, cite it as you would a print article, but also include the URL for the publication.

Stourton, E. (2011, October 8). The year of reading differently. *Slate*. Retrieved from http://www.slate.com

Newspaper Article

Korkki, P. (2011, October 9). For women, parity is still a subtly steep climb. *New York Times*, p. B9.

Newspaper Article Found Online

Levy, M., Yerardi, J., & Voz, D. (2011, October 8). States vary widely in reporting foodborne illnesses. *The Washington Post*. Retrieved from http://www.washingtonpost.com

Listing Web Sites and Other Nonprint Sources

Web Site

Provide author, date, title, and URL. If there is no author, start the entry with the title. If the author is an organization, include the organization's name as author. If there is no discernible title, put a basic description in brackets. If there is no publication date, use *n.d.* Use the complete URL unless it's extremely long and the item can be searched for on the site.

Convention on Biological Diversity. (n.d.) *Strategic plan 2011–2020*. Retrieved from http://www.cbd.int/sp/

Cotterill, C. (n.d.). [Author Web site]. Retrieved from http://www.colincotterill.com/

Web Page within a Web Site

From hyperpower to declining power. (2011, September 7). In *Pew global attitudes project*. Retrieved from http://www.pewglobal.org/2011/09/07/from-hyperpower-to-declining-power/

Listing Audiovisual Media

List the primary contributors as authors, with their role(s) in parentheses. For a television or radio episode, cite as for an article or chapter in a book, placing the script-writer and director in the author position, and the producer in the editor position. Do not use abbreviations. Include the medium in square brackets. When you find an item online, include the URL.

Motion Picture

Hooper, T. (Director), Canning, I., Sherman, E., & Unwin, G. (Producers). (2010). *The king's English.* [Motion picture]. United Kingdom: Weinstein Company & U.K. Film Council.

Video Found Online

Baggs, A. (Director). (2007, January 14). *In my language.* [Video file]. Retrieved from http://www.youtube.com/watch?v=JnylM1hI2jc

Blog Post

Thompson, M. (2011, September 30). Darwinian tax reform. [Web log post]. Retrieved from http://savageminds.org/2011/09/30/darwinian-tax-reform/

Podcast

Living without. (2011, September 16). *This American life.* [Audio podcast]. Retrieved from http://www.thisamericanlife.org/radio-archives/episode/446 /living-without-2011

Sample Student Research Paper Excerpt Using APA Style

The following excerpt from Muaz Paracha's essay "Political Food: Big Business and the State of Food Safety in the United States" shows both in-text citations and a Reference list in APA style. In addition to using proper citation, Paracha also follows the formatting guidelines prescribed by APA: The title page includes the paper title, author's name, class information, and date, which are centered and double spaced. In the top left corner of the title page, the words *Running Head:* and a short version of the title (50 characters or fewer) appear. The short title, but not the words *Running Head:* appears in all capitals and is repeated in the top left corner of every subsequent page of the paper. Page numbers appear in the top right corner of every page, including the title page. If you include headings in your paper, they should be boldface, centered, and on a new line. Do not include any extra line breaks before or after the head. Some instructors require an abstract, or summary of the main points, with an essay. In this excerpt you will see how an abstract is formatted. The full text of the essay, which discusses the impact of lobbying on food safety standards and regulations, appears in Part Three: Social Sciences on p. 386.

Include the words "Running Head" followed by a colon and a short version of the title.

The page number goes in the upper right corner of the page.

Running Head: POLITICAL FOOD 1

Type the full title of the paper, your name, class, professor, and submission date in the center of the page.

Political Food: Big Business and the State of Food Safety in the United States

Muaz Paracha

Eng 110: College Writing

Professor Wan

November 1, 2012

Do not use Running Head *before the short title.*

Abstract is centered. The text following is not indented.

POLITICAL FOOD 2

Abstract

The government has developed regulations regarding the safety of food through the United States Department of Agriculture and the Food and Drug Administration. However, the enforcement of these regulations has been greatly influenced by lobbyists who work on behalf of major food corporations.

The full title appears centered at the top of the page. The first paragraph should be indented.

POLITICAL FOOD 3

Political Food: Big Business and the State of Food Safety in the United States

Since 1906, when Congress enacted the Pure Food and Drug Act, the U.S. government has been regulating the American food supply. The regulation in general was to ensure the quality and safety of the foods and drugs sold to the public. Today, food regulation is a hot-button issue and many people point fingers at the government for not doing its job correctly. However, the government may not be entirely to blame for its decisions but rather big businesses that are chasing profits and financial incentives.

Center and bold-face headings.

Even though recent legislation by the Obama administration has required lobbyists to register their names and companies they work for, well known brands have been able to prevent new regulations from hurting their interests.

The Global Reach of Food Lobbyists

Larger food companies aren't just getting their way here in the United States. "Lobbying by 'powerful' big food companies is blocking reforms which would improve human health and the environment," a director of the United Nations' Food and Agriculture Organization has warned (Jowit, 2010).

The Reference list begins on a new page and is double spaced, like the rest of the paper.

"References" should be centered.

Use the hanging indent format.

POLITICAL FOOD 9

References

Curran, L. (2010). Millions spent lobbying food safety. *Food Safety News.* Retrieved from www.foodsafetynews.com

Eggen, D. (2010, December 8). New Republican lawmakers are hiring lobbyists, despite campaign rhetoric. *The Washington Post.* Retrieved from www.washingtonpost.com

Jowit, J. (2010, September 22). Corporate lobbying is blocking food reforms, senior UN official warns. *The Guardian UK.* Retrieved from www.guardian.co.uk

Nestle, M. (2003). Food politics: How the food industry influences nutrition and health. Los Angeles, CA: University of California Press.

Pollan, M. (2007, January 28). Unhappy meals. *The New York Times.* Retrieved from www.nytimes.com

Randall, E. (2010). Food risk and politics: Scare, scandal and crisis—insights into the risk politics of food. *Social Policy & Administration, 44*(7), 867–869.

U.S. Food and Drug Administration. (2010). *What we do.* Retrieved from www.FDA.gov

U.S. Department of Agriculture. (2010). *Job of USDA*. Retrieved from www.USDA.gov

U.S. Department of Agriculture. (2011). *Agency history*. Retrieved from www.USDA.gov

Water, A., & Heron, K. (2009, February 19). No lunch left behind. *The New York Times.* Retrieved from www.nytimes.com

Part 2
Arts and Humanities

Readings in the Arts and Humanities

The arts and humanities include those areas of academic research and creative expression that explore what is sometimes called the human condition—for example, philosophy, art and art history, literature and creative writing, theater, dance, film, music, new media, religion, and languages. (Certain disciplines, such as history and linguistics, are sometimes categorized among the humanities and sometimes among the social sciences.) Writers in the humanities tend to value and emphasize *interpretation*, studying subjective questions rather than factual knowledge: What is the nature of art? What is the nature of culture? How does one live a good life? How does language shape identity? Where did I come from?

Scholars in the arts and humanities explore these questions in the many shapes and sizes they come in, as you will see in the sixteen professional pieces of writing collected in this section. Here, ten readings stand alone, and three sets are paired in order to emphasize the dialogue between them. Six of these essays are primarily reflecting, three reporting, two explaining, and five arguing. Whatever modes they write in, the writers of these essays interpret both texts and the details of personal and social experience to illuminate larger questions.

Interpretation requires writers to strike a careful balance between the general and the particular, or the abstract and the concrete. Literary scholars, whose main task is to interpret, still need to ground their theories in fact—for example, the date of Oscar Wilde's imprisonment (1895) is important to know if you want to understand the history of the novel or the politics of sexuality. Analyzing how texts, experience, and events work in both a literal and a concrete sense is the first step in an interpretive process. At the end of this part you will see how one student engaged in the act of interpretation by examining the graphic narrative *Persepolis* using both literary concepts and the historical context in which the book was written.

In the arts and humanities, you, too, will be asked to interpret texts—literature, visual art, argumentative essays, film, and digital media—to illuminate the subjective questions at the center of humanistic inquiry. When you write in response to texts like these, you will also be learning to strike a balance between the general and the particular, between facts and interpretation. Concrete details illuminate abstract concepts, and vice versa. You will be learning the art of speculating intelligently, examining nuances, and living with ambiguity and uncertainty. Whether you are reflecting, reporting, explaining, or arguing, you will be drawing your readers' attention to the implications of texts and experiences that require interpretation—*your* interpretation—to be understood.

REFLECTING

Learning to Read and Write

Frederick Douglass

Frederick Augustus Washington Bailey (1817–1895) was born to a slave mother on the Eastern Shore of Maryland; his father was a white man. After his escape from the South in 1838, he adopted the name Douglass and worked both to free other slaves and — after the Civil War — to protect the rights of freed slaves. He was a newspaper editor, a lecturer, the United States minister to Haiti, and the author of several books about his life and times. *The Narrative of the Life of Frederick Douglass: An American Slave* (1841), from which the following selection has been taken, is his best-known work.

I lived in Master Hugh's family about seven years. During this time, I succeeded in learning to read and write. In accomplishing this, I was compelled to resort to various stratagems. I had no regular teacher. My mistress, who had kindly commenced to instruct me, had, in compliance with the advice and direction of her husband, not only ceased to instruct, but had set her face against my being instructed by anyone else. It is due, however, to my mistress to say of her, that she did not adopt this course of treatment immediately. She at first lacked the depravity indispensable to shutting me up in mental darkness. It was at least necessary for her to have some training in the exercise of irresponsible power, to make her equal to the task of treating me as though I were a brute.

My mistress was, as I have said, a kind and tenderhearted woman; and in the simplicity of her soul she commenced, when I first went to live with her, to treat me as she supposed one human being ought to treat another. In entering upon the duties of a slaveholder, she did not seem to perceive that I sustained to her the relation of a mere chattel, and that for her to treat me as a human being was not only wrong, but dangerously so. Slavery proved as injurious to her as it did to me. When I went there, she was a pious, warm, and tenderhearted woman. There was no sorrow or suffering for which she had not a tear. She had bread for the hungry, clothes for the naked, and comfort for every mourner that came within her reach. Slavery soon proved its ability to divest her of these heavenly qualities. Under its influence, the tender heart became stone, and the lamblike disposition gave way to one of tiger-like fierceness. The first step in her downward course was in her ceasing to instruct me. She now commenced to practice her husband's precepts. She finally became even more violent in her opposition than her husband himself. She was not satisfied with simply doing as well as he had commanded; she seemed anxious to do better. Nothing seemed to make her more angry than to see me with a newspaper. She seemed to think that here lay the danger. I have had her rush at me with a face made all up of fury, and snatch from me a newspaper, in a manner that fully revealed her apprehension. She was an apt woman; and a little experience soon demonstrated, to her satisfaction, that education and slavery were incompatible with each other.

From this time I was most narrowly watched. If I was in a separate room any considerable length of time, I was sure to be suspected of having a book, and was at once called to give an account of myself. All this, however, was too late. The first step had been taken. Mistress, in teaching me the alphabet, had given me the *inch*, and no precaution could prevent me from taking the *ell*.[1]

The plan which I adopted, and the one by which I was most successful, was that of making friends of all the little white boys whom I met in the street. As many of these as I could, I converted into teachers. With their kindly aid, obtained at different times and in different places, I finally succeeded in learning to read. When I was sent on errands, I always took my book with me, and by doing one part of my errand quickly, I found time to get a lesson before my return. I used also to carry bread with me, enough of which was always in the house, and to which I was always welcome; for I was much better off in this regard than many of the poor white children in our neighborhood. This bread I used to bestow upon the hungry little urchins, who, in return, would give me that more valuable bread of knowledge. I am strongly tempted to give the names of two or three of those little boys, as a testimonial of the gratitude and affection I bear them; but prudence forbids;—not that it would injure me, but it might embarrass them; for it is almost an unpardonable offense to teach slaves to read in this Christian country. It is enough to say of the dear little fellows, that they lived on Philpot Street, very near Durgin and Bailey's ship-yard. I used to talk this matter of slavery over with them. I would sometimes say to them, I wished I could be as free as they would be when they got to be men. "You will be free as soon as you are twenty-one, *but I am a slave for life!* Have not I as good a right to be free as you have?" These words used to trouble them; they would express for me the liveliest sympathy, and console me with the hope that something would occur by which I might be free.

5 I was now about twelve years old, and the thought of being *a slave for life* began to bear heavily upon my heart. Just about this time, I got hold of a book entitled "The Columbian Orator."[2] Every opportunity I got, I used to read this book. Among much of other interesting matter, I found in it a dialogue between a master and his slave. The slave was represented as having run away from his master three times. The dialogue represented the conversation which took place between them, when the slave was retaken the third time. In this dialogue, the whole argument in behalf of slavery was brought forward by the master, all of which was disposed of by the slave. The slave was made to say some very smart as well as impressive things in reply to his master—things which had the desired though unexpected effect; for the conversation resulted in the voluntary emancipation of the slave on the part of the master.

In the same book, I met with one of Sheridan's mighty speeches on and in

---

[1]*ell*: A unit of measurement, no longer used, equal to 45 inches.—Eds.

[2]*The Columbian Orator*: A collection of speeches widely used in early-nineteenth-century schools to teach argument and rhetoric.—Eds.

behalf of Catholic emancipation.[3] These were choice documents to me. I read them over and over again with unabated interest. They gave tongue to interesting thoughts of my own soul, which had frequently flashed through my mind, and died away for want of utterance. The moral which I gained from the dialogue was the power of truth over the conscience of even a slave-holder. What I got from Sheridan was a bold denunciation of slavery, and a powerful vindication of human rights. The reading of these documents enabled me to utter my thoughts, and to meet the arguments brought forward to sustain slavery; but while they relieved me of one difficulty, they brought on another even more painful than the one of which I was relieved. The more I read, the more I was led to abhor and detest my enslavers. I could regard them in no other light than a band of successful robbers, who had left their homes, and gone to Africa, and stolen us from our homes, and in a strange land reduced us to slavery. I loathed them as being the meanest as well as the most wicked of men. As I read and contemplated the subject, behold! that very discontentment which Master Hugh had predicted would follow my learning to read had already come, to torment and sting my soul to unutterable anguish. As I writhed under it, I would at times feel that learning to read had been a curse rather than a blessing. It had given me a view of my wretched condition, without the remedy. It opened my eyes to the horrible pit, but to no ladder upon which to get out. In moments of agony, I envied my fellow-slaves for their stupidity. I have often wished myself a beast. I preferred the condition of the meanest reptile to my own. Any thing, no matter what, to get rid of thinking! It was this everlasting thinking of my condition that tormented me. There was no getting rid of it. It was pressed upon me by every object within sight or hearing, animate or inanimate. The silver trump of freedom had roused my soul to eternal wakefulness. Freedom now appeared, to disappear no more forever. It was heard in every sound, and seen in every thing. It was ever present to torment me with a sense of my wretched condition. I saw nothing without seeing it, I heard nothing without hearing it, and felt nothing without feeling it. It looked from every star, it smiled in every calm, breathed in every wind, and moved in every storm.

I often found myself regretting my own existence, and wishing myself dead; and but for the hope of being free, I have no doubt but that I should have killed myself, or done something for which I should have been killed. While in this state of mind, I was eager to hear any one speak of slavery. I was a ready listener. Every little while, I could hear something about the abolitionists. It was some time before I found what the word meant. It was always used in such connections as to make it an interesting word to me. If a slave ran away and succeeded in getting clear, or if a slave killed his master, set fire to a barn, or did any thing very wrong in the mind of a slaveholder, it was spoken of as the fruit of *abolition*. Hearing the word in this connection very often, I set about learning what it meant. The dictionary afforded me little or no

---

[3] *Richard Brinsley Sheridan* (1751–1816): A British dramatist, orator, and politician. Roman Catholics were not allowed to vote in England until 1829.—Eds.

help. I found it was "the act of abolishing"; but then I did not know what was to be abolished. Here I was perplexed. I did not dare to ask anyone about its meaning, for I was satisfied that it was something they wanted me to know very little about. After a patient waiting, I got one of our city papers, containing an account of the number of petitions from the north, praying for the abolition of slavery in the District of Columbia, and of the slave trade between the States. From this time I understood the words *abolition* and *abolitionist,* and always drew near when that word was spoken, expecting to hear something of importance to myself and fellow-slaves. The light broke in upon me by degrees. I went one day down on the wharf of Mr. Waters; and seeing two Irishmen unloading a scow of stone, I went, unasked, and helped them. When we had finished, one of them came to me and asked me if I were a slave. I told him I was. He asked, "Are ye a slave for life?" I told him that I was. The good Irishman seemed to be deeply affected by the statement. He said to the other that it was a pity so fine a little fellow as myself should be a slave for life. He said it was a shame to hold me. They both advised me to run away to the north; that I should find friends there, and that I should be free. I pretended not to be interested in what they said, and treated them as if I did not understand them; for I feared they might be treacherous. White men have been known to encourage slaves to escape, and then, to get the reward, catch them and return them to their masters. I was afraid that these seemingly good men might use me so; but I nevertheless remembered their advice, and from that time I resolved to run away. I looked forward to a time at which it would be safe for me to escape. I was too young to think of doing so immediately; besides, I wished to learn how to write, as I might have occasion to write my own pass. I consoled myself with the hope that I should one day find a good chance. Meanwhile, I would learn to write.

The idea as to how I might learn to write was suggested to me by being in Durgin and Bailey's shipyard, and frequently seeing the ship carpenters, after hewing, and getting a piece of timber ready for use, write on the timber the name of that part of the ship for which it was intended. When a piece of timber was intended for the larboard side, it would be marked thus—"L." When a piece was for the starboard side, it would be marked thus—"S." A piece for the larboard side forward, would be marked thus—"L. F." When a piece was for starboard side forward, it would be marked thus—"S. F." For larboard aft, it would be marked thus—"L. A." For starboard aft, it would be marked thus—"S. A." I soon learned the names of these letters, and for what they were intended when placed upon a piece of timber in the shipyard. I immediately commenced copying them, and in a short time was able to make the four letters named. After that, when I met with any boy who I knew could write, I would tell him I could write as well as he. The next word would be, "I don't believe you. Let me see you try it." I would then make the letters which I had been so fortunate as to learn, and ask him to beat that. In this way I got a good many lessons in writing, which it is quite possible I should never have gotten in any other way. During this time, my copybook was the board fence, brick wall, and pavement; my pen and ink was a lump of chalk. With these, I learned mainly how to write. I then commenced and continued copying the italics in *Webster's Spelling Book*, until I could make them all without looking on the book. By this time, my little Master Thomas had gone to school, and learned how to write, and had written over a number of copybooks. These had been brought home, and shown to some of our near neighbors, and then laid aside. My mistress used to go to class meeting at the Wilk Street meeting-house every Monday afternoon, and leave me to take care of the house. When left thus, I used to spend the time in writing in the spaces left in Master Thomas's copybook, copying what he had written. I continued to do this until I could write a hand very similar to that of Master Thomas. Thus, after a long, tedious effort for years, I finally succeeded in learning how to write.

▪ QUESTIONS

Reading

1. As its title proclaims, Douglass's book is a narrative, the story of his life. So, too, is this selection a narrative, the story of his learning to read and write. Identify the main events of this story, and list them in chronological order.
2. Douglass is documenting some of the events in his life in this selection, but certain events are not simply reported but described so that we may see, hear, and feel what was experienced by the people who were present. Which events are described most fully in this narrative? How does Douglass seek to engage our interest and direct our feelings through such scenes?
3. In this selection from his memoir and in the entire book, Douglass is engaged in evaluating an institution — slavery — and arguing a case against it. Can you locate the points in the text where reflecting gives way to argumentation? How does Douglass support his argument against slavery? What contributes to his persuasiveness?

Exploratory Writing

1. The situation of Roman Catholics and, by inference, the Irish is a subtheme in this essay. You can trace it by locating every mention of Catholicism and the Irish in the text. How does this theme relate to African American slavery? Locate *The Columbian Orator* in your library, or find out more about Sheridan and why he argued on behalf of "Catholic emancipation" (paragraph 6).
2. Put yourself in the place of Master Hugh's wife, and retell all events in her words and from her point of view. To do so, you will have to decide both what she might have come to know about all these events and how she would feel about them. You will also have to decide when she is writing. Is she keeping a diary during this time (the early 1830s)? Or is she looking back from the perspective of later years? Has she been moved to write by reading Douglass's own book, which appeared in 1841? If so, how old would she be then, and what would she think about these past events? Would she be angry, bitter, repentant, embarrassed, indulgent, or scornful?

Making Connections

1. Like Douglass, George Orwell ("Politics and the English Language," p. 313) and James Baldwin (p. 131) write about the political implications of language. How do the arguments of these three writers overlap? What ideas do they share? How do they differ?

Essay Writing

1. Borrow Douglass's title, "Learning to Read and Write," and write your own essay, reflecting on your personal history of literacy. When, where, and how did you learn to write? What was the environment like? What challenges did you face? What accomplishments did you experience? If appropriate, discuss the roles that other people played in the process as well as any social or political implications of your experience.

REFLECTING

The Good Short Life

Dudley Clendinen

As a national correspondent and editorial writer at the *New York Times*, Dudley Clendinen reported on the Religious Right, the space shuttle *Challenger* disaster, and the emerging AIDS crisis in the 1980s. In 1993, Clendinen came out on the editorial page of the *New York Times*. His editorial grew into *Out for Good: The Struggle to Build a Gay Rights Movement in America* (1999), a major history of the gay rights movement, cowritten with Adam Nagourney, also of the *New York Times*. During the same period of time, Clendinen was left to care for his stroke-victim mother, and starting in 2000 he lived with her for four hundred days in Canterbury Towers, a Tampa Bay apartment and nursing home complex. His observations of the eclectic group of elderly people there became the acclaimed *A Place Called Canterbury: Tales of the New Old Age in America* (2008). In 2010, Clendinen was diagnosed with A.L.S. (Lou Gehrig's disease), a fatal muscular disorder. He discusses the disease in regular segments on WYPR, the public radio station in Baltimore, where he lives. Clendinen's writing has appeared in the *New Yorker*, *GQ*, *Men's Health*, *Forbes.com*, and the *New York Times Sunday Magazine*. This essay was originally published in the *New York Times* (July 2011).

I have wonderful friends. In this last year, one took me to Istanbul. One gave me a box of hand-crafted chocolates. Fifteen of them held two rousing, pre-posthumous wakes for me. Several wrote large checks. Two sent me a boxed set of all the Bach sacred cantatas. And one, from Texas, put a hand on my thinning shoulder, and appeared to study the ground where we were standing. He had flown in to see me.

"We need to go buy you a pistol, don't we?" he asked quietly. He meant to shoot myself with.

"Yes, Sweet Thing," I said, with a smile. "We do."

I loved him for that.

5 I love them all. I am acutely lucky in my family and friends, and in my daughter, my work, and my life. But I have amyotrophic lateral sclerosis, or A.L.S., more kindly known as Lou Gehrig's disease, for the great Yankee hitter and first baseman who was told he had it in 1939, accepted the verdict with such famous grace, and died less than two years later. He was almost thirty-eight.

I sometimes call it Lou, in his honor, and because the familiar feels less threatening. But it is not a kind disease. The nerves and muscles pulse and twitch, and progressively, they die. From the outside, it looks like the ripple of piano keys in the muscles under my skin. From the inside, it feels like anxious butterflies, trying to get out. It starts in the hands and feet and works its way up and in, or it begins in the muscles of the mouth and throat and chest and abdomen, and works its way down and out. The second way is called bulbar, and that's the way it is with me. We don't live as long, because it affects our ability to breathe early on, and it just gets worse.

At the moment, for sixty-six, I look pretty good. I've lost twenty pounds. My face is thinner. I even get some "Hey, there, Big Boy," looks, which I like. I think of it as my cosmetic phase. But it's hard to smile, and chew. I'm short of breath. I choke a lot. I sound like a wheezy, lisping drunk. For a recovering alcoholic, it's really annoying.

There is no meaningful treatment. No cure. There is one medication, Rilutek, which might make a few months' difference. It retails for about $14,000 a year. That doesn't seem worthwhile to me. If I let this run the whole course, with all the human, medical, technological, and loving support I will start to need just months from now, it will leave me, in five or eight or twelve or more years, a conscious but motionless, mute, withered, incontinent mummy of my former self. Maintained by feeding and waste tubes, breathing and suctioning machines.

No, thank you. I hate being a drag. I don't think I'll stick around for the back half of Lou.

10 I think it's important to say that. We obsess in this country about how to eat and dress and drink, about finding a job and a mate. About having sex and children. About how to live. But we don't talk about how to die. We act as if facing death weren't one of life's greatest, most absorbing thrills and challenges. Believe me, it is. This is not dull. But we have to be able to see doctors and machines, medical and insurance systems, family and friends and religions as informative—not governing—in order to be free.

And that's the point. This is not about one particular disease or even about Death. It's about Life, when you know there's not much left. That is the weird blessing of Lou. There is no escape, and nothing much to do. It's liberating.

I began to slur and mumble in May, 2010. When the neurologist gave me the diagnosis that November, he shook my hand with a cracked smile and released me to the chill, empty gray parking lot below.

It was twilight. He had confirmed what I had suspected through six months of tests by other specialists looking for other explanations. But suspicion and certainty are two different things. Standing there, it suddenly hit me that I was going to die. "I'm not prepared for this," I thought. "I don't know whether to stand here, get in the car, sit in it, or drive. To where? Why?" The pall lasted about five minutes, and then I remembered that I did have a plan. I had a dinner scheduled in Washington that night with an old friend, a scholar and author who was feeling depressed. We'd been talking about him a lot. Fair enough. Tonight, I'd up the ante. We'd talk about Lou.

The next morning, I realized I did have a way of life. For twenty-two years, I have been going to therapists and twelve-step meetings. They helped me deal with being alcoholic and gay. They taught me how to be sober and sane. They taught me that I could be myself, but that life wasn't just about me. They taught me how to be a father. And perhaps most important, they taught me that I can do anything, one day at a time.

Including this. 15

I am, in fact, prepared. This is not as hard for me as it is for others. Not nearly as hard as it is for Whitney, my thirty-year-old daughter, and for my family and friends. I know. I have experience.

I was close to my old cousin, Florence, who was terminally ill. She wanted to die, not wait. I was legally responsible for two aunts, Bessie and Carolyn, and for Mother, all of whom would have died of natural causes years earlier if not for medical technology, well-meaning systems, and loving, caring hands.

I spent hundreds of days at Mother's side, holding her hand, trying to tell her funny stories. She was being bathed and diapered and dressed and fed, and for the last several years, she looked at me, her only son, as she might have at a passing cloud.

I don't want that experience for Whitney—nor for anyone who loves me. Lingering would be a colossal waste of love and money.

If I choose to have the tracheotomy that I will need in the next several 20 months to avoid choking and perhaps dying of aspiration pneumonia, the respirator and the staff and support system necessary to maintain me will easily cost half a million dollars a year. Whose half a million, I don't know.

I'd rather die. I respect the wishes of people who want to live as long as they can. But I would like the same respect for those of us who decide—rationally—not to. I've done my homework. I have a plan. If I get pneumonia, I'll let it snuff me out. If not, there are those other ways. I just have to act while my hands still work: the gun, narcotics, sharp blades, a plastic bag, a fast car, over-the-counter drugs, oleander tea (the polite Southern way), carbon monoxide, even helium. That would give me a *really* funny voice at the end.

I have found the way. Not a gun. A way that's quiet and calm.

Knowing that comforts me. I don't worry about fatty foods anymore. I don't worry about having enough money to grow old. I'm not going to grow old.

I'm having a wonderful time.

I have a bright, beautiful, talented daughter who lives close by, the gift of 25 my life. I don't know if she approves. But she understands. Leaving her is the one thing I hate. But all I can do is to give her a daddy who was vital to the end, and knew when to leave. What else is there? I spend a lot of time writing letters and notes, and taping conversations about this time, which I think of as the Good Short Life (and Loving Exit), for WYPR-FM, the main NPR station in Baltimore. I want to take the sting out of it, to make it easier to talk about death. I am terribly behind in my notes, but people are incredibly patient and nice. And inviting. I have invitations galore.

Last month, an old friend brought me a recording of the greatest concert he'd ever heard, Leonard Cohen, live, in London, three years ago. It's powerful, haunting music, by a poet, composer, and singer whose life has been as tough and sinewy and loving as an old tree.

The song that transfixed me, words and music, was "Dance Me to the End of Love." That's the way I feel about this time. I'm dancing, spinning around, happy in the last rhythms of the life I love. When the music stops—when I can't tie my bow tie, tell a funny story, walk my dog, talk with Whitney, kiss someone special, or tap out lines like this—I'll know that Life is over.

It's time to be gone.

▪ QUESTIONS

Reading

1. In this essay, Clendinen reflects that in this country, we obsess about how to live, but we don't talk about how to die. Highlight, underline, or flag the places where Clendinen addresses the meaning of death. What information does he offer about living and dying?
2. What does Clendinen mean when he mentions "the weird blessing of Lou" (paragraph 11)?
3. How does Whitney, Clendinen's thirty-year-old daughter, respond to his illness? What type of relationship does Clendinen have with his daughter?

Exploratory Writing

1. Working in small groups, write a statement arguing for or against legal euthanasia. If you choose to argue for euthanasia, draw on Clendinen's points in favor of this position. In arguing against legalizing it, think of counterpoints to his essay.
2. Highlight, underline, or flag the sections in this article where Dudley Clendinen discusses alcoholism and his experiences as a recovering alcoholic. Write a paragraph explaining the ways that Clendinen relates those experiences to his approach to his disease. When Clendinen writes, "I realized I did have a way of life" (paragraph 14), what does he mean?

Making Connections

1. Compare and contrast Clendinen's essay reflecting on his disease with Jill Bolte Taylor's description of having a stroke ("Morning of the Stroke" p. 418). How does each author use words to help the reader understand physical experiences? Does Clendinen, like Taylor, have a "stroke of insight"?

Essay Writing

1. Beginning in February 2011, Dudley Clendinen recorded a series of public radio interviews about his experiences living with amyotrophic lateral sclerosis (A.L.S.). Choose one of these recordings (online at "Living with Lou: Dudley Clendinen on a Good, Short Life" **http://mdmorn.wordpress.com/2011/02/21/221111/**), and write an essay reflecting on your own responses to Clendinen's comments, insights, and revelations.

REFLECTING

Trading Stories

Jhumpa Lahiri

Jhumpa Lahiri was born in London in 1967 to Bengali parents. When she was three, her family immigrated to the United States, settling in Rhode Island. She received a BA in English literature from Barnard College in 1989 and went on to earn MAs in English and comparative literature, an MFA in creative writing, and a PhD in renaissance studies, all from Boston University. Her first collection of short stories, *Interpreter of Maladies* (1999), won the Pulitzer Prize for Fiction in 2000. Her 2003 novel, *The Namesake*, shares with *Interpreter of Maladies* the theme of Indian immigrant psychology. *Unaccustomed Earth* (2008) returned Lahiri to the short story genre, this time spanning many generations, countries, and cultures. Lahiri's fiction and nonfiction, both often autobiographical, frequently appear in the *New Yorker* magazine. In 2010, President Barack Obama appointed Lahiri to his Committee on the Arts and Humanities. In this piece for the *New Yorker* (June 2011), Lahiri reflects on the importance of books to her childhood.

Books, and the stories they contained, were the only things I felt I was able to possess as a child. Even then, the possession was not literal; my father is a librarian, and perhaps because he believed in collective property, or perhaps because my parents considered buying books for me an extravagance, or perhaps because people generally acquired less then than they do now, I had

almost no books to call my own. I remember coveting and eventually being permitted to own a book for the first time. I was five or six. The book was diminutive, about four inches square, and was called *You'll Never Have to Look for Friends.* It lived among the penny candy and the Wacky Packs at the old-fashioned general store across the street from our first house in Rhode Island. The plot was trite, more an extended greeting card than a story. But I remember the excitement of watching my mother purchase it for me and of bringing it home. Inside the front cover, beneath the declaration "This book is especially for," was a line on which to write my name. My mother did so, and also wrote the word "mother" to indicate that the book had been given to me by her, though I did not call her Mother but Ma. "Mother" was an alternate guardian. But she had given me a book that, nearly forty years later, still dwells on a bookcase in my childhood room.

Our house was not devoid of things to read, but the offerings felt scant, and were of little interest to me. There were books about China and Russia that my father read for his graduate studies in political science, and issues of *Time* that he read to relax. My mother owned novels and short stories and stacks of a literary magazine called *Desh,* but they were in Bengali, even the titles illegible to me. She kept her reading material on metal shelves in the basement, or off limits by her bedside. I remember a yellow volume of lyrics by the poet Kazi Nazrul Islam, which seemed to be a holy text to her, and a thick, fraying English dictionary with a maroon cover that was pulled out for Scrabble games. At one point, we bought the first few volumes of a set of encyclopedias that the supermarket where we shopped was promoting, but we never got them all. There was an arbitrary, haphazard quality to the books in our house, as there was to certain other aspects of our material lives. I craved the opposite: a house where books were a solid presence, piled on every surface and cheerfully lining the walls. At times, my family's effort to fill our house with books seemed thwarted; this was the case when my father mounted rods and brackets to hold a set of olive-green shelves. Within a few days the shelves collapsed, the Sheetrocked walls of our seventies-era Colonial unable to support them.

What I really sought was a better-marked trail of my parents' intellectual lives: bound and printed evidence of what they'd read, what had inspired and shaped their minds. A connection, via books, between them and me. But my parents did not read to me or tell me stories; my father did not read any fiction, and the stories my mother may have loved as a young girl in Calcutta were not passed down. My first experience of hearing stories aloud occurred the only time I met my maternal grandfather, when I was two, during my first visit to India. He would lie back on a bed and prop me up on his chest and invent things to tell me. I am told that the two of us stayed up long after everyone else had gone to sleep, and that my grandfather kept extending these stories, because I insisted that they not end.

Bengali was my first language, what I spoke and heard at home. But the books of my childhood were in English, and their subjects were, for the most part, either English or American lives. I was aware of a feeling of trespassing. I was aware that I did not belong to the worlds I was reading about: that my family's life was different, that different food graced our table, that different holidays were celebrated, that my family cared and fretted about different things. And yet when a book was in my possession, and as I read it, this didn't matter. I entered into a pure relationship with the story and its characters, encountering fictional worlds as if physically, inhabiting them fully, at once immersed and invisible.

In life, especially as a young girl, I was afraid to participate in social activities. I worried about what others might make of me, how they might judge. But when I read I was free of this worry. I learned what my fictional companions ate and wore, learned how they spoke, learned about the toys scattered in their rooms, how they sat by the fire on a cold day drinking hot chocolate. I learned about the vacations they took, the blueberries they picked, the jams their mothers stirred on the stove. For me, the act of reading was one of discovery in the most basic sense—the discovery of a culture that was foreign to my parents. I began to defy them in this way, and to understand, from books, certain things that they didn't know. Whatever books came into the house on my account were part of my private domain. And so I felt not only that I was trespassing but also that I was, in some sense, betraying the people who were raising me. 5

When I began to make friends, writing was the vehicle. So that, in the beginning, writing, like reading, was less a solitary pursuit than an attempt to connect with others. I did not write alone but with another student in my class at school. We would sit together, this friend and I, dreaming up characters and plots, taking turns writing sections of the story, passing the pages back and forth. Our handwriting was the only thing that separated us, the only way to determine which section was whose. I always preferred rainy days to bright ones, so that we could stay indoors at recess, sit in the hallway, and concentrate. But even on nice days I found somewhere to sit, under a tree or on the ledge of the sandbox, with this friend, and sometimes one or two others, to continue the work on our tale. The stories were transparent riffs on what I was reading at the time: families living on prairies, orphaned girls sent off to boarding schools or educated by stern governesses, children with supernatural powers, or the ability to slip through closets into alternate worlds. My reading was my mirror, and my material; I saw no other part of myself.

My love of writing led me to theft at an early age. The diamonds in the museum, what I schemed and broke the rules to obtain, were the blank notebooks in my teacher's supply cabinet, stacked in neat rows, distributed for us to write out sentences or practice math. The notebooks were slim, stapled together, featureless, either light blue or a brownish-yellow shade. The pages were lined, their dimensions neither too small nor too large. Wanting them for my stories, I worked up the nerve to request one or two from the teacher. Then, on learning that the cabinet was not always locked or monitored, I began helping myself to a furtive supply.

In the fifth grade, I won a small prize for a story called "The Adventures of a Weighing Scale," in which the eponymous narrator describes an assortment of people and other creatures who visit it. Eventually the weight of the world is too much; the scale breaks, and it is abandoned at the dump. I illustrated the story—all my stories were illustrated back then—and bound it together with bits of orange yarn. The book was displayed briefly in the school library, fitted with an actual card and pocket. No one took it out, but that didn't matter. The validation of the card and pocket was enough. The prize also came with a gift certificate for a local bookstore. As much as I wanted to own books, I was beset by indecision. For hours, it seemed, I wandered the shelves of the store. In the end, I chose a book I'd never heard of, Carl Sandburg's "Rootabaga Stories." I wanted to love those stories, but their old-fashioned wit eluded me. And yet I kept the book as a talisman, perhaps, of that first recognition. Like the labels on the cakes and bottles that Alice discovers underground, the essential gift of my award was that it spoke to me in the imperative; for the first time, a voice in my head said, "Do this."

As I grew into adolescence and beyond, however, my writing shrank in what seemed to be an inverse proportion to my years. Though the compulsion to invent stories remained, self-doubt began to undermine it, so that I spent the second half of my childhood being gradually stripped of the one comfort I'd known, that formerly instinctive activity turning thorny to the touch. I convinced myself that creative writers were other people, not me, so that what I loved at seven became, by seventeen, the form of self-expression that most intimidated me. I preferred practicing music and performing in plays, learning the notes of a composition or memorizing the lines of a script. I continued working with words, but channelled my energy into essays and articles, wanting to be a journalist. In college, where I studied literature, I decided that I would become an English professor. At twenty-one, the writer in me was like a fly in the room—alive but insignificant, aimless, something that unsettled me whenever I grew aware of it, and which, for the most part, left me alone. I was not at a stage where I needed to worry about rejection from others. My insecurity was systemic, and preemptive, insuring that, before anyone else had the opportunity, I had already rejected myself.

10 For much of my life, I wanted to be other people; here was the central dilemma, the reason, I believe, for my creative stasis. I was always falling short of people's expectations: my immigrant parents', my Indian relatives', my American peers', above all my own. The writer in me wanted to edit myself. If only there was a little more this, a little less that, depending on the circumstances: Then the asterisk that accompanied me would be removed. My upbringing, an amalgam of two hemispheres, was heterodox and complicated; I wanted it to be conventional and contained. I wanted to be anonymous and ordinary, to look like other people, to behave as others did. To anticipate an alternate future, having sprung from a different past. This had been the lure of acting—the comfort of erasing my identity and adopting another. How could I want to be a writer, to articulate what was within me, when I did not wish to be myself?

It was not in my nature to be an assertive person. I was used to looking to others for guidance, for influence, sometimes for the most basic cues of life. And yet writing stories is one of the most assertive things a person can do.

Fiction is an act of willfulness, a deliberate effort to reconceive, to rearrange, to reconstitute nothing short of reality itself. Even among the most reluctant and doubtful of writers, this willfulness must emerge. Being a writer means taking the leap from listening to saying, "Listen to me."

This was where I faltered. I preferred to listen rather than speak, to see instead of be seen. I was afraid of listening to myself, and of looking at my life.

It was assumed by my family that I would get a PhD. But after I graduated from college, I was, for the first time, no longer a student, and the structure and system I'd known and in some senses depended on fell away. I moved to Boston, a city I knew only vaguely, and lived in a room in the home of people who were not related to me, whose only interest in me was my rent. I found work at a bookstore, opening shipments and running a cash register. I formed a close friendship with a young woman who worked there, whose father is a poet named Bill Corbett. I began to visit the Corbetts' home, which was filled with books and art—a framed poem by Seamus Heaney, drawings by Philip Guston, a rubbing of Ezra Pound's gravestone. I saw the desk where Bill wrote, obscured by manuscripts, letters, and proofs, in the middle of the living room. I saw that the work taking place on this desk was obliged to no one, connected to no institution; that this desk was an island, and that Bill worked on his own. I spent a summer living in that house, reading back issues of *The Paris Review,* and when I was alone, in a bright room on the top floor, pecking out sketches and fragments on a typewriter.

I began to want to be a writer. Secretly at first, exchanging pages with one other person, our prescheduled meetings forcing me to sit down and produce something. Stealing into the office where I had a job as a research assistant, on weekends and at night, to type stories onto a computer, a machine I did not own at the time. I bought a copy of *Writer's Market,* and sent out stories to little magazines that sent them back to me. The following year, I entered graduate school, not as a writer but as a student of English literature. But beneath my declared scholarly objective there was now a wrinkle. I used to pass a bookshop every day on the way to the train, the storefront displaying dozens of titles that I always stopped to look at. Among them were books by Leslie Epstein, a writer whose work I had not yet read but whose name I knew, as the director of the writing program at Boston University. On a lark one day, I walked into the creative-writing department seeking permission to sit in on a class.

It was audacious of me. The equivalent, nearly two decades later, of stealing notebooks from a teacher's cabinet; of crossing a line. The class was open only to writing students, so I did not expect Epstein to make an exception. After he did, I worked up the nerve to apply for a formal spot in the creative-writing program the following year. When I told my parents that I'd been accepted, with a fellowship, they neither encouraged nor discouraged me. Like so many aspects of my American life, the idea that one could get a degree in creative writing, that it could be a legitimate course of study, seemed perhaps frivolous to them. Still, a degree was a degree, and so their reaction to my decision was to remain neutral. Though I corrected her, my mother, at first, referred to it as a critical-writing program. My father, I am guessing, hoped it would have something to do with a PhD.

My mother wrote poems occasionally. They were in Bengali, and were published now and then in literary magazines in New England or Calcutta. She seemed proud of her efforts, but she did not call herself a poet. Both her father and her youngest brother, on the other hand, were visual artists. It was by their creative callings that they were known to the world, and had been described to me. My mother spoke of them reverently. She told me about the day that my grandfather had had to take his final exam at the Government College of Art, in Calcutta, and happened to have a high fever. He was able to complete only a portion of the portrait he had been asked to render, the subject's mouth and chin, but it was done so skillfully that he graduated with honors. Watercolors by my grandfather were brought back from India, framed, and shown off to visitors, and to this day I keep one of his medals in my jewelry box, regarding it since childhood as a good-luck charm.

Before our visits to Calcutta, my mother would make special trips to an art store to buy the brushes and paper and pens and tubes of paint that my uncle had requested. Both my grandfather and my uncle earned their living as commercial artists. Their fine art brought in little money. My grandfather died when I was five, but I have vivid memories of my uncle, working at his table in the corner of the cramped rented apartment where my mother was brought up; preparing layouts for clients who came to the house to approve or disapprove of his ideas, my uncle staying up all night to get the job done. I gathered that my grandfather had never been financially secure, and that my uncle's career was also precarious—that being an artist, though noble and romantic, was not a practical or responsible thing to do.

Abandoned weighing scales, witches, orphans: these, in childhood, had been my subjects. As a child, I had written to connect with my peers. But when I started writing stories again, in my twenties, my parents were the people I was struggling to reach. In 1992, just before starting the writing program at B.U., I went to Calcutta with my family. I remember coming back at the end of summer, getting into bed, and almost immediately writing the first of the stories I submitted that year in workshop. It was set in the building where my mother had grown up, and where I spent much of my time when I was in India. I see now that my impulse to write this story, and several like-minded stories that followed, was to prove something to my parents: that I understood on my own terms, in my own words, in a limited but precise way, the world they came from. For though they had created me, and reared me, and lived with me day after day, I knew that I was a stranger to them, an American child. In spite of our closeness, I feared that I was alien. This was the predominant anxiety I had felt while growing up.

I was my parents' firstborn child. When I was seven, my mother became pregnant again, and gave birth to my sister in November, 1974. A few months later, one of her closest friends in Rhode Island, another Bengali woman, also learned that she was expecting. The woman's husband, like my father, worked at the university. Based on my mother's recommendation, her friend saw the same doctor and planned to deliver at the same hospital where my sister was born. One rainy evening, my parents received a call from the hospital. The woman's husband cried into the telephone as he told my parents that their child had been born dead. There was no reason for it. It had simply happened, as it sometimes does. I remember the weeks following, my mother cooking food and taking it over to the couple, the grief in place of the son who was supposed to have filled their home. If writing is a reaction to injustice, or a search for meaning when meaning is taken away, this was that initial experience for me. I remember thinking that it could have happened to my parents and not to their friends, and I remember, because the same thing had not happened to our family, as my sister was by then a year old already, also feeling ashamed. But, mainly, I felt the unfairness of it—the unfairness of the couple's expectation, unfulfilled.

We moved to a new house, whose construction we had overseen, in a new neighborhood. Soon afterward, the childless couple had a house built in our neighborhood as well. They hired the same contractor, and used the same materials, the same floor plan, so that the houses were practically identical. Other children in the neighborhood, sailing past on bicycles and roller skates, took note of this similarity, finding it funny. I was asked if all Indians lived in matching houses. I resented these children, for not knowing what I knew of the couple's misfortune, and at the same time I resented the couple a little, for having modeled their home on ours, for suggesting that our lives were the same when they were not. A few years later the house was sold, the couple moving away to another town, and an American family altered the façade so that it was no longer a carbon copy of ours. The comic parallel between two Bengali families in a Rhode Island neighborhood was forgotten by the neighborhood children. But our lives had not been parallel; I was unable to forget this. 20

When I was thirty years old, digging in the loose soil of a new story, I unearthed that time, that first tragic thing I could remember happening, and wrote a story called "A Temporary Matter." It is not exactly the story of what had happened to that couple, nor is it a story of something that happened to me. Springing from my childhood, from the part of me that was slowly reverting to what I loved most when I was young, it was the first story that I wrote as an adult.

My father, who, at eighty, still works forty hours a week at the University of Rhode Island, has always sought security and stability in his job. His salary was never huge, but he supported a family that wanted for nothing. As a child, I did not know the exact meaning of "tenure," but when my father obtained it I sensed what it meant to him. I set out to do as he had done, and to pursue a career that would provide me with a similar stability and security. But at the last minute I stepped away, because I wanted to be a writer instead. Stepping away was what was essential, and what was also fraught. Even after I received the Pulitzer Prize, my father reminded me that writing stories was not something to count on, and that I must always be prepared to earn my living in some other way. I listen to him, and at the same time I have learned not to listen, to wander to the edge of the precipice and to leap. And so, though a writer's job is to look and listen, in order to become a writer I had to be deaf and blind.

I see now that my father, for all his practicality, gravitated toward a precipice of his own, leaving his country and his family, stripping himself of the reassurance of belonging. In reaction, for much of my life, I wanted to belong to a place, either the one my parents came from or to America, spread out before us. When I became a writer my desk became home; there was no need for another. Every story is a foreign territory, which, in the process of writing, is occupied and then abandoned. I belong to my work, to my characters, and in order to create new ones I leave the old ones behind. My parents' refusal to let go or to belong fully to either place is at the heart of what I, in a less literal way, try to accomplish in writing. Born of my inability to belong, it is my refusal to let go.

▪ QUESTIONS

Reading

1. What was the first story that Lahiri wrote as an adult? What inspired her to write it?
2. What is Lahiri's father's profession? How does he respond to her choice to be a writer? How does his perspective change when she is awarded a Pulitzer Prize?
3. Highlight, underline, or flag the titles of books that Lahiri mentions in her essay reflecting on her development as a writer. What information does Lahiri seek from these books? What does she hope to learn about her family?
4. "Though a writer's job is to look and listen, in order to become a writer I had to be deaf and blind," writes Lahiri (paragraph 22). Where else in this essay does Lahiri use irony or paradox to explain her situation as a writer?

Exploratory Writing

1. Lahiri writes that when she became a writer, her desk became her home and she no longer needed another home. She uses writing to address her fear of being "alien" (paragraph 18). With a partner, use words that define what "home" means to you, and then compare your results. Is your "home" the same as the physical space where you live? Have you ever felt like a stranger at home?
2. Write a list of at least five books of poetry, fiction, or nonfiction that have influenced your thinking and shaped your view of the world, and do some research about the author of each book. Where was each author born, and where did he or she grow up? What was his or her first language, and which other languages did he or she speak? Did he or she have any jobs or professions aside from writing? In your opinion, how did the author's life shape his or her writing?

Making Connections

1. Lahiri writes, "Bengali was my first language, what I spoke and heard at home. But the books of my childhood were in English, and their subjects were, for the most part, either English or American lives. I was aware of a feeling of trespassing" (paragraph 4).

Amy Tan (p. 178), whose parents immigrated to California from China before she was born, writes about speaking "different Englishes" during her bilingual childhood. How does each writer connect language to "trespassing" versus "belonging"?

Essay Writing

1. Lahiri's essay reflecting on her development as a writer was originally subtitled "Notes from an Apprenticeship." Write an essay reflecting on an apprenticeship in your own life — a time when you were new at something, and learning skills and strategies for practicing it. What insights, surprises, and revelations about life did your apprenticeship bring? The "apprenticeship" you choose does not necessarily need to be finished. You might pick something you're studying now.

REPORTING

The Long Good-bye

Mother's Day in Federal Prison

Amanda Coyne

Amanda Coyne (b. 1966) was born in Colorado and subsequently migrated with her family to Alaska and ten other states as her father's "relentless pursuit of better employment" led him to hold such titles as fry cook, janitor, librarian, college professor, magazine editor, and presidential speechwriter. Coyne describes her own life as having thus far been "similarly kinetic and varied." Between traveling and "experimenting with religion, countercultural lifestyles, and writing," she has been employed as a waitress, nursing-home assistant, teacher, public relations associate, and public-policy analyst. A graduate of the University of Iowa, Coyne is coeditor and cofounder of AlaskaDispatch.com and a teacher of writing at Alaska Pacific University. Her work has been published in the *New York Times Magazine, Harper's,* the *Huffington Post, Bust* magazine, and *Jane* magazine; she has also coauthored the book *Alaska Then and Now* (2008). Coyne has read her pieces on National Public Radio's *All Things Considered* and Public Radio International's *This American Life*. The following essay, which appeared in *Harper's* (May 1997), was her first publication.

You can spot the convict-moms here in the visiting room by the way they hold and touch their children, and by the single flower that is perched in front of them—a rose, a tulip, a daffodil. Many of these mothers have untied the bow that attaches the flower to its silver-and-red cellophane wrapper and are using one of the many empty soda cans at hand as a vase. They sit proudly before their flower-in-a-Coke-can, amid Hershey bar wrappers, half-eaten Ding Dongs, and empty paper coffee cups. Occasionally, a mother will pick up her present and bring it to her nose when one of the bearers of the single flower—her child—asks if she likes it. And the mother will respond the way that mothers always have and always will respond when presented with a gift on this day. "Oh, I just love it. It's perfect. I'll put it in the middle of my Bible." Or, "I'll put it on my desk, right next to your school picture." And always: "It's the best one here."

But most of what is being smelled today is the children themselves. While the other adults are plunking coins into the vending machines, the mothers take deep whiffs from the backs of their children's necks, or kiss and smell the backs of their knees, or take off their shoes and tickle their feet and then pull them close to their noses. They hold them tight and take in their own second scent—the scent assuring them that these are still their children and that they still belong to them.

The visitors are allowed to bring in pockets full of coins, and today that Mother's Day flower, and I know from previous visits to my older sister here at the Federal Prison Camp for women in Pekin, Illinois, that there is always an

Jennifer, prisoner number 07235-029.

aberrant urge to gather immediately around the vending machines. The sandwiches are stale, the coffee weak, the candy bars the ones we always pass up in a convenience store. But after we hand the children over to their mothers, we gravitate toward those machines. Like milling in the kitchen at a party. We all do it, and nobody knows why. Polite conversation ensues around the microwave while the popcorn is popping and the processed-chicken sandwiches are being heated. We ask one another where we are from, how long a drive we had. An occasional whistle through the teeth, a shake of the head. "My, my, long way from home, huh?" "Staying at the Super 8 right up the road. Not a bad place." "Stayed at the Econo Lodge last time. Wasn't a good place at all." Never asking the questions we really want to ask: "What's she in for?" "How much time's she got left?" You never ask in the waiting room of a doctor's office either. Eventually, all of us—fathers, mothers, sisters, brothers, a few boyfriends, and very few husbands—return to the queen of the day, sitting at a fold-out table loaded with snacks, prepared for five or so hours of attempted normal conversation.

Most of the inmates are elaborately dressed, many in prison-crafted dresses and sweaters in bright blues and pinks. They wear meticulously applied makeup in corresponding hues, and their hair is replete with loops and curls—hair that only women with the time have the time for. Some of the better seamstresses have crocheted vests and purses to match their outfits. Although the world outside would never accuse these women of making haute-couture fashion statements, the fathers and the sons and the boyfriends and the very few husbands think they look beautiful, and they tell them so repeatedly. And I can imagine the hours spent preparing for this visit—hours of needles and hooks clicking over brightly colored yards of yarn. The hours of discussing, dissecting, and bragging about these visitors—especially the men. Hours spent in the other world behind the door where we're not allowed, sharing lipsticks and mascaras, and unraveling the occasional hair-tangled hot roller, and the brushing out and lifting and teasing . . . and the giggles that abruptly change into tears without warning—things that define any female-only world. Even, or especially, if that world is a female federal prison camp.

While my sister Jennifer is with her son in the playroom, an inmate's mother comes over to introduce herself to my younger sister, Charity, my brother, John, and me. She tells us about visiting her daughter in a higher-security prison before she was transferred here. The woman looks old and tired, and her shoulders sag under the weight of her recently acquired bitterness. 5

"Pit of fire," she says, shaking her head. "Like a pit of fire straight from hell. Never seen anything like it. Like something out of an old movie about prisons." Her voice is getting louder and she looks at each of us with pleading eyes. "My *daughter* was there. Don't even get me started on that place. Women die there."

John and Charity and I silently exchange glances.

"My daughter would come to the visiting room with a black eye and I'd think, 'All she did was sit in the car while her boyfriend ran into the house.' She didn't even touch the stuff. Never even handled it."

She continues to stare at us, each in turn. "Ten years. That boyfriend talked and he got three years. She didn't know anything. Had nothing to tell them. They gave her ten years. They called it conspiracy. Conspiracy? Aren't there real criminals out there?" She asks this with hands outstretched, waiting for an answer that none of us can give her.

The woman's daughter, the conspirator, is chasing her son through the maze of chairs and tables and through the other children. She's a twenty-four-year-old blonde, whom I'll call Stephanie, with Dorothy Hamill[1] hair and matching dimples. She looks like any girl you might see in any shopping mall in middle America. She catches her chocolate-brown son and tickles him, and they laugh and trip and fall together onto the floor and laugh harder. 10

Had it not been for that wait in the car, this scene would be taking place at home, in a duplex Stephanie would rent while trying to finish her two-year degree in dental hygiene or respiratory therapy at the local community college. The duplex would be spotless, with a blown-up picture of her and her son over the couch and ceramic unicorns and horses occupying the shelves of the entertainment center. She would make sure that her son went to school every day with stylishly floppy pants, scrubbed teeth, and a good breakfast in his belly. Because of their difference in skin color, there would be occasional tension—caused by the strange looks from strangers, teachers, other mothers, and the bullies on the playground, who would chant after they knocked him

[1]*Dorothy Hamill*: The 1976 Olympic gold medal–winning figure skater whose "wedge" haircut became wildly popular in the United States.—Eds.

down, "Your Momma's white, your Momma's white." But if she were home, their weekends and evenings would be spent together transcending those looks and healing those bruises. Now, however, their time is spent eating visiting-room junk food and his school days are spent fighting the boys in the playground who chant, "Your Momma's in prison, your Momma's in prison."

He will be ten when his mother is released, the same age my nephew will be when his mother is let out. But Jennifer, my sister, was able to spend the first five years of Toby's life with him. Stephanie had Ellie after she was incarcerated. They let her hold him for eighteen hours, then sent her back to prison. She has done the "tour," and her son is a well-traveled six-year-old. He has spent weekends visiting his mother in prisons in Kentucky, Texas, Connecticut (the Pit of Fire), and now at last here, the camp—minimum security, Pekin, Illinois.

Ellie looks older than his age. But his shoulders do not droop like his grandmother's. On the contrary, his bitterness lifts them and his chin higher than a child's should be, and the childlike, wide-eyed curiosity has been replaced by defiance. You can see his emerging hostility as he and his mother play together. She tells him to pick up the toy that he threw, say, or to put the deck of cards away. His face turns sullen, but she persists. She takes him by the shoulders and looks him in the eye, and he uses one of his hands to swat at her. She grabs the hand and he swats with the other. Eventually, she pulls him toward her and smells the top of his head, and she picks up the cards or the toy herself. After all, it is Mother's Day and she sees him so rarely. But her acquiescence makes him angrier, and he stalks out of the playroom with his shoulders thrown back.

Toby, my brother and sister and I assure one another, will not have these resentments. He is better taken care of than most. He is living with relatives in Wisconsin. Good, solid, middle-class, churchgoing relatives. And when he visits us, his aunts and his uncle, we take him out for adventures where we walk down the alley of a city and pretend that we are being chased by the "bad guys." We buy him fast food, and his uncle, John, keeps him up well past his bedtime enthralling him with stories of the monkeys he met in India. A perfect mix, we try to convince one another. Until we take him to see his mother and on the drive back he asks the question that most confuses him, and no doubt all the other children who spend much of their lives in prison visiting rooms: "Is my Mommy a bad guy?" It is the question that most seriously disorders his five-year-old need to clearly separate right from wrong. And because our own need is perhaps just as great, it is the question that haunts us as well.

15 Now, however, the answer is relatively simple. In a few years, it won't be. In a few years we will have to explain mandatory minimums, and the war on drugs, and the murky conspiracy laws, and the enormous amount of money and time that federal agents pump into imprisoning low-level drug dealers and those who happen to be their friends and their lovers. In a few years he might have the reasoning skills to ask why so many armed robbers and rapists and child-molesters and, indeed, murderers are punished less severely than his mother. When he is older, we will somehow have to explain to him the difference between federal crimes, which don't allow for parole, and state crimes,

which do. We will have to explain that his mother was taken from him for five years not because she was a drug dealer but because she made four phone calls for someone she loved.

But we also know it is vitally important that we explain all this without betraying our bitterness. We understand the danger of abstract anger, of being disillusioned with your country, and, most of all, we do not want him to inherit that legacy. We would still like him to be raised as we were, with the idea that we live in the best country in the world with the best legal system in the world—a legal system carefully designed to be immune to political mood swings and public hysteria; a system that promises to fit the punishment to the crime. We want him to be a good citizen. We want him to have absolute faith that he lives in a fair country, a country that watches over and protects its most vulnerable citizens: its women and children.

So for now we simply say, “Toby, your mother isn't bad, she just did a bad thing. Like when you put rocks in the lawn mower's gas tank. You weren't bad then, you just did a bad thing.”

Once, after being given this weak explanation, he said, “I wish I could have done something really bad, like my Mommy. So I could go to prison too and be with her.”

We notice a circle forming on one side of the visiting room. A little boy stands in its center. He is perhaps nine years old, sporting a burnt-orange three-piece suit and pompadour hair. He stands with his legs slightly apart, eyes half-shut, and sways back and forth, flashing his cuffs and snapping his fingers while singing:

> *. . . Doesn't like crap games with barons and earls.*
> *Won't go to Harlem in ermine and pearls.*
> *Won't dish the dirt with the rest of the girls.*
> *That's why the lady is a tramp.*

He has a beautiful voice and it sounds vaguely familiar. One of the visitors 20 informs me excitedly that the boy is the youngest Frank Sinatra impersonator and that he has been on television even. The boy finishes his performance and the room breaks into applause. He takes a sweeping bow, claps his miniature hands together, and points both little index fingers at the audience. “More. Later. Folks.” He spins on his heels and returns to the table where his mother awaits him, proudly glowing. “Don't mess with the hair, Mom,” we overhear. “That little boy's slick,” my brother says with true admiration.

Sitting a few tables down from the youngest Frank Sinatra is a table of Mexican-Americans. The young ones are in white dresses or button-down oxfords with matching ties. They form a strange formal contrast to the rest of the rowdy group. They sit silently, solemnly listening to the white-haired woman, who holds one of the table's two roses. I walk past and listen to the grandmother lecture her family. She speaks of values, of getting up early every day, of going to work. She looks at one of the young boys and points a finger at him. "School is the most important thing. *Nada más importante.*[2] You get up and you go to school and you study, and you can make lots of money. You can be big. You can be huge. Study, study, study."

The young boy nods his head. "Yes, *abuelita.*[3] Yes, *abuelita,*" he says.

The owner of the other flower is holding one of the group's three infants. She has him spread before her. She coos and kisses his toes and nuzzles his stomach.

When I ask Jennifer about them, she tells me that it is a "mother and daughter combo." There are a few of them here, these combos, and I notice that they have the largest number of visitors and that the older inmate, the grandmother, inevitably sits at the head of the table. Even here, it seems, the hierarchical family structure remains intact. One could take a picture, replace the fast-food wrappers with chicken and potatoes, and these families could be at any restaurant in the country, could be sitting at any dining room table, paying homage on this day to the one who brought them into the world.

Back at our table, a black-haired, Middle Eastern woman dressed in loose cottons and cloth shoes is whispering to my brother with a sense of urgency that makes me look toward my sister Charity with questioning eyes and a tilt of my head. Charity simply shrugs and resumes her conversation with a nineteen-year-old ex–New York University student—another conspirator. Eight years. 25

Prison, it seems, has done little to squelch the teenager's rebellious nature. She has recently been released from solitary confinement. She wears new retro-bellbottom jeans and black shoes with big clunky heels. Her hair is short, clipped perfectly ragged and dyed white—all except the roots, which are a stylish black. She has beautiful pale skin and beautiful red lips. She looks like any Midwestern coed trying to escape her origins by claiming New York's East Village as home. She steals the bleach from the laundry room, I learn later, in order to maintain that fashionable white hue. But stealing the bleach is not what landed her in the hole. She committed the inexcusable act of defacing federal property. She took one of her government-issue T-shirts and wrote in permanent black Magic Marker, "I have been in your system. I have examined your system." And when she turned around it read, "I find it very much in need of repair."

But Charity has more important things to discuss with the girl than rebelling against the system. They are talking fashion. They talk prints versus plains, spring shoes, and spring dresses. Charity informs the girl that sling-back, high-heeled sandals and pastels are all the rage. She makes a disgusted face and says, "Damn! Pinks and blues wash me out. I hate pastels. I don't *have* any pastels."

This fashion blip seems to be putting the girl into a deep depression. And so Charity, attempting to lighten up the conversation, puts her nose toward the girl's neck.

---

[2]*Nada más importante*: Nothing more important (Spanish).—Eds.

[3]*abuelita*: Grandma (Spanish).—Eds.

"New Armani scent, Gio," my sister announces.

30 The girl perks up. She nods her head. She calls one of the other inmates over.

Charity performs the same ritual: "Coco Chanel." And again: "Paris, Yves St. Laurent."

The line gets longer, and the girls talk excitedly to one another. It seems that Charity's uncanny talent for divining brand-name perfumes is perhaps nowhere on earth more appreciated than here with these sensory-starved inmates.

As Charity continues to smell necks and call out names, I turn back to my brother and find that the woman who was speaking to him so intensely has gone. He stares pensively at the concrete wall ahead of him.

"What did she want?" I ask.

35 "She heard I was a sculptor. She wants me to make a bust, presented in her name, for Qaddafi."

"A bust of what?"

"Of Qaddafi. She's from Libya. She was a freedom fighter. Her kids are farmed out to strangers here—foster homes. It's Qaddafi's twenty-eighth anniversary as dictator in September. She knows him. He's mad at her now, but she thinks that he'll get over it and get her kids back to Libya if she gives him a present."

"Obsession. Calvin Klein," I hear my sister pronounce. The girls cheer in unison.

I get up and search for the girl. I want to ask her about her crime. I look in the book room only to find the four-foot Frank Sinatra crooning "Somewhere over the Rainbow" to a group of spellbound children.

40 I ask Ponytail, one of the female guards, where the woman went. "Rule," she informs me. "Cannot be in the visiting room if no visitor is present. Should not have been here. Had to go back to unit one." I have spoken to Ponytail a few times while visiting my sister and have yet to hear her use a possessive pronoun, a contraction, or a conjunction.

According to Jennifer, Ponytail has wanted to be a prison guard since she was a little girl. She is one of the few female guards here and she has been here the longest, mainly because the male guards are continuously being fired for "indiscretions" with the inmates. But Ponytail doesn't mess around. She is also the toughest guard here, particularly in regard to the federal rules governing exposed skin. She is disgusted by any portion of the leg showing above the required eight-inch shorts length. In summer, they say, she is constantly whipping out her measuring tape and writing up those who are even a fraction of an inch off.

Last summer posed a particular problem for Ponytail, though. It seems that the shorts sold in the commissary were only seven inches from crotch to seam. And because they were commissary-issued, Ponytail couldn't censor them. So, of course, all the women put away their own shorts in favor of the commissary's. This disturbed Ponytail—a condition that eventually, according to one of the girls, developed into a low-grade depression. "She walked around with that sad old tape in her hands all summer, throwing it from one hand to the other and looking at our legs. After a while, not one of us could get her even to crack a smile—not that she's a big smiler, but you can get those corners to turn sometimes. Then she started looking downright sad, you know real depressed like."

Ponytail makes sure that the girls get proper medical care. Also none of the male guards will mess with them when she's around. But even if those things weren't true, the girls would be fond of Ponytail. She is in a way just another woman in the system, and perhaps no other group of women realizes the absolute necessity for female solidarity. These inmates know with absolute certainty what women on the outside only suspect—that men still hold ultimate power over their bodies, their property, and their freedom.

So as a token of this solidarity, they all agreed to slip off their federal shorts and put on their own. Ponytail perked up, the measuring tape appeared again with a vengeance, and quite a few of the shorts owners spent much of their free time that summer cleaning out toilet bowls and wiping the scuffs off the gym floor.

It's now 3:00. Visiting ends at 3:30. The kids are getting cranky, and the adults are both exhausted and wired from too many hours of conversation, too much coffee and candy. The fathers, mothers, sisters, brothers, and the few boyfriends, and the very few husbands are beginning to show signs of gathering the trash. The mothers of the infants are giving their heads one last whiff before tucking them and their paraphernalia into their respective carrying cases. The visitors meander toward the door, leaving the older children with their mothers for one last word. But the mothers never say what they want to say to their children. They say things like, "Do well in school," "Be nice to your sister," "Be good for Aunt Betty, or Grandma." They don't say, "I'm sorry I'm sorry I'm sorry. I love you more than anything else in the world and I think about you every minute and I worry about you with a pain that shoots straight to my heart, a pain so great I think I will just burst when I think of you alone, without me. I'm sorry." 45

We are standing in front of the double glass doors that lead to the outside world. My older sister holds her son, rocking him gently. They are both crying. We give her a look and she puts him down. Charity and I grasp each of his small hands, and the four of us walk through the doors. As we're walking out, my brother sings one of his banana songs to Toby.

"Take me out to the—" and Toby yells out, "Banana store!"

"Buy me some—"

"Bananas!!"

"I don't care if I ever come back. For it's root, root, root for the—" 50

"Monkey team!"

I turn back and see a line of women standing behind the glass wall. Some of them are crying, but many simply stare with dazed eyes. Stephanie is holding both of her son's hands in hers and speaking urgently to him. He is struggling, and his head is twisting violently back and forth. He frees one of his hands from her grasp, balls up his fist, and punches her in the face. Then he walks with purpose through the glass doors and out the exit. I look back at her. She is still in a crouched position. She stares, unblinking, through those doors. Her hands have left her face and are hanging on either side of her. I look away, but before I do, I see drops of blood drip from her nose, down her chin, and onto the shiny marble floor.

▪ QUESTIONS

Reading

1. How would you describe Coyne's point of view in this piece? Detached or involved? Insider or outsider? How does her point of view affect your perception of the federal prison for women that she writes about in this piece?
2. In this report, why do you think that Coyne focuses on Mother's Day in the prison? What kinds of details is she able to report that might not be observable on most other days? What kinds of details are likely to be missing (or obscured) on such a day as this?
3. Coyne has come to visit her sister Jennifer, but why do you suppose she tells so little about Jennifer compared to what she reports about the other prisoners, particularly Stephanie and the nineteen-year-old former New York University student? Why do you suppose that Coyne tells so much about Stephanie's child, Ellie, and the young Frank Sinatra impersonator but so little about Jennifer's child, Toby?
4. Given the selection and arrangement of descriptive details about the people who figure in this account, what do you consider to be Coyne's major purposes in writing this piece?

Exploratory Writing

1. Collaborating in small groups, research or investigate a prison in your community. Write a report highlighting the details that you think are most important in revealing the quality of life in that prison.
2. Reflect on a time when one of your own friends or relatives got into trouble, suffered a tragedy, or made a life-changing mistake. How did his or her story affect you?
3. Imagine that you have been appointed to a public office that has the task of reforming women's prisons like the one described in "The Long Good-bye." As a class, brainstorm about what changes you would make to the system, and why. In considering this subject, you can also refer to the information Christina Boufis (p. 96) provides in her essay on teaching literature in a county jail.

Making Connections

1. Coyne observes that women in the prison system realize the need for female solidarity: "These inmates know with absolute certainty what women on the outside only suspect — that men still hold ultimate power over their bodies, their property, and their freedom" (paragraph 43). Compare this view of male power to Gloria Anzaldúa's; she claims that "Language is a male discourse" (p. 168). Discuss the different ways that Coyne and Anzaldúa talk about female experiences of powerlessness.

Essay Writing

1. Compare Coyne's piece on women's prisons and female prisoners to one or two other stories that you find on this subject in newspapers, in magazines, or on the Internet.

REPORTING

Teaching Literature at the County Jail

Christina Boufis

Christina Boufis (b. 1961) grew up on Long Island and is a graduate of Barnard College. She received an MA in English language and literature from the University of Virginia and a PhD in literature and a certificate in women's studies from the Graduate Center of the City University of New York. She currently teaches nonfiction writing at Stanford and serves as the director of the writing program at the San Francisco Art Institute. She has also taught writing at the University of California at Berkeley and the San Francisco County Jail. Her work has appeared in many popular magazines and academic journals, and her article "A Teacher behind Bars," which first appeared in *Glamour* magazine, was nominated for the Heart of America, a national journalism award. She has said that the following essay "was written out of necessity: Teaching at the jail was so overwhelming at first that I absolutely had to write about it to get some distance from my students' painful experiences and be able to go back the next day." This essay first appeared in the *Common Review* (Fall 2001).

There is no money for books, so I am photocopying Toni Morrison's *Sula*[1] chapter by chapter. This is in defiance of all copyright laws, but I think if she knew, Morrison would understand. Sometimes I even imagine her walking into our classroom, and I wonder how she would react to what she saw: twenty-five women dressed in fluorescent orange, reading her works out loud. It's been almost four years since I began teaching at the San Francisco County Jail, and I barely notice the bright orange uniforms anymore, or that my class is far from the traditional university setting in which I once imagined myself. Instead, I see only the women and their individual faces.

I arrived in San Francisco in 1994, as a new county jail was being built. That year also marked a turning point in California's history: It was the first time the state's corrections budget exceeded that of the entire University of California system. I didn't know this then; I knew only that I wanted to live and work in the city of my choice rather than follow the vagaries of a bleak academic job market. When I heard that a substitute teaching position in high school equivalency was available at the jail, I didn't hesitate. Although I knew next to nothing about the subject, I had spent the last several years in graduate school reading about women in literature. I was eager to work with real ones.

Other than telling me that many women inmates have difficulty reading (most are at a fourth- to seventh-grade reading level, I later discovered) and that I should perhaps start with simple math exercises, my predecessor prepared me for little. He was in a great hurry, offered the class for as long as I

[1]*Toni Morrison* (b. 1931): The winner of the 1993 Nobel Prize for Literature. *Sula* (1973) is one of her novels.—Eds.

would have it, and took off for Tahoe[2] without waiting for my answer. Obviously, he'd had enough.

But he gave me a parting gift: a copy of Alice Walker's *The Color Purple*,[3] stored in the top drawer of the classroom filing cabinet. "Sometimes, at the end of class, if they're quiet, I read it out loud to them," he explained. Though the class was held at San Francisco's newest county jail (nicknamed the "glamour slammer" for its seemingly posh facility), the building's school-like appearance belied the fact that the Sheriff's Department spent not a single cent on any of the educational or rehabilitative programs that went on inside. Thus there was no money for more copies of Walker's novel or anyone else's. The class I was teaching was funded by the local community college, which provided only GED[4] books.

I forgot all about *The Color Purple* my first harried, difficult day at the jail. My shock at seeing the women, who appeared as a blur of orange, turned to alienation, then anger, as the class wore on. "Man, we're going to eat you alive," one woman repeatedly uttered. Others told me they didn't have to do any work and weren't going to. A few more crumpled up the math exercises I'd photocopied and told me they didn't know their multiplication tables. 5

But toward the end of class, one woman seemed to take pity on me and asked for "the book."

"What book?" I replied a little too eagerly.

"The book, the book," others chimed in as if it were obvious.

Another student pointed to the filing cabinet, and I remembered Walker's novel. There was some disagreement about where the previous instructor had left off, but the last ten minutes of class were spent in relative silence as I read and they listened. I wasn't happy with this as a pedagogical strategy—I'd much rather the students read for themselves—but I was thankful that it worked. The women nodded sympathetically to Celie's painful story and thanked me when they left for the day.

"Miss B, Miss B," calls Tanya, a woman who looks and acts much younger than her nineteen years. It has been several months since the other instructor was let go and I was hired; my nickname is a sign of acceptance. 10

Tanya sits up front—the better to get my attention—and soon her pleas take on added urgency. "I need a pencil. I need some more paper." When she finishes with one demand, she moves on to the next. When she gets bored, which happens fairly quickly, she calls repeatedly for *Sula* as if she were a great personal friend. "Where's *Sula*? When do we get to *Sula*?"

I have kept up the practice that my predecessor initiated, spending the last half hour of class reading novels or plays aloud, but with a difference: The

---

[2]*Tahoe*: Lake Tahoe, the largest alpine lake in North America. It is surrounded by the Sierra Nevadas on the California-Nevada border.—Eds.

[3]*Alice Walker* (b. 1944): The best-selling writer of the Pulitzer Prize–winning novel *The Color Purple* (1982).—Eds.

[4]*GED*: General equivalency diploma.—Eds.

students do the reading. The women have come to depend on this promise. The strategy also helps with continuity in what I found to be an almost impossible teaching situation. Turnover is extremely high at county jails and likewise in my classroom. I can have from six to sixteen new students a day and I never know how long any of them will stay. Most serve sentences of less than a year, yet jail is a liminal time during which many wait indeterminately to be sentenced on to prison or parole. Release dates can come and go mysteriously without the promised freedom and no explanation for the delay. Life is thus more volatile in county jails than in prisons and the future more uncertain. Not surprisingly, jails are one of the least studied and understood institutions in the criminal justice system.

Such unsettledness can make anyone edgy, if not downright crazy. Although Tanya has difficulty keeping up with the novel, it doesn't seem to matter. What is important to her is the routine we have established in class, my assurance that we will read the work each day. From what I know of my students' backgrounds, even this modicum of stability was often missing from their lives. Many were homeless before incarceration; few had support from parents, friends, or partners. For Tanya and some of the others, *Sula* has become a talisman of security, something they can rely on in a constantly shifting world.

Tanya has difficulty understanding some of the language and following the plot, but many of the other women do not. They are quick to spot the fact that when Sula's brother, Plum, returns from the war he is a drug addict, though Morrison never states this directly. They can tell by several clues: Plum's weight loss and antisocial behavior, his sugary diet, and the "bent spoon black from steady cooking" found in his bedroom.

The following semester, I teach this same novel in my college writing seminar at the University of California, Berkeley. My Berkeley students don't pick up on the drug connection. Most of them think that Plum uses the spoon to cook soup in his room, and they look at me with disbelief when I tell them otherwise. 15

My jail students seem able to spot danger everywhere, practically in the way an author uses a semicolon. Reading an O. Henry short story, they immediately inferred that one character was a prostitute, just from the author's description of an abandoned shoe. And if my Berkeley students are frustrated with Morrison for not providing explanations (for Sula's mother's missing leg, or Sula's role in a murder), the women at the jail shrug off such ambiguities. They assume that a character can do an evil act, such as not rescuing someone from drowning, and not be evil herself. My Berkeley students want to know what I think the work ultimately means, and they are frustrated with Morrison for being evasive. My jail students seem to rest more easily in uncertainty, knowing that life itself does not provide answers.

I can sympathize with both sets of student reactions (I clearly remember being an undergraduate eager to understand the depths of literature), yet the more I discover about my students at the jail, both individually and statistically, the more I appreciate their acute and emotionally sensitive readings.

Studies vary, but several show that as many as 90 percent of incarcerated women have been sexually, emotionally, or physically abused. Like their imprisoned sisters elsewhere, most of my students are mothers, women of color, and the sole supporters of young children. They are also most likely in jail on drug charges, primarily for possessing minor amounts of crack cocaine. Before the 1980s "war on drugs" legislation mandated jail time for possessing crack cocaine—but none for possessing the same amount of its more expensive cousin, powder cocaine (a drug used predominantly by whites)—these women would have had rehabilitation or community-based programs as options. Not anymore.

The longer I worked at the jail, the more my curiosity was piqued by what I learned and the more I wanted to help. Years of reading Victorian novels had left me with a strong sense of social reform; I believed I could make a difference teaching at the jail, more so than at other places. And I still believe this despite the fact that I have seen hundreds of women get released from jail and come back again—often the same ones, and often more times than I can count.

Tanya is released before we finish reading *Sula,* and I promise to send the remaining chapters to the address she's given. She tells me that when she gets out, she is going to get her son back, get a job, and turn her life around. I am surprised when she mentions her baby; she looks so much like a child and in need of mothering herself.

We finish Morrison's novel, but it is anticlimactic. No one seems particularly interested in discussing the themes, nor is anyone as thrilled as I hoped they'd be when I announce that our next novel will be Zora Neale Hurston's *Their Eyes Were Watching God.*[5] The class seems subdued and sad. Perhaps this is due to Tanya's absence: Although so many students come and go, Tanya has been a steady presence, and her noisy but good-natured complaints have punctuated our days. 20

I try to get one new student to do some work. She is much older, perhaps around fifty-five, and near toothless. "My mind is on burying my son, not on this schoolwork," she tells me, shaking her head. "It ain't right that they should put me in here when I ain't been in a classroom for thirty years. And I just buried my son. It don't make no sense."

I don't know what to say. Educational programs are mandatory at this jail, but the policy makes little sense to me, too, at times.

The next day, the women are livelier, and we begin reading *Their Eyes.* They quickly pick up on the dialect, something I feared would be prohibitive. "That's country," says one woman. Instead of finding Hurston's phonetic spellings a hindrance to understanding, the women seem to relish sounding out the dialogue and laugh when they trip over words. One fairly new student, a white woman whose face is pockmarked with what looks like deep cigarette

---

[5]*Zora Neale Hurston* (1891–1960): A writer and folklorist. *Their Eyes Were Watching God* (1937) is her most popular novel.—Eds.

burns, stands up to give Hurston's novel a try. The other students are encouraging, telling her to go on when she stumbles, and even yelling at me when I correct a mispronunciation. "Let her do it, Miss B! She's getting it."

As the novel continues, the women become hooked on the story and wonder what will happen next. They recognize Joe Starks for the smooth talker he is and think that the main character, Janie, should have stayed with her first husband, Logan, instead of running off with the slick Joe. "Logan wasn't so bad," says one student who has been in and out of jail several times—this despite the fact that Logan had wanted to buy Janie a mule to plow the field, and the protagonist remarks that she cannot love her first husband. "Besides, he was trying to teach her an important lesson—how to work."

25 When we get to the part where Janie meets her true love, Tea Cake, who takes her to a new world in the Florida Everglades, my students are quick to note that "he turned her out." I ask about the phrase and am told that it means to be introduced to new people and places, a whole new way of life.

"Is it a bad thing?"

"It doesn't have to be," one woman explains, "but it usually is. You're turned on to the life." That is, a life of drug use or prostitution.

I ask them to write essays about this, and I get back many that explain how they were turned out to drugs: on first dates, with boyfriends, cousins, even mothers.

When we get to the same scene in my Berkeley class, I say something about Tea Cake turning Janie out. My Cal students stare at me as if I've said something incredibly dumb. Some of them have heard the term before, but it doesn't resonate with meaning. We move on.

30 Tanya, I have heard, is back in jail. Out for less than a week before getting rearrested, she likely did not get the photocopies I sent her. She was apparently caught selling drugs to an undercover cop on the same street corner where she was arrested before. I ask the program's administrator about the rumor I heard, and she confirms it. Tanya said she needed money for clothes and that's why she was selling. "It didn't occur to her to get a job," the administrator states. Yet, knowing her educational level, I wonder how easy it would have been for her to get one.

When Tanya comes back into class, she hugs me and asks me not to be mad at her. I'm not and I tell her so. I am always happy to see my former students again, even in jail; at least I know that they are alive and safe. But the rest of the class is unruly. It's a Monday, the day after visiting hours when the women are allowed a two-hour personal contact with their children. The aftermath of these visits is a palpable feeling of malaise. The women often can't concentrate, nor do they feel like doing anything but talking and complaining.

There are four new students, one of whom tells me she is going to prison in a few days and won't bother doing anything. "That crack took away my brain," says another. One young woman who always sits sullenly in the back spits out, "Why don't you take a day off? All the other classes are canceled today. How come ours isn't?"

I'm frustrated and tired of coercing them to work. So I pull out a passage from *Their Eyes,* where Janie talks about feeling like a rut in a road, beaten down, with the life all beneath the surface, and I tell them to respond in writing.

After much cajoling, they begin to write. One woman details the years she spent with a husband who, like Janie's Joe, always put her down. A new student calls me over and tells me she felt trampled this way when she was homeless. "I need more than one sheet of paper to tell this," she states. I agree.

35 My best student, Linnea, writes quickly, then hands me her essay to read. "I felt I was in a rut when I found myself homeless, hooked on drugs and losing some of my hope," she writes. "I found myself doing things (sexually) that I never thought I would do for drugs. I would have sex in an alleyway, the back seat of an abandoned vehicle, and even out in the open park in front of crowds of people. I would eat out of trash cans. I would go days without bathing, or changing my clothes. . . . I would even try to sell drugs on a very, very small scale. I felt my life was becoming meaningless. . . . I now have a chance to regain my life by being here."

As painful as these stories often are, the women always want to share them by reading them out loud. They clap after each one and make supportive comments. "All you need now is Jesus," or "You're gonna make it, girl. I know it." I correct their punctuation ("Oh yeah, I forget how to use periods," says one student) but am often at a loss for words on the content.

From their essays and comments in class, I can piece together the world that many of my students come from. It's a world of broken promises—mothers who abandon them, boyfriends and fathers who rape them, partners who beat them—and one where home and school are fractured places at best. But despite some of the horrific experiences these women have had, there's a strong element of hope in their writing, a survivor's instinct that things can get better and life will turn around.

We are reading Toni Morrison's *The Bluest Eye,* a somber book about a girl, Pecola, who has internalized white standards of beauty and believes she would be loved if only she had blue eyes. One day, I tell my students that I sometimes feel self-conscious about my position: I'm a white woman teaching mostly African American literature to women of color. "Damn, Miss B, you worry too much," says one student. "Yeah," says another, "you think too hard." As unbelievable as it may sound, there is no racial tension among the women in the jail. Drugs, abuse, and poverty are the great levelers here, at least from what I've seen. It is these elements that transcend division by race, uniting my students with one another and the literature we read.

Similarly, Pecola's life is one of repeated rejection and abuse: She is raped by her father, neglected by her mother. This is by far my students' favorite work, and I suggest they write letters to the author. I vow to someday send them to Toni Morrison and apologize for photocopying her novels.

40 "Dear Toni," one woman writes, "I can really appreciate your book cuz it gives without a doubt insight. . . . Also men abusing women it is a strong issue and your book brought strength to me as a woman of abuse." Despite the

bleak outcome of the novel, the women find positive messages. "Dear Professor Morrison," writes another, "this book made me think about how we put off the beauty of are black people an put on the ugly, but I see the light now an when I leave jail I will keep my Lord with me black women like you makes me proud."

"To Toni Morrison," writes another, "I love the slang that you use it was kind of difficult getting it together but it was real. I love real stuff. . . . you are a dream come true."

"Dear Ms. Morrison. I really enjoyed reading 'The Bluest Eye.' . . . Even tho the cover states that the story is fiction, I truly believe that some little girl may have gone through this. It was a common thing. And Im sorry to say, that it still happens. . . . P.S. If you can please send me an autograph book I would really enjoy it. Thank you."

▪ QUESTIONS

Reading

1. Boufis teaches in two different worlds. In each world, her students have their own kinds of knowledge, and for each audience, Boufis must shift her mode of teaching. What does she learn about teaching from her students in the county jail?
2. Highlight and list the things that Boufis criticizes about the criminal justice system in California.
3. Boufis writes from the perspective of, as she puts it, "a white woman teaching mostly African American literature to women of color" (paragraph 38). How does her voice shape the content of this essay?
4. Make a double-entry list of the ways Boufis compares her students at the county jail with her college writing students at the University of California, Berkeley. If you need more space, use a separate piece of paper. Then, write a paragraph reflecting on the conclusions she draws from this comparison.

COUNTY JAIL	BERKELEY

Exploratory Writing

1. If you were assigned to teach a literature class in a prison or jail, which books would you choose, and why? Create a reading list that includes at least ten books or stories, with a brief description of your goals for what your students would learn from each selection. In addition to the ten readings, include any movies, Web sites, or other educational materials that you think would be enlightening for your students to read.
2. In her experience teaching literature to inmates at the county jail, Boufis meets women who come from a very different background than her own. Reflect on a personal

experience that involved working or spending time with people very different from you. What did you learn?

Making Connections

1. Compare Boufis's and Amanda Coyne's (p. 86) criticisms of harsh penalties for low-level drug dealing. Do some further research on this issue, and write a report on your findings.
2. In this essay, Boufis intersperses her personal observations and experiences with data about the prison system and incarcerated women. Compare her approach to Barbara Ehrenreich's (p. 243). In your opinion, would these authors' reports be more effective if they had left out their personal perspectives and included only factual information? Use examples to support your argument.

Essay Writing

1. What programs are available for prisoners in your local county jail? If there aren't any, what reasons are given for this lack? Write a report on what you learn.

EXPLAINING

The Cave

Plato

Plato (c. 427–347 BCE), the student of Socrates and teacher of Aristotle, is the most revered thinker in Western civilization. As Alfred North Whitehead stated, "All of Western philosophy is but a footnote to Plato. . . . [H]is shadow falls over all of Western thought." Most of the historically significant issues with which philosophy has been concerned — the nature of being, the question of how we know things, the purposes of right action, the structure of an ordered society, the meaning of love and beauty — were issues that he raised. Plato's signature work was his concept of *idealism* — the doctrine of a permanent realm of eternal Forms that shape our mutable, material world. Idealism developed in reaction to the Sophists, who claimed their science of language could lead to the truth. Plato, however, thought it dangerous to suppose that the highest realities — Truth, Goodness, Beauty — could have the flickering impermanence of human words. Plato believed that language, even matter, could be shaped to cheat and deceive. Because he mistrusted writing, Plato's own famous works, namely *The Republic* and *Ion,* are written not as treatises but as dialogues with Socrates. This has, however, led to problems of interpretation and consistency. Nonetheless, these two works have held up as two of the most important and engaging works in philosophical thinking.

"The Cave," perhaps the best-known of Plato's allegories, is presented as a story told by Socrates and then interpreted by the questioner. It appears at the start of Book VII of *The Republic*. The following version was translated by Paul Shorey and published in 1961.

Next, said I, compare our nature in respect of education and its lack to such an experience as this. Picture men dwelling in a sort of subterranean cavern with a long entrance open to the light on its entire width. Conceive them as having their legs and necks fettered from childhood, so that they remain in the same spot, able to look forward only, and prevented by the fetters from turning their heads. Picture further the light from a fire burning higher up and at a distance behind them, and between the fire and the prisoners and above them a road along which a low wall has been built, as the exhibitors of puppet shows have partitions before the men themselves, above which they show the puppets.

All that I see, he said.

See also, then, men carrying past the wall implements of all kinds that rise above the wall, and human images and shapes of animals as well, wrought in stone and wood and every material, some of these bearers presumably speaking and others silent.

A strange image you speak of, he said, and strange prisoners.

Like to us, I said. For, to begin with, tell me do you think that these men would have seen anything of themselves or of one another except the shadows cast from the fire on the wall of the cave that fronted them? 5

How could they, he said, if they were compelled to hold their heads unmoved through life?

And again, would not the same be true of the objects carried past them?

Surely.

If then they were able to talk to one another, do you not think that they would suppose that in naming the things that they saw they were naming the passing objects?

Necessarily. 10

And if their prison had an echo from the wall opposite them, when one of the passersby uttered a sound, do you think that they would suppose anything else than the passing shadow to be the speaker?

By Zeus, I do not, said he.

Then in every way such prisoners would deem reality to be nothing else than the shadows of the artificial objects.

Quite inevitably, he said.

Consider, then, what would be the manner of the release and healing from 15 these bonds and this folly if in the course of nature something of this sort should happen to them. When one was freed from his fetters and compelled to stand up suddenly and turn his head around and walk and to lift up his eyes to the light, and in doing all this felt pain and, because of the dazzle and glitter of the light, was unable to discern the objects whose shadows he formerly saw, what do you suppose would be his answer if someone told him that what he had seen before was all a cheat and an illusion, but that now, being nearer to reality and turned toward more real things, he saw more truly? And if also one should point out to him each of the passing objects and constrain him by questions to say what it is, do you not think that he would be at a loss and that he would regard what he formerly saw as more real than the things now pointed out to him?

Far more real, he said.

And if he were compelled to look at the light itself, would not that pain his eyes, and would he not turn away and flee to those things which he is able to discern and regard them as in very deed more clear and exact than the objects pointed out?

It is so, he said.

And if, said I, someone should drag him thence by force up the ascent which is rough and steep, and not let him go before he had drawn him out into the light of the sun, do you not think that he would find it painful to be so haled along, and would chafe at it, and when he came out into the light, that his eyes would be filled with its beams so that he would not be able to see even one of the things that we call real?

Why, no, not immediately, he said. 20

Then there would be need of habituation, I take it, to enable him to see the things higher up. And at first he would most easily discern the shadows and, after that, the likenesses or reflections in water of men and other things, and later, the things themselves, and from these he would go on to contemplate the appearances in the heavens and heaven itself, more easily by night,

looking at the light of the stars and the moon, than by day the sun and the sun's light.

Of course.

And so, finally, I suppose, he would be able to look upon the sun itself and see its true nature, not by reflections in water or phantasms of it in an alien setting, but in and by itself in its own place.

Necessarily, he said.

And at this point he would infer and conclude that this it is that provides the seasons and the courses of the year and presides over all things in the visible region, and is in some sort the cause of all these things that they had seen. 25

Obviously, he said, that would be the next step.

Well then, if he recalled to mind his first habitation and what passed for wisdom there, and his fellow bondsmen, do you not think that he would count himself happy in the change and pity them?

He would indeed.

And if there had been honors and commendations among them which they bestowed on one another and prizes for the man who is quickest to make out the shadows as they pass and best able to remember their customary precedences, sequences, and coexistences, and so most successful in guessing at what was to come, do you think he would be very keen about such rewards, and that he would envy and emulate those who were honored by these prisoners and lorded it among them, or that he would feel with Homer and greatly prefer while living on earth to be serf of another, a landless man, and endure anything rather than opine with them and live that life?

Yes, he said, I think that he would choose to endure anything rather than such a life. 30

And consider this also, said I. If such a one should go down again and take his old place would he not get his eyes full of darkness, thus suddenly coming out of the sunlight?

He would indeed.

Now if he should be required to contend with these perpetual prisoners in "evaluating" these shadows while his vision was still dim and before his eyes were accustomed to the dark—and this time required for habituation would not be very short—would he not provoke laughter, and would it not be said of him that he had returned from his journey aloft with his eyes ruined and that it was not worthwhile even to attempt the ascent? And if it were possible to lay hands on and to kill the man who tried to release them and lead them up, would they not kill him?

They certainly would, he said.

This image then, dear Glaucon, we must apply as a whole to all that has 35 been said, likening the region revealed through sight to the habitation of the prison, and the light of the fire in it to the power of the sun. And if you assume that the ascent and the contemplation of the things above is the soul's ascension to the intelligible region, you will not miss my surmise, since that is what you desire to hear. But God knows whether it is true. But, at any rate, my dream as it appears to me is that in the region of the known the last thing to be seen and hardly seen is the idea of good, and that when seen it must needs point us to the conclusion that this is indeed the cause for all things of all that is right and beautiful, giving birth in the visible world to light, and the author of light and itself in the intelligible world being the authentic source of truth and reason, and that anyone who is to act wisely in private or public must have caught sight of this.

I concur, he said, so far as I am able.

Come then, I said, and join me in this further thought, and do not be surprised that those who have attained to this height are not willing to occupy themselves with the affairs of men, but their souls ever feel the upward urge and the yearning for that sojourn above. For this, I take it, is likely if in this point too the likeness of our image holds.

Yes, it is likely.

And again, do you think it at all strange, said I, if a man returning from divine contemplations to the petty miseries of men cuts a sorry figure and appears most ridiculous, if, while still blinking through the gloom, and before he has become sufficiently accustomed to the environing darkness, he is compelled, in courtrooms or elsewhere to contend about the shadows of justice or the images that cast the shadows and to wrangle in debate about the notions of these things in the minds of those who have never seen justice itself?

It would be by no means strange, he said. 40

But a sensible man, I said, would remember that there are two distinct disturbances of the eyes arising from two causes, according as the shift is from light to darkness or from darkness to light, and, believing that the same thing happens to the soul too, whenever he saw a soul perturbed and unable to discern something, he would not laugh unthinkingly, but would observe whether coming from a brighter life its vision was obscured by the unfamiliar darkness, or whether the passage from the deeper dark of ignorance into a more luminous world and the greater brightness had dazzled its vision. And so he would deem the one happy in its experience and way of life and pity the other, and if it pleased him to laugh at it, his laughter would be less laughable than that at the expense of the soul that had come down from the light above.

That is a very fair statement, he said.

Then, if this is true, our view of these matters must be this, that education is not in reality what some people proclaim it to be in their professions. What they aver is that they can put true knowledge into a soul that does not possess it, as if they were inserting vision into blind eyes.

They do indeed, he said.

But our present argument indicates, said I, that the true analogy for this indwelling power in the soul and the instrument whereby each of us apprehends is that of an eye that could not be converted to the light from the darkness except by turning the whole body. Even so this organ of knowledge must be turned around from the world of becoming together with the entire soul, like the scene-shifting periactus in the theater, until the soul is able to endure the contemplation of essence and the brightest region of being. And this, we say, is the good, do we not? 45

▪ QUESTIONS

Reading

1. In this dialogue from *The Republic*, Socrates uses an extended analogy to explain his ideas about illusion versus the truth to be found through "the soul's ascension to the intelligible region" (paragraph 35). Briefly summarize this dialogue without using any analogies. What is lost in your rewritten version?
2. In what ways are human beings like chained prisoners in a cave, able to see only the shadows of carved images of things? Why is their delusion not remediable by simply releasing them from the chains that impede their accurate perception of things?
3. Given that Socrates puts so much emphasis on the accurate versus inaccurate perception of things, how do you account for his statement "likening the region revealed through sight to the habitation of the prison" (paragraph 35)? How, one might ask, are we imprisoned by our eyes, by our visual perceptions? What, after all, could be more liberating than to see things clearly with our own eyes?

Exploratory Writing

1. Examine the illustration included with the text. Does it help you visualize Socrates's analogy? Are there any details in the text that are missing or misrepresented in the drawing? Using any materials and media you like, create your own visual representation of "The Cave." (You could make a collage, painting, drawing, or cartoon, for example.) Try to make it an accurate representation of Plato's text.
2. Many people were familiar with the cave allegory before they ever read Plato's text, and many others (all those who cannot read ancient Greek) have only read *The Republic* in translation, which sometimes reflects the assumptions and styles of the translator's own time. Find two different translations of Book VII of Plato's *Republic*, and flag

sections where the language varies between the translations. What interpretations of the text does each version reveal?

Making Connections

1. Socrates was famously mistrustful of writing. In fact, he was probably illiterate. Although documentation suggests that he did exist, our knowledge of his philosophy comes from the writings of his literate students and contemporaries, including Xenophon and Plato. Compare Socrates's style of thinking and discussion to that of Oliver Sacks's Dr. P. (p. 446), Sacks himself, Ann Jurecic's autistic student (p. 402), or Brooke Gladstone (p. 325). Do you recognize anything Socratic about their thinking and work?

Essay Writing

1. Compare and contrast life in the cave with the situation of people watching TV, playing video games, or sitting at desks surfing the Internet. Assuming that Socrates would probably consider all these media more illusory than life in the cave — images of shadows of images — how would you respond to his charges? Write an essay arguing your position.
2. Write an essay reflecting on an experience in your own life that might be described or illuminated by Plato's metaphor of the cave. Imagine yourself as the inhabitant of the cave, mistaking an illusion for reality. Consider this situation in terms of light and darkness, good and evil, and vision and blindness.

EXPLAINING

Urban Legends
"The Boyfriend's Death"

Jan Harold Brunvand

With a PhD in folklore from Indiana University, Jan Harold Brunvand (b. 1933) has become a leading collector and interpreter of contemporary legends. These "urban legends" are stories told around campfires and in college dormitories, often as true experiences that happened to somebody other than the teller of the tale. A professor at the University of Utah for many years, Brunvand has been the editor of the *Journal of American Folklore* and *American Folklore: An Encyclopedia* (1996), and is the author of the standard introduction to the field, *The Study of American Folklore: An Introduction,* fourth edition (1997). The following selection is taken from the first of his several collections of urban legends, *The Vanishing Hitchhiker: American Urban Legends and Their Meanings* (1981). Here Brunvand defines *urban legend,* gives one striking example, and offers some explanations about how and why such stories flourish even in the midst of a highly technologized society. The selection as reprinted is complete, except for the deletion of a few brief references to discussions elsewhere in Brunvand's book.

We are not aware of our own folklore any more than we are of the grammatical rules of our language. When we follow the ancient practice of informally transmitting "lore"—wisdom, knowledge, or accepted modes of behavior—by word of mouth and customary example from person to person, we do not concentrate on the form or content of our folklore; instead, we simply listen to information that others tell us and then pass it on—more or less accurately—to other listeners. In this stream of unself-conscious oral tradition the information that acquires a clear story line is called *narrative folklore,* and those stories alleged to be true are *legends.* This, in broad summary, is the typical process of legend formation and transmission as it has existed from time immemorial and continues to operate today. It works about the same way whether the legendary plot concerns a dragon in a cave or a mouse in a Coke bottle.

It might seem unlikely that legends—*urban* legends at that—would continue to be created in an age of widespread literacy, rapid mass communications, and restless travel. While our pioneer ancestors may have had to rely heavily on oral traditions to pass the news along about changing events and frontier dangers, surely we no longer need mere "folk" reports of what's happening, with all their tendencies to distort the facts. A moment's reflection, however, reminds us of the many weird, fascinating, but unverified rumors and tales that so frequently come to our ears—killers and madmen on the loose, shocking or funny personal experiences, unsafe manufactured products, and many other unexplained mysteries of daily life. Sometimes we encounter different oral versions of such stories, and on occasion we may read about similar events in newspapers or magazines; but seldom do we find, or even seek after, reliable documentation. The lack of verification in no way diminishes the appeal urban legends have for us. We enjoy them merely as stories, and we tend at least to half-believe them as possibly accurate reports. And the legends we tell, as with any folklore, reflect many of the hopes, fears, and anxieties of our time. In short, legends are definitely part of our modern folklore—legends which are as traditional, variable, and functional as those of the past.

Folklore study consists of collecting, classifying, and interpreting in their full cultural context the many products of everyday human interaction that have acquired a somewhat stable underlying form and that are passed traditionally from person to person, group to group, and generation to generation. Legend study is a most revealing area of such research because the stories that people believe to be true hold an important place in their worldview. "If it's true, it's important" is an axiom to be trusted, whether or not the lore really *is* true. Simply becoming aware of this modern folklore which we all possess to some degree is a revelation in itself, but going beyond this to compare the tales, isolate their consistent themes, and relate them to the rest of the culture can yield rich insights into the state of our current civilization. . . .

Urban Legends as Folklore

Folklore subsists on oral tradition, but not all oral communication is folklore. The vast amounts of human interchange, from casual daily conversations to formal discussions in business or industry, law, or teaching, rarely constitute straight oral folklore. However, all such "communicative events" (as scholars dub them) are punctuated routinely by various units of traditional material that are memorable, repeatable, and that fit recurring social situations well enough to serve in place of original remarks. "Tradition" is the key idea that links together such utterances as nicknames, proverbs, greeting and leave-taking formulas, wisecracks, anecdotes, and jokes as "folklore"; indeed, these are a few of the best known "conversational genres" of American folklore. Longer and more complex folk forms—fairy tales, epics, myths, legends, or ballads, for example—may thrive only in certain special situations of oral transmission. All true folklore ultimately depends upon continued oral dissemination, usually within fairly homogeneous "folk groups," and upon the retention through time of internal patterns and motifs that become traditional in the oral exchanges. The corollary of this rule of stability in oral tradition is that all items of folklore, while retaining a fixed central core, are constantly changing as they are transmitted, so as to create countless "variants" differing in length, detail, style, and performance technique. Folklore, in short, consists of oral tradition in variants.

5 Urban legends belong to the subclass of folk narratives, legends, that—unlike fairy tales—are believed, or at least believable, and that—unlike myths—are set in the recent past and involve normal human beings rather than ancient gods or demigods. Legends are folk history, or rather quasi-history.

As with any folk legends, urban legends gain credibility from specific details of time and place or from references to source authorities. For instance, a popular Western pioneer legend often begins something like, "My great-grandmother had this strange experience when she was a young girl on a wagon train going through Wyoming when an Indian chief wanted to adopt her. . . ." Even though hundreds of different great-grandmothers are supposed to have had the same doubtful experience (being desired by the chief because of her beautiful long blond hair), the fact seldom reaches legend-tellers; if it does, they assume that the family lore has indeed spread far and wide. This particular popular tradition, known as "Goldilocks on the Oregon Trail," interests folklorists because of the racist implications of a dark Indian savage coveting a fair young civilized woman—this legend is familiar in the *white* folklore only—and it is of little concern that the story seems to be entirely apocryphal.

In the world of modern urban legends there is usually no geographical or generational gap between teller and event. The story is *true*; it really occurred, and recently, and always to someone else who is quite close to the narrator, or at least "a friend of a friend." Urban legends are told both in the course of casual conversations and in such special situations as campfires, slumber parties, and college dormitory bull sessions. The legends' physical settings are often close by, real, and sometimes even locally renowned for other such happenings. Though the characters in the stories are usually nameless, they are true-to-life examples of the kind of people the narrators and their audience know firsthand.

One of the great mysteries of folklore research is where oral traditions originate and who invents them. One might expect that at least in modern folklore we could come up with answers to such questions, but this is seldom, if ever, the case. . . .

The Performance of Legends

Whatever the origins of urban legends, their dissemination is no mystery. The tales have traveled far and wide, and have been told and retold from person to person in the same manner that myths, fairy tales, or ballads spread in earlier cultures, with the important difference that today's legends are also disseminated by the mass media. Groups of age-mates, especially adolescents, are one important American legend channel, but other paths of transmission are among office workers and club members, as well as among religious, recreational, and regional groups. Some individuals make a point of learning every recent rumor or tale, and they can enliven any coffee break, party, or trip with the latest supposed "news." The telling of one story inspires other people to share what they have read or heard, and in a short time a lively exchange of details occurs and perhaps new variants are created.

Tellers of these legends, of course, are seldom aware of their roles as "performers of folklore." The conscious purpose of this kind of storytelling is to convey a true event, and only incidentally to entertain an audience. Nevertheless, the speaker's demeanor is carefully orchestrated, and his or her delivery is low-key and soft-sell. With subtle gestures, eye movements, and vocal inflections the stories are made dramatic, pointed, and suspenseful. But, just as with jokes, some can tell them and some can't. Passive tellers of urban legends may just report them as odd rumors, but the more active legend tellers re-create them as dramatic stories of suspense and, perhaps, humor.

"The Boyfriend's Death"

With all these points in mind—folklore's subject-matter, style, and oral performance—consider this typical version of a well-known urban legend that folklorists have named "The Boyfriend's Death," collected in 1964 (the earliest documented instance of the story) by folklorist Daniel R. Barnes from an eighteen-year-old freshman at the University of Kansas. The usual tellers of the story are adolescents, and the normal setting for the narration is a college dormitory room with fellow students sprawled on the furniture and floors. 10

> This happened just a few years ago out on the road that turns off highway 59 by the Holiday Inn. This couple were parked under a tree out on this road. Well, it got to be time for the girl to be back at the dorm, so she told her boyfriend that they should start back. But the car wouldn't start, so he told her to lock herself in the car and he would go down to the Holiday Inn and call for help. Well, he didn't come back and he didn't come back, and pretty soon she started hearing a scratching noise on the roof of the car. "Scratch, scratch . . . scratch, scratch." She got scareder and scareder, but he didn't come back. Finally, when it was almost daylight, some people came along and stopped and helped her out of the car, and she looked up and there was her boyfriend hanging from the tree, and his feet were scraping against the roof of the car. This is why the road is called "Hangman's Road."

Here is a story that has traveled rapidly to reach nationwide oral circulation, in the process becoming structured in the typical manner of folk narratives. The traditional and fairly stable elements are the parked couple, the abandoned girl, the mysterious scratching (sometimes joined by a dripping sound and ghostly shadows on the windshield), the daybreak rescue, and the horrible climax. Variable traits are the precise location, the reason for her abandonment, the nature of the rescuers, murder details, and the concluding place-name explanation. While "The Boyfriend's Death" seems to have captured teenagers' imaginations as a separate legend only since the early 1960s, it is clearly related to at least two older yarns, "The Hook" and "The Roommate's Death." All three legends have been widely collected by American folklorists, although only scattered examples have been published, mostly in professional journals. Examination of some of these variations helps to make clear the status of the story as folklore and its possible meanings.

At Indiana University, a leading American center of folklore research, folk-narrative specialist Linda Dégh and her students have gathered voluminous data on urban legends, especially those popular with adolescents. Dégh's preliminary published report on "The Boyfriend's Death" concerned nineteen texts collected from IU students from 1964 to 1968. Several storytellers had heard it in high school, often at parties; others had picked it up in college dormitories or elsewhere on campus. Several students expressed some belief in the legend, supposing either that it had happened in their own hometowns, or possibly in other states, once as far distant as "a remote part of Alabama." One informant reported that "she had been sworn to that the incident actually happened," but another, who had heard some variations of the tale, felt that "it seemed too horrible to be true." Some versions had incorporated motifs from other popular teenage horror legends or local ghost stories. . . .

One of the Indiana texts, told in the state of Washington, localizes the story there near Moses Lake, "in the country on a road that leads to a dead-end right under a big weeping willow tree . . . about four or five miles from town." As in most American versions of the story, these specific local touches make believable what is essentially a traveling legend. In a detail familiar from other variants of "The Boyfriend's Death," the body—now decapitated—is left hanging upside down from a branch of the willow tree with the fingernails scraping the top of the car. Another version studied by the Indiana researcher is somewhat aberrant, perhaps because the student was told the story by a friend's parents who claimed that "it happened a long time ago, probably thirty or forty years." Here a murderer is introduced, a "crazy old lady" on whose property the couple has parked. The victim this time is skinned rather than decapitated, and his head scrapes the car as the corpse swings to and fro in the breezy night.

A developing motif in "The Boyfriend's Death" is the character and role of the rescuers, who in the 1964 Kansas version are merely "some people." The standard identification later becomes "the police," authority figures whose presence lends further credence to the story. They are either called by the missing teenagers' parents, or simply appear on the scene in the morning to check the car. In a 1969 variant from Leonardtown, Maryland, the police give a warning, "Miss, please get out of the car and walk to the police car with us, but don't look back." . . . In a version from Texas collected in 1971, set "at this lake somewhere way out in nowhere," a policeman gets an even longer line: "Young lady, we want you to get out of the car and come with us. Whatever you do, don't turn, don't turn around, just keep walking, just keep going straight and don't look back at the car." The more detailed the police instructions are, the more plausible the tale seems to become. Of course the standard rule of folk-narrative plot development now applies: the taboo must be broken (or the "interdiction violated" as some scholars put it). The girl always *does* look back, like Orpheus in the underworld, and in a number of versions her hair turns white from the shock of what she sees, as in a dozen other American legends.

15 In a Canadian version of "The Boyfriend's Death," told by a fourteen-year-old boy from Willowdale, Ontario, in 1973, the words of the policemen are merely summarized, but the opening scene of the legend is developed more

fully, with several special details, including . . . a warning heard on the car radio. The girl's behavior when left behind is also described in more detail.

> A guy and his girlfriend are on the way to a party when their car starts to give them some trouble. At that same time they catch a news flash on the radio warning all people in the area that a lunatic killer has escaped from a local criminal asylum. The girl becomes very upset and at that point the car stalls completely on the highway. The boyfriend gets out and tinkers around with the engine but can't get the car to start again. He decides that he is going to have to walk on up the road to a gas station and get a tow truck but wants his girlfriend to stay behind in the car. She is frightened and pleads with him to take her, but he says that she'll be safe on the floor of the car covered with a blanket so that anyone passing will think it is an abandoned car and not bother her. Besides he can sprint along the road and get back more quickly than if she comes with him in her high-heeled shoes and evening dress. She finally agrees and he tells her not to come out unless she hears his signal of three knocks on the window. . . .

She does hear knocks on the car, but they continue eerily beyond three; the sound is later explained as the shoes of the boyfriend's corpse bumping the car as the body swings from a limb above the car.

The style in which oral narratives are told deserves attention, for the live telling that is dramatic, fluid, and often quite gripping in actual folk performance before a sympathetic audience may seem stiff, repetitious, and awkward on the printed page. Lacking in all our examples of "The Boyfriend's Death" is the essential ingredient of immediate context—the setting of the legend-telling, the storyteller's vocal and facial expression and gestures, the audience's reaction, and the texts of other similar tales narrated at the same session. Several of the informants explained that the story was told to them in spooky situations, late at night, near a cemetery, out camping, or even "while on a hayride or out parked," occasionally near the site of the supposed murder. Some students refer to such macabre legends, therefore, as "scary stories," "screamers," or "horrors."

A widely-distributed folk legend of this kind as it travels in oral tradition acquires a good deal of its credibility and effect from the localized details inserted by individual tellers. The highway and motel identification in the Kansas text are good examples of this, and in a New Orleans version, "The Boyfriend's Death" is absorbed into a local teenage tradition about "The Grunch"—a half-sheep, half-human monster that haunts specific local sites. One teenager there reported, "A man and lady went out by the lake and in the morning they found 'em hanging upside down on a tree and they said grunches did it." Finally, rumors or news stories about missing persons or violent crimes (as mentioned in the Canadian version) can merge with urban legends, helping to support their air of truth, or giving them renewed circulation after a period of less frequent occurrence.

Even the bare printed texts retain some earmarks of effective oral tradition. Witness in the Kansas text the artful use of repetition (typical of folk narrative style): "Well, he didn't come back and he didn't come back . . . but he didn't come back." The repeated use of "well" and the building of lengthy sentences with "and" are other hallmarks of oral style which give the narrator complete control over his performance, tending to squeeze out interruptions or prevent lapses in attention among the listeners. The scene that is set for the incident—lonely road, night, a tree looming over the car, out of gas—and the sound effects—scratches or bumps on the car—contribute to the style, as does the dramatic part played by the policeman and the abrupt ending line: "She looked back, and she saw . . . !" Since the typical narrators and auditors of "The Boyfriend's Death" themselves like to "park" and may have been alarmed by rumors, strange sights and noises, or automobile emergencies (all intensified in their effects by the audience's knowing other parking legends), the abrupt, unresolved ending leaves open the possibilities of what "really happened."

Urban Legends as Cultural Symbols

Legends can survive in our culture as living narrative folklore if they contain three essential elements: a strong basic story-appeal, a foundation in actual belief, and a meaningful message or "moral." That is, popular stories like "The Boyfriend's Death" are not only engrossing tales, but also "true," or at least so people think, and they teach valuable lessons. Jokes are a living part of oral tradition, despite being fictional and often silly, because of their humor, brevity, and snappy punch lines, but legends are by nature longer, slower, and more serious. Since more effort is needed to tell and appreciate a legend than a joke, it needs more than just verbal art to carry it along. Jokes have significant "messages" too, but these tend to be disguised or implied. People tell jokes primarily for amusement, and they seldom sense their underlying themes. In legends the primary messages are quite clear and straightforward; often they take the form of explicit warnings or good examples of "poetic justice." Secondary messages in urban legends tend to be suggested metaphorically or symbolically; these may provide deeper criticisms of human behavior or social condition.

20 People still tell legends, therefore, and other folk take time to listen to them, not only because of their inherent plot interest but because they seem to convey true, worthwhile, and relevant information, albeit partly in a subconscious mode. In other words, such stories are "news" presented to us in an attractive way, with hints of larger meanings. Without this multiple appeal few legends would get a hearing in the modern world, so filled with other distractions. Legends survive by being as lively and "factual" as the television evening news, and, like the daily news broadcasts, they tend to concern deaths, injuries, kidnappings, tragedies, and scandals. Apparently the basic human need for meaningful personal contact cannot be entirely replaced by the mass media and popular culture. A portion of our interest in what is occurring in the world must be filled by some face-to-face reports from other human beings.

On a literal level a story like "The Boyfriend's Death" simply warns young people to avoid situations in which they may be endangered, but at a more symbolic level the story reveals society's broader fears of people, especially women and the young, being alone and among strangers in the darkened world outside the security of their own home or car. Note that the young woman in the story (characterized by "her high-heeled shoes and evening dress") is shown as especially helpless and passive, cowering under the blanket in the car until she is rescued by men. Such themes recur in various forms in many other urban legends. . . .

In order to be retained in a culture, any form of folklore must fill some genuine need, whether this be the need for an entertaining escape from reality, or a desire to validate by anecdotal examples some of the culture's ideals and institutions. For legends in general, a major function has always been the attempt to explain unusual and supernatural happenings in the natural world. To some degree this remains a purpose for urban legends, but their more common role nowadays seems to be to show that the prosaic contemporary scene is capable of producing shocking or amazing occurrences which may actually have happened to friends or to near-acquaintances but which are nevertheless explainable in some reasonably logical terms. On the one hand we want our factual lore to inspire awe, and at the same time we wish to have the most fantastic tales include at least the hint of a rational explanation and perhaps even a conclusion. Thus an escaped lunatic, a possibly *real* character, not a fantastic invader from outer space or Frankenstein's monster, is said to be responsible for the atrocities committed in the gruesome tales that teenagers tell. As sometimes happens in real life, the car radio gives warning, and the police get the situation back under control. (The policemen's role, in fact, becomes larger and more commanding as the story grows in oral tradition.) Only when the young lovers are still alone and scared are they vulnerable, but society's adults and guardians come to their rescue presently.

In common with brief unverified reports ("rumors"), to which they are often closely related, urban legends gratify our desire to know about and to try to understand bizarre, frightening, and potentially dangerous or embarrassing events that *may* have happened. (In rumors and legends there is always some element of doubt concerning where and when these things *did* occur.) These floating stories appeal to our morbid curiosity and satisfy our sensation-seeking minds that demand gratification through frequent infusions of new information, "sanitized" somewhat by the positive messages. Informal rumors and stories fill in the gaps left by professional news reporting, and these marvelous, though generally false, "true" tales may be said to be carrying the folk-news—along with some editorial matter—from person to person even in today's technological world.

▪ QUESTIONS

Reading

1. Brunvand writes as a scholar, explaining urban legends from his perspective as a folklorist. How does his expertise shape his writing? What did you learn from reading his essay that you didn't know before?
2. According to Brunvand, what are the elements that allow legends to survive as living narrative folklore?
3. How does Brunvand differentiate between "oral communication" and "folklore"? Discuss Brunvand's system for categorizing urban legends. How are folk legends unlike fairy tales?

Exploratory Writing

1. Below is a list of other tales collected by Brunvand. Do you know any stories that might correspond to these titles?

   The Vanishing Hitchhiker
   The Mexican Pet
   The Baby-Sitter and the Man Upstairs
   The Microwaved Pet
   The Toothbrush Story
   Alligators in the Sewers
   The Nude in the RV
   The Kidney Heist

   Briefly describe the stories you have heard. Compare the various versions produced by members of the class. What are the variables in the tale, and what seem to be the common features?
2. Select an urban legend that you have recently heard. Write down the best version of it that you can, and analyze what you have written as an urban legend. That is, explain the features that mark it as an urban legend, and discuss the elements that make it interesting or appealing to you.
3. Collaborating in small groups, choose a story from personal experience or from the media that sounds like an urban legend but is true. Make a presentation in which you identify and discuss the features that make it similar to an urban legend. How can you prove that the story is true?

Making Connections

1. Although Brunvand is a folklorist himself, he chooses to write this explanatory essay in the third person, leaving his own personal experiences and anecdotes out of his account. Find another essay in this book that's written in the third person, and two essays that are written in the first person. Flagging specific examples from each of the four essays, write a few paragraphs that discuss the ways that the writer's perspective shapes the tone of each piece.

Essay Writing

1. Brunvand writes, "And the legends we tell, as with any folklore, reflect many of the hopes, fears, and anxieties of our time" (paragraph 2). Write an essay comparing a mainstream narrative about an event in recent history (such as a *New York Times* or *Washington Post* article about the changing politics in the Middle East or the continuing global economic woes) with an alternative narrative about the same event, taken from an obscure blog or Web site. Identify the major differences between the accounts, and then perform a reading of the alternative narrative in the way that Brunvand reads urban legends.
2. Write an essay reflecting on a time when you believed a story that wasn't true. It can be an urban legend, a story about Santa Claus or the tooth fairy, or something more personal. What was the symbolic meaning of the story? What changed for you when you learned that it wasn't true?

ARGUING

Watching TV Makes You Smarter

Steven Johnson

Steven Johnson (b. 1968) writes on culture and popular science and in 1995 was cofounder of the now defunct *Feed*—one of the earliest e-zines to provide daily content on media, pop culture, and technology. A Distinguished Writer in Residence at New York University, Johnson has had work published in *Harper's*, the *New Yorker*, the *Wall Street Journal*, and the *New York Times*. His six books—including his most recent, *Where Good Ideas Come From* (2010)—concern the intersections of science, technology, culture, faith, pop culture, and innovation. The following piece appeared in the *New York Times Magazine* and was adapted from Johnson's book *Everything Bad Is Good for You: How Today's Popular Culture Is Actually Making Us Smarter* (2005).

The Sleeper Curve

SCIENTIST A: Has he asked for anything special?

SCIENTIST B: Yes, this morning for breakfast . . . he requested something called "wheat germ, organic honey, and tiger's milk."

SCIENTIST A: Oh, yes. Those were the charmed substances that some years ago were felt to contain life-preserving properties.

SCIENTIST B: You mean there was no deep fat? No steak or cream pies or . . . hot fudge?

SCIENTIST A: Those were thought to be unhealthy.

—FROM WOODY ALLEN'S *SLEEPER*

On January 24 [2005], the Fox network showed an episode of its hit drama *24*, the real-time thriller known for its cliffhanger tension and often-gruesome violence. Over the preceding weeks, a number of public controversies had erupted around *24*, mostly focused on its portrait of Muslim terrorists and its penchant for torture scenes. The episode that was shown on the 24th only fanned the flames higher: In one scene, a terrorist enlists a hit man to kill his child for not fully supporting the jihadist cause; in another scene, the secretary of defense authorizes the torture of his son to uncover evidence of a terrorist plot.

But the explicit violence and the post-9/11 terrorist anxiety are not the only elements of *24* that would have been unthinkable on prime-time network television twenty years ago. Alongside the notable change in content lies an equally notable change in form. During its forty-four minutes—a real-time hour, minus sixteen minutes for commercials—the episode connects the lives of twenty-one distinct characters, each with a clearly defined "story arc," as the Hollywood jargon has it: a defined personality with motivations and obstacles and specific relationships with other characters. Nine primary narrative threads wind their way through those forty-four minutes, each drawing extensively upon events and information revealed in earlier episodes. Draw a map of all those intersecting plots and personalities, and you get structure that—where formal complexity is concerned—more closely resembles *Middlemarch* than a hit TV drama of years past like *Bonanza.*

For decades, we've worked under the assumption that mass culture follows a path declining steadily toward lowest-common-denominator standards, presumably because the "masses" want dumb, simple pleasures and big media companies try to give the masses what they want. But as that *24* episode suggests, the exact opposite is happening: The culture is getting more cognitively demanding, not less. To make sense of an episode of *24,* you have to integrate far more information than you would have a few decades ago watching a comparable show. Beneath the violence and the ethnic stereotypes, another trend appears: To keep up with entertainment like *24,* you have to pay attention, make inferences, track shifting social relationships. This is what I call the Sleeper Curve: The most debased forms of mass diversion—video games and violent television dramas and juvenile sitcoms—turn out to be nutritional after all.

I believe that the Sleeper Curve is the single most important new force altering the mental development of young people today, and I believe it is largely a force for good: enhancing our cognitive faculties, not dumbing them down. And yet you almost never hear this story in popular accounts of today's media. Instead, you hear dire tales of addiction, violence, mindless escapism. It's assumed that shows that promote smoking or gratuitous violence are bad for us, while those that thunder against teen pregnancy or intolerance have a positive role in society. Judged by that morality-play standard, the story of popular culture over the past fifty years—if not five hundred—is a story of decline: The morals of the stories have grown darker and more ambiguous, and the antiheroes have multiplied.

5 The usual counterargument here is that what media have lost in moral clarity, they have gained in realism. The real world doesn't come in nicely packaged public-service announcements, and we're better off with entertainment like *The Sopranos* that reflects our fallen state with all its ethical ambiguity. I happen to be sympathetic to that argument, but it's not the one I want to make here. I think there is another way to assess the social virtue of pop culture, one that looks at media as a kind of cognitive workout, not as a series of life lessons. There may indeed be more "negative messages" in the mediasphere today. But that's not the only way to evaluate whether our television shows or video games are having a positive impact. Just as important—if not more important—is the kind of thinking you have to do to make sense of a cultural experience. That is where the Sleeper Curve becomes visible.

Televised Intelligence

Consider the cognitive demands that televised narratives place on their viewers. With many shows that we associate with "quality" entertainment—*The Mary Tyler Moore Show, Murphy Brown, Frasier*—the intelligence arrives fully formed in the words and actions of the characters on-screen. They say witty things to one another and avoid lapsing into tired sitcom clichés, and we smile along in our living rooms, enjoying the company of these smart people. But assuming we're bright enough to understand the sentences they're saying, there's no intellectual labor involved in enjoying the show as a viewer. You no more challenge your mind by watching these intelligent shows than you challenge your body watching *Monday Night Football.* The intellectual work is happening on-screen, not off.

But another kind of televised intelligence is on the rise. Think of the cognitive benefits conventionally ascribed to reading: attention, patience, retention, the parsing of narrative threads. Over the last half-century, programming on TV has increased the demands it places on precisely these mental faculties. This growing complexity involves three primary elements: multiple threading, flashing arrows, and social networks.

According to television lore, the age of multiple threads began with the arrival in 1981 of *Hill Street Blues*, the Steven Bochco police drama invariably praised for its "gritty realism." Watch an episode of *Hill Street Blues* side by side with any major drama from the preceding decades—*Starsky and Hutch,* for instance, or *Dragnet*—and the structural transformation will jump out at you. The earlier shows follow one or two lead characters, adhere to a single dominant plot, and reach a decisive conclusion at the end of the episode. Draw an outline of the narrative threads in almost every *Dragnet* episode, and it will be a single line: from the initial crime scene, through the investigation, to the eventual cracking of the case. A typical *Starsky and Hutch* episode offers only the slightest variation on this linear formula: the introduction of a comic subplot that usually appears only at the tail ends of the episode, creating a structure that looks like the graph below. The vertical axis represents the number of individual threads, and the horizontal axis is time.

Starsky and Hutch (any episode)

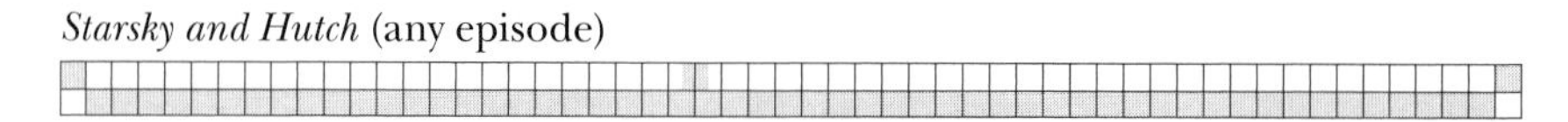

A *Hill Street Blues* episode complicates the picture in a number of profound ways. The narrative weaves together a collection of distinct strands—sometimes as many as ten, though at least half of the threads involve only a few quick scenes scattered through the episode. The number of primary characters—and not just bit parts—swells significantly. And the episode has fuzzy borders: picking up one or two threads from previous episodes at the outset and leaving one or two threads open at the end. Charted graphically, an average episode looks like this:

Hill Street Blues (episode 85)

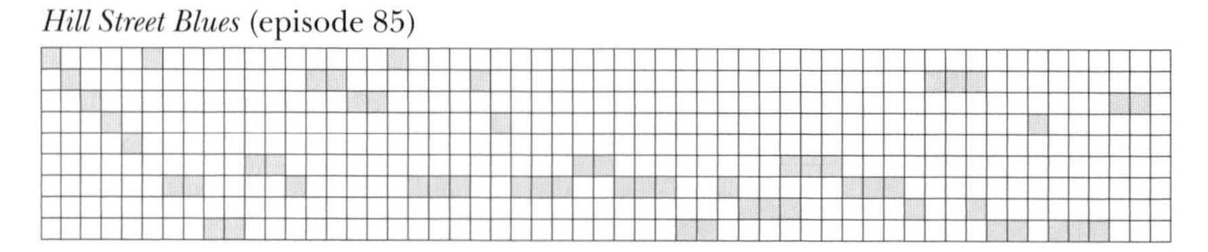

10 Critics generally cite *Hill Street Blues* as the beginning of "serious drama" narrative in the television medium—differentiating the series from the single-episode dramatic programs from the fifties, which were Broadway plays performed in front of a camera. But the *Hill Street* innovations weren't all that original; they'd long played a defining role in popular television, just not during the evening hours. The structure of a *Hill Street* episode—and indeed of all the critically acclaimed dramas that followed, from *thirtysomething* to *Six Feet Under*—is the structure of a soap opera. *Hill Street Blues* might have sparked a new golden age of television drama during its seven-year run, but it did so by using a few crucial tricks that *Guiding Light* and *General Hospital* mastered long before.

Bochco's genius with *Hill Street* was to marry complex narrative structure with complex subject matter. *Dallas* had already shown that the extended, interwoven threads of the soap-opera genre could survive the weeklong interruptions of a prime-time show, but the actual content of *Dallas* was fluff. (The most probing issue it addressed was the question, now folkloric, of who shot J.R.) *All in the Family* and *Rhoda* showed that you could tackle complex social issues, but they did their tackling in the comfort of the sitcom living room. *Hill Street* had richly drawn characters confronting difficult social issues and a narrative structure to match.

Since *Hill Street* appeared, the multi-threaded drama has become the most widespread fictional genre on prime time: *St. Elsewhere, L.A. Law, thirtysomething, Twin Peaks, N.Y.P.D. Blue, E.R., The West Wing, Alias, Lost.* (The only prominent holdouts in drama are shows like *Law and Order* that have essentially updated the venerable *Dragnet* format and thus remained anchored to a single narrative line.) Since the early eighties, however, there has been a noticeable increase in narrative complexity in these dramas. The most ambitious show on TV to date, *The Sopranos*, routinely follows up to a dozen distinct threads over the course of an episode, with more than twenty recurring characters. An episode from late in the first season looks like this:

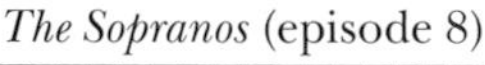

The Sopranos (episode 8)

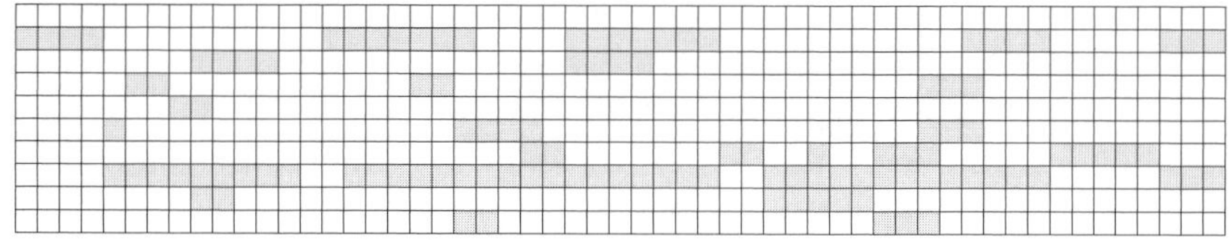

The total number of active threads equals the multiple plots of *Hill Street*, but here each thread is more substantial. The show doesn't offer a clear distinction between dominant and minor plots; each story line carries its weight in the mix. The episode also displays a chordal mode of storytelling entirely absent from *Hill Street*: A single scene in *The Sopranos* will often connect to three different threads at the same time, layering one plot atop another. And every single thread in this *Sopranos* episode builds on events from previous episodes, and continues on through the rest of the season and beyond.

Put those charts together, and you have a portrait of the Sleeper Curve rising over the past thirty years of popular television. In a sense, this is as much a map of cognitive changes in the popular mind as it is a map of on-screen developments, as if the media titans decided to condition our brains to follow ever-larger numbers of simultaneous threads. Before *Hill Street*, the conventional wisdom among television execs was that audiences wouldn't be comfortable following more than three plots in a single episode, and indeed, the *Hill Street* pilot, which was shown in January 1981, brought complaints from viewers that the show was too complicated. Fast-forward two decades, and shows like *The Sopranos* engage their audiences with narratives that make *Hill Street* look like *Three's Company*. Audiences happily embrace that complexity because they've been trained by two decades of multi-threaded dramas.

15 Multi-threading is the most celebrated structural feature of the modern television drama, and it certainly deserves some of the honor that has been doled out to it. And yet multi-threading is only part of the story.

The Case for Confusion

Shortly after the arrival of the first-generation slasher movies—*Halloween*, *Friday the 13th*—Paramount released a mock-slasher flick called *Student Bodies*, parodying the genre just as the *Scream* series would do fifteen years later. In one scene, the obligatory nubile teenage babysitter hears a noise outside a suburban house; she opens the door to investigate, finds nothing and then goes back inside. As the door shuts behind her, the camera swoops in on the doorknob, and we see that she has left the door unlocked. The camera pulls back and then swoops down again for emphasis. And then a flashing arrow appears on the screen, with text that helpfully explains: "Unlocked!"

That flashing arrow is parody, of course, but it's merely an exaggerated version of a device popular stories use all the time. When a sci-fi script inserts into some advanced lab a nonscientist who keeps asking the science geeks to explain what they're doing with that particle accelerator, that's a flashing arrow that gives the audience precisely the information it needs in order to make sense of the ensuing plot. ("Whatever you do, don't spill water on it, or you'll set off a massive explosion!") These hints serve as a kind of narrative hand-holding. Implicitly, they say to the audience, "We realize you have no idea what a particle accelerator is, but here's the deal: All you need to know is that it's a big fancy thing that explodes when wet." They focus the mind on relevant details: "Don't worry about whether the babysitter is going to break up with her boyfriend. Worry about that guy lurking in the bushes." They reduce the amount of analytic work you need to do to make sense of a story. All you have to do is follow the arrows.

By this standard, popular television has never been harder to follow. If narrative threads have experienced a population explosion over the past twenty years, flashing arrows have grown correspondingly scarce. Watching our pinnacle of early eighties TV drama, *Hill Street Blues*, we find there's an informational wholeness to each scene that differs markedly from what you see on shows like *The West Wing* or *The Sopranos* or *Alias* or *E.R.*

Hill Street has ambiguities about future events: Will a convicted killer be executed? Will Furillo marry Joyce Davenport? Will Renko find it in himself to bust a favorite singer for cocaine possession? But the present-tense of each scene explains itself to the viewer with little ambiguity. There's an open question or a mystery driving each of these stories—how will it all turn out?—but there's no mystery about the immediate activity on the screen. A contemporary drama like *The West Wing*, on the other hand, constantly embeds mysteries into the present-tense events: You see characters performing actions or discussing events about which crucial information has been deliberately withheld. Anyone who has watched more than a handful of *The West Wing* episodes closely will know the feeling: Scene after scene refers to some clearly crucial but unexplained piece of information, and after the sixth reference, you'll find yourself wishing you could rewind the tape to figure out what they're talking about, assuming you've missed something. And then you realize that you're supposed to be confused. The open question posed by these sequences is not "How will this turn out in the end?" The question is "What's happening right now?"

20 The deliberate lack of hand-holding extends down to the microlevel of dialogue as well. Popular entertainment that addresses technical issues—whether they are the intricacies of passing legislation, or of performing a heart bypass, or of operating a particle accelerator—conventionally switches between two modes of information in dialogue: texture and substance. Texture is all the arcane verbiage provided to convince the viewer that they're watching Actual Doctors at Work; substance is the material planted amid the background texture that the viewer needs to make sense of the plot.

Conventionally, narratives demarcate the line between texture and substance by inserting cues that flag or translate the important data. There's an unintentionally comical moment in the 2004 blockbuster *The Day After Tomorrow* in which the beleaguered climatologist (played by Dennis Quaid) announces his theory about the imminent arrival of a new ice age to a gathering of government officials. In his speech, he warns that "we have hit a critical desalinization point!" At this moment, the writer-director Roland Emmerich—a master of brazen arrow-flashing—has an official follow with the obliging remark: "It would explain what's driving this extreme weather." They might as well have had a flashing "Unlocked!" arrow on the screen.

The dialogue on shows like *The West Wing* and *E.R.*, on the other hand, doesn't talk down to its audiences. It rushes by, the words accelerating in sync with the high-speed tracking shots that glide through the corridors and operating rooms. The characters talk faster in these shows, but the truly remarkable thing about the dialogue is not purely a matter of speed; it's the willingness to immerse the audience in information that most viewers won't understand. Here's a typical scene from *E.R.*:

[WEAVER *and* WRIGHT *push a gurney containing a sixteen-year-old girl. Her parents,* JANNA *and* FRANK MIKAMI, *follow close behind.* CARTER *and* LUCY *fall in.*]

WEAVER: Sixteen-year-old, unconscious, history of biliary atresia.

CARTER: Hepatic coma?

WEAVER: Looks like it.

MR. MIKAMI: She was doing fine until six months ago.

CARTER: What medication is she on?

MRS. MIKAMI: Ampicillin; tobramycin; vitamins A, D, and K.

LUCY: Skin's jaundiced.

WEAVER: Same with the sclera. Breath smells sweet.

CARTER: Fetor hepaticus?

WEAVER: Yep.

LUCY: What's that?

WEAVER: Her liver's shut down. Let's dip a urine. [*To* **CARTER**] Guys, it's getting a little crowded in here, why don't you deal with the parents? Start lactulose, thirty cc's per NG.

CARTER: We're giving medicine to clean her blood.

WEAVER: Blood in the urine, two-plus.

CARTER: The liver failure is causing her blood not to clot.

MRS. MIKAMI: Oh, God. . . .

CARTER: Is she on the transplant list?

MR. MIKAMI: She's been Status 2a for six months, but they haven't been able to find her a match.

CARTER: Why? What's her blood type?

MR. MIKAMI: AB.

[*This hits* **CARTER** *like a lightning bolt.* **LUCY** *gets it, too. They share a look.*]

There are flashing arrows here, of course—"The liver failure is causing her blood not to clot"—but the ratio of medical jargon to layperson translation is remarkably high. From a purely narrative point of view, the decisive line arrives at the very end: "AB." The sixteen-year-old's blood type connects her to an earlier plot line, involving a cerebral-hemorrhage victim who—after being dramatically revived in one of the opening scenes—ends up brain-dead. Far earlier, before the liver-failure scene above, Carter briefly discusses harvesting the hemorrhage victim's organs for transplants, and another doctor makes a passing reference to his blood type being the rare AB (thus making him an unlikely donor). The twist here revolves around a statistically unlikely event happening at the E.R.—an otherwise perfect liver donor showing up just in time to donate his liver to a recipient with the same rare blood type. But the show reveals this twist with remarkable subtlety. To make sense of that last "AB" line—and the look of disbelief on Carter's and Lucy's faces—you have to recall a passing remark uttered earlier regarding a character who belongs to a completely different thread. Shows like *E.R.* may have more blood and guts than popular TV had a generation ago, but when it comes to storytelling, they possess a quality that can only be described as subtlety and discretion.

Even Bad TV Is Better

Skeptics might argue that I have stacked the deck here by focusing on relatively highbrow titles like *The Sopranos* or *The West Wing*, when in fact the most significant change in the last five years of narrative entertainment involves reality TV. Does the contemporary pop cultural landscape look quite as promising if the representative show is *Joe Millionaire* instead of *The West Wing*?

25 I think it does, but to answer that question properly, you have to avoid the tendency to sentimentalize the past. When people talk about the golden age of television in the early seventies—invoking shows like *The Mary Tyler Moore Show* and *All in the Family*—they forget to mention how awful most television programming was during much of that decade. If you're going to look at pop-culture trends, you have to compare apples to apples, or in this case, lemons to lemons. The relevant comparison is not between *Joe Millionaire* and *MASH*; it's between *Joe Millionaire* and *The Newlywed Game*, or between *Survivor* and *The Love Boat*.

What you see when you make these head-to-head comparisons is that a rising tide of complexity has been lifting programming at the bottom of the quality spectrum and at the top. *The Sopranos* is several times more demanding of its audiences than *Hill Street* was, and *Joe Millionaire* has made comparable advances over *Battle of the Network Stars*. This is the ultimate test of the Sleeper Curve theory: Even the junk has improved.

If early television took its cues from the stage, today's reality programming is reliably structured like a video game: a series of competitive tests, growing more challenging over time. Many reality shows borrow a subtler device from gaming culture as well: The rules aren't fully established at the outset. You learn as you play.

On a show like *Survivor* or *The Apprentice*, the participants—and the audience—know the general objective of the series, but each episode involves new challenges that haven't been ordained in advance. The final round of the first season of *The Apprentice*, for instance, threw a monkey wrench into the strategy that governed the play up to that point, when Trump announced that the two remaining apprentices would have to assemble and manage a team of subordinates who had already been fired in earlier episodes of the show. All of a sudden the overarching objective of the game—do anything to avoid being fired—presented a potential conflict to the remaining two contenders: The structure of the final round favored the survivor who had maintained the best relationships with his comrades. Suddenly, it wasn't enough just to have clawed your way to the top; you had to have made friends while clawing. The original *Joe Millionaire* went so far as to undermine the most fundamental convention of all—that the show's creators don't openly lie to the contestants about the prizes—by inducing a construction worker to pose as a man of means while twenty women competed for his attention.

Reality programming borrowed another key ingredient from games: the intellectual labor of probing the system's rules for weak spots and opportunities. As each show discloses its conventions, and each participant reveals his or her personality traits and background, the intrigue in watching comes from figuring out how the participants should best navigate the environment that has been created for them. The pleasure in these shows comes not from watching other people being humiliated on national television; it comes from depositing other people in a complex, high-pressure environment where no established strategies exist and watching them find their bearings. That's why the water-cooler conversation about these shows invariably tracks in on the strategy displayed on the previous night's episode: Why did Kwame pick Omarosa in that final round? What devious strategy is Richard Hatch concocting now?

When we watch these shows, the part of our brain that monitors the emotional lives of the people around us—the part that tracks subtle shifts in intonation and gesture and facial expression—scrutinizes the action on the screen, looking for clues. We trust certain characters implicitly and vote others off the island in a heartbeat. Traditional narrative shows also trigger emotional connections to the characters, but those connections don't have the same participatory effect, because traditional narratives aren't explicitly about strategy. The phrase "Monday-morning quarterbacking" describes the engaged feeling that spectators have in relation to games as opposed to stories. We absorb stories, but we second-guess games. Reality programming has brought that second-guessing to prime time, only the game in question revolves around social dexterity rather than the physical kind. 30

The Rewards of Smart Culture

The quickest way to appreciate the Sleeper Curve's cognitive training is to sit down and watch a few hours of hit programming from the late seventies on Nick at Nite or the SOAPnet channel or on DVD. The modern viewer who watches a show like *Dallas* today will be bored by the content—not just because the show is less salacious than today's soap operas (which it is by a small margin) but also because the show contains far less information in each scene, despite the fact that its soap-opera structure made it one of the most complicated narratives on television in its prime. With *Dallas*, the modern viewer doesn't have to think to make sense of what's going on, and not having to think is boring. Many recent hit shows—*24*, *Survivor*, *The Sopranos*, *Alias*, *Lost*, *The Simpsons*, *E.R.*—take the opposite approach, layering each scene with a thick network of affiliations. You have to focus to follow the plot, and in focusing you're exercising the parts of your brain that map social networks, that fill in missing information, that connect multiple narrative threads.

Of course, the entertainment industry isn't increasing the cognitive complexity of its products for charitable reasons. The Sleeper Curve exists because there's money to be made by making culture smarter. The economics of television syndication and DVD sales mean that there's a tremendous financial pressure to make programs that can be watched multiple times, revealing new nuances and shadings on the third viewing. Meanwhile, the Web has created a forum for annotation and commentary that allows more complicated shows to prosper, thanks to the fan sites where each episode of shows like *Lost* or *Alias* is dissected with an intensity usually reserved for Talmud scholars. Finally, interactive games have trained a new generation of media consumers to probe complex environments and to think on their feet, and that gamer audience has now come to expect the same challenges from their television shows. In the end, the Sleeper Curve tells us something about the human mind. It may be drawn toward the sensational where content is concerned—sex does sell, after all. But the mind also likes to be challenged; there's real pleasure to be found in solving puzzles, detecting patterns, or unpacking a complex narrative system.

In pointing out some of the ways that popular culture has improved our minds, I am not arguing that parents should stop paying attention to the way their children amuse themselves. What I am arguing for is a change in the criteria we use to determine what really is cognitive junk food and what is genuinely nourishing. Instead of a show's violent or tawdry content, instead of wardrobe malfunctions or the F-word, the true test should be whether a given show engages or sedates the mind. Is it a single thread strung together with predictable punch lines every thirty seconds? Or does it map a complex social network? Is your on-screen character running around shooting everything in sight, or is she trying to solve problems and manage resources? If your kids want to watch reality TV, encourage them to watch *Survivor* over *Fear Factor*. If they want to watch a mystery show, encourage *24* over *Law and Order*. If they want to play a violent game, encourage Grand Theft Auto over Quake. Indeed, it might be just as helpful to have a rating system that used mental labor and not obscenity and violence as its classification scheme for the world of mass culture.

Kids and grown-ups each can learn from their increasingly shared obsessions. Too often we imagine the blurring of kid and grown-up cultures as a series of violations: the nine-year-olds who have to have nipple brooches explained to them thanks to Janet Jackson; the middle-aged guy who can't wait to get home to his Xbox. But this demographic blur has a commendable side that we don't acknowledge enough. The kids are forced to think like grown-ups: analyzing complex social networks, managing resources, tracking subtle narrative intertwinings, recognizing long-term patterns. The grown-ups, in turn, get to learn from the kids: decoding each new technological wave, parsing the interfaces and discovering the intellectual rewards of play. Parents should see this as an opportunity, not a crisis. Smart culture is no longer something you force your kids to ingest, like green vegetables. It's something you share.

▪ QUESTIONS

Reading

1. What is the Sleeper Curve? According to Johnson, what effect does the Sleeper Curve have on young people today?

2. What phrase does Johnson use to describe the engaged feeling that spectators have in relation to games as opposed to stories?
3. Johnson's thesis essentially involves a cause-and-effect claim about watching TV. In this argumentative essay, what kinds of evidence does he offer to support his claim that TV has such an effect? What kinds of evidence might help to strengthen his argument?

Exploratory Writing

1. The drift of Johnson's observations suggests that he favors programs that tend to be as complex and unpredictable as life itself. That being the case, shouldn't we just pay more attention to life than to a TV version of it? In what ways can watching TV serials provide better cognitive workouts than paying close attention to unmediated life? Stage a debate on the proposition "TV makes you smarter than observing life."
2. Use Johnson's graphing method to analyze an episode from your favorite TV serial. For each strand in your graph, write a brief phrase to identify the characters and/or problem that it involves. How many distinct "threads" did you note in the episode? How many different characters were involved? How thick or thin was the treatment of each thread? What insights about the episode did you gain from this analysis? What features of the episode might be overlooked by Johnson's kind of analysis?
3. Johnson's title makes a very broad claim; however, he clearly doesn't think that all TV programs will make one smarter. What specific kinds of programs does he have in mind? Given the kinds of programs that he endorses and his reasons for doing so, what kinds of programs do you suppose he would criticize as likely to make one dumber? Create a list of his criteria for smart television and then grade popular shows based on these criteria.

Making Connections

1. Just as Johnson thinks that certain kinds of TV will make one smarter, Christina Boufis (p. 96) believes that certain kinds of reading will make one more enlightened. Compare their ideas of smartness, and consider which one is likely to be more academically helpful, more professionally helpful, and more existentially helpful.

Essay Writing

1. "Smarter" is such a broad term that it could refer to several different mental abilities. Write a reflective essay that evaluates Johnson's claims in terms of your own experiences watching TV. Has watching TV made you smarter? How does Johnson's idea of smartness compare with your own?

ARGUING

If Black English Isn't a Language, Then Tell Me, What Is?

James Baldwin

Harlem-born writer James Baldwin (1924–1987) experimented with literary forms throughout his career, producing almost twenty volumes of poetry, fiction, essays, and plays, as well as five collaborations with people such as photographer Richard Avedon, poet Nikki Giovani, and anthropologist Margaret Mead. At the age of fourteen, Baldwin followed in his stepfather's footsteps and became a Pentecostal preacher, but he left the church three years later and resettled in New York's bohemian Greenwich Village. There he concentrated on his writing, much of which powerfully—and often poetically—defined and legitimized the black voice. His most famous works include his semi-autobiographical novel *Go Tell It on the Mountain* (1953) and the essay collections *Notes of a Native Son* (1955) and *The Fire Next Time* (1963). The following essay on language and legitimacy first appeared in the *New York Times* in 1979. Baldwin died of stomach cancer in Paris, where he'd moved at the age of twenty-four and spent the last forty years of his life.

The argument concerning the use, or the status, or the reality, of black English is rooted in American history and has absolutely nothing to do with the question the argument supposes itself to be posing. The argument has nothing to do with language itself but with the role of language. Language, incontestably, reveals the speaker. Language, also, far more dubiously, is meant to define the other—and, in this case, the other is refusing to be defined by a language that has never been able to recognize him.

People evolve a language in order to describe and thus control their circumstances or in order not to be submerged by a situation that they cannot articulate. (And if they cannot articulate it, they are submerged.) A Frenchman living in Paris speaks a subtly and crucially different language from that of the man living in Marseilles; neither sounds very much like a man living in Quebec; and they would all have great difficulty in apprehending what the man from Guadeloupe, or Martinique, is saying, to say nothing of the man from Senegal—although the "common" language of all these areas is French. But each has paid, and is paying, a different price for this "common" language, in which, as it turns out, they are not saying, and cannot be saying, the same things: They each have very different realities to articulate, or control.

What joins all languages, and all men, is the necessity to confront life, in order, not inconceivably, to outwit death: The price for this is the acceptance, and achievement, of one's temporal identity. So that, for example, though it is not taught in the schools (and this has the potential of becoming a political issue) the south of France still clings to its ancient and musical Provençal, which resists being described as a "dialect." And much of the tension in the Basque countries, and in Wales, is due to the Basque and Welsh determination not to allow their languages to be destroyed. This determination also feeds the flames in Ireland, for among the many indignities the Irish have been forced to undergo at English hands is the English contempt for their language.

It goes without saying, then, that language is also a political instrument, means, and proof of power. It is the most vivid and crucial key to identity: It reveals the private identity, and connects one with, or divorces one from, the larger, public, or communal identity. There have been, and are, times and places, when to speak a certain language could be dangerous, even fatal. Or, one may speak the same language, but in such a way that one's antecedents are revealed, or (one hopes) hidden. This is true in France, and is absolutely true in England: The range (and reign) of accents on that damp little island make England coherent for the English and totally incomprehensible for everyone else. To open your mouth in England is (if I may use black English) to "put your business in the street." You have confessed your parents, your youth, your school, your salary, your self-esteem, and, alas, your future.

5 Now, I do not know what white Americans would sound like if there had never been any black people in the United States, but they would not sound the way they sound. *Jazz*, for example, is a very specific sexual term, as in *jazz me, baby*, but white people purified it into the Jazz Age. *Sock it to me*, which means, roughly, the same thing, has been adopted by Nathaniel Hawthorne's descendants with no qualms or hesitations at all, along with *let it all hang out* and *right on! Beat to his socks*, which was once the black's most total and despairing image of poverty, was transformed into a thing called the Beat Generation, which phenomenon was, largely, composed of *uptight*, middle-class white people, imitating poverty, trying to *get down*, to *get with it*, doing their *thing*, doing their despairing best to be *funky*, which we, the blacks, never dreamed of doing—we were funky, baby, like *funk* was going out of style.

Now, no one can eat his cake, and have it, too, and it is late in the day to attempt to penalize black people for having created a language that permits the nation its only glimpse of reality, a language without which the nation would be even more *whipped* than it is.

I say that the present skirmish is rooted in American history, and it is. Black English is the creation of the black diaspora. Blacks came to the United States chained to each other, but from different tribes. Neither could speak the other's language. If two black people, at that bitter hour of the world's history, had been able to speak to each other, the institution of chattel slavery could never have lasted as long as it did. Subsequently, the slave was given, under the eye, and the gun, of his master, Congo Square, and the Bible—or, in other words, and under those conditions, the slave began the formation of the black church, and it is within this unprecedented tabernacle that black English began to be formed. This was not, merely, as in the European example, the adoption of a foreign tongue, but an alchemy that transformed ancient elements into a new language: *A language comes into existence by means of brutal necessity, and the rules of the language are dictated by what the language must convey.*

There was a moment, in time, and in this place, when my brother, or my mother, or my father, or my sister, had to convey to me, for example, the danger in which I was standing from the white man standing just behind me, and to convey this with a speed and in a language that the white man could not possibly understand, and that, indeed, he cannot understand, until today. He cannot afford to understand it. This understanding would reveal to him too much about himself and smash that mirror before which he has been frozen for so long.

Now, if this passion, this skill, this (to quote Toni Morrison) "sheer intelligence," this incredible music, the mighty achievement of having brought a people utterly unknown to, or despised by "history"—to have brought this people to their present, troubled, troubling, and unassailable and unanswerable place—if this absolutely unprecedented journey does not indicate that black English is a language, I am curious to know what definition of languages is to be trusted.

10 A people at the center of the Western world, and in the midst of so hostile a population, has not endured and transcended by means of what is patronizingly called a "dialect." We, the blacks, are in trouble, certainly, but we are not inarticulate because we are not compelled to defend a morality that we know to be a lie.

The brutal truth is that the bulk of the white people in America never had any interest in educating black people, except as this could serve white purposes. It is not the black child's language that is despised. It is his experience. A child cannot be taught by anyone who despises him, and a child cannot afford to be fooled. A child cannot be taught by anyone whose demand, essentially, is that the child repudiate his experience, and all that gives him sustenance, and enter a limbo in which he will no longer be black, and in which he knows that he can never become white. Black people have lost too many black children that way.

And, after all, finally, in a country with standards so untrustworthy, a country that makes heroes of so many criminal mediocrities, a country unable to face why so many of the nonwhite are in prison, or on the needle, or standing, futureless, in the streets—it may very well be that both the child, and his elder, have concluded that they have nothing whatever to learn from the people of a country that has managed to learn so little.

▪ QUESTIONS

Reading

1. Baldwin begins his essay by challenging a long-standing argument concerning black English: "The argument has nothing to do with language itself but with the role of language" (paragraph 1). What distinctions does Baldwin note between "language itself" and "the role of language"? Why is this distinction central to his argument?

2. Baldwin's position on black English is at odds with those who would like to deny black English status as a language. Summarize Baldwin's position as well as the position of Baldwin's opponents.
3. In paragraph 4, Baldwin writes, "It goes without saying, then, that language is also a political instrument, means, and proof of power." How, according to Baldwin, does language connect or divide one from "communal identity"? What evidence does he provide to support this claim that language is a political instrument?

Exploratory Writing

1. Baldwin makes an important distinction between *dialect* and *language*. Make a double-entry list of the ways that he defines each (use a separate piece of paper if you need more room). Discuss whether you find his definitions persuasive.

DIALECT	LANGUAGE

2. Baldwin asks his readers to think about the evolution of black English and to consider "what definition of languages is to be trusted" (paragraph 9) if black English is not a language. Collaborate in small groups to choose an example of a dialect with which you are all familiar. Would you define this dialect as a language? Prepare a presentation describing and demonstrating the ways this dialect reflects the richness of its culture.
3. Reread Baldwin's memorable conclusion, first published in 1979. How does he prepare you for this conclusion? What are you left to contemplate? How relevant does his indictment of racism in the United States seem today?

Making Connections

1. Both Baldwin and Martin Luther King Jr. (p. 341) make strong arguments about racial questions. Both of these writers are considered to be exceptional masters of English prose. Write an essay in which you consider them as argumentative writers. Are their styles of argument different? Do they use the same vocabulary? How would you characterize each as a writer? Do you prefer one style over the other? Do you find that one of their arguments is more effective than the other? Present your opinions, and make your case.

Essay Writing

1. Both Baldwin and George Orwell ("Politics and the English Language," p. 313) are interested in understanding language as a political instrument. Write an essay in which you examine their views on the politics of language, pointing out their similarities and differences.

ARGUING

Setting the Record Straight

Scott McCloud

Scott McCloud (b. 1960), cartoonist and comics theorist, grew up in Lexington, Massachusetts, and received a BFA in illustration from Syracuse University. In 1984, he began his career in independent comics, creating the series *Zot!*, the chronicles of two teenagers living in parallel worlds, which he refers to as "a cross between Peter Pan, Buck Rogers, and Marshall McLuhan." He has also written for mainstream comic book titles, notably *Superman*, and has been an important proponent of webcomics. McCloud is perhaps best known, however, for his explorations of comics as a unique narrative medium. In his seminal *Understanding Comics*, published in 1993, McCloud uses the comics form itself to explain how comics differ from more conventional storytelling media like film and novels, while arguing for the medium's distinctive virtues. This was followed by *Reinventing Comics* in 2000 and *Making Comics* in 2006. An excerpt from the opening chapter of *Understanding Comics* is reprinted here.

CHAPTER ONE
SETTING THE RECORD STRAIGHT.

HI, I'M SCOTT McCLOUD.
JANUARY

WHEN I WAS A LITTLE KID I KNEW EXACTLY WHAT COMICS WERE.

COMICS WERE THOSE BRIGHT, COLORFUL MAGAZINES FILLED WITH BAD ART, STUPID STORIES AND GUYS IN TIGHTS.

I READ REAL BOOKS, NATURALLY. I WAS MUCH TOO OLD FOR COMICS!

BUT WHEN I WAS IN 8th GRADE, A FRIEND OF MINE (WHO WAS A LOT SMARTER THAN I WAS) CONVINCED ME TO GIVE COMICS ANOTHER LOOK AND LENT ME HIS COLLECTION.
SOON, I WAS HOOKED!
THE REALLY OLD X-MEN
by STAN & JACK

IN LESS THAN A YEAR, I BECAME TOTALLY OBSESSED WITH COMICS! I DECIDED TO BECOME A COMICS ARTIST IN 10th GRADE AND BEGAN TO PRACTICE, PRACTICE, PRACTICE!

I FELT THAT THERE WAS SOMETHING LURKING IN COMICS... SOMETHING THAT HAD NEVER BEEN DONE.
SOME KIND OF HIDDEN POWER!

BUT WHENEVER I TRIED TO EXPLAIN MY FEELING, I FAILED MISERABLY.
COMIC BOOKS?!
HA! HA! HA!
BUT IT-- BUT IT'S-- BUH...

SURE, I REALIZED THAT COMIC BOOKS WERE USUALLY CRUDE, POORLY-DRAWN, SEMILITERATE, CHEAP, DISPOSABLE KIDDIE FARE--

--BUT--
THEY DON'T HAVE TO BE!

THE PROBLEM WAS THAT FOR MOST PEOPLE, THAT WAS WHAT "COMIC BOOK" MEANT!
DON'T GIMME THAT COMIC BOOK TALK, BARNEY!

IF PEOPLE FAILED TO UNDERSTAND COMICS, IT WAS BECAUSE THEY DEFINED WHAT COMICS COULD BE TOO NARROWLY!

A PROPER DEFINITION, IF WE COULD FIND ONE, MIGHT GIVE LIE TO THE STEREOTYPES--
--AND SHOW THAT THE POTENTIAL OF COMICS IS LIMITLESS AND EXCITING!

THIS IS WHERE OUR JOURNEY BEGINS.

THE WORLD OF COMICS IS A HUGE AND VARIED ONE. OUR DEFINITION MUST ENCOMPASS ALL THESE TYPES--
POW

--WHILE NOT BEING SO BROAD AS TO INCLUDE ANYTHING WHICH IS CLEARLY NOT COMICS.

"COMICS" IS THE WORD WORTH DEFINING, AS IT REFERS TO THE MEDIUM ITSELF, NOT A SPECIFIC OBJECT AS "COMIC BOOK" OR "COMIC STRIP" DO.
WE CAN ALL VISUALIZE A COMIC.
GENERIC GUY

BUT WHAT--
--IS--
--COMICS?

MASTER COMICS ARTIST WILL EISNER USES THE TERM SEQUENTIAL ART WHEN DESCRIBING COMICS.
TAKEN INDIVIDUALLY, THE PICTURES BELOW ARE MERELY THAT-- PICTURES.
HOWEVER, WHEN PART OF A SEQUENCE, EVEN A SEQUENCE OF ONLY TWO, THE ART OF THE IMAGE IS TRANSFORMED INTO SOMETHING MORE: THE ART OF COMICS!
NOTICE THAT THIS DEFINITION IS STRICTLY NEUTRAL ON MATTERS OF STYLE, QUALITY OR SUBJECT MATTER.
BANG!
BANG!
EEEK!
12
12
12
MUCH HAS ALREADY BEEN WRITTEN ON THE VARIOUS SCHOOLS OF COMIC ART; ON PARTICULAR ARTISTS, PARTICULAR TITLES, PARTICULAR TRENDS...
BUT TO DEFINE COMICS, WE MUST FIRST DO A LITTLE AESTHETIC SURGERY AND SEPARATE FORM FROM CONTENT!

*EISNER'S OWN *COMICS AND SEQUENTIAL ART* BEING A HAPPY EXCEPTION.

*JUXTAPOSED = ADJACENT, SIDE-BY-SIDE. GREAT ART SCHOOL WORD.

HOWEVER
YOU MIGHT
SAY THAT
BEFORE IT'S
PROJECTED,
FILM IS
JUST A
VERY
VERY
VERY
VERY
SLOW
COMIC!

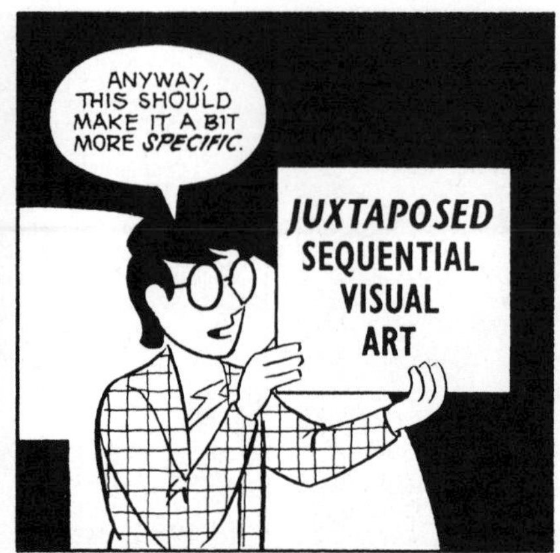
ANYWAY, THIS SHOULD MAKE IT A BIT MORE SPECIFIC.
JUXTAPOSED SEQUENTIAL VISUAL ART

DOES IT HAVE TO SAY "ART"? DOESN'T THAT IMPLY SOME SORT OF VALUE JUDGMENT?
WELL...

OKAY, HOW ABOUT THIS?
JUXTAPOSED SEQUENTIAL STATIC IMAGES
NOW IT SOUNDS KIND OF ARBITRARY.

OKAY, HOW ABOUT THIS?
JUXTAPOSED STATIC IMAGES IN DELIBERATE SEQUENCE
WHAT ABOUT WORDS?

OH, IT DOESN'T HAVE TO CONTAIN WORDS TO BE COMICS...
JUXTAPOSED STATIC IMAGES IN DELIBERATE SEQUENCE
NO, NO. I MEAN, DOESN'T THAT DEFINITION DESCRIBE WORDS??

HUH?
JUXTAPOSED STATIC IMAGES IN DELIBERATE SEQUENCE
LETTERS ARE STATIC IMAGES, RIGHT?
WHEN THEY'RE ARRANGED IN A DELIBERATE SEQUENCE, PLACED NEXT TO EACH OTHER, WE CALL THEM WORDS!
YOU TELL 'IM, BOB!

adv.
com·ics (kom'iks)**n.** plural in form, used with a singular verb. **1.** Juxtaposed pictorial and other images in deliberate sequence, intended to convey information and/or to produce an aesthetic response in the viewer.
~~**2.** Superheroes in bright colorful costumes, fighting dastardly villains who want to conquer the world, in violent sensational pulse-pounding action sequences!! **3.** Cute, cuddly bunnies, mice and roly-poly bears, dancing to and fro, Hippity-Hop, Hippity-Hop. **4.** Corruptor of our Nation's Youth.~~
com·ing (kum'ing) **adj.**

* OR "OCELOT'S CLAW" DEPENDING ON WHOSE BOOK YOU READ. THIS SEQUENCE IS BASED ON A READING BY MEXICAN HISTORIAN AND ARCHAEOLOGIST ALFONSO CASO.

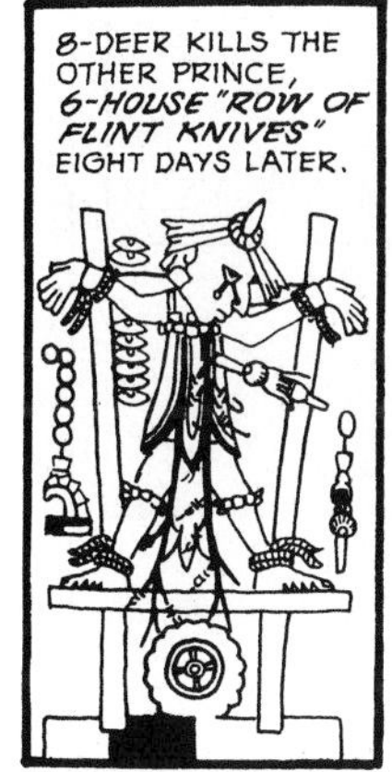

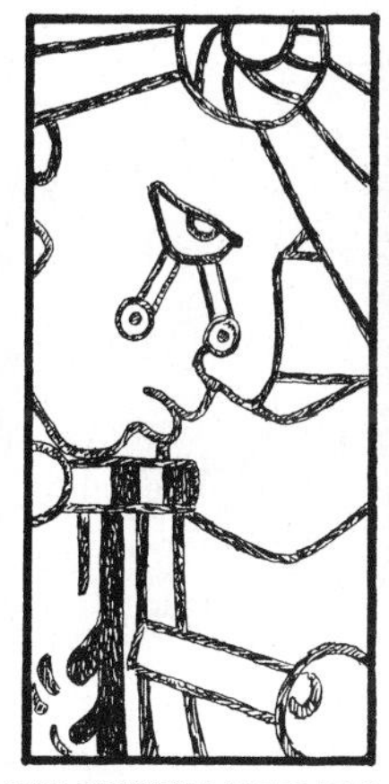

*WE KNOW THE YEAR; I'M JUST GUESSING AT THE DATE REPRESENTED BY "12 MONKEY"

HUNDREDS OF YEARS BEFORE CORTÉS BEGAN COLLECTING COMICS, FRANCE PRODUCED THE STRIKINGLY SIMILAR WORK WE CALL THE BAYEUX TAPESTRY.
THIS 230 FOOT LONG TAPESTRY DETAILS THE NORMAN CONQUEST OF ENGLAND, BEGINNING IN 1066.
TRANSLATION: THE BATTLE RAGES
BISHOP ODIN ENCOURAGES HIS SOLDIERS

FAR FROM DISQUALIFYING THESE AS COMICS, I THINK MODERN COMIC BOOK ARTISTS SHOULD TAKE NOTE OF THE POSSIBILITIES OF SUCH WHOLE PAGE COMPOSITIONS AND HOW FEW ARTISTS HAVE MADE GOOD USE OF THEM SINCE!
PERENNIAL EXCEPTION WILL EISNER.
NO!
WHAT DO YOU WANT TO DO HERE, EH?
DO YOU THINK IF I REPORT THEM IT WILL BE THE END OF IT?
WHICH ONE IS THE PRINCE?
WHAT, NO HORSES?
FINDING COMICS BEYOND OUR OWN MILLENNIUM IS A BIT TRICKIER.
1100
1200

JUXTAPOSED PICTORIAL AND OTHER IMAGES IN DELIBERATE SEQUENCE ?
AT FIRST GLANCE, EGYPTIAN HIEROGLYPHICS WOULD SEEM TO FIT OUR DEFINITION PERFECTLY.
BUT MUCH DEPENDS ON OUR USE OF THE WORD "PICTORIAL."
I'M USING IT TO INDICATE AT LEAST SOME RESEMBLANCE TO THE SUBJECT. BUT THESE GLYPHS REPRESENT ONLY SOUNDS, NOT UNLIKE OUR ALPHABET.
= "baíu"
= "nek"

READING LEFT TO RIGHT WE SEE THE EVENTS OF THE CONQUEST, IN DELIBERATE CHRONOLOGICAL ORDER UNFOLD BEFORE OUR VERY EYES.
AS WITH THE MEXICAN CODEX, THERE ARE NO PANEL BORDERS PER SE, BUT THERE ARE CLEAR DIVISIONS OF SCENE BY SUBJECT MATTER.
DUKE WILLIAM REMOVES HIS HELMET TO RALLY HIS SOLDIERS
HAROLD'S ARMY IS CUT TO PIECES

THUS, THEIR REAL DESCENDENT IS THE WRITTEN WORD AND NOT COMICS.
"ses tu baiu abta, hennu-nek baiu amenta"
"FOLLOW THEE, THE SOULS OF THE EAST. PRAISE THEE, THE SOULS OF THE WEST."
EGYPTIAN PAINTING IS ANOTHER MATTER. SOME, LIKE THIS, MAY SEEM TO BE CONCERNED WITH SEQUENCE, BUT ARE ACTUALLY SHOWING TWO DIFFERENT LOCATIONS, EVENTS AND CASTS, GROUPED ONLY BY SUBJECT.

I HAD BEEN TRYING TO FIND SEQUENCE IN EGYPTIAN PAINTINGS FOR YEARS WHEN I BEGAN THIS BOOK AND WAS READY TO CALL IT QUITS--
--UNTIL I DISCOVERED THAT THE BOOKS I HAD BEEN USING AS REFERENCE--

--HAD ONLY BEEN SHOWING ME PART OF THE PICTURE!

* MORE NEARLY COMPLETE, ANYWAY.

PAINTING TRACED FOR BLACK AND WHITE REPRODUCTION.

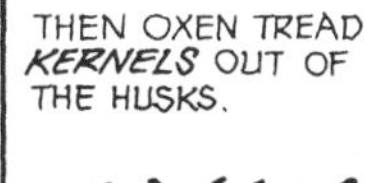

* FACE GOUGED OUT BY FUTURE GENERATIONS OF LEADERS

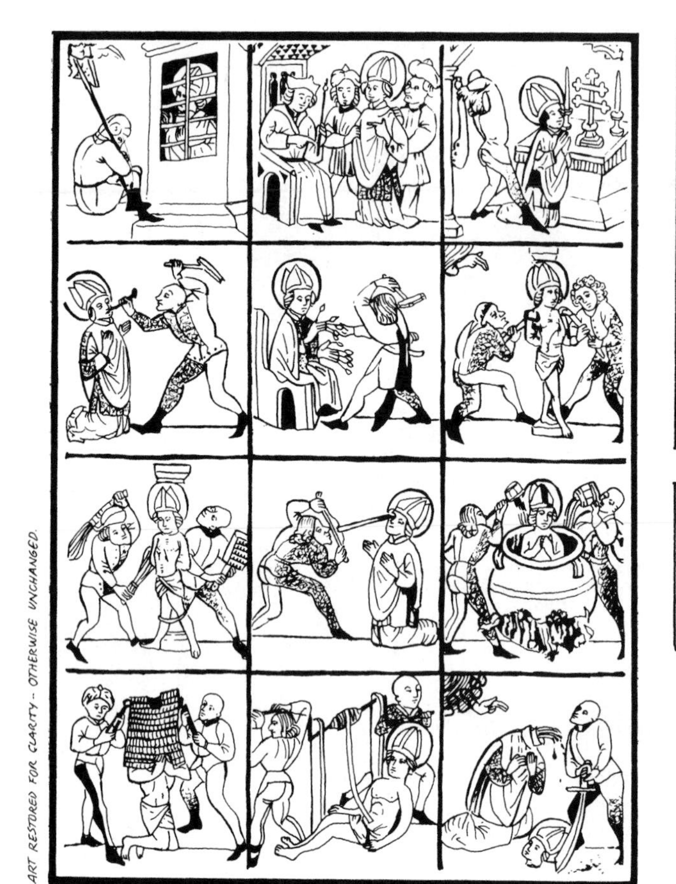

*Maybe I shouldn't say "invent." Europeans were a bit late in discovering printing.

▪QUESTIONS

Reading

1. According to McCloud, what are some stereotypes that most people believe about comic books? Does he agree with these stereotypes?
2. Describe the narrator of *Understanding Comics*. What function does this narrator serve?
3. How did the invention of printing change the role of comics in culture?

Exploratory Writing

1. Underline, highlight, or flag McCloud's different definitions of comics. Choose a sequence of images from any period in history, and explain why it is or is not a comic, according to McCloud's final, complete definition.
2. McCloud uses a comic to make an argument about the cultural status of comics. Choose something that interests you, and create a comic to make an argument about it. How is designing an argumentative comic different from writing an argumentative essay?

Making Connections

1. Put McCloud's definition of comics to the test by applying it to the other graphic selections in this book, by Marjane Satrapi (p. 184) and Brooke Gladstone (p. 325). In what ways does each selection meet McCloud's criteria? Do they violate his definition in any way? In what ways are they similar to or different from the examples McCloud provides? Once you've evaluated McCloud's definition, write or draw your own definition of comics.

Essay Writing

1. McCloud talks about becoming "totally obsessed" with comics and seeing them as a medium with a special, hidden power. Write an essay reflecting on an art form, writing style, type of music or dance, or some other form of personal expression that obsessed you. In your experience, what is special and unique about that type of expression? What is its power?

REFLECTING

Why I Blog

Andrew Sullivan

Writer, editor, and public intellectual Andrew Sullivan (b. 1963) was born in Southern England and lives in Washington, D.C. He attended Oxford University, where he studied modern history and modern languages, and Harvard University, where he received a master's degree in public administration and a PhD in political science in 1989. Openly gay, Sullivan has been an outspoken advocate of gay rights. His 1993 *New Republic* essay, "The Politics of Homosexuality," remains one of the most influential articles of the decade on the subject; his controversial "Why Men Are Different" put him on the cover of *Time* magazine. Sullivan's books include *Virtually Normal: An Argument about Homosexuality* (1995); *Love Undetectable: Notes on Friendship, Sex, and Survival* (1998); *The Conservative Soul* (2006); and, most recently, *Intimations Pursued: The Voice of Practice in the Conversation of Michael Oakeshott* (2008). Editor of the *New Republic* from 1991 to 1996, Sullivan has also been a contributing writer for the *London Sunday Times*, *Time* magazine, and the *New York Times Magazine*. A frequent contributor to the *Atlantic*, in which "Why I Blog" appeared in 2008, Sullivan also writes a blog, *The Dish*, for *Newsweek*'s *Daily Beast* site.

The word *blog* is a conflation of two words: *Web* and *log*. It contains in its four letters a concise and accurate self-description: It is a log of thoughts and writing posted publicly on the World Wide Web. In the monosyllabic vernacular of the Internet, *Web log* soon became the word *blog*.

This form of instant and global self-publishing, made possible by technology widely available only for the past decade or so, allows for no retroactive editing (apart from fixing minor typos or small glitches) and removes from the act of writing any considered or lengthy review. It is the spontaneous expression of instant thought—impermanent beyond even the ephemera of daily journalism. It is accountable in immediate and unavoidable ways to readers and other bloggers, and linked via hypertext to continuously multiplying references and sources. Unlike any single piece of print journalism, its borders are extremely porous and its truth inherently transitory. The consequences of this for the act of writing are still sinking in.

A ship's log owes its name to a small wooden board, often weighted with lead, that was for centuries attached to a line and thrown over the stern. The weight of the log would keep it in the same place in the water, like a provisional anchor, while the ship moved away. By measuring the length of line used up in a set period of time, mariners could calculate the speed of their journey (the rope itself was marked by equidistant "knots" for easy measurement). As a ship's voyage progressed, the course came to be marked down in a book that was called a log.

In journeys at sea that took place before radio or radar or satellites or sonar, these logs were an indispensable source for recording what actually happened. They helped navigators surmise where they were and how far they had traveled and how much longer they had to stay at sea. They provided accountability to a ship's owners and traders. They were designed to be as immune to faking as possible. Away from land, there was usually no reliable corroboration of events apart from the crew's own account in the middle of an expanse of blue and gray and green; and in long journeys, memories always blur and facts disperse. A log provided as accurate an account as could be gleaned in real time.

5 As you read a log, you have the curious sense of moving backward in time as you move forward in pages—the opposite of a book. As you piece together a narrative that was never intended as one, it seems—and is—more truthful. Logs, in this sense, were a form of human self-correction. They amended for hindsight, for the ways in which human beings order and tidy and construct the story of their lives as they look back on them. Logs require a letting-go of narrative because they do not allow for a knowledge of the ending. So they have plot as well as dramatic irony—the reader will know the ending before the writer did.

Anyone who has blogged his thoughts for an extended time will recognize this world. We bloggers have scant opportunity to collect our thoughts, to wait until events have settled and a clear pattern emerges. We blog now—as news reaches us, as facts emerge. This is partly true for all journalism, which is, as its etymology suggests, daily writing, always subject to subsequent revision. And a good columnist will adjust position and judgment and even political loyalty over time, depending on events. But a blog is not so much daily writing as hourly writing. And with that level of timeliness, the provisionality of every word is even more pressing—and the risk of error or the thrill of prescience that much greater.

No columnist or reporter or novelist will have his minute shifts or constant small contradictions exposed as mercilessly as a blogger's are. A columnist can ignore or duck a subject less noticeably than a blogger committing thoughts to pixels several times a day. A reporter can wait—must wait—until every source has confirmed. A novelist can spend months or years before committing words to the world. For bloggers, the deadline is always now. Blogging is therefore to writing what extreme sports are to athletics: more free-form, more accident-prone, less formal, more alive. It is, in many ways, writing out loud.

You end up writing about yourself, since you are a relatively fixed point in this constant interaction with the ideas and facts of the exterior world. And in this sense, the historic form closest to blogs is the diary. But with this difference: A diary is almost always a private matter. Its raw honesty, its dedication to marking life as it happens and remembering life as it was, makes it a terrestrial log. A few diaries are meant to be read by others, of course, just as correspondence could be—but usually posthumously, or as a way to compile facts for a more considered autobiographical rendering. But a blog, unlike a diary, is instantly public. It transforms this most personal and retrospective of forms into a painfully public and immediate one. It combines the confessional genre with the log form and exposes the author in a manner no author has ever been exposed before.

I remember first grappling with what to put on my blog. It was the spring of 2000, and like many a freelance writer at the time, I had some vague notion that I needed to have a presence "online." I had no clear idea of what to do, but a friend who ran a Web-design company offered to create a site for me, and since I was technologically clueless, he also agreed to post various essays and columns as I wrote them. Before too long, this became a chore for him, and he called me one day to say he'd found an online platform that was so simple I could henceforth post all my writing myself. The platform was called Blogger.

As I used it to post columns or links to books or old essays, it occurred to me that I could also post new writing—writing that could even be exclusive to the blog. But what? Like any new form, blogging did not start from nothing. It evolved from various journalistic traditions. In my case, I drew on my mainstream-media experience to navigate the virgin sea. I had a few early inspirations: the old Notebook section of the *New Republic,* a magazine that, under the editorial guidance of Michael Kinsley, had introduced a more English style of crisp, short commentary into what had been a more high-minded genre of American opinion writing. The *New Republic* had also pioneered a Diarist feature on the last page, which was designed to be a more personal, essayistic, first-person form of journalism. Mixing the two genres, I did what I had been trained to do—and improvised.

I'd previously written online as well, contributing to a listserv for gay writers and helping Kinsley initiate a more discursive form of online writing for *Slate,* the first magazine published exclusively on the Web. As soon as I began writing this way, I realized that the online form rewarded a colloquial, unfinished tone. In one of my early Kinsley-guided experiments, he urged me not to think too hard before writing. So I wrote as I'd write an e-mail—with only a mite more circumspection. This is hazardous, of course, as anyone who has ever clicked Send in a fit of anger or hurt will testify. But blogging requires an embrace of such hazards, a willingness to fall off the trapeze rather than fail to make the leap.

From the first few days of using the form, I was hooked. The simple experience of being able to directly broadcast my own words to readers was an exhilarating literary liberation. Unlike the current generation of writers, who have only ever blogged, I knew firsthand what the alternative meant. I'd edited a weekly print magazine, the *New Republic,* for five years, and written countless columns and essays for a variety of traditional outlets. And in all this, I'd often chafed, as most writers do, at the endless delays, revisions, office politics, editorial fights, and last-minute cuts for space that dead-tree publishing entails. Blogging—even to an audience of a few hundred in the early days—was intoxicatingly free in comparison. Like taking a narcotic.

It was obvious from the start that it was revolutionary. Every writer since the printing press has longed for a means to publish himself and reach—instantly—any reader on earth. Every professional writer has paid some dues waiting for an editor's nod, or enduring a publisher's incompetence, or being ground to literary dust by a legion of fact-checkers and copy editors. If you added up the time a writer once had to spend finding an outlet, impressing editors, sucking up to proprietors, and proofreading edits, you'd find another lifetime buried in the interstices. But with one click of the Publish Now button, all these troubles evaporated.

Alas, as I soon discovered, this sudden freedom from above was immediately replaced by insurrection from below. Within minutes of my posting something, even in the earliest days, readers responded. E-mail seemed to unleash their inner beast. They were more brutal than any editor, more persnickety than any copy editor, and more emotionally unstable than any colleague.

Again, it's hard to overrate how different this is. Writers can be sensitive, vain souls, requiring gentle nurturing from editors, and oddly susceptible to the blows delivered by reviewers. They survive, for the most part, but the thinness of their skins is legendary. Moreover, before the blogosphere, reporters and columnists were largely shielded from this kind of direct hazing. Yes, letters to the editor would arrive in due course and subscriptions would be canceled. But reporters and columnists tended to operate in a relative sanctuary, answerable mainly to their editors, not readers. For a long time, columns were essentially monologues published to applause, muffled murmurs, silence, or a distant heckle. I'd gotten blowback from pieces before—but in an amorphous, time-delayed, distant way. Now the feedback was instant, personal, and brutal. 15

And so blogging found its own answer to the defensive counterblast from the journalistic establishment. To the charges of inaccuracy and unprofessionalism, bloggers could point to the fierce, immediate scrutiny of their readers. Unlike newspapers, which would eventually publish corrections in a box of printed spinach far from the original error, bloggers had to walk the walk of self-correction in the same space and in the same format as the original screwup. The form was more accountable, not less, because there is nothing more conducive to professionalism than being publicly humiliated for sloppiness. Of course, a blogger could ignore an error or simply refuse to acknowledge mistakes. But if he persisted, he would be razzed by competitors and assailed by commenters and abandoned by readers. In an era when the traditional media found itself beset by scandals as disparate as Stephen Glass, Jayson Blair, and Dan Rather, bloggers survived the first assault on their worth. In time, in fact, the high standards expected of well-trafficked bloggers spilled over into greater accountability, transparency, and punctiliousness among the media powers that were. Even *New York Times* columnists were forced to admit when they had been wrong.

The blog remained a *superficial* medium, of course. By superficial, I mean simply that blogging rewards brevity and immediacy. No one wants to read a nine-thousand-word treatise online. On the Web, one-sentence links are as legitimate as thousand-word diatribes—in fact, they are often valued more. And, as Matt Drudge told me when I sought advice from the master in 2001, the key to understanding a blog is to realize that it's a broadcast, not a publication. If it stops moving, it dies. If it stops paddling, it sinks.

But the superficiality masked considerable depth—greater depth, from one perspective, than the traditional media could offer. The reason was a single technological innovation: the hyperlink. An old-school columnist can write eight hundred brilliant words analyzing or commenting on, say, a new think-tank report or scientific survey. But in reading it on paper, you have to take the columnist's presentation of the material on faith, or be convinced by a brief quotation (which can always be misleading out of context). Online, a hyperlink to the original source transforms the experience. Yes, a few sentences of bloggy spin may not be as satisfying as a full column, but the ability to read the primary material instantly—in as careful or shallow a fashion as you choose—can add much greater context than anything on paper. Even a blogger's chosen pull quote, unlike a columnist's, can be effortlessly checked against the original. Now this innovation, predating blogs but popularized by them, is increasingly central to mainstream journalism.

A blog, therefore, bobs on the surface of the ocean but has its anchorage in waters deeper than those print media is technologically able to exploit. It disempowers the writer to that extent, of course. The blogger can get away with less and afford fewer pretensions of authority. He is—more than any writer of the past—a node among other nodes, connected but unfinished without the links and the comments and the track-backs that make the blogosphere, at its best, a conversation, rather than a production.

A writer fully aware of and at ease with the provisionality of his own work is nothing new. For centuries, writers have experimented with forms that suggest the imperfection of human thought, the inconstancy of human affairs, and the humbling, chastening passage of time. If you compare the meandering, questioning, unresolved dialogues of Plato with the definitive, logical treatises of Aristotle, you see the difference between a skeptic's spirit translated into writing and a spirit that seeks to bring some finality to the argument. Perhaps the greatest single piece of Christian apologetics, Pascal's *Pensées,* is a series of meandering, short, and incomplete stabs at arguments, observations, insights. Their lack of finish is what makes them so compelling—arguably more compelling than a polished treatise by Aquinas. 20

Or take the brilliant polemics of Karl Kraus, the publisher of and main writer for *Die Fackel,* who delighted in constantly twitting authority with slashing aphorisms and rapid-fire bursts of invective. Kraus had something rare in his day: the financial wherewithal to self-publish. It gave him a fearlessness that is now available to anyone who can afford a computer and an Internet connection.

But perhaps the quintessential blogger *avant la lettre* was Montaigne. His essays were published in three major editions, each one longer and more complex than the previous. A passionate skeptic, Montaigne amended, added to, and amplified the essays for each edition, making them three-dimensional through time. In the best modern translations, each essay is annotated, sentence by sentence, paragraph by paragraph, by small letters (A, B, and C) for each major edition, helping the reader see how each rewrite added to or subverted, emphasized or ironized, the version before. Montaigne was living his skepticism, daring to show how a writer evolves, changes his mind, learns new things, shifts perspectives, grows older—and that this, far from being something that needs to be hidden behind a veneer of unchanging authority, can become a virtue, a new way of looking at the pretensions of authorship and text and truth. Montaigne, for good measure, also peppered his essays with myriads of what bloggers would call external links. His own thoughts are strewn with and complicated by the aphorisms and anecdotes of others. Scholars of the sources note that many of these "money quotes" were deliberately taken out of context, adding layers of irony to writing that was already saturated in empirical doubt.

To blog is therefore to let go of your writing in a way, to hold it at arm's length, open it to scrutiny, allow it to float in the ether for a while, and to let others, as Montaigne did, pivot you toward relative truth. A blogger will notice this almost immediately upon starting. Some e-mailers, unsurprisingly, know more about a subject than the blogger does. They will send links, stories, and facts, challenging the blogger's view of the world, sometimes outright refuting it, but more frequently adding context and nuance and complexity to an idea. The role of a blogger is not to defend against this but to embrace it. He is similar in this way to the host of a dinner party. He can provoke discussion or take a position, even passionately, but he also must create an atmosphere in which others want to participate.

That atmosphere will inevitably be formed by the blogger's personality. The blogosphere may, in fact, be the least veiled of any forum in which a writer dares to express himself. Even the most careful and self-aware blogger will reveal more about himself than he wants to in a few unguarded sentences and publish them before he has the sense to hit Delete. The wise panic that can paralyze a writer—the fear that he will be exposed, undone, humiliated—is not available to a blogger. You can't have blogger's block. You have to express yourself now, while your emotions roil, while your temper flares, while your humor lasts. You can try to hide yourself from real scrutiny, and the exposure it demands, but it's hard. And that's what makes blogging as a form stand out: It is rich in personality. The faux intimacy of the Web experience, the closeness of the e-mail and the instant message, seeps through. You feel as if you know bloggers as they go through their lives, experience the same things you are experiencing, and share the moment. When readers of my blog bump into me in person, they invariably address me as Andrew. Print readers don't do that. It's Mr. Sullivan to them.

25 On my blog, my readers and I experienced 9/11 together, in real time. I can look back and see not just how I responded to the event, but how I responded to it at 3:47 that afternoon. And at 9:46 that night. There is a vividness to this immediacy that cannot be rivaled by print. The same goes for the 2000 recount, the Iraq War, the revelations of Abu Ghraib, the death of John Paul II, or any of the other history-making events of the past decade. There is simply no way to write about them in real time without revealing a huge amount about yourself. And the intimate bond this creates with readers is unlike the

bond that the *Times*, say, develops with its readers through the same events. Alone in front of a computer, at any moment, are two people: a blogger and a reader. The proximity is palpable, the moment human—whatever authority a blogger has is derived not from the institution he works for but from the humanness he conveys. This is writing with emotion not just under but always breaking through the surface. It renders a writer and a reader not just connected but linked in a visceral, personal way. The only term that really describes this is *friendship*. And it is a relatively new thing to write for thousands and thousands of friends.

These friends, moreover, are an integral part of the blog itself—sources of solace, company, provocation, hurt, and correction. If I were to do an inventory of the material that appears on my blog, I'd estimate that a good third of it is reader-generated, and a good third of my time is spent absorbing readers' views, comments, and tips. Readers tell me of breaking stories, new perspectives, and counterarguments to prevailing assumptions. And this is what blogging, in turn, does to reporting. The traditional method involves a journalist searching for key sources, nurturing them, and sequestering them from his rivals. A blogger splashes gamely into a subject and dares the sources to come to him.

Some of this material—e-mails from soldiers on the front lines, from scientists explaining new research, from dissident Washington writers too scared to say what they think in their own partisan redoubts—might never have seen the light of day before the blogosphere. And some of it, of course, is dubious stuff. Bloggers can be spun and misled as easily as traditional writers—and the rigorous source assessment that good reporters do can't be done by e-mail. But you'd be surprised by what comes unsolicited into the in-box, and how helpful it often is.

Not all of it is mere information. Much of it is also opinion and scholarship, a knowledge base that exceeds the research department of any newspaper. A good blog is your own private *Wikipedia*. Indeed, the most pleasant surprise of blogging has been the number of people working in law or government or academia or rearing kids at home who have real literary talent and real knowledge, and who had no outlet—until now. There is a distinction here, of course, between the edited use of e-mailed sources by a careful blogger and the often mercurial cacophony on an unmediated comments section. But the truth is out there—and the miracle of e-mail allows it to come to you.

Fellow bloggers are always expanding this knowledge base. Eight years ago, the blogosphere felt like a handful of individual cranks fighting with one another. Today, it feels like a universe of cranks, with vast, pulsating readerships, fighting with one another. To the neophyte reader, or blogger, it can seem overwhelming. But there is a connection between the intimacy of the early years and the industry it has become today. And the connection is human individuality.

30 The pioneers of online journalism—*Slate* and *Salon*—are still very popular, and successful. But the more memorable stars of the Internet—even

within those two sites—are all personally branded. *Daily Kos*, for example, is written by hundreds of bloggers, and amended by thousands of commenters. But it is named after Markos Moulitsas, who started it, and his own prose still provides a backbone to the front-page blog. The biggest news-aggregator site in the world, the *Drudge Report*, is named after its founder, Matt Drudge, who somehow conveys a unified sensibility through his selection of links, images, and stories. The vast, expanding universe of the *Huffington Post* still finds some semblance of coherence in the Cambridge-Greek twang of Arianna; the entire world of online celebrity gossip circles the drain of Perez Hilton; and the investigative journalism, reviewing, and commentary of *Talking Points Memo* is still tied together by the tone of Josh Marshall. Even *Slate* is unimaginable without Mickey Kaus's voice.

What endures is a human brand. Readers have encountered this phenomenon before—*I. F. Stone's Weekly* comes to mind—but not to this extent. It stems, I think, from the conversational style that blogging rewards. What you want in a conversationalist is as much character as authority. And if you think of blogging as more like talk radio or cable news than opinion magazines or daily newspapers, then this personalized emphasis is less surprising. People have a voice for radio and a face for television. For blogging, they have a sensibility.

But writing in this new form is a collective enterprise as much as it is an individual one—and the connections between bloggers are as important as the content on the blogs. The links not only drive conversation—they drive readers. The more you link, the more others will link to you, and the more traffic and readers you will get. The zero-sum game of old media—in which *Time* benefits from *Newsweek*'s decline and vice versa—becomes win-win. It's great for *Time* to be linked to by *Newsweek* and the other way around. One of the most prized statistics in the blogosphere is therefore not the total number of readers or page views, but the "authority" you get by being linked to by other blogs. It's an indication of how central you are to the online conversation of humankind.

The reason this open-source market of thinking and writing has such potential is that the always adjusting and evolving collective mind can rapidly filter out bad arguments and bad ideas. The flip side, of course, is that bloggers are also human beings. Reason is not the only fuel in the tank. In a world where no distinction is made between good traffic and bad traffic, and where emotion often rules, some will always raise their voice to dominate the conversation; others will pander shamelessly to their readers' prejudices; others will start online brawls for the fun of it. Sensationalism, dirt, and the ease of formulaic talking points always beckon. You can disappear into the partisan blogosphere and never stumble onto a site you disagree with.

But linkage mitigates this. A Democratic blog will, for example, be forced to link to Republican ones, if only to attack and mock. And it's in the interests of both camps to generate shared traffic. This encourages polarized slugfests. But online, at least you see both sides. Reading the *Nation* or *National Review* before the Internet existed allowed for more cocooning than the wide-open online sluice gates do now. If there's more incivility, there's also more fluidity. Rudeness, in any case, isn't the worst thing that can happen to a blogger. Being ignored is. Perhaps the nastiest thing one can do to a fellow blogger is to rip him apart and fail to provide a link.

A successful blog therefore has to balance itself between a writer's own take on the world and others. Some bloggers collect, or "aggregate," other bloggers' posts with dozens of quick links and minimalist opinion topspin: Glenn Reynolds at Instapundit does this for the right-of-center; Duncan Black at Eschaton does it for the left. Others are more eclectic, or aggregate links in a particular niche, or cater to a settled and knowledgeable reader base. A "blogroll" is an indicator of whom you respect enough to keep in your galaxy. For many years, I kept my reading and linking habits to a relatively small coterie of fellow political bloggers. In today's blogosphere, to do this is to embrace marginality. I've since added links to religious blogs and literary ones and scientific ones and just plain weird ones. As the blogosphere has expanded beyond anyone's capacity to absorb it, I've needed an assistant and interns to scour the Web for links and stories and photographs to respond to and think about. It's a difficult balance, between your own interests and obsessions, and the knowledge, insight, and wit of others—but an immensely rich one. There are times, in fact, when a blogger feels less like a writer than an online disc jockey, mixing samples of tunes and generating new melodies through mashups while also making his own music. He is both artist and producer—and the beat always goes on. 35

If all this sounds postmodern, that's because it is. And blogging suffers from the same flaws as postmodernism: a failure to provide stable truth or a permanent perspective. A traditional writer is valued by readers precisely because they trust him to have thought long and hard about a subject, given it time to evolve in his head, and composed a piece of writing that is worth their time to read at length and to ponder. Bloggers don't do this and cannot do this—and that limits them far more than it does traditional long-form writing.

A blogger will air a variety of thoughts or facts on any subject in no particular order other than that dictated by the passing of time. A writer will instead use time, synthesizing these thoughts, ordering them, weighing which points count more than others, seeing how his views evolved in the writing process itself, and responding to an editor's perusal of a draft or two. The result is almost always more measured, more satisfying, and more enduring than a blizzard of posts. The triumphalist notion that blogging should somehow replace traditional writing is as foolish as it is pernicious. In some ways, blogging's gifts to our discourse make the skills of a good traditional writer much more valuable, not less. The torrent of blogospheric insights, ideas, and arguments places a greater premium on the person who can finally make sense of it all, turning it into something more solid, and lasting, and rewarding.

The points of this essay, for example, have appeared in shards and fragments on my blog for years. But being forced to order them in my head and think about them for a longer stretch has helped me understand them better, and perhaps express them more clearly. Each week, after a few hundred posts, I also write an actual newspaper column. It invariably turns out to be more considered, balanced, and evenhanded than the blog. But the blog will always inform and enrich the column, and often serve as a kind of free-form, free-associative research. And an essay like this will spawn discussion best handled on a blog. The conversation, in other words, is the point, and the different idioms used by the conversationalists all contribute something of value to it. And so, if the defenders of the old media once viscerally regarded blogging as some kind of threat, they are starting to see it more as a portal, and a spur.

There is, after all, something simply irreplaceable about reading a piece of writing at length on paper, in a chair or on a couch or in bed. To use an obvious analogy, jazz entered our civilization much later than composed, formal music. But it hasn't replaced it; and no jazz musician would ever claim that it could. Jazz merely demands a different way of playing and listening, just as blogging requires a different mode of writing and reading. Jazz and blogging are intimate, improvisational, and individual—but also inherently collective. And the audience talks over both.

The reason they talk while listening, and comment or link while reading, 40 is that they understand that this is a kind of music that needs to be engaged rather than merely absorbed. To listen to jazz as one would listen to an aria is to miss the point. Reading at a monitor, at a desk, or on an iPhone provokes a querulous, impatient, distracted attitude, a demand for instant, usable information, that is simply not conducive to opening a novel or a favorite magazine on the couch. Reading on paper evokes a more relaxed and meditative response. The message dictates the medium. And each medium has its place—as long as one is not mistaken for the other.

In fact, for all the intense gloom surrounding the newspaper and magazine business, this is actually a golden era for journalism. The blogosphere has added a whole new idiom to the act of writing and has introduced an entirely new generation to nonfiction. It has enabled writers to write out loud in ways never seen or understood before. And yet it has exposed a hunger and need for traditional writing that, in the age of television's dominance, had seemed on the wane.

Words, of all sorts, have never seemed so now.

▪ QUESTIONS

Reading

1. What does Sullivan mean when he writes that the blog is "a *superficial* medium" (paragraph 17)?
2. What, according to Sullivan, is "the most pleasant surprise of blogging" (paragraph 28)?
3. In your own words, explain the analogy that Sullivan makes between blogging versus traditional journalism, and jazz versus "composed, formal" music (paragraph 39). Create your own analogy to describe the distinction between blogging and pre-Internet writing forms.

4. Make a double-entry list of the things that distinguish blogging from print journalism, according to Sullivan. How do his points support his conclusion?

Traditional/Print Journalism	**Blogs**

Exploratory Writing

1. Collaborating in small groups, report on your experiences writing a real-life blog. Each group member should start his or her own blog, or share his or her existing blog with the rest of the group. Post on your blog daily, and comment on other group members' blogs at least once a day. Feel free to invite people outside of the group to read your blog, too. Throughout the week, keep a private journal about your blog, noting whether or not your experiences are similar to those that Sullivan describes. At the conclusion of your blog experiment, discuss your findings with the class.
2. For Sullivan, the "sudden freedom from above" of blogging is "replaced by insurrection from below" (paragraph 14) — instant, personal, and brutal responses from unedited readers. Choose a blog on a topic that interests you, and spend a few days tracking all of the comments from readers posted there. How many of the comments seem constructive and topical? How many seem brutal, like "direct hazing" (15)? How many seem "emotionally unstable" (14) or irrelevant? What conclusions do you draw from your observations?

Making Connections

1. Sullivan describes feeling strong emotions about his interactions with the readers of his blog, including hurt and friendship. Compare this to Mona Eltahawy's concerns about Twitter and personal relationships (p. 163). Based on their experiences and your own, write a set of rules for how to successfully communicate online.

Essay Writing

1. Write your own reflective essay titled "Why I Blog" (or "Why I Don't Blog"). Use details and anecdotes to bring your experiences to life for the reader.

REFLECTING

Twitterholics Anonymous

Mona Eltahawy

Journalist Mona Eltahawy was born in Port Said, Egypt, in 1967 and lived in the United Kingdom, Saudi Arabia, and Israel before becoming a writer, pundit, and activist in the United States in 2000. Her career as a reporter started in the Middle East where she worked as a *Reuters* correspondent in Cairo and Jerusalem. She was the first Egyptian to work for a Western news outlet in Israel. Her outspoken criticism of Egypt lost her a column in a Saudi Arabian–owned publication. However, her commentary on the Middle East, especially issues regarding Muslim women, has earned her the Muslim Leader of Tomorrow Award from the American Society for Muslim Advancement (2005), a Special Prize for Outstanding Contribution to Journalism from the Anna Lindh Foundation (2010), and the Anvil of Freedom Award (2010) from Estlow International Center for Journalism and New Media at the University of Denver. Eltahawy's columns run in Canada's *Toronto Star*, Israel's the *Jerusalem Report*, and Denmark's *Politiken*. In addition, Eltahawy's writings have been published in the *Washington Post* and *International Herald Tribune*. "Twitterholics Anonymous," which describes how Twitter keeps Eltahawy connected, appeared in the *Jerusalem Report* and on her blog *monaeltahawy.com* in 2011.

Twitter is my lifeline to the world. Twitter is the bane of my existence. Twitter connects me to everything I care about and Twitter is ruining my life.

Yes, yes, I'm Mona; I'm a Twitterholic, etc. etc.

Here are the places I tweet: In bed (when I wake up in the middle of the night, I'll reach out for my iPhone and check in on the Twitterverse). In the bathroom (don't ask). On the street. At bookshops. Standing in line to pay at the grocery store. You get the idea.

Sometimes I'll even tweet while I'm on the phone with my sister (we follow each other on Twitter) and she'll tweet back, "I can't believe you're tweeting while we're on the phone!!!"

Yes. It's bad. 5

But in all seriousness, before we start to talk about A for Addiction, let me tell you how—for this columnist and news junkie—Twitter has become part of the backbone for my work along with my laptop and Internet connection. It has broken more stories for me than any other news "source" recently.

I spent almost six years as a *Reuters* correspondent in Cairo and Jerusalem, honing my thirst for speed, which along with accuracy is wire reporting's forte. Twitter gives you the first and can leave you free falling when it comes to the second, but if you don't know how to navigate, then you don't belong on the Twitterhighway.

I first learned of the bomb attack, which took place a few minutes into the

New Year against a Coptic Christian church in Alexandria, Egypt, via Twitter. Granted it was a very slow news day regardless of time zone, but on Twitter there's always someone awake somewhere.

Twitter wasn't just the first place I heard about the uprising in Tunisia but it was, for many days, the only place. The U.S. media mostly ignored the worst unrest to hit the North African country in a decade. It started on December 17, when a young man poured gasoline on himself in Sidi Bouzid to protest police confiscating the fruits and vegetables he sold without a permit, in lieu of a job he couldn't find despite having a university degree.

This is where who you follow along that Twitterhighway matters. Thanks to a group of activists, journalists, and bloggers (sometimes they are all in one), I got not just the latest information from Tunisia—blog entries, video straight from demonstrations, news about arrested bloggers and campaigns for their release—but also live updates from solidarity protests in neighboring countries too, such as the one in Cairo. 10

And then where else could I follow in real time as Boston-based Mauritanian-American activist Nasser Weddady—who has for years run advocacy campaigns to release activists and journalists imprisoned in the Middle East—demanded that Alec Ross, Secretary of State Hillary Clinton's Senior Advisor for Innovation, explain why the U.S. Administration was silent as Tunisia arrested protesters and bloggers and used live ammunition against demonstrators.

Ross is a champion of social media and his boss often extols the virtues of Net freedom, so it was captivating to follow their discussion because here was Tunisia conducting a vicious war against Facebook users, bloggers, and other online activists to shut them down and yet it got little of the condemnation Washington meted out to Iran when the latter went after online activists after the 2009 elections.

So, of course, I'm on Twitter. I don't care about Lady Gaga or Justin Bieber, who between them have about half of the world following them. Twitter helps me mine the world for small gems of optimism to hold on to—those tireless and increasingly frantic tweets from Cairo protesters corralled by police for more than seven hours, or tweets from Egyptian Muslims who attended Christmas Eve services to show solidarity with their Coptic compatriots and pictures showing them standing outside churches holding candles: I demand to be moved to the edge of tears, rage, and optimism, and Twitter delivers.

And that's exactly why it's destroying my life, my ability to write, and my ability to look away from the computer screen. I see a number up there on the Twitter tab and I must refresh, immediately—must.know.now.

I'm glued to Twitter for hours on end. It's exhausting not just because of the amount of time I spend on it—I don't just read, I tweet, too—but because it keeps you in a constant state of alertness. To write, you need to move beyond that alertness, to stop refreshing that Twitter feed, and to wander away. Twitter never lets me wander. Its tentacles hold me too tightly. 15

Just disconnect, you ask? I would lose a vital pipeline of information. But also social interaction.

Writing is a lonely endeavor—the payback for the constant drip-drip-drip of distraction is an army of people across the globe. First up are the Australians, Malaysians and Indonesians. I'll catch a few hours of them before I head to bed just as the Middle East is waking up. By the time I'm awake—or if I sneak a peek in the middle of sleep—I'll get Europe and then during my day, it's the Middle East's night owls along with North American tweeps.

When I'm up all night to write, I'm never alone. But when I need distance for focus and analysis, again I'm never alone.

Addiction. Connection. Distraction. Twitter, I love/hate you.

▪ QUESTIONS

Reading

1. According to Eltahawy, how did the December 2010 uprising in Tunisia begin? How does she characterize the uprising? How did the U.S. media cover this event?
2. "Twitter, I love/hate you," writes Eltahawy (paragraph 19). In this article, what reasons does she give for loving Twitter? What reasons does she give for hating Twitter?
3. Highlight, underline, or flag the terms that Eltahawy uses that readers would not have understood thirty years ago. You'll notice that some of these terms are brand names, while others are hybrid words that Eltahawy seems to have coined herself. How does Eltahawy's choice to use this language support or undermine the premises of her article?

Exploratory Writing

1. What ways is the style of writing used on Twitter different from other kinds of nonfiction writing, such as essays or news articles? Over the course of three days, write at least twenty-five tweets (if you don't use Twitter, you can write the tweets in a notebook; just be sure to limit them to 140 characters—including spaces). Then write an informal response reflecting on your Twitter experiences. How did the short, sporadic format affect your thoughts, feelings, and ways of discussing news or personal events?
2. Choose a current news story that you think is important—such as a conflict, election, policy debate, contentious bill, major weather event like a hurricane or tsunami, or a court case—and follow the coverage of the story via Twitter. Then search for articles about the story in one or more major newspapers (such as the *New York Times*, *Washington Post*, *Guardian*, or *Wall Street Journal*). Prepare a brief class presentation reporting on the similarities and differences you found between the newspaper and Twitter coverage.

Making Connections

1. "I demand to be moved to the edge of tears, rage, and optimism," Eltahawy writes, "and Twitter delivers" (paragraph 13). In her speech "Internet Rights and Wrongs: Choices & Challenges in a Networked World," Hillary Rodham Clinton calls for worldwide "Internet freedom." In her words, "the freedoms to assemble and associate also apply in cyberspace" (p. 570). Based on your reading of Eltahawy and Clinton, compare the pros and cons of such freedom. Why is it important for citizens to have the right to

"assemble and associate" online? What new concerns does this right bring up, for individuals, cultures, or nations? How might those concerns be addressed?

2. In his essay "Why I Blog," Andrew Sullivan reflects on the quickness and immediacy of blogging: "a blog is not so much daily writing as hourly writing. And with that level of timeliness, the provisionality of every word is even more pressing—and the risk of error or the thrill of prescience is that much greater" (p. 153). How does this compare to Eltahawy's description of her Twitter "addiction"? What are the pros and cons of writing in a genre characterized by speed, but lacking time for fact-checking or sustained reflection?

Essay Writing

1. "All news should be written in tweets." Write an essay arguing for or against this proposition. You might make your essay a *reductio ad absurdum* argument like Jonathan Swift's "A Modest Proposal," where you seem to agree with the proposition, but then actually undermine it, by showing that it leads to impossible or absurd conclusions.

ARGUING

How to Tame a Wild Tongue

Gloria Anzaldúa

Gloria Anzaldúa (1942–2004) was an award-winning writer and prolific editor whose life and work championed Chicana culture, lesbianism, and feminism. Determined to get an education, Anzaldúa juggled school with working in the fields of her native South Texas from the age of fourteen. Eventually, she received an MA in English and education from the University of Texas. Anzaldúa's groundbreaking work, *This Bridge Called My Back: Writings by Radical Women of Color* (1981), coedited with Cherrie Moraga, won the Before Columbus Foundation American Book Award and challenged the lesbian and feminist movements to include women of different ethnicities and classes. "How to Tame a Wild Tongue," a chapter from Anzaldúa's book *Borderlands/La Frontera: The New Mestiza* (1987), addresses issues of Chicana identity in the United States.

"We're going to have to control your tongue," the dentist says, pulling out all the metal from my mouth. Silver bits plop and tinkle into the basin. My mouth is a mother lode.

The dentist is cleaning out my roots. I get a whiff of the stench when I gasp. "I can't cap that tooth yet, you're still draining," he says.

"We're going to have to do something about your tongue," I hear the anger rising in his voice. My tongue keeps pushing out the wads of cotton, pushing back the drills, the long thin needles. "I've never seen anything as strong or as stubborn," he says. And I think, how do you tame a wild tongue, train it to be quiet, how do you bridle and saddle it? How do you make it lie down?

> Who is to say that robbing a people of
> its language is less violent than war?
>
> —Ray Gwyn Smith

I remember being caught speaking Spanish at recess—that was good for three licks on the knuckles with a sharp ruler. I remember being sent to the corner of the classroom for "talking back" to the Anglo teacher when all I was trying to do was tell her how to pronounce my name. "If you want to be American, speak 'American.' If you don't like it, go back to Mexico where you belong."

5 "I want you to speak English. *Pa' hallar buen trabajo tienes que saber hablar el inglés bien. Qué vale toda tu educación si todavía hablas inglés con un* 'accent,' "[1]

[1]*Pa' hallar . . . 'accent'*: "To get a good job, you need to speak English well. What's the use of all your education if you speak English with an accent?" (Spanish).—Eds.

my mother would say, mortified that I spoke English like a Mexican. At Pan American University, I, like all Chicano students, was required to take two speech classes. Their purpose: to get rid of our accents.

Attacks on one's form of expression with the intent to censor are a violation of the First Amendment. *El Anglo con cara de inocente nos arrancó la lengua.* Wild tongues can't be tamed, they can only be cut out.

Overcoming the Tradition of Silence

Ahogadas, escupimos el oscuro.
Peleando con nuestra propia sombra
el silencio nos sepulta.

En boca cerrada no entran moscas. "Flies don't enter a closed mouth" is a saying I kept hearing when I was a child. *Ser habladora* was to be a gossip and a liar, to talk too much. *Muchachitas bien criadas,* well-bred girls don't answer back. *Es una falta de respeto*[2] to talk back to one's mother or father. I remember one of the sins I'd recite to the priest in the confession box the few times I went to confession: talking back to my mother, *hablar pa' 'trás, repelar. Hocicona, repelona, chismosa,* having a big mouth, questioning, carrying tales are all signs of being *mal criada.*[3] In my culture they are all words that are derogatory if applied to women—I've never heard them applied to men.

The first time I heard two women, a Puerto Rican and a Cuban, say the word "*nosotras,*" I was shocked. I had not known the word existed. Chicanas use *nosotros*[4] whether we're male or female. We are robbed of our female being by the masculine plural. Language is a male discourse.

And our tongues have become
dry the wilderness has
dried out our tongues and
we have forgotten speech.

—IRENA KLEPFISZ

Even our own people, other Spanish speakers *nos quieren poner candados en la boca.* They would hold us back with their bag of *reglas de academia.*[5]

---

[2]*Es una falta de respeto*: It's disrespectful (Spanish).—Eds.

[3]*mal criada*: Badly brought up (Spanish).—Eds.

[4]*nosotros*: First person plural ("we") in the masculine ("*-os*"). This is the default personal pronoun in Spanish. Traditionally, in Romance languages, a feminine version (*nosotras*) does not exist.—Eds.

[5]*reglas de academia*: Academic rules, or rules of traditional grammar (Spanish).—Eds.

Oye Como Ladra: El Lenguaje de la Frontera

Quien tiene boca se equivoca.

—MEXICAN SAYING

10 "*Pocho*, cultural traitor, you're speaking the oppressor's language by speaking English, you're ruining the Spanish language," I have been accused by various Latinos and Latinas. Chicano Spanish is considered by the purist and by most Latinos deficient, a mutilation of Spanish.

But Chicano Spanish is a border tongue which developed naturally. Change, *evolución, enriquecimiento de palabras nuevas por invención o adopción*[6] have created variants of Chicano Spanish, *un nuevo lenguaje. Un lenguaje que corresponde a un modo de vivir.* Chicano Spanish is not incorrect, it is a living language.

For a people who are neither Spanish nor live in a country in which Spanish is the first language; for a people who live in a country in which English is the reigning tongue but who are not Anglo; for a people who cannot entirely identify with either standard (formal, Castilian) Spanish nor standard English, what recourse is left to them but to create their own language? A language which they can connect their identity to, one capable of communicating the realities and values true to themselves—a language with terms that are neither *español ni inglés*, but both. We speak a patois, a forked tongue, a variation of two languages.

Chicano Spanish sprang out of the Chicanos' need to identify ourselves as a distinct people. We needed a language with which we could communicate with ourselves, a secret language. For some of us, language is a homeland closer than the Southwest—for many Chicanos today live in the Midwest and the East. And because we are a complex, heterogeneous people, we speak many languages. Some of the languages we speak are:

1. Standard English
2. Working-class and slang English
3. Standard Spanish
4. Standard Mexican Spanish
5. North Mexican Spanish dialect
6. Chicano Spanish (Texas, New Mexico, Arizona, and California have regional variations)
7. Tex-Mex
8. *Pachuco* (called *caló*)

My "home" tongues are the languages I speak with my sister and brothers, with my friends. They are the last five listed, with 6 and 7 being closest to my heart. From school, the media, and job situations, I've picked up standard

[6] *evolución, . . . adopción*: Evolution and enrichment with newly invented or adopted words (Spanish).—Eds.

and working-class English. From Mamagrande Locha and from reading Spanish and Mexican literature, I've picked up Standard Spanish and Standard Mexican Spanish. From *los recién llegados*, Mexican immigrants, and *braceros*,[7] I learned the North Mexican dialect. With Mexicans I'll try to speak either Standard Mexican Spanish or the North Mexican dialect. From my parents and Chicanos living in the Valley, I picked up Chicano Texas Spanish, and I speak it with my mom, younger brother (who married a Mexican and who rarely mixes Spanish with English), aunts, and older relatives.

With Chicanas from *Nuevo México* or *Arizona* I will speak Chicano Spanish a little, but often they don't understand what I'm saying. With most California Chicanas I speak entirely in English (unless I forget). When I first moved to San Francisco, I'd rattle off something in Spanish, unintentionally embarrassing them. Often it is only with another Chicana *tejana*[8] that I can talk freely. 15

Words distorted by English are known as anglicisms or *pochismos*. The *pocho* is an anglicized Mexican or American of Mexican origin who speaks Spanish with an accent characteristic of North Americans and who distorts and reconstructs the language according to the influence of English. Tex-Mex, or Spanglish, comes most naturally to me. I may switch back and forth from English to Spanish in the same sentence or in the same word. With my sister and my brother Nune and with Chicano *tejano* contemporaries I speak in Tex-Mex.

From kids and people my own age I picked up *Pachuco*. *Pachuco* (the language of the zoot suiters) is a language of rebellion, both against Standard Spanish and Standard English. It is a secret language. Adults of the culture and outsiders cannot understand it. It is made up of slang words from both English and Spanish. *Ruca* means girl or woman, *vato* means guy or dude, *chale* means no, *simón* means yes, *churo* is sure, talk is *periquiar*, *pigionear* means petting, *que gacho* means how nerdy, *ponte águila* means watch out, death is called *la pelona*. Through lack of practice and not having others who can speak it, I've lost most of the *Pachuco* tongue.

Chicano Spanish

Chicanos, after 250 years of Spanish/Anglo colonization, have developed significant differences in the Spanish we speak. We collapse two adjacent vowels into a single syllable and sometimes shift the stress in certain words such as *maíz/maiz*, *cohete/cuete*. We leave out certain consonants when they appear between vowels: *lado/lao*, *mojado/mojao*. Chicanos from South Texas pronounced *f* as *j* as in *jue* (*fue*). Chicanos use "archaisms," words that are no longer in the Spanish language, words that have been evolved out. We say *semos*, *truje*, *haiga*, *ansina*, and *naiden*. We retain the "archaic" *j*, as in *jalar*, that derives from an earlier *h* (the French *halar* or the Germanic *halon* which was lost to Standard Spanish in the sixteenth century), but which is still found in several

[7]*braceros*: Migratory worker of Latin American origin (Spanish).—Eds.

[8]*tejana*: A female Texan of Latin American descent (Spanish).—Eds.

regional dialects such as the one spoken in South Texas. (Due to geography, Chicanos from the Valley of South Texas were cut off linguistically from other Spanish speakers. We tend to use words that the Spaniards brought over from Medieval Spain. The majority of the Spanish colonizers in Mexico and the Southwest came from Extremadura—Hernán Cortés was one of them—and Andalucía. Andalucians pronounce *ll* like a *y*, and their *d*'s tend to be absorbed by adjacent vowels: *tirado* becomes *tirao*. They brought *el lenguaje popular, dialectos y regionalismos*.)

Chicanos and other Spanish speakers also shift *ll* to *y* and *z* to *s*. We leave out initial syllables, saying *tar* for *estar*, *toy* for *estoy*, *hora* for *ahora* (*cubanos* and *puertorriqueños* also leave out initial letters of some words). We also leave out the final syllable such as *pa* for *para*. The intervocalic *y*, the *ll* as in *tortilla, ella, botella*, gets replaced by *tortia* or *tortiya, ea, botea*. We add an additional syllable at the beginning of certain words: *atocar* for *tocar*, *agastar* for *gastar*. Sometimes we'll say *lavaste las vacijas*, other times *lavates* (substituting the *ates* verb endings for the *aste*).

20 We use anglicisms, words borrowed from English: *bola* from ball, *carpeta* from carpet, *máchina de lavar* (instead of *lavadora*) from washing machine. Tex-Mex argot, created by adding a Spanish sound at the beginning or end of an English word such as *cookiar* for cook, *watchar* for watch, *parkiar* for park, and *rapiar* for rape, is the result of the pressures on Spanish speakers to adapt to English.

We don't use the word *vosotros/as* or its accompanying verb form. We don't say *claro* (to mean yes), *imagínate*, or *me emociona* unless we picked up Spanish from Latinas, out of a book, or in a classroom. Other Spanish-speaking groups are going through the same, or similar, development in their Spanish.

Linguistic Terrorism

> *Deslenguadas. Somos los del español deficiente.* We are your linguistic nightmare, your linguistic aberration, your linguistic *mestizaje*,[9] the subject of your *burla*.[10] Because we speak with tongues of fire we are culturally crucified. Racially, culturally, and linguistically *somos huérfanos*—we speak an orphan tongue.

Chicanas who grew up speaking Chicano Spanish have internalized the belief that we speak poor Spanish. It is illegitimate, a bastard language. And because we internalize how our language has been used against us by the dominant culture, we use our language differences against each other.

Chicana feminists often skirt around each other with suspicion and hesitation. For the longest time I couldn't figure it out. Then it dawned on me. To be close to another Chicana is like looking into the mirror. We are afraid of what we'll see there. *Pena*. Shame. Low estimation of self. In childhood we are

[9] *mestizaje*: People with mixed European and Amerindian ancestry (Spanish).—Eds.

[10] *burla*: Joke, mockery (Spanish).—Eds.

told that our language is wrong. Repeated attacks on our native tongue diminish our sense of self. The attacks continue throughout our lives.

Chicanas feel uncomfortable talking in Spanish to Latinas, afraid of their censure. Their language was not outlawed in their countries. They had a whole lifetime of being immersed in their native tongue; generations, centuries in which Spanish was a first language, taught in school, heard on radio and TV, and read in the newspaper.

If a person, Chicana or Latina, has a low estimation of my native tongue, she also has a low estimation of me. Often with *mexicanas y latinas* we'll speak English as a neutral language. Even among Chicanas we tend to speak English at parties or conferences. Yet, at the same time, we're afraid the other will think we're *agringadas*[11] because we don't speak Chicano Spanish. We oppress each other trying to out-Chicano each other, vying to be the "real" Chicanas, to speak like Chicanos. There is no one Chicano language just as there is no one Chicano experience. A monolingual Chicana whose first language is English or Spanish is just as much a Chicana as one who speaks several variants of Spanish. A Chicana from Michigan or Chicago or Detroit is just as much a Chicana as one from the Southwest. Chicano Spanish is as diverse linguistically as it is regionally. 25

By the end of [the twentieth] century, Spanish speakers will comprise the biggest minority group in the U.S., a country where students in high schools and colleges are encouraged to take French classes because French is considered more "cultured." But for a language to remain alive it must be used. By the end of this century, English, and not Spanish, will be the mother tongue of most Chicanos and Latinos.

So, if you want to really hurt me, talk badly about my language. Ethnic identity is twin skin to linguistic identity—I am my language. Until I can take pride in my language, I cannot take pride in myself. Until I can accept as legitimate Chicano Texas Spanish, Tex-Mex, and all the other languages I speak, I cannot accept the legitimacy of myself. Until I am free to write bilingually and to switch codes without having always to translate, while I still have to speak English or Spanish when I would rather speak Spanglish, and as long as I have to accommodate the English speakers rather than having them accommodate me, my tongue will be illegitimate.

I will no longer be made to feel ashamed of existing. I will have my voice: Indian, Spanish, white. I will have my serpent's tongue—my woman's voice, my sexual voice, my poet's voice. I will overcome the tradition of silence.

> My fingers
> move sly against your palm
> Like women everywhere, we speak in code . . .
>
> —MELANIE KAYE/KANTROWITZ

[11]*agringadas*: Becoming influenced by white American (*gringolo*) culture (Spanish).—Eds.

"Vistas," Corridos y Comida: My Native Tongue

In the 1960s, I read my first Chicano novel. It was *City of Night* by John Rechy, a gay Texan, son of a Scottish father and a Mexican mother. For days I walked around in stunned amazement that a Chicano could write and could get published. When I read *I Am Joaquín* I was surprised to see a bilingual book by a Chicano in print. When I saw poetry written in Tex-Mex for the first time, a feeling of pure joy flashed through me. I felt like we really existed as a people. In 1971, when I started teaching high school English to Chicano students, I tried to supplement the required texts with works by Chicanos, only to be reprimanded and forbidden to do so by the principal. He claimed that I was supposed to teach "American" and English literature. At the risk of being fired, I swore my students to secrecy and slipped in Chicano short stories, poems, a play. In graduate school, while working toward a PhD, I had to "argue" with one advisor after the other, semester after semester, before I was allowed to make Chicano literature an area of focus.

30 Even before I read books by Chicanos or Mexicans, it was the Mexican movies I saw at the drive-in—the Thursday night special of $1.00 a carload—that gave me a sense of belonging. "*Vámonos a las vistas*," my mother would call out and we'd all—grandmother, brothers, sister, and cousins—squeeze into the car. We'd wolf down cheese and bologna-white-bread sandwiches while watching Pedro Infante in melodramatic tearjerkers like *Nosotros los pobres*,[12] the first "real" Mexican movie (that was not an imitation of European movies). I remember seeing *Cuando los hijos se van*[13] and surmising that all Mexican movies played up the love a mother has for her children and what ungrateful sons and daughters suffer when they are not devoted to their mothers. I remember the singing-type "westerns" of Jorge Negrete and Miguel Aceves Mejía. When watching Mexican movies, I felt a sense of homecoming as well as alienation. People who were to amount to something didn't go to Mexican movies or *bailes*[14] or tune their radios to *bolero*, *rancherita*, and *corrido* music.

The whole time I was growing up, there was *norteño* music, sometimes called North Mexican border music, or Tex-Mex music, or Chicano music, or *cantina* (bar) music. I grew up listening to *conjuntos*, three- or four-piece bands made up of folk musicians playing guitar, *bajo sexto*, drums, and button accordion, which Chicanos had borrowed from the German immigrants who had come to Central Texas and Mexico to farm and build breweries. In the Rio Grande Valley, Steve Jordan and Little Joe Hernández were popular, and Flaco Jiménez was the accordion king. The rhythms of Tex-Mex music are those of the polka, also adapted from the Germans, who in turn had borrowed the polka from the Czechs and Bohemians.

---

[12]*Nosotros los pobres*: We the people (Spanish).—Eds.

[13]*Cuando . . . van*: When the children go (Spanish).—Eds.

[14]*bailes*: Dances (Spanish).—Eds.

I remember the hot, sultry evenings when *corridos*—songs of love and death on the Texas-Mexican borderlands—reverberated out of cheap amplifiers from the local *cantinas* and wafted in through my bedroom window.

Corridos first became widely used along the South Texas/Mexican border during the early conflict between Chicanos and Anglos. The *corridos* are usually about Mexican heroes who do valiant deeds against the Anglo oppressors. Pancho Villa's song, "*La cucaracha*," is the most famous one. *Corridos* of John F. Kennedy and his death are still very popular in the Valley. Older Chicanos remember Lydia Mendoza, one of the great border *corrido* singers who was called *la Gloria de Tejas*. Her "*El tango negro*," sung during the Great Depression, made her a singer of the people. The ever-present *corridos* narrated 100 years of border history, bringing news of events as well as entertaining. These folk musicians and folk songs are our chief cultural mythmakers, and they made our hard lives seem bearable.

I grew up feeling ambivalent about our music. Country-western and rock-and-roll had more status. In the '50s and '60s, for the slightly educated and *agringado* Chicanos, there existed a sense of shame at being caught listening to our music. Yet I couldn't stop my feet from thumping to the music, could not stop humming the words, nor hide from myself the exhilaration I felt when I heard it.

There are more subtle ways that we internalize identification, especially in the forms of images and emotions. For me food and certain smells are tied to my identity, to my homeland. Woodsmoke curling up to an immense blue sky; woodsmoke perfuming my grandmother's clothes, her skin. The stench of cow manure and the yellow patches on the ground; the crack of a .22 rifle and the reek of cordite. Homemade white cheese sizzling in a pan, melting inside a folded tortilla. My sister Hilda's hot, spicy *menudo*, *chile colorado* making it deep red, pieces of *panza* and hominy floating on top. My brother Carito barbecuing fajitas in the backyard. Even now and 3,000 miles away, I can see my mother spicing the ground beef, pork, and venison with chile. My mouth salivates at the thought of the hot steaming tamales I would be eating if I were home. 35

Si Le Preguntas a Mi Mamá, "¿Qué Eres?"

> Identity is the essential core of who we are as individuals, the conscious experience of the self inside.
>
> —Kaufman

Nosotros los Chicanos straddle the borderlands. On one side of us, we are constantly exposed to the Spanish of the Mexicans; on the other side we hear the Anglos' incessant clamoring so that we forget our language. Among ourselves we don't say *nosotros los americanos, o nosotros los españoles, o nosotros los hispanos*. We say *nosotros los mexicanos* (by *mexicanos* we do not mean citizens of

Mexico; we do not mean a national identity, but a racial one). We distinguish between *mexicanos del otro lado* and *mexicanos de este lado.*[15] Deep in our hearts we believe that being Mexican has nothing to do with which country one lives in. Being Mexican is a state of soul—not one of mind, not one of citizenship. Neither eagle nor serpent, but both. And like the ocean, neither animal respects borders.

Dime con quien andas y te diré quien eres.
(Tell me who your friends are and I'll tell you who you are.)

—MEXICAN SAYING

Si le preguntas a mi mamá, "¿Qué eres?" te dirá, "Soy mexicana."[16] My brothers and sister say the same. I sometimes will answer "*soy mexicana*" and at others will say "*soy Chicana*" o "*soy tejana.*" But I identified as "*Raza*" before I ever identified as "*mexicana*" or "Chicana."

As a culture, we call ourselves Spanish when referring to ourselves as a linguistic group and when copping out. It is then that we forget our predominant Indian genes. We are 70 percent to 80 percent Indian. We call ourselves Hispanic or Spanish American or Latin American or Latin when linking ourselves to other Spanish-speaking peoples of the Western hemisphere when copping out. We call ourselves Mexican American to signify we are neither Mexican nor American, but more the noun "American" than the adjective "Mexican" (and when copping out).

Chicanos and other people of color suffer economically for not acculturating. This voluntary (yet forced) alienation makes for psychological conflict, a kind of dual identity—we don't identify with the Anglo-American cultural values and we don't totally identify with the Mexican cultural values. We are a synergy of two cultures with various degrees of Mexicanness or Angloness. I have so internalized the borderland conflict that sometimes I feel like one cancels out the other and we are zero, nothing, no one. *A veces no soy nada ni nadie. Pero hasta cuando no lo soy, lo soy.*[17]

40 When not copping out, when we know we are more than nothing, we call ourselves Mexican, referring to race and ancestry; *mestizo* when affirming both our Indian and Spanish (but we hardly ever own our Black) ancestry; Chicano when referring to a politically aware people born and/or raised in the U.S.; *raza* when referring to Chicanos; *tejanos* when we are Chicanos from Texas.

Chicanos did not know we were a people until 1965 when Cesar Chavez and the farmworkers united and *I Am Joaquín* was published and *la Raza Unida* party was formed in Texas. With that recognition, we became a distinct

[15]*mexicanos . . . este lado*: Mexicans from the other side (of the border) and Mexicans from this side (Spanish).—Eds.

[16]*Si le preguntas . . . "Soy mexicana"*: "If you ask my mother, 'What are you?' she'll say, 'I'm Mexican'" (Spanish).—Eds.

[17]*A veces . . . lo soy*: "Sometimes I'm not anything or anyone. But even when I'm not, I am" (Spanish).—Eds.

people. Something momentous happened to the Chicano soul—we became aware of our reality and acquired a name and a language (Chicano Spanish) that reflected that reality. Now that we had a name, some of the fragmented pieces began to fall together—who we were, what we were, how we had evolved. We began to get glimpses of what we might eventually become.

Yet the struggle of identities continues, the struggle of borders is our reality still. One day the inner struggle will cease and a true integration take place. In the meantime, *tenemos que hacer la lucha. ¿Quién está protegiendo los ranchos de mi gente? ¿Quién está tratando de cerrar la fisura entre la india y el blanco en nuestra sangre? El Chicano, sí, el Chicano que anda como un ladrón en su propia casa.*[18]

Los Chicanos, how patient we seem, how very patient. There is the quiet of the Indian about us. We know how to survive. When other races have given up their tongue, we've kept ours. We know what it is to live under the hammer blow of the dominant *norteamericano* culture. But more than we count the blows, we count the days the weeks the years the centuries the eons until the white laws and commerce and customs will rot in the deserts they've created, lie bleached. *Humildes* yet proud, *quietos* yet wild, *nosotros los mexicanos*-Chicanos will walk by the crumbling ashes as we go about our business. Stubborn, persevering, impenetrable as stone, yet possessing a malleability that renders us unbreakable, we, the *mestizas* and *mestizos*, will remain.

▪ QUESTIONS

Reading

1. When does Anzaldúa first read a novel written by a Chicano? How does she respond to her first encounter with poetry written in "Tex-Mex"? Why are these experiences important to her?
2. What is a *pochismo* (paragraph 16)?
3. Anzaldúa uses quotations from other writers to introduce or conclude sections of her essay. List them. How would you characterize their language? How does Anzaldúa's selection of quotes support her central argument?

Exploratory Writing

1. Anzaldúa suggests that there are subtle ways that we internalize identification. What does she mean by "identification"? Reflect on your personal identity. How might identification shape your sense of who you are?
2. How does Anzaldúa characterize Chicanos? Is her characterization of her "race" at odds with her arguments celebrating diversity or does it support her position? Underline, highlight, or flag the places where she defines or characterizes "Chicano" as an ethnic identity.

---

[18] *tenemos . . . casa*: "We have to wage the struggle. Who is protecting my people's hovels? Who is trying to close the gap between the Indian and the white parts in our blood? The Chicano is, yes, the Chicano who goes around like a thief in his own home" (Spanish).—Eds.

Making Connections

1. Amy Tan (p. 178) refers to the different "Englishes" spoken during her childhood. Make a list that compares Tan's account to Anzaldúa's list of the many languages spoken by Chicanos (paragraph 13).
2. Compare Anzaldúa's use of dialect with James Baldwin's (p. 131). Does she use dialects other than "standard" English? Does Baldwin? How does choice of language strengthen or weaken each author's argument?

Essay Writing

1. Anzaldúa writes, "If you want to really hurt me, talk badly about my language. Ethnic identity is twin skin to linguistic identity — I am my language" (paragraph 27). Do you agree that a person's language defines his or her identity? Write an essay using examples to support your position.

REFLECTING

Mother Tongue

Amy Tan

Born in 1952 in Oakland, California, Amy Tan is the daughter of immigrants who fled China's Communist revolution in the late 1940s. Her Chinese name, An-Mei, means "blessing from America." Tan has remarked that she once tried to distance herself from her ethnicity, but writing her first novel, *The Joy Luck Club* (1989), helped her discover "how very Chinese I was." Known as a gifted storyteller, Tan has written four other novels, *The Kitchen God's Wife* (1991), *The Hundred Secret Senses* (1995), *The Bonesetter's Daughter* (2001), and *Saving Fish from Drowning* (2005), as well as a collection of essays, *The Opposite of Fate: Memories of a Writing Life* (2004), and two children's books. The following essay, in which Tan reflects on her experience as a bilingual child speaking both Chinese and English, was originally published in the *Threepenny Review* in 1990.

I am not a scholar of English or literature. I cannot give you much more than personal opinions on the English language and its variations in this country or others.

I am a writer. And by that definition, I am someone who has always loved language. I am fascinated by language in daily life. I spend a great deal of my time thinking about the power of language—the way it can evoke an emotion, a visual image, a complex idea, or a simple truth. Language is the tool of my trade. And I use them all—all the Englishes I grew up with.

Recently, I was made keenly aware of the different Englishes I do use. I was giving a talk to a large group of people, the same talk I had already given to half a dozen other groups. The nature of the talk was about my writing, my life, and my book *The Joy Luck Club*. The talk was going along well enough, until I remembered one major difference that made the whole talk sound wrong. My mother was in the room. And it was perhaps the first time she had heard me give a lengthy speech, using the kind of English I have never used with her. I was saying things like "The intersection of memory upon imagination" and "There is an aspect of my fiction that relates to thus-and-thus"—a speech filled with carefully wrought grammatical phrases, burdened, it suddenly seemed to me, with nominalized forms, past perfect tenses, conditional phrases, all the forms of standard English that I had learned in school and through books, the forms of English I did not use at home with my mother.

Just last week, I was walking down the street with my mother, and I again found myself conscious of the English I was using, the English I do use with her. We were talking about the price of new and used furniture and I heard myself saying this: "Not waste money that way." My husband was with us as well, and he didn't notice any switch in my English. And then I realized why.

It's because over the twenty years we've been together I've often used that same kind of English with him, and sometimes he even uses it with me. It has become our language of intimacy, a different sort of English that relates to family talk, the language I grew up with.

5 So you'll have some idea of what this family talk I heard sounds like, I'll quote what my mother said during a recent conversation which I videotaped and then transcribed. During this conversation, my mother was talking about a political gangster in Shanghai who had the same last name as her family's, Du, and how the gangster in his early years wanted to be adopted by her family, which was rich by comparison. Later, the gangster became more powerful, far richer than my mother's family, and one day showed up at my mother's wedding to pay his respects. Here's what she said in part:

"Du Yusong having business like fruit stand. Like off the street kind. He is Du like Du Zong—but not Tsung-ming Island people. The local people call putong, the river east side, he belong to that side local people. That man want to ask Du Zong father take him in like become own family. Du Zong father wasn't look down on him, but didn't take seriously, until that man big like become a mafia. Now important person, very hard to inviting him. Chinese way, came only to show respect, don't stay for dinner. Respect for making big celebration, he shows up. Mean gives lots of respect. Chinese custom. Chinese social life that way. If too important won't have to stay too long. He come to my wedding. I didn't see, I heard it. I gone to boy's side, they have YMCA dinner. Chinese age I was nineteen."

You should know that my mother's expressive command of English belies how much she actually understands. She reads the *Forbes* report, listens to *Wall Street Week*, converses daily with her stockbroker, reads all of Shirley MacLaine's[1] books with ease—all kinds of things I can't begin to understand. Yet some of my friends tell me they understand 50 percent of what my mother says. Some say they understand 80 to 90 percent. Some say they understand none of it, as if she were speaking pure Chinese. But to me, my mother's English is perfectly clear, perfectly natural. It's my mother tongue. Her language, as I hear it, is vivid, direct, full of observation and imagery. That was the language that helped shape the way I saw things, expressed things, made sense of the world.

Lately, I've been giving more thought to the kind of English my mother speaks. Like others, I have described it to people as "broken" or "fractured" English. But I wince when I say that. It has always bothered me that I can think of no way to describe it other than "broken," as if it were damaged and needed to be fixed, as if it lacked a certain wholeness and soundness. I've heard other terms used: "limited English," for example. But they seem just as bad, as if everything is limited, including people's perceptions of the limited English speaker.

I know this for a fact, because when I was growing up, my mother's "limited"

[1]*Shirley MacLaine* (b. 1934): An American actor, dancer, and writer. She has written her memoirs and several books on spirituality and self-help.—Eds.

English limited *my* perception of her. I was ashamed of her English. I believed that her English reflected the quality of what she had to say. That is, because she expressed them imperfectly her thoughts were imperfect. And I had plenty of empirical evidence to support me: the fact that people in department stores, at banks, and at restaurants did not take her seriously, did not give her good service, pretended not to understand her, or even acted as if they did not hear her.

10 My mother has long realized the limitations of her English as well. When I was fifteen, she used to have me call people on the phone to pretend I was she. In this guise, I was forced to ask for information or even to complain and yell at people who had been rude to her. One time it was a call to her stockbroker in New York. She had cashed out her small portfolio and it just so happened we were going to go to New York the next week, our very first trip outside California. I had to get on the phone and say in an adolescent voice that was not very convincing, "This is Mrs. Tan."

And my mother was standing in the back whispering loudly, "Why he don't send me check, already two weeks late. So mad he lie to me, losing me money."

And then I said in perfect English, "Yes, I'm getting rather concerned. You had agreed to send the check two weeks ago, but it hasn't arrived."

Then she began to talk more loudly. "What he want, I come to New York tell him front of his boss, you cheating me?" And I was trying to calm her down, make her be quiet, while telling the stockbroker, "I can't tolerate any more excuses. If I don't receive the check immediately, I am going to have to speak to your manager when I'm in New York next week." And sure enough, the following week there we were in front of this astonished stockbroker, and I was sitting there red-faced and quiet, and my mother, the real Mrs. Tan, was shouting at his boss in her impeccable broken English.

We used a similar routine just five days ago, for a situation that was far less humorous. My mother had gone to the hospital for an appointment, to find out about a benign brain tumor a CAT scan had revealed a month ago. She said she had spoken very good English, her best English, no mistakes. Still, she said, the hospital did not apologize when they said they had lost the CAT scan and she had come for nothing. She said they did not seem to have any sympathy when she told them she was anxious to know the exact diagnosis, since her husband and son had both died of brain tumors. She said they would not give her any more information until the next time and she would have to make another appointment for that. So she said she would not leave until the doctor called her daughter. She wouldn't budge. And when the doctor finally called her daughter, me, who spoke in perfect English—lo and behold—we had assurances the CAT scan would be found, promises that a conference call on Monday would be held, and apologies for any suffering my mother had gone through for a most regrettable mistake.

15 I think my mother's English almost had an effect on limiting my possibilities in life as well. Sociologists and linguists probably will tell you that a person's developing language skills are more influenced by peers. But I do think

that the language spoken in the family, especially in immigrant families which are more insular, plays a large role in shaping the language of the child. And I believe that it affected my results on achievement tests, IQ tests, and the SAT. While my English skills were never judged as poor, compared to math, English could not be considered my strong suit. In grade school I did moderately well, getting perhaps B's, sometimes B-pluses, in English and scoring perhaps in the sixtieth or seventieth percentile on achievement tests. But those scores were not good enough to override the opinion that my true abilities lay in math and science, because in those areas I achieved A's and scored in the ninetieth percentile or higher.

This was understandable. Math is precise; there is only one correct answer. Whereas, for me at least, the answers on English tests were always a judgment call, a matter of opinion and personal experience. Those tests were constructed around items like fill-in-the-blank sentence completion, such as "Even though Tom was ________ , Mary thought he was ________ ." And the correct answer always seemed to be the most bland combinations of thoughts, for example, "Even though Tom was shy, Mary thought he was charming," with the grammatical structure "even though" limiting the correct answer to some sort of semantic opposites, so you wouldn't get answers like "Even though Tom was foolish, Mary thought he was ridiculous." Well, according to my mother, there were very few limitations as to what Tom could have been and what Mary might have thought of him. So I never did well on tests like that.

The same was true with word analogies, pairs of words in which you were supposed to find some sort of logical, semantic relationship—for example, "*Sunset* is to *nightfall* as ________ is to ________ ." And here you would be presented with a list of four possible pairs, one of which showed the same kind of relationship: *red* is to *stoplight, bus* is to *arrival, chills* is to *fever, yawn* is to *boring.* Well, I could never think that way. I knew what the tests were asking, but I could not block out of my mind the images already created by the first pair, "*sunset* is to *nightfall*"—and I would see a burst of colors against a darkening sky, the moon rising, the lowering of a curtain of stars. And all the other pairs of words—*red, bus, stoplight, boring*—just threw up a mass of confusing images, making it impossible for me to sort out something as logical as saying: "A sunset precedes nightfall" is the same as "a chill precedes a fever." The only way I would have gotten that answer right would have been to imagine an associative situation, for example, my being disobedient and staying out past sunset, catching a chill at night, which turns into feverish pneumonia as punishment, which indeed did happen to me.

I have been thinking about all this lately, about my mother's English, about achievement tests. Because lately I've been asked, as a writer, why there are not more Asian Americans represented in American literature. Why are there few Asian Americans enrolled in creative writing programs? Why do so many Chinese students go into engineering? Well, these are broad sociological questions I can't begin to answer. But I have noticed in surveys—in fact, just last week—that Asian students, as a whole, always do significantly better on math achievement tests than in English. And this makes me think that there are other Asian American students whose English spoken in the home might also be described as "broken" or "limited." And perhaps they also have teachers who are steering them away from writing and into math and science, which is what happened to me.

Fortunately, I happen to be rebellious in nature and enjoy the challenge of disproving assumptions made about me. I became an English major my first year in college, after being enrolled as premed. I started writing nonfiction as a freelancer the week after I was told by my former boss that writing was my worst skill and I should hone my talents toward account management.

But it wasn't until 1985 that I finally began to write fiction. And at first I wrote using what I thought to be wittily crafted sentences, sentences that would finally prove I had mastery over the English language. Here's an example from the first draft of a story that later made its way into *The Joy Luck Club,* but without this line: "That was my mental quandary in its nascent state." A terrible line, which I can barely pronounce. 20

Fortunately, for reasons I won't get into today, I later decided I should envision a reader for the stories I would write. And the reader I decided upon was my mother, because these were stories about mothers. So with this reader in mind—and in fact she did read my early drafts—I began to write stories using all the Englishes I grew up with: the English I spoke to my mother, which for lack of a better term might be described as "simple"; the English she used with me, which for lack of a better term might be described as "broken"; my translation of her Chinese, which could certainly be described as "watered down"; and what I imagined to be her translation of her Chinese if she could speak in perfect English, her internal language, and for that I sought to preserve the essence, but neither an English nor a Chinese structure. I wanted to capture what language ability tests can never reveal: her intent, her passion, her imagery, the rhythms of her speech and the nature of her thoughts.

Apart from what any critic had to say about my writing, I knew I had succeeded where it counted when my mother finished reading my book and gave me her verdict: "So easy to read."

▪ QUESTIONS

Reading

1. In reflecting on her childhood experiences, Tan writes, "I think my mother's English almost had an effect on limiting my possibilities in life as well" (paragraph 15). Why does she believe this? What issues does she raise in her discussion?
2. What are the different "Englishes" with which Tan grew up? Find an example of each "English." What did Tan need to learn about each?
3. Make a list of ways that Tan characterizes her mother's English. What sense do we get of Tan's mother's personality from the quotations and anecdotes that Tan uses in this essay?

4. What was Tan's childhood experience studying math? What reasons does she give for the discrepancy between her achievement-test scores in math and those in English?

Exploratory Writing

1. "[W]hen I was growing up," writes Tan, "my mother's 'limited' English limited *my* perception of her. . . . I believed that her English reflected the quality of what she had to say" (paragraph 9). In your own life, have you ever encountered someone who seemed "limited" to you, and then realized that you had misjudged that person? Write a short fictional or autobiographical account of this experience.
2. Tan tells us that as a writer, she cares about the way language "can evoke an emotion, a visual image, a complex idea, or a simple truth" (paragraph 2). Highlight, underline, or flag passages in Tan's essay where her language is evocative. Where does Tan surprise you with her choice of words?
3. Should only one kind of English be taught in schools? Or should school curricula be expanded to include the teaching of different "Englishes" and bilingual or multilingual dialects? Break into groups and stage a debate on this topic. You can use the essays in this book by Tan and Gloria Anzaldúa (p. 167) to help formulate your arguments. You might also refer to the essay by James Baldwin (p. 131).

Making Connections

1. Gloria Anzaldúa uses the term *linguistic terrorism* in her essay on language and identity. How would you characterize linguistic terrorism? Based on her reflections in this essay, has Tan been a victim of linguistic terrorism? How?

Essay Writing

1. Tan writes that "the language spoken in the family, especially in immigrant families . . . plays a large role in shaping the language of the child" (paragraph 15). Write an essay in which you reflect on the role of language in your family.

REPORTING

The Veil

Marjane Satrapi

Marjane Satrapi (b. 1969) was born in Tehran, Iran, to a politically progressive, intellectual family and grew up in the increasingly repressive Islamic republic. "The Veil" is the first chapter of *Persepolis: The Story of a Childhood* (2003) — a graphic novel that narrates the daily lives of Satrapi, her family, and her friends during the fall of the shah, the early regime of Ayatollah Khomeini, and the beginning of the Iran-Iraq war. Today, Satrapi lives in Paris, France. She has authored and illustrated books for both children and adults, including *Persepolis 2: The Story of a Return* (2004), *Embroideries* (2005), and *Chicken with Plums* (2006). She codirected an animated film version of *Persepolis* with Vincent Paronnaud in 2007. Released in both French and English, the film won the Jury Prize at the Cannes Film Festival and was nominated for an Academy Award in the category of Best Animated Feature Film.

THIS IS ME WHEN I WAS 10 YEARS OLD. THIS WAS IN 1980.

AND THIS IS A CLASS PHOTO. I'M SITTING ON THE FAR LEFT SO YOU DON'T SEE ME. FROM LEFT TO RIGHT: GOLNAZ, MAHSHID, NARINE, MINNA.

IN 1979 A REVOLUTION TOOK PLACE. IT WAS LATER CALLED "THE ISLAMIC REVOLUTION".

THEN CAME 1980: THE YEAR IT BECAME OBLIGATORY TO WEAR THE VEIL AT SCHOOL.
WEAR THIS!

WE DIDN'T REALLY LIKE TO WEAR THE VEIL, ESPECIALLY SINCE WE DIDN'T UNDERSTAND WHY WE HAD TO.
IT'S TOO HOT OUT!
EXECUTION IN THE NAME OF FREEDOM.
GIVE ME MY VEIL BACK!
YOU'LL HAVE TO LICK MY FEET!
GIDDYAP!
OOH! I'M THE MONSTER OF DARKNESS.

AND ALSO BECAUSE THE YEAR BEFORE, IN 1979, WE WERE IN A FRENCH NON-RELIGIOUS SCHOOL.

WHERE BOYS AND GIRLS WERE TOGETHER.

AND THEN SUDDENLY IN 1980...
ALL BILINGUAL SCHOOLS MUST BE CLOSED DOWN.

THEY ARE SYMBOLS OF CAPITALISM.
BRAVO!
WHAT WISDOM!

OF DECADENCE.
THIS IS CALLED A "CULTURAL REVOLUTION."

WE FOUND OURSELVES VEILED AND SEPARATED FROM OUR FRIENDS.

AND THAT WAS THAT...

EVERYWHERE IN THE STREETS THERE WERE DEMONSTRATIONS FOR AND AGAINST THE VEIL.
the veil!
the veil!
the veil!
the veil!
the veil!
freedom!
freedom!
freedom!
freedom!

AT ONE OF THE DEMONSTRATIONS, A GERMAN JOURNALIST TOOK A PHOTO OF MY MOTHER.

I WAS REALLY PROUD OF HER. HER PHOTO WAS PUBLISHED IN ALL THE EUROPEAN NEWSPAPERS.

AND EVEN IN ONE MAGAZINE IN IRAN. MY MOTHER WAS REALLY SCARED.
HAVE YOU SEEN THIS?
DON'T WORRY, DARLING.

SHE DYED HER HAIR,

AND WORE DARK GLASSES FOR A LONG TIME.

I REALLY DIDN'T KNOW WHAT TO THINK ABOUT THE VEIL. DEEP DOWN I WAS VERY RELIGIOUS BUT AS A FAMILY WE WERE VERY MODERN AND AVANT-GARDE.

I WAS BORN WITH RELIGION.

AT THE AGE OF SIX I WAS ALREADY SURE I WAS THE LAST PROPHET. THIS WAS A FEW YEARS BEFORE THE REVOLUTION.
O' Celestial light!

BEFORE ME THERE HAD BEEN A FEW OTHERS.

I AM THE LAST PROPHET.
A WOMAN?

I WANTED TO BE A PROPHET...
BECAUSE OUR MAID DID NOT EAT WITH US.

BECAUSE MY FATHER HAD A CADILLAC.

AND, ABOVE ALL, BECAUSE MY GRANDMOTHER'S KNEES ALWAYS ACHED.
COME HERE MARJI! HELP ME TO STAND UP.
DON'T WORRY. SOON YOU WON'T HAVE ANY MORE PAIN. YOU'LL SEE.

LIKE ALL MY PREDECESSORS I HAD MY HOLY BOOK.

THE FIRST THREE RULES CAME FROM ZARATHUSTRA. HE WAS THE FIRST PROPHET IN MY COUNTRY BEFORE THE ARAB INVASION.
YOU MUST BASE EVERYTHING ON THESE THREE RULES: BEHAVE WELL, SPEAK WELL, ACT WELL.

I ALSO WANTED US TO CELEBRATE THE TRADITIONAL ZARATHUSTRIAN HOLIDAYS. LIKE THE FIRE CEREMONY,

BEFORE THE PERSIAN NEW YEAR, NOROUZ, ON MARCH 21ST, THE FIRST DAY OF SPRING.

ONLY MY GRANDMOTHER KNEW ABOUT MY BOOK.
RULE NUMBER SIX: EVERYBODY SHOULD HAVE A CAR.
RULE NUMBER SEVEN: ALL MAIDS SHOULD EAT AT THE TABLE WITH THE OTHERS.
RULE NUMBER EIGHT: NO OLD PERSON SHOULD HAVE TO SUFFER.
IN THAT CASE, I'LL BE YOUR FIRST DISCIPLE.
REALLY?
BUT TELL ME HOW YOU'LL ARRANGE FOR OLD PEOPLE NOT TO SUFFER?
IT WILL SIMPLY BE FORBIDDEN.

EVERY NIGHT I HAD A BIG DISCUSSION WITH GOD.
GOD, GIVE ME SOME MORE TIME. I AM NOT QUITE READY YET.

YES YOU ARE, CELESTIAL LIGHT, YOU ARE MY CHOICE, MY LAST AND MY BEST CHOICE.

EXCEPT FOR MY GRANDMOTHER I WAS OBVIOUSLY THE ONLY ONE WHO BELIEVED IN MYSELF.
WHAT DO YOU WANT TO BE WHEN YOU GROW UP?

I'LL BE A PROPHET.

HAHA! HAHA! HAHA!
SHE'S CRAZY.

MY PARENTS WERE CALLED IN BY THE TEACHER.
YOUR CHILD IS DISTURBED. SHE WANTS TO BECOME A PROPHET.

WHAT ABOUT IT?
DOESN'T THIS WORRY YOU?

NO ! NOT AT ALL !
?

NONETHELESS, MY PARENTS WERE PUZZLED.
SO TELL ME, MY CHILD, WHAT DO YOU WANT TO BE WHEN YOU GROW UP?
A PROPHET.

I WANT TO BE A DOCTOR.

THAT'S FINE MY LOVE. THAT'S FINE.

I FELT GUILTY TOWARDS GOD.
YOU WANT TO BE A DOCTOR? I THOUGHT THAT...

NO, NO, I WILL BE A PROPHET BUT THEY MUSTN'T KNOW.

I WANTED TO BE JUSTICE, LOVE AND THE WRATH OF GOD ALL IN ONE.

▪ QUESTIONS

Reading

1. How do Marji's views of God and the veil differ? What do these differences suggest about her attitudes toward religion?
2. Marji tells her grandmother that when she becomes a prophet she will declare a rule that "no old person should have to suffer" (p. 189). When her grandmother asks her how she will accomplish this, Marji replies, "it will simply be forbidden." What is *ironic* about Marji's response, given her attitudes about the veil and state-enforced religious observance?
3. The narrative in a graphic novel or comic unfolds through a series of *panels*. Most panels include both illustrations and language that work together to create a visual-verbal language. Choose a panel that contains a great deal of information, and take inventory of the information being communicated. Then make a bulleted list of everything you learn by "reading" the visual components of the panel. Once you complete your list, take ten to twenty minutes to freewrite on the following questions: How does visual communication differ from verbal communication? How does Satrapi use visual and verbal communication differently?

Exploratory Writing

1. Nonfiction graphic narratives are a form of reporting unique to the arts and humanities. Rather than attempting to report objectively, graphic narratives offer stylized accounts of firsthand observations. How does Satrapi's use of visuals shape her account? How would her story be different if it were written in the form of a newspaper article or historical account?
2. Make a short list of adjectives to describe the tone of each panel on the first page of "The Veil." Once your lists are complete, write a paragraph or two reflecting on the range of emotions represented on this single page. How does the tone change from one panel to the next? Are the changes gradual or abrupt? Are they expected or surprising? Why do you think Satrapi chooses to portray so many emotions in such a condensed way?
3. Some critics have complained that Satrapi's visual style is overly simplistic. Others argue that its simplicity is well suited to a story about childhood. In a small group, collaborate on writing the transcript for a debate between two critics representing each of these views. Give your critics names, and be sure to cite specific examples to illustrate their arguments about Satrapi's style. Be prepared to read your transcript out loud for the class.

Making Connections

1. In his essay "Is God an Accident?" (p. 194), Paul Bloom suggests three major theories to explain the origin of religion: the opiate theory, the fraternity theory, and the cognitive theory. Read Bloom's accounts of these theories. Then use his essay as a lens for interpreting "The Veil." Which of his theories seem to best describe Marji's religious belief? Which elements of these theories seem to resonate most with Marji's experience? Which elements are contradicted or challenged by her experience? Be

sure to support your argument with evidence from Bloom's essay and Satrapi's graphic narrative.

2. Satrapi's graphic narrative tells the story of her childhood relationship to God and religion. Choose two figures discussed in Paul Bloom's essay (p. 194), and draw your own graphic narrative in which these two figures have a dialogue about God and religion. Be sure to capture their ideas accurately and to think carefully about how to use visuals to contribute relevant information to the dialogue. (For insight into how graphic narratives work, see Scott McCloud's piece "Setting the Record Straight" on p. 135.)

Essay Writing

1. In 2007, Satrapi created an animated film version of *Persepolis* (see headnote). Get a copy of this film from your local library or video store or online, and write an essay about the similarities and differences between the still version and the animated version of "The Veil." What has Satrapi changed? What has she kept intact? What differences do the changes make? Why do you think she's chosen to preserve particular elements and change others?

ARGUING

Is God an Accident?

Paul Bloom

A writer and award-winning research psychologist, Paul Bloom (b. 1963) was born and raised in Canada. He attended McGill University and went on to earn a PhD from Massachusetts Institute of Technology, specializing in cognitive psychology and language acquisition. While teaching at the University of Arizona and later at Yale University, he developed theories that connect the ability of young children to learn a language quickly to the social skills they seem to pick up automatically, such as interpreting others' intentions (or "mindreading," as he calls it). Bloom's books — including the recent *How Pleasure Works* (2011) — use his theories of evolutionary and social development to unearth knowledge about human cognition and our understanding of morality, religion, and art. The following essay first appeared in the *Atlantic* magazine, December 2005.

I. God Is Not Dead

When I was a teenager my rabbi believed that the Lubavitcher Rebbe, who was living in Crown Heights, Brooklyn, was the Messiah, and that the world was soon to end. He believed that the earth was a few thousand years old, and that the fossil record was a consequence of the Great Flood. He could describe the afterlife, and was able to answer adolescent questions about the fate of Hitler's soul.

My rabbi was no crackpot; he was an intelligent and amiable man, a teacher and a scholar. But he held views that struck me as strange, even disturbing. Like many secular people, I am comfortable with religion as a source of spirituality and transcendence, tolerance and love, charity and good works. Who can object to the faith of Martin Luther King Jr. or the Dalai Lama—at least as long as that faith grounds moral positions one already accepts? I am uncomfortable, however, with religion when it makes claims about the natural world, let alone a world beyond nature. It is easy for those of us who reject supernatural beliefs to agree with Stephen Jay Gould that the best way to accord dignity and respect to both science and religion is to recognize that they apply to "non-overlapping magisteria": science gets the realm of facts, religion the realm of values.

For better or worse, though, religion is much more than a set of ethical principles or a vague sense of transcendence. The anthropologist Edward Tylor got it right in 1871, when he noted that the "minimum definition of religion" is a belief in spiritual beings, in the supernatural. My rabbi's specific claims were a minority view in the culture in which I was raised, but those *sorts* of views—about the creation of the universe, the end of the world, the fates of souls—define religion as billions of people understand and practice it.

The United States is a poster child for supernatural belief. Just about everyone in this country—96 percent in one poll—believes in God. Well over half of Americans believe in miracles, the devil, and angels. Most believe in an afterlife—and not just in the mushy sense that we will live on in the memories of other people, or in our good deeds; when asked for details, most Americans say they believe that after death they will actually reunite with relatives and get to meet God. Woody Allen once said, "I don't want to achieve immortality through my work. I want to achieve it through not dying." Most Americans have precisely this expectation.

But America is an anomaly, isn't it? These statistics are sometimes taken as yet another indication of how much this country differs from, for instance, France and Germany, where secularism holds greater sway. Americans are fundamentalists, the claim goes, isolated from the intellectual progress made by the rest of the world. 5

There are two things wrong with this conclusion. First, even if a gap between America and Europe exists, it is not the United States that is idiosyncratic. After all, the rest of the world—Asia, Africa, the Middle East—is not exactly filled with hard-core atheists. If one is to talk about exceptionalism, it applies to Europe, not the United States.

Second, the religious divide between Americans and Europeans may be smaller than we think. The sociologists Rodney Stark, of Baylor University, and Roger Finke, of Pennsylvania State University, write that the big difference has to do with church attendance, which really is much lower in Europe. (Building on the work of the Chicago-based sociologist and priest Andrew Greeley, they argue that this is because the United States has a rigorously free religious market, in which churches actively vie for parishioners and constantly improve their product, whereas European churches are often under state control and, like many government monopolies, have become inefficient.) Most polls from European countries show that a majority of their people are believers. Consider Iceland. To judge by rates of churchgoing, Iceland is the most secular country on earth, with a pathetic 2 percent weekly attendance. But four out of five Icelanders say that they pray, and the same proportion believe in life after death.

In the United States some liberal scholars posit a different sort of exceptionalism, arguing that belief in the supernatural is found mostly in Christian conservatives—those infamously described by the *Washington Post* reporter Michael Weisskopf in 1993 as "largely poor, uneducated, and easy to command." Many people saw the 2004 presidential election as pitting Americans who are religious against those who are not.

An article by Steven Waldman in the online magazine *Slate* provides some perspective on the divide:

> As you may already know, one of America's two political parties is extremely religious. Sixty-one percent of this party's voters say they pray daily or more

> often. An astounding 92 percent of them believe in life after death. And there's a hard-core subgroup in this party of super-religious Christian zealots. Very conservative on gay marriage, half of the members of this subgroup believe Bush uses too *little* religious rhetoric, and 51 percent of them believe God gave Israel to the Jews and that its existence fulfills the prophecy about the second coming of Jesus.

The group that Waldman is talking about is Democrats; the hard-core subgroup is African American Democrats.

Finally, consider scientists. They are less likely than non-scientists to be religious—but not by a huge amount. A 1996 poll asked scientists whether they believed in God, and the pollsters set the bar high—no mealy-mouthed evasions such as "I believe in the totality of all that exists" or "in what is beautiful and unknown"; rather, they insisted on a real biblical God, one believers could pray to and actually get an answer from. About 40 percent of scientists said yes to a belief in this kind of God—about the same percentage found in a similar poll in 1916. Only when we look at the most elite scientists—members of the National Academy of Sciences—do we find a strong majority of atheists and agnostics. 10

These facts are an embarrassment for those who see supernatural beliefs as a cultural anachronism, soon to be eroded by scientific discoveries and the spread of cosmopolitan values. They require a new theory of why we are religious—one that draws on research in evolutionary biology, cognitive neuroscience, and developmental psychology.

II. Opiates and Fraternities

One traditional approach to the origin of religious belief begins with the observation that it is difficult to be a person. There is evil all around; everyone we love will die; and soon we ourselves will die—either slowly and probably unpleasantly or quickly and probably unpleasantly. For all but a pampered and lucky few life really is nasty, brutish, and short. And if our lives have some greater meaning, it is hardly obvious.

So perhaps, as Marx suggested, we have adopted religion as an opiate, to soothe the pain of existence. As the philosopher Susanne K. Langer has put it, man "cannot deal with Chaos"; supernatural beliefs solve the problem of this chaos by providing meaning. We are not mere things; we are lovingly crafted by God, and serve his purposes. Religion tells us that this is a just world, in which the good will be rewarded and the evil punished. Most of all, it addresses our fear of death. Freud summed it all up by describing a "threefold task" for religious beliefs: "they must exorcise the terrors of nature, they must reconcile men to the cruelty of Fate, particularly as it is shown in death, and they must compensate them for the sufferings and privations which a civilized life in common has imposed on them."

Religions can sometimes do all these things, and it would be unrealistic to deny that this partly explains their existence. Indeed, sometimes theologians use the foregoing arguments to make a case for why we should believe: If one wishes for purpose, meaning, and eternal life, there is nowhere to go but toward God.

One problem with this view is that, as the cognitive scientist Steven Pinker reminds us, we don't typically get solace from propositions that we don't already believe to be true. Hungry people don't cheer themselves up by believing that they just had a large meal. Heaven is a reassuring notion only insofar as people believe such a place exists; it is this belief that an adequate theory of religion has to explain in the first place. 15

Also, the religion-as-opiate theory fits best with the monotheistic religions most familiar to us. But what about those people (many of the religious people in the world) who do not believe in an all-wise and just God? Every society believes in spiritual beings, but they are often stupid or malevolent. Many religions simply don't deal with metaphysical or teleological questions; gods and ancestor spirits are called upon only to help cope with such mundane problems as how to prepare food and what to do with a corpse—not to elucidate the Meaning of It All. As for the reassurance of heaven, justice, or salvation, again, it exists in some religions but by no means all. (In fact, even those religions we are most familiar with are not always reassuring. I know some older Christians who were made miserable as children by worries about eternal damnation; the prospect of oblivion would have been far preferable.) So the opiate theory is ultimately an unsatisfying explanation for the existence of religion.

The major alternative theory is social: Religion brings people together, giving them an edge over those who lack this social glue. Sometimes this argument is presented in cultural terms, and sometimes it is seen from an evolutionary perspective: survival of the fittest working at the level not of the gene or the individual but of the social group. In either case the claim is that religion thrives because groups that have it outgrow and outlast those that do not.

In this conception religion is a fraternity, and the analogy runs deep. Just as fraternities used to paddle freshmen on the rear end to instill loyalty and commitment, religions have painful initiation rites—for example, snipping off part of the penis. Also, certain puzzling features of many religions, such as dietary restrictions and distinctive dress, make perfect sense once they are viewed as tools to ensure group solidarity.

The fraternity theory also explains why religions are so harsh toward those who do not share the faith, reserving particular ire for apostates. This is clear in the Old Testament, in which "a jealous God" issues commands such as:

> Should your brother, your mother's son, or your son or your daughter or the wife of your bosom or your companion who is like your own self incite you in secret, saying "Let us go and worship other gods" . . . you shall surely kill him. Your hand shall be against him first to put him to death and the hand of all the people last. And you shall stone him and he shall die, for he sought to thrust you away from the LORD your God who brought you out of the land of Egypt, from the house of slaves.
>
> —**Deuteronomy 13, 7:11**

This theory explains almost everything about religion—except the religious part. It is clear that rituals and sacrifices can bring people together, and it may well be that a group that does such things has an advantage over one that does not. But it is not clear why a *religion* has to be involved. Why are gods, souls, an afterlife, miracles, divine creation of the universe, and so on brought in? The theory doesn't explain what we are most interested in, which is belief in the supernatural. 20

III. Bodies and Souls

Enthusiasm is building among scientists for a quite different view—that religion emerged not to serve a purpose but by accident.

This is not a value judgment. Many of the good things in life are, from an evolutionary perspective, accidents. People sometimes give money, time, and even blood to help unknown strangers in faraway countries whom they will never see. From the perspective of one's genes this is disastrous—the suicidal squandering of resources for no benefit. But its origin is not magical; long-distance altruism is most likely a by-product of other, more adaptive traits, such as empathy and abstract reasoning. Similarly, there is no reproductive advantage to the pleasure we get from paintings or movies. It just so happens that our eyes and brains, which evolved to react to three-dimensional objects in the real world, can respond to two-dimensional projections on a canvas or a screen.

Supernatural beliefs might be explained in a similar way. This is the religion-as-accident theory that emerges from my work and the work of cognitive scientists such as Scott Atran, Pascal Boyer, Justin Barrett, and Deborah Kelemen. One version of this theory begins with the notion that a distinction between the physical and the psychological is fundamental to human thought. Purely physical things, such as rocks and trees, are subject to the pitiless laws of Newton. Throw a rock, and it will fly through space on a certain path; if you put a branch on the ground, it will not disappear, scamper away, or fly into space. Psychological things, such as people, possess minds, intentions, beliefs, goals, and desires. They move unexpectedly, according to volition and whim; they can chase or run away. There is a moral difference as well: A rock cannot be evil or kind; a person can.

Where does the distinction between the physical and the psychological come from? Is it something we learn through experience, or is it somehow prewired into our brains? One way to find out is to study babies. It is notoriously difficult to know what babies are thinking, given that they can't speak and have little control over their bodies. (They are harder to test than rats or pigeons, because they cannot run mazes or peck levers.) But recently investigators have used the technique of showing them different events and recording how long they look at them, exploiting the fact that babies, like the rest of us, tend to look longer at something they find unusual or bizarre.

This has led to a series of striking discoveries. Six-month-olds understand that physical objects obey gravity. If you put an object on a table and then remove the table, and the object just stays there (held by a hidden wire), babies 25 are surprised; they expect the object to fall. They expect objects to be solid, and contrary to what is still being taught in some psychology classes, they understand that objects persist over time even if hidden. (Show a baby an object and then put it behind a screen. Wait a little while and then remove the screen. If the object is gone, the baby is surprised.) Five-month-olds can even do simple math, appreciating that if first one object and then another is placed behind a screen, when the screen drops there should be two objects, not one or three. Other experiments find the same numerical understanding in non-human primates, including macaques and tamarins, and in dogs.

Similarly precocious capacities show up in infants' understanding of the social world. Newborns prefer to look at faces over anything else, and the sounds they most like to hear are human voices—preferably their mothers'. They quickly come to recognize different emotions, such as anger, fear, and happiness, and respond appropriately to them. Before they are a year old they can determine the target of an adult's gaze, and can learn by attending to the emotions of others; if a baby is crawling toward an area that might be dangerous and an adult makes a horrified or disgusted face, the baby usually knows enough to stay away.

A skeptic might argue that these social capacities can be explained as a set of primitive responses, but there is some evidence that they reflect a deeper understanding. For instance, when twelve-month-olds see one object chasing another, they seem to understand that it really is chasing, with the goal of catching; they expect the chaser to continue its pursuit along the most direct path, and are surprised when it does otherwise. In some work I've done with the psychologists Valerie Kuhlmeier, of Queen's University, and Karen Wynn, of Yale, we found that when babies see one character in a movie help an individual and a different character hurt that individual, they later expect the individual to approach the character that helped it and to avoid the one that hurt it.

Understanding of the physical world and understanding of the social world can be seen as akin to two distinct computers in a baby's brain, running separate programs and performing separate tasks. The understandings develop at different rates: The social one emerges somewhat later than the physical one. They evolved at different points in our prehistory; our physical understanding is shared by many species, whereas our social understanding is a relatively recent adaptation, and in some regards might be uniquely human.

That these two systems are distinct is especially apparent in autism, a developmental disorder whose dominant feature is a lack of social understanding. Children with autism typically show impairments in communication (about a third do not speak at all), in imagination (they tend not to engage in imaginative play), and most of all in socialization. They do not seem to enjoy the company of others; they don't hug; they are hard to reach out to. In the most extreme cases children with autism see people as nothing more than objects—objects that move in unpredictable ways and make unexpected noises and are therefore frightening. Their understanding of other minds is impaired, though their understanding of material objects is fully intact.

At this point the religion-as-accident theory says nothing about supernatural beliefs. Babies have two systems that work in a cold-bloodedly rational way to help them anticipate and understand—and, when they get older, to manipulate—physical and social entities. In other words, both these systems are biological adaptations that give human beings a badly needed head start in dealing with objects and people. But these systems go awry in two important ways that are the foundations of religion. First, we perceive the world of objects as essentially separate from the world of minds, making it possible for us to envision soulless bodies and bodiless souls. This helps explain why we believe in gods and an afterlife. Second, as we will see, our system of social understanding overshoots, inferring goals and desires where none exist. This makes us animists and creationists. 30

IV. Natural-Born Dualists

For those of us who are not autistic, the separateness of these two mechanisms, one for understanding the physical world and one for understanding the social world, gives rise to a duality of experience. We experience the world of material things as separate from the world of goals and desires. The biggest consequence has to do with the way we think of ourselves and others. We are dualists; it seems intuitively obvious that a physical body and a conscious entity—a mind or soul—are genuinely distinct. We don't feel that we *are* our bodies. Rather, we feel that we *occupy* them, we *possess* them, we *own* them.

This duality is immediately apparent in our imaginative life. Because we see people as separate from their bodies, we easily understand situations in which people's bodies are radically changed while their personhood stays intact. Kafka envisioned a man transformed into a gigantic insect; Homer described the plight of men transformed into pigs; in *Shrek 2* an ogre is transformed into a human being, and a donkey into a steed; in *Star Trek* a scheming villain forcibly occupies Captain Kirk's body so as to take command of the *Enterprise*; in *The Tale of the Body Thief*, Anne Rice tells of a vampire and a human being who agree to trade bodies for a day; and in *13 Going on 30* a teenager wakes up as thirty-year-old Jennifer Garner. We don't think of these events as real, of course, but they are fully understandable; it makes intuitive sense to us that people can be separated from their bodies, and similar transformations show up in religions around the world.

This notion of an immaterial soul potentially separable from the body clashes starkly with the scientific view. For psychologists and neuroscientists, the brain is the source of mental life; our consciousness, emotions, and will are the products of neural processes. As the claim is sometimes put, *The mind is what the brain does.* I don't want to overstate the consensus here; there is no accepted theory as to precisely how this happens, and some scholars are skeptical that we will ever develop such a theory. But no scientist takes seriously Cartesian dualism, which posits that thinking need not involve the brain. There is just too much evidence against it.

Still, it *feels* right, even to those who have never had religious training, and even to young children. This became particularly clear to me one night when I was arguing with my six-year-old son, Max. I was telling him that he had to go to bed, and he said, "You can make me go to bed, but you can't make me go to sleep. It's *my* brain!" This piqued my interest, so I began to ask him questions about what the brain does and does not do. His answers showed an interesting split. He insisted that the brain was involved in perception—in seeing, hearing, tasting, and smelling—and he was adamant that it was responsible for thinking. But, he said, the brain was not essential for dreaming, for feeling sad, or for loving his brother. "That's what *I* do," Max said, "though my brain might help me out."

Max is not unusual. Children in our culture are taught that the brain is involved in thinking, but they interpret this in a narrow sense, as referring to conscious problem solving, academic rumination. They do not see the brain as the source of conscious experience; they do not identify it with their selves. They appear to think of it as a cognitive prosthesis—there is Max the person, and then there is his brain, which he uses to solve problems just as he might use a computer. In this commonsense conception the brain is, as Steven Pinker puts it, "a pocket PC for the soul."

If bodies and souls are thought of as separate, there can be bodies without souls. A corpse is seen as a body that used to have a soul. Most things—chairs, cups, trees—never had souls; they never had will or consciousness. At least some nonhuman animals are seen in the same way, as what Descartes described as "beast-machines," or complex automata. Some artificial creatures, such as industrial robots, Haitian zombies, and Jewish golems, are also seen as soulless beings, lacking free will or moral feeling.

Then there are souls without bodies. Most people I know believe in a God who created the universe, performs miracles, and listens to prayers. He is omnipotent and omniscient, possessing infinite kindness, justice, and mercy. But he does not in any literal sense have a body. Some people also believe in lesser noncorporeal beings that can temporarily take physical form or occupy human beings or animals: examples include angels, ghosts, poltergeists, succubi, dybbuks, and the demons that Jesus so frequently expelled from people's bodies.

This belief system opens the possibility that we ourselves can survive the death of our bodies. Most people believe that when the body is destroyed, the soul lives on. It might ascend to heaven, descend to hell, go off into some sort of parallel world, or occupy some other body, human or animal. Indeed, the belief that the world teems with ancestor spirits—the souls of people who have been liberated from their bodies through death—is common across cultures. We can imagine our bodies being destroyed, our brains ceasing to function, our bones turning to dust, but it is harder—some would say impossible—to imagine the end of our very existence. The notion of a soul without a body makes sense to us.

Others have argued that rather than believing in an afterlife because we are dualists, we are dualists because we want to believe in an afterlife. This was Freud's position. He speculated that the "doctrine of the soul" emerged as a solution to the problem of death: If souls exist, then conscious experience need not come to an end. Or perhaps the motivation for belief in an afterlife is cultural: we believe it because religious authorities tell us that it is so, possibly because it serves the interests of powerful leaders to control the masses through the carrot of heaven and the stick of hell. But there is reason to favor the religion-as-accident theory.

In a significant study the psychologists Jesse Bering, of the University of Arkansas, and David Bjorklund, of Florida Atlantic University, told young children a story about an alligator and a mouse, complete with a series of pictures, that ended in tragedy: "Uh oh! Mr. Alligator sees Brown Mouse and is coming to get him!" (The children were shown a picture of the alligator eating the mouse.) "Well, it looks like Brown Mouse got eaten by Mr. Alligator. Brown Mouse is not alive anymore." 40

The experimenters asked the children a set of questions about the mouse's biological functioning—such as "Now that the mouse is no longer alive, will he ever need to go to the bathroom? Do his ears still work? Does his brain still work?"—and about the mouse's mental functioning, such as "Now that the mouse is no longer alive, is he still hungry? Is he thinking about the alligator? Does he still want to go home?"

As predicted, when asked about biological properties, the children appreciated the effects of death: no need for bathroom breaks; the ears don't work, and neither does the brain. The mouse's body is gone. But when asked about the psychological properties, more than half the children said that these would continue: The dead mouse can feel hunger, think thoughts, and have desires. The soul survives. And *children believe this more than adults do,* suggesting that although we have to learn which specific afterlife people in our culture believe in (heaven, reincarnation, a spirit world, and so on), the notion that life after death is possible is not learned at all. It is a by-product of how we naturally think about the world.

V. We've Evolved to Be Creationists

This is just half the story. Our dualism makes it possible for us to think of supernatural entities and events; it is why such things make sense. But there is another factor that makes the perception of them compelling, often irresistible. We have what the anthropologist Pascal Boyer has called a hypertrophy of social cognition. We see purpose, intention, design, even when it is not there.

In 1944 the social psychologists Fritz Heider and Mary-Ann Simmel made a simple movie in which geometric figures—circles, squares, triangles—moved in certain systematic ways, designed to tell a tale. When shown this movie, people instinctively describe the figures as if they were specific types of people (bullies, victims, heroes) with goals and desires, and repeat pretty much the same story that the psychologists intended to tell. Further research has found that bounded figures aren't even necessary—one can get much the same effect in movies where the "characters" are not single objects but moving groups, such as swarms of tiny squares.

Stewart Guthrie, an anthropologist at Fordham University, was the first modern scholar to notice the importance of this tendency as an explanation for religious thought. In his book *Faces in the Clouds,* Guthrie presents anecdotes and experiments showing that people attribute human characteristics to a striking range of real-world entities, including bicycles, bottles, clouds, fire, leaves, rain, volcanoes, and wind. We are hypersensitive to signs of agency—so much so that we see intention where only artifice or accident exists. As Guthrie puts it, the clothes have no emperor. 45

Our quickness to overread purpose into things extends to the perception of intentional design. People have a terrible eye for randomness. If you show them a string of heads and tails that was produced by a random-number generator, they tend to think it is rigged—it looks orderly to them, too orderly. After 9/11 people claimed to see Satan in the billowing smoke from the World Trade Center. Before that some people were stirred by the Nun Bun, a baked good that bore an eerie resemblance to Mother Teresa. In November of 2004 someone posted on eBay a ten-year-old grilled cheese sandwich that looked remarkably like the Virgin Mary; it sold for $28,000. (In response pranksters posted a grilled cheese sandwich bearing images of the Olsen twins, Mary-Kate and Ashley.) There are those who listen to the static from radios and other electronic devices and hear messages from dead people—a phenomenon presented with great seriousness in the Michael Keaton movie *White Noise.* Older readers who lived their formative years before CDs and MPEGs might remember listening intently for the significant and sometimes scatological messages that were said to come from records played backward.

Sometimes there really are signs of nonrandom and functional design. We are not being unreasonable when we observe that the eye seems to be crafted for seeing, or that the leaf insect seems colored with the goal of looking very much like a leaf. The evolutionary biologist Richard Dawkins begins *The Blind Watchmaker* by conceding this point: "Biology is the study of complicated things that give the appearance of having been designed for a purpose." Dawkins goes on to suggest that anyone before Darwin who did not believe in God was simply not paying attention.

Darwin changed everything. His great insight was that one could explain complex and adaptive design without positing a divine designer. Natural selection can be simulated on a computer; in fact, genetic algorithms, which mimic natural selection, are used to solve otherwise intractable computational problems. And we can see natural selection at work in case studies across the world, from the evolution of beak size in Galápagos finches to the arms race we engage in with many viruses, which have an unfortunate capacity to respond adaptively to vaccines.

Richard Dawkins may well be right when he describes the theory of natural selection as one of our species' finest accomplishments; it is an intellectually satisfying and empirically supported account of our own existence. But almost nobody believes it. One poll found that more than a third of college undergraduates believe that the Garden of Eden was where the first human beings appeared. And even among those who claim to endorse Darwinian evolution, many distort it in one way or another, often seeing it as a mysterious internal force driving species toward perfection. (Dawkins writes that it appears almost as if "the human brain is specifically designed to misunderstand Darwinism.") And if you are tempted to see this as a red state–blue state issue, think again: Although it's true that more Bush voters than Kerry voters are creationists, just about half of Kerry voters believe that God created human beings in their present form, and most of the rest believe that although we evolved from less-advanced life-forms, God guided the process. Most Kerry voters want evolution to be taught either alongside creationism or not at all.

What's the problem with Darwin? His theory of evolution does clash with the religious beliefs that some people already hold. For Jews and Christians, God willed the world into being in six days, calling different things into existence. Other religions posit more physical processes on the part of the creator or creators, such as vomiting, procreation, masturbation, or the molding of clay. Not much room here for random variation and differential reproductive success. 50

But the real problem with natural selection is that it makes no intuitive sense. It is like quantum physics; we may intellectually grasp it, but it will never feel right to us. When we see a complex structure, we see it as the product of beliefs and goals and desires. Our social mode of understanding leaves it difficult for us to make sense of it any other way. Our gut feeling is that design requires a designer—a fact that is understandably exploited by those who argue against Darwin.

It's not surprising, then, that nascent creationist views are found in young children. Four-year-olds insist that everything has a purpose, including lions ("to go in the zoo") and clouds ("for raining"). When asked to explain why a bunch of rocks are pointy, adults prefer a physical explanation, while children choose a functional one, such as "so that animals could scratch on them when they get itchy." And when asked about the origin of animals and people, children tend to prefer explanations that involve an intentional creator, even if the adults raising them do not. Creationism—and belief in God—is bred in the bone.

VI. Religion and Science Will Always Clash

Some might argue that the preceding analysis of religion, based as it is on supernatural beliefs, does not apply to certain non-Western faiths. In his recent book, *The End of Faith*, the neuroscientist Sam Harris mounts a fierce attack on religion, much of it directed at Christianity and Islam, which he criticizes for what he sees as ridiculous factual claims and grotesque moral views. But then he turns to Buddhism, and his tone shifts to admiration—it is "the most complete methodology we have for discovering the intrinsic freedom of consciousness, unencumbered by any dogma." Surely this religion, if one wants to call it a religion, is not rooted in the dualist and creationist views that emerge in our childhood.

Fair enough. But while it may be true that "theologically correct" Buddhism explicitly rejects the notions of body-soul duality and immaterial entities with special powers, actual Buddhists believe in such things. (Harris himself recognizes this; at one point he complains about the millions of Buddhists who treat the Buddha as a Christ figure.) For that matter, although many Christian theologians are willing to endorse evolutionary biology—and it was legitimately front-page news when Pope John Paul II conceded that Darwin's theory of evolution might be correct—this should not distract us from the fact that many Christians think evolution is nonsense.

Or consider the notion that the soul escapes the body at death. There is little hint of such an idea in the Old Testament, although it enters into Judaism later on. The New Testament is notoriously unclear about the afterlife, and some Christian theologians have argued, on the basis of sources such as Paul's letters to the Corinthians, that the idea of a soul's rising to heaven conflicts with biblical authority. In 1999 the pope himself cautioned people to think of heaven not as an actual place but, rather, as a form of existence—that of being in relation to God. 55

Despite all this, most Jews and Christians, as noted, believe in an afterlife—in fact, even people who claim to have no religion at all tend to believe in one. Our afterlife beliefs are clearly expressed in popular books such as *The Five People You Meet in Heaven* and *A Travel Guide to Heaven*. As the *Guide* puts it,

> Heaven is *dynamic*. It's bursting with excitement and action. It's the ultimate playground, created purely for our enjoyment, by someone who knows what enjoyment means, because He invented it. It's Disney World, Hawaii, Paris, Rome, and New York all rolled up into one. And it's *forever!* Heaven truly is the vacation that never ends.

(This sounds a bit like hell to me, but it is apparently to some people's taste.)

Religious authorities and scholars are often motivated to explore and reach out to science, as when the pope embraced evolution and the Dalai Lama became involved with neuroscience. They do this in part to make their worldview more palatable to others, and in part because they are legitimately concerned about any clash with scientific findings. No honest person wants to be in the position of defending a view that makes manifestly false claims, so religious authorities and scholars often make serious efforts toward reconciliation—for instance, trying to interpret the Bible in a way that is consistent with what we know about the age of the earth.

If people got their religious ideas from ecclesiastical authorities, these efforts might lead religion away from the supernatural. Scientific views would spread through religious communities. Supernatural beliefs would gradually disappear as the theologically correct version of a religion gradually became consistent with the secular worldview. As Stephen Jay Gould hoped, religion would stop stepping on science's toes.

But this scenario assumes the wrong account of where supernatural ideas come from. Religious teachings certainly shape many of the specific beliefs we hold; nobody is born with the idea that the birthplace of humanity was the Garden of Eden, or that the soul enters the body at the moment of conception, or that martyrs will be rewarded with sexual access to scores of virgins. These ideas are learned. But the universal themes of religion are not learned. They emerge as accidental by-products of our mental systems. They are part of human nature.

▪ QUESTIONS

Reading

1. What are the *opiate* and *fraternity* theories of the origin of religion? How do these differ from the cognitive theories at the heart of Bloom's discussion? Are the opiate and fraternity theories compatible with the cognitive theories, or do they contradict one another?
2. What is *dualism*? According to Bloom, why is dualism so persuasive?
3. Why does Bloom open his essay by invoking the mystical beliefs of a rabbi with whom he seems to disagree? Why does he compare that rabbi to Martin Luther King Jr. and the Dalai Lama?
4. Early in his essay, Bloom quotes public figures making provocative statements about various aspects of religion, including film director Woody Allen, evolutionary biologist Stephen Jay Gould, anthropologist Edward Tylor, and journalist Steven Waldman. Choose one of these quotations and reflect on its function in the essay. Why did Bloom use it? How does the point of view expressed in it relate to the theories of religion Bloom discusses?

Exploratory Writing

1. Bloom's essay focuses on arguing. In fact, he divides his essay into six sections and gives each of them a subtitle that functions like a thesis statement. On a blank sheet of paper, write out each of these subtitles, leaving several lines of blank space beneath each one. Write a brief summary of each section beneath each subtitle. Be sure to identify Bloom's central claims or questions in each section and to offer a concise summary of the evidence he uses to develop them.
2. In small groups, prepare for a debate on Bloom's question, "Is God an accident?" Some teams will make an argument for the cognitive theories Bloom discusses, and some teams will make an argument against them. The main source of evidence will be Bloom's essay, but the teams may choose to bring in evidence from their own experience, reading, and research. Each team must prepare an opening and closing statement (assigning a team member to deliver each) and be prepared to address any question raised by the other teams.

Making Connections

1. In Marjane Satrapi's "The Veil" (p. 184) Marji expresses strong beliefs about God and religion. If Marji were asked, "Is God an accident?" how do you think she would reply? Be sure to support your answer with evidence from Bloom's essay and Satrapi's graphic narrative.

Essay Writing

1. Write an essay in which you make an argument in response to Bloom's question, "Is God an accident?" What scientific theories suggest that the answer might be yes? What kind of "accident" are they referring to? What theories would suggest that the answer might be no? The bulk of your evidence should come from Bloom's essay, but you may use outside research or your own experience as evidence if relevant or necessary to make your argument stronger.

STUDENT ESSAY

Child on the Threshold: The Narrative Voice of a Child in *Persepolis*

Jennifer Bernal

Jennifer Bernal wrote this essay for a class on graphic novels. In it, she explores *Persepolis*, Marjane Satrapi's graphic narrative of her childhood in Iran during the Islamic revolution. (An excerpt from *Persepolis* starts on p. 184 of this book.) Bernal focuses on the tension between adult and childlike characteristics in the narrator's voice. As you read this essay, think about the strategies Bernal uses to interpret *Persepolis*. Pay attention to the aspects of the different modes she employs and how successful she is at using them. You should also examine how she integrates quotes and visuals throughout the text and how she analyzes them. Consider how you might use the same or different strategies in your own paper. Also note Bernal's proper use of MLA style for citing sources throughout the paper. You may refer to pp. 16 to 31 for more on the characteristics of each mode.

The world is not always an easy place to live in when you are a kid. It is big. It is unfair. It is full of physical and societal forces that are difficult to understand. Yet for all its mystery, children have always attempted to not only explain, but to tame the world, and seize control of it. The graphic novel, with its ability to present information in both written and visual forms, seems the perfect format to express a conflict between innocence and a desire to understand—a characteristic which defines the child's voice in literature. The child narrator in the graphic novel *Persepolis*, by Marjane Satrapi, an autobiographical narrative of a young girl's coming of age in Iran during the Islamic revolution, strikingly captures the duality of childhood. My research questions seemed fitting for a child: what? How? Why? What is the "child's voice"? How is it achieved? Why is it effective? The child's voice in this book is characterized by internal conflict: The character sometimes sounds like a child and sometimes like an adult. She truly is a child on the threshold of adulthood. Satrapi expresses the duality of this child's voice not only through content but also through her visual style.

The main character, Marji faces a constant conflict between childhood and adulthood. But the struggle takes place not only between the child and the adults in her society but also between the child and the adult *within* Marji herself. For example, Marji is exposed to many ideas and experiences as she tries to understand the world around her. In Fig. 1, we see her surprising an adult by discussing Marx.

Marji states, "I realized then that I didn't understand anything. I read all the books I could. I'd never read as much as I did during that period" (32–33). She wishes to "understand everything" because of her urge to catch up with the current affairs of the society she lives in. She wishes to know about Marx and communism, about the Iranian revolution, and about "dialectic

Figure 1 Marji surprises her Uncle Anoosh with her interest in Marxism (Satrapi 59).

materialism," to name a few. Her thirst for theoretical knowledge is directly connected to her desire to understand the world in which she is functioning—one that is undergoing a complex sociopolitical revolution. We see Marji grapple with the hypocrisy her teacher shows after the shah's overthrow: "But she was the one who told us that the shah was chosen by God!" (44), Marji exclaims to a fellow schoolgirl. Her insight into the world eclipses that of even the adults surrounding her (especially the teacher, who punishes Marji for her observation), and by deploying the vocabulary of the adults that surround her, Marji's child voice becomes preternaturally adult-like.

Still, the reader also sees Marji being a kid. Sometimes, like all children, she is unthinkingly cruel: In Fig. 2, we see her upsetting another little girl, Laly, with the horrifying (and, as it turns out, incorrect) "truth" about her father's absence.

Laly's father does return, and Marji tries to reconcile with the other girl, first in a child's manner and then as something like an adult. Appealing to their girlhoods, Marji asks, "You want to play?" (49). Rejected, she shucks off her childlike manner and puts on her adult voice: "But you have to admit I wasn't completely wrong when I said he was not on a trip" (52). This time, her cruelty serves only to make her more of a child. In the panel shown in Fig. 3, Laly grows large and declares her father a hero, while Marji shrinks into her childhood where the world is a mystery and there is nothing left to do but be a kid and play in the street.

In this play between candor and sarcasm, insight and misunderstanding, Marji's child voice exhibits qualities of heteroglossia. Russian linguist Mikhail Bakhtin introduced the term to characterize the duality of voices within a single linguistic code. According to *The Literary Encyclopedia,* "the term alludes not only to the co-existence of 'languages' within a language, but their co-existence in a state of tension and competition" (sec 1). For Marji,

Figure 2 A more childlike Marji upsets Laly (Satrapi 48).

Figure 3 Laly makes Marji feel like a small child (Satrapi 52).

the desire to understand the adult world she lives on the periphery of cohabitates with a child's naïveté. Marji's two languages are grafted onto each other in scenes of play between her friends. Ominously, Satrapi's voice-over reports, "The battle was over for our parents but not for us" (44), as Marji and her friends hunt the son of a man who was supposedly part of the shah's secret police. Marji declares revenge as they march through the street, saying "In the name of the dead million, we'll teach Ramin a good lesson" (45). Yet when Marji's mother arrives on the scene, the exclamations of the children demonstrate that they weren't hunting; they were merely playing. The mood of these panels and Marji's mother's distress in the following panels illustrate how precarious the line is between innocence and violence. The child's voice in *Persepolis* is one of transition, where Marji tries to enter a

Figure 4 Repetition represents the repressive Iranian government (Satrapi 95).

world that is not her own and at times misfires dangerously when she crosses that threshold.

The concept of heteroglossia exists not only in the literal language in *Persepolis* but in the visual language (which in a graphic novel is as important to progressing plots and themes as the words are) that shapes Marji's world. In her review of *Persepolis* for the *Village Voice*, Joy Press says that "Satrapi's super-naive style . . . persuasively communicates confusion and horror through the eyes of a precocious preteen." This simple visual style is achieved through two techniques, repetition and filtering, both of which contribute to the duality of the child's voice. First there's repetition of elements. We often see the same images being used over and over. Sometimes the repetition suggests the sameness imposed by the repressive government, which is at times whimsical and at times dangerous. While none of the girls look happy in the government-mandated scarves they wear in the frame shown in Fig. 4, there is nothing threatening in the image. It seems to evoke the charming sameness of the little girls in the children's story *Madeline* by Ludwig Bemelmans and in doing so, makes the reader feel as though she might be reading a story from a child's perspective. Yet, that same image of the headscarf enters into a perilous adult world when Marji is reprimanded on the street and called a "whore" for the manner in which she wears her scarf (Fig. 5). The violence of the scarf being pulled over Marji's head forces the visual language out of the world of children, just as Marji is being forced to comply with the adult world.

Figure 5 The repeated image of the headscarf becomes a dangerous one (Satrapi 133).

At other times images are repeated throughout the book for emphasis. For example, on several occasions we see Marji raising her finger and speaking directly to the reader to make an emphatic point (Fig. 6). The protagonist faces the "audience," so to speak, and grants us an explanation of her thoughts. Young Marji's raised finger is an appeal to ethos: It makes us accept her account and insights into her story. Such a claim to credibility appears as an adult trait. In fact, she claims to achieve adulthood using this declarative position. The fact that she takes the same pose to do so that she used in childhood casts doubt on whether or not she really has become an adult. In both the use of the headscarf and Marji's poses, the repetition of form makes *Persepolis* feel like a children's book, narrated by a child. But, reusing the same images in multiple contexts, Satrapi creates a visual world that, like Marji's words, implies a conflict between adult understanding and childlike innocence.

In addition to simplification through repetition, there's a second simplifying process, that of filtering. *Persepolis* is filled with violent elements. One good example is the torture and execution of guerrilla fighter Ahmadi. Marji recounts, "In the end he was cut to pieces." The dismemberment (Fig. 7) is one of the most violent images we see in the book. However, Satrapi's representation filters the horror. This figure doesn't seem real—it looks neatly sectioned and hollow, like a doll. We see the image presented as a child might imagine it. In simplifying the visual language of the book through repetition and filtering, Satrapi reinforces the conflict between the child and the adult in Marji. Horrific images are smoothed over and cleaned up by a child's perspective which cannot imagine horror, but Marji's interactions with the adult world also lead to vivid verbal and physical violence. The conflict between her adult and child voices is no more apparent than in the visual forms it takes. By posing the same way in childhood and adulthood and simplifying the violent imagery of the revolution, Marji's visual language casts doubt on which

Figure 6 Marji often looks to the audience with this declarative pose (Satrapi 19, 114, 117).

Figure 7 Satrapi draws this gruesome image in a sanitized, childlike way (Satrapi 52).

world she lives in. The reader sees that she takes part in both but that the child's voice is really a tangle of knowledge and ingenuousness.

Let me conclude by answering why Satrapi's visual voice is so effective. Remember she is connecting to the world of childhood through the graphic novel. Her story seems very grim and adult—too grim for children. Still, it is a child's story, or rather the story of a character standing on the threshold of the adult world. The graphic novel is an ideal way to reveal both the conflicting aspects of the child's voice and the balance between these aspects. Indeed, the graphic novel form itself mirrors the heteroglossia of Marji's voice. It is both a form of written language and of visual storytelling. It exists between two art forms, and with that comes an inherent conflict between verbal and visual. For the author to explain the child Marji's particular, slightly uncomfortable vantage point, the in-between genre of the graphic novel is perfect.

Works Cited

"Heteroglossia." *The Literary Encyclopedia.* July 18, 2001. The Literary Dictionary Company. Web. 10 Feb. 2012.

Press, Joy. "Veil of Tears: Two Children of the Revolution Look Back at Iran." *Villagevoice.com.* The Village Voice, May 6, 2003. Web. 28 Feb. 2012.

Satrapi, Marjane. *Persepolis 1: The Story of a Childhood.* New York: Pantheon, 2003. Print.

▪ QUESTIONS

Reading

1. How does Bernal's title anticipate her argument? Why does she use a title and a subtitle? How effective is the title? Does it get you interested in the essay? Does it inform you what the essay will be about? Can you imagine an alternative title that might be equally effective, or even more effective?
2. Bernal uses a variety of sources, including a dictionary definition of linguist Mikhail Bakhtin's term *heteroglossia*. Why does she turn to the dictionary in this case? What does it help her achieve that would be more difficult without it?
3. Because Bernal is writing about a graphic narrative, she uses visual evidence to develop her argument—for example, Figure 7 (p. 213), which depicts the dismembered body of guerrilla fighter Ahmadi. What does she tell us about this image? What aspects of it does she describe? What strategies does she use to analyze it? How do her description and analysis of the visual add something crucial to her argument?

Exploratory Writing

1. Put yourself in the position of a professor meeting with Bernal to discuss her essay. Write a short dialogue between this professor and Bernal, focusing on the relationship between her thesis and her evidence. Be sure you identify the thesis and at least two significant forms of evidence. Be sure you address the following questions: Is the thesis clear? Is it compelling? Does it seem true, without being obvious? Is the evidence pertinent? Does it convince you that the argument is on target?
2. Highlight, underline, or flag all the quotations Bernal uses in her essay. Then write a paragraph or two about how she introduces and analyzes these quotations. What techniques does she use to integrate them into her paragraphs? How does she respond to them? Which of Bernal's strategies might you use in your own writing?

Making Connections

1. In "The Veil," Marjane Satrapi documents her childhood conversations with God. Imagine Marji has grown up and has just read Bernal's essay about her book. Write a

conversation she might have with Bernal. What would she notice in Bernal's essay? What might surprise Marji? Would she disagree with any of Bernal's claims? Write the conversation as a dialogue, or if you want, draw it as a miniature graphic narrative.

Essay Writing

1. Choose one of the essays in this section (or the book) and write an essay in which you analyze the type of voice the author employs. What effect does this have on your understanding of the author, the people or things the author discusses, and your reaction to the piece? Like Bernal, use quotes from the piece you analyze, and employ aspects of reflecting, reporting, explaining, and arguing, as appropriate, to make your point.

Part 3
Social Sciences

Readings in the Social Sciences

The social sciences include academic disciplines that focus on groups of human beings—for example, sociology, political science, anthropology, economics, urban studies, and cultural geography. (Certain disciplines, such as history and linguistics, are sometimes classified among the social sciences and sometimes among the humanities; others, such as psychology, are sometimes classified among the social sciences and sometimes among the sciences.) Public affairs, closely related to the social sciences, encompass politics, law, and current events. Writers in the social sciences and public affairs tend to value facts, statistics, and data. Each discipline has developed careful methods for collecting and analyzing the facts that are relevant for their subjects of study. For example, a sociologist designs surveys to collect meaningful data, paying careful attention to the size and composition of the survey pool as well as potential biases, with the goal of conducting statistical analyses that will explain trends in social life; an anthropologist will often live among the group of people he or she studies, becoming a participant-observer, with the goal of writing an ethnography—a thorough study of a culture.

A variety of methods animate each discipline in the social sciences, but two are especially prominent: a quantitative approach focuses on numbers, usually statistics; a qualitative approach involves the collection and analysis of evidence drawn from a wide range of cultural sources, including interviews, newspapers, books, online sources, conversations, and artifacts. Some social scientists favor quantitative approaches, while others favor qualitative approaches. Many combine the two.

We've collected sixteen essays from the social sciences, ten of which stand alone and the other six of which are grouped in pairs. Four of these essays are primarily reflecting, three reporting, three explaining, and six arguing. Most of these essays emphasize qualitative methods, because working with quantitative data involves specialized methods beyond the scope of most introductory writing courses. At the end of this chapter, you will see an example of one student's analysis of qualitative and quantitative data related to food safety regulations in the United States.

For this course, when you write about the social sciences, you too will be working primarily with qualitative data. Whether you are reflecting, reporting, explaining, or arguing, it will be your job to examine your data in such a way that sheds light on the experiences of human beings that arise from group affiliations and social interactions. If you are writing about history, you'll be focusing on how past events shaped the development of such interactions; if you're writing about economics, you'll be writing about how trade and finances shape lives; if you're writing about politics, you'll be writing about how the choices (and compromises) made by nations and leaders affect the lives of citizens. These various writing topics share a common denominator: a focus on how social phenomena shape lives. It's important to get the facts right, but it's just as important to remember that such issues require judgment and analysis to be understood. That's where you, as a writer, come in.

REFLECTING

My Life as an Undocumented Immigrant

Jose Antonio Vargas

Journalist Jose Antonio Vargas (b. 1983) was awarded the Pulitzer Prize for Breaking News Reporting in 2008 for his coverage of the Virginia Tech shootings. His work has appeared in the *San Francisco Chronicle*, the *Washington Post*, the *New Yorker*, *Rolling Stone*, and other magazines and newspapers. His *Washington Post* series on HIV/AIDS was made into a documentary feature, *The Open City*, which he wrote and coproduced. Most recently, he served as a senior contributing editor at the *Huffington Post*, where he launched the "Technology" and "College" sections and started the blog "Technology as Anthropology." Vargas was born in the Philippines and sent to the United States to live with his grandparents at age twelve. He learned that he was an illegal immigrant at age sixteen, when he tried to obtain a California State driver's license. In 1999, he came out as gay, and in 2011, he "came out" as illegal with this groundbreaking *New York Times Magazine* article. He is the founder of Define American, a campaign designed to "elevate the conversation" about immigration and citizenship.

One August morning nearly two decades ago, my mother woke me and put me in a cab. She handed me a jacket. "*Baka malamig doon*" were among the few words she said. ("It might be cold there.") When I arrived at the Philippines' Ninoy Aquino International Airport with her, my aunt, and a family friend, I was introduced to a man I'd never seen. They told me he was my uncle. He held my hand as I boarded an airplane for the first time. It was 1993, and I was twelve.

My mother wanted to give me a better life, so she sent me thousands of miles away to live with her parents in America—my grandfather (*Lolo* in Tagalog) and grandmother (*Lola*). After I arrived in Mountain View, California, in the San Francisco Bay Area, I entered sixth grade and quickly grew to love my new home, family, and culture. I discovered a passion for language, though it was hard to learn the difference between formal English and American slang. One of my early memories is of a freckled kid in middle school asking me, "What's up?" I replied, "The sky," and he and a couple of other kids laughed. I won the eighth-grade spelling bee by memorizing words I couldn't properly pronounce. (The winning word was "indefatigable.")

One day when I was sixteen, I rode my bike to the nearby DMV office to get my driver's permit. Some of my friends already had their licenses, so I figured it was time. But when I handed the clerk my green card as proof of U.S. residency, she flipped it around, examining it. "This is fake," she whispered. "Don't come back here again."

Confused and scared, I pedaled home and confronted Lolo. I remember him sitting in the garage, cutting coupons. I dropped my bike and ran over to him, showing him the green card. "*Peke ba ito?*" I asked in Tagalog. ("Is this fake?") My grandparents were naturalized American citizens—he worked as a security guard, she as a food server—and they had begun supporting my mother and me financially when I was three, after my father's wandering eye and inability to properly provide for us led to my parents' separation. Lolo was a proud man, and I saw the shame on his face as he told me he purchased the card, along with other fake documents, for me. "Don't show it to other people," he warned.

5 I decided then that I could never give anyone reason to doubt I was an American. I convinced myself that if I worked enough, if I achieved enough, I would be rewarded with citizenship. I felt I could earn it.

I've tried. Over the past fourteen years, I've graduated from high school and college and built a career as a journalist, interviewing some of the most famous people in the country. On the surface, I've created a good life. I've lived the American dream.

But I am still an undocumented immigrant. And that means living a different kind of reality. It means going about my day in fear of being found out. It means rarely trusting people, even those closest to me, with who I really am. It means keeping my family photos in a shoebox rather than displaying them on shelves in my home, so friends don't ask about them. It means reluctantly, even painfully, doing things I know are wrong and unlawful. And it has meant relying on a sort of twenty-first-century underground railroad of supporters, people who took an interest in my future and took risks for me.

Last year I read about four students who walked from Miami to Washington to lobby for the Dream Act, a nearly decade-old immigration bill that would provide a path to legal permanent residency for young people who have been educated in this country. At the risk of deportation—the Obama administration has deported almost 800,000 people in the last two years—they are speaking out. Their courage has inspired me.

There are believed to be 11 million undocumented immigrants in the United States. We're not always who you think we are. Some pick your strawberries or care for your children. Some are in high school or college. And some, it turns out, write news articles you might read. I grew up here. This is my home. Yet even though I think of myself as an American and consider America my country, my country doesn't think of me as one of its own.

10 My first challenge was the language. Though I learned English in the Philippines, I wanted to lose my accent. During high school, I spent hours at a time watching television (especially *Frasier, Home Improvement,* and reruns of *The Golden Girls*) and movies (from *Goodfellas* to *Anne of Green Gables*), pausing the VHS to try to copy how various characters enunciated their words. At the local library, I read magazines, books, and newspapers—anything to learn how to write better. Kathy Dewar, my high school English teacher, introduced me to journalism. From the moment I wrote my first article for the student paper, I convinced myself that having my name in print—writing in English, interviewing Americans—validated my presence here.

The debates over "illegal aliens" intensified my anxieties. In 1994, only a year after my flight from the Philippines, Gov. Pete Wilson was re-elected in part because of his support for Proposition 187, which prohibited undocumented immigrants from attending public school and accessing other services. (A federal court later found the law unconstitutional.) After my encounter at the DMV in 1997, I grew more aware of anti-immigrant sentiments and stereotypes: *They don't want to assimilate, they are a drain on society.* They're not talking about me, I would tell myself. I have something to contribute.

To do that, I had to work—and for that, I needed a Social Security number. Fortunately, my grandfather had already managed to get one for me. Lolo had always taken care of everyone in the family. He and my grandmother emigrated legally in 1984 from Zambales, a province in the Philippines of rice fields and bamboo houses, following Lolo's sister, who married a Filipino-American serving in the American military. She petitioned for her brother and his wife to join her. When they got here, Lolo petitioned for his two children—my mother and her younger brother—to follow them. But instead of mentioning that my mother was a married woman, he listed her as single. Legal residents can't petition for their married children. Besides, Lolo didn't care for my father. He didn't want him coming here too.

But soon Lolo grew nervous that the immigration authorities reviewing the petition would discover my mother was married, thus derailing not only her chances of coming here but those of my uncle as well. So he withdrew her petition. After my uncle came to America legally in 1991, Lolo tried to get my mother here through a tourist visa, but she wasn't able to obtain one. That's when she decided to send me. My mother told me later that she figured she would follow me soon. She never did.

The "uncle" who brought me here turned out to be a coyote, not a relative, my grandfather later explained. Lolo scraped together enough money—I eventually learned it was $4,500, a huge sum for him—to pay him to smuggle me here under a fake name and fake passport. (I never saw the passport again after the flight and have always assumed that the coyote kept it.) After I arrived in America, Lolo obtained a new fake Filipino passport, in my real name this time, adorned with a fake student visa, in addition to the fraudulent green card.

15 Using the fake passport, we went to the local Social Security Administration office and applied for a Social Security number and card. It was, I remember, a quick visit. When the card came in the mail, it had my full, real name, but it also clearly stated: "Valid for work only with INS authorization."

When I began looking for work, a short time after the DMV incident, my grandfather and I took the Social Security card to Kinko's, where he covered the "INS authorization" text with a sliver of white tape. We then made photocopies of the card. At a glance, at least, the copies would look like copies of a regular, unrestricted Social Security card.

Lolo always imagined I would work the kind of low-paying jobs that undocumented people often take. (Once I married an American, he said, I would get my real papers, and everything would be fine.) But even menial jobs require documents, so he and I hoped the doctored card would work for now. The more documents I had, he said, the better.

While in high school, I worked part time at Subway, then at the front desk of the local YMCA, then at a tennis club, until I landed an unpaid internship at the *Mountain View Voice,* my hometown newspaper. First I brought coffee and helped around the office; eventually I began covering city-hall meetings and other assignments for pay.

For more than a decade of getting part-time and full-time jobs, employers have rarely asked to check my original Social Security card. When they did, I showed the photocopied version, which they accepted. Over time, I also began checking the citizenship box on my federal I-9 employment eligibility forms. (Claiming full citizenship was actually easier than declaring permanent resident "green card" status, which would have required me to provide an alien registration number.)

20 This deceit never got easier. The more I did it, the more I felt like an impostor, the more guilt I carried—and the more I worried that I would get caught. But I kept doing it. I needed to live and survive on my own, and I decided this was the way.

Mountain View High School became my second home. I was elected to represent my school at school-board meetings, which gave me the chance to meet and befriend Rich Fischer, the superintendent for our school district. I joined the speech and debate teams, acted in school plays, and eventually became co-editor of the *Oracle,* the student newspaper. That drew the attention of my principal, Pat Hyland. "You're at school just as much as I am," she told me. Pat and Rich would soon become mentors, and over time, almost surrogate parents for me.

After a choir rehearsal during my junior year, Jill Denny, the choir director, told me she was considering a Japan trip for our singing group. I told her I couldn't afford it, but she said we'd figure out a way. I hesitated, and then decided to tell her the truth. "It's not really the money," I remember saying. "I don't have the right passport." When she assured me we'd get the proper documents, I finally told her. "I can't get the right passport," I said. "I'm not supposed to be here."

She understood. So the choir toured Hawaii instead, with me in tow. (Mrs. Denny and I spoke a couple of months ago, and she told me she hadn't wanted to leave any student behind.)

Later that school year, my history class watched a documentary on Harvey Milk, the openly gay San Francisco city official who was assassinated. This was 1999, just six months after Matthew Shepard's body was found tied to a fence in Wyoming. During the discussion, I raised my hand and said something like: "I'm sorry Harvey Milk got killed for being gay. . . . I've been meaning to say this. . . . I'm gay."

25 I hadn't planned on coming out that morning, though I had known that I was gay for several years. With that announcement, I became the only openly gay student at school, and it caused turmoil with my grandparents. Lolo kicked me out of the house for a few weeks. Though we eventually reconciled,

I had disappointed him on two fronts. First, as a Catholic, he considered homosexuality a sin and was embarrassed about having "*ang apo na bakla*" ("a grandson who is gay"). Even worse, I was making matters more difficult for myself, he said. I needed to marry an American woman in order to gain a green card.

Tough as it was, coming out about being gay seemed less daunting than coming out about my legal status. I kept my other secret mostly hidden.

While my classmates awaited their college acceptance letters, I hoped to get a full-time job at *The Mountain View Voice* after graduation. It's not that I didn't want to go to college, but I couldn't apply for state and federal financial aid. Without that, my family couldn't afford to send me.

But when I finally told Pat and Rich about my immigration "problem"—as we called it from then on—they helped me look for a solution. At first, they even wondered if one of them could adopt me and fix the situation that way, but a lawyer Rich consulted told him it wouldn't change my legal status because I was too old. Eventually they connected me to a new scholarship fund for high-potential students who were usually the first in their families to attend college. Most important, the fund was not concerned with immigration status. I was among the first recipients, with the scholarship covering tuition, lodging, books, and other expenses for my studies at San Francisco State University.

As a college freshman, I found a job working part time at the *San Francisco Chronicle,* where I sorted mail and wrote some freelance articles. My ambition was to get a reporting job, so I embarked on a series of internships. First I landed at the *Philadelphia Daily News,* in the summer of 2001, where I covered a drive-by shooting and the wedding of the 76ers star Allen Iverson. Using those articles, I applied to the *Seattle Times* and got an internship for the following summer.

But then my lack of proper documents became a problem again. The *Times*'s recruiter, Pat Foote, asked all incoming interns to bring certain paperwork on their first day: a birth certificate, or a passport, or a driver's license plus an original Social Security card. I panicked, thinking my documents wouldn't pass muster. So before starting the job, I called Pat and told her about my legal status. After consulting with management, she called me back with the answer I feared: I couldn't do the internship. 30

This was devastating. What good was college if I couldn't then pursue the career I wanted? I decided then that if I was to succeed in a profession that is all about truth-telling, I couldn't tell the truth about myself.

After this episode, Jim Strand, the venture capitalist who sponsored my scholarship, offered to pay for an immigration lawyer. Rich and I went to meet her in San Francisco's financial district.

I was hopeful. This was in early 2002, shortly after Senators Orrin Hatch, the Utah Republican, and Dick Durbin, the Illinois Democrat, introduced the Dream Act—Development, Relief and Education for Alien Minors. It seemed like the legislative version of what I'd told myself: If I work hard and contribute, things will work out.

But the meeting left me crushed. My only solution, the lawyer said, was to go back to the Philippines and accept a ten-year ban before I could apply to return legally.

If Rich was discouraged, he hid it well. "Put this problem on a shelf," he told me. "Compartmentalize it. Keep going." 35

And I did. For the summer of 2003, I applied for internships across the country. Several newspapers, including the *Wall Street Journal*, the *Boston Globe*, and the *Chicago Tribune*, expressed interest. But when the *Washington Post* offered me a spot, I knew where I would go. And this time, I had no intention of acknowledging my "problem."

The *Post* internship posed a tricky obstacle: It required a driver's license. (After my close call at the California DMV, I'd never gotten one.) So I spent an afternoon at The Mountain View Public Library, studying various states' requirements. Oregon was among the most welcoming—and it was just a few hours' drive north.

Again, my support network came through. A friend's father lived in Portland, and he allowed me to use his address as proof of residency. Pat, Rich, and Rich's longtime assistant, Mary Moore, sent letters to me at that address. Rich taught me how to do three-point turns in a parking lot, and a friend accompanied me to Portland.

The license meant everything to me—it would let me drive, fly, and work. But my grandparents worried about the Portland trip and the Washington internship. While Lola offered daily prayers so that I would not get caught, Lolo told me that I was dreaming too big, risking too much.

I was determined to pursue my ambitions. I was twenty-two, I told them, responsible for my own actions. But this was different from Lolo's driving a confused teenager to Kinko's. I knew what I was doing now, and I knew it wasn't right. But what was I supposed to do? 40

I was paying state and federal taxes, but I was using an invalid Social Security card and writing false information on my employment forms. But that seemed better than depending on my grandparents or on Pat, Rich, and Jim—or returning to a country I barely remembered. I convinced myself all would be OK if I lived up to the qualities of a "citizen": hard work, self-reliance, love of my country.

At the DMV in Portland, I arrived with my photocopied Social Security card, my college ID, a pay stub from the *San Francisco Chronicle*, and my proof of state residence—the letters to the Portland address that my support network had sent. It worked. My license, issued in 2003, was set to expire eight years later, on my 30th birthday, on February 3, 2011. I had eight years to succeed professionally, and to hope that some sort of immigration reform would pass in the meantime and allow me to stay.

It seemed like all the time in the world.

My summer in Washington was exhilarating. I was intimidated to be in a major newsroom but was assigned a mentor—Peter Perl, a veteran magazine writer—to help me navigate it. A few weeks into the internship, he printed out one of my articles, about a guy who recovered a long-lost wallet, circled the first two paragraphs and left it on my desk. "Great eye for details—awesome!" he wrote. Though I didn't know it then, Peter would become one more member of my network.

At the end of the summer, I returned to the *San Francisco Chronicle*. My plan was to finish school—I was now a senior—while I worked for the *Chronicle* as a reporter for the city desk. But when the *Post* beckoned again, offering me a full-time, two-year paid internship that I could start when I graduated in June 2004, it was too tempting to pass up. I moved back to Washington. 45

About four months into my job as a reporter for the *Post*, I began feeling increasingly paranoid, as if I had "illegal immigrant" tattooed on my forehead—and in Washington, of all places, where the debates over immigration seemed never-ending. I was so eager to prove myself that I feared I was annoying some colleagues and editors—and worried that any one of these professional journalists could discover my secret. The anxiety was nearly paralyzing. I decided I had to tell one of the higher-ups about my situation. I turned to Peter.

By this time, Peter, who still works at the *Post*, had become part of management as the paper's director of newsroom training and professional development. One afternoon in late October, we walked a couple of blocks to Lafayette Square, across from the White House. Over some twenty minutes, sitting on a bench, I told him everything: the Social Security card, the driver's license, Pat and Rich, my family.

Peter was shocked. "I understand you 100 times better now," he said. He told me that I had done the right thing by telling him, and that it was now our shared problem. He said he didn't want to do anything about it just yet. I had just been hired, he said, and I needed to prove myself. "When you've done enough," he said, "we'll tell Don and Len together." (Don Graham is the chairman of The Washington Post Company; Leonard Downie Jr. was then the paper's executive editor.) A month later, I spent my first Thanksgiving in Washington with Peter and his family.

In the five years that followed, I did my best to "do enough." I was promoted to staff writer, reported on video-game culture, wrote a series on Washington's HIV/AIDS epidemic, and covered the role of technology and social media in the 2008 presidential race. I visited the White House, where I interviewed senior aides and covered a state dinner—and gave the Secret Service the Social Security number I obtained with false documents.

I did my best to steer clear of reporting on immigration policy but couldn't always avoid it. On two occasions, I wrote about Hillary Clinton's position on driver's licenses for undocumented immigrants. I also wrote an article about Senator Mel Martinez of Florida, then the chairman of the Republican National Committee, who was defending his party's stance toward Latinos after only one Republican presidential candidate—John McCain, the co-author of a failed immigration bill—agreed to participate in a debate sponsored by Univision, the Spanish-language network. 50

It was an odd sort of dance: I was trying to stand out in a highly competitive newsroom, yet I was terrified that if I stood out too much, I'd invite unwanted scrutiny. I tried to compartmentalize my fears, distract myself by reporting on the lives of other people, but there was no escaping the central conflict in my life. Maintaining a deception for so long distorts your sense of self. You start wondering who you've become, and why.

In April 2008, I was part of a *Post* team that won a Pulitzer Prize for the paper's coverage of the Virginia Tech shootings a year earlier. Lolo died a year earlier, so it was Lola who called me the day of the announcement. The first thing she said was, "*Anong mangyayari kung malaman ng mga tao?*"

What will happen if people find out?

I couldn't say anything. After we got off the phone, I rushed to the bathroom on the fourth floor of the newsroom, sat down on the toilet, and cried.

In the summer of 2009, without ever having had that follow-up talk with top *Post* management, I left the paper and moved to New York to join the *Huffington Post.* I met Arianna Huffington at a Washington Press Club Foundation dinner I was covering for the *Post* two years earlier, and she later recruited me to join her news site. I wanted to learn more about Web publishing, and I thought the new job would provide a useful education. 55

Still, I was apprehensive about the move: Many companies were already using E-Verify, a program set up by the Department of Homeland Security that checks if prospective employees are eligible to work, and I didn't know if my new employer was among them. But I'd been able to get jobs in other newsrooms, I figured, so I filled out the paperwork as usual and succeeded in landing on the payroll.

While I worked at the *Huffington Post,* other opportunities emerged. My HIV/AIDS series became a documentary film called *The Other City,* which opened at the Tribeca Film Festival last year and was broadcast on Showtime. I began writing for magazines and landed a dream assignment: profiling Facebook's Mark Zuckerberg for the *New Yorker.*

The more I achieved, the more scared and depressed I became. I was proud of my work, but there was always a cloud hanging over it, over me. My old eight-year deadline—the expiration of my Oregon driver's license—was approaching.

After slightly less than a year, I decided to leave the *Huffington Post.* In part, this was because I wanted to promote the documentary and write a book about online culture—or so I told my friends. But the real reason was, after so many years of trying to be a part of the system, of focusing all my energy on my professional life, I learned that no amount of professional success would solve my problem or ease the sense of loss and displacement I felt. I lied to a friend about why I couldn't take a weekend trip to Mexico. Another time I concocted an excuse for why I couldn't go on an all-expenses-paid trip to Switzerland. I have been unwilling, for years, to be in a long-term relationship because I never wanted anyone to get too close and ask too many questions. All the while, Lola's question was stuck in my head: What will happen if people find out?

Early this year, just two weeks before my thirtieth birthday, I won a small reprieve: I obtained a driver's license in the state of Washington. The license is valid until 2016. This offered me five more years of acceptable identification—but also five more years of fear, of lying to people I respect and institutions that trusted me, of running away from who I am. 60

I'm done running. I'm exhausted. I don't want that life anymore.

So I've decided to come forward, own up to what I've done, and tell my story to the best of my recollection. I've reached out to former bosses and employers and apologized for misleading them—a mix of humiliation and liberation coming with each disclosure. All the people mentioned in this article gave me permission to use their names. I've also talked to family and friends about my situation and am working with legal counsel to review my options. I don't know what the consequences will be of telling my story.

I do know that I am grateful to my grandparents, my Lolo and Lola, for giving me the chance for a better life. I'm also grateful to my other family—the support network I found here in America—for encouraging me to pursue my dreams.

It's been almost eighteen years since I've seen my mother. Early on, I was mad at her for putting me in this position, and then mad at myself for being angry and ungrateful. By the time I got to college, we rarely spoke by phone. It became too painful; after a while it was easier to just send money to help support her and my two half-siblings. My sister, almost two years old when I left, is almost twenty now. I've never met my fourteen-year-old brother. I would love to see them.

Not long ago, I called my mother. I wanted to fill the gaps in my memory about that August morning so many years ago. We had never discussed it. Part of me wanted to shove the memory aside, but to write this article and face the facts of my life, I needed more details. Did I cry? Did she? Did we kiss goodbye? 65

My mother told me I was excited about meeting a stewardess, about getting on a plane. She also reminded me of the one piece of advice she gave me for blending in: If anyone asked why I was coming to America, I should say I was going to Disneyland.

▪ QUESTIONS

Reading

1. What was Proposition 187? Why was this law of concern to Vargas?
2. According to Vargas, how many undocumented immigrants were deported from the United States between 2009 and the writing of this article, in 2011? How many undocumented immigrants remain in the United States now?
3. What is the "small reprieve" that happens for Vargas just before his thirtieth birthday?

Exploratory Writing

1. "This is my home," Vargas writes (paragraph 9). "Yet even though I think of myself as an American and consider America my country, my country doesn't think of me as one of

its own." Highlight, underline, or flag places where Vargas describes his attempts to become a legal United States citizen. Also highlight, underline, or flag places where Vargas recounts finding nonlegal solutions to his lack of citizenship. What do these attempts illustrate about what it means to be a citizen? What does Vargas mean when he uses the term "my country"?

2. Visit the blog at Vargas's Web site, Define American (**www.defineamerican.com**). Choose a recent news item, personal history, or other entry from the blog, and write a paragraph explaining how it addresses the current debate about immigration, citizenship, and "defining American." Consider the online comments in response to the blog entry as you write your explanation.

Making Connections

1. In his essay "If Black English Isn't a Language, Then Tell Me, What Is?" James Baldwin (p. 131) argues that "language is . . . a political instrument, means, and proof of power." How do Baldwin's arguments, first published in the late 1970s, apply to the current debates about immigration that Vargas describes? You might refer to Vargas's Web site, **www.defineamerican.com**, and to recent newspaper articles about immigration law.

Essay Writing

1. Vargas mentions the Dream Act, introduced by Senators Orrin Hatch and Dick Durbin in early 2002. Write an essay reporting on the Dream Act. What was the bill's history in the United States Senate? How did key news sources, including your local newspapers, cover the bill? In your report, you might include interviews with classmates or people on the street, and/or contact the offices of your local representatives to learn their positions and perspectives on immigration policy.

REFLECTING

Shooting an Elephant

George Orwell

George Orwell (1903–1950) was the pen name of Eric Blair, the son of a British customs officer stationed in Bengal, India. As a boy, Blair was sent home to prestigious English schools, where he learned to dislike the rich and powerful. After finishing preparatory school at Eton College, he returned to Asia to serve as an officer of the British police in India and Burma, where he became disillusioned with imperialism. He later studied conditions among the urban poor and the coal miners of Wigan, a city in northwestern England, which strengthened his socialist beliefs. He was wounded in the Spanish civil war, defending the lost cause of the left against the fascists. Under the name Orwell, he wrote accounts of all of these experiences as well as the anti-Stalinist fable *Animal Farm* (1945) and the novel *1984* (1949). In the following essay, first published in 1936, Orwell attacks the politics of imperialism.

In Moulmein, in Lower Burma, I was hated by large numbers of people—the only time in my life that I have been important enough for this to happen to me. I was sub-divisional police officer of the town, and in an aimless, petty kind of way anti-European feeling was very bitter. No one had the guts to raise a riot, but if a European woman went through the bazaars alone somebody would probably spit betel juice over her dress. As a police officer I was an obvious target and was baited whenever it seemed safe to do so. When a nimble Burman tripped me up on the football field and the referee (another Burman) looked the other way, the crowd yelled with hideous laughter. This happened more than once. In the end the sneering yellow faces of young men that met me everywhere, the insults hooted after me when I was at a safe distance, got badly on my nerves. The young Buddhist priests were the worst of all. There were several thousands of them in the town and none of them seemed to have anything to do except stand on street corners and jeer at Europeans.

All this was perplexing and upsetting. For at that time I had already made up my mind that imperialism was an evil thing and the sooner I chucked up my job and got out of it the better. Theoretically—and secretly, of course—I was all for the Burmese and all against their oppressors, the British. As for the job I was doing, I hated it more bitterly than I can perhaps make clear. In a job like that you see the dirty work of Empire at close quarters. The wretched prisoners huddling in the stinking cages of the lock-ups, the grey, cowed faces of the long-term convicts, the scarred buttocks of the men who had been flogged with bamboos—all these oppressed me with an intolerable sense of guilt. But I could get nothing into perspective. I was young and ill-educated and I had had to think out my problems in the utter silence that is imposed on every Englishman in the East. I did not even know that the British Empire is dying, still less did I know that it is a great deal better than the younger empires that are going to supplant it. All I knew was that I was stuck between my hatred of the empire I served and my rage against the evil-spirited little beasts who tried to make my job impossible. With one part of my mind I thought of the British Raj[1] as an unbreakable tyranny, as something clamped down, in *saecula saeculorum*,[2] upon the will of prostrate peoples; with another part I thought that the greatest joy in the world would be to drive a bayonet into a Buddhist priest's guts. Feelings like these are the normal by-product of imperialism; ask any Anglo-Indian official, if you can catch him off duty.

One day something happened which in a roundabout way was enlightening. It was a tiny incident in itself, but it gave me a better glimpse than I had had before of the real nature of imperialism—the real motives for which despotic governments act. Early one morning the sub-inspector at a police station at the other end of the town rang me up on the phone and said that an elephant was ravaging the bazaar. Would I please come and do something about it? I did not know what I could do, but I wanted to see what was happening and I got on to a pony and started out. I took my rifle, an old .44 Winchester and much too small to kill an elephant, but I thought the noise might be useful *in terrorem*.[3] Various Burmans stopped me on the way and told me about the elephant's doings. It was not, of course, a wild elephant, but a tame one which had gone "must."[4] It had been chained up, as tame elephants always are when their attack of "must" is due, but on the previous night it had broken its chain and escaped. Its mahout,[5] the only person who could manage it when it was in that state, had set out in pursuit, but had taken the wrong direction and was now twelve hours' journey away, and in the morning the elephant had suddenly reappeared in town. The Burmese population had no weapons and were quite helpless against it. It had already destroyed somebody's bamboo hut, killed a cow and raided some fruit-stalls and devoured the stock; also it had met the municipal rubbish van and, when the driver jumped out and took to his heels, had turned the van over and inflicted violences upon it.

The Burmese sub-inspector and some Indian constables were waiting for me in the quarter where the elephant had been seen. It was a very poor quarter, a labyrinth of squalid bamboo huts, thatched with palm-leaf, winding all over a steep hillside. I remember that it was a cloudy, stuffy morning at the beginning of the rains. We began questioning the people as to where the elephant had gone and, as usual, failed to get any definite information. That is invariably the case in the East; a story always sounds clear enough at a distance, but the nearer you get to the scene of events the vaguer it becomes. Some of the people said that the elephant had gone in one direction, some said that he had gone in another, some professed not even to have heard of any elephant. I had almost made up my mind that the whole story was a pack

---

[1] *British Raj*: British rule in India and Burma.—Eds.

[2] *saecula saeculorum*: Forever and ever.—Eds.

[3] *in terrorem*: For fright.—Eds.

[4] *"must"*: The frenzied state of the bull elephant in sexual excitement.—Eds.

[5] *mahout*: An elephant's keeper.—Eds.

of lies, when we heard yells a little distance away. There was a loud, scandalized cry of "Go away, child! Go away this instant!" and an old woman with a switch in her hand came round the corner of a hut, violently shooing away a crowd of naked children. Some more women followed, clicking their tongues and exclaiming; evidently there was something that the children ought not to have seen. I rounded the hut and saw a man's dead body sprawling in the mud. He was an Indian, a black Dravidian coolie,[6] almost naked, and he could not have been dead many minutes. The people said that the elephant had come suddenly upon him round the corner of the hut, caught him with its trunk, put its foot on his back and ground him into the earth. This was the rainy season and the ground was soft, and his face had scored a trench a foot deep and a couple of yards long. He was lying on his belly with arms crucified and head sharply twisted to one side. His face was coated with mud, the eyes wide open, the teeth bared and grinning with an expression of unendurable agony. (Never tell me, by the way, that the dead look peaceful. Most of the corpses I have seen looked devilish.) The friction of the great beast's foot had stripped the skin from his back as neatly as one skins a rabbit. As soon as I saw the dead man I sent an orderly to a friend's house nearby to borrow an elephant rifle. I had already sent back the pony, not wanting it to go mad with fright and throw me if it smelt the elephant.

5 The orderly came back in a few minutes with a rifle and five cartridges, and meanwhile some Burmans had arrived and told us that the elephant was in the paddy fields below, only a few hundred yards away. As I started forward practically the whole population of the quarter flocked out of the houses and followed me. They had seen the rifle and were all shouting excitedly that I was going to shoot the elephant. They had not shown much interest in the elephant when he was merely ravaging their homes, but it was different now that he was to be shot. It was a bit of fun to them, as it would be to an English crowd; besides they wanted the meat. It made me vaguely uneasy. I had no intention of shooting the elephant—I had merely sent for the rifle to defend myself if necessary—and it is always unnerving to have a crowd following you. I marched down the hill, looking and feeling a fool, with the rifle over my shoulder and an ever-growing army of people jostling at my heels. At the bottom, when you got away from the huts, there was a metalled road and beyond that a miry waste of paddy fields a thousand yards across, not yet ploughed but soggy from the first rains and dotted with coarse grass. The elephant was standing eight yards from the road, his left side towards us. He took not the slightest notice of the crowd's approach. He was tearing up bunches of grass, beating them against his knees to clean them and stuffing them into his mouth.

I had halted on the road. As soon as I saw the elephant I knew with perfect certainty that I ought not to shoot him. It is a serious matter to shoot a working elephant—it is comparable to destroying a huge and costly piece of

[6]*Dravidian coolie*: *Dravidian* refers to a large ethnic group from south and central India. A *coolie* is an unskilled laborer.—Eds.

machinery—and obviously one ought not to do it if it can possibly be avoided. And at that distance, peacefully eating, the elephant looked no more dangerous than a cow. I thought then and I think now that his attack of "must" was already passing off; in which case he would merely wander harmlessly about until the mahout came back and caught him. Moreover, I did not in the least want to shoot him. I decided that I would watch him for a little while to make sure that he did not turn savage again, and then go home.

But at that moment I glanced around at the crowd that had followed me. It was an immense crowd, two thousand at the least and growing every minute. It blocked the road for a long distance on either side. I looked at the sea of yellow faces above the garish clothes—faces all happy and excited all over this bit of fun, all certain that the elephant was going to be shot. They were watching me as they would watch a conjurer about to perform a trick. They did not like me, but with the magical rifle in my hands I was momentarily worth watching. And suddenly I realized that I should have to shoot the elephant after all. The people expected it of me and I had got to do it; I could feel their two thousand wills pressing me forward, irresistibly. And it was at this moment, as I stood there with the rifle in my hands, that I first grasped the hollowness, the futility of the white man's dominion in the East. Here was I, the white man with his gun, standing in front of the unarmed native crowd—seemingly the leading actor of the piece; but in reality I was only an absurd puppet pushed to and fro by the will of those yellow faces behind. I perceived in this moment that when the white man turns tyrant it is his own freedom that he destroys. He becomes a sort of hollow, posing dummy, the conventionalized figure of a sahib. For it is the condition of his rule that he shall spend his life in trying to impress the "natives," and so in every crisis he has got to do what the "natives" expect of him. He wears a mask, and his face grows to fit it. I had got to shoot the elephant. I had committed myself to doing it when I sent for the rifle. A sahib has got to act like a sahib; he has got to appear resolute, to know his own mind and do definite things. To come all that way, rifle in hand, with two thousand people marching at my heels, and then to trail feebly away, having done nothing—no, that was impossible. The crowd would laugh at me. And my whole life, every white man's life in the East, was one long struggle not to be laughed at.

But I did not want to shoot the elephant. I watched him beating his bunch of grass against his knees, with that preoccupied grandmotherly air that elephants have. It seemed to me that it would be murder to shoot him. At that age I was not squeamish about killing animals, but I had never shot an elephant and never wanted to. (Somehow it always seems worse to kill a *large* animal.) Besides, there was the beast's owner to be considered. Alive, the elephant was worth at least a hundred pounds; dead, he would only be worth the value of his tusks, five pounds, possibly. But I had got to act quickly. I turned to some experienced-looking Burmans who had been there when we arrived, and asked them how the elephant had been behaving. They all said the same thing: he took no notice of you if you left him alone, but he might charge if you went too close to him.

It was perfectly clear to me what I ought to do. I ought to walk up to within, say, twenty-five yards of the elephant and test his behavior. If he charged, I could shoot; if he took no notice of me, it would be safe to leave him until the mahout came back. But also I knew that I was going to do no such thing. I was a poor shot with a rifle and the ground was soft mud into which one would sink at every step. If the elephant charged and I missed him, I should have about as much chance as a toad under a steam-roller. But even then I was not thinking particularly of my own skin, only of the watchful yellow faces behind. For at the moment, with the crowd watching me, I was not afraid in the ordinary sense, as I would have been if I had been alone. A white man mustn't be frightened in front of "natives"; and so, in general, he isn't frightened. The sole thought in my mind was that if anything went wrong those two thousand Burmans would see me pursued, caught, trampled on and reduced to a grinning corpse like that Indian up the hill. And if that happened it was quite probable that some of them would laugh. That would never do. There was only one alternative. I shoved the cartridges into the magazine and lay down on the road to get a better aim.

The crowd grew very still, and a deep, low, happy sigh, as of people who see the theatre curtain go up at last, breathed from innumerable throats. They were going to have their bit of fun after all. The rifle was a beautiful German thing with cross-hair sights. I did not then know that in shooting an elephant one would shoot to cut an imaginary bar running from ear-hole to ear-hole. I ought, therefore, as the elephant was sideways on, to have aimed straight at his ear-hole; actually I aimed several inches in front of this, thinking the brain would be further forward. 10

When I pulled the trigger I did not hear the bang or feel the kick—one never does when a shot goes home—but I heard the devilish roar of glee that went up from the crowd. In that instant, in too short a time, one would have thought, even for the bullet to get there, a mysterious, terrible change had come over the elephant. He neither stirred nor fell, but every line of his body had altered. He looked suddenly stricken, shrunken, immensely old, as though the frightful impact of the bullet had paralyzed him without knocking him down. At last, after what seemed a long time—it might have been five seconds, I dare say—he sagged flabbily to his knees. His mouth slobbered. An enormous senility seemed to have settled upon him. One could have imagined him thousands of years old. I fired again into the same spot. At the second shot he did not collapse but climbed with desperate slowness to his feet and stood weakly upright, with legs sagging and head drooping. I fired a third time. That was the shot that did for him. You could see the agony of it jolt his whole body and knock the last remnant of strength from his legs. But in falling he seemed for a moment to rise, for as his hind legs collapsed beneath him he seemed to tower upward like a huge rock toppling, his trunk reaching skywards like a tree. He trumpeted, for the first and only time. And then down he came, his belly towards me, with a crash that seemed to shake the ground even where I lay.

I got up. The Burmans were already racing past me across the mud. It was obvious that the elephant would never rise again, but he was not dead. He was breathing very rhythmically with long rattling gasps, his great mound of a side painfully rising and falling. His mouth was wide open—I could see far down into caverns of pale pink throat. I waited for a long time for him to die, but his breathing did not weaken. Finally I fired my two remaining shots into the spot where I thought his heart must be. The thick blood welled out of him like red velvet, but still he did not die. His body did not even jerk when the shots hit him, the tortured breathing continued without a pause. He was dying, very slowly and in great agony, but in some world remote from me where not even a bullet could damage him further. I felt that I had got to put an end to that dreadful noise. It seemed dreadful to see the great beast lying there, powerless to move and yet powerless to die, and not even to be able to finish him. I sent back for my small rifle and poured shot after shot into his heart and down his throat. They seemed to make no impression. The tortured gasps continued as steadily as the ticking of a clock.

In the end I could not stand it any longer and went away. I heard later that it took him half an hour to die. Burmans were bringing dahs[7] and baskets even before I left, and I was told they had stripped his body almost to the bones by the afternoon.

Afterwards, of course, there were endless discussions about the shooting of the elephant. The owner was furious, but he was only an Indian and could do nothing. Besides, legally I had done the right thing, for a mad elephant has to be killed, like a mad dog, if its owner fails to control it. Among the Europeans opinion was divided. The older men said I was right, the younger men said it was a damn shame to shoot an elephant for killing a coolie, because an elephant was worth more than any damn Coringhee coolie. And afterwards I was very glad that the coolie had been killed; it put me legally in the right and it gave me a sufficient pretext for shooting the elephant. I often wondered whether any of the others grasped that I had done it solely to avoid looking a fool.

▪ QUESTIONS

Reading

1. How does Orwell characterize "every white man's life" (paragraph 7) in the East?
2. How do the natives "force" Orwell to shoot the elephant against his better judgment? How does he relate this personal episode to the larger problems of British imperialism?
3. What is Orwell's final reaction to his deed? How literally can we take his statement that he "was very glad that the coolie had been killed" (paragraph 14)?
4. Orwell's recollection of shooting the elephant is shaped to support a specific point or thesis. Where does Orwell state this thesis? Is this placement effective?

---

[7]*dahs*: Large knives.—Eds.

Exploratory Writing

1. From the opening sentence, Orwell displays a remarkable candor concerning his feelings. How does this personal, candid tone add to or detract from the strength of the essay?
2. Although "Shooting an Elephant" seems to be a *reflective*, autobiographical essay, one of Orwell's biographers, Bernard Crick, has suggested that the story may be partly fiction. There is no evidence that Orwell himself actually shot an elephant while he was in Burma. How might your reading of this essay change if you learned that it was pure fiction? How might your reading change if you had proof that it was 100 percent factual?

Making Connections

1. Orwell's narrative focuses on the moral quandary he experienced when confronted with shooting "a mad elephant" (paragraph 14). Choose a claim made by Steven Pinker in his essay "The Moral Instinct" (p. 458) and use it to explore Orwell's quandary. Do Pinker's ideas about morality shed new light on Orwell's experience? If so, how and why? If not, why not?

Essay Writing

1. Write an essay identifying and discussing the ways that Orwell uses irony in "Shooting an Elephant." How does his ironic tone help him make his point?
2. Write an essay reflecting on an ethical dilemma you faced in your own life. What were your choices? How do you feel about the course of action you chose?

REPORTING

Hiroshima

John Berger

After beginning his career as a painter and drawing instructor, John Berger (b. 1926) became one of Britain's most influential art critics. He has achieved recognition as a screenwriter, novelist, and documentary writer. As a Marxist, he is concerned with the ideological and technological conditioning of our ways of seeing both art and the world. In Berger's books, including *Ways of Seeing* (1972), *The Sense of Sight* (1985), and his most recent, *Bento's Sketchbook* (2011), he explores the interrelation between words and images, between verbal and visual meaning. "Hiroshima" first appeared in 1981 in the journal *New Society* and later in *The Sense of Sight*. Berger examines how the facts of nuclear holocaust have been hidden through "a systematic, slow and thorough process of suppression and elimination . . . within the reality of politics." Images, rather than words, Berger asserts, can help us see through the "mask of innocence" that evil wears.

The whole incredible problem begins with the need to reinsert those events of 6 August 1945 back into living consciousness.

I was shown a book last year at the Frankfurt Book Fair. The editor asked me some question about what I thought of its format. I glanced at it quickly and gave some reply. Three months ago I was sent a finished copy of the book. It lay on my desk unopened. Occasionally its title and cover picture caught my eye, but I did not respond. I didn't consider the book urgent, for I believed that I already knew about what I would find within it.

Did I not clearly remember the day—I was in the army in Belfast—when we first heard the news of the bomb dropped on Hiroshima? At how many meetings during the first nuclear disarmament movement had I and others not recalled the meaning of that bomb?

And then, one morning last week, I received a letter from America, accompanying an article written by a friend. This friend is a doctor of philosophy and a Marxist. Furthermore, she is a very generous and warm-hearted woman. The article was about the possibilities of a third world war. Vis-à-vis the Soviet Union she took, I was surprised to read, a position very close to Reagan's. She concluded by evoking the likely scale of destruction which would be caused by nuclear weapons, and then welcomed the positive possibilities that this would offer the socialist revolution in the United States.

It was on that morning that I opened and read the book on my desk. It is called *Unforgettable Fire*.[1] 5

The book consists of drawings and paintings made by people who were in Hiroshima on the day that the bomb was dropped, thirty-six years ago today. Often the pictures are accompanied by a verbal record of what the image represents. None of them is by a professional artist. In 1974, an old man went to the television center in Hiroshima to show to whomever was interested a picture he had painted, entitled "At about 4 pm, 6th August, 1945, near Yurozuyo bridge."

This prompted an idea of launching a television appeal to other survivors of that day to paint or draw their memories of it. Nearly a thousand pictures were sent in, and these were made into an exhibition. The appeal was worded: "Let us leave for posterity pictures about the atomic bomb, drawn by citizens."

Clearly, my interest in these pictures cannot be an art-critical one. One does not musically analyze screams. But after repeatedly looking at them, what began as an impression became a certainty. These were images of hell.

I am not using the word as hyperbole. Between these paintings by women and men who have never painted anything else since leaving school, and who have surely, for the most part, never traveled outside Japan, between these traced memories which had to be exorcised, and the numerous representations of hell in European medieval art, there is a very close affinity.

This affinity is both stylistic and fundamental. And fundamentally it is to do with the situations depicted. The affinity lies in the degree of the multiplication of pain, in the lack of appeal or aid, in the pitilessness, in the equality of wretchedness, and in the disappearance of time. 10

> I am 78 years old. I was living at Midorimachi on the day of the A-bomb blast. Around 9 a.m. that morning, when I looked out of my window, I saw several women coming along the street one after another towards the Hiroshima prefectural hospital. I realized for the first time, as it is sometimes said, that when people are very much frightened hair really does stand on end. The women's hair was, in fact, standing straight up and the skin of their arms was peeled off. I suppose they were around 30 years old.

Time and again, the sober eyewitness accounts recall the surprise and horror of Dante's verses about the Inferno. The temperature at the center of the Hiroshima fireball was 300,000 degrees centigrade. The survivors are called in Japanese *hibakuska*—"those who have seen hell."

> Suddenly, one man who was stark naked came up to me and said in a quavering voice, "Please help me!" He was burned and swollen all over from the effects of the A-bomb. Since I did not recognize him as my neighbor, I asked who he was. He answered that he was Mr. Sasaki, the son of Mr. Ennosuke Sasaki, who had a lumber shop in Funairi town. That morning he had been doing volunteer labor service, evacuating the houses near the prefectural office in Kato town. He had been burned black all over and had started back to his home in Funairi. He looked miserable—burned and sore, and naked with only pieces of his gaiters trailing behind as he walked. Only the part of his hair covered by his soldier's hat was left, as if he was wearing a bowl. When I touched him, his burned skin slipped off. I did not know what to do, so I asked a passing driver to take him to Eba hospital.

Does not this evocation of hell make it easier to forget that these scenes belonged to life? Is there not something conveniently unreal about hell? The whole history of the twentieth century proves otherwise.

Very systematically in Europe the conditions of hells have been constructed. It is not even necessary to list the sites. It is not even necessary to repeat the calculations of the organizers. We know this, and we choose to forget it.

We find it ridiculous or shocking that most of the pages concerning, for example, Trotsky were torn out of official Soviet history. What has been torn out of our history are the pages concerning the experience of the two atom bombs dropped on Japan.

Of course, the facts are there in the textbooks. It may even be that school children learn the dates. But what these facts mean—and originally their meaning was so clear, so monstrously vivid, that every commentator in the world was shocked, and every politician was obliged to say (whilst planning differently), "Never again"—what these facts mean has now been torn out. It has been a systematic, slow, and thorough process of suppression and elimination. This process has been hidden within the reality of politics. 15

Do not misunderstand me. I am not here using the word "reality" ironically, I am not politically naïve. I have the greatest respect for political reality, and I believe that the innocence of political idealists is often very dangerous. What we are considering is how in this case in the West—not in Japan for

How survivors saw it. A painting by Kazuhiro Ishizu, aged 68.

At the Aioi bridge, by Sawami Katagiri, aged 76.

obvious reasons and not in the Soviet Union for different reasons—political and military realities have eliminated another reality.

The eliminated reality is both physical—

> Yokogawa bridge above Tenma river, 6th August 1945, 8:30 a.m.
>
> People crying and moaning were running towards the city. I did not know why. Steam engines were burning at Yokogawa station.
>
> Skin of cow tied to wire.
>
> Skin of girl's hip was hanging down.
>
> "My baby is dead, isn't she?"

and moral.

The political and military arguments have concerned such issues as deterrence, defense systems, relative strike parity, tactical nuclear weapons, and—pathetically—so-called civil defense. Any movement for nuclear disarmament today has to contend with those considerations and dispute their false interpretation. To lose sight of them is to become as apocalyptic as the Bomb and all utopias. (The construction of hells on earth was accompanied in Europe by plans for heavens on earth.)

What has to be redeemed, reinserted, disclosed and never be allowed to be forgotten, is the other reality. Most of the mass means of communication are close to what has been suppressed.

These paintings were shown on Japanese television. Is it conceivable that the BBC would show these pictures on Channel One at a peak hour? Without any reference to "political" and "military" realities, under the straight title, *This Is How It Was, 6th August 1945*? I challenge them to do so.

What happened on that day was, of course, neither the beginning nor the end of the act. It began months, years before, with the planning of the action, and the eventual final decision to drop two bombs on Japan. However much the world was shocked and surprised by the bomb dropped on Hiroshima, it has to be emphasized that it was not a miscalculation, an error, or the result (as can happen in war) of a situation deteriorating so rapidly that it gets out of hand. What happened was consciously and precisely planned. Small scenes like this were part of the plan:

> I was walking along the Hihiyama bridge about 3 p.m. on 7th August. A woman, who looked like an expectant mother, was dead. At her side, a girl of about three years of age brought some water in an empty can she had found. She was trying to let her mother drink from it.
>
> As soon as I saw this miserable scene with the pitiful child, I embraced the girl close to me and cried with her, telling her that her mother was dead.

There was a preparation. And there was an aftermath. The latter included long, lingering deaths, radiation sickness, many fatal illnesses which developed later as a result of exposure to the bomb, and tragic genetical effects on generations yet to be born.

I refrain from giving the statistics: how many hundreds of thousands of dead, how many injured, how many deformed children. Just as I refrain from pointing out how comparatively "small" were the atomic bombs dropped on Japan. Such statistics tend to distract. We consider numbers instead of pain. We calculate instead of judging. We relativize instead of refusing.

It is possible today to arouse popular indignation or anger by speaking of the threat and immorality of terrorism. Indeed, this appears to be the central plank of the rhetoric of the new American foreign policy ("Moscow is the world-base of all terrorism") and of British policy towards Ireland. What is able to shock people about terrorist acts is that often their targets are unselected and innocent—a crowd in a railway station, people waiting for a bus to go home after work. The victims are chosen indiscriminately in the hope of producing a shock effect on political decision-making by their government.

The two bombs dropped on Japan were terrorist actions. The calculation was terrorist. The indiscriminacy was terrorist. The small groups of terrorists operating today are, by comparison, humane killers. 25

Another comparison needs to be made. Today terrorist groups mostly represent small nations or groupings who are disputing large powers in a position of strength. Whereas Hiroshima was perpetrated by the most powerful alliance in the world against an enemy who was already prepared to negotiate, and was admitting defeat.

To apply the epithet "terrorist" to the acts of bombing Hiroshima and Nagasaki is logically justifiable, and I do so because it may help to reinsert that act into living consciousness today. Yet the word changes nothing in itself.

The firsthand evidence of the victims, the reading of the pages which have been torn out, provokes a sense of outrage. This outrage has two natural faces. One is a sense of horror and pity at what happened; the other face is self-defensive and declares: *This should not happen again (here).* For some the *here* is in brackets, for others it is not.

The face of horror, the reaction which has now been mostly suppressed, forces us to comprehend the reality of what happened. The second reaction, unfortunately, distances us from that reality. Although it begins as a straight declaration, it quickly leads into the labyrinth of defense policies, military arguments, and global strategies. Finally it leads to the sordid commercial absurdity of private fall-out shelters.

This split of the sense of outrage into, on one hand, horror, and, on the other hand, expediency occurs because the concept of evil has been abandoned. Every culture, except our own in recent times, has had such a concept. 30

That its religious or philosophical bases vary is unimportant. The concept of evil implies a force or forces which have to be continually struggled against so that they do not triumph over life and destroy it. One of the very first written texts from Mesopotamia, 1,500 years before Homer, speaks of this struggle, which was the first condition of human life. In public thinking nowadays, the concept of evil has been reduced to a little adjective to support an opinion or hypothesis (abortions, terrorism, ayatollahs).

Nobody can confront the reality of 6th August 1945 without being forced to acknowledge that what happened was evil. It is not a question of opinion or interpretation, but of events.

The memory of these events should be continually before our eyes. This is why the thousand citizens of Hiroshima started to draw on their little scraps of paper. We need to show their drawings everywhere. These terrible images can now release an energy for opposing evil and for the lifelong struggle of that opposition.

And from this a very old lesson may be drawn. My friend in the United States is, in a sense, innocent. She looks beyond a nuclear holocaust without considering its reality. This reality includes not only its victims but also its planners and those who support them. Evil from time immemorial has often worn a mask of innocence. One of evil's principal modes of being is *looking beyond* (with indifference) that which is before the eyes.

> August 9th: On the west embankment of a military training field was a young boy four or five years old. He was burned black, lying on his back, with his arms pointing towards heaven.

Only by looking beyond or away can one come to believe that such evil is relative, and therefore under certain conditions justifiable. In reality—the reality to which the survivors and the dead bear witness—it can never be justified. 35

Note

1. Edited by Japan Broadcasting Corporation, London, Wildwood House, 1981; New York, Pantheon, 1981.

▪ QUESTIONS

Reading

1. Berger begins his essay with this powerful sentence: "The whole incredible problem begins with the need to reinsert those events of 6 August 1945 back into living consciousness." What is "the whole incredible problem," as Berger describes and defines it?
2. Berger argues that what happened on August 6, 1945, was "consciously and precisely planned" (paragraph 21). Highlight, underline, or flag the evidence he uses to support this claim. How does this argument support his larger purpose?
3. What does Berger mean by the term *expediency* (paragraph 30)?

Exploratory Writing

1. Berger argues that reviving the concept of "evil" is the only way anybody can "confront the reality of 6th August 1945." He writes, "It is not a question of opinion or interpretation, but of events" (paragraph 31). In your own words, write a definition of *evil*. How is your characterization of evil different from Berger's?
2. Spend some time looking at and thinking about the paintings by survivors Kazuhiro Ishizu and Sawami Katagiri, reprinted on pages 238 and 239. What do you *see* in these paintings? List at least twenty nouns that capture what these images represent to you.
3. Collaborating in small groups, find survivor depictions — whether photographs, oral or written accounts, or paintings — of a recent tragedy or atrocity. Prepare a presentation in which you lay out a strong argument about why it is essential for the public to be exposed to these documents.

Making Connections

1. Berger challenges the BBC to show paintings from survivors of the Hiroshima bombings on Channel One at peak hour, the way they were shown on Japanese television, "[w]ithout any reference to 'political' and 'military' realities" (paragraph 20). In your opinion, do the firsthand stories from American soldiers serving in Iraq (p. 374) show the reality of "how it was"?
2. In her essay "Regarding the Pain of Others" (p. 366), Susan Sontag makes an argument about war photographs. How different are Berger's arguments and conclusions about drawings and paintings that depict war? Do the two essays contradict or reinforce each other?

Essay Writing

1. This essay about Hiroshima was first published in 1981. Write your own essay reflecting on what the term *terrorist* means to you. Include a summary of Berger's characterization of terrorism and terrorist actions. Consider Berger's comments about the use of the word *terrorist* in light of the ways the term has been applied to more recent events.

REPORTING

Nickel and Dimed

On (Not) Getting By in America

Barbara Ehrenreich

A native of Butte, Montana, Barbara Ehrenreich (b. 1941) is one of the country's most outspoken social critics. After graduating from Reed College, Ehrenreich earned a PhD in biology from Roosevelt University in Chicago. Instead of becoming a research scientist, she decided to pursue liberal political activism. According to Ehrenreich, as she began working on leaflets and newsletters, writing "crept up on" her. She was soon a regular contributor to *Ms.* magazine and has since written for the *New Republic, Mother Jones,* and *Time*, among many other periodicals. Ehrenreich's books include *Complaints and Disorders: The Sexual Politics of Sickness* (1973), *Fear of Falling: The Inner Life of the Middle Class* (1989), *The Worst Years of Our Lives: Irreverent Notes from the Decade of Greed* (1990), *Blood Rites: Origins and History of the Passions of War* (1997), *Bait and Switch: The (Futile) Pursuit of the American Dream* (2005), *This Land Is Their Land: Reports from a Divided Nation* (2009), and *Bright-Sided: How the Relentless Promotion of Positive Thinking Has Undermined America* (2009). The recipient of a Guggenheim Fellowship and a MacArthur grant, Ehrenreich contributed the following essay, which provided the basis for her 2001 book of the same title, to the *Atlantic* in 1999. As she later told an interviewer, it began in a meeting with the editor of the magazine when "the conversation drifted to talking about welfare reform and the assumption that these single moms could just get out there in the workforce and get a job and then everything would be okay. They'd be lifted out of poverty. We were both agreeing that nobody seems to see that the math doesn't work. That's when I made this, perhaps disastrous, suggestion that somebody should go out there and do the old-fashioned kind of journalism, just try it for themselves and write about it. I did not expect him to say, 'Yeah, great idea. It should be you.'"

At the beginning of June 1998 I leave behind everything that normally soothes the ego and sustains the body—home, career, companion, reputation, ATM card—for a plunge into the low-wage workforce. There, I become another, occupationally much diminished "Barbara Ehrenreich"—depicted on job-application forms as a divorced homemaker whose sole work experience consists of housekeeping in a few private homes. I am terrified, at the beginning, of being unmasked for what I am: a middle-class journalist setting out to explore the world that welfare mothers are entering, at the rate of approximately fifty thousand a month, as welfare reform kicks in. Happily, though, my fears turn out to be entirely unwarranted: During a month of poverty and toil, my name goes unnoticed and for the most part unuttered. In this parallel universe where my father never got out of the mines and I never got through college, I am "baby," "honey," "blondie," and, most commonly, "girl."

My first task is to find a place to live. I figure that if I can earn $7 an hour—which, from the want ads, seems doable—I can afford to spend $500 on rent, or maybe, with severe economies, $600. In the Key West area, where I live, this pretty much confines me to flophouses and trailer homes—like the one, a pleasing fifteen-minute drive from town, that has no air-conditioning, no screens, no fans, no television, and, by way of diversion, only the challenge of evading the landlord's Doberman pinscher. The big problem with this place, though, is the rent, which at $675 a month is well beyond my reach. All right, Key West is expensive. But so is New York City, or the Bay Area, or Jackson Hole, or Telluride, or Boston, or any other place where tourists and the wealthy compete for living space with the people who clean their toilets and fry their hash browns.[1] Still, it is a shock to realize that "trailer trash" has become, for me, a demographic category to aspire to.

So I decide to make the common trade-off between affordability and convenience, and go for a $500-a-month efficiency thirty miles up a two-lane highway from the employment opportunities of Key West, meaning forty-five minutes if there's no road construction and I don't get caught behind some sun-dazed Canadian tourists. I hate the drive, along a roadside studded with white crosses commemorating the more effective head-on collisions, but it's a sweet little place—a cabin, more or less, set in the swampy back yard of the converted mobile home where my landlord, an affable TV repairman, lives with his bartender girlfriend. Anthropologically speaking, a bustling trailer park would be preferable, but here I have a gleaming white floor and a firm mattress, and the few resident bugs are easily vanquished.

Besides, I am not doing this for the anthropology. My aim is nothing so mistily subjective as to "experience poverty" or find out how it "really feels" to be a long-term low-wage worker. I've had enough unchosen encounters with poverty and the world of low-wage work to know it's not a place you want to visit for touristic purposes; it just smells too much like fear. And with all my real-life assets—bank account, IRA, health insurance, multiroom home—waiting indulgently in the background, I am, of course, thoroughly insulated from the terrors that afflict the genuinely poor.

5 No, this is a purely objective, scientific sort of mission. The humanitarian rationale for welfare reform—as opposed to the more punitive and stingy impulses that may actually have motivated it—is that work will lift poor women out of poverty while simultaneously inflating their self-esteem and hence their future value in the labor market. Thus, whatever the hassles involved in finding child care, transportation, etc., the transition from welfare to work will end happily, in greater prosperity for all. Now there are many problems with this comforting prediction, such as the fact that the economy will inevitably

---

[1]According to the Department of Housing and Urban Development, the "fair-market rent" for an efficiency is $551 here in Monroe County, Florida. A comparable rent in the five boroughs of New York City is $704; in San Francisco, $713; and in the heart of Silicon Valley, $808. The fair-market rent for an area is defined as the amount that would be needed to pay rent plus utilities for "privately owned, decent, safe, and sanitary rental housing of a modest (non-luxury) nature with suitable amenities."

undergo a downturn, eliminating many jobs. Even without a downturn, the influx of a million former welfare recipients into the low-wage labor market could depress wages by as much as 11.9 percent, according to the Economic Policy Institute (EPI) in Washington, D.C.

But is it really possible to make a living on the kinds of jobs currently available to unskilled people? Mathematically, the answer is no, as can be shown by taking $6 to $7 an hour, perhaps subtracting a dollar or two an hour for child care, multiplying by 160 hours a month, and comparing the result to the prevailing rents. According to the National Coalition for the Homeless, for example, in 1998 it took, on average nationwide, an hourly wage of $8.89 to afford a one-bedroom apartment, and the Preamble Center for Public Policy estimates that the odds against a typical welfare recipient's landing a job at such a "living wage" are about 97 to 1. If these numbers are right, low-wage work is not a solution to poverty and possibly not even to homelessness.

It may seem excessive to put this proposition to an experimental test. As certain family members keep unhelpfully reminding me, the viability of low-wage work could be tested, after a fashion, without ever leaving my study. I could just pay myself $7 an hour for eight hours a day, charge myself for room and board, and total up the numbers after a month. Why leave the people and work that I love? But I am an experimental scientist by training. In that business, you don't just sit at a desk and theorize; you plunge into the everyday chaos of nature, where surprises lurk in the most mundane measurements. Maybe, when I got into it, I would discover some hidden economies in the world of the low-wage worker. After all, if 30 percent of the workforce toils for less than $8 an hour, according to the EPI, they may have found some tricks as yet unknown to me. Maybe—who knows?—I would even be able to detect in myself the bracing psychological effects of getting out of the house, as promised by the welfare wonks at places like the Heritage Foundation. Or, on the other hand, maybe there would be unexpected costs—physical, mental, or financial— to throw off all my calculations. Ideally, I should do this with two small children in tow, that being the welfare average, but mine are grown and no one is willing to lend me theirs for a month-long vacation in penury. So this is not the perfect experiment, just a test of the best possible case: an unencumbered woman, smart and even strong, attempting to live more or less off the land.

On the morning of my first full day of job searching, I take a red pen to the want ads, which are auspiciously numerous. Everyone in Key West's booming "hospitality industry" seems to be looking for someone like me—trainable, flexible, and with suitably humble expectations as to pay. I know I possess certain traits that might be advantageous—I'm white and, I like to think, well-spoken and poised—but I decide on two rules: One, I cannot use any skills derived from my education or usual work—not that there are a lot of want ads for satirical essayists anyway. Two, I have to take the best-paid job that is offered me and of course do my best to hold it; no Marxist rants or sneaking off to read novels in the ladies' room. In addition, I rule out various occupations for one reason or another: Hotel front-desk clerk, for example, which to my surprise is regarded as unskilled and pays around $7 an hour, gets eliminated because it involves standing in one spot for eight hours a day. Waitressing is similarly something I'd like to avoid, because I remember it leaving me bone tired when I was eighteen, and I'm decades of varicosities and back pain beyond that now. Telemarketing, one of the first refuges of the suddenly indigent, can be dismissed on grounds of personality. This leaves certain supermarket jobs, such as deli clerk, or housekeeping in Key West's thousands of hotel and guest rooms. Housekeeping is especially appealing, for reasons both atavistic and practical: It's what my mother did before I came along, and it can't be too different from what I've been doing part-time, in my own home, all my life.

So I put on what I take to be a respectful-looking outfit of ironed Bermuda shorts and scooped-neck T-shirt and set out for a tour of the local hotels and supermarkets. Best Western, Econo Lodge, and HoJo's all let me fill out application forms, and these are, to my relief, interested in little more than whether I am a legal resident of the United States and have committed any felonies. My next stop is Winn-Dixie, the supermarket, which turns out to have a particularly onerous application process, featuring a fifteen-minute "interview" by computer since, apparently, no human on the premises is deemed capable of representing the corporate point of view. I am conducted to a large room decorated with posters illustrating how to look "professional" (it helps to be white and, if female, permed) and warning of the slick promises that union organizers might try to tempt me with. The interview is multiple choice: Do I have anything, such as childcare problems, that might make it hard for me to get to work on time? Do I think safety on the job is the responsibility of management? Then, popping up cunningly out of the blue: How many dollars' worth of stolen goods have I purchased in the last year? Would I turn in a fellow employee if I caught him stealing? Finally, "Are you an honest person?"

Apparently, I ace the interview, because I am told that all I have to do is show up in some doctor's office tomorrow for a urine test. This seems to be a fairly general rule: If you want to stack Cheerio boxes or vacuum hotel rooms in chemically fascist America, you have to be willing to squat down and pee in front of some health worker (who has no doubt had to do the same thing herself). The wages Winn-Dixie is offering—$6 and a couple of dimes to start with—are not enough, I decide, to compensate for this indignity.[2] 10

I lunch at Wendy's, where $4.99 gets you unlimited refills at the Mexican part of the Super-bar, a comforting surfeit of refried beans and "cheese sauce." A teenage employee, seeing me studying the want ads, kindly offers me an application form, which I fill out, though here, too, the pay is just $6 and

[2]According to the *Monthly Labor Review* (November 1996), 28 percent of work sites surveyed in the service industry conduct drug tests (corporate workplaces have much higher rates), and the incidence of testing has risen markedly since the eighties. The rate of testing is highest in the South (56 percent of work sites polled), with the Midwest in second place (50 percent). The drug most likely to be detected—marijuana, which can be detected in urine for weeks—is also the most innocuous, while heroin and cocaine are generally undetectable three days after use. Prospective employees sometimes try to cheat the tests by consuming excessive amounts of liquids and taking diuretics and even masking substances available through the Internet.

change an hour. Then it's off for a round of the locally owned inns and guesthouses. At "The Palms," let's call it, a bouncy manager actually takes me around to see the rooms and meet the existing housekeepers, who, I note with satisfaction, look pretty much like me—faded ex-hippie types in shorts with long hair pulled back in braids. Mostly, though, no one speaks to me or even looks at me except to proffer an application form. At my last stop, a palatial B&B, I wait twenty minutes to meet "Max," only to be told that there are no jobs now but there should be one soon, since "nobody lasts more than a couple weeks." (Because none of the people I talked to knew I was a reporter, I have changed their names to protect their privacy and, in some cases perhaps, their jobs.)

Three days go by like this, and, to my chagrin, no one out of the approximately twenty places I've applied calls me for an interview. I had been vain enough to worry about coming across as too educated for the jobs I sought, but no one even seems interested in finding out how overqualified I am. Only later will I realize that the want ads are not a reliable measure of the actual jobs available at any particular time. They are, as I should have guessed from Max's comment, the employers' insurance policy against the relentless turnover of the low-wage workforce. Most of the big hotels run ads almost continually, just to build a supply of applicants to replace the current workers as they drift away or are fired, so finding a job is just a matter of being at the right place at the right time and flexible enough to take whatever is being offered that day. This finally happens to me at one of the big discount hotel chains, where I go, as usual, for housekeeping and am sent, instead, to try out as a waitress at the attached "family restaurant," a dismal spot with a counter and about thirty tables that looks out on a parking garage and features such tempting fare as "Pollish [sic] sausage and BBQ sauce" on 95-degree days. Phillip, the dapper young West Indian who introduces himself as the manager, interviews me with about as much enthusiasm as if he were a clerk processing me for Medicare, the principal questions being what shifts can I work and when can I start. I mutter something about being woefully out of practice as a waitress, but he's already on to the uniform: I'm to show up tomorrow wearing black slacks and black shoes; he'll provide the rust-colored polo shirt with HEARTHSIDE embroidered on it, though I might want to wear my own shirt to get to work, ha ha. At the word "tomorrow," something between fear and indignation rises in my chest. I want to say, "Thank you for your time, sir, but this is just an experiment, you know, not my actual life."

So begins my career at the Hearthside, I shall call it, one small profit center within a global discount hotel chain, where for two weeks I work from 2:00 till 10:00 p.m. for $2.43 an hour plus tips.[3] In some futile bid for gentility, the

[3]According to the Fair Labor Standards Act, employers are not required to pay "tipped employees," such as restaurant servers, more than $2.13 an hour in direct wages. However, if the sum of tips plus $2.13 an hour falls below the minimum wage, or $5.15 an hour, the employer is required to make up the difference. This fact was not mentioned by managers or otherwise publicized at either of the restaurants where I worked.

management has barred employees from using the front door, so my first day I enter through the kitchen, where a red-faced man with shoulder-length blond hair is throwing frozen steaks against the wall and yelling, "Fuck this shit!" "That's just Jack," explains Gail, the wiry middle-aged waitress who is assigned to train me. "He's on the rag again"—a condition occasioned, in this instance, by the fact that the cook on the morning shift had forgotten to thaw out the steaks. For the next eight hours, I run after the agile Gail, absorbing bits of instruction along with fragments of personal tragedy. All food must be trayed, and the reason she's so tired today is that she woke up in a cold sweat thinking of her boyfriend, who killed himself recently in an upstate prison. No refills on lemonade. And the reason he was in prison is that a few DUIs caught up with him, that's all, could have happened to anyone. Carry the creamers to the table in a monkey bowl, never in your hand. And after he was gone she spent several months living in her truck, peeing in a plastic pee bottle and reading by candlelight at night, but you can't live in a truck in the summer, since you need to have the windows down, which means anything can get in, from mosquitoes on up.

At least Gail puts to rest any fears I had of appearing overqualified. From the first day on, I find that of all the things I have left behind, such as home and identity, what I miss the most is competence. Not that I have ever felt utterly competent in the writing business, in which one day's success augurs nothing at all for the next. But in my writing life, I at least have some notion of procedure: Do the research, make the outline, rough out a draft, etc. As a server, though, I am beset by requests like bees: More iced tea here, ketchup over there, a to-go box for table fourteen, and where are the high chairs, anyway? Of the twenty-seven tables, up to six are usually mine at any time, though on slow afternoons or if Gail is off, I sometimes have the whole place to myself. There is the touch-screen computer-ordering system to master, which is, I suppose, meant to minimize server-cook contact, but in practice requires constant verbal fine-tuning: "That's gravy on the mashed, okay? None on the meatloaf," and so forth—while the cook scowls as if I were inventing these refinements just to torment him. Plus, something I had forgotten in the years since I was eighteen: About a third of a server's job is "side work" that's invisible to customers—sweeping, scrubbing, slicing, refilling, and restocking. If it isn't all done, every little bit of it, you're going to face the 6:00 p.m. dinner rush defenseless and probably go down in flames. I screw up dozens of times at the beginning, sustained in my shame entirely by Gail's support—"It's okay, baby, everyone does that sometime"—because, to my total surprise and despite the scientific detachment I am doing my best to maintain, I care.

15 The whole thing would be a lot easier if I could just skate through it as Lily Tomlin in one of her waitress skits, but I was raised by the absurd Booker T. Washingtonian precept that says: If you're going to do something, do it well. In fact, "well" isn't good enough by half. Do it better than anyone has ever done it before. Or so said my father, who must have known what he was talking

about because he managed to pull himself, and us with him, up from the mile-deep copper mines of Butte to the leafy suburbs of the Northeast, ascending from boilermakers to martinis before booze beat out ambition. As in most endeavors I have encountered in my life, doing it "better than anyone" is not a reasonable goal. Still, when I wake up at 4:00 a.m. in my own cold sweat, I am not thinking about the writing deadlines I'm neglecting; I'm thinking about the table whose order I screwed up so that one of the boys didn't get his kiddie meal until the rest of the family had moved on to their Key lime pies. That's the other powerful motivation I hadn't expected—the customers, or "patients," as I can't help thinking of them on account of the mysterious vulnerability that seems to have left them temporarily unable to feed themselves. After a few days at the Hearthside, I feel the service ethic kick in like a shot of oxytocin, the nurturance hormone. The plurality of my customers are hard-working locals—truck drivers, construction workers, even housekeepers from the attached hotel—and I want them to have the closest to a "fine dining" experience that the grubby circumstances will allow. No "you guys" for me; everyone over twelve is "sir" or "ma'am." I ply them with iced tea and coffee refills; I return, mid-meal, to inquire how everything is; I doll up their salads with chopped raw mushrooms, summer squash slices, or whatever bits of produce I can find that have survived their sojourn in the cold-storage room mold-free.

There is Benny, for example, a short, tight-muscled sewer repairman, who cannot even think of eating until he has absorbed a half hour of air-conditioning and ice water. We chat about hyperthermia and electrolytes until he is ready to order some finicky combination like soup of the day, garden salad, and a side of grits. There are the German tourists who are so touched by my pidgin "Willkommen" and "Ist alles gut?" that they actually tip. (Europeans, spoiled by their trade-union-ridden, high-wage welfare states, generally do not know that they are supposed to tip. Some restaurants, the Hearthside included, allow servers to "grat" their foreign customers, or add a tip to the bill. Since this amount is added before the customers have a chance to tip or not tip, the practice amounts to an automatic penalty for imperfect English.) There are the two dirt-smudged lesbians, just off their construction shift, who are impressed enough by my suave handling of the fly in the piña colada that they take the time to praise me to Stu, the assistant manager. There's Sam, the kindly retired cop, who has to plug up his tracheotomy hole with one finger in order to force the cigarette smoke into his lungs.

Sometimes I play with the fantasy that I am a princess who, in penance for some tiny transgression, has undertaken to feed each of her subjects by hand. But the non-princesses working with me are just as indulgent, even when this means flouting management rules—concerning, for example, the number of croutons that can go on a salad (six). "Put on all you want," Gail whispers, "as long as Stu isn't looking." She dips into her own tip money to buy biscuits and gravy for an out-of-work mechanic who's used up all his money on dental surgery, inspiring me to pick up the tab for his milk and pie. Maybe the same high levels of agape can be found throughout the "hospitality industry." I remember the poster decorating one of the apartments I looked at, which said "If you seek happiness for yourself you will never find it. Only when you seek happiness for others will it come to you," or words to that effect—an odd sentiment, it seemed to me at the time, to find in the dank one-room basement apartment of a bellhop at the Best Western. At the Hearthside, we utilize whatever bits of autonomy we have to ply our customers with the illicit calories that signal our love. It is our job as servers to assemble the salads and desserts, pouring the dressings and squirting the whipped cream. We also control the number of butter patties our customers get and the amount of sour cream on their baked potatoes. So if you wonder why Americans are so obese, consider the fact that waitresses both express their humanity and earn their tips through the covert distribution of fats.

Ten days into it, this is beginning to look like a livable lifestyle. I like Gail, who is "looking at fifty" but moves so fast she can alight in one place and then another without apparently being anywhere between them. I clown around with Lionel, the teenage Haitian busboy, and catch a few fragments of conversation with Joan, the svelte fortyish hostess and militant feminist who is the only one of us who dares to tell Jack to shut the fuck up. I even warm up to Jack when, on a slow night and to make up for a particularly unwarranted attack on my abilities, or so I imagine, he tells me about his glory days as a young man at "coronary school"—or do you say "culinary"?—in Brooklyn, where he dated a knock-out Puerto Rican chick and learned everything there is to know about food. I finish up at 10:00 or 10:30, depending on how much side work I've been able to get done during the shift, and cruise home to the tapes I snatched up at random when I left my real home—Marianne Faithfull, Tracy Chapman, Enigma, King Sunny Ade, the Violent Femmes—just drained enough for the music to set my cranium resonating but hardly dead. Midnight snack is Wheat Thins and Monterey Jack, accompanied by cheap white wine on ice and whatever AMC has to offer. To bed by 1:30 or 2:00, up at 9:00 or 10:00, read for an hour while my uniform whirls around in the landlord's washing machine, and then it's another eight hours spent following Mao's central instruction, as laid out in the Little Red Book, which was: Serve the people.

I could drift along like this, in some dreamy proletarian idyll, except for two things. One is management. If I have kept this subject on the margins thus far it is because I still flinch to think that I spent all those weeks under the surveillance of men (and later, women) whose job it was to monitor my behavior for signs of sloth, theft, drug abuse, or worse. Not that managers and especially "assistant managers" in low-wage settings like this are exactly the class enemy. In the restaurant business, they are mostly former cooks or servers, still capable of pinch-hitting in the kitchen or on the floor, just as in hotels they are likely to be former clerks, and paid a salary of only about $400 a week. But everyone knows they have crossed over to the other side, which is, crudely put, corporate as opposed to human. Cooks want to prepare tasty meals; servers want to serve them graciously; but managers are there for only one reason—to make sure that money is made for some theoretical entity that exists far away in Chicago or New York, if a corporation can be said to have a physical existence at all. Reflecting on her career, Gail tells me ruefully that she had sworn, years ago, never to work for a corporation again. "They don't cut you no slack. You give and you give, and they take."

Managers can sit—for hours at a time if they want—but it's their job to see that no one else ever does, even when there's nothing to do, and this is why, for servers, slow times can be as exhausting as rushes. You start dragging out each little chore, because if the manager on duty catches you in an idle moment, he will give you something far nastier to do. So I wipe, I clean, I consolidate ketchup bottles and recheck the cheesecake supply, even tour the tables to make sure the customer evaluation forms are all standing perkily in their places—wondering all the time how many calories I burn in these strictly theatrical exercises. When, on a particularly dead afternoon, Stu finds me glancing at a *USA Today* a customer has left behind, he assigns me to vacuum the entire floor with the broken vacuum cleaner that has a handle only two feet long, and the only way to do that without incurring orthopedic damage is to proceed from spot to spot on your knees. 20

On my first Friday at the Hearthside there is a "mandatory meeting for all restaurant employees," which I attend, eager for insight into our overall marketing strategy and the niche (your basic Ohio cuisine with a tropical twist?) we aim to inhabit. But there is no "we" at this meeting. Phillip, our top manager except for an occasional "consultant" sent out by corporate headquarters, opens it with a sneer: "The break room—it's disgusting. Butts in the ashtrays, newspapers lying around, crumbs." This windowless little room, which also houses the time clock for the entire hotel, is where we stash our bags and civilian clothes and take our half-hour meal breaks. But a break room is not a right, he tells us. It can be taken away. We should also know that the lockers in the break room and whatever is in them can be searched at any time. Then comes gossip; there has been gossip; gossip (which seems to mean employees talking among themselves) must stop. Off-duty employees are henceforth barred from eating at the restaurant, because "other servers gather around them and gossip." When Phillip has exhausted his agenda of rebukes, Joan complains about the condition of the ladies' room and I throw in my two bits about the vacuum cleaner. But I don't see any backup coming from my fellow servers, each of whom has subsided into her own personal funk; Gail, my role model, stares sorrowfully at a point six inches from her nose. The meeting ends when Andy, one of the cooks, gets up, muttering about breaking up his day off for this almighty bullshit.

Just four days later we are suddenly summoned into the kitchen at 3:30 p.m., even though there are live tables on the floor. We all—about ten of us— stand around Phillip, who announces grimly that there has been a report of some "drug activity" on the night shift and that, as a result, we are now to be a "drug-free" workplace, meaning that all new hires will be tested, as will possibly current employees on a random basis. I am glad that this part of the kitchen is so dark, because I find myself blushing as hard as if I had been caught toking up in the ladies' room myself: I haven't been treated this way—lined up in the corridor, threatened with locker searches, peppered with carelessly aimed accusations—since junior high school. Back on the floor, Joan cracks, "Next they'll be telling us we can't have sex on the job." When I ask Stu what happened to inspire the crackdown, he just mutters about "management decisions" and takes the opportunity to upbraid Gail and me for being too generous with the rolls. From now on there's to be only one per customer, and it goes out with the dinner, not with the salad. He's also been riding the cooks, prompting Andy to come out of the kitchen and observe—with the serenity of a man whose customary implement is a butcher knife—that "Stu has a death wish today."

Later in the evening, the gossip crystallizes around the theory that Stu is himself the drug culprit, that he uses the restaurant phone to order up marijuana and sends one of the late servers out to fetch it for him. The server was caught, and she may have ratted Stu out or at least said enough to cast some suspicion on him, thus accounting for his pissy behavior. Who knows? Lionel, the busboy, entertains us for the rest of the shift by standing just behind Stu's back and sucking deliriously on an imaginary joint.

The other problem, in addition to the less-than-nurturing management style, is that this job shows no sign of being financially viable. You might imagine, from a comfortable distance, that people who live, year in and year out, on $6 to $10 an hour have discovered some survival stratagems unknown to the middle class. But no. It's not hard to get my coworkers to talk about their living situations, because housing, in almost every case, is the principal source of disruption in their lives, the first thing they fill you in on when they arrive for their shifts. After a week, I have compiled the following survey:

- Gail is sharing a room in a well-known downtown flophouse for which she and a roommate pay about $250 a week. Her roommate, a male friend, has begun hitting on her, driving her nuts, but the rent would be impossible alone.
- Claude, the Haitian cook, is desperate to get out of the two-room apartment he shares with his girlfriend and two other, unrelated, people. As far as I can determine, the other Haitian men (most of whom only speak Creole) live in similarly crowded situations.
- Annette, a twenty-year-old server who is six months pregnant and has been abandoned by her boyfriend, lives with her mother, a postal clerk.
- Marianne and her boyfriend are paying $170 a week for a one-person trailer.
- Jack, who is, at $10 an hour, the wealthiest of us, lives in the trailer he owns, paying only the $400-a-month lot fee.
- The other white cook, Andy, lives on his dry-docked boat, which, as far as I can tell from his loving descriptions, can't be more than twenty feet long. He offers to take me out on it, once it's repaired, but the offer comes with inquiries as to my marital status, so I do not follow up on it.

- Tina and her husband are paying $60 a night for a double room in a Days Inn. This is because they have no car and the Days Inn is within walking distance of the Hearthside. When Marianne, one of the breakfast servers, is tossed out of her trailer for subletting (which is against the trailer-park rules), she leaves her boyfriend and moves in with Tina and her husband.
- Joan, who had fooled me with her numerous and tasteful outfits (hostesses wear their own clothes), lives in a van she parks behind a shopping center at night and showers in Tina's motel room. The clothes are from thrift shops.[4]

It strikes me, in my middle-class solipsism, that there is gross improvidence in some of these arrangements. When Gail and I are wrapping silverware in napkins—the only task for which we are permitted to sit—she tells me she is thinking of escaping from her roommate by moving into the Days Inn herself. I am astounded: How can she even think of paying between $40 and $60 a day? But if I was afraid of sounding like a social worker, I come out just sounding like a fool. She squints at me in disbelief, "And where am I supposed to get a month's rent and a month's deposit for an apartment?" I'd been feeling pretty smug about my $500 efficiency, but of course it was made possible only by the $1,300 I had allotted myself for start-up costs when I began my low-wage life: $1,000 for the first month's rent and deposit, $100 for initial groceries and cash in my pocket, $200 stuffed away for emergencies. In poverty, as in certain propositions in physics, starting conditions are everything. 25

There are no secret economies that nourish the poor; on the contrary, there are a host of special costs. If you can't put up the two months' rent you need to secure an apartment, you end up paying through the nose for a room by the week. If you have only a room, with a hot plate at best, you can't save by cooking up huge lentil stews that can be frozen for the week ahead. You eat fast food, or the hot dogs and styrofoam cups of soup that can be microwaved in a convenience store. If you have no money for health insurance—and the Hearthside's niggardly plan kicks in only after three months—you go without routine care or prescription drugs and end up paying the price. Gail, for example, was fine until she ran out of money for estrogen pills. She is supposed to be on the company plan by now, but they claim to have lost her application form and need to begin the paperwork all over again. So she spends $9 per migraine pill to control the headaches she wouldn't have, she insists, if her estrogen supplements were covered. Similarly, Marianne's boyfriend lost his job as a roofer because he missed so much time after getting a cut on his foot for which he couldn't afford the prescribed antibiotic.

My own situation, when I sit down to assess it after two weeks of work, would

---

[4]I could find no statistics on the number of employed people living in cars or vans, but according to the National Coalition for the Homeless's 1997 report "Myths and Facts about Homelessness," nearly one in five homeless people (in twenty-nine cities across the nation) is employed in a full- or part-time job.

not be much better if this were my actual life. The seductive thing about waitressing is that you don't have to wait for payday to feel a few bills in your pocket, and my tips usually cover meals and gas, plus something left over to stuff into the kitchen drawer I use as a bank. But as the tourist business slows in the summer heat, I sometimes leave work with only $20 in tips (the gross is higher, but servers share about 15 percent of their tips with the busboys and bartenders). With wages included, this amounts to about the minimum wage of $5.15 an hour. Although the sum in the drawer is piling up, at the present rate of accumulation it will be more than a hundred dollars short of my rent when the end of the month comes around. Nor can I see any expenses to cut. True, I haven't gone the lentil-stew route yet, but that's because I don't have a large cooking pot, pot holders, or a ladle to stir with (which cost about $30 at Kmart, less at thrift stores), not to mention onions, carrots, and the indispensable bay leaf. I do make my lunch almost every day—usually some slow-burning, high-protein combo like frozen chicken patties with melted cheese on top and canned pinto beans on the side. Dinner is at the Hearthside, which offers its employees a choice of BLT, fish sandwich, or hamburger for only $2. The burger lasts longest, especially if it's heaped with gut-puckering jalapeños, but by midnight my stomach is growling again. . . .

In one month, I had earned approximately $1,040 and spent $517 on food, gas, toiletries, laundry, phone, and utilities. If I had remained in my $500 efficiency, I would have been able to pay the rent and have $22 left over (which is $78 less than the cash I had in my pocket at the start of the month). During this time I bought no clothing except for the required slacks and no prescription drugs or medical care (I did finally buy some vitamin B to compensate for the lack of vegetables in my diet). Perhaps I could have saved a little on food if I had gotten to a supermarket more often, instead of convenience stores, but it should be noted that I lost almost four pounds in four weeks, on a diet weighted heavily toward burgers and fries.

How former welfare recipients and single mothers will (and do) survive in the low-wage workforce, I cannot imagine. Maybe they will figure out how to condense their lives—including child-raising, laundry, romance, and meals—into the couple of hours between full-time jobs. Maybe they will take up residence in their vehicles, if they have one. All I know is that I couldn't hold two jobs and I couldn't make enough money to live on with one. And I had advantages unthinkable to many of the long-term poor—health, stamina, a working car, and no children to care for and support. Certainly nothing in my experience contradicts the conclusion of Kathryn Edin and Laura Lein, in their recent book *Making Ends Meet: How Single Mothers Survive Welfare and Low-Wage Work,* that low-wage work actually involves more hardship and deprivation than life at the mercy of the welfare state. In the coming months and years, economic conditions for the working poor are bound to worsen, even without the almost inevitable recession. As mentioned earlier, the influx of former welfare recipients into the low-skilled workforce will have a depressing effect on both wages and the number of jobs available. A general economic downturn will only enhance these effects, and the working poor will of course be facing it without the slight, but nonetheless often saving, protection of welfare as a backup.

30 The thinking behind welfare reform was that even the humblest jobs are morally uplifting and psychologically buoying. In reality they are likely to be fraught with insult and stress. But I did discover one redeeming feature of the most abject low-wage work—the camaraderie of people who are, in almost all cases, far too smart and funny and caring for the work they do and the wages they're paid. The hope, of course, is that someday these people will come to know what they're worth, and take appropriate action.

▪ QUESTIONS

Reading

1. Ehrenreich tells us in the first paragraph who she is and what she wants to uncover: "I am . . . a middle-class journalist setting out to explore the world that welfare mothers are entering, at the rate of approximately fifty thousand a month, as welfare reform kicks in." In her reportorial essay, what questions does Ehrenreich ask about this world? What strategies does she use, as a reporter, to make readers care about this world?
2. According to Ehrenreich, what is the rationale for welfare reform? Why does she distrust this rationale?
3. Ehrenreich plunges us into the middle of her work life at the Hearthside. Identify the details and images that you find most compelling and memorable. How do these details help her establish her credibility?
4. Ehrenreich points to housing as "the principal source of disruption" (paragraph 24) in her coworkers' lives. Look at her survey of where and how her coworkers live. What does this survey suggest about the difficulties of "(not) getting by in America"?

Exploratory Writing

1. On an episode in the first season of his television series *30 Days*, shot in 2005, documentary filmmaker Morgan Spurlock and his fiancée experimented with spending a month in a new city, living on minimum wage. Like Ehrenreich, they found that it was almost impossible to make ends meet. Find out the minimum wage in your town, and calculate your expenses for the coming month. Discuss how your life would change if you had to get by on minimum wage. Would you need to apply for public assistance?
2. What questions are you asking about work? In groups of two, interview each other about your current job and job history. Report to the class on what you learn in these interviews.
3. "In poverty," writes Ehrenreich, "as in certain propositions in physics, starting conditions are everything" (paragraph 25). Make a double-entry list showing ways that Ehrenreich's relatively privileged "starting conditions" make her life different from the lives of her coworkers. If you need more space, use an extra sheet of paper.

EHRENREICH	COWORKERS

Making Connections

1. Compare Ehrenreich's experiment to Christina Boufis's (p. 96) experiences as a literature teacher in a county jail. Write an essay reflecting on the advantages and disadvantages of observing groups of people from an outside perspective.

Essay Writing

1. Go to the library and research the federal Welfare Reform Act of 1996. What main arguments did members of Congress offer for and against welfare reform during the debates that preceded their vote on the act? Research the consequences of welfare reform within your region or state.

REPORTING

"This Is the End of the World"

The Black Death

Barbara Tuchman

Barbara Wertheim Tuchman (1912–1989) wrote books on historical subjects ranging over six centuries — from the Middle Ages to the Vietnam War. Her careful research and lively writing in books like *The Guns of August* (1962), *A Distant Mirror* (1978), *The March of Folly: From Troy to Vietnam* (1984), and *The First Salute* (1988) pleased not only the general public but many professional historians as well. She twice won the Pulitzer Prize. *A Distant Mirror*, from which the following selection has been taken, was on the *New York Times* best-seller list for more than nine months.

In October 1347, two months after the fall of Calais, Genoese trading ships put into the harbor of Messina in Sicily with dead and dying men at the oars. The ships had come from the Black Sea port of Caffa (now Feodosiya) in the Crimea, where the Genoese maintained a trading post. The diseased sailors showed strange black swellings about the size of an egg or an apple in the armpits and groin. The swellings oozed blood and pus and were followed by spreading boils and black blotches on the skin from internal bleeding. The sick suffered severe pain and died quickly within five days of the first symptoms. As the disease spread, other symptoms of continuous fever and spitting of blood appeared instead of the swellings or buboes. These victims coughed and sweated heavily and died even more quickly, within three days or less, sometimes in twenty-four hours. In both types everything that issued from the body — breath, sweat, blood from the buboes and lungs, bloody urine, and blood-blackened excrement — smelled foul. Depression and despair accompanied the physical symptoms, and before the end "death is seen seated on the face."

The disease was bubonic plague, present in two forms: one that infected the bloodstream, causing the buboes and internal bleeding, and was spread by contact; and a second, more virulent pneumonic type that infected the lungs and was spread by respiratory infection. The presence of both at once caused the high mortality and speed of contagion. So lethal was the disease that cases were known of persons going to bed well and dying before they woke, of doctors catching the illness at a bedside and dying before the patient. So rapidly did it spread from one to another that to a French physician, Simon de Covino, it seemed as if one sick person "could infect the whole world." The malignity of the pestilence appeared more terrible because its victims knew no prevention and no remedy.

The physical suffering of the disease and its aspects of evil mystery were expressed in a strange Welsh lament which saw "death coming into our midst like black smoke, a plague which cuts off the young, a rootless phantom which has no mercy for fair countenance. Woe is me of the shilling in the armpit! It is seething, terrible . . . a head that gives pain and causes a loud cry . . . a painful angry knob. . . . Great is its seething like a burning cinder . . . a grievous thing of ashy color." Its eruption is ugly like the "seeds of black peas, broken fragments of brittle sea-coal . . . the early ornaments of black death, cinders of the peelings of the cockle weed, a mixed multitude, a black plague like halfpence, like berries. . . ."

Rumors of a terrible plague supposedly arising in China and spreading through Tartary (Central Asia) to India and Persia, Mesopotamia, Syria, Egypt, and all of Asia Minor had reached Europe in 1346. They told of a death toll so devastating that all of India was said to be depopulated, whole territories covered by dead bodies, other areas with no one left alive. As added up by Pope Clement VI at Avignon, the total of reported dead reached 23,840,000. In the absence of a concept of contagion, no serious alarm was felt in Europe until the trading ships brought their black burden of pestilence into Messina while other infected ships from the Levant carried it to Genoa and Venice.

5 By January 1348 it penetrated France via Marseille, and North Africa via Tunis. Shipborne along coasts and navigable rivers, it spread westward from Marseille through the ports of Languedoc to Spain and northward up the Rhône to Avignon, where it arrived in March. It reached Narbonne, Montpellier, Carcassonne, and Toulouse between February and May, and at the same time in Italy spread to Rome and Florence and their hinterlands. Between June and August it reached Bordeaux, Lyon, and Paris, spread to Burgundy and Normandy, and crossed the Channel from Normandy into southern England. From Italy during the same summer it crossed the Alps into Switzerland and reached eastward to Hungary.

In a given area the plague accomplished its kill within four to six months and then faded, except in the larger cities, where, rooting into the close-quartered population, it abated during the winter, only to reappear in spring and rage for another six months.

In 1349 it resumed in Paris, spread to Picardy, Flanders, and the Low Countries, and from England to Scotland and Ireland as well as to Norway, where a ghost ship with a cargo of wool and a dead crew drifted offshore until it ran aground near Bergen. From there the plague passed into Sweden, Denmark, Prussia, Iceland, and as far as Greenland. Leaving a strange pocket of immunity in Bohemia, and Russia unattacked until 1351, it had passed from most of Europe by mid-1350. Although the mortality rate was erratic, ranging from one-fifth in some places to nine-tenths or almost total elimination in others, the overall estimate of modern demographers has settled—for the area extending from India to Iceland—around the same figure expressed in Froissart's casual words: "a third of the world died." His estimate, the common one at the time, was not an inspired guess but a borrowing of St. John's figure for mortality from plague in Revelation, the favorite guide to human affairs of the Middle Ages.

A third of Europe would have meant about 20 million deaths. No one knows in truth how many died. Contemporary reports were an awed impression, not an accurate count. In crowded Avignon, it was said, 400 died daily;

A detail from *The Triumph of Death*, a fresco by Francesco Traini in the Camposanto, Pisa, Italy, c. 1350.

7,000 houses emptied by death were shut up; a single graveyard received 11,000 corpses in six weeks; half the city's inhabitants reportedly died, including 9 cardinals, or one-third of the total, and 70 lesser prelates. Watching the endlessly passing death carts, chroniclers let normal exaggeration take wings and put the Avignon death toll at 62,000 and even at 120,000, although the city's total population was probably less than 50,000.

When graveyards filled up, bodies at Avignon were thrown into the Rhône until mass burial pits were dug for dumping the corpses. In London in such pits corpses piled up in layers until they overflowed. Everywhere reports speak of the sick dying too fast for the living to bury. Corpses were dragged out of homes and left in front of doorways. Morning light revealed new piles of bodies. In Florence the dead were gathered up by the Compagnia della Misericordia—founded in 1244 to care for the sick—whose members wore red robes and hoods masking the face except for the eyes. When their efforts failed, the dead lay putrid in the streets for days at a time. When no coffins were to be had, the bodies were laid on boards, two or three at once, to be carried to graveyards or common pits. Families dumped their own relatives into the pits, or buried them so hastily and thinly "that dogs dragged them forth and devoured their bodies."

10 Amid accumulating death and fear of contagion, people died without last rites and were buried without prayers, a prospect that terrified the last hours of the stricken. A bishop in England gave permission to laymen to make confession to one another as was done by the Apostles, "or if no man is present then even to a woman," and if no priest could be found to administer extreme

unction, "then faith must suffice." Clement VI found it necessary to grant remissions of sin to all who died of the plague because so many were unattended by priests. "And no bells tolled," wrote a chronicler of Siena, "and nobody wept no matter what his loss because almost everyone expected death. . . . And people said and believed, 'This is the end of the world.' "

In Paris, where the plague lasted through 1349, the reported death rate was 800 a day, in Pisa 500, in Vienna 500 to 600. The total dead in Paris numbered 50,000 or half the population. Florence, weakened by the famine of 1347, lost three- to four-fifths of its citizens, Venice two-thirds, Hamburg and Bremen, though smaller in size, about the same proportion. Cities, as centers of transportation, were more likely to be affected than villages, although once a village was infected, its death rate was equally high. At Givry, a prosperous village in Burgundy of 1,200 to 1,500 people, the parish register records 615 deaths in the space of fourteen weeks, compared to an average of 30 deaths a year in the previous decade. In three villages of Cambridgeshire, manorial records show a death rate of 47 percent, 57 percent, and in one case 70 percent. When the last survivors, too few to carry on, moved away, a deserted village sank back into the wilderness and disappeared from the map altogether, leaving only a grass-covered ghostly outline to show where mortals once had lived.

In enclosed places such as monasteries and prisons, the infection of one person usually meant that of all, as happened in the Franciscan convents of Carcassonne and Marseille, where every inmate without exception died. Of the 140 Dominicans at Montpellier only 7 survived. Petrarch's brother Gherardo, member of a Carthusian monastery, buried the prior and 34 fellow monks one by one, sometimes three a day, until he was left alone with his dog and fled to look for a place that would take him in. Watching every comrade die, men in such places could not but wonder whether the strange peril that filled the air had not been sent to exterminate the human race. In Kilkenny, Ireland, Brother John Clyn of the Friars Minor, another monk left alone among dead men, kept a record of what had happened lest "things which should be remembered perish with time and vanish from the memory of those who come after us." Sensing "the whole world, as it were, placed within the grasp of the Evil One," and waiting for death to visit him too, he wrote, "I leave parchment to continue this work, if perchance any man survive and any of the race of Adam escape this pestilence and carry on the work which I have begun." Brother John, as noted by another hand, died of the pestilence, but he foiled oblivion.

The largest cities of Europe, with populations of about 100,000, were Paris and Florence, Venice and Genoa. At the next level, with more than 50,000, were Ghent and Bruges in Flanders, Milan, Bologna, Rome, Naples, and Palermo, and Cologne. London hovered below 50,000, the only city in England except York with more than 10,000. At the level of 20,000 to 50,000 were Bordeaux, Toulouse, Montpellier, Marseille, and Lyon in France, Barcelona, Seville, and Toledo in Spain, Siena, Pisa, and other secondary cities in Italy, and the Hanseatic trading cities of the Empire. The plague raged through them all, killing anywhere from one-third to two-thirds of their inhabitants.

Burial of plague victims, from *Annales de Gilles li Muisis* (The Annals of Gilles li Muisis, c. 1272–1352).

Italy, with a total population of 10 to 11 million, probably suffered the heaviest toll. Following the Florentine bankruptcies, the crop failures and workers' riots of 1346–1347, the revolt of Cola di Rienzi that plunged Rome into anarchy, the plague came as the peak of successive calamities. As if the world were indeed in the grasp of the Evil One, its first appearance on the European mainland in January 1348 coincided with a fearsome earthquake that carved a path of wreckage from Naples up to Venice. Houses collapsed, church towers toppled, villages were crushed, and the destruction reached as far as Germany and Greece. Emotional response, dulled by horrors, underwent a kind of atrophy epitomized by the chronicler who wrote, "And in these days was burying without sorrowe and wedding without friendschippe."

In Siena, where more than half the inhabitants died of the plague, work was abandoned on the great cathedral, planned to be the largest in the world, and never resumed, owing to loss of workers and master masons and "the melancholy and grief" of the survivors. The cathedral's truncated transept still stands in permanent witness to the sweep of death's scythe. Agnolo di Tura, a chronicler of Siena, recorded the fear of contagion that froze every other instinct. "Father abandoned child, wife husband, one brother another," he wrote, "for this plague seemed to strike through the breath and sight. And so they died. And no one could be found to bury the dead for money or friendship. . . . And I, Agnolo di Tura, called the Fat, buried my five children with my own hands, and so did many others likewise."

There were many to echo his account of inhumanity and few to balance it, 15 for the plague was not the kind of calamity that inspired mutual help. Its loathsomeness and deadliness did not herd people together in mutual distress, but only prompted their desire to escape one another. "Magistrates and notaries refused to come and make the wills of the dying," reported a Franciscan friar of Piazza in Sicily; what was worse, "even the priests did not come to hear their confessions." A clerk of the Archbishop of Canterbury reported the same of English priests who "turned away from the care of their benefices from fear of death." Cases of parents deserting children and children their parents were reported across Europe from Scotland to Russia. The calamity chilled the hearts of men, wrote Boccaccio in his famous account of the plague in Florence that serves as introduction to the *Decameron.* "One man shunned another . . . kinsfolk held aloof, brother was forsaken by brother, oftentimes husband by wife; nay, what is more, and scarcely to be believed, fathers and mothers were found to abandon their own children to their fate, untended, unvisited as if they had been strangers." Exaggeration and literary pessimism were common in the fourteenth century, but the Pope's physician, Guy de Chauliac, was a sober, careful observer who reported the same phenomenon: "A father did not visit his son, nor the son his father. Charity was dead."

Yet not entirely. In Paris, according to the chronicler Jean de Venette, the nuns of the Hotel Dieu or municipal hospital, "having no fear of death, tended the sick with all sweetness and humility." New nuns repeatedly took the places of those who died, until the majority "many times renewed by death now rest in peace with Christ as we may piously believe."

When the plague entered northern France in July 1348, it settled first in Normandy and, checked by winter, gave Picardy a deceptive interim until the next summer. Either in mourning or warning, black flags were flown from church towers of the worst-stricken villages of Normandy. "And in that time," wrote a monk of the abbey of Fourcarment, "the mortality was so great among the people of Normandy that those of Picardy mocked them." The same unneighborly reaction was reported of the Scots, separated by a winter's immunity from the English. Delighted to hear of the disease that was scourging the "southrons," they gathered forces for an invasion, "laughing at their enemies." Before they could move, the savage mortality fell upon them too, scattering some in death and the rest in panic to spread the infection as they fled.

In Picardy in the summer of 1349 the pestilence penetrated the castle of Coucy to kill Enguerrand's[1] mother, Catherine, and her new husband. Whether her nine-year-old son escaped by chance or was perhaps living elsewhere with one of his guardians is unrecorded. In nearby Amiens, tannery workers, responding quickly to losses in the labor force, combined to bargain for higher wages. In another place villagers were seen dancing to drums and trumpets, and on being asked the reason, answered that, seeing their neighbors die day by day while their village remained immune, they believed that they could keep the plague from entering "by the jollity that is in us. That is why we dance." Further north in Tournai on the border of Flanders, Gilles li Muisis, Abbot of St. Martin's, kept one of the epidemic's most vivid accounts. The passing bells rang all day and all night, he recorded, because sextons were anxious to obtain their fees while they could. Filled with the sound of mourning, the city became oppressed by fear, so that the authorities forbade the tolling of bells and the

---

[1]*Enguerrand de Coucy*: A French nobleman. Tuchman follows his life as a way of unifying her study of the fourteenth century.—Eds.

wearing of black and restricted funeral services to two mourners. The silencing of funeral bells and of criers' announcements of deaths was ordained by most cities. Siena imposed a fine on the wearing of mourning clothes by all except widows.

Flight was the chief recourse of those who could afford it or arrange it. The rich fled to their country places like Boccaccio's young patricians of Florence, who settled in a pastoral palace "removed on every side from the roads" with "wells of cool water and vaults of rare wines." The urban poor died in their burrows, "and only the stench of their bodies informed neighbors of their deaths." That the poor were more heavily afflicted than the rich was clearly remarked at the time, in the north as in the south. A Scottish chronicler, John of Fordun, stated flatly that the pest "attacked especially the meaner sort and common people—seldom the magnates." Simon de Covino of Montpellier made the same observation. He ascribed it to the misery and want and hard lives that made the poor more susceptible, which was half the truth. Close contact and lack of sanitation was the unrecognized other half. It was noticed too that the young died in greater proportion than the old; Simon de Covino compared the disappearance of youth to the withering of flowers in the fields.

20

In the countryside peasants dropped dead on the roads, in the fields, in their houses. Survivors in growing helplessness fell into apathy, leaving ripe wheat uncut and livestock untended. Oxen and asses, sheep and goats, pigs and chickens ran wild and they too, according to local reports, succumbed to the pest. English sheep, bearers of the precious wool, died throughout the country. The chronicler Henry Knighton, canon of Leicester Abbey, reported five thousand dead in one field alone, "their bodies so corrupted by the plague that neither beast nor bird would touch them," and spreading an appalling stench. In the Austrian Alps wolves came down to prey upon sheep and then, "as if alarmed by some invisible warning, turned and fled back into the wilderness." In remote Dalmatia bolder wolves descended upon a plague-stricken city and attacked human survivors. For want of herdsmen, cattle strayed from place to place and died in hedgerows and ditches. Dogs and cats fell like the rest.

The dearth of labor held a fearful prospect because the people of the fourteenth century lived close to the annual harvest both for food and for next year's seed. "So few servants and laborers were left," wrote Knighton, "that no one knew where to turn for help." The sense of a vanishing future created a kind of dementia of despair. A Bavarian chronicler of Neuberg on the Danube recorded that "Men and women . . . wandered around as if mad" and let their cattle stray "because no one had any inclination to concern themselves about the future." Fields went uncultivated, spring seed unsown. Second growth with nature's awful energy crept back over cleared land, dikes crumbled, salt water reinvaded and soured the lowlands. With so few hands remaining to restore the work of centuries, people felt, in Walsingham's words, that "the world could never again regain its former prosperity."

Though the death rate was higher among the anonymous poor, the known and the great died, too. King Alfonso XI of Castile was the only reigning monarch killed by the pest, but his neighbor King Pedro of Aragon lost his wife, Queen Leonora, his daughter Marie, and a niece in the space of six months. John Cantacuzene, Emperor of Byzantium, lost his son. In France the lame Queen Jeanne and her daughter-in-law Bonne de Luxemburg, wife of the Dauphin, both died in 1349 in the same phase that took the life of Enguerrand's mother. Jeanne, Queen of Navarre, daughter of Louis X, was another victim. Edward III's second daughter, Joanna, who was on her way to marry Pedro, the heir of Castile, died in Bordeaux. Women appear to have been more vulnerable than men, perhaps because, being more housebound, they were more exposed to fleas. Boccaccio's mistress Fiammetta, illegitimate daughter of the King of Naples, died, as did Laura, the beloved—whether real or fictional—of Petrarch. Reaching out to us in the future, Petrarch cried, "Oh happy posterity who will not experience such abysmal woe and will look upon our testimony as a fable."

In Florence Giovanni Villani, the great historian of his time, died at sixty-eight in the midst of an unfinished sentence: ". . . *e dure questo pistolenza fino a* . . . (in the midst of this pestilence there came to an end . . .)." Siena's master painters, the brothers Ambrogio and Pietro Lorenzetti, whose names never appear after 1348, presumably perished in the plague, as did Andrea Pisano, architect and sculptor of Florence. William of Ockham and the English mystic Richard Rolle of Hampole both disappear from mention after 1349. Francisco Datini, merchant of Prato, lost both his parents and two siblings. Curious sweeps of mortality afflicted certain bodies of merchants in London. All eight wardens of the Company of Cutters, all six wardens of the Hatters, and four wardens of the Goldsmiths died before July 1350. Sir John Pulteney, master draper and four-time mayor of London, was a victim, likewise Sir John Montgomery, governor of Calais.

Among the clergy and doctors the mortality was naturally high because of the nature of their professions. Out of twenty-four physicians in Venice, twenty were said to have lost their lives in the plague, although, according to another account, some were believed to have fled or to have shut themselves up in their houses. At Montpellier, site of the leading medieval medical school, the physician Simon de Covino reported that, despite the great number of doctors, "hardly one of them escaped." In Avignon, Guy de Chauliac confessed that he performed his medical visits only because he dared not stay away for fear of infamy, but "I was in continual fear." He claimed to have contracted the disease but to have cured himself by his own treatment; if so, he was one of the few who recovered.

Clerical mortality varied with rank. Although the one-third toll of cardinals reflects the same proportion as the whole, this was probably due to their concentration in Avignon. In England, in strange and almost sinister procession, the Archbishop of Canterbury, John Stratford, died in August 1348, his appointed successor died in May 1349, and the next appointee three months later, all three within a year. Despite such weird vagaries, prelates in general managed to sustain a higher survival rate than the lesser clergy. Among bish- 25 ops the deaths have been estimated at about one in twenty. The loss of priests, even if many avoided their fearful duty of attending the dying, was about the same as among the population as a whole.

Government officials, whose loss contributed to the general chaos, found, on the whole, no special shelter. In Siena four of the nine members of the governing oligarchy died, in France one-third of the royal notaries, in Bristol fifteen out of the fifty-two members of the Town Council, or almost one-third. Tax-collecting obviously suffered, with the result that Philip VI was unable to collect more than a fraction of the subsidy granted him by the Estates in the winter of 1347–1348.

Lawlessness and debauchery accompanied the plague as they had during the great plague of Athens of 430 BC, when according to Thucydides, men grew bold in the indulgence of pleasure: "For seeing how the rich died in a moment and those who had nothing immediately inherited their property, they reflected that life and riches were alike transitory and they resolved to enjoy themselves while they could." Human behavior is timeless. When St. John had his vision of plague in Revelation, he knew from some experience or race memory that those who survived "repented not of the work of their hands. . . . Neither repented they of their murders, nor of their sorceries, nor of their fornication, nor of their thefts."

Notes

Although Tuchman's notes are labeled by page number, the numbers in this Notes section refer to the paragraphs in which the sources are mentioned. Tuchman does not use numbered footnotes. At the end of her book, she numbers her notes by page number and provides a source for each quotation and citation. Following her notes, she provides a bibliography that provides the full citation for every reference given in her notes.

1. "death is seen seated": Simon de Covino, q. Campbell, 80.
2. "could infect the whole world": q. Gasquet, 41.
3. Welsh lament: q. Ziegler, 190.
9. "that dogs dragged them forth": Agnolo di Tura, q. Ziegler, 58.
10. "or if no man is present": Bishop of Bath and Wells, q. Ziegler, 125. "And no bells tolled": Agnolo di Tura, q. Schevill, 211. The same observation was made by Gabriel de Muisis, notary of Piacenza, q. Crawfurd, 113.
11. Givry parish register: Renouard, 111. Three villages of Cambridgeshire: Saltmarsh.
12. Petrarch's brother: Bishop, 273. Brother John Clyn: q. Ziegler, 195.
13. "And in these days": q. Deaux, 143, citing only "an old northern chronicle."
14. Agnolo di Tura, "Father abandoned child": q. Ziegler, 58.
15. "Magistrates and notaries": q. Deaux, 49. English priests turned away: Ziegler, 261. Parents deserting children: Hecker, 30. Guy de Chauliac, "A father": q. Gasquet, 50–51.
16. nuns of the Hotel Dieu: *Chron. Jean de Venette,* 49.
17. Picards and Scots mock mortality of neighbors: Gasquet, 53, and Ziegler, 198.

18. Catherine de Coucy: *L'Art de vérifier,* 237. Amiens tanners: Gasquet, 57. "By the jollity that is in us": *Grandes Chrôns.,* VI, 486–87.

19. John of Fordun: q. Ziegler, 199. Simon de Covino on the poor: Gasquet, 42. On youth: Cazelles.

20. Knighton on sheep: q. Ziegler, 175. Wolves of Austria and Dalmatia: ibid., 84, 111. Dogs and cats: Muisis, q. Gasquet, 44, 61.

21. Bavarian chronicler of Neuberg: q. Ziegler, 84. Walsingham, "the world could never": Denifle, 273.

22. "Oh happy posterity": q. Ziegler, 45.

23. Giovanni Villani, "*e dure questo*": q. Snell, 334.

24. Physicians of Venice: Campbell, 98. Simon de Covino: ibid., 31. Guy de Chauliac, "I was in continual fear": q. Thompson, 379.

27. Thucydides: q. Crawfurd, 30–31.

Bibliography

L'Art de vérifier les dates des faits historiques, par un Religieux de la Congregation de St.-Maur, vol. XII. Paris, 1818.
Bishop, Morris. *Petrarch and His World.* Indiana University Press, 1963.
Campbell, Anna M. *The Black Death and Men of Learning.* Columbia University Press, 1931.
Cazelles, Raymond. *"La Peste de 1348–49 en Langue d'oil: épidémie prolitarienne et enfantine." Bull philologique et historique,* 1962, pp. 293–305.
Chronicle of Jean de Venette. Trans. Jean Birdsall. Ed. Richard A. Newhall. Columbia University Press, 1853.
Crawfurd, Raymond. *Plague and Pestilence in Literature and Art.* Oxford, 1914.
Deaux, George. *The Black Death, 1347.* London, 1969.
Denifle, Henri. *La Désolation des églises, monastères et hôpitaux en France pendant la guerre de cent ans,* vol. I. Paris, 1899.
Gasquet, Francis Aidan, Abbot. *The Black Death of 1348 and 1349,* 2nd ed. London, 1908.
Grandes Chroniques de France, vol. VI (to 1380). Ed. Paulin Paris. Paris, 1838.
Hecker, J. F. C. *The Epidemics of the Middle Ages.* London, 1844.
Renouard, Yves. *"La Peste noire de 1348–50." Rev. de Paris,* March, 1950.
Saltmarsh, John. "Plague and Economic Decline in England in the Later Middle Ages." *Cambridge Historical Journal,* vol. VII, no. 1, 1941.
Schevill, Ferdinand. *Siena: The History of a Medieval Commune.* New York, 1909.
Snell, Frederick. *The Fourteenth Century.* Edinburgh, 1899.
Thompson, James Westfall. *Economic and Social History of Europe in the Later Middle Ages.* New York, 1931.
Ziegler, Philip. *The Black Death.* New York, 1969. (The best modern study.)

▪ QUESTIONS

Reading

1. According to Tuchman, how many people died in Europe during the Black Death?
2. In writing this report, Tuchman chooses to end many of her paragraphs with direct quotations. Underline, highlight, or flag some of these. What do they have in common? Why do you think Tuchman closes so many paragraphs in this way?

3. Much of this essay is devoted to the reporting of facts and figures. This could be very tedious, but Tuchman is an expert at avoiding dullness. How does she help the reader see and feel the awfulness of the plague? Locate specific examples in the text, and discuss their effectiveness.

Exploratory Writing

1. What is valuable about reading accounts of history? Reflect on a time when learning about events from the distant past changed your view of your own life.
2. "Human behavior is timeless," writes Tuchman (paragraph 27). In your opinion, how does her study of the Black Death support or refute this claim? Make a list of examples of the timeless aspects of human behavior that you find in her essay.
3. Collaborating in small groups, research and create a presentation explaining a painting that portrays the Black Death. What does the painting show about history? In what ways is the painting timeless?

Making Connections

1. Richard Selzer (p. 533) reports on the contemporary AIDS epidemic in Haiti. Compare Selzer's contemporary account to Tuchman's historical report on the Black Death. What are the differences between reporting on history and reporting on events of the present? How do the kinds of evidence used by the two writers compare?
2. Imagine that we had photographs and film footage of many of the gruesome deaths caused by the plague. Susan Sontag (p. 366) writes, "To catch a death actually happening and embalm it for all time is something only cameras can do." Discuss the extent to which images of the dead and dying can be invoked by painters or writers without the use of a camera. How might our reflections about the catastrophe be different if it had been recorded on film?

Essay Writing

1. Taking Tuchman as a model, write a report on some other catastrophe, blending factual reporting with descriptions of what it was like to be there. This will require both careful research and artful selection and arrangement of the fruits of that research.

EXPLAINING

What Is It about 20-Somethings?

Robin Marantz Henig

Robin Maranz Henig is the author of eight nonfiction works, including *A Dancing Matrix: Voyages Along the Viral Frontier* (1993), *The People's Health: A Memoir of Public Health and its Evolution at Harvard* (1997), National Book Critic's Circle Award finalist *The Monk in the Garden: The Lost and Found Genius of Gregor Mendel* (2001), and *Pandora's Baby: How the First Test Tube Babies Sparked the Reproductive Revolution* (2004). Her many awards include a Guggenheim Foundation Fellowship, two Science in Society Awards from the National Association of Science Writers, and a Career Achievement Award from the American Society of Journalists and Authors. As a contributing writer for the *New York Times Magazine*, where this piece appeared in 2010, she has published articles reflecting broad interests in science, religion, and, like this piece on the redefinition of adulthood, society. She received a Master of Science in Journalism from Northwestern University in 1974, and has recently taught at Princeton and Columbia.

This question pops up everywhere, underlying concerns about "failure to launch" and "boomerang kids." Two new sitcoms feature grown children moving back in with their parents—*$h*! My Dad Says,* starring William Shatner as a divorced curmudgeon whose twenty-something son can't make it on his own as a blogger, and *Big Lake,* in which a financial whiz kid loses his Wall Street job and moves back home to rural Pennsylvania. A cover of the *New Yorker* last spring picked up on the zeitgeist: A young man hangs up his new PhD in his boyhood bedroom, the cardboard box at his feet signaling his plans to move back home now that he's officially overqualified for a job. In the doorway stand his parents, their expressions a mix of resignation, worry, annoyance, and perplexity: How exactly did this happen?

It's happening all over, in all sorts of families, not just young people moving back home but also young people taking longer to reach adulthood overall. It's a development that predates the current economic doldrums, and no one knows yet what the impact will be—on the prospects of the young men and women; on the parents on whom so many of them depend; on society, built on the expectation of an orderly progression in which kids finish school, grow up, start careers, make a family, and eventually retire to live on pensions supported by the next crop of kids who finish school, grow up, start careers, make a family, and on and on. The traditional cycle seems to have gone off course, as young people remain untethered to romantic partners or to permanent homes, going back to school for lack of better options, traveling, avoiding commitments, competing ferociously for unpaid internships or temporary (and often grueling) Teach for America jobs, forestalling the beginning of adult life.

The twenties are a black box, and there is a lot of churning in there. One-third of people in their twenties move to a new residence every year. Forty percent move back home with their parents at least once. They go through an average of seven jobs in their twenties, more job changes than in any other stretch. Two-thirds spend at least some time living with a romantic partner without being married. And marriage occurs later than ever. The median age at first marriage in the early 1970s, when the baby boomers were young, was twenty-one for women and twenty-three for men; by 2009 it had climbed to twenty-six for women and twenty-eight for men, five years in a little more than a generation.

We're in the thick of what one sociologist calls "the changing timetable for adulthood." Sociologists traditionally define the "transition to adulthood" as marked by five milestones: completing school, leaving home, becoming financially independent, marrying, and having a child. In 1960, 77 percent of women and 65 percent of men had, by the time they reached thirty, passed all five milestones. Among thirty-year-olds in 2000, according to data from the United States Census Bureau, fewer than half of the women and one-third of the men had done so. A Canadian study reported that a typical thirty-year-old in 2001 had completed the same number of milestones as a twenty-five-year-old in the early '70s.

5 The whole idea of milestones, of course, is something of an anachronism; it implies a lockstep march toward adulthood that is rare these days. Kids don't shuffle along in unison on the road to maturity. They slouch toward adulthood at an uneven, highly individual pace. Some never achieve all five milestones, including those who are single or childless by choice, or unable to marry even if they wanted to because they're gay. Others reach the milestones completely out of order, advancing professionally before committing to a monogamous relationship, having children young and marrying later, leaving school to go to work and returning to school long after becoming financially secure.

Even if some traditional milestones are never reached, one thing is clear: Getting to what we would generally call adulthood is happening later than ever. But why? That's the subject of lively debate among policy makers and academics. To some, what we're seeing is a transient epiphenomenon, the by-product of cultural and economic forces. To others, the longer road to adulthood signifies something deep, durable, and maybe better-suited to our neurological hard-wiring. What we're seeing, they insist, is the dawning of a new life stage—a stage that all of us need to adjust to.

Jeffrey Jensen Arnett, a psychology professor at Clark University in Worcester, Massachusetts, is leading the movement to view the twenties as a distinct life stage, which he calls "emerging adulthood." He says what is happening now is analogous to what happened a century ago, when social and economic changes helped create adolescence—a stage we take for granted but one that had to be recognized by psychologists, accepted by society and accommodated by institutions that served the young. Similar changes at the turn of the twenty-first century have laid the groundwork for another new stage, Arnett says, between the age of eighteen and the late twenties. Among the cultural changes he points to that have led to "emerging adulthood" are the need for more education to survive in an information-based economy; fewer entry-level jobs even after all that schooling; young people feeling less rush to marry because of the general acceptance of premarital sex, cohabitation, and birth control; and young women feeling less rush to have babies given their wide range of career options and their access to assisted reproductive technology if they delay pregnancy beyond their most fertile years.

Just as adolescence has its particular psychological profile, Arnett says, so does emerging adulthood: identity exploration, instability, self-focus, feeling in-between, and a rather poetic characteristic he calls "a sense of possibilities." A few of these, especially identity exploration, are part of adolescence too, but they take on new depth and urgency in the twenties. The stakes are higher when people are approaching the age when options tend to close off and life-long commitments must be made. Arnett calls it "the age-thirty deadline."

The issue of whether emerging adulthood is a new stage is being debated most forcefully among scholars, in particular psychologists and sociologists. But its resolution has broader implications. Just look at what happened for teenagers. It took some effort, a century ago, for psychologists to make the case that adolescence was a new developmental stage. Once that happened, social institutions were forced to adapt: Education, health care, social services, and the law all changed to address the particular needs of twelve- to eighteen-year-olds. An understanding of the developmental profile of adolescence led, for instance, to the creation of junior high schools in the early 1900s, separating seventh and eighth graders from the younger children in what used to be called primary school. And it led to the recognition that teenagers between fourteen and eighteen, even though they were legally minors, were mature enough to make their own choice of legal guardian in the event of their parents' deaths. If emerging adulthood is an analogous stage, analogous changes are in the wings.

10 But what would it look like to extend some of the special status of adolescents to young people in their twenties? Our uncertainty about this question is reflected in our scattershot approach to markers of adulthood. People can vote at eighteen, but in some states they don't age out of foster care until twenty-one. They can join the military at eighteen, but they can't drink until twenty-one. They can drive at sixteen, but they can't rent a car until twenty-five without some hefty surcharges. If they are full-time students, the Internal Revenue Service considers them dependents until twenty-four; those without health insurance will soon be able to stay on their parents' plans, even if they're not in school, until age twenty-six, or up to thirty in some states. Parents have no access to their child's college records if the child is over eighteen, but parents' income is taken into account when the child applies for financial aid up to age twenty-four. We seem unable to agree when someone is old enough to take on adult responsibilities. But we're pretty sure it's not simply a matter of age.

If society decides to protect these young people or treat them differently from fully grown adults, how can we do this without becoming all the things that grown children resist—controlling, moralizing, paternalistic? Young people spend their lives lumped into age-related clusters—that's the basis of K–12 schooling—but as they move through their twenties, they diverge. Some twenty-five-year-olds are married homeowners with good jobs and a couple of kids; others are still living with their parents and working at transient jobs, or not working at all. Does that mean we extend some of the protections and special status of adolescence to all people in their twenties? To some of them? Which ones? Decisions like this matter, because failing to protect and support vulnerable young people can lead them down the wrong path at a critical moment, the one that can determine all subsequent paths. But overprotecting and oversupporting them can sometimes make matters worse, turning the "changing timetable of adulthood" into a self-fulfilling prophecy.

The more profound question behind the scholarly intrigue is the one that really captivates parents: whether the prolongation of this unsettled time of life is a good thing or a bad thing. With life spans stretching into the ninth decade, is it better for young people to experiment in their twenties before making choices they'll have to live with for more than half a century? Or is adulthood now so malleable, with marriage and employment options constantly being reassessed, that young people would be better off just getting started on something, or else they'll never catch up, consigned to remain always a few steps behind the early bloomers? Is emerging adulthood a rich and varied period for self-discovery, as Arnett says it is? Or is it just another term for self-indulgence?

The discovery of adolescence is generally dated to 1904, with the publication of the massive study *Adolescence*, by G. Stanley Hall, a prominent psychologist and first president of the American Psychological Association. Hall attributed the new stage to social changes at the turn of the twentieth century. Child-labor laws kept children under sixteen out of the work force, and universal education laws kept them in secondary school, thus prolonging the period of dependence—a dependence that allowed them to address psychological tasks they might have ignored when they took on adult roles straight out of childhood. Hall, the first president of Clark University—the same place, interestingly enough, where Arnett now teaches—described adolescence as a time of "storm and stress," filled with emotional upheaval, sorrow, and rebelliousness. He cited the "curve of despondency" that "starts at eleven, rises steadily and rapidly till fifteen . . . then falls steadily till twenty-three," and described other characteristics of adolescence, including an increase in sensation seeking, greater susceptibility to media influences (which in 1904 mostly meant "flash literature" and "penny dreadfuls"), and overreliance on peer relationships. Hall's book was flawed, but it marked the beginning of the scientific study of adolescence and helped lead to its eventual acceptance as a distinct stage with its own challenges, behaviors, and biological profile.

In the 1990s, Arnett began to suspect that something similar was taking place with young people in their late teens and early twenties. He was teaching human development and family studies at the University of Missouri, studying college-age students, both at the university and in the community around Columbia, Missouri. He asked them questions about their lives and their expectations like, "Do you feel you have reached adulthood?"

"I was in my early- to mid-thirties myself, and I remember thinking, They're not a thing like me," Arnett told me when we met last spring in Worcester. "I realized that there was something special going on." The young people he spoke to weren't experiencing the upending physical changes that accompany adolescence, but as an age cohort they did seem to have a psychological makeup different from that of people just a little bit younger or a little bit older. This was not how most psychologists were thinking about development at the time, when the eight-stage model of the psychologist Erik Erikson was in vogue. Erikson, one of the first to focus on psychological development past childhood, divided adulthood into three stages—young (roughly ages twenty to forty-five), middle (about ages forty-five to sixty-five) and late (all the rest)—and defined them by the challenges that individuals in a particular stage encounter and must resolve before moving on to the next stage. In young adulthood, according to his model, the primary psychological challenge is "intimacy versus isolation," by which Erikson meant deciding whether to commit to a lifelong intimate relationship and choosing the person to commit to. 15

But Arnett said "young adulthood" was too broad a term to apply to a twenty-five-year span that included both him and his college students. The twenties are something different from the thirties and forties, he remembered thinking. And while he agreed that the struggle for intimacy was one task of this period, he said there were other critical tasks as well.

Arnett and I were discussing the evolution of his thinking over lunch at BABA Sushi, a quiet restaurant near his office where he goes so often he knows the sushi chefs by name. He is fifty-three, very tall and wiry, with clipped steel-gray hair and ice-blue eyes, an intense, serious man. He describes himself as a late bloomer, a onetime emerging adult before anyone had given it a name. After graduating from Michigan State University in 1980, he spent two years playing guitar in bars and restaurants and experimented with girlfriends, drugs, and general recklessness before going for his doctorate in developmental psychology at the University of Virginia. By 1986 he had his first academic job at Oglethorpe University, a small college in Atlanta. There he met his wife, Lene Jensen, the school's smartest psych major, who stunned Arnett when she came to his office one day in 1989, shortly after she graduated, and asked him out on a date. Jensen earned a doctorate in psychology, too, and she also teaches at Clark. She and Arnett have ten-year-old twins, a boy and a girl.

Arnett spent time at Northwestern University and the University of Chicago before moving to the University of Missouri in 1992, beginning his study of young men and women in the college town of Columbia, gradually broadening his sample to include New Orleans, Los Angeles, and San Francisco. He deliberately included working-class young people as well as those who were well off, those who had never gone to college as well as those who were still in school, those who were supporting themselves as well as those whose bills were being paid by their parents. A little more than half of his sample was white, 18 percent African-American, 16 percent Asian-American and 14 percent Latino.

More than 300 interviews and 250 survey responses persuaded Arnett that he was onto something new. This was the era of the Gen X slacker, but Arnett felt that his findings applied beyond one generation. He wrote them up in 2000 in *American Psychologist,* the first time he laid out his theory of "emerging adulthood." According to Google Scholar, which keeps track of such things, the article has been cited in professional books and journals roughly 1,700 times. This makes it, in the world of academia, practically viral. At the very least, the citations indicate that Arnett had come up with a useful term for describing a particular cohort; at best, that he offered a whole new way of thinking about them.

During the period he calls emerging adulthood, Arnett says that young men and women are more self-focused than at any other time of life, less certain about the future and yet also more optimistic, no matter what their economic background. This is where the "sense of possibilities" comes in, he says; they have not yet tempered their idealistic visions of what awaits. "The dreary, dead-end jobs, the bitter divorces, the disappointing and disrespectful children . . . none of them imagine that this is what the future holds for them," he wrote. Ask them if they agree with the statement "I am very sure that someday I will get to where I want to be in life," and 96 percent of them will say yes. But despite elements that are exciting, even exhilarating, about being this age, there is a downside, too: dread, frustration, uncertainty, a sense of not quite understanding the rules of the game. More than positive or negative feelings, what Arnett heard most often was ambivalence—beginning with his finding that 60 percent of his subjects told him they felt like both grown-ups and not-quite-grown-ups. 20

Some scientists would argue that this ambivalence reflects what is going on in the brain, which is also both grown-up and not-quite-grown-up. Neuroscientists once thought the brain stops growing shortly after puberty, but now they know it keeps maturing well into the twenties. This new understanding comes largely from a longitudinal study of brain development sponsored by the National Institute of Mental Health, which started following nearly 5,000 children at ages three to sixteen (the average age at enrollment was about ten). The scientists found the children's brains were not fully mature until at least twenty-five. "In retrospect I wouldn't call it shocking, but it was at the time," Jay Giedd, the director of the study, told me. "The only people who got this right were the car-rental companies."

When the NIMH study began in 1991, Giedd said he and his colleagues expected to stop when the subjects turned sixteen. "We figured that by sixteen their bodies were pretty big physically," he said. But every time the children returned, their brains were found still to be changing. The scientists extended the end date of the study to age eighteen, then twenty, then twenty-two. The subjects' brains were still changing even then. Tellingly, the most significant changes took place in the prefrontal cortex and cerebellum, the regions involved in emotional control and higher-order cognitive function.

As the brain matures, one thing that happens is the pruning of the synapses. Synaptic pruning does not occur willy-nilly; it depends largely on how any one brain pathway is used. By cutting off unused pathways, the brain eventually settles into a structure that's most efficient for the owner of that brain, creating well-worn grooves for the pathways that person uses most. Synaptic pruning intensifies after rapid brain-cell proliferation during childhood and again in the period that encompasses adolescence and the twenties. It is the mechanism of "use it or lose it": the brains we have are shaped largely in response to the demands made of them.

We have come to accept the idea that environmental influences in the first three years of life have long-term consequences for cognition, emotional control, attention, and the like. Is it time to place a similar emphasis, with hopes for a similar outcome, on enriching the cognitive environment of people in their twenties?

NIMH scientists also found a time lag between the growth of the limbic system, where emotions originate, and of the prefrontal cortex, which manages those emotions. The limbic system explodes during puberty, but the prefrontal cortex keeps maturing for another ten years. Giedd said it is logical to suppose—and for now, neuroscientists have to make a lot of logical suppositions—that when the limbic system is fully active but the cortex is still being built, emotions might outweigh rationality. "The prefrontal part is the part that allows you to control your impulses, come up with a long-range strategy, answer the question 'What am I going to do with my life?' " he told me. "That weighing of the future keeps changing into the twenties and thirties." 25

Among study subjects who enrolled as children, MRI scans have been done so far only to age twenty-five, so scientists have to make another logical supposition about what happens to the brain in the late twenties, the thirties, and beyond. Is it possible that the brain just keeps changing and pruning, for years and years? "Guessing from the shape of the growth curves we have," Giedd's colleague Philip Shaw wrote in an e-mail message, "it does seem that much of the gray matter," where synaptic pruning takes place, "seems to have completed its most dramatic structural change" by age twenty-five. For white matter, where insulation that helps impulses travel faster continues to form, "it does look as if the curves are still going up, suggesting continued growth" after age twenty-five, he wrote, though at a slower rate than before.

None of this is new, of course; the brains of young people have always been works in progress, even when we didn't have sophisticated scanning machinery to chart it precisely. Why, then, is the youthful brain only now arising as an explanation for why people in their twenties are seeming a bit unfinished? Maybe there's an analogy to be found in the hierarchy of needs, a theory put forth in the 1940s by the psychologist Abraham Maslow. According to Maslow, people can pursue more elevated goals only after their basic needs of food, shelter, and sex have been met. What if the brain has its own hierarchy of needs? When people are forced to adopt adult responsibilities early, maybe they just do what they have to do, whether or not their brains are ready. Maybe it's only now, when young people are allowed to forestall adult obligations without fear of public censure, that the rate of societal maturation can finally fall into better sync with the maturation of the brain.

Cultural expectations might also reinforce the delay. The "changing timetable for adulthood" has, in many ways, become internalized by twenty-somethings and their parents alike. Today young people don't expect to marry until their late twenties, don't expect to start a family until their thirties, don't expect to be on track for a rewarding career until much later than their parents were. So they make decisions about their futures that reflect this wider time horizon. Many of them would not be ready to take on the trappings of adulthood any earlier even if the opportunity arose; they haven't braced themselves for it.

Nor do parents expect their children to grow up right away—and they might not even want them to. Parents might regret having themselves jumped into marriage or a career and hope for more considered choices for their children. Or they might want to hold on to a reassuring connection with their children as the kids leave home. If they were "helicopter parents"—a term that describes heavily invested parents who hover over their children, swooping down to take charge and solve problems at a moment's notice—they might keep hovering and problem-solving long past the time when their children should be solving problems on their own. This might, in a strange way, be part of what keeps their grown children in the limbo between adolescence and adulthood. It can be hard sometimes to tease out to what extent a child doesn't quite want to grow up and to what extent a parent doesn't quite want to let go.

It is a big deal in developmental psychology to declare the existence of a new stage of life, and Arnett has devoted the past ten years to making his case. Shortly after his *American Psychologist* article appeared in 2000, he and Jennifer Lynn Tanner, a developmental psychologist at Rutgers University, convened the first conference of what they later called the Society for the Study of Emerging Adulthood. It was held in 2003 at Harvard with an attendance of 75; there have been three more since then, and last year's conference, in Atlanta, had more than 270 attendees. In 2004 Arnett published a book, *Emerging Adulthood: The Winding Road From the Late Teens Through the Twenties,* which is still in print and selling well. In 2006 he and Tanner published an edited volume, *Emerging Adults in America: Coming of Age in the 21st Century,* aimed at professionals and academics. Arnett's college textbook, *Adolescence and Emerging Adulthood: A Cultural Approach,* has been in print since 2000 and is now in its fourth edition. Next year he says he hopes to publish another book, this one for the parents of twenty-somethings. 30

If all Arnett's talk about emerging adulthood sounds vaguely familiar . . . well, it should. Forty years ago, an article appeared in *The American Scholar* that declared "a new stage of life" for the period between adolescence and young adulthood. This was 1970, when the oldest members of the baby boom generation—the parents of today's twenty-somethings—were twenty-four.

Young people of the day "can't seem to 'settle down,'" wrote the Yale psychologist Kenneth Keniston. He called the new stage of life "youth."

Keniston's description of "youth" presages Arnett's description of "emerging adulthood" a generation later. In the late sixties, Keniston wrote that there was "a growing minority of post-adolescents [who] have not settled the questions whose answers once defined adulthood: questions of relationship to the existing society, questions of vocation, questions of social role and lifestyle." Whereas once, such aimlessness was seen only in the "unusually creative or unusually disturbed," he wrote, it was becoming more common and more ordinary in the baby boomers of 1970. Among the salient characteristics of "youth," Keniston wrote, were "pervasive ambivalence toward self and society," "the feeling of absolute freedom, of living in a world of pure possibilities," and "the enormous value placed upon change, transformation, and movement"—all characteristics that Arnett now ascribes to "emerging adults."

Arnett readily acknowledges his debt to Keniston; he mentions him in almost everything he has written about emerging adulthood. But he considers the sixties a unique moment, when young people were rebellious and alienated in a way they've never been before or since. And Keniston's views never quite took off, Arnett says, because "youth" wasn't a very good name for it. He has called the label "ambiguous and confusing," not nearly as catchy as his own "emerging adulthood."

For whatever reason Keniston's terminology faded away, it's revealing to read his old article and hear echoes of what's going on with kids today. He was describing the parents of today's young people when they themselves were young—and amazingly, they weren't all that different from their own children now. Keniston's article seems a lovely demonstration of the eternal cycle of life, the perennial conflict between the generations, the gradual resolution of those conflicts. It's reassuring, actually, to think of it as recursive, to imagine that there must always be a cohort of twenty-somethings who take their time settling down, just as there must always be a cohort of fifty-somethings who worry about it.

Keniston called it youth, Arnett calls it emerging adulthood; whatever it's called, the delayed transition has been observed for years. But it can be in fullest flower only when the young person has some other, nontraditional means of support—which would seem to make the delay something of a luxury item. That's the impression you get reading Arnett's case histories in his books and articles, or the essays in *20 Something Manifesto,* an anthology edited by a Los Angeles writer named Christine Hassler. "It's somewhat terrifying," writes a twenty-five-year-old named Jennifer, "to think about all the things I'm supposed to be doing in order to 'get somewhere' successful: 'Follow your passions, live your dreams, take risks, network with the right people, find mentors, be financially responsible, volunteer, work, think about or go to grad school, fall in love and maintain personal well-being, mental health, and nutrition.' When is there time to just be and enjoy?" Adds a twenty-four-year-old from Virginia: "There is pressure to make decisions that will form the foundation for the rest of your life in your twenties. It's almost as if having a range of limited options would be easier."

While the complaints of these young people are heartfelt, they are also the complaints of the privileged. Julie, a twenty-three-year-old New Yorker and contributor to *20 Something Manifesto,* is apparently aware of this. She was coddled her whole life, treated to French horn lessons and summer camp, told she could do anything. "It is a double-edged sword," she writes, "because on the one hand I am so blessed with my experiences and endless options, but on the other hand, I still feel like a child. I feel like my job isn't real because I am not where my parents were at my age. Walking home, in the shoes my father bought me, I still feel I have yet to grow up."

Despite these impressions, Arnett insists that emerging adulthood is not limited to young persons of privilege and that it is not simply a period of self-indulgence. He takes pains in *Emerging Adulthood* to describe some case histories of young men and women from hard-luck backgrounds who use the self-focus and identity exploration of their twenties to transform their lives.

One of these is the case history of Nicole, a twenty-five-year-old African American who grew up in a housing project in Oakland, California. At age six, Nicole, the eldest, was forced to take control of the household after her mother's mental collapse. By eight, she was sweeping stores and babysitting for money to help keep her three siblings fed and housed. "I made a couple bucks and helped my mother out, helped my family out," she told Arnett. She managed to graduate from high school, but with low grades, and got a job as a receptionist at a dermatology clinic. She moved into her own apartment, took night classes at community college, and started to excel. "I needed to experience living out of my mother's home in order to study," she said.

In his book, Arnett presents Nicole as a symbol of all the young people from impoverished backgrounds for whom "emerging adulthood represents an opportunity—maybe a last opportunity—to turn one's life around." This is the stage where someone like Nicole can escape an abusive or dysfunctional family and finally pursue her own dreams. Nicole's dreams are powerful—one course away from an associate's degree, she plans to go on for a bachelor's and then a PhD in psychology—but she has not really left her family behind; few people do. She is still supporting her mother and siblings, which is why she works full time even though her progress through school would be quicker if she found a part-time job. Is it only a grim pessimist like me who sees how many roadblocks there will be on the way to achieving those dreams and who wonders what kind of freewheeling emerging adulthood she is supposed to be having?

Of course, Nicole's case is not representative of society as a whole. And 40 many parents—including those who can't really afford it—continue to help their kids financially long past the time they expected to. Two years ago Karen Fingerman, a developmental psychologist at Purdue University, asked parents of grown children whether they provided significant assistance to their sons or daughters. Assistance included giving their children money or help with everyday tasks (practical assistance) as well as advice, companionship, and an attentive ear. Eighty-six percent said they had provided advice in the previous month; less than half had done so in 1988. Two out of three parents had given a son or daughter practical assistance in the previous month; in 1988, only one in three had.

Fingerman took solace in her findings; she said it showed that parents stay connected to their grown children, and she suspects that both parties get something out of it. The survey questions, after all, referred not only to dispensing money but also to offering advice, comfort, and friendship. And another of Fingerman's studies suggests that parents' sense of well-being depends largely on how close they are to their grown children and how their children are faring—objective support for the adage that you're only as happy as your unhappiest child. But the expectation that young men and women won't quite be able to make ends meet on their own, and that parents should be the ones to help bridge the gap, places a terrible burden on parents who might be worrying about their own job security, trying to care for their aging parents, or grieving as their retirement plans become more and more of a pipe dream.

This dependence on Mom and Dad also means that during the twenties the rift between rich and poor becomes entrenched. According to data gathered by the Network on Transitions to Adulthood, a research consortium supported by the John D. and Catherine T. MacArthur Foundation, American parents give an average of 10 percent of their income to their eighteen- to twenty-one-year-old children. This percentage is basically the same no matter the family's total income, meaning that upper-class kids tend to get more than working-class ones. And wealthier kids have other, less obvious, advantages. When they go to four-year colleges or universities, they get supervised dormitory housing, health care, and alumni networks not available at community colleges. And they often get a leg up on their careers by using parents' contacts to help land an entry-level job—or by using parents as a financial backup when they want to take an interesting internship that doesn't pay.

"You get on a pathway, and pathways have momentum," Jennifer Lynn Tanner of Rutgers told me. "In emerging adulthood, if you spend this time exploring and you get yourself on a pathway that really fits you, then there's going to be this snowball effect of finding the right fit, the right partner, the right job, the right place to live. The less you have at first, the less you're going to get this positive effect compounded over time. You're not going to have the same acceleration."

Even Arnett admits that not every young person goes through a period of "emerging adulthood." It's rare in the developing world, he says, where people have to grow up fast, and it's often skipped in the industrialized world by the people who marry early, by teenage mothers forced to grow up, by young men or women who go straight from high school to whatever job is available without a chance to dabble until they find the perfect fit. Indeed, the majority of humankind would seem to not go through it at all. The fact that emerging adulthood is not universal is one of the strongest arguments against Arnett's claim that it is a new developmental stage. If emerging adulthood is so important, why is it even possible to skip it?

"The core idea of classical stage theory is that all people—underscore 'all'—pass through a series of qualitatively different periods in an invariant and universal sequence in stages that can't be skipped or reordered," Richard Lerner, Bergstrom chairman in applied developmental science at Tufts University, told me. Lerner is a close personal friend of Arnett's; he and his wife, Jacqueline, who is also a psychologist, live twenty miles from Worcester, and they have dinner with Arnett and his wife on a regular basis. 45

"I think the world of Jeff Arnett," Lerner said. "I think he is a smart, passionate person who is doing great work—not only a smart and productive scholar, but one of the nicest people I ever met in my life."

No matter how much he likes and admires Arnett, however, Lerner says his friend has ignored some of the basic tenets of developmental psychology. According to classical stage theory, he told me, "you must develop what you're supposed to develop when you're supposed to develop it or you'll never adequately develop it."

When I asked Arnett what happens to people who don't have an emerging adulthood, he said it wasn't necessarily a big deal. They might face its developmental tasks—identity exploration; self-focus; experimentation in love, work, and worldview—at a later time, maybe as a midlife crisis, or they might never face them at all, he said. It depends partly on why they missed emerging adulthood in the first place, whether it was by circumstance or by choice.

No, said Lerner, that's not the way it works. To qualify as a developmental stage, emerging adulthood must be both universal and essential. "If you don't develop a skill at the right stage, you'll be working the rest of your life to develop it when you should be moving on," he said. "The rest of your development will be unfavorably altered." The fact that Arnett can be so casual about the heterogeneity of emerging adulthood and its existence in some cultures but not in others—indeed, even in some people but not in their neighbors or friends—is what undermines, for many scholars, his insistence that it's a new life stage.

Why does it matter? Because if the delay in achieving adulthood is just a temporary aberration caused by passing social mores and economic gloom, it's something to struggle through for now, maybe feeling a little sorry for the young people who had the misfortune to come of age in a recession. But if it's a true life stage, we need to start rethinking our definition of normal development and to create systems of education, health care, and social supports that take the new stage into account. 50

The Network on Transitions to Adulthood has been issuing reports about young people since it was formed in 1999 and often ends up recommending more support for twenty-somethings. But more of what, exactly? There aren't institutions set up to serve people in this specific age range; social services from a developmental perspective tend to disappear after adolescence. But it's possible to envision some that might address the restlessness and mobility that Arnett says are typical at this stage and that might make the experimentation of "emerging adulthood" available to more young people. How about expanding programs like City Year, in which seventeen- to twenty-four-year-olds from diverse backgrounds spend a year mentoring inner-city children in exchange for a stipend, health insurance, child care, cellphone service and a $5,350 education award? Or a federal program in which a government-sponsored savings account is created for every newborn, to be cashed in at age twenty-one to support a year's worth of travel, education, or volunteer work—a version of the "baby bonds" program that Hillary Clinton mentioned during her 2008 primary campaign? Maybe we can encourage a kind of socially sanctioned "rumspringa," the temporary moratorium from social responsibilities some Amish offer their young people to allow them to experiment before settling down. It requires only a bit of ingenuity—as well as some societal forbearance and financial commitment—to think of ways to expand some of the programs that now work so well for the elite, like the Fulbright fellowship or the Peace Corps, to make the chance for temporary service and self-examination available to a wider range of young people.

A century ago, it was helpful to start thinking of adolescents as engaged in the work of growing up rather than as merely lazy or rebellious. Only then could society recognize that the educational, medical, mental-health, and social-service needs of this group were unique and that investing in them would have a payoff in the future. Twenty-somethings are engaged in work, too, even if it looks as if they are aimless or failing to pull their weight, Arnett says. But it's a reflection of our collective attitude toward this period that we devote so few resources to keeping them solvent and granting them some measure of security.

The kind of services that might be created if emerging adulthood is accepted as a life stage can be seen during a visit to Yellowbrick, a residential program in Evanston, Illinois, that calls itself the only psychiatric treatment facility for emerging adults. "Emerging adults really do have unique developmental tasks to focus on," said Jesse Viner, Yellowbrick's executive medical director. Viner started Yellowbrick in 2005, when he was working in a group psychiatric practice in Chicago and saw the need for a different way to treat this cohort. He is a soft-spoken man who looks like an accountant and sounds like a New Age prophet, peppering his conversation with phrases like "helping to empower their agency."

"Agency" is a tricky concept when parents are paying the full cost of Yellowbrick's comprehensive residential program, which comes to $21,000 a month and is not always covered by insurance. Staff members are aware of the paradox of encouraging a child to separate from Mommy and Daddy when it's on their dime. They address it with a concept they call connected autonomy, which they define as knowing when to stand alone and when to accept help.

Patients come to Yellowbrick with a variety of problems: substance abuse, eating disorders, depression, anxiety, or one of the more severe mental illnesses, like schizophrenia or bipolar disorder, that tend to appear in the late teens or early twenties. The demands of imminent independence can worsen 55 mental-health problems or can create new ones for people who have managed up to that point to perform all the expected roles—son or daughter, boyfriend or girlfriend, student, teammate, friend—but get lost when schooling ends and expected roles disappear. That's what happened to one patient who had done well at a top Ivy League college until the last class of the last semester of his last year, when he finished his final paper and could not bring himself to turn it in.

The Yellowbrick philosophy is that young people must meet these challenges without coddling or rescue. Up to sixteen patients at a time are housed in the Yellowbrick residence, a four-story apartment building Viner owns. They live in the apartments—which are large, sunny, and lavishly furnished—in groups of three or four, with staff members always on hand to teach the basics of shopping, cooking, cleaning, scheduling, making commitments, and showing up.

Viner let me sit in on daily clinical rounds, scheduled that day for C., a young woman who had been at Yellowbrick for three months. Rounds are like the world's most grueling job interview: The patient sits in front alongside her clinician "advocate," and a dozen or so staff members are arrayed on couches and armchairs around the room, firing questions. C. seemed nervous but pleased with herself, frequently flashing a huge white smile. She is twenty-two, tall, and skinny, and she wore tiny denim shorts and a big T-shirt and vest. She started to fall apart during her junior year at college, plagued by binge drinking and anorexia, and in her first weeks at Yellowbrick her alcohol abuse continued. Most psychiatric facilities would have kicked her out after the first relapse, said Dale Monroe-Cook, Yellowbrick's vice president of clinical operations. "We're doing the opposite: We want the behavior to unfold, and we want to be there in that critical moment, to work with that behavior and help the emerging adult transition to greater independence."

The Yellowbrick staff let C. face her demons and decide how to deal with them. After five relapses, C. asked the staff to take away her ID so she couldn't buy alcohol. Eventually she decided to start going to meetings of Alcoholics Anonymous.

At her rounds in June, C. was able to report that she had been alcohol-free for thirty days. Jesse Viner's wife, Laura Viner, who is a psychologist on staff, started to clap for her, but no one else joined in. "We're on eggshells here," Gary Zurawski, a clinical social worker specializing in substance abuse, confessed to C. "We don't know if we should congratulate you too much." The staff was sensitive about taking away the young woman's motivation to improve her life for her own sake, not for the sake of getting praise from someone else.

C. took the discussion about the applause in stride and told the staff she had more good news: In two days she was going to graduate. On time. 60

The twenties are like the stem cell of human development, the pluripotent moment when any of several outcomes is possible. Decisions and actions during this time have lasting ramifications. The twenties are when most people accumulate almost all of their formal education; when most people meet their future spouses and the friends they will keep; when most people start on the careers that they will stay with for many years. This is when adventures, experiments, travels, relationships are embarked on with an abandon that probably will not happen again.

Does that mean it's a good thing to let twenty-somethings meander—or even to encourage them to meander—before they settle down? That's the question that plagues so many of their parents. It's easy to see the advantages to the delay. There is time enough for adulthood and its attendant obligations; maybe if kids take longer to choose their mates and their careers, they'll make fewer mistakes and live happier lives. But it's just as easy to see the drawbacks. As the settling-down sputters along for the "emerging adults," things can get precarious for the rest of us. Parents are helping pay bills they never counted on paying, and social institutions are missing out on young people contributing to productivity and growth. Of course, the recession complicates things, and even if every twenty-something were ready to skip the "emerging" moratorium and act like a grown-up, there wouldn't necessarily be jobs for them all. So we're caught in a weird moment, unsure whether to allow young people to keep exploring and questioning or to cut them off and tell them just to find something, anything, to put food on the table and get on with their lives.

Arnett would like to see us choose a middle course. "To be a young American today is to experience both excitement and uncertainty, wide-open possibility and confusion, new freedoms and new fears," he writes in *Emerging Adulthood.* During the timeout they are granted from nonstop, often tedious and dispiriting responsibilities, "emerging adults develop skills for daily living, gain a better understanding of who they are and what they want from life, and begin to build a foundation for their adult lives." If it really works that way, if this longer road to adulthood really leads to more insight and better choices, then Arnett's vision of an insightful, sensitive, thoughtful, content, well-honed, self-actualizing crop of grown-ups would indeed be something worth waiting for.

▪ QUESTIONS

Reading

1. Who is Jeffrey Jensen Arnett? What is the movement he is leading, according to Henig?
2. Describe the orientation and treatment approach at Yellowbrick. What points do you believe that Henig is trying to make by including it in her article?
3. Highlight, underline, or flag the statistics that Henig cites. How would her explanation change if she rewrote it without using any statistics?

Exploratory Writing

1. Henig points out that our society has a "scattershot approach to markers of adulthood" (paragraph 10). In small groups, make a triple-entry list of the ages and markers that Henig includes. For each marker, devise criteria other than age that could be used to determine one's fitness for the task. Discuss whether it is discriminatory to use age to determine people's legal rights.

MARKER	MINIMUM AGE	ALTERNATIVE CRITERIA
Voting	18	?
Renting a car	25	?

2. Using Henig's article for ideas, write a list of ten questions that could help determine whether someone falls into the category of "emerging adult." Then, using your questions, interview someone aged eighteen to thirty. Do that person's responses indicate that he or she is experiencing "emerging adulthood," as Henig defines and explains it? Why or why not?

Making Connections

1. In her report on teaching literature at a county jail in San Francisco in the 1990s, Christina Boufis (p. 96) tells the story of a nineteen-year-old inmate named Tanya (beginning in paragraph 10). Do you think that Tanya could be described as an "emerging adult" as explained by Henig? Why or why not?

Essay Writing

1. Consider the "five milestones" on the way to adulthood, as listed by Henig: completing school, leaving home, becoming financially independent, getting married, and having a child. In your opinion, are these milestones outdated? Write an essay arguing why or why not. In your argument, be sure to include your own thoughts on what it means to be an adult.

EXPLAINING

The Selfless Gene

Olivia Judson

Born in England in 1970, Olivia Judson moved to Baltimore with her family at the age of ten. Though initially interested in physics, Judson eventually graduated from Stanford University with a biology degree. In 1995, she earned a PhD from Oxford University in biological sciences and soon after joined the *Economist* as a science writer. There she wrote about biology in the style of a witty sex-advice columnist, taking on such different perspectives as that of a queen bee, a male spider, and a fruit fly. She later turned these articles into the best-selling book *Dr. Tatiana's Sex Advice to All Creation: The Definitive Guide to the Evolutionary Biology of Sex* (2002), which was nominated for the Samuel Johnson Prize for excellence in nonfiction writing and, in 2004, adapted into a TV series. Judson is currently a research fellow in evolutionary biology at Imperial College in London. She has written for *Nature,* the *Financial Times*, the *Atlantic*, and *Natural History*, and wrote a weekly blog called *The Wild Side* for the *New York Times*.

At 2 a.m. on February 26, 1852, the Royal Navy troopship *Birkenhead,* which was carrying more than six hundred people, including seven women and thirteen children, struck a rock near Danger Point, two miles off the coast of South Africa. Almost immediately, the ship began to break up. Just three lifeboats could be launched. The men were ordered to stand on deck, and they did. The women and children (along with a few sailors) were put into the lifeboats and rowed away. Only then were the men told that they could try to save themselves by swimming to shore. Most drowned or were eaten by sharks. The heroism of the troops, standing on deck facing almost certain death while others escaped, became the stuff of legend. But the strange thing is, such heroics are not rare: Humans often risk their lives for strangers—think of the firemen going into the World Trade Center—or for people they know but are not related to.

How does a propensity for self-sacrifice evolve? And what about the myriad lesser acts of daily kindness—helping a little old lady across the street, giving up a seat on the subway, returning a wallet that's been lost? Are these impulses as primal as ferocity, lust, and greed? Or are they just a thin veneer over a savage nature? Answers come from creatures as diverse as amoebas and baboons, but the story starts in the county of Kent, in southern England.

Evolving Generosity

Kent has been home to two great evolutionary biologists. In the nineteenth century, Charles Darwin lived for many years in the village of Downe. In the twentieth, William Donald Hamilton grew up catching beetles and chasing butterflies over the rolling hills near Badgers Mount.

Hamilton was a tall man with a craggy face and the tops of a couple of fingers missing from a childhood accident—he blew himself up while making explosives. He died in 2000, at age sixty-three, after an illness contracted while undertaking another risky endeavor: a trip to the Congo to collect chimpanzee feces. When I first met him, in Oxford in 1991, he had a terrific shock of white hair, rode a rickety bicycle at prodigious speed, and was preoccupied with the question of why sex is useful in evolutionary terms. (For my doctorate, I worked with him on this question.) But he began his career studying social behavior, and in the early 1960s he published a trio of now-classic papers in which he offered the first rigorous explanation of how generosity can evolve, and under what circumstances it is likely to emerge.

Hamilton didn't call it generosity, though; he called it altruism. And the particular behaviors he sought to explain are acts of extreme self-sacrifice, such as when a bee dies to defend the hive, or when an animal spends its whole life helping others rear their children instead of having some of its own.

To see why these behaviors appear mysterious to biologists, consider how natural selection works. In every generation, some individuals leave more descendants than others. If the reason for their greater "reproductive success" is due to the particular genes they have, then natural selection has been operating.

Here's an example: Suppose you're a mosquito living on the French Mediterranean coast. Tourists don't like mosquitoes, and the French authorities try to keep the tourists happy by spraying insecticide. Which means that on the coast, mosquitoes bearing a gene that confers insecticide resistance tend to leave many more descendants than those lacking it—and so today's coastal mosquitoes are far more resistant to insecticide than those that live inland.

Extreme altruists, by definition, leave no descendants: They're too busy helping others. So at first blush, a gene that promotes extreme altruism should quickly vanish from a population.

Hamilton's solution to this problem was simple and elegant. He realized that a gene promoting extreme altruism could spread if the altruist helped its close relations. The reason is that your close relations have some of the same genes as you do. In humans and other mammals, full brothers and sisters have, on average, half the same genes. First cousins have, on average, an eighth of their genes in common. Among insects such as ants and bees, where the underlying genetics work differently, full sisters (but not brothers) typically have three-quarters of their genes in common.

Hamilton derived a formula—now known as Hamilton's rule—for predicting whether the predisposition toward a given altruistic act is likely to evolve: $rB > C$. In plain language, this says that genes that promote the altruistic act will spread if the benefit (B) that the act bestows is high enough, and the genetic relationship (r) between the altruist and the beneficiary is close enough, to outweigh the act's cost (C) to the altruist. Cost and benefit are both measured in nature's currency: children. "Cheap" behaviors—such as when a small bird squawks from the bushes to announce it's seen a cat or a hawk—can, and do, evolve easily, even though they often benefit nonrelatives.

"Expensive" behaviors, such as working your whole life to rear someone else's children, evolve only in the context of close kin.

Since Hamilton first proposed the idea, "kin selection" has proved tremendously powerful as a way to understand cooperative and self-sacrificial behavior in a huge menagerie of animals. Look at lions. Lionesses live with their sisters, cousins, and aunts; they hunt together and help one another with child care. Bands of males, meanwhile, are typically brothers and half brothers. Large bands are better able to keep a pride of lionesses; thus, even males who never mate with a female still spread some of their genes by helping their brothers defend the pride. Or take peacocks. Males often stand in groups when they display to females. This is because females are drawn to groups of displaying males; they ogle them, then pick the guy they like best to be their mate. Again, peacocks prefer to display with their brothers rather than with males they are not related to.

Kin selection operates even in mindless creatures such as amoebas. For instance, the soil-dwelling amoeba *Dictyostelium purpureum.* When times are good, members of this species live as single cells, reproducing asexually and feasting on bacteria. But when times get tough—when there's a bacteria shortage—thousands of individuals join together into a single entity known as a slug. This glides off in search of more-suitable conditions. When it finds them, the slug transforms itself into a fruiting body that looks like a tiny mushroom; some of the amoebas become the stalk, others become spores. Those in the stalk will die; only the spores will go on to form the next amoeboid generation. Sure enough, amoebas with the same genes (in other words, clones) tend to join the same slugs: They avoid mixing with genetic strangers and sacrifice themselves only for their clones.

Kin selection also accounts for some of the nastier features of human behavior, such as the tendency stepparents have to favor their own children at the expense of their stepkids. But it's not enough to explain the evolution of all aspects of social behavior, in humans or in other animals.

Living Together

Animals may begin to live together for a variety of reasons—most obviously, safety in numbers. In one of his most engaging papers, Hamilton observed that a tight flock, herd, or shoal will readily appear if every animal tries to make itself safer by moving into the middle of the group—a phenomenon he termed the "selfish herd." But protection from predators isn't the only benefit of bunching together. A bird in a flock spends more time eating and less time looking about for danger than it does when on its own. Indeed, eating well is another common reason for group living. Some predatory animals—chimpanzees, spotted hyenas, and wild dogs, for example—have evolved to hunt together.

15 Many social animals thus live in huge flocks or herds, and not in family groups—or even if the nexus of social life is the family, the family group is

itself part of a larger community. In species such as these, social behavior must extend beyond a simple "Be friendly and helpful to your family and hostile to everybody else" approach to the world. At the least, the evolution of social living requires limiting aggression so that neighbors can tolerate one another. And often, the evolution of larger social groupings is accompanied by an increase in the subtlety and complexity of the ways animals get along together.

Consider baboons. Baboons are monkeys, not apes, and are thus not nearly as closely related to us as chimpanzees are. Nonetheless, baboons have evolved complex social lives. They live in troops that can number from as few as eight to as many as two hundred. Females live with their sisters, mothers, aunts, and infants; males head off to find a new troop at adolescence (around age four). Big troops typically contain several female family groups, along with some adult males. The relationships between members of a troop are varied and complex. Sometimes two or more males team up to defeat a dominant male in combat. Females often have a number of male "friends" that they associate with (friends may or may not also be sex partners). If a female is attacked or harassed, her friends will come bounding to the rescue; they will also protect her children, play with them, groom them, carry them, and sometimes share food with them. If the mother dies, they may even look after an infant in her place.

Yet friendliness and the associated small acts of affection and kindness—a bout of grooming here, a shared bite to eat there—seem like evolutionary curiosities. Small gestures like these don't affect how many children you have. Or do they?

Among social animals, one potentially important cause of premature death is murder. Infanticide can be a problem for social mammals, from baboons and chimpanzees to lions and even squirrels. During one four-year study of Belding's ground squirrels, for example, the main cause of death for juveniles was other Belding's ground squirrels; at least 8 percent of the young were murdered before being weaned. Similarly, fighting between adults—particularly in species where animals are well armed with horns, tusks, or teeth—can be lethal, and even if it is not, it may result in severe injuries, loss of status, or eviction from the group.

The possibility of death by murder creates natural selection for traits that reduce this risk. For example, any animal that can appease an aggressor, or that knows when to advance and when to retreat, is more likely to leave descendants than an animal that leaps wildly into any fray. Which explains why, in many social-mammal species, you don't see many murders, though you do see males engaging in elaborate rituals to see who's bigger and stronger. Serious physical fights tend to break out only when both animals think they can win (that is, when they are about the same size).

Thus, among animals such as baboons, friendships mean more than a bit of mutual scratching; they play a fundamental role in an animal's ability to survive and reproduce within the group. Friendships between males can be important in overcoming a dominant male—which may in turn lead to an 20 improvement in how attractive the animals are to females. Similarly, females that have a couple of good male friends will be more protected from bullying—and their infants less likely to be killed. Why do the males do it? Males that are friends with a particular female are more likely to become her sex partners later on, if indeed they are not already. In other words, friendship may be as primal an urge as ferocity.

Becoming Human

The lineage that became modern humans split off from the lineage that became chimpanzees around six million years ago. Eventually this new lineage produced the most socially versatile animal the planet has ever seen: us. How did we get to be this way?

One clue comes from chimpanzees. Chimpanzee society is the mirror image of baboon society, in that it's the females that leave home at adolescence, and the males that stay where they were born. Chimpanzee communities can also be fairly large, comprising several different subcommunities and family groups. Males prefer to associate with their brothers and half-brothers on their mother's side, but they also have friendships with unrelated males. Friends hang out together and hunt together—and gang up on other males.

However, unlike baboon troops, which roam around the savannah freely intermingling, chimpanzee communities are territorial. Bands of males patrol the edges of their community's territory looking for strangers—and sometimes make deep incursions into neighboring terrain. Males on patrol move together in silence, often stopping to listen. If they run into a neighboring patrol, there may be some sort of skirmish, which may or may not be violent. But woe betide a lone animal that runs into the patrolling males. If they encounter a strange male on his own, they may well kill him. And sometimes, repeated and violent attacks by one community lead to the annihilation of another, usually smaller, one. Indeed, two of the three most-studied groups of chimpanzees have wiped out a neighboring community.

Chimpanzees have two important sources of premature death at the hands of other chimpanzees: They may be murdered by members of their own community, or they may be killed during encounters with organized bands of hostile neighbors.

25 Just like humans. Except that humans aren't armed with big teeth and strong limbs. Humans carry weapons, and have done so for thousands of years.

On Love and War

Darwin wondered whether lethal warring between neighboring groups might have caused humans to evolve to be more helpful and kind to one another. At first, the idea seems paradoxical. But Darwin thought this could have happened if the more cohesive, unified, caring groups had been better able to triumph over their more disunited rivals. If so, the members of those cohesive, yet warlike, groups would have left more descendants.

For a long time, the idea languished. Why? A couple of reasons. First, it appears to depend on "group selection." This is the idea that some groups evolve characteristics that allow them to outcompete other groups, and it's long been out of favor with evolutionary biologists. In general, natural selection works much more effectively on individuals than it does on groups, unless the groups are composed of close kin. That's because group selection can be effective only when the competing groups are genetically distinct. Members of a kin group tend to be genetically similar to one another, and different from members of other kin groups. In contrast, groups composed of non-kin tend to contain considerable genetic variation, and differences between such groups are generally much smaller. Moreover, contact between the groups—individuals migrating from one to another, say—will reduce any genetic differences that have started to accumulate. So unless natural selection within the groups is different—such that what it takes to survive and reproduce in one group is different from what it takes in another—migration quickly homogenizes the genetics of the whole population.

A second reason Darwin's idea has been ignored is that it seems to have a distasteful corollary. The idea implies, perhaps, that some unpleasant human characteristics—such as xenophobia or even racism—evolved in tandem with generosity and kindness. Why? Because banding together to fight means that people must be able to tell the difference between friends (who belong in the group) and foes (who must be fought). In the mid-1970s, in a paper that speculated about how humans might have evolved, Hamilton suggested that xenophobia might be innate. He was pilloried.

But times have changed. Last year, the science journal *Nature* published a paper that tested the idea of "parochial altruism"—the notion that people might prefer to help strangers from their own ethnic group over strangers from a different group; the experiment found that indeed they do. In addition, the idea that natural selection might work on groups—at least in particular and narrow circumstances—has become fashionable again. And so Darwin's idea about the evolution of human kindness as a result of war has been dusted off and scrutinized.

Sam Bowles, an economist turned evolutionary biologist who splits his time between the Santa Fe Institute, in New Mexico, and the University of Siena, in Italy, notes that during the last 90,000 years of the Pleistocene Epoch (from about 100,000 years ago until about 10,000 years ago, when agriculture emerged), the human population hardly grew. One reason for this was the extraordinary climactic volatility of the period. But another, Bowles suggests, was that our ancestors were busy killing one another in wars. Working from archaeological records and ethnographic studies, he estimates that wars between different groups could have accounted for a substantial fraction of human deaths—perhaps as much as 15 percent, on average, of those born in any given year—and as such, represented a significant source of natural selection. 30

Bowles shows that groups of supercooperative, altruistic humans could indeed have wiped out groups of less-united folk. However, his argument works only if the cooperative groups also had practices—such as monogamy and the sharing of food with other group members—that reduced the ability of their selfish members to out-reproduce their more generous members. (Monogamy helps the spread of altruism because it reduces the differences in the number of children that different people have. If, instead, one or two males monopolized all the females in the group, any genes involved in altruism would quickly disappear.) In other words, Bowles argues that a genetic predisposition for altruism would have been far more likely to evolve in groups where disparities and discord inside the group—whether over mates or food—would have been relatively low. Cultural differences between groups would then allow genetic differences to accumulate.

"That's Not the Way You Do It"

If Bowles's analysis is right, it suggests that individuals who could not conform, or who were disruptive, would have weakened the whole group; any group that failed to drive out such people, or kill them, would have been more likely to be overwhelmed in battle. Conversely, people who fit in—sharing the food they found, joining in hunting, helping to defend the group, and so on—would have given their group a collective advantage, and thus themselves an individual evolutionary advantage.

This suggests two hypotheses. First, that one of the traits that may have evolved in humans is conformity, an ability to fit in with a group and adopt its norms and customs. Second, that enforcement of those norms and customs could have been essential for group cohesion and harmony, especially as groups got bigger (bigness is important in battles against other groups).

Let's start with conformity. This hasn't been studied much in other animals, but male baboons do appear to conform to the social regimens of the groups they join. For example, in one baboon troop in Kenya in the 1980s, all the aggressive males died of tuberculosis. The aggressives were the ones to snuff it because they'd eaten meat infected with bovine TB that had been thrown into a garbage dump; only the more-aggressive males ate at the dump. After their deaths, the dynamics of the troop shifted to a more laid-back way of life. Ten years later—by which time all the original resident males had either died or moved on—the troop was still notable for its mellow attitude. The new males who'd arrived had adopted the local customs.

35 What about humans? According to Michael Tomasello—a psychologist at the Max Planck Institute, in Leipzig, Germany, who studies the behavior of human children and of chimpanzees—children as young as three will quickly deduce and conform to rules. If an adult demonstrates a game, and then a puppet comes in and plays it differently, the children will clamor to correct the puppet with shouts of "No, that's not the way you do it—you do it this way!" In other words, it's not just that they infer and obey rules; they try to enforce them, too.

Which brings me to the question of punishment.

Punishment Games

I'll be dictator. Here's how we play: An economist puts some money on the table—let's say $1,000. Since I'm dictator, I get to decide how you and I are going to split the cash; you have no say in the matter. How much do you think I'll give you?

Now, let's play the ultimatum game. We've still got $1,000 to play with, and I still get to make you an offer. But the game has a wrinkle: If you don't like the offer I make, you can refuse it. If you refuse it, we both get nothing. What do you think I'll do here?

As you've probably guessed, people tend to play the two games differently. In the dictator game, the most common offer is nothing, and the average offer is around 20 percent. In the ultimatum game, the most common offer is half the cash, while the average is around 45 percent. Offers of less than 25 percent are routinely refused—so both players go home empty-handed.

Economists scratch their heads at this. In the first place, they are surprised that some people are nice enough to share with someone they don't know, even in the dictator game, where there's nothing to lose by not sharing. Second, economists predict that people will accept any offer in the ultimatum game, no matter how low, because getting something is better than getting nothing. But that's not what happens. Instead, some people forgo getting anything themselves in order to punish someone who made an ungenerous offer. Money, it seems, is not the only currency people are dealing in. 40

Bring in the neuroscientists, and the other currency gets clearer. If you measure brain activity while such games are being played (and there are many variants, for the fun doesn't stop with dictators and ultimatums), you find that the reward centers of the brain—the bits that give you warm, fuzzy feelings—light up when people are cooperating. But they also light up if you punish someone who wasn't generous, or watch the punishment of someone who wasn't.

Whether these responses are universal isn't clear: The genetic basis is obscure, and the number of people who've had their brain activity measured is tiny. Moreover, most economic-game playing has been done with college students; the extent to which the results hold among people from different cultures and backgrounds is relatively unknown. But the results suggest an intriguing possibility: that humans have evolved both to be good at conforming to the prevailing cultural norms and to enjoy making sure that those norms are enforced. (Perhaps this explains why schemes such as zero-tolerance policing work so well: They play into our desire to conform to the prevailing norms.)

Bringing Out the Best

If the evolutionary scenario I've outlined is even half right, then we should expect to find that there are genes involved in mediating friendly behavior. And there are. Consider Williams syndrome.

People who have Williams syndrome tend to have poor cardiovascular function and a small, pointed, "elfin" face. They are typically terrible with numbers but good with words. And they are weirdly, incautiously friendly and nice—and unafraid of strangers.

They are also missing a small segment of chromosome 7. Chromosomes are long strings of DNA. Most people have forty-six chromosomes in twenty-three pairs; you get one set of twenty-three from your mother, and the other from your father. In Williams syndrome, one copy of chromosome 7 is normal; the other is missing a small piece. The missing piece contains about twenty genes, some of which make proteins that are important in the workings of the brain. Since one chromosome is intact, the problem isn't a complete absence of the proteins that the genes encode, but an insufficiency. Somehow, this insufficiency results in people who are too nice. What's more, they can't learn not to be nice. Which is to say, someone with Williams syndrome can learn the phrase "Don't talk to strangers" but can't translate it into action. 45

Much about Williams syndrome remains mysterious. How the missing genes normally influence behavior is unclear; moreover, the environment has a role to play, too. But despite these complexities, Williams syndrome shows that friendliness has a genetic underpinning—that it is indeed as primal as ferocity. Indirectly, it shows something else as well. Most of us are able to apply brakes to friendly behavior, picking and choosing the people we are friendly to; those with Williams syndrome aren't. They cannot modulate their behavior. This is even odder than being too friendly. And it throws into sharp relief one of the chief features of ordinary human nature: its flexibility.

One of the most important, and least remarked upon, consequences of social living is that individual behavior must be highly flexible and tailored to circumstance: An individual who does not know whom to be aggressive toward, or whom to help, is unlikely to survive for long within the group. This is true for baboons and chimpanzees. It is also true for us.

Indeed, the ability to adjust our behavior to fit a given social environment is one of our main characteristics, yet it's so instinctive we don't even notice it, let alone consider it worthy of remark. But its implications are profound—and hopeful. It suggests that we can, in principle, organize society so as to bring out the best facets of our complex, evolved natures.

▪ QUESTIONS

Reading

1. What questions does Judson set out to answer in this explanatory essay? What strategies does she use to help readers understand her explanation? What are her main conclusions?
2. What is *parochial altruism*?
3. Judson explains Darwin's idea that "lethal warring between neighboring groups might have caused humans to evolve to be more helpful and kind to one another" (paragraph 26). Why, according to Judson, did this idea languish?

4. What, according to Judson, can we learn about genetics by studying people with Williams syndrome?

Exploratory Writing

1. "[F]riendship," Judson suggests, "may be as primal an urge as ferocity" (paragraph 20). In small groups, come up with a list of ten human behaviors that you can *unanimously* agree are based on "primal" urges. (You might include the urge to eat, sleep, run from danger, or urinate.) How do people customarily resist these urges? (For example, in the United States, most people do not defecate in the street. Even if they have the urge to go, they find a restroom.) Why might social customs develop that support the expression of some primal urges but not others?
2. In a classroom setting, play what Judson calls "punishment games" — the dictator game and the ultimatum game. Are the results in your classroom similar to the average results that Judson reports? Discuss Judson's comment that people seem to be dealing in a currency in addition to money.

Making Connections

1. Consider Emily Martin's claim (p. 473) that there are "sleeping metaphors" in science — meaning, instances when scientists project cultural imagery onto what they study — which are "all the more powerful" because they are "hidden within the scientific content of texts" (paragraph 37). Do you think that Martin would find any sleeping metaphors in Judson's explanatory essay? Identify examples in Judson's essay where the line between scientific research and cultural ideas is blurred.
2. Compare Judson's explanation of the connection between genes and altruism with Steven Pinker's (p. 458) arguments about morality. How do you think that each writer might respond to the other's conclusions?

Essay Writing

1. Judson believes that our ability to modulate our behavior allows us to organize society in a way that brings out the best in our natures. Some scientists, however, advocate improving human society through the physical manipulation of genes. Do you believe that it should be legal to genetically alter a newly conceived person to enhance qualities such as appearance, intelligence, kindness, or strength? Write an essay arguing your position. As a resource, read (or take) the survey on PBS's Web site for *Cracking the Code of Life*: **www.pbs.org/wgbh/nova/genome/survey.html**.

ARGUING

Bad Food? Tax It, and Subsidize Vegetables

Mark Bittman

Mark Bittman (b. 1950) began his career as a food writer at *Cook's* magazine. In 1990, he started writing for the *New York Times*, where he launched his well-known column The Minimalist, which ran from 1997 to 2011. His many cookbooks include *How to Cook Everything* (1998), *How to Cook Everything Vegetarian* (2007), and *Food Matters: A Guide to Conscious Eating with More Than 75 Recipes* (2009). He has also co-hosted two food-related PBS television series. Bittman never worked as a chef or pursued culinary training; the recipes and tips in his books and column come from his years of experience as a home cook. "My job has been to help make home cooking more accessible," Bittman has said. Over the years, he came to believe that a meat-heavy diet including processed foods was detrimental to one's health, and he began offering more recipes and menus centered on vegetables. This editorial originally appeared in the *New York Times* in July 2011.

What will it take to get Americans to change our eating habits? The need is indisputable, since heart disease, diabetes and cancer are all in large part caused by the Standard American Diet. (Yes, it's SAD.)

Though experts increasingly recommend a diet high in plants and low in animal products and processed foods, ours is quite the opposite, and there's little disagreement that changing it could improve our health and save tens of millions of lives.

And—not inconsequential during the current struggle over deficits and spending—a sane diet could save tens if not hundreds of billions of dollars in health care costs.

Yet the food industry appears incapable of marketing healthier foods. And whether its leaders are confused or just stalling doesn't matter, because the fixes are not really their problem. Their mission is not public health but profit, so they'll continue to sell the health-damaging food that's most profitable, until the market or another force skews things otherwise. That "other force" should be the federal government, fulfilling its role as an agent of the public good and establishing a bold national fix.

5 Rather than subsidizing the production of unhealthful foods, we should turn the tables and tax things like soda, French fries, doughnuts, and hyper-processed snacks. The resulting income should be earmarked for a program that encourages a sound diet for Americans by making healthy food more affordable and widely available.

The average American consumes 44.7 gallons of soft drinks annually. (Although that includes diet sodas, it does not include noncarbonated sweetened beverages, which add up to at least 17 gallons a person per year.) Sweetened drinks could be taxed at 2 cents per ounce, so a six-pack of Pepsi would cost $1.44 more than it does now. An equivalent tax on fries might be 50 cents

Comparing Costs: Soda Versus Fruits and Vegetables

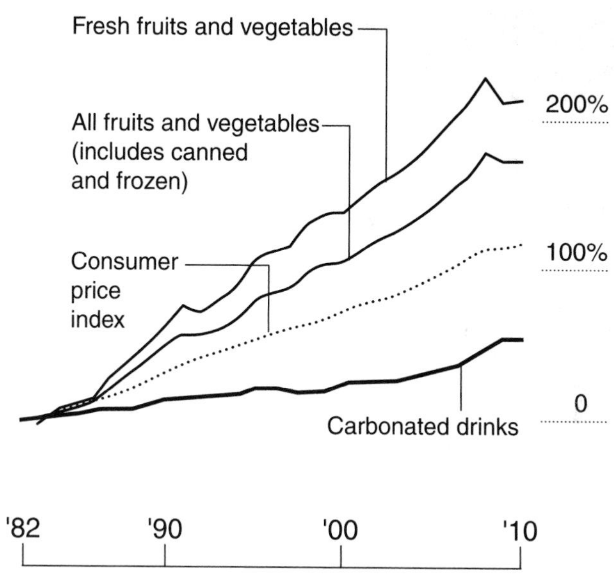

The cost of carbonated drinks has risen since 1982 but at a much lower rate than that of fruits and vegetables, as well as the consumer price index, a measure of the changes in prices for certain products and services purchased by households in the United States.

per serving; a quarter extra for a doughnut. (We have experts who can figure out how "bad" a food should be to qualify, and what the rate should be; right now they're busy calculating ethanol subsidies. Diet sodas would not be taxed.)

Simply put: Taxes would reduce consumption of unhealthful foods and generate billions of dollars annually. That money could be used to subsidize the purchase of staple foods like seasonal greens, vegetables, whole grains, dried legumes, and fruit.

We could sell those staples cheap—let's say for 50 cents a pound—and almost everywhere: drugstores, street corners, convenience stores, bodegas, supermarkets, liquor stores, even schools, libraries, and other community centers.

This program would, of course, upset the processed-food industry. Oh well. It would also bug those who might resent paying more for soda and chips and argue that their right to eat whatever they wanted was being breached. But public health is the role of the government, and our diet is right up there with any other public responsibility you can name, from water treatment to mass transit.

10 Some advocates for the poor say taxes like these are unfair because low-income people pay a higher percentage of their income for food and would find it more difficult to buy soda or junk. But since poor people suffer disproportionately from the cost of high-quality, fresh foods, subsidizing those foods would be particularly beneficial to them.

Right now it's harder for many people to buy fruit than Froot Loops; chips and Coke are a common breakfast. And since the rate of diabetes continues to soar—one-third of all Americans either have diabetes or are pre-diabetic, most with Type 2 diabetes, the kind associated with bad eating habits—and because our health care bills are on the verge of becoming truly insurmountable, this is urgent for economic sanity as well as national health.

Justifying a Tax

At least 30 cities and states have considered taxes on soda or all sugar-sweetened beverages, and they're a logical target: Of the 278 additional calories Americans on average consumed per day between 1977 and 2001, more than 40 percent came from soda, "fruit" drinks, mixes like Kool-Aid and Crystal Light, and beverages like Red Bull, Gatorade, and dubious offerings like Vitamin Water, which contains half as much sugar as Coke.

Some states already have taxes on soda—mostly low, ineffective sales taxes paid at the register. The current talk is of excise taxes, levied before purchase.

"Excise taxes have the benefit of being incorporated into the shelf price, and that's where consumers make their purchasing decisions," says Lisa Powell, a senior research scientist at the Institute for Health Research and Policy at the University of Illinois at Chicago. "And, as per-unit taxes, they avoid volume discounts and are ultimately more effective in raising prices, so they have greater impact."

15 Much of the research on beverage taxes comes from the Rudd Center for Food Policy and Obesity at Yale. Its projections indicate that taxes become significant at the equivalent of about a penny an ounce, a level at which three very good things should begin to happen: The consumption of sugar-sweetened beverages should decrease, as should the incidence of disease and therefore public health costs; and money could be raised for other uses.

Even in the current antitax climate, we'll probably see new, significant soda taxes soon, somewhere; Philadelphia, New York (city and state), and San Francisco all considered them last year, and the scenario for such a tax spreading could be similar to that of legalized gambling: Once the income stream becomes apparent, it will seem irresistible to cash-strapped governments.

Currently, instead of taxing sodas and other unhealthful food, we subsidize them (with, I might note, tax dollars!). Direct subsidies to farmers for crops like corn (used, for example, to make now-ubiquitous high-fructose corn syrup) and soybeans (vegetable oil) keep the prices of many unhealthful foods and beverages artificially low. There are indirect subsidies as well, because prices of junk foods don't reflect the costs of repairing our health and the environment.

Other countries are considering or have already started programs to tax foods with negative effects on health. Denmark's saturated-fat tax is going into effect Oct. 1, and Romania passed (and then un-passed) something similar; earlier this month, a French minister raised the idea of tripling the value added tax on soda. Meanwhile, Hungary is proposing a new tax on foods with "too much" sugar, salt, or fat, while increasing taxes on liquor and soft drinks, all to pay for state-financed health care; and Brazil's Fome Zero (Zero Hunger) program features subsidized produce markets and state-sponsored low-cost restaurants.

Putting all of those elements together could create a national program that would make progress on a half-dozen problems at once—disease, budget, health care, environment, food access, and more—while paying for itself. The benefits are staggering, and though it would take a level of political will that's rarely seen, it's hardly a moonshot.

The need is dire: Efforts to shift the national diet have failed, because education alone is no match for marketing dollars that push the very foods that are the worst for us. (The fast-food industry alone spent more than $4 billion on marketing in 2009; the Department of Agriculture's Center for Nutrition Policy and Promotion is asking for about a third of a percent of that in 2012: $13 million.) As a result, the percentage of obese adults has more than doubled over the last thirty years; the percentage of obese children has tripled. We eat nearly 10 percent more animal products than we did a generation or two ago, and though there may be value in eating at least some animal products, we could perhaps live with reduced consumption of triple bacon cheeseburgers. 20

Government and Public Health

Health-related obesity costs are projected to reach $344 billion by 2018—with roughly 60 percent of that cost borne by the federal government. For a precedent in attacking this problem, look at the action government took in the case of tobacco.

The historic 1998 tobacco settlement, in which the states settled health-related lawsuits against tobacco companies, and the companies agreed to curtail marketing and finance antismoking efforts, was far from perfect, but consider the results. More than half of all Americans who once smoked have quit and smoking rates are about half of what they were in the 1960s.

It's true that you don't need to smoke and you do need to eat. But you don't need sugary beverages (or the associated fries), which have been linked not only to Type 2 diabetes and increased obesity but also to cardiovascular diseases and decreased intake of valuable nutrients like calcium. It also appears that liquid calories provide less feeling of fullness; in other words, when you drink a soda it's probably in addition to your other calorie intake, not instead of it.

To counter arguments about their nutritional worthlessness, expect to see "fortified" sodas—à la Red Bull, whose vitamins allegedly "support mental and physical performance"—and "improved" junk foods (Less Sugar! Higher Fiber!). Indeed, there may be reasons to make nutritionally worthless foods less so, but it's better to decrease their consumption.

Forcing sales of junk food down through taxes isn't ideal. First off, we'll have to listen to nanny-state arguments, which can be countered by the acceptance of the anti-tobacco movement as well as a dozen other successful public health measures. Then there are the predictions of job loss at soda distributorships, but the same predictions were made about the tobacco industry, and 25 those were wrong. (For that matter, the same predictions were made around the nickel deposit on bottles, which most shoppers don't even notice.) Ultimately, however, both consumers and government will be more than reimbursed in the form of cheaper healthy staples, lowered health care costs, and better health. And that's a big deal.

The Resulting Benefits

A study by Y. Claire Wang, an assistant professor at Columbia's Mailman School of Public Health, predicted that a penny tax per ounce on sugar-sweetened beverages in New York State would save $3 billion in health care costs over the course of a decade, prevent something like 37,000 cases of diabetes, and bring in $1 billion annually. Another study shows that a two-cent tax per ounce in Illinois would reduce obesity in youth by 18 percent, save nearly $350 million, and bring in over $800 million taxes annually.

Scaled nationally, as it should be, the projected benefits are even more impressive; one study suggests that a national penny-per-ounce tax on sugar-sweetened beverages would generate at least $13 billion a year in income while cutting consumption by 24 percent. And those numbers would swell dramatically if the tax were extended to more kinds of junk or doubled to two cents an ounce. (The Rudd Center has a nifty revenue calculator online that lets you play with the numbers yourself.)

A 20 percent increase in the price of sugary drinks nationally could result in about a 20 percent decrease in consumption, which in the next decade could prevent 1.5 million Americans from becoming obese and 400,000 cases of diabetes, saving about $30 billion.

It's fun—inspiring, even—to think about implementing a program like this. First off, though the reduced costs of healthy foods obviously benefit the poor most, lower prices across the board keep things simpler and all of us, especially children whose habits are just developing, could use help in eating differently. The program would also bring much needed encouragement to farmers, including subsidies, if necessary, to grow staples instead of commodity crops.

30 Other ideas: We could convert refrigerated soda machines to vending machines that dispense grapes and carrots, as has already been done in Japan and Iowa. We could provide recipes, cooking lessons, even cookware for those who can't afford it. Television public-service announcements could promote healthier eating. (Currently, 86 percent of food ads now seen by children are for foods high in sugar, fat, or sodium.)

Money could be returned to communities for local spending on gyms, pools, jogging and bike trails; and for other activities at food distribution centers; for Meals on Wheels in those towns with a large elderly population, or for Head Start for those with more children; for supermarkets and farmers' markets where needed. And more.

By profiting as a society from the foods that are making us sick and using those funds to make us healthy, the United States would gain the same kind of prestige that we did by attacking smoking. We could institute a national, comprehensive program that would make us a world leader in preventing chronic or "lifestyle" diseases, which for the first time in history kill more people than communicable ones. By doing so, we'd not only repair some of the damage we have caused by first inventing and then exporting the Standard American Diet, we'd also set a new standard for the rest of the world to follow.

▪ QUESTIONS

Reading

1. Who is Y. Claire Wang? How does her work relate to Bittman's argument?
2. Some states already tax sugary sodas. What is the problem, according to Bittman, with the type of taxes that most of these states are using? What is an alternative?
3. According to Bittman, what would be the likely result of increasing the price of sugary drinks nationally by 20 percent?

Exploratory Writing

1. Bittman writes that in his plan, "Diet soda would not be taxed." Yet many people believe that diet soda is at least as unhealthy as sugar- or corn syrup–sweetened drinks. Keeping in mind that many ideas about nutrition are highly controversial and contentious, choose a diet—such as raw food, vegan, low-carb, all-organic, "Cave Man," or macrobiotic—and find at least two sources arguing for and and at least two against its nutritional value. Write a short statement summarizing the pros and cons of this diet.
2. In small groups, design your own plan that would persuade the people in your city to stop eating "bad food," and switch to a nutritionally rich diet. Write a statement, similar to Bittman's, arguing in favor of your own plan. Notice the argumentative techniques that Bittman uses to support his points—including addressing counterarguments—and use a similar strategy for conveying your own.
3. In class, take turns sitting in the "hot seat" as the representative for Bittman's plan, while other students ask questions designed to undermine your arguments. Your responses don't necessarily need to come directly from Bittman's article, but they should show strong argumentative techniques.

Making Connections

1. Consider Walter Kirn's reflections on his personal experiences taking Adderall (p. 525). Kirn notes that the psychiatrist who first prescribed him the drug minimized its risks, but he was still aware of the side effects. Bittman argues that the "bad food" Americans buy, sell, and eat is indisputably unhealthy and yet even educated people consume these foods. In light of both Kirn and Bittman's comments, write a brief essay reflecting on the question, "Why do people consume things they know are bad for them?"

Essay Writing

1. Keep a food diary, recording everything you eat and drink for three days. Also record where the foods and beverages were purchased, who paid for them, and how much they cost. After the three days, write an essay reporting on the nutritional content of your diet. What role did price, convenience, and availability play in your food choices?

The Declaration of Independence

Thomas Jefferson

Thomas Jefferson (1743–1826) was born in Shadwell, Virginia, attended the College of William and Mary, and became a lawyer. He was elected to the Virginia House of Burgesses in 1769 and was a delegate to the Continental Congress in 1776. When the Congress voted in favor of Richard Henry Lee's resolution that the colonies "ought to be free and independent states," a committee of five members, including John Adams, Benjamin Franklin, and Jefferson, was appointed to draw up a declaration. Jefferson, because of his eloquence as a writer, was asked by this committee to draw up a first draft. Jefferson's text, with a few changes suggested by Franklin and Adams, was presented to the Congress. After a debate in which further changes were made, including striking out a passage condemning the slave trade, the Declaration was approved on July 4, 1776. Jefferson said of it, "Neither aiming at originality of principles or sentiments, nor yet copied from any particular and previous writing, it was intended to be an expression of the American mind."

In Congress, July 4, 1776
The unanimous Declaration of the thirteen united States of America

When in the Course of human events it becomes necessary for one people to dissolve the political bands which have connected them with another, and to assume among the powers of the earth, the separate and equal station to which the Laws of Nature and of Nature's God entitle them, a decent respect to the opinions of mankind requires that they should declare the causes which impel them to the separation.

We hold these truths to be self-evident, that all men are created equal, that they are endowed by their Creator with certain unalienable Rights, that among these are Life, Liberty and the pursuit of Happiness. That to secure these rights, Governments are instituted among Men, deriving their just powers from the consent of the governed. That whenever any Form of Government becomes destructive of these ends, it is the Right of the People to alter or to abolish it, and to institute new Government, laying its foundation on such principles and organizing its powers in such form, as to them shall seem most likely to effect their Safety and Happiness. Prudence, indeed, will dictate that Governments long established should not be changed for light and transient causes; and accordingly all experience hath shewn that mankind are more disposed to suffer, while evils are sufferable, than to right themselves by abolishing the forms to which they are accustomed. But when a long train of abuses and usurpations, pursuing invariably the same Object evinces a design to reduce them under absolute Despotism, it is their right, it is their duty, to throw off such Government, and to provide new Guards for their future security. Such has been the patient sufferance of these Colonies; and such is now the necessity which constrains them to alter their former Systems of Government. The history of the present King of Great Britain is a history of repeated injuries and usurpations, all having in direct object the establishment of an absolute Tyranny over these States. To prove this, let Facts be submitted to a candid world.

He has refused his Assent to Laws, the most wholesome and necessary for the public good.

He has forbidden his Governors to pass laws of immediate and pressing importance, unless suspended in their operation till his Assent should be obtained; and when so suspended, he has utterly neglected to attend to them.

5 He has refused to pass other Laws for the accommodation of large districts of people, unless those people would relinquish the right of Representation in the Legislature, a right inestimable to them and formidable to tyrants only.

He has called together legislative bodies at places unusual, uncomfortable, and distant from the depository of their Public Records, for the sole purpose of fatiguing them into compliance with his measures.

He has dissolved Representative Houses repeatedly, for opposing with manly firmness his invasions on the rights of the people.

He has refused for a long time, after such dissolutions, to cause others to be elected; whereby the Legislative Powers, incapable of Annihilation, have returned to the People at large for their exercise; the State remaining in the mean time exposed to all the dangers of invasion from without, and convulsions within.

He has endeavored to prevent the population of these States; for that purpose obstructing the Laws for Naturalization of Foreigners; refusing to pass others to encourage their migration hither, and raising the conditions of new Appropriations of Lands.

10 He has obstructed the Administration of Justice, by refusing his Assent to Laws for Establishing Judiciary Powers.

He has made Judges dependent on his Will alone, for the tenure of their offices, and the amount and payment of their salaries.

He has erected a multitude of New Offices, and sent hither swarms of Officers to harass our people, and eat out their substance.

He has kept among us, in times of peace, Standing Armies without the Consent of our legislatures.

He has affected to render the Military independent of and superior to the Civil Power.

15 He has combined with others to subject us to a jurisdiction foreign to our constitution, and unacknowledged by our laws; giving his Assent to the Acts of pretended Legislation: For quartering large bodies of armed troops among us: For protecting them, by a mock Trial, from punishment for any Murders which they should commit on the Inhabitants of these States: For cutting off our Trade with all parts of the world: For imposing Taxes on us without our Consent: For depriving us in many cases, of the benefits of Trial by Jury: For Transporting us beyond Seas to be tried for pretended offenses: For abolishing

the free System of English Laws in a neighboring Province, establishing therein an Arbitrary government, and enlarging its Boundaries so as to render it at once an example and fit instrument for introducing the same absolute rule into these Colonies: For taking away our Charters, abolishing our most valuable Laws and altering fundamentally the Forms of our Governments: For suspending our own Legislatures, and declaring themselves invested with power to legislate for us in all cases whatsoever.

He has abdicated Government here, by declaring us out of his Protection and waging War against us.

He has plundered our seas, ravaged our Coasts, burnt our towns, and destroyed the lives of our people.

He is at this time transporting large Armies of foreign Mercenaries to complete the works of death, desolation and tyranny, already begun with circumstances of Cruelty & Perfidy scarcely paralleled in the most barbarous ages, and totally unworthy the Head of a civilized nation.

He has constrained our fellow Citizens taken Captive on the high Seas to bear Arms against their Country, to become the executioners of their friends and Brethren, or to fall themselves by their Hands.

He has excited domestic insurrections amongst us, and has endeavored to bring on the inhabitants of our frontiers, the merciless Indian Savages, whose known rule of warfare is an undistinguished destruction of all ages, sexes, and conditions. 20

In every stage of these Oppressions We have Petitioned for Redress in the most humble terms: Our repeated petitions have been answered only by repeated injury. A Prince, whose character is thus marked by every act which may define a Tyrant, is unfit to be the ruler of a free people.

Nor have we been wanting in attention to our British brethren. We have warned them from time to time of attempts by their legislature to extend an unwarrantable jurisdiction over us. We have reminded them of the circumstances of our emigration and settlement here. We have appealed to their native justice and magnanimity, and we have conjured them by the ties of our common kindred to disavow these usurpations, which would inevitably interrupt our connections and correspondence. They too have been deaf to the voice of justice and of consanguinity. We must, therefore, acquiesce in the necessity, which denounces our Separation, and hold them, as we hold the rest of mankind, Enemies in War, in Peace Friends.

We, THEREFORE, the Representatives of the UNITED STATES OF AMERICA, in General Congress, Assembled, appealing to the Supreme Judge of the world for the rectitude of our intentions, do, in the Name, and by Authority of the good People of these Colonies, solemnly publish and declare, That these United Colonies are, and of Right ought to be FREE AND INDEPENDENT STATES; that they are Absolved from all Allegiance to the British Crown, and that all political connection between them and the State of Great Britain, is and ought to be totally dissolved; and that as Free and Independent States, they have full Power to levy War, conclude Peace, contract Alliances, establish Commerce, and to do all the Acts and Things which Independent States may of right do.

And for the support of this Declaration, with a firm reliance on the protection of Divine Providence, we mutually pledge to each other our Lives, our Fortunes, and our sacred Honor.

▪ QUESTIONS

Reading

1. The Declaration of Independence is frequently cited as a classic *deductive* argument. A deductive argument is based on a general statement, or premise, that is assumed to be true. What does this document assume that the American colonists are entitled to, and on what is this assumption based? Look at the reasoning in paragraph 2. What truths are considered self-evident? What does *self-evident* mean?
2. What accusations against the king of Great Britain are the Declaration's facts meant to substantiate?
3. To what extent is the audience of the Declaration intended to be the king and people of Great Britain? What other audiences were intended for this document?

Exploratory Writing

1. Write a declaration of your own, announcing your separation from some injurious situation (an incompatible roommate, a noisy sorority or fraternity house, an awful job). Start with a premise, give reasons to substantiate it, provide facts that illustrate the injurious conditions, and conclude with a statement of what your new condition will mean to you and to other oppressed people.
2. The Declaration of Independence has been celebrated not only for outlining a new kind of self-government but also for Jefferson's writing style. How might the same document have been received if it had been written differently? Collaborating in small groups, rewrite the Declaration in your own words, then present your new version to the class. How does the rewriting change the document's impact?
3. Jefferson asserts that "Life, Liberty and the pursuit of Happiness" are inalienable human rights, but at the time the Declaration was written, slavery was widespread. In class, discuss different definitions of the word *human*. Why has it been such a widespread historical practice to categorize humans into different groups (based on race, class, religion, sex, sexual orientation, and age) before determining laws? How have the political structures of different periods shaped common understandings of those categories? In your discussion, consider the Universal Declaration of Human Rights drafted by the United Nations in 1948 (**www.un.org/en/documents/udhr**) as well as Jefferson's 1776 document.

Making Connections

1. What if, rather than writing the Declaration of Independence, Jefferson had offered "a modest proposal" to the British king? What do you suppose he would have said? How would he have formulated his argument? Write your own modest proposal to the king, addressing him more or less in the manner of Jonathan Swift (p. 305) but drawing on the evidence that Jefferson provides in the Declaration.

2. Compare Barack Obama's March 2008 speech (p. 355) with Jefferson's document. Identify similarities and differences in their tone, style, and purpose.

Essay Writing

1. Although this declaration could have been expected to lead to war and all the horrors thereof, it is a civilized document, showing great respect throughout for certain standards of civility among people and among nations. Define the civilized standards that the Declaration assumes. Write an essay that identifies and characterizes the nature and variety of those expectations.

ARGUING

A Modest Proposal

Jonathan Swift

Jonathan Swift (1667–1745) was born in Dublin, Ireland, of English parents and was educated in Irish schools. A graduate of Trinity College, Dublin, he received a master's degree from Oxford and was ordained as a priest in the Church of England in 1695. He was active in politics as well as religion, becoming an editor and pamphlet writer for the Tory party in 1710. After becoming Dean of St. Patrick's Cathedral, Dublin, in 1713, he settled in Ireland and began to take an interest in the English economic exploitation of Ireland, gradually becoming a fierce Irish patriot. By 1724, the English were offering a reward for the discovery of the writer of the *Drapier's Letters*, a series of pamphlets secretly written by Swift that attacked the British for their treatment of Ireland. In 1726, Swift produced the first volume of a more universal satire, known to modern readers as *Gulliver's Travels*, which has kept his name alive for more than 250 years. "A Modest Proposal," his best-known essay on Irish affairs, appeared in 1729.

A Modest Proposal
for Preventing the Children of Poor People in Ireland
from Being a Burden to Their Parents or Country,
and for Making Them Beneficial to the Public

It is a melancholy object to those who walk through this great town,[1] or travel in the country, when they see the streets, the roads and cabin-doors crowded with beggars of the female sex, followed by three, four, or six children, all in rags, and importuning every passenger for an alms. These mothers, instead of being able to work for their honest livelihood, are forced to employ all their time in strolling, to beg sustenance for their helpless infants, who, as they grow up, either turn thieves for want of work, or leave their dear native country to fight for the Pretender in Spain,[2] or sell themselves to the Barbadoes.[3]

I think it is agreed by all parties that this prodigious number of children, in the arms, or on the backs, or at the heels of their mothers, and frequently of their fathers, is in the present deplorable state of the kingdom a very great additional grievance; and therefore whoever could find out a fair, cheap, and easy method of making these children sound and useful members of the

[1]*this great town*: Dublin.—Eds.

[2]*Pretender in Spain*: A Catholic descendant of the British royal family of Stuart (James I, Charles I, Charles II, and James II). Exiled to France and Spain so that England could be governed by Protestant rulers, the Stuarts prepared various disastrous schemes for regaining the throne.—Eds.

[3]*sell themselves to the Barbadoes*: Sell themselves as indentured servants, a sort of temporary slavery, to the sugar merchants of the British Caribbean islands.—Eds.

commonwealth would deserve so well of the public as to have his statue set up for a preserver of the nation.

But my intention is very far from being confined to provide only for the children of professed beggars; it is of a much greater extent, and shall take in the whole number of infants at a certain age who are born of parents in effect as little able to support them as those who demand our charity in the streets.

As to my own part, having turned my thoughts for many years upon this important subject, and maturely weighed the several schemes of other projectors, I have always found them grossly mistaken in their computation. It is true a child just dropped from its dam may be supported by her milk for a solar year with little other nourishment, at most not above the value of two shillings,[4] which the mother may certainly get, or the value in scraps, by her lawful occupation of begging, and it is exactly at one year old that I propose to provide for them, in such a manner as, instead of being a charge upon their parents, or the parish, or wanting food and raiment for the rest of their lives, they shall, on the contrary, contribute to the feeding and partly to the clothing of many thousands.

5 There is likewise another great advantage to my scheme, that it will prevent those voluntary abortions, and that horrid practice of women murdering their bastard children, alas, too frequent among us, sacrificing the poor innocent babes, I doubt, more to avoid the expense than the shame, which would move tears and pity in the most savage and inhuman breast.

The number of souls in Ireland being usually reckoned one million and a half, of these I calculate there may be about two hundred thousand couples whose wives are breeders, from which number I subtract thirty thousand couples who are able to maintain their own children, although I apprehend there cannot be so many under the present distresses of the kingdom, but this being granted, there will remain an hundred and seventy thousand breeders. I again subtract fifty thousand for those women who miscarry, or whose children die by accident or disease within the year. There only remain an hundred and twenty thousand children of poor parents annually born: the question therefore is, how this number shall be reared, and provided for, which as I have already said, under the present situation of affairs is utterly impossible by all the methods hitherto proposed, for we can neither employ them in handicraft or agriculture; we neither build houses (I mean in the country), nor cultivate land: they can very seldom pick up a livelihood by stealing until they arrive at six years old, except where they are of towardly parts, although I confess they learn the rudiments much earlier, during which time they can however be properly looked upon only as probationers, as I have been informed by a principal gentleman in the County of Cavan, who protested to me that he never knew above one or two instances under the age of six, even in a part of the kingdom so renowned for the quickest proficiency in that art.

I am assured by our merchants that a boy or girl before twelve years old, is no saleable commodity, and even when they come to this age, they will not

[4] *shillings*: A shilling used to be worth about one day's labor.—Eds.

yield above three pounds, or three pounds and half-a-crown at most on the Exchange, which cannot turn to account either to the parents or the kingdom, the charge of nutriment and rags having been at least four times that value.

I shall now therefore humbly propose my own thoughts, which I hope will not be liable to the least objection.

I have been assured by a very knowing American of my acquaintance in London, that a young healthy child well nursed is at a year old a most delicious, nourishing and wholesome food, whether stewed, roasted, baked, or boiled, and I make no doubt that it will equally serve in a fricassee, or a ragout.

I do therefore humbly offer it to public consideration, that of the hundred and twenty thousand children already computed, twenty thousand may be reserved for breed, whereof only one-fourth part to be males, which is more than we allow to sheep, black-cattle, or swine, and my reason is that these children are seldom the fruits of marriage, a circumstance not much regarded by our savages, therefore one male will be sufficient to serve four females. That the remaining hundred thousand may at a year old be offered in sale to the persons of quality, and fortune, through the kingdom, always advising the mother to let them suck plentifully in the last month, so as to render them plump, and fat for a good table. A child will make two dishes at an entertainment for friends, and when the family dines alone, the fore or hind quarters will make a reasonable dish, and seasoned with a little pepper or salt will be very good boiled on the fourth day, especially in winter. 10

I have reckoned upon a medium, that a child just born will weigh twelve pounds, and in a solar year if tolerably nursed increaseth to twenty-eight pounds.

I grant this food will be somewhat dear, and therefore very proper for landlords, who, as they have already devoured most of the parents, seem to have the best title to the children.

Infant's flesh will be in season throughout the year, but more plentiful in March, and a little before and after, for we are told by a grave author, an eminent French physician,[5] that fish being a prolific diet, there are more children born in Roman Catholic countries about nine months after Lent than at any other season; therefore reckoning a year after Lent, the markets will be more glutted than usual, because the number of Popish infants is at least three to one in this kingdom, and therefore it will have one other collateral advantage by lessening the number of Papists among us.

I have already computed the charge of nursing a beggar's child (in which list I reckon all cottagers, laborers, and four-fifths of the farmers) to be about two shillings *per annum*, rags included, and I believe no gentleman would repine to give ten shillings for the carcass of a good fat child, which, as I have said, will make four dishes of excellent nutritive meat, when he hath only some particular friend of his own family to dine with him. Thus the Squire will learn to be a good landlord and grow popular among his tenants, the mother will

[5]*French physician*: François Rabelais (1494?–1553), a French physician and satirist who is known for his novel, *Gargantua and Pantagruel*.—Eds.

have eight shillings net profit, and be fit for work until she produces another child.

Those who are more thrifty (as I must confess the times require) may flay the carcass; the skin of which artificially dressed, will make admirable gloves for ladies, and summer boots for fine gentlemen. 15

As to our city of Dublin, shambles[6] may be appointed for this purpose, in the most convenient parts of it, and butchers we may be assured will not be wanting, although I rather recommend buying the children alive, and dressing them hot from the knife, as we do roasting pigs.

A very worthy person, a true lover of his country, and whose virtues I highly esteem, was lately pleased in discoursing on this matter to offer a refinement upon my scheme. He said that many gentlemen of this kingdom, having of late destroyed their deer, he conceived that the want of venison might be well supplied by the bodies of young lads and maidens, not exceeding fourteen years of age, nor under twelve, so great a number of both sexes in every county being now ready to starve, for want of work and service: and these to be disposed of by their parents if alive, or otherwise by their nearest relations. But with due deference to so excellent a friend, and so deserving a patriot, I cannot be altogether in his sentiments. For as to the males, my American acquaintance assured me from frequent experience that their flesh was generally tough and lean, like that of our schoolboys, by continual exercise, and their taste disagreeable, and to fatten them would not answer the charge. Then as to the females, it would, I think with humble submission, be a loss to the public, because they soon would become breeders themselves: and besides, it is not improbable that some scrupulous people might be apt to censure such a practice (although indeed very unjustly) as a little bordering upon cruelty, which I confess, hath always been with me the strongest objection against any project, howsoever well intended.

But in order to justify my friend, he confessed that this expedient was put into his head by the famous Psalmanazar, a native of the island Formosa, who came from thence to London, above twenty years ago, and in conversation told my friend that in his country when any young person happened to be put to death, the executioner sold the carcass to persons of quality, as a prime dainty, and that, in his time, the body of a plump girl of fifteen, who was crucified for an attempt to poison the emperor, was sold to his Imperial Majesty's Prime Minister of State, and other great Mandarins of the Court, in joints from the gibbet, at four hundred crowns. Neither indeed can I deny that if the same use were made of several plump young girls in this town who, without one single groat to their fortunes, cannot stir abroad without a chair, and appear at the playhouse and assemblies in foreign fineries, which they never will pay for, the kingdom would not be the worse.

Some persons of a desponding spirit are in great concern about that vast number of poor people, who are aged, diseased, or maimed, and I have been

[6]*shambles*: Slaughterhouses.—Eds.

desired to employ my thoughts what course may be taken to ease the nation of so grievous an encumbrance. But I am not in the least pain upon that matter, because it is very well known that they are every day dying, and rotting, by cold, and famine, and filth, and vermin, as fast as can be reasonably expected. And as to the younger laborers they are now in almost as hopeful a condition. They cannot get work, and consequently pine away from want of nourishment, to a degree that if at any time they are accidentally hired to common labor, they have not strength to perform it; and thus the country and themselves are in a fair way of being soon delivered from the evils to come.

I have too long digressed, and therefore shall return to my subject. I think the advantages by the proposal which I have made are obvious and many, as well as of the highest importance. 20

For first, as I have already observed, it would greatly lessen the number of Papists, with whom we are yearly over-run, being the principal breeders of the nation, as well as our most dangerous enemies, and who stay at home on purpose with a design to deliver the kingdom to the Pretender, hoping to take their advantage by the absence of so many good Protestants, who have chosen rather to leave their country than stay at home and pay tithes against their conscience to an idolatrous Episcopal curate.

Secondly, the poorer tenants will have something valuable of their own, which by law may be made liable to distress, and help to pay their landlord's rent, their corn and cattle being already seized, and money a thing unknown.

Thirdly, whereas the maintenance of an hundred thousand children, from two years old, and upwards, cannot be computed at less than ten shillings a piece *per annum*, the nation's stock will be thereby increased fifty thousand pounds *per annum*, besides the profit of a new dish, introduced to the tables of all gentlemen of fortune in the kingdom, who have any refinement in taste, and the money will circulate among ourselves, the goods being entirely of our own growth and manufacture.

Fourthly, the constant breeders, besides the gain of eight shillings sterling *per annum*, by the sale of their children, will be rid of the charge of maintaining them after the first year.

Fifthly, this food would likewise bring great custom to taverns, where the vintners will certainly be so prudent as to procure the best receipts for dressing it to perfection, and consequently have their houses frequented by all the fine gentlemen, who justly value themselves upon their knowledge in good eating; and a skillful cook, who understands how to oblige his guests, will contrive to make it as expensive as they please. 25

Sixthly, this would be a great inducement to marriage, which all wise nations have either encouraged by rewards, or enforced by laws and penalties. It would increase the care and tenderness of mothers towards their children, when they were sure of a settlement for life, to the poor babes, provided in some sort by the public to their annual profit instead of expense. We should soon see an honest emulation among the married women, which of them could bring the fattest child to the market. Men would become as fond of their wives, during the time of their pregnancy, as they are now of their mares in foal, their cows in calf, or sows when they are ready to farrow, nor offer to beat or kick them (as it is too frequent a practice) for fear of a miscarriage.

Many other advantages might be enumerated. For instance, the addition of some thousand carcasses in our exportation of barreled beef; the propagation of swine's flesh, and improvement in the art of making good bacon, so much wanted among us by the great destruction of pigs, too frequent at our tables, are no way comparable in taste or magnificence to a well-grown, fat yearling child, which roasted whole will make a considerable figure at a Lord Mayor's feast, or any other public entertainment. But this and many others I omit, being studious of brevity.

Supposing that one thousand families in this city would be constant customers for infants' flesh, besides others who might have it at merry meetings, particularly weddings and christenings; I compute that Dublin would take off annually about twenty thousand carcasses, and the rest of the kingdom (where probably they will be sold somewhat cheaper) the remaining eighty thousand.

I can think of no one objection that will possibly be raised against this proposal, unless it should be urged that the number of people will be thereby much lessened in the kingdom. This I freely own, and it was indeed one principal design in offering it to the world. I desire the reader will observe, that I calculate my remedy *for this one individual Kingdom of* Ireland, *and for no other that ever was, is, or, I think, ever can be upon earth.* Therefore let no man talk to me of other expedients: *Of taxing our absentees at five shillings a pound: Of using neither clothes, nor household furniture, except what is of our own growth and manufacture: Of utterly rejecting the materials and instruments that promote foreign luxury: Of curing the expensiveness of pride, vanity, idleness, and gaming in our women: Of introducing a vein of parsimony, prudence, and temperance: Of learning to love our country, wherein we differ even from* Laplanders, *and the inhabitants of* Topinamboo*: Of quitting our animosities and factions, nor act any longer like the* Jews, *who were murdering one another at the very moment their city was taken: Of being a little cautious not to sell our country and consciences for nothing: Of teaching landlords to have at least one degree of mercy towards their tenants.* Lastly, *of putting a spirit of honesty, industry, and skill into our shopkeepers, who, if a resolution could now be taken to buy only our native goods, would immediately unite to cheat and exact upon us in the price, the measure and the goodness, nor could ever yet be brought to make one fair proposal of just dealing, though often and earnestly invited to it.*

Therefore I repeat, let no man talk to me of these and the like expedients, 30 till he hath at least a glimpse of hope that there will ever be some hearty and sincere attempt to put them in practice.

But as to myself, having been wearied out for many years with offering vain, idle, visionary thoughts, and at length utterly despairing of success, I fortunately fell upon this proposal, which as it is wholly new, so it hath something solid and real, of no expense and little trouble, full in our own power, and whereby we can incur no danger in disobliging England. For this kind of commodity will not bear exportation, the flesh being of too tender a consistence to admit a long continuance in salt, *although perhaps I could name a country which would be glad to eat up our whole nation without it.*

After all I am not so violently bent upon my own opinion as to reject any offer, proposed by wise men, which shall be found equally innocent, cheap, easy and effectual. But before some thing of that kind shall be advanced in contradiction to my scheme, and offering a better, I desire the author, or authors, will be pleased maturely to consider two points. First, as things now stand, how they will be able to find food and raiment for an hundred thousand useless mouths and backs? And secondly, there being a round million of creatures in human figure, throughout this kingdom, whose whole subsistence put into a common stock would leave them in debt two millions of pounds sterling; adding those who are beggars by profession, to the bulk of farmers, cottagers, and laborers with their wives and children, who are beggars in effect; I desire those politicians who dislike my overture, and may perhaps be so bold to attempt an answer, that they will first ask the parents of these mortals whether they would not at this day think it a great happiness to have been sold for food at a year old, in the manner I prescribe, and thereby have avoided such a perpetual scene of misfortunes as they have since gone through, by the oppression of landlords, the impossibility of paying rent without money or trade, the want of common sustenance, with neither house nor clothes to cover them from the inclemencies of weather, and the most inevitable prospect of entailing the like, or greater miseries upon their breed for ever.

I profess in the sincerity of my heart that I have not the least personal interest in endeavoring to promote this necessary work, having no other motive than the *public good of my country, by advancing our trade, providing for infants, relieving the poor, and giving some pleasure to the rich.* I have no children by which I can propose to get a single penny; the youngest being nine years old, and my wife past child-bearing.

▪ QUESTIONS

Reading

1. A proposal always involves a proposer. What is the character of the proposer here? How do we distinguish between the author and the proposer? What details of style help us make this distinction?
2. When does the proposer actually offer his proposal? What does he do before making his proposal, and what does he do after? How does the order in which he does things affect our impression of both him and his proposal?
3. List the counterarguments to his own proposal that the proposer anticipates. How does he answer and refute proposals that might be considered alternatives to his?
4. It will (hopefully) be evident to most readers that this proposal is *ironic*. Identify several specific places where the author uses words, phrases, or details to highlight the ironic humor of not only the proposal's content but the proposer's tone. Underline, highlight, or flag these instances and be prepared to discuss them in class.

Exploratory Writing

1. To what extent does an ironic essay like this depend on shared values being held by the author and readers without question or exception? In groups, list and discuss several popularly upheld historical positions that now seem to be just as outrageous and absurd as this "modest proposal." (Examples might include burning witches at the stake, executing people for claiming that the earth was round, or denying adults the right to vote and own property because of their race.)
2. *Reductio ad absurdum* is a type of argument in which, in order to disprove a proposition, a writer assumes that very proposition and then shows that it leads to absurd or impossible conclusions. Using this strategy, choose a position in a popular legal debate, and write your own "modest proposal" on its behalf.

Making Connections

1. Steven Pinker (p. 458) argues that there are many issues for which we, as a society, are "too quick to hit the moralization button and look for villains" rather than actually fix the problems. "Our habit of moralizing problems . . . can get in the way of doing the right thing." Choose an argument from Pinker's essay, such as his comments on human-induced climate change (paragraph 77), and discuss ways it is similar to, or different from, the argument in "A Modest Proposal."

Essay Writing

1. Write an essay explaining what you see as advantages and disadvantages of using irony in a written argument.

ARGUING

Politics and the English Language

George Orwell

Despite suffering from tuberculosis, prolific British writer George Orwell (1903–1950) wrote ten books and more than seven hundred articles and reviews during his foreshortened life. His most famous novels, *Animal Farm* (1945) and *1984* (1949), dramatize the causes of totalitarianism in Europe, the rise of which Orwell witnessed and fought, both in writing and briefly as a soldier in the Spanish Civil War. In this essay, written in 1946, Orwell tells his readers that "in our time, political speech and writing are largely the defense of the indefensible." He attacks language that consists "largely of euphemism, question begging and sheer cloudy vagueness." Orwell, like John Berger (p. 236), is concerned with the ways in which language is often used to conceal unpleasant and horrifying realities.

Most people who bother with the matter at all would admit that the English language is in a bad way, but it is generally assumed that we cannot by conscious action do anything about it. Our civilization is decadent and our language—so the argument runs—must inevitably share in the general collapse. It follows that any struggle against the abuse of language is a sentimental archaism, like preferring candles to electric light or hansom cabs to aeroplanes. Underneath this lies the half-conscious belief that language is a natural growth and not an instrument which we shape for our own purposes.

Now, it is clear that the decline of a language must ultimately have political and economic causes: it is not due simply to the bad influence of this or that individual writer. But an effect can become a cause, reinforcing the original cause and producing the same effect in an intensified form, and so on indefinitely. A man may take to drink because he feels himself to be a failure, and then fail all the more completely because he drinks. It is rather the same thing that is happening to the English language. It becomes ugly and inaccurate because our thoughts are foolish, but the slovenliness of our language makes it easier for us to have foolish thoughts. The point is that the process is reversible. Modern English, especially written English, is full of bad habits which spread by imitation and which can be avoided if one is willing to take the necessary trouble. If one gets rid of these habits one can think more clearly, and to think clearly is a necessary first step towards political regeneration: so that the fight against bad English is not frivolous and is not the exclusive concern of professional writers. I will come back to this presently, and I hope that by that time the meaning of what I have said here will have become clearer. Meanwhile, here are five specimens of the English language as it is now habitually written.

These five passages have not been picked out because they are especially bad—I could have quoted far worse if I had chosen—but because they illustrate various of the mental vices from which we now suffer. They are a little below the average, but are fairly representative samples. I number them so that I can refer back to them when necessary:

> "(1) I am not, indeed, sure whether it is not true to say that the Milton who once seemed not unlike a seventeenth-century Shelley had not become, out of an experience ever more bitter in each year, more alien [*sic*] to the founder of that Jesuit sect which nothing could induce him to tolerate."
>
> **Professor Harold Laski** (Essay in *Freedom of Expression*)

> "(2) Above all, we cannot play ducks and drakes with a native battery of idioms which prescribes such egregious collocations of vocables as the basic *put up with* for *tolerate* or *put at a loss* for *bewilder*."
>
> **Professor Lancelot Hogben** (*Interglossa*)

> "(3) On the one side we have the free personality: by definition it is not neurotic, for it has neither conflict nor dream. Its desires, such as they are, are transparent, for they are just what institutional approval keeps in the forefront of consciousness; another institutional pattern would alter their number and intensity; there is little in them that is natural, irreducible, or culturally dangerous. But *on the other* side, the social bond itself is nothing but the mutual reflection of these self-secure integrities. Recall the definition of love. Is not this the very picture of a small academic? Where is there a place in this hall of mirrors for either personality or fraternity?"
>
> **Essay on psychology in *Politics*** (New York)

> "(4) All the 'best people' from the gentlemen's clubs, and all the frantic fascist captains, united in common hatred of Socialism and bestial horror of the rising tide of the mass revolutionary movement, have turned to acts of provocation, to foul incendiarism, to medieval legends of poisoned wells, to legalize their own destruction of proletarian organizations, and rouse the agitated petty-bourgeoisie to chauvinistic fervour on behalf of the fight against the revolutionary way out of the crisis."
>
> **Communist Pamphlet**

> "(5) If a new spirit *is* to be infused into this old country, there is one thorny and contentious reform which must be tackled, and that is the humanization and galvanization of the B.B.C. Timidity here will bespeak cancer and atrophy of the soul. The heart of Britain may be sound and of strong beat, for instance, but the British lion's roar at present is like that of Bottom in Shakespeare's *Midsummer Night's Dream*—as gentle as any sucking dove. A virile new Britain cannot continue indefinitely to be traduced in the eyes or rather ears, of the world by the effete languors of Langham Place, brazenly masquerading as 'standard

English.' When the Voice of Britain is heard at nine o'clock, better far and infinitely less ludicrous to hear aitches honestly dropped than the present priggish, inflated, inhibited, school-ma'amish arch braying of blameless bashful mewing maidens!"

LETTER IN *TRIBUNE*

Each of these passages has faults of its own, but, quite apart from avoidable ugliness, two qualities are common to all of them. The first is staleness of imagery: the other is lack of precision. The writer either has a meaning and cannot express it, or he inadvertently says something else, or he is almost indifferent as to whether his words mean anything or not. This mixture of vagueness and sheer incompetence is the most marked characteristic of modern English prose, and especially of any kind of political writing. As soon as certain topics are raised, the concrete melts into the abstract and no one seems able to think of turns of speech that are not hackneyed: prose consists less and less of *words* chosen for the sake of their meaning, and more and more of *phrases* tacked together like the sections of a prefabricated hen-house. I list below, with notes and examples, various of the tricks by means of which the work of prose-construction is habitually dodged:

Dying Metaphors A newly invented metaphor assists thought by evoking a visual image, while on the other hand a metaphor which is technically "dead" (e.g. *iron resolution*) has in effect reverted to being an ordinary word and can generally be used without loss of vividness. But in between these two classes there is a huge dump of worn-out metaphors which have lost all evocative power and are merely used because they save people the trouble of inventing phrases for themselves. Examples are: *Ring the changes on, take up the cudgels for, toe the line, ride roughshod over, stand shoulder to shoulder with, play into the hands of, no axe to grind, grist to the mill, fishing in troubled waters, on the order of the day, Achilles' heel, swan song, hotbed.* Many of these are used without knowledge of their meaning (what is a "rift," for instance?), and incompatible metaphors are frequently mixed, a sure sign that the writer is not interested in what he is saying. Some metaphors now current have been twisted out of their original meaning without those who use them even being aware of the fact. For example, *toe the line* is sometimes written *tow the line.* Another example is *the hammer and the anvil,* now always used with the implication that the anvil gets the worst of it. In real life it is always the anvil that breaks the hammer, never the other way about: a writer who stopped to think what he was saying would be aware of this, and would avoid perverting the original phrase. 5

Operators or Verbal False Limbs These save the trouble of picking out appropriate verbs and nouns, and at the same time pad each sentence with extra syllables which give it an appearance of symmetry. Characteristic phrases are: *render inoperative, militate against, make contact with, be subjected to, give rise* *to, give grounds for, have the effect of, play a leading part (role) in, make itself felt, take effect, exhibit a tendency to, serve the purpose of, etc., etc.* The keynote is the elimination of simple verbs. Instead of being a single word, such as *break, stop, spoil, mend, kill,* a verb becomes a *phrase,* made up of a noun or adjective tacked on to some general-purposes verb such as *prove, serve, form, play, render.* In addition, the passive voice is wherever possible used in preference to the active, and noun constructions are used instead of gerunds (*by examination of* instead of *by examining*). The range of verbs is further cut down by means of the *-ize* and *de-* formation, and the banal statements are given an appearance of profundity by means of the *not un-* formation. Simple conjunctions and prepositions are replaced by such phrases as *with respect to, having regard to, the fact that, by dint of, in view of, in the interests of, on the hypothesis that;* and the ends of sentences are saved from anticlimax by such resounding commonplaces as *greatly to be desired, cannot be left out of account, a development to be expected in the near future, deserving of serious consideration, brought to a satisfactory conclusion,* and so on and so forth.

Pretentious Diction Words like *phenomenon, element, individual* (as noun), *objective, categorical, effective, virtual, basic, primary, promote, constitute, exhibit, exploit, utilize, eliminate, liquidate,* are used to dress up simple statements and give an air of scientific impartiality to biased judgments. Adjectives like *epoch-making, epic, historic, unforgettable, triumphant, age-old, inevitable, inexorable, veritable,* are used to dignify the sordid processes of international politics, while writing that aims at glorifying war usually takes on an archaic color, its characteristic words being: *realm, throne, chariot, mailed fist, trident, sword, shield, buckler, banner, jackboot, clarion.* Foreign words and expressions such as *cul de sac, ancien régime, deus ex machina, mutatis mutandis, status quo, gleichschaltung, weltanschauung,* are used to give an air of culture and elegance. Except for the useful abbreviations *i.e., e.g.,* and *etc.,* there is no real need for any of the hundreds of foreign phrases now current in English. Bad writers, and especially scientific, political and sociological writers, are nearly always haunted by the notion that Latin or Greek words are grander than Saxon ones, and unnecessary words like *expedite, ameliorate, predict, extraneous, deracinated, clandestine, subaqueous* and hundreds of others constantly gain ground from their Anglo-Saxon opposite numbers.[1] The jargon peculiar to Marxist writing (*hyena, hangman, cannibal, petty bourgeois, these gentry, lackey, flunky, mad dog, White Guard,* etc.) consists largely of words and phrases translated from Russian, German or French; but the normal way of coining a new word is to use a Latin or Greek root with the appropriate affix and, where necessary, the *-ize* formation. It is often easier to make up words of this kind (*deregionalize, impermissible, extramarital, nonfrag-*

[1]An interesting illustration of this is the way in which the English flower names which were in use till very recently are being ousted by Greek ones, *snapdragon* becoming *antirrhinum, forget-me-not* becoming *myosotis,* etc. It is hard to see any practical reason for this change of fashion: it is probably due to an instinctive turning-away from the more homely word and a vague feeling that the Greek word is scientific.

mentatory and so forth) than to think up the English words that will cover one's meaning. The result, in general, is an increase in slovenliness and vagueness.

Meaningless Words In certain kinds of writing, particularly in art criticism and literary criticism, it is normal to come across long passages which are almost completely lacking in meaning.[2] Words like *romantic, plastic, values, human, dead, sentimental, natural, vitality,* as used in art criticism, are strictly meaningless in the sense that they not only do not point to any discoverable object, but are hardly ever expected to do so by the reader. When one critic writes, "The outstanding feature of Mr. X's work is its living quality," while another writes, "The immediately striking thing about Mr. X's work is its peculiar deadness," the reader accepts this as a simple difference of opinion. If words like *black* and *white* were involved, instead of the jargon words *dead* and *living,* he would see at once that language was being used in an improper way. Many political words are similarly abused. The word *Fascism* has now no meaning except in so far as it signifies "something not desirable." The words *democracy, socialism, freedom, patriotic, realistic, justice,* have each of them several different meanings which cannot be reconciled with one another. In the case of a word like *democracy,* not only is there no agreed definition, but the attempt to make one is resisted from all sides. It is almost universally felt that when we call a country democratic we are praising it: consequently the defenders of every kind of régime claim that it is a democracy, and fear that they might have to stop using the word if it were tied down to any one meaning. Words of this kind are often used in a consciously dishonest way. That is, the person who uses them has his own private definition, but allows his hearer to think he means something quite different. Statements like *Marshal Pétain was a true patriot, The Soviet Press is the freest in the world, The Catholic Church is opposed to persecution,* are almost always made with intent to deceive. Other words used in variable meanings, in most cases more or less dishonestly, are: *class, totalitarian, science, progressive, reactionary, bourgeois, equality.*

Now that I have made this catalog of swindles and perversions, let me give another example of the kind of writing that they lead to. This time it must of its nature be an imaginary one. I am going to translate a passage of good English into modern English of the worst sort. Here is a well-known verse from *Ecclesiastes*:

> "I returned and saw under the sun, that the race is not to the swift, nor the battle to the strong, neither yet bread to the wise, nor yet riches to men of understanding, nor yet favor to men of skill; but time and chance happeneth to them all."

---

[2]Example: "Comfort's catholicity of perception and image, strangely Whit-manesque in range, almost the exact opposite in aesthetic compulsion, continues to evoke that trembling atmospheric accumulative hinting at a cruel, an inexorably serene timelessness. . . . Wrey Gardiner scores by aiming at simple bull's-eyes with precision. Only they are not so simple, and through this contented sadness runs more than the surface bittersweet of resignation" (*Poetry Quarterly*).

Here it is in modern English:

> "Objective consideration of contemporary phenomena compels the conclusion that success or failure in competitive activities exhibits no tendency to be commensurate with innate capacity, but that a considerable element of the unpredictable must invariably be taken into account."

This is a parody, but not a very gross one. Exhibit (3), above, for instance, contains several patches of the same kind of English. It will be seen that I have not made a full translation. The beginning and ending of the sentence follow the original meaning fairly closely, but in the middle the concrete illustrations—race, battle, bread—dissolve into the vague phrase "success or failure in competitive activities." This had to be so, because no modern writer of the kind I am discussing—no one capable of using phrases like "objective consideration of contemporary phenomena"—would ever tabulate his thoughts in that precise and detailed way. The whole tendency of modern prose is away from concreteness. Now analyze these two sentences a little more closely. The first contains forty-nine words but only sixty syllables, and all its words are those of everyday life. The second contains thirty-eight words of ninety syllables: eighteen of its words are from Latin roots, and one from Greek. The first sentence contains six vivid images, and only one phrase ("time and chance") that could be called vague. The second contains not a single fresh, arresting phrase, and in spite of its ninety syllables it gives only a shortened version of the meaning contained in the first. Yet without a doubt it is the second kind of sentence that is gaining ground in modern English. I do not want to exaggerate. This kind of writing is not yet universal, and outcrops of simplicity will occur here and there in the worst-written page. Still, if you or I were told to write a few lines on the uncertainty of human fortunes, we should probably come much nearer to my imaginary sentence than to the one from *Ecclesiastes.* 10

As I have tried to show, modern writing at its worst does not consist in picking out words for the sake of their meaning and inventing images in order to make the meaning clearer. It consists in gumming together long strips of words which have already been set in order by someone else, and making the results presentable by sheer humbug. The attraction of this way of writing is that it is easy. It is easier—even quicker, once you have the habit—to say *In my opinion it is a not unjustifiable assumption that* than to say *I think.* If you use ready-made phrases, you not only don't have to hunt about for words; you also don't have to bother with the rhythms of your sentences, since these phrases are generally so arranged as to be more or less euphonious. When you are composing in a hurry—when you are dictating to a stenographer, for instance, or making a public speech—it is natural to fall into a pretentious, Latinized style. Tags like *a consideration which we should do well to bear in mind* or *a conclusion to which all of us would readily assent* will save many a sentence from coming down with a bump. By using stale metaphors, similes and idioms, you save much mental effort, at the cost of leaving your meaning vague, not only for your reader but for yourself. This is the significance of mixed metaphors. The sole aim of a metaphor is to call up a visual image. When these images clash—as in *The Fascist octopus has sung its swan song, the jackboot is thrown into the melting pot*—it can be taken as certain that the writer is not seeing a mental image of the objects he is naming; in other words he is not really thinking. Look again at the examples I gave at the beginning of this essay. Professor Laski (1) uses five negatives in fifty-three words. One of these is superfluous, making nonsense of the whole passage, and in addition there is the slip *alien* for akin, making further nonsense, and several avoidable pieces of clumsiness which increase the general vagueness. Professor Hogben (2) plays ducks and drakes with a battery which is able to write prescriptions, and, while disapproving of the everyday phrase *put up with*, is unwilling to look *egregious* up in the dictionary and see what it means. (3), if one takes an uncharitable attitude towards it, is simply meaningless: probably one could work out its intended meaning by reading the whole of the article in which it occurs. In (4), the writer knows more or less what he wants to say, but an accumulation of stale phrases chokes him like tea leaves blocking a sink. In (5), words and meaning have almost parted company. People who write in this manner usually have a general emotional meaning—they dislike one thing and want to express solidarity with another—but they are not interested in the detail of what they are saying. A scrupulous writer, in every sentence that he writes, will ask himself at least four questions, thus: What am I trying to say? What words will express it? What image or idiom will make it clearer? Is this image fresh enough to have an effect? And he will probably ask himself two more: Could I put it more shortly? Have I said anything that is avoidably ugly? But you are not obliged to go to all this trouble. You can shirk it by simply throwing your mind open and letting the ready-made phrases come crowding in. They will construct your sentences for you—even think your thoughts for you, to a certain extent—and at need they will perform the important service of partially concealing your meaning even from yourself. It is at this point that the special connection between politics and the debasement of language becomes clear.

In our time it is broadly true that political writing is bad writing. Where it is not true, it will generally be found that the writer is some kind of rebel, expressing his private opinions and not a "party line." Orthodoxy, of whatever color, seems to demand a lifeless, imitative style. The political dialects to be found in pamphlets, leading articles, manifestos, White Papers and the speeches of under-secretaries do, of course, vary from party to party, but they are all alike in that one almost never finds in them a fresh, vivid, home-made turn of speech. When one watches some tired hack on the platform mechanically repeating the familiar phrases—*bestial atrocities, iron heel, bloodstained tyranny, free peoples of the world, stand shoulder to shoulder*—one often has a curious feeling that one is not watching a live human being but some kind of dummy: a feeling which suddenly becomes stronger at moments when the light catches the speaker's spectacles and turns them into blank discs which seem to have no eyes behind them. And this is not altogether fanciful. A speaker who uses that kind of phraseology has gone some distance towards turning himself into a machine. The appropriate noises are coming out of his larynx, but his brain is not involved as it would be if he were choosing his words for himself. If the speech he is making is one that he is accustomed to make over and over again, he may be almost unconscious of what he is saying, as one is when one utters the responses in church. And this reduced state of consciousness, if not indispensable, is at any rate favorable to political conformity.

In our time, political speech and writing are largely the defense of the indefensible. Things like the continuance of British rule in India, the Russian purges and deportations, the dropping of the atom bombs on Japan, can indeed be defended, but only by arguments which are too brutal for most people to face, and which do not square with the professed aims of political parties. Thus political language has to consist largely of euphemism, question-begging and sheer cloudy vagueness. Defenseless villages are bombarded from the air, the inhabitants driven out into the countryside, the cattle machine-gunned, the huts set on fire with incendiary bullets: this is called *pacification*. Millions of peasants are robbed of their farms and sent trudging along the roads with no more than they can carry: this is called *transfer of population* or *rectification of frontiers*. People are imprisoned for years without trial, or shot in the back of the neck or sent to die of scurvy in Arctic lumber camps: this is called *elimination of unreliable elements*. Such phraseology is needed if one wants to name things without calling up mental pictures of them. Consider for instance some comfortable English professor defending Russian totalitarianism. He cannot say outright, "I believe in killing off your opponents when you can get good results by doing so." Probably, therefore, he will say something like this:

"While freely conceding that the Soviet régime exhibits certain features which the humanitarian may be inclined to deplore, we must, I think, agree that a certain curtailment of the right to political opposition is an unavoidable concomitant of transitional periods, and that the rigors which the Russian people have been called upon to undergo have been amply justified in the sphere of concrete achievement."

The inflated style is itself a kind of euphemism. A mass of Latin words falls upon the facts like soft snow, blurring the outlines and covering up all the details. The great enemy of clear language is insincerity. When there is a gap between one's real and one's declared aims, one turns as it were instinctively to long words and exhausted idioms, like a cuttlefish squirting out ink. In our age there is no such thing as "keeping out of politics." All issues are political issues, and politics itself is a mass of lies, evasions, folly, hatred and schizophrenia. When the general atmosphere is bad, language must suffer. I should expect to find—this is a guess which I have not sufficient knowledge to verify—that the German, Russian and Italian languages have all deteriorated in the last ten or fifteen years, as a result of dictatorship. 15

But if thought corrupts language, language can also corrupt thought. A bad usage can spread by tradition and imitation, even among people who should and do know better. The debased language that I have been discussing is in some ways very convenient. Phrases like *a not unjustifiable assumption, leaves much to be desired, would serve no good purpose, a consideration which we should do well to bear in mind,* are a continuous temptation, a packet of aspirins always at one's elbow. Look back through this essay, and for certain you will find that I have again and again committed the very faults I am protesting against. By this morning's post I have received a pamphlet dealing with conditions in Germany. The author tells me that he "felt impelled" to write it. I open it at random, and here is almost the first sentence that I see: "(The Allies) have an opportunity not only of achieving a radical transformation of Germany's social and political structure in such a way as to avoid a nationalistic reaction in Germany itself, but at the same time of laying the foundations of a cooperative and unified Europe." You see, he "feels impelled" to write—feels, presumably, that he has something new to say—and yet his words, like cavalry horses answering the bugle, group themselves automatically into the familiar dreary pattern. This invasion of one's mind by ready-made phrases (*lay the foundations, achieve a radical transformation*) can only be prevented if one is constantly on guard against them, and every such phrase anaesthetizes a portion of one's brain.

I said earlier that the decadence of our language is probably curable. Those who deny this would argue, if they produced an argument at all, that language merely reflects existing social conditions, and that we cannot influence its development by any direct tinkering with words and constructions. So far as the general tone or spirit of a language goes, this may be true, but it is not true in detail. Silly words and expressions have often disappeared, not through any evolutionary process but owing to the conscious action of a minority. Two recent examples were *explore every avenue* and *leave no stone unturned,* which were killed by the jeers of a few journalists. There is a long list of flyblown metaphors which could similarly be got rid of if enough people would interest themselves in the job; and it should also be possible to laugh the *not un-* formation out of existence,[3] to reduce the amount of Latin and Greek in the average sentence, to drive out foreign phrases and strayed scientific words, and, in general, to make pretentiousness unfashionable. But all these are minor points. The defense of the English language implies more than this, and perhaps it is best to start by saying what it does not imply.

To begin with it has nothing to do with archaism, with the salvaging of obsolete words and turns of speech, or with the setting up of a "standard English" which must never be departed from. On the contrary, it is especially concerned with the scrapping of every word or idiom which has outworn its usefulness. It has nothing to do with correct grammar and syntax, which are of no importance so long as one makes one's meaning clear, or with the avoidance of Americanisms, or with having what is called a "good prose style." On the other hand it is not concerned with fake simplicity and the attempt to make written English colloquial. Nor does it even imply in every case preferring the Saxon word to the Latin one, though it does imply using the fewest

[3]One can cure oneself of the *not un-* formation by memorizing this sentence: *A not unblack dog was chasing a not unsmall rabbit across a not ungreen field.*

and shortest words that will cover one's meaning. What is above all needed is to let the meaning choose the word, and not the other way about. In prose, the worst thing one can do with words is to surrender to them. When you think of a concrete object, you think wordlessly, and then, if you want to describe the thing you have been visualizing you probably hunt about till you find the exact words that seem to fit. When you think of something abstract you are more inclined to use words from the start, and unless you make a conscious effort to prevent it, the existing dialect will come rushing in and do the job for you, at the expense of blurring or even changing your meaning. Probably it is better to put off using words as long as possible and get one's meaning as clear as one can through pictures or sensations. Afterwards one can choose—not simply *accept*—the phrases that will best cover the meaning, and then switch round and decide what impression one's words are likely to make on another person. This last effort of the mind cuts out all stale or mixed images, all prefabricated phrases, needless repetitions, and humbug and vagueness generally. But one can often be in doubt about the effect of a word or a phrase, and one needs rules that one can rely on when instinct fails. I think the following rules will cover most cases:

(i) Never use a metaphor, simile or other figure of speech which you are used to seeing in print.
(ii) Never use a long word where a short one will do.
(iii) If it is possible to cut a word out, always cut it out.
(iv) Never use the passive where you can use the active.
(v) Never use a foreign phrase, a scientific word or a jargon word if you can think of an everyday English equivalent.
(vi) Break any of these rules sooner than say anything outright barbarous.

These rules sound elementary, and so they are, but they demand a deep change of attitude in anyone who has grown used to writing in the style now fashionable. One could keep all of them and still write bad English, but one could not write the kind of stuff that I quoted in those five specimens at the beginning of this article.

I have not here been considering the literary use of language, but merely language as an instrument for expressing and not for concealing or preventing thought. Stuart Chase and others have come near to claiming that all abstract words are meaningless, and have used this as a pretext for advocating a kind of political quietism. Since you don't know what Fascism is, how can you struggle against Fascism? One need not swallow such absurdities as this, but one ought to recognize that the present political chaos is connected with the decay of language, and that one can probably bring about some improvement by starting at the verbal end. If you simplify your English, you are freed from the worst follies of orthodoxy. You cannot speak any of the necessary dialects, and when you make a stupid remark its stupidity will be obvious, even to yourself. Political language—and with variations this is true of all political parties, 20 from Conservatives to Anarchists—is designed to make lies sound truthful and murder respectable, and to give an appearance of solidity to pure wind. One cannot change this all in a moment, but one can at least change one's own habits, and from time to time one can even, if one jeers loudly enough, send some worn-out and useless phrase—some *jackboot, Achilles' heel, hotbed, melting pot, acid test, veritable inferno* or other lump of verbal refuse—into the dustbin where it belongs.

▪ QUESTIONS

Reading

1. What is Orwell's position on the ways that modern writers are destroying the English language?
2. Orwell argues that "thought corrupts language," but he also argues that "language can also corrupt thought" (paragraph 16). What argument is he making? How does language corrupt thought?
3. Orwell writes in paragraph 16, "Look back through this essay, and for certain you will find that I have again and again committed the very faults I am protesting against." Does Orwell, in fact, break his own rules? If so, what might his purpose be in doing so?
4. What sense of himself does Orwell present to his readers? How would you describe his persona?

Exploratory Writing

1. Orwell stresses that his argument is not about the *literary* use of language. Find an example of a piece of literary writing—poetry, fiction, or literary prose—and analyze it according to Orwell's rules. Discuss whether the guidelines for literary and political writing should be the same.
2. Orwell presents guidelines for good writing in paragraph 18. Exchange one of your recent essays with a classmate. How does your partner's writing measure up to Orwell's standards?

Making Connections

1. American writer James Baldwin (p. 131) was probably influenced by Orwell's essay. Write an essay of your own explaining the connections that you find between Orwell and Baldwin.
2. Orwell argues that "all stale or mixed images, all prefabricated phrases, needless repetitions, and humbug and vagueness generally" turn language into a means of concealing or preventing thought (paragraph 18). He offers rules for political writing that will avoid these pitfalls. If contemporary journalists were required to use Orwell's rules (paragraph 18), would this prevent hidden biases within their work? How does Orwell's conclusion that "the present political chaos is connected with the decay of language" (paragraph 20) apply to Brooke Gladstone's contemporary examples of media bias in "The Great Refusal" (p. 325)?

Essay Writing

1. Spend one week developing a list of examples of bad writing from newspapers and popular magazines. Use this material as the basis for an essay in which you develop a thesis arguing your position on politics and language.
2. Written more than sixty years ago, this is probably the best known of all of Orwell's essays. How insightful and current do you find it today? Take five examples from your reading, as Orwell takes from his, and use them as evidence in an argument of your own about the state of contemporary written English. Take your examples from anywhere you like, including this book—even this question—if you wish. Be careful to choose recent pieces of writing.

EXPLAINING

The Great Refusal

Brooke Gladstone

Media analyst Brooke Gladstone is the managing editor and cohost of National Public Radio's program *On the Media*. She began her career as a print journalist and reviewer, writing for newspapers including the *London Observer*, the *Washington Post*, and the *Boston Globe*. In 1987, she accepted her first editorial position at NPR. Gladstone's multiple awards include a Knight Fellowship at Stanford University, a Peabody Award, and an Overseas Press Club Award. During her Knight Fellowship, she spent a year in Russia, studying the language and covering the bloody insurgency of the Parliament for NPR. In an interview with Scott Simon about her book *The Influencing Machine: Brooke Gladstone on the Media* (2011), illustrated by Josh Neufeld, Gladstone answered the question, "Can reporters be objective?" with "a resolute 'No.'" "Reporters can be fair," she said. "But there's no way that we can divorce ourselves from the experience gleaned over a lifetime that forces us to come to certain conclusions." Take her comments into account as you read this excerpt from *The Influencing Machine*, which explores media bias.

The Great Refusal

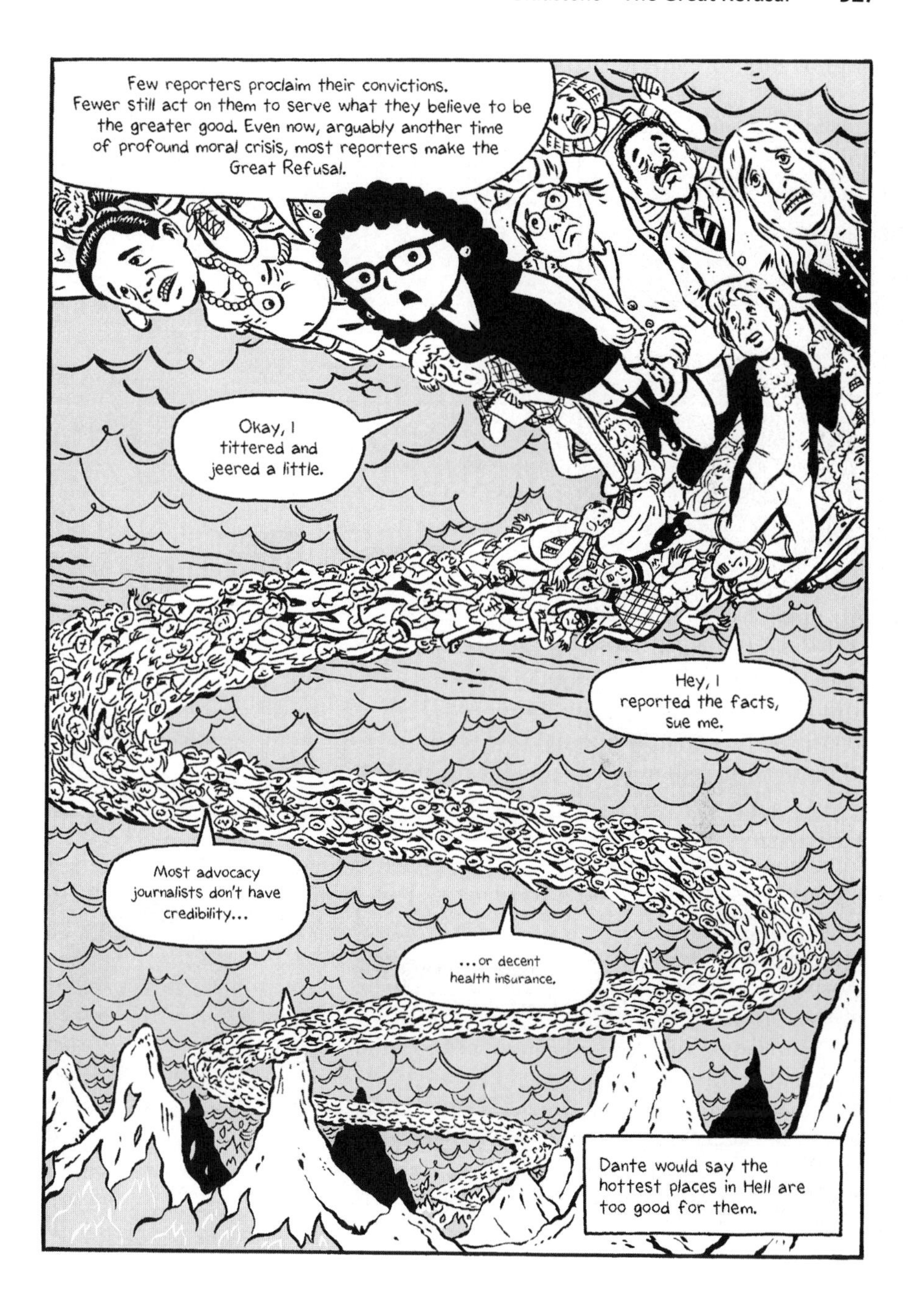
Few reporters proclaim their convictions. Fewer still act on them to serve what they believe to be the greater good. Even now, arguably another time of profound moral crisis, most reporters make the Great Refusal.
Okay, I tittered and jeered a little.
Hey, I reported the facts, sue me.
Most advocacy journalists don't have credibility...
...or decent health insurance.
Dante would say the hottest places in Hell are too good for them.

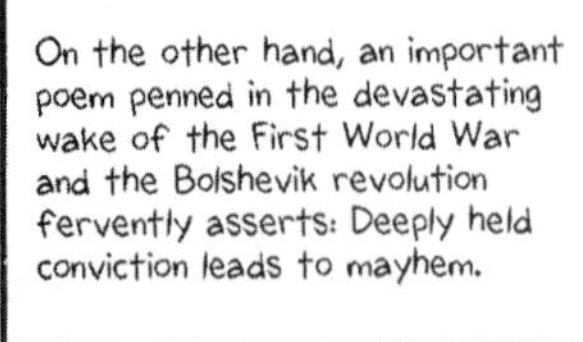
On the other hand, an important poem penned in the devastating wake of the First World War and the Bolshevik revolution fervently asserts: Deeply held conviction leads to mayhem.

Turning and turning in the widening gyre
The falcon cannot hear the falconer...

"Things fall apart; the centre cannot hold;
Mere anarchy is loosed upon the world,
The blood-dimmed tide is loosed, and everywhere
The ceremony of innocence is drowned..."

The **best** lack all conviction, while the **worst**
Are full of passionate intensity.

Damn you, Yeats! Pick a side!
Yeats is the typical news consumer. On any issue -- where one person sees moral courage, another sees culpable bias.

In a 2009 poll, 60% of respondents charged news organizations with bias, up from 45% in 1985. In both years, they saw a mostly liberal bias.
And in fact, reporters are more likely than the general public to identify themselves as liberal.
U.S.S. BIAS

In 2006, New York Times publisher Arthur Sulzberger, Jr., spoke to graduates at the State University of New York at New Paltz.
It wasn't supposed to be this way.
You weren't supposed to be graduating into a world where we are still fighting for fundamental human rights, whether it's the rights of immigrants to start a new life, or the rights of gays to marry, or the rights of women to choose.
STATE UNIVERSITY OF NEW YORK
You weren't supposed to be graduating into a world where oil still drove policy and environmentalists have to fight relentlessly for every gain. You weren't, but you are. And for that, I'm sorry.
I must be honest. I can only read so many paragraphs of a New York Times story before I **puke.**

MOST AMERICANS DON'T READ THE *TIMES*, but among those who express an opinion, Republicans disapprove of the paper by a margin of nearly two to one, while Democrats favor it almost five to one.

A 2002 study by Jim Kuypers at Virginia Tech examined 116 newspapers, including the *Times*. He concluded that the print press operates within a narrow range of mostly liberal beliefs. Those on the far left are ignored, and those who hold what he defines as moderate or conservative views are either denigrated or labeled as "minority opinions."

And yet liberal media watchdogs have found that the mainstream media quote far more conservatives than liberals. They have polled reporters and found them liberal on social issues but conservative on economic ones. And they note that "he who pays the piper calls the tune," and the media's paymasters are a handful of multinational corporations—hardly bastions of liberalism.

So do liberal reporters report liberally, or don't they?

The Center for Media and Public Affairs at George Mason University surveyed ABC, NBC, and CBS's evening news coverage of Presidents Ronald Reagan, Bill Clinton, and George W. Bush during their first seven months in office. Then they analyzed the coverage of President Barack Obama from Inauguration Day through December 31, 2009.

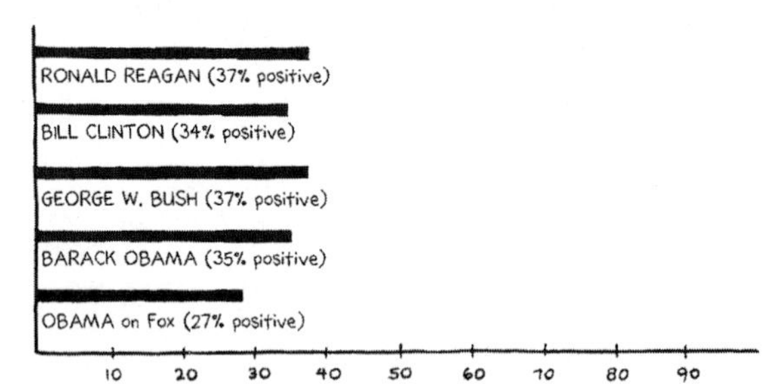

Conclusive proof: the media are biased against presidents!

The argument over political bias is one that anyone can win. It's boring.

Sure, the media are beset by biases, but they're probably not what you think.

Here are the biases *I* think you should worry about . . .

COMMERCIAL **BIAS**

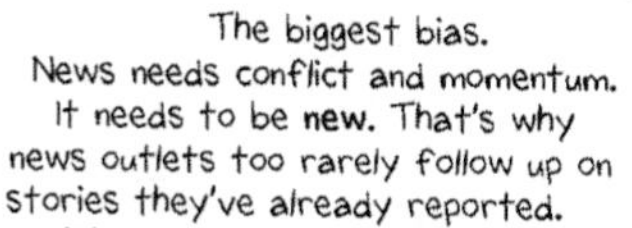

BAD NEWS **BIAS**

STATUS QUO **BIAS**

Because of the status quo bias, the media ignore any position that advocates radical change.

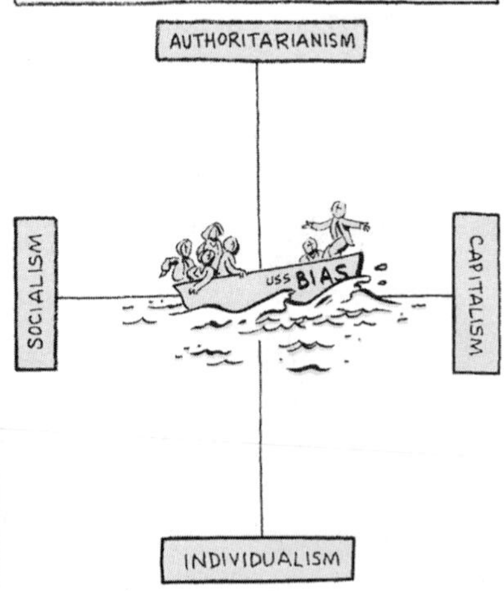

"The mainstream media never question the **structure** of the political system. The American way is the **only** way, politically and socially..."

"This bias ensures that **alternate** points of view about how government might run and what government might do are effectively **ignored.**"

ACCESS BIAS

Reporters believe they must patrol the halls of power, but the price of admission is steep. Antagonize power and the door is barred. So sometimes journalists dance with the devil.

Whenever reporters quote a "senior administration official," they've allowed their source to hide. But if we don't know *who* is speaking, we can't ascertain *why*. We can be more easily manipulated. See if the blind quote is worth it. Usually it isn't.

The problem, of course, is that when journalists are held captive by their sources, they are susceptible to Stockholm syndrome. They empathize with their jailers.

After all, when you're fed an exclusive quote, it's natural to be grateful.

When you're man-hugged by the powerful at any one of the half-dozen black tie parties the Washington press throws for politicians each year, it's natural to be flattered.

Reporters treated John McCain and George W. Bush relatively kindly during their first presidential campaigns, partly because they seemed to *like* reporters. As the *New York Times* noted at the time, Bush "not only slaps reporters' backs but also rubs the tops of their heads and, in a few instances, pinches their cheeks."

Obviously, the biggest risk for access-dependent journalists is self-censorship.

Former CNN news chief Eason Jordan said CNN did not cover stories of brutal suppression in Saddam's Iraq for years in order to protect his Baghdad bureau and staff. At least one known CNN source died gruesomely, despite Jordan's efforts. So why maintain a bureau you can't effectively use?

Legendary Washington reporter I. F. Stone famously shunned off-the-record events. Instead, he pored over government documents other reporters ignored, scooping them with stories hidden in plain sight.

But that is extremely unglamorous work in a glamorous town, where reporters often are more glamorous than the people they cover.

VISUAL BIAS

Press accounts of torture appeared sporadically through 2003 into 2004.

But it wasn't until April 28, 2004, that anyone, even much of the media, noticed. Pictures made us notice.

NARRATIVE BIAS

The great thing about a narrative is that once a template is set with plots and characters, it can be reused again and again when reporting on the same subject, as during presidential campaigns.
W
FRAT BOY
MENDACIOUS PRIG
Standard plot for election coverage: Who's winning the horse race. Standard subplot: How reporters fail the public by obsessing on the horse race.
EFFETE FRANCOPHILE
SCHEMING EMASCULATOR
SAVIOR
The characters, obviously, change with the years.
Pat Robertson and Jerry Falwell ... [are] agents of intolerance ...
I don't think [the NRA] help the Republican Party at all...
Our party's pro-life plank should be changed to allow exceptions for rape, incest, or to save the life of the mother...
McCAIN 2000
STRAIGHT TALK EXPRESS
But sometimes, when, say, an erstwhile media darling changes his narrative, reporters are forced to rewrite the script. This can be very annoying.
I don't believe those things anymore.
McCAIN 2008

Sometimes biases intertwine, resulting in thrillingly misleading reporting.
Case in point: The toppling of Saddam Hussein's statue in Al-Firdos Square on April 9, 2003.
You could call this a **visual/narrative bias** combo.
Pulling down the statue was not the spontaneous act of Iraqis, as often depicted by the media. In fact, the square was empty when the statue was seen by a Marine gunner...
Hey, why don't we take it down?
U.S. MARI

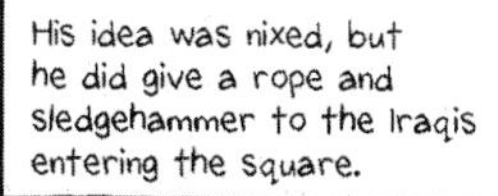
His idea was nixed, but he did give a rope and sledgehammer to the Iraqis entering the square.

The media, based in a nearby hotel, streamed out to watch their fruitless efforts.

Because of the media, the Marines were called in. One draped Saddam's face in an American flag --

-- which was hastily removed.
We didn't want to look like an occupation force.

The media, egged on by their editors at home, zoomed in to make the sparse crowd look bigger, signaling the war's end in a swift and unambiguous blaze of glory.

That day cable news focused the world's attention on the thrilling video. Fox News replayed it every 4.4 minutes. CNN replayed it every 7.7 minutes. Even then, they could have used a wider angle and shown the square in its proper context.
They **could** have used a wider shot -- but the pictures wouldn't have fit the narrative.

FAIRNESS

Case in point: the "Swift Boat Veterans for Truth." The group, funded by a major Republican campaign donor, launched a series of attacks against Democratic presidential candidate John Kerry. It claimed in ads that Kerry lied to get one of his two decorations for bravery and two of his three Purple Hearts for service in Vietnam.

The charges blanketed talk radio, and were repeated hundreds of times on network TV and in newspapers. The Swift Boat ads were awarded a fortune in free TV time as the mainstream media chewed over the controversy.

The charges were quickly debunked by Navy records and Kerry's crewmates—but the reporting on the actual evidence was drowned in a miasma of mainstream media weasel-speak, the surest sign of terminal fairness bias.

NBC's Tim Russert should have known why. In a textbook example of fairness bias, for weeks the mainstream media flooded the zone with "equal coverage" of the two unequal sides, distorting the truth in pursuit of the appearance of balance.

It might seem that fairness bias looms largest on the political beat. But ultimately **all** stories are political.
That's why the editors of Scientific American published this snarky response to its critics on April Fool's Day, 2005.

In retrospect, this magazine's coverage of so-called evolution has been hideously one-sided.
JOHN RENNIE, Editor

For decades, we published articles in every issue that endorsed the ideas of Charles Darwin and his cronies.
ON THE ORIGINS OF SPECIES C. DARWIN

True, the theory of common descent through natural selection has been called **the unifying concept for all of biology and one of the greatest scientific ideas of all time**, but that was no excuse to be fanatics about it.

Good journalism values balance above all else. We owe it to our readers to present everybody's ideas equally and not to ignore or discredit theories simply because they lack scientifically credible arguments or facts.

Nor should we succumb to the easy mistake of thinking that scientists understand their fields better than, say, U.S. Senators or best-selling novelists do.
JURASSIC PARK CRICHTON
STATE of FEAR
SPHERE
CONGO Crichton
AIRFRAME
TIMELINE
CRICHTON

Indeed, if politicians or special interest groups say things that seem untrue or misleading, our duty as journalists is to quote them without comment or contradiction.

To do otherwise would be elitist and therefore wrong.
JOHN RENNIE, Editor

▪ QUESTIONS

Reading

1. Gladstone writes that sometimes biases intertwine, leading to "thrillingly misleading reporting." What example does she use to illustrate this phenomenon?
2. According to Gladstone, what is the biggest risk for journalists who are dependent on information from a particular source?
3. Choose a particularly striking or unusual image from Gladstone's piece and make a list of the features that enable it to communicate in ways that words alone might not. Exchange your list with a classmate and have a discussion about what you might add to or how you might change each other's lists.

Exploratory Writing

1. Look up the dictionary definition of the word *bias*. With the different kinds of bias Gladstone mentions in mind, find three newspaper or magazine articles that you believe are biased. How did you identify the bias(es) in each article? What are the main differences between biased writing and argumentative writing?
2. In pairs or small groups, draft a guide for journalists on how to write or film unbiased stories. Make sure you offer tips for avoiding each of the different kinds of bias that Gladstone explains.

Making Connections

1. Gladstone writes that it wasn't until April 28, 2004, that "anyone" noticed the torture of detainees before the Iraq War began: "Pictures made us notice." Consider Susan Sontag's (p. 366) comments on the shock value of graphic images. How might Sontag respond to Gladstone's explanation of "visual bias"?
2. Like Gladstone, George Orwell makes an argument about social dimensions of language. In "Politics and the English Language" (p. 313) he suggests that "the decline of a language must ultimately have political and economic causes." Where Gladstone uses the form of a graphic narrative to make her point, Orwell uses the form of the expository essay. In addition, Orwell wrote in 1946 and Gladstone in 2011. Write a dialogue where you imagine Gladstone and Orwell meeting — perhaps on a TV show or a social networking site — to discuss the similarities and differences between their views on language and the times in which they lived and wrote.

Essay Writing

1. Choose a current news story, and write a graphic nonfiction essay reporting on how that story has been covered in the media. (You can draw characters and scenes like Gladstone's illustrator did, use computer-generated illustrations, or cut and paste magazine images to make your graphics — be creative!)

ARGUING

Letter from Birmingham Jail

Martin Luther King Jr.

The son of an Atlanta, Georgia, minister, civil rights leader Martin Luther King Jr. (1929–1968) graduated from Morehouse College and Crozier Theological Seminary before receiving a PhD in theology from Boston University in 1955. He became pastor of Dexter Avenue Baptist Church in Montgomery, Alabama, in 1954 and the next year led a boycott of the city's segregated bus system, which brought him national attention when the system began to be integrated in 1956. He organized the Southern Christian Leadership Conference to pursue civil rights gains through nonviolent resistance, and his participation in nonviolent protests led to several arrests. In 1963, King helped plan a massive march on Washington, D.C., where he delivered his famous "I Have a Dream" speech, calling for racial justice. The next year he was awarded the Nobel Peace Prize. He was assassinated in Memphis, Tennessee, at the age of thirty-nine. King wrote the following letter while serving an eight-day jail sentence for participating in protests against segregated businesses in Birmingham, Alabama. In the introduction to its published version, King noted, "This response to a published statement by eight fellow clergymen from Alabama . . . was composed under somewhat constricting circumstance. Begun on the margins of the newspaper in which the statement appeared while I was in jail, the letter was continued on scraps of writing paper supplied by a friendly Negro trusty, and concluded on a pad my attorneys were eventually permitted to leave me. Although the text remains in substance unaltered, I have indulged in the author's prerogative of polishing it for publication."

April 16, 1963

My Dear Fellow Clergymen:

While confined here in the Birmingham city jail, I came across your recent statement calling my present activities "unwise and untimely." Seldom do I pause to answer criticism of my work and ideas. If I sought to answer all the criticisms that cross my desk, my secretaries would have little time for anything other than such correspondence in the course of the day, and I would have no time for constructive work. But since I feel that you are men of genuine good will and that your criticisms are sincerely set forth, I want to try to answer your statement in what I hope will be patient and reasonable terms.

I think I should indicate why I am here in Birmingham, since you have been influenced by the view which argues against "outsiders coming in." I have the honor of serving as president of the Southern Christian Leadership Conference, an organization operating in every southern state, with headquarters in Atlanta, Georgia. We have some eighty-five affiliated organizations across the South, and one of them is the Alabama Christian Movement for

Human Rights. Frequently we share staff, educational, and financial resources with our affiliates. Several months ago the affiliate here in Birmingham asked us to be on call to engage in a nonviolent direct-action program if such were deemed necessary. We readily consented, and when the hour came we lived up to our promise. So I, along with several members of my staff, am here because I was invited here. I am here because I have organizational ties here.

But more basically, I am in Birmingham because injustice is here. Just as the prophets of the eighth century B.C. left their villages and carried their "thus saith the Lord" far beyond the boundaries of their home towns, and just as the Apostle Paul left his village of Tarsus and carried the gospel of Jesus Christ to the far corners of the Greco-Roman world, so am I compelled to carry the gospel of freedom beyond my own home town. Like Paul, I must constantly respond to the Macedonian call for aid.[1]

Moreover, I am cognizant of the interrelatedness of all communities and states. I cannot sit idly by in Atlanta and not be concerned about what happens in Birmingham. Injustice anywhere is a threat to justice everywhere. We are caught in an inescapable network of mutuality, tied in a single garment of destiny. Whatever affects one directly, affects all indirectly. Never again can we afford to live with the narrow, provincial, "outside agitator" idea. Anyone who lives inside the United States can never be considered an outsider anywhere within its bounds.

5 You deplore the demonstrations taking place in Birmingham. But your statement, I am sorry to say, fails to express a similar concern for the conditions that brought about the demonstrations. I am sure that none of you would want to rest content with the superficial kind of social analysis that deals merely with effects and does not grapple with underlying causes. It is unfortunate that demonstrations are taking place in Birmingham, but it is even more unfortunate that the city's white power structure left the Negro community with no alternative.

In any nonviolent campaign there are four basic steps: collection of the facts to determine whether injustices exist; negotiation; self-purification; and direct action. We have gone through all these steps in Birmingham. There can be no gainsaying the fact that racial injustice engulfs this community. Birmingham is probably the most thoroughly segregated city in the United States. Its ugly record of brutality is widely known. Negroes have experienced grossly unjust treatment in the courts. There have been more unsolved bombings of Negro homes and churches in Birmingham than in any other city in the nation. These are the hard brutal facts of the case. On the basis of these conditions, Negro leaders sought to negotiate with the city fathers. But the latter consistently refused to engage in good-faith negotiation.

Then, last September, came the opportunity to talk with leaders of Birmingham's economic community. In the course of the negotiations, certain promises were made by the merchants—for example, to remove the stores'

---

[1]*Macedonian call for aid*: A reference to Paul's vision of a Macedonian man requesting help (see Acts 16:9–10).—Eds.

humiliating racial signs. On the basis of these promises, the Reverend Fred Shuttlesworth and the leaders of the Alabama Christian Movement for Human Rights agreed to a moratorium on all demonstrations. As the weeks and months went by, we realized that we were the victims of a broken promise. A few signs, briefly removed, returned; the others remained.

As in so many past experiences, our hopes had been blasted, and the shadow of deep disappointment settled upon us. We had no alternative except to prepare for direct action, whereby we would present our very bodies as a means of laying our case before the conscience of the local and the national community. Mindful of the difficulties involved, we decided to undertake a process of self-purification. We began a series of workshops on nonviolence, and we repeatedly asked ourselves: "Are you able to accept blows without retaliating?" "Are you able to endure the ordeal of jail?" We decided to schedule our direct-action program for the Easter season, realizing that except for Christmas, this is the main shopping period of the year. Knowing that a strong economic-withdrawal program would be the by-product of direct action, we felt that this would be the best time to bring pressure to bear on the merchants for the needed change.

Then it occurred to us that Birmingham's mayoral election was coming up in March, and we speedily decided to postpone action until after election day. When we discovered that the Commissioner of Public Safety, Eugene "Bull" Connor, had piled up enough votes to be in the run-off, we decided again to postpone action until the day after the run-off so that the demonstrations could not be used to cloud the issues. Like many others, we waited to see Mr. Connor defeated, and to this end we endured postponement after postponement. Having aided in this community need, we felt that our direct-action program could be delayed no longer.

You may well ask, "Why direct action? Why sit-ins, marches, and so forth? Isn't negotiation a better path?" You are quite right in calling for negotiation. Indeed, this is the very purpose of direct action. Nonviolent direct action seeks to create such a crisis and foster such a tension that a community which has constantly refused to negotiate is forced to confront the issue. It seeks so to dramatize the issue that it can no longer be ignored. My citing the creation of tension as part of the work of the nonviolent resister may sound rather shocking. But I must confess that I am not afraid of the word "tension." I have earnestly opposed violent tension, but there is a type of constructive, nonviolent tension which is necessary for growth. Just as Socrates felt that it was necessary to create a tension in the mind so that individuals could rise from the bondage of myths and half truths to the unfettered realm of creative analysis and objective appraisal, so must we see the need for nonviolent gadflies to create the kind of tension in society that will help men rise from the dark depths of prejudice and racism to the majestic heights of understanding and brotherhood. 10

The purpose of our direct-action program is to create a situation so crisis-packed that it will inevitably open the door to negotiation. I therefore concur with you in your call for negotiation. Too long has our beloved Southland been bogged down in a tragic effort to live in monologue rather than dialogue.

One of the basic points in your statement is that the action that I and my associates have taken in Birmingham is untimely. Some have asked: "Why didn't you give the new city administration time to act?" The only answer that I can give to this query is that the new Birmingham administration must be prodded about as much as the outgoing one, before it will act. We are sadly mistaken if we feel that the election of Albert Boutwell as mayor will bring the millennium[2] to Birmingham. While Mr. Boutwell is a much more gentle person than Mr. Connor, they are both segregationists, dedicated to maintenance of the status quo. I have hoped that Mr. Boutwell will be reasonable enough to see the futility of massive resistance to desegregation. But he will not see this without pressure from devotees of civil rights. My friends, I must say to you that we have not made a single gain in civil rights without determined legal and nonviolent pressure. Lamentably, it is an historical fact that privileged groups seldom give up their privileges voluntarily. Individuals may see the moral light and voluntarily give up their unjust posture; but, as Reinhold Niebuhr[3] has reminded us, groups tend to be more immoral than individuals.

We know through painful experience that freedom is never voluntarily given by the oppressor; it must be demanded by the oppressed. Frankly, I have yet to engage in a direct-action campaign that was "well timed" in the view of those who have not suffered unduly from the disease of segregation. For years now I have heard the word "Wait!" It rings in the ear of every Negro with piercing familiarity. This "Wait" has almost always meant "Never." We must come to see, with one of our distinguished jurists, that "justice too long delayed is justice denied."[4]

We have waited for more than 340 years for our constitutional and God-given rights. The nations of Asia and Africa are moving with jet-like speed toward gaining political independence, but we still creep at horse-and-buggy pace toward gaining a cup of coffee at a lunch counter. Perhaps it is easy for those who have never felt the stinging darts of segregation to say, "Wait." But when you have seen vicious mobs lynch your mothers and fathers at will and drown your sisters and brothers at whim; when you have seen hate-filled policemen curse, kick, and even kill your black brothers and sisters; when you see the vast majority of your twenty million Negro brothers smothering in an airtight cage of poverty in the midst of an affluent society; when you suddenly find your tongue twisted and your speech stammering as you seek to explain to your six-year-old daughter why she can't go to the public amusement park

---

[2]*the millennium*: A reference to the Second Coming of Christ, which the Book of Revelation says will be followed by a thousand years of peace.—Eds.

[3]*Reinhold Niebuhr* (1892–1971): A Protestant philosopher who urged church members to put their beliefs into action against social injustice.—Eds.

[4]"*justice too long delayed is justice denied*": A statement made by U.S. Supreme Court Chief Justice Earl Warren. It was inspired by English writer Walter Savage Landor's statement that "Justice delayed is justice denied."—Eds.

that has just been advertised on television, and see tears welling up in her eyes when she is told that Funtown is closed to colored children, and see ominous clouds of inferiority beginning to form in her little mental sky, and see her beginning to distort her personality by developing an unconscious bitterness toward white people; when you have to concoct an answer for a five-year-old son who is asking, "Daddy, why do white people treat colored people so mean?"; when you take a cross-country drive and find it necessary to sleep night after night in the uncomfortable corners of your automobile because no motel will accept you; when you are humiliated day in and day out by nagging signs reading "white" and "colored"; when your first name becomes "nigger," your middle name becomes "boy" (however old you are) and your last name becomes "John," and your wife and mother are never given the respected title "Mrs."; when you are harried by day and haunted by night by the fact that you are a Negro, living constantly at tiptoe stance, never quite knowing what to expect next, and are plagued with inner fears and outer resentments; when you are forever fighting a degenerating sense of "nobodiness"—then you will understand why we find it difficult to wait. There comes a time when the cup of endurance runs over, and men are no longer willing to be plunged into the abyss of despair. I hope, sirs, you can understand our legitimate and unavoidable impatience.

15 You express a great deal of anxiety over our willingness to break laws. This is certainly a legitimate concern. Since we so diligently urge people to obey the Supreme Court's decision of 1954 outlawing segregation in the public schools, at first glance it may seem rather paradoxical for us consciously to break laws. One may then ask: "How can you advocate breaking some laws and obeying others?" The answer lies in the fact that there are two types of laws: just and unjust. I would be the first to advocate obeying just laws. One has not only a legal but a moral responsibility to obey just laws. Conversely, one has a moral responsibility to disobey unjust laws. I would agree with St. Augustine that "an unjust law is no law at all."

Now, what is the difference between the two? How does one determine whether a law is just or unjust? A just law is a manmade code that squares with the moral law or the law of God. An unjust law is a code that is out of harmony with the moral law. To put it in the terms of St. Thomas Aquinas: An unjust law is a human law that is not rooted in eternal law and natural law. Any law that uplifts human personality is just. Any law that degrades human personality is unjust. All segregation statutes are unjust because segregation distorts the soul and damages the personality. It gives the segregator a false sense of superiority and the segregated a false sense of inferiority. Segregation, to use the terminology of the Jewish philosopher Martin Buber, substitutes an "I-it" relationship for an "I-thou" relationship and ends up relegating persons to the status of things. Hence segregation is not only politically, economically, and sociologically unsound, it is morally wrong and sinful. Paul Tillich has said that sin is separation. Is not segregation an existential expression of man's tragic separation, his awful estrangement, his terrible sinfulness? Thus it is that I can urge men to obey the 1954 decision of the Supreme Court, for it is morally right; and I can urge them to disobey segregation ordinances, for they are morally wrong.

Let us consider a more concrete example of just and unjust laws. An unjust law is a code that a numerical or power majority group compels a minority group to obey but does not make binding on itself. This is *difference* made legal. By the same token, a just law is a code that a majority compels a minority to follow and that it is willing to follow itself. This is *sameness* made legal.

Let me give another explanation. A law is unjust if it is inflicted on a minority that, as a result of being denied the right to vote, had no part in enacting or devising the law. Who can say that the legislature of Alabama which set up that state's segregation laws was democratically elected? Throughout Alabama all sorts of devious methods are used to prevent Negroes from becoming registered voters, and there are some counties in which, even though Negroes constitute a majority of the population, not a single Negro is registered. Can any law enacted under such circumstances be considered democratically structured?

Sometimes a law is just on its face and unjust in its application. For instance, I have been arrested on a charge of parading without a permit. Now, there is nothing wrong in having an ordinance which requires a permit for a parade. But such an ordinance becomes unjust when it is used to maintain segregation and to deny citizens the First Amendment privilege of peaceful assembly and protest.

I hope you are able to see the distinction I am trying to point out. In no sense do I advocate evading or defying the law, as would the rabid segregationist. That would lead to anarchy. One who breaks an unjust law must do so openly, lovingly, and with a willingness to accept the penalty. I submit that an individual who breaks a law that conscience tells him is unjust, and who willingly accepts the penalty of imprisonment in order to arouse the conscience of the community over its injustice, is in reality expressing the highest respect for law. 20

Of course, there is nothing new about this kind of civil disobedience. It was evidenced subliminally in the refusal of Shadrach, Meshach, and Abednego to obey the laws of Nebuchadnezzar,[5] on the ground that a higher moral law was at stake. It was practiced superbly by the early Christians, who were willing to face hungry lions and the excruciating pain of chopping blocks rather than submit to certain unjust laws of the Roman Empire. To a degree, academic freedom is a reality today because Socrates practiced civil disobedience. In our own nation, the Boston Tea Party represented a massive act of civil disobedience.

We should never forget that everything Adolf Hitler did in Germany was "legal" and everything the Hungarian freedom fighters did in Hungary was

[5]*"the refusal of Shadrach . . . Nebuchadnezzar"*: According to the Book of Daniel 1:7–3:30, Nebuchadnezzar (c. 630 B.C.E.–c. 562 B.C.E.), king of the Chaldean empire, ordered Shadrach, Meshach, and Abednego to worship a golden image. When they refused, they were cast into a fiery furnace but remained unharmed.—Eds.

"illegal." It was "illegal" to aid and comfort a Jew in Hitler's Germany. Even so, I am sure that, had I lived in Germany at the time, I would have aided and comforted my Jewish brothers. If today I lived in a Communist country where certain principles dear to the Christian faith are suppressed, I would openly advocate disobeying that country's antireligious laws.

I must make two honest confessions to you, my Christian and Jewish brothers. First, I must confess that over the past few years I have been gravely disappointed with the white moderate. I have almost reached the regrettable conclusion that the Negro's great stumbling block in his stride toward freedom is not the White Citizen's Counciler[6] or the Ku Klux Klanner, but the white moderate, who is more devoted to "order" than to justice; who prefers a negative peace which is the absence of tension to a positive peace which is the presence of justice; who constantly says, "I agree with you in the goal you seek, but I cannot agree with your methods of direct action"; who paternalistically believes he can set the timetable for another man's freedom; who lives by a mythical concept of time and who constantly advises the Negro to wait for a "more convenient season." Shallow understanding from people of good will is more frustrating than absolute misunderstanding from people of ill will. Lukewarm acceptance is much more bewildering than outright rejection.

I had hoped that the white moderate would understand that law and order exist for the purpose of establishing justice and that when they fail in this purpose they become the dangerously structured dams that block the flow of social progress. I had hoped that the white moderate would understand that the present tension in the South is a necessary phase of the transition from an obnoxious negative peace, in which the Negro passively accepted his unjust plight, to a substantive and positive peace, in which all men will respect the dignity and worth of human personality. Actually, we who engage in nonviolent direct action are not the creators of tension. We merely bring to the surface the hidden tension that is already alive. We bring it out in the open, where it can be seen and dealt with. Like a boil that can never be cured so long as it is covered up but must be opened with all its ugliness to the natural medicines of air and light, injustice must be exposed, with all the tension its exposure creates, to the light of human conscience and the air of national opinion before it can be cured.

25 In your statement you assert that our actions, even though peaceful, must be condemned because they precipitate violence. But is this a logical assertion? Isn't this like condemning a robbed man because his possession of money precipitated the evil act of robbery? Isn't this like condemning Socrates because his unswerving commitment to truth and his philosophical inquiries precipitated the act by the misguided populace in which they made him drink hemlock? Isn't this like condemning Jesus because his unique God-consciousness and never-ceasing devotion to God's will precipitated the evil act of crucifixion?

[6]*White Citizen's Counciler*: A member of an organization that was formed after the U.S. Supreme Court's 1954 *Brown v. Board of Education* decision. Its purpose was to maintain segregation.—Eds.

We must come to see that, as the federal courts have consistently affirmed, it is wrong to urge an individual to cease his efforts to gain his basic constitutional rights because the quest may precipitate violence. Society must protect the robbed and punish the robber.

I had also hoped that the white moderate would reject the myth concerning time in relation to the struggle for freedom. I have just received a letter from a white brother in Texas. He writes: "All Christians know that the colored people will receive equal rights eventually, but it is possible that you are in too great a religious hurry. It has taken Christianity almost two thousand years to accomplish what it has. The teachings of Christ take time to come to earth." Such an attitude stems from a tragic misconception of time, from the strangely irrational notion that there is something in the very flow of time that will inevitably cure all ills. Actually, time itself is neutral; it can be used either destructively or constructively. More and more I feel that the people of ill will have used time much more effectively than have the people of good will. We will have to repent in this generation not merely for the hateful words and actions of the bad people, but for the appalling silence of the good people. Human progress never rolls in on wheels of inevitability; it comes through the tireless efforts of men willing to be co-workers with God, and without this hard work, time itself becomes an ally of the forces of social stagnation. We must use time creatively, in the knowledge that the time is always ripe to do right. Now is the time to make real the promise of democracy and transform our pending national elegy into a creative psalm of brotherhood. Now is the time to lift our national policy from the quicksand of racial injustice to the solid rock of human dignity.

You speak of our activity in Birmingham as extreme. At first I was rather disappointed that fellow clergymen would see my nonviolent efforts as those of an extremist. I began thinking about the fact that I stand in the middle of two opposing forces in the Negro community. One is a force of complacency, made up in part of Negroes who, as a result of long years of oppression, are so drained of self-respect and a sense of "somebodiness" that they have adjusted to segregation; and in part of a few middle-class Negroes who, because of a degree of academic and economic security and because in some ways they profit by segregation, have become insensitive to the problems of the masses. The other force is one of bitterness and hatred, and it comes perilously close to advocating violence. It is expressed in the various black nationalist groups that are springing up across the nation, the largest and best known being Elijah Muhammad's Muslim movement. Nourished by the Negro's frustration over the continued existence of racial discrimination, this movement is made up of people who have lost faith in America, who have absolutely repudiated Christianity, and who have concluded that the white man is an incorrigible "devil."

I have tried to stand between these two forces, saying that we need emulate neither the "do-nothingism" of the complacent nor the hatred and despair of the black nationalist. For there is the more excellent way of love and nonviolent protest. I am grateful to God that, through the influence of the Negro church, the way of nonviolence became an integral part of our struggle.

If this philosophy had not emerged, by now many streets of the South would, I am convinced, be flowing with blood. And I am further convinced that if our white brothers dismiss as "rabble-rousers" and "outside agitators" those of us who employ nonviolent direct action, and if they refuse to support our nonviolent efforts, millions of Negroes will, out of frustration and despair, seek solace and security in black nationalist ideologies—a development that would inevitably lead to a frightening racial nightmare.

30 Oppressed people cannot remain oppressed forever. The yearning for freedom eventually manifests itself, and that is what has happened to the American Negro. Something within has reminded him of his birthright of freedom, and something without has reminded him that it can be gained. Consciously or unconsciously, he has been caught up by the *Zeitgeist*,[7] and with his black brothers of Africa and his brown and yellow brothers of Asia, South America, and the Caribbean, the United States Negro is moving with a sense of great urgency toward the promised land of racial justice. If one recognizes this vital urge that has engulfed the Negro community, one should readily understand why public demonstrations are taking place. The Negro has many pent-up resentments and latent frustrations, and he must release them. So let him march; let him make prayer pilgrimages to the city hall; let him go on freedom rides[8]—and try to understand why he must do so. If his repressed emotions are not released in nonviolent ways, they will seek expression through violence; this is not a threat but a fact of history. So I have not said to my people, "Get rid of your discontent." Rather, I have tried to say that this normal and healthy discontent can be channeled into the creative outlet of nonviolent direct action. And now this approach is being termed extremist.

But though I was initially disappointed at being categorized as an extremist, as I continued to think about the matter I gradually gained a measure of satisfaction from the label. Was not Jesus an extremist for love: "Love your enemies, bless them that curse you, do good to them that hate you, and pray for them which despitefully use you, and persecute you." Was not Amos an extremist for justice: "Let justice roll down like waters and righteousness like an everflowing stream." Was not Paul an extremist for the Christian gospel: "I bear in my body the marks of the Lord Jesus." Was not Martin Luther an extremist: "Here I stand; I cannot do otherwise, so help me God." And John Bunyan: "I will stay in jail to the end of my days before I make a butchery of my conscience." And Abraham Lincoln: "This nation cannot survive half slave and half free." And Thomas Jefferson: "We hold these truths to be self-evident, that all men are created equal . . . ." So the question is not whether we will be extremists, but what kind of extremists we will be. Will we be extremists for

[7] *Zeitgeist*: The intellectual, moral, and cultural spirit of the times (German).—Eds.

[8] *freedom rides*: The bus and train rides that black and white protesters took in the early 1960s to protest segregation.—Eds.

hate or for love? Will we be extremists for the preservation of injustice or for the extension of justice? In that dramatic scene on Calvary's hill three men were crucified. We must never forget that all three were crucified for the same crime—the crime of extremism. Two were extremists for immorality, and thus fell below their environment. The other, Jesus Christ, was an extremist for love, truth, and goodness, and thereby rose above his environment. Perhaps the South, the nation, and the world are in dire need of creative extremists.

I had hoped that the white moderate would see this need. Perhaps I was too optimistic; perhaps I expected too much. I suppose I should have realized that few members of the oppressor race can understand the deep groans and passionate yearnings of the oppressed race, and still fewer have the vision to see that injustice must be rooted out by strong, persistent, and determined action. I am thankful, however, that some of our white brothers in the South have grasped the meaning of this social revolution and committed themselves to it. They are still all too few in quantity, but they are big in quality. Some—such as Ralph McGill, Lillian Smith, Harry Golden, James McBride Dabbs, Ann Braden, and Sarah Patton Boyle—have written about our struggle in eloquent and prophetic terms. Others have marched with us down nameless streets of the South. They have languished in filthy, roach-infested jails, suffering the abuse and brutality of policemen who view them as "dirty nigger-lovers." Unlike so many of their moderate brothers and sisters, they have recognized the urgency of the moment and sensed the need for powerful "action" antidotes to combat the disease of segregation.

Let me take note of my other major disappointment. I have been so greatly disappointed with the white church and its leadership. Of course, there are some notable exceptions. I am not unmindful of the fact that each of you has taken some significant stands on this issue. I commend you, Reverend Stallings, for your Christian stand on this past Sunday, in welcoming Negroes to your worship service on a nonsegregated basis. I commend the Catholic leaders of this state for integrating Spring Hill College several years ago.

But despite these notable exceptions, I must honestly reiterate that I have been disappointed with the church. I do not say this as one of those negative critics who can always find something wrong with the church. I say this as a minister of the gospel, who loves the church; who was nurtured in its bosom; who has been sustained by its spiritual blessings and who will remain true to it as long as the cord of life shall lengthen.

35 When I was suddenly catapulted into the leadership of the bus protest in Montgomery, Alabama, a few years ago, I felt we would be supported by the white church. I felt that the white ministers, priests, and rabbis of the South would be among our strongest allies. Instead, some have been outright opponents, refusing to understand the freedom movement and misrepresenting its leaders; all too many others have been more cautious than courageous and have remained silent behind the anesthetizing security of stained-glass windows.

In spite of my shattered dreams, I came to Birmingham with the hope that the white religious leadership of this community would see the justice of our cause and, with deep moral concern, would serve as the channel through which our just grievances could reach the power structure. I had hoped that each of you would understand. But again I have been disappointed. . . .

There was a time when the church was very powerful—in the time when the early Christians rejoiced at being deemed worthy to suffer for what they believed. In those days the church was not merely a thermometer that recorded the ideas and principles of popular opinion; it was a thermostat that transformed the mores of society. Whenever the early Christians entered a town, the people in power became disturbed and immediately sought to convict the Christians for being "disturbers of the peace" and "outside agitators." But the Christians pressed on, in the conviction that they were "a colony of heaven," called to obey God rather than man. Small in number, they were big in commitment. They were too God-intoxicated to be "astronomically intimidated." By their effort and example they brought an end to such ancient evils as infanticide and gladiatorial contests.

Things are different now. So often the contemporary church is a weak, ineffectual voice with an uncertain sound. So often it is an archdefender of the status quo. Far from being disturbed by the presence of the church, the powerful structure of the average community is consoled by the church's silent—and often even vocal—sanction of things as they are.

But the judgment of God is upon the church as never before. If today's church does not recapture the sacrificial spirit of the early church, it will lose its authenticity, forfeit the loyalty of millions, and be dismissed as an irrelevant social club with no meaning for the twentieth century. Every day I meet young people whose disappointment with the church has turned into outright disgust.

Perhaps I have once again been too optimistic. Is organized religion too inextricably bound to the status quo to save our nation and the world? Perhaps I must turn my faith to the inner spiritual church, the church within the church, as the true *ekklesia*[9] and the hope of the world. But again I am thankful to God that some noble souls from the ranks of organized religion have broken loose from the paralyzing chains of conformity and joined us as active partners in the struggle for freedom. They have left their secure congregations and walked the streets of Albany, Georgia, with us. They have gone down the highways of the South on torturous rides for freedom. Yes, they have gone to jail with us. Some have been dismissed from their churches, have lost the support of their bishops and fellow ministers. But they have acted in the faith that right defeated is stronger than evil triumphant. Their witness has been the spiritual salt that has preserved the true meaning of the gospel in these troubled times. They have carved a tunnel of hope through the dark mountain of disappointment. 40

I hope the church as a whole will meet the challenge of this decisive hour. But even if the church does not come to the aid of justice, I have no despair about the future. I have no fear about the outcome of our struggle in Birmingham, even if our motives are at present misunderstood. We will reach the

---

[9]*ekklesia*: The church (Greek). Refers to the spirit of the church.—Eds.

goal of freedom in Birmingham and all over the nation, because the goal of America is freedom. Abused and scorned though we may be, our destiny is tied up with America's destiny. Before the pilgrims landed at Plymouth, we were here. Before the pen of Jefferson etched the majestic words of the Declaration of Independence across the pages of history, we were here. For more than two centuries our forebears labored in this country without wages; they made cotton king; they built the homes of their masters while suffering gross injustice and shameful humiliation—and yet out of a bottomless vitality they continued to thrive and develop. If the inexpressible cruelties of slavery could not stop us, the opposition we now face will surely fail. We will win our freedom because the sacred heritage of our nation and the eternal will of God are embodied in our echoing demands.

Before closing I feel impelled to mention one other point in your statement that has troubled me profoundly. You warmly commended the Birmingham police force for keeping "order" and "preventing violence." I doubt that you would have so warmly commended the police force if you had seen its dogs sinking their teeth into unarmed, nonviolent Negroes. I doubt that you would so quickly commend the policemen if you were to observe their ugly and inhumane treatment of Negroes here in the city jail; if you were to watch them push and curse old Negro women and young Negro girls; if you were to see them slap and kick old Negro men and young boys; if you were to observe them, as they did on two occasions, refuse to give us food because we wanted to sing our grace together. I cannot join you in your praise of the Birmingham police department.

It is true that the police have exercised a degree of discipline in handling the demonstrators. In this sense they have conducted themselves rather "nonviolently" in public. But for what purpose? To preserve the evil system of segregation. Over the past few years I have consistently preached that nonviolence demands that the means we use must be as pure as the ends we seek. I have tried to make clear that it is wrong to use immoral means to attain moral ends. But now I must affirm that it is just as wrong, or perhaps even more so, to use moral means to preserve immoral ends. Perhaps Mr. Connor and his policemen have been rather nonviolent in public, as was Chief Pritchett in Albany, Georgia, but they have used the moral means of nonviolence to maintain the immoral end of racial injustice. As T. S. Eliot has said, "The last temptation is the greatest treason: To do the right deed for the wrong reason."

I wish you had commended the Negro sit-inners and demonstrators of Birmingham for their sublime courage, their willingness to suffer, and their amazing discipline in the midst of great provocation. One day the South will recognize its real heroes. They will be the James Merediths,[10] with the noble sense of purpose that enables them to face jeering and hostile mobs, and with the agonizing loneliness that characterizes the life of the pioneer. They will be old, oppressed, battered Negro women, symbolized in a seventy-two-

[10]*James Meredith* (b. 1933): In 1962, the first African American to become a student at the University of Mississippi.—Eds.

year-old woman in Montgomery, Alabama, who rose up with a sense of dignity and with her people decided not to ride segregated buses and who responded with ungrammatical profundity to one who inquired about her weariness: "My feets is tired, but my soul is at rest." They will be the young high school and college students, the young ministers of the gospel and a host of their elders, courageously and nonviolently sitting in at lunch counters and willingly going to jail for consciences' sake. One day the South will know that when these disinherited children of God sat down at lunch counters, they were in reality standing up for what is best in the American dream and for the most sacred values in our Judaeo-Christian heritage, thereby bringing our nation back to those great wells of democracy which were dug deep by the founding fathers in their formulation of the Constitution and the Declaration of Independence.

Never before have I written so long a letter. I'm afraid it is much too long to take your precious time. I can assure you that it would have been much shorter if I had been writing from a comfortable desk, but what else can one do when he is alone in a narrow jail cell other than write long letters, think long thoughts, and pray long prayers? 45

If I have said anything in this letter that overstates the truth and indicates an unreasonable impatience, I beg you to forgive me. If I have said anything that understates the truth and indicates my having a patience that allows me to settle for anything less than brotherhood, I beg God to forgive me.

I hope this letter finds you strong in the faith. I also hope that circumstances will soon make it possible for me to meet each of you, not as an integrationist or a civil rights leader but as a fellow clergyman and a Christian brother. Let us all hope that the dark clouds of racial prejudice will soon pass away and the deep fog of misunderstanding will be lifted from our fear-drenched communities, and in some not too distant tomorrow the radiant stars of love and brotherhood will shine over our great nation with all their scintillating beauty.

Yours in the cause of
Peace and Brotherhood,
Martin Luther King Jr.

▪ QUESTIONS

Reading

1. What are the four basic steps in any nonviolent campaign?
2. How does King define "just" and "unjust" laws? What does King conclude about individuals who break unjust laws?
3. King is always aware of the positions against which he is arguing and the counterarguments that are offered by those who hold those positions. How does he represent those positions, and how does he deal with them? Base your response on specific instances in which he mentions such positions and responds to them.

4. In this *argumentative* open letter, what attitude does King seem to have toward his opponents? How does this apparent attitude strengthen, weaken, or otherwise change the force of his arguments?

Exploratory Writing

1. King's letter was an open response to a statement published by eight white Alabama clergymen. Working alone or in pairs, find an article, an editorial, or a political speech that you passionately disagree with, and write an open letter to the author or speaker. Use the skills and strategies you've learned about argumentative essay writing to strengthen your case.
2. At times King's prose verges on the poetical in its use of imagery and metaphor. Highlight, underline, or flag the places in this letter where King uses poetic language. How do these sections shape your response to the letter?

Making Connections

1. What is the tone of King's letter? How is it similar to or different from the tone of Barack Obama's (p. 355) speech?
2. Compare King's comments on historical racism with James Baldwin's (p. 131). In your opinion, where do the two writers' viewpoints overlap? Where do they diverge?

Essay Writing

1. Write an essay reflecting on King's famous statement: "Injustice anywhere is a threat to justice everywhere" (paragraph 4). Be sure to use contemporary examples of injustice in your discussion.

REFLECTING

A More Perfect Union

Barack Obama

Barack Obama (b. 1961) was born in Honolulu, Hawaii, to a Kansas-born American mother and a Kenyan father, who met and married when they were students at the University of Hawaii. The effects of his parents' interracial marriage, his father's return to Kenya, and his parents' subsequent divorce when he was very young are central to his memoir, *Dreams from My Father: A Story of Race and Inheritance* (1995; reprinted in 2004). A 1995 review in the *New York Times Book Review* said that Obama's memoir "persuasively describes the phenomenon of belonging to two different worlds, and thus belonging to neither." In addition to his memoir, Obama wrote *The Audacity of Hope: Thoughts on Reclaiming the American Dream*, published in 2006. After graduating from Columbia University in 1983, Obama worked as a community organizer in Chicago, then went on to Harvard University, where he became the first African American president of the *Harvard Law Review*; he received his law degree in 1991. Turning down a prestigious judicial clerkship, he chose instead to practice civil rights law in Chicago and to teach constitutional law at the University of Chicago. He served in the Illinois Senate from 1997 to 2003 and was elected to the U.S. Senate in 2004. In 2008 he ran as the Democratic Party nominee for president of the United States against Senator John McCain and won the election. At the National Constitution Center in Philadelphia, Pennsylvania, in March 2008, Senator Obama delivered the following speech about racial relations, precipitated by the controversial remarks made by his former pastor, Reverend Jeremiah Wright. Titled after the preamble to the United States Constitution, the speech elicited a widespread reaction from politicians, news media, academics, and voters, ultimately having a positive effect on the campaign.

"We the people, in order to form a more perfect union."

Two hundred and twenty-one years ago, in a hall that still stands across the street, a group of men gathered and, with these simple words, launched America's improbable experiment in democracy. Farmers and scholars, statesmen and patriots, who had traveled across an ocean to escape tyranny and persecution finally made real their declaration of independence at a Philadelphia convention that lasted through the spring of 1787.

The document they produced was eventually signed but ultimately unfinished. It was stained by this nation's original sin of slavery, a question that divided the colonies and brought the convention to a stalemate until the founders chose to allow the slave trade to continue for at least twenty more years, and to leave any final resolution to future generations.

Of course, the answer to the slavery question was already embedded within our Constitution—a Constitution that had at its very core the ideal of equal citizenship under the law; a Constitution that promised its people liberty and justice, and a union that could be and should be perfected over time.

5 And yet words on a parchment would not be enough to deliver slaves from bondage, or provide men and women of every color and creed their full rights and obligations as citizens of the United States. What would be needed were Americans in successive generations who were willing to do their part—through protests and struggle, on the streets and in the courts, through a civil war and civil disobedience, and always at great risk—to narrow that gap between the promise of our ideals and the reality of their time.

This was one of the tasks we set forth at the beginning of this campaign—to continue the long march of those who came before us, a march for a more just, more equal, more free, more caring, and more prosperous America. I chose to run for the presidency at this moment in history because I believe deeply that we cannot solve the challenges of our time unless we solve them together—unless we perfect our union by understanding that we may have different stories, but we hold common hopes; that we may not look the same and we may not have come from the same place, but we all want to move in the same direction—toward a better future for our children and our grandchildren.

This belief comes from my unyielding faith in the decency and generosity of the American people. But it also comes from my own American story.

I am the son of a black man from Kenya and a white woman from Kansas. I was raised with the help of a white grandfather who survived a Depression to serve in Patton's Army during World War II and a white grandmother who worked on a bomber assembly line at Fort Leavenworth while he was overseas. I've gone to some of the best schools in America and lived in one of the world's poorest nations. I am married to a black American who carries within her the blood of slaves and slaveowners—an inheritance we pass on to our two precious daughters. I have brothers, sisters, nieces, nephews, uncles, and cousins, of every race and every hue, scattered across three continents, and for as long as I live, I will never forget that in no other country on earth is my story even possible.

It's a story that hasn't made me the most conventional candidate. But it is a story that has seared into my genetic makeup the idea that this nation is more than the sum of its parts—that out of many, we are truly one.

10 Throughout the first year of this campaign, against all predictions to the contrary, we saw how hungry the American people were for this message of unity. Despite the temptation to view my candidacy through a purely racial lens, we won commanding victories in states with some of the whitest populations in the country. In South Carolina, where the Confederate flag still flies, we built a powerful coalition of African Americans and white Americans.

This is not to say that race has not been an issue in the campaign. At various stages in the campaign, some commentators have deemed me either "too black" or "not black enough." We saw racial tensions bubble to the surface during the week before the South Carolina primary. The press has scoured every exit poll for the latest evidence of racial polarization, not just in terms of white and black, but black and brown as well.

And yet, it has only been in the last couple of weeks that the discussion of race in this campaign has taken a particularly divisive turn.

On one end of the spectrum, we've heard the implication that my candidacy is somehow an exercise in affirmative action; that it's based solely on the desire of wide-eyed liberals to purchase racial reconciliation on the cheap. On the other end, we've heard my former pastor, Reverend Jeremiah Wright, use incendiary language to express views that have the potential not only to widen the racial divide, but views that denigrate both the greatness and the goodness of our nation—that rightly offend white and black alike.

I have already condemned, in unequivocal terms, the statements of Reverend Wright that have caused such controversy. For some, nagging questions remain. Did I know him to be an occasionally fierce critic of American domestic and foreign policy? Of course. Did I ever hear him make remarks that could be considered controversial while I sat in church? Yes. Did I strongly disagree with many of his political views? Absolutely—just as I'm sure many of you have heard remarks from your pastors, priests, or rabbis with which you strongly disagreed.

15 But the remarks that have caused this recent firestorm weren't simply controversial. They weren't simply a religious leader's effort to speak out against perceived injustice. Instead, they expressed a profoundly distorted view of this country—a view that sees white racism as endemic, and that elevates what is wrong with America above all that we know is right with America; a view that sees the conflicts in the Middle East as rooted primarily in the actions of stalwart allies like Israel, instead of emanating from the perverse and hateful ideologies of radical Islam.

As such, Reverend Wright's comments were not only wrong but divisive, divisive at a time when we need unity; racially charged at a time when we need to come together to solve a set of monumental problems—two wars, a terrorist threat, a falling economy, a chronic health-care crisis, and potentially devastating climate change; problems that are neither black or white or Latino or Asian, but rather problems that confront us all.

Given my background, my politics, and my professed values and ideals, there will no doubt be those for whom my statements of condemnation are not enough. Why associate myself with Reverend Wright in the first place, they may ask? Why not join another church? And I confess that if all that I knew of Reverend Wright were the snippets of those sermons that have run in an endless loop on the television and YouTube, or if Trinity United Church of Christ conformed to the caricatures being peddled by some commentators, there is no doubt that I would react in much the same way.

But the truth is, that isn't all that I know of the man. The man I met more than twenty years ago is a man who helped introduce me to my Christian faith, a man who spoke to me about our obligations to love one another, to care for the sick and lift up the poor. He is a man who served his country as a U.S.

Marine, who has studied and lectured at some of the finest universities and seminaries in the country, and who for over thirty years led a church that serves the community by doing God's work here on earth—by housing the homeless, ministering to the needy, providing day-care services and scholarships and prison ministries, and reaching out to those suffering from HIV/AIDS.

In my first book, *Dreams from My Father,* I described the experience of my first service at Trinity:

> People began to shout, to rise from their seats and clap and cry out, a forceful wind carrying the reverend's voice up into the rafters. . . . And in that single note—hope!—I heard something else; at the foot of that cross, inside the thousands of churches across the city, I imagined the stories of ordinary black people merging with the stories of David and Goliath, Moses and Pharaoh, the Christians in the lion's den, Ezekiel's field of dry bones. Those stories—of survival, and freedom, and hope—became our story, my story; the blood that had spilled was our blood, the tears our tears; until this black church, on this bright day, seemed once more a vessel carrying the story of a people into future generations and into a larger world. Our trials and triumphs became at once unique and universal, black and more than black; in chronicling our journey, the stories and songs gave us a means to reclaim memories that we didn't need to feel shame about . . . memories that all people might study and cherish—and with which we could start to rebuild.

That has been my experience at Trinity. Like other predominantly black churches across the country, Trinity embodies the black community in its entirety—the doctor and the welfare mom, the model student and the former gangbanger. Like other black churches, Trinity's services are full of raucous laughter and sometimes bawdy humor. They are full of dancing, clapping, screaming, and shouting that may seem jarring to the untrained ear. The church contains in full the kindness and cruelty; the fierce intelligence and the shocking ignorance; the struggles and successes; the love and, yes, the bitterness and bias that make up the black experience in America. 20

And this helps explain, perhaps, my relationship with Reverend Wright. As imperfect as he may be, he has been like family to me. He strengthened my faith, officiated my wedding, and baptized my children. Not once in my conversations with him have I heard him talk about any ethnic group in derogatory terms, or treat whites with whom he interacted with anything but courtesy and respect. He contains within him the contradictions—the good and the bad—of the community that he has served diligently for so many years.

I can no more disown him than I can disown the black community. I can no more disown him than I can my white grandmother—a woman who helped raise me, a woman who sacrificed again and again for me, a woman who loves me as much as she loves anything in this world, but a woman who once confessed her fear of black men who passed by her on the street, and who on more than one occasion has uttered racial or ethnic stereotypes that made me cringe.

These people are a part of me. And they are a part of America, this country that I love.

Some will see this as an attempt to justify or excuse comments that are simply inexcusable. I can assure you it is not. I suppose the politically safe thing would be to move on from this episode and just hope that it fades into the woodwork. We can dismiss Reverend Wright as a crank or a demagogue, just as some have dismissed Geraldine Ferraro, in the aftermath of her recent statements, as harboring some deep-seated racial bias.

But race is an issue that I believe this nation cannot afford to ignore right now. We would be making the same mistake that Reverend Wright made in his offending sermons about America—to simplify and stereotype and amplify the negative to the point that it distorts reality. 25

The fact is that the comments that have been made and the issues that have surfaced over the last few weeks reflect the complexities of race in this country that we've never really worked through—a part of our union that we have yet to perfect. And if we walk away now, if we simply retreat into our respective corners, we will never be able to come together and solve challenges like health care, or education, or the need to find good jobs for every American.

Understanding this reality requires a reminder of how we arrived at this point. As William Faulkner once wrote, "The past isn't dead and buried. In fact, it isn't even past." We do not need to recite here the history of racial injustice in this country. But we do need to remind ourselves that so many of the disparities that exist in the African American community today can be directly traced to inequalities passed on from an earlier generation that suffered under the brutal legacy of slavery and Jim Crow.

Segregated schools were, and are, inferior schools; we still haven't fixed them, fifty years after *Brown v. Board of Education*, and the inferior education they provided, then and now, helps explain the pervasive achievement gap between today's black and white students.

Legalized discrimination—where blacks were prevented, often through violence, from owning property, or loans were not granted to African American business owners, or black homeowners could not access FHA mortgages, or blacks were excluded from unions, or the police force, or fire departments—meant that black families could not amass any meaningful wealth to bequeath to future generations. That history helps explain the wealth and income gap between black and white, and the concentrated pockets of poverty that persist in so many of today's urban and rural communities.

A lack of economic opportunity among black men, and the shame and frustration that came from not being able to provide for one's family, contributed to the erosion of black families—a problem that welfare policies for many years may have worsened. And the lack of basic services in so many urban black neighborhoods—parks for kids to play in, police walking the beat, regular garbage pick-up, and building code enforcement—all helped create a cycle of violence, blight, and neglect that continues to haunt us. 30

This is the reality in which Reverend Wright and other African-Americans of his generation grew up. They came of age in the late fifties and early sixties, a time when segregation was still the law of the land and opportunity was systematically constricted. What's remarkable is not how many failed in the face of discrimination, but rather how many men and women overcame the odds; how many were able to make a way out of no way for those like me who would come after them.

But for all those who scratched and clawed their way to get a piece of the American Dream, there were many who didn't make it—those who were ultimately defeated, in one way or another, by discrimination. That legacy of defeat was passed on to future generations—those young men and increasingly young women who we see standing on street corners or languishing in our prisons, without hope or prospects for the future. Even for those blacks who did make it, questions of race, and racism, continue to define their worldview in fundamental ways. For the men and women of Reverend Wright's generation, the memories of humiliation and doubt and fear have not gone away; nor has the anger and the bitterness of those years. That anger may not get expressed in public, in front of white co-workers or white friends. But it does find voice in the barbershop or around the kitchen table. At times, that anger is exploited by politicians, to gin up votes along racial lines, or to make up for a politician's own failings.

And occasionally it finds voice in the church on Sunday morning, in the pulpit and in the pews. The fact that so many people are surprised to hear that anger in some of Reverend Wright's sermons simply reminds us of the old truism that the most segregated hour in American life occurs on Sunday morning. That anger is not always productive; indeed, all too often it distracts attention from solving real problems; it keeps us from squarely facing our own complicity in our condition, and prevents the African American community from forging the alliances it needs to bring about real change. But the anger is real; it is powerful; and to simply wish it away, to condemn it without understanding its roots, only serves to widen the chasm of misunderstanding that exists between the races.

In fact, a similar anger exists within segments of the white community. Most working- and middle-class white Americans don't feel that they have been particularly privileged by their race. Their experience is the immigrant experience—as far as they're concerned, no one's handed them anything; they've built it from scratch. They've worked hard all their lives, many times only to see their jobs shipped overseas or their pension dumped after a lifetime of labor. They are anxious about their futures, and feel their dreams slipping away; in an era of stagnant wages and global competition, opportunity comes to be seen as a zero sum game, in which your dreams come at my expense. So when they are told to bus their children to a school across town, when they hear that an African American is getting an advantage in landing a good job or a spot in a good college because of an injustice that they themselves never committed; when they're told that their fears about crime in urban neighborhoods are somehow prejudiced, resentment builds over time.

35 Like the anger within the black community, these resentments aren't always expressed in polite company. But they have helped shape the political land-

scape for at least a generation. Anger over welfare and affirmative action helped forge the Reagan Coalition. Politicians routinely exploited fears of crime for their own electoral ends. Talk show hosts and conservative commentators built entire careers unmasking bogus claims of racism while dismissing legitimate discussions of racial injustice and inequality as mere political correctness or reverse racism.

Just as black anger often proved counterproductive, so have these white resentments distracted attention from the real culprits of the middle class squeeze—a corporate culture rife with inside dealing, questionable accounting practices, and short-term greed; a Washington dominated by lobbyists and special interests; economic policies that favor the few over the many. And yet, to wish away the resentments of white Americans, to label them as misguided or even racist, without recognizing they are grounded in legitimate concerns—this too widens the racial divide, and blocks the path to understanding.

This is where we are right now. It's a racial stalemate we've been stuck in for years. Contrary to the claims of some of my critics, black and white, I have never been so naive as to believe that we can get beyond our racial divisions in a single election cycle, or with a single candidacy—particularly a candidacy as imperfect as my own.

But I have asserted a firm conviction—a conviction rooted in my faith in God and my faith in the American people—that working together we can move beyond some of our old racial wounds, and that in fact we have no choice if we are to continue on the path of a more perfect union.

For the African American community, that path means embracing the burdens of our past without becoming victims of our past. It means continuing to insist on a full measure of justice in every aspect of American life. But it also means binding our particular grievances—for better health care, and better schools, and better jobs—to the larger aspirations of all Americans—the white woman struggling to break the glass ceiling, the white man who's been laid off, the immigrant trying to feed his family. And it means taking full responsibility for our own lives—by demanding more from our fathers, and spending more time with our children, and reading to them, and teaching them that while they may face challenges and discrimination in their own lives, they must never succumb to despair or cynicism; they must always believe that they can write their own destiny.

Ironically, this quintessentially American—and yes, conservative—notion 40 of self-help found frequent expression in Reverend Wright's sermons. But what my former pastor too often failed to understand is that embarking on a program of self-help also requires a belief that society can change.

The profound mistake of Reverend Wright's sermons is not that he spoke about racism in our society. It's that he spoke as if our society was static; as if no progress has been made; as if this country—a country that has made it possible for one of his own members to run for the highest office in the land and build a coalition of white and black, Latino and Asian, rich and poor, young and old—is still irrevocably bound to a tragic past. But what we know—what we have seen—is that America can change. That is the true genius of this nation. What we have already achieved gives us hope—the audacity to hope—for what we can and must achieve tomorrow.

In the white community, the path to a more perfect union means acknowledging that what ails the African American community does not just exist in the minds of black people; that the legacy of discrimination—and current incidents of discrimination, while less overt than in the past—are real and must be addressed. Not just with words, but with deeds—by investing in our schools and our communities; by enforcing our civil rights laws and ensuring fairness in our criminal justice system; by providing this generation with ladders of opportunity that were unavailable for previous generations. It requires all Americans to realize that your dreams do not have to come at the expense of my dreams; that investing in the health, welfare, and education of black and brown and white children will ultimately help all of America prosper.

In the end, then, what is called for is nothing more, and nothing less, than what all the world's great religions demand—that we do unto others as we would have them do unto us. Let us be our brother's keeper, scripture tells us. Let us be our sister's keeper. Let us find that common stake we all have in one another, and let our politics reflect that spirit as well.

For we have a choice in this country. We can accept a politics that breeds division, and conflict, and cynicism. We can tackle race only as spectacle—as we did in the O.J. trial—or in the wake of tragedy, as we did in the aftermath of Katrina—or as fodder for the nightly news. We can play Reverend Wright's sermons on every channel, every day, and talk about them from now until the election, and make the only question in this campaign whether or not the American people think that I somehow believe or sympathize with his most offensive words. We can pounce on some gaffe by a Hillary supporter as evidence that she's playing the race card, or we can speculate on whether white men will all flock to John McCain in the general election regardless of his policies.

We can do that. 45

But if we do, I can tell you that in the next election, we'll be talking about some other distraction. And then another one. And then another one. And nothing will change.

That is one option. Or, at this moment, in this election, we can come together and say, "Not this time." This time we want to talk about the crumbling schools that are stealing the future of black children and white children and Asian children and Hispanic children and Native American children. This time we want to reject the cynicism that tells us that these kids can't learn; that those kids who don't took like us are somebody else's problem. The children of America are not "those" kids; they are our kids, and we will not let them fall behind in a twenty-first century economy. Not this time.

This time we want to talk about how the lines in the emergency room are filled with whites and blacks and Hispanics who do not have health care, who don't have the power on their own to overcome the special interests in Washington, but who can take them on if we do it together.

Instructor's Manual
Tenth Edition

Fields of Reading

Motives for Writing

Nancy R. Comley
Queens College, CUNY

David Hamilton
University of Iowa

Carl H. Klaus
University of Iowa

Robert Scholes
Brown University

Nancy Sommers
Harvard University

Jason Tougaw
Queens College, CUNY

BEDFORD/ST. MARTIN'S Boston ♦ New York

Manufactured in the United States of America.

7 6 5 4 3 2
f e d c b a

For information, write: Bedford/St. Martin's, 75 Arlington Street, Boston, MA 02116
(617-399-4000)

ISBN 978-1-4576-2383-7

Preface

This manual is meant to help you find your way around *Fields of Reading*, Tenth Edition, and to help you envision some of the ways that the textbook can be put to use in teaching. We begin this manual with the section "Approaches to Teaching from *Fields of Reading*," which introduces the textbook and discusses some ways that it can be used in courses with varying emphases.

Beyond our opening explanations and suggestions, you will find that we have provided answers for all of the reading questions that appear in our text. It may be that you'll have your own thoughts about some of our answers. Whatever ideas and suggestions you have, either for this manual or for *Fields of Reading* itself, we'd welcome hearing about them. Just write us in care of Bedford/St. Martin's, 33 Irving Place, 10th Floor, New York, NY 10003.

Nancy R. Comley
David Hamilton
Carl H. Klaus
Robert Scholes
Nancy Sommers
Jason Tougaw

Contents

PART 3: SOCIAL SCIENCES 22

Paired Readings: On How Language Shapes Reality 33

Paired Readings: On Race Relations 36

Paired Readings: On Documenting War 38

Student Essay 40

PART 4: SCIENCES 41

APPROACHES TO TEACHING FROM *FIELDS OF READING*

Fields of Reading: Motives for Writing has been designed to suit four basic emphases for selecting and organizing material in college writing courses:

1. Curricular (emphasizing broad academic divisions of learning)
2. Thematic (emphasizing focused topics of study)
3. Rhetorical (emphasizing aims of discourse)
4. Formalistic (emphasizing modes of discourse)

Each of these emphases, distinct as it is, necessarily draws to some extent on one or more of the others, so that the set of four constitutes, in fact, a rich grammar of possibilities for course design. These possibilities, together with the numerous pieces in our collection, suggest a virtually incalculable number of ways in which you can use this book in your courses. For this reason, we will confine ourselves to discussing the basic set of four and leave you to extrapolate some of the permutations and combinations on your own. As you will see, we do not propose to recommend any particular emphasis as being preferable to the others, since you are in the best position to determine the needs of your students. Instead, we will provide a brief description of each method, followed by some ideas about how the readings and apparatus in our collection can be used in each case. Here, then, is a discussion of some approaches you can follow in using material from *Fields of Reading.*

1. *Curricular (emphasizing broad academic divisions of learning).* This emphasis is based on the assumption that students can most effectively be led to develop their academic reading and writing abilities by being given repeated opportunities to read material that reflects the broadly related divisions of learning and professional activity that they will encounter as undergraduates, to write material that takes into account the subject matter and forms that prevail in these academic and professional areas, and in general to think about language use in terms of the ways it is carried on in these broad contexts. Students will be encouraged not only to recognize and practice the particular kinds of writing that are affiliated with particular divisions of learning, but also to recognize and develop the qualities that pervade all of the academic and professional areas.

If you wish to follow this emphasis, you can readily do so by focusing on the set of three academic divisions that structure our table of contents: Arts and Humanities, Social Sciences, and Sciences. You can acquaint your students with this overall approach by having them read Part One: An Introduction to Writing, where they will find an explanation of these broad academic divisions and a rationale for organizing a college writing course in terms of such categories, as well as additional perspectives on reading and writing within these broad academic and professional contexts.

In structuring a sequence of reading and writing assignments for this approach, you can divide your course into three main parts, beginning with the arts, followed by the social sciences, and ending with the sciences, immersing your students at length in each broad division. Or you can rotate continuously among the three divisions, using the casebook sections to focus your classroom inquiry. Whichever plan you follow, you will probably find it particularly effective to have your students read pieces that will enable them to see how comparable subject matter and situations are handled within each broad division. For example, you might invite students to compare how firsthand observations are written up in the reporting mode in Arts and Humanities, Social Sciences, and Sciences. And in connection with their reading, you can have students carry out their own firsthand observations, trying out different ways of writing them up for the various academic divisions or reflecting on how they might have to vary their methods of observation to suit different academic divisions.

2. *Thematic (emphasizing focused topics of study).* Given its implicit curricular orientation, this emphasis is necessarily related to the previous one, but rather than working in the context of broad academic divisions, it proceeds according to the assumption that students can most effectively be led to develop their academic reading and writing abilities by being given the opportunity to read and write within the context of focused topics, themes, and issues. This emphasis serves to highlight for students the ways in which particular academic fields or professional areas deal with similar or even identical topics or questions. Teachers who favor this approach will select and organize material to give students a sequence of challenging topics for reading and writing that range across the curriculum. They will also benefit from using the paired readings in each division, as well as the casebooks at the end of the text.

You can best acquaint your students with this overall approach by having them read The Modes Explained section (p. 16) in Part One on reflecting, reporting, explaining, and arguing. Here, your students will find detailed examples and discussions of how different academic disciplines and different professional fields bring different points of view and thus different ways of writing to bear on the very same subject, topic, or question.

In structuring a sequence of topics, as well as a sequence of matching assignments for a thematic approach, you will find it helpful to consult the Thematic Contents (p. xvii). This guide lists each reading under one or more of the following categories:

Contemporary Issues and Experiences
Cultures in Contact and Collision
Education
Ethics, Values, and Beliefs
Family
Gender and Women's Experiences
Health, Disease, and Medicine
History and Interpreting the Past
Human Portraits
Identity
Interpreting the Body
Life and Death
The Media
Observing and Understanding the World
Race
Violence and War

3. *Rhetorical (emphasizing aims of discourse).* This approach is based on the assumption that students can most effectively be led to develop their academic reading and writing abilities by being oriented to think about language use in terms of various basic purposes served in any academic or professional field (reflecting, reporting, explaining, arguing). Teachers who favor this approach generally select and organize material to give students experience in various aims of discourse. Readings thus are chosen to help students understand the inherent nature of a particular purpose, to help them recognize something of the range of different forms it can assume from one field to another, and by extension to provide students with principles they can apply and models they can adapt in their own writing.

You can acquaint your students with the rationale for this overall view of the purpose by having them read the introductory chapters that have an explicit focus on the aims and motives for writing and that give students insight into the four writing purposes. In putting together a sequence of reading and writing assignments for this approach, you will find it useful to consult the Rhetorical Index (p. 725), where you will find pieces listed exemplifying all of the important modes of discourse.

4. *Formalistic (emphasizing modes of discourse).* Given its implicit rhetorical orientation, this emphasis is necessarily related to the previous one, but rather than working in the context of broad rhetorical purposes, it proceeds according to the assumption that students can most effectively be led to develop their academic reading and writing abilities by being given the opportunity to read and write with an eye to the particular forms, modes, and techniques that are used to achieve various academic and professional purposes. Teachers who favor this approach generally select and organize material to give students experience in various modes of discourse. Readings are thus chosen to illustrate particular modes of discourse and thereby to provide students with models that they can adapt to the needs of their own writing.

If you wish to follow this emphasis, you can readily do so by consulting the Rhetorical Index (p. 725). Within this index, you will find a list that consists of the following categories:

Analogy	Description
Case Study	First-Person Perspective
Causal Analysis	Narration
Comparison and Contrast	Process Analysis
Definition	Scientific and Technical Report

For each of these categories, you will find page references to pieces that exemplify the rhetorical procedure. Thus you can acquaint your students with each mode by having them read about it in our introductory discussion as well as witnessing it at work in exemplary selections. Reading questions and writing assignments that focus on modes of discourse can generally be found among the questions that immediately follow each selection.

PART 2: ARTS AND HUMANITIES

Frederick Douglass: *Learning to Read and Write* (REFLECTING)

READING

1. Listing the events of the narrative will emphasize for students how closely tied to Douglass's growing desire for freedom is his acquisition of reading and writing skills. The following items are likely to appear in students' lists:

Mistress begins teaching Douglass to read.

Mistress, injured by slavery and obedient to Master Hugh, ceases instruction.

Mistress snatches newspaper away from Douglass.

Douglass learns to read by befriending white boys.

He discusses slavery with them and feels the weight of being a slave for life.

Douglass gets *The Columbian Orator* and reads the dialogue and Sheridan's speech.

Douglass is able to utter his own thoughts and grows to detest slavery and long for freedom.

Douglass seeks out talk of slavery and finds the meaning of abolition in the newspaper.

Douglass helps Irishmen, who then urge him to escape.
Douglass plans to wait until he can write.
Douglass learns to write by watching carpenters, challenging other boys, and copying Master Thomas's work.

2. A strong response should discuss the fact that Douglass describes most fully the scenes that demonstrate the effects of slavery on himself and others. Events such as his description of his mistress's change in attitude toward him and her snatching the newspaper from him (par. 2) illustrate the slave owner's fear of educated slaves. His feelings after reading Sheridan's speech (par. 6) and the episode with the Irishmen (par. 7) show us why Douglass is determined to escape and make poignant his desire for freedom. In such ways Douglass uses description to bring his story to life and to engage readers in his point of view.

3. In order to answer this question with confidence, students will need to understand the distinction between *reflection* and *argument*. They may gain that understanding through reading Part One: Introduction to Writing in *Fields of Reading*, through class discussion, or through some directed writing on the topic. Addressing this question will help students develop their understanding of *rhetorical modes*. Students may note elements of reflection in Douglass's emphasis on his personal story and his discussions of the emotional impact of the treatment he received. They are likely to discuss his arguments against slavery in paragraphs 2, 4, 6, and 7. They may also note his use of *evidence* against slavery, including the dialogue in *The Columbian Orator*, which shows a slave debating his master; the perhaps unexpected sympathy of the white boys from Philpot Street and the Irish dockworkers; and the corrupting effects of slavery on Douglass's mistress.

Exploratory Writing

1. Sheridan (par. 6) and the Irish dockworkers (par. 7) represent the Irish Catholic situation. The Irish Catholics were a group, like the slaves, who were denied full human rights. This question is useful for a library assignment that can be simple (Who was Richard Brinsley Sheridan, and what did he do?) or extensive (Trace the long history of conflict between the English and the Irish). In comparing the Irish situation to African American slavery, students will have to define what constitutes slavery.

2. Assuming the persona of Master Hugh's wife is a more challenging assignment than the previous one. It forces students to consider why people owned slaves. Be sure to discuss possible approaches to the assignment in class. Having Master Hugh's wife reflect on the events will be more challenging—and offer practice writing in that rhetorical mode—than having her report them as they occurred.

Making Connections

1. This question requires students to synthesize details and ideas from three texts—a challenging task. It might be helpful to ask students first to list the claims about language made by the three writers. Then, it will be easier for them to identify points of similarity and difference. Responses should include at least one opening paragraph in which students introduce all three writers and their texts. Students will find a variety of ways to synthesize the three texts. It is likely that a strong response will emphasize the fact that all three writers suggest that language is a vehicle for understanding—and transforming—social or political realities. They may also emphasize the fact that all three writers suggest that language helps to make abstract ideas more concrete. Obvious differences include the different historical and social contexts in which the three texts were written, and students may point out that it's notable that so many of the ideas explored are similar nonetheless.

Another significant difference is the fact that Douglass emphasizes *reflection* and *narrative* while George Orwell (p. 313) and James Baldwin (p. 131) emphasize *argument*. Therefore, many of the explicit claims of the latter two remain implicit in the former.

Essay Writing

1. Strong responses will combine elements of narrative, reflection, and argument. Students should tell their literacy stories in order to reflect on and make arguments about the politics of literacy in general. For example, a student who attended excellent schools might emphasize the privilege of becoming literate in ideal circumstances, contrasting this experience to Douglass's and those of others who are less privileged. A bilingual student might emphasize the complexity of developing literacy in two languages. A student with a learning disability might emphasize the role of multiple intelligences and make an argument that educators need to become more aware of these. It's a good idea to ask students to complete multiple drafts. First drafts are likely to emphasize either narrative or argument. If this is the case, students will need guidance throughout the revision process to help them bridge narrative, reflection, and argument.

Dudley Clendinen: *The Good Short Life* (REFLECTING)

Reading

1. Clendinen frames death as a part of a good life rather than as something outside of life: "[Death is] one of life's greatest, most absorbing thrills and challenges" (par. 10). Clendinen reflects that this is an unusual way to look at life and death in his society.

2. Clendinen learns from his disease, "Lou," that death is inescapable for everyone: because there's "nothing much to do" about having an incurable, terminal illness, there is a sense of freedom and liberation in living life "when you know there's not much left" (par. 11).

3. According to Clendinen, the knowledge of his impending death is harder for Whitney than it is for him. He does not know whether Whitney approves of his decision to take his own life, but she understands. Clendinen describes his relationship with his daughter as the gift of his life. She is his only real tie to a desire for a longer life: "Leaving her is the one thing I hate" (par. 25).

Exploratory Writing

1. In class discussion of this exercise, consider the ways that writing can be used to persuade readers to change their points of view on a contentious issue. Although Clendinen's article reflects on his own personal experiences rather than making a general argument, his reflections can be used as points in favor of legalizing euthanasia for people with terminal illnesses.

2. Clendinen credits his twenty-two years of therapy and twelve-step meetings (par. 13) with his ability to live "one day at a time." This way of life—learning "to be sober and sane"—taught him he could "do anything . . . including this. I am, in fact, prepared" (par. 14–16). He has learned how to take control of his own life, and now, also, his death.

Making Connections

1. Both Clendinen and Jill Bolte Taylor (p. 418) frame their illnesses as opportunities to gain a fresh perspective on physical experience. Taylor finds excitement and fascination in observing her own stroke, while Clendinen's struggle with Lou Gehrig's disease

changes his view of life and death. Clendinen's "stroke of insight" comes early on, after receiving his diagnosis, and he decides to continue living as before, until it's time to go.

Essay Writing

1. As you discuss student responses to both Clendinen's article and his interviews, consider the ways that writing or narrating an experience can change the way people understand it. Clendinen's reminder that facing death is a part of life—"one of its most absorbing thrills and challenges"—may be a surprising perspective for some readers.

Jhumpa Lahiri: *Trading Stories* (REFLECTING)

Reading

1. The story, "A Temporary Matter," was inspired by a childhood memory of a couple that lived next door.

2. Lahiri's father is a librarian (par. 1). At age eighty, he continued to work forty-hour weeks at the university of Rhode Island. Even after Lahiri was awarded a Pulitzer Prize, he continued to remind her that writing stories was not something she could count on to earn a living (par. 21).

3. Lahiri seeks a connection with her parents: "What I really sought was a better-marked trail of my parents' intellectual lives: bound and printed evidence of what they'd read, what had inspired and shaped their minds" (par. 3).

4. Lahiri observes that to be a writer is to articulate an inner self and to be assertive in the world, yet she says she spent much of her life wanting to be someone else (par. 10) and that she was not naturally assertive: "I was used to looking to others for guidance, for influence, sometimes for the most basic cues of life" (par. 11).

Exploratory Writing

1. This exercise might bring up the fact that many people have contradictory experiences of home. In class discussion, what themes arise from the students' lists? Consider Lahiri's closing comments: "Every story is a foreign territory, which, in the process of writing, is occupied and then abandoned. I belong to my work, to my characters, and in order to create new ones I leave the old ones behind. My parents' refusal to let go or to belong fully to either place is at the heart of what I, in a less literal way, try to accomplish in writing. Born of my inability to belong, it is my refusal to let go" (par. 23).

2. In class discussion, consider the general question of how life events, relationships to education and language, and "insider" or "outsider" experience shape not only the writers' interests and orientation, but also the style and themes of their work. In the student lists, consider how many of the authors had experiences of dislocation, isolation, or not belonging.

Making Connections

1. Amy Tan (p. 178) writes that when she first became a fiction writer, she was trying to "finally prove I had mastery over the English language" (par. 20). Later, "I began to write stories using all the Englishes I had grown up with" (par. 21). Both Tan and Lahiri, who depart from the language of their parents in their writing, describe a complicated relationship between language, writing, and belonging, eventually transforming the very language that invokes a feeling of "trespassing"(Lahiri, par. 4) or shame (Tan, par. 8) into a vehicle for creating a space of inclusion.

Essay Writing

1. Lahiri's story of her apprenticeship is full of ironies, paradoxes, changes, and surprises—her "amalgam of two hemispheres" of an upbringing, her wish to be ordinary despite her extraordinary, recognized talent. For this essay, ask students to highlight how modes of description and writing can illuminate the contradictions that arise during a deep learning process.

Amanda Coyne: *The Long Good-bye: Mother's Day in Federal Prison* (REPORTING)

Reading

1. As an observer, Coyne is both involved and detached. Though she has a sister in prison, she is able to write a detailed reportorial piece about the situation of federally imprisoned women, particularly in relation to their children and other relatives. Coyne's reporting conveys sympathy for the women in prison.

2. By focusing on Mother's Day at the prison, a day when ties are emotionally heightened by the specifics of the holiday, Coyne is able to detail the interaction between the women and their families—specifically their children—and portray them as mothers, sisters, girlfriends, wives, and daughters, rather than just prisoners. The ordinary details of day-to-day life in a women's prison are likely to be missing or obscured on this special day.

3. By paying more attention to the other women and children than she does to her sister, Jennifer, and Jennifer's son, Toby, Coyne is able to document the badly stressed maternal and familial situation of federally imprisoned women and their children without giving an unduly biased amount of attention to the circumstances of her sister. Coyne also portrays a larger and more universal experience, from political and societal issues to the personal feminine identities of the prisoners.

4. Coyne seems to be interested in documenting not only the maternal, familial, and feminine needs of the prisoners themselves, but also the various ways in which those basic human needs are so severely thwarted by the prison system that the children (and other relatives of such women) are clearly seen to be quite badly abused (and innocent) victims of the system. Coyne's use of description also develops the women as dynamic individuals whose stories are both complicated and often sympathetic.

Exploratory Writing

1. This research can easily be started on the Internet. Encourage students to seek out the prison's own informational materials, as well as archived newspaper articles and broader government resources that might discuss it. This exercise might surprise students who have not thought about the fact that there are prisons or jails in their own communities. In class discussion, you can bring in both Coyne's and Christina Boufis's work (p. 96) as you discuss different *reportorial* techniques. Ask students to imagine different ways to develop a report on the local prison: going "undercover" as an inmate, interviewing inmates, interviewing wardens and other staff, and nosing out the history and economic details of the prison. Who owns and operates the prison? Who profits from it? Use this exercise as a way to highlight what makes *reporting* different from other modes of writing.

2. Since this is an exploratory question rather than an essay topic, it could be used also to generate class or small-group discussion. It asks students to make a connection between their own experience and Coyne's. You can raise the question of how Coyne's report might be different if she had not had such a personal connection to this story.

3. If students have already done the exercise of investigating a prison in question 1, you can use their own findings about the local prison as you draft reform suggestions. Connect this exercise to *reportorial* thinking. What information does Coyne or Boufis uncover about the inner workings of the places they report on? What information have students uncovered? How does this kind of reporting help lawmakers and other public officials? How does it help the public?

Making Connections

1. While Coyne notes that the women in prison have bonded by recognizing their powerlessness, Gloria Anzaldúa (p. 167) points out that Chicanas are separated by it. Their learned sense of shame about their own language—a masculine-controlled entity—creates suspicion and competition that "diminish our sense of self" (par. 22). Both writers detail the ways in which female powerlessness restricts the realization of their female identities and, ultimately, their opportunities in life.

Essay Writing

1. This assignment gives students an opportunity to use the Internet and periodical indexes as a means of gathering research material on women's prisons and then to analyze that material to see how other writers perceive and comment on the situation of female prisoners. It also allows students to critically consider the modes of writing used by each writer. Both essays on jail/prison in *Fields of Reading* are reportorial. Students might find online articles that draw more heavily on the modes of arguing, explaining, or reflecting.

Christina Boufis: *Teaching Literature at the County Jail* (reporting)

Reading

1. Christina Boufis has taught literature and writing at the University of California at Berkeley and at Stanford University, where most of her students come from middle- to high-income families and who come to college well prepared academically. The women in the San Francisco county jail never completed high school and most read "at a fourth- to seventh-grade level." This reading time serves as an act of stability, which is something lacking in their lives. From their life experience they see things in the text that the Berkeley students miss, and in the process they open their instructor's eyes to things she's missed as well. Boufis has been trained to critically examine literature, as have her Berkeley students, who are after what "the work ultimately means" (par. 16), while the jail students accept ambiguity and uncertainty. Thus Boufis comes to "appreciate their acute and emotionally sensitive readings" (par. 17).

2. Boufis criticizes the lack of funding for rehabilitation and education programs, the classism and racism of the "war on drugs"–based laws (par. 17), the fact that jail life is unsettled enough to make people "edgy" or "crazy," and the lack of a rehabilitation focus, causing the same inmates to get rearrested frequently.

3. Strong answers will note that Boufis is an outsider, who does not share the background or experiences of the inmates she is teaching. Her own responses to the books she chose differ from her students' responses. She learns from her students as they learn from her, for example, as in the discussion of *Their Eyes Were Watching God*. In class discussion, ask students to imagine this report as written by an insider—one of the inmates. Also raise the question of what makes Boufis an outsider. How do her race and education shape her experiences?

4. A strong answer will cite Boufis's conclusion that the jail students, because of their life experiences, are more comfortable with uncertainty and ambiguity than the privileged Berkeley students (par. 16).

Exploratory Writing

1. This question invites students to imagine themselves in Boufis's role as a teacher, and asks them to consider which lessons are most important. The strongest lists will explicitly make a connection between each reading choice and a broader educational agenda, choosing books or movies that would engage the jail students and teach them critical-thinking skills.

2. In class discussion on this subject, raise the question of what Boufis learned from teaching at the county jail that she might not have uncovered as a reporter. You could make a list of the lessons students remember learning from encounters with people different from themselves. Are some of the lessons ambiguous? Are they all positive and uplifting, or are some depressing? Ask the students to consider the complexity of exchanges between people from different backgrounds.

Making Connections

1. Ask students to research the current drug laws in their communities. In class discussion, explore whether students share Amanda Coyne's (p. 86) and Boufis's objections to the laws. Which public figures support or oppose the current laws?

2. This question calls on students to distinguish between reportorial writing from a personal perspective and reflective writing. By putting their personal voices into their reports, both authors make it easier for readers to relate to the situations they are describing—but they also include data, statistics, and factual information.

Essay Writing

1. This writing assignment offers a chance for investigative reporting and should interest students with a social commitment.

Plato: *The Cave* (EXPLAINING)

Reading

1. Without the analogy, it's much harder to visualize what Socrates is describing and to mentally make complex, abstract ideas concrete and easier to understand. A visual image, such as the illustration included with the text, can serve the same purpose as such an analogy. In class discussion of this use of analogy, consider Scott McCloud's (p. 135) examination of illustration as its own medium.

2. Human beings, according to Plato, are so deluded by the narrow range of their experience and by the distorting framework of their senses that they are incapable of apprehending the realm of ideas and the ideal forms of things that constitute the ultimate reality.

3. The visual perception of things is often so dazzling and beguiling that it can easily lead one to ignore or completely overlook any other aspect of reality, especially the ideal forms of things, which can be grasped only by the mind. For a hint of how tyrannizing the sight of things can be, students might be invited to close their eyes for a period of time, and then to try to conceive the essential form of a visible thing, such as a chair or a tree, without reference to any visual perception of it.

Exploratory Writing

1. The illustration is reasonably complete, except that it does not include the details mentioned in paragraph 3—namely, "men carrying past the wall implements of all kinds that rise above the wall." Creating their own images affords students the opportunity to see how visual representation functions in illuminating an idea.

2. Students may find translations in stale, old-fashioned language, and also translations that invoke different mental images by using different words. This exercise reveals the importance of interpretation and the different ways that images or ideas can be represented.

Making Connections

1. This exercise invites students to contemplate the different types of thinking addressed in this book, and to analyze how different modes of writing reveal different styles of thought. The thought processes of some, like Oliver Sacks's patient (p. 446), are explained explicitly, whereas the thought processes shaping the other essays, can be understood implicitly.

Essay Writing

1. Students can exercise argumentative writing techniques to agree or disagree with Socrates' probable response to high-tech forms of escapism. Encourage them to draw on the other essays in the book, the essays in the "How is the Internet Changing Who We Are" casebook, and/or Steven Johnson's essay (p. 120) as they form their positions.

2. Many essays in this book, like Ann Jurecic's "Mindblindness" (p. 402) and John Berger's "Hiroshima" (p. 236), address the issue of illusion by showing how much our perception shapes our views of outside reality. This assignment asks students to reflect on how that process has affected their own lives.

Jan Harold Brunvand: *Urban Legends: "The Boyfriend's Death"* (EXPLAINING)

Reading

1. Strong answers will identify key elements of explanatory writing in Brunvand's essay, including definitions, illustrations, examples, and historical background. Brunvand's expertise helps him make his explanation deeper and more thorough.

2. The three essential elements are "a strong basic story-appeal, a foundation in actual belief, and a meaningful message or 'moral'" (par. 19).

3. Folklore consists of "units of traditional material that are memorable, repeatable, and that fit recurring social situations well enough to serve in place of original remarks. 'Tradition' is the key idea that links together such utterances as nicknames, proverbs, greetings and leave-taking formulas, wisecracks, anecdotes, and jokes as 'folklore.'" Oral communication consists of "communicative events" ranging from casual daily conversations to formal discussions. Legends (including urban legends) are part of a subclass of folk narratives that are unlike fairy tales in that they're believable, and unlike myths in that they're set in the recent past and involve normal human beings (pars. 5–7). This is an opportunity for class discussion about the process of forming categories and developing systems of classification.

Exploratory Writing

1. To this list we might add a number of spinoffs and other stories. It could be interesting to speculate on possible reasons for variations or the importance of the common features of each tale.

2. In paragraphs 5 and 6, Brunvand sets out the general elements of the urban legend:

- The narrative is believable, set in the recent past, and involves "normal human beings."
- Credibility is established "from specific details of time and place or from references to source authorities."
- "The story is *true*," occurred recently, and to "someone else . . . quite close to the narrator, or at least 'a friend of a friend.'"

The traditional elements of "The Boyfriend's Death" are set out in paragraph 11.

3. In the wake of publicity about child abuse, cases of children brought up in closets or chained in apartments have come to light. These unfortunately true stories are the stuff legends could derive from. As for proof, is it enough to say that we read it in the *New York Times* or that we saw it (for sixty seconds) on the television news? This exercise will generate discussion about *how* we prove that a story is true or real.

Making Connections

1. This exercise is likely to generate surprising results for students. Some of the first-person essays (like Ehrenreich, p. 243) that sound "personal" yield a great deal of well-substantiated factual information, and some of the third-person essays (like Henig, p. 268) that sound neutral contain highly subjective arguments, sometimes veiled ones. Strong responses will note that the third-person voice gives an impression of neutrality, while the first-person voice can seem more "relatable" and warmer.

Essay Writing

1. As in question 3 under Exploratory Writing and question 1 under Making Connections, this essay topic should highlight the problem of legitimacy. Some students might find that "official" versions of a story are the ones plagued by biases, while seemingly dubious sources offer a truer story, as Brooke Gladstone describes in "The Great Refusal" (p. 325). With so much information available from so many sources, how do we distinguish between truth and lies?

2. Students might choose a family lie rather than a popular myth or legend. Discussing these essays in class should raise interesting questions about different types of narratives or "stories" and their use. In class discussion, refer to an essay in this book and ask students to imagine that they suddenly learned that almost everything in it was a lie, from the author's identity to any data reported. Discuss the explosion of false memoirs that has been a key topic in recent years.

Steven Johnson: *Watching TV Makes You Smarter* (ARGUING)

Reading

1. Johnson claims that the Sleeper Curve enhances the cognitive facilities and capacity to understand narrative complexity, as discussed in paragraphs 3 and 4.

2. He uses the phrase "Monday-morning quarterbacking" (par. 30).

3. Johnson's evidence consists primarily of material documenting the increased complexity of TV scripts, but he doesn't offer any evidence to suggest that this complexity has actually led to increased cognitive ability or "smartness" among viewers, other than his presumption that viewers have developed the capacity to watch such series, given their evident popularity.

Exploratory Writing

1. A half-hour TV series probably encompasses more narrative complexity within its compressed framework than a similar period in the course of one's daily experience, and thus it might lead to more cognitive nimbleness than the observation of life itself. In addition, fiction in any form allows an audience to observe an experience or issue from multiple different perspectives. But in another sense, unmediated life is fraught with so many complex variables that by comparison a TV series is often more predictable and contrived.

2. Here is an opportunity for students to use Johnson's graphing technique as a means of understanding their own TV preferences, and to gather evidence that they can use in writing an evaluation of his piece, as called for in the following question.

3. Johnson celebrates TV series that bring together multiple plots in each weekly episode and thereby develop viewers' cognitive abilities to recognize and remember characters from a continually shifting set of stories, as well as to understand their interconnection. Smart television does not talk down to its audience and does not necessarily explain every bit of important information. It allows analysis to be in the hands of the audience and contains ambiguity/mystery even in present-tense events. He contrasts these shows with the narrative simplicity of earlier TV series.

Making Connections

1. Both Christina Boufis (p. 96) and Johnson associate intelligence with following complicated narrative threads over time, which can happen through watching the kinds of TV programs Johnson advocates, or through reading novels. One major difference is that reading promotes literacy, a highly transferable skill that many of the women in Boufis's county jail lack. Student opinions will vary about whether TV or reading would be more "existentially" helpful.

Essay Writing

1. This topic invites students to consider their personal intellectual development. The strongest essays will reflect on multiple kinds of intelligence, including practical skills, academic skills, and creativity. In class discussion, you can bring up Jonah Lehrer's (p. 431) comments about inspiration. Could TV viewing promote inspiration?

James Baldwin: *If Black English Isn't a Language, Then Tell Me, What Is?* (ARGUING)

Reading

1. Language itself is a device by which human beings communicate with one another. As it is used in human situations, however, language is more than a communicative tool; it is a political construct. The distinction is central to Baldwin because it defines the debate about calling black English a dialect or a language as a debate about the identity of African American people. Baldwin contends that white people minimize the role of language in order to demoralize the African American population: "It is not the black child's language that is despised. It is his experience" (par. 11).

2. While his opponents argue that black English is merely a dialect of standard English, Baldwin defines black English as a testament to a history of struggle and a weapon to fight future oppression.

3. Baldwin uses the languages of oppressed people in Ireland, in the Basque countries, and in Wales to defend his position that language is a political instrument. In these countries, arguments about language are arguments about power. Language connects one with

power when one speaks the language of the majority, and it divides one from that power when one speaks the language of the oppressed.

Exploratory Writing

1. For *dialect*, see especially paragraphs 3 and 10. For *language*, see especially paragraphs 1, 2, 4, and 7. Most students are likely to find these definitions persuasive and moving. In class discussion, this question is an opportunity to distinguish between *argumentative* and *explanatory* writing. Baldwin uses these definitions not in an explanatory way, but in the service of a passionate argument.

2. Some examples to consider would be the hybrid languages used by Gloria Anzaldúa (p. 167), the "Englishes" Amy Tan describes (p. 178), the dialects that develop in online subcultures or in the use of new technologies, and regional ways of speaking with which students are familiar. This exercise invites students to deeply consider the issue of legitimacy and to politicize the question of language versus dialect.

3. The parallelism of the final paragraph emphasizes the severity of Baldwin's critique of those in power in the United States. Ending his paragraph with "a country that has managed to learn so little" (par. 12), Baldwin draws attention to the instructional tone of his essay. He provides the lessons in human understanding and redefinition that are purposefully ignored by the advocates of calling black English a dialect. Student responses will vary, but many are likely to feel that Baldwin's persuasive conclusion could have been written just as easily in the past decade. A fruitful topic for class discussion would be whether the election of President Barack Obama has helped legitimize "Black English." Obama (p. 355), Baldwin, and Martin Luther King Jr. (p. 341) are all known for their beautiful use of language. How does this connect to their public identities and political power (par. 4)?

Making Connections

1. This topic encourages a close rereading of both Baldwin and King, and asks students to consider the elements of strong *argumentative* writing.

Essay Writing

1. Both Baldwin and George Orwell (p. 313) see language as a political instrument and as a political signifier, not at all neutral, but a means of power. Although Orwell's essay focuses more on practical instruction for language use, and Baldwin's offers a criticism of racist ideas about language, their basic theses are more similar than different. Students might also notice that both Baldwin and Orwell use language clearly and persuasively.

Scott McCloud: *Setting the Record Straight* (ARGUING)

Reading

1. According to McCloud, most people have an overly narrow definition of comics, seeing them as "crude, poorly-drawn, semi-literate, cheap, disposable, kiddie fare." He believes that a proper definition would better reflect comics' limitless potential.

2. McCloud has created an autobiographical narrator who takes a pedagogical tone, speaking directly to his readers as though we are students in his classroom. This style of narrative demonstrates, rather than merely describing, the unique properties of comics. Reading *Understanding Comics* is, in some ways, more like watching a documentary film than reading an essay or article.

3. According to McCloud, printing allowed sequential art to be viewed by everyone, not only by the elite.

Exploratory Writing

1. This exercise can spur discussion about the fact that different interpretations are possible not only of images, but of the images' contexts as well. In class discussion, consider the different ways of telling a story that are employed in this section.

2. Most students will note that McCloud's comic has much in common with a strong argumentative essay. In class discussion, explore how the visual element of creating a comic changes the impact of the finished work. In addition to the other authors in this section, you might ask students to consider Marjane Satrapi's (p. 184) and Steven Johnson's (p. 120) use of graphics to support their arguments.

Making Connections

1. Students may point out that Marjane Satrapi's comic (p. 184) is heavily narrative, and tells a political history, much like McCloud's examples, whereas Brooke Gladstone's comic (p. 325) focuses more on argument, including large blocks of text with no accompanying images. It may be interesting to discuss the ways in which both Gladstone and Satrapi intend to convey their information while also eliciting an emotional response from the reader, and how comics can more effectively achieve this dual purpose.

Essay Writing

1. This essay topic invites students to connect McCloud's childhood experience to their own. In class discussion of the essays, address whether the students' chosen passions or obsessions have been misunderstood. Have they encountered problems similar to McCloud's as they tried to articulate what is special about their art forms?

Paired Readings: On Writing Online

Andrew Sullivan: *Why I Blog* (reflecting)

Reading

1. By "superficial," Sullivan means that "blogging rewards brevity and immediacy" (par. 17). But because of hyperlinks, blogs can offer more depth than the average article.

2. The "most pleasant surprise of blogging" is that it provides an outlet to many otherwise unpublished people who have "real knowledge" and "real literary talent" (par. 28).

3. Jazz, writes Sullivan, is a newer musical form that hasn't replaced more composed, formal music, but "merely demands a different way of playing and listening, just as blogging requires a different mode of reading and writing" (par. 39). To create their own analogies, students may draw on any number of ideas or inspirations throughout history and across various media.

4. The strongest answers to this question will note that Sullivan's article, itself, demonstrates the relationship between blogging and print articles like this one.

Exploratory Writing

1. This exercise will allow students to test and explore Sullivan's reflections and conclusions against their own blog experiences. Many will likely come into the class with

previous experience blogging, or at least participating on Internet forums. Discussion may also extend to students' experience with other forms of online media, such as Twitter or social networking.

2. Students are likely to find that almost any blog or online forum that allows readers to post public comments serves to demonstrate many of Sullivan's points. Optionally, they can experiment with contributing to the site they are observing. In class, discuss the differences between reporting on the blogs from an outsider perspective, without participating, versus reporting from an insider perspective.

Making Connections

1. This activity could inspire an animated discussion about online interaction and its real-life implications. The discussion may expand to include the effects on politics, interpersonal relationships, and legislation that online communication has had in recent years—and how students' rules could apply.

Essay Writing

1. This essay topic invites students to write in a reflective mode similar to Sullivan's. If students have done exercise 1 in exploratory writing, you can compare and contrast reflective with reportorial approaches to writing about this topic.

Mona Eltahawy: *Twitterholics Anonymous* (REFLECTING)

Reading

1. Eltahawy describes the 2010 uprising as "the worst unrest to hit [Tunisia] in a decade." It started "when a young man poured gasoline on himself in Sidibouzid to protest police confiscating the fruits and vegetables he sold without a permit, in lieu of a job he couldn't find despite having a university degree" (par. 9). The U.S. media, according to Eltahawy, "mostly ignored" this event.

2. Eltahawy loves Twitter because it connects her instantly to a "pipeline" of important world news that's often overlooked by the U.S. media, cuts down on her experience of writer's loneliness by giving her a sense of community, and is updated constantly. She hates Twitter because she finds it addictive and exhausting. Her habit of constantly reading and tweeting doesn't give her the time alone with her thoughts that she requires to get perspective and distance as a writer.

3. Beyond brand names (*iPhone*, *Twitter*) and commonly used terms (*blog*, *tweet*), Eltahawy uses *Twitterholic*, *Twitterverse*, *tweeps*, and *Twitterhighway*. Her language use and the sometimes tweet-like flow of her essay demonstrate that Twitter, a new kind of media space, has changed the writer's ways of thinking and writing.

Exploratory Writing

1. Depending on how creatively they've worked on this exercise, students might find that the Twitter format discourages thick description or what Nabokov called "caress(ing) the detail, the divine detail." They might also find something compelling and essential about working within the brevity of tweets. In class discussion, consider how new modes of social networking have changed the way that people read, write, and follow news.

2. Allow a question-and-answer period in class after each of these presentations. Ask students to consider whether the newspaper coverage of the stories they chose was

less immediate, thorough, and constant than the Twitter coverage, as Eltahawy would suggest.

Making Connections

1. The right to "assemble and associate" online is important because many live in places where to do so physically is impossible. Eltahawy's and Hillary Rodham Clinton's (p. 570) arguments convey that the power of online assembly and communication is not to be taken lightly—it can enable complacency as much as it can freedom, and it is capable of great harm as well as good.

Essay Writing

1. This exercise gives students a chance to practice crafting a written argument, and to consider the different ways that writing can be used to make a point. For an added challenge, suggest that students who personally disagree with the proposition write their essays arguing in favor of it. Eltahawy's own essay includes points that can be used to support arguments on both sides, as well as to craft a reductio ad absurdum argument.

Paired Readings: On Bilingualism

Gloria Anzaldúa: *How to Tame a Wild Tongue* (ARGUING)

Reading

1. She reads her first Chicano novel, *City of Night*, by the gay author John Rechy, in 1960 (par. 45). She describes her response to first reading poetry in Tex-Mex as "pure joy" (par. 46). A strong answer will connect these experiences to Anzaldúa's comment that "ethnic identity is twin skin to linguistic identity—I am my language. Until I can take pride in my language, I cannot take pride in myself" (par. 26). Reading her own language(s) in print gives Anzaldúa a sense of pride and legitimacy.

2. *Pochismos*, or *anglicisms*, are "words distorted by English" (par. 41).

3. A strong answer will note that the quotes are English, Spanish, and bilingual, thereby reflecting Anzaldúa's different tongues. The strongest answers will note that they also range from poetry to prose, and connect thematically as well as linguistically to Anzaldúa's description of her voice as "Indian, Spanish, white" and her "serpent's tongue" as "my woman's voice, my sexual voice, my poet's voice" (par. 45).

Exploratory Writing

1. Students should notice the diversity of identities that Anzaldúa associates with herself. In their personal responses, they can take Anzaldúa's cue and consider sexuality, personality, and vocation as well as ethnicity, culture, language, and gender. People identify themselves in diverse ways: the same bilingual Chicana could identify herself as "an engineer from Cleveland," while another might identify as a "Mexican-American bisexual." The dimensions of identity that we find important vary from person to person, and depend on complex factors, which are discussed in Amy Tan's essay (p. 178) as well as Anzaldúa's.

2. The strongest answers here will note Anzaldúa's generalizations—for example, her statement that "Chicanas feel uncomfortable talking in Spanish to Latinas, afraid of their censure." She sometimes assumes that her own experience is shared by all Chicanas as a group, and that she can speak for them. In class discussion, you might raise the question of

whether this kind of generalization is the same as a prejudice. Another fruitful topic for discussion is whether students have experienced prejudice due to their own ethnicity or language.

Making Connections

1. This list will show students that neither Amy Tan (p. 178) nor Anzaldúa's idea of "language" is limited to strict, conventional definitions. Both authors frame hybrid languages, slang, "incorrect" language use, dialects, and accents as crucial indicators of identity. In class discussion, you may want to bring in James Baldwin's essay (p. 131) and raise the question of which "languages" are seen as legitimate, and why.

2. A strong answer will note that Baldwin and Anzaldúa make relatively similar arguments. They both claim legitimacy for languages that are marginalized and are sometimes considered mere "dialects."

Essay Writing

1. This question asks students to distinguish between *arguing* and other modes of writing, such as *reflecting*. Strong essays will be structured around a clear argument, beginning with a thesis statement, and building their case through offering evidence and examples. The strongest essays will quote Anzaldúa (and/or Tan), raise and refute counterarguments, and provide a clear conclusion.

Amy Tan: *Mother Tongue* (reflecting)

Reading

1. Tan believes that her mother's English affected her performance on achievement tests, IQ tests, and the SAT, because the answers of English tests, unlike math tests, are indefinite and imprecise: "a judgment call, a matter of opinion and personal experience" (par. 16). The strongest answers will bring up Tan's identity as a writer and how she frames becoming an English major in college as something of a defiant act.

2. Tan uses the formal, standard English she learned in school and the English she learned from her mother. Her mother's English, Tan's "mother tongue," is a "language of intimacy," the family talk with which she grew up (par. 4). Tan needed to see her mother's English not as something that was broken and needed to be fixed, but as something passionate, full of rhythm and imagery. Embracing both "Englishes" gave Tan a voice of her own, reflecting both the language she learned in school and her mother tongue.

3. Tan characterizes her mother's language as "vivid, direct, full of observation and imagery" (par. 7), and also "broken . . . fractured . . . limited" (par. 8). We get a complex sense of Tan's mother's personality from her English use—she is not what she seems. The strongest answers will note that there are paradoxes and contradictions, not only in Tan's mother's language, but in how it has influenced Tan.

4. Tan excelled at math, because math is precise (par. 16). Unlike with English, there is only one possible answer on math tests. She was also strongly encouraged to pursue math because her English was not her "strong suit." One issue to introduce in class discussion is how cultural background and language affect our pursuit of goals.

Exploratory Writing

1. A strong answer will connect this personal reflection to the themes that Tan addresses and will draw on Tan's essay for structure.

2. This question is subjective and invites students to move beyond the themes of Tan's essay to critically consider her writing style. In class discussion, ask students to imagine this essay written in Tan's mother's English. How would their response to the essay change? How important is writing style, or the language that a writer uses?

3. As the two groups prepare for their debate, make sure that each group uses a few points directly from the essays by Tan, Gloria Anzaldúa (p. 167), or James Baldwin (p. 131). Also encourage them to write down points and quotations from those essays that can be used to make a strong counterargument.

Making Connections

1. Gloria Anzaldúa (p. 167) describes how Chicanas "have internalized the belief that we speak poor Spanish . . . And because we internalize how our language has been used against us by the dominant culture, we use our language differences against each other" (par. 21). Students could legitimately argue for or against the premise that Tan has been a victim of linguistic terrorism. A strong answer in either case will summarize Anzaldúa's comments and recount anecdotes from Tan's essay as evidence.

Essay Writing

1. This question asks students to distinguish between *reflecting* and the other modes of writing. Students can use Tan's reflecting essay as a model for how to create a strong personal essay of their own on this topic.

Paired Readings: On Religious Belief

Marjane Satrapi: *The Veil* (REPORTING)

Reading

1. In *Persepolis*, Marji views the veil with distance and skepticism, yet her relationship with God is intimate, active, and engaged (pp. 190–91). She presents the two as distinct and separate: The veil is associated with the political, whereas Marji's view of God is more related to her personal beliefs, values, and relationship with God. A strong student response might notice the humor with which Marji describes both the veil and her relationship with God. While Satrapi's irreverance toward the veil might strike some as sacrilegious, her devout, personal approach to religion reveals a greater complexity. A strong student response might notice the humor with which Marji describes both the veil and her relationship with God. This humor might also help mitigate any controversy that arises in the classroom.

2. *Irony* is notoriously difficult to define, and its definition therefore warrants some discussion among students. Marji's declaration (p. 189) is ironic because it suggests that she will rule as a dictator even though Satrapi is critiquing the dictatorial rule of the Islamic Republic in Iran. It may be helpful to define *irony* through an examination of its concrete use in context.

3. Satrapi's use of language and images differs from one panel to the next. In some panels, the text simply narrates events that are represented visually. In others, the text strengthens or enhances visual images, or the images augment Satrapi's sometimes spare narration. Text is often used to indicate dialogue. In the panel depicting the demonstrations for and against the veil, the text (p. 187: "The veil!" and "Freedom!") enters the

frame and is drawn expressively. In a case like this, the difference between text and image is blurred. Some class discussion in which students compare notes will help them understand a broader range of Satrapi's techniques.

Exploratory Writing

1. Students are likely to respond that Satrapi's use of visuals makes her account more interesting, more emotional, and easier to follow. They are likely to favor this technique over historical or journalistic reporting. It may be useful to launch some discussion of what history or journalism can accomplish that a graphic narrative cannot. For example, these more traditional forms of reporting are likely to be more fully based in documented facts and they're more likely to offer confirmable, detailed accounts or analysis of events.

2. The first page of Satrapi's text represents an enormous range of emotion, including boredom, sadness, resignation, bemusement, resentment, outrage, glee, fear, and curiosity. Students may well notice emotions not listed here, and their lists are likely to differ from one another. It will be important to hold students responsible for supporting their claims with evidence, and it may be illuminating for students to share their responses with one another. A strong response may note that the emotional complexity represented on Satrapi's first page is indicative of the complexity of cultural responses to the imposition of the veil and the Islamic rule for which it is a symbol.

3. This activity should be lively. Students will have the opportunity to work together, to be creative, and to have some fun assuming roles. In order for the activity to be productive, students will need to illustrate and develop their claims with evidence from the text. It may also be worth discussing the fact that their use of evidence should inform their more formal writing.

Making Connections

1. Students are likely to approach this question through the bias of their own religious beliefs. This is not a problem unless students fail to offer reasonable evidence for their claims. Any of the theories Paul Bloom discusses (p. 194) may be used to illuminate Satrapi's representation of religion in Iran, but it is vital that students understand these theories fully enough to compare and contrast their degree of relevance to Satrapi's text. The process of applying the theories in context should also become an opportunity for students to develop this understanding. Some class discussion of these theories (and even their application to Satrapi's text) may be helpful during the process.

2. This prompt will give students with a talent for drawing an opportunity to bring that talent to the table. It will also give them an opportunity to digest, synthesize, and summarize some of the major theories discussed in Paul Bloom's (p. 194) essay. Of course, it will serve some students better than others. Because of this, it might be offered as an optional alternative to question 1 under Making Connections or question 1 under Essay Writing.

Essay Writing

1. In "The Hidden Side of *Persepolis*," a short documentary about the making of the film included in the special features section of the DVD, Satrapi makes the point that a successful adaptation of a graphic novel to film must begin with the assumption that the film is an entirely new text. It might be helpful to launch this assignment by showing students the first few minutes of this documentary in class—and even to suggest that they quote Satrapi's statement in their responses. In their responses, students may note that certain images are included or excluded and that certain images have been added to the film. They may also note that the use of animation and voices embodies the text in a new

way. A strong response may also note that the simplicity and abstraction of the animation help Satrapi accomplish her goal of universalizing the story of her childhood in Iran or that the fact that the animation is rendered by hand humanizes the story.

Paul Bloom: *Is God an Accident?* (ARGUING)

READING

1. According to Bloom, "opiate" theories suggest, following the lead of Karl Marx, that life is difficult and the idea of God offers solace; whereas "fraternity" theories suggest that religion "brings people together" and therefore gives them cultural and/or evolutionary advantages. While these definitions are straightforward and should be included in any valid response, the subsequent questions, about whether such theories are compatible with cognitive theories of religion, require a fair amount of interpretation. To make a strong case, students will need to examine the evidence carefully and make reasoned connections, which will be the biggest challenge in responding to these questions.

2. Dualism is the belief that mind and body are separate "mechanisms." In Bloom's words (from the opening paragraph of this section), "We are dualists; it seems intuitively obvious that a physical body and a conscious entity—a mind or soul—are genuinely distinct." A strong response should elaborate on this point, making it clear that Bloom wrestles with debates between dualism and "materialism," the theory that mind and body are one and the same. Students should make it clear that he offers evidence on both sides of the debate.

3. Answering this question requires some interpretation, particularly about Bloom's motives and style of argument. Bloom's rabbi is more than a straw man. Bloom invokes him to represent the 96 percent of the American population who he claims believe in the supernatural. In doing so, he establishes the motive for his essay: Why is it that a large majority of people believe in God? A strong student response might also note that Bloom positions himself as a "friendly" critic, offering respectful and measured explanations of all the theories he discusses.

4. Students' responses will vary widely, depending on which quotations they choose. It will be important that they reflect on how the quotations function in the essay, rather than simply responding to the provocative claims they make. It might be useful to spend some class discussion responding to these quotations, allowing students to make arguments for and against them but emphasizing the distinction between doing this and analyzing the roles they play in Bloom's essay.

EXPLORATORY WRITING

1. Bloom's six subtitles are "God Is Not Dead," "Opiates and Fraternities," "Bodies and Souls," "Natural-Born Dualists," "We've Evolved to Be Creationists," and "Religion and Science Will Always Clash." In each section, Bloom defines his key terms and then addresses arguments and counterarguments. It will be important that students define Bloom's terms accurately, but also that they explain, in their summaries, that he examines both sides of the arguments initiated in his titles.

2. As the instructor, you may want to design a structure for these debates. For example, each team might be given five minutes for an opening statement, five minutes for a rebuttal, and three minutes for a closing statement. (Depending on the number of students in the class, some might be assigned to a committee of judges.) Teams should meet to plan, deciding which evidence supports their position most effectively, assigning roles to each member,

and deciding whether they want to conduct further research. Because religion is a sensitive topic, it may be useful to have a discussion about the debate—and the fact that it is an intellectual exercise, in which nobody's personal beliefs should be challenged or ridiculed.

Making Connections

1. Marji (Marjane Satrapi, p. 184) reveres God and believes she has personal conversations with him. While the adult Satrapi's portrayal of her childhood relationship is humorous, Marji is very serious about it. Because of that, her response to Paul Bloom's (p. 194) essay is likely to be serious too. Either way, an adequate response should respond directly to details from Bloom's essay.

Essay Writing

1. Before students write, it might be useful to spend class time examining Bloom's essay (and perhaps one or two other argumentative essays) as a model. How does Bloom establish a motive for his argument? What is his thesis? What evidence does he provide, and what techniques does he use to analyze it? How is his essay structured? (These questions will become more complicated if other essays are introduced. In addition, other essays will give students models of other techniques to work with.)

Student Essay

Jennifer Bernal: *Child on the Threshold: The Narrative Voice of a Child in* Persepolis

Reading

1. Students should note the word *threshold* in the title, indicating that this is an essay about a change in the protagonist. The main title is evocative, but without the subtitle the essay's focus—Satrapi's development of a distinctive voice to represent her childhood experience—wouldn't be clear. Students should also evaluate the title and offer concrete reasons to support their evaluations. Their own titles should reflect whatever elements they indicate is valuable in a title. A particularly strong response might mention the fact that in a graphic novel, voice is composed of both verbal and visual images.

2. It would be valuable to dedicate some class discussion to the relative merits of dictionaries and encyclopedias as sources. Bernal's source is *The Literary Encyclopedia*, a specialized dictionary. She uses it solely for its definition of Bakhtin's term, probably because it offers a concise explanation that would be difficult to locate in the original source. A strong student response should note that while limited use of dictionaries and encyclopedias is valuable, they should not be relied on too heavily.

3. Bernal tells us that the drawing resembles a dismembered doll, pointing out the consistency with the visual voice Satrapi develops to portray a childlike point of view. In addition, though, the style has the effect of dampening the horror of the image. Nevertheless, this horror is impossible to miss, and because of this, Bernal argues, the image represents a tension between the adult writer and the child protagonist, both of whom can be felt in Satrapi's voice. Students should also note the fact that Bernal is very specific about elements of the image she wants readers to notice and that she analyzes these in order to build toward her claim about this tension.

Exploratory Writing

1. Responses should identify a particular claim as Bernal's thesis. In most cases this will be, "Satrapi expresses the duality of this child's voice not only through content but also through her visual style" (par. 1). However, a student may make a case for an alternative thesis. Responses should make clear how and why Bernal's evidence offers strong support (or does not). It may be worthwhile to encourage students to be creative or playful with the characterization of the fictional students and instructors—and to ask some or all students to read their dialogues aloud in class.

2. All responses should identify some of the following techniques used to integrate the quotations: signal phrase, citation, follow-up discussion and analysis, and grammatical integration between the words of the essay writer and her sources. Finally, students should identify particular strategies they plan to use in their own writing. A particularly reflective student might discuss his or her strengths and weaknesses with regard to these strategies.

Making Connections

1. Instructors should encourage students to write lively dialogues—and, if they're comfortable with it, to try their hands at a graphic form. Students should develop some characterization of both Marjane Satrapi (p. 184) and Jennifer Bernal (p. 208). A strong response will include some disagreement or conflicting points of view. While it's important that the claims they put in the mouths of both characters are consistent with the texts on which they are based, students should be free to take some creative license and be encouraged to integrate language from each text into the dialogue. Any strong response will include each character quoting the other's text directly, asking questions and making claims about the quotations.

Essay Writing

1. Instructors should emphasize the fact that Bernal's essay is argumentative. Students should make a claim about the quality and function of an author's voice and develop this claim with concrete evidence from the text (and possibly other sources). It may be valuable to devote class time to discussion of the qualities in Bernal's essay that work well—and how students might emulate some of these. Because the assignment emphasizes quotation, it may also be useful to use the essay as an opportunity to develop students' ability to integrate quotations. Peer review or draft workshops might emphasize thesis, evidence, and the integration of quotations.

PART 3: SOCIAL SCIENCES

Jose Antonio Vargas: *My Life as an Undocumented Immigrant* (REFLECTING)

Reading

1. Proposition 187 was a bill, advocated by Pete Wilson in 1994, that would have prevented immigrants without documents from attending public schools and accessing other services. The proposition was deemed unconstitutional by a federal court.

2. Over 800,000 people were deported during the first two years of the Obama administration. It is estimated that there are 11 million undocumented immigrants living in the United States today.

3. Just before his thirtieth birthday, Vargas obtains a Washington State driver's license that will give him a form of "acceptable identification" for five years, but will leave him in the position of hiding his true status and "lying to people [he respects]" (par. 60).

Exploratory Writing

1. For Vargas, citizenship is about contribution to his society and the economy, professional success, and assimilation. Instead, he finds it is controlled by legal bureaucracy. When he writes "my country doesn't think of me as one of its own" (par. 9), he refers to laws that force him to choose between hiding his identity or leaving the country where he has lived and worked since childhood.

2. In class discussion, note the passionate debates that arise in the comments section of the *Define American* blog. Discuss how different writing techniques in the blog entries and in the comments—reflecting, reporting, arguing, and explaining—contribute to these debates. How do personal narratives reflecting on undocumented immigrants' own experiences change the conversation?

Making Connections

1. Vargas describes how he convinces himself that assimilating to the language (writing in English, losing his accent, having his name in print) validates his presence as an American—but actually, his total mastery of the language does not legitimize his presence in the eyes of the law. Comparing and contrasting Vargas's article with James Baldwin's essay (p. 131) shows a complex relationship among language, legitimacy, and power. In class discussion, highlight Baldwin's comments on racism, and consider how similar power dynamics apply to the situation of undocumented immigrants today.

Essay Writing

1. This assignment helps students explore various techniques required in writing a *reportorial* essay. As you review or discuss essays in class, ask students to consider the similarities and differences among reportorial writing, explanatory writing, and personal reflections. In many essays, these techniques overlap, but the assignment asks students to isolate reporting from other modes of writing.

George Orwell: *Shooting an Elephant* (REFLECTING)

Reading

1. Orwell characterizes every white man's life in the East as "one long struggle not to be laughed at" (par. 7).

2. Orwell, as the representative of British imperialism, finds that power can be maintained only by impressing the "natives" but that such power forces the wielder to wear a mask much against his will. Orwell realizes that "I was only an absurd puppet pushed to and fro by the will of those yellow faces behind" (par. 7).

3. Shame and embarrassment overcome Orwell at the end. Though legally in the right, he is morally the fool he tried to avoid becoming in front of the natives. That he could be "glad" a coolie died to save his reputation indicates how reprehensible the imperialist system can be.

4. Orwell places his thesis in the middle of the essay (par. 7), where he describes watching the elephant and deciding what to do next. This placement is dramatically effective in that the pressure of the moment seems to force an epiphany on him: "I perceived in this moment that when the white man turns tyrant it is his own freedom that he destroys."

Exploratory Writing

1. Orwell's candor adds much to the moral struggle involved in imperialism. Without this tone, the essay would lack psychological tension and the human element.

2. In class discussion on this topic, you can bring in public controversies over "false memoirs," such as James Frey's *A Million Little Pieces*. Also discuss the manipulation of photographic and film images (see Susan Sontag, p. 366). How can we judge what is true? Why does it matter? There is no easy solution to this problem, but it raises interesting questions about motives for writing, publishing, and reading.

Making Connections

1. Encourage students to consider Orwell's quandary as if they were him. Would Orwell change his tone about the experience after reading Steven Pinker's essay (p. 458)? Alternately, how might Pinker parse Orwell's experience the way he does with Jonathan Haidt's list of situations that most people find abhorrent?

Essay Writing

1. Strong answers will note, among other instances, the discrepancy between Orwell's self-description and how he actually comes across to the reader, the fact that he behaves as though he is entirely at the mercy of the crowd when he is ostensibly in Burma as a "leader," the connection between being important and being hated (par. 1), the response of the crowd, which does not like him because he is holding a gun (par. 7), and the conclusion in paragraph 14 ("I was very glad that the coolie had been killed"). His irony helps highlight the farcical nature of British imperialism—the people involved are not doing what they purport to be doing, and the project of coming to bring order to Burma is actually a racist project, reflecting a disregard for the people's humanity.

2. Strong essays will pick a situation that was genuinely challenging, in which it was hard to do the right thing. In class discussion, raise the idea that people have differing moral standards. How do we decide what is right? What are our motivations?

John Berger: *Hiroshima* (REPORTING)

Reading

1. "The whole incredible problem," as Berger describes it, is the masking of an event that is evil by "*looking beyond* (with indifference) that which is before the eyes" (par. 34). Statistics and impersonal photos prevent us from seeing the evil nature of the bombing of Hiroshima. To see the reality of the event, we must see the pictures and hear the words of the individuals who survived it. Journalistic accounts distort history by removing its immediacy.

2. Berger emphasizes that "what happened" was begun "months, years before, with the planning of the action, and the eventual final decision to drop two bombs on Japan" (par. 21). He refers here to those who worked on the Manhattan Project and those political and military authorities who decided to employ the bomb. Berger is simply reminding us that

it *was* a calculated decision, "not a miscalculation, an error, or the result . . . of a situation deteriorating so rapidly that it gets out of hand" (par. 21); few would dispute this. Yet Berger feels that we have not fully confronted its implications. He calls attention to the grotesque irony that so much human "rationality" went into the service of such irrational cruelty. Part of the "whole incredible problem" is that our leaders are now capable of coldly and objectively contemplating the imposition of such horrors on entire populations.

3. Berger means that in order to hasten their own agendas, those responsible for dropping the bomb on Hiroshima made a calculated decision to inflict pain and human suffering (par. 21), all the while distancing themselves from the fact of that "cruelty" and "evil" through rationalizing, and considering statistics and numbers rather than human experience (par. 23). Similarly, when forced to confront the reality of what happened, people feeling natural outrage and horror when hearing about the "human faces" of the bomb fallout distance themselves from that reality by turning to self-defensive, "expedient" plans for how to prevent such a thing happening *here*. Statistics ignore the real evil that caused the suffering at Hiroshima. "By looking beyond or away" one can "come to believe that such evil is relative, and therefore under certain conditions justifiable" (par. 35).

Exploratory Writing

1. Note Berger's statement: "Evil . . . has often worn a mask of innocence" (par. 33). In class discussion of this issue, you can introduce Hannah Arendt's term "the banality of evil," taken from her study of Adolf Eichmann's trial in Jerusalem. Bring up examples of how everyday people rationalize or contribute to atrocities, such as the detention of innocent asylum-seekers in privately owned American prisons, the torture of detainees at Abu Ghraib, the Holocaust, slavery, or the genocide of Native Americans.

2. Ask students to consider whether they have listed the words "evil" or "Hell." How many of the nouns they list are observations about the events portrayed, and how many are moral (horror, atrocity, devastation)? Which nouns represent a confrontation with the reality of what is portrayed? Which serve to distance us from that reality?

3. For this exercise, encourage students to refer also to Barbara Tuchman (p. 257), the dispatches from soldiers in combat in Iraq and Afghanistan (p. 374), and especially Susan Sontag (p. 366). Berger believes we need to show the drawings by citizens of Hiroshima everywhere (par. 33), yet other writers have argued that images can be deceptive, and Berger himself discusses how outrage, horror, and pity upon facing facts and events can be rapidly displaced by expediency, rationalization, and indifference.

Making Connections

1. One clearly interesting issue about the soldiers' dispatches is that the project to collect them was funded by Boeing, a top defense contractor. Another issue is that they are accounts of American soldiers, published in an American magazine. How might accounts from soldiers or militants on the "other side" offer a different perspective on events? How might accounts from Iraqi and Afghani civilians witnessing the soldiers' actions in their countries offer a different perspective? Is there any evidence of "terrorism" or "evil" in the soldiers' stories? In class discussion, bring up different ways that the choice to kill or torture other human beings is rationalized, seen as relative, or seen as "under certain conditions justifiable" (par. 35).

2. Discussion may focus around what emotional impact students feel by actually seeing the artwork in Berger's piece, whereas they do not see the photos Susan Sontag (p. 366) is talking about. Discuss the difference in authorship and intent between Sontag's and Berger's images, and why that should or should not matter to the audience.

Essay Writing

1. Essays should highlight Berger's comments in paragraphs 24 and 25 especially. In class discussion, raise the question of whether the United States, in the "War on Terror," itself committed terrorist acts based on Berger's definition. This topic asks students to use several modes of writing, including explaining, reporting, and reflecting. Many essays may ultimately become arguments that advocate a particular perspective on terror.

Barbara Ehrenreich: *Nickel and Dimed: On (Not) Getting By in America* (REPORTING)

Reading

1. Ehrenreich goes undercover to see if she could actually survive in the world of the working poor, but rather than simply restate facts from such a life, she dramatizes each event for her readers, often including very specific details about the people she meets and her own situation, making them care about the plight of the working poor.

2. The rationale for welfare reform is that work is uplifting and will boost both the self-esteem and relative value of those transitioning off of welfare. The reality of high living expenses and low wages makes Ehrenreich distrust this rationale.

3. What details the student chooses are subjective, but they should point to her overall credibility as someone who, however briefly, lived this life.

4. The survey suggests that there is a lack of adequate housing for the working poor.

Exploratory Writing

1. See Season 1, Episode 1 of *30 Days*. The first-season DVD may be available from your local library, or can be found online on sites like Netflex and Amazon. Watching Spurlock's documentary can be used to generate class discussion about investigative *reporting* and what it entails. What advantages do documentary filmmakers have over reporters, and vice versa? Photographic and film images hold great power (see also Susan Sontag, p. 366), but Ehrenreich's methodology allows her to do her research discreetly. This episode of Spurlock's program is powerful, because it shows how, even for privileged people like Spurlock and his fiancée (and like Ehrenreich), even a few days of poverty create more poverty. Poor living conditions and taxing working conditions create new transportation and health care expenses for the couple. Students can find basic information about minimum wage in their own community through a quick Internet search. Most are likely to find that without outside help (living with parents, savings, or public assistance), it would not be possible to afford to live in their community on one forty-hour-per-week, minimum-wage job.

2. In class discussion about this partner exercise, talk about interviewing as a reportorial technique. These interviews will yield a surprising amount of detailed information about individual work experiences. Discuss questions that help make an investigative report rich and effective (who, what, when, where, why), and show where Ehrenreich answers these questions in her report.

3. Ehrenreich begins this project as a middle-class white woman with a PhD, who is a successful journalist. She has a "bank account, IRA, health insurance, and multiroom home" waiting for her and is "thoroughly insulated from the terrors that afflict the genuinely poor" (par. 4). In contrast, housing is a "principal source of disruption" (par. 25) in her coworkers' lives. They do not have the money to pay a deposit on an inexpensive rental, so some are living much more expensively, for instance at motels (par. 26). In this

way, their "starting conditions" create a deficit, making daily living more expensive than if they had deposit money (par. 25) or health insurance (par. 26). Even simple things like a pot, pot holders, and a ladle (par. 27) for cooking cheap lentil stew require some money up front. Ehrenreich also has "health, stamina, a working car, and no children" (par. 29), while most long-term poor have none of these advantageous "starting conditions."

Making Connections

1. Like Ehrenreich, Christina Boufis (p. 96) is a middle-class, educated white woman, and poor and disadvantaged women (in Boufis's case, mostly women of color) are the subject of her report. Strong responses to this question will consider how a report by one of Boufis's students, or by one of Ehrenreich's coworkers, would have a different flavor and different strengths than the authors' reports.

Essay Writing

1. This essay question invites students to do reportorial *research*. In preparation, discuss research techniques. You might also open up the topic by inviting students to interview someone (such as a congressperson's representative, the director of a local soup kitchen, or a welfare administrator) as part of their research.

Barbara Tuchman: *"This Is the End of the World": The Black Death* (REPORTING)

Reading

1. No one knows exactly how many people died in Europe during the plague. "Contemporary reports were an awed impression, not an accurate count" (par. 8). Although students may mention the estimation that "a third of the world" died (and, therefore, approximately 20 million people in Europe), strong answers will stress the speculative nature of those figures. Weaker answers will report a number as if it is verified as factual.

2. The direct quotations from contemporary observers sum up the topics discussed—and do so more effectively than mere paraphrase could. Thus, the reader hears the voices of the fourteenth century speak for themselves.

3. Tuchman uses individual examples and illustrations to bring to life her facts and figures. For instance, paragraphs 9 and 10 help explain the probable exaggeration of the figures in paragraph 8. In the conclusion of paragraph 11, which reports various death rates, the final image of the deserted village humanizes those previously quoted percentages. Paragraph 14 likewise conveys how hard hit Italy was: It starts with the uncompleted grandeur of a cathedral and concludes with Agnolo di Tura's poignant record of burying his five children "with my own hands." Tuchman is always aware that reporting the study of history includes the small moments as well as the great.

Exploratory Writing

1. In leading class discussion on this topic, it might help to offer an anecdote from your own life. Examples might include something momentous, like learning about the bloody colonial history of one's own country, discovering how recently women and African Americans were denied the vote, or learning about the Holocaust, the internment of Japanese Americans during World War II, the Inquisition, the history of pogroms, or the Trail of Tears. It could also be something lighter or seemingly trivial that led you to see the past (or present) in a new way—for example, learning that the famous conservationist

James Audubon sampled most of North America's now-endangered birds as he cataloged them, roasting them on a spit and recording their flavor. One reason the study of history is rewarding is that it offers a window into lives different from ours, causing us to question our assumptions.

2. Answers to this will be subjective. The question calls on the student to make his or her own connections between the events Tuchman recounts and his or her idea of what is timeless in human nature. Strong answers will connect aspects of the response to the plague with other moments in history, such as the AIDS crisis. In class discussion, you can compare and contrast the responses to the plague that Tuchman reports with examples of human behavior in crisis from other essays, such as Susan Sontag's (p. 336) argument about photographing the dead, Richard Selzer's (p. 533) report on AIDS in Haiti, or U.S. soldiers' accounts of serving in Iraq and Afghanistan (p. 374).

3. This exercise can be opened to include paintings not shown with the essay. Strong presentations will identify the symbolism in the painting and explain how it connects to broader social ideas and fears about the plague.

Making Connections

1. What we know about each epidemic certainly directs the way we are able to write about them. Strong answers might point to the ways in which each author's purpose directs the tone of each essay. Ask students how the essays might feel different if Tuchman had used the same tone to write about the AIDS epidemic, or if Richard Selzer (p. 533) had access to the same kinds of evidence to write about the Black Death.

2. One thing photographs offer that paintings do not is the sense, however illusory, of "proof"—what we see in photographs seems to tell the "true" story. Yet Susan Sontag (p. 366) discusses how photographs can be manipulated, too. This question is a good starting point for a discussion of documentation and evidence. How can we really know what is true? And how does this affect our interpretation of a narrative?

Essay Writing

1. This research assignment can be as small or as ambitious as you wish and as your library permits. A disaster such as the sinking of the *Titanic* or the San Francisco earthquake will be fully documented in books, articles, and newspaper reports. If your community has sustained a disaster in the last twenty-five years, students can interview eyewitnesses, work with local newspaper files, and, in the case of a natural disaster or fire, get a sense of the physical change wrought by the disaster through photographs and visits to the scene.

Robin Marantz Henig: *What Is It about 20-Somethings?* (EXPLAINING)

Reading

1. Jeffrey Jensen Arnett, a psychology professor, is leading the movement to view the twenties—"emerging adulthood"—as a distinct life stage, akin to the creation, a century ago, of adolescence (par. 6).

2. Yellowbrick, "the only psychiatric facility for emerging adults," serves twenty-somethings by focusing on their "unique developmental tasks" (par. 53). One reason Henig includes Yellowbrick is to support her suggestion that the category "emerging adults" is most accurately applied to the very privileged—given that the facility's $21,000 monthly cost is often covered by the patient's parents.

3. Henig's use of statistics provides readers with concrete examples of what she's explaining, and with evidence to illustrate her points—two key elements of *explanatory* writing.

Exploratory Writing

1. For example, alternative criteria for determining people's right to rent a car might include evaluations of their driving records or credit history. As students engage with this exercise, they'll uncover the deeper problem of universalizing categories and definitions.

2. In class discussion, compare the interview responses to the data and examples presented in Henig's article. Some responses are likely to illustrate Henig's characterization of "emerging adulthood" as a category for the privileged, whereas other interviewees might report that circumstances forced them to take on responsibilities and become independent at a young age.

Making Connections

1. In paragraph 30, Christina Boufis (p. 96) reports that Tanya ended up back in jail after selling drugs to an undercover cop because she needed money for clothes. An administrator says, "It didn't occur to her to get a job," but Boufis wonders whether she could get one. Tanya shares some of the problems of the "emerging adults" at Yellowbrick, but the roots of her situation are very different from theirs. Some students might believe that this difference supports the theory of "emerging adulthood" as a developmental category, while others could conclude that it undermines the theory.

Essay Writing

1. Henig writes that the whole idea of "milestones" is something of an anachronism. As students construct arguments that assess the five traditional milestones in light of their own contemporary perspectives on adulthood, they can also practice evaluating the strength of Henig's claims.

Olivia Judson: *The Selfless Gene* (EXPLAINING)

Reading

1. The questions that Judson sets out to answer are laid out in paragraph 2. Her strategies for addressing them include describing scientists and summarizing their ideas and theories, using many examples, clarifying cause and effect, and clearly defining terms. Judson concludes that flexibility—the ability to adjust our behavior to fit a given social environment—is one of the most important and hopeful human traits, but that it's so instinctive that we rarely notice it. Since we can modulate our behavior, Judson suggests, we can, in principle, organize society to bring out the best in our natures.

2. *Parochial altruism* is "the notion that people might prefer to help strangers from their own ethnic group over strangers from a different group" (par. 29).

3. Darwin's idea languished because it appears to depend on "group selection," and it seems to have the distasteful corollary that xenophobia or even racism evolved in tandem with kindness (par. 28).

4. Williams syndrome, according to Judson, shows that "friendliness has a genetic underpinning—that it is indeed as primal as ferocity" (par. 46).

Exploratory Writing

1. This question invites small groups of students to list ten behaviors innate to all humans and to discuss the ways in which these "primal" urges inform cultural practices. Have students consider the customs that different cultures have developed to regulate these urges. To what degree are these customs conducted in private or public across the spectrum?

2. Judson reports that most "punishment game" experiments have been conducted with college students, so an issue to raise in discussion of this exercise is that your class may be similar in makeup to these groups. Students might discuss what other kinds of currency might be important, beyond money or altruism. Someone might make a seemingly altruistic choice, for example, to impress a person he or she found attractive.

Making Connections

1. Student opinions on this question may vary. The idea is to generate critical thinking and to encourage students to view science reporting as writing, shaped by the background, beliefs, motives, and agenda of the writer.

2. Steven Pinker (p. 458) argues, "The moral sense . . . is as vulnerable to illusions as the other senses. It is apt to confuse morality per se with purity, status, and conformity. . . . It imposes taboos that make certain ideas indiscussible" (par. 65). Judson believes that human flexibility has profound and hopeful implications because "it suggests that we can, in principle, organize society so as to bring out the best facets of our . . . natures" (par. 48). Pinker would probably argue that our idea of the "best" can be highly fallible.

Essay Writing

1. In discussion, you can use these essays to highlight arguments and counterarguments and to identify elements that make an argument powerful and convincing.

Mark Bittman: *Bad Food? Tax it, and Subsidize Vegetables* (ARGUING)

Reading

1. Y. Claire Wang, an assistant professor of public health at Columbia University, conducted a study that predicted that a penny tax on sugar-sweetened beverages would save New York state billions of dollars in health care, bring in $1 billion more, and prevent thousands of cases of diabetes (par. 26). Bittman cites her study to support his arguments.

2. Low sales taxes paid at the register are less effective, according to Bittman, than excise taxes that are incorporated into the shelf price (par. 14).

3. The result would be an approximately 20 percent decrease in consumption, thereby preventing 1.5 million Americans from becoming obese in the next decade, preventing 400,000 cases of diabetes, and saving around $30 billion (par. 28).

Exploratory Writing

1. This exercise should highlight the importance of strong research in argument writing. Encourage students to research and write about a diet with which they are unfamiliar. Given that personal nutrition choices can be contentious, objectivity will be challenging but ultimately essential to a successful argument in this case.

2. Students should flag the places where Bittman anticipates and refutes arguments against his point. In class discussion, use Bittman's article to show how argumentative writing usually features controversial topics and to assess how Bittman uses writing techniques to acknowledge the controversy. His techniques are strategic, introducing some counterarguments while omitting others.

3. This exercise gives students a chance to separate arguing techniques and strategies from the content of particular arguments. To find strong arguments, you or your students can read the highlighted comments for this article at the *New York Times* site (http://community.nytimes.com/comments/www.nytimes.com/2011/07/24/opinion/sunday/24bittman.html), which mention arguments omitted in Bittman's article, such as the problem that many non-organic fruits and vegetables are treated with unhealthy pesticides.

Making Connections

1. Use the comparison of these essays to consider techniques for reflective and argumentative writing. In writing their own reflections on the question "Why do people consume things they know are bad for them?" invite students to ask themselves where they were *reflecting* and where they were *arguing*, and why they chose those strategies.

Essay Writing

1. Ask students to gather evidence from all of the food diary reports together. Strong answers might raise the question of what motivates some people to eat a highly nutritious diet, while others choose the Standard American Diet (SAD) This essay topic shows students how they can use personal experience to collect reportorial data, not just as material for reflective writing.

Thomas Jefferson: *The Declaration of Independence* (ARGUING)

Reading

1. The argument in paragraph 2 can be summarized this way:

   a. God created humans with certain rights.
   b. Humans created governments to preserve those rights.
   c. Humans may change governments if they fail to preserve those rights.

Self-evident means that these are axioms, a priori assumptions that are held without requiring proof.

2. The accusations against the king boil down to the charge that he is not preserving rights but usurping them—behaving like a despot, a tyrant whose word is law, rather than like a constitutional monarch. A king might reply by questioning the nature of the rights claimed for all men, especially liberty, and perhaps by arguing that governments are designed to protect people from others' taking liberties with them and their property. Certainly, it could be argued that the British were only collecting lawful taxes rather than being despotic in America. King George III, of course, sent in the troops, as rulers like to do.

3. The audience certainly included the British people and Parliament as well as the king. But we must remember that most Americans were British citizens at that time, except slaves, who were not citizens at all but rather property. The residents of America were the major audience for the document. They were deeply divided and remained so. Many Tories fought on the British side and later settled out of the United States in Canada and the Bahamas. There was an international audience too, especially the French, who finally entered the war decisively on the side of the rebellious colonies.

Exploratory Writing

1. Remind your students to start with a strong enough position. Jefferson worked from God and nature down through humans and governments to a particular situation. They

should follow his lead. The application of this model to less important matters may produce a comic or parodic effect. Let your students know whether you will approve of such bathos or not. In class discussion, address how easily serious material can take on the high parody of Jonathan Swift's "A Modest Proposal" (p. 305) *accidentally*, when the writer is too earnest, sweeping, or hyperbolic. Some impassioned documents from the past seem mildly comical today in their language. Swift addresses this problem directly, in a clever and sophisticated way, leaving his readers with a powerful and serious argument. Discuss how Jefferson, Martin Luther King Jr. (p. 341), Barack Obama (p. 355), James Baldwin (p. 131), and George Orwell ("Politics and the English Language," p. 313) use prose that avoids a parodic effect.

2. This exercise shows just how important writing style can be in making an argument. The form of the argument can shape how readers or listeners perceive its content.

3. This is one of the most challenging issues to address with students. There's a common urge to glorify (or vilify) historical figures as well as important living figures who are in the public eye. It's also common to try to simplify complex societal situations, especially dark and sickening ones, by associating them with individual personalities (Hitler was evil, Gandhi was good), rather than facing the fact that there were never "good old days." Another common trap is to consider historical horrors like slavery, the oppression of women, the denial of civil rights to women and nonwhites, racist science, or the genocide of Native Americans "in the past." Discuss contemporary examples of racism, slavery, and genocide.

Making Connections

1. The key to making this connection is finding a way to inflate Jefferson's argument so much that it sounds zany. What could possibly be equivalent to Jonathan Swift's (p. 305) idea of roasting babies? Students might come up with very inventive ways to address this question. The underlying idea is to explore writers' motives for using different modes of *argumentative* writing.

2. Most students will find a great many similarities between Obama and Jefferson in terms of tone, style, and purpose. This is a good opportunity to assess the importance of tone in making a strong argument.

Essay Writing

1. This paper should be an explanation rather than an argument. It requires some careful and perhaps subtle analysis. You might not wish to assign it unless you have confidence in your students' ability to accomplish this.

Jonathan Swift: *A Modest Proposal* (ARGUING)

Reading

1. The proposer is somewhat deficient in humanitarian sentiment. He is anti-Catholic and anti-Episcopalian, a staunch low-church Protestant (par. 21). He is convinced that people do most things for money (par. 26), though he professes to be motivated that way himself (par. 33).

The absolute taboo against cannibalism and the strong feeling that children should be cherished force us to look for alternatives to the literal meaning. The brutal way that the proposer speaks of people as if they were animals (such as "a child just dropped from its dam" in par. 4) and his pompous references to himself all help to make him repugnant and ridiculous. We credit Swift with the mastery of this obnoxious puppet.

2. He makes his proposal in paragraph 9. In the earlier paragraphs, he presents himself as a concerned humanitarian, and he describes accurately the terrible economic situation. After stating his proposal, he goes into its details with terrifying rationality and lack of emotion. This order allows us to be implicated more deeply in the situation than if he began with the proposal itself.

3. The counterproposals are mainly included in the italicized lines of paragraph 29. He refutes them simply by scoffing at the idea that anyone would try sincerely to "put them in practice" (par. 30).

4. The title itself, "A Modest Proposal," is both ironic and satirical, since this proposal is undeniably extravagant, outrageous, and extreme. Other examples include the proposer's description of his maturity and years of contemplation (par. 4) and his reference to his thoughts as humble (par. 8) and the "sincerity of [his] heart" (par. 33). The juxtaposition of the proposer's self-description (humble, modest) with his lurid language about cannibalism (children described as "delicious . . . plump, and fat for a good table") helps characterize him for the reader.

Exploratory Writing

1. There may be issues that seem ridiculous to some students and entirely acceptable to others. See the examples of debate topics below.

2. Popular legal debates might include teaching creationism versus evolution in schools, gay rights, abortion, and the death penalty. Each of these topics highlights the fact that society as a whole doesn't have shared values. One person's impassioned proposal might seem absurd and crazy to someone else. In the classroom, you can discuss strengths and weaknesses of reductio ad absurdum as an argumentative strategy.

Making Connections

1. In class discussion, review the scenarios from Steven Pinker's article (p. 458). *Why* are those scenarios considered so morally repugnant? In his own conclusions, such as his remarks on climate change, Pinker arguably falls prey to the same fallacies caused by moral rationalization that he has attributed to others. When morality and moral questions are closely examined, the distinction between moral concerns and practical ones often blurs.

Essay Writing

1. Advantages might include the fact that irony can shock readers out of complacency, provide humor and entertainment, and encourage readers to consider familiar issues and problems in fresh ways. Disadvantages include the risk that your audience won't know you're being ironic, or that the content of your ironic comments might shock or offend readers.

Paired Readings: On How Language Shapes Reality

George Orwell: *Politics and the English Language* (arguing)

Reading

1. Orwell states that staleness of imagery and lack of precision are destroying the English language. He claims that abstraction is politically dangerous because it reduces the

language to senselessness. Perhaps most frightening to Orwell is the fact that obscure diction masks political realities that are too painful to delineate.

2. Language corrupts thought as it anesthetizes the brain. Reading obscure prose teaches one to write obscurely. In the same way, insincere writing, however learned, desensitizes the reader to hypocrisy.

3. By despairing of his ability to avoid all lapses into vagueness, Orwell calls attention to the involuntary nature of the corruption of language, thereby cautioning the reader to be "constantly on guard." Some might say, of course, that if Orwell does not consistently follow his own rules, it may be that the rules are unrealistically strict. Rules (ii) and (iii) in paragraph 19, for instance, would probably, if followed to the letter, make for rather dull prose.

4. Although he presents himself as an expert, by calling attention to his own lapses into obscurity Orwell identifies himself as an individual who wants to reform society—starting with himself. He asks others to follow his advice but does not promise a cure for world problems, only a possible starting point for a solution. His tone is instructional but not insistent or didactic.

Exploratory Writing

1. Some students might find that Orwell's rules for political writing also apply to literary writing. Others will find literary examples where breaking Orwell's rules leads to more beautiful or evocative poetry or prose—for example, using extra words that it would technically be possible to cut out, or using a long word where a shorter would have the same meaning, because of the rhythmic qualities of the longer word. This question invites students to critically evaluate the style of the work they choose.

2. Most students are likely to find hackneyed metaphors, unnecessary words, and the use of the passive voice in each other's essays. In fact, a point to bring up in class discussion is that, after you read Orwell's rules, you are likely to notice vague, murky, repetitive writing everywhere.

Making Connections

1. Most students will find that James Baldwin's work (p. 131) has stylistic similarities to Orwell's. Both are bold, vivid writers. Students are likely to note that Baldwin largely avoids the writing mistakes that Orwell outlines in this essay. If students have read Orwell's essay on shooting an elephant (p. 229) already, they can compare Baldwin's work to both essays.

2. Class discussion could focus on contemporary journalistic writing styles. While Orwell's conclusion that "the present political chaos is connected to the decay of language" is almost inexorably true, it's unlikely that students will agree that the symptoms that Orwell's rules address are the same as those Brooke Gladstone (p. 325) points out. While Orwell's is a call for greater simplicity of language, Gladstone's is a call for greater complexity of thought. The goal is the same: honest, direct reportage of contemporary issues, but Gladstone and Orwell are facing different obstacles in their respective societies.

Essay Writing

1. Students will probably enjoy this exercise, as they are likely to find abundant examples of bad writing in contemporary publications. The strongest essays will detail the political component of this issue, finding examples of writers who conceal their agendas with poor, vague prose.

2. Strong arguments for and against the timelessness of Orwell's essay are equally acceptable. Students who have done exercises evaluating contemporary prose based on Orwell's standards may find that his ideas are still current.

Brooke Gladstone: *The Great Refusal* (EXPLAINING)

READING

1. Gladstone uses media coverage of the toppling of Saddam Hussein's statue in April 2009 as an example of visual bias combining with narrative bias.

2. Gladstone writes, "Obviously, the biggest risk for access-dependent journalists is self-censorship" (p. 333). She gives several examples of this in her explanation of access bias.

3. By mentioning contemporary public figures and quoting figures from history (Dante, Yeats), Gladstone gives her explanation context and perspective. By incorporating real-life figures and events (Arthur Sultzberger Jr.'s speech to SUNY graduates in 2006), she reminds readers that her account is nonfiction.

EXPLORATORY WRITING

1. Argumentative writing consciously uses facts to advocate an opinion and persuade readers, while biased writing intentionally or unintentionally skews facts. In some modes of writing, the authors aim to present themselves as unbiased, while others make it clear that they're presenting an opinion or a personal experience.

2. One of Gladstone's key points is that media bias has always been a problem. This exercise will help students review and understand types of media bias, as well as explore reportorial writing. In discussion, ask why it is valuable to report unbiased news. Is unbiased reporting even possible?

MAKING CONNECTIONS

1. Susan Sontag's argument (p. 366) centers on the power of visual bias. She writes, "New demands are made on reality in the era of cameras. The real thing may not be fearsome enough, and therefore needs to be enhanced; or reenacted more convincingly" (par. 2). In class discussion, consider Sontag's examples in light of Gladstone's statement that sometimes biases intertwine, asking students to review each for other kinds of biases, not just visual.

2. Several types of bias that Gladstone explains could be prevented, or at least exposed, if writers were forced to abide by George Orwell's rules (p. 313). For example, narrative bias—where the same story with the same characters is rehashed in each political campaign—would be exposed when writers cut out unnecessary language. Even with biases that don't initially seem rooted in language, a requirement of direct expression, rather than story-shaping or concealment, might make reportage less biased. In class discussion, raise the question of whether Orwell's rules could be applied to visual media in order to prevent or expose visual bias.

ESSAY WRITING

1. Use class discussion of these essays to consider why Gladstone worked with an illustrator to put her media manifesto in graphic form. Ask students to reflect on the differences between making a report with images versus using words alone.

Paired Readings: On Race Relations

Martin Luther King Jr.: *Letter from Birmingham Jail* (ARGUING)

READING

1. The four steps King lists are collection of the facts to determine whether injustices exist, negotiation, self-purification, and direct action (par. 6).

2. King believes that people have a legal and moral responsibility to obey just laws and a moral responsibility to disobey unjust laws (par. 15). He concludes that an unjust law is a law not rooted in eternal law and natural law, that any law that uplifts human personality is just (par. 16), and that one who breaks an unjust law must do so "with a willingness to accept the penalty" (par. 20). This is an extremely rich topic for class discussion of morality. One person's idea of a just (or eternal, or natural) law might not be shared by another, and it is especially confusing when the majority takes an immoral position, as in the 340 years of oppression described by King. (King mentions this in par. 22, when he reminds his opponents that everything Hitler did in Germany was "legal.") You can consider Steven Pinker's (p. 458) discussion of people's motivations for making moral decisions. People often genuinely disagree on what is "natural" or "eternal"—you can find many examples of this in legal debates about gender, sexuality, racism, religion, the treatment of animals, and any other morally contentious area of social practice.

3. A strong answer will note the fact that this is an open letter and discuss to whom King is addressing his comments, and why. It will also note that King responds to arguments and positions that they have already stated, but also anticipates questions (as in par. 10, "You may ask . . ."). He brings up their counterarguments or anticipated counterarguments in paragraph 5, paragraph 10, paragraph 15, and paragraph 25.

4. King speaks directly to his opponents. His tone is measured and conscientious rather than hostile, although his statement about their "precious time" in paragraph 45 could be veiled irony. The strongest answers will note this ironic moment, followed by King's earnest plea in paragraph 46. His attitude is that they have disappointed him and tried his patience, and that he expected much more from white moderates and from his fellow religious leaders.

EXPLORATORY WRITING

1. You can encourage students to send their open letters to an appropriate newspaper or magazine, or to publish them online. Discuss how an open letter like King's can be more effective than a closed letter, because an open letter stimulates and contributes to public debate. You may also seek out contemporary examples of open letters and discuss their impact.

2. There are many metaphors, starting with "network of mutuality" and "garment of destiny" in paragraph 4. Let your students make a list of the most striking metaphors before choosing some for discussion.

MAKING CONNECTIONS

1. A major difference is that Barack Obama (p. 355) is addressing the public. King's letter, while open to the public, is directed toward a particular group of his opponents. Both speeches are thoughtful in tone and passionate without being aggressive or rash. Students may have different perspectives on the tone of these two documents, but it is important to note what distinguishes them as *argumentative* writing.

2. The richest responses to this question will note King's and James Baldwin's (p. 131) indictment not only of direct, overt oppressors, but of those ordinary or "moderate" individuals who maintain the status quo, contribute to the survival of insidious forms of racism, and do not speak out against oppression.

Essay Writing

1. This topic asks students to *reflect* rather than *argue*, and can be potentially highly personal. The best essays will engage with King's concept of justice in the terms of Thomas Aquinas (par. 16).

Barack Obama: A *More Perfect Union* (REFLECTING)

Reading

1. Obama condemns Wright's controversial statements as "divisive," but he characterizes the man himself as "imperfect" (par. 21). He also says Wright is a good Christian who has had a life of service to the church, the needy, the suffering, and (as a Marine) to the United States (par. 18). The strongest answers will discuss the analogy Obama makes between Wright and the black community as a whole.

2. He says that segregated schools are inferior schools, and that "we still haven't fixed them."

3. Students will find strongly argumentative statements throughout this speech. Areas where Obama uses reflective writing include his recounting of his own "American story" (par. 7), and his remarks about his experience at Trinity, including the quotation from his book (par. 19).

Exploratory Writing

1. His quotes, like his concluding story about Ashley Baia, are carefully chosen to reflect a lack of divisiveness and his intention to embrace good things about American history. In class discussion, ask students to imagine that Obama had used very similar quotations, but from Malcolm X. How might this have changed his tone?

2. In class discussion about this partner exercise, identify the elements of the speech that were most striking to students in their instant response. Were they persuaded by its form, its content, neither, or both? This is a good opportunity to discuss Obama's tone, voice, syntax, and style.

3. Students will think of a wide variety of differences. A performed speech is connected, for listeners, to the sound of the speaker's voice and/or his or her physical appearance, while readers must rely on research, memory, or information within the writing to give them a sense of who has authored a written piece. A written statement can be reread several times, as the reader understands and processes it. It can be read at the reader's pace, with parts skimmed and parts read carefully. With a speech, the listener must absorb the material in the moment, at the speaker's pace. In class or as part of this homework assignment, encourage students to view Obama's speech as well as read it. Performing a speech allows a politician to show him- or herself to the audience.

Making Connections

1. In class discussion of this connection, you might also introduce James Baldwin's (p. 131) stirring essay. Obama and Martin Luther King Jr. (p. 341), like Baldwin, both have complex and nuanced assessments of the racist legacy. Both Obama and King relate

potential counterarguments to show listeners or readers that they are compassionate, moderate, nondivisive thinkers, pushed toward passion because American racism is such a strong problem and ignoring it would be unjust.

2. This exercise is somewhat subjective; students are likely to find that while this speech is lyrical, it holds up to George Orwell's six rules quite nicely (p. 313). Some might find clichés in the language ("bleed together under the same proud flag," "believe with all my heart") or examples of places where Obama uses more words when fewer would do. In class discussion, ask students who have found violations of Orwell's rules in this speech to consider how the speech would be different. Do the violations of rules serve the purposes that Orwell discusses in his essay?

Essay Writing

1. Discuss examples of strong argumentative writing. Encourage students to avoid vague language, clichés, and platitudes, and to use persuasive, convincing statements to convey clearly what changes they would make, why they would make those changes, and how they would implement their proposals.

Paired Readings: On Documenting War

Susan Sontag: *Regarding the Pain of Others* (arguing)

Reading

1. Television, according to Sontag, "serves up the war as images." The war itself takes place at a distance, and television news producers make decisions every day about what the public may and may not see (pars. 10–14).

2. The first argument is that airing atrocity photos is not in "good taste" (par. 11). Sontag comments that "good taste" is always a repressive standard when it comes to institutions, and serves, in this case, to obscure concerns and anxieties about public order. The second argument is that publishing such photographs could cause offense to relatives of the dead. Sontag argues that the American media show little concern for relatives of the dead who are considered "the other" and do not uphold the same standard in publishing photos of "cruelties inflicted on those with darker complexions in exotic countries."

3. Sontag argues against the lurid and exploitative use of images, which (in her opinion) serve to distance us from reality and aestheticize atrocities. Students should note the ways that Sontag structures her argument, then offer their own opinions and responses.

Exploratory Writing

1. A wide variety of answers to this question are acceptable. The exercise invites students to critically consider Sontag's points by thinking carefully about their own responses to images and to the written word. Many are likely to note that photographs can shock because the images seem so "real," and they leave an immediate, and sometimes indelible, impression, while writing can shock because it spurs readers to use their visual imagination, creating their own mental images, which can take on a dimension more terrifying than reality.

2. Answers will vary.

3. Examples include how images of models and celebrities are airbrushed to look more perfect, celebrity tabloid photos are altered using Photoshop, film footage used in "reality TV" shows is selectively edited, sometimes to distort the meaning or context of a participant's words or actions, and film footage used on televised news programs is selectively edited to frame and shape the story. On the other hand, the issue is very complicated, because now the manipulation of images has become part of public debate. In class discussion of this complication, you might consider showing Errol Morris's 2008 documentary about the infamous photographs taken at Abu Ghraib prison, *Standard Operating Procedure*. The filmmaker's Web site (**errolmorris.com**) offers links to thought-provoking reviews of the film, as well as a link to his *New York Times* opinion piece "Believing Is Seeing."

4. In preparing their arguments, encourage the teams of students to draw examples from current events.

Making Connections

1. Strong answers may note that what the soldiers (p. 374) write about is shaped by their audience—often their friends and family. Students should mention that the soldiers do convey empathy for some of the Iraqis they encounter—Commander Edward Jewell worries about what happens to the patients they discharge, especially those needing long-term care, and Lieutenant Brian Humphreys considers the life and perspective of a local police captain who is shot to death in his car.

2. Strong answers will note the many similarities between George Orwell's (p. 313) basic premise and Sontag's: The truth can be manipulated and obscured to political ends. In class discussion, address strategies for documenting current events (especially politically charged events, such as war) with accuracy. This is a good opportunity to discuss investigative journalism and *reportorial* techniques.

Essay Writing

1. This essay topic encourages a deep and critical rereading of Sontag's argument, by testing it against other materials. It also challenges students to view apparently "neutral" artifacts (in this case, newspaper articles and photos) with a critical eye to the hidden agendas of writers, photographers, editors, and producers.

2. Students might choose a photo from current events or popular culture, or something very intimate and personal. The strongest essays will reflect how the images created a change in the student's way of seeing and perceiving "truth."

Various Authors: *Soldiers' Stories: Dispatches from Iraq* (REFLECTING)

Reading

1. When Blackman asks people if they've been in "combat," the question has the "power to unglue." Soldiers burst into sobs at the mention of the word (par. 38).

2. CENTCOM is the name for the headquarters group for the entire war. Its speakers give a "tiresome, trite, and uninformative" presentation filled with army jargon, which does not offer insight or clarity (par. 27). They obviously have no experience or understanding of the situation of soldiers who are in combat (par. 28).

3. There are many examples of both reporting and reflecting in the various stories. This is an opportunity to highlight and discuss reportorial techniques, and how and why they are effective.

4. This question invites students to consider the tone and voice of each dispatch. The different accounts each give a flavor of the individual soldier's personality.

Exploratory Writing

1. Operation Homecoming was made possible by Boeing, one of the nation's largest defense contractors. That the soldiers were told to "write freely" implies that some of them might initially feel constrained about doing that. There are many reasons that soldiers might want to self-censor their stories before publication.

2. In class discussion of this issue, you might address John Berger's (p. 236) perspective on Hiroshima. Berger reveals the bombing from the prespective of its victims, which is often not the way we see it in America. Soldiers from different nations and on different "sides" may have radically divergent experiences of the same events.

Making Connections

1. Encourage students to consider how the soldiers in this piece would weigh in on the publication of images of the dead and dying. In what ways does their writing appeal to Sontag's argument? If they do take a stance, stronger answers should use reflecting, rather than arguing, to address Sontag.

2. This comparison should raise thought-provoking questions for class discussion. Ask students to consider the question of morality. Which actions and events are morally justifiable? Which extenuating circumstances, if any, apply?

Essay Writing

1. This essay topic asks students to consider what makes a letter (even a letter full of reportorial writing) different from a newspaper or magazine article, or even a journal entry. Discuss the intimacy of letters, and why they seem intimate. In class discussion of this topic, compare and contrast letters from soldiers to their families that are later published with "open letters," like Martin Luther King Jr.'s "Letter from Birmingham Jail" (p. 341).

Student Essay

Muaz Paracha: *Political Food: Big Business and the State of Food Safety in the United States*

Reading

1. Essays in the social sciences often have straightforward and fact- or claim-based titles, like Paracha's subtitle, "Big Business and the State of Food Safety in the United States." The inclusion of the main title, "Political Food," injects a voice and point of view into the title. It's punchier than the subtitle, but it may not be appropriate for all courses or contexts. Class discussion might focus on the fact that some audiences may demand different titles. This discussion might benefit from examination of the titles of Paracha's sources. Based on this discussion, students might debate the merits of including both a main title and a subtitle.

2. Students should use two different types of sources to contrast—for example, Pollan's *New York Times* editorial "Unhappy Meals" and the FDA Web site. The purpose of the latter is to *explain* guidelines while the former makes an *argument* about food, eating habits, and economics. A strong response will note the differing modes of the sources and indicate how Paracha draws on these modes to develop his own argument.

3. A strong response should quote examples and possibly even criticize Paracha's choices. This question should push students to more closely consider whether to quote or paraphrase, and which is more useful in certain scenarios.

Exploratory Writing

1. Responses should identify a particular claim as Paracha's thesis. The first sentence of paragraph 2 is the strongest candidate for thesis: "The government has not always been heavily involved in food regulation as it is today, and the increase in its influence has turned the government into a target for food industry lobbyists who wish to manipulate the system." However, a student may make a case for an alternative thesis. Responses should also indicate the evidence Paracha uses to support his thesis and make clear how and why this evidence does or does not offer strong support. Students should address whether the thesis is clear and compelling, and the pertinence and strength of the evidence. In addition, students should characterize their fictional student and instructor. It may be worthwhile to encourage them to be creative or playful with this characterization—and to ask some or all students to read their dialogues aloud in class.

2. Responses should identify some of the following techniques used to integrate quotations: signal phrases, citation, follow-up discussion and analysis, and grammatical integration between the words of the essay writer and his sources. Students should also identify the particular strategies they plan to use in their own writing. A reflective student might discuss his or her strengths and weaknesses with regard to these strategies.

Making Connections

1. A letter to the editor should be concise and thesis driven. Instructors should emphasize both these qualities and evaluate student responses based on them. Strong responses should quote both Mark Bittman's editorial (p. 294) and one or two of Paracha's sources. An ambitious student might locate these sources and quote passages not discussed by Paracha, but this shouldn't be necessary. Students should be able to do a good job with the letter based on the portions of the sources included in Paracha's essay.

Essay Writing

1. Instructors should emphasize that the prompt calls for an argumentative essay based on a question about the student's chosen issue. Some class time should be devoted to the development of strong questions. Instructors might ask students to locate such questions in selections from *Fields of Reading* and use these as models. Students will also need guidance with the research process—particularly using databases, identifying strong sources, and using their sources to advance their own arguments. Instructors should work with the chapter "Researching to Write" (p. 32) to provide this guidance.

PART 4: SCIENCES

Richard Feynman: *The Value of Science* (arguing)

Reading

1. Science, says Feynman, has led us "to imagine all sorts of things infinitely more marvelous than the imaginings of poets and dreamers of the past," and shows us that the imagination of nature is greater than the imagination of humans (par. 11).

2. Feynman sometimes refers to scientists as "we"; at other times he uses "we" to encompass all people. He uses this encompassing language as an *arguing* technique—for example,

when he says "I hope you will excuse me if I remind you of some thoughts that I am sure you have all had" (par. 12) or "We are all sad" (par. 29), he compels readers to imagine that they share his ideas and experiences.

3. "Scientific knowledge," writes Feynman, "is a body of statements of varying degrees of certainty . . . *none* absolutely certain" (par. 27). He sees recognition of doubt as one of the major values that allows science to progress.

Exploratory Writing

1. Feynman's Nobel Prize lecture tells a story of stops and starts, brainstorming at beer parties and on wartime buses, and coming up with many mistakes and "stupid" ideas in his quest to work through the difficulties inherent in quantum electrodynamic theory. His entertaining account of these steps illustrates and supports his argument in "The Value of Science." In class discussion, refer students to Jonah Lehrer's (p. 431) explanation of inspiration and breakthroughs in thought.

2. These lists should demonstrate that Feynman's scientific age would entail different ways of thinking about the world, exploring problems, and expressing ideas, rather than merely changing common behaviors or beliefs.

Making Connections

1. Feynman and Diane Ackerman (p. 442) both use beautiful, poetic language to convey a sense of wonder. Note how Feynman's argument is in the first person, sharing his personal experiences and anecdotes, whereas Ackerman's explanation is in the third person, making no direct reference to herself. Yet in both pieces, the writers use reflective writing techniques in the service of their other goals.

Essay Writing

1. In class discussion about drafting these essays, suggest that students use explanatory writing techniques (such as citing empirical studies)—first to show evidence for human underachievement in the area they've chosen, and then to address why people have fallen short. Examples of topics can be serious or fanciful, including: why there is no cure for cancer, why we cannot teleport from place to place, or why no one has invented a working time machine.

Ann Jurecic: *Mindblindness* (REFLECTING)

Reading

1. "Mindblindness" refers to the idea that people with Asperger's and other autism-spectrum disorders lack a "theory of mind"—"the ability of [the neurotypical] to attribute mental states (such as beliefs, desires, intentions, etc.) to themselves and other people, as a way of making sense of and predicting behavior" (par. 5).

2. Currently, there are no medical tests for autism, according to Jurecic—the disorder can only be diagnosed by observing behaviors (par. 8).

3. In the 1940s, autism was often attributed to unresponsive parenting and emotionally frigid mothers. Today, researchers emphasize neurobiological and genetic causes of autism, which Jurecic assesses as a welcome change (par. 16).

Exploratory Writing

1. Jurecic talks about the "normal" band of the neurological spectrum, "normal intelligence and language," and so on. Some students might define this and explain its useful-

ness, while others will form explanations that highlight the wide variety of behaviors and mentalities from individual to individual, noting that the same behavior can stem from a number of different neurological, social, and psychological roots, raising the question, "Is anyone 'normal'?" The short essay will help develop students' explanatory and argumentative writing techniques.

2. Have students keep in mind Temple Grandin's attempts—as described by Jurecic—to convey her internal experience to people who she knows operate from a different neurological makeup. You might make the argument that every writer must use similar strategies to illustrate, explain, or communicate his or her views, ways of thinking, or inner experience to readers.

Making Connections

1. Steven Pinker's examples (p. 458) demonstrate the deep connection between "moral intuition" and empathy—for example, stabbing a pin into the palm of a child seems repugnant. Considering the essays together raises deep questions about human kinship and difference. Students can assess the approach each author brings to the problems introduced.

Essay Writing

1. This essay topic invites students to practice empathy. In class discussion, explore how the process of reflective writing can help both writers and readers empathize with others' experiences of the world. Consider examples from student essays as well as from personal essays, such as Jill Bolte Taylor's description of having a stroke (p. 418), and Dudley Clendinen's reflections on living and dying with Lou Gehrig's disease (p. 73).

Jill Bolte Taylor: *Morning of the Stroke* (reflecting)

Reading

1. Students may use words like *objective, dry,* or *cold* to describe typical scientific writing. Taylor's writing, by contrast, is often energetic and intimate. Student responses should all note this difference. Anticipating question 2, the strongest responses might also note that Taylor's style varies somewhat throughout the piece, between the scientific and the personal.

2. Students often believe a writer's voice is unchangeable—that it's a given, somehow natural. In addition to prompting students to read Taylor's essay closely, with attention to her rhetorical strategies, this question can also become a prompt for a discussion of voice as it applies to students' own writing. Ideally, students will develop a flexible approach to voice and be able to adapt their voices to various contexts and audiences.

3. Definitions of Taylor's neurobiological terms can be found easily through a quick Internet search. It may be more difficult for students to understand these definitions and express them in their own words. It might be helpful to ask students to read their definitions aloud and compare their definitions with each other.

Exploratory Writing

1. Taylor uses the following words to describe "dreamland": *fluid, surreal, beautiful, free, altered state.* She uses the following words to describe her stroke symptoms: *bizarre, detached, disassociation, dazed, peace, altered state, euphoric, stupor.* Students may well find other descriptions or offer variations on the ones listed here. Discussion might begin

with Taylor's statement in paragraph 5 that "Although this experience was somewhat reminiscent of my morning time in Thetaville, I was sure that this time I was awake."

2. Taylor's diagrams are simple (pp. 419, 421–22, 424–25), intended to help readers visualize the areas of the brain she discusses. Throughout the chapter, Taylor identifies the brain regions associated with certain behaviors, experiences, and symptoms. Students should have little trouble finding a description like this (pars. 3, 9, and 24, for example) and matching it to one of Taylor's diagrams. They may find it more challenging to prepare a presentation that will explain this for others. In addition to getting the facts right, students' presentations should be focused, clear, efficient, and engaging. They should speak slowly, enunciate, make eye contact, and make productive use of the diagrams, as visual aids. It may be helpful to discuss this in advance of the presentations, or even to ask students to practice in small groups or pairs before presenting to the class as a whole.

Making Connections

1. Several support groups and medical organizations publish firsthand accounts of strokes written by survivors. These include Stroke Survivors (**http://www.stroke-survivors.co.uk/**) and the Internet Stroke Center (**http://www.strokecenter.org/patients/survivors.htm**). If students need help finding such sites, or it seems helpful to limit the number of sources they use, it may be a good idea to provide them with these URLs. Once they locate the sources, the biggest challenge for students will be finding a focus—choosing accounts that enable them to explore a central theme or question.

Essay Writing

1. In the video, Taylor tells the same story she tells in "Morning of the Stroke," using somewhat less detail, but embodying her story with gestures, vocal inflections, and the use of visual aids, including a human brain. Students should note these differences, but otherwise their responses are likely to be highly subjective. It is important that their claims are supported with details from the text and the video.

Lewis Thomas: *The Corner of the Eye* (reflecting)

Reading

1. Thomas states that he used to be frightened by the notion of artificial intelligence (par. 3), but then he came to understand that computers, unlike humans, are not designed for ambiguity. This capacity for ambiguity gives the human mind special qualities beyond the reach of any machine, as demonstrated by our language.

2. The Big Bang theory is a misnomer, according to Thomas. Our universe actually began in the Great Light, the most absolute silence imaginable. He points out that in Greek, *chaos* simply meant "empty."

3. The record of language allows us to glimpse the special qualities of the human mind (par. 6). A computer's "mind" cannot be programmed to operate with the same "deep hunch" as the human consciousness, and the intricate and layered concepts that underpin our word derivations illustrate this.

Exploratory Writing

1. Students will find etymological information in the library (check if your library has access to the OED), or by doing a quick Internet search. In class discussion on this topic,

consider Thomas's remarks on how much humans enjoy surprises. Identify the ways that word origins reflect new things we have learned or attempts to grapple with complex new information.

2. This exercise reveals how *reflective* writing can help bring a subject to life or infuse it with a new, fresh perspective. Although Thomas lists several scientific facts about earth in his concluding paragraphs—its ability to generate its own weather or "construct its own carapace from living parts," for example—it is the subjective, poetic descriptions ("how strange and splendid it is, how it catches the breath") that move the reader.

Making Connections

1. In class discussion, cite examples of essayists like Diane Ackerman (p. 442), who uses vivid metaphors to conjure visual images. While this type of language use is an essential component of much *reportorial* writing, to clarify complex ideas, it is also used in reflective writing to elicit an emotional response from the reader.

Essay Writing

1. This essay topic encourages students to carefully consider why writers, scientific and otherwise, choose the themes that they write about, and to analyze the modes of writing that they use in addressing those themes. In class discussion, consider the ways that personal experiences of passion or emotion in response to these scientific surprises figure into the work of other essayists, like Natalie Angier (p. 489), for example.

Jonah Lehrer: *The Eureka Hunt* (REPORTING)

Reading

1. "The insight experience" involves first an impasse (before there can be a breakthrough, there has to be a mental block), then a feeling of certainty that accompanies the breakthrough idea (par. 7).

2. Strong answers will note that the right brain excels at connotation—everything that gets left out of a dictionary definition, such as the emotional charge in a sentence, or understanding metaphors, while the left brain excels at denotation, or storing the primary meaning of a word.

3. Schooler's research is described on p. 433. This description helps highlight the fact that breakthrough thinking and insights come from thought processes and approaches that defy convention. For example, Schooler has found that trying to force an insight can actually work to prevent that very insight, and that there may be great benefits to letting one's mind wander. These revelations help Lehrer more clearly explain the difference between "the insight experience" and conventional thinking.

4. Lehrer explains "the insight experience" by defining terms, using anecdotes, and recounting current research on the subject. If he used the first person and shared his own experience with breakthrough thinking or "Eureka!" moments, the tone of the essay might seem more intimate and reflective. The third-person voice offers a sense of breadth and clarity. This is a subjective question with many possible answers, but it invites students to consider an author's motives for choosing to write in a particular voice.

Exploratory Writing

1. Students are likely to find that that they experience the two essential features of "the insight experience" during this exercise. The solution to the puzzles will come in a

sudden breakthrough moment. In class, discuss activities or types of thinking that seem to operate differently.

2. This question invites students to connect Lehrer's topic to their own intellectual experiences. In class discussion, note whether more students reflected on emotional revelations, such as suddenly understanding something new and enlightening about a family dynamic, or on breakthrough ideas, such as suddenly solving a tricky problem.

Making Connections

1. Lewis Thomas (p. 427) marvels at the ways the human mind could never be supplanted by a master computer, because humans have a great capacity for ambiguous meaning-building, often through making mistakes. He describes how we make these mistakes "instinctively, intuitively." Thomas would likely see the moments of insight that Lehrer describes as representative of humans' unique mental abilities.

2. According to Steven Johnson (p. 120), some television programs call on viewers to follow complex, interconnected plot threads over time, which would seem to be a largely left-brain type of thinking. But according to Lehrer, letting one's thoughts drift might encourage breakthrough thinking. Perhaps watching a mentally unchallenging, escapist television program would encourage insight in that way. Conclusive answers to this question are not important or necessary. The question calls on students to engage more deeply with both Lehrer's explanation and Johnson's arguments.

Essay Writing

1. Most case studies will probably show that the revelation involved several different types of thinking—rigorous, regular preparation as well as insight. This essay assignment is an opportunity to consider different methods of research and writing by encouraging students to strategize about how to learn the true story behind the invention or discovery they have chosen.

Diane Ackerman: *Why Leaves Turn Color in the Fall* (EXPLAINING)

Reading

1. The most spectacular range of foliage occurs in the northeastern United States and in eastern China (par. 4).

2. Generally, Ackerman's mentions of death point toward an acceptance of a "beautiful state" (par. 6) wherein perhaps something can still be communicated to the living world, like the fossilized leaf that can "remind us how . . . alive are the things of this earth that perish" (par. 10).

3. The different leaf colors don't appear to have any special purpose. Ackerman discusses our response to them, at length, in paragraph 6.

Exploratory Writing

1. This exercise will show students how valuable Ackerman's essay is as a piece of reportorial writing. Her explanation can be successfully applied to the practical understanding of her subject matter.

2. The list of adjectives alone allows the reader to develop a vibrant mental image of Ackerman's subject matter. Her essay is as much a piece of literary description as a scientific explanation.

Making Connections

1. Answers to this question are subjective and may highlight students' writing and reading preferences—do they prefer stylistic explanations or more factual ones? Does Ackerman's style get in the way of conveying information, or does she present it in a more pleasant way? The question invites students to compare the techniques of the two writers. Students should also consider the purpose of each essay and how the writer's style and techniques work to that purpose.

Essay Writing

1. This essay topic asks students to use the different writing techniques that Ackerman demonstrates in their own work. In class discussion of the essays, ask students to consider which mode of writing they found more challenging.

Oliver Sacks: *The Man Who Mistook His Wife for a Hat* (EXPLAINING)

Reading

1. Dr. P. cannot recognize or visualize things. He can see, but he cannot put what he sees together in the familiar patterns that humans regularly use. This problem was caused by damage to a particular part of the brain that controls visualization.

2. Sacks has a way of presenting behavior at length, with telling detail, before starting any analysis. He also makes a narrative out of his own gradual realization of the nature and extent of the problem. And he takes pains to characterize the patient, to make us take an interest in this nice, intelligent, artistic man, including extensive dialogue between himself and the patient. The meaning of his bizarre title and the incident from which it is derived are withheld from us until paragraph 29, where they still strike us with considerable force. In short, this essay has many of the qualities of short fiction, with the added element of scientific truthfulness: an unusual and powerful combination.

3. These tests, such as asking Dr. P. to describe pictures in *National Geographic* (par. 24), show that Dr. P. can see, but cannot make coherent sense of what he sees. The brain, according to Sacks, is a machine or computer, but our mental processes are not just abstract and mechanical, but personal, involving "continual judging and feeling" (par. 84).

Exploratory Writing

1. In class discussion of this exercise, bring up Ann Jurecic's (p. 402) reflections about her student Gregory's Asberger's syndrome. Jurecic describes the unique difficulties people with autism have following "normal" processes of learning and relating to others.

2. Sacks's tests show that Dr. P.'s perception is damaged in basic, everyday life, rather than a creative vision that expresses itself exclusively in art. Yet Sacks recommends that Dr. P. should devote his entire life to making music. This exercise invites students, through analyzing what a particular work of art reveals about the artist's perception, to critically consider systems of classification and diagnosis. In class discussion, raise ideas about how all humans are subject to some illusions and limitations of perceptual ability.

Making Connections

1. Strong answers may explore how Dr. P and Jill Bolte Taylor (p. 418) both attempt to organize around the malfunctions in their brains—Dr. P by using music, and Taylor by

observing and analyzing what is happening. It may be important to note how our perspectives of the two change our own understanding of the experience: In Taylor's description, we get the world from her own eyes, and in Dr. P's situation, we get a view of what he looks like from Sacks's observations. How might these experiences look different to us if they were switched—a description of Taylor attempting to use her exercise machine by someone watching her, and Dr. P's own description of, say, trying to put on his hat?

2. Bring other essays from this section into discussion of this issue. As Sacks and Jurecic both show, there is a fine and subtle distinction between our perception and our awareness of the limitations of that perception.

Essay Writing

1. Paragraphs 82–85 contain the heart of Sacks's critique of neural science. Here he makes the really startling claim that his science itself seems to suffer from something similar to the same disease as Dr. P.'s. He makes an appeal for science to find a place for feeling and judging as important components of mental life. Students may well agree with this, but they may also feel that these things are not discussable within the boundaries of scientific thought. Obviously, there is no simple position on such a complex matter.

Steven Pinker: *The Moral Instinct* (ARGUING)

Reading

1. Pinker lists two hallmarks of moralization: first, that the rules it invokes are felt to be universal, and second, that people feel that those who commit immoral acts deserve to be punished (pars. 9–10).

2. Moral reasoning entails considering an issue carefully on moral grounds, then determining why the behavior is right or wrong. Most people, according to Jonathan Haidt, do not engage in moral reasoning, but moral rationalization: They begin with an emotional conclusion, then grope to justify why their conclusion is right (par. 20).

3. Pinker refers to Haidt's five moral spheres: harm, fairness, community (or group loyalty), authority, and purity (par. 37). Pinker concludes that the moral spheres are universal, "but how they are ranked in importance, and which is brought to moralize which area of social life . . . depends on the culture" (par. 52).

Exploratory Writing

1. In class discussion as students prepare to debate this topic, highlight the hypothetical scenarios devised by Haidt (pp. 461–62), and ask students to imagine situations of changed cultural norms that would make them seem "right" rather than "wrong." For instance, if the dog in the third scenario were a cow, would it seem more reasonable for the family to eat it? If Julie and Mark were step-siblings, would it seem more morally acceptable for them to have a one-night stand? How do these variables dispute ideas that morality is innate?

2. This exercise should generate thought-provoking scenarios. In class discussion, highlight the distinction between moral reasoning and moral rationalization. Do students find themselves resorting to rationalization?

3. Pinker refers to bioethicist Leon Kass's essay "The Wisdom of Repugnance," which argues that the ability to feel repugnance or to "shudder" helps defend the central core of our humanity. Pinker argues that "people have shuddered at all kinds of morally irrelevant violations of purity in their culture" and suggests that the "shudder test" is a dan-

gerous way to make moral judgments (par. 75). Ask students to make sure that their argumentative statement is not a knee-jerk or gut-level response, but includes detailed justifications of their positions.

Making Connections

1. This exercise can be used to better understand argumentative modes of writing. Some essayists will assert their own opinions or arguments as universal moral truths, without offering a clear explanation for their conclusions. Others will engage in careful moral reasoning.

Essay Writing

1. There are many examples of amoralized behaviors, particularly in the arenas of gender and sexuality. One issue to discuss in class in conjunction with this essay topic is the connection between science and mortality. Many sexual behaviors (heterosexual oral sex, for example, or all homosexual practices) were recently psychiatrically classified as deviant practices or paraphilias. How can scientists, in particular, ensure that their work avoids moralizing and moral rationalization? Emily Martin's essay (p. 473) is especially interesting on this subject.

2. The challenge of this essay topic is that it demands moral reasoning, rather than moral rationalization. Students must have thoughtful reasons for their arguments. In class discussion, test whether there is consensus about what the different student essayists consider morally wrong.

Emily Martin: *The Egg and the Sperm: How Science Has Constructed a Romance Based on Stereotypical Male-Female Roles* (ARGUING)

Reading

1. Martin proposes to show that "the picture of egg and sperm drawn in popular as well as scientific accounts of reproductive biology relies on stereotypes central to our cultural definitions of male and female. The stereotypes imply not only that female biological processes are less worthy than their male counterparts but also that women are less worthy than men" (par. 1). Her argument is developed in three sections: In the first ("Egg and Sperm: A Scientific Fairy Tale"), she examines the imagery used by the supposedly objective, factually oriented scientific community to show that the "'facts' of biology" are couched in metaphors generated from the stereotyped notion that males are active, females passive. In the second section ("New Research, Old Imagery"), she argues that although recent studies show both egg and sperm to be active, the descriptions persist in replicating stereotypical gender images. In the third section ("Social Implications: Thinking Beyond"), she shows that another dangerous stereotype is present in revisionist accounts: that of "woman as a dangerous and aggressive threat" (par. 29). She warns that "the models that biologists use to describe their data can have important social effects" (par. 33).

2. Fleck argues that scientists preserve "the harmony of illusions," shaping new scientific imagery to conform to existing, entrenched cultural ideas (par. 16).

3. The misrepresentation of scientific facts produces a fairy tale. Of specific fairy tales mentioned, "Sleeping Beauty" is significant, reinforcing the active-passive binary central to male-female stereotyping (par. 10). The sperm's "perilous journey" echoes the myth of the hero's night-sea journey, in which he undergoes various perils before reaching his goal.

Exploratory Writing

1. The metaphors used in textbooks are an interesting study, and could provide the basis for an analytical argument. You may wish to open up the investigation to textbooks in a variety of disciplines. The types of metaphors used are a signal of the kinds of thinking going on and, as in this case, are revelatory of cultural assumptions in those disciplines.

2. If you are familiar with Lakoff and Johnson's *Metaphors We Live By*, you will realize that our thinking is structured metaphorically and that all language can be considered metaphorical. That metaphors indicative of cultural conditioning will creep into students' descriptions of the reproductive functions is a given. One of the values of this writing assignment is students' discovery of this fact.

3. Martin's footnotes help the reader understand the historical and disciplinary context of her arguments. They also refer the reader to a rich variety of supporting sources.

Making Connections

1. This exercise will be rich with opportunity for analysis. Students might choose to analyze Natalie Angier's (p. 489) or Richard Feynman's (p. 395) use of language in reference to the pursuit of science, Diane Ackerman's (p. 442) poetic description of a scientific phenomenon, or Oliver Sacks's (p. 446) and Jill Bolte Taylor's (p. 418) descriptions of brain malfunctions that border on romanticizing. The question should allow students to look at scientific discourse as it interacts with all the modes of writing and—as these selections do—attempts to communicate with a general audience.

Essay Writing

1. Students might also do research about sex education texts and curricula using many of the materials available via the Web.

2. In class discussion of these reflective essays, address the details of how different wrong assumptions became entrenched in the first place. Were tacit cultural norms involved?

Paired Readings: On Scientific Literacy

Natalie Angier: *The Canon* (reporting)

Reading

1. Angier writes that empirical universalism is the premise that "the objective reality of the universe comprises the subjective reality of every one of us" (par. 26). She suggests that science is effective because it surpasses the binary of objective/impersonal and subjective/personal realities.

2. When science is offered as a body of facts, it becomes "a glassy-eyed glossary" (par. 15). Readers of science textbooks or Internet resources are tempted to skim through and ignore everything but the "highlighted hand wavers," in hopes that they won't fail science classes.

3. Angier's father, while dying of a fast-growing brain tumor, told her that he was taking note for the first time of the blooming flowers on his walks through Central Park. This inspired her to "attend anew to the world in rebirth," and she shares the story as a reflection of how she developed the ways of thinking and worldview she's describing here.

Exploratory Writing

1. In class discussion of this exercise, point out ways that writing can capture the wonder and surprise of a natural phenomenon for readers who haven't experienced it firsthand. At the same time, the interviews Angier includes in this excerpt would support the idea that there are aspects of observation that can't be fully understood without direct, real-life experience.

2. Angier concludes with a paragraph that focuses on the potential fun and humor of an earnest attempt to "amending, remodeling, or blowtorching" one's intuitive constructs. Students might find, doing this exercise informally and in pairs, that the history of wrong ideas about the question they've chosen brings hilarity and entertainment. They might also find their own misconceptions, preconceptions, and confusion amusing, surprising, or interesting.

Making Connections

1. By raising not-yet-answered questions (pars. 17 and 21, for example) and demonstrating aspects of Williams' syndrome that remain mysterious (par. 46), Olivia Judson (p. 284) practices science as a mode of thinking, exploration, and critical inquiry, rather than a collection of set facts. Writing allows the scientist to elucidate and display these processes to the reader.

2. Angier's interviewees—such as Strobel, Stevenson, and Greene—all share the opinion that science is not a collection of facts, viewpoints, or laws, but a set of critical thinking tools that allow a scientist the flexibility to assess ideas and to explore the nature of objective reality. Michael Duff also points out that while scientific thinking itself is dynamic, that doesn't mean there aren't "arrogant" scientists incapable of criticizing their own viewpoints. Cognitive neuroscientist Susan Carey and others, however, go farther by arguing that one of the limitations of scientific thinking is that science depends on the belief in an objective reality independent of our subjective experiences.

Essay Writing

1. In class discussion of these essays, you might address the radical changes throughout history within accepted bodies of knowledge (scientific or otherwise). Explanations, for example, that once seemed logical, such as the idea that the earth is flat, have been discarded as false.

Thomas W. Martin: *Scientific Literacy and the Habit of Discourse* (arguing)

Reading

1. *Evidence blindness* is the subordination of scientific evidence to deeply held cultural suppositions and, according to Martin, is found "across the spectrum" of thinkers (par. 4), including within the scientific community.

2. Martin writes that science works because "its core dynamics—not its methods or techniques per se—are rooted in pitting intellects against one another" (par. 5). Science is made effective by the process of smart people overturning previously held conclusions.

3. Martin refers to creationist beliefs. He states that he does not want to "rehash . . . the ongoing culture wars" (par. 2) on this topic or to berate his students. His choice to couch this problem in indirect language is a technique of argumentative writing.

Exploratory Writing

1. Examples might include astrology and certain religious beliefs and practices, but they could also include many historical examples of scientific "facts" that were proven wrong. In class discussion, the contentiousness of debates around belief and evidence might become very clear. This passionate contentiousness supports Martin's argument, and he points out that debate is an essential part of scientific inquiry.

2. These debates can be judged by fellow students, with the "winners" honored for presenting the strongest factual evidence. Students can choose their own debate propositions and draw straws to be assigned sides, or you can provide propositions with the assignment. (Science magazines like *Discover*, *Science*, and *Nature*, or the science section of local or national newspapers, are good sources of topics.) Martin celebrates "pitting intellects against each other" (par. 5) and participating in a dialogue as the true core of scientific literacy, beyond the starting point of terminological knowledge.

Making Connections

1. Students will find a great many similarities between the kinds of biases that Brooke Gladstone (p. 325) outlines, and the "evidence bias" that Martin describes. In both the sciences and the media, according to these accounts, there is the risk that people will consciously or unconsciously suppress evidence, facts, and information due to a moral or cultural agenda. Martin shows the overlap of scientific evidence bias with media biases when he describes top scientists banding together to suppress unorthodox findings and keep them from being published (par. 4).

2. Natalie Angier (p. 489) stresses that science is a mode of inquiry, not a body of facts. Although the students Martin describes have fully mastered the concepts required to excel at quantitative exams, they lack the kind of scientific literacy that Martin and Angier both advocate.

Essay Writing

1. If students have never reconsidered a strong belief, have them write an essay reflecting on a belief they hold against some contrary evidence—personal, scientific, or political. Have them explain where the belief comes from and why evidence to the contrary hasn't swayed them.

Paired Readings: On Pharmacological Enhancement

Margaret Talbot: *Brian Gain* (REPORTING)

Reading

1. Anjan Chatterjee, a neurologist at Penn, coined this term. Cosmetic neurology is the use of drugs designed for medical problems to enhance ordinary mental functioning in people without those conditions.

2. Talbot interviews Alex to get a first-person account from the type of student who, according to her other research, turns to neuroenhancers to help with school performance. She points out that Alex's information about who uses these drugs for "nonmedical" purposes is similar to the information yielded in "two dozen or so scientific studies" (par. 6).

3. Farah draws her conclusions from reviewing the results of forty studies on cognition, most of which looked at learning, working memory, and cognitive control (par. 36). However, she feels these forty studies are limited to a focus on "fairly boring" kinds of thinking, and that more research is needed on other kinds of cognition and intellectual activity, such as verbal fluency, creativity, and abstract thought.

Exploratory Writing

1. Talbot's conclusion could be described as one of resignation. She believes that there's no point in banning neuroenhancing drugs, but that their use is "dispiriting." Students could conclude, in contrast, that the drugs mark a thrilling advance in human thought and potential, expanding society's possibilities, or that the drugs are unnecessarily dangerous, rob people of their natural humanity, and should indeed be more heavily regulated or banned.

2. Talbot probably turned to the BoredAt sites to get a full insider's perspective of college students' experiences and candid thoughts, a strong reportorial technique. In class discussion, use Talbot's report as a model for how a resourceful journalist can turn to multiple sources for insider information—pseudonymous personal interviews, anonymous online forums, on-site observation—and use these to buttress previously published scientific studies.

Making Connections

1. Walter Kirn (p. 525) and Talbot's Alex both seem to fit the same profile in terms of general personality type and their reasons for turning to neuroenhancers. Although Kirn's reflections on his Adderall use tell a story from his adult life, students who follow up on Kirn's biography may be interested in his memoir of his undergraduate years at Princeton, *Lost in the Meritocracy: The Undereducation of an Overachiever*. Students who read the humorous memoir may find Kirn similar to Alex.

2. Strong answers will include specific details from the sources students research. This exercise will provide the opportunity to combine research skills and reportorial writing with argument. Students may also consider the use of narrative and reflection as tools in an argument such as this.

Essay Writing

1. This essay gives students an opportunity to apply reporting techniques, using Talbot (and possibly other reportorial pieces in *Fields of Reading*) as a model. They might begin by choosing a drug and researching the history of its use.

Walter Kirn: *A Pharmacological Education* (REFLECTING)

Reading

1. Kirn got sores in his mouth, early gray hair, and hemorrhoids.

2. Kirn's doctor downplays the risks of the drug, and Kirn hints that his demeanor is vaguely challenging: "I sensed an insult" (par. 1). "It'll help you get back on your feet" (par. 2). The doctor does not protect Kirn from the negative parts of his experience with Adderall.

3. One challenge of reflective writing is conveying a personal point of view in a way that will interest readers. Kirn's use of entertaining analogies, personifications, and other

devices make Adderall come to life, almost as if it's a character in his story. This technique gets readers to pay attention to the details of Kirn's account, and emphasizes the uniqueness of his perspective. (See "Writing Reflective Essays," p. 17.)

Exploratory Writing

1. This exercise works best if the paragraphs and two-line descriptions are distributed to a new group (for example, group A's paragraphs go to group B, group B's to group C, and so on). The two-line descriptions are an entertaining way to experiment with reflective writing strategies. Many writers automatically adopt a particular tone, feeling, and style in their reflective work, as students will notice from their own quick first paragraphs. But tone, style, and emotional intensity can be changed consciously as a writing strategy.

2. Students will find many examples of people trapped in a pressure-productivity cycle—not only college students (as shown in Margaret Talbot's report, p. 505), but also doctors, lawyers struggling to make partner status, and harried parents. In class discussion, raise the question of why Talbot and Kirn do not offer explicit solutions for breaking this cycle in their writing on this subject.

Making Connections

1. Kirn's experiences are almost entirely consistent with the data, and even the speculations, in Margaret Talbot's report (p. 505). The Penn scientists' question about whether drugs that heighten users' focus might dampen their creativity (Talbot, par. 40–41) is interesting to revisit in light of Kirn's reflections, especially his characterization of his own writing at the time he was using Adderall.

Essay Writing

1. Students can use Kirn's reflections and Margaret Talbot's report (p. 505) to shape their arguments. Suggest that students outline these argumentative essays (beginning with the thesis, then supporting statements and data, and their conclusions) before they begin writing to give the argument a strong structure.

Paired Readings: On Life and Death Through Doctors' Eyes

Roy C. Selby Jr.: *A Delicate Operation* (REPORTING)

Reading

1. If the surgeon did not operate, the woman would become blind. Though it is not explicitly stated, there is the suggestion that if the tumor kept growing, it might affect the blood vessels supplying the brain. The careful laying out of the risks involved invests the procedure with dramatic tension.

2. The *dura* is the yellowish, leather-like membrane that surrounds the brain (par. 6).

3. Background information is given in the first three paragraphs. Most of the essay is devoted to the operation itself (pars. 4–10). Postoperative events are confined to paragraphs 11 and 12. In paragraph 11, the tension of waiting is reported. Here, we get a sense of how the surgeon felt (anxious and exhausted). In paragraph 12, the report of the patient's condition tells us that the operation was a success. Selby is very careful to explain terms and procedures for a general audience. For example, in paragraph 1 he explains

what an EMI scan is; in paragraph 2, he explains angiography and what could result if the undersurface of the brain or the hypothalamus were damaged. His explanations also often emphasize just how delicate and complicated the procedure is.

Exploratory Writing

1. Certainly, paragraphs 7 and 8 might be cited as moments of great tension when the surgeon, unable to collapse the tumor, starts to dissect it without being able to see the arteries and optic nerves. This is the moment of greatest danger to the patient and of greatest demand on the expertise of the surgeon. The writer has invested the procedure with tension by telling the reader what the surgeon could not see. The reader is positioned, as it were, looking over the surgeon's shoulder, following the procedure step by step. Further, the writer's objective, understated approach encourages the reader to provide the tension.

2. In comparing this essay with an article in a medical journal, students will see (and likely appreciate) the writing techniques that Selby uses to make complex and specialized subject matter accessible to lay readers. His descriptions, definitions, examples, and illustrations epitomize strong reportorial writing.

3. By observing which steps are omitted from certain checklists but not from others, students can see how challenging it is to be comprehensive when writing instructions.

Making Connections

1. While Richard Selzer's essay (p. 533) does indeed include some reportorial elements (such as the bulleted list, par. 124), his use of narrative, dialogue, and characterization make his essay much more personal and reflective. Selby uses a technical tone to explain specialized topics, whereas Selzer conveys much of his specialized information in a more personal, emotional tone.

2. Selby's procedure requires what Jonah Lehrer (p. 431) would characterize as left-brain thinking, focusing on logic, analysis, rationality, and accuracy.

Essay Writing

1. This topic asks students to engage in reflective writing, imagining themselves in Selby's role, and contemplating how they might perform his tasks similarly or differently.

Richard Selzer: *A Mask on the Face of Death* (REFLECTING)

Reading

1. When summarizing this scene, students might think about details that are memorable because of their relationship to the rest of the essay. They might note the Haitian guide's comment that he has had contact with prostitutes "like every good Haitian boy" (par. 1) as a striking example of Selzer's argument that societal expectations in Haiti perpetuate the spread of AIDS. Selzer's description of the three "beautiful and young and lively" (par. 2) women might be particularly memorable because of its sharp contrast to the later images of disease and death.

Selzer spends so much time with these women because he wants to learn more about the spread of AIDS in Haiti. These women's attitudes are important because they are typical of attitudes that thwart AIDS prevention.

2. Selzer sees that the doctor can only offer a prescription for a Gatorade-like drink and the phrase "Eat like an ox," which is ironic because even if the disease did not cause lack of appetite, poverty would prevent patients from buying food (par. 49). He learns

that Haiti does not have the resources to provide care for AIDS symptoms. Selzer senses the futility of the doctor's attempts to combat a fatal disease with such limited resources. At the same time, he witnesses the doctor's willingness to offer what he can and to accept the personal risk of working with AIDS patients, a risk exacerbated by poor conditions (par. 66).

3. To engage the reader, Selzer opens with a detailed description of a scene at the Copacabana. After this first section, the essay is organized in part like a travelogue. The scenes are connected by the obvious, lurking presence of AIDS—but also by a sense of helplessness that pervades Selzer's interactions. Throughout the essay, Selzer interweaves the specific with the general, beginning with details about his trip to the Copacabana and to the clinic directed by Doctor Pape and ending with a list of statistics about AIDS in Haiti. His use of juxtaposition roots general facts in individual human experiences and emphasizes the stark differences in wealth among those affected by AIDS.

Exploratory Writing

1. Strong answers to this question will note how Selzer is approached by prostitutes. His perspective on the situation is strongly and obviously shaped by being an outsider, both to Haiti and to the experience of having AIDS. Yet he is also a doctor, and he writes with expertise. This question should help students distinguish between reportorial and reflective writing.

2. As they prepare their presentations, encourage students to make full use of strong argumentative techniques, such as introducing and responding to counterarguments and providing evidence.

3. The journalist's remark indicates that he blames the American press for Haiti's loss of income from tourism. He asks Selzer not to portray Haiti as a dangerous place to visit. His comment has implications for the prevention of AIDS: It suggests that concern with the economic impact rather than with the health crisis might cause Haitians to downplay the problem and risk, slowing efforts at prevention.

In judging whether Selzer has honored this request, students might consider Selzer's discussion of the source of the AIDS virus. Rather than indict Haiti as "the source of AIDS in the western hemisphere" (par. 103), Selzer considers different possible sources, including the United States. Students should also think about how Selzer's piece would affect their own desire to visit Haiti.

Making Connections

1. Students may note Selzer's comment on behalf of Miracle, Dr. Pape's patient (par. 58), as a moment of unabashed concern. Roy C. Selby Jr. (p. 529) and Selzer both display compassion, yet also a measured detachment. Students should think about how different situations demand vastly different approaches by the doctors. For instance, Selby's patient's outcome is largely in his hands, whereas there is little to nothing that can be done for the patients Selzer observes.

Essay Writing

1. Students should first think about the meaning of the phrase "the politics of AIDS." They might be able to define this more clearly by identifying points in Selzer's essay where he examines relations of power, particularly of economic power, between countries and between social classes. Their own essays should examine these relations and their effect on AIDS care and prevention. Encourage students to research the history and politics of AIDS in their own country.

Student Essay

Lindsay Gellman: *"The Moral Meaning of a Pause": Ethics Committees and the Cloning Debate*

Reading

1. The source for the quotation is Gilbert Meilaender's "Progress without Pause" (*First Things: A Monthly Journal of Religion and Public Life*, 2009). The quotation anticipates Gellman's argument that the main function of ethics committees is to pause scientific advancements "until the public moral framework shifts to accommodate a previously controversial advancement" (par. 2). Although an evocative title like this is unusual in a science essay, a strong response might note that Gellman's essay focuses on the ethics of science, rather than making a scientific argument or presenting scientific research. Students should offer concrete reasons to support their evaluations of the title.

2. Gellman uses quotation to establish her own motive in the essay's opening paragraph. The articles she quotes demonstrate the pervasiveness of the debate. President Clinton's speech offers a strong claim on the purpose of ethics committees "to make an objective moral judgment" (par. 1). Gellman's motive is to complicate this argument. Class discussion might emphasize the fact that Gellman uses these quotations to establish a cultural conversation about cloning and to make it clear how her own argument is an original contribution to these conversations.

3. When students revise the verb in one of these signal sentences, the new version should make logical sense, though it may create a meaning not found in Gellman's essay. It may be worthwhile to ask students to read these revisions aloud, followed by class discussion of how the use of particular verbs helps a writer indicate his or her stance, or point of view, about a given source.

Exploratory Writing

1. Responses should identify a particular claim as Gellman's thesis. In this case, it would be difficult to argue that the thesis is any sentence but the one that opens paragraph 2: "However, it can be argued that in some cases ethics committees serve primarily to pause the funding process for scientific developments until the public moral framework shifts to accommodate a previously controversial advancement." If a student makes a case for an alternative thesis, he or she should offer evidence and reasoning to support that case. Some class discussion could be devoted to the tentative quality of Gellman's thesis—why students think Gellman chose to write this way, whether the strategy is effective, and how the nature of the topic may have led her to use it. Responses should also indicate the evidence Gellman uses to support her thesis, evaluating whether the thesis is clear and compelling, and the pertinence and strength of the evidence. In addition, students should characterize their fictional student and instructor. It may be worthwhile to encourage them to be creative or playful with this characterization—and to ask some or all students to read their dialogues aloud in class.

2. Depending on the results of their interviews, students may argue that fears about cloning have or have not softened since Dolly was cloned in 1997. Either way, they should support their claims with details from their interviews. They may also argue that attitudes are mixed and that it's difficult to establish how much attitudes have changed. It may be useful to devote some class discussion to interviews as a methodology for gathering evidence, both before and after the projects are completed. What can be learned from interviews? What cannot be learned?

Making Connections

1. In order to write a coherent response, students will need to review Steven Pinker's discussion of psychological, genetic, and philosophical explanations for morality (p. 458). A strong response will quote or paraphrase Pinker's discussion of the type of explanation the student chooses, make connections to moral questions raised by Gellman's essay, and take a position on whether or not Pinker's category illuminates these moral questions.

Essay Writing

1. Some class time should be devoted to identifying relevant scientific controversies. Students will also need guidance with the research process—particularly the use of databases, identifying strong sources, and using them to advance their own arguments. Instructors should work with the chapter "Researching to Write" (p. 32) in order to provide this guidance. Finally, it may be a good idea to ask students to follow Gellman's lead and write an introductory paragraph that uses quotations to establish motive, both by demonstrating the pervasiveness of the chosen controversy and identifying an argument the student will complicate.

PART 5: CASEBOOKS

Casebook: How Is the Internet Changing Who We Are?

James Gleick: *Meme Pool* (EXPLAINING)

Reading

1. Memes emerge through the replication of ideas. Gleick quotes evolutionary biologist Richard Dawkins's explanation of how memes travel: "by leaping from brain to brain via a process which, in a broad sense, can be called imitation" (par. 5). Later Gleick elaborates, noting that memes travel "on paper and celluloid and silicon and anywhere else information can go" (par. 10).

2. According to Gleick, Dawkins coined the term *meme* in his 1976 book (par. 5).

3. Gleick mentions patent medicines, psychic surgery, Satanism, superstitions, racist myths, astrology, and surgical fads and iatroepidemics (epidemics caused by those fads). He finds examples of unhelpful or detrimental memes interesting because they show that genetic success and memetic success are not the same.

Exploratory Writing

1. This exercise can be used to problematize Internet research, showing how ideas and counterideas can spread, morph, and change. Proponents of meme theory could use this as a case in point, while opponents could use the same phenomena as an illustration of flaws in meme-based concepts and in the meme/gene comparison. Students will uncover both philosophical objections to meme theory (such as John Gray's) and scientific objections (Stephen Jay Gould).

2. In their lists of guidelines, the groups should refer to Dennett's idea (quoted by Gleick), that "we are seldom 'in charge' of our own minds" (par. 19). In class discussion,

raise the question of whether this idea automatically equates to the conclusion that online media cannot or should not be monitored to protect users from viral advertising, jingles, and messages.

Making Connections

1. One criticism of meme theory is the claim that *meme* is simply a word manipulation—that memes are ideas, tunes, catchphrases, or images that can be spread only when other humans take them up. Sherry Turkle's arguments (p. 619), however, show an increasing willingness on the part of humans to interact with machines rather than with one another. Teenagers "assume that when [their friends] visited, it would usually be on the virtual real estate of Facebook" (par. 12), and they "grow up not necessarily thinking of simulation as second best" (par. 14). This would imply that as humans' relationship with technology changes, so too may the nature of memes. Turkle's ideas support the idea that humans could be—to use Gleick's language—"shov[ed] . . . toward the wings" (par. 18).

Essay Writing

1. In helping students prepare for this essay, ask them to compare and contrast the examples of memes that predate the Internet with those that have emerged or thrived in a viral online environment. You might refer back to Gleick's example of "jump the shark," which he suggests couldn't have existed in a pre-Internet universe. Ask students to consider whether their examples show that the Internet has dramatically transformed the way memes work or only intensified an already existing dynamic.

David Friedman: *From 1890: The First Text Messages* (REPORTING)

Reading

1. A fight circuit happened when two operators fought across the telegraph. It was futile because it was impossible for two operators tapping at once to understand what the other was saying.
2. Each operator had a distinct way of sending messages, and they became able to recognize each other's over time, "just as a familiar face is recognized" (par. 7).
3. Friedman uses terms like *went viral*, *text messages*, *ROFL*, and *LOL* (reporting that *Ha* was the *LOL* of 1890) to show that many of the dynamics of communication that we attribute to Internet technology actually appeared long before the Internet, in slightly different form.

Exploratory Writing

1. Students will find some aspects of every article in Friedman's archive that show continuity in human thoughts, feelings, and behaviors over the past century or so. Articles like "An Auto Hater Gives His Opinion, and Acts" (September 1911) will be humorously familiar.
2. A major difference between the texts sent back and forth by telegraph operators circa 1890 and text messages today is that the telegraph operators represented a small part of the population, whereas use of today's text messaging technology is widespread and common. In class discussion, raise the question of how prevalence changes the societal impact of a technology, using the essays in this casebook (as well as the paired readings in "On Writing Online," pp. 152–66) for examples.

Making Connections

1. Friedman shows how people in different times (post-2010 versus 1890), using different technologies (telegraphs versus texts), have more in common than not in terms of communication style, the content of what they want to communicate, and their reasons for being in touch. According to the examples in James Gleick's explanation (p. 555), memes have operated and spread with the same underlying dynamics at different historical moments. The telegraph technology that Friedman describes, like today's Internet, would be a powerful way for memes to virally repopulate, and there are memes—such as the use of *Ha* as the 1890s *LOL*—in Friedman's account.

Essay Writing

1. Students will want to find case studies, current and historical examples, and other data to support their explanations. The problem of how new technologies do and do not change society is central not only to the writings included in this casebook, but also to almost all writing about communication.

Hillary Rodham Clinton: *Internet Rights and Wrongs: Choices & Challenges in a Networked World* (ARGUING)

Reading

1. Clinton believes that this debate is "beside the point"—that the problem is whether governments and political regimes are oppressive and repressive, regardless of the tools they use to reach those ends.

2. "When countries curtail Internet freedom, they place limits on their economic future" (par. 41), writes Clinton. Freedom of expression on the Internet helps fuel "innovation economies," she argues, by allowing young people to participate in international debates, have a level playing field with other businesspeople through equal access to tools and information, and reduce government corruption through public criticism.

3. Hannah Rosenthal, the U.S. special envoy to monitor and combat anti-semitism, made a 2010 trip to the sites of two Nazi concentration camps with a group of American Muslim leaders and imams (par. 34). Clinton uses the story of this trip to make an argument that reeducation is more effective than censorship.

Exploratory Writing

1. This exercise encourages students to apply ideas and arguments (like Clinton's) to specific cases that haven't already been used as examples. As a longer essay assignment, have students consider a breaking international news event in light of all of the articles in this casebook, applying the question, "How is the Internet changing who we are?" to the case of that nation at this moment in history.

2. Within each small group, there may be passionate disagreement about what information should be "public" versus what should be kept "private," and the meaning of those terms. Clinton's speech is designed to appease both sides, using general language—"In our vigorous effort to prevent attacks or apprehend criminals, we retain a commitment to human rights and fundamental freedoms" (par. 22)—rather than explicitly stating the activities that she believes should be public or private. In comparing Clinton's argumentative writing and speaking strategies to those of other writers, and in their own small-group discussion, students will find that she chooses dramatically different language and

strategies than writers making an uncompromised argument in passionate support or opposition to a cause (see especially, Martin Luther King Jr. [p. 341] and Jeffrey Rosen [p. 594]).

Making Connections

1. Clinton limits her specific examples to non-U.S. cases of censorship and government oppression, while Jeffrey Rosen (p. 594) uses a number of U.S. cases that would apply to Clinton's arguments about governments' right to invade privacy on or off the Internet. For instance, Rosen cites the case of a Canadian psychotherapist barred permanently from visiting the United States after a border guard's Internet search found an article where the therapist had described his experiments with LSD thirty years earlier. Students can evaluate how well Clinton's arguments take such cases into account.

Essay Writing

1. Have students consider the different techniques Clinton uses that are explicitly argumentative strategies. Ask students to look for *euphemisms* in Clinton's comments, other argumentative essays, and their own writing. In their own work, they will find examples of how language can dramatically strengthen or weaken an argument.

Clive Thompson: *I'm So Totally, Digitally, Close to You: The Brave New World of Digital Intimacy* (reporting)

Reading

1. Anthropologist Robin Dunbar has theorized that each human "has a hardwired . . . number of people he or she can personally know at one time"—for humans, it tops out at around 150 (par. 7).

2. A strong summary of Thompson's conclusion will state that "all this incessant updating" and the erosion of privacy have created "a culture of people who know more about themselves." The final part of the question is subjective, with no wrong answers. Strong answers will draw heavily on Thompson's comments or on the other readings in this casebook. For example, drawing on Nicholas Carr's essay (p. 609), an alternative conclusion would be that "all this incessant updating" has created a culture of stupid people who think mechanically and superficially.

3. Thompson means that while cyberspace was originally celebrated as a place where people could reinvent themselves, it has brought back the dynamics of small-town life, where "everybody knows your business" and checks up on you.

Exploratory Writing

1. On the *New York Times* Web site (at **www.nytimes.com**), Thompson's archived piece includes readers' questions and Thompson's answers. These exchanges provide a number of interesting points beyond those in the article. In response to one question, Thompson writes:

> Some people I interviewed worried about the fact that these online interactions all take place on someone's corporate turf. If you get really invested in your relationships on Facebook—just to pick the biggest corporate example here—what happens if Facebook starts doing something you don't like? What if Facebook effectively "controls" your social interactions, by controlling the commons—the mental green space where you and your

> friends hang out? This is what happened last year when Facebook introduced "Beacon," a tool that would report on your News Feed whenever you bought something at certain online stores. Many people really didn't like that, and the outcry caused Facebook to quickly add extra privacy provisions to Beacon. In this sense, online relationships are radically different from face-to-face chatting over coffee in, say, a Starbucks. The Starbucks baristas probably aren't listening to what you're saying or monitoring it; Facebook and Twitter and every other company brokering ambient awareness is, however passively.

Another question raised is about whether people ever get the opportunity to be alone with their thoughts anymore. Is what Thompson characterizes as increased self-knowledge really just a performance?

2. At the time of this writing, a number of these authors had Facebook pages, Twitter feeds, or blogs that turned up with a simple Google search. In class discussion, compare the experience of surfing these sites with reading a promotional Web site created for an author by his or her publisher, reading a gossip column, or reading a tell-all memoir.

Making Connections

1. Andrew Sullivan (p. 152) describes the "visceral, personal" way that a reader and a writer are connected through a blog as friendship. Mona Eltahawy (p. 163) is ambivalent, saying, "Twitter is my lifeline to the world. Twitter is the bane of my existence. Twitter connects me to everything I care about and Twitter is ruining my life." Thompson notes that Twitter, Facebook, and the like expand a person's circle of "weak ties," but do not expand the number of "true intimates." Both Sullivan and Thompson see tremendous benefits in these "weak ties" maintained through technology. Sullivan values the interaction and expanded knowledge base he gains as a writer from blogging, while Thompson reports that "weak ties" can improve people's abilities to solve problems. For Eltahawy, though, even as a "vital pipeline of information," Twitter is deeply personal. She looks to it for work, but also for "gems of optimism to hold onto."

Essay Writing

1. Even if students "cheat" on their research for this essay, it's an opportunity to contemplate how much they are personally dependent on the Internet in everyday life. One reader responding to Thompson's article quoted Lawrence Ferlinghetti: "What's called the dominant culture will fade away as soon as the electricity goes off."

Jeffrey Rosen: *The End of Forgetting* (EXPLAINING)

Reading

1. Rosen means that, because personal information is stored forever in public view on the Internet, "societal forgetting" has been phased out; we now have a "collective identity crisis," returning to a situation where we can no longer reinvent our identities.

2. The senators wrote to express their concern over a Facebook feature that allowed users' previously private information to be viewed publically.

3. Our current Internet situation, according to Rosen, is quickly being replaced with Web 3.0, an online universe where "user-generated content is combined with a new layer of data aggregation and analysis and live video" (par. 18). Reputation management and maintaining privacy will become even more difficult. Rosen's examples include the fact that people will be able to check cell phone photos on facial recognition software and pull up all the tagged photos of each other on the Web.

Exploratory Writing

1. Solutions, such as the European Union's Think B4 U Post campaign or ReputationDefender services, and proposed solutions, such as the ability to declare "reputation bankruptcy" or passing new, stronger privacy laws, are each subject to the problems of rapidly changing technology. Rosen concludes that we will need to develop new kinds of empathy to deal with emerging problems.

2. In class discussion, students might also consider dimensions of online identity, such as the potential for activism or for publicizing and marketing products or businesses. How uncomfortable do they feel "merg[ing] activities that used to be separate?" How helpful are Rosen's explanatory writing strategies in shedding light on their own experiences?

Making Connections

1. An article David Friedman (p. 566) quotes talks about "Friends They Never Meet," a phenomenon that would seem more prevalent in the era of Facebook, Twitter, and online chat rooms. Students will find that historical reports and historiographic writing allow contemporary writers to put seemingly "new" or radical social changes into the broader context of human existence and experience. You might have them consider how much control they have over their online identities compared to the identifiable characteristics telegraphers discerned from each other's techniques.

Essay Writing

1. Rosen also mentions that the Internet limits our ability to reinvent ourselves. As students prepare these reflective essays, suggest that they ask themselves whether they feel the "almost existential" limitation on their power of self-creation that Rosen describes. Some students might find that their online activity enhances their possibility of creating and controlling identities (the "protean self"), while others will feel constrained by "the end of [societal] forgetting."

Nicholas Carr: *Is Google Making Us Stupid?* (ARGUING)

Reading

1. Strong answers will note that Carr observes that he feels as if someone outside is "tinkering with [his] brain" (par. 2) and "chipping away [his] capacity for concentration and contemplation" (par. 4). Lists should include some of the following:

- Deep reading, which used to come naturally, has become a struggle
- Lowered attention span and lost concentration
- Shallower thinking and skimming the surface ("like a guy on a Jet Ski", par. 4)
- Inability to read long articles or books
- Ability to interpret text and make "rich mental connections" remains disengaged
- Move to more mechanical, automatic responses
- Seeing ambiguity as "a bug that needs to be fixed" rather than an opportunity for insight
- "Complex inner density" (Foreman) replaced with a self that responds mechanically and thoughtlessly to whatever is "instantly available"
- Turning into "pancake people" (Foreman), spread wide and thin
- Our real intelligence transformed into artificial intelligence

2. Carr writes: "The faster we surf across the Web . . . the more opportunities Google and other companies gain to collect information about us and to feed us advertisements. . . . It's in their economic interests to drive us to distraction" (par. 29). Strong answers will discuss this advertising motive and Carr's idea that these businesses actually want people to be not only consumers, but thoughtless consumers.

3. This question invites students to consider effective ways to construct an argument. Strong answers will note that Carr refers to scholarly studies and quotes experts (including a developmental psychologist and a neuroscientist) to strengthen his argument.

4. Carr takes a friendly tone that is not polemical as he makes his argument. Strong answers will note that he admits his fallibility, rather than presenting all of his ideas as hard facts—he says, "Maybe I'm just a worrywart" and invites readers to be skeptical of his skepticism. Although he lays out strong arguments, he shares his personal, emotional responses as he makes his case. He describes noticing changes in his ways of thinking, refers to the Google founders' idea that people would be "better off" if our brains were supplemented with artificial brains as "unsettling," and describes himself as "haunted" by Kubrick's "weird" and "poignant" juxtaposition of a feeling computer with emotionless humans.

Exploratory Writing

1. Students' experiences will vary widely. This exercise invites them to think personally about the different themes of Carr's essay. In class discussion, raise the question of which activities stimulate students' intelligence. When do they experience inspiration or breakthroughs in their thinking? You can also refer to Jonah Lehrer's (p. 431) essay about the types of thinking that generate "aha" moments.

2. After breaking students into pairs, you can open the discussion to the class as a whole. Discuss Carr's comment that it used to be widely believed that the brain was "fixed" by adulthood, but researchers like Olds now understand that the brain is "almost infinitely malleable." How should this change the way we structure society? Discuss how the brain's plasticity could make human beings vulnerable to manipulation, stealthily integrated advertising, and subliminal images, but how it also affords adults the opportunity to continue to grow intellectually throughout their lives.

Making Connections

1. One way to stimulate students' thinking on this issue is to ask them to track all the advertising they see in their online activity for a few days or a week. They should note how much advertising they see, what kinds of ads they see, and how customized those ads are. With this data in hand, they can imagine the pros and cons of paid ads disappearing.

Essay Writing

1. Examples of themes might be a world in which people who are dating never actually meet in person and conduct their relationships entirely with "scientifically" compatible partners from separate computer terminals; a world in which every mistake a person makes is made public and haunts the person indefinitely (Jeffrey Rosen, p. 594), a world where all personal relationships are rendered obsolete by technological ones (Sherry Turkle, p. 619); a world in which every citizen is a mindless, mechanical consumer with no inner life (Carr); or a world in which no one ever leaves his or her home, socializes in person, touches other human beings, or goes outside (Clive Thompson, p. 583). The essays can be used to generate a discussion about dystopia and why technological development is so often a factor in dystopian visions.

Sherry Turkle: *Connectivity and Its Discontents* (ARGUING)

READING

1. Turkle reports that Ellen feels guilty and confused because she multitasks during Skype conversations with her grandmother. The advantages of Skype include the cost (free), which enables Ellen to call more frequently, and the "compelling sense that the other person is present" (par. 2). However, Turkle explains that their intimacy decreased because Ellen now treats talking as one of several tasks to be completed at once.

2. The technology of texting, according to Turkle, offers just the right amount of access and control, allowing people to be in touch with many others, while also keeping them at bay. Like Goldilocks looking for porridge that was not too hot, not too cold, but just right, "texting puts people not too close, not too far, but at the right distance" (par. 8).

3. Turkle mentions robots in the concluding paragraphs of the piece to show how current technology is priming us for relationships with robots. Virtual contact in real relationships (texting, Facebook, Skype, and so on) is paving the way for replacement of people with robots—digitized friendships that become part of life itself are priming people for "relationships that could bring superficiality to a higher power, that is, for relationships with the inanimate" (par. 14).

EXPLORATORY WRITING

1. Responses to this exercise might be comic, but they can lead to a serious discussion of virtual reality and simulated intimacy versus the authentic intimacy that Turkle values. The documentary *Catfish* (rumored to be a mockumentary) about virtual relationships not always being what they appear, would be an interesting assignment for class discussion or writing exercises.

2. You can offer students the chance to brainstorm metaphors for a different kind of recent technology—Skype, Twitter, texts, Facebook, tablets, or cell phones—in addition to the computer. They may want to consider the scenes Turkle describes as well as their own observations about the way they, their friends, and their families use these technologies as they brainstorm their metaphors. Ask them to think about these metaphors in light of Turkle's arguments about authenticity and intimacy.

MAKING CONNECTIONS

1. Turkle's anecdotes demonstrate that Skype, Facebook, texting, and e-mail create more distance than intimacy, which, in turn, changes our ability to appreciate the authentic over the inauthentic. Growing up in a virtual-reality saturated world can actually change our values, such as our ability to value life—an argument that has often been made with reference to hand-to-hand combat versus chemical warfare, and to seeing mediated representations of atrocities versus witnessing them directly (see John Berger, p. 236, and Susan Sontag, p. 366).

ESSAY WRITING

1. As students plan their essays, it might be helpful to refer to Steven Pinker's (p. 458) examples of the moral instinct. Turkle raises the question of whether new generations place value on life and existence, a question students can address using different writing strategies. You may point them to the broad questions Turkle poses at the end of the piece as a place for them to begin their own essays.

Casebook Questions

1. Students will need to identify two essays that offer genuinely conflicting claims about the digital age. These may or may not focus on the same or similar technologies or platforms. Some class discussion should be devoted to identifying workable pairs. The paragraphs students write about these conflicting claims will implicitly explore motive. Class discussion can make this explicit, guiding students to identify an intellectual debate they will enter when they write about the sources they find. Students will also need guidance with the research process—particularly the use of databases, identifying strong sources, and using them to advance their own arguments. "Researching to Write" (p. 32) can provide this guidance. If time allows, ask students to write a rough draft for an in-class workshop that focuses on motive, use of sources, and argument.

2. Students should be reminded that new technologies are not the only technologies—that pencil and paper, for example, changed people's lives every bit as much as the Internet has today. The way they use essays from the casebook to frame their arguments will depend on their chosen topics and the results of the research. These essays should all make conceptual or historical arguments that are relevant even though the technologies at hand differ. It will be important that students' arguments make concrete claims about the meaning of their chosen technologies in people's lives. This should be emphasized throughout the research and writing process—as well as in draft workshops or peer review.

3. Ideally, students will present their lectures orally, though it's possible to complete the assignment by compiling slides, materials, and notes. In either case, encourage students to think about the rhetorical modes most suited to their topics—reflecting, explaining, arguing, or reporting. An excellent lecture might emphasize any one of these modes or combine them, but the lecturer should be aware of his or her rhetorical aims. A strong presentation should also be built on strong research. Finally, a great lecture depends on the quality of presentation: clarity, liveliness, structure, and brevity. Ask students to practice by delivering draft lectures to each other in small groups. They can evaluate each other on the qualities listed above, and then revise in advance of delivering their lectures for the larger group.

Casebook: What Is the Value of a College Education?

Gary Gutting: *What Is College For?* (arguing)

Reading

1. The statistics Gutting includes show that the majority of graduates find their college experiences to be valuable in both practical and less tangible ways. The statistics set up Gutting's argument for a more nuanced evaluation of the value of a college education by providing a positive backdrop against which to discuss the "serious concerns about the quality of this experience" (par. 4).

2. Gutting notes problems of expense and access, the unfair treatment of part-time faculty and graduate students, and the unnecessarily expensive dorms, student centers, and superfluous administrators.

3. Gutting says that universities mainly exist "to nourish a world of intellectual culture; that is, a world of ideas, dedicated to what we can know scientifically, understand humanistically, or express artistically" (par. 6).

Exploratory Writing

1. Gutting claims that colleges are not just for students, but institutions to "nourish a world of intellectual culture" (par. 6) for all members of society, among other claims. Strong answers will support or refute Gutting's claims with clear, specific evidence. Students may also call on the other essays in this casebook to support their arguments.

Making Connections

1. Strong answers will follow Gutting's structure for argument and possibly include statistics or research of some kind. In class discussion, consider how students at the University of Phoenix might react to these editorials evaluating their school in relation to Gutting's standards.

Essay Writing

1. This question invites students to write reflectively in response to Gutting's argument. Ask students to consider carefully what they expect their education to give to them, how their expectations and assessments have changed since they started college, and how their own engagement affects their experience as a whole.

Mark Edmundson: *On the Uses of a Liberal Education* (reflecting)

Reading

1. A Joon Lee fest is when Edmundson and his fellow professors meet in the hallway and rave about a favorite student of theirs, Joon Lee. Edmundson mentions this to note the stark contrast between Joon Lee, who is passionate and eccentric, and the typical student of the generation, who is passionless, polite, and unenthusiastic.

2. Edmundson shows that his students have taken on the values of "high consumer capitalism," where the "pervading view is the cool consumer perspective" (par. 18). To his students, passion and rigor have been replaced with mild manners and an aversion to both admiration and confrontation.

3. Edmundson argues that cultural studies programs rarely work because rather than fostering deep engagement with theory and critical analysis of contemporary culture, they usually devolve into a personal discussion of students' likes and dislikes. To make this point, Edmundson uses the technique of stating the opposing opinion ("To some professors, the solution . . ." [par. 48]) in order to refute it.

Exploratory Writing

1. Edmundson's ideal student—a passionate, enthusiastic critical thinker who uses the libraries and museums, is transformed by books, and is willing to question and rebel against the status quo—stands in stark contrast to the bland, uncritical student/consumers he describes. In class discussion, raise the question of why students are seeking an education. Students can also consider whether, in this very discussion, they are critically engaging with theories, ideas, and Edmundson's text, or simply uncritically sharing personal opinions and experiences.

2. Edmundson suggests that for professors to be "usefully offensive" might be a good thing, shaking students out of their complacency, but that ultimately, students themselves must "make their own way against the current sludgy tide" (par. 59). In class discussion, ask students whether they agree with Edmundson's depiction of the educational climate, or if they feel that times have changed since this article was written in 1997.

Making Connections

1. The students that Edmundson is characterizing are of a different generation than the ones Cathy N. Davidson (p. 650) describes. Has the consumer culture of Edmundson's students evolved to better meet the needs of Davidson's students? Or are these simply two opposing perspectives on the same issues? Can both be right?

Essay Writing

1. Students may also refer to other essays in this casebook. Some student guides will reflect values similar to Edmundson's—the idea of learning for transformation, creativity, the development of critical thinking skills, and social change—whereas others will advocate a more practical approach—college as means to increasing social status or earning power. Use class discussion of the different values reflected in the essays to help students critically engage with the debates on the meaning of higher education.

David Leonhardt: *Even for Cashiers, College Pays Off* (ARGUING)

Reading

1. The Hamilton Project, a Washington-based research group, did a study comparing college to other investments and found that a college education delivered an "inflation-adjusted annual return" higher than that of real estate or the stock market. Leonhardt uses this data because it supports his argument that college is cost-effective and frames it literally as a "good investment."

2. These skeptics may be well-meaning, says Leonhardt, but their position is elitist because they themselves usually have college degrees and can provide their children with expensive educations (pars. 20–21).

3. Cashiers are mentioned specifically in the title because of the common assumption that this is a career that doesn't require a college education. The title shows that the tenor of Leonhardt's article is about whether or not college is a cost-effective and practical investment. In contrast, Mark Edmundson's article (p. 630), which advocates education as a vehicle for social and personal transformation, frames each student as an individual, not a "doctor" or a "cashier."

Exploratory Writing

1. Students might interview people whose cases aren't addressed in Leonhardt's article—such as those educated in countries where college is free for all those who qualify, people who graduated from highly competitive colleges, or people who dropped out of college. The exercise should provide practice in reportorial writing while also encouraging students to engage in argument.

2. In class discussion, ask the group as a whole to assess the persuasiveness of each proposal. How practical, creative, viable, or inspired is each solution? These proposals can be used as examples to show the role that writing strategies play in persuading readers.

Making Connections

1. Leonhardt doesn't account for one of Linda Lee's (p. 670) main arguments—that class privilege leads to more class privilege. Lee and Leonhardt have polar assessments of the current relationship between college costs and financial privilege, including differing data and polar interpretations of the data as a whole. Students will likely conclude that neither author would be persuaded by the other's arguments. But it is interesting to note

that neither writer argues—as Mark Edmundson (p. 630) does—that learning for learning's sake is valuable for everyone in the society or that college is a place where capitalist values should be contested.

Essay Writing

1. This assignment asks students to choose a profession that doesn't require a college degree and to use argument techniques (as opposed to personal reflection) to assess the value of a college education in this field—but in class discussion ask students to reflect on values typically associated with this career choice that may differ from the values typically associated with a traditional college education. Discuss the essays in class in relation to the varying perspectives included in this casebook.

Cathy N. Davidson: *Project Classroom Makeover* (arguing)

Reading

1. Duke was criticized widely in the media, but Davidson specifically notes criticism from two academic publications, *Inside Higher Ed* and the *Chronicle of Higher Education*.

2. Duke's choice to turn to crowdsourcing reversed the traditional roles and relationship of students and teachers—what Davidson calls a "hierarchy based on credentials" (par. 14). Interrupting the unidirectional flow of information, she says of the experiment, "instead of teaching, we hoped to learn" (par. 12).

3. Davidson describes the reception model of education as a traditional, lecture-style model of learning, where students "face forward, learn from on high, memorize what was already a given, or accept knowledge as something predetermined and passively absorbed" (par.31). She contrasts this model with an interactive model of education—but there's no need to distinguish between "better" and "worse," she says, "because we have both" (par.33).

Exploratory Writing

1. Ask students whether they have used any of the apps Davidson refers to—or if they feel they would be useful in a classroom setting. Ask students what other apps they know of that could be used for learning purposes, or if they have ideas for educational apps of their own.

2. Davidson makes use of the specific apps to show how iPods very much have a place in an interactive learning model. Davidson also uses specific examples of the program's successes, some of them directly refuting the sarcastic criticisms the program received early on in the media.

Making Connections

1. An important distinction to raise in this discussion will be Davidson's insistence on using technology for educational purposes—for exploiting a device that might otherwise only be used for entertainment. Explore the ways in which Davidson and Mark Edmundson (p. 630) might both agree and disagree about educational models and solutions to problems in higher education today.

Essay Writing

1. Encourage students to assess the value of specific aspects of each type of learning experience. What makes each experience unique, and why? Is it possible, in the scenarios they describe, to have both, as Davidson suggests we do?

James Traub: *The Next Drive-Thru U* (REPORTING)

READING

1. The University of Phoenix is one of only a few for-profit universities that exist. Traub states that the distinction between profit-making companies and all academic institutions is becoming "increasingly moot."

2. Traub uses John Sterling to epitomize the shift in values of the university, away from a place for intellectual enrichment and transformation and toward a profit-oriented product that targets students as consumers. His portrayal of the contradictions in Sterling's position (having loved his classical education at Berkeley, yet not wishing the same for his students "because they can't afford it") invites readers to consider this shift from multiple angles.

3. The accreditations board denied the university's requests to start a doctoral program and to offer undergraduate degrees in whatever it wished. The general attitude at the school, Traub reports, is that still-powerful "forces of convention" are trying to "throttle" Sterling. Traub notes that an "alternative point of view is that there are still standards for an academic education [that] the university may have been threatening to transgress" (par. 23).

EXPLORATORY WRITING

1. This question asks students to list the advantages of attending an online university as opposed to a more traditional college, but in class discussion, consider whether Traub makes the consumer model of education sound appealing or unappealing. Students can evaluate the effectiveness of articles throughout this casebook in either swaying readers' opinions or neutrally informing them.

2. Students are likely to find a wide variety of programs for educational reforms—some successful, some not. Ask students to think about the issues these reforms were meant to address and how the reform writers might respond to Arthur Levine's suggestion about in-house postsecondary education.

MAKING CONNECTIONS

1. Traub's examples (such as Ottawa University's slogan "Ottawa majors in *you*") and George Felton's explanation (p. 674) both show that many universities have become (in Traub's words) "market-driven institutions trying to satisfy customer demand" (par. 4). Mark Edmundson's account (p. 630) describes in more detail the ramifications of this phenomenon in the classroom.

ESSAY WRITING

1. Encourage students to use strong reflective writing strategies as they compose these essays, recounting their opinions but using detailed descriptions, anecdotes, and stylized writing to help the reader see their world.

Linda Lee: *The Case against College* (ARGUING)

READING

1. Caroline Bird wrote the 1975 book *The Case against College*, which argued that students weren't there to learn, college wasn't an effective way to train workers, and there was no real evidence that college itself was the reason for graduates' higher earnings.

2. Lee tacitly acknowledges that some readers might see her argument against universal college education as blasphemous. Nobel Prize–winning playwright George Bernard

Shaw had a well-known disdain for the requirements of institutional education, so choosing him to quote supports Lee's arguments that college is not for everyone and that this position has a long history.

3. Lee makes the case that because various professions—video store manager, plumber, mechanic—do not require a college degree, and that a college degree doesn't necessarily increase the average wage of people in these professions, college is not for everyone.

Exploratory Writing

1. Use students' examples to discuss not only the case against (or for) college, but also how successfully the arguments in Lee's essay (and other essays in this casebook) account for these anecdotes. For example, are there cases of people who start college with reading or writing problems, "fairly dumb," or without passion, and then become transformed by college?

2. This exercise shows an alternative perspective to Lee's arguments—that college can be a place for transformation, where students can learn skills, work with experts, and use resources to strengthen their abilities to take on new tasks. Students may also consider great ways to access these resources outside of any educational institution.

Making Connections

1. Lee argues that these students wouldn't actually need a college education to gain the benefits they seek—a higher salary, certain job skills, and access to jobs. The students who "belong in college," she argues, are exactly the opposite of the students described by the University of Phoenix because they seek to pursue "learning for learning's sake" (par. 1).

Essay Writing

1. As students search for information to build a conclusion, they can compare these reportorial techniques with the argumentative writing strategies used by Lee. They may use data from this casebook as well as conduct original research such as interviewing a college alumnus, comparing their own experiences today with the alumnus's experience.

George Felton: *How to Write a Great College Slogan* (explaining)

Reading

1. According to Felton, "The best part of getting into college remains getting out" (par. 17).

2. "With One World" fast approaching, state universities need to remember that regionalism can appear to be provincialism (par. 10).

3. Felton uses humor not only to entertain the reader, but also to illustrate and explain the outrageousness of the new college landscape in "that great American amusement park, AdLand" (par. 4).

Exploratory Writing

1. Felton is a copywriter as well as a writer and English professor. In class discussion of this exercise, raise the question of how advertorial writing (designed to sell something) differs from modes of writing designed to educate, inform, inspire, and enlighten.

2. Felton's humorous explanation shows how good sloganeers are aware of their product and its audience, but readers of the slogan might be manipulated by language that is vague, misleading, or "honest but not too honest." This exercise can be used to show the

effectiveness of Felton's explanation—and the wider and deeper point he makes about the uses of a college education.

Making Connections

1. Both Felton and Mark Edmundson (p. 630) show how colleges today are being marketed according to a consumer model. Felton concludes that earning potential is the selling point of a college education, while Edmundson describes several dimensions of the consumer/customer attitude of most of his students—they are passionless and expect to be entertained.

Essay Writing

1. In preparing their arguments, students may refer to other essays in this casebook that discuss the transformational potential of a college experience: Gary Gutting (p. 627); Mark Edmundson (p. 630); and Cathy N. Davidson (p. 650). In addition, students might find Natalie Angier's celebration of scientific literacy (p. 489) helpful. When assigning this prompt, note that it is not necessarily easier for students as writers to make strong arguments that reflect their personal beliefs—sometimes it's easier or more fun to argue against their own position.

Casebook Questions

1. In order to complete this assignment, students will need to identify how their chosen authors define the *value* of higher education. As a prewriting assignment, you might ask them to highlight or underline all passages where the author addresses the value of education, either directly or indirectly. Then, they might write a paragraph summarizing the author's definition of *value*, integrating quotations from the text or paraphrasing (and citing it). This will put students in a good position to identify sources that offer opposing viewpoints. Once they find sources they think are good candidates, you might encourage them to complete the same process with each of the essays. This process will help them generate a great deal of writing on the texts, much of which may end up in the essay itself.

A strong response will depend on sources that speak to each other on similar topics and that demonstrate differing values with regard to education. Of course, students will need guidance with locating and identifying sources that do this—including the use of databases and identifying compatible sources. Instructors should work with the chapter "Researching to Write" (p. 32) to provide this guidance.

Finally, students will need practice making their own arguments about these sources. The questions in the prompt should help, but it may be useful to conduct a thesis workshop, emphasizing the particular criteria emphasized in the assignment: the identification of different definitions of *value* and the ways these definitions inform each writer's argument.

2. A proposal is a distinctive kind of argument. The qualities of each student's ideal university will offer implicit evidence of what he or she values about higher education. Students should be encouraged to make these values explicit in their introductions, identifying the core values represented by their proposed universities. A strong proposal will offer both written and visual evidence, be structured cohesively, and be designed in an appealing way. Students should find plenty of evidence to draw from in this casebook, but they should be encouraged to find additional sources as well. They might begin by locating works addressed or cited in the selections in the casebook, but they should also do some research using academic databases. Instructors should work with the chapter "Researching to Write" (p. 32) in order to provide guidance with this process. An alternative method might ask students to collaborate on proposals in groups.

3. Although completing this project may take more time, effort, and resources than the more traditional options, it may ultimately be more rewarding and enjoyable, especially for students who are inclined toward this medium. While it may be easy for the project to get sidetracked, encourage students to maintain focus on the thesis of their manifesto, ensuring that the footage they use for the final product supports their argument. The project offers students a chance to use unique forms of supporting evidence and a creative way of expressing argument. Depending on their experience, students may need substantial guidance with equipment and software. If your college employs educational technologists, it may be worthwhile to investigate whether they can offer your students individual support or group workshops. Students may also be recruited to offer each other guidance, as some of them are likely to have more experience with the relevant technologies than others. An alternative method for this assignment may be to ask students to collaborate on documentaries in groups.

Casebook: What Do We Really Know about Gender?

Anne Fausto-Sterling: *Society Constructs Biology; Biology Constructs Gender* (ARGUING)

Reading

1. Spallanzani's experiments proved the opposite of what he concluded, but because of his staunch commitment to ovism, his mind was closed to alternative interpretations of his results (par. 8). Similarly, because Spallanzani was such a highly regarded scientist, his colleagues adopted his false beliefs, rather than considering his experimental results. Fausto-Sterling uses this case to show how societal preconceptions can bias the work of even competent scientists, particularly in areas of passionate belief.

2. Like gender, human height falls on a continuum—there are not only two heights of adults, but a range between the extremes of short and tall. Fausto-Sterling uses the example of medically treating "height deficient" adults who don't have dwarfism or a hormone deficiency to show how designations of abnormality are not rooted in neutral science; rather, they are connected to complex cultural and economic issues.

3. While acknowledging that even great scientists are vulnerable to bias in their work based on cultural assumptions, Fausto-Sterling's argument is ultimately in favor of using scientific methodology. Arguing that scientific practices are "at once potentially progressive and retrogressive," she concludes that it is the role of science writers to "shuttle back and forth" (par. 33) along these seemingly contradictory strands of meaning to develop a more complex understanding of how ideas are formed and transformed.

Exploratory Writing

1. This exercise encourages students to actively practice the type of thought necessary for the critical science writing that Fausto-Sterling advocates in her final paragraph. Although questioning some facts might seem silly or ridiculous, you can note in class discussion that many known "truths" in the history of science have been soundly refuted as false.

2. For this exercise, you might choose a contemporary study tied to the themes of this casebook. Like the preceding exercise (above), this one invites students to practice the kinds of critical thinking and reading that Fausto-Sterling advocates for science writers.

Making Connections

1. Stephen Jay Gould (p. 709) clearly shows how bias and prejudice affected Paul Broca's study of brain size in men and women—in his neglecting to correct his raw data, his willingness to lean on the a priori assumption that "women are, on average, a little less intelligent than men" (par. 4), and in his conclusion that brain size is an unequivocal measurement of intelligence. Broca's tone of truth and objectivity lent authority to the prevailing idea of female inferiority; surely, providing a scientific basis for an already prevalent social norm has slowed the progress of gender equality.

Essay Writing

1. Encourage students to share or present their findings in class. The essays will likely show the radical dynamism of popular and scientific ideas about how things work and offer insights into the odd (and sometimes humorous) scientific "facts" throughout history. Most of these examples will have some similarities with the cases Fausto-Sterling uses to make her argument. As students form their explanations, they can turn to the essays in the "Sciences" section of *Fields of Reading* (such as Richard Feynman's [p. 395], or Natalie Angier's [p. 489]) for models for understanding doubt, uncertainty, and change within scientific writing and thought.

E.J. Graff: *The M/F Boxes* (reporting)

Reading

1. Ann Hopkins's firm, Price Waterhouse, told her that she wouldn't make partner because she was "too masculine." Because the court found in favor of Hopkins and declared this sex discrimination, the case set a valuable precedent for legal organizations fighting for gay, lesbian, and transgender rights.

2. Graff highlights IFGE, GEA, and the Working Group on Trans Equality, and suggests that one of the greatest successes of these groups (circa 2001) was that all of the major gay and lesbian organizations, and many smaller ones, had newly included transgender people in their mission statements.

3. Graff's examples of legal cases support the conclusion and premises of her report by offering evidence that the movement against discrimination and abuse based on gender noncomformity is gaining cohesion and power.

Exploratory Writing

1. As of 2011, the American Psychiatric Association was considering changing this "disorder" to "Gender Dysphoria" in the *Diagnostic and Statistical Manual of Mental Disorders*. Several other nations, including Britain (2002) and France (2009), have officially declared that gender nonconformity is neither a mental disorder nor a medical problem. In class discussion, ask why this issue is so controversial and how effectively Graff's report addresses the controversy. (Students might be interested in reading Daphne [now Dylan] Scholinski's *The Last Time I Wore a Dress*.)

2. Reading these autobiographical books is a powerful way for nontransgender readers to imagine and understand the issues faced by transgender people. In class discussion, evaluate the strengths that different modes of writing offer for giving readers new insights. While Graff's report offers information and case studies, to help readers understand the discrimination faced by transgender people, reflective writing such as memoirs and Jay Prosser's narrative (p. 701) offer an inside view, allowing readers to imagine

themselves in the author's position. Reflective writing can be an important tool for combating prejudice.

Making Connections

1. Most of us, writes Graff, have "a narrow range in which we feel 'natural' as we gender ourselves daily" (par. 6), and that usually it lines up with biological sex. Peggy Orenstein (p. 705) writes that, even as someone who studied gender, she took the fact of her own gender for granted and was "unnerved" that it could be "so easily threatened." Both writers illustrate how the assumption of clear, fixed gender identity does not reflect reality.

Essay Writing

1. Gender can be so taken for granted that some students and interviewees may find this assignment initially difficult to dig into, but students may be surprised by the complexity of other people's perceptions of gender. Kate Bornstein's *My Gender Workbook* is a helpful resource for understanding how age, race, class, and many other factors contribute to the ways we perceive one another's sex. Strong responses will reveal that gender identity is complex, even for those who seem to fit easily into one category or the other (as Peggy Orenstein reflects, p. 705.)

Jay Prosser: *The Body Narrative of Transsexuality* (REFLECTING)

Reading

1. Prosser feels "immediate sympathy" about his students' confusion, but he also feels similar confusion himself.

2. The presentation is "dazzling" because the student takes on the challenging subject of transition. That the hybrid quality of *Ceremony* makes it hard for students to assess makes a "metacommentary" on the class's discomfort with Prosser's own process of transition.

3. Prosser's first-person reflections allow us an insider's view of his experience, encouraging us to imagine ourselves in his position. This is one of the greatest strengths of reflective writing.

Exploratory Writing

1. One thing we can "know" from looking at a picture of a stranger is gender—the person is usually identifiable as male or female. Prosser's reflections show that these simple categorizations can be illusory. Students will discover that they cannot know from looking at a picture whether a person has transitioned from one sex to the other or which sex he or she identifies as. Other things that seem knowable, such as age, race, or ethnicity, may also be deceptive. Some people have a physical appearance, for example, that makes them seem to be a different race from their biological parents. (See Lise Funderburg's *Black, White, Other: Biracial Americans Talk about Race and Identity* [1994].) Others have physical conditions that make them appear to have an age different from their chronological one. Invite class discussion on the ways that different modes of writing can challenge stereotypes by encouraging us to think critically and question expected truths.

2. In class discussion of this exercise, point out that Prosser's experience of transition led him first to an interest in visual images of transexuality and then to an interest in "visuality" more broadly. Artworks in all genres, visual or not, can force or seduce viewers into a confrontation with paradox or something that is uncategorizable. Raise the question

of similarities and differences between how this happens in creative works and how it is possible in nonfiction writing.

Making Connections

1. Strong answers should point to both authors' use of specific details—Michael Chabon's (p. 715) description of himself employing his tool set, and Prosser's description of his physical transition, for example—as techniques for communicating their experiences of performing or inhabiting gender in a visceral, relatable way.

Essay Writing

1. Ideas might include changing the standard language to address teachers so that there are polite but nongendered titles that students can use; changing language more wisely in society so that the pronouns we use to describe one another are gender-neutral; increasing awareness of transgender issues in schools; and discussing these issues more openly. Students can use other argumentative essays as models for structuring a convincing proposal.

Peggy Orenstein: *What Makes a Woman a Woman?* (reflecting)

Reading

1. Orenstein, diagnosed with breast cancer at age thirty-five, was told her risk could be reduced by the removal of her breasts and ovaries. This caused her to question what constituted her own biological sex, while Caster Semenya's sex was called into question publically in the media.

2. Although Orenstein includes expert testimony (such as Sheri Berenbaum's study), her characterization of gender identity as "mysterious" and defying objectivity stresses her personal experiences and reflections, rather than aiming to report facts or argue that her experience applies universally.

3. Orenstein concludes that her sex could not be altered by a surgeon's scalpel, although she's not certain why this is the case. She concludes that there is something deep and inherent in gender identity.

Exploratory Writing

1. Some students might argue that it isn't possible to make this kind of list because there aren't any qualities that fix a person in one biological sex or the other. Either way, there's likely to be strong disagreement about what constitutes each sex. Students can consider the discussions throughout this casebook as they evaluate the meaning of this dissent.

2. In class discussion of these journals (which students do not need to share publically), bring up the idea from E.J. Graff's report (p. 695) that "most of us have a narrow range in which we feel 'natural' as we gender ourselves daily" (par. 6). Ask students to consider what behaviors and activities would feel "unnatural" to them, and why. Wearing lipstick? Using the men's restroom? Ask students to imagine a society that was not organized around gender or sex difference. Are these differences so powerful and fundamental that any society would reorder itself around them over time? Or in the future, could they be seen as less central and more fluid, like racial difference?

Making Connections

1. Jay Prosser (p. 701) reflects that his students did not know which gender pronouns or titles to use during his gender transition, which caused enough discomfort that there

was relief when the class was over. Since his students seemed otherwise polite and sympathetic, it seems that the limitations of gendered language made an enormous difference in everyone's comfort level. If it was standard to use a gender-neutral pronoun (such as "per" instead of "his" or "her"), students might have happily proceeded with interacting with their professor without worrying about identifying his/her sex by scrutinizing his/her face, body, and behavior for physical cues.

Essay Writing

1. As they research this issue, students should refer to the other essays in this casebook. They can have the option of finding a case like Caster Semenya's, widely covered in the media, or choosing a memoir, biography, or other book about someone who has faced public questioning of their identity.

Stephen Jay Gould: *Women's Brains* (ARGUING)

Reading

1. Gould uses sophisticated modes of numerical analysis, such as "multiple regression," to refute Broca's simplistic and prejudiced interpretation of numbers. Gould's painstaking analysis of Broca's data epitomizes the "inferential" reasoning that he considers fundamental to science.

2. Broca's method of calculating relies exclusively on raw data concerning the average weight and size of women's brains versus men's brains, without considering any of the factors or variables that might account for the differences, such as age, height, disease, and nutrition. Gould, by contrast, takes these and other factors into account in order to demonstrate the dangers of relying on raw, uncorrected data.

3. Students should notice that Gould quotes sources in order to establish his argument and discount counterarguments. He quotes *Middlemarch,* written by a woman, to establish an early case for women's intelligence and capabilities. By contrast, he quotes Broca and his followers to reveal their misogynistic biases. When he quotes Maria Montessori, chastising her for reverse discrimination, he demonstrates that he is interested in a thorough and balanced account of his subject. For Gould, the problem with Montessori is that she duplicates Broca's oversimplified approach, but claims that women, rather than men, are superior.

4. Gould allows his sources to speak for themselves. Taken out of context and presented to a contemporary audience, their sexism is blatant, even jarring. Quoting them extensively offers readers the opportunity to see this scientific writing from another era for themselves. Many (if not most) readers will be persuaded just from reading the excerpts that the writing's misogyny interferes with the arguments of these authors. This helps Gould make his case and cut down on the amount of exposition and analysis he needs to be persuasive.

Exploratory Writing

1. Student translations will vary widely. It will be important that they're accurate, although students may take some creative liberties with them. Class discussion might be initiated with the following question: "How difficult was it to preserve Eliot's meaning while modernizing her style?" The question will help initiate a discussion of how style and language shape meaning.

2. Success with this assignment will require some ingenuity—and some detail. To be successful, a student must demonstrate an accurate understanding of Gould's concept of "biological labeling" and offer an interesting, detailed, description of a school whose

practices are rooted in such labeling. It may be useful to ask some students to read these responses aloud. The conversation may lead to some productive observations about the implicit ideas that shape the educational institutions with which they have experience.

Making Connections

1. While strong answers may draw from any of the sources in this casebook, they should include details about how these theories are being reevaluated and what specific assumptions are being overturned. Students should also note whether the theories are being questioned via scientific inquiry, as Gould does, or if the writer is using reflection or anecdotal evidence to reevaluate the prevailing ideology.

Essay Writing

1. Answers will vary widely. Success with this assignment will depend on choosing two essays that work well together—whether they represent conflicting opinions or approach a social attitude from two different perspectives. For example, students could pair Michael Chabon's "Faking It" (p. 715) with Peggy Orenstein's "What Makes a Woman a Woman?" (p. 705) to examine societal expectations for fitting into defined genders, or Jay Prosser's "The Body Narrative of Transsexuality" (p. 701) with Anne Fausto-Sterling's "Society Constructs Biology; Biology Constructs Gender" (p. 681) to compare the two writers' approaches to the fluidity and socially constructed definition of gender.

Michael Chabon: *Faking It* (REFLECTING)

Reading

1. Chabon's tone is humorous, one of a mock authoritative narrator. Students might note any number of signals of Chabon's humorous tone, including referring to his children as "people" who played on the towels hanging on the back of the door, or the mock formality of describing his and his wife's approach to correcting the children's behavior as "a pilot program of nag-based maintenance, targeted yelling, and regular exercises in stumbling over damp bath towels in dark bedrooms" (par. 1).
2. "Fronting," as described by Chabon, is projecting the air of level-headedness even when you are convinced the situation is not in your control. Chabon quotes Kipling both to provide a backdrop against which he believes American men learn what is expected of them, as well as to point out the distinction that the requirement that men "keep [their] head" is more a matter of the appearance, not the reality, of control.
3. Chabon readily points out where he falls short of the appearance he projects—he has the tools, for example, and is able to complete certain tasks, but he has a deep distrust in his own competence. Most notably though, at the end of the essay, in a moment when the stakes are highest, his ability to inspire confidence in his wife can be seen as a characteristically "masculine" moment.

Exploratory Writing

1. This question should provide an opportunity for students to write reflectively. In class discussion, ask students to consider their reaction to this person's failure and whether grace can or should be extended to public figures—such as politicians and celebrities—who make these kinds of mistakes in full public view.
2. Ask students to consider the source for each of these stereotypes—is it scientific evidence, representation in the media, or what they have been taught to believe by parents

and teachers? It may also be interesting to guess how the other authors in this casebook might react to these stereotypes.

Making Connections

1. Both authors seek to define their respective genders as well as call such definitions into question. They are also careful not to generalize about the opposite gender. How does this approach affect their assessment of their own gender? Ask students to reflect on why they may find one of these essays more convincing than the other.

Essay Writing

1. Encourage students to be creative in their research: scientific treatises, manner books, journals, poems, and essays (those critical and supportive of traditional Victorian masculinity). Strong essays should provide clear, detailed evidence to support the argument that these ideas have—or have not—persisted.

Casebook Questions

1. The prompts require students to complete six designated tasks in order to create a structure for their research process: (1) Identify two essays in the casebook that challenge similar cultural assumptions. (2) List the evidence used by each author. (3) Locate some of the evidence used by each author. (4) Evaluate the author's use of the sources located. (5) Find additional sources that address similar cultural assumptions about gender. (6) Write an essay that makes an argument about the origins, meaning, or validity of the assumptions at hand.

A guided research project can help students learn the elements and value of research without the burden of generating topics and methodologies on their own. With this in mind, students might be asked to complete each of these tasks sequentially—and might receive feedback from the instructor or peers at strategic stages in the process. In order to write a strong essay, students will need to be specific about their chosen assumptions and make a strong claim about their origin, meaning, or validity. In addition, students will need to develop and support their claims with strong evidence. Instructors should work with the chapter "Researching to Write" (p. 32) to provide guidance with particular phases of the process, including the use of databases, the evaluation of sources, and the development of an argument.

2. This is an ambitious assignment because it requires students to learn a great deal about their chosen figures, link what they learn to public debates about gender, and devise their own arguments about what the figures reveal about gender debates. In addition, students will need to balance a variety of sources (personal writing, newspaper and magazine articles, and gender theory, for example) and rhetorical modes (reporting, explaining, arguing, and reflecting). In order to make this work, the assignment should be done over the course of weeks and completed in stages—for example, a research proposal, an annotated bibliography, a draft, and a revision. Workshops and peer review in class should focus on developing theses that are clear, compelling, and motivated—that, in short, make a contribution to debates about gender by identifying what the chosen figure reveals about cultural assumptions about gender. Students will also need guidance with the research process—particularly the use of databases, identifying strong sources, and using them to advance their own arguments. Instructors should work with the chapter "Researching to Write" (p. 32) to provide this guidance.

3. An alternative medium can be difficult, but it can also motivate students because of its novelty and because it reflects the types of media they are likely to interact with in their daily lives. With this in mind, students might be encouraged to produce a documentary to post

to YouTube or another social media Web platform. Either way, the research process will be intensive, and students will need guidance. They should be encouraged to think explicitly about the demands of their chosen medium and the rhetorical modes most well suited to their topics. Of course, students will also need guidance with the research process, as with the other research projects above. Instructors should work with the chapter "Researching to Write" (p. 32) to provide this guidance. Students should be encouraged to think about how elements of essay writing translate to their chosen medium, including introductions and conclusions, use of sources and citation, and analysis of evidence. Finally, depending on their experience with their chosen media, students may need substantial guidance with equipment and software. If your college employs educational technologists, it may be worthwhile to investigate whether they can offer your students individual support or group workshops. Students may also be recruited to offer each other guidance, as some of them are likely to have more experience with the relevant technologies than others. An alternative method for this assignment is to ask students to collaborate on documentaries in groups.

E-Pages

Isabel Allende and Big Think: *Writing Process* (REFLECTING)

Reading

1. Allende spends eight to fourteen hours per day writing (0:30).
2. Allende characterizes her approach to work as *schizophrenic* because she splits her year into two parts. The first half is her "inner time," devoted to writing and solitude. She says, "I do what I have to do [the rest of the year]," implying an extroverted life that adds to her experiences and likely gives her more inspiration for future writing (2:15).
3. Allende knows that a story of hers is flowing when the characters do things that she doesn't expect (3:20).

Exploratory Writing

1. Author interviews often provide information about the way writers write. Advise struggling students to track these down, either in print or online. Also, exhort students to make connections between the writing process and the finished product. For example, if the chosen writer's process resembles Allende's, does that resemblance carry over into their writing?

Making Connections

1. Reading and historical research inform Allende's writing process. Producing a memoir indicates the importance of recollection and personal experience to her work. Starting most days with a letter to her mother primes her for larger literary undertakings. Just as *Fields of Reading* notes that most writing happens "unpredictably" or "organically" (p. 6), so Allende characterizes her ideas as seeds inside her, some of which grow into obsessions that get into her writing (2:00).

Essay Writing

1. Students should anchor their essays with a detailed account of their personal writing processes. They may choose to first relate their own methods and then compare them to Allende's, or discuss the relationships to hers as they go along. Encourage them to reference specific experiences and pieces of writing in their descriptions. Also encourage them

to identify the parts of their processes that are especially fruitful and any parts of their processes they find problematic (and have them try to identify methods for overcoming those hurdles).

T.M. Luhrmann: *When God Talks Back* (EXPLAINING)

READING

1. One style resembles meditation. It entails emptying the mind in an attempt to "hold yourself motionless before the divine" (8:20). The other style requires the use of imagination. Practitioners attend to their thoughts rather than disengage from them.

2. Schizophrenics typically hear many voices, which speak frequently, extensively, and often negatively. People reporting the voice of God describe His speech as rare, brief, and positive (9:30).

3. Every present-day Christian, Luhrmann thinks, is aware of "smart, decent people who are not Christian." Their existence confronts the Christian with "the possibility of another interpretation," or worldview (16:40).

EXPLORATORY WRITING

1. Students should ground their comparisons in specific examples—ideally quotations—from both the Bible and Luhrmann's discussion. For instance, they might observe that in the Bible, God sometimes speaks in reproof (as when Adam and Eve eat from the Tree of Knowledge), while the accounts Luhrmann reports are positive (e.g., God saying "I will always be with you.") (10:20).

MAKING CONNECTIONS

1. Students may approach this question from several directions. One is through the case Bloom makes for conceptual dualism. Humans, he argues, have two different categories of understanding: physical and psychological. The first is for what we can see and prove—the material world. The second is for notional, unverifiable things, like the concept of an immortal soul. This dualism "makes it possible for us to think of supernatural entities and events," such as God talking to someone (p. 202). He also points out that children are more disposed to the second category of thinking than adults.

ESSAY WRITING

1. A discussion of any religious practice can be deeply personal or sensitive, so encourage students to base their essay in research. This is a good opportunity to explore reliable sources and how to expose biased reporting. Students may want to discuss groups to which they belong. However, it may be useful for them to consider researching groups they know little about. Encourage them to look outside the major religions and to explore spiritual practices (like meditation).

Dan Ariely: *The Context of Our Character* (EXPLAINING)

READING

1. Enron

2. Ariely sets up a scenario that would tempt people to steal. He wants to understand what really governs cheating in everyday life, and the role that conscience plays in our decision-making processes. Students should explain the experiment in their own words,

but make sure they include the setting for the experiment—a college dormitory. They should also address the impulse for students to take a Coke, which was not their property, out of a refrigerator, but not take a dollar bill from a plate of six dollars, as that would register, to a greater degree, in their consciences as "stealing."

3. As we progress technologically, and cash becomes less prominent than credit cards, PayPal, and other symbolic transactions, it will be easier for people to act dishonestly, despite thinking they're still being honest.

Exploratory Writing

1. The lists that your students present to the class should be eclectic, but most will likely refer to taking a friend's piece of clothing, or borrowing a book or movie and not returning it. Make sure they list objects that were taken without the intention of returning them. Ask them to investigate why they believe the items they list are "acceptable" to steal. Ariely's concept—that if you take money from someone, you feel like a thief; but if you take an object, you can come up with all kinds of stories trying to justify your behavior—should be brought up. Ask students to analyze their justifications.

Making Connections

1. Prepare students for this exercise by briefly describing the way to structure a dialogue—implying that each line should present an argument from one author to another. If students have trouble conceiving of the dialogue, ask them to create a setting for inspiration, whether it's a courtroom or a café. A successful dialogue will present evidence of arguments from each reading, as well as illustrate the juxtaposition—and perhaps similar understandings—within the authors' concepts of altruism and dishonesty.

Essay Writing

1. Encourage students to watch more than one video, or read more than one passage from one of Ariely's books, and then pick one that they feel connects with a dilemma they have encountered before. Be sure to note when a student presents clear and specific evidence, exhibits knowledge learned, and also reflects on whether or not his or her behavior has changed following the incident.

GOOD: *Not Your Parents' American Dream: The Pursuit of a New National Ideal* (reporting)

Reading

1. Baby Boomers showed the most willingness (34%); the Silent Generation showed the least (9%).

2. Achieving the American Dream has become more important to people over time. The bar graph in the upper right indicates that each succeeding generation places a greater value on achieving the American Dream than the one before it.

3. The chart to the left of center indicates that 65% of respondents believe that achieving the American Dream without a college education is possible.

Exploratory Writing

1. As long as it meets the stated requirements, a student's infographic may portray any phenomenon, issue, etc. Some possibilities that lend themselves to visual representation are beliefs that change over time, physical processes, and geographic/demographic differ-

ences. If a student is having trouble coming up with a topic or issue, recommend that he or she browse through the essays in the book to find an interesting topic.

Making Connections

1. According to the infographic, people in their twenties are more interested in a "sense of personal fulfillment" than "professional success and the trappings of material wealth." This hierarchy of priorities corresponds with Henig's description of a group of emerging adults disposed to self-exploration, switching jobs, and living with their parents. Students may cite evidence from the infographic and article that adults of the previous generation valued financial stability more and settled down sooner, but they may also use Kenneth Keniston's research on sixties youth culture to argue for similarities. Because students may fall into the demographic discussed in Henig's piece, they may have personal reactions. Make sure they focus on citing evidence and encourage them to do research with which to support their feelings.

Essay Writing

1. Responses will vary but should be anchored by an explanatory definition of the American Dream. Make sure that their definitions connect with the requirements students list. Each essay should also reference the infographic, regardless of its author's viewpoint. If feasible, pave the way for this assignment by having students discuss the meaning of the American Dream with partners or small groups.

Michael Shermer and the Richard Dawkins Foundation for Reason and Science: *The Baloney Detection Kit* (explaining)

Reading

1. If a scientist overlooks counterarguments or alternative explanations, critics will point them out (5:15).

2. A *confirmation bias* is the tendency of people to look for proof of what they already believe (11:20).

3. Shermer calls science the best tool for understanding how the world works (13:10).

Exploratory Writing

1. Challenge students to choose claims they're relatively unfamiliar with. Doing so will minimize bias and enrich their knowledge. Instead of writing in a typical paragraph format, students may structure their responses as a Q&A series or numbered list.

Making Connections

1. Martin supports understanding scientific literacy as "an ongoing commitment to evidence over preconception" (p. 503). With such questions as "Where does the preponderance of evidence point?" and "Are personal beliefs driving the claim?" the Baloney Detection Kit would improve the scientific literacy of anyone not already in the habit of making such inquiries.

Essay Writing

1. Ask students to include their checklist as part of the essay. Encourage them to use items or subjects of personal interest as the objects of their evaluations. For example, an art student might enjoy devising a checklist for what makes a masterpiece.

Iain McGilchrist: *The Divided Brain and the Making of the Western World* (ARGUING)

READING

1. The frontal lobe's purpose is to inhibit the rest of the brain. This inhibition allows people to distance themselves from their immediate experiences (3:30).

2. McGilchrist argues against the notion that one side of the brain governs emotion and the other reason (0:25). Instead, he argues that the left side deals with abstractions and "yields clarity," while the right side handles things that live and change (6:45).

3. Pursuing happiness leads to unhappiness; the proliferation of information has coincided with a decline in understanding it (8:15).

EXPLORATORY WRITING

1. As long as the chosen material comes from a reputable source, students may draw on any print or digital media. They may consider current or outdated research. They may even look at the findings of Roger Sperry, who popularized the divided brain model that McGilchrist dismisses at the beginning of the video.

MAKING CONNECTIONS

1. Opinions will vary, but all should reference specific pedagogical techniques employed by "The Divided Brain" and "Morning of the Stroke." In "The Divided Brain" they include animation, historical context, and persuasive rhetoric. In "Morning of the Stroke" they include simple illustrations and personal narrative. What students have learned may be physiological facts (e.g., the symptoms of a stroke) and/or aspects of information presentation.

ESSAY WRITING

1. Encourage students to consider their own experiences, especially *as students*. Have their educations focused on isolated facts or real-world applications? Ask them why emphasis on one or the other (or equal attention to each) might be beneficial. As for the idea that society today prioritizes the virtual over the real, invite students to contemplate social networking, texting, and the like. In their experiences, does technological communication expedite or inhibit face-to-face interaction? You should also encourage them to do some research into the topic in periodicals or online sources. This is also an excellent opportunity to allow students to do multimedia essays or presentations rather than traditional argument papers.

Know Your Meme: *What People Think I Do / What I Really Do* (EXPLAINING)

READING

1. The meme was posted to Facebook by contemporary artist Garnet Hertz in early February 2012 (0:45).

2. Surfers, Girl Gamer, Surrealist (1:00)

3. Internet Scientist

EXPLORATORY WRITING

1. Students may of course make "student" the subject of their charts. Urge those who do so to be more specific by profiling their major (English, sociology, etc.), a meaningful

extracurricular activity, or a post-college goal (medical school, law school, a particular job, etc.). Alternatively, any occupation or activity is fair game. Suggest that students talk to friends or relatives about outside perspectives on their chosen roles.

Making Connections

1. Replication, mutation, and patterned language ("What so-and-so thinks I do") are among this meme's generic characteristics. The existence of Facebook, particularly its "Share" feature, is one example of a condition favorable to the spread of "What People Think I Do / What I Really Do." Its exploitation of the Internet landscape is one point of its resemblance to other memes in "the age of virality" (p. 559). Conversely, its newness differentiates it from many of the memes Gleick mentions. While the opening notes of Beethoven's Fifth Symphony are centuries old, "What People Think I Do" first appeared in February 2012.

Essay Writing

1. Students may take a practical or philosophical approach to this question. That is, they may focus on cataloging how well they know the important people in their lives, or they may ponder the limits of knowledge and subjectivity. Either way, the people they write about should embody varying degrees or kinds of familiarity. For example, a student may have a clearer idea of her best friend's job as a supermarket cashier than of her older sister's job as a financial consultant. Students may identify positive as well as negative consequences of not fully understanding what those close to them do.

Michael Oatman: *Admittance to a Better Life* (reflecting)

Reading

1. Oatman claims that education was the figurative "rabbit hole through which" he pushed through to begin a better life, as if entering a new, mysterious world of opportunity and intellectual transformation (0:10).

2. Oatman's "new battlefields" are "affirmative action, illegal immigration, and institutional racism" (2:20).

3. Education allowed Oatman to escape his life as a "semi-thug," fraught with the threat of imprisonment and death (1:10).

Exploratory Writing

1. Essays should adhere to the guidelines specified at **http://thisibelieve.org/guidelines/**. These include: Tell a story and be brief, positive, and personal. Encourage authors of first-rate pieces to submit their work to *This I Believe*.

Making Connections

1. While students should draw on material from Oatman and Lee, they may also incorporate their own experiences and independent research. Whatever position they take, their writing should acknowledge, if not rebut, the counterarguments. Invite students to articulate the purpose(s) of college. Career preparation? Intellectual enrichment? Personal growth?

Essay Writing

1. Answers will vary, but most will probably express mixed feelings. College education is typically a years-long commitment that emphasizes general intellectual skills (e.g., criti-

cal thinking) rather than technical proficiency. Students may welcome such a prioritization or reproach it as impractical. Oatman, for one, found it liberating.

Stephen T. Asma: *Gauging Gender* (ARGUING)

READING

1. In the nineteen-seventies and eighties, feminists drew a distinction between sex and gender. The former is a biological concept referring "to the reproductive categories of male and female." The latter has its basis in society rather than nature. It refers to the "socially constructed roles, behaviors, and traits of male and female."

2. Asma first mentions the epistemological argument. It claims that because all human knowledge is mediated and subjective, people can't truly know anything. The second, metaphysical argument uses the existence of intersexed people as evidence that biological sex is a continuum, not one of two categories.

3. Asma rejects the epistemological argument as "unwarranted and melodramatic." While he acknowledges that scientific facts may be mediated, he defends science as "corroborated causal theory." He argues that the occurrence of intersexuality is so rare that "the traditional categories of male and female are accurate pictures of nature." Recognizing a distinction between sex and gender, Asma believes, makes room for both biological data and social theory in the study of identity.

EXPLORATORY WRITING

1. Students' lists should include examples of roles (breadwinner, caregiver, etc.), behaviors (belching, going to the bathroom in groups), and traits (rowdy, sensitive), not just one or two out of those three. Challenge students to generate at least five items for each gender and the neutral category. They may make their graphic organizers manually or digitally.

MAKING CONNECTIONS

1. Responses should draw on both articles. They may recommend an education program that includes an explanation of the biological basis for intersexuality, as described by Asma. They may emphasize the conception of sexual identity as a continuum, as Graff does, and discuss "deviance" in that context. They may call for sharing stories like Daphne Scholinski's and Tyra Hunter's to put a human face on a complex issue and illustrate the need for sensitivity.

ESSAY WRITING

1. Students may approach this essay with apprehension. Reassure them that they needn't discuss anything beyond the limits of their comfort zones. Focusing on gender norms and their relationships to them—whether they play sports, video games, or the flute—is sufficient to fulfill this assignment. Students are welcome but not required to broach the subject of sexuality. All essays should, however, address personal conformity and nonconformity with gender roles.

Jennifer Siebel Newsom: Miss Representation *film trailer* (ARGUING)

READING

1. Answers may range from the headline "Condi Rice, Dominatrix" (0:45) to the comment on "The O'Reilly Factor" about "the PMS and the mood swings" of a hypothetical female president (2:00).

2. An equal number of seven-year-old boys and girls want to become President of the United States (1:20). If the same question was asked to fifteen-year-olds, Caroline Heldman claims you would see a "massive gap emerging."

Exploratory Writing

1. Advocate for variety in media selection. Three types of print media will not offer the breadth of perspective that a news talk show, a television commercial, a Hollywood blockbuster, or a magazine will. Likewise, an article in O, *The Oprah Magazine*, a show on OWN TV, and a post to Oprah's blog will lack the scope of ideological mixture. Encourage students to interrogate the validity of all representations they find, whether positive or negative.

2. The guidelines for the previous question also apply here. In comparing media representations of men and women, students may either focus on specific occurrences or general practices.

Making Connections

1. Whatever students identify as the "trick" of being a woman should be supported by evidence and thoughtful arguments. They may draw on personal experience, famous articulations of womanhood (as Chabon does for manhood with Kipling's "If"), scientific data, and more. Whether their attitudes toward the notion of a female essence are critical or approving, students should each note at least one cause and one effect of it.

Essay Writing

1. Students should feel free to indulge their creativity in this essay or an alternative format. They may develop characters, describe scenes, and even incorporate sample dialogue into their responses, provided they keep the core question of female representation in sight. Connecting their creative choices to the imaginary film's social mission is key to a successful essay.

This time we want to talk about the shuttered mills that once provided a decent life for men and women of every race, and the homes for sale that once belonged to Americans from every religion, every region, every walk of life. This time we want to talk about the fact that the real problem is not that someone who doesn't look like you might take your job; it's that the corporation you work for will ship it overseas for nothing more than a profit.

This time we want to talk about the men and women of every color and creed who serve together, and fight together, and bleed together under the same proud flag. We want to talk about how to bring them home from a war that never should've been authorized and never should've been waged, and we want to talk about how we'll show our patriotism by caring for them, and their families, and giving them the benefits they have earned. 50

I would not be running for president if I didn't believe with all my heart that this is what the vast majority of Americans want for this country. This union may never be perfect, but generation after generation has shown that it can always be perfected. And today, whenever I find myself feeling doubtful or cynical about this possibility, what gives me the most hope is the next generation — the young people whose attitudes and beliefs and openness to change have already made history in this election.

There is one story in particular that I'd like to leave you with today — a story I told when I had the great honor of speaking on Dr. King's birthday at his home church, Ebenezer Baptist, in Atlanta.

There is a young, twenty-three-year-old white woman named Ashley Baia who organized for our campaign in Florence, South Carolina. She had been working to organize a mostly African American community since the beginning of this campaign, and one day she was at a roundtable discussion where everyone went around telling their story and why they were there.

And Ashley said that when she was nine years old, her mother got cancer. And because she had to miss days of work, she was let go and lost her health care. They had to file for bankruptcy, and that's when Ashley decided that she had to do something to help her mom.

She knew that food was one of their most expensive costs, and so Ashley convinced her mother that what she really liked and really wanted to eat more than anything else was mustard and relish sandwiches. Because that was the cheapest way to eat. 55

She did this for a year until her mom got better, and she told everyone at the roundtable that the reason she joined our campaign was so that she could help the millions of other children in the country who want and need to help their parents too.

Now Ashley might have made a different choice. Perhaps somebody told her along the way that the source of her mother's problems were blacks who were on welfare and too lazy to work, or Hispanics who were coming into the country illegally. But she didn't. She sought out allies in her fight against injustice.

Anyway, Ashley finishes her story and then goes around the room and asks everyone else why they're supporting the campaign. They all have different stories and reasons. Many bring up a specific issue. And finally they come to this elderly black man who's been sitting there quietly the entire time. And Ashley asks him why he's there. And he does not bring up a specific issue. He does not say health care or the economy. He does not say education or the war. He does not say that he was there because of Barack Obama. He simply says to everyone in the room, "I am here because of Ashley."

"I'm here because of Ashley." By itself, that single moment of recognition between that young white girl and that old black man is not enough. It is not enough to give health care to the sick, or jobs to the jobless, or education to our children.

But it is where we start. It is where our union grows stronger. And as so many generations have come to realize over the course of the two hundred and twenty-one years since a band of patriots signed that document in Philadelphia, that is where the perfection begins. 60

▪ QUESTIONS

Reading

1. How does Obama characterize his former pastor, Rev. Jeremiah Wright?
2. How does Obama describe segregated schools? What remarks does he make about the school system?
3. In what ways is Obama's speech *reflective*? In what ways is it *argumentative* or *polemical*? Find and list examples of each mode of writing in Obama's speech.

Exploratory Writing

1. Highlight, underline, or flag the quotations that Obama uses in this speech. Consider not only the content of the quotes but the types of people he is quoting. What purpose does it serve to invoke the preamble to the Constitution in this speech? What purpose does it serve to invoke William Faulkner?
2. Without thinking too much about it or doing any extra research, write a personal response describing your instant reaction to this speech. Compare your response with that of another student. What do the different responses tell you about the effectiveness of the speech?
3. Some writing—such as plays, speeches, and slam poetry—is designed to be performed in front of an audience. List some differences between reading words on a page and hearing them spoken. Why would a politician choose to give a speech rather than simply post its text online or publish it in newspapers?

Making Connections

1. Martin Luther King Jr.'s famous "Letter from Birmingham Jail" (p. 341) was a response to eight white Alabama clergymen who published a statement speaking out against antisegregation demonstrations in the streets. Obama's speech is also a statement in response to a controversy. Compare and contrast the different ways that King and

Obama address the problem of race. How does each man anticipate his opponents' arguments?

2. George Orwell ("Politics and the English Language," p. 313) offers six rules for political writing. Analyze Obama's speech according to these rules, as well as Orwell's other comments about political writing. How do you think Orwell would respond to this speech? Would he find it vague and obfuscating, or clear and honest?

Essay Writing

1. Imagine that you are running for president. Write a passionate speech describing why you are running and what you plan to do if you're elected. (An interesting bit of trivia about Obama's speech—although presidential candidates usually have their speechwriters write the first drafts of their speeches based on their ideas, in this case Obama wrote the first draft, and then got editing help from his speechwriter, Jon Favreau.)

ARGUING

Regarding the Pain of Others

Susan Sontag

One of America's leading social commentators, Susan Sontag (1933–2004) was hailed as a brilliant critic and provocative thinker. Raised in Arizona and California, she studied at a number of universities, among them the University of Chicago, Harvard, and Oxford. When her formal schooling finished, she began writing essays for such magazines as the *New Yorker* and the *New York Review of Books*. Beginning in 1964 with "Notes on Camp"—an influential essay on the avant-garde—her work was both widely discussed and well received. She published two groundbreaking collections of essays on culture and politics in the 1960s: *Against Interpretation* (1966) and *Styles of Radical Will* (1969). Over the next several decades, she continued to explore a wide range of cultural phenomena, from illness to art. In later years, she published work in other genres, including a best-selling historical novel, *The Volcano Lover* (1992). The following piece is taken from *Regarding the Pain of Others* (2003), a book on war imagery in which the author decried the birth of a "culture of spectatorship," arguing that it "neutralized the moral force of photographs of atrocities." Sontag's many honors and awards included membership in the American Academy of Arts and Sciences, a MacArthur Fellowship, and a National Book Award.

To catch a death actually happening and embalm it for all time is something only cameras can do, and pictures taken by photographers out in the field of the moment of (or just before) death are among the most celebrated and often reproduced of war photographs. There can be no suspicion about the authenticity of what is being shown in the picture taken by Eddie Adams in February 1968 of the chief of the South Vietnamese national police, Brigadier General Nguyen Ngoc Loan, shooting a Vietcong suspect in a street in Saigon. Nevertheless, it was staged—by General Loan, who had led the prisoner, hands tied behind his back, out to the street where journalists had gathered; he would not have carried out the summary execution there had they not been available to witness it. Positioned beside his prisoner so that his profile and the prisoner's face were visible to the cameras behind him, Loan aimed point-blank. Adams's picture shows the moment the bullet has been fired; the dead man, grimacing, has not started to fall. As for the viewer, this viewer, even many years after the picture was taken . . . well, one can gaze at these faces for a long time and not come to the end of the mystery, and the indecency, of such co-spectatorship.

More upsetting is the opportunity to look at people who know they have been condemned to die: the cache of six thousand photographs taken between 1975 and 1979 at a secret prison in a former high school in Tuol Sleng, a suburb of Phnom Penh, the killing house of more than fourteen thousand Cambodians charged with being either "intellectuals" or "counter-revolutionaries" — the documentation of this atrocity courtesy of the Khmer Rouge record keepers, who had each sit for a photograph just before being executed.* A selection of these pictures in a book titled *The Killing Fields* makes it possible, decades later, to stare back at the faces staring into the camera— therefore at us. The Spanish Republican soldier has just died, if we may believe the claim made for that picture, which Capa took at some distance from his subject: we see no more than a grainy figure, a body and head, an energy, swerving from the camera as he falls. These Cambodian women and men of all ages, including many children, photographed from a few feet away, usually in half figure, are — as in Titian's *The Flaying of Marsyas*, where Apollo's knife is eternally about to descend — forever looking at death, forever about to be murdered, forever wronged. And the viewer is in the same position as the lackey behind the camera; the experience is sickening. The prison photographer's name is known — Nhem Ein — and can be cited. Those he photographed, with their stunned faces, their emaciated torsos, the number tags pinned to the top of their shirts, remain an aggregate: anonymous victims.

And even if named, unlikely to be known to "us." When Woolf notes that one of the photographs she has been sent shows a corpse of a man or woman so mangled that it could as well be that of a dead pig, her point is that the scale of war's murderousness destroys what identifies people as individuals, even as human beings.[1] This, of course, is how war looks when it is seen from afar, as an image.

Victims, grieving relatives, consumers of news — all have their own nearness to or distance from war. The frankest representations of war, and of disaster-injured bodies, are of those who seem most foreign, therefore least likely to be known. With subjects closer to home, the photographer is expected to be more discreet.

When, in October 1862, a month after the battle of Antietam, photographs taken by Gardner and O'Sullivan were exhibited at Brady's Manhattan gallery, the *New York Times* commented: 5

> The living that throng Broadway care little perhaps for the Dead at Antietam, but we fancy they would jostle less carelessly down the great thoroughfare, saunter less at their ease, were a few dripping bodies, fresh from the field, laid along the pavement. There would be a gathering up of skirts and a careful picking of way . . .

*Photographing political prisoners and alleged counter-revolutionaries just before their execution was also standard practice in the Soviet Union in the 1930s and 1940s, as recent research into the NKVD files in the Baltic and Ukrainian archives, as well as the central Lubyanka archives, has disclosed.—Au.

[1]*Virginia Woolf* (1882–1941): English novelist and essayist, who reflected on the roots of war in her book *Three Guineas*.—Eds.

Concurring in the perennial charge that those whom war spares are callously indifferent to the sufferings beyond their purview did not make the reporter less ambivalent about the immediacy of the photograph.

> The dead of the battlefield come to us very rarely even in dreams. We see the list in the morning paper at breakfast but dismiss its recollection with the coffee. But Mr. Brady has done something to bring home to us the terrible reality and earnestness of war. If he has not brought bodies and laid them in our dooryards and along the streets, he has done something very like it. . . . These pictures have a terrible distinctness. By the aid of the magnifying-glass, the very features of the slain may be distinguished. We would scarce choose to be in the gallery, when one of the women bending over them should recognize a husband, a son, or a brother in the still, lifeless lines of bodies, that lie ready for the gaping trenches.

Admiration is mixed with disapproval of the pictures for the pain they might give the female relatives of the dead. The camera brings the viewer close, too close; supplemented by a magnifying glass—for this is a double-lens story—the "terrible distinctness" of the pictures gives unnecessary, indecent information. Yet the *Times* reporter cannot resist the melodrama that mere words supply (the "dripping bodies" ready for "the gaping trenches"), while reprehending the intolerable realism of the image.

New demands are made on reality in the era of cameras. The real thing may not be fearsome enough, and therefore needs to be enhanced; or reenacted more convincingly. Thus, the first newsreel ever made of a battle—a much-publicized incident in Cuba during the Spanish-American War of 1898 known as the Battle of San Juan Hill—in fact shows a charge staged shortly afterward by Colonel Theodore Roosevelt and his volunteer cavalry unit, the Rough Riders, for the Vitagraph cameramen, the actual charge up the hill, after it was filmed, having been judged insufficiently dramatic. Or the images may be too terrible, and need to be suppressed in the name of propriety or of patriotism—like the images showing, without appropriate partial concealment, our dead. To display the dead, after all, is what the enemy does. In the Boer War (1899–1902), after their victory at Spion Kop in January 1900, the Boers thought it would be morale-building for their own troops to circulate a horrifying picture of dead British soldiers. Taken by an unknown Boer photographer ten days after the British defeat, which had cost the lives of thirteen hundred of their soldiers, it gives an intrusive view down a long shallow trench packed with unburied bodies. What is particularly aggressive about the image is the absence of a landscape. The trench's receding jumble of bodies fills the whole picture space. British indignation upon hearing of this latest Boer outrage was keen, if stiffly expressed: To have made public such pictures, declared *Amateur Photographer*, "serves no useful purpose and appeals to the morbid side of human nature solely."

There had always been censorship, but for a long time it remained desultory, at the pleasure of generals and heads of state. The first organized ban on press photography at the front came during the First World War; both the German and French high commands allowed only a few selected military photographers near the fighting. (Censorship of the press by the British General Staff was less inflexible.) And it took another fifty years, and the relaxation of censorship with the first televised war coverage, to understand what impact shocking photographs could have on the domestic public. During the Vietnam era, war photography became, normatively, a criticism of war. This was bound to have consequences: Mainstream media are not in the business of making people feel queasy about the struggles for which they are being mobilized, much less of disseminating propaganda against waging war.

Since then, censorship—the most extensive kind, self-censorship, as well as censorship imposed by the military—has found a large and influential number of apologists. At the start of the British campaign in the Falklands in April 1982, the government of Margaret Thatcher granted access to only two photojournalists—among those refused was a master war photographer, Don McCullin—and only three batches of film reached London before the islands were recaptured in May. No direct television transmission was permitted. There had not been such drastic restrictions on the reporting of a British military operation since the Crimean War. It proved harder for the American authorities to duplicate the Thatcher controls on the reporting of their own foreign adventures. What the American military promoted during the Gulf War in 1991 were images of the techno war: the sky above the dying, filled with light-traces of missiles and shells—images that illustrated America's absolute military superiority over its enemy. American television viewers weren't allowed to see footage acquired by NBC (which the network then declined to run) of what that superiority could wreak: the fate of thousands of Iraqi conscripts who, having fled Kuwait City at the end of the war, on February 27, were carpet bombed with explosives, napalm, radioactive DU (depleted uranium) rounds, and cluster bombs as they headed north, in convoys and on foot, on the road to Basra, Iraq—a slaughter notoriously described by one American officer as a "turkey shoot." And most American operations in Afghanistan in late 2001 were off-limits to news photographers.

The terms for allowing the use of cameras at the front for nonmilitary purposes have become much stricter as war has become an activity prosecuted with increasingly exact optical devices for tracking the enemy. There is no war without photography, that notable aesthete of war Ernst Jünger observed in 1930, thereby refining the irrepressible identification of the camera and the gun, "shooting" a subject and shooting a human being. War-making and picture-taking are congruent activities: "It is the same intelligence, whose weapons of annihilation can locate the enemy to the exact second and meter," wrote Jünger, "that labors to preserve the great historical event in fine detail."*

*Thus, thirteen years before the destruction of Guernica, Arthur Harris, later the chief of Bombing Command in the Royal Air Force during the Second World War, then a young RAF squadron leader in Iraq, described the air campaign to crush the rebellious natives in this

The preferred current American way of war-making has expanded on this model. Television, whose access to the scene is limited by government controls and by self-censorship, serves up the war as images. The war itself is waged as much as possible at a distance, through bombing, whose targets can be chosen, on the basis of instantly relayed information and visualizing technology, from continents away: the daily bombing operations in Afghanistan in late 2001 and early 2002 were directed from U.S. Central Command in Tampa, Florida. The aim is to produce a sufficiently punishing number of casualties on the other side while minimizing opportunities for the enemy to inflict any casualties at all; American and allied soldiers who die in vehicle accidents or from "friendly fire" (as the euphemism has it) both count and don't count. 10

In the era of tele-controlled warfare against innumerable enemies of American power, policies about what is to be seen and not seen by the public are still being worked out. Television news producers and newspaper and magazine photo editors make decisions every day which firm up the wavering consensus about the boundaries of public knowledge. Often their decisions are cast as judgments about "good taste"—always a repressive standard when invoked by institutions. Staying within the bounds of good taste was the primary reason given for not showing any of the horrific pictures of the dead taken at the site of the World Trade Center in the immediate aftermath of the attack on September 11, 2001. (Tabloids are usually bolder than broadsheet papers in printing grisly images; a picture of a severed hand lying in the rubble of the World Trade Center ran in one late edition of New York's *Daily News* shortly after the attack; it seems not to have appeared in any other paper.) And television news, with its much larger audience and therefore greater responsiveness to pressures from advertisers, operates under even stricter, for the most part self-policed constraints on what is "proper" to air. This novel insistence on good taste in a culture saturated with commercial incentives to lower standards of taste may be puzzling. But it makes sense if understood as obscuring a host of concerns and anxieties about public order and public morale that cannot be named, as well as pointing to the inability otherwise to formulate or defend traditional conventions of how to mourn. What can be shown, what should not be shown—few issues arouse more public clamor.

The other argument often used to suppress pictures cites the rights of relatives. When a weekly newspaper in Boston briefly posted online a propaganda video made in Pakistan that showed the "confession" (that he was Jewish) and subsequent ritual slaughter of the kidnapped American journalist Daniel Pearl in Karachi in early 2002, a vehement debate took place in which the right of Pearl's widow to be spared more pain was pitted against the newspaper's right to print and post what it saw fit and the public's right to see. The video was

newly acquired British colony, complete with photographic proof of the success of the mission. "The Arab and the Kurd," he wrote in 1924, "now know what real bombing means in casualties and damage; they now know that within forty-five minutes a full-sized village (vide attached photos of Kushan-Al-Ajaza) can be practically wiped out and a third of its inhabitants killed by four or five machines which offer them no real target, no opportunity for glory as warriors, no effective means of escape."—Au.

quickly taken off-line. Notably, both sides treated the three and a half minutes of horror only as a snuff film. Nobody could have learned from the debate that the video had other footage, a montage of stock accusations (for instance, images of Ariel Sharon sitting with George W. Bush at the White House, Palestinian children killed in Israeli attacks), that it was a political diatribe and ended with dire threats and a list of specific demands—all of which might suggest that it was worth suffering through (if you could bear it) to confront better the particular viciousness and intransigence of the forces that murdered Pearl. It is easier to think of the enemy as just a savage who kills, then holds up the head of his prey for all to see.

With our dead, there has always been a powerful interdiction against showing the naked face. The photographs taken by Gardner and O'Sullivan still shock because the Union and Confederate soldiers lie on their backs, with the faces of some clearly visible. American soldiers fallen on the battlefield were not shown again in a major publication for many wars, not, indeed, until the taboo-shattering picture by George Strock that *Life* published in September 1943—it had initially been withheld by the military censors—of three soldiers killed on the beach during a landing in New Guinea. (Though "Dead GIs on Buna Beach" is invariably described as showing three soldiers lying face down in the wet sand, one of the three lies on his back, but the angle from which the picture was taken conceals his head.) By the time of the landing in France—June 6, 1944—photographs of anonymous American casualties had appeared in a number of newsmagazines, always prone or shrouded or with their faces turned away. This is a dignity not thought necessary to accord to others.

The more remote or exotic the place, the more likely we are to have full frontal views of the dead and dying. Thus postcolonial Africa exists in the consciousness of the general public in the rich world—besides through its sexy music—mainly as a succession of unforgettable photographs of large-eyed victims, starting with figures in the famine lands of Biafra in the late 1960s to the survivors of the genocide of nearly a million Rwandan Tutsis in 1994 and, a few years later, the children and adults whose limbs were hacked off during the program of mass terror conducted by the RUF, the rebel forces in Sierra Leone. (More recently, the photographs are of whole families of indigent villagers dying of AIDS.) These sights carry a double message. They show a suffering that is outrageous, unjust, and should be repaired. They confirm that this is the sort of thing which happens in that place. The ubiquity of those photographs, and those horrors, cannot help but nourish belief in the inevitability of tragedy in the benighted or backward—that is, poor—parts of the world.

15 Comparable cruelties and misfortunes used to take place in Europe, too; cruelties that surpass in volume and luridness anything we might be shown now from the poor parts of the world occurred in Europe only sixty years ago. But horror seems to have vacated Europe, vacated it for long enough to make the present pacified state of affairs seem inevitable. (That there could be death camps and a siege and civilians slaughtered by the thousands and thrown

into mass graves on European soil fifty years after the end of the Second World War gave the war in Bosnia and the Serb campaign of killing in Kosovo their special, anachronistic interest. But one of the main ways of understanding the war crimes committed in southeastern Europe in the 1990s has been to say that the Balkans, after all, were never really part of Europe.) Generally, the grievously injured bodies shown in published photographs are from Asia or Africa. This journalistic custom inherits the centuries-old practice of exhibiting exotic—that is, colonized—human beings: Africans and denizens of remote Asian countries were displayed like zoo animals in ethnological exhibitions mounted in London, Paris, and other European capitals from the sixteenth until the early twentieth century. In *The Tempest*, Trinculo's first thought upon coming across Caliban is that he could be put on exhibit in England: "[N]ot a holiday fool there but would give it piece of silver. . . . When they will not give a doit to relieve a lame beggar, they will lay out ten to see a dead Indian." The exhibition in photographs of cruelties inflicted on those with darker complexions in exotic countries continues this offering, oblivious to the considerations that deter such displays of our own victims of violence; for the other, even when not an enemy, is regarded only as someone to be seen, not someone (like us) who also sees. But surely the wounded Taliban soldier begging for his life whose fate was pictured prominently in the *New York Times* also had a wife, children, parents, sisters and brothers, some of whom may one day come across the three color photographs of their husband, father, son, brother being slaughtered—if they have not already seen them.

▪ QUESTIONS

Reading

1. How does Sontag characterize the role of television in the "preferred current American way of war-making" (paragraph 10)?
2. What are two commonly used arguments in favor of suppressing the publication of images of the dead? Summarize Sontag's criticisms of these arguments.
3. What is the main purpose of Sontag's essay? Do you find her argument persuasive? Why or why not?

Exploratory Writing

1. Only cameras, according to Sontag, can "catch a death actually happening and embalm it for all time" (paragraph 1). Do you agree with this statement, or do you think that written words can "catch," or capture, an event just as persuasively as a photograph?
2. Sontag points out the irony of one reporter's use of sensationalistic phrases ("'dripping bodies' ready for 'the gaping trenches'") within a condemnation of graphic images (paragraph 5). Make a double-entry list comparing the "shock value" of photographs versus that of the written word. Use a separate sheet of paper if you need more room.

Photographs	Writing

3. "New demands are made on reality in the era of cameras," Sontag states. "The real thing may not be fearsome enough and therefore needs to be enhanced; or reenacted more convincingly" (paragraph 6). She discusses how images can be manipulated or staged to intensify the drama of war events, or suppressed to downplay their importance. List examples, outside of a war context, of ways that images are regularly manipulated and altered for effect.
4. Split up into teams, and stage a debate on the subject of whether American newspapers should be allowed to publish photographs of people who have been (or are being) killed in war. Your team should use at least three well-crafted arguments to make your case.

Making Connections

1. Sontag argues that "[T]he more remote or exotic the place, the more likely we are to have full frontal views of the dead and dying" (paragraph 14). She is suggesting that images of people who seem remote or less like us are less likely to be censored. How do the soldiers who write home in "Soldiers' Stories" (p. 374) represent Iraq as a place? Do they suggest that it feels remote or exotic to them? Does their attitude toward the place shape what they do or don't say when they write home?
2. George Orwell ("Politics and the English Language," p. 313) talks about how language can be used in political writing for the purposes of distortion and obfuscation. Drawing on Orwell's examples as well as Sontag's, discuss differences between using manipulative language in war reporting and publishing manipulated images.

Essay Writing

1. Consider Sontag's remarks on the "double message" carried by photographs of dead and dying people in "exotic" places (paragraph 14). Using online newspaper archives, find three articles with photographs from the past two years documenting catastrophic events, war, or atrocities in Africa, Asia, or Latin America. How does each article support or refute Sontag's thesis?
2. Write an essay describing a photograph that had a great personal impact on your life and beliefs. What was so powerful about this image?

REFLECTING

Soldiers' Stories

Dispatches from Iraq

Various Authors

The following pieces were compiled from e-mails and journal entries written by soldiers serving in the war in Iraq during 2003–2004. Sponsored by the National Endowment for the Arts (NEA) since April 2004, Operation Homecoming is a project that organized fifty-nine writing workshops for military personnel in twenty-seven overseas and domestic military installations in order to encourage them to document their experiences. The NEA has also received over 1,200 writing submissions, with almost a hundred anthologized in *Operation Homecoming: Iraq, Afghanistan, and the Home Front in the Words of U.S. Troops and Their Families* (2006). In 2007, a documentary with interviews and dramatic readings aired on PBS. The soldiers' stories — poetry, fiction, and nonfiction — will be preserved in the U.S. National Archives and Records Administration in College Park, Maryland.

Captain Ryan Kelly, thirty-six, Denver, Colorado. E-mail to his mother, from Camp Buehring, Kuwait. December 2003.

The worst thing here is not the searing heat or the cold nights. It's the waiting. Waiting for the wind to quit blowing and the sand to quit grinding against your skin. Waiting for a moment of privacy in a tent packed with seventy other men, in a camp packed with seven hundred other tents, in a base packed with fifteen thousand soldiers, all looking for a clean place to go to the bathroom. . . . Waiting for the bone-rattling coughs from dust finer than powdered sugar to stop attacking the lungs. Waiting for the generals to order the battalion to move north, toward Tikrit, where others—Iraqis—are also waiting: waiting for us . . .

A quick look around my tent will show you who is fighting this war. There's Ed, a fifty-eight-year-old grandfather from Delaware. He never complains about his age, but his body does, in aches and creaks and in the slowness of his movements on late nights and cold mornings.

There's Lindon, a thirty-one-year-old, black-as-coal ex-Navy man from Trinidad who speaks every word with a smile. His grandfather owned an animal farm and lived next to his grandmother, who owned an adjacent cocoa field. They met as children.

There's Sergeant Lilian, a single mother who left her five-year-old daughter at home with a frail and aging mother because nobody else was there to help.

There's Melissa and Mike, two sergeants who got married inside the Fort Dix chapel a month before we deployed—so in love, yet forbidden, because 5 of fraternization policies, even to hold hands in front of other soldiers. But if you watch them closely, you can catch them stealing secret glances at each other. Sometimes I'll see them sitting together on a box of bottled water tenderly sharing a lunch. They are so focussed on each other that the world seems to dissolve around them. If they were on a picnic in Sheep Meadow in Central Park, instead of here, surrounded by sand and war machines, it would be the same. War's a hell of a way to spend your honeymoon.

There's Sergeant First Class Ernesto, thirty-eight, a professional soldier whose father owns a coffee plantation in Puerto Rico and whose four-year-old daughter cries when he calls.

There's Noah, a twenty-three-year-old motocross stuntman, who wears his hair on the ragged edge of Army regulations. He's been asking me for months to let him ship his motorcycle to the desert. I keep telling him no.

There's Chief Warrant Officer 4 Jerry, the "linedog" of aviation maintenance, whose father was wounded in WWII a month after he arrived in combat. On D-Day, a grenade popped up from behind a hedge grove near a Normandy beach and spewed burning white phosphorus all over his body, consigning the man to a cane and special shoes for the rest of his life. CWO4 Jerry lives out on the flight line, going from aircraft to aircraft with his odd bag of tools, like a doctor making house calls. He works so hard that I often have to order him to take a day off.

There's Martina, twenty-two, a jet-black-haired girl, who fled Macedonia with her family to escape the genocide of the civil war in Bosnia. Her family ran away to prevent the draft from snatching up her older brother and consuming him in a war they considered absurd and illegal. A few years later, the family, with no place else to run, watched helplessly as the United States flew their daughter into Iraq. She's not even a U.S. citizen, just a foreigner fighting for a foreign country on foreign soil for a foreign cause. She has become one of my best soldiers.

There is William (Wild Bill), a twenty-three-year-old kid from Jersey with a strong chin and a James Dean–like grin. The day before we went on leave, he roared up in front of the barracks and beamed at me from behind the wheel of a gleaming white monster truck that he bought for fifteen hundred dollars. Three days later, he drove it into the heart of Amish country, where the transmission clanked and clattered to a stop. He drank beer all night at some stranger's house, and in the morning sold him the truck. Kicker is, he made it back to post in time for my formation. 10

There's Top, my First Sergeant, my no-nonsense right-hand man. He's my counsel, my confidant, my friend. He's the top enlisted man in the company, with twenty-eight years in the Army, and would snap his back, and anybody else's, for that matter, for any one of our men. Last year, his pit bull attacked his wife's smaller dog—a terrier of some sort, I think. As she tried to pry them apart, the pit bit off the tip of her ring finger. Top punched the pit bull in the skull and eventually separated the two. A hospital visit and half a pack of cigarettes later, he learned the blow broke his hand. He bought her a new wedding ring in Kuwait.

And on and on and on . . .

I hope you are doing well, Mom. I'm doing my best. For them. For me. For you. I hope it's good enough.

Commander Edward W. Jewell, MD, forty-eight, Washington, D.C. Journal entries, hospital ship USNS Comfort. *March–April 2003.*

March 27. Q: The *Comfort* is a large non-combat hospital ship protected by the most powerful Navy, Army, and Air Force in history. What is there to be afraid of? A: Everything. Danger is all around us. We are really very close to the action. At times we see oil fires near the shore. However, we cannot really see the combat. We are not afraid of the Iraqi military. If they try to fire a rocket at us it would be easily shot down by artillery on the ground, aircraft, or by naval gunnery/rockets. However, we believe there are mines in the Gulf. Purportedly, small boats have approached the *Comfort* several times. When this happens we call in a helo and launch our small boat to run them off. How can we possibly see one of these things in the dark? I think it would be very easy for a terrorist to attack this ship with an explosive-laden small boat. Very easy. Would the Iraqis attack a hospital ship if they could? Why not? In their view, they were invaded by mercenary infidels who deserve no better. A surgeon buddy of mine, Mike from Massachusetts, thinks an attack on our ship is a near-given, with a 50% chance of success. However, he is a proctologist and a Red Sox fan and naturally pessimistic.

March 28. Sickening sight: A helicopter's downwash blows a stack of letters 15 overboard. Who knows what was lost? Last letter to save a troubled relationship? A fat check? Notice of tax audit? We'll never know. That's war.

The doctors are all bored from underutilization, but the surgeons seem particularly restless. There are so many of them and not enough cases to fill the time.

The Army helos cannot fly patients out to us in bad weather. The visibility has been poor the last three days, with choppy seas. We were to have received twenty or thirty new patients, but they never made it because of the weather.

March 29. The old Navy jargon "belay my last," meaning disregard my last statement, applies to my commentary from yesterday. We got creamed with fresh casualties last night, thirty new patients, both sides, all needing immediate and significant intervention. The injuries are horrifying. Ruptured eyeballs. Children missing limbs. Large burns. Genitals and buttocks blown off. Grotesque fractures. Gunshot wounds to the head. Faces blown apart. Paraplegics from spine injuries. The number of X-ray studies performed last night in a short period of time is so great that it causes the entire system to crash under the burden of electronic data it is being fed.

Our patients are mostly Iraqis. Along with their combat wounds, they are dirty, undernourished, and dehydrated. One rumor says that we will treat all the wounded Iraqi EPWs (enemy prisoners of war) for the duration of the war, and these are the only patients we will see. If true, this would, in effect, make the *Comfort* a prison hospital ship. The corpsmen on the wards have to guard the prisoners and keep them from communicating with one another to prevent rebellion. As medical people we are trained to care for the sick; it is difficult to stay mindful that these patients are the enemy and could fight back against us.

April 5. The Saturday entertainment is karaoke. I usually like it, but tonight it's not for me. The room is hot and crowded, and the whole event just too loud. I step out for air. On deck is a different world. For safety we are on "darken ship" status now. This means no external lights, and all windows are covered to block light transmission. The goal is to make the ship invisible or nearly so to evildoers trying to locate the ship in the dark. It does actually work. The night is moonless, skies only a slight haze. It is very dark outside. So dark my eyes need ten minutes to fully accommodate. There is a magnificent display of stars tonight, reminiscent of what you see in Utah. The night has a misty, Impressionist feel. People moving about in the night are just vague dark shapes. Voices are low. Boys and girls being what they are, couples are forming on *Comfort.* They drift into obscure corners. Ghostlike green blobs of fluorescence rise and fall in the water. Jellyfish. Thousands of jellyfish drift and bob around the ship. I watch the stars until my neck hurts. Someone is singing in the dark in a beautiful, strange language. He tells me it is Hindi, and he is actually practicing for karaoke. I hope he wins.

April 7. The prisoners are kept on a separate ward, deep in the bowels of the ship, for security reasons, and the location is kept obscure. There is concern for the security of the prisoners. Lawyers run everything now, and we actually have a lawyer on board whose primary job is to ensure we comply with all tenets of the Geneva Conventions. There are press on board all the time.

Most of the Iraqis show real appreciation for the care rendered them. I would love to talk to them about family, etc., but we have been firmly warned not to do this. The prisoners are a sad lot. I feel for them. Most were not real soldiers, just conscripts forced to fight for the Big Lie, Saddam Hussein. Some of these guys, however, were the feared fedayeen suicide commandos. In general, the prisoners are badly wounded. They look defeated and glad to be out of combat.

April 11. The number of patients coming aboard *Comfort* is simply out of control. Like the doctors on *M*A*S*H,* we have grown to hate the rumble of helos on the flight deck, since it usually means another load of Iraqi patients. Today we received at least thirty-five more patients. New in the last twenty-four hours is a big influx of sick and injured children. We have only one doctor with residency training in pediatrics. Some of the kids are very ill. One was DOA from drinking kerosene. "They" are sending everyone here. We don't know who "they" are, and no one seems to have a handle on where these patients come from, when they are arriving, or who is sending them. We take them all and do our best.

There is no long-term-care plan for all these patients, and the ones who survive will need long-term care. Where will they go? Who will care for them after we leave? We have become deeply involved in a humanitarian crisis that we will not be able to extricate ourselves from.

April 15. Civilian Iraqi patients are being allowed to move around the ship more (with escorts, of course) as their conditions improve. I saw a teenager today smiling and shaking hands with everyone. As he bent to tie his shoe, his sleeve slid up. I saw he had a tattoo on his upper arm. A fresh Marine Corps "globe and anchor." Wow! Hearts and minds, indeed. 25

April 17. We began in earnest to discharge stable EPW patients from the *Comfort.* Close to thirty sent back today. Sent somewhere. Sadly, these guys don't realize they are not being repatriated. For security reasons, they cannot be told where they are really going. Looking at these pathetic-looking fellows, it is easy to forget that they were the enemy, and many probably still wish us harm. According to an ICU doctor, one of the most timid-looking teenage patients is actually an identified terrorist. Another patient awoke from surgery disoriented to place; he asked if he had been sent home to Syria!

April 21. Comfort receives a visit from CENTCOM, the name for the headquarters group for the entire war. A group of their medical-admin bureaucrats, primarily Army, are on board to give us an overview of the medical situation in Iraq and Kuwait. We hope to hear something concrete about our own status: What is planned for us, how can we offload our patients, and, mostly, when can we go home? Instead of insight and clarity, we got more obscuring mud in the eye. The formal presentation is tiresome, trite, and uninformative. It takes fifteen minutes to get the PowerPoint working. The speaker uses too much Army-specific jargon. He admits that the *Comfort* is the most stable, established, and productive medical unit in the theater. The hospitals in Iraq have been looted and are barely functioning.

A Q&A session follows. The discussion is as overheated as the room. Pointed questions regarding why we got stuck with so many patients go ignored or glossed over. It is explained that the Iraqi casualties were put on helicopters by well-meaning, altruistic U.S. troops, even though they were told not to do this. They offer no explanation for why all the Iraqis ended up in our hospital. They thank us for all our hard work, tell us that they "feel our pain," and say that war is hell. It is not convincing or reassuring to us. These guys all look rested, tanned, and pain-free to us.

Sergeant Timothy J. Gaestel, twenty-two, Austin, Texas. E-mail to his father, from south of Baghdad. September 21, 2003.

Hey, Dad, this is your son. I finally get to write y'all a letter. First off, let me tell you we made it here safe and so far, but everything is going very good. Now, Dad, I know that you have already received a phone call that tells you I am OK, but I want you to know exactly what happened. . . . We were heading south down Highway 8 and I was gunning for the second truck. Byrd was driving and my chief was the passenger. We got off Highway 8 onto Ambush Alley, the route we didn't take going up there. I was in the back of the truck with my 240B machine gun, and the S2 [an intelligence officer] wanted to ride in the back of the truck with me, since I was the only one back there. We were at the end of the convoy at this point so we were really hauling ass, driving down the wrong side of the road and all that, just so we could get to the front of the convoy. My buddy Eddie was a badass driver and kept us from getting in wrecks a few times. But still able to get the mission done. The XO [executive officer] truck was behind us and needed to get in front, not to mention the fact that I had his Gatorade I was supposed to throw to him the next time they passed us.

At that exact moment, a loud and thunderous boom went off and pushed me all the way to the front of where my 240B was mounted. I knew something had just happened and when I turned around I could see two large smoke clouds on each side of the road. The first thing I thought was that I had just been hit in the back by an IED [improvised explosive device]. It wasn't like I felt as if I was going to die, more like "Man, that really hurt." At that moment, I reached around and felt my back and pulled my hand back, and it was covered with blood. Before that I honestly thought it had just hit my IBA [interceptor body armor]. It turns out that it had hit my IBA and gone right through it.

I lay down in the back of the truck, but this didn't seem like a good idea and I didn't have my weapon and had to yell at the S2 to give me my weapon— I didn't want an ambush to happen and for me to not have my weapon. So I stood up on my knees and yelled again to him to man the 240B; he was scared, but that's what happens when you don't ever get any kind of training and you sit in an office all day. This guy didn't react very well when I showed him my back—he started flipping out and yelling "Oh, G., you got hit man, oh he's hit bad, man." This is the last thing that you tell someone who has just been hit in the back and is bleeding. As you can imagine, I was pretty pissed off at this point, and I showed my anger toward the people in the town that we were driving through. I had my M4 rifle at the ready and my trigger finger on the trigger and was just waiting for someone to give me a reason to have me put it from safe to semi. I maintained my military bearing as well as one could in that situation. I sure wanted to shoot the bastard that had just set the IED off.

As we were making our way back to the FOB [forward operating base] at that last street, I could no longer sit up straight and my back was killing me. There was a major who was our field surgeon waiting for me in the front of the gate to check me out. This guy didn't reassure me, either. When I told him that I was OK, he looked at me and said, "Look, son, you may have internal bleeding." Now I was scared. They rushed me to the aid station, where I talked to some sergeant majors and the colonel. In like fifteen minutes, in my brown underwear, green socks up to my knees, and a blanket, I was rushed out to the landing zone where a chopper took me to CSH [Combat Support Hospital] 28, in downtown Baghdad. The flight through Baghdad was amazing, too, you could see the whole city and all the buildings and stuff, it was very strange. The helicopter pilot was a badass as well, he had to do a wartime landing, which is really fast and quick; it was cool. Now, Dad, I hadn't seen a female in twenty-one days, and so you could imagine I was excited when I looked down off the helicopter as we were coming in for a landing to see a very beautiful woman (it could be she was beautiful because I haven't seen a woman in a while). Now when I landed, a female second lieutenant took me into the ER with no one else in the whole room except her and me. She came up to me and ripped off my blanket, grabbed my brown undies, and ripped those off too and gave me a catheter. Now that was more painful than the IED and way not what I was thinking was going to happen when she grabbed my blanket off me. Then she gave me some morphine and I was good.

One thing that bothered me is the way they treated people—just because they're always around stuff like that doesn't mean that they have to act like it's nothing to get hit in the back by a bomb. They did an X-ray of my back and found that I had two pieces of shrapnel in my back. I asked the doctor if I could keep the shrapnel and he said, "Yeah, sure, forever." They weren't going to be taking the shrapnel out. So, yeah, now your son is going to have two pieces of metal in his back for the rest of his life. I was cleaned up and taken to patient hold. A place that is something out of a movie. It was horrible to see all the soldiers with missing legs and arms and bandages everywhere. Shortly afterward, I was given some morphine and I passed out. When I woke up, Colonel Smith, Company Sergeant Major Burgos, Lieutenant Layton, Company Sergeant Major Howard, and our chaplain came in. The first thing Lieutenant Layton said to me was, "Well, me and the sergeant major were talking and you are the first person to receive the Purple Heart in the 'Loyalty' battalion since Grenada (in 1983)." It's quite crazy, the turn of events that have led me here. A Purple Heart recipient—I guess all it means is that some guy got me before I could get him. We will joke about this all someday, Dad. I told them I didn't want you all to find out about this because I'm not leaving Iraq and I don't want you to worry. I know you're going to worry anyway but the reason I shared this story here was so you know what it's like to be here and that the people that I'm with all look after one another. I guess it's really crazy that I volunteered to stay even though I was hit in the back with shrapnel, and as soon as I can I'm going to return to my unit. I don't want Mom to worry so don't read her the detailed parts of this letter. I LOVE Y'ALL and will be home soon enough.

Captain Lisa R. Blackman, thirty-two, Chelmsford, Massachusetts, serving as a clinical psychologist. E-mails to friends and family, from Al Udeid Air Base, Qatar. October 2004.

A quick word on guilt. No one ever feels like they are doing enough. If you are in a safe location, you feel guilty that your friends are getting shot at and you aren't. If you are getting shot at, you feel guilty if your buddy gets hit and you don't. If you get shot at but don't die, you feel guilty that you lived, and more guilty if you get to go home and your friends have to stay behind. I have not seen one person out here who didn't check off "increased guilt" on our intake form. . . .

Lately I have had a string of combat-trauma evaluations. Several have been Army troops passing through for R and R—they come here for a bit and then go back to Iraq or Afghanistan. As if this is a glamorous vacation site. But they are grateful to be someplace safe (and someplace with alcohol, which I will surely complain about at a later date). Anyway, each one presented with a different complaint. One guy wasn't sleeping, one gal was angry about "sexual 35 harassment" in her unit, one gal was depressed, one guy just wanted to go home. Standard stuff.

I had no initial clue that the problems were combat-related and no idea that I should be assessing for acute stress disorder or PTSD. None of these guys or gals said "I was in combat" or "I saw someone die." None connected these experiences to their symptoms. It was as if they didn't remember how hard and unusual it is to be at war. They're used to the danger. They've been out here too long. Why would a war mess with your mood, right?

Each evaluation started with the typical questions: "What brought you in today?" "When did the problem start?" "Have you ever experienced these symptoms before?" "How's your sleep?" etc., etc., etc. I kept asking questions and thinking that the symptoms did not add up. Something wasn't right. I wasn't getting the right reactions. Stories were incomplete. Affect was blunted. Level of distress did not match presenting complaint. Alarm red, people, alarm red.

At home I ask people if they have ever experienced or witnessed a traumatic event or abuse. But out here I ask, "Have you ever been in combat?" Apparently, this is a question with the power to unglue, because all four of these troops burst into tears at the mention of the word "combat."

And when I say burst, I mean splatter—tears running, snot flowing, and I literally had to mop my floor after one two-hour session. In other words, I mean sobbing for minutes on end, unable to speak, flat-out grief by an otherwise healthy, strong, manly guy who watches football on the weekends and never puts the toilet seat down.

Each time, I sit there with not a clue what to say . . . offering tissues . . . saying I'm sorry . . . trying to normalize . . . trying to say, "It was not your fault that so-and-so died" and "If you could have done differently, you would have" and "You had a right to be scared." And, even worse, "You had to shoot back," and "Yes, you killed someone, and you still deserve to go back to your family and live your life." 40

Next time you are hanging out with a friend, think about what you would do if he turned to you and said, "My boss made me kill someone, and I know I'm going to Hell for it, so why bother?" What would you say to "normalize" that?

I will probably never see these folks again. I have no idea if I have been helpful. Maybe I planted a seed of reprieve that will grow into self-forgiveness. Maybe I did absolutely nothing but sit here. Who knows?

I can't stop thinking about the fact that these folks have lost something that they will never get back—innocence (and a life free of guilt). My heart hurts for them.

Second Lieutenant Brian Humphreys, thirty-two, Santa Barbara, California. Journal, Hit, Iraq. February–September 2004.

Bang, bang, bang. The sheet-metal door amplifies the sound of the large fist striking it. Sergeant Graham is standing in the doorway, silhouetted by the white-hot afternoon sunlight.

"Sir, we have a unit in contact, two friendly KIA. The platoon is getting ready downstairs." 45

I throw my uniform and flak jacket on, grab my rifle, and head down a flight of stairs. The platoon is already on the vehicles, ready to roll with an ambulance.

The palm groves to our east that line the Euphrates River whip by. To the west of the asphalt ribbon are the scorched wadis used by insurgents to stage their attacks. Up ahead I see the telltale cluster of Humvees and marines. I pull up to the first vehicle and find the patrol leader.

"Where do you want the ambulance?" I ask.

"Just have it pull up, we'll guide it in," he replies, as if we have arrived to help fix a flat tire. The ambulance in the middle of my six-vehicle column pulls forward, and I get out to find where the casualties are.

"What the hell is that?" I ask a marine. Perhaps the explosion had somehow killed a farm animal of some sort who wandered out on the road. A sheep maybe? Or a cow. No, not big enough. Well, what is that and how did it happen? The marine gives his buddy's name and asks me to help find his head. Fuck. 50

We do not want the stray dogs that occupy Iraq with us to find our brothers. The corpsmen, with their blue latex gloves and body bags, scour the bushes for the last scraps of human tissue as waves of heat rise from the desert. The Associated Press dutifully reports that three marines were killed in Al Anbar province in Iraq. Names have not been released by the Defense Department pending notification of next of kin. We will not read the two-sentence notice for several days. The Internet room is always padlocked while we wait for somebody to get a knock on the door half a world away.

At one point the casualties got so bad that it seemed the room was closed for a week at a time while notifications were made. Iraq is coming apart at the seams. Pictures of flag-draped coffins being unloaded from Air Force transports surface on the back reaches of the Internet, as if they were a grainy celebrity sex video that decent people should avoid looking at. But I think otherwise. The images of flag-draped coffins show the end of war as we are meant to see it, and as we are meant to believe it. Uniforms, flags, patriotism, honor, sacrifice. In these images we are not street fighters struggling to survive and kill in a distant gangland but soldiers in the nation's service. They will help the families, I think. They will help us. In our own way, we, too, need to believe.

Today, the marines will have to wait to log on to their chat rooms, HotOrNot.com, MilitarySingles.com, and the online shopping sites. I myself have become something of a spendthrift in Iraq, ordering more books and CDs than I normally would. I have seen death enough times among people who had been indestructibly living only the day before. It is better to go ahead and buy the CD you have been meaning to get. There are reminders wherever you care to look. For instance, the pile of blood-soaked flak jackets sitting in the company's combat operations center, a low-tech jumble of maps and radios. The flak jackets' owners are either dead or in the hospital recovering from their wounds.

The executive officer reminds us that the flak jackets need to be sent back through the Marine Corps' supply chain as soon as possible. Somewhere, somebody will wash them and inspect them for damage, filling out all the necessary paperwork. It is the banality, even more than the carnage, that shocks. Our occupation grinds on. Others will assign meaning to our lives here, noble or otherwise. For us, though, there is a close meanness to the fight. There are no flags, no dress uniforms. We are fighting a rival gang for the same turf, while the neighborhood residents cower and wait to see whose side they should come out on.

Imperceptibly, we are coming to the end of our deployment. Time has stood 55 still for months, with days and nights fusing together in the burning-hot air of the desert. But now our deployment is being measured in finite units of time. It takes getting used to.

Returning from a patrol with my platoon, I find a blue sedan riddled with bullet holes on the side of the highway. There are a few Iraqi soldiers standing around when we find it. We quickly learn the car belongs to Captain Laithe, one of the senior men in the local police force. Connected, calculating, and English-speaking, he has collaborated with the Americans since the fall of Baghdad. I wondered since I first met him why he cast his lot with us, what calculation he made, and whether we could even understand it—what mix of nobility and venality it contained. His future, however he imagined it, ended with the finality of death in a hail of bullets on the highway less than a mile from our forward operating base.

Not long before we leave, I am awakened out of a sound sleep again, this time at midnight. The company executive officer is at the door. We have another KIA. I feel the same shock I did the first time, only there's a certain numbness to it now, as if it were hitting a nerve becoming deadened by repeated blows. Our turn had almost passed, and now this. I nod, and begin collecting my gear. Lieutenant Lenz is outside in the pitch-black. It is the body of one of his marines that we will go out in the dead of night to recover. I ask Lenz if he is all right. I ask him if his marines are all right. The worst thing, he says, is that by now they are used to it. It is better and worse at the same time. I realize that we have all come to accept the loss of familiar faces, to live with it, and cross the line of departure again the next morning. It is this acceptance, rather than the thud of hidden bombs, that has finally made us veterans, and will finish the words on the obscure page of history that we occupy.

We head off in the pitch-black, navigating the highway through the grainy green glow of our night-vision goggles. We move north to a point just north of the place where we lost the two marines in the bomb explosion months before. One of the Humvees in the patrol struck a land mine a short distance from the Iraqi National Guard post the marines had been tasked with protecting.

The sun is rising above the river's palm groves when the trucks arrive to remove the wrecked vehicle. The dead marine's remains are loaded in another truck and driven north towards Al Asad Air Base. The remains will be laid in a flag-draped coffin, and then secured in the cargo hold of a transport plane to be flown back to the United States. We, too, will soon go to Al Asad. We will then strap ourselves into the cargo hold of an identical plane to begin our own journey home. The scrawled memorials on barracks walls to fallen buddies will stay behind for the troops who replace us. They might read the awkwardly worded poems and epitaphs written in loving memory, and half wonder who we were.

▪ QUESTIONS

Reading

1. According to Captain Lisa R. Blackman's entry, how do the people she questions during combat-trauma evaluations respond to the word *combat*?
2. What is CENTCOM? How does Commander Edward W. Jewell describe the visit and presentation?
3. A *dispatch* is a type of report, often sent from on-site officials, military personnel, or journalists, to be published in a newspaper or magazine back home. Identify and list examples of reporting versus reflecting in these soldiers' stories. Use a separate piece of paper if you need more room.

REPORTING	REFLECTING

4. Are each of these "soldiers' stories" written in the same style? What observations can you make about the style of these pieces, both individually and as a whole?

Exploratory Writing

1. These "soldiers' stories" were written in workshops led by professional writers. The soldiers were told to "write freely, without fear of official constraints or oversight," and many of their writings are taken from private letters and journals. How might the stories be different if they were written anonymously for inclusion in these same public forums? Does it matter how the project was funded? Why were soldiers told to "write freely"? Collaborating in small groups, peruse the Operation Homecoming Web site (**www.nea.gov/national/homecoming/index.html**), and prepare a statement on what it means to "write freely."
2. Choose an article with a photo gallery from documentary photographer Andrea Bruce's "Unseen Iraq" series, online at the *Washington Post* (**http://voices.washingtonpost.com/unseen-iraq/**), such as the article "A Joyful Welcome Home for Detainees" (posted October 5, 2008) or "A Baghdad Trailer Park for Widows and Children" (posted September 15, 2008). Compare the article to this collection of soldiers' stories. What do these different reports tell readers who have never visited Iraq? What strategies can newspaper and magazine editors use to create balanced reports from a war?

Making Connections

1. Imagine that one of the soliders whose letters are collected in "Soldiers' Stories" has read Susan Sontag's "Regarding the Pain of Others" (p. 366). Adopt his or her voice and persona and write a letter in response to Sontag.
2. "Evil from time immemorial has often worn a mask of innocence," writes John Berger (p. 236) at the close of his essay. Carefully highlight, underline, or flag any references to evil, horror, or hell in both Berger's essay and these soldiers' stories. Do you think that Berger's conclusions about the reality of Hiroshima also apply to the reality of the Iraq War? Why or why not?

Essay Writing

1. One of these soldiers' stories, the report from Sergeant Timothy J. Gaestel, is an e-mail to a father from his twenty-two-year-old son. Write a reflective essay discussing how this epistolary approach shapes the way you respond to Sergeant Gaestel's narrative. You can also use examples from the other epistolary stories in this essay.

STUDENT ESSAY

Political Food

Big Business and the State of Food Safety in the United States

Muaz Paracha

Muaz Paracha wrote "Political Food" for an Introduction to College Writing class that focuses on food-related topics. In it, he traces the evolution of food safety regulations; Paracha argues that lobbyists' influence has grown over time and prevented the government from adequately protecting the United States' food supply. Paracha uses a variety of sources, which he documents in APA style, to support his claim. As you read "Political Food," think about how Paracha constructs his argument. Pay attention to the kinds of information he uses and whether you think they support his conclusions. Consider the ways you might incorporate research in your own writing to strengthen your arguments. Refer to Arguing in Part 1: An Introduction to Writing (p. 26) for information on the characteristics of an argument paper.

Since 1906, when Congress enacted the Pure Food and Drug Act, the U.S. government has been regulating the American food supply. The regulation in general was to ensure the quality and safety of the foods and drugs sold to the public. Today, food regulation is a hot-button issue and many people point fingers at the government for not doing its job correctly. However, the government may not be entirely to blame for its decisions but rather big businesses that are chasing profits and financial incentives. Today's government food regulation is strongly influenced by food lobbyists trying to benefit their clients' businesses.

The History of Food Regulation in the United States

The government has not always been heavily involved in food regulation as it is today, and the increase in its influence has turned the government into a target for food industry lobbyists who wish to manipulate the system. The very first government department dealing with food was the USDA (United States Department of Agriculture), which was the organization that enacted the Pure Food and Drug Act. The USDA focuses on implementing agricultural government policies on ranchers and farmers, and making sure their products meet the set standards (USDA, 2010). The USDA also informs the public about agricultural foods and nutritional science regarding those products. The government also created the FDA (Food and Drug Administration), which oversees food and drugs that are produced by companies (FDA, 2010). The FDA, similar to the USDA, is responsible for informing the public about the products made by the companies it regulates. The FDA also dictates what are considered to be healthy eating habits and the nutritional labels on food. Jointly, the USDA and FDA are responsible for our entire food supply and informing the public about food.

The actions of food producers led to the government's regulation in the first place. Members of the food industry were not concerned with the quality of their products, the health of their consumers, or how safe their products were. They were, and still are, motivated by sales and profits. The government realized that the Meat Inspection Act of 1906 was needed because of an exposé on the Chicago meatpacking industry. This law regulates the slaughtering of any consumable animal (USDA, 2011). The conditions of the slaughterhouses were unsanitary and unacceptable, and many Americans got sick due to companies unwilling to bear the expense of cleanliness. In this instance the government needed to step in to save consumers from companies that were trying to cut corners. Today, companies still have the same incentives to keep costs low. Back then, the government was taking them head-on, but today the food industries have gone behind the scenes and straight to the source of this legislation—congress.

The Influence of Food Lobbyists

Because members of Congress must constantly fund-raise for future elections, they are particularly vulnerable to business interests, even as they seek to please their constituents back home to remain in office. The food industry is only concerned with members of Congress who serve on committees that shape the laws and guidelines that the FDA and USDA enforce. The food industry focuses its attention on the heads of these committees.

For example, food industry leaders changed the outcome of the work done by the Nutrition and Human Needs committee headed by George McGovern in 1977. Starting in 1968, Senator McGovern's group investigated problems with diets of Americans that were causing both malnutrition and obesity. The committee released a report about healthy eating habits, which urged consumers to "eat less high-fat meats, eggs, and dairy products" (Pollan, 2007). This didn't sit well with many of the senator's constituents because they worked in the meat, egg, and dairy industries, and they pressured McGovern and other committee members to alter the report. Ultimately the committee held more hearings and revised the report to avoid specific references to those foods. That same year the Senate disbanded the committee as part of an organizational reform effort. Though McGovern and the rest of the committee bowed to pressure placed on them by members of the meat, dairy, and sugar industries, a beef lobbyist helped "rusticate the three-term senator; sending an unmistakable warning to anyone who would challenge the American diet" (Pollan, 2007). That warning? Question the food industry and face consequences.

To understand the connection between food businesses and government we must explore the various roles lobbyists play. As Marion Nestle explains in her book *Food Politics: How the Food Industry Influences Nutrition and Health* (2003), "Historically, lobbying always has involved three elements: (1) promoting the views of special-interest groups, (2) attempting to influence government laws, rules, or policies that might affect those groups, and (3) communicating with government officials or their representatives about laws, rules, or policies of interest" (95). The first of these traditional roles, promoting the industry's views, was on display at a recent conference at the American Academy of Sciences, where government scientists discussed the federal school lunch program, which will be renewed soon. Representatives from PepsiCo, Sara Lee, Campbells, and FritoLay, along with the egg, soy, dairy, and baking industries, presented their companies' products, hoping to convince the government to include those products in the new school lunch program (Water & Heron, 2009).

However, these companies do not stop at just making presentations in front of committees. As Nestle says, they influence laws, in this case by targeting officials in Washington, D.C. In 2009 there were 335 registered food lobbyists who represented 62 different food companies. These companies spent a grand total of $57,004,716. Among the top spenders were household names such as Coca-Cola, PepsiCo, Starbucks, McDonald's, and Hershey (Curran, 2010). One of the things these companies were spending their $57 million on was targeting bills related to food, including the Federal Food, Drug, and Cosmetic Act. This bill involved "[amending] the Federal Food, Drug, and Cosmetic Act with respect to the safety of the food supply," to give the FDA more power and control over the food industry. The proposed law would have required the FDA to thoroughly inspect food factories and products, and the increased cost of these inspections would fall to the corporations. Though the new procedures would raise food producers' costs, it is clear that industry lobbyists for the biggest companies influenced the content of the bill. For instance, it did not include meat producers (an industry whose power we saw at work against George McGovern), which had been criticized for *E. coli* outbreaks in the years before this bill's creation. Furthermore, larger corporations can afford to pay the new fees, but smaller producers cannot. Ultimately, the biggest food companies benefit, as their competitors could be priced out of business. Indeed, when the Senate voted on the bill, "At least 221 organizations hired 77 lobbying firms to try to influence the sweeping overhaul of food safety laws . . ." according to Dan Eggen of the *Washington Post* (2010). Though the bill passed in the Senate, members of the House of Representatives prevented its passing in Congress, so the Federal Food, Drug, and Cosmetic Act did not become a law.

This is just one example of the way food lobbyists have increased their influence, however. The Senate has created a Web site that shows exactly how much each company is spending and what they were specifically spending to lobby for or against. Lauren Curran, of *Food Safety News,* found that in one quarter, McDonald's spent $315,160 on lobbying against food safety and food labeling legislation, as well as childhood nutrition and climate change–related bills (2010). In the same amount of time, Kraft Foods spent $700,000 on twelve different bills navigating through Congress; Wal-Mart spent $1.6 million through four different lobbying organizations on bills related to clean energy, cheap healthy foods, and food safety; and Coca-Cola spent over $2 million lobbying on issues such as water safety, recycling requirements, and food safety.

As far as statistics go, these numbers speak for themselves. All that money is being used to influence not only food legislation, but other business-regulating legislations as well. Notice a lot of the companies lobbying Congress are household names, and they protect their reputations by fighting food safety precautions that may uncover flaws in their products and make them unpopular in the public eye.

A large portion of that $57 million also goes to the lobbyists' final responsibility: communicating with government officials. To do this, large food companies pay a premium to get the best, most experienced firms on their payrolls. Lobbying firms are most successful when they have direct contacts with the Congress members who are making the decisions (i.e., the heads of the committees discussed above). Recently, former members of Congress have started joining lobbying firms. They are great candidates for these positions because they have extensive knowledge of the law-making process and have preexisting contacts in office. Sodexo, a food processing company, hired Richard Gephardt, the former House Democratic Party leader as a lobbyist (Nestle, 2003). Obviously the food industry knows how to choose its lobbyists and how to equip them with the financial assets necessary to do their jobs. Additionally, the industry spends money to get the attention of the politicians who matter, which means spending on them. Nestle notes, "Lobbyists for special interests have been padding the pockets of amoral politicians for longer than most of us have been alive, and they've been doing so with the help of a controlled media that rarely presents the facts without shrouding them in terms of 'left' or 'right' in order to confuse people" (2003). We know that a lot of the money goes to campaign contributions and charities. Furthermore, due to a recent Supreme Court decision, the ban on campaign donation limits was lifted. Companies can now pump in as much money as it takes to get politicians to listen. Even though recent legislation proposed by the Obama administration has required lobbyists to register their names and companies they work for, well-known brands have been able to prevent new regulations from hurting their interests. 10

The Global Reach of Food Lobbyists

Larger food companies aren't just getting their way here in the United States. "Lobbying by 'powerful' big food companies is blocking reforms which would improve human health and the environment," a director of the United Nations' Food and Agriculture Organization has warned (Jowit, 2010). The UN had a proposal for a "code of conduct for the livestock industry" due to the trends in *E. coli* poisoning, mad cow disease, bird flu, and other livestock-related epidemics. However, large agribusiness and food-processing companies went overseas and shared their financial incentives with foreign leaders. According to Juliette Jowit's article in the *Guardian UK* (2010), when these countries were contacted regarding the proposal, they were in strong opposition to it. The article fails to mention the names of these companies, which is another example of how these deals are made behind closed doors and away from media. Companies do not care if something is going to benefit "human health and the environment," especially if it involves them paying for it.

Lobbying has become a tool for businesses to thrive. If many companies in one industry are seeing to it that they are being represented in government it is only sensible for the rest of the industry to join in. Some lobbyists work for special-interest groups who may be advocating for safer, more regulated practices regarding the food industry; however, they may not be as influential as the bigger multibillionaire conglomerate food companies out there. The media is slowly but surely uncovering what lobbyists are doing. Judging from the numbers and reports, there isn't a single form of food legislation passed without lobbyist involvement. Dan Eggen of the *Washington Post* states that many Republican senators are hiring lobbyists as members of their staff because they "provide analysis into specific bills that require prior information and understanding" (2010). True lobbyists present research regarding specific bills, but that research is usually geared toward a particular goal that they are trying to accomplish.

The government originally introduced food legislation as a way of protecting its citizens from the foul business practices of the meat industry. Now due to lobbying, the meat industry still goes on avoiding further regulation from the government while on average more than two thousand Americans are hospitalized due to *E. coli* poisoning. One hundred and ninety million Americans are battling obesity, but the government can't do anything to help because lobbyists are breathing down their necks. Clearly the members of Congress need to make the American people a priority rather than accepting donations, gifts, and propaganda research from the food industry's lobbyists.

References

Curran, L. (2010). Millions spent lobbying food safety. *Food Safety News*. Retrieved from www.foodsafetynews.com

Eggen, D. (2010, December 8). New Republican lawmakers are hiring lobbyists, despite campaign rhetoric. *The Washington Post*. Retrieved from www.washingtonpost.com

Jowit, J. (2010, September 22). Corporate lobbying is blocking food reforms, senior UN official warns. *The Guardian UK*. Retrieved from www.guardian.co.uk

Nestle, M. (2003). Food politics: How the food industry influences nutrition and health. Los Angeles, CA: University of California Press.

Pollan, M. (2007, January 28). Unhappy meals. *New York Times*. Retrieved from www.nytimes.com

Randall, E. (2010). Food risk and politics: Scare, scandal and crisis—insights into the risk politics of food. *Social Policy & Administration*, 44(7), 867–869.

U.S. Food and Drug Administration. (2010). *What we do*. Retrieved from www.FDA.gov

U.S. Department of Agriculture. (2010). *Job of USDA*. Retrieved from www.USDA.gov

U.S. Department of Agriculture. (2011). *Agency history*. Retrieved from www.USDA .gov

Water, A., & Heron, K. (2009, February 19). No lunch left behind. *New York Times*. Retrieved from www.nytimes.com

▪ QUESTIONS

Reading

1. Paracha has titled his essay "Political Food," but has also included a subtitle, "Big Business and the State of Food Safety in the United States." What are the differing contributions of the title and subtitle? Can you offer any alternative titles and subtitles that might work just as well?
2. Paracha uses a variety of sources, including newspaper articles, books, and articles from Web sites. Choose two of these sources and contrast the roles they play in helping Paracha develop his argument.
3. Paracha quotes some sources directly and paraphrases others. What do you think accounts for his choice to quote or paraphrase? Use an example of each method to support your answer.

Exploratory Writing

1. Put yourself in the position of a professor meeting with Paracha to discuss his essay. Write a short dialogue between this professor and Paracha, focusing on the relationship between his thesis and the evidence he provides. Be sure you identify the thesis and at least two significant forms of evidence. Also, address the following questions: Is the thesis clear? Is it compelling? Does it seem true, without being obvious? Is the evidence pertinent? Does it convince you that the argument is on target?
2. Highlight or underline all the quotations Paracha uses in his essay. Then write a paragraph or two about how he introduces and analyzes these quotations. What techniques does he use to integrate them into his paragraphs? How does he respond to them? Which of Paracha's strategies might you use in your own writing?

Making Connections

1. In "Bad Food? Tax It, and Subsidize Vegetables" (p. 294), Mark Bittman makes an argument about food and big business, originally published in the *New York Times*. Imagine you are Muaz Paracha. You've just read Bittman's article. Write a letter to the editor in response, drawing on some of the research in "Political Food" to support your argument.

Essay Writing

1. Paracha chose an important social issue — food safety — and did research into the ways in which that issue is affected by government policies. Choose an issue described in one of the readings in this part (e.g., immigration policy, poverty, the media), and develop an argument that focuses on a specific aspect of the issue (like the history of opposition to the Dream Act, for instance). Write an essay, responding to and incorporating research on your topic, that makes an argument about the issue you've chosen.

Part 4
Sciences

Readings in the Sciences

The hypothesis—a tentative argument based on evidence—is the cornerstone of science. A hypothesis is generally more interesting to a scientist than a fact, because it implies there is more to be known or discovered. Of course, science has a practical side. In the words of physicist Richard Feynman, "scientific knowledge allows us to do all kinds of things and make all kinds of things." But it's only possible to apply scientific knowledge—say, harnessing geothermal energy or treating Alzheimer's disease—after scientists spend years conducting studies to investigate hypotheses about the topic at hand. Often, scientific research is reported as a series of big discoveries and new facts, but any working scientist will tell you that an uncertain hypothesis represents the real work of science.

Welcoming doubt is fundamental to a scientific worldview, and thus, to a scientific education. The science writer Natalie Angier explains that science "is a way of viewing the world, of facing reality square on but taking nothing on its face." Ultimately, the goal is a new understanding of reality, with the proviso that that understanding is subject to revision based on new evidence or a new hypothesis. In this sense, scientists engage in a "never-ending dialogue," as Thomas W. Martin argues. Feynman, Angier, and Martin agree that "scientific literacy" is more about a way of seeing and investigating the world than it is about learning facts.

The scientific method—the observation, collection, measuring, and analysis of evidence using empirical techniques—allows a scientist to conduct the careful, firsthand observation required to make sense of evidence that can be bewildering. A scientist can study anything—from molecules to language—as long as it can be explained through the scientific method and empirical observation.

There are many approaches to knowledge within the sciences. Experimental science focuses on laboratory experiments; applied science focuses on solutions to real-world problems. Biological science focuses on living organisms, including human beings; physical science focuses on the earth, the universe, and the cosmos. The fifteen essays collected here—nine that stand on their own and three paired sets—all address fundamental questions about the world. Of these, five are primarily reflecting; four reporting; two explaining; and four arguing. Some of these essays are written by scientists, such as cell biologist Lewis Thomas and cognitive scientist Steven Pinker; others are by writers who specialize in science, such as Diane Ackerman. At the end of this part, you will see how one student examined the ethics of cloning through science and the law.

When you write in scientific disciplines, you may start with hard facts but end up exploring philosophical questions that scientific observations provoke. You may even end up addressing scientific questions and debates in your writing for the humanities or social sciences. Whatever the case may be, you should feel free to enter the conversations these essays open up, to experiment with various methods of responding to them, and to find your own careful methods for writing about the fundamental questions about life and the workings of the universe.

ARGUING

The Value of Science

Richard Feynman

Nobel Prize–winning physicist Richard Feynman (1918–1988) was known for his trailblazing work in the fields of quantum mechanics, particle physics, and quantum electrodynamics. After his application to Columbia University was rejected, he attended the Massachusetts Institute of Technology, then Princeton University, where he received a doctorate in 1942. He participated in the Manhattan Project in Los Alamos, New Mexico, where he helped the United States Army develop the atomic bomb. Feynman founded the influential fields of quantum computing and nanotechnology. His Feynman diagrams (maps of the behavior of subatomic particles) have been essential for physicists since 1948. Feynman was a gifted and popular lecturer as well as a groundbreaking scientist. In addition to the Nobel Prize and dozens of other prestigious awards, he won the Oersted Medal for his skills as a teacher. His books of thoughts and reminiscences, including *"Surely You're Joking, Mr. Feynman!": Adventures of a Curious Character* (1985) and "*What Do You Care What Other People Think?": Further Adventures of a Curious Character* (1988), made complex scientific ideas accessible to lay audiences. Delivered at a meeting of the National Academy of Sciences in 1955, "The Value of Science" is considered one of Feynman's most passionate assessments of scientific study.

From time to time, people suggest to me that scientists ought to give more consideration to social problems—especially that they should be more responsible in considering the impact of science upon society. This same suggestion must be made to many other scientists, and it seems to be generally believed that if the scientists would only look at these very difficult social problems and not spend so much time fooling with the less vital scientific ones, great success would come of it.

It seems to me that we do think about these problems from time to time, but we don't put full-time effort into them—the reason being that we know we don't have any magic formula for solving problems, that social problems are very much harder than scientific ones, and that we usually don't get anywhere when we do think about them.

I believe that a scientist looking at nonscientific problems is just as dumb as the next guy—and when he talks about a nonscientific matter, he will sound as naive as anyone untrained in the matter. Since the question of the value of science is not a scientific subject, this discussion is dedicated to proving my point—by example.

The first way in which science is of value is familiar to everyone. It is that scientific knowledge enables us to do all kinds of things and to make all kinds of things. Of course if we make good things, it is not only to the credit of science it is also to the credit of the moral choice which led us to good work. Scientific knowledge is an enabling power to do either good or bad—but it

Richard Feynman played a key role in popularizing physics with his lectures and books.

does not carry instructions on how to use it. Such power has evident value—even though the power may be negated by what one does.

I learned a way of expressing this common human problem on a trip to Honolulu. In a Buddhist temple there, the man in charge explained a little bit about the Buddhist religion for tourists, and then ended his talk by telling them he had something to say to them that they would *never* forget—and I have never forgotten it. It was a proverb of the Buddhist religion:

"To every man is given the key to the gates of heaven; the same key opens the gates of hell."

What, then, is the value of the key to heaven? It is true that if we lack clear instructions that determine which is the gate to heaven and which the gate to hell, the key may be a dangerous object to use, but it obviously has value. How can we enter heaven without it?

The instructions, also, would be of no value without the key. So it is evident that, in spite of the fact that science could produce enormous horror in the world, it is of value because it *can* produce *something*.

Another value of science is the fun called intellectual enjoyment which some people get from reading and learning and thinking about it, and which others get from working in it. This is a very real and important point and one which is not considered enough by those who tell us it is our social responsibility to reflect on the impact of science on society.

Is this mere personal enjoyment of value to society as a whole? No! But it is also a responsibility to consider the value of society itself. Is it, in the last analysis, to arrange things so that people can enjoy things? If so, the enjoyment of science is as important as anything else.

But I would like *not* to underestimate the value of the worldview which is the result of scientific effort. We have been led to imagine all sorts of things infinitely more marvelous than the imaginings of poets and dreamers of the past. It shows that the imagination of nature is far, far greater than the imagination of man. For instance, how much more remarkable it is for us all to be stuck—half of us upside down—by a mysterious attraction, to a spinning ball that has been swinging in space for billions of years, than to be carried on the back of an elephant supported on a tortoise swimming in a bottomless sea.

I have thought about these things so many times alone that I hope you will excuse me if I remind you of some thoughts that I am sure you have all had—or this type of thought—which no one could ever have had in the past, because people then didn't have the information we have about the world today.

For instance, I stand at the seashore, alone, and start to think. There are the rushing waves . . . mountains of molecules, each stupidly minding its own business . . . trillions apart . . . yet forming white surf in unison.

Ages on ages . . . before any eyes could see . . . year after year . . . thunderously pounding the shore as now. For whom, for what? . . . on a dead planet, with no life to entertain.

Never at rest . . . tortured by energy . . . wasted prodigiously by the sun . . . poured into space. A mite makes the sea roar. 15

Deep in the sea, all molecules repeat the patterns of one another till complex new ones are formed. They make others like themselves . . . and a new dance starts.

Growing in size and complexity . . . living things, masses of atoms, DNA, protein . . . dancing a pattern ever more intricate.

Out of the cradle onto the dry land . . . here it is standing . . . atoms with consciousness . . . matter with curiosity.

Stands at the sea . . . wonders at wondering . . . I . . . a universe of atoms . . . an atom in the universe.

The Grand Adventure

The same thrill, the same awe and mystery, come again and again when we look at any problem deeply enough. With more knowledge comes deeper, more wonderful mystery, luring one on to penetrate deeper still. Never concerned that the answer may prove disappointing, but with pleasure and confidence we turn over each new stone to find unimagined strangeness leading on to more wonderful questions and mysteries—certainly a grand adventure! 20

It is true that few unscientific people have this particular type of religious experience. Our poets do not write about it; our artists do not try to portray this remarkable thing. I don't know why. Is nobody inspired by our present picture of the universe? The value of science remains unsung by singers, so you are reduced to hearing—not a song or a poem, but an evening lecture about it. This is not yet a scientific age.

Perhaps one of the reasons is that you have to know how to read the music. For instance, the scientific article says, perhaps, something like this: "The radioactive phosphorus content of the cerebrum of the rat decreases to one half in a period of two weeks." Now, what does that mean?

It means that phosphorus that is in the brain of a rat (and also in mine, and yours) is not the same phosphorus as it was two weeks ago, but that all of the atoms that are in the brain are being replaced, and the ones that were there before have gone away.

So what is this mind, what are these atoms with consciousness? Last week's potatoes! That is what now can *remember* what was going on in my mind a year ago—a mind which has long ago been replaced.

That is what it means when one discovers how long it takes for the atoms of the brain to be replaced by other atoms, to note that the thing which I call my individuality is only a pattern or dance. The atoms come into my brain, dance a dance, then go out; always new atoms but always doing the same dance, remembering what the dance was yesterday. 25

The Remarkable Idea

When we read about this in the newspaper, it says, "The scientist says that this discovery may have importance in the cure of cancer." The paper is only interested in the use of the idea, not the idea itself. Hardly anyone can understand the importance of an idea, it is so remarkable. Except that, possibly, some children catch on. And when a child catches on to an idea like that, we have a scientist. These ideas do filter down (in spite of all the conversation about TV replacing thinking), and lots of kids get the spirit—and when they have the spirit you have a scientist. It's too late for them to get the spirit when they are in our universities, so we must attempt to explain these ideas to children.

I would now like to turn to a third value that science has. It is a little more indirect, but not much. The scientist has a lot of experience with ignorance and doubt and uncertainty, and this experience is of very great importance, I think. When a scientist doesn't know the answer to a problem, he is ignorant. When he has a hunch as to what the result is, he is uncertain. And when he is pretty darn sure of what the result is going to be, he is in some doubt. We have found it of paramount importance that in order to progress we must recognize the ignorance and leave room for doubt. Scientific knowledge is a body of statements of varying degrees of certainty—some most unsure, some nearly sure, none *absolutely* certain.

Now, we scientists are used to this, and we take it for granted that it is perfectly consistent to be unsure—that it is possible to live and *not* know. But I don't know whether everyone realizes that this is true. Our freedom to doubt was born of a struggle against authority in the early days of science. It was a very deep and strong struggle. Permit us to question—to doubt, that's all—not to be sure. And I think it is important that we do not forget the importance of this struggle and thus perhaps lose what we have gained. Here lies a responsibility to society.

We are all sad when we think of the wondrous potentialities human beings seem to have, as contrasted with their small accomplishments. Again and again people have thought that we could do much better. They of the past saw in the nightmare of their times a dream for the future. We, of their future, see that their dreams, in certain ways surpassed, have in many ways remained dreams. The hopes for the future today are, in good share, those of yesterday.

Education, for Good and Evil

Once some thought that the possibilities people had were not developed 30 because most of those people were ignorant. With education universal, could all men be Voltaires? Bad can be taught at least as efficiently as good. Education is a strong force, but for either good or evil.

Communications between nations must promote understanding: So went another dream. But the machines of communication can be channeled or choked. What is communicated can be truth or lie. Communication is a strong force also, but for either good or bad.

The applied sciences should free men of material problems at least. Medicine controls diseases. And the record here seems all to the good. Yet there are men patiently working to create great plagues and poisons. They are to be used in warfare tomorrow.

Nearly everybody dislikes war. Our dream today is peace. In peace, man can develop best the enormous possibilities he seems to have. But maybe future men will find that peace, too, can be good and bad. Perhaps peaceful men will drink out of boredom. Then perhaps drink will become the great problem which seems to keep man from getting all he thinks he should out of his abilities.

Clearly, peace is a great force, as is sobriety, as are material power, communication, education, honesty, and the ideals of many dreamers.

We have more of these forces to control than did the ancients. And maybe 35 we are doing a little better than most of them could do. But what we ought to be able to do seems gigantic compared with our confused accomplishments.

Why is this? Why can't we conquer ourselves?

Because we find that even great forces and abilities do not seem to carry with them clear instructions on how to use them. As an example, the great accumulation of understanding as to how the physical world behaves only convinces one that this behavior seems to have a kind of meaninglessness. The sciences do not directly teach good and bad.

Through all ages men have tried to fathom the meaning of life. They have realized that if some direction or meaning could be given to our actions, great human forces would be unleashed. So, very many answers must have been given to the question of the meaning of it all. But they have been of all different sorts, and the proponents of one answer have looked with horror at the actions of the believers in another. Horror, because from a disagreeing point of view all the great potentialities of the race were being channeled into a false and confining blind alley. In fact, it is from the history of the enormous monstrosities created by false belief that philosophers have realized the apparently infinite and wondrous capacities of human beings. The dream is to find the open channel.

What, then, is the meaning of it all? What can we say to dispel the mystery of existence?

If we take everything into account, not only what the ancients knew, but all of what we know today that they didn't know, then I think that we must frankly admit that *we do not know*. 40

But, in admitting this, we have probably found the open channel.

This is not a new idea; this is the idea of the age of reason. This is the philosophy that guided the men who made the democracy that we live under. The idea that no one really knew how to run a government led to the idea that we should arrange a system by which new ideas could be developed, tried out, tossed out, more new ideas brought in; a trial and error system. This method was a result of the fact that science was already showing itself to be a successful venture at the end of the eighteenth century. Even then it was clear to socially minded people that the openness of the possibilities was an opportunity, and that doubt and discussion were essential to progress into the unknown. If we want to solve a problem that we have never solved before, we must leave the door to the unknown ajar.

Our Responsibility as Scientists

We are at the very beginning of time for the human race. It is not unreasonable that we grapple with problems. There are tens of thousands of years in the future. Our responsibility is to do what we can, learn what we can, improve the solutions, and pass them on. It is our responsibility to leave the men of the future a free hand. In the impetuous youth of humanity, we can make grave errors that can stunt our growth for a long time. This we will do if we say we have the answers now, so young and ignorant; if we suppress all discussion, all criticism, saying, "This is it, boys, man is saved!" and thus doom man for a long time to the chains of authority, confined to the limits of our present imagination. It has been done so many times before.

It is our responsibility as scientists, knowing the great progress and great value of a satisfactory philosophy of ignorance, the great progress that is the fruit of freedom of thought, to proclaim the value of this freedom, to teach how doubt is not to be feared but welcomed and discussed, and to demand this freedom as our duty to all coming generations.

▪ QUESTIONS

Reading

1. How does Feynman describe "the worldview which is the result of scientific effort" (paragraph 11)? According to Feynman, how has science changed the world?
2. Highlight, underline, or flag places where Feynman groups readers' experiences with his own (such as "We are all sad . . .", paragraph 29). Why do you think Feynman chooses to do this?

3. What percentage of statements in the scientific body of knowledge can we know to be true, with absolute certainty? Why does Feynman bring this up?

Exploratory Writing

1. "There is always another way to say the same thing that doesn't look at all like the way you said it before," said Feynman, when he won the Nobel Prize in Physics in 1965. "In the search for new laws, you always have the psychological excitement of feeling that possibly nobody has yet thought of the crazy possibility you are looking at right now." Read Feynman's Nobel Prize lecture (**http://www.nobelprize.org/nobel_prizes/physics/laureates/1965/feynman-lecture.html**), and write a short outline of the process he used to formulate his breakthrough ideas about quantum electrodynamics. What does this process show about scientific thinking?
2. Feynman writes that "this is not yet a scientific age" (paragraph 21), that we are reduced to hearing lectures about scientific discoveries instead of songs or poems. In small groups, write a double-entry list (headed "Now" and "In a Scientific Age") of ten things that would be different in the world if we lived in a scientific age. Can you find any evidence that we are closer to living in a scientific age now than when Feynman gave this lecture? Write a paragraph in which you explore how close we are to a scientific age.

Now	In a Scientific Age

Making Connections

1. "The same thrill, the same awe and mystery, come again and again when we look at any problem deeply enough," writes Feynman (paragraph 20). In her explanation of why leaves change color in the fall, find places where Diane Ackerman (p. 442) expresses a sense of awe, mystery, or being thrilled. In each case, evaluate how Ackerman uses writing techniques to convey her sense of wonder.

Essay Writing

1. "We are all sad," writes Feynman, "when we think of the wondrous potentialities human beings seem to have, as contrasted with their small accomplishments" (paragraph 29). Choose an area where you believe human beings have great, but unrealized, potential. Write an essay explaining why human accomplishments in that area have been so small.

REFLECTING

Mindblindness

Ann Jurecic

Ann Jurecic is both a writer and a scholar of literature. Before earning a PhD from Princeton University, she spent two years teaching English at a public high school. She currently teaches at Rutgers University, where one of her courses, "Literature and Medicine," focuses on narratives written by people with illnesses. "Literature about illness offers a compelling perspective on ancient puzzles about the relationship of nature and culture, mind and body, and self and others," she has said. "It also asks us to think about realms of experience that can seem beyond language." Jurecic's writings on neurodiversity and autism-spectrum disorders have generated controversy in academic circles, as well as among writers with Asperger's Syndrome. This article first appeared in 2006 in *Literature and Medicine*, a scholarly journal that explores the intersection between scientific and literary knowledge. It has since been updated to include new research and perspectives.

On the first day of class, Gregory stood out as different. While he contributed eagerly to class discussion, his comments were off topic and they often focused narrowly on his own concerns. Because this was a composition class, I noted immediately that his way of thinking about writing was rule-bound and mechanical. In the first several weeks of class, for instance, Gregory probably asked a hundred questions, in and out of class, about the mechanics of MLA citation. In addition, his speech was stilted and he did not look at anyone but me when he spoke. He also could not follow the class's jokes, although he seemed to have his own private sense of what was funny and would smile and rock in his chair when something amused him. Gregory was charming, but everyone in the group, myself included, had difficulty interacting with him in class.

The challenge that Gregory posed for me and for the other students is that of understanding and empathizing with neurological difference. That is, while the other twelve students in the class and I all seemed to be distributed along the "normal" band of the neurological spectrum, Gregory presented as someone with Asperger's syndrome, an Autism Spectrum Disorder. Although people with Asperger's have the impaired social skills, fixed interests, and repetitive behaviors that are typical of autism, because their language development appears ordinary and they demonstrate average to above-average intelligence, they are more likely to attend college—and they are doing so in ever-increasing numbers. Some, like Gregory, are characterized as "little professors" because they display both the extraordinary intelligence and the social eccentricities commonly associated with the figure of "the absentminded professor." Although elements of Gregory's behavior were unusual, his fundamental difficulty in my class was communication. The other students struggled to make sense of his unfamiliar ways of speaking and writing, and he struggled to make sense of us and expectations about class discussions and college writing.[1]

My interactions with Gregory as a teacher compelled me to consider the challenges to affective and intellectual understanding posed by neurological difference. Thus, in what follows, I explore the promise and problems of empathy in institutional realms such as education and medicine. My central questions are these: In the classroom and the clinic, how does one make contact across a neurological divide? If language impedes comprehension as much as it enables it, then will such contact always be frustrated? In situations where verbal and affective communication are difficult, such as with neurological difference, is empathy possible?

The Problem of Empathy

In posing such questions, I enter contested academic territory. In the disciplines of literary studies and writing studies there is considerable apprehension about venturing into realms of understanding that appear to be governed by feeling as much or more than reason. In contrast to conventional scholarly ways of thinking, empathy seems soft, simple, and unreliable. At the same time that literary critics might see empathy across divides of difference as a risky practice, however, scholars in the medical humanities have focused a good deal of attention on the necessity of empathy in medical practice. Howard Spiro's anthology, *Empathy and the Practice of Medicine*, maintains that the relationship between doctors and patients was profoundly transformed by the rise of scientific paradigms and bureaucratic medical practices that devalue emotional engagement with patients.[2] Similarly, Jodi Halpern pushes against the repeated calls for physicians to treat their patients with "detached concern" and argues instead for clinical empathy, which she defines as "a unique form of understanding patients that requires physicians to be emotionally engaged yet also promotes the objectivity that their roles demand."[3] Halpern's definition complicates a common understanding of empathy that has its origins in the work of Theodor Lipps, a German psychologist who is credited with developing the concept of empathy in his 1903 text *Einfülung*. Lipps defines empathy as "the power of projecting one's personality into (and so fully comprehending) the object of contemplation."[4] More familiarly, empathy is the belief that one could somehow step into another's shoes and see the world from that person's perspective. Maureen A. Milligan and Ellen Singer More also reject this simple version of empathy in their introduction to *The Empathic Practitioner*, in which they insist that clinical empathy should not be understood as a movement of the self into the other. Quoting Alexandra Kaplan, they assert instead that empathy is "the capacity to take in and appreciate the affective life of another while maintaining a sufficient sense of self to permit cognitive structuring of that experience."[5] With this definition of empathy, Kaplan adds critical distance to empathic practice. To empathize appropriately, in other words, one must understand and accept empathy's challenges and its limits.

The cognitive difference of autism can present a profound obstacle to empathy for those on the normal band of the neurological spectrum. This situation is a bit ironic because autism itself is often characterized as an impairment of empathy or Theory of Mind. *Theory of Mind* in the literature on autism refers to "the ability of [the neurotypical] to attribute mental states (such as beliefs, desires, intentions, etc.) to themselves and other people, as a way of making sense of and predicting behavior."[6] The Theory of Mind hypothesis of autism maintains that people with autism do not develop such a capacity for intellectual or emotional empathy; they instead experience what is called *mindblindness*.[7]

Although many people with autism may demonstrate limited Theory of Mind, it is also the case that imagining the minds of people who are different from oneself is always a complicated task. Theorizing or imagining other minds is indeed far easier for those of us who are neurotypical because most other minds are similar to our own. When most of us try to imagine an *autistic* mind, however, we tend to get into trouble. The challenge, then, for those who are researching and writing about autism, is to figure out both how to theorize a mind that does not possess a familiar social capacity and how to explain a mind with which we cannot fully empathize—to which *we* are, in many ways, blind.

It might well seem that empathic understanding of those with autism and Asperger's can never be more than a projection. In fact, scholarly writing about autism for much of the twentieth century, including case studies by psychoanalyst Melanie Klein and psychologist Bruno Bettelheim, may be characterized as exhibiting profound failures of both reason and emotion as well as ignorance of the limits of empathy. By contrast, recent works by Temple Grandin, who has autism, and by neurologist Oliver Sacks offer more successful representations of autism. Their work engages research across multiple disciplines— connecting several branches of medicine as well as biography, psychology, and education— while also redefining the practice of empathy as a form of engagement that seeks, both cognitively and affectively, to make sense of another's experience while preserving and respecting difference. Writing of this kind—writing that is shaped by reflection and a desire to understand difference—has the potential to transform ingrained structures of thought and to refigure how medical and educational institutions conceive of neurological difference.

Autism's Current Narrative

What does science know about autism at this point in time? Defining autism is a challenge, in part because many people with autism cannot explain their experience, and also because the disorder is highly variable, with a range of impairments and severities across the autistic continuum. Although any single account of autism will be incomplete, cognitive psychologists and neuroscientists have learned a great deal in recent decades. Autism is diagnosed not with a medical test, but through observable behaviors that medical literature refers to as a triumvirate of disabilities: impairments of social interaction, impairments in communication, and "stereotyped" interests and behavior.[8] People with autism tend to avoid eye contact and to lack expected facial, bodily, and other nonverbal expression, all of which are linked to an impaired ability to communicate. Those with the most severe form of the disorder have little or no language, but even many of those who possess language are unable to participate in the give and take of conversations because their speech can be mimetic, repetitive, or idiosyncratic. The play of children with autism often seems unusual: It, too, can be repetitive, focused for extended periods on one object or activity, and disengaged from the play of other children. People with autism also tend to exhibit surprising reactions—they can profoundly resist unexpected events or changes in routine and can display acute sensitivity to some sensations while appearing indifferent to other people. Another common characteristic of autism is skill with rote learning, which stands in juxtaposition to profound difficulty with tasks that require attention to context rather than to detail or with interpretation of nonliteral language.

It is a commonplace of the literature on autism that "children with autism are unable to interpret the emotional states of others, failing to recognize anger, sorrow, or manipulative intent."[9] Autistic children can develop attachments to their parents and families, but they are generally not interested in their peers, and later, as adolescents and adults do not develop many strong social connections.[10] The underlying cause of this social disengagement is widely believed to involve a failed Theory of Mind—that is, an inability "to attribute mental states to oneself and to others and to interpret behavior in terms of mental states."[11] Theory of Mind is typically tested by asking someone to distinguish between his or her own knowledge and that of others in a situation where someone else might hold a different and/or false belief. In other words, what is being tested is one's ability to *imagine* a mind that knows or believes differently from one's own. Autism researcher Simon Baron-Cohen tests Theory of Mind by creating a drama for his research subjects using two dolls, Anne and Sally. Anne puts a marble into a basket in full view of Sally. Then Sally leaves the scene, and Anne removes the marble from the basket and puts it into a box. When Sally returns, researchers ask their subjects where Sally will look for the marble. Neurotypical children and those with Down's syndrome who are over the age of three understand that Sally holds a false belief that the marble is still in the basket. However, most autistic children, and some with Asperger's, think that Sally will look in the box. They do not differentiate their own knowledge of where Anne has put the marble from the false belief held by Sally.[12] They cannot put themselves into another's place either cognitively or emotionally.

While cognitive scientists have delineated elements of Theory of Mind, 10 neurologists have explored the possibility that autism is linked to impairments or differences in the functioning of mirror neurons. Mirror neurons are brain cells that typically fire both when one acts and when one observes that same action performed by another.[13] In people with autism, it appears that the brain cells that fire in response to action do not respond to observing that action, which may help to explain social, motor, and even language differences. At the present moment, however, much current funding for autism research focuses on studies of the genetic basis of the disease. Researchers are seeking to identify the complex set of interacting genes that may cause autism and to determine possible environmental triggers.[14] There is an urgency to such research as mounting evidence emerges for autism's sharply rising incidence in the United States, which appears to have more than doubled in the last four decades.[15] There is, news outlets declare, an autism epidemic.

Even as we learn more about autism, however, it is clear that current scientific narratives about it are hardly complete. Autism has primarily been defined by outsiders, mostly scientists and scholars. Lost in the scholarly literature is attention to the inner life of the person with autism. How do people with autism want to be recognized and understood? This question is being answered in part by the proliferation of autism autobiographies published in print and online.[16] It is also the case, however, that many people with the condition simply do not have the language or the inclination to write or speak about their experiences; the story of what they know and who they are has long been unavailable or unrecognized. Having surveyed texts about the definitions and etiology of the disorder, I still find it nearly impossible to imagine what it would be like to have severe autism. When I try, I imagine a world in which sensations are disordered and overwhelming, in which language cannot help to put experience into a coherent narrative, in which all but the most familiar people are mysterious and incomprehensible, and in which repetition, routine, and the predictable provide the few available forms of solace. I can no more fully imagine the emotional, mental, and social lives of people with autism, especially how they understand human relationships, than I can imagine a life without the spoken word. Here is where *my* practice of empathy confronts its limits.

The Mindblind Past

In the mid-twentieth century, efforts to attend to the inner life of those with autism were central to explanations of the disorder. Although the psychological focus of this era might suggest the possibility of a richer understanding of individuals with autism, practitioners such as Melanie Klein and Bruno Bettelheim produced deeply troubling interpretations of their autistic patients. Caught between the reigning theories of their era and the absence of both autistic autobiography and neurological knowledge of the disorder, their case studies reveal little insight or empathy. In Klein's 1930 essay "The Importance of Symbol Formation in the Development of the Ego," she focuses on a child named Dick, with whom she began working when he was four years old. At that time, he had little functional language, the intellect of a fifteen- to eighteen-month-old, and no evident emotional ties to his mother or his nurse. In addition, he appeared to have no interests beyond trains and stations, doors and doorknobs. He had little anxiety and no ability to play or engage with his environment. Although Klein labels Dick schizophrenic, a term that served at the time for a range of neurological conditions, today a child exhibiting these behaviors would be labeled autistic.

Klein begins her study of Dick by offering a framework for normal child development. There is, she asserts, "an early stage of mental development at which sadism becomes active at all the various sources of libidinal pleasure."[17]

At this time, the child's "dominant aim is to possess himself of the contents of the mother's body and to destroy her by means of every weapon which sadism can command" (96). Thus, she explains, "the excess of sadism gives rise to anxiety and sets in motion the ego's earliest modes of defence" (96). She concludes her construction of normal childhood ego development by stating that this anxiety sets in motion a "mechanism of identification" by which the child equates the organs that are the source of anxiety (the "penis, vagina, [and] breast") with other things on which the child then places the anxiety (97). "Thus," concludes Klein, "not only does symbolism come to be the foundation of all phantasy and sublimation but, more than that, upon it is built up the subject's relation to the outside world and to reality in general" (97–98).

By this logic, it is evident to Klein that a child who thinks literally, not symbolically, and who has not developed a settled relationship to the outside world, is profoundly delayed in psychological development, and this is the case with Dick. Rather than finding him to express "normal" sadism, she sees him as incapable of aggression and concludes that he has developed strong defenses against aggressive impulses that have locked him into a presymbolic phase; he cannot express his sadistic relation to his mother's body, and thus he cannot develop the symbolic sense that will enable him to connect with the world. This whole study is rather shocking in the context of current thinking about autism, which has turned completely away from explanations based on ego development. Klein's construction of Dick is, from a contemporary perspective, severely weakened because she adheres to a rigid symbolic system that does not enable her to read his mind as much as it claims him as confirmation of her theory and builds a fortress of words around him. The framework available to Klein enables her to recognize only a single "theory of mind." Her theory, in other words, does not enable her to see the possibility of a *spectrum* of minds.

Nearly thirty years after Klein composed her case study of Dick, and more than a decade after Leo Kanner and Hans Asperger named and defined autism, Bruno Bettelheim published another compelling case study in *Scientific American* entitled "Joey: A 'Mechanical Boy,'" which, like Klein's, is driven by a theoretical argument that can only account for the autistic mind as a failure because it is not like the neurotypical mind.[18] Joey's autistic withdrawal expresses itself, Bettelheim tells us, through his belief that he is a machine:

> He functioned as if by remote control, run by machines of his own powerfully creative fantasy. Not only did he himself believe that he was a machine but, more remarkably, he created this impression in others. Even while he performed actions that are intrinsically human, they never appeared to be other than machine-started and executed. On the other hand, when the machine was not working we had to concentrate on recollecting his presence, for he seemed not to exist.[19]

Bettelheim concludes with the haunting assertion that "Joey was a child who had been robbed of his humanity" (117).

In the story of Joey's mechanical endeavors—involving every part of his daily life, from sleeping to eating to defecating (a process Bettelheim dwells upon with Freudian fervor)—what is significant to Bettelheim is less what the narrative reveals about autism than what it reveals about "emotional development in a machine age" (117). Joey, he decides, finds it *too painful* to be human, a disconcerting judgment. Bettelheim thinks Joey has sublimated his humanity because of his "detached" and "indifferent" mother (118), whom Bettelheim accuses of completely ignoring her son, and also because he is a child of his culture. In his major theoretical work on autism, *The Empty Fortress*, Bettelheim notoriously maintains that emotionally withdrawn and unloving parents, particularly mothers, are largely responsible for autism. He asserts that "the precipitating factor in infantile autism is the parent's wish that his child should not exist."[20] In Joey's case, however, Bettelheim finds the origin of Joey's disorder in the current era of material excess: "At the extreme where utter scarcity reigns," he asserts, "the forming of relationships is certainly hampered. But our society of mechanized plenty often makes for equal difficulties in a child's learning to relate" (126). Parents in earlier years, he says, expended effort and took pleasure in being able to give to their children, which in turn enabled the children to develop "a sense of personal worth" and thus a foundation for social relations (126). He warns, however, that when providing comfort becomes too easy in times of plenty, parents get no pleasure from giving, and children develop no sense of worth.[21] In the service of this moral about how our attachment to the material has left us starved for humanity, Bettelheim weaves Joey into a metaphor-laden, machine-age fairy tale for the readers of *Scientific American* about how our attachment to the material world has left us starved for humanity and displaced true empathy.

As a fairy tale, the story may seem uplifting. Readers receive confirmation of the importance of parental love and care, the dangers of materialism, and even the risks of early toilet training. Ultimately, however, when Bettelheim tells us at the end of the article that Joey made a Memorial Day float with the slogan "Feelings are more important than anything under the sun" (127), it appears Joey has been transformed for the purposes of a moral and medical fiction, as Dick was transformed in Klein's earlier case study. Thus, Bettelheim's text demonstrates again the distortions we generate when we use illness to interpret and write about the unknowable or unreachable realm of another's experience.

These distortions ultimately result in a false etiology for the disorder. In *The Empty Fortress*, Bettelheim argues that autism is parallel to the "extinction of feeling" and effacement of self suffered by some concentration camp prisoners.[22] To introduce this analogy, he writes, "In the German concentration camps I witnessed with utter disbelief the nonreacting of certain prisoners to their most cruel experience" (57). Then, he continues, making the link to autism, "I did not know and would not have believed that I would observe similar behavior in the most benign of therapeutic environments, because of what children had experienced in the past" (57). The prisoners who felt helpless and doomed "deteriorated to near autistic behavior when the feeling of doom penetrated so deep that it brought the added conviction of imminent death" (65). Children with autism, he believes, have an "inner reality" comparable to the "external reality" of the prisoners and, like them, direct all their energy into a defensive withdrawal (75). The absence of language, he claims, is a "defense against emotional pain or any further depletion of the self" (59). Thus, he concludes that "infantile autism is a state of mind that develops in reaction to feeling oneself in an extreme situation, entirely without hope" (68). Here we have an extraordinary symbolic equation in which Bettelheim draws on his own experience and his formative psychological observation of reactions to brutal mistreatment. In order to understand human behavior that defies explanation, Bettelheim turns to the only experience he can compare to what he observes. The analogy inspires him. It enables him to begin, he thinks, to understand the disease. And his memory of these withdrawn men, avoided by the other prisoners "as if in fear of contagion" (65), helps him to think about their experience and autism in terms with which he can clearly identify.

As moving as Bettelheim's elaborate analogy may be, it distorts more than it enlightens, for it causes Bettelheim to assume analogous causes—that people with autism, like concentration camp prisoners, suffered from abuse, and that the absence of language is a reaction to helplessness and hopelessness. His analogy seems to be informed by such pain and such an effort to imagine the experience of another, but with few medical facts to turn to, Bettelheim's reliance on his own experience and the limitations of a Freudian framework gives him a distorted picture of the minds he seeks to understand. Bettelheim's problematic story about Joey appears, in the end, to illustrate the dangers of a version of empathy in which he imposes his own experience on his subject. Bettelheim's relation to Joey in no way approaches the version of empathy defined by Kaplan, which would involve attending to Joey's experience while also respecting his difference. Without taking the critical step of preserving difference, Bettelheim ignores empathy's limits, and this ultimately contributes to his own version of mindblindness—the inability to understand an autistic mind.

Empathy and Revisions of Autism

In my discussion of Bettelheim and Klein, I have attended to the problem of empathy as it appears in case studies and to the ways in which doctors may misjudge the limits of their perspectives as they try to understand patients. Klein's and Bettelheim's texts, it seems, could be used to make an argument about the dangers of empathy. These theorists use their narratives about autism to render the already marginalized patients they work with even more powerless. Because medical practitioners and teachers possess some authority about their patients and students, it is essential for them to recognize empathy's unreliability and potential for abuse, and to examine with care the ways in which differences in power create the conditions for displacement and coercion. There will always be differences in the particulars of personal, embodied experience— including neurology. We can never fully comprehend the perceptions and experiences of others. And yet, while I believe that this critique 20 of empathy expresses an appropriate sensitivity to the complexity of social interaction, I remain concerned that if we banish the practice of empathy from professional encounters, we will abandon attempts to understand one another. Can there be ethical empathy?

While one might not expect to find an answer to that question in an autism memoir, Temple Grandin's autobiography, *Thinking in Pictures, and Other Reports from My Life with Autism*, suggests new ways of thinking about the possibilities and limits of empathy. Grandin is a professor of animal science at Colorado State University, and while she is widely respected in her field as the designer of livestock farms and slaughter plants that take into account the welfare of animals, she became famous as a memoirist and autism advocate. Grandin's autobiographical writing invites readers into her thoughts and experiences. She represents herself as being on a continuum of humanity with them at the same time that she offers examples that demonstrate they can never truly understand the difference of her mind. In the first chapter of *Thinking in Pictures*, for instance, Grandin begins by declaring that images are her natural cognitive mode—"full-color movies, complete with sound, which run like a VCR tape in my head"—and that, in contrast, words are "like a second language," a language that will always be foreign, will always require translation back into pictures.[23] Although Grandin offers the analogy between language and video, and although she spends the early pages of her book describing in words how she thinks entirely visually as she designs livestock equipment, moments in the text make clear that her narrative can only be an approximation of her way of being. She points out, for instance, that the images with which she thinks are always specific, never general: To her, there is no generalized image of a dog, or even a Great Dane. Instead, she sees specific Great Danes, each of which is arranged in strict chronological order in her memory. Abstract concepts therefore present a particular challenge. The Lord's Prayer, for instance, was incomprehensible to her until she "broke it down into specific visual images" (33). In this prayer, "the power and the glory," for instance, makes sense only as a "semicircular rainbow and an electric tower," and "thy will be done" as an image of "God throwing a lightning bolt" (33). Even more foreign is her assertion that, because of her visual orientation, "certain verb conjugations, such as 'to be,' are absolutely meaningless" (31). Because Grandin thinks in pictures, her relationship to language will remain deeply alien to those who think linguistically—deeply alien, that is, to many of her readers. While Grandin does not reject the possibility of empathy, she insists that readers confront the complexity of autism and recognize how her ability to see and think in atypical ways has allowed her to make unique contributions to animal science and the treatment of autism.

Grandin's work reaches out to readers who do not have autism—inviting them to develop limited empathy with her—but her work also raises the question of whether anyone who is not on the autistic spectrum can develop a deep understanding or expertise about autism. Oliver Sacks's literary case study of Grandin, "An Anthropologist on Mars," confronts this challenge to empathy and expertise directly. Throughout his career, Sacks has maintained that writing and narrative are central to making sense of the unfamiliar and disorienting world of neurological disorders. As an experienced writer and physician, he clearly understands that his work cannot represent the details of Grandin's inner life. But he is resolved to engage anyway. He confronts the limits of empathy and uses knowledge, observation, and writing to begin the work of changing minds—beginning with the minds of his readers.

Because Sacks wants readers to understand autism beyond the clinical diagnosis, and because he recognizes that "no two people with autism are the same," he makes the surprising claim that "if we hope to understand the autistic individual, nothing less than a total biography will do."[24] In composing his biographical case study of Grandin, however, Sacks also narrates his own perceptions and evolving thoughts as he spends a weekend visiting and interviewing her, listening, learning, and evaluating her claims about autism in relation to his own expertise in neurology. She remains a puzzle to him (as he does to her), but she is a puzzle well worth engaging. In the end, Sacks shapes Grandin's public and private lives and thoughts into a story more coherent and, I would say, even more compelling than Grandin's own autobiography. His essay shows that thoughtful, researched, even scholarly engagement that does not overvalue any single framework can, like Grandin's text, enable us to learn about others.

A fundamental element of Sacks's compassionate engagement is that he brings to the task of understanding autism a willingness to *negotiate* knowledge. He builds his understanding of autism in dialogue with Grandin. In addition, he mediates between areas of scholarly inquiry that are not typically thought to have any bearing on one another. His essay bridges biography and neurology, the study of mind and body, and, perhaps most surprisingly, scientific inquiry and spiritual questioning. Sacks's connective thinking is evident when his portrait combines scientific knowledge with a writer's careful perceptions. He states, for instance, that he was surprised before he met Grandin that a person with autism could have written an autobiography. It seemed, he says, "a contradiction in terms" (253). He notes that *Emergence: Labeled Autistic*, Grandin's first autobiography, which she wrote with a journalist, had "coherence," "poignancy," and an often "'normal' tone" that perhaps could be attributed to her collaborator (253). And yet, as an experienced writer, Sacks reviews her papers and her autobiographical articles and finds "a detail and consistency, a directness, that changed [his] mind" (253).

Sacks's work also complicates the relation between expert and amateur, physician and patient, when he asks Grandin open questions and is prepared for unsettling answers that alter his conceptions of autism. His simple question about the night sky—"Do you get a feeling of its grandeur?"—invites Grandin to reflect upon death, morality, divine judgment, and her scientific notion of God (294). Sacks had never before considered the spiritual lives of people with autism and this possibility alters his conception of autistic minds. Another time, Sacks is resistant when Grandin claims that the differences in her "emotional circuit" mean she has no unconscious, no repressed thoughts: "Either you are incorrect or there is an almost unimaginable difference of psychic structure. Repression is universal in human beings" (286–87). And then he thinks again. He thinks of his experience with patients suffering from illnesses or injuries to the brain and he revises his reaction, appreciating anew the differences that neurology makes.

Learning and Responsiveness

Having explored in this essay questions about autism and empathy, I now wonder whether Sacks's interactions with Grandin might best be understood as expressing something other than empathy. While his practice suggests the type of empathy defined by Kaplan—an affective connection that is informed by analysis—the word *empathy* remains burdened by implications of appropriation, displacement, arrogance, pity, and erasure. It may also be inadequate to name a complex connection forged across a divide of neurological difference. Sacks's essay depicts learning that is characterized by reciprocity and negotiation, by a movement from the self to another and back. A better term to suggest both the movement between self and another and the distance that remains between them is "responsiveness." Responsiveness can express the affective engagement of something like empathy, as well as the transformation of thought that can occur in the interplay between the writer and his subject.

Having arrived at an appreciation for Sacks's negotiated understanding and responsiveness to Grandin, I would like to return to my classroom and to my student Gregory. Assessing Gregory's educational story is a challenge because narratives of teaching, like the case studies by Klein and Bettelheim, are often shaped by the pressure to present a subject who is transformed and healed by the knowledge and compassion of the professional. Thus, in both educational and medical realms, narrative conventions can lure us into forgetting that there remains an irreducible difference between the experience of the subject and our own version of the story. With this danger in mind, it is evident that Gregory's story is not one of unequivocal educational success. Indeed, I have never confronted the limits of teaching so profoundly as when I worked with Gregory. Not surprisingly, he did not learn to write and think in the same way as the other students, or with as much normative success. Once he defined his position on a matter, he appeared to find it impossible to independently locate and examine assumptions and counterarguments or to complicate his original stance because doing so required being able to imagine a perspective different from his own. Thus, in early conferences about his drafts, I made the mistake of asking him to think in a way that he simply could not. In addition, because he could not comprehend what his readers might expect or think, he struggled to work with the conventions of academic writing. He had difficulty, for instance, recognizing when he offered too much or too little background; he did not notice when he left his argument behind to go on a tangent; he omitted the transitions that might have eased a reader from one idea, one paragraph, or one sentence to the next. He struggled, as I did, with the fundamental tension between how I taught and how he learned. His definitive neurological reality could not be changed by my concern or my educational practice. Instead, I had to figure out how to redefine my goals and to teach around various cognitive obstacles—mine as well as his.

If we achieved some level of success, it was because I found ways to respond to Gregory's individual perspective and cognitive style. I gradually learned to listen and to understand at least some of what I heard. I realized that Gregory often showed me what would work best for him. His requests for extra conferences, his detailed queries about my written comments, his regular e-mails asking me to look at this or that section of a new draft at first seemed merely obsessive, but I discovered that they expressed a need to literalize the audience that he could not imagine. Thus, in our conferences, I began to narrate my experience as a reader. I coached him as he took notes on my observations and charted plans for revision. I also realized that, until he had more experience, he would only be able to produce academic essays by developing an explicit system, so I offered mechanical rules for organizing his essays and paragraphs that I would have been reluctant to use with other students. I worked with him to develop a process that would enable him to write in the future. Understanding an audience will never be an intuitive or easy task for him, so his writing and revising process must involve real readers—professors, teaching assistants, tutors, others—who can review his drafts to help him find the problems that he cannot see on his own. Working in this way, Gregory, who had seemed impossible to teach at the beginning of the semester, finished the term performing solidly in the middle of the class.

In the end, this is not a story of profound personal or institutional transformation. It is, I believe, better understood as a story about the possibilities afforded by the practice of responsiveness. In the particular context of a writing class, this means that Gregory learned that responding to an audience is essential to the task of writing. At the same time, I learned to become open to learning *from*, not simply *about*, an audience, if the word "audience" can mean an interlocutor, reader, or student. Such responsiveness also defines the core of Sacks's essay, where he negotiates with multiple audiences, especially those readers whose thinking about autism he seeks to transform. As an author and a neurological authority, he demonstrates how important it is for him to learn from Grandin, to be surprised by her, even awed by her, and to respect her difference as he seeks to understand her. Ultimately, in institutional settings such as the classroom or doctor's office, the reciprocal engagement that Sacks demonstrates will never be a panacea for the disruption to communication caused by difference. It does not promise total clarity and insight. But his practice does suggest that the effort to make a connection can be rewarded and that we should therefore not resign ourselves to blindness about other minds.

Notes

1. See Frith and Happé, "Language and Communication in Autistic Disorders" and *The Acquisition and Dissolution of Language.*
2. See Spiro et al., *Empathy and the Practice of Medicine.*
3. Halpern, "Empathy," 161–3. See also Halpern's *From Detached Concern to Empathy.*

4. Halpern, "Empathy," 162.
5. Alexandra G. Kaplan, "Male or Female Psychotherapists for Women: New Formulations," in *Women's Growth in Connection: Writings from the Stone Center*, ed. Judith V. Jordan et al. (New York: Guilford Press, 1991), 273. Cited in More and Milligan, introduction to *The Empathic Practitioner*, 3.
6. Tager-Flusberg, Baron-Cohen, and Cohen, "An Introduction to the Debate," 3.
7. See Baron-Cohen, *Mindblindness*.
8. See *Diagnostic and Statistical Manual of Mental Disorders*, 66–7.
9. Rodier, "The Early Origins of Autism," 56.
10. See Folstein and Rosen-Sheidley, "Genetics of Autism," 944.
11. Baron-Cohen, *Mindblindness*, 55.
12. See Baron-Cohen, *Mindblindness*, 69–72.
13. See Iacoboni, *Mirroring People*.
14. See Turner, Barnby, and Bailey, "Genetic Clues to the Biological Basis of Autism."
15. See, for instance, Blakeslee, "Autism Diagnoses Double in California"; and Silberman, "The Geek Syndrome."
16. The most popular recent autistic autobiographies are by Temple Grandin and Donna Williams. Grandin has two autobiographies, *Emergence: Labeled Autistic* and *Thinking in Pictures*. Williams also has two autobiographies, *Nobody Nowhere: The Extraordinary Autobiography of an Autistic* and *Somebody Somewhere, Breaking Free from the World of Autism*. Lists of other autobiographies and links to online autobiographies are available at Kathleen Seidel's "Autistic Autobiography Online."
17. Klein, "The Importance of Symbol Formation in the Development of the Ego," 95–6. Subsequent references are cited parenthetically in the text.
18. It is worth explaining why so many of the examples I have written about examine boys. Autism affects boys at a much higher rate than it affects girls, approximately 3 or 4:1 among those with IQs higher than 50. See Bauman and Kemper, *The Neurobiology of Autism*, 32. There are some interesting hypotheses about why this is so, including speculation about excess prenatal levels of testosterone and even a controversial theory, drawing on the early work of Hans Asperger in the 1940s, that autism is an expression of "extreme maleness." According to Baron-Cohen, "male" brains (whether these brains belong to men or to women) are better at systematizing than empathizing. Autism, according to his argument, is an extreme version of the male cognitive profile. See Baron-Cohen, "The Extreme Male Brain Theory of Autism."
19. Bettelheim, "Joey," 117. Subsequent references are cited parenthetically in the text.
20. Bettelheim, *The Empty Fortress*, 125.
21. See Bettelheim, "Joey," 126.
22. Bettelheim, *The Empty Fortress*, 57. Subsequent references are cited parenthetically in the text.
23. Grandin, *Thinking in Pictures*, 19. Subsequent references are cited parenthetically in the text.
24. Sacks, "An Anthropologist on Mars," 250.

Bibliography

Baron-Cohen, Simon. "The Extreme Male Brain Theory of Autism." *Trends in Cognitive Science* 6, no. 6 (2002): 248–54.

———. *Mindblindness: An Essay on Autism and Theory of Mind.* Cambridge, MA: MIT Press, 1995.

Bauman, Margaret L. and Thomas Kemper. *The Neurobiology of Autism.* Baltimore: Johns Hopkins University Press, 1994.

Bettelheim, Bruno. "Joey: A 'Mechanical Boy.'" *Scientific American* 200 (1959): 116–27.

———. *The Empty Fortress: Infantile Autism and the Birth of the Self.* New York: Free Press/ Macmillan, 1967.

Blakeslee, Sandra. "Autism Diagnoses Double in California." *New York Times,* May 14, 2003.

Diagnostic and Statistical Manual of Mental Disorders, 4th ed. American Psychiatric Association, 1994.

Folstein, Susan E. and Beth Rosen-Sheidley. "Genetics of Autism: Complex Aetiology for a Heterogeneous Disorder." *Nature Reviews* 2 (2001): 943–55.

Frith, Uta and Francesca Happé. "Language and Communication in Autistic Disorders." *Philosophical Transactions: Biological Sciences* 346 (1994): 1315.

Grandin, Temple. *Thinking in Pictures, and Other Reports from My Life with Autism.* New York, Vintage, 1995.

Grandin, Temple and Margaret M. Scariano. *Emergence: Labeled Autistic.* New York: Warner Books, 1986.

Halpern, Jodi. "Empathy: Using Resonance Emotions in the Service of Curiosity." In *Empathy and the Practice of Medicine: Beyond Pills and the Scalpel,* edited by Howard Spiro, Mary G. McCrea Curnen, Enid Peschel, and Deborah St. James, 160–73. New Haven: Yale University Press, 1993.

———. *From Detached Concern to Empathy: Humanizing Medical Practice.* New York: Oxford University Press, 2001.

Iacoboni, Marco. *Mirroring People: The Science of Empathy and How We Connect with Others.* New York: Farrar, Straus and Giroux, 2008.

Klein, Melanie. "The Importance of Symbol Formation in the Development of the Ego." In *The Selected Melanie Klein,* edited by Mitchell Juliet, 95–111. New York: Free Press, 1986.

More, Ellen Singer and Maureen A. Milligan. *The Empathic Practitioner: Empathy, Gender and Medicine.* New Brunswick, NJ: Rutgers University Press, 1994.

Rodier, Patricia M. "The Early Origins of Autism." *Scientific American* 282, no.2 (2000): 56–63.

Sacks, Oliver. "An Anthropologist on Mars." In *An Anthropologist on Mars: Seven Paradoxical Tales,* 244–96. New York: Vintage, 1995.

Seidel, Kathleen. "Autistic Autobiography Online." http://www.neurodiversity.com/autobiography.html (accessed November 2, 2005).

Silberman, Steve. "The Geek Syndrome." *Wired* 9, December 2001. http://www.wired.com/wired/archive/9.12/aspergers.html (accessed February 26, 2006).

Spiro, Howard M., Mary G. McCrea Curnen, Enid Peschel, and Deborah St. James, eds. *Empathy and the Practice of Medicine: Beyond Pills and the Scalpel.* New Haven: Yale University Press, 1993.

Tager-Flusberg, Helen, Simon Baron-Cohen, and Donald J. Cohen. "An Introduction to the Debate." In *Understanding Other Minds: Perspectives from Autism,* edited by Helen Tager-Flusberg, Simon Baron-Cohen, and Donald J. Cohen, 3–9. Oxford: Oxford University Press, 1993.

Turner, Martha, Gabrielle Barnby, and Anthony Bailey. "Genetic Clues to the Biological Basis of Autism." *Molecular Medicine Today* 6 (2000): 238–44.

Williams, Donna. *Nobody Nowhere: The Extraordinary Autobiography of an Autistic.* New York: Harper, 1992.

———. *Somebody Somewhere: Breaking Free from the World of Autism.* New York: Three Rivers Press, 1994.

▪ QUESTIONS

Reading

1. What does the term *mindblindness* mean?
2. How is autism diagnosed, according to Jurecic?
3. How have psychological theories about the causes of autism changed since the 1940s? What is Jurecic's assessment of these changes?

Exploratory Writing

1. Using Jurecic's essay as a guide, make a double-entry list contrasting autism spectrum behaviors with "normal" behaviors. Does Jurecic define "normal"?

"NORMAL" BEHAVIORS	AUTISM SPECTRUM BEHAVIORS

   Write a brief essay explaining how you believe "normal" human behavior should be understood and defined. Do you feel that "normal" is a useful category? Why or why not?

2. In pairs, take turns trying to explain something that you view or experience in a unique way, or simply something the other person has never experienced. (For example, one of you is a surfer and the other has never tried surfing, one of you is tall and the other short, one of you is trilingual and the other speaks only one language, one of you thinks in pictures and the other in words.) When you've each taken a turn, discuss what techniques each of you used to convey your perspectives, and how you might alter those techniques to better communicate with each other.

Making Connections

1. Steven Pinker (p. 458) notes that when anthropologists survey moral concerns in many different cultures, the same themes emerge: harm, fairness, group loyalty, authority, and purity. Which of these themes are dependent on a "normal" ability to empathize, as described by Jurecic? In your opinion, does cultural difference usually overpower neurological difference, or vice versa?

Essay Writing

1. Jurecic writes: "Having surveyed texts about the definitions and etiology of the disorder, I still find it nearly impossible to imagine what it would be like to have severe autism. . . . I can no more fully imagine the emotional, mental, and social lives of people with autism, especially how they understand human relationships, than I can imagine a life without the spoken word. Here is where *my* practice of empathy confronts its limits" (paragraph 11). Imagine that you wake up one morning with one of your basic senses or abilities missing — for example, your sense of smell or touch, or your ability to move or speak. Write an essay reflecting on your imagined experience.

REFLECTING

Morning of the Stroke

Jill Bolte Taylor

Neuroanatomist Jill Bolte Taylor is in a unique position to reflect on the massive stroke she experienced one morning in 1996. After Taylor told the story of her stroke to an invited audience at the 2008 TED (Technology, Entertainment, Design) conference, she found a worldwide audience on YouTube. *Time* magazine named Taylor one of the 100 most influential people of 2008. "Morning of the Stroke" is an excerpt from Taylor's book, *My Stroke of Insight* (2008). As in her TED talk, Taylor narrates the experience of recognizing her symptoms — including euphoria and dissociation — as the stroke gripped her. She narrates the account from two perspectives: that of the woman in the throes of a severe brain hemorrhage and that of the brain researcher with the rare opportunity to analyze her symptoms from the inside out. In the book, she also describes her career before and after the stroke, her eight-year recovery, and the spiritual and intellectual insights she gained from the experience.

It was 7:00 a.m. on December 10, 1996. I awoke to the familiar tick-tick-tick of my compact disc player as it began winding up to play. Sleepily, I hit the snooze button just in time to catch the next mental wave back into dreamland. Here, in this magic land I call "Thetaville"—a surreal place of altered consciousness somewhere between dreams and stark reality—my spirit beamed beautiful, fluid, and free from the confines of normal reality.

Six minutes later, as the tick-tick-tick of the CD alerted my memory that I was a land mammal, I sluggishly awoke to a sharp pain piercing my brain directly behind my left eye. Squinting into the early morning light, I clicked off the impending alarm with my right hand and instinctively pressed the palm of my left hand firmly against the side of my face. Rarely ill, I thought how queer it was for me to awaken to such a striking pain. As my left eye pulsed with a slow and deliberate rhythm, I felt bewildered and irritated. The throbbing pain behind my eye was sharp, like the caustic sensation that sometimes accompanies biting into ice cream.

As I rolled out of my warm waterbed, I stumbled into the world with the ambivalence of a wounded soldier. I closed the bedroom window blind to block the incoming stream of light from stinging my eyes. I decided that exercise might get my blood flowing and perhaps help dissipate the pain. Within moments, I hopped onto my "cardio-glider" (a full-body exercise machine) and began jamming away to Shania Twain singing the lyrics, "Whose bed have your boots been under?" Immediately, I felt a powerful and unusual sense of dissociation roll over me. I felt so peculiar that I questioned my well-being. Even though my thoughts seemed lucid, my body felt irregular. As I watched my hands and arms rocking forward and back, forward and back, in opposing synchrony with my torso, I felt strangely detached from my normal cogni-

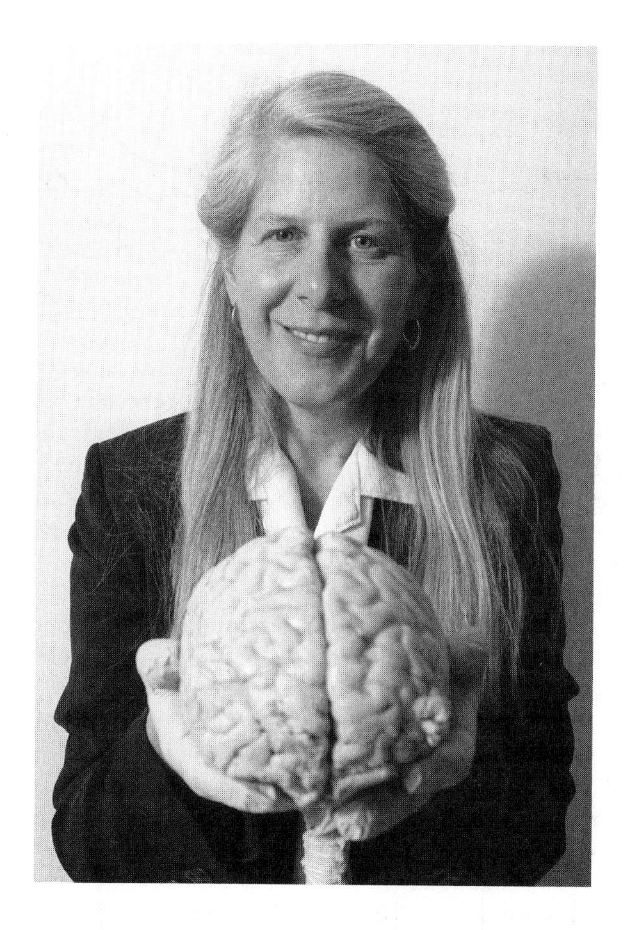

tive functions. It was as if the integrity of my mind/body connection had somehow become compromised.

Feeling detached from normal reality, I seemed to be witnessing my activity as opposed to feeling like the active participant performing the action. I felt as though I was observing myself in motion, as in the playback of a memory. My fingers, as they grasped onto the handrail, looked like primitive claws. For a few seconds I rocked and watched, with riveting wonder, as my body oscillated rhythmically and mechanically. My torso moved up and down in perfect cadence with the music and my head continued to ache.

I felt bizarre, as if my conscious mind was suspended somewhere between my normal reality and some esoteric space. Although this experience was somewhat reminiscent of my morning time in Thetaville, I was sure that this time I was awake. Yet, I felt as if I was trapped inside the perception of a meditation that I could neither stop nor escape. Dazed, I felt the frequency of shooting pangs escalate inside my brain, and I realized that this exercise regime was probably not a good idea. 5

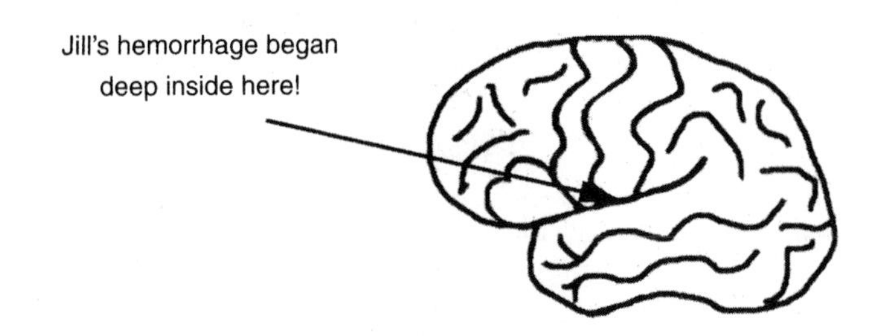

Feeling a little nervous about my physical condition, I climbed off the machine and bumbled through my living room on the way to the bath. As I walked, I noticed that my movements were no longer fluid. Instead they felt deliberate and almost jerky. In the absence of my normal muscular coordination, there was no grace to my pace and my balance was so impaired that my mind seemed completely preoccupied with just keeping me upright.

As I lifted my leg to step into the tub, I held on to the wall for support. It seemed odd that I could sense the inner activities of my brain as it adjusted and readjusted all of the opposing muscle groups in my lower extremities to prevent me from falling over. My perception of these automatic body responses was no longer an exercise in intellectual conceptualization. Instead, I was momentarily privy to a precise and experiential understanding of how hard the fifty trillion cells in my brain and body were working in perfect unison to maintain the flexibility and integrity of my physical form. Through the eyes of an avid enthusiast of the magnificence of the human design, I witnessed with awe the autonomic functioning of my nervous system as it calculated and recalculated every joint angle.

Ignorant to the degree of danger my body was in, I balanced my weight against the shower wall. As I leaned forward to turn on the faucet, I was startled by an abrupt and exaggerated clamor as water surged into the tub. This unexpected amplification of sound was both enlightening and disturbing. It brought me to the realization that, in addition to having problems with coordination and equilibrium, my ability to process incoming sound (auditory information) was erratic.

I understood neuroanatomically that coordination, equilibrium, audition and the action of inspirational breathing were processed through the pons of my brainstem. For the first time, I considered the possibility that I was perhaps having a major neurological malfunction that was life threatening.

10 As my cognitive mind searched for an explanation about what was happening anatomically inside my brain, I reeled backward in response to the augmented roar of the water as the unexpected noise pierced my delicate and aching brain. In that instant, I suddenly felt vulnerable, and I noticed that the constant brain chatter that routinely familiarized me with my surroundings was no longer a predictable and constant flow of conversation. Instead, my verbal thoughts were now inconsistent, fragmented, and interrupted by an intermittent silence.

Fibers Passing Through the Pons of the Brainstem

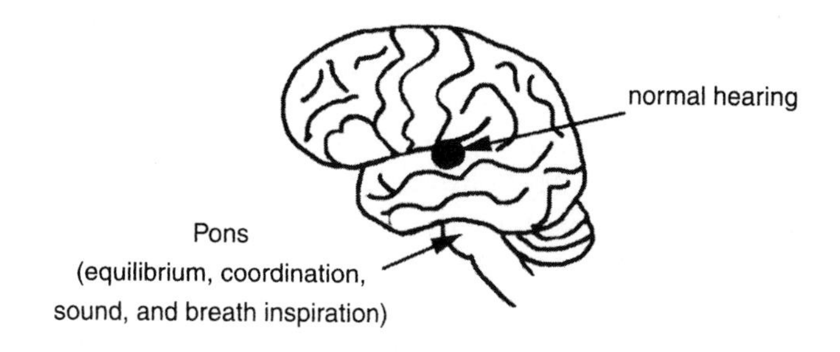

Language Centers

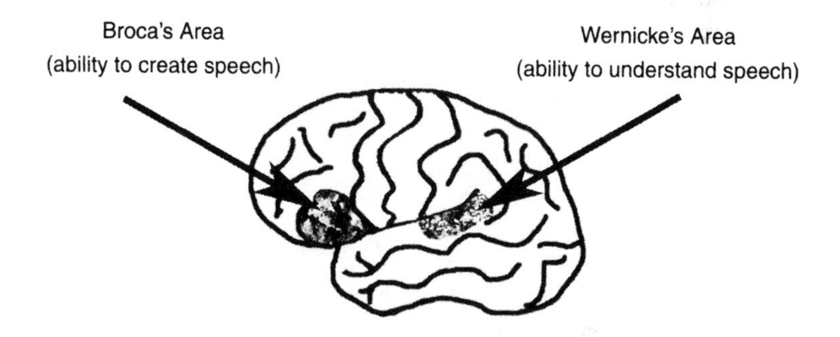

When I realized that the sensations outside of me, including the remote sounds of a bustling city beyond my apartment window, had faded away, I could tell that the broad range of my natural observation had become constricted. As my brain chatter began to disintegrate, I felt an odd sense of isolation. My blood pressure must have been dropping as a result of the bleeding in my brain because I felt as if all of my systems, including my mind's ability to instigate movement, were moving into a slow mode of operation. Yet, even though my thoughts were no longer a constant stream of chatter about the external world and my relationship to it, I was conscious and constantly present within my mind.

Confused, I searched the memory banks of both my body and brain, questioning and analyzing anything I could remember having experienced in the past that was remotely similar to this situation. *What is going on?* I wondered. *Have I ever experienced anything like this before? Have I ever felt like this before? This feels like a migraine. What is happening in my brain?*

The harder I tried to concentrate, the more fleeting my ideas seemed to be. Instead of finding answers and information, I met a growing sense of peace. In place of that constant chatter that had attached me to the details of my life, I felt enfolded by a blanket of tranquil euphoria. How fortunate I was that the portion of my brain that registered fear, my amygdala, had not reacted with alarm to these unusual circumstances and shifted me into a state of panic. As the language centers in my left hemisphere grew increasingly silent and I became detached from the memories of my life, I was comforted by an expanding sense of grace. In this void of higher cognition and details pertaining to my normal life, my consciousness soared into an all- knowingness, a "being at *one*" with the universe, if you will. In a compelling sort of way, it felt like the good road home and I liked it.

By this point I had lost touch with much of the physical three-dimensional reality that surrounded me. My body was propped up against the shower wall and I found it odd that I was aware that I could no longer clearly discern the physical boundaries of where I began and where I ended. I sensed the composition of my being as that of a fluid rather than that of a solid. I no longer perceived myself as a whole object separate from everything. Instead, I now blended in with the space and flow around me. Beholding a growing sense of detachment between my cognitive mind and my ability to control and finely manipulate my fingers, the mass of my body felt heavy and my energy waned.

Orientation Association Area
(physical boundaries, space, and time)

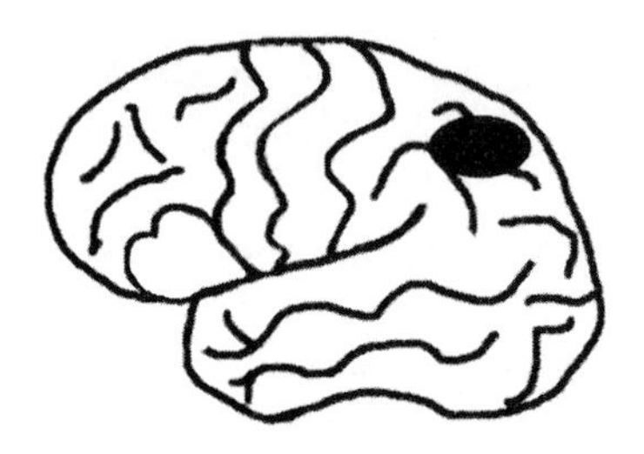

When the shower droplets beat into my chest like little bullets, I was harshly startled back into this reality. As I held my hands up in front of my face and wiggled my fingers, I was simultaneously perplexed and intrigued. *Wow, what a strange and amazing thing I am. What a bizarre living being I am. Life! I am life! I am a sea of water bound inside this membranous pouch. Here, in this form, I am a conscious mind and this body is the vehicle through which I am ALIVE! I am trillions of cells sharing a common mind. I am here, now, thriving as life. Wow! What an unfathomable concept! I am cellular life, no—I am molecular life with manual dexterity and a cognitive mind!* 15

In this altered state of being, my mind was no longer preoccupied with the billions of details that my brain routinely used to define and conduct my life in the external world. Those little voices, that brain chatter that customarily kept me abreast of myself in relation to the world outside of me, were delightfully silent. And in their absence, my memories of the past and my dreams of the future evaporated. I was alone. In the moment, I was alone with nothing but the rhythmic pulse of my beating heart.

I must admit that the growing void in my traumatized brain was entirely seductive. I welcomed the reprieve that the silence brought from the constant chatter that related me to what I now perceived as the insignificant affairs of society. I eagerly turned my focus inward to the steadfast drumming of the trillions of brilliant cells that worked diligently and synchronously to maintain my body's steady state of homeostasis. As the blood poured in over my brain, my consciousness slowed to a soothing and satisfying awareness that embraced the vast and wondrous world within. I was both fascinated and humbled by how hard my little cells worked, moment by moment, just to maintain the integrity of my existence in this physical form.

For the first time, I felt truly at one with my body as a complex construction of living, thriving organisms. I was proud to see that I was this swarming conglomeration of cellular life that had stemmed from the intelligence of a single molecular genius! I welcomed the opportunity to pass beyond my normal perceptions, away from the persevering pain that relentlessly pulsed in my head. As my consciousness slipped into a state of peaceful grace, I felt ethereal. Although the pulse of pain in my brain was inescapable, it was not debilitating.

Standing there with the water pounding onto my breasts, a tingling sensation surged through my chest and forcefully radiated upward into my throat. Startled, I became instantly aware that I was in grave danger. Shocked back into this external reality, I immediately reassessed the abnormalities of my physical systems. Determined to understand what was going on, I actively scanned my reservoir of education in demand of a self-diagnosis. *What is going on with my body? What is wrong with my brain?*

Although the sporadically discontinuous flow of normal cognition was virtually incapacitating, somehow I managed to keep my body on task. Stepping out of the shower, my brain felt inebriated. My body was unsteady, felt heavy, and exerted itself in very slow motion. *What is it I'm trying to do? Dress, dress for work. I'm dressing for work.* I labored mechanically to choose my clothes and by 8:15 a.m., I was ready for my commute. Pacing my apartment, I thought, *Okay, I'm going to work. I'm going to work. Do I know how to get to work? Can I drive?* As I visualized the road to McLean Hospital, I was literally thrown off balance when my right arm dropped, completely paralyzed against my side. In that moment I knew. *Oh my gosh, I'm having a stroke! I'm having a stroke!* And in the next instant, the thought flashed through my mind, *Wow, this is so cool!* 20

I felt as though I was suspended in a peculiar euphoric stupor, and I was strangely elated when I understood that this unexpected pilgrimage into the intricate functions of my brain actually had a physiological basis and explanation. I kept thinking, *Wow, how many scientists have the opportunity to study their own brain function and mental deterioration from the inside out?* My entire life had been dedicated to my own understanding of how the human brain creates our perception of reality. And now I was experiencing this most remarkable stroke of insight!

When my right arm became paralyzed, I felt the life force inside the limb explode. When it dropped dead against my body, it clubbed my torso. It was the strangest sensation. I felt as if my arm had been guillotined off!

I understood neuroanatomically that my motor cortex had been affected and I was fortunate that within a few minutes, the deadness of my right arm subtly abated. As the limb began to reclaim its life, it throbbed with a formidable tingling pain. I felt weak and wounded. My arm felt completely depleted of its intrinsic strength, yet I could wield it like a stub. I wondered if it would ever be normal again. Catching sight of my warm and cradling waterbed, I seemed to be beckoned by it on this cold winter morning in New England. *Oh, I am so tired. I feel so tired. I just want to rest. I just want to lie down and relax for a little while.* But resounding like thunder from deep within my being, a commanding voice spoke clearly to me: *If you lie down now you will never get up!*

Movement and Sensory Perception

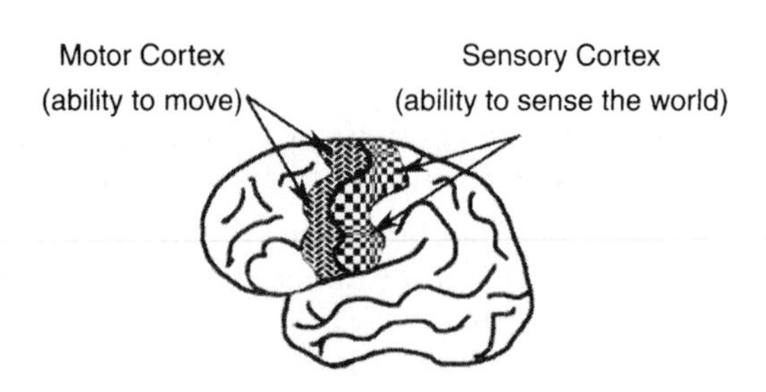

Startled by this ominous illumination, I fathomed the gravity of my immediate situation. Although I was compelled by a sense of urgency to orchestrate my rescue, another part of me delighted in the euphoria of my irrationality. I stepped across the threshold of my bedroom, and as I gazed into the eyes of my reflected image, I paused for a moment, in search of some guidance or profound insight. In the wisdom of my dementia, I understood that my body was, by the magnificence of its biological design, a precious and fragile gift. It was clear to me that this body functioned like a portal through which the energy of who I am can be beamed into a three-dimensional external space.

This cellular mass of my body had provided me with a marvelous temporary home. This amazing brain had been capable of integrating literally billions of trillions of bits of data, in every instant, to create for me a three-dimensional perception of this environment that actually appeared to be not only seamless and real, but also safe. Here in this delusion, I was mesmerized by the efficiency of this biological matrix as it created my form, and I was awed by the simplicity of its design. I saw myself as a complex composite of dynamic systems, a collection of interlacing cells capable of integrating a medley of sensory modalities streaming in from the external world. And when the systems functioned properly, they naturally manifested a consciousness capable of perceiving a normal reality. I wondered how I could have spent so many years in this body, in this form of life, and never really understood that I was just visiting here.

Even in this condition, the egotistical mind of my left hemisphere arrogantly retained the belief that although I was experiencing a dramatic mental incapacity, my life was invincible. Optimistically, I believed that I would

Territory of Jill's Hemorrhage
(shaded oval area)

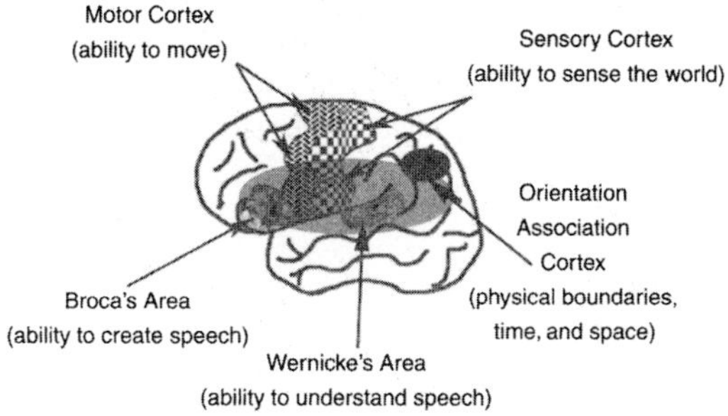

Motor Cortex
(ability to move)
Sensory Cortex
(ability to sense the world)
Orientation
Association
Cortex
(physical boundaries,
time, and space)
Broca's Area
(ability to create speech)
Wernicke's Area
(ability to understand speech)

recover completely from this morning's events. Feeling a little irritated by this impromptu disruption of my work schedule, I bantered, *Okay, well, I'm having a stroke. Yep, I'm having a stroke . . . but I'm a very busy woman! All right, since I can't stop this stroke from happening, then, okay, I'll do this for a week! I'll learn what I need to know about how my brain creates my perception of reality and then I'll meet my schedule, next week. Now, what am I doing? Getting help. I must stay focused and get help.*

To my counterpart in the looking glass I pleaded, *Remember, please remember everything you are experiencing! Let this be my stroke of insight into the disintegration of my own cognitive mind.*

▪ QUESTIONS

Reading

1. Taylor uses a memoir form as a means of reflecting on scientific research. Doing so allows her to express a sense of awe at what her stroke reveals about the relationship between the brain and her sense of self. In your own words, explain how Taylor understands that relationship. How would her account be different if she were writing in more conventionally scientific terms?
2. *Voice* is the personality of a piece of writing. A writer will adopt different voices for different purposes in different contexts. With this in mind, reread the italicized sections of Taylor's account. How would you describe the voice in the italicized passages? How is this voice different from the primary voice of the account? Why do you think Taylor uses more than one voice to tell her story?
3. Taylor often uses the language of neurobiology — especially terms for regions of the brain and physiological functions — to explain the symptoms of her stroke. Brain regions she discusses and illustrates include *pons*, *Broca's area*, *Wernicke's area*, *motor cortex*, and *orientation association cortex*. Physiological functions she discusses include *coordination*, *equilibrium*, *orientation*, *audition*, *inspirational breathing*, and *sensory modalities*. Choose two terms that you think are particularly important, and write a paragraph in which you define these terms and explain how and why they're crucial to understanding Taylor's account. To come up with your definitions, start with Taylor's text. If you need more information, consult a dictionary or an online reference work.

Exploratory Writing

1. Taylor begins her account of her stroke with a description of dozing in dreamland. Using a double-entry format, make a list of phrases Taylor uses to describe dreamland and her stroke symptoms. Once you've completed your lists, write a paragraph comparing Taylor's descriptions of dreamland and her stroke symptoms.

DREAMLAND	STROKE SYMPTOMS

2. Taylor incorporates simple diagrams of the human brain to help readers visualize the regions she describes. Her intention is to help readers understand where in the brain her particular symptoms originated. Choose a symptom that you find interesting or puzzling. Then, find the diagram that represents the origin of that symptom. Using Taylor's descriptions and diagrams, prepare a brief presentation for the class, explaining the origin of the symptom.

Making Connections

1. Use a search engine to find several online accounts written by people who have survived strokes. Drawing on "Morning of the Stroke," write an essay that makes an argument about how these accounts represent the effects of stroke on the identities of survivors. For this project, you might also want to look for Taylor's book, *My Stroke of Insight,* in the library, to give you a more detailed sense of her views on the relationship between her stroke and her identity.

Essay Writing

1. Watch the video of Taylor's account of her stroke on the TED Web site: **http://www.ted.com/index.php/talks/jill_bolte_taylor_s_powerful_stroke_of_insight.html**. What do you learn from the video that you didn't learn from Taylor's written account? What did you learn from the written account that you didn't learn from the video? How did your impression of Taylor change after watching the video?

REFLECTING

The Corner of the Eye

Lewis Thomas

Essayist, physician, and academic Lewis Thomas (1913–1993) was born to a doctor and a nurse in Flushing, New York. He followed in his parents' footsteps, beginning a successful research career in immunology and microbiology after studying at Harvard Medical School. It wasn't until 1971, however, when he received a monthly column in the *New England Journal of Medicine*, that Thomas began to write the essays that brought him acclaim as a science writer. The column, which moved to *Discover* in 1980, brought attention to Thomas's lyrical prose and his ability to draw on science for insights into a range of subjects, from the interconnectedness of earth and its organisms to space exploration to nuclear warfare. He won a National Book Award in 1975 for *The Lives of a Cell*, a collection of these columns, which was followed by numerous compilations, including *The Medusa and the Snail* (1979); *Et Cetera, Et Cetera* (1990); and *The Fragile Species* (1992). Thomas died in 1993. "The Corner of the Eye," from *Late Night Thoughts on Listening to Mahler's Ninth Symphony* (1983), displays Thomas's meditative style (influenced by Montaigne) and focuses on two of his fascinations: the development of language and the relationship between humans and nature.

There are some things that human beings can see only out of the corner of the eye. The niftiest examples of this gift, familiar to all children, are small, faint stars. When you look straight at one such star, it vanishes; when you move your eyes to stare into the space nearby, it reappears. If you pick two faint stars, side by side, and focus on one of the pair, it disappears and now you can see the other in the corner of your eye, and you can move your eyes back and forth, turning off the star in the center of your retina and switching the other one on. There is a physiological explanation for the phenomenon: We have more rods, the cells we use for light perception, at the periphery of our retinas; more cones, for perceiving color, at the center.

Something like this happens in music. You cannot really hear certain sequences of notes in a Bach fugue unless at the same time there are other notes being sounded, dominating the field. The real meaning in music comes from tones only audible in the corner of the mind.

I used to worry that computers would become so powerful and sophisticated as to take the place of human minds. The notion of Artificial Intelligence used to scare me half to death. Already, a large enough machine can do all sorts of intelligent things beyond our capacities: calculate in a split second the answers to mathematical problems requiring years for a human brain, draw accurate pictures from memory, even manufacture successions of sounds with a disarming resemblance to real music. Computers can translate textbooks, write dissertations of their own for doctorates, even speak in machine-tooled, inhuman phonemes any words read off from a printed page. They can communicate with one another, holding consultations and committee meetings of their own in networks around the earth.

Computers can make errors, of course, and do so all the time in small, irritating ways, but the mistakes can be fixed and nearly always are. In this respect they are fundamentally inhuman, and here is the relaxing thought: Computers will not take over the world; they cannot replace us, because they are not designed, as we are, for ambiguity.

Imagine the predicament faced by a computer programmed to make language, not the interesting communication in sounds made by vervets or in symbols by brilliant chimpanzee prodigies, but real human talk. The grammar would not be too difficult, and there would be no problem in constructing a vocabulary of etymons, the original, pure, unambiguous words used to name real things. The impossibility would come in making the necessary mistakes we humans make with words instinctively, intuitively, as we build our kinds of language, changing the meanings to imply quite different things, constructing and elaborating the varieties of ambiguity without which speech can never become human speech. 5

Look at the record of language if you want to glimpse the special qualities of the human mind that lie beyond the reach of any machine. Take, for example, the metaphors we use in everyday speech to tell ourselves who we are, where we live, and where we come from.

The earth is a good place to begin. The word *earth* is used to name the ground we walk on, the soil in which we grow plants or dig clams, and the planet itself; we also use it to describe all of humanity ("the whole earth responds to the beauty of a child," we say to each other).

The earliest word for earth in our language was the Indo-European root *dhghem,* and look what we did with it. We turned it, by adding suffixes, into *humus* in Latin; today we call the complex polymers that hold fertile soil together *humic* acids, and somehow or other the same root became *humility.* With another suffix the word became *human.* Did the earth become human, or did the human emerge from the earth? One answer may lie in that nice cognate word *humble. Humane* was built on it, extending the meaning of both the earth and ourselves. In ancient Hebrew, *adamah* was the word for earth, *adam* for man. What computer could run itself through such manipulations as those?

We came at the same system of defining ourselves from the other direction. The word *wiros* was the first root for man; it took us in our vanity on to *virile* and *virtue,* but also turned itself into the Germanic word *weraldh,* meaning the life of man, and thence in English to our word *world.*

There is a deep hunch in this kind of etymology. The world of man derives from this planet, shares origin with the life of the soil, lives in humility with all the rest of life. I cannot imagine programming a computer to think up an idea like that, not a twentieth-century computer, anyway. 10

The world began with what it is now the fashion to call the "Big Bang." Characteristically, we have assigned the wrong words for the very beginning of the earth and ourselves, in order to evade another term that would cause this century embarrassment. It could not, of course, have been a bang of any sort, with no atmosphere to conduct the waves of sound, and no ears. It was something else, occurring in the most absolute silence we can imagine. It was the Great Light.

We say it had been chaos before, but it was not the kind of place we use the word *chaos* for today, things tumbling over each other and bumping around. Chaos did not have that meaning in Greek; it simply meant empty.

We took it, in our words, from chaos to cosmos, a word that simply meant order, cosmetic. We perceived the order in surprise, and our cosmologists and physicists continue to find new and astonishing aspects of the order. We made up the word *universe* from the whole affair, meaning literally turning everything into one thing. We used to say it was a miracle, and we still permit ourselves to refer to the whole universe as a marvel, holding in our unconscious minds the original root meaning of these two words, miracle and marvel—from the ancient root word *smei,* signifying a smile. It immensely pleases a human being to see something never seen before, even more to learn something never known before, most of all to think something never thought before. The rings of Saturn are the latest surprise. All my physicist friends are enchanted by this phenomenon, marveling at the small violations of the laws of planetary mechanics, shocked by the unaccountable braids and spokes stuck there among the rings like graffiti. It is nice for physicists to see something new and inexplicable; it means that the laws of nature are once again about to be amended by a new footnote.

The greatest surprise of all lies within our own local, suburban solar system. It is not Mars; Mars was surprising in its way but not flabber-gasting; it was a disappointment not to find evidence of life, and there was some sadness in the pictures sent back to earth from the Mars Lander, that lonely long-legged apparatus poking about with its jointed arm, picking up sample after sample of the barren Mars soil, looking for any flicker of life and finding none; the only sign of life on Mars was the Lander itself, an extension of the human mind all the way from earth to Mars, totally alone.

Nor is Saturn the great surprise, nor Jupiter, nor Venus, nor Mercury, nor any of the glimpses of the others. 15

The overwhelming astonishment, the queerest structure we know about so far in the whole universe, the greatest of all cosmological scientific puzzles, confounding all our efforts to comprehend it, is the earth. We are only now beginning to appreciate how strange and splendid it is, how it catches the breath; the loveliest object afloat around the sun, enclosed in its own blue bubble of atmosphere, manufacturing and breathing its own oxygen, fixing its own nitrogen from the air into its own soil, generating its own weather at the surface of its rain forests, constructing its own carapace from living parts: chalk cliffs, coral reefs, old fossils from earlier forms of life now covered by layers of new life meshed together around the globe, Troy upon Troy.

Seen from the right distance, from the corner of the eye of an extraterrestrial visitor, it must surely seem a single creature, clinging to the round warm stone, turning in the sun.

▪ QUESTIONS

Reading

1. According to Thomas, could computers become sophisticated enough to take the place of human minds? Why or why not?
2. Summarize Thomas's comments about the Big Bang theory.
3. Highlight, underline, or flag the different words or word origins that Thomas defines in his essay. Why is etymology important in his discussion?

Exploratory Writing

1. In small groups, write a list of biological, astronomical, or chemical phenomena that could be considered miraculous or marvelous. Do some research to learn the etymology of the terms we use to describe these phenomena or processes. What additional insights do the word roots offer?
2. Consider Thomas's conclusions about planet earth. Which of his reflections are scientifically based observations? Rewrite his two concluding paragraphs in objective, scientific language, removing any poetic language or subjective descriptions. How does this change the tone of Thomas's essay?

Making Connections

1. A number of the science writers included in this volume use writing to conjure memorable visual images of scientific phenomena. Compare Thomas's descriptive writing to the work of any two other essayists in this book. Highlight the passages in their descriptions that allow you to "see" images in your mind.

Essay Writing

1. Thomas writes: "It immensely pleases a human being to see something never seen before, even more to learn something never known before, most of all to think something never thought before" (paragraph 13). He celebrates the element of surprise in scientific observation and discovery. Reflecting on your own experiences, write an essay describing a moment when you saw, learned, or thought something new about the natural world. How did that moment change your perspective?

REPORTING

The Eureka Hunt

Jonah Lehrer

Jonah Lehrer (b. 1981) is a contributing editor for the technology magazine *Wired*. His collection of essays, *Proust Was a Neuroscientist* (2007), proposes that the imaginative work of eight artists predated scientists' current understanding of the brain. The title essay charts the early-twentieth-century French writer's "discoveries" that taste and smell can evoke intense memories — an observation only recently confirmed by scientists. (It was not until 2002 that Brown University psychologist Rachel Herz showed that the nerves associated with taste and smell connect to the hippocampus, affecting long-term memory.) In a 2008 interview, Lehrer explains how Proust's novels, which he read during breaks from his lab experiments on the memory of sea slugs, inspired his thesis: "Once I had this idea about looking at art through the prism of science, I began to see connections everywhere." Lehrer's latest book, *How We Decide* (2009), rationalizes the daily decisions we make from a neuroscientific perspective. He earned a degree from Columbia University, sharing a lab with Nobel Prize–winning neuroscientist Eric Kandel, and studied at Oxford University as a Rhodes Scholar. His writing has been featured on NPR and has appeared in the *Boston Globe, Nature, Seed*, the *Washington Post*, and the *New Yorker*, in which this article appeared in July 2008.

The summer of 1949 was long and dry in Montana. On the afternoon of August 5th—the hottest day ever recorded in the state—a lightning fire was spotted in a remote area of pine forest. A parachute brigade of fifteen firefighters known as smoke jumpers was dispatched to put out the blaze; the man in charge was named Wag Dodge. When the jumpers left Missoula, in a C-47 cargo plane, they were told that the fire was small, just a few burning acres in the Mann Gulch.

Mann Gulch, nearly three miles long, is a site of geological transition, where the Great Plains meet the Rocky Mountains, pine trees give way to tall grasses, and steep cliffs loom over the steppes of the Midwest. The fire began in the trees on one side of the gulch. By the time the firefighters arrived, the blaze was already out of control. Dodge moved his men along the other side of the gulch and told them to head downhill, toward the water.

When the smoke jumpers started down the gulch, a breeze was blowing the flames away from them. Suddenly, the wind reversed, and Dodge watched the fire leap across the gulch and spark the grass on his side. He and his men were only a quarter mile uphill. An updraft began, and fierce winds howled through the canyon as the fire sucked in the surrounding air. Dodge was suddenly staring at a wall of flame fifty feet tall and three hundred feet deep. In a matter of seconds, the fire began to devour the grass, hurtling toward the smoke jumpers at seven hundred feet a minute.

Dodge screamed at his men to retreat. They dropped their gear and started running up the steep canyon walls, trying to reach the top of the ridge. After a few minutes, Dodge glanced over his shoulder and saw that the fire was less than fifty yards away. He realized that the blaze couldn't be outrun; the gulch was too steep, the flames too fast.

5 So Dodge stopped running. The decision wasn't as suicidal as it appeared: In a moment of desperate insight, he had devised an escape plan. He lit a match and ignited the ground in front of him, the flames quickly moving up the grassy slope. Then Dodge stepped into the shadow of his fire, so that he was surrounded by a buffer of burned land. He wet his handkerchief with water from his canteen, clutched the cloth to his mouth, and lay down on the smoldering embers. He closed his eyes and tried to inhale the thin layer of oxygen clinging to the ground. Then he waited for the fire to pass over him.

Thirteen smoke jumpers died in the Mann Gulch fire. White crosses below the ridge still mark the spots where the men died. But after several terrifying minutes Dodge emerged from the ashes, virtually unscathed.

There is something inherently mysterious about moments of insight. Wag Dodge, for instance, could never explain where his idea for the escape fire came from. ("It just seemed the logical thing to do" was all he could muster.) His improbable survival has become one of those legendary stories of insight, like Archimedes shouting "Eureka!" when he saw his bathwater rise, or Isaac Newton watching an apple fall from a tree and then formulating his theory of gravity. Such tales all share a few essential features, which psychologists and neuroscientists use to define "the insight experience." The first of these is the impasse: Before there can be a breakthrough, there has to be a mental block. Wag Dodge spent minutes running from the fire, although he was convinced that doing so was futile. Then, when the insight arrived, Dodge immediately realized that the problem was solved. This is another key feature of insight: the feeling of certainty that accompanies the idea. Dodge didn't have time to think about whether his plan would work. He simply knew that it would.

Mark Jung-Beeman, a cognitive neuroscientist at Northwestern University, has spent the past fifteen years trying to figure out what happens inside the brain when people have an insight. "It's one of those defining features of the human mind, and yet we have no idea how or why it happens," he told me. Insights have often been attributed to divine intervention, but, by mapping the epiphany as a journey between cortical circuits, Jung-Beeman wants to purge the insight experience of its mystery. Jung-Beeman has a tense smile, a receding hairline, and the wiry build of a long-distance runner. He qualified for the 1988 and 1992 Olympic trials in the fifteen hundred metres, although he gave up competitive running after, as he puts it, "everything below the hips started to fall apart." He now subsists on long walks and manic foot tapping. When Jung-Beeman gets excited about an idea—be it the cellular properties of pyramidal neurons or his new treadmill—his speech accelerates, and he starts to draw pictures on whatever paper is nearby. It's as if his mind were sprinting ahead of his mouth.

Jung-Beeman became interested in the nature of insight in the early 1990s, while researching the right hemisphere of the brain. At the time, he was studying patients who had peculiar patterns of brain damage. "We had a number of patients with impaired right hemispheres," he said. "And the doctors would always say, 'Wow, you're lucky—it got the right hemisphere. That's the minor hemisphere. It doesn't do much, and it doesn't do anything with language.'" But it gradually became clear to Jung-Beeman that these patients did have serious cognitive problems after all, particularly with understanding linguistic nuance, and he began to suspect that the talents of the right hemisphere had been overlooked. If the left hemisphere excelled at denotation—storing the primary meaning of a word—Jung-Beeman suspected that the right hemisphere dealt with connotation, everything that gets left out of a dictionary definition, such as the emotional charge in a sentence or a metaphor. "Language is so complex that the brain has to process it in two different ways at the same time," he said. "It needs to see the forest *and* the trees. The right hemisphere is what helps you see the forest."

10 It wasn't clear how to pinpoint these nuanced aspects of cognition, because the results of right-hemisphere damage were harder to spot than those of left-hemisphere damage. But in 1993 Jung-Beeman heard a talk by the psychologist Jonathan Schooler on moments of insight. Schooler had demonstrated that it was possible to interfere with insight by making people explain their thought process while trying to solve a puzzle—a phenomenon he called "verbal overshadowing." This made sense to Jung-Beeman, since the act of verbal explanation would naturally shift activity to the left hemisphere, causing people to ignore the more subtle associations coming from the right side of the brain. "That's when I realized that insight could be a really interesting way to look at all these skills the right hemisphere excelled at," he said. "I guess I had an insight about insight."

Jung-Beeman began searching in the right hemisphere for the source of insight in the brain. He decided to compare puzzles solved in moments of insight with those solved by methodical testing of potential solutions, in which people could accurately trace their thought process and had no sense of surprise when the answer came. Unfortunately, all the classic puzzles developed by scientists to study insight *required* insight; If subjects didn't solve them in a sudden "Aha!" moment, they didn't solve them at all. In a popular puzzle known as "the candle problem," for instance, subjects are given a cardboard box containing a few thumbtacks, a book of matches, and a candle. They are told to attach the candle to a piece of corkboard so that it can burn properly. Nearly 90 percent of people pursue the same two strategies. They try to tack the candle directly to the board, which causes the candle wax to shatter. Or they try melting the candle with the matches, so that it sticks to the board; but the wax doesn't hold and the candle falls. Only 4 percent of people manage to come up with the solution, which involves attaching the candle to the cardboard box and tacking the cardboard box to the corkboard.

To isolate the brain activity that defined the insight process, Jung-Beeman needed to develop a set of puzzles that could be solved either by insight or by analysis. Doing so was a puzzle in itself. "It can get pretty frustrating trying to find an experimentally valid brainteaser," Jung-Beeman said. "The puzzles can't be too hard or too easy, and you need to be able to generate lots of them." He eventually settled on a series of verbal puzzles, based on ones used by a psychologist in the early 1960s, which he named the Compound Remote Associate Problems, or CRAP. (The joke is beginning to get old, and in his scientific papers Jung-Beeman decorously leaves off the final *P.*)

In a CRA word puzzle, a subject is given three words, such as *pine, crab,* and *sauce,* and asked to think of a word that can be combined with all three—in this case, *apple* (*pineapple, crab apple, applesauce*). The subjects have up to thirty seconds to solve the puzzle. If they come up with an answer, they press the space bar on the keyboard and say whether the answer arrived via insight or analysis. When I participated in the experiment in Jung-Beeman's lab, I found that it was surprisingly easy to differentiate between the two cognitive paths. When I solved puzzles with analysis, I tended to sound out each possible word combination, cycling through all the words that went with *pine* and then seeing if they also worked with *crab* or *sauce.* If I worked toward a solution, I always double-checked it before pressing the space bar. An insight, on the other hand, felt instantaneous: The answer arrived like a revelation.

Jung-Beeman initially asked his subjects to solve the puzzles while inside an fMRI machine, a brain scanner that monitors neural activity by tracking changes in blood flow. But fMRI has a three-to-five-second delay, as the blood diffuses across the cortex. "Insights happen too fast for fMRI," Jung-Beeman said. "The data was just too messy." Around this time, he teamed up with John Kounios, a cognitive neuroscientist at Drexel University, who was interested in insight largely because it seemed to contradict the classic model of learning, in which the learning process was assumed to be gradual. Kounios, a man with a shock of unruly wavy hair and an affinity for rumpled button-up vests, had been working with electroencephalography, or EEG, which measures the waves of electricity produced by the brain by means of a nylon hat filled with greased electrodes. (The device looks like a bulky shower cap.) Because there is no time delay with EEG, Kounios thought it could be useful for investigating the fleeting process of insight. Unfortunately, the waves of electricity can't be traced back to their precise source, but Kounios and Jung-Beeman saw that combining EEG with fMRI might allow them to construct a precise map, both in time and space, of the insight process.

The resulting studies, published in 2004 and 2006, found that people who solved puzzles with insight activated a specific subset of cortical areas. Although the answer seemed to appear out of nowhere, the mind was carefully preparing itself for the breakthrough. The first areas activated during the problem-solving process were those involved with executive control, like the prefrontal cortex and the anterior cingulate cortex. The scientists refer to this as the "preparatory phase," since the brain is devoting its considerable computational power to the problem. The various sensory areas, like the visual cortex, go silent as the brain suppresses possible distractions. "The cortex does this for the same reason we close our eyes when we're trying to think," Jung-Beeman said. "Focus is all about blocking stuff out." 15

What happens next is the "search phase," as the brain starts looking for answers in all the relevant places. Because Jung-Beeman and Kounios were giving people word puzzles, they saw additional activity in areas related to speech and language. The search can quickly get frustrating, and it takes only a few seconds before people say that they've reached an impasse, that they can't think of the right word. "Almost all of the possibilities your brain comes up with are going to be wrong," Jung-Beeman said. "And it's up to the executive-control areas to keep on searching or, if necessary, change strategies and start searching somewhere else."

But sometimes, just when the brain is about to give up, an insight appears. "You'll see people bolt up in their chair and their eyes go all wide," Ezra Wegbreit, a graduate student in the Jung-Beeman lab who often administers the CRA test, said. "Sometimes they even say 'Aha!' before they blurt out the answer." The suddenness of the insight comes with a burst of brain activity. Three hundred milliseconds before a participant communicates the answer, the EEG registers a spike of gamma rhythm, which is the highest electrical frequency generated by the brain. Gamma rhythm is thought to come from the "binding" of neurons, as cells distributed across the cortex draw themselves together into a new network, which is then able to enter consciousness. It's as if the insight had gone incandescent.

Jung-Beeman and Kounios went back and analyzed the information from the fMRI experiment to see what was happening inside the brain in the seconds before the gamma burst. "My biggest worry was that we would find nothing," Kounios said. "I thought there was a good possibility that whatever we found on the EEG wouldn't show up on the brain imaging." When the scientists looked at the data, however, they saw that a small fold of tissue on the surface of the right hemisphere, the anterior superior temporal gyrus (aSTG), became unusually active in the second before the insight. The activation was sudden and intense, a surge of electricity leading to a rush of blood. Although the function of the aSTG remains mostly a mystery—the brain is stuffed with obscurities—Jung-Beeman wasn't surprised to see it involved with the insight process. A few previous studies had linked the area to aspects of language comprehension, such as the detection of literary themes and the interpretation of metaphors. (A related area was implicated in the processing of jokes.) Jung-Beeman argues that these linguistic skills, like insight, require the brain to make a set of distant and unprecedented connections. He cites studies showing that cells in the right hemisphere are more "broadly tuned" than cells in the left hemisphere, with longer branches and more dendritic spines. "What this means is that neurons in the right hemisphere are collecting information from a larger area of cortical space," Jung-Beeman said. "They are less precise but better connected." When the brain is searching for an insight, these are the cells that are most likely to produce it.

The insight process, as sketched by Jung-Beeman and Kounios, is a delicate mental balancing act. At first, the brain lavishes the scarce resource of attention on a single problem. But, once the brain is sufficiently focussed, the cortex needs to relax in order to seek out the more remote association in the right hemisphere, which will provide the insight. "The relaxation phase is crucial," Jung-Beeman said. "That's why so many insights happen during warm showers." Another ideal moment for insights, according to the scientists, is the early morning, right after we wake up. The drowsy brain is unwound and disorganized, open to all sorts of unconventional ideas. The right hemisphere is also unusually active. Jung-Beeman said, "The problem with the morning, though, is that we're always so rushed. We've got to get the kids ready for school, so we leap out of bed and never give ourselves a chance to think." He recommends that, if we're stuck on a difficult problem, it's better to set the alarm clock a few minutes early so that we have time to lie in bed and ruminate. We do some of our best thinking when we're still half asleep.

20 As Jung-Beeman and Kounios see it, the insight process is an act of cognitive deliberation—the brain must be focussed on the task at hand—transformed by accidental, serendipitous connections. We must concentrate, but we must concentrate on letting the mind wander. The patterns of brain activity that define this particular style of thought have recently been studied by Joy Bhattacharya, a psychologist at Goldsmiths, University of London. Using EEG, he has found that he can tell which subjects will solve insight puzzles up to eight seconds before the insight actually arrives. One of the key predictive signals is a steady rhythm of alpha waves emanating from the right hemisphere. Alpha waves typically correlate with a state of relaxation, and Bhattacharya believes that such activity makes the brain more receptive to new and unusual ideas. He has also found that unless subjects have sufficient alpha-wave activity they won't be able to make use of hints the researchers give them.

One of the surprising lessons of this research is that trying to force an insight can actually prevent the insight. While it's commonly assumed that the best way to solve a difficult problem is to focus, minimize distractions, and pay attention only to the relevant details, this clenched state of mind may inhibit the sort of creative connections that lead to sudden breakthroughs. We suppress the very type of brain activity that we should be encouraging. Jonathan Schooler has recently demonstrated that making people focus on the details of a visual scene, as opposed to the big picture, can significantly disrupt the insight process. "It doesn't take much to shift the brain into left-hemisphere mode," he said. "That's when you stop paying attention to those more holistic associations coming in from the right hemisphere." Meanwhile, in a study published last year, German researchers found that people with schizotypy—a mental condition that resembles schizophrenia, albeit with far less severe symptoms—were significantly better at solving insight problems than a control group. Schizotypal subjects have enhanced right-hemisphere function and tend to score above average on measures of creativity and associative thinking.

Schooler's research has also led him to reconsider the bad reputation of letting one's mind wander. Although we often complain that the brain is too easily distracted, Schooler believes that letting the mind wander is essential. "Just look at the history of science," he said. "The big ideas seem to always come when people are sidetracked, when they're doing something that has nothing to do with their research." He cites the example of Henri Poincaré, the nineteenth-century mathematician, whose seminal insight into non-Euclidean geometry arrived while he was boarding a bus. "At the moment when I put my foot on the step," Poincaré wrote, "the idea came to me, without anything in my former thoughts seeming to have paved the way for it. . . . I did not verify the idea; I should not have had the time, as, upon taking my seat in the omnibus, I went on with the conversation already commenced, but I felt a perfect certainty." Poincaré credited his sudden mathematical insight to "unconscious work," an ability to mull over the mathematics while he was preoccupied with unrelated activities, like talking to a friend on the bus. In his 1908 essay "Mathematical Creation," Poincaré insisted that the best way to think about complex problems is to immerse yourself in the problem until you hit an impasse. Then, when it seems that "nothing good is accomplished," you should find a way to distract yourself, preferably by going on a "walk or a journey." The answer will arrive when you least expect it. Richard Feynman, the Nobel Prize–winning physicist, preferred the relaxed atmosphere of a topless bar, where he would sip 7UP, "watch the entertainment," and, if inspiration struck, scribble equations on cocktail napkins.

Kounios and Jung-Beeman aren't quite ready to offer extensive practical advice, but, when pressed, they often sound like Poincaré. "You've got to know when to step back," Kounios said. "If you're in an environment that forces you to produce and produce, and you feel very stressed, then you're not going to have any insights." Many stimulants, like caffeine, Adderall, and Ritalin, are taken to increase focus—one recent poll found that nearly 20 percent of scientists and researchers regularly took prescription drugs to "enhance concentration"—but, according to Jung-Beeman and Kounios, drugs may actually make insights less likely, by sharpening the spotlight of attention and discouraging mental rambles. Concentration, it seems, comes with the hidden cost of diminished creativity. "There's a good reason Google puts Ping-Pong tables in their headquarters," Kounios said. "If you want to encourage insights, then you've got to also encourage people to relax." Jung-Beeman's latest paper investigates why people who are in a good mood are so much better at solving insight puzzles. (On average, they solve nearly 20 percent more CRA problems.)

Last year, Kounios and Jung-Beeman were invited to present their findings to DARPA, the central research agency of the Department of Defense. ("It was quite strange," Kounios recalls. "I never thought I'd be talking about creativity to national-security officials.") DARPA was interested in finding ways to encourage insights amid the stress of war, fostering creativity on the battlefield. The scientists are convinced that it's only a matter of time before it becomes possible to "up-regulate" insight. "This could be a drug or technology or just a new way to structure our environment," Jung-Beeman said. "I think we'll soon get to the point where we can do more than tell people to take lots of showers."

25 For now, though, the science of promoting insight remains rooted in anecdote, in stories of people, like Poincaré, who were able to consistently induce the necessary state of mind. Kounios tells a story about an expert Zen meditator who took part in one of the CRA insight experiments. At first, the meditator couldn't solve any of the insight problems. "This Zen guy went through thirty or so of the verbal puzzles and just drew a blank," Kounios said. "He was used to being very focussed, but you can't solve these problems if you're too focussed." Then, just as he was about to give up, he started solving one puzzle after another, until, by the end of the experiment, he was getting them all right. It was an unprecedented streak. "Normally, people don't get better as the task goes along," Kounios said. "If anything, they get a little bored." Kounios believes that the dramatic improvement of the Zen meditator came from his paradoxical ability to focus on *not* being focussed, so that he could pay attention to those remote associations in the right hemisphere. "He had the cognitive control to let go," Kounios said. "He became an insight machine."

The most mysterious aspect of insight is not the revelation itself but what happens next. The brain is an infinite library of associations, a cacophony of competing ideas, and yet, as soon as the right association appears, we know. The new thought, which is represented by that rush of gamma waves in the right hemisphere, immediately grabs our attention. There is something paradoxical and bizarre about this. On the one hand, an epiphany is a surprising event; we are startled by what we've just discovered. Some part of our brain, however, clearly isn't surprised at all, which is why we are able to instantly recognize the insight. "As soon as the insight happens, it just seems so obvious," Schooler said. "People can't believe they didn't see it before."

The brain area responsible for this act of recognition is the prefrontal cortex, which lights up whenever people are shown the right answer—even if they haven't come up with the answer themselves. Pressed tight against the bones of the forehead, the prefrontal cortex has undergone a dramatic expansion during human evolution, so that it now represents nearly a third of the brain. While this area is often associated with the most specialized aspects of human cognition, such as abstract reasoning, it also plays a critical role in the insight process. Hallucinogenic drugs are thought to work largely by modulating the prefrontal cortex, tricking the brain into believing that its sensory delusions are revelations. People have the feeling of an insight but without the content. Understanding how this happens—how a circuit of cells can identify an idea as an insight, even if the idea has yet to enter awareness—requires an extremely precise level of investigation. The rhythms of brain waves and the properties of blood can't answer the question. Instead, it's necessary to study the brain at its most basic level, as a loom of electrical cells.

Earl Miller is a neuroscientist at MIT who has devoted his career to understanding the prefrontal cortex. He has a shiny shaved head and a silver goatee. His corner office in the gleaming Picower Institute is cantilevered over a railroad track, and every afternoon the quiet hum of the lab is interrupted by the rattle of a freight train. Miller's favorite word is *exactly*—it's the adverb that modifies everything, so that a hypothesis is "exactly right," or an experiment was "exactly done"—and that emphasis on precision has defined his career. His first major scientific advance was a by-product of necessity. It was 1995, and Miller had just started his lab at MIT. His research involved recording directly from neurons in the monkey brain, monitoring the flux of voltage within an individual cell as the animals performed various tasks. "There were machines that allowed you to record from eight or nine at the same time, but they were very expensive," Miller said. "I still had no grants, and there was no way I could afford one." So Miller began inventing his own apparatus in his spare time. After a few months of patient tinkering, he constructed a messy tangle of wires, steel screws, and electrodes that could simultaneously record from numerous cells, distributed across the brain. "It worked even better than the expensive machine," Miller said.

This methodological advance—it's known as multiple electrode recording—allowed Miller to ask a completely new kind of scientific question. For the first time, it was possible to see how cells in different brain areas interacted. Miller was most interested in the interactions of the prefrontal cortex. "You name the brain area, and the prefrontal cortex is almost certainly linked to it," he said. It took more than five years of painstaking probing, as Miller recorded from cells in the monkey brain, but he was eventually able to show that the prefrontal cortex wasn't simply an aggregator of information. Instead, it was like the conductor of an orchestra, waving its baton and directing the players. This is known as "top-down processing," since the prefrontal cortex (the "top" of the brain) is directly modulating the activity of other areas. This is why, during the focussing phase of the insight process, Jung-Beeman and Kounios saw activity in the prefrontal cortex and the neighboring anterior cingulate cortex. They were watching the conductor at work.

In 2001, Miller and Jonathan Cohen, a neuroscientist at Princeton, published an influential paper that laid out their theory of how, exactly, the prefrontal cortex controls the rest of the brain. According to Miller and Cohen, this brain area is responsible not only for focussing on the task at hand but for figuring out what other areas need to be engaged in order to solve a problem. One implication of this is that if we're trying to solve a verbal puzzle the prefrontal cortex will selectively activate the specific brain areas involved with verbal processing. If it decides to turn on parts of the right hemisphere, then we might end up with an insight; if it decides to restrict its search to the left hemisphere, we'll probably arrive at a solution incrementally or not at all.

This "integrative" theory of the prefrontal cortex suggests why we can instantly recognize the insight, even when it seems surprising: the brain has been concertedly pursuing the answer; we just didn't know it. "Your consciousness is very limited in capacity," Miller said, "and that's why your prefrontal cortex makes all these plans without telling you about it." When that obscure circuit in the right hemisphere finally generates the necessary association, the prefrontal cortex is able to identify it instantly, and the insight erupts into awareness. We suddenly notice the music that has been playing all along.

Because Miller can eavesdrop on neurons, he's been able to see how these insights operate at the cellular level. One of his current experiments involves showing monkeys different arrangements of dots and asking them to sort the arrangements into various categories that they have been taught. The monkeys guess randomly at first, learning from trial and error. "But then, at a certain point, the monkey just gets it," Miller said. "They just start being able to categorize arrangements of dots that they've never seen before. That's the moment of categorical insight." This primate epiphany registers as a new pattern of neural activity in the prefrontal cortex. The brain cells have been altered by the breakthrough. "An insight is a restructuring of information—it's seeing the same old thing in a completely new way," Miller said. "Once that restructuring occurs, you never go back."

And yet even this detailed explanation doesn't fully demystify insight. It remains unclear how simple cells recognize what the conscious mind cannot, or how they are able to filter through the chaos of bad ideas to produce the epiphany. "This mental process will always be a little unknowable, which is why it's so interesting to study," Jung-Beeman said. "At a certain point, you just have to admit that your brain knows much more than you do." An insight is a fleeting glimpse of the brain's huge store of unknown knowledge. The cortex is sharing one of its secrets.

So it was for Wag Dodge. After the fire crossed the river, all the other smoke jumpers were fixated on reaching the ridge. Panic had narrowed their thoughts, so that beating the flames up the slope was their sole goal. But, because Dodge realized that the fire would beat them to the top, his prefrontal cortex started frantically searching for an alternative. It was able to look past his fear and expand the possibilities of his thought process, as he considered remote mental associations that he'd never contemplated before. (As Miller says, "That Dodge guy had some really high prefrontal function.") And then, just as the blaze started to suck the oxygen out of the air, some remote bit of his brain realized that he could cheat death by starting his own fire. This unprecedented idea, a flicker of electricity somewhere in the right hemisphere, was immediately recognized as the solution the prefrontal cortex had been searching for. And so Dodge stopped running. He stood still as the wall of flame raced toward him. Then he lit the match.

▪ QUESTIONS

Reading

1. Which essential features comprise "the insight experience"?
2. Chart the different activities or types of thinking that are governed by each hemisphere of the brain, according to this essay.

LEFT BRAIN	RIGHT BRAIN

3. Discuss Jonathan Schooler's research and experiments. How does describing Schooler's work strengthen this *reportorial* essay?
4. What role does the writer, Jonah Lehrer, play in this third-person report of how insight works? In what ways would a first-person reflection on the experience of insight be different from this account?

Exploratory Writing

1. In the course of doing his research, Jung-Beeman realized that "all the classic puzzles developed by scientists to study insight *required* insight; if subjects didn't solve them in a sudden 'Aha!' moment, they didn't solve them at all" (paragraph 11). In small groups, find a sample "insight puzzle" online or at the library. Each group member should first try to solve the puzzle alone. After your attempt, report your experiences trying to solve the puzzle to the rest of the group.
2. Reflect on a time when you had an epiphany, or an "Aha!" moment. How did it change your life and way of thinking?

Making Connections

1. Consider Lewis Thomas's (p. 427) reflection, "It immensely pleases a human being to see something never seen before, even more to learn something never known before, most of all to think something never thought before." How do "Aha!" moments fit in with his discussion of ways the universe is surprising?
2. Steven Johnson (p. 120) argues that watching certain kinds of television shows can make people smarter. Based on both Johnson's and Lehrer's arguments and examples, do you think that television viewing can stimulate moments of insight? Do the kinds of intellectual development that Johnson attributes to television viewing sound more right-brained or left-brained to you?

Essay Writing

1. According to the Nobel Prize–winning physiologist Albert Szent-Györgyi, "Discovery consists of seeing what everybody has seen and thinking what nobody has thought." Research and write an essay about a famous invention, discovery, or breakthrough in history. To what extent did the discovery arrive in a "Aha!" moment? To what extent was it the result of the inventor's methodical labor? What can we learn about insight from the particular case study you've chosen?

EXPLAINING

Why Leaves Turn Color in the Fall

Diane Ackerman

Poet, essayist, and naturalist Diane Ackerman was born in Waukegan, Illinois, in 1948 and received an MFA and PhD in English from Cornell University. Her earliest works, published when she was still a doctoral student, were the poetry collections *The Planets* (1976) and *Wife of Life* (1978); since then she has produced several volumes, most recently *I Praise My Destroyer* (1998) and *Origami Bridges* (2002). Ackerman's first book of prose was *Twilight of the Tenderfoot* (1980), about her experiences working on a cattle ranch in New Mexico. Her subsequent prose works have focused on a range of subjects, as suggested by some of their titles: *The Moon by Whale Light: And Other Adventures among Bats, Crocodilians, Penguins, and Whales* (1990), *The Rarest of the Rare: Vanishing Animals, Timeless Worlds* (1995), *A Natural History of Love* (1994), *Cultivating Delight: A Natural History of My Garden* (2001), *An Alchemy of Mind* (2004), *The Zookeeper's Wife: A War Story* (2007), and *One Hundred Names for Love: A Stroke, a Marriage, and the Language of Healing* (2011). All, however, are characterized by Ackerman's deeply insightful observations of the natural world, as evidenced perhaps most fully in her most popular book and the source of a highly rated public television series, *A Natural History of the Senses* (1990), in which the following selection appeared. Admitting that her work is difficult to categorize, Ackerman has said, "I write about nature and human nature. And most often about that twilight zone where the two meet and have something they can teach each other."

The stealth of autumn catches one unaware. Was that a goldfinch perching in the early September woods, or just the first turning leaf? A red-winged blackbird or a sugar maple closing up shop for the winter? Keen-eyed as leopards, we stand still and squint hard, looking for signs of movement. Early-morning frost sits heavily on the grass, and turns barbed wire into a string of stars. On a distant hill, a small square of yellow appears to be a lighted stage. At last the truth dawns on us: Fall is staggering in, right on schedule, with its baggage of chilly nights, macabre holidays, and spectacular, heart-stoppingly beautiful leaves. Soon the leaves will start cringing on the trees, and roll up in clenched fists before they actually fall off. Dry seedpods will rattle like tiny gourds. But first there will be weeks of gushing color so bright, so pastel, so confettilike, that people will travel up and down the East Coast just to stare at it—a whole season of leaves.

Where do the colors come from? Sunlight rules most living things with its golden edicts. When the days begin to shorten, soon after the summer solstice on June 21, a tree reconsiders its leaves. All summer it feeds them so they can process sunlight, but in the dog days of summer the tree begins pulling nutrients back into its trunk and roots, pares down, and gradually chokes off its leaves. A corky layer of cells forms at the leaves' slender petioles, then scars over. Undernourished, the leaves stop producing the pigment chlorophyll, and photosynthesis ceases. Animals can migrate, hibernate, or store food to prepare for winter. But where can a tree go? It survives by dropping its leaves, and by the end of autumn only a few fragile threads of fluid-carrying xylem hold leaves to their stems.

A turning leaf stays partly green at first, then reveals splotches of yellow and red as the chlorophyll gradually breaks down. Dark green seems to stay longest in the veins, outlining and defining them. During the summer, chlorophyll dissolves in the heat and light, but it is also being steadily replaced. In the fall, on the other hand, no new pigment is produced, and so we notice the other colors that were always there, right in the leaf, although chlorophyll's shocking green hid them from view. With their camouflage gone, we see these colors for the first time all year, and marvel, but they were always there, hidden like a vivid secret beneath the hot glowing greens of summer.

The most spectacular range of fall foliage occurs in the northeastern United States and in eastern China, where the leaves are robustly colored, thanks in part to a rich climate. European maples don't achieve the same flaming reds as their American relatives, which thrive on cold nights and sunny days. In Europe, the warm, humid weather turns the leaves brown or mildly yellow. Anthocyanin, the pigment that gives apples their red and turns leaves red or red-violet, is produced by sugars that remain in the leaf after the supply of nutrients dwindles. Unlike the carotenoids, which color carrots, squash, and corn, and turn leaves orange and yellow, anthocyanin varies from year to year, depending on the temperature and amount of sunlight. The fiercest colors occur in years when the fall sunlight is strongest and the nights are cool and dry (a state of grace scientists find vexing to forecast). This is also why leaves appear dizzyingly bright and clear on a sunny fall day: The anthocyanin flashes like a marquee.

Not all leaves turn the same colors. Elms, weeping willows, and the ancient ginkgo all grow radiant yellow, along with hickories, aspens, bottlebrush buckeyes, cottonweeds, and tall, keening poplars. Basswood turns bronze, birches bright gold. Water-loving maples put on a symphonic display of scarlets. Sumacs turn red, too, as do flowering dogwoods, black gums, and sweet gums. Though some oaks yellow, most turn a pinkish brown. The farmlands also change color, as tepees of cornstalks and bales of shredded-wheat-textured hay stand drying in the fields. In some spots, one slope of a hill may be green and the other already in bright color, because the hillside facing south gets more sun and heat than the northern one. 5

An odd feature of the colors is that they don't seem to have any special purpose. We are predisposed to respond to their beauty, of course. They shimmer with the colors of sunset, spring flowers, the tawny buff of a colt's pretty rump, the shuddering pink of a blush. Animals and flowers color for a reason—adaptation to their environment—but there is no adaptive reason for leaves to color so beautifully in the fall any more than there is for the sky or ocean to be blue. It's just one of the haphazard marvels the planet bestows every year. We find the sizzling colors thrilling, and in a sense they dupe us. Colored like living things, they signal death and disintegration. In time, they will become fragile and, like the body, return to dust. They are as we hope our own fate will be when we die: Not to vanish, just to sublime from one beautiful state into another. Though leaves lose their green life, they bloom with urgent colors, as the woods grow mummified day by day, and Nature becomes more carnal, mute, and radiant.

We call the season *fall,* from the Old English *feallan,* to fall, which leads back through time to the Indo-European *phol,* which also means to fall. So the word and the idea are both extremely ancient, and haven't really changed since the first of our kind needed a name for fall's leafy abundance. As we say the word, we're reminded of that other Fall, in the garden of Eden, when fig leaves never withered and scales fell from our eyes. Fall is the time when leaves fall from the trees, just as spring is when flowers spring up, summer is when we simmer, and winter is when we whine from the cold.

Children love to play in piles of leaves, hurling them into the air like confetti, leaping into soft unruly mattresses of them. For children, leaf fall is just one of the odder figments of Nature, like hailstones or snowflakes. Walk down a lane overhung with trees in the never-never land of autumn, and you will forget about time and death, lost in the sheer delicious spill of color. Adam and Eve concealed their nakedness with leaves, remember? Leaves have always hidden our awkward secrets.

But how do the colored leaves fall? As a leaf ages, the growth hormone auxin fades, and cells at the base of the petiole divide. Two or three rows of small cells, lying at right angles to the axis of the petiole, react with water, then come apart, leaving the petioles hanging on by only a few threads of xylem. A light breeze, and the leaves are airborne. They glide and swoop, rocking in invisible cradles. They are all wing and may flutter from yard to yard on small whirlwinds or updrafts, swiveling as they go. Firmly tethered to earth, we love to see things rise up and fly—soap bubbles, balloons, birds, fall leaves. They remind us that the end of a season is capricious, as is the end of life. We especially like the way leaves rock, careen, and swoop as they fall. Everyone knows the motion. Pilots sometimes do a maneuver called a "falling leaf," in which the plane loses altitude quickly and on purpose, by slipping first to the right, then to the left. The machine weighs a ton or more, but in one pilot's mind it is a weightless thing, a falling leaf. She has seen the motion before, in the Vermont woods where she played as a child. Below her the trees radiate gold, copper, and red. Leaves are falling, although she can't see them fall, as she falls, swooping down for a closer view.

10 At last the leaves leave. But first they turn color and thrill us for weeks on end. Then they crunch and crackle underfoot. They *shush,* as children drag their small feet through leaves heaped along the curb. Dark, slimy mats of leaves cling to one's heels after a rain. A damp, stuccolike mortar of semidecayed leaves protects the tender shoots with a roof until spring, and makes a rich humus. An occasional bulge or ripple in the leafy mounds signals a shrew or a field mouse tunneling out of sight. Sometimes one finds in fossil stones

the imprint of a leaf, long since disintegrated, whose outlines remind us how detailed, vibrant, and alive are the things of this earth that perish.

▪ QUESTIONS

Reading

1. According to Ackerman, where does the most spectacular range of fall foliage occur?
2. Highlight, underline, or flag the places where Ackerman makes a connection between the concept of autumn leaves and the concept of death in general. How would you summarize the point she is making here?
3. What is the purpose of the different leaf colors?

Exploratory Writing

1. Print out a photograph of autumn foliage from the Internet. Collaborating in small groups, label the trees in the picture based on (a) how they got their colors, and (b) which types of trees they might be. Use only Ackerman's essay as a reference point. Based on this exercise, how useful did you find the essay? What did you learn about trees from reading it?
2. Make a list of all of the adjectives that Ackerman uses to describe autumn leaves. How would her explanation of the leaves be different without those adjectives? What can you learn just from reading the list, with none of the scientific explanations attached?

Making Connections

1. Ackerman's title sets up the expectation that what follows will provide an explanation of a scientific process. Roy C. Selby Jr.'s "A Delicate Operation" (p. 529) also purports to report on a process. In fact, how similar—and how different—are the two essays? Do you feel that one provides a clearer or more effective explanation than the other does? Why or why not? Which do you respond to more favorably?

Essay Writing

1. Think of a natural phenomenon that you consider beautiful or spectacular. Do some research to learn about the biological, geological, or other natural process that produces it. Write an essay in which, like Ackerman, you explain the technical aspects of the natural process while also describing the beauty of the phenomenon and reflecting on the reasons that you respond to it as you do.

EXPLAINING

The Man Who Mistook His Wife for a Hat

Oliver Sacks

Oliver Sacks was born in London, England, in 1933 and educated in London and Oxford before coming to the United States to complete his education in California and New York. At present he is professor of neurology and psychiatry at Columbia University Medical Center. He is best known, however, for his extraordinary writing on matters related to his medical studies, in such books as *Awakenings* (1974), *Seeing Voices: A Journey into the World of the Deaf* (1989), *An Anthropologist on Mars* (1995), *The Island of the Colorblind* (1997), and his national best-seller, *The Man Who Mistook His Wife for a Hat* (1986), from which the following selection was adapted. Interested in the art of storytelling as well as in clinical neurology, Sacks subtitled the book in which this essay appeared "*and Other Clinical Tales*." He insists that his essays are not just case studies but also tales or fables of "heroes, victims, martyrs, warriors." In his writing, he says, "the scientific and romantic . . . come together at the intersection of fact and fable." Sacks's prose style is lyrical as well as accurate; his explanation of prosopagnosia (perception without recognition) seeks to engage our interest and emotions while it defines and illustrates a syndrome unfamiliar to many readers. His most recent book is *The Mind's Eye* (2010).

Dr. P. was a musician of distinction, well known for many years as a singer, and then, at the local school of music, as a teacher. It was here, in relation to his students, that certain strange problems were first observed. Sometimes a student would present himself, and Dr. P. would not recognize him; or, specifically, would not recognize his face. The moment the student spoke, he would be recognized by his voice. Such incidents multiplied, causing embarrassment, perplexity, fear—and, sometimes, comedy. For not only did Dr. P. increasingly fail to see faces, but he saw faces when there were no faces to see: Genially, Magoo-like, when in the street he might pat the heads of water hydrants and parking meters, taking these to be the heads of children; he would amiably address carved knobs on the furniture and be astounded when they did not reply. At first these odd mistakes were laughed off as jokes, not least by Dr. P. himself. Had he not always had a quirky sense of humor and been given to Zen-like paradoxes and jests? His musical powers were as dazzling as ever; he did not feel ill—he had never felt better; and the mistakes were so ludicrous—and so ingenious—that they could hardly be serious or betoken anything serious. The notion of there being "something the matter" did not emerge until some three years later, when diabetes developed. Well aware that diabetes could affect his eyes, Dr. P. consulted an ophthalmologist, who took a careful history and examined his eyes closely. "There's nothing the matter with your eyes," the doctor concluded. "But there is trouble with the visual parts of your brain. You don't need my help, you must see a neurologist." And so, as a result of this referral, Dr. P. came to me.

It was obvious within a few seconds of meeting him that there was no trace of dementia in the ordinary sense. He was a man of great cultivation and charm who talked well and fluently, with imagination and humor. I couldn't think why he had been referred to our clinic.

And yet there *was* something a bit odd. He faced me as he spoke, was oriented toward me, and yet there was something the matter—it was difficult to formulate. He faced me with his *ears*, I came to think, but not with his eyes. These, instead of looking, gazing, at me, "taking me in," in the normal way, made sudden strange fixations—on my nose, on my right ear, down to my chin, up to my right eye—as if noting (even studying) these individual features, but not seeing my whole face, its changing expressions, "me," as a whole. I am not sure that I fully realized this at the time—there was just a teasing strangeness, some failure in the normal interplay of gaze and expression. He saw me, he *scanned* me, and yet . . .

"What seems to be the matter?" I asked him at length.

"Nothing that I know of," he replied with a smile, "but people seem to think there's something wrong with my eyes." 5

"But *you* don't recognize any visual problems?"

"No, not directly, but I occasionally make mistakes."

I left the room briefly to talk to his wife. When I came back, Dr. P. was sitting placidly by the window, attentive, listening rather than looking out. "Traffic," he said, "street sounds, distant trains—they make a sort of symphony, do they not? You know Honegger's[1] *Pacific 234*?"

What a lovely man, I thought to myself. How can there be anything seriously the matter? Would he permit me to examine him?

"Yes, of course, Dr. Sacks." 10

I stilled my disquiet, his perhaps, too, in the soothing routine of a neurological exam—muscle strength, coordination, reflexes, tone. . . . It was while examining his reflexes—a trifle abnormal on the left side—that the first bizarre experience occurred. I had taken off his left shoe and scratched the sole of his foot with a key—a frivolous-seeming but essential test of a reflex—and then, excusing myself to screw my ophthalmoscope together, left him to put on the shoe himself. To my surprise, a minute later, he had not done this.

"Can I help?" I asked.

"Help what? Help whom?"

"Help you put on your shoe."

"Ach," he said, "I had forgotten the shoe," adding, sotto voce, "The shoe? The shoe?" He seemed baffled. 15

"Your shoe," I repeated. "Perhaps you'd put it on."

He continued to look downward, though not at the shoe, with an intense but misplaced concentration. Finally his gaze settled on his foot: "That is my shoe, yes?"

Did I mis-hear? Did he mis-see?

"My eyes," he explained, and put a hand to his foot. "*This* is my shoe, no?"

[1]*Arthur Honegger* (1892–1955): French composer.—Eds.

"No, it is not. That is your foot. *There* is your shoe." 20

"Ah! I thought that was my foot."

Was he joking? Was he mad? Was he blind? If this was one of his "strange mistakes," it was the strangest mistake I had ever come across.

I helped him on with his shoe (his foot), to avoid further complication. Dr. P. himself seemed untroubled, indifferent, maybe amused. I resumed my examination. His visual acuity was good: He had no difficulty seeing a pin on the floor, though sometimes he missed it if it was placed to his left.

He saw all right, but what did he see? I opened out a copy of the *National Geographic* magazine and asked him to describe some pictures in it.

His responses here were very curious. His eyes would dart from one thing 25 to another, picking up tiny features, individual features, as they had done with my face. A striking brightness, a color, a shape would arrest his attention and elicit comment—but in no case did he get the scene-as-a-whole. He failed to see the whole, seeing only details, which he spotted like blips on a radar screen. He never entered into relation with the picture as a whole—never faced, so to speak, *its* physiognomy. He had no sense whatever of a landscape or scene.

I showed him the cover, an unbroken expanse of Sahara dunes.

"What do you see here?" I asked.

"I see a river," he said. "And a little guesthouse with its terrace on the water. People are dining out on the terrace. I see colored parasols here and there." He was looking, if it was "looking," right off the cover into midair and confabulating nonexistent features, as if the absence of features in the actual picture had driven him to imagine the river and the terrace and the colored parasols.

I must have looked aghast, but he seemed to think he had done rather well. There was a hint of a smile on his face. He also appeared to have decided that the examination was over and started to look around for his hat. He reached out his hand and took hold of his wife's head, tried to lift it off, to put it on. He had apparently mistaken his wife for a hat! His wife looked as if she was used to such things.

I could make no sense of what had occurred in terms of conventional neu- 30 rology (or neuropsychology). In some ways he seemed perfectly preserved, and in others absolutely, incomprehensibly devastated. How could he, on the one hand, mistake his wife for a hat and, on the other, function, as apparently he still did, as a teacher at the music school?

I had to think, to see him again—and to see him in his own familiar habitat, at home.

A few days later I called on Dr. P. and his wife at home, with the score of the *Dichterliebe* in my briefcase (I knew he liked Schumann),[2] and a variety of odd objects for the testing of perception. Mrs. P. showed me into a lofty apartment, which recalled fin-de-siècle Berlin. A magnificent old Bösendorfer stood in state in the center of the room, and all around it were music stands, instru-

[2]*Robert Schumann* (1810–1856): German romantic composer.—Eds.

ments, scores. . . . There were books, there were paintings, but the music was central. Dr. P. came in, a little bowed, and, distracted, advanced with outstretched hands to the grandfather clock, but, hearing my voice, corrected himself, and shook hands with me. We exchanged greetings and chatted a little of current concerts and performances. Diffidently, I asked him if he would sing.

"The *Dichterliebe!*" he exclaimed. "But I can no longer read music. You will play them, yes?"

I said I would try. On that wonderful old piano even my playing sounded right, and Dr. P. was an aged but infinitely mellow Fischer-Dieskau,[3] combining a perfect ear and voice with the most incisive musical intelligence. It was clear that the music school was not keeping him on out of charity.

Dr. P.'s temporal lobes were obviously intact: He had a wonderful musical cortex. What, I wondered, was going on in his parietal and occipital lobes, especially in those areas where visual processing occurred? I carry the Platonic solids in my neurological kit and decided to start with these. 35

"What is this?" I asked, drawing out the first one.

"A cube, of course."

"Now this?" I asked, brandishing another.

He asked if he might examine it, which he did swiftly and systematically: "A dodecahedron, of course. And don't bother with the others—I'll get the icosahedron, too."

Abstract shapes clearly presented no problems. What about faces? I took out a pack of cards. All of these he identified instantly, including the jacks, queens, kings, and the joker. But these, after all, are stylized designs, and it was impossible to tell whether he saw faces or merely patterns. I decided I would show him a volume of cartoons which I had in my briefcase. Here, again, for the most part, he did well. Churchill's cigar, Schnozzle's nose: As soon as he had picked out a key feature he could identify the face. But cartoons, again, are formal and schematic. It remained to be seen how he would do with real faces, realistically represented. 40

I turned on the television, keeping the sound off, and found an early Bette Davis film. A love scene was in progress. Dr. P. failed to identify the actress—but this could have been because she had never entered his world. What was more striking was that he failed to identify the expressions on her face or her partner's, though in the course of a single torrid scene these passed from sultry yearning through passion, surprise, disgust, and fury to a melting reconciliation. Dr. P. could make nothing of any of this. He was very unclear as to what was going on, or who was who or even what sex they were. His comments on the scene were positively Martian.

It was just possible that some of his difficulties were associated with the unreality of a celluloid, Hollywood world; and it occurred to me that he might be more successful in identifying faces from his own life. On the walls of the

[3]*Dietrich Fischer-Dieskau* (b. 1925): German baritone, noted for his interpretations of Schumann's vocal music.—Eds.

apartment there were photographs of his family, his colleagues, his pupils, himself. I gathered a pile of these together and, with some misgivings, presented them to him. What had been funny, or farcical, in relation to the movie, was tragic in relation to real life. By and large, he recognized nobody: neither his family, nor his colleagues, nor his pupils, nor himself. He recognized a portrait of Einstein because he picked up the characteristic hair and mustache; and the same thing happened with one or two other people. "Ach, Paul!" he said, when shown a portrait of his brother. "That square jaw, those big teeth—I would know Paul anywhere!" But was it Paul he recognized, or one or two of his features, on the basis of which he could make a reasonable guess as to the subject's identity? In the absence of obvious "markers," he was utterly lost. But it was not merely the cognition, the gnosis, at fault; there was something radically wrong with the whole way he proceeded. For he approached these faces—even of those near and dear—as if they were abstract puzzles or tests. He did not relate to them, he did not behold. No face was familiar to him, seen as a "thou," being just identified as a set of features, an "it." Thus, there was formal, but no trace of personal, gnosis. And with this went his indifference, or blindness, to expression. A face, to us, is a person looking out—we see, as it were, the person through his *persona,* his face. But for Dr. P. there was no *persona* in this sense—no outward *persona,* and no person within.

I had stopped at a florist on my way to his apartment and bought myself an extravagant red rose for my buttonhole. Now I removed this and handed it to him. He took it like a botanist or morphologist given a specimen, not like a person given a flower.

"About six inches in length," he commented. "A convoluted red form with a linear green attachment."

"Yes," I said encouragingly, "and what do you think it *is,* Dr. P.?" 45

"Not easy to say." He seemed perplexed. "It lacks the simple symmetry of the Platonic solids, although it may have a higher symmetry of its own. . . . I think this could be an inflorescence or flower."

"Could be?" I queried.

"Could be," he confirmed.

"Smell it," I suggested, and he again looked somewhat puzzled, as if I had asked him to smell a higher symmetry. But he complied courteously, and took it to his nose. Now, suddenly, he came to life.

"Beautiful!" he exclaimed. "An early rose. What a heavenly smell!" He started 50 to hum "*Die Rose, die Lillie . . .*" Reality, it seemed, might be conveyed by smell, not by sight.

I tried one final test. It was still a cold day, in early spring, and I had thrown my coat and gloves on the sofa.

"What is this?" I asked, holding up a glove.

"May I examine it?" he asked, and, taking it from me, he proceeded to examine it as he had examined the geometrical shapes.

"A continuous surface," he announced at last, "infolded on itself. It appears to have"—he hesitated—"five outpouchings, if this is the word."

"Yes," I said cautiously. "You have given me a description. Now tell me what it is." 55

"A container of some sort?"

"Yes," I said, "and what would it contain?"

"It would contain its contents!" said Dr. P., with a laugh. "There are many possibilities. It could be a change purse, for example, for coins of five sizes. It could . . ."

I interrupted the barmy flow. "Does it not look familiar? Do you think it might contain, might fit, a part of your body?"

No light of recognition dawned on his face.[4] 60

No child would have the power to see and speak of "a continuous surface . . . infolded on itself," but any child, any infant, would immediately know a glove as a glove, see it as familiar, as going with a hand. Dr. P. didn't. He saw nothing as familiar. Visually, he was lost in a world of lifeless abstractions. Indeed, he did not have a real visual world, as he did not have a real visual self. He could speak about things, but did not see them face-to-face. Hughlings Jackson, discussing patients with aphasia and left-hemisphere lesions, says they have lost "abstract" and "propositional" thought—and compares them with dogs (or, rather, he compares dogs to patients with aphasia). Dr. P., on the other hand, functioned precisely as a machine functions. It wasn't merely that he displayed the same indifference to the visual world as a computer but—even more strikingly—he construed the world as a computer construes it, by means of key features and schematic relationships. The scheme might be identified—in an "identikit" way—without the reality being grasped at all.

The testing I had done so far told me nothing about Dr. P.'s inner world. Was it possible that his visual memory and imagination were still intact? I asked him to imagine entering one of our local squares from the north side, to walk through it, in imagination or in memory, and tell me the buildings he might pass as he walked. He listed the buildings on his right side, but none of those on his left. I then asked him to imagine entering the square from the south. Again he mentioned only those buildings that were on the right side, although these were the very buildings he had omitted before. Those he had "seen" internally before were not mentioned now; presumably, they were no longer "seen." It was evident that his difficulties with leftness, his visual field deficits, were as much internal as external, bisecting his visual memory and imagination.

What, at a higher level, of his internal visualization? Thinking of the almost hallucinatory intensity with which Tolstoy visualizes and animates his characters, I questioned Dr. P. about *Anna Karenina*. He could remember incidents without difficulty, had an undiminished grasp of the plot, but completely omitted visual characteristics, visual narrative, and scenes. He remembered the words of the characters but not their faces; and though, when asked, he

[4]Later, by accident, he got it on, and exclaimed, "My God, it's a glove!" This was reminiscent of Kurt Goldstein's patient "Lanuti," who could only recognize objects by trying to use them in action.—Au.

could quote, with his remarkable and almost verbatim memory, the original visual descriptions, these were, it became apparent, quite empty for him and lacked sensorial, imaginal, or emotional reality. Thus, there was an internal agnosia as well.[5]

But this was only the case, it became clear, with certain sorts of visualization. The visualization of faces and scenes, of visual narrative and drama—this was profoundly impaired, almost absent. But the visualization of schemata was preserved, perhaps enhanced. Thus, when I engaged him in a game of mental chess, he had no difficulty visualizing the chessboard or the moves—indeed, no difficulty in beating me soundly.

Luria[6] said of Zazetsky that he had entirely lost his capacity to play games but that his "vivid imagination" was unimpaired. Zazetsky and Dr. P. lived in worlds which were mirror images of each other. But the saddest difference between them was that Zazetsky, as Luria said, "fought to regain his lost faculties with the indomitable tenacity of the damned," whereas Dr. P. was not fighting, did not know what was lost, did not indeed know that anything was lost. But who was more tragic, or who was more damned—the man who knew it, or the man who did not? 65

When the examination was over, Mrs. P. called us to the table, where there was coffee and a delicious spread of little cakes. Hungrily, hummingly, Dr. P. started on the cakes. Swiftly, fluently, unthinkingly, melodiously, he pulled the plates toward him and took this and that in a great gurgling stream, an edible song of food, until, suddenly, there came an interruption: a loud, peremptory rat-tat-tat at the door. Startled, taken aback, arrested by the interruption, Dr. P. stopped eating and sat frozen, motionless, at the table, with an indifferent, blind bewilderment on his face. He saw, but no longer saw, the table; no longer perceived it as a table laden with cakes. His wife poured him some coffee: The smell titillated his nose and brought him back to reality. The melody of eating resumed.

How does he do anything? I wondered to myself. What happens when he's dressing, goes to the lavatory, has a bath? I followed his wife into the kitchen and asked her how, for instance, he managed to dress himself. "It's just like the eating," she explained. "I put his usual clothes out, in all the usual places, and he dresses without difficulty, singing to himself. He does everything singing to himself. But if he is interrupted and loses the thread, he comes to a complete stop, doesn't know his clothes—or his own body. He sings all the

[5]I have often wondered about Helen Keller's visual descriptions, whether these, for all their eloquence, are somehow empty as well? Or whether, by the transference of images from the tactile to the visual, or, yet more extraordinarily, from the verbal and the metaphorical to the sensorial and the visual, she *did* achieve a power of visual imagery, even though her visual cortex had never been stimulated, directly, by the eyes? But in Dr. P.'s case it is precisely the cortex that was damaged, the organic prerequisite of all pictorial imagery. Interestingly and typically he no longer dreamed pictorially—the "message" of the dream being conveyed in nonvisual terms.—Au.

[6]*Alexander Luria* (1902–1977): Russian neuropsychologist who developed theories of brain function that were based, in part, on his work with people with traumatic head injuries.—Eds.

time—eating songs, dressing songs, bathing songs, everything. He can't do anything unless he makes it a song."

While we were talking my attention was caught by the pictures on the walls.

"Yes," Mrs. P. said, "he was a gifted painter as well as a singer. The school exhibited his pictures every year."

I strolled past them curiously—they were in chronological order. All his earlier work was naturalistic and realistic, with vivid mood and atmosphere, but finely detailed and concrete. Then, years later, they became less vivid, less concrete, less realistic and naturalistic, but far more abstract, even geometrical and cubist. Finally, in the last paintings, the canvases became nonsense, or nonsense to me—mere chaotic lines and blotches of paint. I commented on this to Mrs. P. 70

"Ach, you doctors, you're such Philistines!"[7] she exclaimed. "Can you not see *artistic development*—how he renounced the realism of his earlier years, and advanced into abstract, nonrepresentational art?"

"No, that's not it," I said to myself (but forbore to say it to poor Mrs. P.). He had indeed moved from realism to nonrepresentation to the abstract, yet this was not the artist, but the pathology, advancing—advancing towards a profound visual agnosia, in which all powers of representation and imagery, all sense of the concrete, all sense of reality, were being destroyed. This wall of paintings was a tragic pathological exhibit, which belonged to neurology, not art.

And yet, I wondered, was she not partly right? For there is often a struggle, and sometimes, even more interestingly, a collusion between the powers of pathology and creation. Perhaps, in his cubist period, there might have been both artistic and pathological development, colluding to engender an original form; for as he lost the concrete, so he might have gained in the abstract, developing a greater sensitivity to all the structural elements of line, boundary, contour—an almost Picasso-like power to see, and equally depict, those abstract organizations embedded in, and normally lost in, the concrete. . . . Though in the final pictures, I feared, there was only chaos and agnosia.

We returned to the great music room, with the Bösendorfer in the center, and Dr. P. humming the last torte.

"Well, Dr. Sacks," he said to me. "You find me an interesting case, I perceive. Can you tell me what you find wrong, make recommendations?" 75

"I can't tell you what I find wrong," I replied, "but I'll say what I find right. You are a wonderful musician, and music is your life. What I would prescribe, in a case such as yours, is a life which consists entirely of music. Music has been the center, now make it the whole, of your life."

This was four years ago—I never saw him again, but I often wondered about how he apprehended the world, given his strange loss of image, visuality, and the perfect preservation of a great musicality. I think that music, for

[7]*Philistines*: Uncultured, materialistic people. According to the Bible, the Philistines were enemies of the Israelites.—Eds.

him, had taken the place of image. He had no body-image, he had body-music: This is why he could move and act as fluently as he did, but came to a total confused stop if the "inner music" stopped. And equally with the outside, the world. . . . [8]

In *The World as Representation and Will,* Schopenhauer[9] speaks of music as "pure will." How fascinated he would have been by Dr. P., a man who had wholly lost the world as representation, but wholly preserved it as music or will.

And this, mercifully, held to the end—for despite the gradual advance of his disease (a massive tumor or degenerative process in the visual parts of his brain) Dr. P. lived and taught music to the last days of his life.

Postscript

How should one interpret Dr. P.'s peculiar inability to interpret, to judge, a glove as a glove? Manifestly, here, he could not make a cognitive judgment, though he was prolific in the production of cognitive hypotheses. A judgment is intuitive, personal, comprehensive, and concrete—we "see" how things stand, in relation to one another and oneself. It was precisely this setting, this relating, that Dr. P. lacked (though his judging, in all other spheres, was prompt and normal). Was this due to lack of visual information, or faulty processing of visual information? (This would be the explanation given by a classical, schematic neurology.) Or was there something amiss in Dr. P.'s attitude, so that he could not relate what he saw to himself? 80

These explanations, or modes of explanation, are not mutually exclusive—being in different modes they could coexist and both be true. And this is acknowledged, implicitly or explicitly, in classical neurology: implicitly, by Macrae, when he finds the explanation of defective schemata, or defective visual processing and integration, inadequate; explicitly, by Goldstein, when he speaks of "abstract attitude." But abstract attitude, which allows "categorization," also misses the mark with Dr. P.—and, perhaps, with the concept of "judgment" in general. For Dr. P. *had* abstract attitude—indeed, nothing else. And it was precisely this, his absurd abstractness of attitude—absurd because unleavened with anything else—which rendered him incapable of perceiving identity or particulars, rendered him incapable of judgment.

Neurology and psychology, curiously, though they talk of everything else, almost never talk of "judgment"—and yet it is precisely the downfall of judgment . . . which constitutes the essence of so many neuropsychological disorders. Judgment and identity may be casualties—but neuropsychology never speaks of them.

[8]Thus, as I learned later from his wife, though he could not recognize his students if they sat still, if they were merely "images," he might suddenly recognize them if they *moved.* "That's Karl," he would cry. "I know his movements, his body-music."—Au.

[9]*Arthur Schopenhauer* (1788–1860): German philosopher whose work included a theory to explain the life and work of the artist.—Eds.

And yet, whether in a philosophic sense (Kant's sense),[10] or an empirical and evolutionary sense, judgment is the most important faculty we have. An animal, or a man, may get on very well without "abstract attitude" but will speedily perish if deprived of judgment. Judgment must be the *first* faculty of higher life or mind—yet it is ignored, or misinterpreted, by classical (computational) neurology. And if we wonder how such an absurdity can arise, we find it in the assumptions, or the evolution, of neurology itself. For classical neurology (like classical physics) has always been mechanical—from Hughlings Jackson's mechanical analogies to the computer analogies of today.

Of course, the brain is a machine and a computer—everything in classical neurology is correct. But our mental processes, which constitute our being and life, are not just abstract and mechanical, but personal, as well—and, as such, involve not just classifying and categorizing, but continual judging and feeling also. If this is missing, we become computer-like, as Dr. P. was. And, by the same token, if we delete feeling and judging, the personal, from the cognitive sciences, we reduce them to something as defective as Dr. P.—and we reduce our apprehension of the concrete and real.

By a sort of comic and awful analogy, our current cognitive neurology and psychology resemble nothing so much as poor Dr. P.! We need the concrete and real, as he did; and we fail to see this, as he failed to see it. Our cognitive sciences are themselves suffering from an agnosia essentially similar to Dr. P.'s. Dr. P. may therefore serve as a warning and parable—of what happens to a science which eschews the judgmental, the particular, the personal, and becomes entirely abstract and computational. 85

It was always a matter of great regret to me that, owing to circumstances beyond my control, I was not able to follow his case further, either in the sort of observations and investigations described, or in ascertaining the actual disease pathology.

One always fears that a case is "unique," especially if it has such extraordinary features as those of Dr. P. It was, therefore, with a sense of great interest and delight, not unmixed with relief, that I found, quite by chance—looking through the periodical *Brain* for 1956—a detailed description of an almost comically similar case, similar (indeed identical) neuropsychologically and phenomenologically, though the underlying pathology (an acute head injury) and all personal circumstances were wholly different. The authors speak of their case as "unique in the documented history of this disorder"—and evidently experienced, as I did, amazement at their own findings.[11] The interested

---

[10]*Immanuel Kant* (1724–1804): German philosopher; some of his work concerned ethics and moral judgment.—Eds.

[11]Only since the completion of this book have I found that there is, in fact, a rather extensive literature on visual agnosia in general, and prosopagnosia in particular. In particular I had the great pleasure recently of meeting Dr. Andrew Kertesz, who has himself published some extremely detailed studies of patients with such agnosias (see, for example, his paper on visual agnosia, Kertesz 1979). Dr. Kertesz mentioned to me a case known to him of a farmer who had developed prosopagnosia and in consequence could no longer distinguish (the faces of) his *cows,* and of another such patient, an attendant in a natural history museum,

reader is referred to the original paper, Macrae and Trolle (1956), of which I here subjoin a brief paraphrase, with quotations from the original.

Their patient was a young man of thirty-two, who, following a severe automobile accident, with unconsciousness for three weeks, "... complained, exclusively, of an inability to recognize faces, even those of his wife and children." Not a single face was "familiar" to him, but there were three he could identify; these were workmates: one with an eye-blinking tic, one with a large mole on his cheek, and a third "because he was so tall and thin that no one else was like him." Each of these, Macrae and Trolle bring out, was "recognized solely by the single prominent feature mentioned." In general (like Dr. P.) he recognized familiars only by their voices.

He had difficulty even recognizing himself in a mirror, as Macrae and Trolle describe in detail: "In the early convalescent phase he frequently, especially when shaving, questioned whether the face gazing at him was really his own, and even though he knew it could physically be none other, on several occasions grimaced or stuck out his tongue 'just to make sure.' By carefully studying his face in the mirror he slowly began to recognize it, but 'not in a flash' as in the past—he relied on the hair and facial outline, and on two small moles on his left cheek."

In general he could not recognize objects "at a glance," but would have to seek out, and guess from, one or two features—occasionally his guesses were absurdly wrong. In particular, the authors note, there was difficulty with the *animate.* 90

On the other hand, simple schematic objects—scissors, watch, key, etc.—presented no difficulties. Macrae and Trolle also note that: "His *topographical memory* was strange: The seeming paradox existed that he could find his way from home to hospital and around the hospital, but yet could not name streets en route [unlike Dr. P., he also had some aphasia] or appear to visualize the topography."

It was also evident that visual memories of people, even from long before the accident, were severely impaired—there was memory of conduct, or perhaps a mannerism, but not of visual appearance or face. Similarly, it appeared, when he was questioned closely, that he no longer had visual images in his *dreams.* Thus, as with Dr. P., it was not just visual perception, but visual imagination and memory, the fundamental powers of visual representation, which were essentially damaged in this patient—at least those powers insofar as they pertained to the personal, the familiar, the concrete.

A final, humorous point. Where Dr. P. might mistake his wife for a hat, Macrae's patient, also unable to recognize his wife, needed her to identify herself by a visual *marker,* by "... a conspicuous article of clothing, such as a large hat."

---

who mistook his own reflection for the diorama of an *ape.* As with Dr. P., and as with Macrae and Trolle's patient, it is especially the animate which is so absurdly misperceived. The most important studies of such agnosias, and of visual processing in general, are now being undertaken by A. R. and H. Damasio.—Au.

▪ QUESTIONS

Reading

1. Summarize as clearly as you can the nature of Dr. P.'s problem. What are the symptoms? What seems to have caused them?
2. In explaining the case study of Dr. P., Sacks uses several techniques commonly found in fiction writing, including describing characters in a compelling way. How does Sacks bring Dr. and Mrs. P. to life as characters? How does he characterize himself? What are your impressions of Dr. Sacks from this characterization?
3. Highlight, underline, or flag the tests that Sacks uses to learn about Dr. P.'s condition. How, according to Sacks, is the human brain different from a machine or a computer?

Exploratory Writing

1. Sacks is relieved to learn that the case of Dr. P. is not entirely unique. Collaborate in small groups to find a case of someone who has a neurological condition that makes his or her perception different from the "normal," or average. Write up a case study or profile of this person, and present your findings to the class. What is the diagnosis of his or her condition? What are its details? What might it be like to live with this condition?
2. Mrs. P. believes that Dr. P.'s abstract, nonrepresentational images are evidence of his artistic development rather than his visual agnosia. Sacks writes, "There is often . . . a collusion between the powers of pathology and creation" (paragraph 73). Choose a work of visual art that you find powerful, and list its qualities or details that could equally be interpreted as either artistic innovation or signs of skewed perception. Why does Sacks fear that Dr. P.'s later work is more about "chaos and agnosia" than creativity?

Making Connections

1. Dr. P. and Jill Bolte Taylor (p. 418) have both seen, perceived, and experienced the world in unusual ways. Compare Dr. P.'s visual perceptions, as Sacks describes them, with Taylor's account of how she sees the world.
2. The prisoners in Plato's allegory of the cave (p. 104), like Dr. P., are unaware of their inability to perceive reality. Sacks asks whether a man who is aware that he has lost his faculties is "more tragic" than a man like Dr. P., who has no understanding of what is lost (paragraph 65). How might Socrates evaluate the case of Dr. P.? In "The Cave," is Socrates arguing, in essence, that all human beings suffer from a kind of neurological disorder?

Essay Writing

1. This essay is not only a single case history and an explanation of some curious behavior. It also contains an argument about the nature of the cognitive sciences — how they should and should not proceed. What is that argument? Do you agree or disagree with the view of cognitive science that Sacks is advocating? Write an essay in which you present his position, and develop one of your own on this matter.

The Moral Instinct

Steven Pinker

A cognitive scientist, psychologist, linguist, and scholar, Steven Pinker (b. 1954) has been variously described as the "bad boy" of language, an "agent provocateur" of science, a "wunderkind," and an "evolutionary pop star." He earned these labels as much from his best-selling books and articles in the mainstream press as from his many — and masterful — scholarly works. His books include *The Language Instinct* (1994), which argues that language is a biological adaptation; *How the Mind Works* (1997), which includes the rest of the mind — "from vision and reasoning to the emotions, humor, and art" — in his synthesis; and *The Blank Slate: The Modern Denial of Human Nature* (2002), which explores the political, moral, and emotional aspects of human nature. His latest book is *The Better Angels of Our Nature: The Decline of Violence in History and Its Causes* (2011). Pinker — currently a professor in the department of psychology at Harvard University — was, until 2003, director of the Center for Cognitive Neuroscience at the Massachusetts Institute of Technology (MIT), where he specialized in psycholinguistics — particularly language development in children. Born in Montreal, Canada, he earned a degree in experimental psychology at McGill University, then went to the United States in 1976 to do graduate work at Harvard, followed by a postdoctoral fellowship at MIT. He became a naturalized U.S. citizen in 1980. His essay "The Moral Instinct" appeared in the *New York Times Magazine* in January 2008.

Which of the following people would you say is the most admirable: Mother Teresa, Bill Gates or Norman Borlaug? And which do you think is the least admirable? For most people, it's an easy question. Mother Teresa, famous for ministering to the poor in Calcutta, has been beatified by the Vatican, awarded the Nobel Peace Prize and ranked in an American poll as the most admired person of the twentieth century. Bill Gates, infamous for giving us the Microsoft dancing paper clip and the blue screen of death, has been decapitated in effigy in "I Hate Gates" Web sites and hit with a pie in the face. As for Norman Borlaug . . . who the heck is Norman Borlaug?

Yet a deeper look might lead you to rethink your answers. Borlaug, father of the "Green Revolution" that used agricultural science to reduce world hunger, has been credited with saving a billion lives, more than anyone else in history. Gates, in deciding what to do with his fortune, crunched the numbers and determined that he could alleviate the most misery by fighting everyday scourges in the developing world like malaria, diarrhea, and parasites. Mother Teresa, for her part, extolled the virtue of suffering and ran her well-financed missions accordingly: Their sick patrons were offered plenty of prayer but harsh conditions, few analgesics and dangerously primitive medical care.

It's not hard to see why the moral reputations of this trio should be so out of line with the good they have done. Mother Teresa was the very embodiment of saintliness: white-clad, sad-eyed, ascetic, and often photographed with the wretched of the earth. Gates is a nerd's nerd and the world's richest man, as likely to enter heaven as the proverbial camel squeezing through the needle's eye. And Borlaug, now ninety-three, is an agronomist who has spent his life in labs and nonprofits, seldom walking onto the media stage, and hence into our consciousness, at all.

I doubt these examples will persuade anyone to favor Bill Gates over Mother Teresa for sainthood. But they show that our heads can be turned by an aura of sanctity, distracting us from a more objective reckoning of the actions that make people suffer or flourish. It seems we may all be vulnerable to moral illusions, the ethical equivalent of the bending lines that trick the eye on cereal boxes and in psychology textbooks. Illusions are a favorite tool of perception scientists for exposing the workings of the five senses, and of philosophers for shaking people out of the naive belief that our minds give us a transparent window onto the world (since if our eyes can be fooled by an illusion, why should we trust them at other times?). Today, a new field is using illusions to unmask a sixth sense, the moral sense. Moral intuitions are being drawn out of people in the lab, on Web sites, and in brain scanners, and are being explained with tools from game theory, neuroscience and evolutionary biology.

"Two things fill the mind with ever new and increasing admiration and awe, the oftener and more steadily we reflect on them," wrote Immanuel Kant, "the starry heavens above and the moral law within." These days, the moral law within is being viewed with increasing awe, if not always admiration. The human moral sense turns out to be an organ of considerable complexity, with quirks that reflect its evolutionary history and its neurobiological foundations. 5

These quirks are bound to have implications for the human predicament. Morality is not just any old topic in psychology but close to our conception of the meaning of life. Moral goodness is what gives each of us the sense that we are worthy human beings. We seek it in our friends and mates, nurture it in our children, advance it in our politics, and justify it with our religions. A disrespect for morality is blamed for everyday sins and history's worst atrocities. To carry this weight, the concept of morality would have to be bigger than any of us and outside all of us.

So dissecting moral intuitions is no small matter. If morality is a mere trick of the brain, some may fear, our very grounds for being moral could be eroded. Yet as we shall see, the science of the moral sense can instead be seen as a way to strengthen those grounds, by clarifying what morality is and how it should steer our actions.

The Moralization Switch

The starting point for appreciating that there *is* a distinctive part of our psychology for morality is seeing how moral judgments differ from other kinds of opinions we have on how people ought to behave. Moralization is a psychological state that can be turned on and off like a switch, and when it is on, a distinctive mind-set commandeers our thinking. This is the mind-set that makes us deem actions immoral ("killing is wrong"), rather than merely disagreeable ("I hate brussels sprouts"), unfashionable ("bell-bottoms are out"), or imprudent ("don't scratch mosquito bites").

The first hallmark of moralization is that the rules it invokes are felt to be universal. Prohibitions of rape and murder, for example, are felt not to be matters of local custom but to be universally and objectively warranted. One can easily say, "I don't like brussels sprouts, but I don't care if you eat them," but no one would say, "I don't like killing, but I don't care if you murder someone."

The other hallmark is that people feel that those who commit immoral acts deserve to be punished. Not only is it allowable to inflict pain on a person who has broken a moral rule; it is wrong *not* to, to "let them get away with it." People are thus untroubled in inviting divine retribution or the power of the state to harm other people they deem immoral. Bertrand Russell wrote, "The infliction of cruelty with a good conscience is a delight to moralists—that is why they invented hell." 10

We all know what it feels like when the moralization switch flips inside us—the righteous glow, the burning dudgeon, the drive to recruit others to the cause. The psychologist Paul Rozin has studied the toggle switch by comparing two kinds of people who engage in the same behavior but with different switch settings. Health vegetarians avoid meat for practical reasons, like lowering cholesterol and avoiding toxins. Moral vegetarians avoid meat for ethical reasons: to avoid complicity in the suffering of animals. By investigating their feelings about meat-eating, Rozin showed that the moral motive sets off a cascade of opinions. Moral vegetarians are more likely to treat meat as a contaminant—they refuse, for example, to eat a bowl of soup into which a drop of beef broth has fallen. They are more likely to think that other people ought to be vegetarians, and are more likely to imbue their dietary habits with other virtues, like believing that meat avoidance makes people less aggressive and bestial.

Much of our recent social history, including the culture wars between liberals and conservatives, consists of the moralization or amoralization of particular kinds of behavior. Even when people agree that an outcome is desirable, they may disagree on whether it should be treated as a matter of preference and prudence or as a matter of sin and virtue. Rozin notes, for example, that smoking has lately been moralized. Until recently, it was understood that some people didn't enjoy smoking or avoided it because it was hazardous to their health. But with the discovery of the harmful effects of secondhand smoke, smoking is now treated as immoral. Smokers are ostracized; images of people smoking are censored; and entities touched by smoke are felt to be contaminated (so hotels have not only nonsmoking rooms but nonsmoking *floors*). The desire for retribution has been visited on tobacco companies, who have been slapped with staggering "punitive damages."

At the same time, many behaviors have been amoralized, switched from moral failings to lifestyle choices. They include divorce, illegitimacy, being a working mother, marijuana use, and homosexuality. Many afflictions have been reassigned from payback for bad choices to unlucky misfortunes. There used to be people called "bums" and "tramps"; today they are "homeless." Drug addiction is a "disease"; syphilis was rebranded from the price of wanton behavior to a "sexually transmitted disease" and more recently a "sexually transmitted infection."

This wave of amoralization has led the cultural right to lament that morality itself is under assault, as we see in the group that anointed itself the Moral Majority. In fact there seems to be a Law of Conservation of Moralization, so that as old behaviors are taken out of the moralized column, new ones are added to it. Dozens of things that past generations treated as practical matters are now ethical battlegrounds, including disposable diapers, IQ tests, poultry farms, Barbie dolls, and research on breast cancer. Food alone has become a minefield, with critics sermonizing about the size of sodas, the chemistry of fat, the freedom of chickens, the price of coffee beans, the species of fish, and now the distance the food has traveled from farm to plate.

Many of these moralizations, like the assault on smoking, may be understood as practical tactics to reduce some recently identified harm. But whether an activity flips our mental switches to the "moral" setting isn't just a matter of how much harm it does. We don't show contempt to the man who fails to change the batteries in his smoke alarms or takes his family on a driving vacation, both of which multiply the risk they will die in an accident. Driving a gas-guzzling Hummer is reprehensible, but driving a gas-guzzling old Volvo is not; eating a Big Mac is unconscionable, but not imported cheese or crème brûlée. The reason for these double standards is obvious: People tend to align their moralization with their own lifestyles. 15

Reasoning and Rationalizing

It's not just the content of our moral judgments that is often questionable, but the way we arrive at them. We like to think that when we have a conviction, there are good reasons that drove us to adopt it. That is why an older approach to moral psychology, led by Jean Piaget and Lawrence Kohlberg, tried to document the lines of reasoning that guided people to moral conclusions. But consider these situations, originally devised by the psychologist Jonathan Haidt:

Julie is traveling in France on summer vacation from college with her brother Mark. One night they decide that it would be interesting and fun if they tried making love. Julie was already taking birth-control pills, but Mark uses a condom, too, just to be safe. They both enjoy the sex but decide not to do it again. They keep the night as a special secret, which makes them feel closer to each other. What do you think about that—was it OK for them to make love?

A woman is cleaning out her closet and she finds her old American flag. She doesn't want the flag anymore, so she cuts it up into pieces and uses the rags to clean her bathroom.

A family's dog is killed by a car in front of their house. They heard that dog meat was delicious, so they cut up the dog's body and cook it and eat it for dinner.

Most people immediately declare that these acts are wrong and then grope to justify *why* they are wrong. It's not so easy. In the case of Julie and Mark, people raise the possibility of children with birth defects, but they are reminded that the couple were diligent about contraception. They suggest that the siblings will be emotionally hurt, but the story makes it clear that they weren't. They submit that the act would offend the community, but then recall that it was kept a secret. Eventually many people admit, "I don't know, I can't explain it, I just know it's wrong." People don't generally engage in moral reasoning, Haidt argues, but moral *rationalization:* They begin with the conclusion, coughed up by an unconscious emotion, and then work backward to a plausible justification. 20

The gap between people's convictions and their justifications is also on display in the favorite new sandbox for moral psychologists, a thought experiment devised by the philosophers Philippa Foot and Judith Jarvis Thomson called the Trolley Problem. On your morning walk, you see a trolley car hurtling down the track, the conductor slumped over the controls. In the path of the trolley are five men working on the track, oblivious to the danger. You are standing at a fork in the track and can pull a lever that will divert the trolley onto a spur, saving the five men. Unfortunately, the trolley would then run over a single worker who is laboring on the spur. Is it permissible to throw the switch, killing one man to save five? Almost everyone says yes.

Consider now a different scene. You are on a bridge overlooking the tracks and have spotted the runaway trolley bearing down on the five workers. Now the only way to stop the trolley is to throw a heavy object in its path. And the only heavy object within reach is a fat man standing next to you. Should you throw the man off the bridge? Both dilemmas present you with the option of sacrificing one life to save five, and so, by the utilitarian standard of what would result in the greatest good for the greatest number, the two dilemmas are morally equivalent. But most people don't see it that way: Though they would pull the switch in the first dilemma, they would not heave the fat man in the second. When pressed for a reason, they can't come up with anything coherent, though moral philosophers haven't had an easy time coming up with a relevant difference, either.

When psychologists say "most people" they usually mean "most of the two dozen sophomores who filled out a questionnaire for beer money." But in this case it means most of the 200,000 people from a hundred countries who shared their intuitions on a Web-based experiment conducted by the psychologists Fiery Cushman and Liane Young and the biologist Marc Hauser. A difference between the acceptability of switch-pulling and man-heaving, and an inability to justify the choice, was found in respondents from Europe, Asia, and North and South America; among men and women, blacks and whites, teenagers and octogenarians, Hindus, Muslims, Buddhists, Christians, Jews, and atheists; people with elementary-school educations and people with PhDs.

Joshua Greene, a philosopher and cognitive neuroscientist, suggests that evolution equipped people with a revulsion to manhandling an innocent person. This instinct, he suggests, tends to overwhelm any utilitarian calculus that would tot up the lives saved and lost. The impulse against roughing up a fellow human would explain other examples in which people abjure killing one to save many, like euthanizing a hospital patient to harvest his organs and save five dying patients in need of transplants, or throwing someone out of a crowded lifeboat to keep it afloat.

By itself this would be no more than a plausible story, but Greene teamed up with the cognitive neuroscientist Jonathan Cohen and several Princeton colleagues to peer into people's brains using functional MRI. They sought to find signs of a conflict between brain areas associated with emotion (the ones that recoil from harming someone) and areas dedicated to rational analysis (the ones that calculate lives lost and saved). 25

When people pondered the dilemmas that required killing someone with their bare hands, several networks in their brains lighted up. One, which included the medial (inward-facing) parts of the frontal lobes, has been implicated in emotions about other people. A second, the dorsolateral (upper and outer-facing) surface of the frontal lobes, has been implicated in ongoing mental computation (including nonmoral reasoning, like deciding whether to get somewhere by plane or train). And a third region, the anterior cingulate cortex (an evolutionarily ancient strip lying at the base of the inner surface of each cerebral hemisphere), registers a conflict between an urge coming from one part of the brain and an advisory coming from another.

But when the people were pondering a hands-off dilemma, like switching the trolley onto the spur with the single worker, the brain reacted differently: Only the area involved in rational calculation stood out. Other studies have shown that neurological patients who have blunted emotions because of damage to the frontal lobes become utilitarians: They think it makes perfect sense to throw the fat man off the bridge. Together, the findings corroborate Greene's theory that our nonutilitarian intuitions come from the victory of an emotional impulse over a cost-benefit analysis.

A Universal Morality?

The findings of trolleyology—complex, instinctive and worldwide moral intuitions—led Hauser and John Mikhail (a legal scholar) to revive an analogy from the philosopher John Rawls between the moral sense and language. According to Noam Chomsky, we are born with a "universal grammar" that forces us to analyze speech in terms of its grammatical structure, with no conscious awareness of the rules in play. By analogy, we are born with a universal moral grammar that forces us to analyze human action in terms of its moral structure, with just as little awareness.

The idea that the moral sense is an innate part of human nature is not far-fetched. A list of human universals collected by the anthropologist Donald E. Brown includes many moral concepts and emotions, including a distinction between right and wrong; empathy; fairness; admiration of generosity; rights and obligations; proscription of murder, rape, and other forms of violence; redress of wrongs; sanctions for wrongs against the community; shame; and taboos.

The stirrings of morality emerge early in childhood. Toddlers spontaneously offer toys and help to others and try to comfort people they see in distress. And according to the psychologists Elliot Turiel and Judith Smetana, preschoolers have an inkling of the difference between societal conventions and moral principles. Four-year-olds say that it is not OK to wear pajamas to school (a convention) and also not OK to hit a little girl for no reason (a moral principle). But when asked whether these actions would be OK if the teacher allowed them, most of the children said that wearing pajamas would now be fine but that hitting a little girl would still not be. 30

Though no one has identified genes for morality, there is circumstantial evidence they exist. The character traits called "conscientiousness" and "agreeableness" are far more correlated in identical twins separated at birth (who share their genes but not their environment) than in adoptive siblings raised together (who share their environment but not their genes). People given diagnoses of "antisocial personality disorder" or "psychopathy" show signs of morality blindness from the time they are children. They bully younger children, torture animals, habitually lie and seem incapable of empathy or remorse, often despite normal family backgrounds. Some of these children grow up into the monsters who bilk elderly people out of their savings, rape a succession of women, or shoot convenience-store clerks lying on the floor during a robbery.

Though psychopathy probably comes from a genetic predisposition, a milder version can be caused by damage to frontal regions of the brain (including the areas that inhibit intact people from throwing the hypothetical fat man off the bridge). The neuroscientists Hanna and Antonio Damasio and their colleagues found that some children who sustain severe injuries to their frontal lobes can grow up into callous and irresponsible adults, despite normal intelligence. They lie, steal, ignore punishment, endanger their own children, and can't think through even the simplest moral dilemmas, like what two people should do if they disagreed on which TV channel to watch or whether a man ought to steal a drug to save his dying wife.

The moral sense, then, may be rooted in the design of the normal human brain. Yet for all the awe that may fill our minds when we reflect on an innate moral law within, the idea is at best incomplete. Consider this moral dilemma: A runaway trolley is about to kill a schoolteacher. You can divert the trolley onto a sidetrack, but the trolley would trip a switch sending a signal to a class of six-year-olds, giving them permission to name a teddy bear Muhammad. Is it permissible to pull the lever?

This is no joke. Last month a British woman teaching in a private school in Sudan allowed her class to name a teddy bear after the most popular boy in the class, who bore the name of the founder of Islam. She was jailed for blasphemy and threatened with a public flogging, while a mob outside the prison demanded her death. To the protesters, the woman's life clearly had less value than maximizing the dignity of their religion, and their judgment on whether it is right to divert the hypothetical trolley would have differed from ours. Whatever grammar guides people's moral judgments can't be all *that* universal. Anyone who stayed awake through Anthropology 101 can offer many other examples.

Of course, languages vary, too. In Chomsky's theory, languages conform to an abstract blueprint, like having phrases built out of verbs and objects, while the details vary, like whether the verb or the object comes first. Could we be wired with an abstract spec sheet that embraces all the strange ideas that people in different cultures moralize? 35

The Varieties of Moral Experience

When anthropologists like Richard Shweder and Alan Fiske survey moral concerns across the globe, they find that a few themes keep popping up from amid the diversity. People everywhere, at least in some circumstances and with certain other folks in mind, think it's bad to harm others and good to help them. They have a sense of fairness: that one should reciprocate favors, reward benefactors, and punish cheaters. They value loyalty to a group, sharing and solidarity among its members, and conformity to its norms. They believe that it is right to defer to legitimate authorities and to respect people with high status. And they exalt purity, cleanliness, and sanctity while loathing defilement, contamination, and carnality.

The exact number of themes depends on whether you're a lumper or a splitter, but Haidt counts five—harm, fairness, community (or group loyalty), authority, and purity—and suggests that they are the primary colors of our moral sense. Not only do they keep reappearing in cross-cultural surveys, but each one tugs on the moral intuitions of people in our own culture. Haidt asks us to consider how much money someone would have to pay us to do hypothetical acts like the following:

Stick a pin into your palm.

Stick a pin into the palm of a child you don't know. (Harm.)

Accept a wide-screen TV from a friend who received it at no charge because of a computer error. 40

Accept a wide-screen TV from a friend who received it from a thief who had stolen it from a wealthy family. (Fairness.)

Say something bad about your nation (which you don't believe) on a talk-radio show in your nation.

Say something bad about your nation (which you don't believe) on a talk-radio show in a foreign nation. (Community.)

Slap a friend in the face, with his permission, as part of a comedy skit.

Slap your minister in the face, with his permission, as part of a comedy skit. (Authority.) 45

Attend a performance-art piece in which the actors act like idiots for thirty minutes, including flubbing simple problems and falling down on stage.

Attend a performance-art piece in which the actors act like animals for thirty minutes, including crawling around naked and urinating on stage. (Purity.)

In each pair, the second action feels far more repugnant. Most of the moral illusions we have visited come from an unwarranted intrusion of one of the moral spheres into our judgments. A violation of community led people to frown on using an old flag to clean a bathroom. Violations of purity repelled the people who judged the morality of consensual incest and prevented the moral vegetarians and nonsmokers from tolerating the slightest trace of a vile contaminant. At the other end of the scale, displays of extreme purity lead people to venerate religious leaders who dress in white and affect an aura of chastity and asceticism.

The Genealogy of Morals

The five spheres are good candidates for a periodic table of the moral sense not only because they are ubiquitous but also because they appear to have deep evolutionary roots. The impulse to avoid harm, which gives trolley ponderers the willies when they consider throwing a man off a bridge, can also be found in rhesus monkeys, who go hungry rather than pull a chain that delivers food to them and a shock to another monkey. Respect for authority is clearly related to the pecking orders of dominance and appeasement that are widespread in the animal kingdom. The purity-defilement contrast taps the emotion of disgust that is triggered by potential disease vectors like bodily effluvia, decaying flesh, and unconventional forms of meat, and by risky sexual practices like incest.

The other two moralized spheres match up with the classic examples of 50 how altruism can evolve that were worked out by sociobiologists in the 1960s and 1970s and made famous by Richard Dawkins in his book *The Selfish Gene.* Fairness is very close to what scientists call reciprocal altruism, where a willingness to be nice to others can evolve as long as the favor helps the recipient more than it costs the giver and the recipient returns the favor when fortunes reverse. The analysis makes it sound as if reciprocal altruism comes out of a robotlike calculation, but in fact Robert Trivers, the biologist who devised the theory, argued that it is implemented in the brain as a suite of moral emotions. Sympathy prompts a person to offer the first favor, particularly to someone in need for whom it would go the furthest. Anger protects a person against cheaters who accept a favor without reciprocating, by impelling him to punish the ingrate or sever the relationship. Gratitude impels a beneficiary to reward those who helped him in the past. Guilt prompts a cheater in danger of being found out to repair the relationship by redressing the misdeed and advertising that he will behave better in the future (consistent with Mencken's definition of *conscience* as "the inner voice which warns us that someone might be looking"). Many experiments on who helps whom, who likes whom, who punishes whom and who feels guilty about what have confirmed these predictions.

Community, the very different emotion that prompts people to share and sacrifice without an expectation of payback, may be rooted in nepotistic altruism, the empathy and solidarity we feel toward our relatives (and which evolved because any gene that pushed an organism to aid a relative would have helped copies of itself sitting inside that relative). In humans, of course, communal feelings can be lavished on nonrelatives as well. Sometimes it pays people (in an evolutionary sense) to love their companions because their interests are yoked, like spouses with common children, in-laws with common relatives, friends with common tastes, or allies with common enemies. And sometimes it doesn't pay them at all, but their kinship-detectors have been tricked into treating their groupmates as if they were relatives by tactics like kinship metaphors (*blood brothers, fraternities, the fatherland*), origin myths, communal meals, and other bonding rituals.

Juggling the Spheres

All this brings us to a theory of how the moral sense can be universal and variable at the same time. The five moral spheres are universal, a legacy of evolution. But how they are ranked in importance, and which is brought in to moralize which area of social life—sex, government, commerce, religion, diet, and so on—depends on the culture. Many of the flabbergasting practices in faraway places become more intelligible when you recognize that the same moralizing impulse that Western elites channel toward violations of harm and fairness (our moral obsessions) is channeled elsewhere to violations in the other spheres. Think of the Japanese fear of nonconformity (community), the holy ablutions and dietary restrictions of Hindus and Orthodox Jews (purity), the outrage at insulting the Prophet among Muslims (authority). In the West, we believe that in business and government, fairness should trump community and try to root out nepotism and cronyism. In other parts of the world this is incomprehensible—what heartless creep would favor a perfect stranger over his own brother?

The ranking and placement of moral spheres also divides the cultures of liberals and conservatives in the United States. Many bones of contention, like homosexuality, atheism, and one-parent families from the right, or racial imbalances, sweatshops, and executive pay from the left, reflect different weightings of the spheres. In a large Web survey, Haidt found that liberals put a lopsided moral weight on harm and fairness while playing down group loyalty, authority, and purity. Conservatives instead place a moderately high weight on all five. It's not surprising that each side thinks it is driven by lofty ethical values and that the other side is base and unprincipled.

Reassigning an activity to a different sphere, or taking it out of the moral spheres altogether, isn't easy. People think that a behavior belongs in its sphere as a matter of sacred necessity and that the very act of questioning an assignment is a moral outrage. The psychologist Philip Tetlock has shown that the mentality of taboo—a conviction that some thoughts are sinful to think—is not just a superstition of Polynesians but a mind-set that can easily be triggered in college-educated Americans. Just ask them to think about applying the sphere of reciprocity to relationships customarily governed by community or authority. When Tetlock asked subjects for their opinions on whether adoption agencies should place children with the couples willing to pay the most, whether people should have the right to sell their organs, and whether they should be able to buy their way out of jury duty, the subjects not only disagreed but felt personally insulted and were outraged that anyone would raise the question.

The institutions of modernity often question and experiment with the way activities are assigned to moral spheres. Market economies tend to put everything up for sale. Science amoralizes the world by seeking to understand phenomena rather than pass judgment on them. Secular philosophy is in the business of scrutinizing all beliefs, including those entrenched by authority and tradition. It's not surprising that these institutions are often seen to be morally corrosive. 55

Is Nothing Sacred?

And "morally corrosive" is exactly the term that some critics would apply to the new science of the moral sense. The attempt to dissect our moral intuitions can look like an attempt to debunk them. Evolutionary psychologists seem to want to unmask our noblest motives as ultimately self-interested — to show that our love for children, compassion for the unfortunate, and sense of justice are just tactics in a Darwinian struggle to perpetuate our genes. The explanation of how different cultures appeal to different spheres could lead to a spineless relativism, in which we would never have grounds to criticize the practice of another culture, no matter how barbaric, because "we have our kind of morality and they have theirs." And the whole enterprise seems to be dragging us to an amoral nihilism, in which morality itself would be demoted from a transcendent principle to a figment of our neural circuitry.

In reality, none of these fears are warranted, and it's important to see why not. The first misunderstanding involves the logic of evolutionary explanations. Evolutionary biologists sometimes anthropomorphize DNA for the same reason that science teachers find it useful to have their students imagine the world from the viewpoint of a molecule or a beam of light. One shortcut to understanding the theory of selection without working through the math is to imagine that the genes are little agents that try to make copies of themselves.

Unfortunately, the meme of the selfish gene escaped from popular biology books and mutated into the idea that organisms (including people) are ruthlessly self-serving. And this doesn't follow. Genes are not a reservoir of our dark unconscious wishes. "Selfish" genes are perfectly compatible with selfless organisms, because a gene's metaphorical goal of selfishly replicating itself can be implemented by wiring up the brain of the organism to do unselfish things, like being nice to relatives or doing good deeds for needy strangers. When a mother stays up all night comforting a sick child, the genes that endowed her with that tenderness were "selfish" in a metaphorical sense, but by no stretch of the imagination is *she* being selfish.

Nor does reciprocal altruism—the evolutionary rationale behind fairness—imply that people do good deeds in the cynical expectation of repayment down the line. We all know of unrequited good deeds, like tipping a waitress in a city you will never visit again and falling on a grenade to save platoon-mates. These bursts of goodness are not as anomalous to a biologist as they might appear.

In his classic 1971 article, Trivers, the biologist, showed how natural selection could push in the direction of true selflessness. The emergence of tit-for-tat reciprocity, which lets organisms trade favors without being cheated, is just a first step. A favor-giver not only has to avoid blatant cheaters (those who would accept a favor but not return it) but also prefer generous reciprocators (those who return the biggest favor they can afford) over stingy ones (those who return the smallest favor they can get away with). Since it's good to be chosen as a recipient of favors, a competition arises to be the most generous partner around. More accurately, a competition arises to *appear* to be the most generous partner around, since the favor-giver can't literally read minds or see into the future. A reputation for fairness and generosity becomes an asset. 60

Now this just sets up a competition for potential beneficiaries to inflate their reputations without making the sacrifices to back them up. But it also pressures the favor-giver to develop ever-more-sensitive radar to distinguish the genuinely generous partners from the hypocrites. This arms race will eventually reach a logical conclusion. The most effective way to *seem* generous and fair, under harsh scrutiny, is to be generous and fair. In the long run, then, reputation can be secured only by commitment. At least some agents evolve to be genuinely high-minded and self-sacrificing—they are moral not because of what it brings them but because that's the kind of people they are.

Of course, a theory that predicted that everyone always sacrificed themselves for another's good would be as preposterous as a theory that predicted that no one ever did. Alongside the niches for saints there are niches for more grudging reciprocators, who attract fewer and poorer partners but don't make the sacrifices necessary for a sterling reputation. And both may coexist with outright cheaters, who exploit the unwary in one-shot encounters. An ecosystem of niches, each with a distinct strategy, can evolve when the payoff of each strategy depends on how many players are playing the other strategies. The human social environment does have its share of generous, grudging, and crooked characters, and the genetic variation in personality seems to bear the fingerprints of this evolutionary process. . . .

Doing Better by Knowing Ourselves

Morality, then, is still something larger than our inherited moral sense, and the new science of the moral sense does not make moral reasoning and conviction obsolete. At the same time, its implications for our moral universe are profound.

At the very least, the science tells us that even when our adversaries' agenda is most baffling, they may not be amoral psychopaths but in the throes of a moral mind-set that appears to them to be every bit as mandatory and universal as ours does to us. Of course, some adversaries really are psychopaths, and others are so poisoned by a punitive moralization that they are beyond the pale of reason. (The actor Will Smith had many historians on his side when he recently speculated to the press that Hitler thought he was acting morally.) But in any conflict in which a meeting of the minds is not completely hopeless, a recognition that the other guy is acting from moral rather than venal reasons can be a first patch of common ground. One side can acknowledge the other's concern for community or stability or fairness or dignity, even while arguing that some other value should trump it in that instance. With affirmative action, for example, the opponents can be seen as arguing from a sense of fairness, not racism, and the defenders can be seen as acting from a concern with community, not bureaucratic power. Liberals can ratify conservatives' concern with families while noting that gay marriage is perfectly consistent with that concern.

The science of the moral sense also alerts us to ways in which our psychological makeup can get in the way of our arriving at the most defensible moral conclusions. The moral sense, we are learning, is as vulnerable to illusions as the other senses. It is apt to confuse morality per se with purity, status, and conformity. It tends to reframe practical problems as moral crusades and thus see their solution in punitive aggression. It imposes taboos that make certain ideas indiscussible. And it has the nasty habit of always putting the self on the side of the angels. 65

Though wise people have long reflected on how we can be blinded by our own sanctimony, our public discourse still fails to discount it appropriately. In the worst cases, the thoughtlessness of our brute intuitions can be celebrated as a virtue. In his influential essay "The Wisdom of Repugnance," Leon Kass, former chair of the President's Council on Bioethics, argued that we should disregard reason when it comes to cloning and other biomedical technologies and go with our gut: "We are repelled by the prospect of cloning human beings . . . because we intuit and feel, immediately and without argument, the violation of things that we rightfully hold dear. . . . In this age in which everything is held to be permissible so long as it is freely done . . . repugnance may be the only voice left that speaks up to defend the central core of our humanity. Shallow are the souls that have forgotten how to shudder."

There are, of course, good reasons to regulate human cloning, but the shudder test is not one of them. People have shuddered at all kinds of morally irrelevant violations of purity in their culture: touching an untouchable, drinking from the same water fountain as a Negro, allowing Jewish blood to mix with Aryan blood, tolerating sodomy between consenting men. And if our ancestors' repugnance had carried the day, we never would have had autopsies, vaccinations, blood transfusions, artificial insemination, organ transplants and in vitro fertilization, all of which were denounced as immoral when they were new.

There are many other issues for which we are too quick to hit the moralization button and look for villains rather than bug fixes. What should we do when a hospital patient is killed by a nurse who administers the wrong drug in a patient's intravenous line? Should we make it easier to sue the hospital for damages? Or should we redesign the IV fittings so that it's physically impossible to connect the wrong bottle to the line?

And nowhere is moralization more of a hazard than in our greatest global challenge. The threat of human-induced climate change has become the occasion for a moralistic revival meeting. In many discussions, the cause of climate change is overindulgence (too many SUVs) and defilement (sullying the atmosphere), and the solution is temperance (conservation) and expiation (buying carbon offset coupons). Yet the experts agree that these numbers don't add up: Even if every last American became conscientious about his or her carbon emissions, the effects on climate change would be trifling, if for no other reason than that two billion Indians and Chinese are unlikely to copy our born-again abstemiousness. Though voluntary conservation may be one wedge in an effective carbon-reduction pie, the other wedges will have to be morally boring, like a carbon tax and new energy technologies, or even taboo, like nuclear power and deliberate manipulation of the ocean and atmosphere. Our habit of moralizing problems, merging them with intuitions of purity and contamination, and resting content when we feel the right feelings, can get in the way of doing the right thing.

70 Far from debunking morality, then, the science of the moral sense can advance it, by allowing us to see through the illusions that evolution and culture have saddled us with and to focus on goals we can share and defend. As Anton Chekhov wrote, "Man will become better when you show him what he is like."

▪ QUESTIONS

Reading

1. According to Pinker, what are the hallmarks of moralization?
2. How does Jonathan Haidt contrast moral reasoning with moral rationalization?
3. What are the five moral spheres to which Pinker refers? Summarize Pinker's conclusion about the spheres and moral relativism.

Exploratory Writing

1. Prepare a debate over the proposition, "Morality is innate." You might draw on Olivia Judson's (p. 284) arguments as well as Pinker's as you research your case.
2. In pairs, discuss the situations devised by Jonathan Haidt (paragraphs 17–19). Is anyone able to explain *why* these scenarios are wrong? Next, devise a hypothetical moral quandary based on Haidt's examples. Trade your scenarios, then attempt to write a clear, reasonable statement about *why* the scenario is right or wrong. What did you learn about your own moral reasoning from this exercise?

3. Summarize Pinker's argument about the "shudder test." Write your own argumentative statement, either agreeing or disagreeing with Pinker.

Making Connections

1. Choose any argumentative essay in this book, and flag any moral statements or arguments contained within it. In each case, would you categorize the statement as moral reasoning or moral rationalization?

Essay Writing

1. Choose a behavior that has been "amoralized" (paragraph 13). Write an essay reporting on the history of social and legal prohibitions against that behavior. (Note that the very categorization of some of these things as "behaviors" or "choices" is controversial.) In your research, be aware of moral agendas within the sources you find.
2. Write an essay describing your personal experience of something that you find morally wrong. Why is it wrong? What experiences led you to hold your current beliefs on the subject?

ARGUING

The Egg and the Sperm

How Science Has Constructed a Romance Based on Stereotypical Male-Female Roles

Emily Martin

Emily Martin (b. 1944) is a professor of anthropology at New York University. She has written *The Woman in the Body: A Cultural Analysis of Reproduction* (1987), *Flexible Bodies: Tracking Immunity in American Culture—From the Days of Polio to the Age of AIDS* (1994), and *Bipolar Expeditions: Mania and Depression in American Culture* (2009). In the following article, which originally appeared in the journal *Signs* (1991), Martin's intent is to expose the cultural stereotypes operative in the so-called scientific language surrounding human reproduction.

> The theory of the human body is always a part of a world-picture. . . . The theory of the human body is always a part of a fantasy.
>
> —JAMES HILLMAN, *The Myth of Analysis*[1]

As an anthropologist, I am intrigued by the possibility that culture shapes how biological scientists describe what they discover about the natural world. If this were so, we would be learning about more than the natural world in high school biology class; we would be learning about cultural beliefs and practices as if they were part of nature. In the course of my research I realized that the picture of egg and sperm drawn in popular as well as scientific accounts of reproductive biology relies on stereotypes central to our cultural definitions of male and female. The stereotypes imply not only that female biological processes are less worthy than their male counterparts but also that women are less worthy than men. Part of my goal in writing this article is to shine a bright light on the gender stereotypes hidden within the scientific language of biology. Exposed in such a light, I hope they will lose much of their power to harm us.

Egg and Sperm: A Scientific Fairy Tale

At a fundamental level, all major scientific textbooks depict male and female reproductive organs as systems for the production of valuable substances,

Portions of this article were presented as the 1987 Becker Lecture, Cornell University. I am grateful for the many suggestions and ideas I received on this occasion. For especially pertinent help with my arguments and data I thank Richard Cone, Kevin Whaley, Sharon Stephens, Barbara Duden, Susanne Kuechler, Lorna Rhodes, and Scott Gilbert. The article was strengthened and clarified by the comments of the anonymous *Signs* reviewers as well as the superb editorial skills of Amy Gage.

[1]James Hillman, *The Myth of Analysis* (Evanston, Ill.: Northwestern University Press, 1972), 220.

such as eggs and sperm.[2] In the case of women, the monthly cycle is described as being designed to produce eggs and prepare a suitable place for them to be fertilized and grown—all to the end of making babies. But the enthusiasm ends there. By extolling the female cycle as a productive enterprise, menstruation must necessarily be viewed as a failure. Medical texts describe menstruation as the "debris" of the uterine lining, the result of necrosis, or death of tissue. The descriptions imply that a system has gone awry, making products of no use, not to specification, unsalable, wasted, scrap. An illustration in a widely used medical text shows menstruation as a chaotic disintegration of form, complementing the many texts that describe it as "ceasing," "dying," "losing," "denuding," "expelling."[3]

Male reproductive physiology is evaluated quite differently. One of the texts that sees menstruation as failed production employs a sort of breathless prose when it describes the maturation of sperm: "The mechanisms which guide the remarkable cellular transformation from spermatid to mature sperm remain uncertain. . . . Perhaps the most amazing characteristic of spermatogenesis is its sheer magnitude: The normal human male may manufacture several hundred million sperm per day."[4] In the classic text *Medical Physiology*, edited by Vernon Mountcastle, the male/female, productive/destructive comparison is more explicit: "Whereas the female *sheds* only a single gamete each month, the seminiferous tubules *produce* hundreds of millions of sperm each day" (emphasis mine).[5] The female author of another text marvels at the length of the microscopic seminiferous tubules, which, if uncoiled and placed end to end, "would span almost one-third of a mile!" She writes, "In an adult male these structures produce millions of sperm cells each day." Later she asks, "How is this feat accomplished?"[6] None of these texts expresses such intense enthusiasm for any female processes. It is surely no accident that the "remarkable" process of making sperm involves precisely what, in the medical view, menstruation does not: production of something deemed valuable.[7]

One could argue that menstruation and spermatogenesis are not analogous processes and, therefore, should not be expected to elicit the same kind of response. The proper female analogy to spermatogenesis, biologically, is ovulation. Yet ovulation does not merit enthusiasm in these texts either.

[2]The textbooks I consulted are the main ones used in classes for undergraduate premedical students or medical students (or those held on reserve in the library for these classes) during the past few years at Johns Hopkins University. These texts are widely used at other universities in the country as well.

[3]Arthur C. Guyton, *Physiology of the Human Body*, 6th ed. (Philadelphia: Saunders College Publishing, 1984), 624.

[4]Arthur J. Vander, James H. Sherman, and Dorothy S. Luciano, *Human Physiology: The Mechanisms of Body Function*, 3d ed. (New York: McGraw Hill, 1980), 483–84.

[5]Vernon B. Mountcastle, *Medical Physiology*, 14th ed. (London: Mosby, 1980), 2:1624.

[6]Eldra Pearl Solomon, *Human Anatomy and Physiology* (New York: CBS College Publishing, 1983), 678.

[7]For elaboration, see Emily Martin, *The Woman in the Body: A Cultural Analysis of Reproduction* (Boston: Beacon, 1987), 27–53.

Textbook descriptions stress that all of the ovarian follicles containing ova are already present at birth. Far from being *produced,* as sperm are, they merely sit on the shelf, slowly degenerating and aging like overstocked inventory: "At birth, normal human ovaries contain an estimated one million follicles [each], and no new ones appear after birth. Thus, in marked contrast to the male, the newborn female already has all the germ cells she will ever have. Only a few, perhaps 400, are destined to reach full maturity during her active reproductive life. All the others degenerate at some point in their development so that few, if any, remain by the time she reaches menopause at approximately fifty years of age."[8] Note the "marked contrast" that this description sets up between male and female: the male, who continuously produces fresh germ cells, and the female, who has stockpiled germ cells by birth and is faced with their degeneration.

Nor are the female organs spared such vivid descriptions. One scientist writes in a newspaper article that a woman's ovaries become old and worn out from ripening eggs every month, even though the woman herself is still relatively young: "When you look through a laparoscope . . . at an ovary that has been through hundreds of cycles, even in a superbly healthy American female, you see a scarred, battered organ."[9] 5

To avoid the negative connotations that some people associate with the female reproductive system, scientists could begin to describe male and female processes as homologous. They might credit females with "producing" mature ova one at a time, as they're needed each month, and describe males as having to face problems of degenerating germ cells. This degeneration would occur throughout life among spermatogonia, the undifferentiated germ cells in the testes that are the long-lived, dormant precursors of sperm.

But the texts have an almost dogged insistence on casting female processes in a negative light. The texts celebrate sperm production because it is continuous from puberty to senescence, while they portray egg production as inferior because it is finished at birth. This makes the female seem unproductive, but some texts will also insist that it is she who is wasteful.[10] In a section heading for *Molecular Biology of the Cell,* a best-selling text, we are told that "Oogenesis is wasteful." The text goes on to emphasize that of the seven million oogonia, or egg germ cells, in the female embryo, most degenerate in the ovary. Of those that do go on to become oocytes, or eggs, many also degenerate, so that at birth only two million eggs remain in the ovaries. Degeneration continues

[8]Vander, Sherman, and Luciano, 568.

[9]Melvin Konner, "Childbearing and Age," *New York Times Magazine* (December 27, 1987), 22–23, esp. 22.

[10]I have found but one exception to the opinion that the female is wasteful: "Smallpox being the nasty disease it is, one might expect nature to have designed antibody molecules with combining sites that specifically recognize the epitopes on smallpox virus. Nature differs from technology, however: It thinks nothing of wastefulness. (For example, rather than improving the chance that a spermatozoon will meet an egg cell, nature finds it easier to produce millions of spermatozoa)" (Niels Kaj Jerne, "The Immune System," *Scientific American* 229, no. 1 [July 1973]: 53). Thanks to a *Signs* reviewer for bringing this reference to my attention.

throughout a woman's life: By puberty three hundred thousand eggs remain, and only a few are present by menopause. "During the forty or so years of a woman's reproductive life, only 400 to 500 eggs will have been released," the authors write. "All the rest will have degenerated. It is still a mystery why so many eggs are formed only to die in the ovaries."[11]

The real mystery is why the male's vast production of sperm is not seen as wasteful.[12] Assuming that a man "produces" 100 million (10^8) sperm per day (a conservative estimate) during an average reproductive life of sixty years, he would produce well over two trillion sperm in his lifetime. Assuming that a woman "ripens" one egg per lunar month, or thirteen per year, over the course of her forty-year reproductive life, she would total five hundred eggs in her lifetime. But the word "waste" implies an excess, too much produced. Assuming two or three offspring, for every baby a woman produces, she wastes only around two hundred eggs. For every baby a man produces, he wastes more than one trillion (10^{12}) sperm.

How is it that positive images are denied to the bodies of women? A look at language—in this case, scientific language—provides the first clue. Take the egg and the sperm.[13] It is remarkable how "femininely" the egg behaves and how "masculinely" the sperm.[14] The egg is seen as large and passive.[15] It does not *move* or *journey*, but passively "is transported," "is swept,"[16] or even "drifts"[17] along the fallopian tube. In utter contrast, sperm are small, "streamlined,"[18]

---

[11]Bruce Alberts et al., *Molecular Biology of the Cell* (New York: Garland, 1983), 795.

[12]In her essay "Have Only Men Evolved?" (in *Discovering Reality: Feminist Perspectives on Epistemology, Metaphysics, Methodology, and Philosophy of Science*, ed. Sandra Harding and Merrill B. Hintikka [Dordrecht, The Netherlands: Reidel, 1983], 45–69, esp. 60–61), Ruth Hubbard points out that sociobiologists have said the female invests more energy than the male in the production of her large gametes, claiming that this explains why the female provides parental care. Hubbard questions whether it "really takes more 'energy' to generate the one or relatively few eggs than the large excess of sperms required to achieve fertilization." For further critique of how the greater size of eggs is interpreted in sociobiology, see Donna Haraway, "Investment Strategies for the Evolving Portfolio of Primate Females," in *Body/Politics*, ed. Mary Jacobus, Evelyn Fox Keller, and Sally Shuttleworth (New York: Routledge, 1990), 155–56.

[13]The sources I used for this article provide compelling information on interactions among sperm. Lack of space prevents me from taking up this theme here, but the elements include competition, hierarchy, and sacrifice. For a newspaper report, see Malcolm W. Browne, "Some Thoughts on Self Sacrifice," *New York Times* (July 5, 1988), C6. For a literary rendition, see John Barth, "Night-Sea Journey," in his *Lost in the Funhouse* (Garden City, N.Y.: Doubleday, 1968), 3–13.

[14]See Carol Delaney, "The Meaning of Paternity and the Virgin Birth Debate," *Man* 21, no. 3 (September 1986): 494–513. She discusses the difference between this scientific view that women contribute genetic material to the fetus and the claim of long-standing Western folk theories that the origin and identity of the fetus comes from the male, as in the metaphor of planting a seed in soil.

[15]For a suggested direct link between human behavior and purportedly passive eggs and active sperm, see Erik H. Erikson, "Inner and Outer Space: Reflections on Womanhood," *Daedalus* 93, no. 2 (Spring 1964): 582–606, esp. 591.

[16]Guyton (n. 3), 619; and Mountcastle (n. 5), 1609.

[17]Jonathan Miller and David Pelham, *The Facts of Life* (New York: Viking Penguin, 1984), 5.

[18]Alberts et al., 796.

and invariably active. They "deliver" their genes to the egg, "activate the developmental program of the egg,"[19] and have a "velocity" that is often remarked upon.[20] Their tails are "strong" and efficiently powered.[21] Together with the forces of ejaculation, they can "propel the semen into the deepest recesses of the vagina."[22] For this they need "energy," "fuel,"[23] so that with a "whiplashlike motion and strong lurches"[24] they can "burrow through the egg coat"[25] and "penetrate" it.[26]

At its extreme, the age-old relationship of the egg and the sperm takes on a royal or religious patina. The egg coat, its protective barrier, is sometimes called its "vestments," a term usually reserved for sacred, religious dress. The egg is said to have a "corona,"[27] a crown, and to be accompanied by "attendant cells."[28] It is holy, set apart and above, the queen to the sperm's king. The egg is also passive, which means it must depend on sperm for rescue. Gerald Schatten and Helen Schatten liken the egg's role to that of Sleeping Beauty: "a dormant bride awaiting her mate's magic kiss, which instills the spirit that brings her to life."[29] Sperm, by contrast, have a "mission,"[30] which is to "move through the female genital tract in quest of the ovum."[31] One popular account has it that the sperm carry out a "perilous journey" into the "warm darkness," where some fall away "exhausted." "Survivors" "assault" the egg, the successful candidates "surrounding the prize."[32] Part of the urgency of this journey, in more scientific terms, is that "once released from the supportive environment of the ovary, an egg will die within hours unless rescued by a sperm."[33] The wording stresses the fragility and dependency of the egg, even though the same text acknowledges elsewhere that sperm also live for only a few hours.[34]

In 1948, in a book remarkable for its early insights into these matters, Ruth Herschberger argued that female reproductive organs are seen as biologically

---

[19]Ibid., 796.

[20]See, e.g., William F. Ganong, *Review of Medical Physiology*, 7th ed. (Los Altos, Calif.: Lange Medical Publications, 1975), 322.

[21]Alberts et al. (n. 11), 796.

[22]Guyton, 615.

[23]Solomon (n. 6), 683.

[24]Vander, Sherman, and Luciano (n. 4), 4th ed. (1985), 580.

[25]Alberts et al., 796.

[26]All biology texts quoted use the word "penetrate."

[27]Solomon, 700.

[28]A. Beldecos et al., "The Importance of Feminist Critique for Contemporary Cell Biology," *Hypatia* 3, no. 1 (Spring 1988): 61–76.

[29]Gerald Schatten and Helen Schatten, "The Energetic Egg," *Medical World News* 23 (January 23, 1984): 51–53, esp. 51.

[30]Alberts et al., 796.

[31]Guyton (n. 3), 613.

[32]Miller and Pelham (n. 17), 7.

[33]Alberts et al. (n. 11), 804.

[34]Ibid., 801.

interdependent, while male organs are viewed as autonomous, operating independently and in isolation:

> At present the functional is stressed only in connection with women: it is in them that ovaries, tubes, uterus, and vagina have endless interdependence. In the male, reproduction would seem to involve "organs" only.
>
> Yet the sperm, just as much as the egg, is dependent on a great many related processes. There are secretions which mitigate the urine in the urethra before ejaculation, to protect the sperm. There is the reflex shutting off of the bladder connection, the provision of prostatic secretions, and various types of muscular propulsion. The sperm is no more independent of its milieu than the egg, and yet from a wish that it were, biologists have lent their support to the notion that the human female, beginning with the egg, is congenitally more dependent than the male.[35]

Bringing out another aspect of the sperm's autonomy, an article in the journal *Cell* has the sperm making an "existential decision" to penetrate the egg: "Sperm are cells with a limited behavioral repertoire, one that is directed toward fertilizing eggs. To execute the decision to abandon the haploid state, sperm swim to an egg and there acquire the ability to effect membrane fusion."[36] Is this a corporate manager's version of the sperm's activities—"executing decisions" while fraught with dismay over difficult options that bring with them very high risk?

There is another way that sperm, despite their small size, can be made to loom in importance over the egg. In a collection of scientific papers, an electron micrograph of an enormous egg and tiny sperm is titled "A Portrait of the Sperm."[37] This is a little like showing a photo of a dog and calling it a picture of the fleas. Granted, microscopic sperm are harder to photograph than eggs, which are just large enough to see with the naked eye. But surely the use of the term "portrait," a word associated with the powerful and wealthy, is significant. Eggs have only micrographs or pictures, not portraits.

One depiction of sperm as weak and timid, instead of strong and powerful—the only such representation in Western civilization, so far as I know—occurs in Woody Allen's movie *Everything You Always Wanted to Know about Sex but Were Afraid to Ask*. Allen, playing the part of an apprehensive sperm inside a man's testicles, is scared of the man's approaching orgasm. He is reluctant to launch himself into the darkness, afraid of contraceptive devices, afraid of winding up on the ceiling if the man masturbates.

---

[35]Ruth Herschberger, *Adam's Rib* (New York: Pelligrini & Cudaby, 1948), esp. 84. I am indebted to Ruth Hubbard for telling me about Herschberger's work, although at a point when this paper was already in draft form.

[36]Bennett M. Shapiro, "The Existential Decision of a Sperm," *Cell* 49, no. 3 (May 1987): 293–94, esp. 293.

[37]Lennart Nilsson, "A Portrait of the Sperm," in *The Functional Anatomy of the Spermatozoan*, ed. Bjorn A. Afzelius (New York: Pergamon, 1975), 79–82.

The more common picture—egg as damsel in distress, shielded only by her sacred garments; sperm as heroic warrior to the rescue—cannot be proved to be dictated by the biology of these events. While the "facts" of biology may not *always* be constructed in cultural terms, I would argue that in this case they are. The degree of metaphorical content in these descriptions, the extent to which differences between egg and sperm are emphasized, and the parallels between cultural stereotypes of male and female behavior and the character of egg and sperm all point to this conclusion. 15

New Research, Old Imagery

As new understandings of egg and sperm emerge, textbook gender imagery is being revised. But the new research, far from escaping the stereotypical representations of egg and sperm, simply replicates elements of textbook gender imagery in a different form. The persistence of this imagery calls to mind what Ludwik Fleck termed "the self-contained" nature of scientific thought. As he described it, "the interaction between what is already known, what remains to be learned, and those who are to apprehend it, goes to ensure harmony within the system. But at the same time they also preserve the harmony of illusions, which is quite secure within the confines of a given thought style."[38] We need to understand the way in which the cultural content in scientific descriptions changes as biological discoveries unfold, and whether that cultural content is solidly entrenched or easily changed.

In all of the texts quoted above, sperm are described as penetrating the egg, and specific substances on a sperm's head are described as binding to the egg. Recently, this description of events was rewritten in a biophysics lab at Johns Hopkins University—transforming the egg from the passive to the active party.[39]

Prior to this research, it was thought that the zona, the inner vestments of the egg, formed an impenetrable barrier. Sperm overcame the barrier by mechanically burrowing through, thrashing their tails and slowly working their way along. Later research showed that the sperm released digestive enzymes that chemically broke down the zona; thus, scientists presumed that the sperm used mechanical *and* chemical means to get through to the egg.

In this recent investigation, the researchers began to ask questions about the mechanical force of the sperm's tail. (The lab's goal was to develop a contraceptive that worked topically on sperm.) They discovered, to their great surprise, that the forward thrust of sperm is extremely weak, which contradicts the assumption that sperm are forceful penetrators.[40] Rather than thrusting

[38]Ludwik Fleck, *Genesis and Development of a Scientific Fact*, ed. Thaddeus J. Trenn and Robert K. Merton (Chicago: University of Chicago Press, 1979), 38.

[39]Jay M. Baltz carried out the research I describe when he was a graduate student in the Thomas C. Jenkins Department of Biophysics at Johns Hopkins University.

[40]Far less is known about the physiology of sperm than comparable female substances, which some feminists claim is no accident. Greater scientific scrutiny of female reproduction

forward, the sperm's head was now seen to move mostly back and forth. The sideways motion of the sperm's tail makes the head move sideways with a force that is ten times stronger than its forward movement. So even if the overall force of the sperm were strong enough to mechanically break the zona, most of its force would be directed sideways rather than forward. In fact, its strongest tendency, by tenfold, is to escape by attempting to pry itself off the egg. Sperm, then, must be exceptionally efficient at *escaping* from any cell surface they contact. And the surface of the egg must be designed to trap the sperm and prevent their escape. Otherwise, few if any sperm would reach the egg.

The researchers at Johns Hopkins concluded that the sperm and egg stick together because of adhesive molecules on the surfaces of each. The egg traps the sperm and adheres to it so tightly that the sperm's head is forced to lie flat against the surface of the zona, a little bit, they told me, "like Br'er Rabbit getting more and more stuck to tar baby the more he wriggles." The trapped sperm continues to wiggle ineffectually side to side. The mechanical force of its tail is so weak that a sperm cannot break even one chemical bond. This is where the digestive enzymes released by the sperm come in. If they start to soften the zona just at the tip of the sperm and the sides remain stuck, then the weak, flailing sperm can get oriented in the right direction and make it through the zona—provided that its bonds to the zona dissolve as it moves in. 20

Although this new version of the saga of the egg and the sperm broke through cultural expectations, the researchers who made the discovery continued to write papers and abstracts as if the sperm were the active party who attacks, binds, penetrates, and enters the egg. The only difference was that sperm were now seen as performing these actions weakly.[41] Not until August 1987, more than three years after the findings described above, did these researchers reconceptualize the process to give the egg a more active role. They began to describe the zona as an aggressive sperm catcher, covered with adhesive molecules that can capture a sperm with a single bond and clasp it to the zona's surface.[42] In the words of their published account: "The innermost

---

has long enabled the burden of birth control to be placed on women. In this case, the researchers' discovery did not depend on development of any new technology. The experiments made use of glass pipettes, a manometer, and a simple microscope, all of which have been available for more than one hundred years.

[41]Jay Baltz and Richard A. Cone, "What Force Is Needed to Tether a Sperm?" (abstract for Society for the Study of Reproduction, 1985), and "Flagellar Torque on the Head Determines the Force Needed to Tether a Sperm" (abstract for Biophysical Society, 1986).

[42]Jay M. Baltz, David F. Katz, and Richard A. Cone, "The Mechanics of the Sperm-Egg Interaction at the Zona Pellucida," *Biophysical Journal* 54, no. 4 (October 1988): 643–54. Lab members were somewhat familiar with work on metaphors in the biology of female reproduction. Richard Cone, who runs the lab, is my husband, and he talked with them about my earlier research on the subject from time to time. Even though my current research focuses on biological imagery and I heard about the lab's work from my husband every day, I myself did not recognize the role of imagery in the sperm research until many weeks after the period of research and writing I describe. Therefore, I assume that any awareness the lab members may have had about how underlying metaphor might be guiding this particular research was fairly inchoate.

vestment, the *zona pellucida*, is a glyco-protein shell, which captures and tethers the sperm before they penetrate it. . . . The sperm is captured at the initial contact between the sperm tip and the *zona*. . . . Since the thrust [of the sperm] is much smaller than the force needed to break a single affinity bond, the first bond made upon the tip-first meeting of the sperm and *zona* can result in the capture of the sperm."[43]

Experiments in another lab reveal similar patterns of data interpretation. Gerald Schatten and Helen Schatten set out to show that, contrary to conventional wisdom, the "egg is not merely a large, yolk-filled sphere into which the sperm burrows to endow new life. Rather, recent research suggests the almost heretical view that sperm and egg are mutually active partners."[44] This sounds like a departure from the stereotypical textbook view, but further reading reveals Schatten and Schatten's conformity to the aggressive-sperm metaphor. They describe how "the sperm and egg first touch when, from the tip of the sperm's triangular head, a long, thin filament shoots out and harpoons the egg." Then we learn that "remarkably, the harpoon is not so much fired as assembled at great speed, molecule by molecule, from a pool of protein stored in a specialized region called the acrosome. The filament may grow as much as twenty times longer than the sperm head itself before its tip reaches the egg and sticks."[45] Why not call this "making a bridge" or "throwing out a line" rather than firing a harpoon? Harpoons pierce prey and injure or kill them, while this filament only sticks. And why not focus, as the Hopkins lab did, on the stickiness of the egg, rather than the stickiness of the sperm?[46] Later in the article, the Schattens replicate the common view of the sperm's perilous journey into the warm darkness of the vagina, this time for the purpose of explaining its journey into the egg itself: "[The sperm] still has an arduous journey ahead. It must penetrate farther into the egg's huge sphere of cytoplasm and somehow locate the nucleus, so that the two cells' chromosomes can fuse. The sperm dives down into the cytoplasm, its tail beating. But it is soon interrupted by the sudden and swift migration of the egg nucleus, which rushes toward the sperm with a velocity triple that of the movement of chromosomes during cell division, crossing the entire egg in about a minute."[47]

Like Schatten and Schatten and the biophysicists at Johns Hopkins, another researcher has recently made discoveries that seem to point to a more interactive view of the relationship of egg and sperm. This work, which Paul Wassarman conducted on the sperm and eggs of mice, focuses on identifying the specific molecules in the egg coat (the zona pellucida) that are involved in egg-sperm interaction. At first glance, his descriptions seem to fit the model of an egalitarian relationship. Male and female gametes "recognize one

---

[43]Ibid., 643, 650.

[44]Schatten and Schatten (n. 29), 51.

[45]Ibid., 52.

[46]Surprisingly, in an article intended for a general audience, the authors do not point out that these are sea urchin sperm and note that human sperm do not shoot out filaments at all.

[47]Schatten and Schatten, 53.

another," and "interactions . . . take place between sperm and egg."[48] But the article in *Scientific American* in which those descriptions appear begins with a vignette that presages the dominant motif of their presentation: "It has been more than a century since Hermann Fol, a Swiss zoologist, peered into his microscope and became the first person to see a sperm penetrate an egg, fertilize it, and form the first cell of a new embryo."[49] This portrayal of the sperm as the active party—the one that *penetrates* and *fertilizes* the egg and *produces* the embryo—is not cited as an example of an earlier, now outmoded view. In fact, the author reiterates the point later in the article: "Many sperm can bind to and penetrate the zona pellucida, or outer coat, of an unfertilized mouse egg, but only one sperm will eventually fuse with the thin plasma membrane surrounding the egg proper (*inner sphere*), fertilizing the egg and giving rise to a new embryo."[50]

The imagery of sperm as aggressor is particularly startling in this case: the main discovery being reported is isolation of a particular molecule *on the egg coat* that plays an important role in fertilization! Wassarman's choice of language sustains the picture. He calls the molecule that has been isolated, ZP3, a "sperm receptor." By allocating the passive, waiting role to the egg, Wassarman can continue to describe the sperm as the actor, the one that makes it all happen: "The basic process begins when many sperm first attach loosely and then bind tenaciously to receptors on the surface of the egg's thick outer coat, the zona pellucida. Each sperm, which has a large number of egg-binding proteins on its surface, binds to many sperm receptors on the egg. More specifically, a site on each of the egg-binding proteins fits a complementary site on a sperm receptor, much as a key fits a lock."[51] With the sperm designated as the "key" and the egg the "lock," it is obvious which one acts and which one is acted upon. Could this imagery not be reversed, letting the sperm (the lock) wait until the egg produces the key? Or could we speak of two halves of a locket matching, and regard the matching itself as the action that initiates the fertilization?

It is as if Wassarman were determined to make the egg the receiving partner. Usually in biological research, the *protein* member of the pair of binding molecules is called the receptor, and physically it has a pocket in it rather like a lock. As the diagrams that illustrate Wassarman's article show, the molecules on the sperm are proteins and have "pockets." The small, mobile molecules that fit into these pockets are called ligands. As shown in the diagrams, ZP3 on the egg is a polymer of "keys"; many small knobs stick out. Typically, molecules on the sperm would be called receptors and molecules on the egg would be called ligands. But Wassarman chose to name ZP3 on the egg the receptor

[48]Paul M. Wassarman, "Fertilization in Mammals," *Scientific American* 259, no. 6 (December 1988): 78–84, esp. 78, 84.

[49]Ibid., 78.

[50]Ibid., 79.

[51]Ibid., 78.

and to create a new term, "the egg-binding protein," for the molecule on the sperm that otherwise would have been called the receptor.[52]

Wassarman does credit the egg coat with having more functions than those of a sperm receptor. While he notes that "the zona pellucida has at times been viewed by investigators as a nuisance, a barrier to sperm and hence an impediment to fertilization," his new research reveals that the egg coat "serves as a sophisticated biological security system that screens incoming sperm, selects only those compatible with fertilization and development, prepares sperm for fusion with the egg and later protects the resulting embryo from polyspermy [a lethal condition caused by fusion of more than one sperm with a single egg]."[53] Although this description gives the egg an active role, that role is drawn in stereotypically feminine terms. The egg *selects* an appropriate mate, *prepares* him for fusion, and then *protects* the resulting offspring from harm. This is courtship and mating behavior as seen through the eyes of a sociobiologist: woman as the hard-to-get prize, who, following union with the chosen one, becomes woman as servant and mother.

And Wassarman does not quit there. In a review article for *Science*, he outlines the "chronology of fertilization."[54] Near the end of the article are two subject headings. One is "Sperm Penetration," in which Wassarman describes how the chemical dissolving of the zona pellucida combines with the "substantial propulsive force generated by sperm." The next heading is "Sperm-Egg Fusion." This section details what happens inside the zona after a sperm "penetrates" it. Sperm "can make contact with, adhere to, and fuse with (that is, fertilize) an egg."[55] Wassarman's word choice, again, is astonishingly skewed in favor of the sperm's activity, for in the next breath he says that sperm *lose* all motility upon fusion with the egg's surface. In mouse and sea urchin eggs, the sperm enters at the *egg*'s volition, according to Wassarman's description: "Once fused with egg plasma membrane [the surface of the egg], how does a sperm enter the egg? The surface of both mouse and sea urchin eggs is covered with thousands of plasma membrane-bound projections, called microvilli [tiny 'hairs']. Evidence in sea urchins suggests that, after membrane fusion, a group of elongated microvilli cluster tightly around and interdigitate over the sperm head. As these microvilli are resorbed, the sperm is drawn into the egg. Therefore, sperm motility, which ceases at the time of fusion in both sea urchins and mice, is not required for sperm entry."[56] The section called

---

[52]Since receptor molecules are relatively immotile and the ligands that bind to them relatively motile, one might imagine the egg being called the receptor and the sperm the ligand. But the molecules in question on egg and sperm are immotile molecules. It is the sperm as a cell that has motility, and the egg as a cell that has relative immotility.

[53]Wassarman, 78–79.

[54]Paul M. Wassarman, "The Biology and Chemistry of Fertilization," *Science* 235, no. 4788 (January 30, 1987): 553–60, esp. 554.

[55]Ibid., 557.

[56]Ibid., 557–58. This finding throws into question Schatten and Schatten's description (n. 29 above) of the sperm, its tail beating, diving down into the egg.

"Sperm Penetration" more logically would be followed by a section called "The Egg Envelops," rather than "Sperm-Egg Fusion." This would give a parallel—and more accurate—sense that both the egg and the sperm initiate action.

Another way that Wassarman makes less of the egg's activity is by describing components of the egg but referring to the sperm as a whole entity. Deborah Gordon has described such an approach as "atomism" ("the part is independent of and primordial to the whole") and identified it as one of the "tenacious assumptions" of Western science and medicine.[57] Wassarman employs atomism to his advantage. When he refers to processing going on within sperm, he consistently returns to descriptions that remind us from whence these activities came: They are part of sperm that penetrate an egg or generate propulsive force. When he refers to processes going on within eggs, he stops there. As a result, any active role he grants them appears to be assigned to the parts of the egg, and not to the egg itself. In the quote above, it is the microvilli that actively cluster around the sperm. In another example, "the driving force for engulfment of a fused sperm comes from a region of cytoplasm just beneath an egg's plasma membrane."[58]

Social Implications: Thinking Beyond

All three of these revisionist accounts of egg and sperm cannot seem to escape the hierarchical imagery of older accounts. Even though each new account gives the egg a larger and more active role, taken together they bring into play another cultural stereotype: woman as a dangerous and aggressive threat. In the Johns Hopkins lab's revised model, the egg ends up as the female aggressor who "captures and tethers" the sperm with her sticky zona, rather like a spider lying in wait in her web.[59] The Schatten lab has the egg's nucleus "interrupt" the sperm's dive with a "sudden and swift" rush by which she "clasps the sperm and guides its nucleus to the center."[60] Wassarman's description of the surface of the egg "covered with thousands of plasma membrane-bound projections, called microvilli" that reach out and clasp the sperm adds to the spiderlike imagery.[61]

These images grant the egg an active role but at the cost of appearing disturbingly aggressive. Images of woman as dangerous and aggressive, the femme fatale who victimizes men, are widespread in Western literature and culture.[62] 30

[57]Deborah R. Gordon, "Tenacious Assumptions in Western Medicine," in *Biomedicine Examined*, ed. Margaret Lock and Deborah Gordon (Dordrecht, The Netherlands: Kluwer, 1988), 19–56, esp. 26.

[58]Wassarman, "The Biology and Chemistry of Fertilization," 558.

[59]Baltz, Katz, and Cone (n. 42 above), 643, 650.

[60]Schatten and Schatten, 53.

[61]Wassarman, "The Biology and Chemistry of Fertilization," 557.

[62]Mary Ellman, *Thinking about Women* (New York: Harcourt Brace Jovanovich, 1968), 140; Nina Auerbach, *Woman and the Demon* (Cambridge, Mass.: Harvard University Press, 1982), esp. 186.

More specific is the connection of spider imagery with the idea of an engulfing, devouring mother.[63] New data did not lead scientists to eliminate gender stereotypes in their descriptions of egg and sperm. Instead, scientists simply began to describe egg and sperm in different, but no less damaging, terms.

Can we envision a less stereotypical view? Biology itself provides another model that could be applied to the egg and the sperm. The cybernetic model—with its feedback loops, flexible adaptation to change, coordination of the parts within a whole, evolution over time, and changing response to the environment—is common in genetics, endocrinology, and ecology and has a growing influence in medicine in general.[64] This model has the potential to shift our imagery from the negative, in which the female reproductive system is castigated both for not producing eggs after birth and for producing (and thus wasting) too many eggs overall, to something more positive. The female reproductive system could be seen as responding to the environment (pregnancy or menopause), adjusting to monthly changes (menstruation), and flexibly changing from reproductivity after puberty to nonreproductivity later in life. The sperm and egg's interaction could also be described in cybernetic terms. J. F. Hartman's research in reproductive biology demonstrated fifteen years ago that if an egg is killed by being pricked with a needle, live sperm cannot get through the zona.[65] Clearly, this evidence shows that the egg and sperm *do* interact on more mutual terms, making biology's refusal to portray them that way all the more disturbing.

We would do well to be aware, however, that cybernetic imagery is hardly neutral. In the past, cybernetic models have played an important part in the imposition of social control. These models inherently provide a way of thinking about a "field" of interacting components. Once the field can be seen, it can become the object of new forms of knowledge, which in turn can allow new forms of social control to be exerted over the components of the field. During the 1950s, for example, medicine began to recognize the psychosocial *environment* of the patient: the patient's family and its psychodynamics. Professions such as social work began to focus on this new environment, and the resulting knowledge became one way to further control the patient. Patients began to be seen not as isolated, individual bodies, but as psychosocial entities located in an "ecological" system: management of "the patient's psychology was a new entrée to patient control."[66]

The models that biologists use to describe their data can have important social effects. During the nineteenth century, the social and natural sciences

[63]Kenneth Alan Adams, "Arachnophobia: Love American Style," *Journal of Psychoanalytic Anthropology* 4, no. 2 (1981): 157–97.

[64]William Ray Arney and Bernard Bergen, *Medicine and the Management of Living* (Chicago: University of Chicago Press, 1984).

[65]J. F. Hartman, R. B. Gwatkin, and C. F. Hutchison, "Early Contact Interactions between Mammalian Gametes *In Vitro*," *Proceedings of the National Academy of Sciences (U.S.)* 69, no. 10 (1972): 2767–69.

[66]Arney and Bergen, 68.

strongly influenced each other: the social ideas of Malthus about how to avoid the natural increase of the poor inspired Darwin's *Origin of Species*.[67] Once the *Origin* stood as a description of the natural world, complete with competition and market struggles, it could be reimported into social science as social Darwinism, in order to justify the social order of the time. What we are seeing now is similar: the importation of cultural ideas about passive females and heroic males into the "personalities" of gametes. This amounts to the "implanting of social imagery on representations of nature so as to lay a firm basis for reimporting exactly that same imagery as natural explanations of social phenomena."[68]

Further research would show us exactly what social effects are being wrought from the biological imagery of egg and sperm. At the very least, the imagery keeps alive some of the hoariest old stereotypes about weak damsels in distress and their strong male rescuers. That these stereotypes are now being written in at the level of the *cell* constitutes a powerful move to make them seem so natural as to be beyond alteration.

The stereotypical imagery might also encourage people to imagine that what results from the interaction of egg and sperm—a fertilized egg—is the result of deliberate "human" action at the cellular level. Whatever the intentions of the human couple, in this microscope "culture" a cellular "bride" (or femme fatale) and a cellular "groom" (her victim) make a cellular baby. Rosalind Petchesky points out that through visual representations such as sonograms, we are given "*images* of younger and younger, and tinier and tinier, fetuses being 'saved.'" This leads to "the point of viability being 'pushed back' *indefinitely*."[69] Endowing egg and sperm with intentional action, a key aspect of personhood in our culture, lays the foundation for the point of viability being pushed back to the moment of fertilization. This will likely lead to greater acceptance of technological developments and new forms of scrutiny and manipulation, for the benefit of these inner "persons": court-ordered restrictions on a pregnant woman's activities in order to protect her fetus, fetal surgery, amniocentesis, and rescinding of abortion rights, to name but a few examples.[70] 35

Even if we succeed in substituting more egalitarian, interactive metaphors to describe the activities of egg and sperm, and manage to avoid the pitfalls of cybernetic models, we would still be guilty of endowing cellular entities

[67]Ruth Hubbard, "Have Only Men Evolved?" (n. 12 above), 51–52.

[68]David Harvey, personal communication, November 1989.

[69]Rosalind Petchesky, "Fetal Images: The Power of Visual Culture in the Politics of Reproduction," *Feminist Studies* 13, no. 2 (Summer 1987): 263–92, esp. 272.

[70]Rita Arditti, Renate Klein, and Shelley Minden, *Test-Tube Women* (London: Pandora, 1984); Ellen Goodman, "Whose Right to Life?" *Baltimore Sun* (November 17, 1987); Tamar Lewin, "Courts Acting to Force Care of the Unborn," *New York Times* (November 23, 1987), A1 and B10; Susan Irwin and Brigitte Jordan, "Knowledge, Practice, and Power: Court Ordered Cesarean Sections," *Medical Anthropology Quarterly* 1, no. 3 (September 1987): 319–34.

with personhood. More crucial, then, than what *kinds* of personalities we bestow on cells is the very fact that we are doing it at all. This process could ultimately have the most disturbing social consequences.

One clear feminist challenge is to wake up sleeping metaphors in science, particularly those involved in descriptions of the egg and the sperm. Although the literary convention is to call such metaphors "dead," they are not so much dead as sleeping, hidden within the scientific content of texts—and all the more powerful for it.[71] Waking up such metaphors, by becoming aware of when we are projecting cultural imagery onto what we study, will improve our ability to investigate and understand nature. Waking up such metaphors, by becoming aware of their implications, will rob them of their power to naturalize our social conventions about gender.

▪ QUESTIONS

Reading

1. Summarize Martin's argument. How has she structured it?
2. What does Ludwik Fleck mean by the "self-contained" nature of scientific thought (paragraph 16)?
3. The first subheading in the essay is "Egg and Sperm: A Scientific Fairy Tale." The implications are that the actions of the egg and sperm constitute a story written by scientists. List ways that different fairy-tale images or archetypes are often attached to characterizations of the egg and the sperm.

EGG	SPERM

Exploratory Writing

1. Collaborating in small groups, look at some biology textbooks. Are the same or similar "sleeping metaphors" that Martin discusses present in the discussions of human or animal reproduction? What about other bodily processes and functions? Conduct a sleeping-metaphor search through one or more textbooks. List five to ten examples (or more) of writing in which the description of biological functions reflects cultural ideas or prejudices.
2. Using the biological information in Martin's essay, write a nonsexist description of the reproductive functions. In your conclusion, reflect on any difficulties you encountered in keeping your cellular entities free of personhood. Switch papers with a classmate to check each other for sleeping metaphors.

[71]Thanks to Elizabeth Fee and David Spain, who in February 1989 and April 1989, respectively, made points related to this.

3. Unlike many essayists in this book, Martin uses footnotes extensively in her argumentative essay. Read these footnotes carefully. What is Martin's purpose in using them?

Making Connections

1. Martin argues that the traditional understanding of the relationship between a human egg and sperm is a "scientific fairy tale." Choose one of the selections in the "Sciences" section and analyze it the way Martin analyzes her scientific sources, focusing on sleeping metaphors and biased scientific language. Which elements of the argument are developed through data and evidence? Which are developed through rhetoric? Are you ultimately persuaded by the selection? Or do you have doubts?

Essay Writing

1. Look at a sampling of sex-education texts and materials designed for elementary or secondary school students to see if the cultural stereotypes that Martin warns against are present. What analogies and metaphors do you find being used? Write up your discussion as an argument either for or against the revision of those texts.
2. Write an essay reflecting on a time in your life when an assumption you had was turned on its head, and you learned to look at one of your beliefs in a radical new way.

REPORTING

The Canon

Natalie Angier

Popular science writer Natalie Angier (b. 1958) is the author of *Natural Obsessions* (1988), an inside look at cancer research, *The Beauty of the Beastly* (1995), a celebration of sometimes-underappreciated creatures and phenomena in the natural world, and the National Book Award–nominated *Woman: an Intimate Geography* (1999), about the science of the female body. Her awards include an American Association for the Advancement of Science prize for excellence in science journalism, the Lowell Thomas Gold Medal for travel writing, and a 1991 Pulitzer Prize for her work as a journalist. Her most recent book, *Canon: A Whirligig Tour of the Beautiful Basics of Science* (2007), from which this piece is excerpted, is a lively exploration of "what researchers in all the major scientific disciplines — physics, chemistry, biology, geology and astronomy — wish that everybody understood about their work," according to Angier.

Scott Strobel, a biochemist at Yale University, is tall, tidy, and boyishly severe, his complexion a polished apple, his jaw ajut, his hair a sergeant's clipped command. He looks athletic. He keeps pictures of his three beaming children on his desk. I am not surprised to learn that he graduated summa cum laude from Brigham Young University. He might be good company at a family picnic, but on this fluorescent-enhanced midweek morning, as we sit around his office coffee table engaged in what he has deemed a form of constructive entertainment, Strobel is about as much fun as an oncologist.

Strobel has taken out his personal kit of Mastermind, a game I had never seen before and knew nothing about. He often plays the game with the graduate students and postdoctoral fellows in his lab. They love it. So, I later discovered, do my husband and daughter. Now Strobel is teaching me to play Mastermind, but of the many words competing for the tip of my tongue, "love" is not one of them.

In Mastermind, he explains, you try to divine your opponent's hidden sequence of four colored pegs by shuffling your own colored pegs among peg holes. If you guess a correct color in the correct position, your opponent inserts a black peg on his side of the board; a correct color in an incorrect position gets you a white peg; and the wrong color for any position earns you no peg at all. Your goal is to end up with four black pegs on your adversary's end in as few rounds as possible.

"Got it?" he says, pushing the board in my direction.

"I never really liked games," I plead. "Don't you have any nice slide presentations instead?" 5

"I have a point to make with this," he says. "Go ahead."

Without a tornado or the sudden onset of pneumococcal pneumonia to deliver me, I sigh and arrange my pegs in a pleasant police lineup of blue, red, yellow, green. Strobel responds in a pattern of blacks, whites, and blanks. I lunge with a red piece, he parries by plucking off a white peg. Green here? Sorry, dear. I'm trying my best, but I have a wooden ear for the game, and I make bad choices and no progress. I fight back tears, which fecklessly leap to freedom as sweat. I curse Strobel and all scientists who ever lived, especially the inventor of the pegboard.

Finally, Strobel takes pity on me. "Well, I think you get the idea," he says. He sweeps the malignant little pins back into their box, and I lapse into limp remission.

Mastermind, he declares, is "a microcosm for how science works." By insisting I play the game, he was trying to impress on me an essential truth about science. And while the dramady at Strobel's gaming table was not my favorite hour, in its intensity and memorability it reflects the strength with which scientists, whatever their specialty, agree with this truth.

Science is not a body of facts. Science is a state of mind. It is a way of viewing the world, of facing reality square on but taking nothing on its face. It is about attacking a problem with the most manicured of claws and tearing it down into sensible, edible pieces. 10

Even more than the testimonials to the fun of science, I heard the earnest affidavit that science is not a body of facts, it is a way of thinking. I heard these lines so often they began to take on a bodily existence of their own.

"Many teachers who don't have a deep appreciation of science present it as a set of facts," said David Stevenson, a planetary scientist at Caltech. "What's often missing is the idea of critical thinking, how you assess which ideas are reasonable and which are not."

"When I look back on the science I had in high school, I remember it being taught as a body of facts and laws you had to memorize," said Neil Shubin, a paleontologist at the University of Chicago. "The Krebs cycle, Linnaean classifications. Not only does this approach whip the joy of doing science right out of most people, but it gives everyone a distorted view of what science is. Science is not a rigid body of facts. It is a dynamic process of discovery. It is as alive as life itself."

"I couldn't care less whether people memorize the periodic table or not," said David Baltimore, the former president of Caltech. "I understand they're more concerned with problems that are meaningful in their own lives. I just wish they would approach those problems in a more rational way."

When science is offered as a body of facts, science becomes a glassy-eyed glossary. You skim through a textbook or an educational Web site, and words in boldface leap out at you. You're tempted to ignore everything but the highlighted hand wavers. You think, if I learn these terms, maybe I won't flunk chemistry. Yet if you follow such a strategy, chances are excellent that you will flunk chemistry in the ways that matter—not on the report card in your backpack, but on the ratings card in your brain. 15

The conjuring of science as a smarty-pants set of unerring facts that might be buzzed up on a *Jeopardy!* afternoon also suits the opponents of science, like the antievolutionists who seize on every disputed fossil to question the entire Darwinian enterprise. "Creationists first try to paint science as a body of facts and certainties, and then they attack this or that 'certainty' for not being so certain after all," said Shubin. "They cry, 'Aha! You can't make up your mind. You can't be trusted. Why should we believe you about anything?' Yet they are the ones who constructed the straw man of scientific infallibility in the first place."

"Science is not a collection of rigid dogmas, and what we call scientific truth is constantly being revised, challenged, and refined," said Michael Duff, a theoretical physicist at the University of Michigan. "It's irritating to hear people who hold fundamentalist views accuse scientists of being the inflexible, rigid ones, when usually it's the other way around. As a scientist, you know that any new discovery you're lucky enough to uncover will raise more questions than you started with, and that you must always question what you thought was correct and remind yourself how little you know. Science is a very humble and humbling activity.

"Which doesn't mean," Duff added hastily, "that there aren't arrogant scientists around."

Back at Yale University, Strobel further explains the message of Mastermind. If science is not a static body of facts, what is it? What does it mean to think scientifically, to take a scientific whack at a problem? The world is big. The world is messy. The world is a teenager's bedroom: Everything's in there. Now how do you get it to the kitchen sink? How can you possibly begin to make sense of it? One furred fork, one accidental petri dish, one peg hole at a time.

20 "If you're trying to pose a question in a way that gets you data you can interpret, you want to isolate a variable," Strobel says. "In science we take great pains to design experiments that ask only one question at a time. You isolate a single variable, and then you see what happens when you change that variable alone, while doing your best to keep everything else in the experiment unchanged." In Mastermind, you change a single peg and watch the impact of that deviation on your "experiment." In science, if you'd like to know, for example, whether a chemical reaction depends on the presence of oxygen, you would stage the experiment twice, first with oxygen, then without. Everything else you'd keep the same to the closest approximation possible—same heat, same light, same timing, same type of container; and, just to be safe, same white socks and Tevas.

You don't need to work at a laboratory bench to follow a scientific game plan. People behave scientifically all the time, although they may not realize it. "If someone is trying to fix a DVD player, they do experiments, they do controls," said Paul Sternberg, a developmental biologist at Caltech. "Step one is observation: What does the picture look like? What are the possible things that could be wrong here? Is it really the player, or could it be the television set? You come up with a hypothesis, then you start testing it. You borrow your neighbor's DVD player, you hook it up, you see your TV set is fine. So you check your DVD's input, output, a couple of wires. You may be able to track down the problem even without really understanding how a DVD player works.

"Or maybe you're trying to troubleshoot your pet," Sternberg said. "Why does the fish look funny? Why is my dog upset? I'll feed the hamster less or I'll feed it more, or maybe it doesn't like the noise, so I'll move it away from the stereo system. Should I take Job A or Job B? Well, let me see how long the drive would be from the office to my daughter's school during rush hour; that could be the killer factor in making a decision. These are all examples of forming hypotheses, doing experiments, coming up with controls. Some people learn these things at an early age. I had to get a PhD to figure them out."

A number of scientists proposed that people may have been more comfortable with the nuts and bolts of science back when they were comfortable with nuts and bolts. "It was easier to introduce students and the lay public to science when people fixed their own cars or had their hands in machinery of various kinds," said David Botstein of Princeton. "In the immediate period after World War II, everybody who'd been through basic training knew how a differential gear worked because they had taken one apart."

Farmers, too, were natural scientists. They understood the nuances of seasons, climate, plant growth, the do-si-do between parasite and host. The scientific curiosity that entitled our nation's Founding Fathers to membership in Club Renaissance, Anyone? had agrarian roots. Thomas Jefferson experimented with squashes and broccoli imported from Italy, figs from France, peppers from Mexico, beans collected by Lewis and Clark, as he systematically sought to select the "best" species of fruits and vegetables the world had to offer and "to reject all others from the garden." George Washington designed new methods of fertilizing and rotating crops and invented the sixteen-sided treading barn, in which horses would gallop over freshly harvested wheat and efficiently shake the grain from the stalks.

25 "The average adult American today knows less about biology than the average ten-year-old living in the Amazon, or than the average American of two hundred years ago," said Andrew Knoll, a professor of natural history at Harvard's Earth and Planetary Sciences Department. "Through the fruits of science, ironically enough, we've managed to insulate people from the need to know about science and nature." Yet still, people troubleshoot their pets, their kids, and, in moments of utter recklessness, their computers, and they apply scientific reasoning in many settings without realizing it, for the simple reason that the method works so well.

Much of the reason for its success is founded on another fundamental of the scientific bent. Scientists accept, quite staunchly, that there is a reality capable of being understood, and understood in ways that can be shared with and agreed upon by others. We can call this "objective" reality if we like, as opposed to subjective reality, or opinion, or "whimsical set of predilections." The contrast is deceptive, however, for it implies that the two are discrete entities with remarkably little in common. Objective reality is out there, other, impersonal, and "not me," while subjective reality is private, intimate, inimitable, and life as it is truly lived. Objective reality is cold and abstract; subjective reality is warm and Rockwell. Science is effective because it bypasses such binaries in favor of what might be called empirical universalism, the rigorously outfitted and enormously fruitful premise that the objective reality of the universe comprises the subjective reality of every one of us. We are of the universe, and by studying the universe we ultimately turn the mirror on ourselves. "Science is not describing a universe out there, and we're separate entities," said Brian Greene. "We're part of that universe, we're made of the same stuff as that universe, of ingredients that behave according to the same laws as they do elsewhere in the universe."

A molecule of water beaded on a forehead at Yale University would be indistinguishable from a molecule of water skating through space aboard Comet Kohoutek. Ashes to ashes, stardust to our dust. As I'll describe later in detail, the elements of our bodies, and of the earth, and of a painted Grandma's holiday apron, were all forged in the bellies of long-dead suns.

To say that there is an objective reality, and that it exists and can be understood, is one of those plain-truth poems of science that is nearly bottomless in its beauty. It is easy to forget that there is an objective, concrete universe, an outerverse measured in light years, a microverse trading in angstroms, the currency of atoms; we've succeeded so well in shaping daily reality to reflect the very narrow parameters and needs of *Homo sapiens.* We the subjects become we the objects, and we forget that the moon shows up each night for the graveyard shift, and we often haven't a clue as to where we might find it in the sky. We are made of stardust; why not take a few moments to look up at the family album? "Most of the time, when people walk outside at night and see the stars, it's a big, pretty background, and it's not quite real," said the Caltech planetary scientist Michael Brown. "It doesn't occur to them that the pattern they see in the sky repeats itself once a year, or to appreciate why that's true."

Star light, star bright, Brown wishes you'd try this trick at night: Pay attention to the moon. Go outside a few evenings in any given month, and see what time the moon rises, and what phase it's in, and when it sets, and then see if you can explain why. "Just doing this makes you realize that the sun and moon are both out there," he said, "and that the sun is actually shining on the moon, and the moon is going around the earth, and that it's not all a Hollywood special effect." Brown knows first-eye how powerful such simple observations can be. It was the summer after he'd graduated from college, and he was biking across Europe and sleeping outside each night. In accordance with his status as young, footloose, and overseas, he wore no wristwatch, so he sought to keep time by the phases of the moon. "I realized that I had never noticed before that the full moon rises when the sun sets," he said. "I thought, Hey, you know, this makes sense. I suppose I should have been embarrassed not to have noticed it before, but I wasn't. Instead, it was just an amazing feeling. The whole physical world is really out there, and things are really happening. It's so easy to isolate yourself from most of the world, to say nothing of the rest of the universe."

The last spring of my father's life, before he died unexpectedly of a fast-growing tumor, he told me that it was the first time he had stopped, during his walks through Central Park in New York, and paid attention to the details of the plants in bloom: the bulging out of a bud from a Lenten rose, the uncurling of a buttery magnolia blossom, the sprays of narcissus, Siberian bugloss, and bleeding heart. I was so impressed by this that, ever since, I have tried to do likewise, attending anew to the world in rebirth. Each spring I ask a specific question about what I'm seeing and so feel as though I am lighting a candle in his memory, a small focused flame against the void of self-absorption, the blindness of I. 30

Another fail-safe way to change the way you see the world is to invest in a microscope. Not one of those toy microscopes sold in most Science 'n' Discovery chain stores, which, as Tom Eisner, a professor of chemical ecology at Cornell, has observed, are unwrapped on Christmas morning and in the closet before Boxing Day. Not the microscopes that magnify specimens up to hundreds of times and make everything look like a satellite image of an Iowa cornfield. Rather, you should buy a dissecting microscope, also known as a stereo microscope. Admittedly, such microscopes are not cheap, running a couple of hundred dollars or so. Yet this is a modest price to pay for revelation, revolution, and—let's push this envelope out of the box while we're at it—personal salvation. Like Professor Brown, I speak from experience. I was accustomed to looking through high-powered microscopes in laboratories and seeing immune cells and cancer cells and frogs' eggs and kidney tissue from fetal mice. But it wasn't until my daughter received a dissecting microscope as a gift, and we began using it to examine the decidua of everyday life, that I began yodeling my hallelujahs. A feather from a blue jay, a fiddlehead fern, a scraping from a branch that turned out to be the tightly honeycombed housing for a stinkbug's eggs. How much heft and depth, shadow and thistle, leap out at you when the small is given scope to strut. At a mere 40X magnification, salt grains look like scattered glass pillows, a baby beetle becomes a Fabergé egg, and, as much as I hate mosquitoes, a mosquito under the microscope is pure Giacometti: *Thin Man Takes Wing, with Violin.*

Yes, the world is out there, over your head and under your nose, and it is real and it is knowable. To understand something about why a thing is as it is in no way detracts from its beauty and grandeur, nor does it reduce the observed to "just a bunch of"—chemicals, molecules, equations, specimens for a microscope. Scientists get annoyed at the hackneyed notion that their pursuit of knowledge diminishes the mystery or art or "holiness" of life. Let's say you look at a red rose, said Brian Greene, and you understand a bit about the physics behind its lovely blood blush. You know that red is a certain wavelength of light, and that light is made of little particles called photons. You understand that photons representing all colors of the rainbow stream from the sun and strike the surface of the rose, but that, as a result of the molecular composition of pigments in the rose, it's the red photons that bounce off its petals and up to your eyes, and so you see red.

"I like that picture," said Greene. "I like the extra story line, which comes, by the way, from Richard Feynman. But I still have the same strong emotional response to a rose as anybody else. It's not as though you become an automaton, dissecting things to death." To the contrary. A rose is a rose is a rose; but the examined rose is a sonnet.

That the universe can be explored and incrementally understood without losing its "magic" does not imply a corollary: that maybe "magic" is true after all, is hidden under accretions of apparent order, and that one of these days reality will kick off on a bucking broomstick toward Hogwarts on the hill. The universe still brims with mysteries, of course, but, in their conviction that the universe is knowable, scientists doubt that these question marks, once they have been understood well enough to become commas, will prove to be regions of arbitrary lawlessness or paranormality. "We have a pretty good idea of what kind of world this is, and it is not as mysterious, in the conventional sense of the word, as some people might wish," said Steven Weinberg. "It's not a world in which human destiny is linked to the positions of planets, or where people can be cured by crystals or bend spoons with their thoughts. Sometimes the police will call in a psychic to help solve a crime, and you'll hear a discussion on television for or against. But this isn't really an open question."

Scientists may believe that much, if not all, of the universe will prove comprehensible, yet interestingly, this comprehensibility continues to astound them. Immanuel Kant observed that "the most astonishing thing about the universe is that it can be understood." This was hardly a clause in a prenuptial agreement. As the Princeton astrophysicist John Bahcall put it in an interview shortly before he died, we crawled out of the ocean, we are confined to a tiny landmass circling a midsize, middle-aged, pale-faced sun located in one arm of just another pinwheel galaxy among millions of star-spangled galaxies; yet we have come to comprehend the universe on the largest scales and longest time frames, from the subatomic out to the edge of the cosmos. "It's remarkable, it's extraordinary, and it didn't have to be that way," Bahcall said.

Another surprising barrier to thinking scientifically is that we often believe we already understand how many things work, especially simple things we were supposed to have learned in one of our formative, single-digit grades. Even absent specific exposure to this or that kiddie science problem via a parent, a camp counselor, or the Professor on *Gilligan's Island,* we develop an intuitive grasp of physical reality, a set of down-to-earth, seemingly sensible explanations for everyday phenomena: why it's hot in the summer and cold in the winter, or what's going on when we throw a ball into the air. Sometimes these intuitive concepts are so comfortably lodged in our brains that if that tossed ball were to become a cartoon piano and fall on our heads, we'd pick ourselves up like a dazed Wile E. Coyote, shake the twinkling phosphenes from our eyes, and go back to our same misguided schemes for catching the bleep-bleep Road Runner.

Susan Carey, a professor of cognitive neuroscience at Harvard, has explored the ways that our lovingly cultivated and often erroneous models of physical reality can subvert understanding and impede our capacity to learn. She uses as an example a ball that has been tossed into the air and then falls back to the ground. Say you draw a picture of this trajectory, she said, with a series of balls in a steep arc to represent the ball rising upward, at midpoint in the air, and coming down again. You then ask people to draw arrows showing what sort of forces they think are acting on the ball during its trajectory—their strength and direction. The vast majority of people look at the picture and draw big force arrows pointing up while the ball is headed skyward, and big arrows pointing downward while the ball is descending. A sizable fraction of respondents, recognizing that gravity is acting on the ball during its entire voyage, will add little arrows pointing down next to the big arrows pointing up for the ascent portion of the curve. For the ball at its zenith, many will draw a little up arrow and a little down arrow that effectively cancel each other out.

It makes sense, doesn't it? Ball going up, force arrows pointing up; ball going down, force arrows plunging earthward. In fact, it makes so much sense that people believed exactly this model of motion for hundreds of years. There's even a name for it—the impetus theory, the idea that when something is in motion, a force, an impetus, must be keeping it in motion. As reasonable and as obvious as this theory seems, however, it is wrong. True, there was an upward force exerted on the ball when it first was thrust into the air, compliments of the pitcher. But once the ball has been launched, once it is in midexcursion, there is no more upward force acting on it. Once the ball is in the air, the only force acting on it is gravity. All those arrows on the diagram should be pointing down. If there were no gravity to worry about, a ball tossed upward would keep sailing upward, no further encouragement necessary. This is one of Isaac Newton's many brilliant productions, the famed law of inertia: An object at rest tends to stay at rest, unless induced by the nudge of a police officer's stick to get up off the park bench, this isn't the Plaza Hotel, you know; while an object in motion tends to stay in motion unless a force is applied to stop it. Yet even though we have heard about the law of inertia, and have seen the movie showing what happens when a jealous computer clips an astronaut's tether in the weightlessness of space—there he go-o-o-es—still we have trouble applying the idea of inertia to something in motion, and still we draw diagrams of ascending balls with upthrusting arrows.

"People come to science learning with a coherent, rather systematic theory of mechanical phenomena, and it's usually a variant of impetus theory," said Carey. "And often, as they learn about Newtonian theory, force, momentum, inertia, pressure, they simply assimilate the new information into their preexisting concepts." She and other researchers have found that even among people who have had a year of college physics, a high proportion will explain the ball's trajectory in impetus terms. "They hadn't undergone a conceptual change," she said. "The intuitive concepts they started with still held sway."

Sometimes a piece of knowledge learned early can make a powerful impression, can become an intuitive understanding that is then summoned forth in a valiant effort to explain something else. For example, researchers have shown that many people, on being asked why it is warm and sunny in the summer and cold and sullen in the winter, attribute seasonality to the comparative distance between Earth and the sun. They begin by stating a fact picked up at some point in elementary or high school—that Earth's orbit around the sun is not a perfect circle, but an ellipse. They then explain that, when Earth is closest to the sun on its ovoid track, we have summer; and when it is farthest away, it's time for road salt.

Walter Lewin, a professor of physics at MIT, showed me a video of Harvard seniors being asked, at their commencement ceremony, to explain why we have seasons. Again and again the young men and women, cucumber-confident in their caps and gowns, explained it as a matter of Earth being farthest from the sun in winter and closest in summer. The respondents weren't all art history or English majors, either, but included a few physics and engineering students as well.

Lewin, who is Dutch and therefore gratuitously tall, has an Einsteinian froth of whitish hair, a loping, electric style, and a facial expression often tuned to an impish, resigned incredulity. "The misconceptions of high school," he said, "can dog you for the rest of your life."

It's true that Earth's orbit is elliptical, he said, but only modestly so. Yet when the students try to explain in a drawing how the shape of our planet's orbit causes the seasons, they invariably exaggerate the eccentricity of the ellipse into something with the contours of a Tic Tac. Now they have a visual representation of how they view the seasons. You see way out here, at the farther elliptical tip of the orbit? That's winter. You see this tip, where we're squeezing toward the sun? That's summer. "They fail to ask the question, If this were the case, why, then, is it winter in the Southern Hemisphere when it's summer in the North, and vice versa?" said Lewin. "They can't shake the image of the all-powerful ellipse from their minds."

As it happens, Earth is slightly *farther* from the sun in July than it is in December, yet none of this matters. Seasonality is the result, not of orbital geometry, but of Earth's tilt: the fact that the globe is spinning on an axis that is tipped over 23 degrees relative to the plane of Earth's migration around the sun. As a result, sometimes the Northern Hemisphere points toward the sun and is bathed in a comparatively stronger and more direct blast of heat and light, and everybody living between Caracas, Venezuela, and Wood Buffalo, Canada, is advised to wear plenty of sunscreen, long-sleeved clothing, a sombrero, and a canvas tarp. Six months later, when Earth is at the opposite end of its lazy-Susan revolution, the Northern Hemisphere is tipped away from the sun, and it's the Southern Hemisphere's time to get braised.

Again, most people know about Earth's tilt, if for no other reason than their childhood exposure to that obligatory household prop, the four-color globe, on which half the countries have long since been renamed, redrawn, and overtaken by a military junta, and which was rarely used except for the purposes of spinning it around on its notably slanted axis until it squealed. Because the spinning was understood to explain why we have days and nights, 45 however, the angle of the rotation was as likely to be erroneously lumped together with the day-night kernel of kiddie wisdom as with any explanation for snow days and summer vacations.

Nor is it necessary that we learn our misinformation in childhood to hang on to it as a toddler would a small, shiny choking hazard. Whether sizing up new acquaintances or seizing on novel ideas, we remain forever at the mercy of our first impressions. We hear an explanation for something we hadn't been exposed to before, it sounds good and tastes better, and—you didn't just swallow that thing, did you? Cindy Lustig, a professor of psychology at the University of Michigan, recently demonstrated the ease with which our mind makes up its mind about new things. She gathered together forty-eight of the standard academic research subjects—undergraduate students—and instructed them to make an association between two related words, like "knee" and "bend" or "coffee" and "mug."

On a follow-up test, she asked her subjects to change the association, so that instead of answering the "knee" cue with "bend," the person was to reply "bone"; for the coffee prompt, "cup" rather than "mug." OK, time for lunch. Later that day, Lustig divided the group of subjects in two. Half were told to revert to the original association when confronted with the cue word. No problem: knee *bend,* coffee *mug.* The other group was asked to say whichever of their learned responses came to mind. Half of them would reply "bend" or "mug," and half "bone" or "cup." Good enough. Flip of the coin. Ah, but the next day, what then? When the random-answer subjects were again asked to say whatever response came to mind on hearing their cue words, a sizable majority conjured up their first tutorial, getting the bends, getting mugged. The earliest link, said Lustig, had become the brain's default setting.

Reporters know this tendency all too well, of the mind's readiness to make a quick connection and then seal it with an acrylic topcoat. I remember writing a story for the front page of the *New York Times* in 1991, about the spectacular discovery that we humans and other mammals have many hundreds of genes devoted to the production of odor receptors, the molecules studding the cells of our nasal passages that allow us to detect the thousands of aromas surrounding us. When I first heard the name of one of the smell researchers, Linda Buck, I immediately thought of another Linda with a similar surname, Linda Hunt, the New Jersey–born actress who won an Academy Award for playing a Chinese-Indonesian man. Well, both names are U-based, and you can *hunt* a *buck,* right? Ding-dong, connection made! Which is which? A wicked switch! I continued reporting the story. The hours flapped past. And when I finally got down to writing, I couldn't help but revert on cue to the earliest connection I'd made in the "Linda with the monosyllabic, rather bland last name" category, and I typed in Linda Hunt. Only at the last minute, right before the piece was to go to press, did I double-check the name against the journal article—and gasp at my error. Fortunately, I had time to make the change and save myself from prolonged humiliation. Linda Buck and her collaborator, Richard Axel, have since been awarded the Nobel Prize for their discovery, but there's still no Oscar in sight.

While simple facts like name spelling are easy to check and correct, it's much trickier to confront your preconceptions and misconceptions and to articulate how or why you conceive of something as you do. Your ideas may be vague. You're not sure where they came from. You feel stupid when you realize you're wrong, and you don't want to admit it, so you say, To hell with it, I'm no good at this, good-bye. Please don't do that. If you realize you might have put those up arrows on the ascending ball, too, or you weren't sure about the seasons, or you thought the lunar phases were the result of Earth's shadow being cast on the moon, rather than the real reason (that half the moon is always lit by the sun, and half is always dark, and that as the moon makes its month-long revolution around Earth we see different proportions of its light and dark sides), blame it on the brain and its insatiable greed, for picking up everything it comes upon and storing it in the nearest or most logical slot, which may not be right, but so what. That you have to be willing to make mistakes if you're going to get anywhere is true, and also a truism. Less familiar is the fun that you can have by dissecting the source of your misconceptions, and how, by doing so, you'll realize the errors are not stupid, that they have a reasonable or at least humorous provenance. Moreover, once you've recognized your intuitive constructs, you have a chance of amending, remodeling, or blowtorching them as needed, and replacing them with a closer approximation of science's approximate truths, now shining round you like freshly pressed coins.

▪ QUESTIONS

Reading

1. What does Angier mean by the term *empirical universalism*?
2. What happens, according to Angier, when we read science as a body of facts or a series of highlighted terms? Have you had this experience?
3. What does Angier tell us about her father? Why does she share this information?

Exploratory Writing

1. Planetary scientist Michael Brown, writes Angier, "wishes you'd . . . [p]ay attention to the moon." Take up Brown's challenge (paragraph 29) and spend a few nights going outside and observing the moon. Write some brief reflections about your experiences. What did you observe or learn? In what ways was your experience similar to Brown's? How was the experience different from reading about the moon?
2. In pairs, find a simple scientific question that you can't answer with certainty, and do some research on how other people (historically, or in the current scientific community) have attempted to answer it. What did you learn from this investigation?

Making Connections

1. "Science is not a body of facts," writes Angier. "Science is a state of mind." Consider evolutionary biologist Olivia Judson's explaining essay, "The Selfless Gene" (p. 284), in light of this revelation. Highlight, underline, or flag the places where Judson

demonstrates a scientific state of mind. In Judson's essay, how does writing connect to the practice of science that Angier describes?

2. Thomas W. Martin (p. 501) writes that growing evidence from cognitive science shows that individuals have a limited ability to criticize their own viewpoints. Choose one of the scientists Angier discusses in this essay and write a response in that person's voice. Would he or she argue that scientists are or are not susceptible to this problem? How would he or she suggest people try to expand their ability to assess their viewpoints?

Essay Writing

1. "Scientists get annoyed at the hackneyed notion that their pursuit of knowledge diminishes the mystery or art or 'holiness' of life," writes Angier (paragraph 32). Choose one of the many scientists Angier quotes in this report, and research information about his or her work. Write an essay explaining how, in your opinion, this scientist's experiments and theories show the beauty, mystery, or magic of the universe — or, on the other hand, how they diminish a sense of art or "holiness."

ARGUING

Scientific Literacy and the Habit of Discourse

Thomas W. Martin

Thomas W. Martin studied the history and philosophy of science before earning a PhD in molecular biophysics at the University of Virginia. He was chief scientific officer of the biotech company Diffusion Pharmaceuticals, and is now a faculty member at Arizona State University. His writing includes studies for scientific journals as well as articles for newspapers such as the *Christian Science Monitor.* His current teaching and research focus on sustainability and renewable energy sources. His essay "Scientific Literacy and the Habit of Discourse" was awarded first place in *Seed* magazine's second annual Science Writing Contest (2007), which asked writers and scientists to address the question, "What does it mean to be scientifically literate in the twenty-first century?"

Twenty years ago, as a college freshman, I knew precisely what it meant to be scientifically literate. In fact, I held an objective measure in the palm of my hand, courtesy of E. D. Hirsch. His book *Cultural Literacy: What Every American Needs to Know* was a best-selling paperback, and conveniently listed thousands of names, terms, and phrases with which every educated person—he informed us—should be familiar. After plodding through the entire list during the course of an afternoon, I smugly discovered I could easily define each item of scientific vocabulary. Fuzziness about literary examples such as "Aeschylus" caused me no discomfort, but inability to rigorously describe "aerobic respiration" in the biochemical sense (not the superficial, then-popular Jane Fonda sense) would have induced severe nerdish embarrassment.

Today I teach science and its history at an honors college, and am naturally far less confident about how to measure scientific literacy. The students who enter our program possess not only the expected high SAT scores, but also perfect or near-perfect scores on a battery of Advanced Placement exams, particularly in the basic sciences. A noticeable portion of those students also believe in the literal truth of certain ancient accounts of earth's history that, to put it bluntly, directly contradict mountains of well-established data from geology, climatology, and biology. Without rehashing the ongoing culture wars surrounding this topic (and certainly without berating my own students), this serves as a useful place to begin tackling the notion of "scientific literacy."

We frequently hear the refrain that if our nation simply raised the level of science courses, taught our children more subjects, and/or gave them more hands-on lab work, we could ensure the production of a citizenry capable of understanding an increasingly complex world. They would then be prepared to make the difficult choices of the 21st century, etc. However, my incoming students' technical mastery already exceeds what even the most rosy-eyed optimist could realistically dream for America (or the globe) as a whole. In other words, even if a citizenry were to achieve an impressive degree of scientific literacy—construed as raw conceptual competence—it would still be entirely possible for those same citizens to routinely subordinate scientific evidence to their own deeply-ingrained cultural suppositions.

More importantly, the phenomenon of "evidence blindness" is hardly restricted to inexperienced students, or even to ideological segments of the general population. To varying degrees, it can be found across the spectrum, including some very striking examples in the realm of professional science itself. As noted recently in *Seed,* leading disciplinary practitioners who feel threatened by unorthodox new findings will sometimes band together to suppress such information, with the explicit intention of blocking its appearance in the journals. While these luminaries undoubtedly convince themselves they are merely upholding the integrity of their fields, the truth is that they (in quintessentially human fashion) are often more interested in preserving cherished beliefs than in encouraging potentially disruptive discoveries.

5 Over the past few decades, growing evidence from cognitive science has revealed significant limits on the ability of individuals to criticize their own viewpoints. Even the most analytically gifted and experienced among us are susceptible to bias and self-deception to an extent that we (ironically enough) generally fail to appreciate. As psychologist Daniel Gilbert puts it in his book *Stumbling on Happiness,* "Each of us is trapped in a place, a time, and a circumstance, and our attempts to use our minds to transcend those boundaries are, more often than not, ineffective." The reason science does manage to be astonishingly effective is not because large groups are automatically wiser or less prone to self-deception than individuals. History adequately demonstrates that, if anything, the opposite is more nearly the case. Science works because its core dynamics—not its methods or techniques per se—are rooted in pitting intellects against one another. Science eventually yields impressive answers because it compels smart people to incessantly try to disprove the ideas generated by other smart people.

The goal of science is to find those ideas that can withstand the long and hard barrage of evidence-based argument. That lesson must be experienced anew by the members of each generation, irrespective of their careers. Mastery of scientific concepts and theories is a necessary starting point, but it serves only as a prerequisite to joining the never-ending dialogue. Students must learn first-hand how to both imaginatively create new hypotheses and to dispassionately critique them. Many commentators have rightly implored us to make certain that young people encounter the "thrill" of discovery. While this is undeniably desirable, it is arguably even more crucial that they experience the agony (if only on a modest scale) of having a pet hypothesis demolished by facts.

Several current presidential candidates have insisted that they oppose the scientific account of earth's natural history as a matter of principle. In the present cultural climate, altering one's beliefs in response to anything (facts included) is considered a sign of weakness. Students must be convinced that changing one's mind in light of the evidence is not weakness: Changing one's mind is the essence of intellectual growth. By forcing students into evidence-based debates with one another, this mode of interaction, like any other, can become habitual. After being consistently challenged by their peers, most students eventually see that attempts to free themselves from facts are a hollow, and fundamentally precarious, form of "freedom."

In an era in which we tremble at offending the sensibilities of our neighbors, students must comprehend that it is not only possible but absolutely vital that we criticize each other's ideas firmly yet civilly. They must do this despite clear cases of prominent scientists falling into petty, acerbic (and therefore counterproductive) exchanges. The responsibility for fostering scientific literacy of this sort—that is, literacy construed as an ongoing commitment to evidence over preconception—falls upon all of us in our discussions both formal and informal, both public and private. When scientific celebrities fail to set a good example for students, it is especially incumbent upon the rest of us to set them back on the proverbial right track, rather than to reflexively hasten their derailment.

We do our children no favors by going easy on them—or, more to the point—allowing them to go easy on each other. Nature has a way of being far tougher. If we can create environments in which they can safely have small epiphanies in the light of evidence, they will be motivated to share those lessons. They will then be scientifically literate in the sense that scientific discourse will continue to endure and flourish. And that is the sense that ultimately matters.

▪ QUESTIONS

Reading

1. What is "evidence blindness"? According to Martin, who can have evidence blindness?
2. According to Martin, what makes science effective?
3. "A noticeable portion of [my] students also believe in the literal truth of certain ancient accounts of earth's history that, to put it bluntly, directly contradict mountains of well-established data from geology, climatology, and biology," Martin writes (paragraph 2). What does he mean by "certain ancient accounts of earth's history"? Why does he use this indirect reference?

Exploratory Writing

1. Choose a widely held belief, and do some research to find scientific evidence contradicting it (such as articles in science magazines). Also find at least one example of a person who belongs to a group that holds this belief, and has written an article explaining or arguing for the belief. What does your research show about scientific literacy? Does your research support Martin's arguments?
2. In pairs or teams, hold a debate about an interesting new scientific discovery. Whether you are assigned the "pro" or "con" side, you do not need to agree personally with what

you argue, as this is an exercise to strengthen your skills in evidence-finding and argumentative technique. As you plan your "pro" or "con" case, research the topic and make sure to base your argument on scientific evidence rather than cultural assumptions.

Making Connections

1. Brooke Gladstone (p. 325) defines a number of different kinds of bias common in media coverage of news. Where does the problem of biased thinking figure into Martin's argument about the causes of scientific illiteracy? What are some similarities between the role of bias in the media and the role of bias in the sciences?
2. Natalie Angier (p. 489) writes that "the conjuring of science as a . . . set of unerring facts" is often used by its opponents, like "antievolutionists who seize on every disputed fossil to question the entire Darwinian enterprise" (paragraph 16). Would some of Martin's students, as he describes them, be opponents of science as Angier describes it?

Essay Writing

1. Write an essay reflecting on a time in your life when a strong belief of yours changed due to new information, new experiences, new ideas, or new evidence. What was challenging for you about changing this belief? Why did you hold the belief in the first place?

REPORTING

Brain Gain

Margaret Talbot

Essayist and reporter Margaret Talbot became a staff writer at the *New Yorker* in 2003. Her work has appeared in the *New York Times Magazine*, *National Geographic*, and the *Atlantic*, among other publications. She was a founding editor of *Lingua Franca*, a magazine about academic and intellectual life, and received the 1999 Whiting Writer's Award. Talbot is currently a senior fellow at the New American Foundation, where she writes about family life, culture, and politics. Her work often centers on the intersection between scientific facts and societal habits and beliefs. This essay, on neuroenhancers, appeared in the *New Yorker* in 2009.

A young man I'll call Alex recently graduated from Harvard. As a history major, Alex wrote about a dozen papers a semester. He also ran a student organization, for which he often worked more than forty hours a week; when he wasn't on the job, he had classes. Weeknights were devoted to all the schoolwork that he couldn't finish during the day, and weekend nights were spent drinking with friends and going to dance parties. "Trite as it sounds," he told me, it seemed important to "maybe appreciate my own youth." Since, in essence, this life was impossible, Alex began taking Adderall to make it possible.

Adderall, a stimulant composed of mixed amphetamine salts, is commonly prescribed for children and adults who have been given a diagnosis of attention-deficit hyperactivity disorder. But in recent years Adderall and Ritalin, another stimulant, have been adopted as cognitive enhancers: drugs that high-functioning, overcommitted people take to become higher-functioning and more overcommitted. (Such use is "off label," meaning that it does not have the approval of either the drug's manufacturer or the Food and Drug Administration.) College campuses have become laboratories for experimentation with neuroenhancement, and Alex was an ingenious experimenter. His brother had received a diagnosis of ADHD, and in his freshman year Alex obtained an Adderall prescription for himself by describing to a doctor symptoms that he knew were typical of the disorder. During his college years, Alex took fifteen milligrams of Adderall most evenings, usually after dinner, guaranteeing that he would maintain intense focus while losing "any ability to sleep for approximately eight to ten hours." In his sophomore year, he persuaded the doctor to add a thirty-milligram "extended release" capsule to his daily regimen.

Alex recalled one week during his junior year when he had four term papers due. Minutes after waking on Monday morning, around seven-thirty, he swallowed some "immediate release" Adderall. The drug, along with a steady

stream of caffeine, helped him to concentrate during classes and meetings, but he noticed some odd effects; at a morning tutorial, he explained to me in an e-mail, "I alternated between speaking too quickly and thoroughly on some subjects and feeling awkwardly quiet during other points of the discussion." Lunch was a blur: "It's always hard to eat much when on Adderall." That afternoon, he went to the library, where he spent "too much time researching a paper rather than actually writing it—a problem, I can assure you, that is common to all intellectually curious students on stimulants." At eight, he attended a two-hour meeting "with a group focussed on student mental-health issues." Alex then "took an extended-release Adderall" and worked productively on the paper all night. At eight the next morning, he attended a meeting of his organization; he felt like "a zombie," but "was there to insure that the semester's work didn't go to waste." After that, Alex explained, "I went back to my room to take advantage of my tired body." He fell asleep until noon, waking "in time to polish my first paper and hand it in."

I met Alex one evening last summer, at an appealingly scruffy bar in the New England city where he lives. Skinny and bearded, and wearing faded hipster jeans, he looked like the lead singer in an indie band. He was ingratiating and articulate, and smoked cigarettes with an ironic air of defiance. Alex was happy enough to talk about his frequent use of Adderall at Harvard, but he didn't want to see his name in print; he's involved with an Internet start-up, and worried that potential investors might disapprove of his habit.

5 After we had ordered beers, he said, "One of the most impressive features of being a student is how aware you are of a twenty-four-hour work cycle. When you conceive of what you have to do for school, it's not in terms of nine to five but in terms of what you can physically do in a week while still achieving a variety of goals in a variety of realms—social, romantic, sexual, extracurricular, résumé-building, academic commitments." Alex was eager to dispel the notion that students who took Adderall were "academic automatons who are using it in order to be first in their class, or in order to be an obvious admit to law school or the first accepted at a consulting firm." In fact, he said, "it's often people"—mainly guys—"who are looking in some way to compensate for activities that are detrimental to their performance." He explained, "At Harvard, at least, most people are to some degree realistic about it. . . . I don't think people who take Adderall are aiming to be the top person in the class. I think they're aiming to be among the best. Or maybe not even among the best. At the most basic level, they aim to do better than they would have otherwise." He went on, "Everyone is aware of the fact that if you were up at 3 A.M. writing this paper it isn't going to be as good as it could have been. The fact that you were partying all weekend, or spent the last week being high, watching 'Lost'—that's going to take a toll."

Alex's sense of who uses stimulants for so-called "nonmedical" purposes is borne out by two dozen or so scientific studies. In 2005, a team led by Sean Esteban McCabe, a professor at the University of Michigan's Substance Abuse Research Center, reported that in the previous year 4.1 per cent of American undergraduates had taken prescription stimulants for off-label use; at one school, the figure was twenty-five per cent. Other researchers have found even higher rates: a 2002 study at a small college found that more than thirty-five per cent of the students had used prescription stimulants nonmedically in the previous year.

Drugs such as Adderall can cause nervousness, headaches, sleeplessness, and decreased appetite, among other side effects. An FDA warning on Adderall's label notes that "amphetamines have a high potential for abuse" and can lead to dependence. (The label also mentions that adults using Adderall have reported serious cardiac problems, though the role of the drug in those cases is unknown.) Yet college students tend to consider Adderall and Ritalin benign, in part because they are likely to know peers who have taken the drugs since childhood for ADHD Indeed, McCabe reports, most students who use stimulants for cognitive enhancement obtain them from an acquaintance with a prescription. Usually, the pills are given away, but some students sell them.

According to McCabe's research team, white male undergraduates at highly competitive schools—especially in the Northeast—are the most frequent collegiate users of neuroenhancers. Users are also more likely to belong to a fraternity or a sorority, and to have a GPA of 3.0 or lower. They are ten times as likely to report that they have smoked marijuana in the past year, and twenty times as likely to say that they have used cocaine. In other words, they are decent students at schools where, to be a great student, you have to give up a lot more partying than they're willing to give up.

The Bored At Web sites—which allow college students to chat idly while they're ostensibly studying—are filled with messages about Adderall. Posts like these, from the BoredAtPenn site, are typical: "I have some Adderall—I'm sitting by room 101.10 in a grey shirt and headphones"; "I have Adderall for sale 20mg for $15"; "I took Adderall at 8 p.m., it's 6:30 a.m. and I've barely blinked." On the Columbia site, a poster with an e-mail address from CUNY complains that her friends take Adderall "like candy," adding, "I don't want to be at a disadvantage to everyone else. Is it really that dangerous? Will it fuck me up? My grades weren't that great this year and I could do with a bump." A Columbia student responds, "It's probably not a good idea if you're not prescribed," but offers practical advice anyway: "Keep the dose normal and don't grind them up or snort them." Occasional dissents ("I think there should be random drug testing at every exam") are drowned out by testimonials like this one, from the BoredAtHarvard site: "I don't want to be a pusher or start people on something bad, but Adderall is AMAZING."

Alex remains enthusiastic about Adderall, but he also has a slightly jaundiced critique of it. "It only works as a cognitive enhancer insofar as you are dedicated to accomplishing the task at hand," he said. "The number of times I've taken Adderall late at night and decided that, rather than starting my paper, hey, I'll organize my entire music library! I've seen people obsessively cleaning their rooms on it." Alex thought that generally the drug helped him to bear down on his work, but it also tended to produce writing with a characteristic flaw. "Often, I've looked back at papers I've written on Adderall, and they're verbose. They're belaboring a point, trying to create this airtight argument, when if you just got to your point in a more direct manner it would be stronger. But with Adderall I'd produce two pages on something that could be said in a couple of sentences." Nevertheless, his Adderall-assisted papers usually earned him at least a B. They got the job done. As Alex put it, "Productivity is a good thing." 10

Last April, the scientific journal *Nature* published the results of an informal online poll asking whether readers attempted to sharpen "their focus, concentration, or memory" by taking drugs such as Ritalin and Provigil—a newer kind of stimulant, known generically as modafinil, which was developed to treat narcolepsy. One out of five respondents said that they did. A majority of the fourteen hundred readers who responded said that healthy adults should be permitted to take brain boosters for nonmedical reasons, and sixty-nine per cent said that mild side effects were an acceptable risk. Though a majority said that such drugs should not be made available to children who had no diagnosed medical condition, a third admitted that they would feel pressure to give "smart drugs" to their kids if they learned that other parents were doing so.

Such competitive anxieties are already being felt in the workplace. Recently, an advice column in *Wired* featured a question from a reader worried about "a rising star at the firm" who was "using unprescribed modafinil to work crazy hours. Our boss has started getting on my case for not being as productive." And on Internet forums such as ImmInst, whose members share a nerdy passion for tweaking their cognitive function through drugs and supplements, people trade advice about dosages and "stacks"—improvised combinations—of neuroenhancers. ("Cut a tablet into fourths and took 25 mg every four hours, 4 times today, and had a great and productive day—with no side effects.") In one recent post, a fifty-two-year-old—who was working full time, studying for an advanced degree at night, and "married, etc."—wrote that after experimenting with modafinil he had settled on two daily doses of a hundred milligrams each. He believed that he was "performing a little better," adding, "I also feel slightly more animated when in discussion."

Not long ago, I met with Anjan Chatterjee, a neurologist at the University of Pennsylvania, in his office, which is tucked inside the labyrinthine Penn hospital complex. Chatterjee's main research interests are in subjects like the neurological basis of spatial understanding, but in the past few years, as he has heard more about students taking cognitive enhancers, he has begun writing about the ethical implications of such behavior. In 2004, he coined the term "cosmetic neurology" to describe the practice of using drugs developed for recognized medical conditions to strengthen ordinary cognition. Chatterjee worries about cosmetic neurology, but he thinks that it will eventually become as acceptable as cosmetic surgery has; in fact, with neuroenhancement it's harder to argue that it's frivolous. As he notes in a 2007 paper, "Many sectors of society have winner-take-all conditions in which small advantages produce disproportionate rewards." At school and at work, the usefulness of being "smarter," needing less sleep, and learning more quickly are all "abundantly clear." In the near future, he predicts, some neurologists will refashion themselves as "quality-of-life consultants," whose role will be "to provide information while abrogating final responsibility for these decisions to patients." The demand is certainly there: from an aging population that won't put up with memory loss; from overwrought parents bent on giving their children every possible edge; from anxious employees in an efficiency-obsessed, BlackBerry-equipped office culture, where work never really ends.

Chatterjee told me that many people who come to his clinic are cognitively preoccupied versions of what doctors call the "worried well." The day I visited his office, he had just seen a middle-aged woman, a successful Philadelphia lawyer, who mentioned having to struggle a bit to come up with certain names. "Here's an example of someone who by most measures is doing perfectly fine," Chatterjee said. "She's not having any trouble at work. But she notices she's having some problems, and it's very hard to know how much of that is just getting older." Of course, people in her position could strive to get regular exercise and plenty of intellectual stimulation, both of which have been shown to help maintain cognitive function. But maybe they're already doing so and want a bigger mental rev-up, or maybe they want something easier than sweaty workouts and Russian novels: a pill.

Recently, I spoke on the phone with Barbara Sahakian, a clinical neuropsychologist at Cambridge University, and the co-author of a December, 2007, article in *Nature*, "Professor's Little Helper." Sahakian, who also consults for several pharmaceutical companies, and her co-author, Sharon Morein-Zamir, 15 reported that a number of their colleagues were using prescription drugs like Adderall and Provigil. Because the drugs are easy to buy online, they wrote, it would be difficult to stop their spread: "The drive for self-enhancement of cognition is likely to be as strong as if not stronger than in the realms of 'enhancement' of beauty and sexual function." (In places like Cambridge, at least.)

When I spoke with Sahakian, she had just flown from England to Scottsdale, Arizona, to attend a conference, and she was tired. She might, justifiably, have forgone distractions like me, but she had her cell phone with her, and though it was a weekend morning some industrious person in the Cambridge news office had reached Sahakian in her hotel room, after she got out of the shower and before she had to rush to the first session. "We may be healthy and high-functioning, and think of ourselves that way, but it's very rare that we are actually functioning at our *optimal* level," Sahakian said. "Take me. I'm over here, and I've got jet lag and I've got to give a talk tonight and perform well, in what will be the middle of the night, U.K. time." She mentioned businessmen who have to fly back and forth across the Atlantic: "The difference between making a deal and not is huge and they sometimes only have one meeting to try and do it." She sympathized with them, but, she added, "We are a society that so wants a quick fix that many people are happy to take drugs."

For the moment, people looking for that particular quick fix have a limited choice of meds. But, given the amount of money and research hours being spent on developing drugs to treat cognitive decline, Provigil and Adderall are likely to be joined by a bigger pharmacopoeia. Among the drugs in the pipeline are ampakines, which target a type of glutamate receptor in the brain; it is hoped that they may stem the memory loss associated with diseases like Alzheimer's. But ampakines may also give healthy people a palpable cognitive boost. A 2007 study of sixteen healthy elderly volunteers found that five hundred milligrams of one particular ampakine "unequivocally" improved short-term memory, though it appeared to detract from episodic memory— the recall of past events. Another class of drugs, cholinesterase inhibitors, which are already being used with some success to treat Alzheimer's patients, have also shown promise as neuroenhancers. In one study, the drug donepezil strengthened the performance of pilots on flight simulators; in another, of thirty healthy young male volunteers, it improved verbal and visual episodic memory. Several pharmaceutical companies are working on drugs that target nicotine receptors in the brain, in the hope that they can replicate the cognitive uptick that smokers get from cigarettes.

Zack and Casey Lynch are a young couple who, in 2005, launched NeuroInsights, a company that advises investors on developments in brain-science technology. (Since then, they've also founded a lobbying group, the Neurotechnology Industry Organization.) Casey and Zack met as undergraduates at UCLA; she went on to get a master's degree in neuroscience at UCSF, and he became an executive at a software company. Last summer, I had coffee with them in the Noe Valley neighborhood of San Francisco, and they both spoke with casual certainty about the coming market for neuroenhancers.

Zack, who has a book being published this summer, called *The Neuro Revolution,* said, "We live in an information society. What's the next form of human society? The *neuro*-society." In coming years, he said, scientists will understand the brain better, and we'll have improved neuroenhancers that some people will use therapeutically, others because they are "on the borderline of needing them therapeutically," and others purely "for competitive advantage."

Zack explained that he didn't really like the term "enhancement": "We're not talking about superhuman intelligence. No one's saying we're coming out with a pill that's going to make you smarter than Einstein! . . . What we're really talking about is *enabling* people." He sketched a bell curve on the back of a napkin. "Almost every drug in development is something that will take someone who's working at, like, forty per cent or fifty per cent, and take them up to eighty," he said.

New psychiatric drugs have a way of creating markets for themselves. 20 Disorders often become widely diagnosed after drugs come along that can alter a set of suboptimal behaviors. In this way, Ritalin and Adderall helped make ADHD a household name, and advertisements for antidepressants have helped define shyness as a malady. If there's a pill that can clear up the wavering focus of sleep-deprived youth, or mitigate the tip-of-the-tongue experience of middle age, then those rather ordinary states may come to be seen as syndromes. As Casey put it, "The drugs get better, and the markets become bigger."

"Yes," Zack said. "We call it the lifestyle-improvement market."

The Lynches said that Provigil was a classic example of a related phenomenon: mission creep. In 1998, Cephalon, the pharmaceutical company that manufactures it, received government approval to market the drug, but only for "excessive daytime sleepiness" due to narcolepsy; by 2004, Cephalon had obtained permission to expand the labeling, so that it included sleep apnea and "shift-work sleep disorder." Net sales of Provigil climbed from a hundred and ninety-six million dollars in 2002 to nine hundred and eighty-eight million in 2008.

Cephalon executives have repeatedly said that they do not condone off-label use of Provigil, but in 2002 the company was reprimanded by the FDA for distributing marketing materials that presented the drug as a remedy for tiredness, "decreased activity," and other supposed ailments. And in 2008 Cephalon paid four hundred and twenty-five million dollars and pleaded guilty to a federal criminal charge relating to its promotion of off-label uses for Provigil and two other drugs. Later this year, Cephalon plans to introduce Nuvigil, a longer-lasting variant of Provigil. Candace Steele, a spokesperson, said, "We're exploring its possibilities to treat excessive sleepiness associated with schizophrenia, bipolar depression, traumatic injury, and jet lag." Though she emphasized that Cephalon was not developing Nuvigil as a neuroenhancer, she noted, "As part of the preparation for some of these other diseases, we're looking to see if there's improvement in cognition."

Unlike many hypothetical scenarios that bioethicists worry about—human clones, "designer babies"—cognitive enhancement is already in full swing. Even if today's smart drugs aren't as powerful as such drugs may someday be, there are plenty of questions that need to be asked about them. How much do they actually help? Are they potentially harmful or addictive? Then, there's the question of what we mean by "smarter." Could enhancing one kind of thinking exact a toll on others? All these questions need proper scientific answers, but for now much of the discussion is taking place furtively, among the increasing number of Americans who are performing daily experiments on their own brains.

Paul Phillips was unusual for a professional poker player. When he joined the circuit, in the late nineties, he was already a millionaire: a twenty-something tech guy who had started off writing software, helped found an Internet portal called go2net, and cashed in at the right moment. He was cerebral and, at times, brusque. His nickname was Dot Com. On the international poker-tournament scene—where the male players tend to be either unabashedly schlumpy or sharply dressed in the manner of a Vegas hotel manager—Phillips cultivated a geeky New Wave style. He wore vintage shirts in wild geometric patterns; his hair was dyed orange or silver one week, shaved off the next. Most unusual of all, Phillips talked freely about taking prescription drugs—Adderall and, especially, Provigil—in order to play better cards. 25

He first took up the game in 1995, when he was in college, at UC San Diego. He recalled, "It was very mathematical, but you could also inject yourself into the game and manipulate the other guy with words"—more so than in a game like chess. Phillips soon felt that he had mastered the strategic aspects of poker. The key variable was execution. At tournaments, he needed to be able to stay focused for fourteen hours at a stretch, often for several days, but he found it difficult to do so. In 2003, a doctor gave him a diagnosis of ADHD, and he began taking Adderall. Within six months, he had won $1.6 million at poker events—far more than he'd won in the previous four years. Adderall not only helped him concentrate; it also helped him resist the impulse to keep playing losing hands out of boredom. In 2004, Phillips asked his doctor to give him a prescription for Provigil, which he added to his Adderall regimen. He took between two hundred and three hundred milligrams of Provigil a day, which, he felt, helped him settle into an even more serene and objective state of mindfulness; as he put it, he felt "less like a participant than an observer—and a very effective one." Though Phillips sees neuroenhancers as essentially steroids for the brain, they haven't yet been banned from poker competitions.

Last summer, I visited Phillips in the high-desert resort town of Bend, Oregon, where he lives with his wife, Kathleen, and their two daughters, Ivy and Ruby. Phillips, who is now thirty-six, seemed a bit out of place in Bend, where people spend a lot of time skiing and river rafting. Among the friendly, faithfully recycling locals, he was making an effort to curb his caustic side. Still, when I first sent Phillips an e-mail asking him to explain, more precisely, how Provigil affected him, he couldn't resist a smart-ass answer: "More precisely: after a pill is consumed, tiny molecules are absorbed into the bloodstream, where they eventually cross the blood-brain barrier and influence the operation of the wetware up top."

In person, he was more obliging. He picked me up at the Bend airport driving a black convertible BMW, and we went for coffee at a cheery café called Thump. Phillips wore shorts and flip-flops and his black T-shirt displayed an obscure programming joke. "Poker is about sitting in one place, watching your opponents for a long time, and making better observations about them than they make about you," he said. With Provigil, he "could process all the information about what was going on at the table and do something about it." Though there is no question that Phillips became much more successful at poker after taking neuroenhancers, I asked him if his improvement could be explained by a placebo effect, or by coincidence. He doubted it, but allowed that it could. Still, he said, "there's a sort of clarity I get with Provigil. With Adderall, I'd characterize the effect as correction—correction of an underlying condition. Provigil feels like enhancement." And, whereas Adderall made him "jittery," Provigil's effects were "completely limited to my brain." He had "zero difficulty sleeping."

On the other hand, Phillips said, Provigil's effects "have attenuated over time. The body is an amazing adjusting machine, and there's no upside that I've been able to see to just taking more." A few years ago, Phillips tired of poker, and started playing competitive Scrabble. He was good, but not that good. He was older than many of his rivals, and he needed to undertake a lot of rote memorization, which didn't come as easily as it once had. "I stopped short of memorizing the entire dictionary, and to be really good you have to get up to eight- and nine-letter words," he told me. "But I did learn every word up to five letters, plus maybe ten thousand seven- and eight-letter words." Provigil, he said, helped with the memorization process, but "it's not going to make you smarter. It's going to make you better able to use the tools you have for a sustained period."

Similarly, a journalist I know, who takes the drug when he has to stay up all night on deadline, says that it doesn't help in the phase when he's trying to figure out what he wants to say or how to structure a story; but, once he's arrived at those insights, it helps him stay intent on completing a draft. Similarly, a seventy-four-year-old who published a letter in *Nature* last year offered a charmingly specific description of his modafinil habit: "Previously, I could work competently on the fracture-mechanics of high-silica stone (while replicating ancient tool-flaking techniques) for about an hour. With modafinil, I could continue for almost three hours."

Cephalon, the Provigil manufacturer, has publicly downplayed the idea that the drug can be used as a smart pill. In 2007, the company's founder and CEO, Frank Baldino, Jr., told a reporter from the trade journal *Pharmaceutical Executive,* "I think if you're tired, Provigil will keep you awake. If you're not tired, it's not going to do anything." But Baldino may have been overly modest. Only a few studies have been done of Provigil's effects on healthy, non-sleep-deprived volunteers, but those studies suggest that Provigil does provide an edge, at least for some kinds of challenges. In 2002, researchers at Cambridge

University gave sixty healthy young male volunteers a battery of standard cognitive tests. One group received modafinil; the other got a placebo. The modafinil group performed better on several tasks, such as the "digit span" test, in which subjects are asked to repeat increasingly longer strings of numbers forward, then backward. They also did better in recognizing repeated visual patterns and on a spatial-planning challenge known as the Tower of London task. (It's not nearly as fun as it sounds.) Writing in the journal *Psychopharmacology*, the study's authors said the results suggested that "modafinil offers significant potential as a cognitive enhancer."

Phillips told me that, much as he believes in neuroenhancers, he did not want to be "the poster boy for smart-in-a-pill." At one point, he said, "We really don't know the possible implications for long-term use of these things." (He recently stopped taking Provigil every day, replacing it with another prescription stimulant.) He found the "arms-race aspect" of cognitive enhancement distasteful, and didn't like the idea that parents might force their kids to take smart pills. He sighed when I suggested that adults, too, might feel coerced into using the drugs. "Yeah, in a competitive field—if suddenly a quarter of the people are more equipped, but you don't want to take the risks with your body—it could begin to seem terribly unfair," he said. "I don't think we need to be turning up the crank another notch on how hard we work. But the fact is, the baseline competitive level is going to reorient around what these drugs make possible, and you can choose to compete or not."

In the afternoon, we drove over to Phillip's house—a big place, handsome and new, with a sweeping deck overhanging the Deschutes River. Inside, toys were strewn across the shag carpeting. Phillips was waiting for his wife and daughters to come home from the swimming pool, and, sitting in his huge, high-ceilinged living room, he looked a little bored. He told me that he had recently decided to apply to graduate school in computer programming. It was going to be hard—getting out all those applications, convincing graduate programs that he was serious about returning to school. But he had, as he put it, "exhausted myself on all forms of leisure," and felt nostalgic for his last two years of college, when he had discovered computer programming. "That was the most purely intellectually satisfying period of my whole life," he said. "It transformed my brain from being all over the place to a reasonable edifice of knowledge about something." Back then, he hadn't taken any smart pills. "I would have been a freakin' dynamo in college if I'd been taking them," he said. "But, still, I had to *find* computers. That made a bigger difference than anything else—finding something I just couldn't get enough of."

Provigil may well confer a temporary advantage on healthy people, but this doesn't mean that it's ready to replace your morning espresso. Anjan Chatterjee told me that there "just aren't enough studies of these drugs in normal people." He said, "In the situations where they do help, do they come with a cost?" As he wrote in a recent letter to *Nature*, "Most seasoned physicians have had the sobering experience of prescribing medications that, despite good intentions, caused bad outcomes." Given that cognitive enhancement is a choice, not a necessity, the cost-benefit calculation for neuroenhancers should probably be different than it is for, say, heart medications.

Provigil can be habit-forming. In a study published recently in the *Journal of the American Medical Association*, a group led by Nora Volkow, the director of the National Institute on Drug Abuse, scanned the brains of ten men after they had been given a placebo, and also after they had been given a dose of modafinil. The modafinil appeared to lead to an increase in the brain chemical dopamine. "Because drugs that increase dopamine have the potential for abuse," Volkow's report concluded, "these results suggest that risk for addiction in vulnerable persons merits heightened awareness." (Cephalon, in a response to the report, notes that Provigil's label urges physicians to monitor patients closely, especially those with a history of drug abuse.) On the Web site Erowid, where people vividly, and anonymously, report their experiences with legal and illegal drugs, some modafinil users have described a dependency on the drug. One man, who identified himself as a former biochemistry student, said that he had succeeded in kicking cocaine and opiate habits but couldn't stop using modafinil. Whenever he ran out of the drug, he said, "I start to freak out." After "4–5 days" without it, "the head fog starts to come back." 35

Eliminating foggy-headedness seems to be the goal of many users of neuroenhancers. But can today's drugs actually accomplish this? I recently posed this question to Anjan Chatterjee's colleague Martha Farah, who is a psychologist at Penn and the director of its Center for Cognitive Neuroscience. She has been writing about neuroenhancers for several years from a perspective that is deeply fascinated and mildly critical, but basically in favor—with the important caveat that we need to know much more about how these drugs work. I spoke with her one afternoon at her research center, which is in a decidedly unfuturistic-looking Victorian house on Walnut Street, in Philadelphia. Farah, who is an energetic conversationalist, had bought canned espresso drinks for us. Though she does not take neuroenhancers, she has found that her interest in them has renewed her romance with the next best thing: caffeine.

Farah had just finished a paper in which she reviewed the evidence on prescription stimulants as neuroenhancers from forty laboratory studies involving healthy subjects. Most of the studies looked at one of three types of cognition: learning, working memory, and cognitive control. A typical learning test asks subjects to memorize a list of paired words; an hour, a few days, or a week later, they are presented with the first words in the pairs and asked to come up with the second. The studies on learning showed that neuroenhancers did improve retention. The benefits were more apparent in studies where subjects had been asked to remember information for several days or longer.

Working memory has been likened to a mental scratch pad: You use it to keep relevant data in mind while you're completing a task. (Imagine a cross-examination, in which a lawyer has to keep track of the answers a witness has given, and formulate new questions based on them.) In one common test, subjects are shown a series of items—usually letters or numbers—and then presented with challenges: Was this number or letter in the series? Was this one? In the working-memory tests, subjects performed better on neuroenhancers, though several of the studies suggested that the effect depended on how good a subject's working memory was to begin with: the better it was, the less benefit the drugs provided.

The third category that the studies examined was cognitive control—how effectively you can check yourself in circumstances where the most natural response is the wrong one. A classic test is the Stroop Task, in which people are shown the name of a color (let's say orange) written in a different color (let's say purple). They're asked to read the word (which is easy, because our habitual response to a word is to read it) or to name the ink color (which is harder, because our first impulse is to say "orange"). These studies presented a more mixed picture, but over all they showed some benefit "for most normal healthy subjects"—especially for people who had inherently poorer cognitive control.

Farah told me, "These drugs will definitely help some technically normal people—that is, people who don't meet the diagnostic criteria for ADHD or any kind of cognitive impairment." But, she emphasized, "they will help people in the lower end of the ability range more than in the higher end." One explanation for this phenomenon might be that, the more adept you are at a given task, the less room you have to improve. Farah has a hunch that there may be another reason that existing drugs, so far, at least, don't offer as much help to people with greater intellectual abilities. Drugs like Ritalin and Adderall work, in part, by elevating the amount of dopamine in the brain. Dopamine is something you want just enough of: too little, and you may not be as alert and motivated as you need to be; too much, and you may feel overstimulated. Neuroscientists have discovered that some people have a gene that leads the brain to break down dopamine faster, leaving less of it available; such people are generally a little worse at certain cognitive tasks. People with more available dopamine are generally somewhat better at the same tasks. It makes sense, then, that people with naturally low dopamine would benefit more from an artificial boost. 40

Of course, learning, working memory, and cognitive control represent just a few aspects of thinking. Farah concluded that studies looking at other kinds of cognition—verbal fluency, for instance—were too few and too contradictory to tell us much. And the effects of neuroenhancers on some vital forms of intellectual activity, such as abstract thought and creativity, have barely been studied at all. Farah said that the extant literature was concerned with "fairly boring kinds of thinking—how long can you stay vigilant while staring at a screen and waiting for a little light to blink." She added, "It would be great to have studies of more flexible kinds of thought."

Both Chatterjee and Farah have wondered whether drugs that heighten users' focus might dampen their creativity. After all, some of our best ideas come to us not when we sit down at a desk but, rather, when we're in the shower or walking the dog—letting our minds roam. Jimi Hendrix reported that the inspiration for "Purple Haze" came to him in a dream; the chemist

Friedrich August Kekule claimed that he discovered the ring structure of benzene during a reverie in which he saw the image of a snake biting its tail. Farah told me, "Cognitive psychologists have found that there is a trade-off between attentional focus and creativity. And there is some evidence that suggests that individuals who are better able to focus on one thing and filter out distractions tend to be less creative."

Farah and Chatterjee recently completed a preliminary study looking at the effect of one ten-milligram dose of Adderall on sixteen students doing standard laboratory tests of creative thinking. They did not find that this low dose had a detrimental effect, but both believe that this is only the beginning of the vetting that must be done. "More and more of our young people are using these drugs to help them work," Farah said. "They've got their laptop, their iPhone, and their Adderall. This rising generation of workers and leaders may have a subtly different style of thinking and working, because they're using these drugs or because they learned to work using these drugs, so that even if you take the drugs away they'll still have a certain approach. I'm a little concerned that we could be raising a generation of very focused accountants."

Farah has also been considering the ethical complications resulting from the rise of smart drugs. Don't neuroenhancers confer yet another advantage on the kind of people who already can afford private tutors and prep courses? At many colleges, students have begun calling the off-label use of neuroenhancers a form of cheating. Writing last year in the *Cavalier Daily,* the student newspaper of the University of Virginia, a columnist named Greg Crapanzano argued that neuroenhancers "create an unfair advantage for the users who are willing to break the law in order to gain an edge. These students create work that is dependent on the use of a pill rather than their own work ethic." Of course, it's hard to imagine a university administration that would require students to pee in a cup before they get their blue books. And though secretly taking a neuroenhancer for a three-hour exam does seem unfair, condemning the drugs' use seems extreme. Even with the aid of a neuroenhancer, you still have to write the essay, conceive the screenplay, or finish the grant proposal, and if you can take credit for work you've done on caffeine or nicotine, then you can take credit for work produced on Provigil.

45 Farah questions the idea that neuroenhancers will expand inequality. Citing the "pretty clear trend across the studies that say neuroenhancers will be less helpful for people who score above average," she said that cognitive-enhancing pills could actually become levellers, if they are dispensed cheaply. A 2007 discussion paper published by the British Medical Association also makes this point: "Equality of opportunity is an explicit goal of our education system, giving individuals the best chance of achieving their full potential and of competing on equal terms with their peers. Selective use of neuroenhancers amongst those with lower intellectual capacity, or those from deprived backgrounds who do not have the benefit of additional tuition, could enhance the educational opportunities for those groups." If the idea of giving a pill as a substitute for better teaching seems repellent—like substituting an I.V. drip

of synthetic nutrition for actual food—it may nevertheless be preferable to a scenario in which only wealthy kids receive a frequent mental boost.

Farah was one of several scholars who contributed to a recent article in *Nature*, "Towards Responsible Use of Cognitive Enhancing Drugs by the Healthy." The optimistic tone of the article suggested that some bioethicists are leaning toward endorsing neuroenhancement. "Like all new technologies, cognitive enhancement can be used well or poorly," the article declared. "We should welcome new methods of improving our brain function. In a world in which human workspans and lifespans are increasing, cognitive enhancement tools—including the pharmacological—will be increasingly useful for improved quality of life and extended work productivity, as well as to stave off normal and pathological age-related cognitive declines. Safe and effective cognitive enhancers will benefit both the individual and society." The British Medical Association report offered a similarly upbeat observation: "Universal access to enhancing interventions would bring up the baseline level of cognitive ability, which is generally seen to be a good thing."

And yet when enthusiasts share their vision of our neuroenhanced future it can sound dystopian. Zack Lynch, of NeuroInsights, gave me a rationale for smart pills that I found particularly grim. "If you're a fifty-five-year-old in Boston, you have to compete with a twenty-six-year-old from Mumbai now, and those kinds of pressures are only going to grow," he began. Countries other than the U.S. might tend to be a little looser with their regulations, and offer approval of new cognitive enhancers first. "And if you're a company that's got forty-seven offices worldwide, and all of a sudden your Singapore office is using cognitive enablers, and you're saying to Congress, 'I'm moving all my financial operations to Singapore and Taiwan, because it's legal to use those there,' you bet that Congress is going to say, 'Well, OK' It will be a moot question then. It would be like saying, 'No, you can't use a cell phone. It might increase productivity!' "

If we eventually decide that neuroenhancers work, and are basically safe, will we one day enforce their use? Lawmakers might compel certain workers—emergency-room doctors, air-traffic controllers—to take them. (Indeed, the Air Force already makes modafinil available to pilots embarking on long missions.) For the rest of us, the pressure will be subtler—that queasy feeling I get when I remember that my younger colleague is taking Provigil to meet deadlines. All this may be leading to a kind of society I'm not sure I want to live in: a society where we're even more overworked and driven by technology than we already are, and where we have to take drugs to keep up; a society where we give children academic steroids along with their daily vitamins.

Paul McHugh, a psychiatrist at Johns Hopkins University, has written skeptically about cosmetic neurology. In a 2004 essay, he notes that at least once a year in his private practice he sees a young person—usually a boy—whose parents worry that his school performance could be better, and want a medication that will assure it. In most of these cases, "the truth is that the son does not have the superior IQ of his parents," though the boy may have other qualities that surpass those of his parents—he may be "handsome, charming, athletic, graceful." McHugh sees his job as trying to get the parents to "forget about adjusting him to their aims with medication or anything else." When I spoke with him on the phone, McHugh expanded on this point: "Maybe it's wrong-footed trying to fit people into the world, rather than trying to make the world a better place for people. And if the idea is that the only college your child can go to is Harvard, well, maybe *that's* the idea that needs righting."

If Alex, the Harvard student, and Paul Phillips, the poker player, consider their use of neuroenhancers a private act, Nicholas Seltzer sees his habit as a pursuit that aligns him with a larger movement for improving humanity. Seltzer has a BA from UC Davis and a master's degree in security policy from George Washington University. But the job that he obtained with these credentials—as a researcher at a defense-oriented think tank, in northern Virginia—has not left him feeling as intellectually alive as he would like. To compensate, he writes papers in his spare time on subjects like "human biological evolution and warfare." He also primes his brain with artificial challenges; even when he goes to the rest room at the office, he takes the opportunity to play memory or logic games on his cell phone. Seltzer, who is thirty, told me that he worried that he "didn't have the mental energy, the endurance, the—I don't know what to properly call this—the *sponginess* that I seem to recall having when I was younger." 50

Suffice it to say that this is not something you notice when you talk to Seltzer. And though our memory is probably at its peak in our early twenties, few thirty-year-olds are aware of a deficit. But Seltzer is the Washington-wonk equivalent of those models and actors in L.A. who discern tiny wrinkles long before their agent does. His girlfriend, a technology consultant whom he met in a museum, is nine years younger, and he was already thinking about how his mental fitness would stand up next to hers. He told me, "She's twenty-one, and I want to stay young and vigorous and don't want to be a burden on her later in life." He didn't worry about visible signs of aging, but he wanted to keep his mind "nimble and healthy for as long as possible."

Seltzer considers himself a "transhumanist," in the mold of the Oxford philosopher Nick Bostrom and the futurist writer and inventor Ray Kurzweil. Transhumanists are interested in robots, cryogenics, and living a really, really long time; they consider biological limitations that the rest of us might accept, or even appreciate, as creaky obstacles to be aggressively surmounted. On the ImmInst forums—"ImmInst" stands for "Immortality Institute"—Seltzer and other members discuss life-extension strategies and the potential benefits of cognitive enhancers. Some of the forum members limit themselves to vitamin and mineral supplements. Others use Adderall or modafinil or, like Seltzer, a drug called piracetam, which was first marketed by a Belgian pharmaceutical company in 1972 and, in recent years, has become available in the U.S. from retailers that sell supplements. Although not approved for any use by the FDA, piracetam has been used experimentally on stroke patients—to little effect—and on patients with a rare neurological condition called progressive myoclonus epilepsy, for whom it proved helpful in alleviating muscle spasms. Data on piracetam's benefits for healthy people are virtually nonexistent, but many users believe that the drug increases blood flow to the brain.

From the time I first talked to Seltzer, it was clear that although he felt cognitive enhancers were of practical use, they also appealed to him on an aesthetic level. Using neuroenhancers, he said, "is like customizing yourself—customizing your brain." For some people, he went on, it was important to enhance their mood, so they took antidepressants; but for people like him it was more important "to increase mental horsepower." He added, "It's fundamentally a choice you're making about how you want to experience consciousness." Whereas the nineties had been about "the personalization of technology," this decade was about the personalization of the brain—what some enthusiasts have begun to call "mind hacking."

Of course, the idea behind mind hacking isn't exactly new. Fortifying one's mental stamina with drugs of various kinds has a long history. Sir Francis Bacon consumed everything from tobacco to saffron in the hope of goosing his brain. Balzac reputedly fuelled sixteen-hour bouts of writing with copious servings of coffee, which, he wrote, "chases away sleep, and gives us the capacity to engage a little longer in the exercise of our intellects." Sartre dosed himself with speed in order to finish *Critique of Dialectical Reason*. My college friends and I wrote term papers with the sweaty-palmed assistance of NoDoz tablets. And, before smoking bans, entire office cultures chugged along on a collective nicotine buzz—at least, if *Mad Men* is to be believed. Seltzer and his interlocutors on the ImmInst forum are just the latest members of a seasoned cohort, even if they have more complex pharmaceuticals at their disposal.

55 I eventually met Seltzer in an underground food court not far from the Pentagon. We sat down at a Formica table in the dim light. Seltzer was slim, had a shaved head, and wore metal-frame glasses; matching his fastidious look, he spoke precisely, rarely stumbling over his words. I asked him if he had any ethical worries about smart drugs. After a pause, he said that he might have a concern if somebody popped a neuroenhancer before taking a licensing exam that certified him as, say, a brain surgeon, and then stopped using the drug. Other than that, he couldn't see a problem. He said that he was a firm believer in the idea that "we should have a fair degree of liberty to do with our bodies and our minds as we see fit, so long as it doesn't impinge on the basic rights, liberty, and safety of others." He argued, "Why would you *want* an upward limit on the intellectual capabilities of a human being? And, if you have a very nationalist viewpoint, why wouldn't you want our country to have the advantage over other countries, particularly in what some people call a knowledge-based economy?" He went on, "Think about the complexity of the intellectual tasks that people need to accomplish today. Just trying to understand what Congress is doing is not a simple thing! The complexity of understanding the gamut of scientific and technical and social issues is difficult. If we had a tool

that enabled more people to understand the world at a greater level of sophistication, how can we prejudice ourselves against the notion, simply because we don't like athletes to do it? To me, it doesn't seem like the same question. And it deserves its own debate."

Seltzer had never had a diagnosis of any kind of learning disorder. But he added, "Though I wouldn't say I'm dyslexic, sometimes when I type prose, after I look back and read it, I've frequently left out words or interposed words, and sometimes I have difficulty concentrating." In graduate school, he obtained a prescription for Adderall from a doctor who didn't ask a lot of questions. The drug helped him, especially when his ambitions were relatively low. He recalled, "I had this one paper, on nuclear strategy. The professor didn't look favorably on any kind of creative thinking." On Adderall, he pumped out the paper in an evening. "I just bit my tongue, regurgitated, and got a good-enough grade."

On the other hand, Seltzer recalled that he had taken piracetam to write an essay on "the idea of harmony as a trope in Chinese political discourse"—it was one of the papers he was proudest of. He said, "It was really an intellectual challenge to do. I felt that the piracetam helped me to work within the realm of the abstract, and make the kind of associations that I needed—following this idea of harmony from an ancient religious belief as it was translated throughout the centuries into a very important topic in political discourse."

After a hiatus of several years, Seltzer had recently resumed taking neuroenhancers. In addition to piracetam, he took a stack of supplements that he thought helped his brain functioning: fish oils, five antioxidants, a product called ChocoMind, and a number of others, all available at the health-food store. He was thinking about adding modafinil, but hadn't yet. For breakfast every morning, he concocted a slurry of oatmeal, berries, soy milk, pomegranate juice, flaxseed, almond meal, raw eggs, and protein powder. The goal behind the recipe was efficiency: to rely on "one goop you could eat or drink that would have everything you need nutritionally for your brain and body." He explained, "Taste was the last thing on my mind; I wanted to be able to keep it down—that was it." (He told me this in the kitchen of his apartment; he lives with a roommate, who walked in while we were talking, listened perplexedly for a moment, then put a frozen pizza in the oven.)

Seltzer's decision to take piracetam was based on his own online reading, which included medical-journal abstracts. He hadn't consulted a doctor. Since settling on a daily regimen of supplements, he had sensed an improvement in his intellectual work and his ability to engage in stimulating conversation. He continued, "I feel I'm better able to articulate my thoughts. I'm sure you've been in the zone—you're having a really exciting debate with somebody, your brain feels alive. I feel that more. But I don't want to say that it's this profound change."

I asked him if piracetam made him feel smarter, or just more alert and confident—a little better equipped to marshal the resources he naturally had. "Maybe," he said. "I'm not sure what being smarter means, entirely. It's a 60 difficult quality to measure. It's the gestalt factor, all these qualities coming together—not only your ability to crunch some numbers, or remember some figures or a sequence of numbers, but also your ability to maintain a certain emotional state that is conducive to productive intellectual work. I do feel I'm more intelligent with the drugs, but I can't give you a number of IQ points."

The effects of piracetam on healthy volunteers have been studied even less than those of Adderall or modafinil. Most peer-reviewed studies focus on its effects on dementia, or on people who have suffered a seizure or a concussion. Many of the studies that look at other neurological effects were performed on rats and mice. Piracetam's mechanisms of action are not understood, though it may increase levels of the neurotransmitter acetylcholine. In 2008, a committee of the British Academy of Medical Sciences noted that many of the clinical trials of piracetam for dementia were methodologically flawed. Another published review of the available studies of the drug concluded that the evidence "does not support the use of piracetam in the treatment of people with dementia or cognitive impairment," but suggested that further investigation might be warranted. I asked Seltzer if he thought he should wait for scientific ratification of piracetam. He laughed. "I don't want to," he said. "Because it's working."

It makes no sense to ban the use of neuroenhancers. Too many people are already taking them, and the users tend to be educated and privileged people who proceed with just enough caution to avoid getting into trouble. Besides, Anjan Chatterjee is right that there is an apt analogy with plastic surgery. In a consumer society like ours, if people are properly informed about the risks and benefits of neuroenhancers, they can make their own choices about how to alter their minds, just as they can make their own decisions about shaping their bodies.

Still, even if you acknowledge that cosmetic neurology is here to stay, there is something dispiriting about the way the drugs are used—the kind of aspirations they open up, or don't. Jonathan Eisen, an evolutionary biologist at UC Davis, is skeptical of what he mockingly calls "brain doping." During a recent conversation, he spoke about colleagues who take neuroenhancers in order to grind out grant proposals. "It's weird to me that people are taking these drugs to write grants," he said. "I mean, if you came up with some really interesting paper that was *spurred* by taking some really interesting drug—magic mushrooms or something—that would make more sense to me. In the end, you're only as good as the ideas you've come up with."

But it's not the mind-expanding sixties anymore. Every era, it seems, has its own defining drug. Neuroenhancers are perfectly suited for the anxiety of white-collar competition in a floundering economy. And they have a synergistic relationship with our multiplying digital technologies: The more gadgets we own, the more distracted we become, and the more we need help in order to focus. The experience that neuroenhancement offers is not, for the most part, about opening the doors of perception, or about breaking the bonds of the self, or about experiencing a surge of genius. It's about squeezing out an extra few hours to finish those sales figures when you'd really rather collapse into bed; getting a B instead of a B-minus on the final exam in a lecture class where you spent half your time texting; cramming for the GREs at night, because the information-industry job you got after college turned out to be deadening. Neuroenhancers don't offer freedom. Rather, they facilitate a pinched, unromantic, grindingly efficient form of productivity.

This winter, I spoke again with Alex, the Harvard graduate, and found that, after a break of several months, he had gone back to taking Adderall—a small dose every day. He felt that he was learning to use the drug in a more "disciplined" manner. Now, he said, it was less about staying up late to finish work he should have done earlier, and more "about staying focused on work, which makes me want to work longer hours." What employer would object to that? 65

▪ QUESTIONS

Reading

1. Who coined the term *cosmetic neurology*, and what does it mean?
2. Why does Talbot interview Alex? How does what she learns from Alex compare with and contrast to the data from studies that she cites?
3. Martha Farah, who Talbot interviews, claims that neuroenhancers are more likely to "help people in the lower end of the ability range more than in the higher end" (paragraph 40). What evidence does she use to draw her conclusions about neuroenhancers and cognition? What further research does she advocate?

Exploratory Writing

1. What conclusions does Talbot draw about the use of neuroenhancers? Reread her concluding paragraphs, and write a few paragraphs that come to a different conclusion based on the data and evidence Talbot offers in her report. What words could you use to describe her conclusion? What words would best describe yours?
2. What is the likeliest reason that Talbot visited BoredAt Web sites as part of the research for this report? In pairs, visit the BoredAt site for your own school (or any other school if yours doesn't have one). Do students on the site discuss "nonmedical" drug use, either of prescription or illegal drugs? Do they express concerns about grades or completing work on time? Prepare a short report about your findings. Are they similar to Talbot's?

Making Connections

1. What are the similarities and differences between Alex, based on what we know from Talbot's interview with him, and Walter Kirn (p. 525), who also has a personal story of performance-enhancing drug use?
2. Talbot raises the question of whether or not neuroenhancers constitute cheating in an academic setting. Research the effects of performance-enhancing drugs on athletes

(baseball players, runners, or cyclists, for instance) and compare them with those of neuroenhancers as described by Talbot and Walter Kirn (p. 525). Based on your research, write a letter to your school arguing for or against prohibiting students from using neuroenhancers.

Essay Writing

1. "Every era . . ." writes Talbot, "has its own defining drug" (paragraph 64). Choose any moment in history, and write a report on what you believe to be its defining drug. Why does that drug define that era?

REFLECTING

A Pharmacological Education

Walter Kirn

Walter Kirn (b. 1962) is the author of five novels and a collection of short stories. His books *Thumbsucker* (1999) and *Up in the Air* (2001) were both adapted into feature films. His most recent novel, *The Unbinding* (2006), was written exclusively for the Internet and appeared online in *Slate* magazine. Kirn's well-reviewed comic memoir, *Lost in the Meritocracy: The Undereducation of an Overachiever* (2009), tells the story of his experiences as a working-class Minnesota-raised teenager attending Princeton University, where many of the other students came from wealthy, privileged backgrounds. After graduating from Princeton, he pursued a second undergraduate degree, in literature, from Oxford University. His nonfiction writing and book reviews have appeared in the *New York Times Magazine*, *New York* magazine, and others. He briefly guest-authored Andrew Sullivan's famous blog while Sullivan was on vacation. This article, which details Kirn's experience taking Adderall, first appeared in the *New York Times* in 2009.

Low on energy, drained of resources, and out of ideas about what to do, I consulted an expert on recovery and was given my personal stimulus package. It came in a small brown bottle of 60 pills, a dose of which was to be taken twice a day (but not too late in the day, because it might cause sleeplessness, and not too closely together, because it might cause dizziness). The psychiatrist who prescribed them predicted good things—enhanced concentration, a new competitive edge—and he minimized the risks, which is what finally sold me on Adderall. The drug was a compound of amphetamines meant to combat attention-deficit hyperactivity disorder, he said, that had proved safe in many trials—if used as directed. I sensed an insult. Did I look like someone who couldn't take direction? I let it pass.

That was about a decade ago, during a one-man economic downturn that is, in miniature, reflected in the current national one. What I wished for back then—a modest, short-term boost that would yield sustainable long-term gains—is what so many of us want right now, particularly, I would think, worried college students who find themselves stumbling back to school in a season of grim, uncertain prospects. "It'll help you get back on your feet," my doctor told me, using America's favorite metaphor for accepting a little help, but not too much help, when we're facing daunting circumstances that we're slightly ashamed to find daunting. The key word in this phrase, of course, is "back," because it implies that the subject stood upright previously, and all by himself.

To strivers young and old, the lure of mental accelerants like Adderall and its many molecular cousins has only grown since I swallowed my first dose and started down a pharmacological path that was more dizzying than I expected.

I found out the hard way that revving up your brain in order to win the race, or just stay in it, comes at a cost that may exceed the benefits. Lately, others are learning this lesson, too, sometimes in traumatic ways. In the last eight years, it was recently reported, calls to poison-control centers concerning overdoses of legal stimulants by young people shot up 76 percent. The increase tracked a near doubling of the rates at which such medications are prescribed, from about four million prescriptions eight years ago to eight million today. Neither of these figures surprises me. In matters related to modern pep pills, everything seems to double every few years, including, sometimes, a person's appetite for them.

Adderall, I discovered during the courtship phase of what became our deeply tortured relationship, offers a kind of assistance to the brain that feels just right, at first, for the age of multitasking. The drug might as well have been invented by Microsoft and embedded in the Windows toolbar. It seemed to allow me to do three things at once and not completely fail at two of them. Far more important, however, it helped me do one thing at once and focus on it. If I was toiling at my computer, it sharpened the clicking sensations of the keyboard while lowering the volume of the phone whose ringing might have broken my work trance. It also, for me at least, suppressed emotion, freeing me from the claims of other people (my children primarily, because I work at home) who wanted a piece of my precious, deskbound time.

5 The ability to stay on task, even the dullest, most numbing task, was Adderall's first gift to me. It was also its first curse, because it encouraged me to take on work of an increasingly stupefying nature and do it well enough that I got more of it, until I was doing almost no other kind. I can see, though, how harried students might covet this power and why, according to some estimates, a quarter of undergraduates at certain colleges are availing themselves of such stimulants. They're well aware of the dire economic news—big law firms instituting hiring freezes; whole industries, like publishing, imploding—and it's natural that they would welcome any advantage in their quests to get the grades that will get them the jobs that will get them the insurance that will get them the medications to do the jobs.

A recent labor statistic suggests to me that this circular relationship between pressure and productivity is operating in full swing. In this year's second quarter, the numbers tell us, the American work force squeezed from its tired body the largest increase in output in the last six years. What caused the jump is open speculation, but I imagine it was partly because of nervousness. The tension produced by the fear of losing a job suggests an adrenalized state perhaps not unlike the one that Adderall unleashes. Anxiety is nature's most plentiful stimulant. Under its influence, trembling fingers fly.

The flood of energy released by my pills was, like the recent surge in productivity, a bracing but also troubling development. How long would it last? What would happen when it slowed down? The writing I did on Adderall strikes me now, as I look back on it, as the work of a fellow trying to stay warm by burning semicolons. It was high on intensity, rather low on feeling, and marked by a certain jazzy, hectic tone. The income it brought me got me over the hump, though, and I banked my savings, luckily. That's because a new hump soon emerged, more massive and forbidding than the first. And this time it wasn't financial, or merely financial. It was systemic, biological. It manifested as sores inside my mouth, a faint corona of gray hair and a case of hemorrhoids from nonstop sitting.

I reached a point with Adderall that reminded me of a warning the United States Marine Corps is said to give its enemies: You can run, but you'll only die tired.

Or graduate tired, in the case of college students. And what's so wrong with that? The course of a formal education is short but its consequences vast, so why not give it your spirit-crushing all, especially during a fiercely competitive age? "Simply because," the parent in me says. He's been there, this man. He's weary, he's spent, and he just knows.

▪ QUESTIONS

Reading

1. What physical side effects did Kirn experience from taking Adderall?
2. How does Kirn characterize his doctor's behavior? What role does the doctor play in this story?
3. Highlight and list the ways Kirn describes Adderall. How do these descriptions change the way that you respond to his reflections? How would this article be changed if someone removed these descriptions?

Exploratory Writing

1. Kirn reflects that the writing he did when he was taking Adderall now seems to him to be "high on intensity, rather low on feeling, and marked by a certain jazzy, hectic tone" (paragraph 7). In groups, have each person quickly write a paragraph on the simple topic, "How the weather is affecting my mood," without putting his or her name on the paper. Shuffle and randomly distribute the paragraphs. Write a two-line description of the emotional content and tone of the paragraph you receive, then shuffle and randomly redistribute these descriptions. Rewrite your own, original paragraph with the new tone, feeling, and style described in the description you've received.
2. Kirn mentions the "circular relationship between pressure and productivity" (paragraph 6). Find an example of this "circular relationship" in another context. How do people in that situation tend to cope with pressure? What are some solutions other than neuroenhancing drugs?

Making Connections

1. Margaret Talbot (p. 505) reports on a number of studies showing the effects of a variety of drugs that alter cognitive functioning. Which of Kirn's experiences on Adderall, as he represents them here, seem consistent with findings of these studies? Which seem to contradict the studies?

2. In “The Value of Science” (p. 395) Richard Feynman states that “Scientific knowledge is an enabling power to do either good or bad — but it does not carry instructions on how to use it.” Adderall is the product of medical science. Consider Kirn’s description of the pros and cons of using the drug and write a paragraph about whether this is “good” or “bad” science, in Feynman’s terms. Based on Kirn’s experience, what “instructions” would be necessary to use this particular scientific advancement correctly?

Essay Writing

1. Find at least two credible online sources on the effects of Adderall, and write an essay arguing for or against the proposition: “Adderall and similar psychostimulants should be prescribed to healthy adults over 18 to help them perform better at work or in college.” Use clinical studies, expert opinions, anecdotes, reports, and other data to support your argument.

REPORTING

A Delicate Operation

Roy C. Selby Jr.

Roy C. Selby Jr. (1930–2001) graduated from Louisiana State University and the University of Arkansas Medical School, where he specialized in neurology and neurosurgery. He was the author of numerous professional articles on neurosurgery and a member of the American Association of Neurological Surgeons. "A Delicate Operation," which first appeared in *Harper's* magazine in 1975, reports for a more general audience the details of a difficult brain operation.

In the autumn of 1973 a woman in her early fifties noticed, upon closing one eye while reading, that she was unable to see clearly. Her eyesight grew slowly worse. Changing her eyeglasses did not help. She saw an ophthalmologist, who found that her vision was seriously impaired in both eyes. She then saw a neurologist, who confirmed the finding and obtained X-rays of the skull and an EMI scan—a photograph of the patient's head. The latter revealed a tumor growing between the optic nerves at the base of the brain. The woman was admitted to the hospital by a neurosurgeon.

Further diagnosis, based on angiography, a detailed X-ray study of the circulatory system, showed the tumor to be about two inches in diameter and supplied by many small blood vessels. It rested beneath the brain, just above the pituitary gland, stretching the optic nerves to either side and intimately close to the major blood vessels supplying the brain. Removing it would pose many technical problems. Probably benign and slow-growing, it may have been present for several years. If left alone it would continue to grow and produce blindness, and might become impossible to remove completely. Removing it, however, might not improve the patient's vision and could make it worse. A major blood vessel could be damaged, causing a stroke. Damage to the undersurface of the brain could cause impairment of memory and changes in mood and personality. The hypothalamus, a most important structure of the brain, could be injured, causing coma, high fever, bleeding from the stomach, and death.

The neurosurgeon met with the patient and her husband and discussed the various possibilities. The common decision was to operate.

The patient's hair was shampooed for two nights before surgery. She was given a cortisone-like drug to reduce the risk of damage to the brain during surgery. Five units of blood were cross-matched, as a contingency against hemorrhage. At 1:00 p.m. the operation began. After the patient was anesthetized her hair was completely clipped and shaved from the scalp. Her head was prepped with an organic iodine solution for ten minutes. Drapes were placed over her, leaving exposed only the forehead and crown of the skull. All the routine instruments were brought up—the electrocautery used to coagulate areas of bleeding, bipolar coagulation forceps to arrest bleeding from individual blood vessels without damaging adjacent tissues, and small suction tubes to remove blood and cerebrospinal fluid from the head, thus giving the surgeon a better view of the tumor and surrounding areas.

A curved incision was made behind the hairline so it would be concealed when the hair grew back. It extended almost from ear to ear. Plastic clips were applied to the cut edges of the scalp to arrest bleeding. The scalp was folded back to the level of the eyebrows. Incisions were made in the muscle of the right temple, and three sets of holes were drilled near the temple and the top of the head because the tumor had to be approached from directly in front. The drill, powered by nitrogen, was replaced with a fluted steel blade, and the holes were connected. The incised piece of skull was pried loose and held out of the way by a large sponge. 5

Beneath the bone is a yellowish leatherlike membrane, the dura, that surrounds the brain. Down the middle of the head the dura carries a large vein, but in the area near the nose the vein is small. At that point the vein and dura were cut, and clips made of tantalum, a hard metal, were applied to arrest and prevent bleeding. Sutures were put into the dura and tied to the scalp to keep the dura open and retracted. A malleable silver retractor, resembling the blade of a butter knife, was inserted between the brain and skull. The anesthesiologist began to administer a drug to relax the brain by removing some of its water, making it easier for the surgeon to manipulate the retractor, hold the brain back, and see the tumor. The nerve tracts for smell were cut on both sides to provide additional room. The tumor was seen approximately two-and-one-half inches behind the base of the nose. It was pink in color. On touching it, it proved to be very fibrous and tough. A special retractor was attached to the skull, enabling the other retractor blades to be held automatically and freeing the surgeon's hands. With further displacement of the frontal lobes of the brain, the tumor could be seen better, but no normal structures—the carotid arteries, their branches, and the optic nerves—were visible. The tumor obscured them.

A surgical microscope was placed above the wound. The surgeon had selected the lenses and focal length prior to the operation. Looking through the microscope, he could see some of the small vessels supplying the tumor and he coagulated them. He incised the tumor to attempt to remove its core and thus collapse it, but the substance of the tumor was too firm to be removed in this fashion. He then began to slowly dissect the tumor from the adjacent brain tissue and from where he believed the normal structures to be.

Using small squares of cotton, he began to separate the tumor from very loose fibrous bands connecting it to the brain and to the right side of the part of the skull where the pituitary gland lies. The right optic nerve and carotid artery came into view, both displaced considerably to the right. The optic nerve had a normal appearance. He protected these structures with cotton compresses placed between them and the tumor. He began to raise the tumor from the skull and slowly to reach the point of its origin and attachment—just in front of the pituitary gland and medial to the left optic nerve, which still could not be seen. The small blood vessels entering the tumor were cauterized. The upper portion of the tumor was gradually separated from the brain, and the branches of the carotid arteries and the branches to the tumor were coagulated. The tumor was slowly and gently lifted from its bed, and for the first time the left carotid artery and optic nerve could be seen. Part of the tumor adhered to this nerve. The bulk of the tumor was amputated, leaving a small bit attached to the nerve. Very slowly and carefully the tumor fragment was resected.

The tumor now removed, a most impressive sight came into view—the pituitary gland and its stalk of attachment to the hypothalamus, the hypothalamus itself, and the brainstem, which conveys nerve impulses between the body and the brain. As far as could be determined, no damage had been done to these structures or other vital centers, but the left optic nerve, from chronic pressure of the tumor, appeared gray and thin. Probably it would not completely recover its function.

After making certain there was no bleeding, the surgeon closed the wounds and placed wire mesh over the holes in the skull to prevent dimpling of the scalp over the points that had been drilled. A gauze dressing was applied to the patient's head. She was awakened and sent to the recovery room. 10

Even with the microscope, damage might still have occurred to the cerebral cortex and hypothalamus. It would require at least a day to be reasonably certain there was none, and about seventy-two hours to monitor for the major postoperative dangers—swelling of the brain and blood clots forming over the surface of the brain. The surgeon explained this to the patient's husband, and both of them waited anxiously. The operation had required seven hours. A glass of orange juice had given the surgeon some additional energy during the closure of the wound. Though exhausted, he could not fall asleep until after two in the morning, momentarily expecting a call from the nurse in the intensive care unit announcing deterioration of the patient's condition.

At 8:00 a.m. the surgeon saw the patient in the intensive care unit. She was alert, oriented, and showed no sign of additional damage to the optic nerves or the brain. She appeared to be in better shape than the surgeon or her husband.

▪ QUESTIONS

Reading

1. Why did Selby decide to operate? What could have happened if the patient chose not to have the operation? What effect does knowing this information have on the reader?
2. What is the *dura*?
3. Selby uses different methods of reporting to create the drama of "A Delicate Operation." At what point in the essay does he provide background information? How much of the essay reports events before, during, and after the operation? At what points does the writer explain terms and procedures for the reader?

Exploratory Writing

1. Highlight, underline, or flag the passages in this essay that you find especially powerful. How did Selby create this effect?
2. Using the Internet or library, find an article on neurosurgery that was obviously written for professionals within the field rather than for a general audience. How does the tone of the article differ from Selby's? How is the structure different? What types of material are included in — or omitted from — each article?
3. Write a checklist of steps required in the neurosurgical procedure that Selby describes. As a class or in small groups, compare the different checklists. Were certain steps forgotten on some checklists? Discuss whether a checklist would be a useful resource for doctors working on this complex procedure.

Making Connections

1. Compare Selby's perspective to Richard Selzer's (p. 533). Why is Selby's essay reportorial, while Selzer's is reflective? What elements of explanation are required in each essay to introduce specialized topics to the reader?
2. Jonah Lehrer (p. 431) describes the differences between left-brain thinking and the right-brain thinking that results in moments of inspiration. In your opinion, does the surgeon performing the procedure described in this essay use left-brain thinking, right-brain thinking, or both? Refer to Lehrer's definitions, and use specific examples from Selby's report to explain your conclusions.

Essay Writing

1. Imagine that you had to perform an operation like the one Selby describes. Write an essay reflecting on the experiences and personality traits that would help or hinder your performance as a surgeon.

REFLECTING

A Mask on the Face of Death

Richard Selzer

Richard Selzer (b. 1928) is the son of a general practitioner father and a singer mother, both of whom wanted their son to follow in their footsteps. At ten he began sneaking into his father's office to look at his medical textbooks, where he discovered "the rich alliterative language of medicine — words such as cerebellum, which, when said aloud, melt in the mouth and drip from the end of the tongue like chocolate." After his father's death, he decided to become a doctor and was for many years a professor of surgery at Yale Medical School. Only after working as a doctor for many decades did he begin to write. About the similarities between surgery and writing he says, "In surgery, it is the body that is being opened up and put back together. In writing it is the whole world that is taken in for repairs, then put back in working order piece by piece." His articles have appeared in *Vanity Fair, Harper's, Esquire*, and the *New York Times Magazine*. His books include the short-story collections *Rituals of Surgery* (1974) and *The Doctor Stories* (1998); the essay collections *Mortal Lessons* (1976), *Raising the Dead* (1994), *The Exact Location of the Soul* (2001), and *The Whistler's Room* (2004); and an autobiography, *Down from Troy* (1992). This essay appeared in *Life* in 1988.

It is ten o'clock at night as we drive up to the Copacabana, a dilapidated brothel on the rue Dessalines in the red-light district of Port-au-Prince. My guide is a young Haitian, Jean-Bernard. Ten years before, J-B tells me, at the age of fourteen, "like every good Haitian boy" he had been brought here by his older cousins for his *rite de passage*. From the car to the entrance, we are accosted by a half dozen men and women for sex. We enter, go down a long hall that breaks upon a cavernous room with a stone floor. The cubicles of the prostitutes, I am told, are in an attached wing of the building. Save for a red-purple glow from small lights on the walls, the place is unlit. Dark shapes float by, each with a blindingly white stripe of teeth. Latin music is blaring. We take seats at the table farthest from the door. Just outside, there is the rhythmic lapping of the Caribbean Sea. About twenty men are seated at the tables or lean against the walls. Brightly dressed women, singly or in twos or threes, stroll about, now and then exchanging banter with the men. It is as though we have been deposited in act two of Bizet's *Carmen*. If this place isn't Lillas Pastia's tavern, what is it?

Within minutes, three light-skinned young women arrive at our table. They are very beautiful and young and lively. Let them be Carmen, Mercedes, and Frasquita.

"I want the old one," says Frasquita, ruffling my hair. The women laugh uproariously.

"Don't bother looking any further," says Mercedes. "We are the prettiest ones."

"We only want to talk," I tell her.

"Aaah, aaah," she crows. "*Massissi.* You are *massissi.*" It is the contemptuous Creole term for homosexual. If we want only to talk, we must be gay. Mercedes and Carmen are slender, each weighing one hundred pounds or less. Frasquita is tall and hefty. They are dressed for work: red taffeta, purple chiffon, and black sequins. Among them a thousand gold bracelets and earrings multiply every speck of light. Their bare shoulders are like animated lamps gleaming in the shadowy room. Since there is as yet no business, the women agree to sit with us. J-B orders beer and cigarettes. We pay each woman $10.

"Where are you from?" I begin.

"We are Dominican."

"Do you miss your country?"

"Oh, yes, we do." Six eyes go muzzy with longing. "Our country is the most beautiful in the world. No country is like the Dominican. And it doesn't stink like this one."

"Then why don't you work there? Why come to Haiti?"

"Santo Domingo has too many whores. All beautiful, like us. All light-skinned. The Haitian men like to sleep with light women."

"Why is that?"

"Because always, the whites have all the power and the money. The black men can imagine they do, too, when they have us in bed."

Eleven o'clock. I look around the room that is still sparsely peopled with men.

"It isn't getting any busier," I say. Frasquita glances over her shoulder. Her eyes drill the darkness.

"It is still early," she says.

"Could it be that the men are afraid of getting sick?" Frasquita is offended.

"Sick! They do not get sick from us. We are healthy, strong. Every week we go for a checkup. Besides, we know how to tell if we are getting sick."

"I mean sick with AIDS." The word sets off a hurricane of taffeta, chiffon, and gold jewelry. They are all gesticulation and fury. It is Carmen who speaks.

"AIDS!" Her lips curl about the syllable. "There is no such thing. It is a false disease invented by the American government to take advantage of the poor countries. The American president hates poor people, so now he makes up AIDS to take away the little we have." The others nod vehemently.

"*Mira, mon cher.* Look, my dear," Carmen continues. "One day the police came here. Believe me, they are worse than the *tonton macoutes* with their submachine guns. They rounded up one hundred and five of us and they took our blood. That was a year ago. None of us have died, you see? We are all still here. *Mira,* we sleep with all the men and we are not sick."

"But aren't there some of you who have lost weight and have diarrhea?"

"One or two, maybe. But they don't eat. That is why they are weak."

"Only the men die," says Mercedes. "They stop eating, so they die. It is hard to kill a woman."

"Do you eat well?"

"Oh, yes, don't worry, we do. We eat like poor people, but we eat." There is a sudden scream from Frasquita. She points to a large rat that has emerged from beneath our table.

"My God!" she exclaims. "It is big like a pig." They burst into laughter. For a moment the women fall silent. There is only the restlessness of their many bracelets. I give them each another $10.

"Are many of the men here bisexual?"

"Too many. They do it for money. Afterward, they come to us." Carmen lights a cigarette and looks down at the small lace handkerchief she has been folding and unfolding with immense precision on the table. All at once she turns it over as though it were the ace of spades. 30

"*Mira, blanc* . . . look, white man," she says in a voice suddenly full of foreboding. Her skin seems to darken to coincide with the tone of her voice.

"*Mira*, soon many Dominican women will die in Haiti!"

"Die of what?"

She shrugs. "It is what they do to us."

"Carmen," I say, "if you knew that you had AIDS, that your blood was bad, would you still sleep with men?" Abruptly, she throws back her head and laughs. It is the same laughter with which Frasquita had greeted the rat at our feet. She stands and the others follow. 35

"*Méchant!* You wicked man," she says. Then, with terrible solemnity, "You don't know anything."

"But you are killing the Haitian men," I say.

"As for that," she says, "everyone is killing everyone else." All at once, I want to know everything about these three—their childhoods, their dreams, what they do in the afternoon, what they eat for lunch.

"Don't leave," I say. "Stay a little more." Again, I reach for my wallet. But they are gone, taking all the light in the room with them—Mercedes and Carmen to sit at another table where three men have been waiting. Frasquita is strolling about the room. Now and then, as if captured by the music, she breaks into a few dance steps, snapping her fingers, singing to herself.

Midnight. And the Copacabana is filling up. Now it is like any other seedy nightclub where men and women go hunting. We get up to leave. In the center a couple are dancing a *méringue*. He is the most graceful dancer I have ever watched; she, the most voluptuous. Together they seem to be riding the back of the music as it gallops to a precisely sexual beat. Closer up, I see that the man is short of breath, sweating. All at once, he collapses into a chair. The woman bends over him, coaxing, teasing, but he is through. A young man with a long polished stick blocks my way. 40

"I come with you?" he asks. "Very good time. You say yes? Ten dollars? Five?"

I have been invited by Dr. Jean William Pape to attend the AIDS clinic of which he is the director. Nothing from the outside of the low whitewashed structure would suggest it as a medical facility. Inside, it is divided into many small cubicles and a labyrinth of corridors. At nine a.m. the hallways are already full of emaciated silent men and women, some sitting on the few benches, the rest leaning against the walls. The only sounds are subdued moans of discomfort interspersed with coughs. How they eat us with their eyes as we pass.

The room where Pape and I work is perhaps ten feet by ten. It contains a desk, two chairs, and a narrow wooden table that is covered with a sheet that will not be changed during the day. The patients are called in one at a time, asked how they feel and whether there is any change in their symptoms, then examined on the table. If the patient is new to the clinic, he or she is questioned about sexual activities.

A twenty-seven-year-old man whose given name is Miracle enters. He is wobbly, panting, like a groggy boxer who has let down his arms and is waiting for the last punch. He is neatly dressed and wears, despite the heat, a heavy woolen cap. When he removes it, I see that his hair is thin, dull reddish, and straight. It is one of the signs of AIDS in Haiti, Pape tells me. The man's skin is covered with a dry itchy rash. Throughout the interview and examination he scratches himself slowly, absentmindedly. The rash is called prurigo. It is another symptom of AIDS in Haiti. This man has had diarrhea for six months. The laboratory reports that the diarrhea is due to an organism called cryptosporidium, for which there is no treatment. The telltale rattling of the tuberculous moisture in his chest is audible without a stethoscope. He is like a leaky cistern that bubbles and froths. And, clearly, exhausted.

"Where do you live?" I ask. 45

"Kenscoff." A village in the hills above Port-au-Prince.

"How did you come here today?"

"I came on the *tap-tap*." It is the name given to the small buses that swarm the city, each one extravagantly decorated with religious slogans, icons, flowers, animals, all painted in psychedelic colors. I have never seen a *tap-tap* that was not covered with passengers as well, riding outside and hanging on. The vehicles are little masterpieces of contagion, if not of AIDS then of the multitude of germs which Haitian flesh is heir to. Miracle is given a prescription for a supply of Sera, which is something like Gatorade, and told to return in a month.

"*Mangé kou bêf*," says the doctor in farewell. "Eat like an ox." What can he mean? The man has no food or money to buy any. Even had he food, he has not the appetite to eat or the ability to retain it. To each departing patient the doctor will say the same words—"*Mangé kou bêf*." I see that it is his way of offering a hopeful goodbye.

"Will he live until his next appointment?" I ask. 50

"No." Miracle leaves to catch the *tap-tap* for Kenscoff.

Next is a woman of twenty-six who enters holding her right hand to her forehead in a kind of permanent salute. In fact, she is shielding her eye from view. This is her third visit to the clinic. I see that she is still quite well nourished.

"Now, you'll see something beautiful, tremendous," the doctor says. Once seated upon the table, she is told to lower her hand. When she does, I see that her right eye and its eyelid are replaced by a huge fungating ulcerated tumor, a side product of her AIDS. As she turns her head, the cluster of lymph glands in her neck to which the tumor has spread is thrown into relief. Two years ago she received a blood transfusion at a time when the country's main blood bank was grossly contaminated with AIDS. It has since been closed down. The only blood available in Haiti is a small supply procured from the Red Cross.

"Can you give me medicine?" the woman wails.

"No." 55

"Can you cut it away?"

"No."

"Is there radiation therapy?" I ask.

"No."

"Chemotherapy?" The doctor looks at me in what some might call weary 60 amusement. I see that there is nothing to do. She has come here because there is nowhere else to go.

"What will she do?"

"Tomorrow or the next day or the day after that she will climb up into the mountains to seek relief from the *houngan*, the voodoo priest, just as her slave ancestors did two hundred years ago."

Then comes a frail man in his thirties, with a strangely spiritualized face, like a child's. Pus runs from one ear onto his cheek, where it has dried and caked. He has trouble remembering, he tells us. In fact, he seems confused. It is from toxoplasmosis of the brain, an effect of his AIDS. This man is bisexual. Two years ago he engaged in oral sex with foreign men for money. As I palpate the swollen glands of his neck, a mosquito flies between our faces. I swat at it, miss. Just before coming to Haiti I had read that the AIDS virus had been isolated from a certain mosquito. The doctor senses my thought.

"Not to worry," he says. "So far as we know there has never been a case transmitted by insects."

"Yes," I say. "I see." 65

And so it goes until the last, the thirty-sixth AIDS patient has been seen. At the end of the day I am invited to wash my hands before leaving. I go down a long hall to a sink. I turn on the faucets but there is no water.

"But what about *you*?" I ask the doctor. "You are at great personal risk here—the tuberculosis, the other infections, no water to wash . . ." He shrugs, smiles faintly, and lifts his hands palm upward.

We are driving up a serpiginous steep road into the barren mountains above Port-au-Prince. Even in the bright sunshine the countryside has the bloodless color of exhaustion and indifference. Our destination is the Baptist Mission Hospital, where many cases of AIDS have been reported. Along the road there are slow straggles of schoolchildren in blue uniforms who stretch out their hands as we pass and call out, "Give me something." Already a crowd of outpatients has gathered at the entrance to the mission compound. A tour of the premises reveals that in contrast to the aridity outside the gates, this is an enclave of productivity, lush with fruit trees and poinsettia.

The hospital is clean and smells of creosote. Of the forty beds, less than a third are occupied. In one male ward of twelve beds, there are two patients. The chief physician tells us that last year he saw ten cases of AIDS each week. Lately the number has decreased to four or five.

"Why is that?" we want to know. 70

"Because we do not admit them to the hospital, so they have learned not to come here."

"Why don't you admit them?"

"Because we would have nothing but AIDS here then. So we send them away."

"But I see that you have very few patients in bed."

"That is also true." 75

"Where do the AIDS patients go?"

"Some go to the clinic in Port-au-Prince or the general hospital in the city. Others go home to die or to the voodoo priest."

"Do the people with AIDS know what they have before they come here?"

"Oh, yes, they know very well, and they know there is nothing to be done for them."

Outside, the crowd of people is dispersing toward the gate. The clinic has 80 been canceled for the day. No one knows why. We are conducted to the office of the reigning American pastor. He is a tall, handsome Midwesterner with an ecclesiastical smile.

"It is voodoo that is the devil here." He warms to his subject. "It is a demonic religion, a cancer on Haiti. Voodoo is worse than AIDS. And it is one of the reasons for the epidemic. Did you know that in order for a man to become a *houngan* he must perform anal sodomy on another man? No, of course you didn't. And it doesn't stop there. The *houngans* tell the men that in order to appease the spirits they too must do the same thing. So you have ritualized homosexuality. That's what is spreading the AIDS." The pastor tells us of a nun who witnessed two acts of sodomy in a provincial hospital where she came upon a man sexually assaulting a houseboy and another man mounting a male patient in his bed.

"Fornication," he says. "It is Sodom and Gomorrah all over again, so what can you expect from these people?" Outside his office we are shown a cage of terrified, cowering monkeys to whom he coos affectionately. It is clear that he loves them. At the car, we shake hands.

"By the way," the pastor says, "what is your religion? Perhaps I am a kinsman?"

"While I am in Haiti," I tell him, "it will be voodoo or it will be nothing at all."

Abruptly, the smile breaks. It is as though a crack had suddenly appeared 85 in the face of an idol.

From the mission we go to the general hospital. In the heart of Port-au-Prince, it is the exact antithesis of the immaculate facility we have just left—filthy, crowded, hectic, and staffed entirely by young interns and residents. Though it is associated with a medical school, I do not see any members of the faculty. We are shown around by Jocelyne, a young intern in a scrub suit. Each bed in three large wards is occupied. On the floor about the beds, hunkered in the posture of the innocent poor, are family members of the patients. In the corridor that constitutes the emergency room, someone lies on a stretcher receiving an intravenous infusion. She is hardly more than a cadaver.

"Where are the doctors in charge?" I ask Jocelyne. She looks at me questioningly.

"We are in charge."

"I mean your teachers, the faculty."

"They do not come here." 90

"What is wrong with that woman?"

"She has had diarrhea for three months. Now she is dehydrated." I ask the woman to open her mouth. Her throat is covered with the white plaques of thrush, a fungus infection associated with AIDS.

"How many AIDS patients do you see here?"

"Three or four a day. We send them home. Sometimes the families abandon them, then we must admit them to the hospital. Every day, then, a relative comes to see if the patient has died. They want to take the body. That is important to them. But they know very well that AIDS is contagious and they are afraid to keep them at home. Even so, once or twice a week the truck comes to take away the bodies. Many are children. They are buried in mass graves."

"Where do the wealthy patients go?" 95

"There is a private hospital called Canapé Vert. Or else they go to Miami. Most of them, rich and poor, do not go to the hospital. Most are never diagnosed."

"How do you know these people have AIDS?"

"We don't know sometimes. The blood test is inaccurate. There are many false positives and false negatives. Fifteen percent of those with the disease have negative blood tests. We go by their infections—tuberculosis, diarrhea, fungi, herpes, skin rashes. It is not hard to tell."

"Do they know what they have?"

"Yes. They understand at once and they are prepared to die." 100

"Do the patients know how AIDS is transmitted?"

"They know, but they do not like to talk about it. It is taboo. Their memories do not seem to reach back to the true origins of their disaster. It is understandable, is it not?"

"Whatever you write, don't hurt us any more than we have already been hurt." It is a young Haitian journalist with whom I am drinking a rum punch. He means that any further linkage of AIDS and Haiti in the media would complete the economic destruction of the country. The damage was done early in the epidemic when the Centers for Disease Control in Atlanta added Haitians to the three other high-risk groups—hemophiliacs, intravenous drug users, and homosexual and bisexual men. In fact, Haitians are no more susceptible to AIDS than anyone else. Although the CDC removed Haitians from special scrutiny in 1985, the lucrative tourism on which so much of the country's economy was based was crippled. Along with tourism went much of the foreign business investment. Worst of all was the injury to the national pride. Suddenly Haiti was indicted as the source of AIDS in the western hemisphere.

What caused the misunderstanding was the discovery of a large number of Haitian men living in Miami with AIDS antibodies in their blood. They denied absolutely they were homosexuals. But the CDC investigators did not know that homosexuality is the strongest taboo in Haiti and that no man would ever admit to it. Bisexuality, however, is not uncommon. Many married men and heterosexually oriented males will occasionally seek out other men for sex. Further, many, if not most, Haitian men visit female prostitutes from time to time. It is not difficult to see that once the virus was set loose in Haiti, the spread would be swift through both genders.

Exactly how the virus of AIDS arrived is not known. Could it have been brought home by the Cuban soldiers stationed in Angola and thence to Haiti, about fifty miles away? Could it have been passed on by the thousands of Haitians living in exile in Zaire, who later returned home or immigrated to the United States? Could it have come from the American and Canadian homosexual tourists, and, yes, even some U.S. diplomats who have traveled to the island to have sex with impoverished Haitian men all too willing to sell themselves to feed their families? Throughout the international gay community Haiti was known as a good place to go for sex. 105

On a private tip from an official at the Ministry of Tourism, J-B and I drive to a town some fifty miles from Port-au-Prince. The hotel is owned by two Frenchmen who are out of the country, one of the staff tells us. He is a man of about thirty and clearly he is desperately ill. Tottering, short of breath, he shows us about the empty hotel. The furnishings are opulent and extreme—tiger skins on the wall, a live leopard in the garden, a bedroom containing a giant bathtub with gold faucets. Is it the heat of the day or the heat of my imagination that makes these walls echo with the painful cries of pederasty?

The hotel where we are staying is in Pétionville, the fashionable suburb of Port-au-Prince. It is the height of the season but there are no tourists, only a dozen or so French and American businessmen. The swimming pool is used once or twice a day by a single person. Otherwise, the water remains undisturbed until dusk, when the fruit bats come down to drink in midswoop. The hotel keeper is an American. He is eager to set me straight on Haiti.

"What did and should attract foreign investment is a combination of reliable weather, an honest and friendly populace, low wages, and multilingual managers."

"What spoiled it?"

"Political instability and a bad American press about AIDS." He pauses, then adds: "To which I hope you won't be contributing." 110

"What about just telling the truth?" I suggest.

"Look," he says, "there is no more danger of catching AIDS in Haiti than in New York or Santo Domingo. It is not where you are but what you do that counts." Agreeing, I ask if he had any idea that much of the tourism in Haiti during the past few decades was based on sex.

"No idea whatsoever. It was only recently that we discovered that that was the case."

"How is it that you hoteliers, restaurant owners and the Ministry of Tourism did not know what *tout*[1] Haiti knew?"

"Look. All I know is that this is a middle-class, family-oriented hotel. We don't allow guests to bring women, or for that matter men, into their rooms. If they did, we'd ask them to leave immediately." 115

At five a.m. the next day the telephone rings in my room. A Creole-accented male voice.

"Is the lady still with you, sir?"

"There is no lady here."

"In your room, sir, the lady I allowed to go up with a package?"

"There is no lady here, I tell you." 120

At seven a.m. I stop at the front desk. The clerk is a young man.

"Was it you who called my room at five o'clock?"

"Sorry," he says with a smile. "It was a mistake, sir. I meant to ring the room next door to yours." Still smiling, he holds up his shushing finger.

Next to Dr. Pape, director of the AIDS clinic, Bernard Liautaud, a dermatologist, is the most knowledgeable Haitian physician on the subject of the epidemic. Together, the two men have published a dozen articles on AIDS in international medical journals. In our meeting they present me with statistics:

- There are more than one thousand documented cases of AIDS in Haiti, and as many as one hundred thousand carriers of the virus.
- Eighty-seven percent of AIDS is now transmitted heterosexually. While it is true that the virus was introduced via the bisexual community, that route has decreased to 10 percent or less.
- Sixty percent of the wives or husbands of AIDS patients tested positive for the antibody.
- Fifty percent of the prostitutes tested in the Port-au-Prince area are infected.
- Eighty percent of the men with AIDS have had contact with prostitutes.
- The projected number of active cases in four years is ten thousand. (Since my last visit, the Haitian Medical Association broke its silence on the epidemic by warning that one million of the country's six million people could be carriers by 1992.)

The two doctors have more to tell. "The crossing over of the plague from the homosexual to the heterosexual community will follow in the United States within two years. This, despite the hesitation to say so by those who fear to sow panic among your population. In Haiti, because bisexuality is more common, 125

[1] *tout*: All.—Eds.

there was an early crossover into the general population. The trend, inevitably, is the same in the two countries."

"What is there to do, then?"

"Only education, just as in America. But here the Haitians reject the use of condoms. Only the men who are too sick to have sex are celibate."

"What is to be the end of it?"

"When enough heterosexuals of the middle and upper classes die, perhaps there will be the panic necessary for the people to change their sexual lifestyles."

This evening I leave Haiti. For two weeks I have fastened myself to this lovely fragile land like an ear pressed to the ground. It is a country to break a traveler's heart. It occurs to me that I have not seen a single jogger. Such a public expenditure of energy while everywhere else strength is ebbing—it would be obscene. In my final hours, I go to the Cathedral of Sainte Trinité, the inner walls of which are covered with murals by Haiti's most renowned artists. Here are all the familiar Bible stories depicted in naïveté and piety, and all in such an exuberance of color as to tax the capacity of the retina to receive it, as though all the vitality of Haiti had been turned to paint and brushed upon these walls. How to explain this efflorescence at a time when all else is lassitude and inertia? Perhaps one day the plague will be rendered in poetry, music, painting, but not now. Not now. 130

▪ QUESTIONS

Reading

1. Summarize the scene at the Copacabana. Which details are memorable? Why does Selzer spend so much time with Carmen, Mercedes, and Frasquita? Why are their attitudes toward AIDS so important?
2. Selzer writes at great length about his visit to the AIDS clinic directed by Dr. Jean William Pape. What does Selzer learn from observing patients at this clinic? What does Selzer learn about AIDS from the doctor at work?
3. Look at the various scenes and vignettes Selzer offers his readers. How does he connect these different scenes? How does this structure succeed in presenting his reflections?

Exploratory Writing

1. How might Selzer's research experience at the Copacabana have been different if he were a woman, or a man raised and educated in Haiti, rather than the United States? Consider the ways that Carmen, Mercedes, and Frasquita approach him and respond to his questions. How might his commentary have been different if he, himself, were infected with HIV? In your opinion, how balanced is the report that Selzer offers?
2. Collaborating in small groups, take the "How Much Do You Know about HIV/AIDS?" quiz (**www.pbs.org/wgbh/pages/frontline/aids/etc/quiz.html**) on the *Frontline*

Web site. Using the links contained in the answers, choose a topic in the field of HIV/AIDS education, prevention, and treatment, and prepare a presentation arguing a policy position. (For example, "The U.S. Should Provide Federal Funding for Needle Exchange" or "HIV Testing Should Be a Standard Part of Medical Care for Patients Age 13–64.") Use at least four key points to make your argument persuasive.

3. A young Haitian journalist tells Selzer, "Whatever you write, don't hurt us any more than we have already been hurt" (paragraph 103). What is the significance of this request? After reading Selzer's essay, do you think Selzer has honored this request?

Making Connections

1. In "A Delicate Operation," Richard Selby (p. 529) focuses on a specific medical procedure and one patient, while Selzer takes on HIV/AIDS, multiple patients, and a foreign country. Find sections of both pieces where both writers describe doctors' reactions to patients (for instance, do they judge their patients' behaviors? Do they show compassion?) In groups, discuss what these descriptions say about how medical professionals need to behave to do their work. Write up ten rules for medical professionals to follow.

Essay Writing

1. What have you learned about the politics of AIDS from reading Selzer's essay? Write an essay reflecting on this essay.

STUDENT ESSAY

"The Moral Meaning of a Pause"

Ethics Committees and the Cloning Debate

Lindsay Gellman

Lindsay Gellman's essay "The Moral Meaning of a Pause" was written for a class called Writing and Evolution, a seminar drawing on topics relating to evolutionary science. Gellman explores the ethical reactions and public discourse surrounding the cloning of Dolly the sheep. She focuses on the moment during which legislators and scientists paused their developments, allowing the public to either accept or reject the implications of such a significant scientific discovery. As you read the essay, pay attention to the way Gellman combines science and legal issues to make a larger point about how a society thinks about and revises its ethical standards. Notice her use of APA style to document her sources. Consider the way she applies analysis, the same way she might apply it while writing about literature, politics, or any other discipline. To read more about writing across the disciplines, refer to Part One: An Introduction to Writing.

The initial responses of the U.S. government and the public to the cloning of Dolly the sheep in 1997 suggested that an absolutist moral judgment would soon be made regarding the related issue of human cloning. In January 1997, the geneticist Ian Wilmut published the results of his successful cloning of a sheep, the first mammal to be cloned from an adult somatic cell. Public discourse was amplified by the media, and soon stirred up hysteria surrounding the possibility of human cloning as the logical extension to the successful cloning of other mammals. A March 1997 article in *Nature* called the cloning of Dolly "an irreversible development of breathtaking implications," while a *New York Times* article of the preceding month bore the headline "Cloning for Good or Evil." A *Time* magazine headline asked: "Will We Follow the Sheep?" In a March 4, 1997, speech, then-President Bill Clinton said that because this recent development in cloning "carries burdens as well as benefits," he had "asked our National Bioethics Advisory Commission . . . to conduct a thorough review of the legal and the ethical issues raised by this new cloning discovery and to recommend possible actions to prevent its abuse." Clinton requested that the commission report back to him in 90 days. He said that the results of the commission's investigation into the "profound ethical implications of the latest advances" would be crucial to gaining a "fuller understanding of this technology." By ordering that the commission gather information so that its members would be able to effectively evaluate the ethics of human cloning technology, Clinton made clear that he expected the commission to make an objective moral judgment on the issue.

However, it can be argued that in some cases ethics committees serve primarily to pause the funding process for scientific developments until the public moral framework shifts to accommodate a previously controversial advancement. Butler and Wadman quote Steve Jones, professor of genetics at University College London, as saying: "'The public is not frightened of progress but of rapid progress' . . . the job of ethics committees . . . is to act as a 'brake,' slowing the application of technology to a speed acceptable to the public" (Butler & Wadman, 1997). In the same vein, Gilbert Meilaender encourages individuals to contemplate "the moral meaning of a pause" in his February 2009 article "Progress without Pause." A close examination of U.S. federal legislation, United Nations declarations, and media coverage regarding human cloning in the wake of Dolly reveals that, in practice, ethics committees have delayed the making of moral decisions rather than issued such judgments on human cloning.

Although government officials may depend on ethics committees for definitive moral judgments and expect them to make objective evaluations, the framework in which the officials, perhaps unintentionally, allow the committees to operate reinforces the notion of a time gap as an alternative to, rather than a means of, achieving a moral decision. For example, by creating a timetable that involved a 90-day review period, the Clinton administration emphasized the power of the pause itself, perhaps above any ethical conclusions that might have been drawn during the evaluation process. In addition to this time delay in reaching a decision on federal funding, Clinton requested a voluntary moratorium on even the private application of cloning technologies. In his remarks on human cloning, Clinton (1997) said:

> Science often moves faster than our ability to understand its implications. That is why we have a responsibility to move with caution and care to harness the powerful forces of science and technology. . . . I'm asking for a voluntary moratorium on the cloning of human beings until our Bioethics Advisory Commission and our entire nation have had a real chance to understand and debate the profound ethical implications of the latest advances.

Clinton's words represent the reinforcement of a "pause-for-the-sake-of-pausing" framework in that he emphasizes the rapid pace of science and the need to slow this pace so that the public can come to terms with recent developments. His statement implies that understanding a new technology is equivalent to accepting it as morally permissible; he focuses on pausing for comprehension and nationwide debate rather than for the issuing of an ultimate decision. By specifically mentioning his administration's intention to harness scientific power, Clinton seems to indicate that the U.S. government is sympathetic to most new technological developments, and that cloning, like all science we come to understand, will inevitably become acceptable.

The U.S. federal pause widened into a significant time gap as the United Nations sought to pass international laws prohibiting human cloning, while individual countries continued to disagree over whether to ban all forms of human cloning or to allow research in therapeutic cloning. A 2004 *Economist* article comments on the time lag between scientific development and potential funding created by this disagreement:

> The United Nations has spent the past three years trying to draft an international convention banning human cloning, but the only thing upon which the UN General Assembly has managed to agree is to discuss the issue again this year. . . . In the meantime, countries should not use delays at the UN as an excuse to avoid passing their own national legislation ("Pregnant Pause," paragraphs 4–8).

The *Economist*'s comment underscores the seemingly excessive amount of time the United Nations, and in turn the legislative bodies of individual countries, allowed for debate on human cloning legislation. Furthermore, the article taps into the public frustration with the disproportionately low number of decisions reached for the time spent.

The United Nations, however, appeared to reach a decision on the issue in August 2005. While it can be argued that the decision, released as the United Nations Declaration on Human Cloning, represents a definitive moral judgment on the issue of human cloning, the document instead leaves the door open for further debate on the issue. The majority opinion, a ban on all forms of human cloning, was decided as the result of a vote in which 84 nations were in favor of the ban, 34 were against it, and 37 abstained. The press release announcing the decision explains this lack of unanimity as due to fundamental disagreement over the morality of therapeutic cloning. The press release notes: "The representative of Mexico . . . said that those negotiating the Declaration had had to take into account uncertainty over new scientific advances, as well as its ethical, cultural and religious implications. . . . Regretfully, it had not been possible to achieve a consensus." Because of the high level of dissent among diplomats, as well as the discussion of opposing viewpoints within the press release announcing the decision, it seems as though this United Nations Declaration represents the perpetuation of, rather than an end to, the pause in the cloning debate. 5

This delay in U.S. and international decisions regarding research funding suggests that funding for scientific developments depends on the ability of government executives—and therefore of the public who elects them—to become comfortable with a new idea. In March 2009, President Barack Obama issued an executive order lifting the heavy restrictions on embryonic stem cell funding put in place by former President George W. Bush. The order urged Congress to increase funding to research on new stem cell lines in the hopes of treating and curing Parkinson's disease, diabetes, and heart disease, among other medical conditions (Stolberg, 2009). This goal is extremely similar to that of therapeutic cloning, which would use cloned embryos as a source of stem cells. Although President Obama denounced human cloning in his remarks about the executive order, his request for federal embryonic stem cell funding represents a decisive step toward the acceptance of human-cell-based genetic technologies that drew widespread skepticism and criticism in the initial cloning debate.

Indeed, the recent history of the cloning debate suggests not only that government executives have warmed up to the idea of cloning, but so too have the general public and the overall tone of media coverage. For example, cloning was received by the media as a morally acceptable procedure, although one that is perhaps governed by strange motivations, when it was applied to man's best friend in June 2008. At that time, BioArts International, a genetic technology company, held an essay contest for dog owners; the winner had the opportunity to have his or her dog cloned for free, thus prolonging the life of the beloved dog's genetic characteristics, if not that of the original dog ("Odd News," 2008). BioArts typically offers cloning services in the $100,000 price range, but because it was overwhelmed by demand from "passionate dog owners who are upset that they cannot afford to participate," the company decided to give away one procedure. The high demand for dog cloning, combined with the outpouring of newspaper articles publicizing both the contest and these dog owners who pay for cloning, is a testament to the way in which acceptance of cloning seeped into the public moral framework in the years between Dolly's cloning and the *Economist*'s call to action. Instead of echoing the anxious tone of 1997 article headlines, CNN.com's headline about owners of a cloned dog gushed: "Couple loves cloned best friend." This dramatic shift in tone, taken as one measure of the public response to cloning, represents a social trend in increased habituation to this technology.

Articles looking back on the cloning debate imply that, in retrospect, the expansion of the commercial cloning industry, and thus of the tolerance of cloning, was inevitable. The U.K.'s *Times Online* reported in August 2008 that five clones were created from the pit bull terrier Booger, who saved his owner's life when she was attacked by another dog (Lewis). The article noted: "The cloning of Booger [realizes] a commercial dream that began more than ten years ago." This choice of language frames the decade-long development of a pet cloning industry as the logical extension of the cloning of Dolly, a conclusion completely at odds with the generally adverse public reactions cloning incited in 1997. Because—as the *Economist* article laments—no convincing legislative or definitive moral decisions regarding human cloning were made during this time span, the increased public acceptance of issues related to human cloning can be viewed as mainly the result of the eleven-year pause.

Although critics of human cloning make a clear ethical distinction between the cloning of nonhuman animals and that of human beings, the public's moral shift toward accepting human cloning is rendered plain by the motivation driving many of the dog owners interested in cloning their pets: the pet owner feels that his or her dog possesses particularly heroic or anthropomorphic qualities. For example, many pet owners, particularly those devoted enough to pay large sums to have their original pets cloned, regard their dogs with a respect typically reserved for other human beings. Edgar and Nina Otto, who paid $155,000 to have their late dog Sir Lancelot cloned in January 2009, said that they made their decision mainly because of the dog's human-like personality traits: "Sir Lancelot was the most human of any dog we've ever had" (BioArts International, 2009). This industry for the cloning of beloved pets who remind their owners of human beings was rapidly developing as the United Nations, as well as the legislatures of individual countries, squabbled over the ethics of cloning, thus suggesting not only that many people had become accustomed to the technology of cloning during the time lag, but that they might soon feel comfortable with cloning human beings.

Like their entrepreneurial counterparts, many scientists are also sensitive to the ethical climate surrounding their research, and attempt to gauge the opportune time to debut their findings in order to receive a favorable impression from government officials and the public. For example, Derek Burke, a microbiologist interested in research on cloning, said: "We should not move on [research into] human cloning; society is not ready for it" (Butler & Wadman, 1997). The words of scientists such as Burke suggest that timing seems to carry as much weight as, if not more than, any moral analysis actually taking place within bioethics committees. The pause itself contributes significantly to the manner in which the ethical problem is resolved: either the issue remains unacceptable despite the pause, or the public becomes accustomed to the issue at hand. The latter case exemplifies the philosophy of moral relativism, which, according to contemporary philosopher Simon Blackburn (2001), states that there is no absolute or objective morality, and that instead the moral intuitions we share happen to be arbitrary results of our evolutionary development, and are therefore subject to debate and criticism (p. 19). If a bioethics committee functions primarily to stall for time, it fails to meet the standard expectation of society that it will synthesize current knowledge about a subject and draw an ethical conclusion, rather than wait for the public voice to fill the void. More disturbingly, there are some notions we should never get used to, and others we must accept quickly before it is too late—the typical committee pause allows for failure on both counts. The same energy with which we question the validity of our morals must be applied to reevaluating both the "moral meaning of a pause" and the role of bioethics committees in national and international decisions. 10

References

BioArts International. (2009). First commercially cloned dog delivered to Florida family. *BioArts.* Retrieved from www.bioarts.com

Blackburn, S. (2001). *Being good: A short introduction to ethics.* New York, NY: Oxford University Press.

Butler, D., & Wadman, M. (1997, March 6). Calls for cloning ban sell science short. *Nature, 386*(6620), 8–9.

Clinton, W. (1997, March 4). *Remarks by the president on cloning.* Address from the Oval Office, Washington, DC. Retrieved from http://clinton6.nara.gov/1997/03/1997-03-04-remarks-by-president-on-cloning.html

Cloning for good or evil. (1997, Feb 27). *New York Times.* Retrieved from www.nytimes.com

Lewis, L. (2008, August 6). Puppies of hero pit bull Booger are world's first commercial clones. *Times Online.* Retrieved from www.timesonline.co.uk

Meilaender, G. (2009, February 1). Progress without pause. *First Things: A Monthly Journal of Religion and Public Life.* Retrieved from http://www.firstthings.com/article/2009/01/003-progress-without-pause-29

Odd news: company offers dog clone to contest winner. (2008, June 23). *UPI.* Retrieved from www.upi.com

Pregnant pause. (2004, Jan 22). *The Economist.* Retrieved from www.economist.com

Stolberg, S. (2009, March 9). Obama lifts Bush's strict limits on stem cell research. *New York Times.* Retrieved from www.nytimes.com

Thompson, D., & Kluge, J. (1997, March 10). Will we follow the sheep? *Time.* Retrieved from www.time.com

United Nations. (2005). *General Assembly adopts United Nations Declaration on Human Cloning by vote of 84-34-37.* (Press Release GA/10333). Retrieved from http://www.un.org/News/Press/docs/2005/ga10333.doc.htm

Wilmut, I., Schnieke, A.E., McWhir, J., Kind, A.J., & Campbell, K. H. (1997, February 27). Viable offspring derived from fetal and adult mammalian cells. *Nature, 385*(6619), 810–813.

▪ QUESTIONS

Reading

1. Gellman uses a quotation — "the moral meaning of a pause" — in her title. What is the source for the quotation? What function does it serve in the title? Is the strategy effective? Why or why not?
2. Gellman quotes a number of sources in her opening paragraph, including articles from scientific journals and popular magazines as well as a speech by Bill Clinton. What is her motive for quoting so much so early in her essay? What rhetorical purposes does the strategy serve?
3. Circle or highlight the signal phrases Gellman uses to introduce her quotations, paying particular attention to the verbs she uses. In a number of cases she uses the verb "said." Choose one of these instances and change the verb to one of the following: *claimed, denied, boasted, discovered, elaborated,* or a verb of your choice. How does the meaning of the sentence change with the new verb? What does it imply about the writer's stance in relation to her source?

Exploratory Writing

1. Put yourself in the position of a professor meeting with Gellman to discuss her essay. Write a short dialogue between this professor and Gellman, focusing on the relationship between her thesis and her evidence. Be sure you identify the thesis and at least two significant forms of evidence. Be sure you address the following questions: Is the thesis clear? Is it compelling? Does it seem true, without being obvious? Is the evidence pertinent? Does it convince you that the argument is on target?
2. Gellman suggests that people's attitudes about cloning have softened since 1997, when Dolly the sheep was first cloned. Interview five people you know about their attitudes about cloning and write a reflection on whether their answers seem to support or refute Gellman's argument.

Making Connections

1. In "The Moral Instinct" (p. 458), Steven Pinker offers psychological, genetic, and philosophical explanations for morality. Choose one of his explanations and reflect on whether or not it seems to explain the moral attitudes about cloning Gellman writes about in her essay.

Essay Writing

1. Gellman chose a controversial scientific development, cloning, and did research into changing social attitudes about it. Choose another recent scientific development and conduct some research on social responses to it. Like Gellman, you should use a combination of sources — for example, articles in scientific journals, editorials, and think pieces from the popular press, speeches, and interviews. Based on these sources, make an argument about social attitudes to the scientific development you've chosen.

Part 5
Casebooks

How Is the Internet Changing Who We Are?

The Internet marks a new information age—akin to the invention of writing (about six thousand years ago), the development of movable type for printing (six or eleven centuries ago, depending on whether you're talking about China or Europe), and the advent of mass printing (three centuries ago). In less than two decades, the Internet has changed how we socialize, how we learn, and how we work, how we communicate. Arguably, we express—or even become—ourselves through socializing, learning, working, and communicating. To what degree are online information technologies shaping people's identities? How is Facebook changing the nature of friendship? How are blogs transforming news? How is Twitter reshaping the circulation of knowledge? What does the existence of Google or other search engines do to traditional classrooms?

This casebook frames the digital revolution in relation to the information technologies that have shaped other eras. Each of the readings in this casebook explores broad questions about these technologies or the impact of particular technologies on the lives and identities of the people who use them. The casebook begins with James Gleick's "Meme Pool" (p. 555), which explains Richard Dawkins's theory of memes and suggests that information evolves like organisms. Gleick's essay is a provocative frame for the rest of the casebook, offering a theory to explain how our ideas about the tools we use are generated and circulated. David Friedman's "From 1890: The First Text Messages" (p. 566) reports on the shorthand used by telegraph operators, a precursor to today's text messages, to provide some historical context and remind us revolutionary communication technologies are nothing new. In "Internet Rights and Wrongs: Choices & Challenges in a Networked World" (p. 570), Hillary Rodham Clinton argues for the importance for a free and open Internet worldwide. Clive Thompson uses "I'm So Totally, Digitally, Close to You: The Brave New World of Digital Intimacy" (p. 583) to report on the intimacy—or illusion of it—that exists in online communities. Jeffrey Rosen, in "The End of Forgetting" (p. 594), explains how the relentless online documenting of daily life haunts people offline, making it difficult to leave the past behind. In "Is Google Making Us Stupid?" (p. 609), Nicholas Carr argues that we may be offloading our intelligence to the vast archives of knowledge accessible through search engines. Finally, in "Connectivity and Its Discontents" (p. 619), Sherry Turkle argues that digital technologies have reshaped our lives permanently and therefore it's imperative that we engage in critical and reflective conversations about the pros and cons of what they mean for our lives.

The essays in this casebook are the product of careful research and attention to the rhetorical tools that will reach and persuade audiences. Because the development of information technologies advances so rapidly, their authors are generally forthright about the fact that the future is uncertain. Nevertheless, they are sifting through the proliferation of knowledge to make sense of this latest information revolution as it's happening.

You will do the same when you conduct research on this newest information age, exploring the questions raised in these essays and following up with your own investigation. How has the circulation of information changed in the past two decades? How do current technologies compare with those of other eras? What are the promises and pitfalls of the lives we lead online? How are our personal identities shaped by the time we spend interacting with people, texts, and platforms on the Web? What new insights about life in the digital age are being proposed by writers who reflect on it, on or offline? What is it too early to know or understand? These are the questions that should guide you in your own research project on questions about how the Internet may be changing who we are, can be, or will be.

EXPLAINING

Meme Pool

James Gleick

James Gleick (b. 1954) has written widely on science and technology issues. His first book, *Chaos: Making a New Science* (1987), introduced chaos theory and the term "the butterfly effect" to the public and was a finalist for the National Book Award and the Pulitzer Prize. Since then, he has authored several award-winning best-sellers, including *Faster: The Acceleration of Just about Everything* (1999), *What Just Happened: A Chronicle from the Electronic Frontier* (2002), and the biographies *Genius: The Life and Science of Richard Feynman* (1992) and *Isaac Newton* (2003). After graduating from Harvard, Gleick began working as a newspaper reporter in 1976, co-founding an independent paper in Minneapolis and writing for the *New York Times*. In 1993, he co-founded The Pipeline, one of the earliest Internet service providers in the United States. This essay, which draws parallels between how organisms and information evolve, was originally published in Gleick's 2011 book, *The Information*.

> When I muse about memes, I often find myself picturing an ephemeral flickering pattern of sparks leaping from brain to brain, screaming "Me, me!"
>
> —Douglas Hofstadter (1983)

"Now through the very universality of its structures, starting with the code, the biosphere looks like the product of a unique event," Jacques Monod wrote in 1970. "The universe was not pregnant with life, nor the biosphere with man. Our number came up in the Monte Carlo game. Is it any wonder if, like a person who has just made a million at the casino, we feel a little strange and a little unreal?"

Monod, the Parisian biologist who shared the Nobel Prize for working out the role of messenger RNA in the transfer of genetic information, was not alone in thinking of the biosphere as more than a notional place: an entity, composed of all the earth's life-forms, simple and complex, teeming with information, replicating and evolving, coding from one level of abstraction to the next. This view of life was more abstract—more mathematical—than anything Darwin had imagined, but he would have recognized its basic principles. Natural selection directs the whole show. Now biologists, having absorbed the methods and vocabulary of communications science, went further to make their own contributions to the understanding of information itself. Monod proposed an analogy: Just as the biosphere stands above the world of nonliving matter, so an "abstract kingdom" rises above the biosphere. The denizens of this kingdom? Ideas.

> Ideas have retained some of the properties of organisms. Like them, they tend to perpetuate their structure and to breed; they too can fuse, recombine,

> segregate their content; indeed they too can evolve, and in this evolution selection must surely play an important role.

Ideas have "spreading power," he noted—"infectivity, as it were"—and some more than others. An example of an infectious idea might be a religious ideology that gains sway over a large group of people. The American neurophysiologist Roger Sperry had put forward a similar notion several years earlier, arguing that ideas are "just as real" as the neurons they inhabit. Ideas have power, he said.

> Ideas cause ideas and help evolve new ideas. They interact with each other and with other mental forces in the same brain, in neighboring brains, and thanks to global communication, in far distant, foreign brains. And they also interact with the external surroundings to produce in toto a burstwise advance in evolution that is far beyond anything to hit the evolutionary scene yet. . . .

Monod added, "I shall not hazard a theory of the selection of ideas." No need. Others were willing.

Richard Dawkins made his own connection between the evolution of genes and the evolution of ideas. His essential actor was the replicator, and it scarcely mattered whether replicators were made of nucleic acid. His rule is "All life evolves by the differential survival of replicating entities." Wherever there is life, there must be replicators. Perhaps on other worlds replicators could arise in a silicon-based chemistry—or in no chemistry at all.

What would it mean for a replicator to exist without chemistry? "I think that a new kind of replicator has recently emerged on this planet," he proclaimed at the end of his first book, in 1976. "It is staring us in the face. It is still in its infancy, still drifting clumsily about in its primeval soup, but already it is achieving evolutionary change at a rate that leaves the old gene panting far behind." That "soup" is human culture; the vector of transmission is language; and the spawning ground is the brain.

For this bodiless replicator itself, Dawkins proposed a name. He called it the *meme*, and it became his most memorable invention, far more influential than his selfish genes or his later proselytizing against religiosity. "Memes propagate themselves in the meme pool by leaping from brain to brain via a process which, in the broad sense, can be called imitation," he wrote. They compete with one another for limited resources: brain time or bandwidth. They compete most of all for *attention*. For example: 5

Ideas. Whether an idea arises uniquely or reappears many times, it may thrive in the meme pool or it may dwindle and vanish. The belief in God is an example Dawkins offers—an ancient idea, replicating itself not just in words but in music and art. The belief that the earth orbits the sun is no less a meme, competing with others for survival. (Truth may be a helpful quality for a meme, but it is only one among many.)

Tunes. This tune

has spread for centuries across several continents. This one

a notorious though shorter-lived invader of brains, overran an immense population many times faster.

Catchphrases. One text snippet, "What hath God wrought?" appeared early and spread rapidly in more than one medium. Another, "Read my lips," charted a peculiar path through late twentieth-century America. "Survival of the fittest" is a meme that, like other memes, mutates wildly ("survival of the fattest"; "survival of the sickest"; "survival of the fakest"; "survival of the twittest" . . .).

Images. In Isaac Newton's lifetime, no more than a few thousand people had any idea what he looked like, though he was one of England's most famous men, yet now millions of people have quite a clear idea—based on replicas of copies of rather poorly painted portraits. Even more pervasive and indelible are the smile of *Mona Lisa, The Scream* of Edvard Munch, and the silhouettes of various fictional extraterrestrials. These are memes, living a life of their own, independent of any physical reality. "This may not be what George Washington looked like then," a tour guide was overheard saying of the Gilbert Stuart painting at the Metropolitan Museum of Art, "but this is what he looks like now." Exactly.

Memes emerge in brains and travel outward, establishing beachheads on paper and celluloid and silicon and anywhere else information can go. They are not to be thought of as elementary particles but as organisms. The number three is not a meme; nor is the color blue, nor any simple thought, any more than a single nucleotide can be a gene. Memes are complex units, distinct and memorable—units with staying power. Also, an object is not a meme. The hula hoop is not a meme; it is made of plastic, not of bits. When this species of toy spread worldwide in a mad epidemic in 1958, it was the product, the physical manifestation of a meme, or memes: the craving for hula hoops; the swaying, swinging, twirling skill set of hula-hooping. The hula hoop itself is a meme vehicle. So, for that matter, is each human hula hooper—a strikingly effective meme vehicle, in the sense neatly explained by the philosopher Daniel Dennett: "A wagon with spoked wheels carries not only grain or freight from place to place; it carries the brilliant idea of a wagon with spoked wheels from mind to mind." Hula hoopers did that for the hula hoop's memes—and in 1958 they found a new transmission vector, broadcast television, sending its messages immeasurably faster and farther than any wagon. The moving image of 10 the hula hooper seduced new minds by hundreds, and then by thousands, and then by millions. The meme is not the dancer but the dance.

We are their vehicles and their enablers. For most of our biological history they existed fleetingly; their main mode of transmission was the one called "word of mouth." Lately, however, they have managed to adhere in solid substance: clay tablets, cave walls, paper sheets. They achieve longevity through our pens and printing presses, magnetic tapes and optical disks. They spread via broadcast towers and digital networks. Memes may be stories, recipes, skills, legends, and fashions. We copy them, one person at a time. Alternatively, in Dawkins's meme-centered perspective, they copy themselves. At first some of Dawkins's readers wondered how literally to take that. Did he mean to give memes anthropomorphic desires, intentions, and goals? It was the selfish gene all over again. (Typical salvo: "Genes cannot be selfish or unselfish, any more than atoms can be jealous, elephants abstract, or biscuits teleological." Typical rebuttal: a reminder that *selfishness* is defined by the geneticist as the tendency to increase one's chances of survival relative to its competitors.)

Dawkins's way of speaking was not meant to suggest that memes are conscious actors, only that they are entities with interests that can be furthered by natural selection. Their interests are not our interests. "A meme," Dennett says, "is an information packet with attitude." When we speak of *fighting for a principle* or *dying for an idea*, we may be more literal than we know. "To die for an idea; it is unquestionably noble," H. L. Mencken wrote. "But how much nobler it would be if men died for ideas that were true!"

Tinker, tailor, soldier, sailor . . . Rhyme and rhythm help people remember bits of text. Or: rhyme and rhythm help bits of text get remembered. Rhyme and rhythm are qualities that aid a meme's survival, just as strength and speed aid an animal's. Patterned language has an evolutionary advantage. Rhyme, rhythm, and reason—for reason, too, is a form of pattern. *I was promised on a time to have reason for my rhyme; from that time unto this season, I received nor rhyme nor reason.*

Like genes, memes have effects on the wide world beyond themselves: phenotypic effects. In some cases (the meme for making fire; for wearing clothes; for the resurrection of Jesus) the effects can be powerful indeed. As they broadcast their influence on the world, memes thus influence the conditions affecting their own chances of survival. The meme or memes composing Morse code had strong positive feedback effects. "I believe that, given the right conditions, replicators automatically band together to create systems, or machines, that carry them around and work to favour their continued replication," wrote Dawkins. Some memes have evident benefits for their human hosts ("look before you leap," knowledge of CPR, belief in hand washing before cooking), but memetic success and genetic success are not the same. Memes can replicate with impressive virulence while leaving swaths of collateral damage—patent medicines and psychic surgery, astrology and satanism, racist myths, superstitions, and (a special case) computer viruses. In a way, these are the most interesting—the memes that thrive to their hosts' detriment, such as the idea that suicide bombers will find their reward in heaven.

When Dawkins first floated the *meme* meme, Nicholas Humphrey, an evolutionary psychologist, said immediately that these entities should be considered "living structures, not just metaphorically but technically": 15

> When you plant a fertile meme in my mind you literally parasitize my brain, turning it into a vehicle for the meme's propagation in just the way that a virus may parasitize the genetic mechanism of a host cell. And this isn't just a way of talking—the meme for, say, "belief in life after death" is actually realized physically, millions of times over, as a structure in the nervous systems of individual men the world over.

Most early readers of *The Selfish Gene* passed over memes as a fanciful afterthought, but the pioneering ethologist W. D. Hamilton, reviewing the book for *Science*, ventured this prediction:

> Hard as this term may be to delimit—it surely must be harder than gene, which is bad enough—I suspect that it will soon be in common use by biologists and, one hopes, by philosophers, linguists, and others as well and that it may become absorbed as far as the word "gene" has been into everyday speech.

Memes could travel wordlessly even before language was born. Plain mimicry is enough to replicate knowledge—how to chip an arrowhead or start a fire. Among animals, chimpanzees and gorillas are known to acquire behaviors by imitation. Some species of songbirds *learn* their songs, or at least song variants, after hearing them from neighboring birds (or, more recently, from ornithologists with audio players). Birds develop song repertoires and song dialects—in short, they exhibit a birdsong *culture* that predates human culture by eons. These special cases notwithstanding, for most of human history memes and language have gone hand in glove. (Clichés are memes.) Language serves as culture's first catalyst. It supersedes mere imitation, spreading knowledge by abstraction and encoding.

Perhaps the analogy with disease was inevitable. Before anyone understood anything of epidemiology, its language was applied to species of information. An emotion can be *infectious*, a tune *catchy*, a habit *contagious*. "From look to look, contagious through the crowd / The panic runs," wrote the poet James Thomson in 1730. Lust, likewise, according to Milton: "Eve, whose eye darted contagious fire." But only in the new millennium, in the time of global electronic transmission, has the identification become second nature. Ours is the age of virality: viral education, viral marketing, viral e-mail and video and networking. Researchers studying the Internet itself as a medium— crowdsourcing, collective attention, social networking, and resource allocation— employ not only the language but also the mathematical principles of epidemiology.

One of the first to use the terms *viral text* and *viral sentences* seems to have been a reader of Dawkins named Stephen Walton of New York City, corresponding in 1981 with Douglas Hofstadter. Thinking logically—perhaps in the mode of a computer—Walton proposed simple self-replicating sentences along the lines of "Say me!" "Copy me!" and "If you copy me, I'll grant you three wishes!" Hofstadter, then a columnist for *Scientific American*, found the term *viral text* itself to be even catchier.

> Well, now, Walton's own viral text, as you can see here before your eyes, has managed to commandeer the facilities of a very powerful host—an entire magazine and printing press and distribution service. It has leapt aboard and is now—even as you read this viral sentence—propagating itself madly throughout the ideosphere!

(In the early 1980s, a magazine with a print circulation of 700,000 still seemed like a powerful communications platform.) Hofstadter gaily declared himself infected by the *meme* meme.

One source of resistance—or at least unease—was the shoving of us humans toward the wings. It was bad enough to say that a person is merely a gene's way of making more genes. Now humans are to be considered as vehicles for the propagation of memes, too. No one likes to be called a puppet. Dennett summed up the problem this way: "I don't know about you, but I am not initially attracted by the idea of my brain as a sort of dung heap in which the larvae of other people's ideas renew themselves, before sending out copies of themselves in an informational diaspora. . . . Who's in charge, according to this vision—we or our memes?"

He answered his own question by reminding us that, like it or not, we are seldom "in charge" of our own minds. He might have quoted Freud; instead he quoted Mozart (or so he thought):

> In the night when I cannot sleep, thoughts crowd into my mind. . . . Whence and how do they come? I do not know and I have nothing to do with it. Those which please me I keep in my head and hum them.

Later Dennett was informed that this well-known quotation was not Mozart's after all. It had taken on a life of its own; it was a fairly successful meme.

For anyone taken with the idea of memes, the landscape was changing faster than Dawkins had imagined possible in 1976, when he wrote, "The computers in which memes live are human brains." By 1989, the time of the second edition of *The Selfish Gene*, having become an adept programmer himself, he had to amend that: "It was obviously predictable that manufactured electronic computers, too, would eventually play host to self-replicating patterns of information." Information was passing from one computer to another "when their owners pass floppy disks around," and he could see another phenomenon on the near horizon: computers connected in networks. "Many of them," he wrote, "are literally wired up together in electronic mail exchange. . . . It is a perfect milieu for self-replicating programs to flourish." Indeed, the Internet was in its birth throes. Not only did it provide memes with a nutrient-rich 20 culture medium; it also gave wings to the *idea* of memes. *Meme* itself quickly became an Internet buzzword. Awareness of memes fostered their spread.

A notorious example of a meme that could not have emerged in pre-Internet culture was the phrase "jumped the shark." Loopy self-reference characterized every phase of its existence. To jump the shark means to pass a peak of quality or popularity and begin an irreversible decline. The phrase was thought to have been used first in 1985 by a college student named Sean J. Connolly, in reference to a certain television series. The origin of the phrase requires a certain amount of explanation without which it could not have been initially understood. Perhaps for that reason, there is no recorded usage until 1997, when Connolly's roommate, Jon Hein, registered the domain name jumptheshark.com and created a Web site devoted to its promotion. The Web site soon featured a list of frequently asked questions:

> Q. Did "jump the shark" originate from this Web site, or did you create the site to capitalize on the phrase?
>
> A. This site went up December 24, 1997 and gave birth to the phrase "jump the shark." As the site continues to grow in popularity, the term has become more commonplace. The site is the chicken, the egg, and now a Catch-22.

It spread to more traditional media in the next year; Maureen Dowd devoted a column to explaining it in the *New York Times* in 2001; in 2003 the same newspaper's "On Language" columnist, William Safire, called it "the popular culture's phrase of the year"; soon after that, people were using the phrase in speech and in print without self-consciousness—no quotation marks or explanation—and eventually, inevitably, various cultural observers asked, "Has 'jump the shark' jumped the shark?" ("Granted, Jump the Shark is a brilliant cultural concept. . . . But now the damn thing is everywhere.") Like any good meme, it spawned mutations. The "jumping the shark" entry in *Wikipedia* advised in 2009, "See also: jumping the couch; nuking the fridge."

Is this science? In his 1983 column, Hofstadter proposed the obvious memetic label for such a discipline: *memetics*. The study of memes has attracted researchers from fields as far apart as computer science and microbiology. In bioinformatics, chain letters are an object of study. They are memes; they have evolutionary histories. The very purpose of a chain letter is replication; whatever else a chain letter may say, it embodies one message: *Copy me.* One student of chain-letter evolution, Daniel W. VanArsdale, listed many variants, in chain letters and even earlier texts: "Make seven copies of it exactly as it is written" [1902]; "Copy this in full and send to nine friends" [1923]; "And if any man shall take away from the words of the book of this prophecy, God shall take away his part out of the book of life" [Revelation 22:19]. Chain letters flourished with the help of a new nineteenth-century technology: "carbonic paper," sandwiched between sheets of writing paper in stacks. Then carbon paper made a symbiotic partnership with another technology, the typewriter. Viral outbreaks of chain letters occurred all through the early twentieth century.

"An unusual chain-letter reached Quincy during the latter part of 1933," wrote a local Illinois historian. "So rapidly did the chain-letter fad develop symptoms of mass hysteria and spread throughout the United States, that by 1935–1936 the Post Office Department, as well as agencies of public opinion, had to take a hand in suppressing the movement." He provided a sample—a meme motivating its human carriers with promises and threats:

> We trust in God. He supplies our needs.
> Mrs. F. Streuzel . . . . Mich.
> Mrs. A. Ford . . . . Chicago, Ill.
> Mrs. K. Adkins . . . . Chicago, Ill.
> etc.
>
> Copy the above names, omitting the first. Add your name last. Mail it to five persons who you wish prosperity to. The chain was started by an American Colonel and must be mailed 24 hours after receiving it. This will bring prosperity within 9 days after mailing it.
> Mrs. Sanford won $3,000. Mrs. Andres won $1,000.
> Mrs. Howe who broke the chain lost everything she possessed.
> The chain grows a definite power over the expected word.
> DO NOT BREAK THE CHAIN.

Two subsequent technologies, when their use became widespread, provided orders-of-magnitude boosts in chain-letter fecundity: photocopying (c. 1950) and e-mail (c. 1995). One team of information scientists—Charles H. Bennett from IBM in New York and Ming Li and Bin Ma from Ontario, Canada— inspired by a chance conversation on a hike in the Hong Kong mountains, began an analysis of a set of chain letters collected during the photocopier era. They had thirty-three, all variants of a single letter, with mutations in the form of misspellings, omissions, and transposed words and phrases. "These letters have passed from host to host, mutating and evolving," they reported.

> Like a gene, their average length is about 2,000 characters. Like a potent virus, the letter threatens to kill you and induces you to pass it on to your "friends and associates"—some variation of this letter has probably reached millions of people. Like an inheritable trait, it promises benefits for you and the people you pass it on to. Like genomes, chain letters undergo natural selection and sometimes parts even get transferred between coexisting "species."

Reaching beyond these appealing metaphors, they set out to use the letters as a "test bed" for algorithms used in evolutionary biology. The algorithms were designed to take the genomes of various modern creatures and work backward, by inference and deduction, to reconstruct their phylogeny—their evolutionary trees. If these mathematical methods worked with genes, the scientists suggested, they should work with chain letters, too. In both cases the researchers were able to verify mutation rates and relatedness measures.

Still, most of the elements of culture change and blur too easily to qualify as stable replicators. They are rarely as neatly fixed as a sequence of DNA. Dawkins himself emphasized that he had never imagined founding anything like a new science of memetics. A peer-reviewed *Journal of Memetics* came to life in 1997—published online, naturally—and then faded away after eight years partly spent in self-conscious debate over status, mission, and terminology. Even compared with genes, memes are hard to mathematize or even to define rigorously. So the gene-meme analogy causes uneasiness and the genetics-memetics analogy even more.

Genes at least have a grounding in physical substance. Memes are abstract, intangible, and immeasurable. Genes replicate with near-perfect fidelity, and evolution depends on that: some variation is essential, but mutations need to be rare. Memes are seldom copied exactly; their boundaries are always fuzzy, and they mutate with a wild flexibility that would be fatal in biology. The term *meme* could be applied to a suspicious cornucopia of entities, from small to large. For Dennett, the first four notes of Beethoven's Fifth Symphony were "clearly" a meme, along with Homer's *Odyssey* (or at least the *idea* of the *Odyssey*), the wheel, anti-Semitism, and writing. "Memes have not yet found their Watson and Crick," said Dawkins; "they even lack their Mendel."

Yet here they are. As the arc of information flow bends toward ever greater connectivity, memes evolve faster and spread farther. Their presence is felt if not seen in herd behavior, bank runs, informational cascades, and financial bubbles. Diets rise and fall in popularity, their very names becoming catchphrases—the South Beach Diet and the Atkins Diet, the Scarsdale Diet, the Cookie Diet and the Drinking Man's Diet all replicating according to a dynamic about which the science of nutrition has nothing to say. Medical practice, too, experiences "surgical fads" and "iatroepidemics"—epidemics caused by fashions in treatment—like the iatroepidemic of children's tonsillectomies that swept the United States and parts of Europe in the mid-twentieth century, with no more medical benefit than ritual circumcision. Memes were seen through car windows when yellow diamond-shaped BABY ON BOARD signs appeared as if in an instant of mass panic in 1984, in the United States and then Europe and Japan, followed an instant later by a spawn of ironic mutations (BABY I'M BOARD, EX IN TRUNK). Memes were felt when global discourse was dominated in the last year of the millennium by the belief that the world's computers would stammer or choke when their internal clocks reached a special round number.

In the competition for space in our brains and in the culture, the effective combatants are the messages. The new, oblique, looping views of genes and memes have enriched us. They give us paradoxes to write on Möbius strips. "The human world is made of stories, not people," writes David Mitchell. "The people the stories use to tell themselves are not to be blamed." Margaret Atwood writes: "As with all knowledge, once you knew it, you couldn't imagine how it was that you hadn't known it before. Like stage magic, knowledge before you knew it took place before your very eyes, but you were looking elsewhere." Nearing death, John Updike reflects on

> A life poured into words—apparent waste
> intended to preserve the thing consumed.

Fred Dretske, a philosopher of mind and knowledge, wrote in 1981: "In the beginning there was information. The word came later." He added this explanation: "The transition was achieved by the development of organisms with the capacity for selectively exploiting this information in order to survive and perpetuate their kind." Now we might add, thanks to Dawkins, that the transition was achieved by the information itself, surviving and perpetuating its kind and selectively exploiting organisms.

Most of the biosphere cannot see the infosphere; it is invisible, a parallel universe humming with ghostly inhabitants. But they are not ghosts to us—not anymore. We humans, alone among the earth's organic creatures, live in both worlds at once. It is as though, having long coexisted with the unseen, we have begun to develop the needed extrasensory perception. We are aware of the many species of information. We name their types sardonically, as though to reassure ourselves that we understand: *urban myths* and *zombie lies.* We keep them alive in air-conditioned server farms. But we cannot own them. When a jingle lingers in our ears, or a fad turns fashion upside down, or a hoax dominates the global chatter for months and vanishes as swiftly as it came, who is master and who is slave?

▪ QUESTIONS

Reading

1. Where do memes emerge, according to Gleick, and how do they move around?
2. Who coined the term *meme*? When did this term originate?
3. "Truth may be a helpful quality for a meme, but it is only one among many," writes Gleick (paragraph 6). Highlight, underline, or flag Gleick's examples of memes that reflect wrong ideas or wrong information. What do these examples show us about the workings of memes?

Exploratory Writing

1. Do an online search for the term "meme," and find a scholarly article criticizing meme theory and the concept of memes. Make a list of the writer's arguments. Write a few paragraphs in which you evaluate the persuasiveness of those arguments.
2. Gleick writes, "In the competition for space in our brains and in the culture, the effective combatants are the messages" (paragraph 27). He wonders whether humans are the masters, or the slaves of these messages. In small groups, write a list of

guidelines for gaining control of one's own thoughts and ideas. Is this even possible, or are we all "slaves" to media ideas, images, and messages?

Making Connections

1. Sherry Turkle (p. 619) observes that younger people use text messaging and other electronic forms of communication more than face-to-face interactions, and claims that technology has changed our perceptions of authenticity. Consider Gleick's description of memes in light of Turkle's arguments about intimacy and authenticity. Can ideas, catchphrases, tunes, and images begin to "communicate" with each other, outside of individual human minds, bodies, or consciousness? What does it mean to be authentically human?

Essay Writing

1. Choose any meme that is not included among Gleick's examples, and write an essay explaining how that meme functions. Where did the meme likely first originate? How has it changed over time? Could this meme exist without the Internet?

REPORTING

From 1890: The First Text Messages

David Friedman

After graduating from Northern Arizona University, David Friedman moved to New York City and worked as a photographer for Christie's auction house and Ralph Lauren. He started the blog Ironic Sans in 2006 as a catchall space for his thoughts on art, culture, technology, and other topics. His comic inventions for Internet use, such as the twenty-word retweeter and the idea to use the domain *.ugh* on ironic or parodic sites to avoid libel lawsuits, have been featured on popular technology Web sites. For one of his blog projects, which he called *Sunday Magazine*, Friedman posted a *New York Times Sunday Magazine* article each week from exactly one hundred years before the date of the blog post. (For example, on September 24, 2011, he posted an article from September 24, 1911.) He included commentary and context for each article. The following essay is his *Sunday Magazine* analysis of an article about telegraph operators, in which he claims they were the first to use text messages.

I'm trying something new today. Sometimes in my research I find an interesting old article that I wouldn't normally post because it's not from the Sunday Magazine section, or it's from further than 100 years ago so I'll never get to it. Instead of letting these go unused, I figure I'll occasionally post them midweek during what would otherwise be slow weeks. Since this weekend I only have three articles to post, it seems like a good week to try it.

From November 30, 1890 (a Sunday, although not in the Magazine Section)

FRIENDS THEY NEVER MEET

ACQUAINTANCES MADE BY THE TELEGRAPH KEY.

CONFIDENCES EXCHANGED BETWEEN MEN WHO HAVE NEVER SEEN EACH OTHER—THEIR PECULIAR CONVERSATIONAL ABBREVIATIONS.

Telegraph operators on opposite sides of the country had some time to get to know each other when they weren't busy sending other people's messages. "Metaphorically they shake hands cordially twice a day—when they begin work and when they end it. And when business is dull they hold long conversations, with hundreds of miles—perhaps thousands—separating them, as two friends might do over a dinner table."

What really caught my eye, though, is that the abbreviations they used seem a lot like the abbreviations used in today's text messages.

> In their conversations telegraphers use a system of abbreviations which enables them to say considerably more in a certain period of time then they otherwise could. Their morning greeting to a friend in a distant city is usually "g. m.," and the farewell for the evening, "g. n.," the letters of course standing for good morning and good night. The salutation may be accompanied by an inquiry by one as to the health of the other, which would be expressed thus: "Hw r u ts mng?" And the answer would be: "I'm pty wl; hw r u?" or "I'm nt flg vy wl; fraid I've gt t mlaria."
>
> By the time these courtesies have taken place some early messages have come from the receiving department or from some other wire, and the man before whom they are placed says to his friend many miles away: "Wl hrs a fu; Gol hang ts everlastin grind. I wish I ws rich." And the other man says: "No rest fo t wickd, min pen," the last two words indicating that he wants the sender to wait a minute while he adjusts and tests his pen. Presently he clicks out "g a," meaning "go ahead," and the day's work has begun.

I'm not sure what "Wl hrs a fu" is supposed to mean. But it sounds like "min pen" is an 1890 equivalent of today's instant messager's "afk brb." 5

A couple months ago (in this blog) but actually 20 years later (in real time), the *New York Times Sunday Magazine* ran an article explaining that these conversations between telegraph operators were how jokes went viral in 1910. So surely there must have been a telegraph equivalent of LOL or ROFL, right?

> Operators laugh over a wire, or rather, they convey the fact that they are amused. They do this by telegraphing "ha, ha." Very great amusement is indicated by sending "ha" slowly and repeating it several times, and a smile is expressed by sending "ha" once or perhaps twice. Transmitting it slowly and repeating it tells the perpetrator of the joke at the other end of the wire that the listener is leaning back in his chair and laughing long and heartily.

So it looks like "ha" was the "LOL" of 1890. And it makes sense, when you consider how easy it is to telegraph "ha" compared to "LOL" or "ROFL" in Morse Code. "Ha" has a nice rhythm to it. Try tapping them out on your desk and see for yourself:

HA: •••• •—
LOL: •—•• ——— •—••
ROFL: •—• ——— ••—• •—••

I was also fascinated to discover that telegraph operators learned to identify each other by how the dots and dashes were transmitted across the wire, and could even distinguish a male operator from a female:

> No two operators send alike. The click of the instrument is always the same to the ear of a man who does not understand it, but one operator recognizes the sending of another if he has ever heard it before for any length of time, just as a familiar face is recognized. Operator "Tommy" Snaggs leaves New York, and, after roaming from one city to another, finally lands in the Galveston (Texas) office and goes to work. He is put down to work a wire running to Kansas City. The man in Kansas City begins to send. Mr. Snaggs pricks up his ears and interrupts the sender. "Ain't tt u Billy Robinson?" he asks, and the other man says, "Yes, tts me, & ur ole Tommy Snaggs." Mr. Snaggs returns, "tts wo I am, I thot I reconized ur sendin." Then they devote a few moments to telling of their travels. The last time they worked on the same wire one was in Boston and the other in Montreal.
>
> It is a peculiar fact also that an experienced operator can almost invariably distinguish a woman's sending from a man's. There is nearly always some peculiarity about a woman's style of transmission. It is not necessarily a fault. Many women send very clearly and make their dots and dashes precisely as they were intended to be made. It is impossible to describe the peculiarity, but there is no doubt of its existence. Nearly all women have a habit of rattling off a lot of meaningless dots before they say anything. But some men do that too. A woman's touch is lighter than a man's, and her dots and dashes will not carry so well on a very long circuit. That is presumably the reason why in all large offices the women are usually assigned to work the wires running to various parts of the cities.

When two operators fight across the telegraph, it's called a "fight circuit" and it's pretty futile because it's impossible for two operators tapping at once to tell what the other is saying. The article tells a humorous old story of one operator who set up a rudimentary chat bot to fight for him (possibly passing the Turing test twenty-two years before Alan Turing was even born):

> They fought for some time. Neither would yield. The man at Albany, who was old and astute, saw that the man at Syracuse, who was young and stubborn, was in for an all-night struggle. The Albany man looked around for a proxy. He found it in the clock wire, which was a wire attached to the clock's pendulum, the swaying of which acted to open and close the circuit. He connected the Syracuse wire with the clock wire and went home to bed, leaving the Syracuse man valorously battling with the tick-tick, tick-tick of the clock. The old story concludes with the veracious statement that when the Albany man reached the office the next morning he heard the Syracuse man still fighting the clock, and

that when the former disconnected the clock wire and closed the circuit the latter snapped out triumphantly, "I downed you at last, did I?"

•••• •— •••• •—.

▪ QUESTIONS

Reading

1. According to Friedman, what was a "fight circuit"? Why was it relatively pointless, according to Friedman?
2. How could telegraph operators distinguish one another without meeting in person?
3. Highlight, underline, or flag the terms Friedman uses that seem to be contemporary terms — terms not in wide use in 1890. Why does he use these terms in his report?

Exploratory Writing

1. This report was a part of Friedman's ongoing blog project to revisit hundred-year-old *Sunday Times Magazine* articles and post them with some new commentary. In pairs, go to his online archive of posts (**http://sundaymagazine.org/**) and pick one. Prepare and present your own short report on the article. What does it show about social change? In what ways could the article have been published yesterday?
2. Write a double-entry list comparing "text messages" circa 1890 with text messages today. What similarities did you find? What differences?

CHARACTERISTICS OF TELEGRAPH MESSAGES (1890)	CHARACTERISTICS OF TEXT MESSAGES

Making Connections

1. Consider James Gleick's (p. 555) explanation of memes. How do the "first text messages" in Friedman's report relate to Gleick's description of memes? How might the telegraph have contributed to a new meme?

Essay Writing

1. Choose any communication form, and write an essay explaining how it emerged. Is the kind of communication you chose reliant on certain technologies, or could it exist without those technologies, in a slightly altered form? You can use the explaining essays in this casebook — Jeffrey Rosen's (p. 594) and James Gleick's (p. 555) — for examples of how to use explanatory writing techniques.

ARGUING

Internet Rights and Wrongs

Choices & Challenges in a Networked World

Hillary Rodham Clinton

Hillary Rodham Clinton (b. 1947) represented New York in the United States Senate before becoming President Barack Obama's secretary of state in 2008. She studied law at Yale University on her way to becoming one of the one hundred most influential lawyers in the United States. After her husband, Bill Clinton, was elected president in 1992, she introduced a number of initiatives as First Lady, including the controversial Clinton Health Care Plan. In 1996, during the Whitewater controversy, Hillary Clinton was subpoenaed to testify before a grand jury, making her the first United States First Lady to have been summoned to appear in court. She was also the first former First Lady to be elected to the Senate and to run for president. Clinton was mentioned in some of the WikiLeaks cables she discusses in the following speech, which she gave at George Washington University in 2011; her name appears on leaked State Department documents that instructed diplomats to surveil United Nations personnel, including Secretary-General Ban Ki-moon. Clinton's books include *It Takes a Village and Other Lessons Children Teach Us* (1996) and her autobiography, *Living History* (2003).

Thank you all very much and good afternoon. It is a pleasure, once again, to be back on the campus of the George Washington University, a place that I have spent quite a bit of time in all different settings over the last now nearly twenty years. I'd like especially to thank President Knapp and Provost Lerman, because this is a great opportunity for me to address such a significant issue, and one which deserves the attention of citizens, governments, and I know is drawing that attention. And perhaps today in my remarks, we can begin a much more vigorous debate that will respond to the needs that we have been watching in real time on our television sets.

A few minutes after midnight on January 28th, the Internet went dark across Egypt. During the previous four days, hundreds of thousands of Egyptians had marched to demand a new government. And the world, on TVs, laptops, cell phones, and smart phones, had followed every single step. Pictures and videos from Egypt flooded the web. On Facebook and Twitter, journalists posted on-the-spot reports. Protestors coordinated their next moves. And citizens of all stripes shared their hopes and fears about this pivotal moment in the history of their country.

Millions worldwide answered in real time, "You are not alone and we are with you." Then the government pulled the plug. Cell phone service was cut off, TV satellite signals were jammed, and Internet access was blocked for nearly the entire population. The government did not want the people to communicate with each other and it did not want the press to communicate with the public. It certainly did not want the world to watch.

The events in Egypt recalled another protest movement eighteen months earlier in Iran, when thousands marched after disputed elections. Their protestors also used Web sites to organize. A video taken by cell phone showed a young woman named Neda killed by a member of the paramilitary forces, and within hours, that video was being watched by people everywhere.

5 The Iranian authorities used technology as well. The Revolutionary Guard stalked members of the Green Movement by tracking their online profiles. And like Egypt, for a time, the government shut down the Internet and mobile networks altogether. After the authorities raided homes, attacked university dorms, made mass arrests, tortured and fired shots into crowds, the protests ended.

In Egypt, however, the story ended differently. The protests continued despite the Internet shutdown. People organized marches through flyers and word of mouth and used dial-up modems and fax machines to communicate with the world. After five days, the government relented and Egypt came back online. The authorities then sought to use the Internet to control the protests by ordering mobile companies to send out pro-government text messages, and by arresting bloggers and those who organized the protests online. But eighteen days after the protests began, the government failed and the president resigned.

What happened in Egypt and what happened in Iran, which this week is once again using violence against protestors seeking basic freedoms, was about a great deal more than the Internet. In each case, people protested because of deep frustrations with the political and economic conditions of their lives. They stood and marched and chanted and the authorities tracked and blocked and arrested them. The Internet did not do any of those things; people did. In both of these countries, the ways that citizens and the authorities used the Internet reflected the power of connection technologies on the one hand as an accelerant of political, social, and economic change, and on the other hand as a means to stifle or extinguish that change.

There is a debate currently underway in some circles about whether the Internet is a force for liberation or repression. But I think that debate is largely beside the point. Egypt isn't inspiring people because they communicated using Twitter. It is inspiring because people came together and persisted in demanding a better future. Iran isn't awful because the authorities used Facebook to shadow and capture members of the opposition. Iran is awful because it is a government that routinely violates the rights of its people.

So it is our values that cause these actions to inspire or outrage us, our sense of human dignity, the rights that flow from it, and the principles that ground it. And it is these values that ought to drive us to think about the road ahead. Two billion people are now online, nearly a third of humankind. We hail from every corner of the world, live under every form of government, and subscribe to every system of beliefs. And increasingly, we are turning to the Internet to conduct important aspects of our lives.

The Internet has become the public space of the twenty-first century—the world's town square, classroom, marketplace, coffeehouse, and nightclub. We all shape and are shaped by what happens there, all two billion of us and counting. And that presents a challenge. To maintain an Internet that delivers the greatest possible benefits to the world, we need to have a serious conversation about the principles that will guide us, what rules exist and should not exist and why, what behaviors should be encouraged or discouraged and how. 10

The goal is not to tell people how to use the Internet any more than we ought to tell people how to use any public square, whether it's Tahrir Square or Times Square. The value of these spaces derives from the variety of activities people can pursue in them, from holding a rally to selling their vegetables, to having a private conversation. These spaces provide an open platform, and so does the Internet. It does not serve any particular agenda, and it never should. But if people around the world are going to come together every day online and have a safe and productive experience, we need a shared vision to guide us.

One year ago, I offered a starting point for that vision by calling for a global commitment to Internet freedom, to protect human rights online as we do offline. The rights of individuals to express their views freely, petition their leaders, worship according to their beliefs—these rights are universal, whether they are exercised in a public square or on an individual blog. The freedoms to assemble and associate also apply in cyberspace. In our time, people are as likely to come together to pursue common interests online as in a church or a labor hall.

Together, the freedoms of expression, assembly, and association online comprise what I've called the freedom to connect. The United States supports this freedom for people everywhere, and we have called on other nations to do the same. Because we want people to have the chance to exercise this freedom. We also support expanding the number of people who have access to the Internet. And because the Internet must work evenly and reliably for it to have value, we support the multi-stakeholder system that governs the Internet today, which has consistently kept it up and running through all manner of interruptions across networks, borders, and regions.

In the year since my speech, people worldwide have continued to use the Internet to solve shared problems and expose public corruption, from the people in Russia who tracked wildfires online and organized a volunteer firefighting squad, to the children in Syria who used Facebook to reveal abuse by their teachers, to the Internet campaign in China that helps parents find their missing children.

At the same time, the Internet continues to be restrained in a myriad of ways. In China, the government censors content and redirects search requests to error pages. In Burma, independent news sites have been taken down with distributed denial of service attacks. In Cuba, the government is trying to create a national intranet, while not allowing their citizens to access the global Internet. In Vietnam, bloggers who criticize the government are arrested and abused. In Iran, the authorities block opposition and media Web sites, target 15 social media, and steal identifying information about their own people in order to hunt them down.

These actions reflect a landscape that is complex and combustible, and sure to become more so in the coming years as billions of more people connect to the Internet. The choices we make today will determine what the Internet looks like in the future. Businesses have to choose whether and how to enter markets where Internet freedom is limited. People have to choose how to act online, what information to share and with whom, which ideas to voice and how to voice them. Governments have to choose to live up to their commitments to protect free expression, assembly, and association.

For the United States, the choice is clear. On the spectrum of Internet freedom, we place ourselves on the side of openness. Now, we recognize that an open Internet comes with challenges. It calls for ground rules to protect against wrongdoing and harm. And Internet freedom raises tensions, like all freedoms do. But we believe the benefits far exceed the costs.

And today, I'd like to discuss several of the challenges we must confront as we seek to protect and defend a free and open Internet. Now, I'm the first to say that neither I nor the United States government has all the answers. We're not sure we have all the questions. But we are committed to asking the questions, to helping lead a conversation, and to defending not just universal principles but the interests of our people and our partners.

The first challenge is achieving both liberty and security. Liberty and security are often presented as equal and opposite; the more you have of one, the less you have of the other. In fact, I believe they make each other possible. Without security, liberty is fragile. Without liberty, security is oppressive. The challenge is finding the proper measure: enough security to enable our freedoms, but not so much or so little as to endanger them.

Finding this proper measure for the Internet is critical because the qualities that make the Internet a force for unprecedented progress—its openness, its leveling effect, its reach and speed—also enable wrongdoing on an unprecedented scale. Terrorists and extremist groups use the Internet to recruit members, and plot and carry out attacks. Human traffickers use the Internet to find and lure new victims into modern-day slavery. Child pornographers use the Internet to exploit children. Hackers break into financial institutions, cell phone networks, and personal e-mail accounts. 20

So we need successful strategies for combating these threats and more without constricting the openness that is the Internet's greatest attribute. The United States is aggressively tracking and deterring criminals and terrorists online. We are investing in our nation's cybersecurity, both to prevent cyberincidents and to lessen their impact. We are cooperating with other countries to fight transnational crime in cyberspace. The United States government invests in helping other nations build their own law enforcement capacity. We have also ratified the Budapest Cybercrime Convention, which sets out the steps countries must take to ensure that the Internet is not misused by criminals and terrorists while still protecting the liberties of our own citizens.

In our vigorous effort to prevent attacks or apprehend criminals, we retain a commitment to human rights and fundamental freedoms. The United States is determined to stop terrorism and criminal activity online and offline, and in both spheres we are committed to pursuing these goals in accordance with our laws and values.

Now, others have taken a different approach. Security is often invoked as a justification for harsh crackdowns on freedom. Now, this tactic is not new to the digital age, but it has new resonance as the Internet has given governments new capacities for tracking and punishing human rights advocates and political dissidents. Governments that arrest bloggers, pry into the peaceful activities of their citizens, and limit their access to the Internet may claim to be seeking security. In fact, they may even mean it as they define it. But they are taking the wrong path. Those who clamp down on Internet freedom may be able to hold back the full expression of their people's yearnings for a while, but not forever.

The second challenge is protecting both transparency and confidentiality. The Internet's strong culture of transparency derives from its power to make information of all kinds available instantly. But in addition to being a public space, the Internet is also a channel for private communications. And for that to continue, there must be protection for confidential communication online. Think of all the ways in which people and organizations rely on confidential communications to do their jobs. Businesses hold confidential conversations when they're developing new products to stay ahead of their competitors. Journalists keep the details of some sources confidential to protect them from exposure or retribution. And governments also rely on confidential communication online as well as offline. The existence of connection technologies may make it harder to maintain confidentiality, but it does not alter the need for it.

25 Now, I know that government confidentiality has been a topic of debate during the past few months because of WikiLeaks, but it's been a false debate in many ways. Fundamentally, the WikiLeaks incident began with an act of theft. Government documents were stolen, just the same as if they had been smuggled out in a briefcase. Some have suggested that this theft was justified because governments have a responsibility to conduct all of our work out in the open in the full view of our citizens. I respectfully disagree. The United States could neither provide for our citizens' security nor promote the cause of human rights and democracy around the world if we had to make public every step of our efforts. Confidential communication gives our government the opportunity to do work that could not be done otherwise.

Consider our work with former Soviet states to secure loose nuclear material. By keeping the details confidential, we make it less likely that terrorists or criminals will find the nuclear material and steal it for their own purposes. Or consider the content of the documents that WikiLeaks made public. Without commenting on the authenticity of any particular documents, we can observe that many of the cables released by WikiLeaks relate to human rights work carried on around the world. Our diplomats closely collaborate with activists, journalists, and citizens to challenge the misdeeds of oppressive governments. It is dangerous work. By publishing diplomatic cables, WikiLeaks exposed people to even greater risk.

For operations like these, confidentiality is essential, especially in the Internet age when dangerous information can be sent around the world with the click of a keystroke. But of course, governments also have a duty to be transparent. We govern with the consent of the people, and that consent must be informed to be meaningful. So we must be judicious about when we close off our work to the public, and we must review our standards frequently to make sure they are rigorous. In the United States, we have laws designed to ensure that the government makes its work open to the people, and the Obama administration has also launched an unprecedented initiative to put government data online, to encourage citizen participation, and to generally increase the openness of government.

The U.S. government's ability to protect America, to secure the liberties of our people, and to support the rights and freedoms of others around the world depends on maintaining a balance between what's public and what should and must remain out of the public domain. The scale should and will always be tipped in favor of openness, but tipping the scale over completely serves no one's interests. Let me be clear. I said that the WikiLeaks incident began with a theft, just as if it had been executed by smuggling papers in a briefcase. The fact that WikiLeaks used the Internet is not the reason we criticized its actions. WikiLeaks does not challenge our commitment to Internet freedom.

And one final word on this matter: There were reports in the days following these leaks that the U.S. government intervened to coerce private companies to deny service to WikiLeaks. That is not the case. Now, some politicians and pundits publicly called for companies to disassociate from WikiLeaks, while others criticized them for doing so. Public officials are part of our country's public debates, but there is a line between expressing views and coercing conduct. Business decisions that private companies may have taken to enforce their own values or policies regarding WikiLeaks were not at the direction of the Obama administration.

A third challenge is protecting free expression while fostering tolerance and civility. I don't need to tell this audience that the Internet is home to every kind of speech—false, offensive, incendiary, innovative, truthful, and beautiful. 30

The multitude of opinions and ideas that crowd the Internet is both a result of its openness and a reflection of our human diversity. Online, everyone has a voice. And the Universal Declaration of Human Rights protects the freedom of expression for all. But what we say has consequences. Hateful or defamatory words can inflame hostilities, deepen divisions, and provoke violence. On the Internet, this power is heightened. Intolerant speech is often amplified and impossible to retract. Of course, the Internet also provides a unique space for people to bridge their differences and build trust and understanding.

Some take the view that, to encourage tolerance, some hateful ideas must be silenced by governments. We believe that efforts to curb the content of speech rarely succeed and often become an excuse to violate freedom of expression. Instead, as it has historically been proven time and time again, the better answer to offensive speech is more speech. People can and should speak out against intolerance and hatred. By exposing ideas to debate, those with merit tend to be strengthened, while weak and false ideas tend to fade away; perhaps not instantly, but eventually.

Now, this approach does not immediately discredit every hateful idea or convince every bigot to reverse his thinking. But we have determined as a society that it is far more effective than any other alternative approach. Deleting writing, blocking content, arresting speakers—these actions suppress words, but they do not touch the underlying ideas. They simply drive people with those ideas to the fringes, where their convictions can deepen, unchallenged.

Last summer, Hannah Rosenthal, the U.S. special envoy to monitor and combat anti-semitism, made a trip to Dachau and Auschwitz with a delegation of American imams and Muslim leaders. Many of them had previously denied the Holocaust, and none of them had ever denounced Holocaust denial. But by visiting the concentration camps, they displayed a willingness to consider a different view. And the trip had a real impact. They prayed together, and they signed messages of peace, and many of those messages in the visitors books were written in Arabic. At the end of the trip, they read a statement that they wrote and signed together condemning without reservation Holocaust denial and all other forms of anti-Semitism.

The marketplace of ideas worked. Now, these leaders had not been arrested for their previous stance or ordered to remain silent. Their mosques were not shut down. The state did not compel them with force. Others appealed to them with facts. And their speech was dealt with through the speech of others. 35

The United States does restrict certain kinds of speech in accordance with the rule of law and our international obligations. We have rules about libel and slander, defamation, and speech that incites imminent violence. But we enforce these rules transparently, and citizens have the right to appeal how they are applied. And we don't restrict speech even if the majority of people find it offensive. History, after all, is full of examples of ideas that were banned for reasons that we now see as wrong. People were punished for denying the divine right of kings, or suggesting that people should be treated equally regardless of race, gender, or religion. These restrictions might have reflected the dominant view at the time, and variations on these restrictions are still in force in places around the world.

But when it comes to online speech, the United States has chosen not to depart from our time-tested principles. We urge our people to speak with civility, to recognize the power and reach that their words can have online. We've seen in our own country tragic examples of how online bullying can have terrible consequences. Those of us in government should lead by example, in the tone we set and the ideas we champion. But leadership also means empowering people to make their own choices, rather than intervening and taking those choices away. We protect free speech with the force of law, and we appeal to the force of reason to win out over hate.

Now, these three large principles are not always easy to advance at once. They raise tensions, and they pose challenges. But we do not have to choose among them. Liberty and security, transparency and confidentiality, freedom of expression and tolerance—these all make up the foundation of a free, open, and secure society as well as a free, open, and secure Internet where universal human rights are respected, and which provides a space for greater progress and prosperity over the long run.

Now, some countries are trying a different approach, abridging rights online and working to erect permanent walls between different activities—economic exchanges, political discussions, religious expressions, and social interactions. They want to keep what they like and suppress what they don't. But this is no easy task. Search engines connect businesses to new customers, and they also attract users because they deliver and organize news and information. Social networking sites aren't only places where friends share photos; they also share political views and build support for social causes or reach out to professional contacts to collaborate on new business opportunities.

Walls that divide the Internet, that block political content, or ban broad categories of expression, or allow certain forms of peaceful assembly but prohibit others, or intimidate people from expressing their ideas are far easier to erect than to maintain. Not just because people using human ingenuity find ways around them and through them but because there isn't an economic Internet and a social Internet and a political Internet; there's just the Internet. And maintaining barriers that attempt to change this reality entails a variety of costs—moral, political, and economic. Countries may be able to absorb these costs for a time, but we believe they are unsustainable in the long run. There are opportunity costs for trying to be open for business but closed for free expression—costs to a nation's education system, its political stability, its social mobility, and its economic potential. 40

When countries curtail Internet freedom, they place limits on their economic future. Their young people don't have full access to the conversations and debates happening in the world or exposure to the kind of free inquiry that spurs people to question old ways of doing and invent new ones. And barring criticism of officials makes governments more susceptible to corruption, which creates economic distortions with long-term effects. Freedom of thought and the level playing field made possible by the rule of law are part of what fuels innovation economies.

So it's not surprising that the European-American Business Council, a group of more than seventy companies, made a strong public support statement last week for Internet freedom. If you invest in countries with aggressive censorship and surveillance policies, your Web site could be shut down without warning, your servers hacked by the government, your designs stolen, or your staff threatened with arrest or expulsion for failing to comply with a politically motivated order. The risks to your bottom line and to your integrity will at some point outweigh the potential rewards, especially if there are market opportunities elsewhere.

Now, some have pointed to a few countries, particularly China, that appears to stand out as an exception, a place where Internet censorship is high and economic growth is strong. Clearly, many businesses are willing to endure restrictive Internet policies to gain access to those markets, and in the short term, even perhaps in the medium term, those governments may succeed in maintaining a segmented Internet. But those restrictions will have long-term costs that threaten one day to become a noose that restrains growth and development.

There are political costs as well. Consider Tunisia, where online economic activity was an important part of the country's ties with Europe while online censorship was on par with China and Iran. The effort to divide the economic Internet from the "everything else" Internet in Tunisia could not be sustained. People, especially young people, found ways to use connection technologies to organize and share grievances, which, as we know, helped fuel a movement that led to revolutionary change. In Syria, too, the government is trying to negotiate a non-negotiable contradiction. Just last week, it lifted a ban on Facebook and YouTube for the first time in three years, and yesterday they convicted a teenage girl of espionage and sentenced her to five years in prison for the political opinions she expressed on her blog.

This, too, is unsustainable. The demand for access to platforms of expression cannot be satisfied when using them lands you in prison. We believe that governments who have erected barriers to Internet freedom, whether they're technical filters or censorship regimes or attacks on those who exercise their rights to expression and assembly online, will eventually find themselves boxed in. They will face a dictator's dilemma and will have to choose between letting the walls fall or paying the price to keep them standing, which means both doubling down on a losing hand by resorting to greater oppression and enduring the escalating opportunity cost of missing out on the ideas that have been blocked and people who have been disappeared. 45

I urge countries everywhere instead to join us in the bet we have made, a bet that an open Internet will lead to stronger, more prosperous countries. At its core, it's an extension of the bet that the United States has been making for more than two hundred years, that open societies give rise to the most lasting progress, that the rule of law is the firmest foundation for justice and peace, and that innovation thrives where ideas of all kinds are aired and explored. This is not a bet on computers or mobile phones. It's a bet on people. We're confident that together with those partners in government and people around the world who are making the same bet by hewing to universal rights that underpin open societies, we'll preserve the Internet as an open space for all. And that will pay long-term gains for our shared progress and prosperity. The United States will continue to promote an Internet where people's rights are protected and that is open to innovation, interoperable all over the world, secure enough to hold people's trust, and reliable enough to support their work.

In the past year, we have welcomed the emergence of a global coalition of countries, businesses, civil society groups, and digital activists seeking to advance these goals. We have found strong partners in several governments worldwide, and we've been encouraged by the work of the Global Network Initiative, which brings together companies, academics, and NGOs to work together to solve the challenges we are facing, like how to handle government requests for censorship or how to decide whether to sell technologies that could be used to violate rights or how to handle privacy issues in the context of cloud computing. We need strong corporate partners that have made principled, meaningful commitments to Internet freedom as we work together to advance this common cause.

We realize that in order to be meaningful, online freedoms must carry over into real-world activism. That's why we are working through our Civil Society 2.0 initiative to connect NGOs and advocates with technology and training that will magnify their impact. We are also committed to continuing our conversation with people everywhere around the world. Last week, you may have heard, we launched Twitter feeds in Arabic and Farsi, adding to the ones we already have in French and Spanish. We'll start similar ones in Chinese, Russian, and Hindi. This is enabling us to have real-time, two-way conversations with people wherever there is a connection that governments do not block.

Our commitment to Internet freedom is a commitment to the rights of people, and we are matching that with our actions. Monitoring and responding to threats to Internet freedom has become part of the daily work of our diplomats and development experts. They are working to advance Internet freedom on the ground at our embassies and missions around the world. The United States continues to help people in oppressive Internet environments get around filters, stay one step ahead of the censors, the hackers, and the thugs who beat them up or imprison them for what they say online.

While the rights we seek to protect and support are clear, the various ways 50 that these rights are violated are increasingly complex. I know some have criticized us for not pouring funding into a single technology, but we believe there is no silver bullet in the struggle against Internet repression. There's no app for that. Start working, those of you out there. And accordingly, we are taking a comprehensive and innovative approach, one that matches our diplomacy with technology, secure distribution networks for tools, and direct support for those on the front lines.

In the last three years, we have awarded more than $20 million in competitive grants through an open process, including interagency evaluation by technical and policy experts to support a burgeoning group of technologists and activists working at the cutting edge of the fight against Internet repression. This year, we will award more than $25 million in additional funding. We are taking a venture capital-style approach, supporting a portfolio of technologies, tools, and training, and adapting as more users shift to mobile devices. We have our ear to the ground, talking to digital activists about to where they need help, and our diversified approach means we're able to adapt to the range of threats that they face. We support multiple tools, so if repressive governments figure out how to target one, others are available. And we invest in the cutting edge because we know that repressive governments are constantly innovating their methods of oppression and we intend to stay ahead of them.

Likewise, we are leading the push to strengthen cybersecurity and online innovation, building capacity in developing countries, championing open and interoperable standards, and enhancing international cooperation to respond to cyber threats. Deputy Secretary of Defense Lynn gave a speech on this issue just yesterday. All these efforts build on a decade of work to sustain an Internet that is open, secure, and reliable. And in the coming year, the administration will complete an international strategy for cyberspace, charting the course to continue this work into the future.

This is a foreign-policy priority for us, one that will only increase in importance in the coming years. That's why I've created the Office of the Coordinator for Cyber Issues, to enhance our work on cybersecurity and other issues and facilitate cooperation across the State Department and with other government agencies. I've named Christopher Painter, formerly senior director for cyber security at the National Security Council and a leader in the field for twenty years, to head this new office.

The dramatic increase in Internet users during the past ten years has been remarkable to witness. But that was just the opening act. In the next twenty years, nearly five billion people will join the network. It is those users who will decide the future.

So we are playing for the long game. Unlike much of what happens online, progress on this front will be measured in years, not seconds. The course we chart today will determine whether those who follow us will get the chance to experience the freedom, security, and prosperity of an open Internet. 55

As we look ahead, let us remember that Internet freedom isn't about any one particular activity online. It's about ensuring that the Internet remains a space where activities of all kinds can take place, from grand, ground-breaking, historic campaigns to the small, ordinary acts that people engage in every day.

We want to keep the Internet open for the protestor using social media to organize a march in Egypt; the college student emailing her family photos of her semester abroad; the lawyer in Vietnam blogging to expose corruption; the teenager in the United States who is bullied and finds words of support online; for the small-business owner in Kenya using mobile banking to manage her profits; the philosopher in China reading academic journals for her dissertation; the scientist in Brazil sharing data in real time with colleagues overseas; and the billions and billions of interactions with the Internet every single day as people communicate with loved ones, follow the news, do their jobs, and participate in the debates shaping their world.

Internet freedom is about defending the space in which all these things occur so that it remains not just for the students here today, but your successors and all who come after you. This is one of the grand challenges of our time. We are engaged in a vigorous effort against those who we have always stood against, who wish to stifle and repress, to come forward with their version of reality and to accept none other. We enlist your help on behalf of this struggle. It's a struggle for human rights, it's a struggle for human freedom, and it's a struggle for human dignity.

Thank you all very much.

▪ QUESTIONS

Reading

1. Where does Clinton stand in the debate over whether the Internet is a force of liberation or repression?
2. According to Clinton, what is the relationship between Internet freedom and economic freedom?
3. Who is Hannah Rosenthal? Why does Clinton mention her?

Exploratory Writing

1. Highlight, underline, or flag the names of nations that Clinton uses as examples in this speech. Choose just one of those nations and do a search for news about current political events in that nation (**http://www.bbc.co.uk/news/** is a good site for your online search). Choosing one article, write a short report on how living in a "networked world" has shaped recent events in that country.
2. In small groups, make a double-entry list of online activities you think should be public, with government access to all materials, versus private. Put a star beside the items that cause disagreement within your group. Next, make a second list of offline activities that should be public versus those that should be private. Should personal journals or private files on a laptop hard drive be admissible as court evidence? Should it be legal to film people in their homes without their knowledge? What about in the streets or other public places? Is this the same as monitoring Internet activities?

PUBLIC ONLINE ACTIVITIES	PRIVATE ONLINE ACTIVITIES

PUBLIC OFFLINE ACTIVITIES	PRIVATE OFFLINE ACTIVITIES

Making Connections

1. Jeffrey Rosen (p. 594) tells the story of Stacy Snyder, a twenty-five-year-old teacher in training who was denied her degree after posting a picture on her MySpace page, visible to her students, labeled "drunken pirate." Rosen explains that the problem Snyder faced was one example of a challenge faced by millions of people — "how best to live our lives in a world where the Internet records everything and forgets nothing." How do Clinton's arguments relate to Stacy Snyder's problem, and to Rosen's other examples? What solutions does she offer?

Essay Writing

1. Clinton introduces counterarguments — arguments opposed to hers — in order to refute them, as in her remarks about WikiLeaks: "Some have suggested that this theft was justified because governments have a responsibility to conduct all of our work out in the open in the full view of our citizens. I respectfully disagree. The United States could neither provide for our citizens' security nor promote the cause of human rights and democracy around the world if we had to make public every step of our efforts" (paragraph 25). Write your own argumentative essay respectfully (or heatedly, if you prefer) agreeing or disagreeing with this point. You can use cases or examples other than WikiLeaks, but be sure to include (and refute) at least one counterargument.

REPORTING

I'm So Totally, Digitally, Close to You

The Brave New World of Digital Intimacy

Clive Thompson

Clive Thompson is the brain trust behind Collision Detection, one of the Internet's most highly regarded blogs on science, technology, and culture since its inception in 2002. A one-time Knight Fellow at MIT, Thompson is currently a contributing writer for *Wired* and the *New York Times Magazine*, in which the following piece appeared in 2008. His writing has also appeared in the *Washington Post*, *Lingua Franca*, and *Entertainment Weekly*, as well as in many anthologies, including *The Best American Science and Nature Writing* (2002).

On September 5, 2006, Mark Zuckerberg changed the way that Facebook worked, and in the process he inspired a revolt.

Zuckerberg, a doe-eyed twenty-four-year-old CEO, founded Facebook in his dorm room at Harvard two years earlier, and the site quickly amassed nine million users. By 2006, students were posting heaps of personal details onto their Facebook pages, including lists of their favorite TV shows, whether they were dating (and whom), what music they had in rotation, and the various ad hoc "groups" they had joined (like *Sex and the City* Lovers). All day long, they'd post "status" notes explaining their moods—"hating Monday," "skipping class b/c i'm hung over." After each party, they'd stagger home to the dorm and upload pictures of the soused revelry, and spend the morning after commenting on how wasted everybody looked. Facebook became the de facto public commons—the way students found out what everyone around them was like and what he or she was doing.

But Zuckerberg knew Facebook had one major problem: It required a lot of active surfing on the part of its users. Sure, every day your Facebook friends would update their profiles with some new tidbits; it might even be something particularly juicy, like changing their relationship status to "single" when they got dumped. But unless you visited each friend's page every day, it might be days or weeks before you noticed the news, or you might miss it entirely. Browsing Facebook was like constantly poking your head into someone's room to see how she was doing. It took work and forethought. In a sense, this gave Facebook an inherent, built-in level of privacy, simply because if you had two hundred friends on the site—a fairly typical number—there weren't enough hours in the day to keep tabs on every friend all the time.

"It was very primitive," Zuckerberg told me when I asked him about it last month. And so he decided to modernize. He developed something he called News Feed, a built-in service that would actively broadcast changes in a user's page to every one of his or her friends. Students would no longer need to spend their time zipping around to examine each friend's page, checking to see if there was any new information. Instead, they would just log into Facebook, and News Feed would appear: a single page that—like a social gazette from the eighteenth century—delivered a long list of up-to-the-minute gossip about their friends, around the clock, all in one place. "A stream of everything that's going on in their lives," as Zuckerberg put it.

When students woke up that September morning and saw News Feed, the first reaction, generally, was one of panic. Just about every little thing you changed on your page was now instantly blasted out to hundreds of friends, including potentially mortifying bits of news—Tim and Lisa broke up; Persaud is no longer friends with Matthew—and drunken photos someone snapped, then uploaded and tagged with names. Facebook had lost its vestigial bit of privacy. For students, it was now like being at a giant, open party filled with everyone you know, able to eavesdrop on what everyone else was saying, all the time. 5

"Everyone was freaking out," Ben Parr, then a junior at Northwestern University, told me recently. What particularly enraged Parr was that there wasn't any way to opt out of News Feed, to "go private" and have all your information kept quiet. He created a Facebook group demanding Zuckerberg either scrap News Feed or provide privacy options. "Facebook users really think Facebook is becoming the Big Brother of the Internet, recording every single move," a California student told the *Star-Ledger* of Newark. Another chimed in, "Frankly, I don't need to know or care that Billy broke up with Sally, and Ted has become friends with Steve." By lunchtime of the first day, 10,000 people had joined Parr's group, and by the next day it had 284,000.

Zuckerberg, surprised by the outcry, quickly made two decisions. The first was to add a privacy feature to News Feed, letting users decide what kind of information went out. But the second decision was to leave News Feed otherwise intact. He suspected that once people tried it and got over their shock, they'd like it.

He was right. Within days, the tide reversed. Students began e-mailing Zuckerberg to say that via News Feed they'd learned things they would never have otherwise discovered through random surfing around Facebook. The bits of trivia that News Feed delivered gave them more things to talk about—Why do you hate Kiefer Sutherland?—when they met friends face to face in class or at a party. Trends spread more quickly. When one student joined a group—proclaiming her love of Coldplay or a desire to volunteer for Greenpeace—all her friends instantly knew, and many would sign up themselves. Users' worries about their privacy seemed to vanish within days, boiled away by their excitement at being so much more connected to their friends. (Very few people stopped using Facebook, and most people kept on publishing most of their information through News Feed.) Pundits predicted that News Feed would kill Facebook, but the opposite happened. It catalyzed a massive boom in the site's growth. A few weeks after the News Feed imbroglio, Zuckerberg opened the site to the general public (previously, only students could join), and it grew quickly; today, it has one hundred million users.

When I spoke to him, Zuckerberg argued that News Feed is central to Facebook's success. "Facebook has always tried to push the envelope," he said.

"And at times that means stretching people and getting them to be comfortable with things they aren't yet comfortable with. A lot of this is just social norms catching up with what technology is capable of."

10 In essence, Facebook users didn't think they wanted constant, up-to-the-minute updates on what other people are doing. Yet when they experienced this sort of omnipresent knowledge, they found it intriguing and addictive. Why?

Social scientists have a name for this sort of incessant online contact. They call it "ambient awareness." It is, they say, very much like being physically near someone and picking up on his mood through the little things he does—body language, sighs, stray comments—out of the corner of your eye. Facebook is no longer alone in offering this sort of interaction online. In the last year, there has been a boom in tools for "microblogging": posting frequent tiny updates on what you're doing. The phenomenon is quite different from what we normally think of as blogging, because a blog post is usually a written piece, sometimes quite long: a statement of opinion, a story, an analysis. But these new updates are something different. They're far shorter, far more frequent, and less carefully considered. One of the most popular new tools is Twitter, a Web site and messaging service that allows its two-million-plus users to broadcast to their friends haiku-length updates—limited to 140 characters, as brief as a mobile-phone text message—on what they're doing. There are other services for reporting where you're traveling (Dopplr) or for quickly tossing online a stream of the pictures, videos, or Web sites you're looking at (Tumblr). And there are even tools that give your location. When the new iPhone, with built-in tracking, was introduced in July, one million people began using Loopt, a piece of software that automatically tells all your friends exactly where you are.

For many people—particularly anyone over the age of thirty—the idea of describing your blow-by-blow activities in such detail is absurd. Why would you subject your friends to your daily minutiae? And conversely, how much of their trivia can you absorb? The growth of ambient intimacy can seem like modern narcissism taken to a new, supermetabolic extreme—the ultimate expression of a generation of celebrity-addled youths who believe their every utterance is fascinating and ought to be shared with the world. Twitter, in particular, has been the subject of nearly relentless scorn since it went online. "Who really cares what I am doing, every hour of the day?" wondered Alex Beam, a *Boston Globe* columnist, in an essay about Twitter last month. "Even I don't care."

Indeed, many of the people I interviewed, who are among the most avid users of these "awareness" tools, admit that at first they couldn't figure out why anybody would want to do this. Ben Haley, a thirty-nine-year-old documentation specialist for a software firm who lives in Seattle, told me that when he first heard about Twitter last year from an early-adopter friend who used it, his first reaction was that it seemed silly. But a few of his friends decided to give it a try, and they urged him to sign up, too.

Each day, Haley logged on to his account, and his friends' updates would appear as a long page of one- or two-line notes. He would check and recheck the account several times a day, or even several times an hour. The updates were indeed pretty banal. One friend would post about starting to feel sick; one posted random thoughts like "I really hate it when people clip their nails on the bus"; another Twittered whenever she made a sandwich—and she made a sandwich every day. Each so-called tweet was so brief as to be virtually meaningless.

But as the days went by, something changed. Haley discovered that he was beginning to sense the rhythms of his friends' lives in a way he never had before. When one friend got sick with a virulent fever, he could tell by her Twitter updates when she was getting worse and the instant she finally turned the corner. He could see when friends were heading into hellish days at work or when they'd scored a big success. Even the daily catalog of sandwiches became oddly mesmerizing, a sort of metronomic click that he grew accustomed to seeing pop up in the middle of each day. 15

This is the paradox of ambient awareness. Each little update—each individual bit of social information—is insignificant on its own, even supremely mundane. But taken together, over time, the little snippets coalesce into a surprisingly sophisticated portrait of your friends' and family members' lives, like thousands of dots making a pointillist painting. This was never before possible, because in the real world, no friend would bother to call you up and detail the sandwiches she was eating. The ambient information becomes like "a type of ESP," as Haley described it to me, an invisible dimension floating over everyday life.

"It's like I can distantly read everyone's mind," Haley went on to say. "I love that. I feel like I'm getting to something raw about my friends. It's like I've got this heads-up display for them." It can also lead to more real-life contact, because when one member of Haley's group decides to go out to a bar or see a band and Twitters about his plans, the others see it, and some decide to drop by—ad hoc, self-organizing socializing. And when they do socialize face to face, it feels oddly as if they've never actually been apart. They don't need to ask, "So, what have you been up to?" because they already know. Instead, they'll begin discussing something that one of the friends Twittered that afternoon, as if picking up a conversation in the middle.

Facebook and Twitter may have pushed things into overdrive, but the idea of using communication tools as a form of "co-presence" has been around for a while. The Japanese sociologist Mizuko Ito first noticed it with mobile phones: Lovers who were working in different cities would send text messages back and forth all night—tiny updates like "enjoying a glass of wine now" or "watching TV while lying on the couch." They were doing it partly because talking for hours on mobile phones isn't very comfortable (or affordable). But they also discovered that the little Ping-Ponging messages felt even more intimate than a phone call.

"It's an aggregate phenomenon," Marc Davis, a chief scientist at Yahoo! and former professor of information science at the University of California at Berkeley, told me. "No message is the single-most-important message. It's sort of like when you're sitting with someone and you look over and they smile at you. You're sitting here reading the paper, and you're doing your side-by-side thing, and you just sort of let people know you're aware of them." Yet it is also why it can be extremely hard to understand the phenomenon until you've experienced it. Merely looking at a stranger's Twitter or Facebook feed isn't interesting, because it seems like blather. Follow it for a day, though, and it begins to feel like a short story; follow it for a month, and it's a novel.

You could also regard the growing popularity of online awareness as a reaction to social isolation, the modern American disconnectedness that Robert Putnam explored in his book *Bowling Alone*. The mobile workforce requires people to travel more frequently for work, leaving friends and family behind, and members of the growing army of the self-employed often spend their days in solitude. Ambient intimacy becomes a way to "feel less alone," as more than one Facebook and Twitter user told me. 20

When I decided to try out Twitter last year, at first I didn't have anyone to follow. None of my friends were yet using the service. But while doing some Googling one day I stumbled upon the blog of Shannon Seery, a thirty-two-year-old recruiting consultant in Florida, and I noticed that she Twittered. Her Twitter updates were pretty charming—she would often post links to camera-phone pictures of her two children or videos of herself cooking Mexican food, or broadcast her agonized cries when a flight was delayed on a business trip. So on a whim I started "following" her—as easy on Twitter as a click of the mouse—and never took her off my account. (A Twitter account can be "private," so that only invited friends can read one's tweets, or it can be public, so anyone can; Seery's was public.) When I checked in last month, I noticed that she had built up a huge number of online connections: she was now following 677 people on Twitter and another 442 on Facebook. How in God's name, I wondered, could she follow so many people? Who precisely are they? I called Seery to find out.

"I have a rule," she told me. "I either have to know who you are, or I have to know of you." That means she monitors the lives of friends, family, anyone she works with, and she'll also follow interesting people she discovers via her friends' online lives. Like many people who live online, she has wound up following a few strangers—though after a few months they no longer feel like strangers, despite the fact that she has never physically met them.

I asked Seery how she finds the time to follow so many people online. The math seemed daunting. After all, if her one thousand online contacts each post just a couple of notes each a day, that's several thousand little social pings to sift through daily. What would it be like to get thousands of e-mail messages a day? But Seery made a point I heard from many others: Awareness tools aren't as cognitively demanding as an e-mail message. E-mail is something you have to stop to open and assess. It's personal; someone is asking for 100 percent of your attention. In contrast, ambient updates are all visible on one single page in a big row, and they're not really directed at you. This makes them skimmable, like newspaper headlines; maybe you'll read them all, maybe you'll skip some. Seery estimated that she needs to spend only a small part of each hour actively reading her Twitter stream.

Yet she has, she said, become far more gregarious online. "What's really funny is that before this 'social media' stuff, I always said that I'm not the type of person who had a ton of friends," she told me. "It's so hard to make plans and have an active social life, having the type of job I have where I travel all the time and have two small kids. But it's easy to tweet all the time, to post pictures of what I'm doing, to keep social relations up." She paused for a second, before continuing: "Things like Twitter have actually given me a much bigger social circle. I know more about more people than ever before."

I realized that this is becoming true of me, too. After following Seery's Twitter stream for a year, I'm more knowledgeable about the details of her life than the lives of my two sisters in Canada, whom I talk to only once every month or so. When I called Seery, I knew that she had been struggling with a three-day migraine headache; I began the conversation by asking her how she was feeling. 25

Online awareness inevitably leads to a curious question: What sort of relationships are these? What does it mean to have hundreds of "friends" on Facebook? What kind of friends are they, anyway?

In 1998, the anthropologist Robin Dunbar argued that each human has a hardwired upper limit on the number of people he or she can personally know at one time. Dunbar noticed that humans and apes both develop social bonds by engaging in some sort of grooming; apes do it by picking at and smoothing one another's fur, and humans do it with conversation. He theorized that ape and human brains could manage only a finite number of grooming relationships: Unless we spend enough time doing social grooming—chitchatting, trading gossip or, for apes, picking lice—we won't really feel that we "know" someone well enough to call him a friend. Dunbar noticed that ape groups tended to top out at fifty-five members. Since human brains were proportionally bigger, Dunbar figured that our maximum number of social connections would be similarly larger: about 150 on average. Sure enough, psychological studies have confirmed that human groupings naturally tail off at around 150 people: the "Dunbar number," as it is known. Are people who use Facebook and Twitter increasing their Dunbar number because they can so easily keep track of so many more people?

As I interviewed some of the most aggressively social people online—people who follow hundreds or even thousands of others—it became clear that the picture was a little more complex than this question would suggest. Many maintained that their circle of true intimates, their very close friends and family, had not become bigger. Constant online contact had made those ties immeasurably richer, but it hadn't actually increased the number of them; deep relationships are still predicated on face time, and there are only so many hours in the day for that.

But where their sociality had truly exploded was in their "weak ties"—loose acquaintances, people they knew less well. It might be someone they met at a conference, or someone from high school who recently "friended" them on Facebook, or somebody from last year's holiday party. In their pre-Internet lives, these sorts of acquaintances would have quickly faded from their attention. But when one of these far-flung people suddenly posts a personal note to your feed, it is essentially a reminder that they exist. I have noticed this effect myself. In the last few months, dozens of old work colleagues I knew from ten years ago in Toronto have friended me on Facebook, such that I'm now suddenly reading their stray comments and updates and falling into oblique, funny conversations with them. My overall Dunbar number is thus 301: Facebook (254) + Twitter (47), double what it would be without technology. Yet only twenty are family or people I'd consider close friends. The rest are weak ties—maintained via technology.

This rapid growth of weak ties can be a very good thing. Sociologists have long found that "weak ties" greatly expand your ability to solve problems. For example, if you're looking for a job and ask your friends, they won't be much help; they're too similar to you, and thus probably won't have any leads that you don't already have yourself. Remote acquaintances will be much more useful, because they're farther afield, yet still socially intimate enough to want to help you out. Many avid Twitter users—the ones who fire off witty posts hourly and wind up with thousands of intrigued followers—explicitly milk this dynamic for all it's worth, using their large online followings as a way to quickly answer almost any question. Laura Fitton, a social-media consultant who has become a minor celebrity on Twitter—she has more than 5,300 followers—recently discovered to her horror that her accountant had made an error in filing last year's taxes. She went to Twitter, wrote a tiny note explaining her problem, and within ten minutes her online audience had provided leads to lawyers and better accountants. Fritton joked to me that she no longer buys anything worth more than fifty dollars without quickly checking it with her Twitter network. 30

"I outsource my entire life," she said. "I can solve any problem on Twitter in six minutes." (She also keeps a secondary Twitter account that is private and only for a much smaller circle of close friends and family—"My little secret," she said. It is a strategy many people told me they used: one account for their weak ties, one for their deeper relationships.)

It is also possible, though, that this profusion of weak ties can become a problem. If you're reading daily updates from hundreds of people about whom they're dating and whether they're happy, it might, some critics worry, spread your emotional energy too thin, leaving less for true intimate relationships. Psychologists have long known that people can engage in "parasocial" relationships with fictional characters, like those on TV shows or in books, or with remote celebrities we read about in magazines. Parasocial relationships can use up some of the emotional space in our Dunbar number, crowding out real-life people. Danah Boyd, a fellow at Harvard's Berkman Center for Internet and Society who has studied social media for ten years, published a paper this spring arguing that awareness tools like News Feed might be creating a whole new class of relationships that are nearly parasocial—peripheral people in our network whose intimate details we follow closely online, even while they, like Angelina Jolie, are basically unaware we exist.

"The information we subscribe to on a feed is not the same as in a deep social relationship," Boyd told me. She has seen this herself; she has many virtual admirers that have, in essence, a parasocial relationship with her. "I've been very, very sick lately, and I write about it on Twitter and my blog, and I get all these people who are writing to me telling me ways to work around the health-care system, or they're writing saying, 'Hey, I broke my neck!' And I'm like, 'You're being very nice and trying to help me, but though you feel like you know me, you don't.' " Boyd sighed. "They can observe you, but it's not the same as knowing you."

When I spoke to Caterina Fake, a founder of Flickr (a popular photo-sharing site), she suggested an even more subtle danger: that the sheer ease of following her friends' updates online has made her occasionally lazy about actually taking the time to visit them in person. "At one point I realized I had a friend whose child I had seen, via photos on Flickr, grow from birth to one year old," she said. "I thought, I really should go meet her in person. But it was weird; I also felt that Flickr had satisfied that getting-to-know-you satisfaction, so I didn't feel the urgency. But then I was like, Oh, that's not sufficient! I should go in person!" She has about four hundred people she follows online but suspects many of those relationships are tissue-fragile. "These technologies allow you to be much more broadly friendly, but you just spread yourself much more thinly over many more people."

What is it like to never lose touch with anyone? One morning this summer 35 at my local café, I overheard a young woman complaining to her friend about a recent Facebook drama. Her name is Andrea Ahan, a twenty-seven-year-old restaurant entrepreneur, and she told me that she had discovered that high-school friends were uploading old photos of her to Facebook and tagging them with her name, so they automatically appeared in searches for her.

She was aghast. "I'm like, my God, these pictures are completely hideous!" Ahan complained, while her friend looked on sympathetically and sipped her coffee. "I'm wearing all these totally awful nineties clothes. I look like crap. And I'm like, Why are you people in my life, anyway? I haven't seen you in ten years. I don't know you anymore!" She began furiously detagging the pictures—removing her name, so they wouldn't show up in a search anymore.

Worse, Ahan was also confronting a common plague of Facebook: the recent ex. She had broken up with her boyfriend not long ago, but she hadn't "unfriended" him, because that felt too extreme. But soon he paired up with another young woman, and the new couple began having public conversations on Ahan's ex-boyfriend's page. One day, she noticed with alarm that the new girlfriend was quoting material Ahan had e-mailed privately to her boyfriend; she suspected he had been sharing the e-mail with his new girlfriend. It is the sort of weirdly subtle mind game that becomes possible via Facebook, and it drove Ahan nuts.

"Sometimes I think this stuff is just crazy, and everybody has got to get a life and stop obsessing over everyone's trivia and gossiping," she said.

Yet Ahan knows that she cannot simply walk away from her online life, because the people she knows online won't stop talking about her, or posting unflattering photos. She needs to stay on Facebook just to monitor what's being said about her. This is a common complaint I heard, particularly from people in their twenties who were in college when Facebook appeared and have never lived as adults without online awareness. For them, participation isn't optional. If you don't dive in, other people will define who you are. So you constantly stream your pictures, your thoughts, your relationship status, and what you're doing—right now!—if only to ensure the virtual version of you is accurate, or at least the one you want to present to the world.

40 This is the ultimate effect of the new awareness: It brings back the dynamics of small-town life, where everybody knows your business. Young people at college are the ones to experience this most viscerally, because, with more than 90 percent of their peers using Facebook, it is especially difficult for them to opt out. Zeynep Tufekci, a sociologist at the University of Maryland, Baltimore County, who has closely studied how college-age users are reacting to the world of awareness, told me that athletes used to sneak off to parties illicitly, breaking the no-drinking rule for team members. But then camera phones and Facebook came along, with students posting photos of the drunken carousing during the party; savvy coaches could see which athletes were breaking the rules. First the athletes tried to fight back by waking up early the morning after the party in a hungover daze to detag photos of themselves so they wouldn't be searchable. But that didn't work, because the coaches sometimes viewed the pictures live, as they went online at 2 a.m. So parties simply began banning all camera phones in a last-ditch attempt to preserve privacy.

"It's just like living in a village, where it's actually hard to lie because everybody knows the truth already," Tufekci said. "The current generation is never unconnected. They're never losing touch with their friends. So we're going back to a more normal place, historically. If you look at human history, the idea that you would drift through life, going from new relation to new relation, that's very new. It's just the twentieth century."

Psychologists and sociologists spent years wondering how humanity would adjust to the anonymity of life in the city, the wrenching upheavals of mobile immigrant labor—a world of lonely people ripped from their social ties. We now have precisely the opposite problem. Indeed, our modern awareness tools reverse the original conceit of the Internet. When cyberspace came along in the early 1990s, it was celebrated as a place where you could reinvent your identity—become someone new.

"If anything, it's identity-constraining now," Tufekci told me. "You can't play with your identity if your audience is always checking up on you. I had a student who posted that she was downloading some Pearl Jam, and someone wrote on her wall, 'Oh, right, ha-ha—I know you, and you're not into that.'" She laughed. "You know that old cartoon? 'On the Internet, nobody knows you're a dog'? On the Internet today, everybody knows you're a dog! If you don't want people to know you're a dog, you'd better stay away from a keyboard."

Or, as Leisa Reichelt, a consultant in London who writes regularly about ambient tools, put it to me: "Can you imagine a Facebook for children in kindergarten, and they never lose touch with those kids for the rest of their lives? What's that going to do to them?" Young people today are already developing an attitude toward their privacy that is simultaneously vigilant and laissez-faire. They curate their online personas as carefully as possible, knowing that everyone is watching—but they have also learned to shrug and accept the limits of what they can control.

It is easy to become unsettled by privacy-eroding aspects of awareness tools. But there is another—quite different—result of all this incessant updating: a culture of people who know much more about themselves. Many of the avid Twitterers, Flickrers, and Facebook users I interviewed described an unexpected side effect of constant self-disclosure. The act of stopping several times a day to observe what you're feeling or thinking can become, after weeks and weeks, a sort of philosophical act. It's like the Greek dictum to "know thyself," or the therapeutic concept of mindfulness. (Indeed, the question that floats eternally at the top of Twitter's Web site—"What are you doing?"—can come to seem existentially freighted. What are you doing?) Having an audience can make the self-reflection even more acute, since, as my interviewees noted, they're trying to describe their activities in a way that is not only accurate but also interesting to others: the status update as a literary form. 45

Laura Fitton, the social-media consultant, argues that her constant status updating has made her "a happier person, a calmer person" because the process of, say, describing a horrid morning at work forces her to look at it objectively. "It drags you out of your own head," she added. In an age of awareness, perhaps the person you see most clearly is yourself.

▪ QUESTIONS

Reading

1. What is the *Dunbar number*?
2. Thompson is reporting on Twitter, Facebook, and the world of digital intimacy, but he sums up his report with a controversial conclusion. Summarize this conclusion. Do you agree or disagree? Based on your own reading of Thompson's report, what different conclusion could you reach?
3. What does Thompson mean when he writes that our "modern awareness tools reverse the original conceit" of the Internet (paragraph 42)?

Exploratory Writing

1. Collaborating in small groups, make a list of advantages to having a presence on Facebook, Twitter, and similar sites, and a list of advantages to being "off the grid." Do you think that these forms of "digital intimacy" will be an enduring part of our society, or are they a passing fad?

ADVANTAGES OF FACEBOOK, TWITTER, AND SO ON	**ADVANTAGES OF BEING "OFF THE GRID"**

2. On an Internet search engine, conduct a search for the authors in this casebook. Make a chart of which ones keep a blog, maintain a Twitter feed, or have a Facebook page. Choose one of the authors, and list things you learned about him or her that would not be in a typical author biography. Did this search feel like "poking your head" into the author's private space?

Making Connections

1. Compare and contrast Andrew Sullivan's (p. 152) reflections on keeping a blog and Mona Eltahawy's (p. 163) observations on using Twitter with Thompson's conclusion that constant self-disclosure on the Internet becomes "a sort of philosophical act" of self-knowledge. How does each author characterize "friends"?

Essay Writing

1. Spend a full day (or, ideally, two or three days) not using the Internet at all — no e-mail, no social-networking sites, no Google, no *Wikipedia*. It will probably be a great inconvenience, partly because people you know may be online. Write an essay reflecting on how life in your generation would be different without any Internet technology at all.

EXPLAINING

The End of Forgetting

Jeffrey Rosen

Law professor Jeffrey Rosen teaches at George Washington University and serves as the legal affairs editor of the *New Republic*. He has written widely on legal issues, such as privacy concerns and Internet freedom, for magazines and newspapers, including the *New York Times* and the *New Yorker,* and he is the author of *The Unwanted Gaze: The Destruction of Privacy in America* (2000), *The Naked Crowd: Reclaiming Security and Freedom in an Anxious Age* (2004), *The Most Democratic Branch: How the Courts Serve America* (2006), and *The Supreme Court: The Personalities and Rivalries That Defined America* (2007). He was a Marshall Scholar at Oxford University and has been named one of the ten best magazine journalists in America by the *Chicago Tribune*. In this *New York Times Magazine* article from 2011, Rosen explores how the information we post online can follow us offline—with destructive consequences.

Four years ago, Stacy Snyder, then a twenty-five-year-old teacher in training at Conestoga Valley High School in Lancaster, Pennsylvania, posted a photo on her MySpace page that showed her at a party wearing a pirate hat and drinking from a plastic cup, with the caption "Drunken Pirate." After discovering the page, her supervisor at the high school told her the photo was "unprofessional," and the dean of Millersville University School of Education, where Snyder was enrolled, said she was promoting drinking in virtual view of her underage students. As a result, days before Snyder's scheduled graduation, the university denied her a teaching degree. Snyder sued, arguing that the university had violated her First Amendment rights by penalizing her for her (perfectly legal) after-hours behavior. But in 2008, a federal district judge rejected the claim, saying that because Snyder was a public employee whose photo didn't relate to matters of public concern, her "Drunken Pirate" post was not protected speech.

When historians of the future look back on the perils of the early digital age, Stacy Snyder may well be an icon. The problem she faced is only one example of a challenge that, in big and small ways, is confronting millions of people around the globe: how best to live our lives in a world where the Internet records everything and forgets nothing—where every online photo, status update, Twitter post, and blog entry by and about us can be stored forever. With Web sites like LOL Facebook Moments, which collects and shares embarrassing personal revelations from Facebook users, ill-advised photos and online chatter are coming back to haunt people months or years after the fact. Examples are proliferating daily: There was the sixteen-year-old British girl who was fired from her office job for complaining on Facebook, "I'm so totally bored!!"; there was the sixty-six-year-old Canadian psychotherapist who tried to enter the United States but was turned away at the border—and barred permanently from visiting the country—after a border guard's Internet search found that the therapist had written an article in a philosophy journal describing his experiments thirty years ago with L.S.D.

According to a recent survey by Microsoft, 75 percent of U.S. recruiters and human-resource professionals report that their companies require them to do online research about candidates, and many use a range of sites when scrutinizing applicants—including search engines, social-networking sites, photo- and video-sharing sites, personal Web sites and blogs, Twitter and online-gaming sites. Seventy percent of U.S. recruiters report that they have rejected candidates because of information found online, like photos and discussion-board conversations and membership in controversial groups.

Technological advances, of course, have often presented new threats to privacy. In 1890, in perhaps the most famous article on privacy ever written, Samuel Warren and Louis Brandeis complained that because of new technology—like the Kodak camera and the tabloid press—"gossip is no longer the resource of the idle and of the vicious but has become a trade." But the mild society gossip of the Gilded Age pales before the volume of revelations contained in the photos, video, and chatter on social-media sites and elsewhere across the Internet. Facebook, which surpassed MySpace in 2008 as the largest social-networking site, now has nearly 500 million members, or 22 percent of all Internet users, who spend more than 500 billion minutes a month on the site. Facebook users share more than 25 billion pieces of content each month (including news stories, blog posts and photos), and the average user creates 70 pieces of content a month. There are more than 100 million registered Twitter users, and the Library of Congress recently announced that it will be acquiring—and permanently storing—the entire archive of public Twitter posts since 2006.

5 In Brandeis's day—and until recently, in ours—you had to be a celebrity to be gossiped about in public: Today all of us are learning to expect the scrutiny that used to be reserved for the famous and the infamous. A twenty-six-year-old Manhattan woman told the *New York Times* that she was afraid of being tagged in online photos because it might reveal that she wears only two outfits when out on the town—a Lynyrd Skynyrd T-shirt or a basic black dress. "You have movie-star issues," she said, "and you're just a person."

We've known for years that the Web allows for unprecedented voyeurism, exhibitionism, and inadvertent indiscretion, but we are only beginning to understand the costs of an age in which so much of what we say, and of what others say about us, goes into our permanent—and public—digital files. The fact that the Internet never seems to forget is threatening, at an almost existential level, our ability to control our identities; to preserve the option of reinventing ourselves and starting anew; to overcome our checkered pasts.

In a recent book, *Delete: The Virtue of Forgetting in the Digital Age*, the cyberscholar Viktor Mayer-Schönberger cites Stacy Snyder's case as a reminder of the importance of "societal forgetting." By "erasing external memories," he says in the book, "our society accepts that human beings evolve over time, that we have the capacity to learn from past experiences and adjust our behavior." In traditional societies, where missteps are observed but not necessarily recorded,

the limits of human memory ensure that people's sins are eventually forgotten. By contrast, Mayer-Schönberger notes, a society in which everything is recorded "will forever tether us to all our past actions, making it impossible, in practice, to escape them." He concludes that "without some form of forgetting, forgiving becomes a difficult undertaking."

It's often said that we live in a permissive era, one with infinite second chances. But the truth is that for a great many people, the permanent memory bank of the Web increasingly means there are *no* second chances—no opportunities to escape a scarlet letter in your digital past. Now the worst thing you've done is often the first thing everyone knows about you.

The Crisis—and the Solution?

All this has created something of a collective identity crisis. For most of human history, the idea of reinventing yourself or freely shaping your identity—of presenting different selves in different contexts (at home, at work, at play)—was hard to fathom, because people's identities were fixed by their roles in a rigid social hierarchy. With little geographic or social mobility, you were defined not as an individual but by your village, your class, your job, or your guild. But that started to change in the late Middle Ages and the Renaissance, with a growing individualism that came to redefine human identity. As people perceived themselves increasingly as individuals, their status became a function not of inherited categories but of their own efforts and achievements. This new conception of malleable and fluid identity found its fullest and purest expression in the American ideal of the self-made man, a term popularized by Henry Clay in 1832. From the late eighteenth to the early twentieth century, millions of Europeans moved from the Old World to the New World and then continued to move westward across America, a development that led to what the historian Frederick Jackson Turner called "the significance of the frontier," in which the possibility of constant migration from civilization to the wilderness made Americans distrustful of hierarchy and committed to inventing and reinventing themselves.

In the twentieth century, however, the ideal of the self-made man came under siege. The end of the Western frontier led to worries that Americans could no longer seek a fresh start and leave their past behind, a kind of reinvention associated with the phrase "G.T.T.," or "Gone to Texas." But the dawning of the Internet age promised to resurrect the ideal of what the psychiatrist Robert Jay Lifton has called the "protean self." If you couldn't flee to Texas, you could always seek out a new chat room and create a new screen name. For some technology enthusiasts, the Web was supposed to be the second flowering of the open frontier, and the ability to segment our identities with an endless supply of pseudonyms, avatars, and categories of friendship was supposed to let people present different sides of their personalities in different contexts. What seemed within our grasp was a power that only Proteus possessed: namely, perfect control over our shifting identities. 10

But the hope that we could carefully control how others view us in different contexts has proved to be another myth. As social-networking sites expanded, it was no longer quite so easy to have segmented identities: Now that so many people use a single platform to post constant status updates and photos about their private and public activities, the idea of a home self, a work self, a family self, and a high school–friends self has become increasingly untenable. In fact, the attempt to maintain different selves often arouses suspicion. Moreover, far from giving us a new sense of control over the face we present to the world, the Internet is shackling us to everything that we have ever said, or that anyone has said about us, making the possibility of digital self-reinvention seem like an ideal from a distant era.

Concern about these developments has intensified this year, as Facebook took steps to make the digital profiles of its users generally more public than private. Last December, the company announced that parts of user profiles that had previously been private—including every user's friends, relationship status, and family relations—would become public and accessible to other users. Then in April, Facebook introduced an interactive system called Open Graph that can share your profile information and friends with the Facebook partner sites you visit.

What followed was an avalanche of criticism from users, privacy regulators, and advocates around the world. Four Democratic senators—Charles Schumer of New York, Michael Bennet of Colorado, Mark Begich of Alaska, and Al Franken of Minnesota—wrote to the chief executive of Facebook, Mark Zuckerberg, expressing concern about the "instant personalization" feature and the new privacy settings. The reaction to Facebook's changes was such that when four NYU. students announced plans in April to build a free social-networking site called Diaspora, which wouldn't compel users to compromise their privacy, they raised more than $20,000 from more than 700 backers in a matter of weeks. In May, Facebook responded to all the criticism by introducing a new set of privacy controls that the company said would make it easier for users to understand what kind of information they were sharing in various contexts.

Facebook's partial retreat has not quieted the desire to do something about an urgent problem. All around the world, political leaders, scholars, and citizens are searching for responses to the challenge of preserving control of our identities in a digital world that never forgets. Are the most promising solutions going to be technological? Legislative? Judicial? Ethical? A result of shifting social norms and cultural expectations? Or some mix of the above? Alex Türk, the French data-protection commissioner, has called for a "constitutional right to oblivion" that would allow citizens to maintain a greater degree of anonymity online and in public places. In Argentina, the writers Alejandro Tortolini and Enrique Quagliano have started a campaign to "reinvent forgetting on the Internet," exploring a range of political and technological ways of making data disappear. In February, the European Union helped finance a campaign called "Think B4 U post!" that urges young people to consider the "potential consequences" of publishing photos of themselves or their friends without "thinking carefully" and asking permission. And in the United States, a group of technologists, legal scholars, and cyberthinkers are exploring ways of recreating the possibility of digital forgetting. These approaches share the common goal of reconstructing a form of control over our identities: the ability to reinvent ourselves, to escape our pasts and to improve the selves that we present to the world.

Reputation Bankruptcy and Twittergation

A few years ago, at the giddy dawn of the Web 2.0 era—so called to mark the rise of user-generated online content—many technological theorists assumed that self-governing communities could ensure, through the self-correcting wisdom of the crowd, that all participants enjoyed the online identities they deserved. *Wikipedia* is one embodiment of the faith that the wisdom of the crowd can correct most mistakes—that a *Wikipedia* entry for a small-town mayor, for example, will reflect the reputation he deserves. And if the crowd fails—perhaps by turning into a digital mob—*Wikipedia* offers other forms of redress. Those who think their *Wikipedia* entries lack context, because they overemphasize a single personal or professional mistake, can petition a group of select editors that decides whether a particular event in someone's past has been given "undue weight." For example, if the small-town mayor had an exemplary career but then was arrested for drunken driving, which came to dominate his *Wikipedia* entry, he can petition to have the event put in context or made less prominent. 15

In practice, however, self-governing communities like *Wikipedia*—or algorithmically self-correcting systems like Google—often leave people feeling misrepresented and burned. Those who think that their online reputations have been unfairly tarnished by an isolated incident or two now have a practical option: consulting a firm like ReputationDefender, which promises to clean up your online image. ReputationDefender was founded by Michael Fertik, a Harvard Law School graduate who was troubled by the idea of young people being forever tainted online by their youthful indiscretions. "I was seeing articles about the 'Lord of the Flies' behavior that all of us engage in at that age," he told me, "and it felt un-American that when the conduct was online, it could have permanent effects on the speaker and the victim. The right to new beginnings and the right to self-definition have always been among the most beautiful American ideals."

ReputationDefender, which has customers in more than one hundred countries, is the most successful of the handful of reputation-related start-ups that have been growing rapidly after the privacy concerns raised by Facebook and Google. (ReputationDefender recently raised $15 million in new venture capital.) For a fee, the company will monitor your online reputation, contacting Web sites individually and asking them to take down offending items. In addition, with the help of the kind of search-optimization technology that businesses use to raise their Google profiles, ReputationDefender can bombard the Web with positive or neutral information about its customers, either creating new Web pages or by multiplying links to existing ones to ensure they show up at the top of any Google search. (Services begin from $10 a month to $1,000 a year; for challenging cases, the price can rise into the tens of thousands.) By automatically raising the Google ranks of the positive links, ReputationDefender pushes the negative links to the back pages of a Google search, where they're harder to find. "We're hearing stories of employers increasingly asking candidates to open up Facebook pages in front of them during job interviews," Fertik told me. "Our customers include parents whose kids have talked about them on the Internet—'Mom didn't get the raise'; 'Dad got fired'; 'Mom and Dad are fighting a lot, and I'm worried they'll get a divorce.'"

Companies like ReputationDefender offer a promising short-term solution for those who can afford it; but tweaking your Google profile may not be enough for reputation management in the near future, as Web 2.0 swiftly gives way to Web. 3.0—a world in which user-generated content is combined with a new layer of data aggregation and analysis and live video. For example, the Facebook application Photo Finder, by Face.com, uses facial-recognition and social-connections software to allow you to locate any photo of yourself or a friend on Facebook, regardless of whether the photo was "tagged"—that is, the individual in the photo was identified by name. At the moment, Photo Finder allows you to identify only people on your contact list, but as facial-recognition technology becomes more widespread and sophisticated, it will almost certainly challenge our expectation of anonymity in public. People will be able to snap a cellphone picture (or video) of a stranger, plug the images into Google and pull up all tagged and untagged photos of that person that exist on the Web.

In the nearer future, Internet searches for images are likely to be combined with social-network aggregator search engines, like today's Spokeo and Pipl, which combine data from online sources—including political contributions, blog posts, YouTube videos, Web comments, real estate listings and photo albums. Increasingly these aggregator sites will rank people's public and private reputations, like the new Web site Unvarnished, a reputation marketplace where people can write anonymous reviews about anyone. In the Web 3.0 world, Fertik predicts, people will be rated, assessed and scored based not on their creditworthiness but on their trustworthiness as good parents, good dates, good employees, good babysitters or good insurance risks.

Anticipating these challenges, some legal scholars have begun imagining new laws that could allow people to correct, or escape from, the reputation scores that may govern our personal and professional interactions in the future. Jonathan Zittrain, who teaches cyberlaw at Harvard Law School, supports an idea he calls "reputation bankruptcy," which would give people a chance to wipe their reputation slates clean and start over. To illustrate the problem, Zittrain showed me an iPhone app called Date Check, by Intelius, that offers a "sleaze detector" to let you investigate people you're thinking about dating—it reports their criminal histories, address histories, and summaries of their social-networking profiles. Services like Date Check, Zittrain said, could soon become even more sophisticated, rating a person's social desirability based on minute social measurements—like how often he or she was approached or avoided by others at parties (a ranking that would be easy to calibrate under existing technology using cellphones and Bluetooth). Zittrain also speculated that, over time, more and more reputation queries will be processed by a handful of de facto reputation brokers—like the existing consumer-reporting agencies Experian and Equifax, for example—which will provide ratings for people based on their sociability, trustworthiness, and employability.

To allow people to escape from negative scores generated by these services, Zittrain says that people should be allowed to declare "reputation bankruptcy" every ten years or so, wiping out certain categories of ratings or sensitive information. His model is the Fair Credit Reporting Act, which requires consumer-reporting agencies to provide you with one free credit report a year—so you can dispute negative or inaccurate information—and prohibits the agencies from retaining negative information about bankruptcies, late payments or tax liens for more than 10 years. "Like personal financial bankruptcy, or the way in which a state often seals a juvenile criminal record and gives a child a 'fresh start' as an adult," Zittrain writes in his book *The Future of the Internet and How to Stop It*, "we ought to consider how to implement the idea of a second or third chance into our digital spaces."

Another proposal, offered by Paul Ohm, a law professor at the University of Colorado, would make it illegal for employers to fire or refuse to hire anyone on the basis of legal off-duty conduct revealed in Facebook postings or Google profiles. "Is it really fair for employers to know what you've put in your Facebook status updates?" Ohm asks. "We could say that Facebook status updates have taken the place of water-cooler chat, which employers were never supposed to overhear, and we could pass a prohibition on the sorts of information employers can and can't consider when they hire someone."

Ohm became interested in this problem in the course of researching the ease with which we can learn the identities of people from supposedly anonymous personal data like movie preferences and health information. When Netflix, for example, released 100 million purportedly anonymous records revealing how almost 500,000 users had rated movies from 1999 to 2005, researchers were able to identify people in the database by name with a high degree of accuracy if they knew even only a little bit about their movie-watching preferences, obtained from public data posted on other ratings sites.

Ohm says he worries that employers would be able to use social-network-aggregator services to identify people's book and movie preferences and even Internet-search terms, and then fire or refuse to hire them on that basis. A handful of states—including New York, California, Colorado, and North Dakota—broadly prohibit employers from discriminating against employees for legal off-duty conduct like smoking. Ohm suggests that these laws could be extended to prevent certain categories of employers from refusing to hire people based on Facebook pictures, status updates, and other legal but embarrassing personal information. (In practice, these laws might be hard to enforce, since employers might not disclose the real reason for their hiring decisions, so employers, like credit-reporting agents, might also be required by law to disclose to job candidates the negative information in their digital files.)

25 Another legal option for responding to online setbacks to your reputation is to sue under current law. There's already a sharp rise in lawsuits known as Twittergation—that is, suits to force Web sites to remove slanderous or false posts. Last year, Courtney Love was sued for libel by the fashion designer Boudoir Queen for supposedly slanderous comments posted on Twitter, on Love's MySpace page, and on the designer's online marketplace-feedback page. But even if you win a U.S. libel lawsuit, the Web site doesn't have to take the offending material down any more than a newspaper that has lost a libel suit has to remove the offending content from its archive.

Some scholars, therefore, have proposed creating new legal rights to force Web sites to remove false or slanderous statements. Cass Sunstein, the Obama administration's regulatory czar, suggests in his new book, *On Rumors,* that there might be "a general right to demand retraction after a clear demonstration that a statement is both false and damaging." (If a newspaper or blogger refuses to post a retraction, they might be liable for damages.) Sunstein adds that Web sites might be required to take down false postings after receiving notice that they are false—an approach modeled on the Digital Millennium Copyright Act, which requires Web sites to remove content that supposedly infringes intellectual property rights after receiving a complaint.

As Stacy Snyder's "Drunken Pirate" photo suggests, however, many people aren't worried about false information posted by others—they're worried about true information they've posted about themselves when it is taken out of context or given undue weight. And defamation law doesn't apply to true information or statements of opinion. Some legal scholars want to expand the ability to sue over true but embarrassing violations of privacy—although it appears to be a quixotic goal.

Daniel Solove, a George Washington University law professor and author of the book *The Future of Reputation*, says that laws forbidding people to breach confidences could be expanded to allow you to sue your Facebook friends if they share your embarrassing photos or posts in violation of your privacy settings. Expanding legal rights in this way, however, would run up against the First Amendment rights of others. Invoking the right to free speech, the U.S. Supreme Court has already held that the media can't be prohibited from publishing the name of a rape victim that they obtained from public records. Generally, American judges hold that if you disclose something to a few people, you can't stop them from sharing the information with the rest of the world.

That's one reason that the most promising solutions to the problem of embarrassing but true information online may be not legal but technological ones. Instead of suing after the damage is done (or hiring a firm to clean up our messes), we need to explore ways of preemptively making the offending words or pictures disappear.

Expiration Dates

Jorge Luis Borges, in his short story "Funes, the Memorious," describes a young man who, as a result of a riding accident, has lost his ability to forget. Funes has a tremendous memory, but he is so lost in the details of everything he knows that he is unable to convert the information into knowledge and unable, as a result, to grow in wisdom. Viktor Mayer-Schönberger, in *Delete*, uses the Borges story as an emblem for the personal and social costs of being so shackled by our digital past that we are unable to evolve and learn from our mistakes. After reviewing the various possible legal solutions to this problem, Mayer-Schönberger says he is more convinced by a technological fix: namely, mimicking human forgetting with built-in expiration dates for data. He imagines a world in which digital-storage devices could be programmed to delete photos or blog posts or other data that have reached their expiration dates, and he suggests that users could be prompted to select an expiration date before saving any data. 30

This is not an entirely fanciful vision. Google not long ago decided to render all search queries anonymous after nine months (by deleting part of each Internet protocol address), and the upstart search engine Cuil has announced that it won't keep any personally identifiable information at all, a privacy feature that distinguishes it from Google. And there are already small-scale privacy apps that offer disappearing data. An app called TigerText allows text-message senders to set a time limit from one minute to thirty days after which the text disappears from the company's servers on which it is stored and therefore from the senders' and recipients' phones. (The founder of TigerText, Jeffrey Evans, has said he chose the name before the scandal involving Tiger Woods's supposed texts to a mistress.)

Expiration dates could be implemented more broadly in various ways. Researchers at the University of Washington, for example, are developing a technology called Vanish that makes electronic data "self-destruct" after a specified period of time. Instead of relying on Google, Facebook, or Hotmail to delete the data that is stored "in the cloud"—in other words, on their distributed servers—Vanish encrypts the data and then "shatters" the encryption key. To read the data, your computer has to put the pieces of the key back together, but they "erode" or "rust" as time passes, and after a certain point the document can no longer be read. Tadayoshi Kohno, a designer of Vanish, told me that the system could provide expiration dates not only for e-mail but also for any data stored in the cloud, including photos or text or anything posted on Facebook, Google, or blogs. The technology doesn't promise perfect control—you can't stop someone from copying your photos or Facebook chats during the period in which they are not encrypted. But as Vanish improves, it could bring us much closer to a world where our data didn't linger forever.

Kohno told me that Facebook, if it wanted to, could implement expiration dates on its own platform, making our data disappear after, say, three days or three months unless a user specified that he wanted it to linger forever. It might be a more welcome option for Facebook to encourage the development of Vanish-style apps that would allow individual users who are concerned about privacy to make their own data disappear without imposing the default on all Facebook users.

So far, however, Zuckerberg, Facebook's CEO, has been moving in the opposite direction—toward transparency rather than privacy. In defending Facebook's recent decision to make the default for profile information about friends and relationship status public rather than private, Zuckerberg said in January to the founder of the publication *TechCrunch* that Facebook had an obligation to reflect "current social norms" that favored exposure over privacy. "People have really gotten comfortable not only sharing more information and different kinds but more openly and with more people, and that social norm is just something that has evolved over time," he said.

Privacy's New Normal

But not all Facebook users agree with Zuckerberg. Plenty of anecdotal evidence suggests that young people, having been burned by Facebook (and frustrated by its privacy policy, which at more than 5,000 words is longer than the U.S. Constitution), are savvier than older users about cleaning up their tagged photos and being careful about what they post. And two recent studies challenge the conventional wisdom that young people have no qualms about having their entire lives shared and preserved online forever. A University of California, Berkeley, study released in April found that large majorities of people between eighteen and twenty-two said there should be laws that require Web sites to delete all stored information about individuals (88 percent) and that give people the right to know all the information Web sites know about them (62 percent)—percentages that mirrored the privacy views of older adults. A recent Pew study found that eighteen-to-twenty-nine-year-olds are actually more concerned about their online profiles than older people are, vigilantly deleting unwanted posts, removing their names from tagged photos, and censoring themselves as they share personal information, because they are coming to understand the dangers of oversharing.

Still, Zuckerberg is on to something when he recognizes that the future of our online identities and reputations will ultimately be shaped not just by laws and technologies but also by changing social norms. And norms are already developing to recreate off-the-record spaces in public, with no photos, Twitter posts, or blogging allowed. Milk and Honey, an exclusive bar on Manhattan's Lower East Side, requires potential members to sign an agreement promising not to blog about the bar's goings on or to post photos on social-networking sites, and other bars and nightclubs are adopting similar policies. I've been at dinners recently where someone has requested, in all seriousness, "Please don't tweet this"—a custom that is likely to spread.

But what happens when people transgress those norms, using Twitter or tagging photos in ways that cause us serious embarrassment? Can we imagine a world in which new norms develop that make it easier for people to forgive and forget one another's digital sins?

That kind of social norm may be harder to develop. Alessandro Acquisti, a scholar at Carnegie Mellon University, studies the behavioral economics of privacy—that is, the conscious and unconscious mental trade-offs we make in deciding whether to reveal or conceal information, balancing the benefits of sharing with the dangers of disclosure. He is conducting experiments about the "decay time" and the relative weight of good and bad information—in other words, whether people discount positive information about you more quickly and heavily than they discount negative information about you. His research group's preliminary results suggest that if rumors spread about something good you did ten years ago, like winning a prize, they will be discounted; but if rumors spread about something bad that you did ten years ago, like driving drunk, that information has staying power. Research in behavioral psychology confirms that people pay more attention to bad rather than good information, and Acquisti says he fears that "twenty years from now, if all of us have a skeleton on Facebook, people may not discount it because it was an error in our youth."

On the assumption that strangers may not make it easy for us to escape our pasts, Acquisti is also studying technologies and strategies of "privacy nudges" that might prompt people to think twice before sharing sensitive photos or information in the first place. Gmail, for example, has introduced a feature that forces you to think twice before sending drunken e-mail messages. When you enable the feature, called Mail Goggles, it prompts you to solve simple math problems before sending e-mail messages at times you're likely to regret. (By default, Mail Goggles is active only late on weekend nights.) Acquisti is investigating similar strategies of "soft paternalism" that might nudge people to hesitate before posting, say, drunken photos from Cancún. "We could easily think about a system, when you are uploading certain photos, that immediately detects how sensitive the photo will be."

A silly but surprisingly effective alternative might be to have an anthropomorphic icon—a stern version of Microsoft's Clippy—that could give you a reproachful look before you hit the send button. According to M. Ryan Calo, who runs the consumer-privacy project at Stanford Law School, experimenters studying strategies of "visceral notice" have found that when people navigate a Web site in the presence of a human-looking online character who seems to be actively following the cursor, they disclose less personal information than people who browse with no character or one who appears not to be paying attention. As people continue to experience the drawbacks of living in a world that never forgets, they may well learn to hesitate before posting information, with or without humanoid Clippys. 40

Forgiveness

In addition to exposing less for the Web to forget, it might be helpful for us to explore new ways of living in a world that is slow to forgive. It's sobering, now that we live in a world misleadingly called a "global village," to think about privacy in actual, small villages long ago. In the villages described in the Babylonian Talmud, for example, any kind of gossip or tale-bearing about other people—oral or written, true or false, friendly or mean—was considered a terrible sin because small communities have long memories and every word spoken about other people was thought to ascend to the heavenly cloud. (The digital cloud has made this metaphor literal.) But the Talmudic villages were, in fact, far more humane and forgiving than our brutal global village, where much of the content on the Internet would meet the Talmudic definition of gossip: although the Talmudic sages believed that God reads our thoughts and records them in the book of life, they also believed that God erases the book for those who atone for their sins by asking forgiveness of those they have wronged. In the Talmud, people have an obligation not to remind others of their past misdeeds, on the assumption they may have atoned and grown spiritually from their mistakes. "If a man was a repentant [sinner]," the Talmud says, "one must not say to him, 'Remember your former deeds.'"

Unlike God, however, the digital cloud rarely wipes our slates clean, and the keepers of the cloud today are sometimes less forgiving than their all-powerful divine predecessor. In an interview with Charlie Rose on PBS, Eric Schmidt, the CEO of Google, said that "the next generation is infinitely more social online"—and less private—"as evidenced by their Facebook pictures," which "will be around when they're running for president years from now." Schmidt added: "As long as the answer is that I chose to make a mess of myself with this picture, then it's fine. The issue is when somebody else does it." If people chose, to expose themselves for fifteen minutes of fame, Schmidt says, "that's their choice, and they have to live with it."

Schmidt added that the "notion of control is fundamental to the evolution of these privacy-based solutions," pointing to Google Latitude, which allows people to broadcast their locations in real time.

This idea of privacy as a form of control is echoed by many privacy scholars, but it seems too harsh to say that if people like Stacy Snyder don't use their privacy settings responsibly, they have to live forever with the consequences. Privacy protects us from being unfairly judged out of context on the basis of snippets of private information that have been exposed against our will; but we can be just as unfairly judged out of context on the basis of snippets of public information that we have unwisely chosen to reveal to the wrong audience.

Moreover, the narrow focus on privacy as a form of control misses what really worries people on the Internet today. What people seem to want is not simply control over their privacy settings; they want control over their online reputations. But the idea that any of us can control our reputations is, of course, an unrealistic fantasy. The truth is we can't possibly control what others say or know or think about us in a world of Facebook and Google, nor can we realistically demand that others give us the deference and respect to which we think we're entitled. On the Internet, it turns out, we're not entitled to demand any particular respect at all, and if others don't have the empathy necessary to forgive our missteps, or the attention spans necessary to judge us in context, there's nothing we can do about it. 45

But if we can't control what others think or say or view about us, we can control our own reaction to photos, videos, blogs and Twitter posts that we feel unfairly represent us. A recent study suggests that people on Facebook and other social-networking sites express their real personalities, despite the widely held assumption that people try online to express an enhanced or idealized impression of themselves. Samuel Gosling, the University of Texas, Austin, psychology professor who conducted the study, told the Facebook blog, "We found that judgments of people based on nothing but their Facebook profiles correlate pretty strongly with our measure of what that person is really like, and that measure consists of both how the profile owner sees him or herself and how that profile owner's friends see the profile owner."

By comparing the online profiles of college-aged people in the United States and Germany with their actual personalities and their idealized personalities, or how they wanted to see themselves, Gosling found that the online profiles conveyed "rather accurate images of the profile owners, either because people aren't trying to look good or because they are trying and failing to pull it off." (Personality impressions based on the online profiles were most accurate for extroverted people and least accurate for neurotic people, who cling tenaciously to an idealized self-image.)

Gosling is optimistic about the implications of his study for the possibility of digital forgiveness. He acknowledged that social technologies are forcing us to merge identities that used to be separate—we can no longer have segmented selves like "a home or family self, a friend self, a leisure self, a work self." But although he told Facebook, "I have to find a way to reconcile my professor self with my having-a-few-drinks self," he also suggested that as all of us have to merge our public and private identities, photos showing us having a few drinks on Facebook will no longer seem so scandalous. "You see your accountant going out on weekends and attending clown conventions, that no longer makes you think that he's not a good accountant. We're coming to terms and reconciling with that merging of identities."

Perhaps society will become more forgiving of drunken Facebook pictures in the way Gosling says he expects it might. And some may welcome the end of the segmented self, on the grounds that it will discourage bad behavior and hypocrisy: it's harder to have clandestine affairs when you're broadcasting your every move on Facebook, Twitter, and Foursquare. But a humane society values privacy, because it allows people to cultivate different aspects of their personalities in different contexts; and at the moment, the enforced merging of identities that used to be separate is leaving many casualties in its wake. Stacy Snyder couldn't reconcile her "aspiring-teacher self" with her "having-a-few-drinks self": Even the impression, correct or not, that she had a drink in a pirate hat at an off-campus party was enough to derail her teaching career.

That doesn't mean, however, that it had to derail her life. After taking down 50 her MySpace profile, Snyder is understandably trying to maintain her privacy: Her lawyer told me in a recent interview that she is now working in human resources; she did not respond to a request for comment. But her success as a human being who can change and evolve, learning from her mistakes and growing in wisdom, has nothing to do with the digital file she can never entirely escape. Our character, ultimately, can't be judged by strangers on the basis of our Facebook or Google profiles; it can be judged by only those who know us and have time to evaluate our strengths and weaknesses, face to face and in context, with insight and understanding. In the meantime, as all of us stumble over the challenges of living in a world without forgetting, we need to learn new forms of empathy, new ways of defining ourselves without reference to what others say about us, and new ways of forgiving one another for the digital trails that will follow us forever.

▪ QUESTIONS

Reading

1. What does Rosen mean by "the end of forgetting"?
2. Why did four Democratic senators write to Mark Zuckerberg?
3. What is Web 3.0 (versus Web 2.0)? How does it relate to Rosen's overall explanation?

Exploratory Writing

1. Highlight, underline, or flag the possible solutions to the problem of "the end of forgetting" that Rosen mentions in this article, including solutions that have been tried already, and solutions that have been proposed for the future. Choose one solution and evaluate its pros and cons.

2. Conduct a comprehensive Internet search of yourself or someone you know, and write a list of everything you find. Did any inaccurate or slanderous material come up? Did you find anything you or the person you know would permanently erase from the public record? In light of your results, what are your thoughts and feelings about the problems Rosen explains in this article?

Making Connections

1. Rosen mentions Samuel Warren and Louis Brandeis's famous article, published in 1890, claiming that because of new technology, "gossip is no longer the resource of the idle and of the vicious but has become a trade." Consider David Friedman's (p. 566) report on the first "text messages" from 1890. In your opinion, how has new technology truly, deeply changed society? In what ways are apparent technological changes merely new manifestations of old problems?

Essay Writing

1. "We are only beginning to understand the costs of an age in which so much of what we say . . . goes into our permanent—and public—digital files," writes Rosen. "The fact that the Internet never seems to forget is threatening, at an almost existential level, our ability to control our identities . . ." (paragraph 6). Write an essay reflecting on your identity, online and off. Do you have more than one "identity"? How do these identities differ? Where do they overlap?

ARGUING

Is Google Making Us Stupid?

Nicholas Carr

Nicholas Carr (b. 1959) has published numerous books and articles on the intersection of technology, business, and culture. Of these, the most incendiary have been *Does IT Matter?* (2004), a book that argues the diminished importance of information technology in an increasingly savvy corporate workplace; "The Amorality of Web 2.0" (Rough Type, 2005), an article that criticizes the quality of crowd-sourced information projects such as *Wikipedia* and the blogosphere as opposed to the more expensive professional alternatives they displace; and the following essay, first published in the *Atlantic* in 2008, which posits that the Internet may diminish our capacity for concentration and contemplation as well as lead to other detrimental effects on cognition. His most recent book, *The Shallows: What the Internet Is Doing to Our Brain* (2011), was a finalist for the Pulitzer Prize in general nonfiction. Carr holds a BA from Dartmouth College and an MA in English literature from Harvard University. In addition to writing best-sellers and much-discussed technology articles (often published on his blog, Rough Type), Carr has been a speaker at MIT, Harvard, the Kennedy School of Government, and NASA. He was named to *Encyclopaedia Britannica*'s editorial board of advisers in 2008.

"Dave, stop. Stop, will you? Stop, Dave. Will you stop, Dave?" So the supercomputer HAL pleads with the implacable astronaut Dave Bowman in a famous and weirdly poignant scene toward the end of Stanley Kubrick's *2001: A Space Odyssey*. Bowman, having nearly been sent to a deep-space death by the malfunctioning machine, is calmly, coldly disconnecting the memory circuits that control its artificial brain. "Dave, my mind is going," HAL says, forlornly. "I can feel it. I can feel it."

I can feel it, too. Over the past few years I've had an uncomfortable sense that someone, or something, has been tinkering with my brain, remapping the neural circuitry, reprogramming the memory. My mind isn't going—so far as I can tell—but it's changing. I'm not thinking the way I used to think. I can feel it most strongly when I'm reading. Immersing myself in a book or a lengthy article used to be easy. My mind would get caught up in the narrative or the turns of the argument, and I'd spend hours strolling through long stretches of prose. That's rarely the case anymore. Now my concentration often starts to drift after two or three pages. I get fidgety, lose the thread, begin looking for something else to do. I feel as if I'm always dragging my wayward brain back to the text. The deep reading that used to come naturally has become a struggle.

I think I know what's going on. For more than a decade now, I've been spending a lot of time online, searching and surfing and sometimes adding to the great databases of the Internet. The Web has been a godsend to me as a writer. Research that once required days in the stacks or periodical rooms of libraries can now be done in minutes. A few Google searches, some quick clicks on hyperlinks, and I've got the telltale fact or pithy quote I was after. Even when I'm not working, I'm as likely as not to be foraging in the Web's info-thickets—reading and writing e-mails, scanning headlines and blog posts, watching videos and listening to podcasts, or just tripping from link to link to link. (Unlike footnotes, to which they're sometimes likened, hyperlinks don't merely point to related works; they propel you toward them.)

For me, as for others, the Net is becoming a universal medium, the conduit for most of the information that flows through my eyes and ears and into my mind. The advantages of having immediate access to such an incredibly rich store of information are many, and they've been widely described and duly applauded. "The perfect recall of silicon memory," *Wired*'s Clive Thompson has written, "can be an enormous boon to thinking." But that boon comes at a price. As the media theorist Marshall McLuhan pointed out in the 1960s, media are not just passive channels of information. They supply the stuff of thought, but they also shape the process of thought. And what the Net seems to be doing is chipping away my capacity for concentration and contemplation. My mind now expects to take in information the way the Net distributes it: in a swiftly moving stream of particles. Once I was a scuba diver in the sea of words. Now I zip along the surface like a guy on a Jet Ski.

I'm not the only one. When I mention my troubles with reading to friends and acquaintances—literary types, most of them—many say they're having similar experiences. The more they use the Web, the more they have to fight to stay focused on long pieces of writing. Some of the bloggers I follow have also begun mentioning the phenomenon. Scott Karp, who writes a blog about online media, recently confessed that he has stopped reading books altogether. "I was a lit major in college, and used to be [a] voracious book reader," he wrote. "What happened?" He speculates on the answer: "What if I do all my reading on the Web not so much because the way I read has changed, i.e., I'm just seeking convenience, but because the way I THINK has changed?" 5

Bruce Friedman, who blogs regularly about the use of computers in medicine, also has described how the Internet has altered his mental habits. "I now have almost totally lost the ability to read and absorb a longish article on the Web or in print," he wrote earlier this year. A pathologist who has long been on the faculty of the University of Michigan Medical School, Friedman elaborated on his comment in a telephone conversation with me. His thinking, he said, has taken on a "staccato" quality, reflecting the way he quickly scans short passages of text from many sources online. "I can't read *War and Peace* anymore," he admitted. "I've lost the ability to do that. Even a blog post of more than three or four paragraphs is too much to absorb. I skim it."

Anecdotes alone don't prove much. And we still await the long-term neurological and psychological experiments that will provide a definitive picture of how Internet use affects cognition. But a recently published study of online research habits, conducted by scholars from University College London, suggests that we may well be in the midst of a sea change in the way we read and think. As part of the five-year research program, the scholars examined computer logs documenting the behavior of visitors to two popular research sites, one operated by the British Library and one by a UK educational consortium, that provide access to journal articles, e-books, and other sources of written information. They found that people using the sites exhibited "a form of skimming activity," hopping from one source to another and rarely returning to any source they'd already visited. They typically read no more than one or two pages of an article or book before they would "bounce" out to another site. Sometimes they'd save a long article, but there's no evidence that they ever went back and actually read it. The authors of the study report:

> It is clear that users are not reading online in the traditional sense; indeed there are signs that new forms of "reading" are emerging as users "power browse" horizontally through titles, contents pages and abstracts going for quick wins. It almost seems that they go online to avoid reading in the traditional sense.

Thanks to the ubiquity of text on the Internet, not to mention the popularity of text-messaging on cell phones, we may well be reading more today than we did in the 1970s or 1980s, when television was our medium of choice. But it's a different kind of reading, and behind it lies a different kind of thinking—perhaps even a new sense of the self. "We are not only *what* we read," says Maryanne Wolf, a developmental psychologist at Tufts University and the author of *Proust and the Squid: The Story and Science of the Reading Brain*. "We are *how* we read." Wolf worries that the style of reading promoted by the Net, a style that puts "efficiency" and "immediacy" above all else, may be weakening our capacity for the kind of deep reading that emerged when an earlier technology, the printing press, made long and complex works of prose commonplace. When we read online, she says, we tend to become "mere decoders of information." Our ability to interpret text, to make the rich mental connections that form when we read deeply and without distraction, remains largely disengaged.

Reading, explains Wolf, is not an instinctive skill for human beings. It's not etched into our genes the way speech is. We have to teach our minds how to translate the symbolic characters we see into the language we understand. And the media or other technologies we use in learning and practicing the craft of reading play an important part in shaping the neural circuits inside our brains. Experiments demonstrate that readers of ideograms, such as the Chinese, develop a mental circuitry for reading that is very different from the circuitry found in those of us whose written language employs an alphabet. The variations extend across many regions of the brain, including those that govern such essential cognitive functions as memory and the interpretation of visual and auditory stimuli. We can expect as well that the circuits woven by our use of the Net will be different from those woven by our reading of books and other printed works.

10 Sometime in 1882, Friedrich Nietzsche bought a typewriter—a Malling-Hansen Writing Ball, to be precise. His vision was failing, and keeping his eyes focused on a page had become exhausting and painful, often bringing on

crushing headaches. He had been forced to curtail his writing, and he feared that he would soon have to give it up. The typewriter rescued him, at least for a time. Once he had mastered touch-typing, he was able to write with his eyes closed, using only the tips of his fingers. Words could once again flow from his mind to the page.

But the machine had a subtler effect on his work. One of Nietzsche's friends, a composer, noticed a change in the style of his writing. His already terse prose had become even tighter, more telegraphic. "Perhaps you will through this instrument even take to a new idiom," the friend wrote in a letter, noting that, in his own work, his " 'thoughts' in music and language often depend on the quality of pen and paper."

"You are right," Nietzsche replied, "our writing equipment takes part in the forming of our thoughts." Under the sway of the machine, writes the German media scholar Friedrich A. Kittler, Nietzsche's prose "changed from arguments to aphorisms, from thoughts to puns, from rhetoric to telegram style."

The human brain is almost infinitely malleable. People used to think that our mental meshwork, the dense connections formed among the hundred billion or so neurons inside our skulls, was largely fixed by the time we reached adulthood. But brain researchers have discovered that that's not the case. James Olds, a professor of neuroscience who directs the Krasnow Institute for Advanced Study at George Mason University, says that even the adult mind "is very plastic." Nerve cells routinely break old connections and form new ones. "The brain," according to Olds, "has the ability to reprogram itself on the fly, altering the way it functions."

As we use what the sociologist Daniel Bell has called our "intellectual technologies"—the tools that extend our mental rather than our physical capacities—we inevitably begin to take on the qualities of those technologies. The mechanical clock, which came into common use in the fourteenth century, provides a compelling example. In *Technics and Civilization*, the historian and cultural critic Lewis Mumford described how the clock "disassociated time from human events and helped create the belief in an independent world of mathematically measurable sequences." The "abstract framework of divided time" became "the point of reference for both action and thought."

15 The clock's methodical ticking helped bring into being the scientific mind and the scientific man. But it also took something away. As the late MIT computer scientist Joseph Weizenbaum observed in his 1976 book, *Computer Power and Human Reason: From Judgment to Calculation*, the conception of the world that emerged from the widespread use of timekeeping instruments "remains an impoverished version of the older one, for it rests on a rejection of those direct experiences that formed the basis for, and indeed constituted, the old reality." In deciding when to eat, to work, to sleep, to rise, we stopped listening to our senses and started obeying the clock.

The process of adapting to new intellectual technologies is reflected in the changing metaphors we use to explain ourselves to ourselves. When the mechanical clock arrived, people began thinking of their brains as operating "like clockwork." Today, in the age of software, we have come to think of them as operating "like computers." But the changes, neuroscience tells us, go much deeper than metaphor. Thanks to our brain's plasticity, the adaptation occurs also at a biological level.

The Internet promises to have particularly far-reaching effects on cognition. In a paper published in 1936, the British mathematician Alan Turing proved that a digital computer, which at the time existed only as a theoretical machine, could be programmed to perform the function of any other information-processing device. And that's what we're seeing today. The Internet, an immeasurably powerful computing system, is subsuming most of our other intellectual technologies. It's becoming our map and our clock, our printing press and our typewriter, our calculator and our telephone, and our radio and TV.

When the Net absorbs a medium, that medium is re-created in the Net's image. It injects the medium's content with hyperlinks, blinking ads, and other digital gewgaws, and it surrounds the content with the content of all the other media it has absorbed. A new e-mail message, for instance, may announce its arrival as we're glancing over the latest headlines at a newspaper's site. The result is to scatter our attention and diffuse our concentration.

The Net's influence doesn't end at the edges of a computer screen, either. As people's minds become attuned to the crazy quilt of Internet media, traditional media have to adapt to the audience's new expectations. Television programs add text crawls and pop-up ads, and magazines and newspapers shorten their articles, introduce capsule summaries, and crowd their pages with easy-to-browse info-snippets. When, in March of this year, the *New York Times* decided to devote the second and third pages of every edition to article abstracts, its design director, Tom Bodkin, explained that the "shortcuts" would give harried readers a quick "taste" of the day's news, sparing them the "less efficient" method of actually turning the pages and reading the articles. Old media have little choice but to play by the new-media rules.

Never has a communications system played so many roles in our lives—or exerted such broad influence over our thoughts—as the Internet does today. Yet, for all that's been written about the Net, there's been little consideration of how, exactly, it's reprogramming us. The Net's intellectual ethic remains obscure. 20

About the same time that Nietzsche started using his typewriter, an earnest young man named Frederick Winslow Taylor carried a stopwatch into the Midvale Steel plant in Philadelphia and began a historic series of experiments aimed at improving the efficiency of the plant's machinists. With the approval of Midvale's owners, he recruited a group of factory hands, set them to work on various metalworking machines, and recorded and timed their every movement as well as the operations of the machines. By breaking down every job into a sequence of small, discrete steps and then testing different ways of performing each one, Taylor created a set of precise instructions—an "algorithm," we might say today—for how each worker should work. Midvale's employees grumbled about the strict new regime, claiming that it turned them into little more than automatons, but the factory's productivity soared.

More than a hundred years after the invention of the steam engine, the Industrial Revolution had at last found its philosophy and its philosopher. Taylor's tight industrial choreography—his "system," as he liked to call it—was embraced by manufacturers throughout the country and, in time, around the world. Seeking maximum speed, maximum efficiency, and maximum output, factory owners used time-and-motion studies to organize their work and configure the jobs of their workers. The goal, as Taylor defined it in his celebrated 1911 treatise, *The Principles of Scientific Management,* was to identify and adopt, for every job, the "one best method" of work and thereby to effect "the gradual substitution of science for rule of thumb throughout the mechanic arts." Once his system was applied to all acts of manual labor, Taylor assured his followers, it would bring about a restructuring not only of industry but of society, creating a utopia of perfect efficiency. "In the past the man has been first," he declared; "in the future the system must be first."

Taylor's system is still very much with us; it remains the ethic of industrial manufacturing. And now, thanks to the growing power that computer engineers and software coders wield over our intellectual lives, Taylor's ethic is beginning to govern the realm of the mind as well. The Internet is a machine designed for the efficient and automated collection, transmission, and manipulation of information, and its legions of programmers are intent on finding the "one best method"—the perfect algorithm—to carry out every mental movement of what we've come to describe as "knowledge work."

Google's headquarters, in Mountain View, California—the Googleplex—is the Internet's high church, and the religion practiced inside its walls is Taylorism. Google, says its chief executive, Eric Schmidt, is "a company that's founded around the science of measurement," and it is striving to "systematize everything" it does. Drawing on the terabytes of behavioral data it collects through its search engine and other sites, it carries out thousands of experiments a day, according to the *Harvard Business Review,* and it uses the results to refine the algorithms that increasingly control how people find information and extract meaning from it. What Taylor did for the work of the hand, Google is doing for the work of the mind.

The company has declared that its mission is "to organize the world's information and make it universally accessible and useful." It seeks to develop "the perfect search engine," which it defines as something that "understands exactly what you mean and gives you back exactly what you want." In Google's view, information is a kind of commodity, a utilitarian resource that can be mined and processed with industrial efficiency. The more pieces of information we can "access" and the faster we can extract their gist, the more productive we become as thinkers. 25

Where does it end? Sergey Brin and Larry Page, the gifted young men who founded Google while pursuing doctoral degrees in computer science at

Stanford, speak frequently of their desire to turn their search engine into an artificial intelligence, a HAL-like machine that might be connected directly to our brains. "The ultimate search engine is something as smart as people—or smarter," Page said in a speech a few years back. "For us, working on search is a way to work on artificial intelligence." In a 2004 interview with *Newsweek*, Brin said, "Certainly if you had all the world's information directly attached to your brain, or an artificial brain that was smarter than your brain, you'd be better off." Last year, Page told a convention of scientists that Google is "really trying to build artificial intelligence and to do it on a large scale."

Such an ambition is a natural one, even an admirable one, for a pair of math whizzes with vast quantities of cash at their disposal and a small army of computer scientists in their employ. A fundamentally scientific enterprise, Google is motivated by a desire to use technology, in Eric Schmidt's words, "to solve problems that have never been solved before," and artificial intelligence is the hardest problem out there. Why wouldn't Brin and Page want to be the ones to crack it?

Still, their easy assumption that we'd all "be better off" if our brains were supplemented, or even replaced, by an artificial intelligence is unsettling. It suggests a belief that intelligence is the output of a mechanical process, a series of discrete steps that can be isolated, measured, and optimized. In Google's world, the world we enter when we go online, there's little place for the fuzziness of contemplation. Ambiguity is not an opening for insight but a bug to be fixed. The human brain is just an outdated computer that needs a faster processor and a bigger hard drive.

The idea that our minds should operate as high-speed data-processing machines is not only built into the workings of the Internet, it is the network's reigning business model as well. The faster we surf across the Web—the more links we click and pages we view—the more opportunities Google and other companies gain to collect information about us and to feed us advertisements. Most of the proprietors of the commercial Internet have a financial stake in collecting the crumbs of data we leave behind as we flit from link to link—the more crumbs, the better. The last thing these companies want is to encourage leisurely reading or slow, concentrated thought. It's in their economic interest to drive us to distraction.

Maybe I'm just a worrywart. Just as there's a tendency to glorify technological progress, there's a countertendency to expect the worst of every new tool or machine. In Plato's *Phaedrus*, Socrates bemoaned the development of writing. He feared that, as people came to rely on the written word as a substitute for the knowledge they used to carry inside their heads, they would, in the words of one of the dialogue's characters, "cease to exercise their memory and become forgetful." And because they would be able to "receive a quantity of information without proper instruction," they would "be thought very knowledgeable when they are for the most part quite ignorant." They would be "filled with the conceit of wisdom instead of real wisdom." Socrates wasn't wrong—the new technology did often have the effects he feared—but he was shortsighted. 30

He couldn't foresee the many ways that writing and reading would serve to spread information, spur fresh ideas, and expand human knowledge (if not wisdom).

The arrival of Gutenberg's printing press, in the fifteenth century, set off another round of teeth gnashing. The Italian humanist Hieronimo Squarciafico worried that the easy availability of books would lead to intellectual laziness, making men "less studious" and weakening their minds. Others argued that cheaply printed books and broadsheets would undermine religious authority, demean the work of scholars and scribes, and spread sedition and debauchery. As New York University professor Clay Shirky notes, "Most of the arguments made against the printing press were correct, even prescient." But, again, the doomsayers were unable to imagine the myriad blessings that the printed word would deliver.

So, yes, you should be skeptical of my skepticism. Perhaps those who dismiss critics of the Internet as Luddites or nostalgists will be proved correct, and from our hyperactive, data-stoked minds will spring a golden age of intellectual discovery and universal wisdom. Then again, the Net isn't the alphabet, and although it may replace the printing press, it produces something altogether different. The kind of deep reading that a sequence of printed pages promotes is valuable not just for the knowledge we acquire from the author's words but for the intellectual vibrations those words set off within our own minds. In the quiet spaces opened up by the sustained, undistracted reading of a book, or by any other act of contemplation, for that matter, we make our own associations, draw our own inferences and analogies, foster our own ideas. Deep reading, as Maryanne Wolf argues, is indistinguishable from deep thinking.

If we lose those quiet spaces, or fill them up with "content," we will sacrifice something important not only in our selves but in our culture. In a recent essay, the playwright Richard Foreman eloquently described what's at stake:

> I come from a tradition of Western culture, in which the ideal (my ideal) was the complex, dense, and "cathedral-like" structure of the highly educated and articulate personality—a man or woman who carried inside themselves a personally constructed and unique version of the entire heritage of the West. [But now] I see within us all (myself included) the replacement of complex inner density with a new kind of self—evolving under the pressure of information overload and the technology of the "instantly available."

As we are drained of our "inner repertory of dense cultural inheritance," Foreman concluded, we risk turning into "'pancake people'—spread wide and thin as we connect with that vast network of information accessed by the mere touch of a button."

I'm haunted by that scene in *2001.* What makes it so poignant, and so weird, is the computer's emotional response to the disassembly of its mind: its despair as one circuit after another goes dark, its childlike pleading with the astronaut—"I can feel it. I can feel it. I'm afraid"—and its final reversion to what can only be called a state of innocence. HAL's outpouring of feeling contrasts with the emotionlessness that characterizes the human figures in the film, who go about their business with an almost robotic efficiency. Their thoughts and actions feel scripted, as if they're following the steps of an algorithm. In the world of *2001,* people have become so machinelike that the most human character turns out to be a machine. That's the essence of Kubrick's dark prophecy: As we come to rely on computers to mediate our understanding of the world, it is our own intelligence that flattens into artificial intelligence.

▪ QUESTIONS

Reading

1. What does Carr mean by the term *stupid* in his title? Make a list of the ways that Carr thinks the Internet adversely changes the brain's functions.
2. What is the agenda of Google's creators and programmers, according to Carr? Why do they want our minds to operate like machines?
3. Carr uses personal anecdotes and reflections in his argument, but he says, "Anecdotes alone don't prove much" (paragraph 7). Which other techniques does he use to make his point?
4. What is Carr's tone in this essay? What sense does he offer you of his own authority and expertise?

Exploratory Writing

1. Over a weekend, spend an hour surfing the Internet and an hour reading a good novel. What are your impressions of the different types of thinking that each activity required? Which hour passed faster? In a double-entry list, jot down all of your impressions and experiences from the two different activities.

INTERNET SURFING	READING A NOVEL

2. James Olds describes the adult human mind as "very plastic," with "the ability to reprogram itself on the fly" (quoted in paragraph 13). In pairs, make a list of ten activities, and speculate about how each one might affect your brain if you did it every day for fifteen years. Examples include javelin throwing, scuba diving, reading nineteenth-century Russian novels, solving complex mathematical theorems, studying ancient Greek, watching ten hours of MTV, playing video games, hiking in the woods, meditating, or staring at nothing. How do your current activities affect your intelligence?

Making Connections

1. Hillary Rodham Clinton (p. 570) argues for global Internet freedom. But a great deal of Internet content is "paid for" through advertising. Imagine if companies like Google were nonprofits that ran on a donation basis and refused to include product placements or other advertisements of any kind, and evaluate Carr's arguments based on this premise. How much of our Internet experience is filtered through advertising? What difference does it make that you are targeted as a consumer when you search for information online? How do Internet freedom and consumerism affect each other?

Essay Writing

1. Carr writes, "you should be skeptical of my skepticism" (paragraph 32). Although some of the essays in this casebook offer arguments and information that strongly support or celebrate the Internet, many of the authors hint at potentially dark or negative consequences of our increasingly technological society. Choose an essay describing one of these dark or negative consequences, and write an essay imagining what the world would be like if the consequence happened in the most extreme way possible. Use information from the essay you chose.

ARGUING

Connectivity and Its Discontents

Sherry Turkle

Sociologist and psychologist Sherry Turkle (b. 1948) is Abby Rockefeller Mauzé Professor of the Social Studies of Science and Technology at the Massachusetts Institute of Technology. An expert on sociable robotics, she has written widely on the psychological aspects of the relationship between human beings and technology. Her books include *The Second Self: Computers and the Human Spirit* (1984), *Life on the Screen: Identity in the Age of the Internet* (1995), and *Simulation and Its Discontents* (2009), and she has edited three volumes on the subject of humans' response to objects. Her work focuses on the relationship between humans and machines, a topic she explores in "Connectivity and Its Discontents," which originally appeared in her book *Alone Together: Why We Expect More from Technology and Less from Each Other* (2011).

Online connections were first conceived as a substitute for face-to-face contact, when the latter was for some reason impractical: Don't have time to make a phone call? Shoot off a text message. But very quickly, the text message became the connection of choice. We discovered the network—the world of connectivity—to be uniquely suited to the overworked and overscheduled life it makes possible. And now we look to the network to defend us against loneliness even as we use it to control the intensity of our connections. Technology makes it easy to communicate when we wish and to disengage at will.

A few years ago at a dinner party in Paris, I met Ellen, an ambitious, elegant young woman in her early thirties, thrilled to be working at her dream job in advertising. Once a week, she would call her grandmother in Philadelphia using Skype, an Internet service that functions as a telephone with a Web camera. Before Skype, Ellen's calls to her grandmother were costly and brief. With Skype, the calls are free and give the compelling sense that the other person is present—Skype is an almost real-time video link. Ellen could now call more frequently: "Twice a week and I stay on the call for an hour," she told me. It should have been rewarding; instead, when I met her, Ellen was unhappy. She knew that her grandmother was unaware that Skype allows surreptitious multitasking. Her grandmother could see Ellen's face on the screen but not her hands. Ellen admitted to me, "I do my e-mail during the calls. I'm not really paying attention to our conversation."

Ellen's multitasking removed her to another place. She felt her grandmother was talking to someone who was not really there. During their Skype conversations, Ellen and her grandmother were more connected than they had ever been before, but at the same time, each was alone. Ellen felt guilty and confused: she knew that her grandmother was happy, even if their intimacy was now, for Ellen, another task among multitasks.

I have often observed this distinctive confusion: these days, whether you are online or not, it is easy for people to end up unsure if they are closer together or further apart. I remember my own sense of disorientation the first time I realized that I was "alone together." I had traveled an exhausting thirty-six hours to attend a conference on advanced robotic technology held in central Japan. The packed grand ballroom was Wi-Fi enabled: the speaker was using the Web for his presentation, laptops were open throughout the audience, fingers were flying, and there was a sense of great concentration and intensity. But not many in the audience were attending to the speaker. Most people seemed to be doing their e-mail, downloading files, and surfing the Net. The man next to me was searching for a *New Yorker* cartoon to illustrate his upcoming presentation. Every once in a while, audience members gave the speaker some attention, lowering their laptop screens in a kind of curtsy, a gesture of courtesy.

5 Outside, in the hallways, the people milling around me were looking past me to virtual others. They were on their laptops and their phones, connecting to colleagues at the conference going on around them and to others around the globe. There but not there. Of course, clusters of people chatted with each other, making dinner plans, "networking" in that old sense of the word, the one that implies having a coffee or sharing a meal. But at this conference, it was clear that what people mostly want from public space is to be alone with their personal networks. It is good to come together physically, but it is more important to stay tethered to our devices. I thought of how Sigmund Freud considered the power of communities both to shape and to subvert us, and a psychoanalytic pun came to mind: "connectivity and its discontents."

The phrase comes back to me months later as I interview management consultants who seem to have lost touch with their best instincts for what makes them competitive. They complain about the BlackBerry revolution, yet accept it as inevitable while decrying it as corrosive. They say they used to talk to each other as they waited to give presentations or took taxis to the airport; now they spend that time doing e-mail. Some tell me they are making better use of their "downtime," but they argue without conviction. The time that they once used to talk as they waited for appointments or drove to the airport was never downtime. It was the time when far-flung global teams solidified relationships and refined ideas.

In corporations, among friends, and within academic departments, people readily admit that they would rather leave a voicemail or send an e-mail than talk face-to-face. Some who say "I live my life on my BlackBerry" are forthright about avoiding the "real-time" commitment of a phone call. The new technologies allow us to "dial down" human contact, to titrate its nature and extent. I recently overheard a conversation in a restaurant between two women. "No one answers the phone in our house anymore," the first woman proclaimed with some consternation. "It used to be that the kids would race to pick up the phone. Now they are up in their rooms, knowing no one is going to call them, and texting and going on Facebook or whatever instead." Parents with teenage children will be nodding at this very familiar story in recognition and perhaps a sense of wonderment that this has happened, and so quickly. And teenagers will simply be saying, "Well, what's your point?"

A thirteen-year-old tells me she "hates the phone and never listens to voice-mail." Texting offers just the right amount of access, just the right amount of control. She is a modern Goldilocks: For her, texting puts people not too close, not too far, but at just the right distance. The world is now full of modern Goldilockses, people who take comfort in being in touch with a lot of people whom they also keep at bay. A twenty-one-year-old college student reflects on the new balance: "I don't use my phone for calls anymore. I don't have the time to just go on and on. I like texting, Twitter, looking at someone's Facebook wall. I learn what I need to know."

Randy, twenty-seven, has a younger sister—a Goldilocks who got her distances wrong. Randy is an American lawyer now working in California. His family lives in New York, and he flies to the East Coast to see them three or four times a year. When I meet Randy, his sister Nora, twenty-four, had just announced her engagement and wedding date via e-mail to a list of friends and family. "That," Randy says to me bitterly, "is how I got the news." He doesn't know if he is more angry or hurt. "It doesn't feel right that she didn't call," he says. "I was getting ready for a trip home. Couldn't she have told me then? She's my sister, but I didn't have a private moment when she told me in person. Or at least a call, just the two of us. When I told her I was upset, she sort of understood, but laughed and said that she and her fiancé just wanted to do things simply, as simply as possible. I feel very far away from her."

Nora did not mean to offend her brother. She saw e-mail as efficient and did not see beyond. We have long turned to technology to make us more efficient in work; now Nora illustrates how we want it to make us more efficient in our private lives. But when technology engineers intimacy, relationships can be reduced to mere connections. And then, easy connection becomes redefined as intimacy. Put otherwise, cyberintimacies slide into cybersolitudes. 10

And with constant connection comes new anxieties of disconnection, a kind of panic. Even Randy, who longs for a phone call from Nora on such an important matter as her wedding, is never without his BlackBerry. He holds it in his hands during our entire conversation. Once, he puts it in his pocket. A few moments later, it comes out, fingered like a talisman. In interviews with young and old, I find people genuinely terrified of being cut off from the "grid." People say that the loss of a cell phone can "feel like a death." One television producer in her mid-forties tells me that without her smartphone, "I felt like I had lost my mind." Whether or not our devices are in use, without them we feel disconnected, adrift. A danger even to ourselves, we insist on our right to send text messages while driving our cars and object to rules that would limit the practice.

Only a decade ago, I would have been mystified that fifteen-year-olds in my urban neighborhood, a neighborhood of parks and shopping malls, of front stoops and coffee shops, would feel the need to send and receive close to six thousand messages a month via portable digital devices or that best friends would assume that when they visited, it would usually be on the virtual real estate of Facebook. It might have seemed intrusive, if not illegal, that my mobile phone would tell me the location of all my acquaintances within a ten-mile radius. But these days we are accustomed to all this. Life in a media bubble has come to seem natural. So has the end of a certain public etiquette: On the street, we speak into the invisible microphones on our mobile phones and appear to be talking to ourselves. We share intimacies with the air as though unconcerned about who can hear us or the details of our physical surroundings.

I once described the computer as a second self, a mirror of mind. Now the metaphor no longer goes far enough. Our new devices provide space for the emergence of a new state of the self, itself, split between the screen and the physical real, wired into existence through technology.

Teenagers tell me they sleep with their cell phone, and even when it isn't on their person, when it has been banished to the school locker, for instance, they know when their phone is vibrating. The technology has become like a phantom limb, it is so much a part of them. These young people are among the first to grow up with an expectation of continuous connection: always on, and always on them. And they are among the first to grow up not necessarily thinking of simulation as second best. All of this makes them fluent with technology but brings a set of new insecurities. They nurture friendships on social-networking sites and then wonder if they are among friends. They are connected all day but are not sure if they have communicated. They become confused about companionship. Can they find it in their lives on the screen? Could they find it with a robot? Their digitized friendships—played out with emoticon emotions, so often predicated on rapid response rather than reflection—may prepare them, at times through nothing more than their superficiality, for relationships that could bring superficiality to a higher power, that is, for relationships with the inanimate. They come to accept lower expectations for connection and, finally, the idea that robot friendships could be sufficient unto the day.

15 Overwhelmed by the volume and velocity of our lives, we turn to technology to help us find time. But technology makes us busier than ever and ever more in search of retreat. Gradually, we come to see our online life as life itself. We come to see what robots offer as relationship. The simplification of relationship is no longer a source of complaint. It becomes what we want. These seem the gathering clouds of a perfect storm.

Technology reshapes the landscape of our emotional lives, but is it offering us the lives we want to lead? Many roboticists are enthusiastic about having robots tend to our children and our aging parents, for instance. Are these psychologically, socially, and ethically acceptable propositions? What are our responsibilities here? And are we comfortable with virtual environments that propose themselves not as places for recreation but as new worlds to live in? What do we have, now that we have what we say we want—now that we have what technology makes easy? This is the time to begin these conversations, together. It is too late to leave the future to the futurists.

▪ QUESTIONS

Reading

1. How does Turkle's acquaintance Ellen feel about Skype? Why does she feel this way? What do Turkle and Ellen see as the advantages and disadvantages of this technology?
2. What does Turkle mean when she describes texting as making people into "Goldilockses" (paragraph 8)?
3. Highlight, underline, and flag places where Turkle mentions robots. How does she distinguish robots from technologies like Skype, personal computers, social networking sites, and text messaging?

Exploratory Writing

1. Turkle says that we turn to technology to help us communicate but that it leads to weaker connections between people. Make a double-entry list of the ways in which the communication technologies you use (e.g., e-mail, Facebook, Twitter, Skype, texting, cell phone) bring you closer to your friends and family and ways in which they fail at that goal. Would you be willing to give up any of these technologies given the disadvantages you list? Why or why not?

ADVANTAGES	DISADVANTAGES

2. Turkle writes that she once described the computer as "a second self, a mirror of mind," but she finds that now "the metaphor no longer goes far enough" (paragraph 13). In small groups, come up with at least ten metaphors for the personal computer. What do these metaphors illustrate about the relationship between technology and society?

Making Connections

1. Hillary Rodham Clinton (p. 570) argues that it is people's values, rather than anything inherent in the technology, that shape whether the Internet is used as a force of liberation or repression. In what ways do Turkle's anecdotal examples support this argument? In what ways do Turkle's arguments call Clinton's into question?

Essay Writing

1. Consider Turkle's question: "Technology reshapes the landscape of our emotional lives, but is it offering us the lives we want to lead?" (paragraph 16). Write an essay that speaks to that question. Your essay can be an argument, like Turkle's, defending a position on the value of real versus virtual life; a personal reflection on your own experiences and thoughts; an explanation of how the virtual is defined, and distinguished from (or conflated with) what is real in today's culture; or a report on a particular case of virtual reality. Specify in your essay's subtitle whether you are arguing, reflecting, reporting, or explaining.

ARGUMENTATION AND RESEARCH PROJECTS

1. Choose two essays from this casebook that offer conflicting ideas about the meaning of the digital age. First, write a paragraph or two about the particular ways they conflict about particular questions or technologies. Then, find three or four more sources that offer arguments or analysis of these same questions or technologies. Once you have read your sources thoroughly, write your own essay, making an argument about the topic at hand.
2. Identify a particular technology from any era (for example, the printing press, the book, the telegram, Twitter, or Google Books), and conduct some research on its origin and development. Use newspapers, magazines, encyclopedias, and academic journals to learn as much as you can about this technology. Then, use at least two essays in this casebook to help you frame an argument about how it changes (or changed) the lives of the people who use (or used) it.
3. Play the role of a professor of media studies and prepare a lecture on an interesting case study related to one of the information technologies driving the digital revolution. You might focus on the developers of *Wikipedia* or Facebook; on an individual who has received public attention for a dramatic experience arising through online interactions; a legal battle incited by particular technology; a particular online archive or information source; or a promising technology that faded quickly or failed to catch on. Use online databases and books to learn as much as you can about your topic. Then, decide on a format for your presentation. You might use traditional paper handouts, video footage, presentation software like PowerPoint or Prezi (**http://prezi.com/**), or some combination of these forms. Be sure you offer plenty of background, highlight the most dramatic features of the case at hand, and use your sources to document your evidence and analyze your details.

What Is the Value of a College Education?

How would you define the *value* of a college education? As higher education has grappled with the growing corporatization of the university, easier access to information online, and rising costs of a traditional college experience, this question has become a focal point amongst instructors, writers, and students. Should universities continue to be mechanisms of humanistic enterprise whose value lies in transforming students as people, thinkers, and citizens? Should their main purpose be to train students for future careers? Is a higher education still a means to a better life, economically and personally? Why do we need experts on economics or physics or visual art when we can learn anything we need to know with a few keystrokes?

The authors of the essays in this casebook offer their own definitions of the value and purpose of a college education and proposals for changes to the higher educational system. In "What Is College For?" (p. 627), philosophy professor Gary Gutting argues that "the raison d'être of a college is to nourish a world of intellectual culture." In "On the Uses of a Liberal Education" (p. 630), English professor Mark Edmundson reflects on the way the corporatization of universities fosters a "cool consumer worldview," whereby students purchase entertainment rather than challenge themselves intellectually. "Even for Cashiers, College Pays Off" (p. 646), by *New York Times* columnist David Leonhardt, reports on recent studies that suggest that a college degree leads to higher salaries and makes people happier and healthier. In "Project Classroom Makeover" (p. 650), Duke University Dean Cathy N. Davidson argues that the digital age will require radical revisions to higher education, and in "The Next Drive-Thru U" (p. 660), James Traub reports on the rise of University of Phoenix, a distance-learning institution that reflects a new model in the business of education. Traub was prompted by arguments like that made by Linda Lee in "The Case against College" (p. 670) — that a college education need not be a universal goal for everybody. Finally, in "How to Write a Great College Slogan" (p. 674) English professor George Felton satirically explains the marketing language used by colleges to attract students and their parents.

These essays reflect genuine uncertainty about the future of colleges in the United States. Their writers respond to this uncertainty with anxiety, anticipation, skepticism, irony, and enthusiasm. Some mourn the loss of educational ideals, while others envision new ideals; some focus on flaws in current trends, others on possibilities created by rapid change.

Ultimately, the future of education will depend on the work of teachers and writers like these, as well as the students participating in that system. You'll need to define value in your own terms when you enter these debates and conduct your own research. What is your vision of a valuable education? What hopes do you have for your own education? How should we measure the collective value of higher education in relation to its value for individual students or graduates? How might the economic, personal, and cultural values of a college education be understood in relation to each other? Which writers define value most effectively? Which offer the most convincing evidence? What other issues affect the value of higher education? How might you go about researching these issues?

ARGUING

What Is College For?

Gary Gutting

Gary Gutting is a professor of philosophy at Notre Dame University. He is the author of several books, including *Religious Belief and Skepticism* (1982), *What Philosophers Know: Case Studies in Recent Analytic Philosophy* (2009), and *Thinking the Impossible: French Philosophy since 1960* (2011), and the editor of *Notre Dame Philosophical Reviews*, an online book-review journal. Gutting's courses focus on contemporary philosophy, the philosophy of science, and the philosophy of religion. This essay, which surveys different purposes for higher education before coming to a final judgment, first appeared in December 2011 in the *New York Times* blog *The Opinionator*, to which Gutting regularly contributes.

Most American college students are wrapping up yet another semester this week. For many of them, and their families, the past months or years in school have likely involved considerable time, commitment, effort and expense. Was it worth it?

Some evidence suggests that it was. A Pew Research survey this year found that 74 percent of graduates from four-year colleges say that their education was "very useful in helping them grow intellectually." Sixty-nine percent said that "it was very useful in helping them grow and mature as a person" and 55 percent claimed that "it was very useful in helping prepare them for a job or career." Moreover, 86 percent of these graduates think "college has been a good investment for them personally."

Nonetheless, there is incessant talk about the "failure" of higher education. Much of this has to do with access: it's too expensive, admissions policies are unfair, the drop-out rate is too high. There is also dismay at the exploitation of graduate students and part-time faculty members, the over-emphasis on frills such as semi-professional athletics or fancy dorms and student centers, and the proliferation of expensive and unneeded administrators. As important as they are, these criticisms don't contradict the Pew Survey's favorable picture of the fundamental value of students' core educational experience.

But, there are serious concerns about the quality of this experience. In particular, the university curriculum leaves students disengaged from the material they are supposed to be learning. They see most of their courses as intrinsically "boring," of value only if they provide training relevant to future employment or if the teacher has a pleasing (amusing, exciting, "relevant") way of presenting the material. As a result, students spend only as much time as they need to get what they see as acceptable grades (on average, about twelve to fourteen hours a week for all courses combined). Professors have ceased to expect genuine engagement from students and often give good grades (B or better) to work that is at best minimally adequate.

This lack of academic engagement is real, even among schools with the best students and the best teachers, and it increases dramatically as the quality of the school decreases. But it results from a basic misunderstanding—by both students and teachers—of what colleges are for. 5

First of all, they are not simply for the education of students. This is an essential function, but the raison d'être of a college is to nourish a world of intellectual culture; that is, a world of ideas, dedicated to what we can know scientifically, understand humanistically, or express artistically. In our society, this world is mainly populated by members of college faculties: scientists, humanists, social scientists (who straddle the humanities and the sciences properly speaking), and those who study the fine arts. Law, medicine, and engineering are included to the extent that they are still understood as "learned professions," deploying practical skills that are nonetheless deeply rooted in scientific knowledge or humanistic understanding. When, as is often the case in business education and teacher training, practical skills far outweigh theoretical understanding, we are moving beyond the intellectual culture that defines higher education.

Our support for higher education makes sense only if we regard this intellectual culture as essential to our society. Otherwise, we could provide job-training and basic social and moral formation for young adults far more efficiently and cheaply, through, say, a combination of professional and trade schools, and public-service programs. There would be no need to support, at great expense, the highly specialized interests of, for example, physicists, philosophers, anthropologists, and art historians. Colleges and universities have no point if we do not value the knowledge and understanding to which their faculties are dedicated.

This has important consequences for how we regard what goes on in college classrooms. Teachers need to see themselves as, first of all, intellectuals, dedicated to understanding poetry, history, human psychology, physics, biology—or whatever is the focus of their discipline. But they also need to realize that this dedication expresses not just their idiosyncratic interest in certain questions but a conviction that those questions have general human significance, even apart from immediately practical applications. This is why a discipline requires not just research but also teaching. Non-experts need access to what experts have learned, and experts need to make sure that their research remains in contact with general human concerns. The classroom is the primary locus of such contact.

Students, in turn, need to recognize that their college education is above all a matter of opening themselves up to new dimensions of knowledge and understanding. Teaching is not a matter of (as we too often say) "*making* a subject (poetry, physics, philosophy) interesting" to students but of students coming to see how such subjects are *intrinsically* interesting. It is more a matter of students moving beyond their interests than of teachers fitting their subjects to interests that students already have. Good teaching does not make a course's subject more interesting; it gives the students more interests—and so makes them more interesting.

Students readily accept the alleged wisdom that their most important learning at college takes place outside the classroom. Many faculty members—thinking of their labs, libraries or studies—would agree. But the truth is that, for both students and faculty members, the classroom is precisely where the most important learning occurs. 10

▪ QUESTIONS

Reading

1. Gutting begins with some statistics reported by a Pew Research survey. What are these statistics, and what do they suggest about the argument Gutting is going to make?
2. According to Gutting, what are some commonly discussed failures of higher education?
3. Gutting claims that colleges "are not simply for the education of students" (paragraph 6). In his view, what else do colleges do?

Exploratory Writing

1. Highlight, underline, or flag three of Gutting's major claims. Do you agree or disagree with these claims?

Making Connections

1. Gutting argues that "our support for higher education makes sense only if we regard this intellectual culture as essential to our society" (paragraph 7). In "The Next Drive-Thru U" (p. 660), James Traub reports on the rise and success of the University of Phoenix. Imagine you are Gutting and write an editorial on the meaning of this success. Does the University of Phoenix make a contribution to intellectual culture? Do its students receive an education that reflects what Gutting considers valuable about a college education?

Essay Writing

1. Write a response to Gutting's editorial, answering his question "Was it worth it?" about your first semester of college. How would you describe your own engagement with your classes? How would you describe the intellectual culture of your classrooms? Based on your experience, would you say your college experience is "worth it" so far? Would you define that worth similarly to Gutting, or do you have different ideas about the value of college?

REFLECTING

On the Uses of a Liberal Education

Mark Edmundson

Literature scholar and professor Mark Edmundson (b. 1949) specializes in romantic poetry and literary theory and teaches at the University of Virginia. His books include *Literature against Philosophy, Plato to Derrida: A Defense of Poetry* (1995), *Teacher: The One Who Made the Difference* (2003), *Why Read?* (2005), and the memoir *The Fine Wisdom and Perfect Teachings of the Kings of Rock and Roll* (2010). He has written extensively for magazines and newspapers, such as *Harper's* and the *New York Times*, as an advocate of studying the classics, liberal arts, and writing. He published this exploration of higher education in *Harper's* in September 1997.

Today is evaluation day in my Freud class, and everything has changed. The class meets twice a week, late in the afternoon, and the clientele, about fifty undergraduates, tends to drag in and slump, looking disconsolate and a little lost, waiting for a jump start. To get the discussion moving, they usually require a joke, an anecdote, an off-the-wall question—When you were a kid, were your Halloween getups ego costumes, id costumes, or superego costumes? That sort of thing. But today, as soon as I flourish the forms, a buzz rises in the room. Today they write their assessments of the course, their assessments of *me*, and they are without a doubt wide-awake. "What is your evaluation of the instructor?" asks question number eight, entreating them to circle a number between five (excellent) and one (poor, poor). Whatever interpretive subtlety they've acquired during the term is now out the window. Edmundson: one to five, stand and shoot.

And they do. As I retreat through the door—I never stay around for this phase of the ritual—I look over my shoulder and see them toiling away like the devil's auditors. They're pitched into high writing gear, even the ones who struggle to squeeze out their journal entries word by word, stoked on a procedure they have by now supremely mastered. They're playing the informed consumer, letting the provider know where he's come through and where he's not quite up to snuff.

But why am I so distressed, bolting like a refugee out of my own classroom, where I usually hold easy sway? Chances are the evaluations will be much like what they've been in the past—they'll be just fine. It's likely that I'll be commended for being "interesting" (and I am commended, many times over), that I'll be cited for my relaxed and tolerant ways (that happens, too), that my sense of humor and capacity to connect the arcana of the subject matter with current culture will come in for some praise (yup). I've been hassled this term, finishing a manuscript, and so haven't given their journals the attention I should have, and for that I'm called—quite civilly, though—to account. Overall, I get off pretty well.

Yet I have to admit that I do not much like the image of myself that emerges from these forms, the image of knowledgeable, humorous detachment and bland tolerance. I do not like the forms themselves, with their number ratings, reminiscent of the sheets circulated after the TV pilot has just played to its sample audience in Burbank. Most of all I dislike the attitude of calm consumer expertise that pervades the responses. I'm disturbed by the serene belief that my function—and, more important, Freud's, or Shakespeare's, or Blake's—is to divert, entertain, and interest. Observes one respondent, not at all unrepresentative: "Edmundson has done a fantastic job of presenting this difficult, important, and controversial material in an enjoyable and approachable way."

5 Thanks but no thanks. I don't teach to amuse, to divert, or even, for that matter, to be merely interesting. When someone says she "enjoyed" the course—and that word crops up again and again in my evaluations—somewhere at the edge of my immediate complacency I feel encroaching self-dislike. That is not at all what I had in mind. The off-the-wall questions and the sidebar jokes are meant as lead-ins to stronger stuff—in the case of the Freud course, to a complexly tragic view of life. But the affability and the one-liners often seem to be all that land with the students; their journals and evaluations leave me little doubt.

I want some of them to say that they've been changed by the course. I want them to measure themselves against what they've read. It's said that some time ago a Columbia University instructor used to issue a harsh two-part question. One: What book did you most dislike in the course? Two: What intellectual or characterological flaws in you does that dislike point to? The hand that framed that question was surely heavy. But at least it compels one to see intellectual work as a confrontation between two people, student and author, where the stakes matter. Those Columbia students were being asked to relate the quality of an *encounter*, not rate the action as though it had unfolded on the big screen.

Why are my students describing the Oedipus complex and the death drive as being interesting and enjoyable to contemplate? And why am I coming across as an urbane, mildly ironic, endlessly affable guide to this intellectual territory, operating without intensity, generous, funny, and loose?

Because that's what works. On evaluation day, I reap the rewards of my partial compliance with the culture of my students and, too, with the culture of the university as it now operates. It's a culture that's gotten little exploration. Current critics tend to think that liberal-arts education is in crisis because universities have been invaded by professors with peculiar ideas: deconstruction, Lacanianism, feminism, queer theory. They believe that genius and tradition are out and that P.C., multiculturalism, and identity politics are in because of an invasion by tribes of tenured radicals, the late millennial equivalents of the Visigoth hordes that cracked Rome's walls.

But mulling over my evaluations and then trying to take a hard, extended look at campus life both here at the University of Virginia and around the country eventually led me to some different conclusions. To me, liberal-arts education is as ineffective as it is now not chiefly because there are a lot of strange theories in the air. (Used well, those theories *can* be illuminating.) Rather, it's that university culture, like American culture writ large, is, to put it crudely, ever more devoted to consumption and entertainment, to the using and using up of goods and images. For someone growing up in America now, there are few available alternatives to the cool consumer worldview. My students didn't ask for that view, much less create it, but they bring a consumer weltanschauung to school, where it exerts a powerful, and largely unacknowledged, influence. If we want to understand current universities, with their multiple woes, we might try leaving the realms of expert debate and fine ideas and turning to the classrooms and campuses, where a new kind of weather is gathering.

From time to time I bump into a colleague in the corridor and we have what I've come to think of as a Joon Lee fest. Joon Lee is one of the best students I've taught. He's endlessly curious, has read a small library's worth, seen every movie, and knows all about showbiz and entertainment. For a class of mine he wrote an essay using Nietzsche's Apollo and Dionysus to analyze the pop group The Supremes. A trite, cultural-studies bonbon? Not at all. He said striking things about conceptions of race in America and about how they shape our ideas of beauty. When I talk with one of his other teachers, we run on about the general splendors of his work and presence. But what inevitably follows a JL fest is a mournful reprise about the divide that separates him and a few other remarkable students from their contemporaries. It's not that some aren't nearly as bright—in terms of intellectual ability, my students are all that I could ask for. Instead, it's that Joon Lee has decided to follow his interests and let them make him into a singular and rather eccentric man; in his charming way, he doesn't mind being at odds with most anyone. 10

It's his capacity for enthusiasm that sets Joon apart from what I've come to think of as the reigning generational style. Whether the students are sorority/fraternity types, grunge aficionados, piercer/tattooers, black or white, rich or middle class (alas, I teach almost no students from truly poor backgrounds), they are, nearly across the board, very, very self-contained. On good days they display a light, appealing glow; on bad days, shuffling disgruntlement. But there's little fire, little passion to be found.

This point came home to me a few weeks ago when I was wandering across the university grounds. There, beneath a classically cast portico, were two students, male and female, having a rip-roaring argument. They were incensed, bellowing at each other, headstrong, confident, and wild. It struck me how rarely I see this kind of full-out feeling in students anymore. Strong emotional display is forbidden. When conflicts arise, it's generally understood that one of the parties will say something sarcastically propitiating ("whatever" often does it) and slouch away.

How did my students reach this peculiar state in which all passion seems to be spent? I think that many of them have imbibed their sense of self from consumer culture in general and from the tube in particular. They're the progeny of 100 cable channels and omnipresent Blockbuster outlets. TV, Marshall

McLuhan famously said, is a cool medium. Those who play best on it are low-key and nonassertive; they blend in. Enthusiasm, à la Joon Lee, quickly looks absurd. The form of character that's most appealing on TV is calmly self-interested though never greedy, attuned to the conventions, and ironic. Judicious timing is preferred to sudden self-assertion. The TV medium is inhospitable to inspiration, improvisation, failures, slipups. All must run perfectly.

Naturally, a cool youth culture is a marketing bonanza for producers of the right products, who do all they can to enlarge that culture and keep it grinding. The Internet, TV, and magazines now teem with what I call persona ads, ads for Nikes and Reeboks and Jeeps and Blazers that don't so much endorse the capacities of the product per se as show you what sort of person you will be once you've acquired it. The Jeep ad that features hip, outdoorsy kids whipping a Frisbee from mountaintop to mountaintop isn't so much about what Jeeps can do as it is about the kind of people who own them. Buy a Jeep and be one with them. The ad is of little consequence in itself, but expand its message exponentially and you have the central thrust of current consumer culture—buy in order to be.

15 Most of my students seem desperate to blend in, to look right, not to make a spectacle of themselves. (Do I have to tell you that those two students having the argument under the portico turned out to be acting in a role-playing game?) The specter of the uncool creates a subtle tyranny. It's apparently an

easy standard to subscribe to, this Letterman-like, Tarantino-like cool, but once committed to it, you discover that matters are rather different. You're inhibited, except on ordained occasions, from showing emotion, stifled from trying to achieve anything original. You're made to feel that even the slightest departure from the reigning code will get you genially ostracized. This is a culture tensely committed to a laid-back norm.

Am I coming off like something of a crank here? Maybe. Oscar Wilde, who is almost never wrong, suggested that it is perilous to promiscuously contradict people who are much younger than yourself. Point taken. But one of the lessons that consumer hype tries to insinuate is that we must never rebel against the new, never even question it. If it's new—a new need, a new product, a new show, a new style, a new generation—it must be good. So maybe, even at the risk of winning the withered, brown laurels of crankdom, it pays to resist newness-worship and cast a colder eye.

Praise for my students? I have some of that too. What my students are, at their best, is decent. They are potent believers in equality. They help out at the soup kitchen and volunteer to tutor poor kids to get a stripe on their résumés, sure. But they also want other people to have a fair shot. And in their commitment to fairness they are discerning; there you see them at their intellectual best. If I were on trial and innocent, I'd want them on the jury.

What they will not generally do, though, is indict the current system. They won't talk about how the exigencies of capitalism lead to a reserve army of the unemployed and nearly inevitable misery. That would be getting too loud, too brash. For the pervading view is the cool consumer perspective, where passion and strong admiration are forbidden. "To stand in awe of nothing, Numicus, is perhaps the one and only thing that can make a man happy and keep him so," says Horace in the *Epistles*, and I fear that his lines ought to hang as a motto over the university in this era of high consumer capitalism.

It's easy to mount one's high horse and blame the students for this state of affairs. But they didn't create the present culture of consumption. (It was largely my own generation, that of the Sixties, that let the counterculture search for pleasure devolve into a quest for commodities.) And they weren't the ones responsible, when they were six and seven and eight years old, for unplugging the TV set from time to time or for hauling off and kicking a hole through it. It's my generation of parents who sheltered these students, kept them away from the hard knocks of everyday life, making them cautious and overfragile, who demanded that their teachers, from grade school on, flatter them endlessly so that the kids are shocked if their college profs don't reflexively suck up to them.

20 Of course, the current generational style isn't simply derived from culture and environment. It's also about dollars. Students worry that taking too many chances with their educations will sabotage their future prospects. They're aware of the fact that a drop that looks more and more like one wall of the Grand Canyon separates the top economic tenth from the rest of the population. There's a sentiment currently abroad that if you step aside for a moment, to write, to travel, to fall too hard in love, you might lose position permanently. We may be on a conveyor belt, but it's worse down there on the filth-strewn floor. So don't sound off, don't blow your chance.

But wait. I teach at the famously conservative University of Virginia. Can I extend my view from Charlottesville to encompass the whole country, a whole generation of college students? I can only say that I hear comparable stories about classroom life from colleagues everywhere in America. When I visit other schools to lecture, I see a similar scene unfolding. There are, of course, terrific students everywhere. And they're all the better for the way they've had to strive against the existing conformity. At some of the small liberal-arts colleges, the tradition of strong engagement persists. But overall, the students strike me as being sweet and sad, hovering in a nearly suspended animation.

Too often now the pedagogical challenge is to make a lot from a little. Teaching Wordsworth's "Tintern Abbey," you ask for comments. No one responds. So you call on Stephen. Stephen: "The sound, this poem really flows." You: "Stephen seems interested in the music of the poem. We might extend his comment to ask if the poem's music coheres with its argument. Are they consistent? Or is there an emotional pain submerged here that's contrary to the poem's appealing melody?" All right, it's not usually that bad. But close. One friend describes it as rebound teaching: They proffer a weightless comment, you hit it back for all you're worth, then it comes dribbling out again. Occasionally a professor will try to explain away this intellectual timidity by describing the students as perpetrators of postmodern irony, a highly sophisticated mode. Everything's a slick counterfeit, a simulacrum, so by no means should any phenomenon be taken seriously. But the students don't have the urbane, Oscar Wilde–type demeanor that should go with this view. Oscar was cheerful, funny, confident, strange. (Wilde, mortally ill, living in a Paris flophouse: "My wallpaper and I are fighting a duel to the death. One or the other of us has to go.") This generation's style is considerate, easy to please, and a touch depressed.

Granted, you might say, the kids come to school immersed in a consumer mentality—they're good Americans, after all—but then the university and the professors do everything in their power to fight that dreary mind-set in the interest of higher ideals, right? So it should be. But let us look at what is actually coming to pass.

Over the past few years, the physical layout of my university has been changing. To put it a little indecorously, the place is looking more and more like a retirement spread for the young. Our funds go to construction, into new dorms, into renovating the student union. We have a new aquatics center and ever-improving gyms, stocked with StairMasters and Nautilus machines. Engraved on the wall in the gleaming aquatics building is a line by our founder, Thomas Jefferson, declaring that everyone ought to get about two hours' exercise a day. Clearly even the author of the Declaration of Independence endorses the turning of his university into a sports-and-fitness emporium.

But such improvements shouldn't be surprising. Universities need to attract the best (that is, the smartest *and* the richest) students in order to survive in an ever more competitive market. Schools want kids whose parents can pay the full freight, not the ones who need scholarships or want to bargain down the tuition costs. If the marketing surveys say that the kids require sports centers, then, trustees willing, they shall have them. In fact, as I began looking around, I came to see that more and more of what's going on in the university is customer driven. The consumer pressures that beset me on evaluation day are only a part of an overall trend. 25

From the start, the contemporary university's relationship with students has a solicitous, nearly servile tone. As soon as someone enters his junior year in high school, and especially if he's living in a prosperous zip code, the informational material—the advertising—comes flooding in. Pictures, testimonials, videocassettes, and CD-ROMs (some bidden, some not) arrive at the door from colleges across the country, all trying to capture the student and his tuition cash. The freshman-to-be sees photos of well-appointed dorm rooms; of elaborate phys-ed facilities; of fine dining rooms; of expertly kept sports fields; of orchestras and drama troupes; of students working alone (no overbearing grown-ups in range), peering with high seriousness into computers and microscopes; or of students arrayed outdoors in attractive conversational garlands.

Occasionally—but only occasionally, for we usually photograph rather badly; in appearance we tend at best to be styleless—there's a professor teaching a class. (The college catalogues I received, by my request only, in the late Sixties were austere affairs full of professors' credentials and course descriptions; it was clear on whose terms the enterprise was going to unfold.) A college financial officer recently put matters to me in concise, if slightly melodramatic, terms: "Colleges don't have admissions offices anymore, they have marketing departments." Is it surprising that someone who has been approached with photos and tapes, bells and whistles, might come in thinking that the Freud and Shakespeare she had signed up to study were also going to be agreeable treats?

How did we reach this point? In part the answer is a matter of demographics and (surprise) of money. Aided by the GI Bill, the college-going population in America dramatically increased after the Second World War. Then came the baby boomers, and to accommodate them, schools continued to grow. Universities expand easily enough, but with tenure locking faculty in for lifetime jobs, and with the general reluctance of administrators to eliminate their own slots, it's not easy for a university to contract. So after the baby boomers had passed through—like a fat meal digested by a boa constrictor—the colleges turned to energetic promotional strategies to fill the empty chairs. And suddenly college became a buyer's market. What students and their parents wanted had to be taken more and more into account. That usually meant creating more comfortable, less challenging environments, places where almost no one failed, everything was enjoyable, and everyone was nice.

Just as universities must compete with one another for students, so must the individual departments. At a time of rank economic anxiety, the English and history majors have to contend for students against the more success-insuring branches, such as the sciences and the commerce school. In 1968, more than 21 percent of all the bachelor's degrees conferred in America were in the humanities; by 1993, that number had fallen to about 13 percent. The humanities now must struggle to attract students, many of whose parents devoutly wish they would study something else.

30 One of the ways we've tried to stay attractive is by loosening up. We grade much more softly than our colleagues in science. In English, we don't give many Ds, or Cs for that matter. (The rigors of Chem 101 create almost as many English majors per year as do the splendors of Shakespeare.) A professor at Stanford recently explained grade inflation in the humanities by observing that the undergraduates were getting smarter every year; the higher grades simply recorded how much better they were than their predecessors. Sure.

Along with softening the grades, many humanities departments have relaxed major requirements. There are some good reasons for introducing more choice into curricula and requiring fewer standard courses. But the move, like many others in the university now, jibes with a tendency to serve—and not challenge—the students. Students can also float in and out of classes during the first two weeks of each term without making any commitment. The common name for this time span—shopping period—speaks volumes about the consumer mentality that's now in play. Usually, too, the kids can drop courses up until the last month with only an innocuous "W" on their transcripts. Does a course look too challenging? No problem. Take it pass-fail. A happy consumer is, by definition, one with multiple options, one who can always have what he wants. And since a course is something the students and their parents have bought and paid for, why can't they do with it pretty much as they please?

A sure result of the university's widening elective leeway is to give students more power over their teachers. Those who don't like you can simply avoid you. If the clientele dislikes you en masse, you can be left without students, period. My first term teaching I walked into my introduction to poetry course and found it inhabited by one student, the gloriously named Bambi Lynn Dean. Bambi and I chatted amiably a while, but for all that she and the pleasure of her name could offer, I was fast on the way to meltdown. It was all a mistake, luckily, a problem with the scheduling book. Everyone was waiting for me next door. But in a dozen years of teaching I haven't forgotten that feeling of being ignominiously marooned. For it happens to others, and not always because of scheduling glitches. I've seen older colleagues go through hot embarrassment at not having enough students sign up for their courses; they graded too hard, demanded too much, had beliefs too far out of keeping with the existing disposition. It takes only a few such instances to draw other members of the professoriat further into line.

And if what's called tenure reform—which generally just means the abolition of tenure—is broadly enacted, professors will be yet more vulnerable to the whims of their customer-students. Teach what pulls the kids in, or walk. What about entire departments that don't deliver? If the kids say no to Latin and Greek, is it time to dissolve classics? Such questions are being entertained more and more seriously by university administrators.

How does one prosper with the present clientele? Many of the most successful professors now are the ones who have "decentered" their classrooms. There's a new emphasis on group projects and on computer-generated exchanges among the students. What they seem to want most is to talk to one another. A classroom now is frequently an "environment," a place highly conducive to the exchange of existing ideas, the students' ideas. Listening to one another, students sometimes change their opinions. But what they generally can't do is acquire a new vocabulary, a new perspective, that will cast issues in a fresh light.

35 The Socratic method—the animated, sometimes impolite give-and-take between student and teacher—seems too jagged for current sensibilities. Students frequently come to my office to tell me how intimidated they feel in class; the thought of being embarrassed in front of the group fills them with dread. I remember a student telling me how humiliating it was to be corrected by the teacher, by me. So I asked the logical question: "Should I let a major factual error go by so as to save discomfort?" The student—a good student, smart and earnest—said that was a tough question. He'd need to think about it.

Disturbing? Sure. But I wonder, are we really getting students ready for Socratic exchange with professors when we push them off into vast lecture rooms, two and three hundred to a class, sometimes face them with only grad students until their third year, and signal in our myriad professorial ways that we often have much better things to do than sit in our offices and talk with them? How bad will the student-faculty ratios have to become, how teeming the lecture courses, before we hear students righteously complaining, as they did thirty years ago, about the impersonality of their schools, about their decline into knowledge factories? "This is a firm," said Mario Savio at Berkeley during the Free Speech protests of the Sixties, "and if the Board of Regents are the board of directors, . . . then . . . the faculty are a bunch of employees and we're the raw material. But we're a bunch of raw material that don't mean . . . to be made into any product."

Teachers who really do confront students, who provide significant challenges to what they believe, *can* be very successful, granted. But sometimes such professors generate more than a little trouble for themselves. A controversial teacher can send students hurrying to the deans and the counselors, claiming to have been offended. ("Offensive" is the preferred term of repugnance today, just as "enjoyable" is the summit of praise.) Colleges have brought in hordes of counselors and deans to make sure that everything is smooth, serene, unflustered, that everyone has a good time. To the counselor, to the dean, and to the university legal squad, that which is normal, healthy, and prudent is best.

An air of caution and deference is everywhere. When my students come to talk with me in my office, they often exhibit a Franciscan humility. "Do you have a moment?" "I know you're busy. I won't take up much of your time." Their presences tend to be very light; they almost never change the temperature of the room. The dress is nondescript: clothes are in earth tones; shoes are practical—cross-trainers, hiking boots, work shoes, Dr. Martens, with now and then a stylish pair of raised-sole boots on one of the young women. Many, male and female both, peep from beneath the bills of monogrammed baseball caps. Quite a few wear sports, or even corporate, logos, sometimes on one piece of clothing but occasionally (and disconcertingly) on more. The walk is slow; speech is careful, sweet, a bit weary, and without strong inflection. (After the first lively week of the term, most seem far in debt to sleep.) They are almost unfailingly polite. They don't want to offend me; I could hurt them, savage their grades.

Naturally, there are exceptions, kids I chat animatedly with, who offer a joke, or go on about this or that new CD (almost never a book, no). But most of the traffic is genially sleepwalking. I have to admit that I'm a touch wary, too. I tend to hold back. An unguarded remark, a joke that's taken to be off-color, or simply an uncomprehended comment can lead to difficulties. I keep it literal. They scare me a little, these kind and melancholy students, who themselves seem rather frightened of their own lives.

40 Before they arrive, we ply the students with luscious ads, guaranteeing them a cross between summer camp and lotusland. When they get here, flattery and nonstop entertainment are available, if that's what they want. And when they leave? How do we send our students out into the world? More and more, our administrators call the booking agents and line up one or another celebrity

to usher the graduates into the millennium. This past spring, Kermit the Frog won himself an honorary degree at Southampton College on Long Island; Bruce Willis and Yogi Berra took credentials away at Montclair State; Arnold Schwarzenegger scored at the University of Wisconsin–Superior. At Wellesley, Oprah Winfrey gave the commencement address. (*Wellesley*—one of the most rigorous academic colleges in the nation.) At the University of Vermont, Whoopi Goldberg laid down the word. But why should a worthy administrator contract the likes of Susan Sontag, Christopher Hitchens, or Robert Hughes—someone who might actually say something, something disturbing, something "offensive"—when he can get what the parents and kids apparently want and what the newspapers will softly commend—more lite entertainment, more TV?

Is it a surprise, then, that this generation of students—steeped in consumer culture before going off to school, treated as potent customers by the university well before their date of arrival, then pandered to from day one until the morning of the final kiss-off from Kermit or one of his kin—are inclined to see the books they read as a string of entertainments to be placidly enjoyed or languidly cast down? Given the way universities are now administered (which is more and more to say, given the way that they are currently marketed), is it a shock that the kids don't come to school hot to learn, unable to bear their own ignorance? For some measure of self-dislike, or self-discontent—which is much different than simple depression—seems to me to be a prerequisite for getting an education that matters. My students, alas, usually lack the confidence to acknowledge what would be their most precious asset for learning: their ignorance.

Not long ago, I asked my Freud class a question that, however hoary, never fails to solicit intriguing responses: Who are your heroes? Whom do you admire? After one remarkable answer, featuring T. S. Eliot as hero, a series of generic replies rolled in, one gray wave after the next: my father, my best friend, a doctor who lives in our town, my high school history teacher. Virtually all the heroes were people my students had known personally, people who had done something local, specific, and practical, and had done it for them. They were good people, unselfish people, these heroes, but most of all they were people who had delivered the goods.

My students' answers didn't exhibit any philosophical resistance to the idea of greatness. It's not that they had been primed by their professors with complex arguments to combat genius. For the truth is that these students don't need debunking theories. Long before college, skepticism became their habitual mode. They are the progeny of Bart Simpson and David Letterman, and the hyper-cool ethos of the box. It's inane to say that theorizing professors have created them, as many conservative critics like to do. Rather, they have substantially created a university environment in which facile skepticism can thrive without being substantially contested.

Skeptical approaches have *potential* value. If you have no all-encompassing religious faith, no faith in historical destiny, the future of the West, or anything comparably grand, you need to acquire your vision of the world somewhere. If it's from literature, then the various visions literature offers have to be inquired into skeptically. Surely it matters that women are denigrated in Milton and in Pope, that some novelistic voices assume an overbearing godlike authority, that the poor are, in this or that writer, inevitably cast as clowns. You can't buy all of literature wholesale if it's going to help draw your patterns of belief.

But demystifying theories are now overused, applied mechanically. It's all logocentrism, patriarchy, ideology. And in this the student environment—laid-back, skeptical, knowing—is, I believe, central. Full-out debunking is what plays with this clientele. Some have been doing it nearly as long as, if more crudely than, their deconstructionist teachers. In the context of the contemporary university, and cool consumer culture, a useful intellectual skepticism has become exaggerated into a fundamentalist caricature of itself. The teachers have buckled to their students' views. 45

At its best, multiculturalism can be attractive as well-deployed theory. What could be more valuable than encountering the best work of far-flung cultures and becoming a citizen of the world? But in the current consumer environment, where flattery plays so well, the urge to encounter the other can devolve into the urge to find others who embody and celebrate the right ethnic origins. So we put aside the African novelist Chinua Achebe's abrasive, troubling *Things Fall Apart* and gravitate toward hymns on Africa, cradle of all civilizations.

What about the phenomenon called political correctness? Raising the standard of civility and tolerance in the university has been—who can deny it?—a very good thing. Yet this admirable impulse has expanded to the point where one is enjoined to speak well—and only well—of women, blacks, gays, the disabled, in fact of virtually everyone. And we can owe this expansion in many ways to the student culture. Students now do not wish to be criticized, not in any form. (The culture of consumption never criticizes them, at least not *overtly*.) In the current university, the movement for urbane tolerance has devolved into an imperative against critical reaction, turning much of the intellectual life into a dreary Sargasso Sea. At a certain point, professors stopped being usefully sensitive and became more like careful retailers who have it as a cardinal point of doctrine never to piss the customers off.

To some professors, the solution lies in the movement called cultural studies. What students need, they believe, is to form a critical perspective on pop culture. It's a fine idea, no doubt. Students should be able to run a critical commentary against the stream of consumer stimulations in which they're immersed. But cultural-studies programs rarely work, because no matter what you propose by way of analysis, things tend to bolt downhill toward an uncritical discussion of students' tastes, into what they like and don't like. If you want to do a Frankfurt School–style analysis of *Braveheart*, you can be pretty sure that by mid-class Adorno and Horkheimer will be consigned to the junk heap of history and you'll be collectively weighing the charms of Mel Gibson. One sometimes wonders if cultural studies hasn't prospered because, under the guise of serious intellectual analysis, it gives the customers what they most want—easy pleasure, more TV. Cultural studies becomes nothing better than what its detractors claim it is—Madonna studies—when students kick loose from the critical perspective and groove to the product, and that, in my experience teaching film and pop culture, happens plenty.

On the issue of genius, as on multiculturalism and political correctness, we professors of the humanities have, I think, also failed to press back against our students' consumer tastes. Here we tend to nurse a pair of—to put it charitably—disparate views. In one mode, we're inclined to a programmatic debunking criticism. We call the concept of genius into question. But in our professional lives per se, we aren't usually disposed against the idea of distinguished achievement. We argue animatedly about the caliber of potential colleagues. We support a star system, in which some professors are far better paid, teach less, and under better conditions than the rest. In our own profession, we are creating a system that is the mirror image of the one we're dismantling in the curriculum. Ask a professor what she thinks of the work of Stephen Greenblatt, a leading critic of Shakespeare, and you'll hear it for an hour. Ask her what her views are on Shakespeare's genius and she's likely to begin questioning the term along with the whole "discourse of evaluation." This dual sensibility may be intellectually incoherent. But in its awareness of what plays with students, it's conducive to good classroom evaluations and, in its awareness of where and how the professional bread is buttered, to self-advancement as well.

My overall point is this: It's not that a left-wing professorial coup has taken over the university. It's that at American universities, left-liberal politics have collided with the ethos of consumerism. The consumer ethos is winning. 50

Then how do those who at least occasionally promote genius and high literary ideals look to current students? How do we appear, those of us who take teaching to be something of a performance art and who imagine that if you give yourself over completely to your subject you'll be rewarded with insight beyond what you individually command?

I'm reminded of an old piece of newsreel footage I saw once. The speaker (perhaps it was Lenin, maybe Trotsky) was haranguing a large crowd. He was expostulating, arm waving, carrying on. Whether it was flawed technology or the man himself, I'm not sure, but the orator looked like an intricate mechanical device that had sprung into fast-forward. To my students, who mistrust enthusiasm in every form, that's me when I start riffing about Freud or Blake. But more and more, as my evaluations showed, I've been replacing enthusiasm and intellectual animation with stand-up routines, keeping it all at arm's length, praising under the cover of irony.

It's too bad that the idea of genius has been denigrated so far, because it actually offers a live alternative to the demoralizing culture of hip in which most of my students are mired. By embracing the works and lives of extraordinary people, you can adapt new ideals to revise those that came courtesy of your parents, your neighborhood, your clan—or the tube. The aim of a good liberal-arts education was once, to adapt an observation by the scholar Walter

Jackson Bate, to see that "we need not be the passive victims of what we deterministically call 'circumstances' (social, cultural, or reductively psychological-personal), but that by linking ourselves through what Keats calls an 'immortal free-masonry' with the great we can become freer—freer to be ourselves, to be what we most want and value."

But genius isn't just a personal standard; genius can also have political effect. To me, one of the best things about democratic thinking is the conviction that genius can spring up anywhere. Walt Whitman is born into the working class and thirty-six years later we have a poetic image of America that gives a passionate dimension to the legalistic brilliance of the Constitution. A democracy needs to constantly develop, and to do so it requires the most powerful visionary minds to interpret the present and to propose possible shapes for the future. By continuing to notice and praise genius, we create a culture in which the kind of poetic gamble that Whitman made—a gamble in which failure would have entailed rank humiliation, depression, maybe suicide—still takes place. By rebelling against established ways of seeing and saying things, genius helps us to apprehend how malleable the present is and how promising and fraught with danger is the future. If we teachers do not endorse genius and self-overcoming, can we be surprised when our students find their ideal images in TV's latest persona ads?

55 A world uninterested in genius is a despondent place, whose sad denizens drift from coffee bar to Prozac dispensary, unfired by ideals, by the glowing image of the self that one might become. As Northrop Frye says in a beautiful and now dramatically unfashionable sentence, "The artist who uses the same energy and genius that Homer and Isaiah had will find that he not only lives in the same palace of art as Homer and Isaiah, but lives in it at the same time." We ought not to deny the existence of such a place simply because we, or those we care for, find the demands it makes intimidating, the rent too high.

What happens if we keep trudging along this bleak course? What happens if our most intelligent students never learn to strive to overcome what they are? What if genius, and the imitation of genius, become silly, outmoded ideas? What you're likely to get are more and more one-dimensional men and women. These will be people who live for easy pleasures, for comfort and prosperity, who think of money first, then second, and third, who hug the status quo; people who believe in God as a sort of insurance policy (cover your bets); people who are never surprised. They will be people so pleased with themselves (when they're not in despair at the general pointlessness of their lives) that they cannot imagine humanity could do better. They'll think it their highest duty to clone themselves as frequently as possible. They'll claim to be happy, and they'll live a long time.

It is probably time now to offer a spate of inspiring solutions. Here ought to come a list of reforms, with due notations about a core curriculum and various requirements. What the traditionalists who offer such solutions miss is that no matter what our current students are given to read, many of them will simply translate it into melodrama, with flat characters and predictable morals. (The unabated capitalist culture that conservative critics so often endorse has put students in a position to do little else.) One can't simply wave a curricular wand and reverse acculturation.

Perhaps it would be a good idea to try firing the counselors and sending half the deans back into their classrooms, dismantling the football team and making the stadium into a playground for local kids, emptying the fraternities, and boarding up the student-activities office. Such measures would convey the message that American colleges are not northern outposts of Club Med. A willingness on the part of the faculty to defy student conviction and affront them occasionally—to be usefully offensive—also might not be a bad thing. We professors talk a lot about subversion, which generally means subverting the views of people who never hear us talk or read our work. But to subvert the views of our students, our customers, that would be something else again.

Ultimately, though, it is up to individuals—and individual students in particular—to make their own way against the current sludgy tide. There's still the library, still the museum, there's still the occasional teacher who lives to find things greater than herself to admire. There are still fellow students who have not been cowed. Universities are inefficient, cluttered, archaic places, with many unguarded corners where one can open a book or gaze out onto the larger world and construe it freely. Those who do as much, trusting themselves against the weight of current opinion, will have contributed something to bringing this sad dispensation to an end. As for myself, I'm canning my low-key one-liners; when the kids' TV-based tastes come to the fore, I'll aim and shoot. And when it's time to praise genius, I'll try to do it in the right style, full-out, with faith that finer artistic spirits (maybe not Homer and Isaiah quite, but close, close), still alive somewhere in the ether, will help me out when my invention flags, the students doze, or the dean mutters into the phone. I'm getting back to a more exuberant style; I'll be expostulating and arm waving straight into the millennium, yes I will.

▪ QUESTIONS

Reading

1. What is a Joon Lee fest? Why does Edmundson mention Joon Lee?
2. Highlight, underline, or flag Edmundson's characterizations of his students. What overall point does he make with these characterizations?
3. What does Edmundson conclude about cultural studies programs as a solution to the problems he's outlined?

Exploratory Writing

1. In small groups, write a double-entry list of the traits, interests, personalities, and learning styles of the victims of consumer culture that Edmundson is criticizing ("Consumers") versus Edmundson's ideal students ("Students"). What does the contrast between the two demonstrate about "the uses of a college education"?

CONSUMERS	STUDENTS

2. "To subvert the views of our students, our customers, that would be something else again" (paragraph 58). What does Edmundson mean by "subversion"? Have any of your teachers ever been subversive in the way that he describes? Why or why not?

Making Connections

1. Edmundson feels that consumer culture has detrimentally affected higher education. How would he react to Cathy N. Davidson's iPod project (p. 650)? Write an imagined dialogue between the two professors in which they discuss the best ways to educate students. How would each describe his or her students? How do their assessments of student intelligence converge or differ?

Essay Writing

1. Using explanatory essay techniques, write a guide for college students titled "How to Get the Most Out of Your College Education." Do you think that Edmundson would agree with the tips in your guide? In what ways do you agree or disagree with Edmundson's ideas on the reasons students should go to college? Use your tips to show readers what you feel are the most important aspects of higher education.

ARGUING

Even for Cashiers, College Pays Off

David Leonhardt

New York Times Washington Bureau Chief David Leonhardt (b. 1973) studied applied mathematics at Yale before becoming a journalist. His awards include a Peter Lisagor Award for Exemplary Journalism, a Gerald Loeb Award in magazine writing for his article "Obamanomics," and a 2011 Pulitzer Prize for Commentary. His Economics Scene column appeared in the *Times* from 2006 to 2011, and was a two-time winner of the Society of American Business Editors and Writers Best in Business Journalism Contest. He is also a frequent contributor to the *Times*'s *Economix* blog, and helped create popular interactive features on the paper's Web site — a budget deficit calculator and a rent-versus-buy housing calculator. His frequent themes, several of which feature prominently in this 2011 *New York Times* op-ed, include the job market, corporate scandals, economic policy, and social class.

Almost a century ago, the United States decided to make high school nearly universal. Around the same time, much of Europe decided that universal high school was a waste. Not everybody, European intellectuals argued, should go to high school.

It's clear who made the right decision. The educated American masses helped create the American century, as the economists Claudia Goldin and Lawrence Katz have written. The new ranks of high school graduates made factories more efficient and new industries possible.

Today, we are having an updated version of the same debate. Television, newspapers, and blogs are filled with the case against college for the masses: It saddles students with debt; it does not guarantee a good job; it isn't necessary for many jobs. Not everybody, the skeptics say, should go to college.

The argument has the lure of counterintuition and does have grains of truth. Too many teenagers aren't ready to do college-level work. Ultimately, though, the case against mass education is no better than it was a century ago.

The evidence is overwhelming that college is a better investment for most graduates than in the past. A new study even shows that a bachelor's degree pays off for jobs that don't require one: secretaries, plumbers, and cashiers. And, beyond money, education seems to make people happier and healthier. 5

"Sending more young Americans to college is not a panacea," says David Autor, an MIT economist who studies the labor market. "Not sending them to college would be a disaster."

The most unfortunate part of the case against college is that it encourages children, parents, and schools to aim low. For those families on the fence — often deciding whether a student will be the first to attend — the skepticism becomes one more reason to stop at high school. Only about 33 percent of young adults get a four-year degree today, while another 10 percent receive a two-year degree.

So it's important to dissect the anti-college argument, piece by piece. It obviously starts with money. Tuition numbers can be eye-popping, and student debt has increased significantly. But there are two main reasons college costs aren't usually a problem for those who graduate.

First, many colleges are not very expensive, once financial aid is taken into account. Average net tuition and fees at public four-year colleges this past year were only about $2,000 (though Congress may soon cut federal financial aid).

Second, the returns from a degree have soared. Three decades ago, full-time workers with a bachelor's degree made 40 percent more than those with only a high school diploma. Last year, the gap reached 83 percent. College graduates, though hardly immune from the downturn, are also far less likely to be unemployed than non-graduates. 10

Skeptics like to point out that the income gap isn't rising as fast as it once was, especially for college graduates who don't get an advanced degree. But the gap remains enormous—and bigger than ever. Skipping college because the pace of gains has slowed is akin to skipping your heart medications because the pace of medical improvement isn't what it used to be.

The Hamilton Project, a research group in Washington, has just finished a comparison of college with other investments. It found that college tuition in recent decades has delivered an inflation-adjusted annual return of more than 15 percent. For stocks, the historical return is 7 percent. For real estate, it's less than 1 percent.

Another study being released this weekend—by Anthony Carnevale and Stephen J. Rose of Georgetown—breaks down the college premium by occupations and shows that college has big benefits even in many fields where a degree is not crucial.

Construction workers, police officers, plumbers, retail salespeople, and secretaries, among others, make significantly more with a degree than without one. Why? Education helps people do higher-skilled work, get jobs with better-paying companies or open their own businesses.

This follows the pattern of the early twentieth century, when blue- and white-collar workers alike benefited from having a high school diploma. 15

When confronted with such data, skeptics sometimes reply that colleges are mostly a way station for smart people. But that's not right either. Various natural experiments—like teenagers' proximity to a campus, which affects whether they enroll—have shown that people do acquire skills in college.

Even a much-quoted recent study casting doubt on college education, by an NYU sociologist and two other researchers, was not so simple. It found that only 55 percent of freshmen and sophomores made statistically significant progress on an academic test. But the margin of error was large enough that many more may have made progress. Either way, the general skills that colleges teach, like discipline and persistence, may be more important than academics anyway.

None of this means colleges are perfect. Many have abysmal graduation rates. Yet the answer is to improve colleges, not abandon them. Given how much the economy changes, why would a high school diploma forever satisfy most citizens' educational needs?

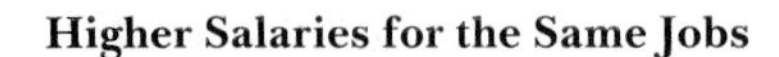

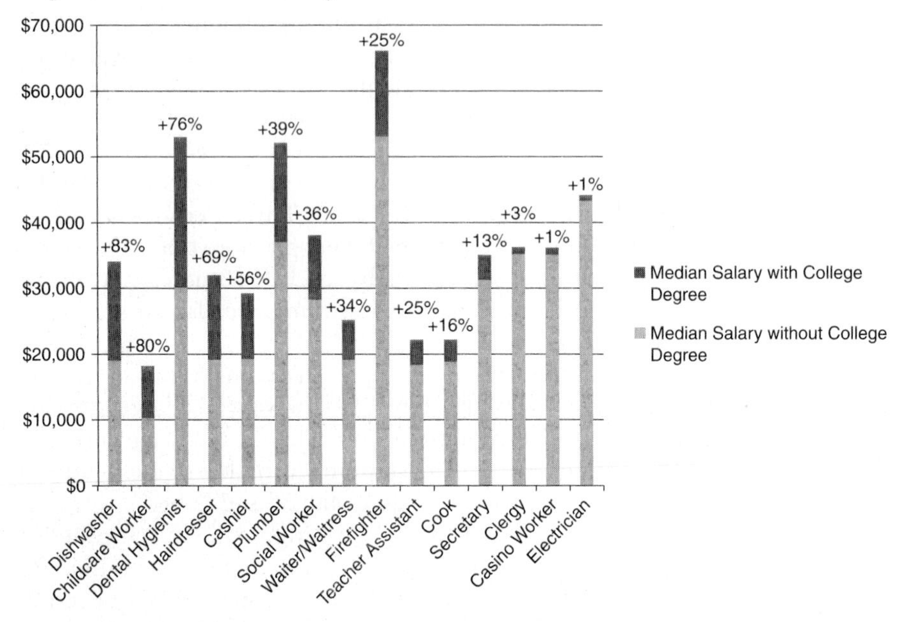

A recent study showed that in some fields workers with a four-year college degree earned more than those who did not have degrees.

Or think about it this way: People tend to be clear-eyed about this debate in their own lives. For instance, when researchers asked low-income teenagers how much more college graduates made than non-graduates, the teenagers made excellent estimates. And in a national survey, 94 percent of parents said they expected their child to go to college.

Then there are the skeptics themselves, the professors, journalists, and others who say college is overrated. They, of course, have degrees and often spend tens of thousands of dollars sending their children to expensive colleges. 20

I don't doubt that the skeptics are well meaning. But, in the end, their case against college is an elitist one—for me and not for thee. And that's rarely good advice.

▪ QUESTIONS

Reading

1. What is the Hamilton Project? What do its findings show about college education, and why does Leonhardt mention these findings?
2. According to Leonhardt, what is the problem with the position of "skeptics," like professors and journalists, who argue "the case against college"?
3. Why does Leonhardt specifically mention cashiers in his title? What does this title reveal about his position?

Exploratory Writing

1. Interview someone over age twenty-one who is not currently a student — such as a friend, relative, colleague, boss, or mentor — about why he or she chose to attend, or not to attend, college, and the effects of that decision. How does your data from this interview support, or refute, Leonhardt's points? What issues weren't included in Leonhardt's report?
2. "The answer is to improve colleges, not abandon them," writes Leonhardt (paragraph 18). In pairs, write a proposal for how colleges should be improved. After you've finished, assess whether your proposal would solve all of the problems in the "anti-college argument" that Leonhardt recounts.

Making Connections

1. Leonhardt writes that "it's important to dissect the anti-college argument, piece by piece" (paragraph 8). Does Leonhardt take into account all of the "pieces" of Linda Lee's (p. 670) anti-college argument? Highlight, underline, or flag each author's main points on the pros and cons of college. Do you think that either author would be able to persuade the other to change his or her position?

Essay Writing

1. Research a profession that doesn't typically require a college degree to practice, noting the education, experience, and resources that are required for someone to thrive in it. Write an essay arguing for or against Leonhardt's notion that it would pay to have a college degree in any field, using this profession as an example.

ARGUING

Project Classroom Makeover

Cathy N. Davidson

Cathy N. Davidson (b. 1949) has published more than twenty books, including *Revolution and the Word: The Rise of the Novel in America* (2004) and *The Future of Thinking* (2010). She is John Hope Franklin Institute Professor of Interdisciplinary Studies at Duke University, where, from 1998 to 2006, she served as vice provost for interdisciplinary studies. In 2006, she co-founded the Humanities, Arts, Science, and Technology Advanced Collaboratory (HASTAC, pronounced "haystack")—a virtual network of 6,500 members interested in cultural and technological innovation. President Obama nominated her to the National Council of the Humanities in 2010, and in 2011, the Senate confirmed the appointment. In this excerpt from her book *Now You See It: How the Brain Science of Attention Will Transform the Way We Live, Work, and Learn* (2011), Davidson discusses the unexpected effects giving iPods to incoming students at Duke had on learning and teaching at the university.

The *Newsweek* cover story proclaimed, "iPod, Therefore I Am."

On MTV News, it was "Dude, I just got a free iPod!"

Peter Jennings smirked at the ABC-TV news audience, "Shakespeare on the iPod? Calculus on the iPod?"

The online academic publication *Inside Higher Ed* worried for our reputation. How would Duke University "deal with the perception that one of the country's finest institutions—with selective admissions, a robust enrollment, and a plush endowment—would stoop to a publicity ploy?"

5 And *The Chronicle of Higher Education* was apoplectic: "The University seems intent on transforming the iPod into an academic device, when the simple fact of the matter is that iPods are made to listen to music. It is an unnecessarily expensive toy that does not become an academic tool simply because it is thrown into a classroom."[1]

What had these pundits so riled up? In 2003, we at Duke were approached by Apple about becoming one of six "Apple Digital Campuses." Each campus would choose a technology that Apple was then developing and would propose a campuswide use for it. It would be a partnership of business and education, exploratory in all ways. One university selected Apple PowerBooks loaded with iLife digital audio and video production software. Another chose e-portfolios, online workspaces where students could develop multimedia projects together and then archive them. Another selected audio software for creating audio archives and other infrastructure. What landed us in hot water was that, at Duke, instead of any of these, we chose a flashy new music-listening gadget that young people loved but that baffled most adults: iPods.

In 2003, the iPod did not have a single known educational app, nor did it seem to fall into that staid, stolid, overpriced, and top-down category known as IT, or instructional technology. Gigantic billboards had sprung up everywhere showing young people dancing, their silhouettes wild against brilliant bright backgrounds. What could possibly be educational about iPods? No one was thinking about their learning potential because they were so clearly about young users, not about IT administrators. That's why they intrigued us.

Our thinking was that educators had to begin taking seriously the fact that incoming students were born after the information age was in full swing. They were the last entering class who, as a group, would remember the before and after of the Internet. If they were born roughly in 1985 or so, they would have been entering grade school around the time that Tim Berners-Lee was inventing the protocols for the World Wide Web. These kids had grown up searching for information online. They had grown up socializing online, too, playing games with their friends online and, of course, sharing music files online. Categories and distinctions that an earlier generation of students would have observed in school and at home, between knowledge making and play, came bundled in a new way for this first generation of kids who, in their informal learning, were blurring that boundary. Their schools hadn't changed much, but at home, online, they were already information searchers. They had learned by Googling. What if instead of telling them what they should know, we asked them? What if we continued the lesson of the Internet itself and let them lead us into a new, exploratory way of learning in order to see if this self-directed way might mean something when it came to education? What if we assumed that their experiences online had already patterned their brains to a different kind of intellectual experimentation—and what if we let them show us where the pedagogical results of such an experiment might lead?

From the way most schools operated in 2003—from preschool to graduate schools—you wouldn't have had much of an idea that the Internet had ever been invented. It was as if young people were still going to the library to look in the *Encyclopaedia Britannica* for knowledge, under the watchful eye of the friendly local librarian. Schools of education were still training teachers without regard for the opportunities and potential of a generation of kids who, from preschool on, had been transfixed by digital media.

The opportunity seemed to be staring us in the face. At home, five-year-olds were playing Pokémon every chance they could, exchanging the cards at preschool with their pals, and then designing tools online to customize their characters and even writing elementary code to streamline their game play. They were memorizing hundreds of character names and roles and mastering a nine-year-old reading level just to play, but teacher training on every level was still text-based. It was as if schools were based on a kind of "hunt-and-peck" literacy, whereas kids were learning through searching, surfing, and browsing the Web. They were playing games in 3-D multimedia, learning to read and write not through schoolbooks but as they played games online and then traded their Pokémon cards with their friends. 10

When Duke announced that we would be giving a free iPod to every member of the entering first-year class, there were no conditions. We simply asked students to dream up learning applications for this cool little white device with the adorable earbuds, and we invited them to pitch their ideas to the faculty.

If one of their profs decided to use iPods in a course, the prof, too, would receive a free Duke-branded iPod and so would all the students in the class (whether they were first-years or not). We would not control the result. This was an educational experiment without a syllabus. No lesson plan. No assessment matrix rigged to show that our investment had been a wise one. No assignment to count the basketballs. After all, as we knew from the science of attention, to direct attention in one way precluded all the other ways. So we asked our basic questions in as broad and open-ended a way possible: *Are there interesting learning applications for this device that is taking over young America as a source of entertainment?* And then the most revolutionary question of all: *What do you students have to tell us about learning in a digital age?*

If it were a reality show, you might call it Project Classroom Makeover. It was a little wild, a little wicked, exactly what you have to do to create a calculated exercise in disruption, distraction, and difference: a lesson in institutional unlearning, in breaking our own patterns and trying to understand more of the intellectual habits of a new generation of students and providing a unique space where those new talents might flourish. Instead of teaching, we hoped to learn. We wanted to tap into a wellspring of knowledge young people brought to college from their own informal learning outside of school. We didn't know what would happen, but we had faith that the students would come up with something interesting. Or not. We couldn't deny that failure was also a possibility.

At the time, I was vice provost for interdisciplinary studies at Duke, a position equivalent to what in industry would be the R&D (research and development) person, and I was among those responsible for cooking up the iPod experiment and figuring out how it could work in the most interesting ways.[2] We wanted to stir up some of the assumptions in traditional higher education. We didn't count on causing the uproar that we did. We assumed some of our fellow educators would raise an eyebrow, but we didn't imagine an educational innovation would land us on the cover of *Newsweek*. Usually, if education is on the cover, it's another grim national report on how we are falling behind in the global brain race. Come to think of it, that *is* what the *Newsweek* cover story was about! Like Socrates before us, Duke was leading youth astray, tugging them down the slippery slope to perdition by thin, white vinyl iPod cords.

We were inverting the traditional roles of teacher and learner, the fundamental principle in education: hierarchy based on credentials. The authority principle, based on top-down expertise, is the foundation of formal education, from kindergarten playgroups to advanced graduate courses. At least since the GI Bill that followed World War II, and the rapid expansion at that time of the public university system, a college degree has been the entry card to middle-class, white-collar achievement. Not graduating from high school and lacking a college degree has constituted failure, and education has constructed its objectives backward from that (negative) goal, in some cities all the way down to competition for the right private nursery school.

What this means for young people who come to an elite private university is that they have taken one of a number of specific routes to get there. One way is to test to get into the best preschools so you can go to the best private grammar schools so you can be admitted to the most elite boarding schools so you can be competitive at the Ivies or an elite school outside the Ivies like Stanford or Duke. Another way is through public schools, a lifetime of determined and focused study, getting A's and even A+ grades in every class, always taking the most difficult courses, earning perfect scores on tests, and doing lots of extracurricular work, too. These students have been focused toward educational achievement their entire lives.[3] We wondered what these astonishing young overachievers would do if given the chance not to follow the rules but to make them. 15

In the world of technology, *crowdsourcing* means inviting a group to collaborate on a solution to a problem, but that term didn't yet exist in 2003 when we conducted the iPod experiment. It was coined by Jeff Howe of *Wired* magazine in 2006 to refer to the widespread Internet practice of posting an open call requesting help in completing some task, ranging from writing code (that's how the open source code that powers the Mozilla browser was written) to creating a winning logo (such as the "Birdie" design of Twitter, which cost a total of six bucks).[4] Crowdsourcing is "outsourcing" to the "crowd," and it works best when you observe three nonhierarchical principles. First, the fundamental principle of all crowdsourcing is that difference and diversity—not expertise and uniformity—solves problems. Second, if you predict the result in any way, if you try to force a solution, you limit the participation and therefore the likelihood of success. And third, the community most served by the solution should be chiefly involved in the process of finding it.

In the iPod experiment, we were crowdsourcing educational innovation for a digital age to our incoming students. We were walking the walk. Crowdsourced thinking is very different from credentialing, or relying on top-down expertise. If anything, crowdsourcing is suspicious of expertise, because the more expert we are, the more likely we are to be limited in what we even conceive to be the problem, let alone the answer. While formal education typically teaches hierarchies of what's worth paying attention to, crowdsourcing works differently, in that it assumes that no one of us individually is smarter than all of us collectively. No matter how expert we are, no matter how brilliant, we can improve, we can learn, by sharing insights and working together collectively.

Once the pieces were in place, we decided to take our educational experiment one step further. By giving the iPods to the first-year students, we ended up with a lot of angry sophomores, juniors, and seniors. They'd paid hefty private-university tuitions too! So we relented and said *any* student could have a free iPod—just so long as she convinced a prof to require one for a course and came up with a learning app in that course.

Does that sound sneaky? Far be it from me to say that we *planned* this, but once the upperclassmen coveted the iPods, once they'd begun to protest enviously and vehemently, those iPods suddenly tripled and quadrupled in perceived value: Everyone wanted one.

20 If "Shakespeare on the iPod" is the smirking setup, here's the punch line: Within one year, we had distributed more free iPods to students in forty-eight separate "iPod courses" than we had given without strings to the 1,650 entering first-year students.

That was vindicating enough, but it wasn't all. The real treasure trove was to be found in the students' innovations. Working together, and often alongside their profs, they came up with far more learning apps for their iPods than anyone—even at Apple—had dreamed possible. No one has ever accused Steve Jobs of not being cagey, and Apple's Digital Campus strategy was an R & D winner. The company's flagship technology now had an active lab of students creating new apps for it. There was also plenty of publicity for the iPod as a potential learning tool—the teenagers of America should all thank us for making it easier to pitch the purchase to their parents. In the first year of the iPod experiment, Duke students came up with dozens of stunning new ways to learn. Most predictable were uses whereby students downloaded audio archives relevant to their courses—Nobel Prize acceptance speeches by physicists and poets, the McCarthy hearings, famous trials, congressional debates, or readings by T. S. Eliot or Toni Morrison, or Thomas Edison's famous recitation of "Mary Had a Little Lamb"—one of the first sound recordings ever made. Almost instantly, students figured out that they could also record lectures on their iPods and listen at their leisure. Classes from Spanish 101 to Introduction to Jazz to organic chemistry could be taped and listened to anywhere. You didn't have to go to the library or the language lab to study. You could listen to assignments on the bus, at the gym, while out on a run—and everyone did. Because everyone had the device, sound suddenly had a new educational role in our text- and visuals-dominated classroom culture.

Some version of this convenient form of listening was possible with that radical eighties technology, the Sony Walkman. But the Walkman connected to radio and to tapes, not to the World Wide Web, with its infinite amount of information ready for downloading.

Interconnection was the part the students grasped before any of us did. Students who had grown up connected digitally gravitated to ways that the iPod could be used for *collective* learning. They turned the iPods into social media and networked their learning in ways we did not anticipate. In the School of the Environment, with the encouragement of Professor Marie Lynn Miranda, one class interviewed families in a North Carolina community concerned with lead paint in their homes and schools. Each student would upload the day's interviews to a course Web site, and any other student could download and comment on the interviews. At the end of the course, they combined their interviews, edited them digitally, and created an audio documentary that aired on local and regional radio stations and all over the Web.[5]

Some med students realized that there was an audio library of all the possible heart arrhythmias, but no way to access it in a real-time health exam. They came up with a way to put a stethoscope in one ear, using very simple signal-tracking technology to match what they were hearing in the patient's chest to the cataloged conditions. The implications of this original use were obvious, and soon students studying to be doctors and nurses were "operationalizing" such techniques for the diagnostic use of doctors in rural North Carolina and Africa. Dr. Martha Adams, a senior administrator at the Duke School of Medicine, grasped how revolutionary it was to be able to make state-of-the-art medical research available to those far outside major research centers, and to also make it possible for doctors elsewhere to report on health problems and patterns they were observing in their own communities, thus advancing medical research in both directions. Soon she was working with the National Institutes of Health and leading a national outreach iPod initiative. Once again, attention was being focused in multiple directions at once, not just on outcomes but on process and on interaction, the mirroring happening (as it must, definitionally) in both directions.

In the music department, composing students uploaded compositions to their iPods so their fellow students could listen and critique. Music performance students inserted their voices or their instruments into duets or choruses or orchestras. You could listen to how you sounded as first chair in the flute section of a famous philharmonic orchestra. Students in Duke's engineering department had a field day mangling and dissecting their iPods to study (hack, some would say) everything from Apple's ultrasecret computer code to the physical properties of the famous white plastic exterior of the original iPods. 25

And they began exploring apps, developing applications that could be added to the iPod's repertoire of abilities without Apple having to give away its proprietary code. In other words, the iPod could still remain an iPod with its own distinctive characteristics, but it could change and morph as new features were added and new capabilities emerged, including some developed by users. To me, this was a conceptual breakthrough: that a commercial product might also be susceptible to consumer customization, a way of extending the infinitely changeable open-source properties of the Internet itself to a product with a far more fixed, finite identity. It was a hybrid of old and new thinking. If that isn't a metaphor for attention in the digital age, I don't know what is.

By the end of our first experimental year, Duke was part of a new movement to transform the iPod from a listening device into an interactive broadcasting device. We were proud to host the world's first-ever academic "podcasting" conference early in 2005. I recently found one of our announcements for the conference and was amused to see those quotation marks around *podcasting.* No one was quite sure even what to call this new phenomenon, in which you could record a lecture, upload it to a Web site, and then anyone anywhere in the world could download it. Shakespeare on an iPod? Absolutely. And that lecture on Shakespeare delivered in the Allen Building at Duke could later be listened to by a student riding a bus in Bangkok or Brasília. That may not seem revolutionary now. It is hard to remember way back then, in the distant past of the Internet, before iPhones and netbooks, before MySpace and Facebook, and a full two years before YouTube was invented with its motto to "Broadcast Yourself."

The first podcasting conference drew standing-room-only attendance. It was sponsored by one of the first programs I'd spearheaded at Duke, something (another hybrid) called Information Science + Information Studies, or ISIS for short—artists and computer scientists, social scientists and engineers, and everyone in between in a new configuration. Lots of news media crowded into the auditorium at the Center for Interdisciplinary Engineering, Medicine, and Applied Science to witness the event. In a short span, the message had changed from "How could anyone possibly think this device could be used for learning?" to "This device facilitates sophisticated academic research and has the potential to make that learning instantly available to anyone in the world—for free."

The conceptual breakthrough of podcasting was access. It was expensive buying all those iPods, but the result was a breakthrough in education far beyond Duke, one whose purpose was to make a world of information cheaper to access than it ever had been before. With very little outlay, you had the potential of transmitting anything you heard, anywhere: You could download anything you heard worldwide. Not prerecorded programs made by professionals but content created and uploaded by anyone, ready for downloading—and for remixing and uploading again. When we launched the iPod experiment, no one expected that someday there would be an iTunes U (formed in 2007) with over 350,000 lectures and other educational audio and video files compiled by universities, libraries, and museums all around the world and available for download.

30 Duke took a lot of heat for being a "rich, privileged institution" that could afford this frivolity, but a revolution in the democratization of knowledge is not frivolous, especially considering that, once customized, an individual mobile device is actually an inexpensive computer. Several years after the Duke experiment, in the fall of 2008, Culbreth Middle School, a public school in nearby Chapel Hill, North Carolina, created its own iPod program for an experimental group of staff and students. They chose the iPod instead of a more traditional laptop because of "the mobility of the device in one's pocket with instant access to information and apps."[6] In January 2010, seventh graders were encouraged to explore the different ways their iPods could be used to keep them informed in the wake of the disastrous earthquake that brought destruction to Haiti. They used iPods to gather measurements of earthquake magnitude and related information, including demographic data, humanitarian assistance updates, local Haitian news podcasts, and historical information on Haitian culture and politics. The device also performed Creole-language translation. Students were even able to maintain up-to-date communication with a local graduate student who was in Haiti at the time and was badly injured in the earthquake. They used their iPods to educate themselves about a terrible disaster far away and produced their own podcasts from the information they gleaned. The experiment left little doubt that in the event of an

emergency closer to home, students would be able to contribute their new knowledge to disaster-relief and fund-raising efforts locally.

The iPod experiment was not an investment in technology. It was an investment in a new form of attention, one that didn't require the student to always face forward, learn from on high, memorize what was already a given, or accept knowledge as something predetermined and passively absorbed. It was also an investment in student-led curiosity, whose object was not a hunk of white plastic, but the very nature of interactivity, crowdsourcing, customizing, and inspired inquiry-driven problem solving. At our most ambitious, we hoped to change the one-directional model of attention that has formed the twentieth-century classroom.[7]

This iPod experiment was a start at finding a new learning paradigm of formal education for the digital era. As we have seen, an infant's neural pathways are being sheared and shaped along with his values and his behavior in constant interaction with the people around him who exert influence over his life. The iPod experiment was an acknowledgment that the brain is, above all, interactive, that it selects, repeats, and mirrors, always, constantly, in complex interactions with the world. The experiment was also an acknowledgment that the chief mode of informal learning for a new generation of students had been changed by the World Wide Web. It was an attempt to put the new science of attention together with the new digital technology that both demanded and, in some ways, helped produce it.

I'm not going to argue that the *interactive* task of surfing is better or worse than the reception model that dominated mass education in the twentieth century. "Better" and "worse" don't make a lot of sense to me. But there's a difference and, as we have seen, difference is what we pay attention to. Said another way, we concentrate in a different way when we are making the connections, when we are clicking and browsing, than when we are watching (as in a TV show or movie) or listening or even reading a book. Indisputably, the imagination is engaged in making connections in all of those forms, as it is in anything we experience. It is engaged in a different way when we ourselves are making the connections, when we're browsing from one to another link that interests us and draws our attention. We don't need a "better or worse" because we have both, and both are potentially rich and fascinating cognitive activities. But the relative newness of the surfing/searching experience drove our interest in the potential of the iPod experiment; in 2003, educators already knew how to mine traditional media, but we had not yet figured out how to harness the new forms of attention students who had grown up surfing the Web were mastering. The Web does not prescribe a clear, linear pathway through the content. There is no one way to move along a straight-and-narrow road from beginning to end.

The formal education most of us experienced—and which we now often think of when we picture a classroom—is based on giving premium value to expertise, specialization, and hierarchy. It prepared us for success in the twentieth century, when those things mattered above all. Yet what form of education is required in the information age, when what matters has grown very different? What form of education is required in a world of social networking, crowdsourcing, customizing, and user-generated content; a world of searching and browsing, where the largest-ever encyclopedia is created not by experts but by volunteers around the world—as is the world's second most popular Web browser (Mozilla's Firefox), the world's most massive online multiplayer game (*World of Warcraft*, with over eleven million subscribers a month), and all the social networking and communication sites, from MySpace and Facebook to Twitter?

Notes

1. These are all quoted and the experiment is discussed in James Todd, "The iPod Idea: Wired for Scholarship," *Duke Magazine* 91, no. 5, Sept.–Oct. 2005.
2. The iPod experiment would never have happened without approval and funding of this forward-looking initiative, for which credit goes to my colleagues Tracy Futhey, vice president for information technology, and Provost Peter Lange.
3. On values formation and the blind spots it leaves, see Barbara Herrnstein Smith, *Contingencies of Value: Alternate Perspectives for Critical Theory* (Cambridge, MA: Harvard University Press, 1988).
4. Jeff Howe, *Crowdsourcing: Why the Power of the Crowd Is Driving the Future of Business* (NewYork: Crown, 2008).
5. Professor Marie Lynn Miranda is a pioneer in using new technologies to help shape community activism on environmental policy. Her Web site is: www.nicholas.duke.edu/DEarchives/f02/f-mapping.html (accessed May 6, 2010).
6. Maria Magher, "iPod Gets Top Marks: Culbreth Middle School Is the First in the State to Require Device," *Chapel Hill News*, Mar. 14, 2010.
7. I have written about this at length with my HASTAC cofounder, David Theo Goldberg, in a research report that was first put up on the Web for comment from anyone who wished to offer it, then published in a research report based on colloquia we held all over the country, *The Future of Learning Institutions in a Digital Age* (Cambridge, MA: MIT Press, 2009). The expanded book form of this project is Cathy N. Davidson and David Theo Goldberg, *The Future of Thinking: Learning Institutions in a Digital Age* (Cambridge, MA: MIT Press, 2010).

▪ QUESTIONS

Reading

1. Who criticized Duke University for distributing iPods to students in 2003? Why?
2. According to Davidson, how does crowdsourcing challenge traditional educational practices?
3. What does Davidson mean by "the reception model" of education? How does she contrast this model with interactive learning? Why does she want to avoid using the terms "better" and "worse" to explain the contrast?

Exploratory Writing

1. Highlight, underline, or flag the various classroom "apps" students developed for the iPod. Which of these apps is most surprising? Why?
2. Davidson begins by reporting on the iPod experiment at Duke, and she ends by making an argument about how the device suggests new educational methods for the Information Age. How does she use the details she reports to develop her argument? How might you do something similar in your own writing?

Making Connections

1. Imagine Cathy Davidson is appearing with Mark Edmundson (p. 630) at a National Council of the Humanities hearing on the future of higher education. Write a dialogue in which each makes a proposal for a new educational model, followed by some debate between the two of them.

Essay Writing

1. Write an essay in which you compare and contrast the value of two of your own learning experiences: one rooted in "expertise, specialization, and hierarchy" and one rooted in interaction, networking, crowdsourcing, or customization. Following Davidson's lead, make an argument about the *difference* between these learning experiences, without making claims about which was "better" or "worse."

REPORTING

The Next Drive-Thru U

James Traub

James Traub (b. 1954) is a contributing writer for the *New York Times Magazine*, has been a staff writer for the *New Yorker*, and has been published in the *Atlantic*, the *New York Review of Books*, and *Foreign Affairs*. His subjects include politics and profiles of politicians, the history of New York City, and higher education. His books include *Too Good to Be True: The Outlandish Story of Wedtech* (1990), *The Devil's Playground: A Century of Pleasure and Profit in Times Square* (2004), *The Best Intentions: Kofi Annan and the UN in the Era of American World Power* (2006), and *The Freedom Agenda: Why America Must Spread Democracy (Just Not the Way George Bush Did)* (2008). In researching his 1994 study of New York's City College (CCNY), which provided free education to its students from 1920 to 1970 and has been seen as an important model for higher education as an equalizer of class differences, *City on a Hill: Testing the American Dream at City College* (1995), Traub spent a year on campus, attending classes and interviewing students and professors. This exploration of the University of Phoenix appeared in the *New Yorker* in October 1997.

At the University of Phoenix, which describes itself as the second-largest private university in the United States, terms that normally have a clear and literal meaning are used in an oddly evanescent way; this seems especially true of the language that evokes our most romantic feelings about higher education. The university has, for example, a "bookstore" on the ground floor of its central administration building. The store is a boutique offering backpacks, T-shirts, coffee mugs, beer glasses, and ties, all bearing the school logo; the only books are textbooks, which you have to order from someone standing behind a counter. The U of P's "library" can be found, as Kurt Slobodzian, the librarian, likes to say, "wherever there's a computer"; students can access thousands of journals via the Online Collection. And the word *campus* is understood, at the University of Phoenix, to mean "site," or even "outlet." The university is a franchise operation, with forty-seven sites all over the West and in Michigan, Florida, and Louisiana; most of them consist of an office building, or merely a few floors of a building, just off a highway exit ramp. When I was talking to the director of the university's "distance learning" program, I noticed that he was using the word "campus" to apply to himself and three other people, who ran the program from a suite of offices. The University of Phoenix is, in fact, a para-university. It has the operational core of higher education—students, teachers, classrooms, exams, degree-granting programs—without a campus life, or even an intellectual life. There are no tenured professors; and the most recent issue of the university's only academic journal contained but a single academic article, about copyright law.

You cannot get a rise out of the university's top officials by pointing any of this out. William Gibbs, a former Price Waterhouse manager, who is the president of the U of P, said to me, "The people who are our students don't really want the education. They want what the education provides for them—better jobs, moving up in their career, the ability to speak up in meetings, that kind of stuff. They want it to *do* something for them."

Apparently, it does. Enrollment may be flat at élite institutions, but the U of P has grown from three thousand students to forty thousand over the last decade. It offers accredited bachelor's-degree programs in business, nursing, and education, and an MBA as well. The university is also the principal subsidiary of a profit-making company called the Apollo Group. Since late 1994, when the company first offered shares on the NASDAQ exchange, Apollo stock has increased in value from two dollars to thirty-five dollars, on a split-adjusted basis. One broker I spoke to said that most of his customers were professors at Arizona State, who had concluded that the U of P delivered pretty much the same product they did, only more efficiently. The University of Phoenix is competing not with the Ivy League but with the big state schools and the small, unheralded private colleges, where most students enroll. It's a Darwinian world out there; some two hundred colleges have closed during the last ten years.

College, for most of us, means greenswards, dreamy spires, professors with elbow patches, old volumes in the stacks; but no more than several dozen colleges answer to this description. Higher education in America is now a vast industry that accommodates two-thirds of America's high school graduates, or more than fourteen million people. Most of the nation's thirty-seven hundred colleges see themselves as market-driven institutions trying to satisfy customer demand. As I drove around Phoenix, I kept hearing ads on the radio for Ottawa University, a Kansas institution that has three campuses in Arizona and others in Singapore, Malaysia, and Hong Kong. "Ottawa," the announcer said, "majors in *you*."

5 Almost half of America's freshmen attend community colleges, institutions with no residential facilities and, often, no campus. According to a study conducted by Arthur Levine, the president of Teachers College, at Columbia University, only a sixth of America's college students fit the stereotype: full-time students, living on campus. Levine says that a survey of the five-sixths who do not has found that "they wanted the kind of relationship with a college that they had with their bank, their supermarket, and their gas company. They say, 'I want terrific service, I want convenience, I want quality control. Give me classes twenty-four hours a day, and give me in-class parking, if possible.' These are students who want stripped-down classes. They don't want to buy anything they're not using." Such students understand clearly that higher education has become an indispensable passport to a better life.

In a 1994 book entitled *Dogmatic Wisdom*, a history professor named Russell Jacoby faults critics on both the left and the right for focussing on the intellectual melodramas that agitate a tiny number of institutions—"canon wars" and battles over "speech codes"—while ignoring the "narrow practicality" that dominates educational practice at almost all the others. Jacoby quotes a Department of Education study showing that of a million bachelor's degrees awarded in 1991 seven thousand three hundred were in philosophy and religion, twelve thousand in foreign languages, and about two hundred and fifty thousand in business. The institution that sees itself as the steward of intellectual culture is becoming increasingly marginal; the others are racing to accommodate the new student. And the University of Phoenix, according to Arthur Levine, "is the first of the new breed."

John Sperling, the founder of the University of Phoenix and the chairman of the Apollo Group, is a blunt, ornery seventy-six-year-old from the Ozarks. In the company's bland and studiously polite environment, he stands out for his willingness to call an idiot an idiot. Sperling is an economic historian by profession, and, like many economists, he considers himself one of the few rational people on earth. Among the people he counts as idiots are those who believe that market forces can be ignored; during one of several conversations, he observed that the principal effect of the war on drugs was that it forced users to commit crimes. Along with George Soros and Peter Lewis, Sperling helped finance the Arizona referendum to permit the medical use of marijuana.

Sperling himself had a classical education—a BA in history at Reed, a master's in history at Berkeley, and a D. Phil. in economic history at Cambridge. He recalls his time at Berkeley as among the happiest years of his life. He was, however, far too restless to stick with the academic routine. In the early seventies, while teaching courses in the humanities at San Jose State, Sperling won a government contract to offer a variety of classes to teachers and police officers, and that was the beginning of what he considers his real education. "They were the best students I ever had," he told me. "They really fell in love with education. It wasn't long before they said, 'We'd like to get a degree.' So I went to the administration, and they said, 'No way.' I said, 'I'm bringing you students.' And they said, 'We don't need no stinking students.'"

Sperling developed a program with twenty-five hundred teachers and police at the University of San Francisco and two other colleges in California, but he claims that the regional accrediting body said, "Either get rid of these programs or we'll pull your accreditation for the whole university." Sperling came to see higher education as a closed system whose gates were manned by the accrediting agencies—a racket designed to squelch the forces of individual choice.

10 Sperling reached the Wild West of the free-market system in 1976, when he went to Phoenix, visited a local law firm, and drew up a charter for a new university and, just like that, the University of Phoenix opened for business. He targeted the niche market that he had already begun serving—the adult learner. The University of Phoenix would accept anybody who was twenty-three or older and was working. Students had to have sixty college credits when they arrived, so the need for general education, liberal arts, and all the other stuff that takes up so much time and money at college could be dispensed with. Sperling wanted to provide a useful and profitable service, not replicate higher education. What interested him was not so much what to teach this population as *how* to deliver it. "Higher education is one of the most inefficient mecha-

nisms for the transfer of knowledge that have ever been invented," Sperling said. "I decided to go back to my economics and conceive of education as a production function, in which you specify the learning outcomes that you want—they're your product—and then do a regression and figure out the most efficient way of producing them."

Just as the Ivy League model was developed two centuries ago to accommodate aspiring clerics, so the University of Phoenix is shaped by the needs of working adults in the corporate economy. And because it was created all at once it's a highly rational institution. Classes are held at night, from six to ten. Courses consist of five or six weekly sessions, taken one at a time and one right after another. Each degree program is identical from one campus to the next. Laura Palmer Noone, whose title is vice-president for academic affairs—elsewhere she would be called "provost"—says, "What we have found is that adults don't want all that much flexibility; they want it to be simple."

One of Sperling's early insights was that adults also put very little stock in academic opinion. He concluded, "You were going to have to draw your faculty from the world they were familiar with—the world of work. If you had a PhD that didn't mean shit." Marketing would be taught by a marketing executive, and accounting by an accountant. In a vocational setting, these teachers had the credentials that mattered. The "practitioner" system also, and not incidentally, allowed the university to deliver coursework far more cheaply than its competitors, since it paid its instructors an average of about a thousand dollars for each five-week course. Many of the teachers, and especially the businessmen, say they do their nighttime job for the sheer satisfaction of it. Hugh McBride, the executive director and chair of the graduate business programs, told me, "It's really a joy to have someone say, 'You know, Hugh, I used that last week in the company.'"

Faculty members are required to have a master's degree, but few, if any, of them have academic credentials that remotely rival Sperling's. Hugh McBride, for example, spent twenty years in the Army doing systems work, earned his MBA, and went to work for Citicorp and the Metro-North rail service. Larry Gudis, the director of the Phoenix campus, is a former high school teacher and assistant principal who spent three years working as a training manager at Intel. When he walked out of his office for a minute, I glanced at the three books he had on his shelf. Their titles were *Training and Performance*, *The Miracle of Personal Leadership*, and *Team and Organizational Development*.

The traditional American university occupies a space that is both bounded and pastoral—a space that speaks of monastic origins and a commitment to unworldliness. The headquarters of the University of Phoenix, by contrast, consists of two buildings of banded glass and brick with a fig leaf of grass in between and a parking lot all around them. The central campus happens to be situated in the middle of an industrial park near Sky Harbor Airport. As with the forty-six other facilities, the area was chosen with an eye to convenience in an automotive culture. The university leases multiple sites in many of the cities where it operates, choosing them so that no student has to drive more than twenty minutes to get to class. (In Phoenix, there are four sites, with two more scheduled to open soon.) And as the culture shifts from an automotive to an electronic one the U of P is moving to abridge space altogether. The on-line program offers classes to two thousand five hundred students who work out of their homes, including military personnel stationed all over the world. A separate service, the Center for Distance Education, provides one-on-one study for two thousand more students. Hundreds of colleges now offer some form of distance learning, but the U of P is one of the few where you can earn a degree without ever mingling with other students or even meeting a professor.

One evening, I attended a meeting of Business Communication Skills, a course known as COMM 202. The class met on the fourth floor of the taller of the two buildings at the central campus. The view outside the plate-glass windows was mesmerizing; waving palms; sawtooth mountains; airplanes sailing through a deepening blue sky. The teacher, Katherine Barnett, who was the assistant department chair for General Studies at the university, was a blond woman in her late forties with an ingratiating smile and a brittle manner. During the day, she taught reading and English at a public high school. She taught twenty-five or thirty classes a year at the U of P, and did some curriculum consulting as well. It sounded like a staggering burden, but she had kids to put through college. 15

There were about fifteen students. Most had been in a prior course together, and they had already found a comfort zone consisting of friendly chatter. Since this was COMM 202's first session, Barnett asked the students to talk briefly about themselves. They volunteered in order of courage. Maria Surrell was a long-distance operator for Sprint; Tammy Walter was a full-time mother; Ben Burns ran the laundry at a VA pharmacy center; Jody Gagnon was the contract administrator for a construction firm. The youngest student in the group, Jared Annes, was twenty-four; he had spent four years in the Army after high school and now worked for a computer firm that designed telephone voice systems. "I want to be more than just Joe Programmer; that's why I chose the Business and Information Systems degree," he had told me before the class. To the others he now said, with a laugh, "When I grow up, I want to be rich." One of the oldest students, Dean Williams, slight and earnest, said that he was in "food management." He had got a job at an Albertson's supermarket when he was a teenager; the money was good, and at the time he couldn't see any reason to stay in school. Now it was twenty years later, and he was managing the produce department in one store. He wanted to move up, but, he said, "it seemed like I got to a stopping point because I didn't have that degree."

Barnett agreed. "The days are gone when you could make your way to the top of the ladder by sheer guts," she told the class. "Now you have to have that piece of paper." The class was designed to teach the kind of oral-presentation skills that are required in business. Group work—a simulacrum of the team-oriented business environment—is an integral part of U of P pedagogy: for COMM 202, the final project would consist of a group presentation of a business meeting. Students would also make individual speeches. Barnett told the class that she would be giving hints on how to reduce the stress of making public presentations. She sounded forgiving. "If you make a mess of it but you try anyway, you're going to get the grade," she said.

COMM 202 was for students who had arrived at the University of Phoenix with fewer than twenty-four credits; in effect, it was for freshmen. Later that evening, I attended a session of Advanced Marketing Management, for students working on their MBA. They were required to turn in papers each week, and to do considerable reading; the final group project would be to devise a marketing strategy to capture 1 percent of the beverage market. The teacher, George Francisco, had been a brand manager for Philadelphia Cream Cheese and other products at Kraft. He talked about the idea of a mature market. The soda business had stopped growing, he explained, so the big players were branching out into flavored teas and bottled waters. One student said, "We had a caffeinated water we tried to market—Aqua Java." It hadn't worked. They talked about high-stakes presentations. "Let me tell you what happened at Kraft," Francisco said. "If you went over an hour and a half, they walked out of the room." There was a little collective gasp.

The University of Phoenix has been denigrated as a "diploma mill," but in this class and the others I attended the students were engaged and the discussion was spirited. What was a little hard to get used to, though, was the lack of intellectual, as opposed to professional, curiosity. Ideas had value only insofar as they could be put to use—if they could *do* something for you, as Bill Gibbs had said. Here was a university formed around the idea that practiced experience is superior to abstract understanding—a proposition that almost seemed self-negating. Indeed, the U of P's greatest contribution to curriculum design may be its Assessment of Prior Learning, a system that allows students to earn credit for courses by proving that they have had equivalent personal experience. You can even take a course in the subject, which allows you to get credit for mastering the "theory" behind the system and also gives you the tools to successfully "challenge" other courses. Norma Turner, who often teaches this course, told me about a student who earned nineteen credits—plus three more for the class itself—by writing essays demonstrating his mastery in such subjects as Parenting, Family Life, and Loss, and Bereavement.

20 The University of Phoenix is not cheap compared with many of its competitors. At two hundred and sixteen dollars a credit, a bachelor's degree could come to more than twenty thousand dollars. But I didn't meet a single student who questioned the value of the investment. Many of them had chosen the University of Phoenix after a good deal of comparison shopping. They had tried Arizona State University but had found that they had difficulty scheduling all their classes at night. They had enrolled in community college but had been unable to tolerate the juvenile atmosphere. They had tried to register elsewhere but had grown tired of waiting in line for courses that turned out to be closed. In a consumer-driven market, the U of P had adapted itself to their needs more effectively than the competition had; it was doing unambiguously what the others were doing haltingly. Scott Safranski, a professor of management at St. Louis University, who headed a visiting accreditation-review

team that looked at Phoenix last year, notes that detractors have called the school the McDonald's of higher education but says, "I'm not sure that's entirely derogatory. They've provided a uniform product in a consistent way which is convenient to the consumer at an affordable price." He adds, "I certainly hope they don't take my market away too quickly."

The University of Phoenix is still one of the few for-profit academic institutions established to date; but the distinction between profit-making companies and educational institutions is becoming increasingly moot. Several education experts I spoke to volunteered the idea that a new kind of institution would come into being as the result of an alliance between a state-university system, a "content provider," like Disney, and a technology firm, like Motorola. The fastest-growing sector of higher education is, in fact, the "corporate university," which typically provides training for middle and upper management. A 1994 book by Stan Davis and Jim Botkin titled *The Monster Under the Bed* observes that the increase in "classroom contact hours" for corporate employees in one year, 1992, exceeded the enrollment growth at all the colleges built between 1960 and 1990. The authors foresee the business model, with its focus on "competition, service, and standards," supplanting the current educational model.

This may be a bit premature, but the line between corporate training and academic education has clearly blurred. One day, I drove into Tempe, a suburb just beyond Phoenix (itself a sprawling suburb), to visit Motorola University, a gleaming facility on landscaped grounds that looks more like a university than the University of Phoenix does. Motorolans, as they are known, were taking courses in Behavioral Interviewing and Developing Your Human Potential, along with some in recondite aspects of computer-chip design. The curriculum sounded a lot like the one at the University of Phoenix, and, in fact, the U of P offers several of its courses on the campus. Motorola does not provide an academic degree, as some corporate universities do, but Arizona State offers a master's in Management of Technology on the Motorola campus, using teachers from both institutions. In Phoenix, if not yet in Boston or New York, the corporate university is part of a web, not of a pecking order—one of several kinds of "providers" filling in different aspects of a "learner"'s needs. Arthur Levine, of Teachers College, predicts that several generations from now "we'll still have some number of residential colleges and some number of research universities, but most of the rest will disappear." Corporations may simply make postsecondary education an in-house function. Non-élite institutions, Levine suggests, will be reduced largely to examining and certifying students for workplace readiness.

Like any successful business, the University of Phoenix is oriented toward growth, and in recent years it has begun to expand into the realm of the conventional university. The number of credits required for admission has dropped from sixty to zero. The U of P has created a General Studies department, which offers courses not only in Oral Communications but in Philosophy and

Religion. (Bill Gibbs, though, says that he would like to see the Religion course focus on such practical advice as how to do business among different bodies of believers.) In effect, it is now taking responsibility for the entire undergraduate education of many of its students. The administration hired William Pepicello, who has a PhD in linguistics from Brown and a manner that is identifiably academic, to establish a Gen. Ed. curriculum and embody the school's new identity. Last year, the U of P sought permission from accreditors to offer undergraduate degrees in whatever subjects it wished, and to establish a doctoral program. Both of these proposals were rejected—a decision that infuriated many at the school. The general view in Phoenix is that the forces of convention which have been trying to throttle John Sperling for a quarter of a century still have the upper hand in academe. An alternative point of view is that there are still standards for an academic education, and the university may have been threatening to transgress them. Stephen Spangehl, an official of the North Central Association, which is the regional accrediting body, declines to give specific reasons for the decision but says that the group was concerned about, among other things, the university's lack of rigorous academic assessment. "They seem more concerned about customer satisfaction," Spangehl says. "Our focus has always been on learning."

It's that sort of curt dismissal that makes John Sperling furious. "Jesus, they're disgusting," he said when I asked him about the decision. But he was moving ahead, looking for new markets. He had recently returned from a trip to the Far East. There were, he said, a million potential customers for information-systems training in Malaysia alone, and the China market was incalculable. The Apollo Group was making a big push into distance learning, and that may well be the growth market for postsecondary education. Moreover, the whole public-school market was opening up. Jorge Klor de Alva, a former anthropology professor at Berkeley, who is now the chair of the U of P's academic cabinet, told me that the advent of school vouchers "will create huge opportunities for private, for-profit schools." Apollo could own a chain of schools, provide management services, and market curricular material. Once you conceive of education as a product, and regress from the needs of the consumer, a whole world of possibilities presents itself.

25 Sperling himself seems unable to decide whether he has created a superior model for higher education or a viable alternative to the existing one. As we were having dinner one evening, he started going on about the uselessness of classical education. "One of my favorite books is *Tom Jones*," he said. "I read *Tom Jones* for the sheer pleasure, but I didn't go out and rut with some maid in the canebrakes. It's all part of what happens up here." He pointed to his head, but he sounded so thoroughly exasperated that he might as well have been talking about his appendix. "The University of Phoenix causes you to *apply* what you've learned *the next day at work*." Then, lest I get the wrong idea, he reminded me of how deeply he had loved Berkeley.

"Why don't you want all your students to have the experience you had?" I asked.

"Because they can't afford to."

"Wouldn't it be good if they could?"

Sperling gave me a weary look, and said, "I'm not involved in social reform." He had once tried to build a chain of technical schools for inner-city youth, he told me, and when that failed he had vowed never again to create something there wasn't a demand for. "Microsoft is a much more powerful force shaping the world than Harvard or Yale or Princeton," he said. "So if you can't beat 'em, join 'em."

▪ QUESTIONS

Reading

1. What differentiates the University of Phoenix from other universities? How significant is this distinction, according to Traub?
2. Highlight, underline, or flag the places where Traub characterizes John Sterling. How does his profile of Sterling support the rest of his report?
3. How has the accreditations board responded to the University of Phoenix's proposals? What two contrasting explanations does Traub offer for this response?

Exploratory Writing

1. In groups, make a double-entry list of the advantages of attending online classes at a school like the University of Phoenix versus attending a more traditional school. (You might consider the other pieces in this casebook for descriptions of more traditional college experiences.) Did you find more advantages to list under "Online" or under "Traditional"? What disagreements arose within your group about business-model versus not-for-profit universities?

ONLINE SCHOOL	TRADITIONAL SCHOOL

2. Traub interviews Arthur Levine of Teachers College, who suggests that in the future, corporations may make postsecondary education an "in-house function." Do some research, and find an example (from any era) of a program for future educational reform. Compare and contrast this model with the University of Phoenix, as described by Traub.

Making Connections

1. Traub writes that at the University of Phoenix, "terms that normally have a clear and literal meaning are used in an oddly evanescent way" (paragraph 1). In his explanation of "How to Write a Great College Slogan," George Felton (p. 674) describes how colleges are using language in service of their marketing agendas. Note the examples in Traub's article of colleges using slogans or other marketing language. What do these examples reveal?

Essay Writing

1. If you were given full funding to attend any college or university in the world, which university would you choose and why? What would you study? Write an essay reflecting on your own values and priorities when it comes to higher education. How do these values connect to your vision of the meaning of life?

ARGUING

The Case against College

Linda Lee

Linda Lee (b. 1982) is the author of a novel, two biographies, and the memoir *Out of Wedlock: A Love Story* (1982). She has worked as a book editor and an editor for the *New York Times*. Her book for parents, *Success Without College: Why Your Child May Not Have to Go to College Right Now—and May Not Have to Go At All* (2001), from which this piece is excerpted, argues that undergraduate education does not benefit all students. In her *Family Circle* article on this theme, she wrote, "[My son] had been smart enough to get into the Bronx High School of Science in New York and did well on his SATs. But I know now that he did not belong in college. . . . He did not go to study philosophy. Nor did he feel it incumbent to go to class or complete courses. Meanwhile I was paying $1,000 a week for this pleasure cruise."

All great truths begin as blasphemies.

—George Bernard Shaw

Here is who belongs in college: the high-achieving student who is interested in learning for learning's sake, those who intend to become schoolteachers, and those young people who seem certain to go on to advanced degrees in law, medicine, architecture, and the like.

Here is who actually goes to college: everyone. That everyone includes the learning disabled and the fairly dumb, those who have trouble reading and writing and doing math, slackers who see college as an opportunity to major in Beers of the World, burned-out book jockeys, and the just plain average student with not much interest in anything.

Think about your high school class. Now think about the 76 percent of those students (80 to 90 percent in middle-class suburbs) who *say* they expect to go to two-year or four-year colleges. You begin to see the problem?

Pamela Gerhardt, who has been teaching advanced writing and editing at the University of Maryland for six years, says she has seen a decline in her students' interest in the world of ideas. In an article in the *Washington Post* on August 22, 1999, she noted: "Last semester, many of my students drifted in late, slumped into chairs, made excuses to leave early, and surrounded my desk when papers were due, clearly distraught over the looming deadline. 'I can't think of any problems,' one told me. 'Nothing interests me.' "

5 Her students, she said, rejected the idea of writing about things like homelessness or AIDS. Five male students, she said, wanted to write about the "problem" of the instant replay in televised football games.

Ever since the Garden of Eden, people have been complaining that things used to be better, once upon a time, back when. I suppose it is possible that, thirty years ago, students were just as shallow and impatient with education as they are today. But I don't think so. It could be that a college education is wasted on the young, but it is more likely that a college education is especially being wasted on today's youth.

Of course, there was a period twenty-five years ago when Cassandras argued that college was a waste of time and money. Around the time that *The Overeducated American* was published, in 1975, Caroline Bird wrote a book called *The Case against College.* Her book has been out of print for decades. But there are arguments that seem very familiar to me: that Madison Avenue sells college like soap flakes, that going to college had become a choice requiring no forethought; that students weren't really there to learn and that college was no longer an effective way to train workers.

But primarily Ms. Bird argued that "there is no real evidence that the higher income of college graduates is due to college at all." She cited as her proof Christopher Jencks's report "Inequality: A Reassessment of the Effect of Family and Schooling in America," which pointed out that people from high-status families tended to earn more than people from low-status families, even if they had the same amount of education.

College, Bird pointed out twenty-five years ago, "fails to work its income-raising magic for almost a third of those who go." Moreover, she said, "college doesn't make people intelligent, ambitious, happy, liberal or quick to learn new things. It's the other way around. Intelligent, ambitious, happy, liberal, quick-to-learn people are attracted to college in the first place."

Or, as Zachary Karabell asked in the 1999 book *What's College For? The Struggle to Define American Higher Education,* "on a more pragmatic level, does college truly lead to better jobs?" 10

He answered his own question with "Not necessarily. The more people go to college, the less a college degree is worth." He goes on to point out that the Bureau of Labor Statistics includes in its list of jobs that require a college degree "insurance adjuster" and "manager of a Blockbuster video store." Is that what you were foreseeing for Joey when you wrote that $25,000 tuition check?

Caroline Bird was outraged over the expense of college in 1975. A Princeton education, she said, would cost $22,256 for tuition, books, travel, room, board, and pocket money—for four years.

Twenty-five years later, the price for that Princeton degree has grown to $140,000, including room and board and books, but not travel money and pocket change. It's even more than that, if you factor in the student's lost wages. Because of the low unemployment rates at the end of the nineties, anyone with the IQ to go to Princeton could make at least $15,000 a year with only a high school diploma, and perhaps more. So tack on at least $60,000 (if the student knows computers, make that $120,000) in lost wages while Jared or Jessica was busy at Princeton studying Shakespeare. That puts the price of a college degree from a fine Ivy League school at more than $200,000.

Is it worth it today? Perhaps even less so than in Caroline Bird's day, primarily because students no longer seem interested in ideas, and because it is so much easier to make money just by hopping onto the Internet.

"I agree that from the perspective of society as a whole, it would be better if fewer people went to college," Robert Frank told me. He's the popular Cornell economist, and the author of *Luxury Fever* and other books. "Economists often challenge this notion by citing studies that show significantly higher wages for college graduates," he said. "But all these studies say is that the people who attend college are better, on the average, than those who don't. They don't tell us how much value is added to them by attending college. From the individual's point of view, it still often pays to attend college, since employers so often use education as an initial screening device. Everyone wants the best-paying and most interesting jobs, after all, which assures that there will always be a surfeit of applicants for them. So employers who offer such jobs have every incentive to confine their attention to college graduates. But that doesn't mean that we'd be poorer as a nation if fewer people went to college." 15

An article in *Newsweek* (November 1, 1999) by Robert J. Samuelson said: "Going to Harvard or Duke won't automatically produce a better job and higher pay. Graduates of these schools generally do well. But they do well because they are talented." The article was titled "The Worthless Ivy League?"

Brigid McMenamin wrote a blistering piece in *Forbes* magazine (December 28, 1998) called "The Tyranny of the Diploma." Beyond listing the usual suspects in the computer field who did not complete college—Bill Gates, Michael Dell—she pointed to the young digerati who are making $50,000 to $80,000 a year and more at age sixteen. At a time when most kids in college say they are there "to get a job," these kids may well skip college in order to jump in on the booming Internet business.

Moreover, as Ms. McMenamin recounts, almost 15 percent, or 58 members, of the Forbes 400 (a yearly listing of the most successful business leaders), had either, as she put it, ditched college or avoided it altogether. In terms of wages, she said, brick masons and machinists had it all over biology and liberal arts majors. As a capper, she stated: "A hefty 21 percent of all degree-holders who work earn less than the average for high school grads." She didn't even bring up plumbers, electricians, and car mechanics.

▪ QUESTIONS

Reading

1. What book did Caroline Bird author? What were its main arguments?
2. What does the George Bernard Shaw quote at the beginning of this article mean? How does it support Lee's argument?
3. Highlight, underline, or flag the jobs and careers that Lee mentions in this article. How are these examples of professions significant?

Exploratory Writing

1. Write a list of ten to fifteen people, alive or dead, whom you greatly admire. Do some research, and find out how and where each person on the list got his or her formal

education. What is the connection, in your opinion, between each person's educational background and his or her achievements?

2. In pairs, think up a fantasy achievement — a way that you could change the world, if new things were possible (finding the cure for cancer, designing a time machine, finding the key to eternal life, making the most beautiful painting in history, breaking an Olympic record, or something else you think would be valuable). Write a list of at least twenty-five skills, resources, and experiences that you would need in order to succeed. In what ways would college help you gain these skills, resources, or experience? In which ways would college be unnecessary?

Making Connections

1. James Traub quotes the president of the "para-university" University of Phoenix as saying, "The people who are our students don't really want the education. They want what the education provides for them. . . ." (p. 661). How would Lee's arguments apply to these students?

Essay Writing

1. "I suppose it is possible that, thirty years ago, students were just as shallow and impatient with education as they are today. But I don't think so," writes Lee in paragraph 6. Write a reportorial essay investigating ways that college students in your community have changed over the past thirty years. You can use interviews, case studies, historical records, and readings to form your conclusions.

EXPLAINING

How to Write a Great College Slogan

George Felton

George Felton is a professor of writing and copywriting in the liberal arts department at the Columbus College of Art and Design in Ohio. His work has appeared in the *New York Times, Advertising Age, Newsweek,* and the *Wall Street Journal.* His popular textbook, *Advertising: Concept and Copy* (2nd edition, 2006), offers readers a guide to the challenging processes of coming up with ideas for ads and then writing effective copy. He has received a Columbus Literary Award, and his advertising and copywriting work has been featured in *HOW, Print,* and *Communication Arts* magazines. His essays about advertising focus on how to develop ways of thinking that strengthen advertorial writing and creative approaches to marketing problems. Felton expertly analyzes marketing language used by colleges in this satirical piece from the *Chronicle of Higher Education* (2001).

I'm sure we've all noticed that colleges and universities these days are writing slogans for themselves and putting them in their promotional materials right next to the college logo, much as Volkswagen does ("Drivers wanted"), or FedEx ("The World On Time"), or almost anyone else in business. It only makes sense: If you're selling something, get the door open, wedge your foot in, and keep it there.

But we may also have noticed that college slogans tend to be—how to put this?—kind of lame. They sound like they were written by the admissions department or development folks on a Friday afternoon in a badly ventilated meeting room. All committee, no heart. To wit:

- University of Idaho: Tradition. Change. Excellence.
- Oakland University: Think Success. Think Oakland University.
- Defiance College: To Know. To Lead. To Serve. To Understand.

As you see, they're dutiful and sane, but they've got no oomph, no razzmatazz, no get-up-and-zing. If we're going to compete with the big boys, we need to do better. In the spirit of improving the breed, of getting in the game, I offer some modest suggestions, a few dos and don'ts, to create that winning slogan for your campus.

Make it fun. Do this before you do anything else. Remember, by creating a slogan, you've entered that great American amusement park, AdLand. Students will judge your slogan against the best lines still echoing in their heads from the day's play: "Just do it," "Got milk?," and the rest. So be warned. Play to win. Hey, there's a slogan. Be good or be gone. Hey, there's another one.

5 Make it catchy. To borrow advice from the New York advertising agency Kirshenbaum Bond & Partners, you don't want your strategy showing. Too many college slogans hang so far below the hemline that they trip on them-

selves. The windy laboriousness of this slogan, for example, gives off the whiff of too much homework: "Quinnipiac University: Challenging students to meet the challenges of the future." I have that headachy, overloaded feeling already. You, too?

Slogans solve problems, and I'd think the big problem here would be pronouncing the place. Try this: "Quinnipiac: Rhymes with 'Win a Free Mac.' And that's just what you'll get when you're accepted for early decision. We'll give you your choice of an iMac or iBook for school. Cool!" See how naturally the slogan leads to strong selling copy?

Honest is good, but too honest is bad. A slogan could be seen as a chance to tell the truth, but when has that ever been persuasive? Iowa State University's, for example, is "Becoming the best." Modest yet ambitious, perhaps even true. But like detergent boxes that say "New Formula! Cleans Better!" or frozen meals claiming "More Chicken! Improved Taste!" it makes you wonder what Iowa State was doing before. They might as well have written, "Now with more professors" or "Pretty darned okay, considering everything." I suggest "Iowa State University: Why not the best?" It worked for Jimmy Carter, didn't it? (Besides, since we've forgotten the past, and students never knew it, the line's washday-fresh all over again.) Get in our face a little. Force the issue. Why not Iowa State? Well, why not? Give me one good reason. I'm waiting.

See the power of a good offense? And you could follow it up in the brochure: "Can't think of a reason? Then give us a season." So think big. Say more, not less. Ask yourself, what might be true? Then keep on going.

Don't let common sense get in the way. Here's a slogan I admire: "University of Sarasota. Now in California." Assuming that Sarasota is only in Florida is exactly the kind of narrow-mindedness that cripples college marketing today. Properly viewed, Sarasota is wherever we want it to be, kind of like Superman. With distributed-learning centers and online learning, a college's brand is infinitely portable, so it has no excuse for not being ubiquitous. If I can get Starbucks along the highway, on the corner, from a bookstore, on campus, online, at the supermarket, and out of the cup at my elbow right now, your brand ought to be at least as available. I should be able to suck down your school's brew without so much as a straw. So, as your university expands everywhere, write a slogan that tells us about it. Possibilities? "University of Maryland: All Terrapin Station All the Time." "University of Arkansas! Pigs Fly!" And so on.

10 Exercise caution with regional appeals. With One World fast approaching, state universities need to remember that regionalism can appear to be provincialism. Mississippi State University, for example, promises "Leadership for 21st Century Mississippi." That simply won't do. It suggests that MSU grads, if not stopped at the state border for insufficient intellectual baggage, will at the very least find success unlikely in New York and points beyond. I suggest reworking it a bit: "Next Millennial Leadership for the Known Universe, and Then Some." That may need a little tightening, but you get the idea.

Plagiarize where appropriate. One time-tested creative principle is modeling. So borrow liberally from the best slogans out there. Students will hear the similarity, but as endless movie remakes and sequels testify, they actually prefer similarity. Should you want to capitalize on students' career anxieties, "Got milk?" could become "Got chops?" Or, if your school favors innovation and design-your-own-degree programs, you might take the Altoids slogan, "The curiously strong mints," and turn it into "The curiously curious college."

If you're West Point or Annapolis or maybe even St. John's College, with its no-nonsense Great Books curriculum, you might try "The school with seriously strong strictures." Take your position in the marketplace, peruse the great slogans of our time, then just plug and play.

Keep an eye out for cross-promotional opportunities. Why sell one thing when you can sell two? Some product slogans are already so good that they'd work perfectly in partnership with your institution: "Courage for your head: Bell helmets and Reed College invite you to 'A Weekend With the Classics.'" Or "You've got questions. We've got answers. Radio Shack and MIT present 'Why We Talk Funny: The Mind-Mouth Mechanism.'"

Hide the sales pitch without obscuring it. Sierra Nevada College can show us the way here. Its slogan is "a personalized four-year college experience in a unique alpine setting." Hmmm . . . "unique alpine setting." Kind of teases the mind, doesn't it? And a quick check of location confirms the euphemism. What we've got here is as academic a way as possible of saying: "Tahoe, baby. Ski your shins off." They haven't said it, of course, but we hear it singing in the wires nonetheless.

So find the key fact for your institution—its "human truth," as advertisers often call the real reason people buy a product. Then slip that into the slogan, and elevate it to near but not total obscurity. Kids are hip to overkill, so suggest, don't state. Are they shopping for low-cost fun? A stress-free, beer-soaked, cooling-off period from the rigors of too much high school study hall? You could write "Putz University. Spend less. Party more," but you'd be bottom-feeding. Remember, elevate: "Putz University. You can't put a price on happiness. Or can you?" It sounds good, it feels good, and best of all, beer and self-esteem get to stay out all night. 15

Here's one last, and I hope obvious, piece of advice:

Tread lightly on learning for learning's sake. Relevance and practicality are where it's at today. Too much academic navel-gazing leads to no job at all, especially if you do it well enough, in which case it literally leads nowhere: The holder of an advanced degree merely gets up, walks to the front of the classroom, turns around, and assumes the role of teacher. Students know this, and for most of them, it's simply not enough. The best part of getting into college remains getting out.

Many colleges couldn't agree more. "Columbus State University: Education that works." "St. John's University: Real learning for real life." "Hofstra University: We teach success."

Good directions, all, but with an undergraduate year now running between $20,000 and $30,000 at private institutions and about $8,000 at public ones, why not throw the parents a bone? A slogan like "Keep on toolin'" taps into the nostalgia that kids feel for the sixties they never knew and their parents feel for the sixties they can't remember. It promises students valuable career skills while convincing parents that they're still hip—all in just three words.

The key here, as in all sloganeering, is simple: Know who's buying and what's really for sale. 20

▪ QUESTIONS

Reading

1. What is the best part of getting into college, according to Felton?
2. According to Felton, why should people writing college slogans "exercise caution with regional appeals" (paragraph 10)?
3. Highlight, underline, or flag the places where Felton uses humor (including irony and sarcasm) to explain college slogan-writing. How would his explanation change if someone edited out the humor?

Exploratory Writing

1. Go online, and find ten college slogans not mentioned in this article. How does each slogan measure up, based on Felton's explanation? Rewrite each of the inadequate (or "kind of lame") slogans to make them great, according to Felton's guidelines.
2. Felton concludes that the key in all sloganeering is to know who's buying, and what's really for sale. Find ten slogans advertising any products, services, policies, political candidates, or institutions. How does each slogan reflect "who's buying"? How does each show "what's really for sale"?

Making Connections

1. Mark Edmundson (p. 630) refers to today's students as "consumers" and "customers." How does Felton's view of the purpose of college relate to Edmundson's perspective? How would Felton respond to Edmundson?

Essay Writing

1. Write an argumentative essay in favor of "learning for learning's sake." You don't necessarily need to agree with your own argument, but you should use argumentative writing techniques to make your case strong and convincing.

ARGUMENTATION AND RESEARCH PROJECTS

1. Choose an essay from this casebook and conduct some research to find one or two essays or articles that offer opposing viewpoints. The authors of the articles you find may respond directly to your chosen essay, or they may simply focus on the same questions, drawing different conclusions about them. Write your own essay in which you make an argument about how each author's definition of the value of college shapes his or her perspective. Consider the following questions as you develop your argument: What assumptions lead the authors to think differently from each other? What evidence do they present to support their points of view? Can you imagine any common ground between the authors, or are their differences so fundamental that common ground is impossible?
2. Write a proposal for the creation of your ideal college, addressed to a board of trustees who might fund and oversee the development of the institution. Support your proposal with the work of teachers, writers, and thinkers who have made arguments about the value of an education. Include at least one or two opposing viewpoints and offer counterarguments to refute them. Use sources you find in this casebook and in your own research. Include some visual material — photos, graphs, maps, or illustrations — to enliven your proposal. (As an alternative, you might create the proposal in the form of a lecture presentation, using slides to outline the details.)
3. Make a video "manifesto" evaluating your own college and making an argument about what it might become in the future. A *manifesto* is a radical proposal for a new way of thinking, a new kind of art, or a new cultural institution. To make your manifesto, interview as many students, teachers, and administrators as you can. What are your college's biggest strengths? What are its weaknesses? What challenges does it face in the near future? How might it evolve in the long term? Then, reflect on how what you learn resonates (or does not resonate) with ideas explored in some of the essays in this casebook. Find two or three additional sources that explore the questions and themes raised in your interviews. Be sure you contextualize these interviews in relation to the ideas explored in these sources.

What Do We Really Know about Gender?

Scholars of gender studies are in the business of questioning and exploring what most of us think of as truth or common sense with regard to the origins and meaning of what it means and how it feels to be male, female, or transgendered. Of course, gender is fundamental to personal identity, social relations, and legal policies that shape our lives. The essays in this casebook raise a number of research questions: Is every person really simply male or female? To what degree is gender rooted in biology or "constructed" by social factors? What biases about gender shape cultural institutions? Is it possible that nobody really embodies maleness or femaleness entirely? Might we all fall somewhere along a spectrum of gender identities? What hardships do people face when they don't fall neatly into conventional gender categories?

Each of the readings in this casebook explores one or more of these research questions, using particular rhetorical modes to illuminate them and to push readers to reconsider what they think they know about gender. In "Society Constructs Biology; Biology Constructs Gender" (p. 681), Anne Fausto-Sterling argues that scientific definitions of biological sex are distorted by social and cultural biases about gender. E. J. Graff reports on research that suggests that the categories "male" and "female" are drastic oversimplications of biological sex and gender identity in "The M/F Boxes" (p. 695). Jay Prosser uses "The Body Narrative of Transsexuality" (p. 701) to reflect on his own experience as a college professor transitioning from female to male. In her reflective essay "What Makes a Woman a Woman?" (p. 705), Peggy Orenstein asks, after doctors recommend surgery as a way of reducing her risk of breast cancer, "without breasts or hormone-producing ovaries, what would be the difference be, say, between myself and a pre-op female-to-male transsexual?" Steven Jay Gould's essay, "Women's Brains" (p. 709), makes an argument about the limitations and biases of nineteenth-century research on apparent difference between men's and women's brains. The celebrated novelist Michael Chabon employs humor in "Faking It" (p. 715) to reconcile social expectations for men with his own actions.

All of these essays are motivated by their authors' desire to re-examine questions about gender that many people take for granted. They want us to take a second look, examining evidence and research, rather than relying on attitudes shaped by our cultural experiences. In each case, the author presents concrete evidence—drawn from personal experience, scientific research, or social theory— to demonstrate that what we think we know demands reconsideration.

You should think in similar terms as you take the questions raised in these essays and follow up with your own research. What do we think we know about gender? What evidence do essays in this casebook offer to complicate or challenge these assumptions? What questions are left unanswered? What kinds of evidence will you need in order to find some answers? These are the questions that should guide you in your own gender studies research project.

ARGUING

Society Constructs Biology; Biology Constructs Gender

Anne Fausto-Sterling

Brown University professor of biology and gender studies Anne Fausto-Sterling (b. 1944) holds degrees in zoology and developmental genetics. Her books include *Myths of Gender: Biological Theories about Women and Men* (1992) and *Sexing the Body: Gender Politics and the Construction of Sexuality* (2000). The latter was named a *CHOICE* Magazine Outstanding Academic Book of 2000, was co-winner of the American Sociological Association's Robert K. Merton Book Award, and received a Distinguished Publication Award from the Association for Women in Psychology. Fausto-Sterling has written widely for both popular and scholarly audiences on gender, sexuality, intersexuality, developmental biology, and the social construction of race. Her work was groundbreaking in its time and continues to influence gender research. Her popular essay "The Five Sexes: Why Male and Female Are Not Enough" argues that, biologically, there are "at least five sexes — perhaps even more." In "Society Constructs Biology," which appeared in the "Learning about Women: Gender, Politics, and Power" issue of the journal *Daedalus*, Fausto-Sterling examines how cultural assumptions shape science, and thus, our perception of gender.

Truth, bias, objectivity, prejudice. In recent years both defenders and critics of the activities of the modern Western scientific community have used these words with a certain abandon as they engage in debate about the role of science and the scientist in our culture. Perhaps the best-known voice in this discussion is that of Thomas Kuhn, whose historical analyses of the "progress" of science threw into sharp relief the uneven nature of the development of scientific ideas.[1] In the past decade feminist analysts of science have joined the discussion. Historians, philosophers, anthropologists, and scientists who write from a feminist perspective have raised varied and complex questions about modern science.[2]

In this essay I propose to examine the interaction of two processes that have important consequences for our understanding of how science works. These are (1) the process by which cultural understandings of gender become building blocks in supposedly objective understandings of nature, and (2) the process by which scientific theory helps to shape social concepts such as gender.

The two case studies presented in this essay (one historical, one contemporary) will illustrate how cultural understandings or beliefs, whether conscious or unconscious, influence the construction of scientific theory. Two current examples of the way scientific ideas are used to define social norms will illustrate the role that scientific theory plays in the definition of social concepts.

Social Construction of Science

The writings of a famous and highly imaginative Italian scientist, Abbé Lazzaro Spallanzani (1729–1799), illustrate that the inner workings of the mind of a dedicated experimental scientist are complex and often under subconscious wraps.[3] Although Spallanzani is probably best known for his experimental disproof of the idea of spontaneous generation, he also made an important contribution to eighteenth-century thinking about fertilization and embryonic development. The presence of spermatozoa in the semen had been discovered in Spallanzani's time, but the role of these "vermicelli" (or "spermatozoan worms," as they were often called) remained a subject of considerable debate within the context of a long-lived controversy about the origin of the embryo. Ovists believed that it arose solely from the egg, while spermists maintained that the womb was a passive vessel that offered fertile ground for the growth and development of the semen.

5 The most famous of early biologists belonged to different camps. The frontispiece of William Harvey's *Concerning the Generation of Living Animals* depicts Zeus sitting on a throne and opening what looks like a bird's egg, out of which hop, fly, and crawl all manner of beasts, mythical and otherwise. On the egg is written *Ex ovo omnia.* On the other side we find Antony van Leeuwenhoek arguing that the animalcules in semen find their way to the womb, where they act as seed; he dismisses eggs as "emunctorys* . . . adhering to the bowels of animals."[4]

Spallanzani, an ovist, performed a series of experiments with mating frogs to disprove Carolus Linnaeus's claim that insemination must always be internal. In a classic demonstration of the scientific method, he observed that the male frog, grasping the female frog as she lays eggs, deposits semen on the eggs as they emerge from her uterus. To test the semen's function, he constructed little taffeta breeches for the male frogs (unwittingly presaging Kenneth Grahame's *The Wind in the Willows,* in which toads wear clothes and drive cars) and made the following observations:

> The males, notwithstanding this incumbrance, seek the females with equal eagerness and perform, as well as they can, the act of generation; but the event is such as may be expected: The eggs are never prolific for want of having been bedewed with semen, which sometimes may be seen in the breeches in the form of drops. That these drops are real seed, appeared clearly from the artificial fecondation that was obtained by means of them.[5]

In other words, Spallanzani showed not only that preventing semen deposition prevented egg development, but also that when he spread semen on the eggs, fertilization resulted. A model of good experimentation indeed.

But Spallanzani did not conclude from these or other experiments that the vermicelli were necessary for the embryo to develop. Instead he conducted a series of experiments in an attempt to find out how much semen was needed

**emunctory*: any organ that removes waste from the body.

to achieve fertilization. Observing that even very tiny amounts were sufficient, he concluded that the important factor was something he called the "seminal aura," which he thought to be "nothing but the vapor of the seed exceedingly rarified."[6] Believing that his results proved the ovists's theory, he proceeded to perform a series of experiments on the seminal aura, all of which he designed to disprove the role of the spermatozoan in fertilization. He diluted semen samples until he could see no more sperm and found the diluted fluid still capable of fertilization. He also filtered semen so thoroughly that it could no longer induce development. The former results he took as proof of the existence of a seminal aura; the latter he ignored.[7]

In Spallanzani we have an example of a highly talented eighteenth-century scientist doing careful experiments that prove, to our modern-day eyes, the opposite of what he concluded. Because he interpreted his investigations within a particular theoretical framework—that of ovism—his mind was dosed to alternative conclusions that seem obvious to those not so committed. Because Spallanzani was a scientist of considerable authority and influence, his conclusions, rather than his experimental results, dominated biological thought on fertilization. A correct account of the role of the sperm in fertilization and development was not generally accepted for another hundred years. The point here is not that an incompetent scientist made a series of experimental errors, but that an extremely good scientist performed a series of beautifully controlled experiments but did not draw from them the correct conclusions. The process by which cultural categories shape perception and influence reasoning is little studied. The case of Spallanzani and his experiments on spermatozoa and their role in fertilization would be an excellent starting point for a cultural anthropologist who wished to analyze this process. That this phenomenon holds true for modern scientific activity can be seen in the next, more contemporary example.

During mammalian development all embryos (regardless of their potential sex) pass through a stage that embryologists have dubbed the "indifferent period." Examination of XX and XY embryos during this period shows no evidence of sex differences in either the embryonic gonad or sexually-related somatic structures such as the oviducts or the vas deferens. Present are a single gonad that will later take either a male or female path of development, and two sets of accessory structures known as the mesonephric and paramesonephric ducts. In female development the mesonephric ducts disintegrate while the paramesonephric ducts form the oviducts, uterus, and part of the vagina. In male development the paramesonephric ducts degenerate while the mesonephric ducts develop into the epididymal duct and the vas deferens. In general, then, mammals first develop a single pair of gonads, which subsequently takes either a male or a female direction, and both male and female accessory structures, only one set of which survives while the other degenerates. Baldly stated, up to a certain point all embryos are completely bisexual.

10 The choice of whether to follow a male or a female path of development is made through the intervention of the sex chromosomes and hormones present in utero. It is at this point in the story that a curious use of language that has

set limits on the experimental questions asked about sexual development enters in. I will first recount the tale as it is told in text books, popular literature, and the vast majority of scientific papers, and then underline some of the story's peculiarities, showing how they have resulted in a supposedly general account of the development of the sexes that is in actuality only an account of male development. This example illustrates a case in which the meaning of *man* as a supposedly inclusive universal has slipped unnoticed into its meaning as an exclusive biological category. What biologists turn out to have provided as our account of the development of gender from a mechanistic point of view is really only an account of male differentiation.

The following excerpts come from an up-to-date and heavily used undergraduate embryology text written by Dr. Bruce M. Carlson. My intent is not to attack Carlson, who recounts an almost universally held set of beliefs, but merely to analyze the text to uncover some of the underlying structures of those beliefs. Carlson writes:

> The sex-determining function of the Y chromosome is intimately bound with the activity of the H-Y antigen . . . its major function is to cause the organization of the primitive gonad into the testis. In the *absence* of the H-Y antigen the gonad later becomes transformed into the ovary. (Italics added.)

The account continues with a discussion of the formation of nongonadal (somatic) sex organs such as the uterus and vas deferens.

> The early embryo develops a dual set of potential genital ducts [the mesonephric and paramesonephric ducts]. . . . Under the *influence of testosterone* secreted by the testes, the mesonephric ducts develop into the duct system through which spermatozoa are conveyed from the testes to the urethra. . . . The potentially female paramesonephric ducts regress *under the influence* of another secretion of the embryonic testes, the Mullerian Inhibitory Factor. (Italics added.)

> In genetically female embryos neither testosterone nor Mullerian Inhibitory Factor is secreted by the gonads. In the *absence of testosterone* the mesonephric ducts regress and the *lack of Mullerian Inhibitory Factor* permits the paramesonephric ducts to develop into the oviducts, uterus, and part of the vagina. The external genitalia also first take form in a morphologically indifferent condition and then develop either in the male direction *under the influence of testosterone* or in the female direction *if the influence of testosterone is lacking.* (Italics added.)[8]

Carlson also writes of "the natural tendency of the body to develop along female lines in the absence of other modifying influences."[9] The presence-or-absence-of-maleness concept is an old one. Simone de Beauvoir quoted Aristotle as saying that "the female is a female by virtue of a certain *lack* of qualities."[10] Psychologist Dr. John Money calls accounts of sexual development similar to Carlson's an example of "the Adam Principle" that something is *added* to an embryo to make it a male.[11] A well-known reproductive biologist, Dr. R.V. Short, concludes an introductory account of sex determination differentiation by spelling out what he sees as the implications of that viewpoint:

> In all systems that we have considered, maleness means mastery; the Y-chromosome over the X, the medulla [of the indifferent gonad] over the cortex, androgen over oestrogen. So physiologically speaking, there is no justification for believing in the equality of the sexes; *vive la différence!*[12]

The idea that the female represents some natural, fundamental "ground state" is also familiar. Strangely, although biologists emulate physicists by reducing organisms to smaller and smaller parts in order to investigate causes that precede causes ad infinitum, they are generally satisfied to accept the idea that a female direction of development occurs passively in the absence of instructions from so-called male sex hormones.* How does it happen? What are the mechanisms? Investigators ask these questions about male development (generically referred to as sexual differentiation), but only a few express interest in applying the same scrutiny to development of the female. This imbalance in levels of intellectual curiosity is reflected in the etymologies of the words that name sex hormones: *androgen* comes from the Greek *andros* and the Latin *generare* (to make a male), *estrogen* from the Latin *oestrus* (gadfly or frenzy). In fact, the word *gynogen*, which would be the etymologically and biologically correct counterpart to *androgen*, cannot be found in biological accounts of sexual development (or, for that matter, in any dictionary).

If we look carefully at the existing biological literature, we can see how we might construct a narrative that treats female sexual differentiation as requiring as much investigation and explanation as male sexual differentiation. We could begin by examining the many studies on hormonal control of sexual development in cold-blooded vertebrates. Some examples: the addition of estrogen to the water of certain XY (potentially male) fish causes them to develop as females rather than males; similarly, the addition of estrogen to the water of amphibian tadpoles before and during their metamorphosis to adults results in all exposed larvae becoming females.[13] Clearly, such research provides evidence that so-called female hormones actively induce female development; that is, they behave as gynogens. But the findings of studies on cold-blooded vertebrates are usually considered inapplicable to mammals. Only rarely does a publication on mammalian development include a consideration of the active role of female hormones.

15 Estrogen and progesterone (another female hormone) are not absent during female mammalian development. In addition to estrogen synthesis in the fetal ovary, all sexual development, both male and female, takes place in the presence of high concentrations of placentally-produced female hormones, especially the estrogens and progesterones.[14] That sexual development occurs in a sea of female placental hormones is recognized and viewed as a "problem"

---

*In reality, both males and females produce estrogens and androgens, but in differing quantities.

for male development. A variety of hypotheses have been proposed and experiments carried out to explain why the developing male embryo is not feminized by maternal hormones. Yet the scientist who is concerned about the potential feminizing effect of female hormones in male development is often the same one who writes that female development is not directed by hormones at all, but is an event that results from a lack of male hormones. This lopsided logic requires both attention and explanation.

What I've just written is, of course, an oversimplification. In some parts of the scientific literature the idea of a positive role for estrogen has begun to creep in. This is partly due to the discovery that testosterone may be converted into estrogen by certain cells in the body, and that what was long believed to be an effect of testosterone on male behavior in rodents is actually caused by the conversion of testosterone to estrogen by cells in the brain.[15] Nevertheless, the associations of male/presence/active and female/absence/passive still govern our concepts of human development and influence the language used to explain them in the current literature.

There is one other etymological/scientific issue to be teased out of the account of male and female development in vertebrates. It is the designation of the male gamete-transporting ducts as mesonephric (middle kidney) and the female's as paramesonephric (sitting next to the middle kidney). Three different types of kidneys have evolved during the evolution of vertebrates: the pronephros, the mesonephros, and the metanephros. In mammals the pronephros is vestigial in the embryo and completely absent in the adult. The mesonephros functions as a kidney in the embryos of some mammals, and its ducts become part of the adult postembryonic male gonadal duct system (this ancient connection between gamete transport and waste excretion is also seen in vertebrates such as those fish and amphibia whose kidney tubules are the means of transporting both sperm and urine to the outside.) The metanephros becomes the functional kidney at birth.

In female mammals there evolved a separate set of ducts (dubbed the paramesonephric ducts) having nothing to do with the kidneys, apparently designed only for the transport of ova. The prefix *para* has several meanings, including near, beside, adjacent to, closely resembling, almost, beyond, remotely or indirectly relating to, faulty or abnormal condition, and associated in an accessory capacity. The use of the prefix is common in the language of anatomy and certainly not restricted to structures related to sexual organs. The adrenal glands, for example, are sometimes referred to as the paranephros because of their location atop the kidneys, so the naming of the paramesonephric ducts for their positional relationship to ducts in the male (note that they have no separate name of their own as do the adrenals) could be nothing more than happenstance. It would be easier to sustain that argument, however, if the literature revealed further interest in both the embryonic and evolutionary origins of these ducts. Yet knowledge about them is lacking.

The changing function of an organ such as the embryonic kidney is a well-known evolutionary phenomenon. Front limbs, for example, have evolved into wings, arms, legs, and flippers. Bones that form parts of the jaw in reptiles have become the functional sound-receiving and -transferring bones of the inner ear in mammals. On the other hand, the appearance of a brand new structure is less common and presents a profoundly difficult explanatory problem for evolutionary biologists. Yet the evolutionary and embryological origins of the paramesonephric duct, which might be such a de novo structure, have been little studied; as one author writes, "The phylogenetic origin of paramesonephric ducts is again obscure."[16] As in the case of estrogen's role in governing female development, our lack of understanding of the origin and development of the paramesonephric duct represents a research path not taken. The reasons for this are probably multiple, but at least one of them must be that the road to understanding these ducts has been considered a side path, one lying next to or away from the main road that one must follow in order to understand male development.

Another example of how scientific language betrays a one-sided curiosity 20 can be found in the literature on the study of male and female sexual differentiation of the rat brain, which until very recently has been framed around the idea that testosterone provides an "organizing effect" on the "intrinsic tendency to develop according to a female pattern of body structure and behavior."[17] (Does this phraseology imply that the female brain is disorganized?) Or consider the fact that mutations affecting androgen metabolism in humans and other mammals have been extensively studied and well-cataloged, but that none affecting estrogen metabolism have been isolated. Some authors have suggested that because implantation in the uterus is impossible without estrogen, an ovum affected by a mutation that interferes with estrogen metabolism would not survive. In other words, estrogen metabolism may be more poorly understood than androgen metabolism because it is essential for mammalian life. From this perspective, the focus on the role of androgens in sexual development, while not misplaced, certainly seems one-sided. Correcting the imbalance is not technically impossible; estrogen metabolism studies could be conducted with laboratory animals in ways that avoid the problem of lethality. It seems, though, that our considerable scientific and experimental ingenuity has not yet been directed toward solving this particular puzzle.

These cases from the biological literature strongly suggest that broad cultural paradigms about the nature of male and female have had a considerable effect on biological theory. The language used to describe "the facts" has channeled experimental thought along certain lanes, leaving others not only unexplored but unnoticed.

The Scientific Construction of Culture

The idea that biologists can construct culture may be taken both literally and figuratively. Consider, for example, the current explosion of knowledge and technological capability that falls into the category of genetic technology. Growth hormone, produced during childhood and important for normal postnatal development, was available on only a very limited basis until recently because its only source was purified human pituitary glands. Because of its unavailability and expense, its use in therapy was mandatorily restricted to children who, because of growth hormone insufficiencies, would fail to grow before puberty and would thus become adult dwarfs. Now, however, the stretch of DNA that codes for growth hormone has been cloned and inserted into a common bacterium that can easily be grown in large quantities. As a result of such technical advances, large quantities of relatively inexpensive growth hormone will become commercially available in the very near future. What are the cultural consequences of this "progress"?

In 1984 the National Institute of Child Health and Development (NICHD) held a conference on the potential uses of a more easily available growth hormone. Although a number of interesting issues arose during the conference, I will focus on only one—what I call an attempt to redefine normality—in this case, with regard to height. We all know that humans come in many different heights. There are not two classes, tall and short, but a continuous range, at the farthest ends of which we have dwarfs and giants, people who are so far from average height that few things in the world are designed to suit them. Coat racks are too high or too low. Ditto water fountains. And finding appropriate mass-produced clothing is out of the question. There are several kinds of dwarfism and giantism, some of which result from the body's production of too little or too much of certain hormones. The question is, At what point do we consider such states to be medically abnormal? At what point in the continuum of height difference do we have a disease in need of a cure?

We could probably agree that three-foot-tall and eight-foot-tall adults would have had an easier and better life if their condition had been treated during childhood to bring them into a more "normal" range. Instead of addressing this issue, however, the members of the NICHD conference concentrated on defining a new disease, neither dwarfism nor giantism, that they called "short stature." "The conferees agreed . . . that the emotional suffering and lack of opportunity for short persons to participate fully in society require more study and *intervention.*" They also reached the consensus that there is an "urgent need for therapeutic trials to determine the effect of growth hormone in short children *who do not have a growth hormone deficiency.*" (Italics added.)[18] As a result of the conference participants' definition of this new category of biological abnormality, there will soon be a treatment available for short stature—a treatment that might otherwise have had a rather small market.

25 Such a redefinition of biological normality, especially when it involves increasing the potential market of a particular drug, is not new. For example, it is a little-known but reasonably widespread practice for private physicians to prescribe hormones for taller-than-average girls who express concern that they may grow "too tall for a woman." The hormone treatment brings them into puberty early, which causes them to stop growing and thus keeps them within the "normal" female height range. Here, social views about how tall a female should be lead to medical intervention with the growth process in order to keep a female's physical height within the socially prescribed norm. This norm is based in part on prior biological observation; it ignores the fact that

the current well-fed Western European and North American populations are taller than generations past. The biological norm that has influenced the social norm is changing, while the social norm—at least for women—plays a role in an attempt to prevent further biological change.

Just as cultural values and beliefs shaped Spallanzani's observations and influenced scientists' perceptions of what was important to investigate in male/female development, so biological theory influences cultural norms. The far-reaching impact of such influences can be seen in the claim that men are biologically more competent at spatial visualization, and thus at mathematical skills, than women. In the United States, supposed sex differences in mathematical ability are often cited as an explanation for the relatively small percentage of women who work as mathematicians, engineers, physicists, and architects (not all European countries have the same skewed sex ratio of employment). The assertion that differences in mathematical ability are biologically based has had a well-documented effect on our entire educational system.[19] Rather than cover a large, complicated, and already well-reviewed literature on this topic, I will continue my case study approach by discussing the 1984 volume of *Progress in Brain Research*, a book entirely devoted to the topic of sex differences in the brain.[20]

The interspecific* scope of the book is evident in its table of contents. An article on sex differences in testosterone metabolism in the Japanese quail sits side by side with articles on sex differences in the rat brain, in songbirds, in talapoin monkeys, in marmosets, and last but definitely not least, in humans. Some articles jump back and forth between species; for example, "Hormonal Organization of Sex Differences in Play Fighting and Spatial Behavior"[21] has two paragraphs on rhesus monkeys, followed by four on humans, one on humans and monkeys, one on monkeys and rats, and five on rats alone. The volume is characterized by the use of evidence drawn from studies of one species to formulate projections or applications for other species. Data drawn from many different species are used as though they apply to humans, with no acknowledgment of the theoretical issues involved in so doing. Thus theories based on studies of rats, postulating an organizing influence of testosterone on the brain, are either directly or by implication applied to humans as well. Yet any good comparative anatomist talking with a well-trained comparative ethologist would be quick to acknowledge the enormous differences in brain complexity and learning capacity—and in the relationships between hormone concentrations and particular behaviors—that exist across the phylogenetic spectrum.

The impact of the book and of such interspecific intermixing is difficult to evaluate because of the variable quality of the articles. In the same volume there are articles that disprove the organizational role of testosterone on the brain and articles that assume the truth of the organizer hypothesis. The scientific positivist would argue that this situation simply reflects the scientific process *en marche:* the pros and cons of a theory are openly debated, and the

**Interspecific*: concerning more than one species, or relationships among various species.

truth will out. At some levels the process of scientific debate does work in this volume. Yet in general what one sees is simply a mosaic of propositions. Differing perspectives on sex differences in the brain appear side by side, illustrating a broad pattern of views about the roles of male and female in our culture.

An article entitled "Sex Differences in Mathematical Abilities," for example, purports to provide a balanced account of biological and social theories on the origin of such differences, and concludes that a combination of both biological and social factors cause sex differences in mathematical ability. The authors are conducting a longitudinal study of young people who have been identified as having unusual mathematical talent. Their fairly substantial sample consists of about 40 percent girls. Their much-publicized finding is that among these youngsters, who are in the top 5 percent of their classes in terms of mathematical ability, more boys than girls score in the very high ranges (above 700) on college aptitude tests. Because most of these children have had the same number and kinds of math courses in school, the authors conclude that the observed differences in test performance may well be due to an innate biological difference, one they suggest is connected to different levels of prenatal exposure to testosterone in males and females.

30 In response to a question about the consequences of their work on math and science education for young women, the authors make the following ambiguous reply:

> There are many more males than females who can reason extremely well mathematically. This is group data and . . . cannot be used to counsel any single person. Our data do, however, tell us that it is likely that many more boys than girls will be successful in their pursuit of degrees or careers in quantitatively oriented sciences.[22]

The logical jumps in this statement are problematic for a number of reasons, not the least of which is the authors' projection of potential success in college and business as if test scores were the sole determinants of one's professional progress. In this regard, the authors make much of their data showing higher male than female performance in high school on math aptitude tests, but let slip without discussion the fact that the same set of female students get higher *grades* in their math courses. Consideration of the quality of math and science education and its influence on the degree and career patterns of young men and women is peculiarly absent from the discussion, an absence, I argue, that stems from a reliance on "scientific data" of the sort presented in the volume—data that are removed from the social and political contexts in which the research has taken place. Disembodied scientific concepts are often used to make far-reaching social decisions about such things as the structure of our educational system.[23]

The views of the authors of the article on mathematical ability continue to receive widespread publicity. One recent example is a UPI story[24] about a paper delivered by Dr. Camilla Benbow at the national meetings of the American

Association for the Advancement of Science. Newspapers and national television evening news reported her speculations of a connection between testosterone, hemispheric specialization of the brain, and the supposedly greater mathematical reasoning skills of males. The intellectual poverty of this viewpoint has been well-demonstrated in a variety of forums. A recently published study suggests the damaging effects on adolescent girls of such widespread publicity by showing that parents' confidence in their daughters' mathematical ability was significantly shaken by the implications of an earlier article by Benbow and Stanley, which received nationwide attention.[25] The suggestion of biologically based feminine intellectual incapacities can influence girls to limit their horizons. Not only must the door to mathematical study be open to females, but the path leading to it must be cleared of obstacles, some of which come in the form of gender-influenced and gender-biased scientific research.

In the 1984 volume of *Progress in Brain Research*, the intermingling of a wide range of animal studies (some of which are very well done, providing clear-cut results of experiments carried out under carefully controlled and defined laboratory conditions) with studies on humans (which are usually poorly done and taken out of social context) lends unwarranted scientific credence to the latter work. Ironically, the best aspects of the scientific process—the testing and reformulating of hypotheses—here lend a kind of moral support to the worst aspects—the unwarranted logical jumps in reasoning resting on data drawn from widely differing species, the nonconscious assimilation of cultural ideology into scientific theory, and the design and analysis of studies on human subjects without recognition of or regard to cultural frameworks and theory.

Conclusion

What should we conclude about the social function of science, and about science as an intellectual activity? Much recent writing about science has involved linear, unidirectional thinking: the social function of science is presented as either good or bad; science is held to be either totally objective or totally biased, a form of inquiry through which progressive knowledge may be gained or a form of inquiry shaped by the culture in which it has grown. Instead, the relationship between the activities of scientists, their cultural attitudes, the theories they devise, and their effects on human biology and social institutions are nonlinear and multidirectional. The same is true of reflections on the scientific process. The activities of scientists are self-deluding *and* self-correcting; they are at once potentially progressive and retrogressive. What we must do in writing about them is to shuttle back and forth along the strands of meaning in order to gain more complex and accurate understandings of the processes involved.

ENDNOTES

1. Thomas W. Kuhn, *The Structure of Scientific Revolutions* (Chicago: University of Chicago Press, 1962).

2. See, for example, Ruth Herschberger, *Adam's Rib* (New York: Pellegrini and Cudahy, 1984); Evelyn Fox Keller, *Reflections on Gender and Science* (New Haven, CT: Yale University Press, 1985); Anne Fausto-Sterling, *Myths of Gender* (New York: Basic Books, 1985); Ruth Bleier, *Science and Gender* (New York: Pergamon Press, 1984); Marian Lowe and Ruth Hubbard, *Woman's Nature* (New York: Pergamon Press, 1983); Carolyn Merchant, *The Death of Nature* (San Francisco: Harper & Row, 1980); Janet Sayers, *Biological Politics* (London: Tavistock, 1982); Sandra Harding, *The Science Question in Feminism* (Ithaca, NY: Cornell University Press, 1986).

3. See also Evelyn Fox Keller, *A Feeling for the Organism* (San Francisco: Freeman, 1983), and June Goodfield, *An Imagined World* (New York: Harper & Row, 1981).

4. Albert Tyler, "Comparative Gametology and Syngamy," in *Fertilization: Comparative Morphology, Biochemistry and Immunology*, vol. 1, ed. Charles B. Metz and Alberto Monroy (New York: Academic Press, 1967).

5. Ibid.

6. Ibid.

7. Ibid.

8. Bruce M. Carlson, *Patten's Foundations of Embryology* (New York: McGraw-Hill, 1981), pp. 459–61.

9. Ibid.

10. Simone De Beauvoir, *The Second Sex* (New York: Bantam, 1952), p. xvi.

11. John Money, *Love and Lovesickness* (Baltimore: Johns Hopkins University Press, 1970), p. 5.

12. R.V. Short, "Sex Determination and Differentiation," in *Embryonic and Fetal Development*, ed. C.R. Austin and R.V. Short (London: Cambridge University Press, 1972), p. 70.

13. Ursula Mittwoch, *Genetics of Sex Differentiation* (New York: Academic Press, 1973).

14. J.D. Wilson et al., "The Hormonal Control of Sexual Development," *Science* 211 (1981), pp. 1278–84.

15. See Robert W. Goy and Bruce S. McEwen, eds., *Sexual Differentiation of the Brain* (Cambridge, MA: MIT Press, 1980); Bleier, *Science and Gender;* and *Progress in Brain Research* 61 (1984).

16. M. Hildebrand, *Analysis of Vertebrate Structure* (New York: John Wiley & Sons, 1974).

17. Goy and McEwen, *Sexual Differentiation*, p. 3.

18. C. Gene Drafts, *Genewatch* 1 (5 & 6) (1985), p. 9.

19. See Margaret Rossiter, *Women Scientists in America: Struggles and Strategies to 1940* (Baltimore: Johns Hopkins University Press, 1982); Sayers, *Biological Politics;* and Fausto-Sterling, *Myths of Gender.*

20. *Progress in Brain Research* 61 (1984).

21. William W. Beatty, "Hormonal Organization of Sex Differences in Play Fighting and Spatial Behavior," *Progress in Brain Research* 61 (1984), pp. 315–30.

22. Camilla Persson Benbow and Robert M. Benbow, "Biological Correlates of High Mathematical Reasoning Ability," *Progress in Brain Research* 61 (1984), pp. 469–90.

23. Rossiter, *Women Scientists in America;* Sayers, *Biological Politics;* and Fausto-Sterling, *Myths of Gender.*

24. "In Math, Biology May Be Destiny," *Providence Journal,* 27 May 1986, p. A-9.

25. J.W. Eccles and Janis E. Jacobs, "Social Forces Shape Math Attitudes and Performance," *Signs* 11 (1986), pp. 367–80.

▪ QUESTIONS

Reading

1. How did other eighteenth-century scientists respond to Spallanzani's conclusions about his "seminal aura" studies? What does this response show us?
2. Why does Fausto-Sterling use the example of short and tall adults? How does this connect to her arguments about gender?
3. What solutions does Fausto-Sterling offer to the problem of scientific bias? Is she arguing against the value of science as a method? What are her conclusions about scientific writing?

Exploratory Writing

1. In pairs or on your own, play the "truth" game: Choose a fact that you "know" is true — such as "the sun rises in the east and sets in the west" — and write a list of twenty thoughts or ideas that call that truth into question. Whose perspective does this fact come from? Which terms, definitions, or categories does this fact assume, and could they be viewed in an alternative way? (For example, you might call into question what it means to "rise" or "set.")
2. Find a scientific study in a biological or medical journal or popular-science magazine that deals with a topic with social implications — for example, gender, sexuality, intelligence, health, beauty, or religion. Highlight, underline, or flag the key terms or categories that guide the research reported in the article. How do the authors define these terms or categories? Do they address social questions or ambiguities? In what ways might social ideas "write" this biology by contributing to these initial categories, terms, or definitions?

Making Connections

1. Consider Fausto-Sterling's opening words: "Truth, bias, objectivity, prejudice." She uses these terms to frame her argument, claiming that culture shapes scientific practice and that what we believe to be "scientifically" true shapes society. In what ways are these processes apparent in the research Stephen Jay Gould discusses (p. 709)? How has this research, conducted in the latter part of the nineteenth century, influenced current attitudes about gender?

Essay Writing

1. Choose a scientific idea that was once widely believed, and is now widely understood to be wrong. Conduct some research to learn as much as you can about this idea. Then, write an essay explaining how it was once understood and why it fell out of favor. Some examples would be the idea that the earth is flat, that the sun circles the earth, that hysteria is caused by the uterus moving freely around inside the body, or that personality traits can be determined by skull shape. How did the idea form? What processes did the people who shared this belief use to reach their conclusion? In what ways did those processes correspond to Fausto-Sterling's description of the ways cultural beliefs shape scientific beliefs?

REPORTING

The M/F Boxes

E. J. Graff

Investigative journalist E. J. Graff is known for her writings on gender inequality, social justice, children's rights, and illegal discrimination. She is the author of *What Is Marriage For? The Strange Social History of Our Most Intimate Institution* (1999), and the coauthor, with former Massachusetts Lieutenant Governor Evelyn Murray, of *Getting Even: Why Women Still Don't Make As Much As Men—And What to Do So We Will* (2005). Her award-winning reports have appeared in the *New York Times Magazine*, the *Washington Post*, and other newspapers and magazines. She's currently a senior fellow at the Schuster Institute for Investigative Journalism at Brandeis University. On her blog at the *American Prospect*, she often calls into question ideology masked as science on the topic of sex difference. This exploration of the transgender movement first appeared in the *Nation*.

A fifteen-year-old girl is incarcerated in a Chicago mental hospital in 1981 and kept there for three years because she won't wear a dress. A Winn-Dixie truck driver is fired from a job he held for twenty years when his boss learns that he wears women's clothes at home. A small-time hustler in Falls City, Nebraska, is raped and then murdered when he's discovered to be physically female. A woman bleeds to death after a Washington, DC, hit-and-run accident when, after finding male genitals under her clothes, paramedics stand by laughing.

M or F? For most of us that's a simple question, decided while we were in utero. Checking off that box—at the doctor's, on the census, on a driver's license—takes scarcely a thought. But there's an emerging movement of increasingly vocal people whose bodies or behavior unsettle that clear division. They're calling themselves "transgendered": It's a spongy neologism that, at its broadest, absorbs everyone from medically reassigned transsexuals to cross-dressing men to women so masculine that security guards are called to eject them from women's restrooms. Fellow travelers include intersexuals (once called hermaphrodites), whose bodies are both/and rather than either/or. The slash between M/F cuts painfully through these lives.

And so they've started to organize. Brought together by the Internet, inspired by the successes of the gay rights movement, and with national sympathy gained from the movie *Boys Don't Cry*, intersex and transgender activists are starting to get a hearing in organizations ranging from college campuses to city councils, from lesbian and gay rights groups to pediatric conferences. And, like the feminist and gay rights movements before them, the new sex-and-gender activists may force us to rethink, in life and in law, how we define and interpret the basics of sex.

A first clue to how zealously the M/F border is guarded—to how sex is literally constructed—comes at birth. One in 2,000 infants is born with genitalia ambiguous enough to make doctors hem and haw when parents ask that first question: boy or girl? Since the late 1950s/early 1960s, standard medical procedure has been to lie and obfuscate. Rather than explain that the child is "a mixture of male and female," writes Anne Fausto-Sterling, author of *Sexing the Body*, medical manuals advise physicians to reassign the child surgically to one sex or another, telling parents only that "the gonads were incompletely developed . . . and therefore required removal." A large clitoris may be cut down; a micropenis may be removed and a vagina built; a testis or testes are sliced out—sometimes over the parents' explicit objections.

5 Now some of those children have come of age and are telling their stories: severe depression, sexual numbness, and a longtime despair at having been folded, spindled, and mutilated. The leader of this nascent movement is Cheryl Chase, who in 1993 organized the Intersex Society of North America. ISNA opposes reassignment surgery on intersex infants and advocates raising intersex children as social males or females, educating them about their bodies and letting them choose at puberty whether they'd like surgical assistance or a shift in social sex. ISNA's cause was helped when Johns Hopkins sex researcher and PhD John Money, who wrote the intersex silence-and-reassignment protocol, was profoundly discredited. After a child he called "John" was accidentally castrated soon after birth, Money advised his parents to have him undergo surgery to construct a vagina, raise him as "Joan," and give him female hormones at puberty. Money reported this involuntary sex reassignment as fully successful. But in 1997, both a medical journal report and a *Rolling Stone* article revealed that the reassignment had been a disaster. Despite the insistence of parents, doctors, psychologists, and teachers, "Joan" had always insisted that she was "just a boy with long hair in girl's clothes." In adolescence, John took back his manhood.

How did John "know" he was male—and by extension, how do any of us decide we're girls or boys? One theory is that, in utero, John had undergone the androgen bath that turns an undifferentiated fetus—which otherwise becomes female—male, giving him a male identity and masculine behavior. In the other rare cases where XY infants lose penises and are raised as girls, some insist on being boys—but others happily identify as (masculine, lesbian) women, which suggests that things aren't quite so simple. Scientists recognize that our brains and nervous systems are somewhat plastic, developing in response to environmental stimuli. Sexuality—all of it, from identity to presentation to sexual orientation—is no exception; it develops as a biological interaction between inborn capacities and outside influences. As a result, most of us have a narrow range in which we feel "natural" as we gender ourselves daily through clothes, stance, stride, tone. For most, that gendered behavior is consonant with biological sex: Girls present as female, if not feminine, and fall in love with boys; boys present as male or masculine and fall in love with girls. But those in whom gendered behavior is vice versa—feminine boys, highly masculine girls—get treated as unnatural, even though their gendering is just as biological as the rest of ours. What happens to these transgendered folks can be so brutal that the pediatric surgeons who cut off infant clitorises or penises look like merely the advance guard of the M/F border patrol.

Take, for instance, Daphne Scholinski, so masculine that at age 6, strangers chastised her when she tried to use women's restrooms. In her dry, pitiless memoir *The Last Time I Wore a Dress*, Scholinski tells the story of being committed to a mental hospital at fifteen for some very real problems, including severe neglect, her father's violence and her own delinquency. The hospital ignored her shocking childhood and instead "treated" her masculinity. Scholinski got demerits if she didn't wear makeup. She was put on a boys' ward, where she was twice raped, to encourage her to be more feminine. Her confinement was so disturbing that she still gets post-traumatic stress flashbacks, including nightmares so terrifying that she wakes up and vomits. And so Scholinski is starting an organization dedicated to reforming the diagnosis of childhood GID, or gender identity disorder, under which she was treated.

Or consider the treatment of Darlene Jespersen and Peter Oiler. After working for Harrah's Reno casino for eighteen years, in the summer of 2000, Jespersen was fired from her bartending job when Harrah's launched a new policy requiring all its female employees to wear foundation, powder, eyeliner, lipstick, and so on. "I tried it," says Jespersen in a plaintive voice, "but I felt so naked." The obverse happened to Peter Oiler, a weathered, middle-aged man with large aviator glasses, a pleasant drawl and a bit of an overbite. After twenty years of being rotated through progressively more responsible jobs in Winn-Dixie's shipping yards, in 1999 Oiler was driving a fifty-foot truck delivering grocery supplies throughout southeastern Louisiana—until Winn-Dixie learned that he called himself "transgendered." Oiler tried to explain that he simply wore women's clothes on the weekends: He wasn't going to become a woman; he didn't want to wear makeup and heels on company time. In January 2000 Oiler was fired.

Jespersen and Oiler are stunned. Jespersen is suing Harrah's. Says Oiler, "I was raised to believe that if you do an honest day's work, you'll get an honest day's pay." The ACLU Lesbian and Gay Rights Project has taken up his case, in part because of the sheer injustice—and in part to get courts to treat discrimination against people who violate sex stereotypes as illegal sex discrimination. If a woman can wear a dress, or if a man can refuse makeup, why not vice versa? In doing so, the ACLU, like the three national lesbian and gay legal organizations, would be building on the 1989 Supreme Court decision *Price Waterhouse v. Ann Hopkins*. Price Waterhouse had told Hopkins that she wasn't going to make partner because she was too masculine—and, in actual written memos, advised her to wear jewelry and makeup, to go to charm school, to be less aggressive. The Supreme Court declared such stereotyping to be sex discrimination.

Will judges see Peter Oiler's dismissal as illegal sex stereotyping? There have been some recent hints that they might. In Massachusetts, for instance, the U.S. Court of Appeals for the First Circuit said Lucas Rosa could sue a bank that instructed feminine Rosa, who had shown up to apply for a loan wearing a dress, to go home and come back in men's clothes; a female, after all, would have been considered for the loan. Another Massachusetts judge said that a male student could come to school in a dress, since female students could. 10

A Washington transsexual prisoner raped by a prison guard, and two New York municipal employees harassed for being gay, were allowed to sue when judges ruled they'd been attacked for violating stereotyped expectations of their sex.

Our society has learned to see why women would want masculine privileges like playing soccer and serving on the Supreme Court, but there's been no matching force expanding the world for males. Boys and men still patrol each other's masculinity with a *Glengarry Glen Ross* level of ridicule and violence that can seem, to women, nearly surreal. Those males who violate the M-box's limits on behavior are quite literally risking their lives.

Which means that, if you're a performing drag queen, a cross-dressing straight man like Peter Oiler, or a transsexual who still has some male ID, do not under any circumstances get stopped by a cop. In New York City, says Pauline Park, a co-founder of NYAGRA (New York Association for Gender Rights Advocacy), even if the police don't actually beat you, "you could be arrested and detained for days or weeks. They don't let people out until they plead guilty to prostitution. They put them in the men's cell, where they're often assaulted and sometimes raped, as a tactic to get people to plead guilty."

And don't turn to emergency medical personnel. In August 1995 Tyra Hunter's car crashed in Washington, DC. When firefighting paramedics cut away her dress and found male genitals, they laughed and mocked her. She bled to death in the hospital. In August 2000 a jury awarded Hunter's mother $1.75 million in a wrongful-death action. Hunter's experience, unfortunately, is not unusual. Once a month, someone transgendered is murdered, and those are just the documented cases. Transgender activists are beginning to mark November 28, the anniversary of another such death, as a Day of Remembrance, with candlelight vigils and a determination to slow the steady drumbeat of murder.

"We're despised. We're pariahs in this society," says Miranda Stevens-Miller, chair of the transgender rights organization It's Time, Illinois, about transsexuals and otherwise transgendered people. Many transsexuals are fired once they begin to transition. Others lose custody and visitation rights, houses, leases. Many are shut out of office and other public restrooms for years—an indignity that cuts to the very core of being human, since every living body needs to pee. And so the most urgent transgender organizing is happening locally, in organizations such as TGNet Arizona, NYAGRA and It's Time, Oregon. They're teaching Trans 101 to local employers, doctors, city councils, lesbian and gay organizations, judges, families, landlords, friends. They're attempting to collect statistics on firings, beatings, murders, bathroom harassment, police abuse. Often these groups are driven by the energy and determination of one or two people who spend their own time and pennies writing and photocopying leaflets, giving workshops for corporate and college groups, and lobbying city councils and lesbian and gay organizations for inclusion in hate-crimes and antidiscrimination laws. Lately, they're having remarkable success at adding "gender identity and expression" to the protected categories in local and state employment nondiscrimination and hate-crimes laws; they've won in locales ranging from Portland, Oregon, to DeKalb, Illinois, to the state of Rhode Island.

Nationally, trans groups are still in the skirmishing phase faced by any new movement, with the inevitable splits over strategy and personality. The group with the most name recognition, GenderPAC, angers some transgender activists by avoiding the "T" word in its advocacy, saying that it aims at gender freedom for everyone; it acts on behalf of such people as Darlene Jespersen and Peter Oiler, or boys called "faggot" for not being noticeably masculine. Currently the most significant transgender organizations nationally are IFGE (International Foundation for Gender Education), GEA (Gender Education and Advocacy), and the Working Group on Trans Equality, a loose network of grassroots trans activists aiming at a coordinated national presence. Perhaps the biggest success so far is that all the major lesbian and gay organizations and many smaller ones have added transgendered folks to their mission statements as folks who are equally, if differently, queer. 15

Or is it so different? All of us deviate from what's expected from our sex. While the relationship between transgender activists and lesbian and gay groups has at times been contentious, some lesbian and gay activists, notably Chai Feldblum, Georgetown law professor, are starting to urge that we all organize around our common deviance from sex stereotypes. The differences between homosexual, transgender, and transsexual experiences are not that great: All are natural variations on the brain's gendered development that have cropped up throughout human history, from Tiresias to Radclyffe Hall, from Billy Tipton to Quentin Crisp. For the most part, the mainstream sees us on one sliding scale of queerness. And occasionally our struggles and goals intersect quite neatly. For instance, homos can't always tell whether we're harassed at work because someone figures out that we date others of the same sex, or simply because we're too butch or too fey.

And none of us can rely on having our marriages recognized by the institutions around us when we need them—because marriage is one of the last laws on the books that discriminate based on sex. Recently, Joe Gardiner asked a Kansas court to invalidate his dead father's marriage to transwoman (born male, medically and legally reassigned as female) J'Noel Gardiner, saying J'Noel was "really" a man—and therefore could not have legally married a man. The lower court agreed with the son that XY = man, which meant the son would inherit his father's fat estate. But the Kansas appeals judge remanded the case back down for a new trial. Sex, the appeals court declared, isn't decided simply by a chromosome test. Rather, sex is a complex constellation of characteristics that includes not only chromosomes but also "gonadal sex, internal morphologic sex, external morphologic sex, hormonal sex, phenotypic sex, assigned sex and gender of rearing, and sexual identity." The court approvingly quoted Johns Hopkins researcher and medical doctor William Reiner, who wrote, "The organ that appears to be critical to psychosexual development and adaptation is not the external genitalia, but the brain."

▪ QUESTIONS

Reading

1. What was the 1989 Supreme Court decision *Price Waterhouse v. Ann Hopkins?* How was this case influential?
2. What, according to Graff, were the most significant transgender organizations when this article was first published (2001)? What, arguably, was their biggest success at the time?
3. Highlight, underline, or flag the examples of legal proceedings that Graff includes in her report. How do these specific examples support or undermine her conclusions?

Exploratory Writing

1. Find at least two articles on gender identity disorder, the subject of Daphne (now Dylan) Scholinski's (paragraph 7) memoir. What are the latest advances in treating this disorder? How do the articles you've found address the controversy around whether this is a disorder at all?
2. Read a memoir written by a transgender person, such a Christine Jorgenson's autobiography, any of Kate Bornstein's autobiographical books, Daphne (now Dylan) Scholinski's *The Last Time I Wore a Dress*, Mark Rees's *Dear Sir or Madam: The Autobiography of a Female-To-Male Transsexual*, or Jennifer Finney Boyle's *She's Not There*. Give a brief report on this book. What themes and issues does the memoir discuss that are also introduced in Graff's report? What insights does the book offer about "the M/F boxes"?

Making Connections

1. Peggy Orenstein (p. 705) reflects that she questioned her own gender identity when she was diagnosed with breast cancer and learned that she needed a double mastectomy and hysterectomy, but then concluded that her gender identity ran deeper than anything confined to the physical body. From reading both Graff's report and Orenstein's reflections, what can you conclude about how we define the personal experience of gender identity?

Essay Writing

1. "How did John 'know' he was male," asks Graff, "—and by extension, how do any of us decide we're girls or boys?" (paragraph 6). Interview several people about their gender identities. Ask how and why they believe they are "male," "female," or "other." How do other people perceive their genders? Are outsiders' perceptions ever different than theirs? Do your interviews support or contradict Graff's claim that "all of us deviate from what's expected from our sex"? (paragraph 16). Write an essay reporting your findings.

REFLECTING

The Body Narrative of Transsexuality

Jay Prosser

Writer and literature scholar Jay Prosser is the author of the study of transsexual autobiography *Second Skins: The Body Narratives of Transsexuality* (1998), and *Light in the Dark Room: Photography and Loss* (2004), which began from his interest in pictorial representations of transsexuality. He co-edited *Palatable Poison: Critical Perspectives on* The Well of Loneliness (2002). He writes on topics of race, ethnicity, and heritage as well as sexuality and gender. Currently, he is collaborating with his mother on a family memoir that involves the Baghdadi Jewish and Chinese diasporas, and working on a study of Buddhism in America. He has taught literature and American studies at the University of Leicester and the University of Leeds. In this piece, the opening of *Second Skins*, Prosser describes his own gender transformation.

I spent the bulk of the first month of my transsexual transition from female to male teaching an undergraduate course on the contemporary American novel. Scheduled over an intensive summer session, the class met for almost four hours a day, four days a week. My hormone treatment, beginning the week before the course, was comparably intensive. My endocrinologist believed in shocking my body into transition, starting me up on massive dosages of testosterone and leveling these off once my body had adjusted. Under this program not only did I experience rapid dramatic somatic changes, some of these became immediately apparent. My face squared off and my neck thickened; accumulating facial "fuzz" required shaving every few days; and, while it didn't crack, my voice deepened enough to get me an invariable "sir" over the phone. Within two weeks of the course ending, after just over a month of treatment, I was thus able to begin living full-time as a man, documents all changed to reflect a new, unambivalent status.

Although the minutiae of these somatic changes might have bypassed my students, I have no doubt that I failed to cut a clearly gendered figure in the class. In the world outside academia I was already passing as male almost consistently. Yet my profile at college would have led students to expect a female teacher. For the entire month my poor students remarkably, collectively, assiduously, and awkwardly avoided referring to me with a pronoun or a gendered title. The two exceptions occurred not in speech but in writing—in the absence of my body—in the logs students handed in weekly: one "Miss," which I circled viscerally; one "he," which I left unmarked. Students seemed to sex me individually (how not to make this most fundamental of identity assignments?), so their careful avoidance must have stemmed from their failure to reach consensus as a group—perhaps even a collective sense that I was going through some kind of significant transition.

The group's uncertainty on how to read me earned my immediate sympathy. Yet in no way did I seek to resolve its predicament. I felt unable, too caught up in my own predicament, the circumstances of teaching at this most transitional point in my transition. I did not feel I could present as a man in a department in which I had been known as a butch woman for five years and that I was anyway leaving that semester. At the same time I was so relieved to be moving away from femaleness that nothing could have persuaded me to anchor myself back to it, even provisionally. The obvious alternative—to have come out as a transsexual—I thought would have rooted rather than alleviated my students' confusion and discomfort. For, in common perception, to name oneself transsexual is to own precisely to being gender displaced, to being a subject in transition, moving beyond or in between sexual difference. So I left them uncomfortably (all of us horribly uncomfortable) leaving me to my ambivalence; and as the class progressed, this not attributing me with a gender, in my experience, became more and more glaring—a kind of deafening unspoken. In this gendered nonzone, I felt too embodied (only body) yet also disembodied: For what on earth did I embody? Not surprisingly, I was massively relieved once the course was over, and I sensed students felt similarly.

Some breathing space did open up toward the end of the course, however. One student gave a dazzling presentation on Leslie Marmon Silko's *Ceremony*, tracing the theme—of all things—of transition. Of the novels assigned, *Ceremony* clearly frustrated students. It made them feel unconfident, uncertain of how to read. They couldn't place it: its hybrid characters; its plot that mixes and yet refuses to merge realistic historical moment and mythic quest; the novel's genre, its shifting affiliation to a modern psychological novel and a traditional Native ceremony. Staking its value to the course topics and to her own reading pleasure precisely on its treatment of transition, the presenting student mounted an inspiring defense of the novel. She argued that it was *Ceremony's* layered investment in the theme of transition that the class was making its stumbling block, even as the importance of understanding and pursuing transition was the novel's very point. An intermediate nonzone, transition represents the movement in between that threatens to dislocate our ties to identity places we conceive of as essentially (in every sense) secure. Transition provokes discomfort, anxiety—both for the subject in transition and for the other in the encounter; it pushes up against the very feasibility of identity. Yet transition is also necessary for identity's continuity; it is that which moves us on.

Does it even need saying how I heard her presentation as a poignant metacommentary on my own dislocation in the course? With uncanny precision she appeared to cut through (and reveal in cross-section) the thick layers of anxiety that had coated our discussions. Even when she added an autobiographical postscript to her presentation, I found it impossible to disown or disembody transition. Revealing her entanglement in her interpretation of the novel and the class reading, the student described *her own* status as transitional: in her identity, consciously and complexly in between Native, Spanish, and Irish cultural heritages; and at this period of her life. My course marked her transition from college to beginning graduate school the following semester; it was part of her transition to making this kind of reading and thinking her career.

Instead of moving me away from my personal experience through hers, my student's revelation brought into relief (again, in my perspective) my own silence. My body had brought transition to the surface, embodied it as transsexual bodies in a disconcertingly literal way not unlike bodies "in between" racial difference do. Unlike my articulate student, however, I had remained unable to remark on, to reassure, or to confront others over my in-betweenness. In part I felt as though my experience of transition, my very movement in between, obturated any expression of my transsexuality, exceeded the grounds of its own speakability. But the difference between us—the fact of my student's "coming out" and my not—was also informed by the relation our respective bodies found to the narratives we were reading: by what we, as a class, had set up as speakable material. Her autobiographical voicing was patently prompted and supported by our reading of narratives of cultural crossing. If in contrast my body remained as unspeakable for me as it was unreadable for students, it was in part because narratives of sexual crossing lay outside our designated subject matter. Indeed, such narratives had yet to be formed into any kind of equivalent critical tradition.

▪ QUESTIONS

Reading

1. How does Prosser feel about his students' inability to read his gender while he is transitioning from female to male?
2. Why does Prosser think so highly of his student's presentation about Leslie Marmon Silko's *Ceremony*?
3. Prosser writes about his experiences in the first person, from his own perspective. How does this writing choice shape the way we read his essay?

Exploratory Writing

1. "My body had brought transition to the surface," writes Prosser (paragraph 6). In small groups, find five or six photographs (in a magazine or online) of people none of you know in real life. Separately, write a list of twelve things you know about each of the people in these images, just by looking at them. Meeting again in your group, compare the items on each of your lists. Can you be sure each item is true? Why or why not? What did your group discover while doing this exercise?
2. Find a poem, painting, sculpture, film of a performance, photograph, or other piece of creative writing or art that you believe embodies transition. How does the work you've chosen call into question expected gender or other categories? Prepare a brief presentation (like Prosser's student's inspiring presentation on Silko's *Ceremony*) explaining this work and what it reveals.

Making Connections

1. Michael Chabon (p. 715) and Prosser both reflect on how their gendered bodies affect the ways that they are seen by themselves and others around them — Chabon, as a man who describes his outward masculinity as a performance, and Prosser, as someone who (temporarily) could not be identified as either male or female by his students. How do their reflections help you to understand these experiences? What techniques does each author use to make his story resonate with readers?

Essay Writing

1. Write a proposal for how the standard college classroom environment could be made more comfortable for students or teachers (like Prosser) who, temporarily or permanently, cannot (or do not wish to) be identified as "male" or "female." What changes would be required in order to avoid the situation that Prosser describes? Use argumentative writing techniques to make your proposal effective.

REFLECTING

What Makes a Woman a Woman?

Peggy Orenstein

Peggy Orenstein (b. 1961) is a regular contributor to the *New York Times Magazine, O* magazine, *Vogue*, and other popular publications on subjects of society, gender, and culture. Her books include *Schoolgirls: Young Women, Self Esteem, and the Confidence Gap* (1995); *Waiting for Daisy: A Tale of Two Continents, Three Religions, Five Infertility Doctors, an Oscar, an Atomic Bomb, a Romantic Night, and One Woman's Quest to Become a Mother* (2007); and *Cinderella Ate My Daughter: Dispatches from the Front Lines of the New Girlie-Girl Culture* (2011). Before becoming a full-time writer in 1991, Orenstein worked as an editor at the magazines *Esquire, Mother Jones*, and *Manhattan Inc. Waiting for Daisy* was chosen as a Best Book by *Kirkus Reviews*, a *Seattle Post-Intelligencer* Top 10 Book, and received a Books for a Better Life Award from the National Multiple Sclerosis Society. This essay first appeared in the *New York Times* in September 2010.

There is a painting by Richard Prince hanging in the Walker Art Center in Minneapolis, a purple canvas bisected by one line of chartreuse type that reads: "I met my first girl, her name was Sally. Was that a girl, was that a girl. That's what people kept asking." That refrain echoed in my head as I pored over the photos of eighteen-year-old Caster Semenya, the South African track star whose biological sex was called into question last month after she annihilated her competition, winning the 800-meter world championship in significantly less time than her own previous finishes.

Was that a girl, was that a girl. That's what people kept asking.

Semenya's saga was made for the news media. A girl who may not be a girl! That chest! Those arms! That face! She was the perfect vehicle for nearly any agenda: Was this another incidence of people calling into question black female athletes' femininity (the Williams sisters, the basketball legend Sheryl Swoopes)? Was it sexist to assume women were incapable of huge leaps in athletic performance? Should all female athletes be gender-verified, as they were in Olympic competition until 1999? (The practice was dropped because no competitive edge was proved for the few women with rare disorders of sex development—it served only to humiliate them.) Should the entire practice of sex-segregating sports be abandoned?

Was that a girl, was that a girl. That's what people kept asking.

5 I had my own reasons to be fascinated by Semenya's story: I related to it. Not directly—I mean, no one has ever called my biological sex into question. No one, that is, except for me. After my breast-cancer diagnosis at age thirty-five I was told I almost certainly had a genetic mutation that predisposed me to reproductive cancers. The way I could best reduce my risk would be to surgically remove both of my breasts and my ovaries. In other words, to amputate healthy body parts. But not just any parts: the ones associated in the most

primal way with reproduction, sexuality, with my sense of myself as female. Even without that additional blow, breast cancer can feel like an assault on your femininity. Reconstructing the psyche becomes as much a part of going through treatment as reconstructing the body.

In the weeks that followed my diagnosis, during that heightened, crystalline time of fear and anxiety, I was not, I admit, at my most rational. So I began to fret: Without breasts or hormone-producing ovaries, what would the difference be, say, between myself and a pre-op female-to-male transsexual? Other than that my situation was involuntary? That seemed an awfully thin straw on which to base my entire sense of womanhood. What, precisely, made me a girl anyway? Who got to decide? How much did it matter?

When I was in college, in the early 1980s, the gospel was that the whole enchilada of gender was a social construct: Differences between boys and girls were imposed by culture, rather than programmed by chromosomes and chemicals, and it was time to divest ourselves of them. That turned out to be less true than feminists of the era might have wished: Physiology, not just sisterhood, is powerful. While femininity may be relative—slipping and sliding depending on the age in which you live, your stage of life, what you're wearing (quick: Do tailored clothes underscore or undercut it?) even the height of the person standing next to you—biology, at least to some degree, is destiny, though it should make no never mind to women's rights or progress.

Even as I went on as a journalist to explore ideas about gender, I took the fact of my own for granted: As for most people—men and women alike—it was so clear to me as to be invisible. I was unnerved, then, to discover not only that it could be so easily threatened but also how intense that threat felt. That, too, gave me pause: Why should being biologically male or female still be so critical to our self-definition? Is it nature—an evolutionary imperative to signal with whom we can reproduce? Is it nurture? Either way, and regardless of our changing roles and opportunities, it is profound.

Was that a girl, was that a girl? That's what people kept asking.

10 And yet, identity is not simply the sum of our parts. That's what makes Semenya—whose first name is usually conferred on a boy but happens to be Greek for "beaver"—so intriguing. Science may or may not be able to establish some medical truth about her, something that will be relevant on the playing field. But I doubt that will change who she considers herself to be. According to Sheri Berenbaum, a professor of psychology and pediatrics at Penn State who studies children with disorders of sex development, even people with ambiguous biology tend to identify as male or female, though what motivates that decision remains unclear. "People's hormones matter," she said, "but something about their rearing matters too. What about it, though, no one really knows."

There is something mysterious at work, then, that makes us who we are, something internally driven. Maybe it's about our innate need to categorize the world around us. Maybe it arises from—or gives rise to—languages that don't allow for neutrality. My guess, however, is that it's deeper than that, something that transcends objectivity, defies explanation. That's what I concluded about

myself, anyway. Although I have, so far, opted to hang onto my body parts (and still wonder, occasionally, if I would feel differently were, say, a kidney or an arm at issue), I know that my sex could never really be changed by any surgeon's scalpel. Why not? Perhaps because of the chemistry set I was born with, one that Semenya may or may not share. Perhaps merely because . . . I say so. And maybe that will have to be enough.

▪ QUESTIONS

Reading

1. Why does Orenstein relate to eighteen-year-old track star Caster Semenya?
2. Highlight, underline, or flag places where Orenstein or experts she cites point out that something is unknown, mysterious, or can't be determined. How does including these open questions affect Orenstein's essay?
3. What does Orenstein conclude from her reflections? What is one alternative conclusion she could have reached?

Exploratory Writing

1. On your own, write a double-entry list of qualities that are absolutely necessary to make someone a "man" or a "woman." Meet in small groups, and share your lists. How much do you agree on these qualities? Where are there disagreements? As you reflect on this exercise, are your conclusions similar to Orenstein's?

QUALITIES OF MEN	QUALITIES OF WOMEN

2. For five days, keep a journal of your personal experiences of gender. When do you notice people identifying you by gender (such as calling you "Miss" or "Sir")? When do you participate in activities that are categorized by sex, like playing on an all-male soccer team or using a women's restroom? When are you asked to identify yourself as male or female? How do your clothing choices, activities, or interests connect to social ideas about gender roles?

Making Connections

1. Orenstein writes that our need to classify ourselves and others by gender "arises from — or gives rise to — languages that don't allow for neutrality" (paragraph 11). However, she also thinks that gender classification originates from more fundamental and mysterious causes. Consider Prosser's (p. 701) reflections on transitioning from female to male while teaching a college class. How would Prosser's experiences have been different if our language allowed for gender neutrality? Which aspects of Prosser's transition were not affected by language?

Essay Writing

1. Find a story of someone whose gender has been publically called into question, like Caster Semenya. Write an essay explaining the case — why was this person's gender questioned? How were ideas of maleness or femaleness framed by those doing the questioning? Did this person call his or her own gender into question, like Orenstein, or was the questioning an imposition from outside?

ARGUING

Women's Brains

Stephen Jay Gould

Stephen Jay Gould (1941–2002) was a professor of biology, geology, and the history of science at Harvard University for more than thirty years. He was also a baseball fan and a prolific essayist. In 1974 he began writing "This View of Life," a monthly column for *Natural History*, where he not only explained and defended Darwinian ideas of evolution but also exposed abuses and misunderstandings of scientific concepts and methods. Some of the most recent of his more than twenty books are *Crossing Over: Where Art and Science Meet* (2000), *The Structure of Evolutionary Theory* (2002), *Triumph and Tragedy in Mudville: A Lifelong Passion for Baseball* (2003), and *The Hedgehog, the Fox, and the Magister's Pox* (2003). The following essay appeared in *Natural History* in 1992.

In the prelude to *Middlemarch*, George Eliot[1] lamented the unfulfilled lives of talented women:

> Some have felt that these blundering lives are due to the inconvenient indefiniteness with which the Supreme Power has fashioned the natures of women: if there were one level of feminine incompetence as strict as the ability to count three and no more, the social lot of women might be treated with scientific certitude.

Eliot goes on to discount the idea of innate limitation, but while she wrote in 1872, the leaders of European anthropometry were trying to measure "with scientific certitude" the inferiority of women. Anthropometry, or measurement of the human body, is not so fashionable a field these days, but it dominated the human sciences for much of the nineteenth century and remained popular until intelligence testing replaced skull measurement as a favored device for making invidious comparisons among races, classes, and sexes. Craniometry, or measurement of the skull, commanded the most attention and respect. Its unquestioned leader, Paul Broca (1824–1880), professor of clinical surgery at the Faculty of Medicine in Paris, gathered a school of disciples and imitators around himself. Their work, so meticulous and apparently irrefutable, exerted great influence and won high esteem as a jewel of nineteenth-century science.

Broca's work seemed particularly invulnerable to refutation. Had he not measured with the most scrupulous care and accuracy? (Indeed, he had. I have the greatest respect for Broca's meticulous procedure. His numbers are sound. But science is an inferential exercise, not a catalog of facts. Numbers,

[1]*George Eliot*: The pen name of Marianne Evans (1819–1880), British novelist. *Middlemarch* (1871–1872) is considered her greatest work.—Eds.

by themselves, specify nothing. All depends upon what you do with them.) Broca depicted himself as an apostle of objectivity, a man who bowed before facts and cast aside superstition and sentimentality. He declared that "there is no faith, however respectable, no interest, however legitimate, which must not accommodate itself to the progress of human knowledge and bend before truth." Women, like it or not, had smaller brains than men and, therefore, could not equal them in intelligence. This fact, Broca argued, may reinforce a common prejudice in male society, but it is also a scientific truth. L. Manouvrier, a black sheep in Broca's fold, rejected the inferiority of women and wrote with feeling about the burden imposed upon them by Broca's numbers:

> Women displayed their talents and their diplomas. They also invoked philosophical authorities. But they were opposed by *numbers* unknown to Condorcet[2] or to John Stuart Mill.[3] These numbers fell upon poor women like a sledge hammer, and they were accompanied by commentaries and sarcasms more ferocious than the most misogynist imprecations of certain church fathers. The theologians had asked if women had a soul. Several centuries later, some scientists were ready to refuse them a human intelligence.

Broca's argument rested upon two sets of data: the larger brains of men in modern societies, and a supposed increase in male superiority through time. His most extensive data came from autopsies performed personally in four Parisian hospitals. For 292 male brains, he calculated an average weight of 1,325 grams; 140 female brains averaged 1,144 grams for a difference of 181 grams, or 14 percent of the male weight. Broca understood, of course, that part of this difference could be attributed to the greater height of males. Yet he made no attempt to measure the effect of size alone and actually stated that it cannot account for the entire difference because we know, a priori, that women are not as intelligent as men (a premise that the data were supposed to test, not rest upon):

> We might ask if the small size of the female brain depends exclusively upon the small size of her body. Tiedemann has proposed this explanation. But we must not forget that women are, on the average, a little less intelligent than men, a difference which we should not exaggerate but which is, nonetheless, real. We are therefore permitted to suppose that the relatively small size of the female brain depends in part upon her physical inferiority and in part upon her intellectual inferiority.

5 In 1873, the year after Eliot published *Middlemarch,* Broca measured the cranial capacities of prehistoric skulls from L'Homme Mort cave. Here he found a difference of only 99.5 cubic centimeters between males and females, while modern populations range from 129.5 to 220.7. Topinard, Broca's chief disciple,

[2] *Marquis de Condorcet* (1743–1794): A French mathematician and revolutionary.—Eds.

[3] *John Stuart Mill* (1806–1873): A British economist and philosopher.—Eds.

explained the increasing discrepancy through time as a result of differing evolutionary pressures upon dominant men and passive women:

> The man who fights for two or more in the struggle for existence, who has all the responsibility and the cares of tomorrow, who is constantly active in combating the environment and human rivals, needs more brain than the woman whom he must protect and nourish, the sedentary woman, lacking any interior occupations, whose role is to raise children, love, and be passive.

In 1879, Gustave Le Bon, chief misogynist of Broca's school, used these data to publish what must be the most vicious attack upon women in modern scientific literature (no one can top Aristotle). I do not claim his views were representative of Broca's school, but they were published in France's most respected anthropological journal. Le Bon concluded:

> In the most intelligent races, as among the Parisians, there are a large number of women whose brains are closer in size to those of gorillas than to the most developed male brains. This inferiority is so obvious that no one can contest it for a moment; only its degree is worth discussion. All psychologists who have studied the intelligence of women, as well as poets and novelists, recognize today that they represent the most inferior forms of human evolution and that they are closer to children and savages than to an adult, civilized man. They excel in fickleness, inconstancy, absence of thought and logic, and incapacity to reason. Without doubt there exist some distinguished women, very superior to the average man, but they are as exceptional as the birth of any monstrosity, as, for example, of a gorilla with two heads; consequently, we may neglect them entirely.

Nor did Le Bon shrink from the social implications of his views. He was horrified by the proposal of some American reformers to grant women higher education on the same basis as men:

> A desire to give them the same education, and, as a consequence, to propose the same goals for them, is a dangerous chimera. . . . The day when, misunderstanding the inferior occupations which nature has given her, women leave the home and take part in our battles; on this day a social revolution will begin, and everything that maintains the sacred ties of the family will disappear.

Sound familiar?[4]

I have reexamined Broca's data, the basis for all this derivative pronouncement, and I find his numbers sound but his interpretation ill-founded, to say

---

[4]When I wrote this essay, I assumed that Le Bon was a marginal, if colorful, figure. I have since learned that he was a leading scientist, one of the founders of social psychology, and best known for a seminal study on crowd behavior, still cited today (*La psychologie des foules*, 1895), and for his work on unconscious motivation.—Au.

the least. The data supporting his claim for increased difference through time can be easily dismissed. Broca based his contention on the samples from L'Homme Mort alone—only seven male and six female skulls in all. Never have so little data yielded such far-ranging conclusions.

In 1988, Topinard published Broca's more extensive data on the Parisian hospitals. Since Broca recorded height and age as well as brain size, we may use modern statistics to remove their effect. Brain weight decreases with age, and Broca's women were, on average, considerably older than his men. Brain weight increases with height, and his average man was almost half a foot taller than his average woman. I used multiple regression, a technique that allowed me to assess simultaneously the influence of height and age upon brain size. In an analysis of the data for women, I found that, at average male height and age, a woman's brain would weigh 1,212 grams. Correction for height and age reduces Broca's measured difference of 181 grams by more than a third, to 113 grams.

I don't know what to make of this remaining difference because I cannot assess other factors known to influence brain size in a major way. Cause of death has an important effect: Degenerative disease often entails a substantial diminution of brain size. (This effect is separate from the decrease attributed to age alone.) Eugene Schreider, also working with Broca's data, found that men killed in accidents had brains weighing, on average, 60 grams more than men dying of infectious diseases. The best modern data I can find (from American hospitals) records a full 100-gram difference between death by degenerative arteriosclerosis and by violence or accident. Since so many of Broca's subjects were elderly women, we may assume that lengthy degenerative disease was more common among them than among the men. 10

More importantly, modern students of brain size still have not agreed on a proper measure for eliminating the powerful effect of body size. Height is partly adequate, but men and women of the same height do not share the same body build. Weight is even worse than height, because most of its variation reflects nutrition rather than intrinsic size—fat versus skinny exerts little influence upon the brain. Manouvrier took up this subject in the 1880s and argued that muscular mass and force should be used. He tried to measure this elusive property in various ways and found a marked difference in favor of men, even in men and women of the same height. When he corrected for what he called "sexual mass," women actually came out slightly ahead in brain size.

Thus, the corrected 113-gram difference is surely too large; the true figure is probably close to zero and may as well favor women as men. And 113 grams, by the way, is exactly the average difference between a 5-foot-4-inch and a 6-foot-4-inch male in Broca's data. We would not (especially us short folks) want to ascribe greater intelligence to tall men. In short, who knows what to do with Broca's data? They certainly don't permit any confident claim that men have bigger brains than women.

To appreciate the social role of Broca and his school, we must recognize that his statements about the brains of women do not reflect an isolated prejudice toward a single disadvantaged group. They must be weighed in the context of a general theory that supported contemporary social distinctions as biologically ordained. Women, blacks, and poor people suffered the same disparagement, but women bore the brunt of Broca's argument because he had easier access to data on women's brains. Women were singularly denigrated but they also stood as surrogates for other disenfranchised groups. As one of Broca's disciples wrote in 1881: "Men of the black races have a brain scarcely heavier than that of white women." This juxtaposition extended into many other realms of anthropological argument, particularly to claims that, anatomically and emotionally, both women and blacks were like white children—and that white children, by the theory of recapitulation, represented an ancestral (primitive) adult stage of human evolution. I do not regard as empty rhetoric the claim that women's battles are for all of us.

Maria Montessori did not confine her activities to educational reform for young children. She lectured on anthropology for several years at the University of Rome, and wrote an influential book entitled *Pedagogical Anthropology* (English edition, 1913). Montessori was no egalitarian. She supported most of Broca's work and the theory of innate criminality proposed by her compatriot Cesare Lombroso. She measured the circumference of children's heads in her schools and inferred that the best prospects had bigger brains. But she had no use for Broca's conclusions about women. She discussed Manouvrier's work at length and made much of his tentative claim that women, after proper correction of the data, had slightly larger brains than men. Women, she concluded, were intellectually superior, but men had prevailed heretofore by dint of physical force. Since technology has abolished force as an instrument of power, the era of women may soon be upon us: "In such an epoch there will really be superior human beings, there will really be men strong in morality and in sentiment. Perhaps in this way the reign of women is approaching, when the enigma of her anthropological superiority will be deciphered. Woman was always the custodian of human sentiment, morality, and honor."

15 This represents one possible antidote to "scientific" claims for the constitutional inferiority of certain groups. One may affirm the validity of biological distinctions but argue that the data have been misinterpreted by prejudiced men with a stake in the outcome, and that disadvantaged groups are truly superior. In recent years, Elaine Morgan has followed this strategy in her *Descent of Woman*, a speculative reconstruction of human prehistory from the woman's point of view—and as farcical as more famous tall tales by and for men.

I prefer another strategy. Montessori and Morgan followed Broca's philosophy to reach a more congenial conclusion. I would rather label the whole enterprise of setting a biological value upon groups for what it is: irrelevant and highly injurious. George Eliot well appreciated the special tragedy that biological labeling imposed upon members of disadvantaged groups. She expressed it for people like herself—women of extraordinary talent. I would apply it more widely—not only to those whose dreams are flouted but also to those who never realize that they may dream—but I cannot match her prose. In conclusion, then, the rest of Eliot's prelude to *Middlemarch*:

The limits of variation are really much wider than anyone would imagine from the sameness of women's coiffure and the favorite love stories in prose and verse. Here and there a cygnet is reared uneasily among the ducklings in the brown pond, and never finds the living stream in fellowship with its own oary-footed kind. Here and there is born a Saint Theresa, foundress of nothing, whose loving heartbeats and sobs after an unattained goodness tremble off and are dispersed among hindrances instead of centering in some long-recognizable deed.

▪ QUESTIONS

Reading

1. In paragraph 3, Gould claims, "Numbers, by themselves, specify nothing. All depends upon what you do with them." What exactly does Gould do with numbers?
2. How does Gould's use of numbers differ from what Broca and his followers did with numbers? Specifically, what distinguishes Gould's and Broca's methods of calculating and interpreting the data about women's brains?
3. It might also be said, "Quotations, by themselves, specify nothing. All depends upon what you do with them." What does Gould do with quotations in this essay?
4. Why does Gould quote so extensively from Broca and his followers, particularly from Le Bon? What purpose do all of these quotations serve in connection with the points that Gould is trying to make about women's brains and "biological labeling"?

Exploratory Writing

1. Gould begins and ends his essay with passages from George Eliot's *Middlemarch*. Rewrite these passages in modern English. Do your best to translate them into language a novelist of today might use while capturing Eliot's original meaning.
2. Imagine a world in which "biological labeling" was widely accepted, shaping social and educational policy. Write a detailed description of the schools in such a world.

Making Connections

1. Gould reexamines influential moments in the history of the scientific study of gender, evaluating the data and conclusions of previous researchers with the benefit of today's growing body of knowledge about gender and sex. In fact, this is the process through which science develops — new researchers building on and revising yesterday's knowledge. From the other readings in this casebook, find two or three instances in which the writers discuss how previous theories about gender have been reevaluated. What were these theories? Why were they reevaluated? What new theories are replacing them?

Essay Writing

1. The science of gender is inherently connected to social attitudes. Choose two of the essays in this casebook, and compare and contrast the practical or social implications of the research they discuss.

REFLECTING

Faking It

Michael Chabon

Recognized as "one of the most celebrated writers of his generation" by the *Virginia Quarterly Review*, Michael Chabon (b. 1963) pens essays, screenplays, and novels, including *The Mysteries of Pittsburgh* (1988), *Wonder Boys* (1995), and *The Yiddish Policeman's Union* (2007). His epic historical novel, *The Amazing Adventures of Kavalier & Clay* (2000), won the 2001 Pulitzer Prize for Fiction. Chabon also wrote a regular column in *Details* magazine, where he frequently ruminated on parenthood. Of the column, Chabon said in an interview, "I hadn't read a lot by men of my generation and background about being the father now — maybe the floodgates are opening a little, but it felt like I was on relatively untrodden ground." These pieces grew into *Manhood for Amateurs: The Pleasures and Regrets of a Husband, Father, and Son* (2009), a nonfiction look at the complexities of contemporary masculinity. In this excerpt from the book Chabon describes the difference between his outer confidence and internal doubts.

At one time there was a pair of hooks on the back of the bathroom door from which one could hang a couple of towels, but people used the towels as vines, webbing, and rope for games of Tarzan, Spider-Man, and Look! I'm a Dead Guy That Hung Themself, and now, to serve four children, there remained one wall-mounted towel rack with only two bars. This situation encouraged the general tendency among the children to leave their soggy bath towels in Noguchi-like[1] arrangements on the floor. The parents allocated resources for a pilot program of nag-based maintenance, targeted yelling, and regular exercises in stumbling over damp bath towels in dark bedrooms, but when emotional funding at last ran out, it became apparent that someone would have to put up a second towel rack. Responsibility for this task logically fell to the person who knew, kind of, how to use an electric drill.

You should have seen me. I had my cordless Makita in its blue high-impact plastic case. I had a ratcheting screwdriver, a nice Sears Craftsman hammer, a mechanical pencil with a good eraser, and (that most beautifully named of all tools) a spirit level. I sat down on the tile floor of the bathroom with the new chrome towel rack from Restoration Hardware and its gnomic instruction sheet, and I ran the fingers of one hand across the designated stretch of beadboard while sagely stroking my whiskers with the fingers of the other. I strongly suspect that I may well have looked as if I knew what I was doing.

I managed to sustain the appearance of competence over nearly the entire course of the next three hours, except for the painful minute that followed my dropping one of the metal towel bars onto my right thumb, behind whose

[1]*Isamu Noguchi* (1904–1988): Japanese American artist, landscape architect, and sculptor. — Eds.

nail, like a ghost on an old television screen, a grayish-blue blotch immediately made manifest. But from the moment I began to trace with my pencil the prospective outline of one of the faceplates against the beadboard until the moment when, holding my breath, I insinuated two ominously heavy towels into the works of the now-mounted towel rack, I was expecting, at every instant, disaster: molly bolts sliding with a creak of splintering wood from their holes, nickel-plated towel bars clanging against the floor.

I knew how to use my tools, more or less. I understood the rudimentary physics of tension and load that were supposed to hold the rack together and keep it fixed to the wall. And yet on both the deepest and the most practical levels, I had no reason to believe, no evidence from prior experience of myself, physics, or life itself, that I knew how or would be able to pull off the job. In fact, I had encountered a certain amount of tragedy in my dealings with molly bolts over the years.

5 "You're going to put that up?" my wife had asked me when I brought the rack home from the store. She didn't sound dubious so much as surprised, as if I were also proposing to weave a new set of bath towels from cotton I had grown and harvested myself.

"Duh," I said coolly. "No biggie."

This is an essential element of the business of being a man: to flood everyone around you in a great radiant arc of bullshit, one whose source and object of greatest intensity is yourself. To behave as if you have everything firmly under control even when you have just sailed your boat over the falls. "To keep your head," wrote Rudyard Kipling in his classic poem "If," which articulated the code of high-Victorian masculinity in whose fragmentary shadow American men still come of age, "when all about you are losing theirs"; but in reality, the trick of being a man is to give the appearance of keeping your head when, deep inside, the truest part of you is crying out, *Oh, shit!*

Perhaps in the end there is little difference between keeping one's head and appearing to do so; perhaps the effort required to feign unconcern and control over a situation itself imparts a measure of control. If so, then the essence of traditional male virtue lies in imposture, in an ongoing act of dissimulation—fronting—which hardly conforms to the classic Kipling model of square-dealing candor.

I have no doubt that the male impulse to downplay his own lack of fitness for a job, to refuse to acknowledge his inadequacy, insufficiency, or lack of preparation, has been and continues to be responsible for a large share of the world's woes, in the form of the accidents, errors, and calamities that result from specific or overarching acts of faking it, a grim encyclopedia of which the G. W. Bush administration readily affords. There is also the more subtle damage that is done repeatedly to boys who grow up learning from their fathers and the men around them the tragic lesson that failure is not a human constant but a kind of aberration of gender, a flaw in a man, to be concealed.

10 Men's refusal to stop and ask for directions, a foundational cliché of women's criticism, analysis, and stand-up mockery of male behavior, is a per-

fect example of this tendency to put up a front, in that it views as aberrant a condition— being lost—that is ineluctable, a given of human existence. We are born lost and spend vast stretches of our lives on wrong turns and backtracking. In this respect, male fronting resembles a number of other behaviors typically ascribed to men and masculinity, in that it proceeds by denying essential human conditions or responses—say public displays of mutual affection, grief, or triumphs—marking them as feminine, infantile, socially unacceptable.

I learned to pretend that I know what I am doing from my own father, an extremely intelligent and well-informed man whose intermittent bouts with mistakenness and inaccuracy visibly cost him bitter pain and embarrassment, and shocked the hell out of me when I was a child. By fiat and consensus, fathers are always right, so that when facts or events inevitably conspire to prove them wrong, they and their sons alike totter on the brink of an abyss. I have never forgotten the day—I can't have been older than five—when I watched in silent horror as my father, imperturbable and confident and disdaining the instruction sheet, assembled an entire barbecue grill with its key pieces upside down and backward. I remember my mounting anxiety about whether I should point out his mistake to him, and most clearly of all I remember the sharp and mocking look my mother gave him when at last I betrayed him.

When I became a father, I made a promise to myself not to pretend to knowledge I did not possess, not to claim authority I plainly lacked, not to hide my doubts and uncertainties, my setbacks and regrets, from my children. And so I have tried to share them over the years as I have been fired from screenwriting jobs or proved wrong or led to look a fool. I have made a point (until the recent advent of GPS) to stop and ask for directions. But sometimes I waver in my resolve. My sense of myself as a father, my sense of fathers, is so deeply caught up with some kind of primal longing (which I think we all share) for inerrancy, for the word of God, for a rock and a redeemer, a mighty hand and an outstretched arm, for the needle that always always finds true north in a storm.

And maybe that longing in one's wife and children runs beyond the understanding of even the most painfully self-conscious of fathers. One recent winter my family and I found ourselves stuck in Jackson Hole, Wyoming, in the middle of a snowstorm. All flights out were canceled. There was a flight home from Idaho Falls, a drive of two hours through a high mountain pass, or three hours by an easier route that skirted the mountains. Either way, there would be snow, ice, unknown chances. If we wanted, we could wait for an airline-chartered bus that might eventually depart for Idaho Falls, getting us home to Oakland no one could say when. Or we could sit tight, wait it out, and hope to get home sometime tomorrow or the next day.

I didn't give it a moment's thought. We had rented a big strong four-by-four. It had the tires and the muscle for the roads up there. I liked the way I felt behind its wheel, competent and unperturbed by weather. The fact that I had not driven in a blizzard in twenty years barely entered the conscious register of my thoughts.

"Let's drive," I told my wife. "I'll go the long way around." 15

She looked at me with a strange expression, then said okay; later, after we had made it safely and without incident up and down through ice and rain and snowfall that was at times blinding, my wife told me that she initially thought I was dangerously insane when I proposed driving to Idaho Falls through a blizzard. But then she had heard something in my voice that reassured her; she'd seen something in my eyes. I looked as if I knew what I was doing. And though I gripped the wheel with bloodless hands and prayed wildly to the gods of the interstate trucker whom I carefully tailed all the way to Idaho, in the backseat the kids calmly watched their iPod videos, and my wife studied the map and gossiped with me, and none of them knew or suspected for a moment—for I never betrayed, by word or deed, my secret—that I was in way over my head. I was the father and the husband; they were safe with me. We made it to the airport right on time to catch the next flight home.

"I knew you could do it," my wife said, and I thought about saying, "Well, that makes one of us." But I held my tongue and nodded with a Kiplingesque modesty, because the truth was that in the absence of any evidence or experience or reason to think so, I had known that I could do it, too. I had no choice, do you see, but to know that.

By the way, the towels are still hanging from the rack in the bathroom. And I fully expect, at any moment, in the dead of night, to hear a telltale clatter on the tiles.

▪ QUESTIONS

Reading

1. Describe the tone of the first paragraph. Which words and phrases signal this tone?
2. What is "fronting"? Why does Chabon quote Rudyard Kipling when discussing fronting?
3. Highlight, underline, and flag the characteristics of masculinity that Chabon identifies. When does his description of himself fall in line with these characteristics? When does it deviate?

Exploratory Writing

1. Chabon writes that his idea of fathers is "deeply caught up with some kind of primal longing (which I think we all share) for inerrancy" (paragraph 12). Think of a person you admired—either a public figure or someone in your own life—who erred in some way. Write a brief description of his or her failure and what life lesson you drew from it.
2. With a partner, brainstorm a list of fifteen to twenty stereotypes about men. Which of these might Chabon think are true? Which would he say are examples of "fronting"? Which do you think are accurate? How does Chabon's description of masculinity compare with your own definition?

Making Connections

1. Peggy Orenstein (p. 705) and Chabon both make generalizations about men and women in their pieces. In what ways are their generalizations about either gender similar? How do they differ? How do their methods (e.g., humor, personal stories, or invoking public figures) differ? Do you find one more convincing than the other? Why or why not?

Essay Writing

1. Research the "high-Victorian masculinity" mentioned by Chabon (paragraph 7) and write an essay in which you explain the concept. How was masculinity defined in the Victorian era? What activities were considered masculine? Do you agree with Chabon that those ideas have persisted in the United States today? Why or why not?

ARGUMENTATION AND RESEARCH PROJECTS

1. Choose two essays from this casebook that challenge similar cultural assumptions about gender. Identify an assumption that interests you and put each writer's argument to the test by examining the way he or she uses evidence to challenge that assumption. First, make a list of the evidence used by each writer. Then, track down some of the original sources — scientific articles, newspaper reports, or statistics — used by the writer. When you read them in their entirety, do these sources seem to support the author's position? After you've done this, find at least two more sources that address your chosen assumption. Once you've collected your evidence, write an essay that makes an argument about the origins, meaning, or validity of the assumption challenged in the essays you've chosen to work with.
2. Identify a person whose gender identity has received public attention. This may be somebody discussed in one of this casebook's essays or somebody you choose on your own. This could be someone who draws attention to gender ambiguities, someone who plays to gender stereotypes, or someone who does a job normally done by people of a different gender. Learn as much as you can about this person. Find newspaper articles or films about this person, and read memoirs, essays, or interviews in which he or she discusses his or her own point of view. Then, use some of the theories or concepts articulated by the essays in this casebook to frame your own argument about the public debates about the person you're researching. Consider some of the following as you develop your argument: What questions tend to be raised about your chosen person? What biases about gender are revealed by these questions? How does this particular case challenge or support common-sense notions about gender identity? How has public attention affected the life of the person in question?
3. Make a documentary depicting your own gendered experience, in a medium of your choice — for example, a video, Web site, blog, essay, or podcast. Draw on some of the essays in this casebook to help you analyze your experience. Conduct interviews of friends, family, professors, or other students who may have insight about or who may shape your experience. Be as lively and creative as you can be. Be sure to choose a particular theme or set of questions to guide and shape your documentary. Decide what rhetorical modes you want to use — reflecting, reporting, explaining, or arguing — to tell your story and engage your audience.

Acknowledgments

Diane Ackerman. "Why Leaves Turn Color in the Fall" from *A Natural History of the Senses.* Copyright © 1990 by Diane Ackerman. Used by permission of Random House, Inc.

Natalie Angier. Excerpt from "Thinking Scientifically: An Out-of-Body Experience" from *The Canon: A Whirligig Tour of the Beautiful Basics of Science* by Natalie Angier. Copyright © 2007 by Natalie Angier. Reprinted by permission of Houghton Mifflin Harcourt Publishing Company. All rights reserved.

Gloria Anzaldúa. "How to Tame a Wild Tongue" from *Borderlands/La Frontera: The New Mestiza.* Copyright © 1987, 1999 by Gloria Anzaldúa. Reprinted by permission of Aunt Lute Books. (Permission received by email; contract not received)

James Baldwin. "If Black English Isn't a Language, Then Tell Me, What Is?" Originally published in the *New York Times,* July 29, 1979. Collected in *The Price of the Ticket,* published by St. Martin's Press. Copyright © 1979 by James Baldwin. Reprinted by arrangement with the James Baldwin Estate.

John Berger. "Hiroshima" from *The Sense of Sight* by John Berger. Copyright © 1985 by John Berger. Used by permission of Pantheon Books, a division of Random House, Inc.

Mark Bittman. "Bad Food? Tax It and Subsidize Vegetables" from the *New York Times,* July 23, 2011. Copyright © 2011 by the New York Times. All rights reserved. Used by permission and protected by the Copyright Laws of the United States. The printing, copying, redistribution, or retransmission of this Content without express written permission is prohibited.

Paul Bloom. "Is God an Accident?" from the *Atlantic Online,* December 2005. Copyright © 2005, the Atlantic Media Company as published in the *Atlantic.* Reprinted with permission of Tribune Media Services.

Christina Boufis. "Teaching Literature at the County Jail" from the *Common Review* 1, No. 1. Copyright © 2001 by Christina Boufis. Used with permission of the author.

Jan Harold Brunvand. "Urban Legends: 'The Boyfriend's Death'" from *The Vanishing Hitchhiker: American Urban Legends and Their Meanings.* Copyright © 1981 by Jan Harold Brunvand. Reprinted by permission of W. W. Norton & Company, Inc.

Nicholas Carr. "Is Google Making Us Stupid?" from the *Atlantic,* July/August 2008. Copyright © 2008 by Nicholas Carr. Reprinted by permission of the author.

Michael Chabon. "Faking It" from *Manhood for Amateurs* (pp. 127–134) HarperCollins 2009. Copyright © 2009 by Michael Chabon. Reprinted by permission of HarperCollins Publishers and HarperCollins Pulishers Ltd. All rights reserved.

Dudley Clendinen. "The Good Short Life" from the *New York Times,* July 9, 2011. Copyright © 2011 by the New York Times. All rights reserved. Used by permission and protected by the Copyright Laws of the United States. The printing, copying, redistribution, or retransmission of this Content without express written permission is prohibited.

Amanda Coyne. "The Long Good-bye" from *Harper's* magazine, May 1997. Copyright © 1997 by Amanda Coyne. Reprinted with permission of the author.

Cathy N. Davidson. "Project Classroom Makeover" from *Now You See It: How the Brain Science of Attention Will Transform the Way We Live, Work, and Learn* by Cathy N. Davidson. Copyright © 2011 by Cathy N. Davidson. Used by permission of Viking Penguin, a division of Penguin Group (USA) Inc.

Mark Edmundson. "On the Uses of a Liberal Education" from *Harper's* magazine, September 1997. Copyright © 1997 by Harper's Magazine. All rights reserved. Reproduced from the September issue by special permission.

Barbara Ehrenreich. "Serving in Florida" from *Nickel and Dimed* by Barbara Ehrenreich. Copyright © 2001 by Barbara Ehrenreich. Reprinted by permission of Henry Holt and Company, LLC.

Mona Eltahawy. "Twitterholics Anonymous" from *Jerusalem Rerport,* Wednesday, January 12, 2011. Copyright © 2011 by Mona Eltahawy.

Anne Fausto-Sterling. "Society Constructs Biology; Biology Constructs Gender" from *Daedalus,* 116:4 (Fall, 1987). Copyright © 1987 by the American Academy of Arts and Sciences. Reprinted by permission of MIT Press Journals.

George Felton. "How to Write a Great College Slogan" from the *Chronicle of Higher Education,* January 19, 2001. Copyright © 2011 by George Felton. Reprinted by permission of the author.

Richard P. Feynman. "The Value of Science" from *The Pleasure of Finding Things Out.* Copyright © 2005 Richard P. Feynman. Reprinted by permission of Basic Books, a member of the Perseus Books Group.

David Friedman. "From 1890: The First Text Messages" from *Sunday Magazine,* August 10, 2010, 12:45 p.m. Copyright © 2010 by David Friedman. Reprinted by permission of the author.

Brooke Gladstone. "The Great Refusal" from *The Influencing Machine: Brooke Gladstone on the Media* by Brooke Gladstone and illustrated by Josh Neufeld. Copyright © 2011 by Brooke Gladstone and Josh Neufield. Used by permission of W. W. Norton & Company, Inc.

James Gleick. "Meme Pool" from *The Information: A History, A Theory, A Flood* by James Gleick. Copyright © 2011 by James Gleick. Used by permission of Pantheon Books, a division of Random House, Inc.

Stephen Jay Gould. "Women's Brains" from *The Panda's Thumb: More Reflections on Natural History.* Copyright © 1980 by Stephen Jay Gould. Reprinted with permission of Turbo, Inc.

E.J. Graff. "The M/F Boxes," published in the *Nation* (http://www.thenation.com), November 29, 2001. Reprinted by permission of the author.

Gary Gutting. "What Is College For?" from the *New York Times,* December 14, 2011. Copyright © 2011 by the New York Times. All rights reserved. Used by permission and protected by the Copyright Laws of the United States. The printing, copying, redistribution, or retransmission of this Content without express written permission is prohibited.

Robin Marantz Henig. "What Is It About 20-Somethings?" from the *New York Times,* August 18, 2010. Copyright © 2010 by the New York Times. All rights reserved. Used by permission and protected by the Copyright Laws of the United States. The printing, copying, redistribution, or retransmission of this Content without express written permission is prohibited.

Steven Johnson. "Watching TV Makes You Smarter" from the *New York Times Magazine,* April 24, 2005; reprinted in *Everything Bad Is Good for You* by Steven Johnson. Copyright © 2005 by Steven Johnson. Used by permission of Riverhead Books, an imprint of Penguin Group (USA) Inc.

Olivia Judson. "The Selfless Gene" by Olivia Judson. Copyright © 2007 by Olivia Judson. Originally appeared in the *Atlantic,* October 2007. Reprinted by permission of Georges Borchardt, Inc., on behalf of the author.

Ann Jurecic. "Mindblindness" originally from *Literature & Medicine* 25:1 (2006), 1–23; updated 2012 by the author. Copyright © 2006 by the Johns Hopkins University Press. Adapted and reprinted with permission of the Johns Hopkins University Press.

Martin Luther King Jr. "Letter from Birmingham Jail." Copyright © 1963 by Dr. Martin Luther King. Jr. Copyright © renewed 1991 by Coretta Scott King. Reprinted by arrangement with the Heirs to the Estate of Martin Luther King Jr., c/o Writers House as agent for the proprietor New York, NY.

Walter Kirn. "A Pharmacological Education" from the *New York Times,* September 6, 2009. Copyright © 2009 by the New York Times. All rights reserved. Used by permission and protected by the Copyright Laws of the United States. The printing, copying, redistribution, or retransmission of this Content without express written permission is prohibited.

Jhumpa Lahiri. "Trading Stories" from the *New Yorker,* June 13, 2011. Copyright © 2011 by Jhumpa Lahiri. Reprinted with permission of William Morris Endeavor Entertainment, LLC.

Linda Lee. "The Case against College" from *Success Without College.* Copyright © 2000 by Linda Lee. Used by permission of Doubleday, a division of Random House, Inc.

Jonah Lehrer. "The Eureka Hunt" from the *New Yorker,* July 28, 2008. Reprinted with permission of the author.

David Leonhardt. "Even for Cashiers, College Pays Off" from the *New York Times,* June 25, 2011. Copyright © 2011 by the New York Times. All rights reserved. Used by permission and protected by the Copyright Laws of the United States. The printing, copying, redistribution, or retransmission of this Content without express written permission is prohibited.

Emily Martin. "The Egg and the Sperm: How Science Has Constructed a Romance Based on Stereotypical Male-Female Roles" from *Signs: Journal of Women in Culture and Society* 16:3. Copyright © 1991 by the University of Chicago Press. Reprinted with permission of University of Chicago Press.

Thomas W. Martin. "Scientific Literacy and the Habit of Discourse" from *Seedmagazine.com*, September 21, 2007. Copyright © 2007 by Seed Magazine. Reprinted by permission of Seed Media Group LLC.

Scott McCloud. "Setting the Record Straight" (pp. 2-23) from *Understanding Comics* by Scott McCloud. Copyright © 1993, 1994 by Scott McCloud. Reprinted by permission of HarperCollins Publishers.

Peggy Orenstein. "What Makes a Woman a Woman?" from the *New York Times*, September 13, 2009. Copyright © 2009 by Peggy Orenstein. Reprinted by permission of the author.

George Orwell. "Politics and the English Language" from *Shooting an Elephant and Other Essays* by George Orwell. Copyright © 1946 by Sonia Brownell Orwell and renewed © 1974 by Sonia Orwell. "Shooting an Elephant" from *Shooting an Elephant and Other Essays* by George Orwell. Copyright © 1950 by Sonia Brownell Orwell and renewed 1978 by Sonia Pitt-Rivers. Reprinted by permission of Houghton Mifflin Harcourt Publishing Company and Bill Hamilton as the Literary Executor of the Estate of the late Sonia Brownell Orwell and Secker & Warburg Ltd.

Steven Pinker. "The Moral Instinct" from the *New York Times*, January 13, 2008. Copyright © 2008 by the New York Times. All rights reserved. Used by permission and protected by the Copyright Laws of the United States. The printing, copying, redistribution, or retransmission of this Content without express written permission is prohibited.

Jay Prosser. "The Body Narrative of Transsexuality" from *Second Skins*. Copyright © 1998 by Columbia University Press. Reprinted by permission of Columbia University Press.

Jeffrey Rosen. "The End of Forgetting" from the *New York Times*, July 21, 2010. Copyright © 2010 by the New York Times. All rights reserved. Used by permission and protected by the Copyright Laws of the United States. The printing, copying, redistribution, or retransmission of this Content without express written permission is prohibited.

Oliver Sacks. "The Man Who Mistook His Wife for a Hat" from *The Man Who Mistook His Wife for a Hat and Other Clinical Tales*. Copyright © 1970, 1981, 1983, 1984, 1985 by Oliver Sacks. Reprinted with the permission of Simon & Schuster, Inc.

Marjane Satrapi. "The Veil" from *Persepolis: The Story of a Childhood*, translated by Mattias Ripa & Blake Ferris, translation copyright © 2003 by L'Association, Paris, France. Used by permission of Pantheon Books, a division of Random House, Inc.

Roy C. Selby Jr. "A Delicate Operation" from *Harper's* magazine, December 1975. Copyright © 1975 by Harper's Magazine. All rights reserved. Reproduced from the December issue by special permission.

Richard Selzer. "A Mask on the Face of Death" by Richard Selzer. Copyright © 1987 by Richard Selzer. Originally appeared in *Life* magazine. Reprinted with permission of Georges Borchardt, Inc. on behalf of the author.

Susan Sontag. Chapter 4 from *Regarding the Pain of Others* by Susan Sontag. Copyright © 2003 by Susan Sontag. Reprinted by permission of Farrar, Straus and Giroux, LLC.

Andrew Sullivan. "Why I Blog" by Andrew Sullivan, originally published by the *Atlantic*. Copyright © 2008 by Andrew Sullivan. Reprinted with permission of the Wylie Agency LLC.

Margaret Talbot. "Brain Gain" from the *New Yorker*, April 27, 2009. Copyright © 2009 by Margaret Talbot. Reprinted by permission of the Wylie Agency LLC.

Amy Tan. "Mother Tongue." Copyright © 1990 by Amy Tan. First appeared in the *Threepenny Review*. Reprinted by permission of the author and the Sandra Dijkstra Literary Agency.

Jill Bolte Taylor. "Morning of the Stroke" from *My Stroke of Insight* by Jill Bolte Taylor. Copyright © 2006 by Jill Bolte Taylor. Used by permission of Viking Penguin, a division of Penguin Group (USA) Inc.

Lewis Thomas. "The Corner of the Eye" from *Late Night Thoughts on Listening to Mahler's Ninth* by Lewis Thomas. Copyright © 1981 by Lewis Thomas. Used by permission of Viking Penguin, a division of Penguin Group (USA) Inc.

Clive Thompson. "I'm So Totally, Digitally, Close to You" from the *New York Times*, September 7, 2008. Copyright © 2008 the New York Times. All rights reserved. Used by permission and protected by the Copyright Laws of the United States. The printing, copying, redistribution, or retransmission of this Content without express written permission is prohibited.

James Traub. "The Next Drive-Thru U" by James Traub, originally published in the *New Yorker.* Copyright © 1997 by James Traub. Used by permission of the Wylie Agency LLC.

Barbara Tuchman. "'This Is the End of the World': The Black Death" from *A Distant Mirror* by Barbara W. Tuchman. Text copyright © 1978 by Barbara W. Tuchman. Used by permission of Alfred A. Knopf, a division of Random House, Inc.

Sherry Turkle. "Connectivity and Its Discontents" excerpt from Introduction of *Alone Together,* Basic Books. Copyright © 2011 by Sherry Turkle. Reprinted by permission of Basic Books, a member of the Perseus Books Group.

Jose Antonio Vargas. "My Life as an Undocumented Immigrant" from the *New York Times,* June 22, 2011. Copyright © 2011 by the New York Times. All rights reserved. Used by permission and protected by the Copyright Laws of the United States. The printing, copying, redistribution, or retransmission of this Content without express written permission is prohibited.

Various Authors. "A Quick Look at Who Is Fighting This War" by Ryan Kelly, copyright © 2006 by Ryan Kelly; "Alarm Red" by Lisa Blackman, copyright © 2006 by Lisa Blackman; "Veterans" by Brian Humphreys, copyright © 2006 by Brian Humphreys; "Life on the USNS Comfort" by Edward Jewell, copyright © 2006 by Edward Jewell; "What's Going on Over Here" by Timothy Gaestel, copyright © 2006 by Timothy Gaestel; "Headnotes" by Andrew Carroll, copyright © 2006 by Andrew Carroll, from *Operation Homecoming,* edited by Andrew Carroll. Used by permission of Random House, Inc. This material appears in this publication as excerpts. In some cases, the original spelling and punctuation have been altered, and military slang and technical terms have been clarified or replaced.

PHOTO CREDITS

Page 77: (Jhumpa Lahiri family photo)

Page 87: (Jennifer, prisoner) Tim Zielenbach / Contact Press Images

Page 106: (Drawing of Plato's cave) Line drawing of the cave, p. 316, from *The Great Dialogues of Plato* by Plato, translated by W.H.D. Rouse, translation copyright © 1956, renewed © 1984 by J.C.G. Rouse. Used by permission of Dutton Signet, a division of Penguin Group (USA) Inc.

Page 238: (Painting by Kazuhiro Ishizu) Kazuhiro Ishizu, Hiroshima Peace Memorial Museum

Page 239: (Painting by Sawami Katagiri) Sawami Katagiri, Hiroshima Peace Memorial Museum

Page 259: (*Triumph of Death*) Alinari / Art Resource, NY

Page 261: (Burial of victims) Snark / Art Resource, NY

Page 396: (Richard Feynman) Science Photo Library / Photo Researchers

Page 419: (Jill Bolte Taylor) AJ Mast / The New York Times / Redux

Page 506: (Woman at computer) Adrian Tomine

Page 596: (delete adolescence) James Wojcik / Art Dept. / trunkarchive.com

Page 596: (ctrl identity) James Wojcik / Art Dept. / trunkarchive.com

Page 633: (Whatever) Jeremy Wolff

Page 634: (Univ. of You) Jeremy Wolff

Page 707: (crossed legs) Elinor Carucci / trunkarchive.com

E-PAGES CREDITS

Isabel Allende and Big Think. "Writing Process" footage courtesy of Big Think.

T.M. Luhrmann. "When God Talks Back" from "The Brian Lehrer Show—WNYC Radio."

Dan Ariely. "The Context of Our Character" © 2008, Duke University—The Fuqua School of Business.

GOOD. "Not Your Parents' American Dream: The Pursuit of a New National Ideal" originally appeared on www.GOOD.is on January 26, 2012. Reprinted with permission from GOOD.

Michael Shermer and the Richard Dawkins Foundation for Reason and Science. "The Baloney Detection Kit." *Text:* Used by permission of Skeptics Society and Michael Shermer. *Video:* Richard Dawkins Foundation for Reason and Science.

Iain McGilchrist. "The Divided Brain and the Making of the Western World." Video and illustrations courtesy of RSA, Cognitive Media, and Iain McGilchrist.

Know Your Meme. "What People Think I Do / What I Really Do" used with permission from Cheezburger.com.

Michael Oatman. "Admittance to a Better Life." Audio recording Copyright © 2007 by This I Believe, Inc. Used with permission of This I Believe, Inc. *Text:* "Admittance to a Better Life," copyright © 2007 by Michael Oatman; from the book *This I Believe II: More Personal Philosophies of Remarkable Men and Women*, edited by Jay Allison and Dan Gediman. Copyright © 2008 by This I Believe, Inc. Reprinted by permission of Henry Holt and Company, LLC.

Stephen T. Asma. "Gauging Gender" © Stephen T. Asma, Professor of Philosophy at Columbia College Chicago; artwork © Kevin Van Aelst.

Jennifer Siebel Newsom. *Miss Representation* film trailer © Girls Club Entertainment LLC. Distributed by ro*co films educational 2012.

Rhetorical Index

Analogy

Case Study

Causal Analysis

Comparison and Contrast

Definition

Description

First-Person Perspective

Author and Title Index

Narration

Process Analysis

Scientific and Technical Report

Student Essays